# THE OXFORD HANDBOOK OF

# ELECTORAL
# SYSTEMS

# THE OXFORD HANDBOOK OF

# ELECTORAL

# SYSTEMS

*Edited by*

ERIK S. HERRON,

ROBERT J. PEKKANEN,

*and*

MATTHEW S. SHUGART

OXFORD

UNIVERSITY PRESS

# OXFORD
## UNIVERSITY PRESS

Oxford University Press is a department of the University of Oxford. It furthers
the University's objective of excellence in research, scholarship, and education
by publishing worldwide. Oxford is a registered trade mark of Oxford University
Press in the UK and certain other countries.

Published in the United States of America by Oxford University Press
198 Madison Avenue, New York, NY 10016, United States of America.

Library of Congress Cataloging-in-Publication Data
Names: Herron, Erik S., editor. | Pekkanen, Robert, editor. |
Shugart, Matthew Soberg, 1960– editor.
Title: The Oxford handbook of electoral systems / edited by Erik S. Herron,
Robert J. Pekkanen, and Matthew S. Shugart.
Other titles: Handbook of electoral systems
Description: New York, NY : Oxford University Press, 2018. |
Includes bibliographical references.
Identifiers: LCCN 2017038798 | ISBN 9780190258658 (hardback) |
ISBN 9780197564714 (paperback)
Subjects: LCSH: Elections. | Elections—Case studies. | Representative
government and representation. | Representative government and
representation—Case studies. | Comparative politics. | BISAC: POLITICAL
SCIENCE / History & Theory. | POLITICAL SCIENCE / Political Process / Elections.
Classification: LCC JF1001 .O94 2018 | DDC 324.6—dc23
LC record available at https://lccn.loc.gov/2017038798

# CONTENTS

## PART I FOUNDATIONS OF ELECTORAL SYSTEMS

## PART II ISSUES AND REPRESENTATION

# PART III  ELECTORAL SYSTEMS AND THE WIDER POLITICAL SYSTEM

# PART IV  ELECTORAL SYSTEMS AND RESEARCH DESIGN

# PART V  HOLDING ELECTIONS

# PART VI  ELECTORAL SYSTEMS IN CONTEXT

## PART VII ELECTORAL SYSTEMS IN THE CONTEXT OF REFORM

## PART VIII ELECTORAL SYSTEMS IN THE CONTEXT OF NEW DEMOCRACIES

# About the Editors

Erik S. Herron is the Eberly Family Distinguished Professor of Political Science at West Virginia University. His research focuses on political institutions, especially electoral systems. Erik has traveled extensively in Eastern Europe and Eurasia, including a term as a Fulbright scholar in Ukraine and fifteen election observation missions. He has published research in the *American Journal of Political Science,* the *Journal of Politics, World Politics, Comparative Political Studies, Electoral Studies*, and other journals, as well as three books: *Mixed Electoral Systems: Contamination and Its Consequences* (with Federico Ferrara and Misa Nishikawa), *Elections and Democracy after Communism,* and *Normalizing Corruption: Failures of Accountability in Ukraine.*

Robert J. Pekkanen is Professor at the Henry M. Jackson School of International Studies, Adjunct Professor of Political Science, and Adjunct Professor of Sociology at the University of Washington. He received his PhD in political science from Harvard University in 2002. His research interests lie in electoral systems, political parties, and civil society. He has published articles in political science journals such as the *American Political Science Review,* the *British Journal of Political Science,* and *Comparative Political Studies*, as well as six books on American nonprofit advocacy, Japanese civil society, and Japanese elections and political parties.

Matthew S. Shugart is Distinguished Professor of Political Science at the University of California, Davis, and Affiliated Professor at the University of Haifa. He is a world-renowned scholar of democratic institutions. He is a two-time winner of the George H. Hallet Award, given annually by the Representation and Electoral Systems Section of the American Political Science Association for a book published at least ten years ago that has made a lasting contribution to the field. He won it first for his collaboration with Rein Taagepera (*Seats and Votes,* 1989) and again for *Presidents and Assemblies* (1992, with John M. Carey). He has participated as an advisor on electoral-system reform and constitutional design in several countries, including Albania, Bulgaria, Colombia, Estonia, and Israel.

# CONTRIBUTORS

James F. Adams, University of California, Davis, United States

Nathan Allen, St. Francis Xavier University, Canada

Audrey André, Vrije Universiteit Brussel, Belgium

Shaun Bowler, University of California, Riverside, United States

John M. Carey, Dartmouth College, United States

Josep M. Colomer, Georgetown University, United States

Gary W. Cox, Stanford University, United States

Brian F. Crisp, Washington University in St. Louis, United States

Sam Depauw, Vrije Universiteit Brussel, Belgium

Dominik Duell, University of Essex, United Kingdom

Benjamin Ferland, University of Ottawa, Canada

Karen E. Ferree, University of California, San Diego, United States

Michael Gallagher, Trinity College Dublin, Ireland

Jennifer Gandhi, Emory University, United States

Matt Golder, Pennsylvania State University, United States

Thad E. Hall, Fors Marsh Group, United States

Lisa Handley, Oxford Brookes University, United Kingdom

Reuven Y. Hazan, Hebrew University, Jerusalem, Israel

Abigail L. Heller, Emory University, United States

Verónica Hoyo, University of California, San Diego, United States

Reut Itzkovitch-Malka, Open University of Israel

Kristof Jacobs, Ratboud University, Netherlands

Joel W. Johnson, Colorado State University, Pueblo, United States

Mark P. Jones, Rice University, United States

**Ken Kollman,**  University of Michigan, United States

**Mona Lena Krook,**  Rutgers University, United States

**David Lublin,**  American University, United States

**Thomas Carl Lundberg,**  University of Glasgow, United Kingdom

**Toni Makkai,**  Australian National University, Australia

**Michael Marsh,**  Trinity College Dublin, Ireland

**Shane Martin,**  University of Essex, United Kingdom

**Louis Massicotte,**  Laval University, Canada

**Ian McAllister,**  Australian National University, Australia

**Paul Mitchell,**  London School of Economics, United Kingdom

**Robert G. Moser,**  University of Texas, Austin, United States

**Kuniaki Nemoto,**  Musashi University, Japan

**Misa Nishikawa,**  Ball State University, United States

**Pippa Norris,**  Harvard University, United States, and University of Sydney, Australia

**Gianluca Passarelli,**  Sapienza University, Rome, Italy

**Matt Qvortrup,**  Coventry University, United Kingdom

**Gideon Rahat,**  Hebrew University, Jerusalem, Israel

**Alan Renwick,**  University College London, United Kingdom

**Nathan J. Rexford,**  University of California, Davis, United States

**Ethan Scheiner,**  University of California, Davis, United States

**William M. Simoneau,**  Washington University in St. Louis, United States

**Daniel M. Smith,**  Harvard University, United States

**Heather Stoll,**  University of California, Santa Barbara, United States

**Rein Taagepera,**  University of California, Irvine, United States

**Steven L. Taylor,**  Troy University, United States

**Joshua A. Tucker,**  New York University, United States

**Åsa von Schoultz (née Bengtsson),**  Mid Sweden University, Sweden

**Jack Vowles,**  Victoria University, New Zealand

**Adam Ziegfeld,**  Temple University, United States

**Thomas Zittel,**  University of Frankfurt, Germany

# Acknowledgments

We are indebted to a host of colleagues and friends for their support while we developed the *Oxford Handbook of Electoral Systems*. While naming everyone would make this already sizable volume even longer, we would like to acknowledge a few groups and individuals to whom we owe a special debt.

The origins of the volume can be traced back to our collaboration on a research project funded by the National Science Foundation (SES-0751662 and SES-0751436). The project on electoral systems and party personnel decisions not only brought the three coeditors together but also introduced them to some of the contributors, and produced ideas and data featured in the *Handbook*.

The community of electoral systems scholars was incredibly responsive to our requests for participation in the volume. Our volume includes over fifty outstanding contributors, and we have benefited from interactions with them during the production of the *Handbook*. The field of electoral studies features even more great scholars we could not include in the volume, but who will continue to advance the field, supporting and challenging arguments in the book.

We are grateful to Oxford University Press for its encouragement and patience in the development process. We would especially like to thank Molly Balikov, Alyssa Callan, and David Pervin at OUP, and Meghana Antony at Newgen, for all of their efforts to take this volume from an idea to a fully realized handbook. Saadia Pekkanen also offered guidance at an early stage as we conceived the project. Colleagues at our home universities—West Virginia University, University of Washington, and University of California, Davis—helped us to carve out the time needed to craft the volume, and we thank them for their support. Robert thanks the Japan Studies Program at the University of Washington for support. We also thank J. D. Mussel for reading several chapters and for offering numerous helpful comments.

Finally, we would like to thank our families (Lea and Carter Herron, Saadia and Sophia Pekkanen, and Merry Shugart) for their steadfast support.

CHAPTER 1

.............................................................................

# TERMINOLOGY AND BASIC RULES OF ELECTORAL SYSTEMS

.............................................................................

ERIK S. HERRON, ROBERT J. PEKKANEN,
AND MATTHEW S. SHUGART

No subject is more central to the study of political science than elections. All across the globe, elections are a focal point for citizens, the media, and politicians long before—and sometimes well after—they occur. Indeed, as scholars have long known, electoral systems—the rules determining how voters' preferences are translated into election results—profoundly shape important political outcomes, including party systems, the diversity of public officials, and policy choices. Electoral systems have accordingly been a hot topic in established democracies from the United Kingdom and Italy to New Zealand and Japan. Even in the United States, events like the 2000 and 2016 presidential elections and court decisions such as *Citizens United* have sparked advocates to promote change in the Electoral College, redistricting, and campaign finance rules. Elections and electoral systems have also intensified as a field of academic study, with groundbreaking work sharpening our understanding of how electoral systems fundamentally shape the connections among citizens, government, and policy.

For decades, research on electoral systems has been noted as the best example of the accumulation of knowledge in political science (Riker 1982). The field of inquiry has been far from static, however, with the development of new election rules, the establishment of new democratic systems, and the discovery of new theoretical and empirical regularities characterizing the field over recent decades. However, these developments have not been accompanied by a volume that synthesizes the field's collective knowledge and makes it accessible to a wide audience. This volume provides an in-depth exploration of the origins and effects of electoral systems. Contributions from top scholars in the field cover the design and adoption of election rules; how rules influence representation, policy, and the functions of other institutions; and the emerging horizons of

electoral systems research. The book addresses key theoretical questions and methodological approaches that will guide electoral systems research in the decades to come and
should serve as a key resource for scholars, students, and practitioners.

# THE TOPIC OF ELECTORAL SYSTEMS

Electoral systems are the set of rules for taking votes in any given election and determining the seats in the representative assembly[1] or other elected institution, including
a presidency where one is elected. We say "set" of rules because if we were to speak of
"electoral rules," we would be implying narrower features, such as specific provisions
defining the allocation of seats (e.g., proportional formulas, which we review later in
this chapter) or minimum vote percentages required to earn seats (i.e., legal thresholds).
Thus, *electoral system* is a broader concept than *electoral rules*. At the same time, the
electoral system is narrower than a country's (or other jurisdiction's) *electoral laws*; the
latter term could refer to provisions on who is eligible to vote, the criteria for candidacy,
whether voting is mandatory, the day(s) on which voting is held, how disputes are to be
resolved, campaign financing, and other legal matters that are not specifically about the
votes-to-seats conversion process.[2]

Within the definition of the process of turning votes into seats, the electoral system
works on two dimensions that have been identified in previous scholarship (Lijphart
1985; Shugart 2001; Colomer 2011): *interparty* and *intraparty*. Over many decades, the
greater bulk of work has been on the interparty dimension, and has been concerned
with how the electoral system shapes the number of parties, the likelihood of a majority party existing in the assembly, and the degree of correspondence between votes and
seats for individual parties (i.e., proportionality).

The effects of the electoral system on the interparty dimension are often seen as
most fundamental, because they have further effects on the nature of governance. For
instance, if the executive format of a democracy is parliamentary,[3] the electoral system
will shape the likelihood of a single-party majority government, coalition government,
or other more consensual governance involving cooperation among two or more parties (Lijphart 1999). This relationship occurs because it is unusual in most democracies
for one party to win a majority of the vote,[4] but the electoral system may boost one of
the largest parties' seats into a majority of the representative assembly. In presidential
systems, there are at least two national institutions with their own electoral systems
(three if there is an elected second chamber of the assembly), because there must also
be a set of rules for electing the president. Moreover, the electoral system for the assembly shapes the likelihood that the president will have a majority (or nearly so) for his
or her own party, face opposition control, or have to deal with a fragmented body in
attempting to pass legislation. Thus, electoral systems, and their effects on the interparty
dimension, are fundamental to the pattern of competition and governance the polity
will experience.

Electoral systems also shape the intraparty dimension, which refers to the extent to which candidates and representatives of the same party are in competition with one another, as well as with those of other parties. The intraparty dimension also includes features of the electoral system that give candidates more or less incentive to connect with constituents as individuals through a "personal vote." In fact, these aspects of the intraparty dimension are directly related: if copartisans must compete for votes, they are more likely to advertise what they can do for voters themselves, rather than emphasize primarily what the party can do.

Thus, the *Oxford Handbook of Electoral Systems* that you are reading explores why different sets of rules are selected, how they function, and what consequences they produce.

## Basic Rules: Plurality versus Proportional (but No Sharp Break)

To understand differences among sets of rules, the common tendency is to divide the world into two kinds of electoral systems: plurality (or "majoritarian") and proportional. This classic dichotomy remains useful for certain purposes. However, it can be misleading because, in fact, there is no sharp break between these basic categories, as we shall demonstrate in this section and the next. Where it remains most useful is on a basic question belonging to the interparty dimension: if we use one set of rules, are we likely to have a "two-party system," making majority-party government likely, or are we likely to have a "multiparty system," leading to coalition governance? A question of this sort sets up an implicit causal path:

$$\text{Electoral System} \rightarrow \text{Party System}$$

Even if we acknowledge that the political world is not this simple, and many other factors intervene, we at least need good measures of "electoral system" and "party system" to carry out the analysis. The "dependent variable" in this simple causal path, the party system, is often measured through a quantity called the "effective number of parties" ($N$). Shugart and Taagepera's chapter in this volume provides a detailed definition and discussion of $N$; a brief introduction to the concept will suffice here. The "effective" number is an index that summarizes the number and relative sizes of parties by weighting each party's share (of either votes or seats) by itself.[5] In this way, two equal-sized parties yield $N = 2.0$, three equal-sized parties yield $N = 3.0$, but three parties of unequal size would likely have a value of $N$ between 2.0 and 3.0.

The effective number is thus a quasi-continuous index that summarizes the competition among parties. While other measures may be useful for specific questions, the effective number of parties has become the standard since its first introduction by Laakso and Taagepera (1979). This way of measuring party system "size" thus gets us beyond the overly sharp break implied by the classic categories of "two-party system" and "multiparty system." In this volume, when the effective number is calculated on seat-winning parties, we will designate it $N_S$, and when it is calculated on vote-earning parties, $N_V$.[6]

The question of how to measure the "independent variable"—the electoral system—is far more complex, but again we should be cautious about breaking down electoral systems into two basic categories, as implied by the notion of "plurality versus proportional." Electoral systems come in numerous categories that go by various proper names. However, just as our party-system-dependent variable can start with blunt categories (two-party vs. multiparty) and then be reconceptualized through a scale (the effective number), so too can a key characteristic of electoral systems be put on a scale.

Often with electoral systems we are concerned with how "restrictive" or "permissive" they are, meaning the extent to which they inhibit or facilitate the representation of small parties. If this is our primary concern with electoral systems, the scale we recommend using is the *seat product*, which combines two key institutional variables into one: *district magnitude* and *assembly size*. The district magnitude is how many seats are allocated in a given electoral district, and we abbreviate it as $M$.[7] The assembly size is the total number of seats in a representative body (a national legislative chamber, a city council, etc.),[8] abbreviated $S$. Multiply them together and we have the seat product. Shugart and Taagepera's chapter in this volume shows that there is a clear deductive logic and strong empirical support for the Seat Product Model (SPM) of the effective number of parties:

$$N_S = (MS)^{1/6}$$

In words, the effective number of seat-winning parties tends to be, on average, the sixth root of the product of average district magnitude and assembly size.[9] The SPM formula calls our attention to the fact that there is not a sharp break between "plurality" and "proportional." In fact, a system using plurality ($M = 1$, because every district elects one member of the assembly) for 250 seats should tend to have approximately the same effective number of parties, on average, as a "proportional" system in which a 50-seat assembly is divided into ten districts. In the latter case, the average district magnitude is five (50/10), and the resulting seat product is 250 (5 × 50). In analyzing electoral systems and their impact on party systems, it is much more fruitful to develop scales than to use categories, because the scales allow us to make more precise quantitative predictions about likely effects.

Nonetheless, a desire for making predictions about the scale of effects of electoral systems on party systems does not obviate all advantages that might reside in dealing with categories. For one thing, the impact on the number and relative sizes of parties is far from the only outcome of interest. For another, finer details of the electoral system may have their own impact on the party system (and other outputs), either modifying or potentially overriding for a specific case something as broad and generalizable as the SPM. Thus, there will always be need for clear categories to define different features of electoral systems. One prominent dimension that is not clearly scalable, but rather is categorical, is the *allocation formula*.

## Allocation Formula

In describing an electoral system, as already noted, we need to go beyond the blunt categories of plurality and proportional. We focus this section initially on the simplest categories of systems, proportional representation (PR) in a single round of voting in which the voter makes a single "categorical" choice. This means an election in which there is no second vote held in the event the contest did not produce a decision in the first round; "simple" rules are decisive in one round, by definition. Moreover, a voter has no opportunity to rank-order his or her preferences across several candidates (or parties); the ballot is thus not "ordinal" but "categorical." We discuss these alternative possibilities further later, and the distinctions among ballot types are taken up in more detail in Gallagher and Mitchell's chapter.

A reader might wonder, what has happened to plurality? We started with "plurality versus proportional" and now we say we will focus on PR rules. Do not worry: plurality has not disappeared. It has been *subsumed*. Plurality is just a *special case of PR*; any simple "proportional" formula reduces to plurality when applied in a district of magnitude equal to one. This is why there is no sharp break between the common blunt categories of plurality and PR.

We start with an illustration of two common proportional allocation formulas: (1) *D'Hondt divisors* and (2) *Hare quota with largest remainders*. We take up D'Hondt first.[10] Take the hypothetical distribution of party vote percentages in Table 1.1. Under D'Hondt, every party's votes[11] are divided by a series of divisors, which are successive integers

**Table 1.1  Allocation by D'Hondt Divisors to Hypothetical Constellation of Parties**

| Divisor | Party A | Party B | Party C | Party D | Party E |
|---------|---------|---------|---------|---------|---------|
| 1 | 43 (1) | 20 (3) | 17 (4) | 13 (6) | 7 (12) |
| 2 | 21.5 (2) | 10 (8) | 8.5 (10) | 6.5 (14) | 3.5 |
| 3 | 14.3 (5) | 6.7 (13) | 5.67 | 4.3 | |
| 4 | 10.75 (7) | 5 | 4.25 | | |
| 5 | 8.6 (9) | 4.0 | | | |
| 6 | 7.17 (11) | | | | |
| 7 | 6.14 (15) | | | | |

The number in parentheses shows the order in which seats are assigned.

(1, 2, 3, 4 . . . ). The party with the largest quotient gets the first seat. Of course, in our example this is party A, as its votes have been divided by one, and hence remain unaltered. If this were a district of magnitude equal to one, we would be done! In other words, using the D'Hondt formula for proportional allocation when there is just one seat is precisely the same as using "plurality" (as long as the "list" has no more candidates than the district: one[12]).

Now, suppose there are two seats. Who gets the second one? In our example this would also be party A, because even after division by two, its quotient is greater than party B's initial votes. The process continues for however many seats are at stake. In the table, we indicate, with the numbers in parentheses, the quotients in order. From these numbers, we can see that if there were three seats, party A would have two and party B one. If there were five seats, party A would have three, and parties B and C would have one each. Party D does not get a seat unless the district magnitude is at least six, and only when magnitude reaches twelve does party E earn a seat, given the relative sizes of the parties in our example.

In Table 1.1 we include the counting of D'Hondt quotients out to fifteen, at which point we have seven seats earned by party A, three by party B, two each for C and D, and one for E. The fifteen-seat allocation means 46.7 percent for a party with 43 percent of the vote, and 6.7 percent of seats for party E (which has 7 percent of the vote); it is thus relatively "proportional" because the percentages of votes and seats are roughly equivalent for each party. However, the lower-magnitude outcomes can be quite disproportional; for instance, the largest party has at least half the seats for any magnitude smaller than eleven in this example. While the example is contrived, it demonstrates two key points: (1) D'Hondt, while a "proportional" allocation formula, tends to favor the largest party, and (2) as the district magnitude is reduced, the actual outcome becomes more "majoritarian" down to the limiting case of one seat, where it is identical to plurality (as indeed it was *in this example* even with two available seats).

Another common formula for proportional allocation is the Hare quota with largest remainders (also known as LR-Hare). First, we need to determine what the quota is by taking the votes and dividing them by the number of seats to be allocated. Because we are using percentages, we can think of a Hare (also called "simple") quota as being 100 percent/$M$. LR-Hare is demonstrated in Table 1.2, using the same hypothetical constellation of votes for five parties as we used in Table 1.1.

First, the procedure is to determine how many times the quota can be divided into each party's votes. The table shows examples of allocation at three different district magnitudes: one, three, and fifteen. The formula initially allocates a seat for each *quota's* worth of votes a party has, discarding any fractions (because seats come only in integers). Once we have this number for each party, we deduct the votes it has "spent" on whatever number of seats it has won thus far from its original votes, leaving each party with a *remainder*. If, as is usually the case, seats remain unfilled, we turn to the "largest remainders" stage of the allocation. At this stage, we sort the parties in descending order by their remainders and give each one a seat until all remaining seats are filled.

Table 1.2  Allocation by Hare Quota and Largest Remainders to Hypothetical
          Constellation of Parties

| Hare Quota For … | Party A | Party B | Party C | Party D | Party E | Seats Filled at Quota Stage | Seats to Be Filled at Remainder Stage |
|---|---|---|---|---|---|---|---|
| | 43 | 20 | 17 | 13 | 7 | | |
| **1 seat**: 100% | 0 | 0 | 0 | 0 | 0 | 0 | 1 |
| Remaining votes (seats) | 43 (1) | 0 | 0 | 0 | 0 | | |
| Total | 1 | 0 | 0 | 0 | 0 | | |
| **3 seats**: 33.3% | 1 | 0 | 0 | 0 | 0 | 1 | 2 |
| Remaining votes (seats) | 9.7 | 20 (1) | 17 (1) | 13 | 6 | | |
| Total | 1 | 1 | 1 | | | | |
| **15 seats**: 6.67% | 6 | 3 | 2 | 1 | 0 | 12 | 3 |
| Remaining votes (seats) | 3 | 0 | 3.7 (1) | 6.3 (1) | 7 (1) | | |
| Total | 6 | 3 | 3 | 2 | 1 | | |

The number, 1, in parentheses indicates a seat won by largest remainders.

If the magnitude is one ($M = 1$), what is the Hare quota? It is 100 percent of the votes. In any competitive election, clearly no party (or candidate) will obtain this quota. Thus, each party has a "remainder" equivalent to its original vote total. The largest party gets the one seat "remaining" to be filled. In other words, LR-Hare is plurality when $M = 1$.

In the three-seat example, we see that only party A has more than a quota's worth of votes, leaving two seats to be filled by remainders. The largest remainders belong to parties B and C. Thus, the three largest parties each get a seat. Notice how different this is from the application of D'Hondt to the same party votes in Table 1.1, where the largest party won two of the three seats. The allocation formula thus can make a material difference in the result. This is especially so when district magnitude is low—as long as it is not the lowest possible, given that with $M = 1$ either formula becomes plurality.

The third example in Table 1.2 is for $M = 15$. In this case, with a Hare quota of 6.67 percent of votes, twelve seats are allocated at the quota stage: six for party A, three for party B, two for party C, and one for party D. The three seats remaining after the quota stage go to parties C, D, and E. Both parties A and B used up too many votes on their quota seats to have enough left over for remainder seats. As a result, whereas D'Hondt awarded the largest party seven out of fifteen seats, LR-Hare awards it six.

The two allocation rules reviewed here are basic representations of two families of formula: *divisor rules* and *largest-remainder* rules. Within the family, the divisor sequence can be altered, for instance, to cut large parties' votes down faster and thereby open up earlier seat-winning possibilities to small parties. One way to achieve this outcome is to employ the so-called Ste.-Laguë divisors, which use the sequence 1, 3, 5, 7 . . . ; another sequence used in some Scandinavian countries is 1.4, 3, 5, 7 . . . ; this "modified Ste.-Laguë" formula shifts the balance slightly in favor of middle-sized parties.[13]

In the family of largest-remainder systems, smaller quotas can be used. Perhaps paradoxically, a smaller quota is more favorable to big parties. When the quota is smaller, fewer votes are used up in the quota allocation stage, making it more likely that larger parties have sufficient votes left over to participate in the stage of allocation via largest remainders. A prominent example is the Droop quota, defined as

$$Q = \left[ V / (M+1) \right] + 1,$$

where $Q$ is the quota, $V$ is the total number of votes, and $M$ is the magnitude of the district. Because we use shares for shorthand, we can replace V with 1. The formula may look odd, but it directly reduces to the definition of majority (or "absolute majority") when $M = 1$: it yields half the votes, plus one vote. Thus, it ensures that there could not be two parties with sufficient votes for our one seat, thus resulting in overallocation.[14] If we did not add the +1 at the end of the preceding formula, we would get 50 percent, which, of course, two parties (or candidates) could have. This is a general feature of the Droop quota: it prevents more than $M$ winners from having a quota's worth of votes.

If Droop were applied to the example in Table 1.2, the quota for three seats would be 25 percent[15] and the quota for fifteen seats would be 6.25 percent. If we were to follow the procedure through, we would find that Droop and largest remainders (LR-Droop) for this example would yield the same outcome as D'Hondt. This is often the case, but is not a general rule. The general rule is that the largest party will tend to use up fewer votes on quota seats compared to when a Hare quota is used, and hence is more likely to participate in the remainder stage, which is indeed the case with our example. In his chapter in this volume, Carey refers to remainder seats under Hare as being bought "wholesale," whereas quota seats are purchased at "retail" price. He offers several examples of how the use of LR-Hare versus D'Hondt (or other systems) can be consequential, with focus on newer democracies, where seemingly small differences can be especially critical to the development of democracy.

In this section we have seen that there are various "proportional" allocation formulas. They can be consequential for just how seats are divided up among parties when $M > 1$, that is, when a district elects more than one seat. However, when they are used in districts electing just one seat, they all give the vote to the party with the most votes. In other words, there is no sharp break between proportional and plurality. A system in which one seat is at stake and is allocated to whoever gets the highest votes (in one round of casting categorical ballots) is just a PR formula applied to the smallest possible district magnitude.[16]

# ELECTORAL SYSTEMS TERMINOLOGY

Both the academic literature and popular commentary on electoral systems are littered with conflicting and sometimes confusing terms. Acronyms proliferate. For this reason, no introduction to the topic of electoral systems would be complete without some guide through the thickets, and an effort to provide a path forward that is clearer about terms and what they mean. We are not under illusions that we will proffer the last word on the topic. Nor have we imposed a single standard on our contributors, although it is possible that some of them may feel that we were unusually authoritarian in editing chapters that are (mostly) about democratic rules.

## What to Call a Common Electoral System That Features Plurality Rule

We can start with the common Anglo-American electoral system because it demonstrates so many of the problems with terminology. We saw in the last section how any common "proportional" formula becomes "plurality" when applied to the election of a single winner. In this section, we are interested in a different question: What do we term a system in which an entire assembly is characterized by employing the rule that the candidate with the most votes wins the seat in each of several districts, one per assembly member? If this is not a straightforward question, what in the field of electoral systems could be?

Yet, the system in question goes by various common proper names, including single-member plurality, first past the post (FPTP), and relative majority. Each name has problems. In this volume, we have a preference for "FPTP," but some contributors have objections to the term, and the objections are sensible enough. For one, why should a common example of our topic area be defined by a phrase that comes from horse-racing? That is, after all, what the term conjures up: which horse got to the finishing post first? Some students of electoral systems object on the basis that the "post" is not even fixed when the rule is "most votes wins," because one can win 50.1 percent to 49.9 percent or, just as well, 30 percent to 20 percent (with various smaller parties divvying up the rest). The second example is a bigger margin, for sure, but that a candidate can win with a smaller absolute vote percentage in one field of competition than in another illustrates the nonfixed nature of the "post"; you need only the most, and what this share needs to be depends on the rest of the competition.

Then why use the term "FPTP" at all? One reason is that it is well established and understood. We should acknowledge that this, by itself, might not be a good reason. Just because journalists and the general public use it does not mean we, as scientists, have to follow along. After all, in few sciences are the terms used in analysis the same as those used by the public. If you get a minor but irritating respiratory condition, the medical professionals might say it is pharyngitis. But most of us would just say we have a cold. Nonetheless, we political scientists are probably more likely to be accused of obscuring common things by fancy jargon than of failing to be precise. There is little, if anything, about the term "FPTP" that is nonprecise. It works. However, maybe other terms are better.

Scientifically, the way to approach the problem should be to designate a system by its critical components. We should aim to get away from thick description—what Taagepera (2007, 9) referred to as our equivalent of zoology—and aim instead for the precision of molecular biology. None of the various terms in common use for the electoral system in question, even among political scientists, meets this standard. *Single-member plurality*, often abbreviated SMP, comes close to this "molecular" standard but fails to serve well in other respects, to which we turn now.

The term "plurality" is fairly precise as a designator for the largest share (not necessarily a majority, in the sense of more than half).[17] The objection to "SMP" starts with the middle word in the term, "member." It is reasonable to think of membership in a collective body, such as a legislature or a political party. In this sense, "member," per se, is not an objectionable term. However, the designation here refers to the *district magnitude*—the number of seats per district, which is one. Electoral formulas (here, plurality) convert votes into seats, whatever number might be elected in the district. Those who win the seats gain membership in the assembly and, usually, a given party caucus. The rules do not allocate *members*, per se. Therefore, we prefer to speak of districts by the number of *seats*, and the term "single-seat district" is much more straightforward than single-member district.

There is a second, more pragmatic, reason for favoring "seat" over "member" in this context. If a district elects more than one seat, it is often called a multimember district. This invites use of the acronym "MMD," just as the single-member district is often called SMD. Yet we also have a common acronym designating an electoral system in which there are overlapping components (or "tiers") of districts, with one component consisting of all single-seat districts and the other being one or more multiseat districts. Depending on the precise relationship used to connect these overlapping components (see Gallagher and Mitchell's chapter), the system in question might be called mixed-member proportional, abbreviated MMP. Here, the middle term, "member," has a logic to it. The system's full proper name signifies that the *members* of the assembly are elected under a *mix*[18] of rules (and further, in this case, that the overall rule is to achieve some degree of proportionality).

A prominent case of MMP is New Zealand, which adopted the system only in the mid-1990s after decades of using the common Anglo-American system—yes, the very system that some folks like to call SMP. So New Zealand changed from SMP to MMP. If our names and acronyms are to be part of any logical systematic nomenclature—which we believe is essential for both clarity and scientific precision—then logically, this would imply that New Zealand changed one thing: "S" to "M" in its otherwise "MP" system. Of course, it did nothing of the sort, because the "P" means different things in these acronyms too. Yet, we have heard political scientists—even specialists in this field—accidentally refer to MMP as "multimember proportional" (as though there were any other kind). This is precisely the problem: when New Zealand changed its system to introduce overall proportionality as a goal, it needed to adopt one or more multiseat districts. Or, as most would say, it adopted multimember districts, also known as MMDs. In other words (or other acronyms), it needed MMDs to implement MMP as a change from SMP, which had only SMDs. Sometimes that first "M" means member; sometimes it means multi.[19] These inconsistencies generate confusion, as we have witnessed first-hand at conferences, as well as in the classroom.

For the reasons just articulated, one of us codrafted an appendix to a book (Shugart and Wattenberg 2001) that advocated for referring to district magnitude categories as single-seat districts and multiseat districts (instead of "-member"), which in acronym terms (if we must) would be, respectively, SSD and MSD. More than fifteen years later, these alternatives have not caught on, but we keep trying. For the most part, throughout the chapters of this volume, these will be the terms used.

If it were entirely up to us, we would go further. The idea of a dichotomous division of the world of electoral systems into those in which districts have one seat and those in which districts have two or more seats is often a hindrance to serious analysis. An electoral system in which all districts elect two or three seats has much more in common with one that has all single-seat districts than it has with the Netherlands, where there is one district electing all 150 members in one chamber of parliament. Yet the conventional dichotomy places the two-seat and three-seat systems in the same box with the Netherlands as systems using multiseat (multimember) districts. Nonetheless, the distinction of one versus many is useful for some purposes, and to a degree we will employ such a division in organizing some of the chapters of this volume (as explained later). We simply ask that scholars, advocates, and others use this dichotomy sparingly and carefully.

A common careless use of the common "SMD" acronym is to treat it as if it refers to an electoral system when in fact it tells us only the district magnitude (one). Thus, someone perusing the electoral systems literature might read that some body (or tier) is elected via an "SMD system." But there is no such *system*. There are several systems that use single-"member" districts, but using different *rules* to determine the one winner. Examples include plurality, two-round majority, alternative vote, and various others; in this volume there are chapters representing several countries using these different SMD or—as we prefer—SSD *systems*. If one is talking about district magnitude and finds "$M = 1$ districts" clumsy (though it certainly is precise), one might use "SSD"; but if one wants to define an electoral system, one needs a more precise term.

The need for precision takes us back to the use of the term "FPTP" and its alternatives. We have stated why we object to both "single-member plurality" and "SMP," but why use

"FPTP" instead? The answer might start with another question: what are the alternatives? We could advocate single-seat district plurality, which would be SSDP. Or it could be "SSP" for single-seat plurality. But the last thing we need in this literature is another acronym! Thus, we refrain from advocating it, even though if we were starting with a clean slate, this might just be our preference.

If we want an encapsulating term to designate a system in which every member is elected by plurality in a unique district, the term "FPTP" is well understood and designates just those features that we are interested in identifying. It thus is probably the worst of all possible names for this electoral system, aside from all the others that have been tried from time to time. As Shugart and Taagepera (2017, 33) point out, it is a neutral term between proportional and plurality. Because most PR formulas reduce to plurality when applied in a single-seat district, it is useful to avoid drawing a sharp distinction. A large-assembly FPTP system can be quite "permissive" to small parties,[20] more so than many "PR" systems that use relatively small district magnitudes and assembly sizes (and perhaps also a further restrictive rule, such as a legal threshold). The most restrictive systems are not actually those using FPTP to elect a fairly large assembly, but rather the election of a single "member" nationwide, such as presidential elections. More restrictive still would be the election of an entire assembly by plurality in one district (which no country has ever done, to our knowledge). The term "FPTP" thus reminds us that it is not either plurality or proportional on a systemic basis, but simply the application of the same rule that defines PR (the first seat in a district goes to the largest party) within districts of the minimum possible magnitude (single-seat districts, or SSDs).

## Terminology beyond "PR" and "FPTP"

In the previous section we suggested that "FPTP" was not ideal but nonetheless preferred for the common system of single-seat districts (SSDs) in which the candidate with the most votes (plurality) wins in any given district. A wider preference would be to avoid proper names (and their inevitable acronyms) altogether, but we recognize this would be a drastic solution with no chance of catching on. Political scientists and electoral system advocates are a bit like animal watchers: we enjoy the zoo with all its many distinct species on display.

What, then, about proper names and acronyms for other systems? We already have discussed mixed-member proportional (MMP) in the context of discussing FPTP: under MMP, one "tier" of seats is typically elected in SSDs by plurality, whereas another exists for the purpose of bringing the overall membership of the assembly into proportionality with party votes. See this volume's chapter on New Zealand by Vowles or the one on Germany by Zittel for illustrations of MMP.[21] In this section, we turn our attention to names and acronyms beyond PR and FPTP.

Most PR systems allocate seats to party lists, but this leaves out the question of what kind of list is used, a question that sits squarely on the intraparty dimension of electoral systems. It also leaves out the possibility of PR without lists per se. The first set of questions—list type—concerns how the candidates are elected from the list submitted by the party. The main types are *closed lists* and *open lists*, although intermediate types are common. These main types are sometimes abbreviated as CLPR and OLPR, respectively. When lists are closed, voters have no opportunity to favor one or more candidates over others. They simply endorse the list as a whole, and any seats the party wins are filled in the priority order established by the party before the election. For an example of such a system in context, see the chapter on Israel by Hazan, Malka, and Rahat or the chapter on South Africa by Ferree.

When lists are open, voters may (or must, depending on specific rules) vote for one or more individual candidates. Seats are still allocated to the lists according to their collective vote totals (as under CLPR), but the candidates elected from a list are ordered according to the total votes they have obtained as individuals ("preference votes"). If the system is genuinely OLPR, candidate preference votes are the sole criterion for determining candidates' order of election from their lists. OLPR systems are discussed in the chapters in this volume on Finland (by von Schoultz), Indonesia (by Allen), and Colombia (by Taylor and Shugart[22]). Other list PR systems allow (or require) preference votes to be cast, but mix in both these votes and a pre-election priority order when determining final order of election. While these can be grouped with open lists under a category of "preferential list" (Shugart 2008), they should not be conflated with OLPR systems. The latter term should be reserved for those systems in which preference votes alone set the final list order. Systems that use intermediate or mixed criteria to order lists are often referred to as "flexible" or "semiopen" lists.

There is one common nonlist form of PR: *single transferable vote*, abbreviated STV. Under this system, voters give ranked preferences to individual candidates. Because many parties tend to nominate more than one candidate per multiseat district, candidates of the same party are competing for ranked preferences. Thus, the concerns of the intraparty dimension are prominent here, as candidates look for ways to appeal to voters as more than simply a party representative. The way STV allocates seats is as follows. Candidates who obtain a stipulated quota (typically the aforementioned Droop quota) of first-preference votes are elected, but if there are fewer such candidates than the district magnitude—as there often are—then second and lower-ranked preferences for the individual candidates are taken into account. Any candidate with more votes than the quota has some of his or her votes "transferred" to the candidate listed second on the ballots whose voters marked him or her first. These transferred "surplus" votes may put some other candidate over the quota, leading to another seat being filled. If still more remain to be filled, then the weakest candidate is eliminated, and votes are transferred based, again, on the indicated second preferences.[23] The process of sequential elimination continues until all seats are filled (or ballots are "exhausted," meaning no more preferences for noneliminated candidates remain, in which case the top vote earners get the remaining seats). For a discussion of STV in context, see the chapter in this volume by Marsh on Ireland.

It should be noted that STV can be used in a single-seat district (including for a single office, such as a president, governor, or mayor). When it is used in this way, the Droop quota for election would be majority, and if no one has obtained this quota in first preferences, the weakest is eliminated and that candidate's votes are transferred to second preferences. The process continues until some candidate hits the quota (or all ballots are exhausted). When STV is used with single-seat districts, it is usually not called "STV" but rather "alternative vote" or "instant runoff." However, it is the same allocation procedure, just a different name. Thus, we see again a reason that it would be best to shy away from overuse of unique proper names and from dichotomizing the world into systems of single-seat districts and those of multiseat districts. The allocation rule, STV, can be applied in any district magnitude, but when the magnitude is one, we usually call it something else.

If there are transferable votes, there must also be *nontransferable* votes. Indeed, recognizing such a possibility takes us down a path to yet another section of the electoral system zoo. A vote is nontransferable when it stays only with the candidate for whom it is cast, and neither "pools" to others of the same party (as in a list system) nor can be transferred (as under STV).[24] This "NTV" class of formulas refers to those employed generally in multiseat districts, with a ballot that does not permit the voter to rank-order, although if the specific rules allow the voter to cast multiple votes, they need not be for candidates of the same party.[25]

The best-known variant of this set of rules actually provides each voter with only one vote, and is known as the *single nontransferable vote*, or SNTV. It was formerly used in Japan, and is discussed in the chapter in this volume by Nemoto. While generally treated as a class all its own, SNTV is actually a direct generalization of LR-Hare. As we noted in the preceding section, when no party obtains sufficient votes for a quota,[26] the $M$ seats would go to the $M$ parties with the highest vote totals (i.e., the largest remainders). If we replace "party" with "candidate," we have SNTV: each voter gets one vote, and the $M$ candidates with the highest votes win. It is this feature that has led some LR-Hare systems to function almost precisely as if they were SNTV, where parties or "camps" present multiple lists, none of which tends to win sufficient votes for more than one seat. This pattern can be observed in Hong Kong (see Carey's chapter) and formerly in Colombia (see the chapter by Taylor and Shugart).

When SNTV generalizes to cases in which the voter may cast more than one vote, it sensibly should be called *multiple nontransferable votes* (MNTV). However, such systems go by a plethora of other names; we will leave aside this detail here (see Shugart and Taagepera 2017), other than to mention one relatively common variant. If the voter has $M$ votes and the top $M$ vote earners get the seats, it is commonly called "block vote." The name is misleading, however, inasmuch as the votes need not be cast "in block," that is, with all the voters' available votes cast for candidates of the same party. The voter may split across parties, vote for independents,[27] or partially abstain. Thus, MNTV is a more descriptive term, as well as one that identifies it as a member of the same family as SNTV—the family in which voters may vote for some (stipulated maximum) number of candidates and the top $M$ candidates win. Systems that can be considered MNTV are common at the local level in Canada, the United States, and the United Kingdom (as the chapters on those countries in this volume discuss), and are found in a few national elections.[28] What if nontransferable votes are used when there is only one seat? Assuming the voter has $M$ votes, this is plurality! Thus, once again, we see an entire family of systems that encompasses the single-seat variant commonly known as FPTP as one end of a continuum rather than as a distinct category.

Clarifying electoral systems terminology is another task that the *Oxford Handbook of Electoral Systems* is designed to address. De-emphasizing dichotomies and focusing instead on the fundamental features that link electoral systems together allows the development of a streamlined lexicon that renders discussions in our branch of science more precise.

# A GUIDE TO THE HANDBOOK

This volume features forty-four chapters (including this introduction) covering fundamental theoretical issues, methodological challenges, and practical applications in the electoral systems literature. It builds upon the rich history of electoral studies to familiarize readers with core issues that scholars have investigated for decades and also points to the promising future for learning more about how electoral systems function. The remaining chapters are organized into eight parts that reflect key thematic topics within the wider subject area.

The chapters in part I cover the foundations of electoral systems. Michael Gallagher and Paul Mitchell (chapter 2) delve further than this chapter has into variation in electoral system families, providing a key typology and set of definitions that should interest both novice and expert psephologists. The importance of institutions in determining critical outcomes, such as the number of political parties and disproportionality, forms the core of Matthew S. Shugart and Rein Taagepera's chapter (chapter 3); they demonstrate how the seat product (district magnitude times assembly size) is fundamental to predicting the shape of party systems. Josep M. Colomer (chapter 4) provides a counterpoint, arguing that political forces determine the contours of electoral systems in an endogenous process. Together, these chapters provide a theoretical road map, building upon the established framework of electoral studies. John M. Carey (Chapter 5) evaluates electoral system choice as societies transition from autocracy to democracy and subsequently mature as democratic systems, and provides several brief case studies of choices of rules that had important consequences for the subsequent functioning of a new democracy. Alan Renwick's chapter (chapter 6) extends this discussion, investigating four core issues in the design and redesign of electoral institutions with a focus primarily on more established democracies.

Chapters in part II investigate the effects of electoral systems on representation of social groups. A key consideration is the interplay of the electoral system and underlying patterns of social diversity, highlighted by Robert G. Moser, Ethan Scheiner, and

Heather Stoll (chapter 7). David Lublin and Shaun Bowler (chapter 8) take up the closely related theme of how electoral systems affect the representation of ethnic minority groups, while Mona Lena Krook (chapter 9) focuses on implications for the representation of women. Electoral systems also influence voter turnout (Daniel M. Smith, chapter 10) and the fit between ideological positions of citizens and elites (Matt Golder and Benjamin Ferland, chapter 11), as well as the polarization of political parties on issues (James F. Adams and Nathan J. Rexford, chapter 12).

Part III consists of several chapters that explore the ways in which the electoral system interacts with the wider political system. Here we find chapters on portfolio maximization in parliamentary elections (Gary W. Cox, chapter 13) and on presidential elections and their impact on the legislature (Mark P. Jones, chapter 14). Then we have three chapters that concern ways in which the electoral system shapes legislative bodies and the activities of legislators themselves; each of these includes a significant focus on the intra-party dimension: legislative organization (Shane Martin, chapter 15), legislator roles (Audrey André and Sam Depauw, chapter 16), and constituency service (Brian F. Crisp and William M. Simoneau, chapter 17). While electoral systems are generally mechanisms for selecting representatives in democracy, elections can also be mechanisms for direct democracy, as Matt Qvortrup (chapter 18) explains, and are employed in many countries in which the wider political system is nondemocratic, as covered by Jennifer Gandhi and Abigail L. Heller (chapter 19).

Chapters in part IV explore several aspects of research design, illustrating how the complexities of election data may be harnessed to generate new findings (Ken Kollman, chapter 20), discussing how experimental methods may be incorporated into electoral studies (Joshua A. Tucker and Dominik Duell, chapter 21), and adjudicating disputes about the ways in which scholars analyze mixed-member electoral systems (Erik S. Herron, Kuniaki Nemoto, and Misa Nishikawa, chapter 22).

Part V focuses on several aspects of the process of holding elections, including election administration (Thad E. Hall, chapter 23), the integrity of the process (Pippa Norris, chapter 24), redistricting (Lisa Handley, chapter 25), and campaign finance (Joel W. Johnson, chapter 26).

In addition to evaluating core issues in the study of electoral systems, the volume provides illustrative applications in countries all over the world. The purpose of these chapters is to represent the range of electoral system diversity, although we also have aimed for a sample that is reasonably representative of geographic and cultural backgrounds. We have grouped these case studies into three additional parts that make up the remainder of the volume.

In the first of these sections, part VI, the case studies focus on countries that have used essentially unchanged sets of electoral rules for the first chamber (lower house) of their assemblies for several decades. These chapters are sorted in order by their seat products ($MS$, as introduced earlier in this chapter), starting with the largest and working down to the smallest—with one exception, to be explained. We order them in this way because of the centrality of $MS$ to shaping the effective number of seat-winning parties. But, of course, individual countries may deviate from their $MS$-derived expectation; that is, after all, precisely the reason for having chapters that explain electoral systems *in context*. We start from our highest *MS* examples because these are in a crucial respect the simplest of all: they take the votes across the entire country and employ a proportional seat allocation formula. In these countries, there is no districting or regionalization of party support to consider, because the entire assembly is elected in one large nationwide district. These countries are the flexible-list PR case of the Netherlands (Kristof Jacobs, chapter 27) and the closed-list PR case of Israel (Reuven Y. Hazan, Reut Itzkovich-Malka, and Gideon Rahat, chapter 28).

All of the remaining cases in part VI employ districts in one way or another. Our largest seat product of any districted system is the open-list PR case of Finland (Åsa von Schoultz, chapter 29). We next present the largest assembly employing exclusively SSDs for its elected national parliament, the United Kingdom (Thomas Carl Lundberg, chapter 30), followed by another PR country that employs relatively low-magnitude districts, Ireland (Michael Marsh, chapter 31). These two countries have approximately the same seat product, thereby reminding us that there is no sharp break between FPTP and PR.

We proceed to five other countries that use exclusively SSDs for their main national assembly chamber: France (Verónica Hoyo, chapter 32); India (Adam Ziegfeld, chapter 33); the United States (Steven L. Taylor, chapter 34); Canada (Louis Massicotte, chapter 35); and the country with the smallest *MS* in our set, Australia (Ian McAllister and Toni Makkai, chapter 36). These countries represent different allocation formulas despite the use of SSDs—a reminder that there is no such thing as an SSD (SMD) system per se: France with two-round majority-plurality and Australia with the alternative vote (with FPTP in the other three countries). Finally, we conclude the countries of part VI with a democracy that has used throughout the post–World War II period a hybrid with SSDs in one tier and PR in the other, the MMP system of Germany (Thomas Zittel, chapter 37). Several of the countries covered in part VI use different systems either for other national offices (e.g., a PR system in the Australian Senate) or for subnational assemblies (e.g., MMP in Scotland and Wales within the United Kingdom; MNTV in various bodies in the United States and United Kingdom; various list systems in France), and thus, where appropriate, these chapters also address intracountry variation.

In part VII, we turn our attention to established democracies that have carried out major electoral reforms, serving as context-rich case studies of the topic of Renwick's chapter in part I. These chapters cover the move from FPTP to MMP in New Zealand (Jack Vowles, chapter 38), SNTV to MMM in Japan (Kuniaki Nemoto, chapter 39), open-list PR to a form of MMM and then a majority-bonus PR system in Italy (Gianluca Passarelli, chapter 40), and an LR-Hare system (that, as discussed earlier, worked like SNTV) to D'Hondt list PR in Colombia (Steven L Taylor and Matthew S. Shugart, chapter 41).

In part VIII, we have several chapters on electoral system choice and functioning in new democracies, serving as context-rich case studies of the topic of Carey's chapter in part I. These chapters cover Ukraine (Erik S. Herron, chapter 42), a large formerly Communist country that has gone from two rounds in SSDs to MMM to the largest-ever assembly to be elected by nationwide PR and back to MMM; Indonesia (Nathan Allen, chapter 43), the largest mainly Muslim democracy and a case study of the adoption of open-list PR; and South Africa (Karen E. Ferree, chapter 44), where one of the most extremely proportional systems ever in use demonstrates, perhaps better than any other case could, the importance of context when assessing the performance of an electoral system.

The *Oxford Handbook of Electoral Systems* surely will not be the final word in the study of electoral systems and their effects. Our hope is that the volume sparks ongoing conversations about how we can advance knowledge in a more comprehensive and precise manner on a topic situated in the core of the political science discipline.

## Notes

1. We say "assembly" rather than "legislature" because the latter refers to a role beyond the scope of the electoral system. That is, the electoral system allocates seats in a collective body whose members assemble for various tasks. Lawmaking is only one of those tasks, and in some systems it may be a subordinate or even nonexistent one. For instance, many nondemocratic political systems have assemblies that are elected, albeit with restrictions on effective choice (see the chapter by Gandhi and Heller), but the members of these bodies devote little or none of their time to actual legislating.
2. The volume covers several topics about the relationship of the electoral system to broader electoral laws, for example, the chapters by Johnson, Norris, and Smith.
3. By "parliamentary," we mean that the head of the government (prime minister) and cabinet are dependent on the assembly majority, and no elected president (or one with no significant powers) is present.
4. Among the few large democracies where an electoral majority is common are South Africa (see Ferree's chapter in this volume) and the United States (see Taylor's chapter). For a comparative analysis of the frequency of majority parties, see Li (2017).
5. The formula is $N = 1 / \Sigma \left( p_i \right)^2$, where $p_i$ is the $i$th party's share (of either votes or seats) and the summation is over all $i$ parties in the system.
6. Contributors may occasionally use other terms, such as effective number of "parliamentary" or "electoral" parties. We have asked all contributors to eschew the acronyms "ENPP" and "ENEP" on the grounds that acronyms have proliferated too much in this literature and that systematic scientific notation such as $N$ with an appropriate subscript is more elegant.
7. By "district," we mean geographically bounded areas in which votes are cast and, through the application of the electoral rules, seats are allocated. In individual countries other terms may be used, such as constituency, electorate, or riding. There may be one district for the entire country (as in Israel and the Netherlands), or every member of the representative assembly may be from a unique district, each of which has one seat.
8. Prior to Taagepera (2007) most works neglected assembly size as a key feature of the electoral system. A prominent exception is Lijphart (1994).
9. For two-tier systems (see the chapter by Gallagher and Mitchell for definition), there is an extended version of the SPM, which is shown in the chapter by Shugart and Taagepera.
10. Many works spell the formula "d'Hondt"; however, the Belgian mathematician after whom it is named was Viktor D'Hondt, and thus the capitalized "D" is the correct version (see Gallagher and Mitchell 2008, 632).

11. In actual applications, the raw votes would be used. We speak of vote percentages solely because it makes illustration more convenient.

12. Usually in party-list PR, lists can have no more candidates than the district magnitude. However, there are PR systems that allow a greater number.

13. One can also go the other way: Imperiali divisors have the sequence 1, 1.5, 2, 2.5, and thus are more favorable to the largest party. This (rarely used) sequence thus favors the largest party; it should not be confused with Imperiali *quota* (see Passarelli's chapter).

14. If, with one seat, no candidate earns the absolute majority of votes, we turn to largest remainders. Hence, once again, we have plurality if Droop quota and largest remainders is applied to $M = 1$.

15. Technically, the quota would be 25 percent, plus one vote. We ignore the "plus one" for simplicity. There is also a quota called Hagenbach-Bischoff that does not have the "plus one"; in practice, the results are almost always the same.

16. What happens if we approach the question from the other direction, and generalize plurality allocation to districts electing more than one seat? We get a system in which *all* seats go to the largest party. The most prominent application of such a rule is at the state level in the US Electoral College. For instance, California allocates more than fifty "electors" to the candidate with the most votes, regardless of how close the contest is or how many significant competitors there may be. This is the ultimate "restrictive" system, for any given district magnitude. Thus, while PR becomes equivalent to "plurality" when magnitude is reduced to its lowest possible value, plurality defined as "winner takes all" remains plurality at any magnitude.

17. Nonetheless, "plurality" can also mean "many," as in "a plurality of different names for the same old electoral system." We agree with Fowler (1965) that largest share should be "plurity" (which is also easier to say); however, the word is not in common use and might therefore confuse more than it would enlighten.

18. We prefer "mixed-member" over the oft-used "mixed" as the latter might refer to any number of ways of mixing different rules. On the other hand, a mixed-member system is one with two overlapping components, each using a different principle of representation (usually plurality and proportional). There are other types of "mixed-member" systems aside from MMP. See the chapters in this volume by Gallagher and Mitchell and by Herron, Nemoto, and Nishikawa for details.

19. Moreover, by itself, $M$ means magnitude, as in $M = 1$ for "SMD" and $M > 1$ for "MMD" and a mix of members elected under both for MMP.

20. See this volume's chapters on India (by Ziegfeld) and the United Kingdom (by Lundberg).

21. There is hardly a general statement about electoral system types that does not come with a caveat, and the one about overall proportionality of MMP is no exception. Instead of calculating the overall seats for parties on a nationwide basis, it is possible for an MMP system to do so in a series of regions. This approach tends to result in a less proportional allocation. An example is the electoral system for the Scottish Parliament (see Lundberg's chapter on the United Kingdom).

22. In Colombia, parties have the option of presenting either closed or open lists, as Taylor and Shugart explain.

23. The third preference comes into effect only if the candidate marked as second preference is already elected or eliminated, and so on.

24. The distinction between pooling and transferring votes is from Cox (1997, 41–42).

25. In the sense of allowing the voter to divide his or her vote across two or more parties, the vote is *dividual* in the terminology laid out in the chapter by Gallagher and Mitchell.

26. Or more precisely for the sake of our example, some may obtain the votes for a quota but not also for a remainder (hence qualifying for only one seat).
27. All NTV systems, as well as STV, may be applied in elections without parties. List systems, on the other hand (except when $M = 1$), require that there be parties—or at least groups that band together to present lists of candidates—and thus are de facto parties whether or not they call themselves such.
28. For example, MNTV has been used for the National Assembly of Mauritius and for Senate elections in the Philippines.

## REFERENCES

Colomer, Josep M., ed. *Personal Representation: The Neglected Dimension of Electoral Systems.* Essex: ECPR Press, 2011.

Cox, Gary W. *Making Votes Count: Strategic Coordination in the World's Electoral Systems.* New York: Cambridge University Press, 1997.

Fowler, H. W. *Fowler's Modern English Usage.* Revised and edited by Sir Ernest Gowers. Oxford: Oxford University Press, 1965.

Gallagher, Michael, and Mitchell, Paul, eds. *The Politics of Electoral Systems.* Oxford: Oxford University Press, 2008.

Laakso, Markku, and Taagepera, Rein. "'Effective' Number of Parties: A Measure with Application to Western Europe." *Comparative Political Studies* 12, no. 1 (1979): 3–27.

Li, Yuhui. "Electoral System Effects Re-Examined Using the Largest Vote Share Variable." *Democratization* (2017).

Lijphart, Arend. "The field of electoral systems research: A critical survey", *Electoral Studies* 4, no. 1 (1985): 3–14.

Lijphart, Arend. *Electoral Systems and Party Systems: A Study of Twenty-Seven Democracies, 1945–1990.* Oxford: Oxford University Press, 1994.

Lijphart, Arend. 1999, *Patterns of Democracy: Government Forms and Performance in Thirty-Six Democracies.* New Haven, CT: Yale University Press.

Riker, William. "The Two-Party System and Duverger's Law: An Essay on the History of Political Science." *American Journal of Political Science* 76, no. 4 (1982): 753–766.

Shugart, Matthew S. "'Extreme' Electoral Systems and the Appeal of the Mixed-Member Alternative." In *Mixed-Member Electoral Systems: The Best of Both Worlds?*, edited by Matthew Soberg Shugart and Martin P. Wattenberg. Oxford: Oxford University Press, 2001.

Shugart, Matthew S. "Comparative Electoral Systems Research: The Maturation of a Field and New Challenges Ahead." In *The Politics of Electoral Systems*, edited by Michael Gallagher and Paul Mitchell. Oxford: Oxford University Press, 2008.

Shugart, Matthew S., and Rein Taagepera. *Votes from Seats: Logical Models of Electoral Systems.* Cambridge: Cambridge University Press, 2017.

Shugart, Matthew S., and Martin P. Wattenberg. *Mixed-Member Electoral Systems: The Best of Both Worlds?* Oxford: Oxford University Press, 2001.

Taagepera, Rein. *Predicting Party Sizes: The Logic of Simple Electoral Systems.* Oxford: Oxford University Press, 2007.

# PART I

# FOUNDATIONS OF ELECTORAL SYSTEMS

CHAPTER 2

..............................................................................................

# DIMENSIONS OF VARIATION IN ELECTORAL SYSTEMS

..............................................................................................

## MICHAEL GALLAGHER AND PAUL MITCHELL

ELECTORAL systems matter. They are a crucial link in the chain connecting the preferences of citizens to the policy choices made by governments. They are chosen by political actors and, once in existence, have political consequences for those actors. In all but the smallest-scale societies, government is representative government, in which the people do not govern themselves directly but rather delegate the task of political decision making to a smaller set of public officials. In democratic societies these representatives are elected, and it is the question of how they are elected that is of principal interest. In particular, we wish to explore variations in these methods of election, and to try to ascertain whether, and in what ways, it makes a difference how they are elected. The method of election is, quite obviously, a crucial link in the chain of representative democracy.

First, we need to start with a definition. By an "electoral system" we mean the set of rules that structure how votes are cast at elections for a representative assembly or for a single office such as a president, and how these votes are then converted into seats (or the one seat, if a presidency). This chapter will focus on rules for elections to assemblies—parliaments, councils, and so forth. Given a set of votes, an electoral system determines the composition of the assembly. The electoral system is narrower than what we term the "electoral regulations," by which we mean the wider set of rules concerning elections. Such rules—concerning, for example, ease of access to the ballot for would-be candidates, the right to vote, the fairness of the administration of the election, and the transparency of the counting of the votes—are all very important in determining the significance and legitimacy of an election. However, they should not be confused with the more narrowly defined concept of the electoral system itself.

Sceptical readers faced with large books on electoral systems thus defined might wonder whether it really matters so much which electoral system a country adopts. Why should anyone care whether a country opts for the D'Hondt or the Sainte-Laguë method of allocating seats?[1] What difference does it make if the weight of preference votes is increased or decreased? Anecdotal evidence suggests that many practicing politicians do, indeed, frequently react with bored indifference to what they see as trivial technicalities, which can be left to the anoraks in the back room to sort out while they decide the really important questions. Ordinary citizens too might wonder whether they need to know much about electoral systems. The choices might seem obscure, the terminology arcane, the issues at stake unclear. Does it really matter?

Needless to say, we believe these questions do matter. Moreover, even a little bit of reflection should be enough to convince anyone that electoral systems can make a difference. Even those who don't feel they need to understand the distinction between highest averages and largest remainders methods of seat allocation realize that there is a big difference between single-seat district systems (such as "first past the post," often called FPTP) and proportional representation systems. That is one choice that very few politicians would be willing to leave to someone else to decide.

To illustrate this, consider the history of British government since the late 1970s. Throughout the 1980s, the Conservative Party under Margaret Thatcher enjoyed huge parliamentary majorities and implemented a series of radical right-wing changes to economic and social policy. In 1997 and 2001, the Labour Party under Tony Blair achieved equally large majorities in the House of Commons.[2] Yet, each of these majority governments was elected on 41 to 43 percent of the votes. If Britain had a proportional representation (PR) system then, even if there was no change to the way votes were cast, the pattern of government would have been very different. In 2001, for example, Labour, having won 41 percent of the votes, would have had either to negotiate a coalition with the third-placed Liberal Democrats or to try to form a minority government on its own. Under either option, Tony Blair would not have been nearly as free to commit British troops to the war in Iraq in 2003. Individuals will have their own opinions as to whether this would have been a good thing or a bad thing—what cannot be disputed is that a different electoral system would have made a big difference to policy output.

Electoral systems matter in other ways too, as we shall see. They may make a big difference to the shape of the party system, to the nature of government (coalition or single party), to the kind of choices facing voters at elections, to the ability of voters to hold their representative(s) personally accountable, to the behavior of parliamentarians, to the degree to which a parliament contains people from all walks of life and backgrounds, to the amount of democracy and cohesion within political parties—and of course to the quality of government, and hence to the quality of life of the citizens ruled by that government.

First, we will present a brief overview of the various "families" of electoral systems.

## DIMENSIONS OF ELECTORAL SYSTEMS

"It is the easiest thing in the world to get inextricably tangled among the complexities of electoral systems," wrote Harry Eckstein over half a century ago (1963, 249). Here, we

Table 2.1  Categories of Electoral System

| Broad Category | Specific Types | Country Examples |
| --- | --- | --- |
| Single-seat constituency systems | Single-member plurality (also known as first past the post or FPTP) | Canada, India, United Kingdom, United States |
| | Alternative vote (AV) | Australia |
| | Two-round system (2RS) | France |
| Mixed-member systems | Mixed-member proportional | Germany, New Zealand |
| | Mixed-member majoritarian | Hungary, Japan, Russia, Thailand |
| Closed-list systems | — | Israel, South Africa, Spain |
| Preferential list systems | Open list | Chile, Denmark, Finland |
| | Flexible list | Austria, Belgium, Netherlands |
| PR-STV | — | Ireland, Malta |

outline some broad categories into which electoral systems fall. For the purposes of this chapter, we have assigned electoral systems to one of five categories, listed in Table 2.1, although in some cases there is considerable variation within these.

The first category consists of those systems under which all seats are allocated within single-seat districts[3] (SSDs), also known as single-member districts (SMDs). There are many different ways of allocating a single seat, but since such systems have a lot in common in terms of their effects, it makes sense to treat them as a single broad category. The second broad category is that of mixed-member systems (Shugart and Wattenberg 2003a), in which some members of parliament (MPs) are elected by a plurality or majority formula (usually from SSDs) and others are elected by PR. Then, list systems are based on the idea of parties presenting lists of candidates within each multiseat constituency. They are conventionally divided into two types: those using closed lists, in which the voter cannot express a choice for individual candidates on the list, and those based on preferential lists, where voters can do so. Finally, under PR-single transferable vote (STV), voters are able to rank order all candidates within each multiseat constituency.

The main task of this chapter is to outline more fully the main dimensions on which electoral systems differ, and these are set out in Table 2.2.

## District Magnitude

The first dimension is district magnitude, the number of seats per constituency. This is not just a useful taxonomic aid but a factor that makes a big difference to the effects of an electoral system and thus to a country's politics. Measuring average district magnitude is straightforward in countries where all constituencies are of the same size: single-seat constituency systems such as Australia, Canada, France, India, the United Kingdom, and the United States, or those few other countries where all the constituencies are multimember and of uniform size such as Chile prior to 2017 (2) and Malta (5). In a few countries there is only one (national) constituency, so the number of seats is the district magnitude in the Netherlands (150), Israel (120), and Slovakia (150).

In some other countries district magnitude varies, but we can easily work out an average value. For example, in Spain, 350 MPs are returned from fifty-two constituencies, so average district magnitude equals 6.7, while in Ireland there are forty constituencies and 158 MPs and district magnitude is 3.95. We might wonder, though, whether it matters how this mean is arrived at. In Ireland, as it happens, all constituencies return either 3, 4, or 5 MPs—but suppose its 158 MPs were instead returned from 38 two-seat constituencies and two 41 seat constituencies? Would this make any difference to the kind of outcomes we could expect? Simulations conducted by Taagepera and Shugart (1989, 264–266) suggest that in many ways it would not make a difference, and it does not change the "seat product" (mean magnitude times assembly size), which Shugart and Taagepera (2017; see also their chapter in this volume) show is the dominant institutional factor in shaping the "effective" number of parties.[4] Nonetheless, small parties can expect to fare better if there are at least a few really large constituencies. More detailed study by Monroe and Rose of the consequences of this "magnitude variation" concludes that this factor is more important than generally recognized and, because district magnitude in urban areas is usually larger than in rural areas, the effect is to disadvantage large parties with a predominantly urban base (Monroe and Rose 2002). We might also wonder whether the number of constituencies, as well as their average size, makes a difference. The simple answer is that it does, and this question is explored more fully in Gallagher and Mitchell (2008, appendix C).[5]

Things become a bit trickier when there is more than one "tier" of seat allocation, but since we have not discussed that dimension yet, we will postpone the full consideration of district magnitude until the end of this section.

## Number of Votes Cast

Since "one person one vote" is a hallmark of a democratic system, why would we encounter any variation here? The reason is simple: giving people more than one vote does not violate democratic principles provided everyone still has the same number of votes. Having just one vote is very much the norm, but in most cases within the family termed "mixed-member systems," everyone has two votes. For example, when voters in Germany or New Zealand go to the polling station on election day, they are confronted with a ballot paper that invites them to cast one vote for a candidate to represent their local single-seat constituency and another vote for a party in the contest for seats awarded at the national level.

## Table 2.2  Dimensions on Which Electoral Systems Vary

| Dimension of Variation | Value | Examples |
|---|---|---|
| District magnitude (number of seats per constituency) | 1 | *Single-member plurality* (Canada, India, United Kingdom, United States)<br>*Alternative vote* (Australia)<br>*Two-round system* (France) |
| | More than 1 | *PR list systems* (Israel, Spain, South Africa, Austria, Belgium, Chile, Denmark, Finland, Netherlands)<br>*Mixed-member systems* (Germany, Hungary, Japan, New Zealand, Russia)<br>*PR-STV* (Ireland) |
| How many votes can voter cast? | 2 | *Most mixed-member systems* (Germany, Hungary, Japan, New Zealand, Russia) |
| | 1 | All other systems |
| Ballot structure | Categorical (also termed "nominal" or "integral") | *Single-member plurality* (Canada, India, United Kingdom, United States)<br>*Two-round system* (France)<br>*Virtually all PR list systems* |
| | Dividual: can "divide" vote among different parties | *Most mixed-member systems* (Germany, Hungary, Japan, New Zealand, Russia)<br>*PR list with panachage* (Luxembourg, Switzerland) |
| | Ordinal: can rank order candidates | *Alternative vote* (Australia)<br>*PR-STV* (Ireland) |
| How much choice does voter have regarding individual candidates? | No choice of candidate within party | *Single-member constituency systems* (Australia, Canada, France, India, United Kingdom, United States)<br>*Most mixed-member systems* (Germany, Hungary, Japan, New Zealand, Russia)<br>*Closed-list PR systems* (Israel, South Africa, Spain) |
| | Choice of candidate within party | *Preferential-list PR systems* (Austria, Belgium, Denmark, Finland, Netherlands, Switzerland) |

*(continued)*

**Table 2.2  Continued**

| Dimension of Variation | Value | Examples |
|---|---|---|
| | Choice of candidate without regard to party | *PR-STV* (Ireland) |
| How many levels of seat allocation does electoral system have? | 1 | *Single-member plurality* (Canada, India, United Kingdom, United States)<br>*Alternative vote* (Australia)<br>*Two-round system* (France)<br>*Some PR list systems* (Belgium, Chile, Finland, Israel, Netherlands, Spain)<br>*PR-STV* (Ireland) |
| | 2 (compensatory; also termed corrective or MMP) | *Some mixed-member systems* (Germany, New Zealand)<br>*Some PR list systems* (Denmark, South Africa) |
| | 2 (parallel; also termed MMM) | *Some mixed-member systems* (Japan, Russia) |
| | 3 (compensatory) | *Some mixed-member systems* (Hungary—partially compensatory)<br>*Some PR list systems* (Austria) |
| Measures to limit the degree of proportionality | Small district magnitude (M) | M = 1 (Australia, Canada, France, India, United Kingdom, United States)<br>M = average 4 (Ireland, Paraguay)<br>M is in effect small in mixed-member systems when list seat allocation is separate from single-seat constituency outcomes (Japan, Russia) |
| | Significant vote thresholds that parties need to cross to get any (or "fair") representation | Germany, Hungary, New Zealand |
| | Malapportionment | United States (Senate), Spain, Canada, France, India |

*Source:* Chapters 4–25 of Gallagher and Mitchell (2008). The classification scheme draws in particular on the ideas and discussions of André Blais and Louis Massicotte (2002), Gary Cox (1997, 37–68), David Farrell (2001, 4–10), Arend Lijphart (1994, 10–56), and Rein Taagepera and Matthew Shugart (1989, 19–37).

# Ballot Structure

Douglas Rae was the first to introduce a distinction between ballot papers under which voters must cast a vote for one and only one party, which he termed "categorical" or "nominal," and those under which the voter can rank order the parties or candidates, which he called "ordinal" (Rae 1971, 17–18). The significance of the distinction is explained by Rae in this way: "categorical systems channel each parcel of electoral strength into the grasp of a single party, while ordinal balloting may disperse each parcel of electoral strength among a number of competing parties" (Rae 1971, 18). Unfortunately, Rae seemingly did not realize that this "clarification" goes beyond his initial definition and leaves considerable confusion about how we should classify ballot structures that allow the voter to "divide" his or her vote between two or more parties but not to do any rank ordering.

The first category, at least, is clear enough. It covers ballot papers in most countries. In these cases the voter expresses support for the sole candidate of a party (under single-member plurality), for a party list (Spain, Israel), or for one candidate (Finland, the Netherlands, and others) or perhaps several candidates (pre-1994 Italy) on one party's list.

Rae's "ordinal" category, as we have said, is a little confusing, and does not cover all the systems in which the ballot structure is not categorical. Rae's own treatment of such systems does not clear up the confusion, and Lijphart has already called attention to Rae's "errors of classification" here (Lijphart 1994, 119). Rae (1971, 42–44) describes the German two-vote system as categorical (even though voters can cast their two votes for different parties, thus "dividing" their vote, in his terms). Logically, then, we might expect him to deal similarly with those PR systems under which voters are provided with the facility termed "panachage," where they have a number of preference votes at their disposal and can distribute these among candidates on more than one party's list. This system, also called "free list," is used in Luxembourg and Switzerland and has subsequently been adopted in Honduras and El Salvador. Inconsistently, though, Rae describes these as ordinal systems, even though the voter cannot rank the options.

In reality, Rae's classification would have been more useful with three categories, thus allowing us to distinguish systems permitting rank ordering from those permitting simple vote splitting. The latter we term "dividual," since they enable votes to be "divided" among more than one party.[6] This category includes mixed systems in which voters may, if they wish, cast their constituency vote for a candidate of one party and their list vote for a different party, an option exercised by many voters in New Zealand and by rather fewer in Germany. In a two-round system, voters may switch from one party at the first round to a different one at the second—though since voters cannot split their vote in any one round, and only one of their votes can contribute toward the election of a candidate, this is probably better classified as categorical. PR list systems with the option of panachage belong in the dividual category in that voters can split their votes among different parties, whereas systems under which voters are confined to an intraparty choice are categorical.

Ordinal voting, correctly defined, permits voters to rank order the candidates on the ballot paper. This is a central feature of both the alternative vote and PR-STV. In each case, voters are faced with a list of all candidates in the constituency and may rank all (or, at least, as many as they wish, depending on the specific electoral laws) in order of their choice.

## Choice of Candidate within Parties

The structure of the ballot will also make clear whether voters have any power to choose among the candidates of their party. This facility is self-evidently unavailable under single-seat constituency systems, when parties do not offer more than one candidate in the first place.[7]

PR-list systems differ on this dimension. Some, broadly termed preferential list systems, enable the voter to indicate a preference for one candidate (or in many cases several candidates) on their party's list, and these preference votes then play a role in determining which candidates fill the seats that the party receives. Some preferential list systems are more open than others: a distinction can be drawn between fully open lists, where the voters alone determine which candidates receive the seats, and flexible lists, where the party's initial ordering of the candidates determines the outcome unless sufficient numbers of voters combine to overturn this (see Shugart 2008). How much of a role the preference votes play therefore varies from case to case. In some countries, under fully open lists, they completely determine it (if the party wins three seats, for example, the seats go to the three candidates with the highest numbers of preference votes). In others, using flexible lists, the impact of preference votes is muffled by the details of the rules. Finland and Kosovo epitomize the former approach, Belgium and the Netherlands the latter. The sweeping generalization of Sartori (1997, 17–18), based on Italian experience, according to whom party "machine bosses" can manipulate preference voting to ensure that they and their favored candidates are elected no matter how apparently "open" the lists are, does not stand up to empirical scrutiny as a broad proposition.

Other PR list systems, in contrast, employ "closed lists," in which the voter can choose among parties but not among candidates within parties, and the order of candidates' names that is decided by the party determines which of them receive its seats. As it happens, in most of the mixed-member systems used to elect national parliaments, the list element employs closed lists, though this is not an essential feature of mixed systems and in principle the lists could be open, which is an option parties can use in Lithuania. It is possible to see two different concepts of representation underlying the choice to be made between preferential list and closed-list systems, a distinction that emerged when the question of which variant to adopt was discussed in Sweden in the 1990s. According to one concept, the purpose of elections is to enable the direct representation of the people, and consequently preferential list systems, allowing the people to choose their own representatives, are more appropriate. According to the other, representation takes place through the political parties and the purpose of elections is to enable the parties to secure their proper share of representation; consequently, closed lists are more appropriate than open ones because the parties' candidate selectors are better judges than the voters of who is best able to realize the ideas and goals of the parties (Petersson et al., 1999, 117–123). In "principal–agent" terms, MPs are the agents; closed-list systems seem to assume that parties are the sole principals, while open-list systems assume that MPs have two principals, parties and voters (see discussion in Carey 2009).

Finally, PR-STV gives voters a choice not only among their party's candidates but also across party lines; voters are not constrained by party lines when deciding how to rank order the names of all the candidates on the ballot paper.

## Levels of Seat Allocation

Most of the dimensions that we have looked at so far are fairly straightforward, but all too often it is when we get on to levels of seat allocation that those not instinctively enthused by the subject of electoral systems find their eyes glazing over. This would be a pity because, even though the details of specific systems can be complicated to master, the basic principles are easy enough to grasp.

In many countries there is only one level of seat allocation. In other words, each voter casts a vote in a constituency; seats in that constituency are awarded, in accordance with the rules, to parties (and candidates); and each party's national total of seats is simply the sum of the seats it won in each of the constituencies. There is, by definition, only one level of seat allocation in single-seat constituency systems such as Australia, Canada, France, India, the United Kingdom, and the United States. There is also just one level in many PR systems such as in Belgium, Chile, Finland, and Spain (see Table 2.2).

Why, then, complicate matters by having more than one level or "tier" of seat allocation? There are various reasons for doing this, perhaps the most common of which is that it gets around the problem caused by one of the most robust findings in electoral systems research, namely, that the smaller the average district magnitude, the greater the disproportionality. This relationship is unfortunate, because it points to a tradeoff between two desirable properties of electoral systems, namely, ensuring a close correspondence between the overall levels of electoral support and seats in parliament for parties, and providing a local constituency representative for voters. With just one tier, the two poles are a single-seat constituency system, which scores well on the local representation dimension but poorly on proportionality, and a PR system with just one constituency covering the whole country (as in Israel and the Netherlands), which gives excellent proportionality but no direct representation for localities. With only one level of seat allocation, we are forced to sacrifice a bit of one desirable property to get more of the other.

Having more than one level means that we might be able to have our cake and eat it too. Archetypal mixed-member proportional (MMP) systems, such as that in

New Zealand, illustrate the point. Here, around 60 percent of the MPs are elected from single-seat constituencies (71 out of 120 at the 2017 election), while the rest are elected from party lists; in Germany, the first country to adopt this system, there is an even balance.[8] The list seats are awarded to parties in such a way as to ensure that the total number of seats received by each party is proportional to its share of the list vote. Hence, the system delivers a high degree of overall proportionality, while at the same time each voter has a local constituency MP. Mixed-member systems have thus been described as being, at least at first sight (and with an often-missed question mark after the title of the book that uses the phrase), "the best of both worlds" (Shugart and Wattenberg 2003c, 595; see also Plescia 2016), though another analysis dubs them "the worst of both worlds" (Doorenspleet 2010). In mixed-member systems voters typically have two votes, though in some, such as Lesotho, voters cast a single ballot, which counts both as a vote for a constituency candidate and as a vote for that candidate's party nationally, which eliminates any possibility of vote splitting. While the details differ greatly, the same kind of thinking (i.e., supplying both proportionality and local representation) underlies the choice of a two-tiered or even three-tiered seat allocation in some other countries too: those using mixed-member systems, such as Japan and New Zealand, and single-vote systems, such as Austria and Denmark.

Of course, in the real world, there are also less noble reasons to have higher (or "upper") tiers. Sometimes these tiers mainly have the effect of giving additional benefit to the larger parties, as in the so-called reinforced PR used in Cyprus and Greece in the past, because of the high threshold (17 percent in Greece in 1981 and 1985, for example) that a party needed to pass to qualify for any of the higher-tier seats. In Hungary the existence of three tiers is not, as those confronted by the system might initially suppose, designed to confuse and to ensure that only a handful of initiates really understand what's going on but, as explained in Benoit (2008), reflects the outcome of bargaining at the time of the transition to democracy in the late 1980s coupled with a degree of inertia.

In all MMP systems the higher tier is conventionally[9] termed "compensatory" or corrective, because the seats awarded at the higher tier(s) are used to compensate the parties that were underrepresented at the lower level and to correct disproportionalities that arose there.[10] In Germany, for example, the smaller parties such as the Greens and the Free Democratic Party (FDP) win few if any of the single-seat constituencies and are brought up to their "fair" overall share by being given the appropriate number of list seats. In other cases, though, the two "tiers" are "parallel"; really, each is on the same level and neither can be seen as higher or lower. In the mixed-member majoritarian (MMM) systems used in Japan and Russia, for example, voters each have two votes just as in Germany and New Zealand, but the list seats are awarded in proportion to the list votes only, without any regard for the seats that the parties won in the single-seat constituency section of the election, so large parties retain the seat bonus that they usually achieve in the SSD component. The approach of the system used in Hungary, like that of Italy between 1993 and 2005, is somewhere between the two, having elements of parallel allocation but also providing for a degree of compensation, so it can be seen as partly compensatory. In the terms of Shugart and Wattenberg, such systems provide for "vote linkage" rather than "seat linkage" between the PR and SSD components, in that parties' list vote totals are in effect reduced for each SSD seat that they win (Shugart and Wattenberg 2003b, 14–15; Benoit 2008; D'Alimonte 2008). In mixed-member majoritarian systems, the overrepresentation of the large parties in the single-seat districts is only partially "corrected" by the list seats and proportionality is typically very low (Gallagher 2014, 20).

## Limitations on Proportionality

Proportionality is generally regarded as a "good thing"—in moderation. Few electoral systems go for broke on the proportionality dimension; most have, in practice, some way of limiting it.

The most explicit entry barrier is the use of thresholds. Many PR systems employ some kind of threshold that prevents the smallest parties getting their "fair" share of the seats. In Germany, for example, the only parties that qualify for any list seats are those that either win 5 percent of the list votes or win three single-seat constituencies. In a number of postcommunist countries (Czech Republic, Latvia, Poland, Slovakia), parties receive no seats at all unless they win 5 percent of the national votes (Rose and Munro 2003). This discrimination against small parties and their supporters is usually justified in terms of preventing excessive fragmentation and thereby making it easier to form stable governments, a particular concern in postcommunist countries given their usually weakly structured party systems.

Non-PR systems generally don't have rules specifying a threshold, mainly because they don't need to. As has often been pointed out in the electoral systems literature, in practice there is always an "effective threshold" that makes it next to impossible for parties below a certain size to win a seat. This effective threshold is determined above all by the district magnitude, with the seat allocation formula also playing a part. While we cannot specify a formula that will tell us the effective threshold in all circumstances, Lijphart (1997, 74) and Taagepera (1998, 394) concur that it can best be estimated by the formula $(75/(M + 1))$, where M refers to the district magnitude. In other words, in a constituency with ten seats, for example, the effective threshold equals $75/(10 + 1)$, that is, $75/11$, or 6.8—meaning that a party with fewer than 6.8 percent of the votes in such a constituency is unlikely to win a seat.[11] Hence, if there is a formal threshold that is fixed at a level lower than 6.8 percent, then it is likely to prove superfluous, while if it is higher than 6.8 percent, it may well prove meaningful. In a two-seat constituency the effective threshold is $75/3$, that is, 25 percent, meaning that only parties above this level of strength have a realistic chance of gaining representation. Thus, the effective threshold imposed by small district magnitude is usually even more deadly to small parties than a legal threshold in a PR system. In single-seat constituency systems, certainly, proportionality is already virtually certain to be low, so there is no need for formal thresholds. Proportionality increases as district magnitude increases (when a PR formula is being used, that is), but even when district magnitude is in the two to four range we can expect a significant deviation from complete proportionality.

Another way of building in a limit to proportionality is through malapportionment: awarding some areas of a country more seats in relation to population than others.[12] For example, one analysis found that Chile and Spain both featured in the "top twenty" most malapportioned lower houses of parliaments, with Canada, France, and India not very far behind—and malapportionment in the US Senate is over twice as high as in Chile's Chamber of Deputies (Samuels and Snyder 2001, 660–662). Malapportionment might be effected by the party in power for blatantly partisan reasons—obviously, it would then give more seats to the areas where it is strongest—but that is not always why it occurs. Small, peripheral, predominantly rural regions of a country where population density is lowest and contact between voters and MPs may be relatively difficult to bring about are the areas most likely to receive generous representation—although, of course, this usually has political consequences, with parties of the left typically losing out since they are weak in such regions. The constitution or laws in many countries place some constraints on how far the ratio of representation in each constituency can deviate from the national average figure, but even so, the range of variation within a country is often surprising (see also the chapters in Grofman and Lijphart 2002).

## District Magnitude Revisited

As we noted at the start of this section, it is easy to calculate average district magnitude in single-tier systems but more complicated when there are two or more tiers. For example, of the 598 MPs in Germany, 299 are elected in single-seat constituencies, while the other 299 are returned from lists.[13] The list seats are awarded in such a way as to ensure that the *total* number of seats (not the list seats) received by each party is proportional to its share of the list votes it received. So, should we regard district magnitude in Germany as being 1.99 (598 divided by 300, i.e., the 299 single-seat constituencies plus the one national constituency), or as being 598 (on the grounds that all 598 seats are shared out in a single allocation among the parties in proportion to their votes)? Or should we settle on a plausible-looking value somewhere in between?

Rae (1971, 20–21) adopts the first of these approaches, but, perhaps inevitably for a pioneering study, his work contained flaws that subsequent researchers were able to identify—though, unfortunately, this particular error is one that persists even in some contemporary literature. Lijphart observes that in many instances, Rae's method produces a result that is simply logically impossible, being even smaller than the lower-tier district magnitude (Lijphart 1990, 486). The correct calculation of district magnitude in two-tiered systems (and, by extension, systems with more than two tiers) depends on which tier is decisive in determining seat allocations, and this depends on the specific rules in each case. A key factor is the relative number of seats awarded at the two levels. In a compensatory or corrective two-tiered system, the question is whether the number of higher-tier seats is sufficient to "correct" the disproportionalities arising at the lower level. Taagepera and Shugart (1989, 129) claimed, "The magnitude of the basic district becomes irrelevant to the final votes-to-seats conversion, if sufficient numbers of remainder seats or compensatory seats are allocated at a second stage, so that they compensate for district-level deviation from PR."

In Germany, the 50 percent of seats returned from lists have proved enough to correct these deviations, so if there were no legal thresholds restricting access to the share-out of these seats, we might treat Germany as having a district magnitude of 598. If, on the other hand, Germany had 588 single-seat constituencies and just ten upper-tier seats, it is obvious that district magnitude would in effect be very little different from one.

In their more recent work, Shugart and Taagepera (2017) have found that the district magnitude of the lower (or "basic") tier, as well as the total number of seats in this tier,[14] are not irrelevant after all for the proportionality of a two-tier compensatory system. Nonetheless, the size of the upper, or higher, tier is crucial in reducing the overall disproportionality below what it would be from the lower tier alone. What remains unanswered is just how many higher-tier seats are needed to overcome the disproportionalities arising at the lower level. The aim would be to find the function of M (district magnitude at the lower tier) that generates an equation telling us what proportion of seats need to be reserved for the higher tier if we are to reduce disproportionality to the bare minimum; an equation that would have the form

$$\frac{HTS}{TS} = \frac{1}{f(M)},$$

where HTS is the number of higher-tier seats and TS the total number of seats. For example, the equation

$$\frac{HTS}{TS} = \frac{1}{M+1}$$

would mean that when single-seat constituencies are employed at the lower tier, half the total number of seats needs to be allocated at the higher tier, while if average district magnitude at the lower tier is nine, then only 10 percent of seats need to be reserved for the higher tier. A refined version could start with an agreed "acceptable level" of disproportionality and a predetermined average district magnitude at the lower tier, to establish how many higher-tier seats need to be provided to ensure that disproportionality is unlikely to exceed the set limit.

Preliminary investigation suggests that the number of upper-tier seats needed is probably lower than would be produced by the formula given previously. The biggest component in the total amount of disproportionality is usually generated by the over-representation of the largest party, so in practice the seats:votes ratio of the largest party is a key variable.[15] Even under plurality (FPTP) systems, this is rarely significantly in excess of 3:2. Hence, higher-tier seats would need to amount only to a third of the total number to ensure something close to full proportionality even when the lower-tier seats are filled in SSDs, since the largest party's SSD seats would now amount to something very close to its "fair" share of the total number of seats. This suggests that

$$\frac{\text{HTS}}{\text{TS}} = \frac{1}{2M+1}$$

might produce a reasonable estimate of the number of higher-tier seats needed to achieve near-complete proportionality in a compensatory two-tier system.

Even in the absence (for the time being) of a more precise formula, it seems safe to say that in most countries the higher tier ends up more decisive than the lower tier in determining proportionality. In New Zealand, as in Germany, there are enough higher-tier seats to ensure that (again leaving aside thresholds) district magnitude is in effect equivalent to the number of seats in parliament. In Denmark, although the number of higher-tier seats is smaller (40 out of a total of 175), the lower tier itself does not generate much disproportionality (135 MPs elected in seventeen constituencies each with an average district magnitude of 7.9), so the 40 higher-tier seats are quite sufficient to ensure that the overall results are highly proportional.[16] The exception is the system that operated in Italy until 2005, where only a quarter of the 630 seats were available at the higher tier, the rest being awarded by plurality in single-seat constituencies—and, moreover, the higher-tier seats were only partially compensatory rather than fully compensatory, as we noted earlier.

We should mention two further aspects of two-tier seat allocations. The first is that, as Lijphart (1994, 32) points out, upper-tier seats may be either adjustment-seats or remainder-pooling systems. Those discussed previously (Germany, New Zealand, Denmark) are adjustment-seat cases, in that the number of upper-tier seats is fixed and preset. In remainder-pooling systems, in contrast, all seats are in theory available to be awarded at the lowest tier, but in practice this never happens. Usually, in the lower-tier constituencies, each party receives a seat for each "quota" of votes it wins, and any remaining votes the parties win over and above their full quotas, along with any seats not awarded, are transferred to and pooled at the higher tier. What happens at the higher tier depends on the precise rules in a particular country. In Austria, for example, seats are awarded in such a way as to make the outcome proportional in terms of the *total* number of votes (not just the higher-tier, or remainder, votes) won by each party, and so district magnitude, again leaving aside the thresholds in operation, is in effect the number of seats in parliament: 183.[17]

The second aspect concerns MMM systems where, as we have said, the two components of the election—the single-seat constituency section and the list section—are on the same level rather than constituting different tiers. In Japan, for example, 295 MPs are elected from single-seat constituencies and the other 180 from eleven multiseat constituencies. In analytic terms it makes perfect sense to treat this as if the country were divided into two, with single-seat constituencies used in one part and a PR list system in the other. Here, then, it may be valid for once to employ Rae's approach and to calculate district magnitude simply by dividing the total number of seats (475) by the total number of constituencies (306), giving a district magnitude of 1.6. Likewise, in Russia average district magnitude at the 2016 election equaled the number of seats (450) divided by the number of constituencies (226), that is, 2.0. The complexities inherent in MMM systems mean that it is difficult to know what would be the "real" impact of a given number of seats in each component on overall representation.

# Conclusion

The previous account indicates in broad terms how the main electoral systems and formulae operate. We have reviewed the main dimensions of electoral systems—in particular district magnitude, ballot structure, intraparty choice of candidates, the existence of more than one tier of allocation, and legal thresholds and effective thresholds—and have discussed the ways in which particular choices on each of these dimensions need to be made when an electoral system is designed. It can be seen that the range of actual systems is wide, and the range of possible ones is virtually infinite. The chapters in this *Handbook* explore the consequences of such variation.

# Author's Note

This chapter is closely based upon Chapter 1 in Gallagher and Mitchell (2008).

# Notes

1. See the introduction to this volume for explanation of some basic terms such as these.
2. The Labour Party surpassed this electoral alchemy in 2005 when it converted 35 percent of the votes nationally into 55 percent of the seats.
3. We will use "district" and "constituency" interchangeably. These and other terms are used in different countries of the English-speaking world (as noted in the introduction to this volume).
4. The effective number of parties is explained briefly in the introduction to this volume and in more detail in the chapter by Shugart and Taagepera.
5. For a fixed assembly size, the mean magnitude and the number of districts do not vary independently. Thus, a greater number of districts, given a constant mean district magnitude, would raise assembly size and therefore the seat product.
6. "Dividual" is defined by the Oxford English Dictionary as meaning "capable of being divided into parts, divisible, divided into parts, fragmentary, divided or distributed among a number."
7. As so often, an exception can be found even to this apparently solid generalization: in Japan the Liberal Democratic Party (LDP) in safe seats sometimes allows two candidates

to run and then admits the victor to its parliamentary party, treating the election in effect as a primary (see Reed 2008, 277–293). Cases of a party running two or more candidates in safe single-seat constituencies also have occurred occasionally in the Philippines.

8. This is a somewhat simplified account of the German system, omitting details such as the threshold, *Überhangmandate* (overhang seats), and *Ausgleichsmandate* (balance seats), which are explained fully in Saalfeld (2008).

9. This is something of an overstatement given the terminological profusion in the field.

10. In most countries compensatory seats correct some or all of the disproportionalities that were introduced in the lower tiers. Unusually, since 2005 Italy has awarded "bonus seats" to the largest party, such that the "correction" is majority inducing. The current (2017) electoral system guarantees an absolute majority (55 percent of the total seats) to a list that obtains at least 40 percent of the votes (see D'Alimonte 2015; for a critique Pasquino 2015). The electoral system of Italy's tiny neighbor San Marino also guarantees an overall majority (58 percent of the seats) to the largest party or coalition. Greece too awards such "plurality bonus" seats: at its 2015 elections, 250 of the 300 seats were allocated proportionately among all parties reaching the 3 percent threshold, and the remaining 50 are awarded to the largest party.

11. It should be emphasized that this relationship applies only within an individual constituency. It does not purport to tell us the effective national threshold in a country whose parliament is elected from a large number of ten-seat constituencies. It is also worth noting that just as the effective threshold can be computed from a known district magnitude, so an effective magnitude can be computed from a known threshold. See Gallagher and Mitchell (2008, appendix C) for a fuller discussion.

12. A related concept—in that both usually result in some parties paying a higher "price" in terms of votes per seat than others—is gerrymandering. While it is possible that in particular circumstances the impact of malapportionment could be to increase proportionality, the principle of awarding more seats per person to some parts of a country than to others runs counter to the underlying philosophy of proportional representation.

13. To be more precise, we should say that at least 598 members of the Bundestag are elected in this manner. The total number of seats is now normally higher—it was 631 after the 2013 election, and 709 after that of 2017 for example—due to the additional overhang and balance seats.

14. That is, its "seat product"; see Shugart and Taagepera's chapter in this volume.

15. To be precise, the important variable in achieving full proportionality is technically the highest seats:votes ratio achieved by any party. Of course, this might not be the largest party; a party with 0.6 percent of the votes might win 1.2 percent of the seats and thus achieve a ratio of 2, which would require there to be as many upper-tier seats as lower-tier seats, with this party receiving no upper-tier seats to bring its lower-tier seats down to 0.6 percent of the total seats. However, a small party can be left with a high seats:votes ratio without doing much damage to overall proportionality (because it has only a seat or two more than its entitlement), whereas a large party, even if its seats:votes ratio is "only" 3:2, is likely to have tens or hundreds of seats more than its "fair" share. Hence, in practical terms, the seats:votes ratio of the largest party is what matters.

16. More precisely, this 175-seat total is for mainland Denmark and excludes an additional 4 seats (two each for Greenland and the Faroe Islands).

17. For a detailed account see Müller (2008) on Austria. Another example is South Africa, for which see Gouws and Mitchell (2008).

# References

Benoit, Kenneth. "Hungary: Holding back the Tiers". In *The Politics of Electoral Systems*, edited by Michael Gallagher and Paul Mitchell, 231–252. Oxford University Press, 2008.

Blais, André, and Louis Massicotte. "Electoral Systems." In *Comparing Democracies 2: New Challenges in the Study of Elections and Voting*, edited by Lawrence LeDuc, Richard G. Niemi, and Pippa Norris, 40–69. London: Sage, 2002.

Carey, John M. *Legislative Voting and Accountability*. Cambridge: Cambridge University Press, 2009.

Cox, Gary. *Making Votes Count: Strategic Coordination in the World's Electoral Systems*. Cambridge: Cambridge University Press, 1997.

D'Alimonte, Roberto. "Italy: A Case of Fragmented Bipolarism." In *The Politics of Electoral Systems*, edited by Michael Gallagher and Paul Mitchell, 253–276. Oxford University Press, 2008.

D'Alimonte, Roberto. "The New Italian Electoral System: Majority-Assuring but Minority-Friendly." *Contemporary Italian Politics* 7, no. 3 (2015): 286–292.

Doorenspleet, Renske. "Electoral Systems and Democratic Quality: Do Mixed Systems Combine the Best or the Worst of Both Worlds? An Explorative Quantitative Cross-National Study." *Acta Politica* 40, no. 1 (2010): 28–49.

Eckstein, Harry. "The Impact of Electoral Systems on Representative Government." In *Comparative Politics: A Reader*, edited by Harry Eckstein and David E. Apter, 247–254. London: Collier-Macmillan, 1963.

Farrell, David. *Electoral Systems: A Comparative Introduction*. Basingstoke: Palgrave, 2001.

Gallagher, Michael. "Electoral Institutions and Representation." In *Comparing Democracies 4*, edited by Lawrence LeDuc, Richard Niemi, and Pippa Norris, 11–31. London: Sage, 2014.

Gallagher, Michael, and Paul Mitchell, eds. *The Politics of Electoral Systems*. Oxford: Oxford University Press, 2008.

Gouws, Amanda, and Paul Mitchell. "South Africa: One Party Dominance Despite Perfect Proportionality". In *The Politics of Electoral Systems*, edited by Michael Gallagher and Paul Mitchell, 353–373. Oxford University Press, 2008.

Grofman, Bernard, and Arend Lijphart, eds. *The Evolution of Electoral and Party Systems in the Nordic Countries*. New York: Agathon Press, 2002.

Lijphart, Arend. "The Political Consequences of Electoral Laws, 1945–85." *American Political Science Review* 84, no. 2 (1990): 481–496.

Lijphart, Arend. *Electoral Systems and Party Systems: A Study of Twenty-Seven Democracies, 1945–1990*. Oxford: Oxford University Press, 1994.

Lijphart, Arend. "The Difficult Science of Electoral Systems: A Commentary on the Critique by Alberto Penadés." *Electoral Studies* 16, no. 1 (1997): 73–77.

Monroe, Burt L., and Amanda G. Rose. "Electoral Systems and Unimagined Consequences: Partisan Effects of Districted Proportional Representation." *American Journal of Political Science* 46, no. 1 (2002): 67–89.

Müller, Wolfgang C. "Austria: A Complex Electoral System with Subtle Effects". In *The Politics of Electoral Systems*, edited by Michael Gallagher and Paul Mitchell, 397–432. Oxford University Press, 2008.

Pasquino, Gianfranco. "Italia Has Yet Another Electoral Law." *Contemporary Italian Politics* 7, no. 3 (2015): 293–300.

Petersson, Olof, Klaus von Beyme, Lauri Karvonen, Birgitta Nedelmann, and Eivind Smith. *Report from the Democratic Audit of Sweden 1999: Democracy the Swedish Way.* Stockholm: SNS Förlag, 1999.

Plescia, Carolina. *Split-Ticket Voting in Mixed-Member Electoral Systems.* Colchester: ECPR Press, 2016.

Rae, Douglas W. *The Political Consequences of Electoral Laws.* Rev. ed. New Haven, CT, and London: Yale University Press, 1971.

Reed, Steven R. "Japan: Haltingly toward a Two-Party System." In *The Politics of Electoral Systems*, edited by Michael Gallagher and Paul Mitchell, 277–293. Oxford: Oxford University Press, 2008.

Rose, Richard, and Neil Munro. *Elections and Parties in New European Democracies.* Washington DC: CQ Press, 2003.

Saalfeld, Thomas. "Germany: Stability and Strategy in a Mixed-Member Proportional System." In *The Politics of Electoral Systems*, edited by Michael Gallagher and Paul Mitchell, 209–229. Oxford: Oxford University Press, 2008.

Samuels, David, and Richard Snyder. "The Value of a Vote: Malapportionment in Comparative Perspective." *British Journal of Political Science* 31, no. 4 (2001): 651–671.

Sartori, Giovanni. *Comparative Constitutional Engineering: An Inquiry into Structures, Incentives and Outcomes.* 2nd ed. Basingstoke: Macmillan, 1997.

Shugart, Matthew Soberg. "Comparative Electoral Systems Research: The Maturation of a Field and New Challenges Ahead." In *The Politics of Electoral Systems*, edited by Michael Gallagher and Paul Mitchell, 25–55. Oxford: Oxford University Press, 2008.

Shugart, Matthew S., and Rein Taagepera. *Votes from Seats: Logical Models of Electoral Systems.* New York: Cambridge University Press, 2017.

Shugart, Matthew Soberg, and Martin P. Wattenberg, eds. *Mixed-Member Electoral Systems: The Best of Both Worlds?* Oxford: Oxford University Press, 2003a.

Shugart, Matthew Soberg, and Martin P. Wattenberg. "Mixed-Member Electoral Systems: A Definition and Typology." In *Mixed-Member Electoral Systems: The Best of Both Worlds?*, edited by Matthew Soberg Shugart and Martin P. Wattenberg, 10–24. Oxford: Oxford University Press, 2003b.

Shugart, Matthew Soberg, and Martin P. Wattenberg. "Conclusion: Are Mixed-Member Systems the Best of Both Worlds?" In *Mixed-Member Electoral Systems: The Best of Both Worlds?*, edited by Matthew Soberg Shugart and Martin P. Wattenberg, 571–596. Oxford: Oxford University Press, 2003c.

Taagepera, Rein. "Effective Magnitude and Effective Thresholds." *Electoral Studies* 17, no. 4 (1998): 393–404.

Taagepera, Rein, and Matthew Soberg Shugart. *Seats and Votes: The Effects and Determinants of Electoral Systems.* New Haven, CT: Yale University Press, 1989.

CHAPTER 3

······························································

# ELECTORAL SYSTEM EFFECTS
# ON PARTY SYSTEMS

······························································

MATTHEW S. SHUGART AND REIN TAAGEPERA

## ELECTORAL SYSTEM EFFECTS ON PARTY
## SYSTEMS

······························································

THE question of how electoral systems shape party systems has been central to the literature on elections for about as long as there have been elections. At one time, elections were almost universally conducted by some form of majority voting system. Late in the nineteenth century, and especially throughout the twentieth century, more and more countries began to adopt other rules for distributing seats in national assemblies and other elected bodies. These systems include proportional representation (PR).

Some nineteenth-century writers promoted various PR systems on the grounds that they would produce assemblies more reflective of the range of opinion in the society (e.g., Droop 2012 [1869]; Hare 1859). As mass political parties developed, interest turned to whether the number of parties systematically varied across different electoral systems. The most famous statement of this connection between rules and parties is the set of propositions that have come to be known as Duverger's law. The so-called law states that the use of plurality rule in districts electing one member tends to produce a two-party system. With various restatements and refinements, this basic proposition has been the dominant way of thinking about the nexus between electoral systems and party systems.

Notwithstanding its vaunted status as a "law," this central proposition of the literature on electoral systems fails to meet the basic standards of a scientific law. In this chapter, rather than offer a review of the "law" itself, we will trace an alternative means of quantifying party systems and how they are connected to electoral systems and other institutions. We take the heretical stance that it is time to retire the notion of a "Duverger's law" and to build and refine more quantitatively precise models instead.

# Counting and Measuring

In this section, we review two key quantitative indicators that are by now well established in the analysis of party systems: the "effective number of parties," which is a size-weighted count of how many parties there are, and "deviation from proportionality," which measures the degree to which votes and seats shares differ from one another in a given party system.

## Counting Parties: The Effective Number

Counting parties turns out to be not so simple as just counting parties. We may not find it very interesting that five parties won seats in Canada's national election of 2015. After all, one of them had more than half the seats, and one of the remaining four had only 1 of the 338 total seats. The outcome of this election may or may not qualify as a "two-party system." It depends on what one means by that concept. Two parties combined for 83 percent of the seats, but only 71.4 percent of the votes. However, the third party had 19.7 percent of votes and 44 seats. This is certainly not a "two-party system" in the same way that Jamaica's is. In the latter country's 2016 election, there were only two parties that won seats (one with 32, the other with 31), and these two together combined for 99.8 percent of the votes.

Perhaps we could say that in both Canada and Jamaica there are only two "significant" parties. Yet this too runs into trouble. Why is the third party in the Canadian example, with nearly a fifth of the votes and an eighth of the seats, "insignificant"?

The difficulty of making sense of real-world election systems by just a simple count of parties or arbitrarily deciding which subset of parties is "significant" leads to the desire to have some sort of weighted count. This is where the concept of an "effective number," first introduced by Laakso and Taagepera (1979), comes in.

The effective number of parties is an index that aims to summarize the unequal-sized parties into a single number. It is a weighted count in that its calculation ensures that a large party contributes more to the index than any smaller one contributes. It accomplishes this aim by squaring each party's share of either seats or votes. The formula for calculating the effective number of seat-winning parties (which we can designate $N_S$) is

$$N_S = 1 / \sum \left( s_i \right)^2 = \text{inverse sum of squared fractional shares}$$

In words, we square the seat shares for each of $i$ parties—however many there are, starting with the seat share for the largest party, $s_1$. Then we sum up all the squares. Once we have this sum, we take the reciprocal. In this way, the index weights each party by its own size. The squaring results in a large party contributing more to the final index value than does a small one. For instance, suppose the largest party has half the seats, $s_1 = 0.5$; thus, we have $0.5^2 = 0.25$. Now suppose among several remaining parties the smallest (the $i$th) one has only 5 percent of the seats. We take the share, 0.05, and square it, and get 0.0025. In this way, when we sum up the squared shares of all the parties, the smallest one has counted for much less than the largest. This is precisely what we want—a size-weighted count of how many parties there are.

Alternatively, we could calculate our index on vote shares, giving us the effective number of vote-earning parties ($N_V$):

$$N_V = 1 / \sum (v_i)^2$$

Here $v_i$ stands for the fractional *vote* share of the $i$th party. Thus, for any given election result, we have two effective numbers: $N_S$ for the seats and $N_V$ for the votes. These numbers are sometimes referred to as ENPP (effective number of parliamentary parties)[1] and ENEP (effective number of electoral parties), respectively. However, given our interest in systematically constructing logical models, we adopt the approach more typical of scientific notation: single symbols with subscripts.[2]

A useful feature of the index is that it will always yield the actual number of parties (or other components) if they are equal in size. If, as is usually the case, the parties vary in size, the effective number will be smaller than the actual number. For instance, take a case of four equal-sized parties, meaning each has 25 percent of the seats (or votes):

$$\begin{aligned} N_S &= 1 / \sum (s_i)^2 = 1 / \left[ 0.25^2 + 0.25^2 + 0.25^2 + 0.25^2 \right] \\ &= 1 / \left[ 0.0625 + 0.0625 + 0.0625 + 0.0625 \right] \\ &= 1 / 0.25 = 4 \end{aligned}$$

Precisely as it should, the index yields $N = 4$ for this constellation of four same-sized parties. Now, suppose one of them splits in two, so that we have

25%, 25%, 25%, 12.5%, 12.5%

We now have five parties, but they are no longer equal in seats. The effective number logically should be some value greater than four but less than five. If we repeat the calculation procedure with this new constellation, we get $N_S = 4.57$. Now suppose one of the small ones merges with one of the bigger parties. We are now back to four parties, but they are unequal:

37.5%, 25%, 25%, 12.5%

The calculation will result in $N_S = 3.56$, suggesting, accurately, that this constellation has a degree of fragmentation somewhere roughly equidistant between one with three equal-sized parties and one with four equal-sized parties.

The effective number of seat-winning parties is directly related to the index of fractionalization ($F$) of party seat shares:

$$F = 1 - \sum \left(s_i\right)^2 = 1 - (1/N_S)$$

The index, $F$, has a long pedigree in economics and was also the measure of fragmentation used by Rae (1967) in the first major cross-national quantitative study of the impact of electoral systems on party systems.[3] It seems to have fallen into disuse. The effective $N$ has become dominant.

Notwithstanding the dominance of $N$, it is not without its flaws, critics, and suggested alternatives (Molinar 1991; Dunleavy and Boucek 2003; Golosov 2009). No single measure can summarize everything we would want to know about a given constellation of party sizes. One drawback that is relevant to the electoral systems literature is the ambiguity of its measures of how closely a constellation conforms to a "two-party system" (Gaines and Taagepera 2013). Given how central this notion of two-party versus multiparty is to the literature on electoral systems, the fact that some distributions of party systems might have a considerable degree of "two-partyness" yet have $N$ near 3 might lead to faulty interpretations. An example would be two parties each having 40 percent, and two others with 10 percent each. By any reasonable standard, this hypothetical constellation features competition between two equal parties, with the others clearly out of the running for the first position. Yet it yields $N = 2.94$.

Similarly, values of $N$ near 2 can result from constellations that are not in any meaningful sense "two party." Consider a case of a party with 60 percent and two other parties with 20 percent each. This results in $N = 2.27$. Yet, given such a strongly dominant party, no one could call that a "two-party system."

Despite these drawbacks and various efforts to propose alternatives, the effective number has become the dominant index, by far. It is easy to calculate, as sketched earlier, and has a solid logical foundation. Like any tool, it needs to be used for its proper purpose. It is a measure of fragmentation, not, for instance, a proxy for the number of "serious" parties.[4] As long as we do not try to read more into it than it is capable of telling us (Taagepera 1999), it is a fine measure of how fragmented a party system is.[5] For this reason, like most of the related literature, we will continue using it. We find that the effective number lends itself well to generalizations about the institutional effects on party systems, which is the main focus of this chapter. First, however, we briefly describe another important index that summarizes an aspect of how electoral systems affect political parties—measures of disproportionality.

## Measuring Deviation from Proportionality

As with quantitatively summarizing the variable sizes of parties in an assembly or in the electorate, there are also various measures in use for characterizing how "proportional" the seats–votes relationship is. We will refer to such indices as measures of "deviation from proportionality." Two main measures dominate.[6] Both start with the difference between seat and vote shares, for each party, but then they process these differences in different ways.

Loosemore and Hanby (1971) introduced into the literature on electoral systems an index of deviation that we'll designate as $D_1$, following the systematics of Taagepera (2007, 76–79). For deviation from proportionality, it is

$$D_1 = \frac{1}{2} \sum |s_i - v_i|$$

Here $s_i$ is the $i$th party's seat share, and $v_i$ is its vote share. The index can range in principle from 0 to 1 (or 100 percent). Note that $|s_i \text{-} v_i| = |v_i \text{-} s_i|$ is never negative. $D_1$ dominated until Gallagher (1991) introduced what we'll designate as $D_2$:

$$D_2 = \left[ \frac{1}{2} \sum (s_i - v_i)^2 \right]^{1/2}$$

It has often been designated as the "least square" index, but this is a misnomer. The index does involve squaring a difference but no minimization procedure so as to find some "least" squares. $D_2$ can range from 0 to 1 (100 percent), but whenever more than two parties have nonzero deviations, the upper limit actually remains below 1. The value of $D_1$ will be greater than or equal to that for $D_2$.

Gallagher's $D_2$ rapidly displaced $D_1$ during the 1990s as the more widely used index,[7] despite grounds for doubting whether it is the best of the various measures (Taagepera and Grofman 2003; Taagepera 2007, 76–78).

## INSTITUTIONAL EFFECTS

By now there exists a substantial body of work that seeks to explain how electoral systems and other institutional rules shape party systems. Most of this work has used the effective number of parties as its principal outcome variable, and we will focus our attention on that outcome as well. Many studies have recognized district magnitude as one of the key input variables, but various works differ in what other inputs are considered. We will review some of this prior work later, but the primary purpose of what follows is not to review the literature per se, but rather to demonstrate the substantial explanatory power of just two basic institutional parameters: *district magnitude* (the number of seats in an electoral district) and *assembly size* (the total number of seats in the main national representative body).

There really is no better way to demonstrate the power of a simple institutional effect than with a graph, and accordingly we will show several in this chapter. Strikingly, most works in the related literature have few or no graphs—or those they present include no actual data.[8] Partly the reason for the absence of data graphs in many works is the preference of authors for multivariate regressions, which do not lend themselves well to graphing.[9] More important, the regressions found in most of these works typically produce widely varying coefficient estimates on key variables like magnitude, depending on which other variables are included and on which specific sample selection criteria are used.[10] The authors of these works typically are not troubled by such variance in their own estimates, because they are testing merely *directional* hypotheses—for instance: the effective number of parties *increases* as magnitude *increases*, conditional on (various factors). As political scientists interested in electoral systems effects, we can do better than this. We can offer a specific numerical estimate of the effect, grounded in logic.

To do so, we start with the fragmentation of seats and only then extend to predicting the fragmentation of votes. The reason for doing so is actually straightforward, but it is contrary to what most other authors have done. That is, it is typically the case that authors (e.g., Amorim Neto and Cox 1997; Cox 1997; Clark and Golder 2006) first estimate the contribution of various inputs, including the electoral system but also a measure of social diversity, to the effective number of *vote-earning* parties ($N_V$) at the national level. This relationship is estimated through a regression. They then take the $N_V$ to be an input into a second regression, in which the electoral system is the primary independent variable and the outcome to be explained is the effective number of seat-winning parties ($N_S$).

The method of estimating the votes first and then the seats is sensible. After all, parties earn votes before they earn seats. The votes are cast, and then the electoral authorities calculate how many seats each party wins by applying the electoral law to the known distribution of votes. However, as Taagepera (2007) notes, this method proved to be a dead end for theory building. For the logic of institutional effects on party systems, it is much more fruitful to start at the other end—the seats. The logic for doing so is elementary, in that it is found within the famous so-called Duverger's law. Duverger (1951, 1954) claimed that the electoral system—specifically first past the post (FPTP)—first worked through a "mechanical" effect, whereby the *available seats* constrained which parties actually could win. Only then did a "psychological" effect kick in, encouraging voters and other actors to avoid "wasting" votes on parties that could not possibly win.

By the same logic, attempts to predict how electoral systems and party systems are related should start with the quantity that is more constrained—the seats. It is the number of available seats that directly limits the feasible number of (seat-winning) parties. The number of parties earning votes is only indirectly constrained. By this logic, we can develop a model of how seats—both in a district and in the national assembly as a whole—shape the party system through what we term the Seat Product Model. In the next section, we sketch the steps in this model, summarizing Shugart and Taagepera (2017). The inputs into the Seat Product Model are strictly institutional; later we will return to the question of whether inclusion of a factor like social diversity might improve the predictive power of the model.

# The Seat Product Model: How We Can Predict Party Systems from Seats

The concept of the *seat product* was introduced by Taagepera (2007) and refers to the mathematical product of a country's mean district magnitude ($M$) and its assembly size ($S$). Through a series of logical steps and application of algebra, it allows us to derive formulas predicting what a given output quantity, such as the effective number of seat-winning parties ($N_S$), can be expected to be, on average, for a given seat product. The formulas then can be tested, both via visual inspection through graphing and by statistical regression.

In Figure 3.1, we show a data plot in which the effective number of seat-winning parties ($N_S$) is on the y-axis and the "seat product" ($MS$) is on the x-axis. The data points represent country-level means, for all democracies that have at least three post–World War II elections in our dataset,[11] for which the electoral system meets Taagepera's (2007) definition of "simple." A simple electoral system is one in which all seats are allocated in districts, meaning there are no "upper tiers" (see Gallagher and Mitchell's chapter).[12] Moreover, the seat allocation formula must be a basic proportional one in a single round of voting. Importantly, FPTP is included in the definition of a simple system, because all proportional formulas that are used in party list systems[13] reduce to FPTP (plurality) when $M = 1$.

On logical grounds introduced in Taagepera (2007) and summarized later in this chapter, we expect

$$N_S = (MS)^{1/6} \qquad \text{(Equation 1);}$$

in words, the effective number of seat-winning parties equals, on average, the seat product, raised to the power, one-sixth. Equation 1, it must be emphasized, is not a mere regression result. Rather, it is derived from logic, which we summarize later. When we do test it via regression, we almost perfectly confirm it;[14] the solid line in Figure 3.1 represents Equation 1. Countries are labeled if their actual mean value is either greater than 1.33 times the value predicted by Equation 1 or less than three-quarters the predicted value.[15]

In Figure 3.1, we differentiate parliamentary and presidential systems, because much of the literature, starting from Amorim Neto and Cox (1997) and Cox (1997), argues that the assembly party system can be explained only via regression designs in which the observed effective number of presidential candidates is entered as an "independent" variable. Our data plot gives scant reason to claim the pattern is different for presidential systems. There is one significant outlier—Brazil, represented by the data point with the highest $N_S$ in Figure 3.1—but as a group, the presidential and parliamentary systems fit within a common trend represented by Equation 1.[16]

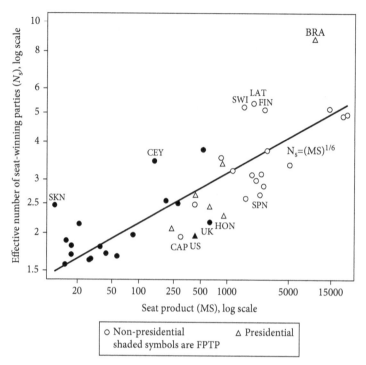

**FIGURE 3.1.** Relation of the nationwide effective number of seat-winning parties ($N_S$) to the seat product (*MS*), both on logarithmic scales.

Note: Abbreviations for relatively deviant cases: BRA (Brazil), CAP (Cap Verde), CEY (Ceylon to 1970), HON (Honduras), FIN (Finland), LAT (Latvia), SKN (St. Kitts and Nevis), SPN (Spain), SWI (Switzerland), UK (United Kingdom), US (United States).

Source: Unless otherwise indicated, data in the tables and figures in this chapter are authors' calculations on original data drawn from Struthers et al. (2018). Data points represent country averages over several elections.

Further, our symbol patterns in Figure 3.1 differentiate FPTP systems (where every district elects just one member, via plurality rule) from PR systems (in which mean *M* > 1). Once again, there is scant evidence for any need to treat FPTP and PR as if they were distinct categories. We see some intermixing of PR systems (open symbols) and FPTP systems (filled in) at moderate levels of *MS*. The range of *MS* from about 200 to 1,000 includes both FPTP and PR, as well as both parliamentary and presidential.

Thus, for example, were a given country to have *MS* = 625, we would predict from Equation 1 that it would tend to have $N_S$ = 2.92, regardless of its executive type and regardless of whether the system consisted of 625 single-seat districts (*M* = 1, *S* = 625),[17] a PR system with a single 25-seat district (*M* = *S* = 25), or any intermediate combination (say, mean *M* = 5, *S* = 125). For any given country or election, we can expect some deviation from the predicted value, due to various factors other than the seat product.

We will refer to Equation 1 as the Seat Product Model (SPM). The section that follows describes its logical derivation.

# The Logic behind the Seat Product Model

The SPM for the effective number of seat-winning parties ($N_S$) starts with a basic question: how many parties would we expect to win at least one seat in a district electing $M$ seats? We can designate the number of parties, of any size, that win representation in a given district as $N'_{S0}$, where the prime mark indicates that we are referring to a district-level quantity instead of nationwide and the zero indicates that this is the unweighted count (i.e., the actual number rather than the effective number, which is the size-weighted count).

Taagepera and Shugart (1993) first proposed that the relationship should be

$$N'_{S0} = M^{1/2}$$ (Equation 2).

Figure 3.2 shows that it is a reasonable approximation. The figure plots our two quantities against each other on logarithmic scales; data points represent individual elections at the district level in a large number of democracies. The light gray diagonal line represents Equation 2. While data points are somewhat scattered, Equation 2 captures the average trend. Like Equation 1, it is important to emphasize, this is not a best-fit regression line. It is derived from logic, which we now explain.

The logic that leads to Equation 2 starts with the boundary conditions. What are the ranges in which the data *could not possibly occur*? Asking this basic question can be a good starting point for figuring out what the average relationship should be, on logical grounds. In our case, the minimum number of parties that could win a seat in any district is clearly one; the thick horizontal line in Figure 3.2 at $N'_{S0} = 1$ is thus a lower limit. For any given $M$ the feasible maximum is $N'_{S0} = M$, in which case each party has exactly one of the district's seats. This is the thick black diagonal line above which the graph space is shaded gray. Data points in the range $N'_{S0} > M$ are thus impossible, hence the labeling of this region as a "forbidden area."

Between these boundaries, any value of the number of parties between one and $M$ is feasible. Yet we note that there is considerable white space in the feasible area, where no data points are found. We can express the average trend by taking the mean of our plausible extremes; in logarithmic space, this is the geometric average, and it leads us to Equation 2:

$$N'_{S0} = \left[ M^0 * M^1 \right]^{1/2} = M^{1/2}$$

If we then want to develop expressions for the nationwide outcomes, we can start with the simplest case, which is when there is a single nationwide district, so that we have $M = S$. A few countries have had such districts, including Israel and the Netherlands. By Equation 2 and the condition of $M = S$, we have[18]

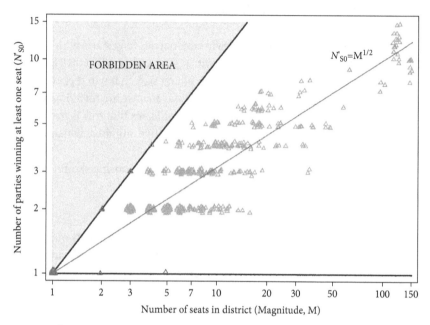

**FIGURE 3.2.** The relationship between district magnitude (*M*) and the number of seat-winning parties ($N'_{S0}$).

Data source: Struthers et al. (2018).

$$N_{S0} = (MS)^{1/4} \qquad \text{(Equation 3)}.$$

Equation 3 should be generalizable to any mean *M* and any *S*, including simple districted systems in which *S* seats in the assembly are divided across some plural number of districts with mean *M*.[19] When tested graphically or by regression, it is confirmed.

Figure 3.3 shows the data plot. Clearly the fit is quite strong, despite a few prominent outliers.[20] Similarly to Figure 3.1, countries are labeled if their actual mean value is either greater than 1.33 times the value predicted by Equation 3 or less than three-quarters the predicted value. All subsequent figures similarly have labels for countries outside this range of the predictions for the graphed quantity. Remarkably, the United Kingdom and Spain deviate from average expectation in both Figures 3.1 and 3.3, but in opposite directions. Unexpectedly, many parties win seats, yet the effective number of parties is low. This is the signature of a country with one or two unusually dominant parties and a profusion of tiny (often regional) ones. In contrast, the United States is low on both accounts. Inspecting our graphs helps in pinning down which countries share some oddities, and to what extent.

If we want to proceed from the number of parties (of any size) to the effective number, we can go by way of the share of the largest party, $s_1$. This share is the one that most strongly affects $N_S$, by virtue of the squaring (weighting by size). Taagepera (2007) first

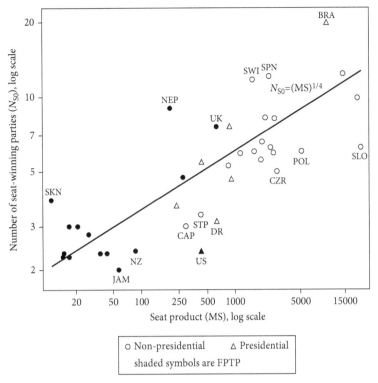

**FIGURE 3.3.** How the actual number of seat-winning parties ($N_{S0}$) relates to the seat product ($MS$), national level.

> Note: Abbreviations for relatively deviant cases: BRA (Brazil), CAP (Cap Verde), CZR (Czechia), DR (Dominican Republic), JAM (Jamaica), NEP (Nepal), NZ (New Zealand), POL (Poland), SKN (St. Kitts and Nevis), SPN (Spain), STP (Sao Tome and Principe), SVK (Slovakia), SWI (Switzerland), UK (United Kingdom), US (United States).

suggested that the same logic of considering boundary conditions, described earlier for deriving Equation 2, could work for estimating $s_1$, as follows. The minimum $s_1$ for any given $N_{S0}$ is $s_1 = 1 / N_{S0}$. This minimum is reached when all parties are equal in size. The maximum is almost $s_1 = 1$; more precisely, it is as close as possible to one party having all seats as can be, while leaving seats for each of the $N_{S0} - 1$ remaining parties. To keep it simple, we can take the approximation

$$s_1 = \left[ N_{S0}^{-1} * N_{S0}^{0} \right]^{1/2} = N_{S0}^{-1/2} \qquad \text{(Equation 4)}.$$

In Figure 3.4, we see the scatterplot. Once again, the fit is overall quite strong, despite a few cases that are somewhat more distant from the line representing Equation 4 than the rest.[21] The United Kingdom and Spain again stand out.

Having connected the largest seat share to the actual number of parties, which in turn connects to the seat product (Figure 3.3), we now have only one more step to get us back

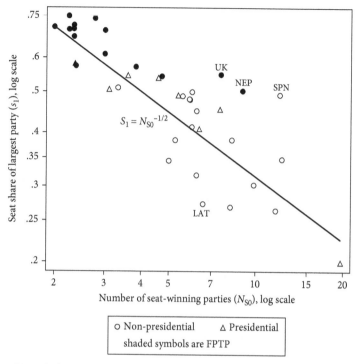

**FIGURE 3.4.** How the largest seat share ($s_1$) relates to the number of seat-winning parties ($N_{S0}$).

Note: Abbreviations for relatively deviant cases: LAT (Latvia), NEP (Nepal), SPN (Spain), UK (United Kingdom).

to Equation 1 (and Figure 3.1): how are the largest share and the effective number related? Taagepera (2007) offers a logic leading to the following average expectation:

$$N_S = s_1^{-4/3}$$

(Equation 5).

Figure 3.5 shows this to be a strong approximation to our country means, with nearly all cases close to the line representing Equation 5.[22]

The series of steps and graphs shown so far complete the major steps in the logical chain extending from the number of parties to expect in a single district to the Seat Product Model of the nationwide effective number of seat-winning parties. What remains to be done is the connection to votes, which we take up in the next section.

## From Seats to Votes

So far we have summarized the derivation of Equation 1, the Seat Product Model for the effective number of seat-winning parties ($N_S$). Here, we show that this can be extended to votes. When a given number of parties wins seats in a representative assembly, how many more are likely to try their luck? How are these two numbers connected logically?

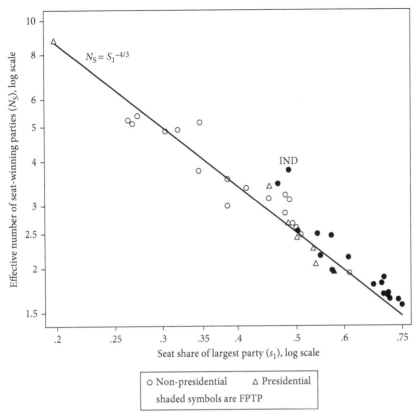

**FIGURE 3.5.** Relationship of the effective number of seat-winning parties ($N_S$) to the largest seat share ($s_1$).

Note: Abbreviations for relatively deviant case: IND (India).

The answer that Shugart and Taagepera (2017) propose is that the number of "pertinent" vote-earning parties should tend to be the number of actual seat-winning parties, plus one close loser: *strivers are winners plus one.*

The now fairly well-established idea of an "$M + 1$ rule" for the number of "serious" or "viable" *candidates* offers a useful starting point. This rule was elaborated by Reed (1990, 2003) and Cox (1997). A recent review summarizes it as follows: "The $M+1$ rule, whereby the number of parties or candidates in a district is capped by the district magnitude ($M$) plus one" (Ferree, Powell, and Scheiner 2013, 812). This "parties *or* candidates" becomes problematic when $M$ is large and the number of parties is thus sure to be smaller than $M$.

The original notion behind the $M + 1$ rule was that it generalized the so-called Duverger's law. When $M = 1$, it hardly matters whether we think of the competing agents as parties or candidates—each party generally presents just one candidate, so the concepts merge. Duverger's law predicts two parties (two candidates) when $M = 1$. Reed's contribution was to say that under single nontransferable vote (SNTV) rules formerly used in Japan (see Nemoto's chapter), the number of "serious" candidates also was near $M + 1$. Reed operationalized "serious" via the effective number,[23] and he explicitly meant candidates, not parties. Under SNTV, larger parties typically nominate more than one candidate per district (but fewer than $M$—see Bergman et al. 2013). Because there are $M$ winners, and they are those with the highest individual vote totals regardless of party, there are $M + 1$ viable candidates,[24] according to Reed's argument. In other words, the district has $M$ winners and one close loser. The rest tend to fall farther behind, at least under certain conditions specified by Reed and extended by Cox.

Cox himself recognizes the limits of applicability of the $M + 1$ rule to larger magnitudes and to the (effective) number of parties, saying it specifies an "upper bound" rather than a prediction. It is obvious that it would be a poor prediction of the number of parties. For instance, in the single nationwide district of $M = 150$ seats in the Netherlands, 151 parties is overkill. Above some moderate level of $M$—Cox (1997, 100) suggests "about five" seats—the $M + 1$ rule is not the principal factor limiting proliferation of parties (Cox 1997, 122). Further, Cox (1997, 102n) states that the application of the $M + 1$ rule to lists in PR systems is "substantially less compelling." Thus, he concludes, "something else" other than the strategic voting that leads to $M + 1$ viable candidates under FPTP and SNTV must be at work when we are concerned with the number of vote-earning parties in PR systems (Cox 1997, 110).[25]

For making sense of the number of viable vote-earning parties, Shugart and Taagepera agree that the "plus one" is an important logical building block. However, the "plus one" should be added to the *number of seat-winning parties* ($N_{S0}$), not the total number of seats allocated in a district ($M$). The Reed and Cox notion of viability being conditioned by competition for seats is logically correct, but further progress comes when we put this "plus one" after the number of seat-winning parties, instead of after the magnitude. This leads to an expression,

$$N_{V0} = N_{S0} + 1 \qquad \text{(Equation 6)},$$

where $N_{V0}$ is the "number of pertinent vote-earning parties" and $N_{S0}$ is the actual (not effective) number of seat-winning parties. Then, given Equation 3, we can replace $N_{S0}$ with the seat product:

$$N_{V0} = (MS)^{1/4} + 1 \qquad \text{(Equation 7)}.$$

Only one step remains to get us to the outcome of interest, the effective number of vote-earning parties, $N_{V0}$. We need to specify a relationship between $N_V$ and $N_{V0}$. We can do so with the basic observation that the relationship should be, logically, the same as for seats, that is, between $N_S$ and $N_{S0}$. As outlined in the preceding section, the equations[26] already imply

$$N_S = N_{S0}^{2/3},$$

and thus we should also have

$$N_V = N_{V0}^{\,2/3}.$$

We can substitute in and derive the following prediction for $N_V$:

$$N_V = \left[ (MS)^{1/4} + 1 \right]^{2/3} \qquad \text{(Equation 8)}.$$

This is testable, and confirmed by both regression analysis and the data plot of Figure 3.6.

The data plot in Figure 3.6 shows that Equation 8 (the solid curve) is a reasonable fit, despite the scatter of the actual data. The dashed curve is the result of a regression on these data points. It is only slightly off, giving a slope of 0.75. The expected slope of two-thirds is grounded in logic, and as the data plot shows, the result is hardly different. Moreover, if we leave out the one extreme data point, Brazil, with the exceedingly high $N_V = 9.6$, we obtain a nearly precise estimate of our coefficient, 0.682.[27] Here the United Kingdom and Spain do not stand out as extreme outliers. This means their vote structure is closer to ordinary for the given seat product $MS$; it's at the seat level that strong surprises emerge, compared to other FPTP and PR countries.

Compared to our criterion for major deviations (off by a factor of four-thirds), Figure 3.3 has the most deviations (fifteen). This implies that the actual number of seat-winning parties is most at the mercy of tiny parties winning a single seat or failing to do so. Effective numbers are more stable. In the logical chain of reasoning they are far removed from seat product $MS$, and deviations occur—ten cases in both Figures 3.1 and 3.6. Remarkably, proceeding from seats to votes does not increase scatter, as one might expect. As expected, scatter is much lower when factors graphed are just one step removed from one another in the logical chain—from $N_{S0}$ to $s_1$ in Figure 3.4 (four deviant cases), and from $s_1$ to $N_S$ in Figure 3.5 (one deviant case).

When doing statistics of green peas the average size may be just an empirical given, and the extra large and small ones may be seen as mere anonymous statistical outliers. Here this is not so. First, the average output is not empirical but a logically grounded expectation, almost bafflingly confirmed by empirics. Second, countries have identities that peas don't (at least for us). In our graphs the most frequent outliers, each in a somewhat different way, were Brazil, Cape Verde, Latvia, St. Kitts and Nevis, Spain, Switzerland, the United Kingdom, and the United States. While most of the forty-nine countries considered (because they have "simple" electoral systems) fall closer to expectations, why do those eight deviate in the various ways they do? Pinning down country-specific features is a major payoff of the study described here. We have not just an elegant completed edifice but also starting points for more country-specific studies, now that we know how these countries stand out against the benchmark.

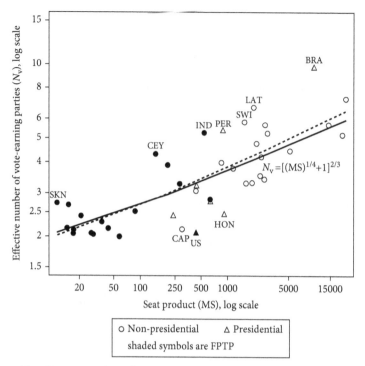

**FIGURE 3.6.** The effective number of vote-earning parties and the seat product.

Note: Abbreviations for relatively deviant cases: BRA (Brazil), CAP (Cape Verde), CEY (Ceylon to 1970), HON (Honduras), IND (India), LAT (Latvia), PER (Peru), SKN (St. Kitts and Nevis), SWI (Switzerland), US (United States).

## COMPLEX SYSTEMS AND ETHNIC FACTORS

In this section, we consider two additional factors: (1) how institutions affect party fragmentation when the electoral system is not "simple" and (2) whether considering the ethnic fragmentation of a country can improve our ability to predict the party system beyond what we can get from the seat product model.

Considering these two additional factors is important for two reasons. First, a significant percentage of the world's democratic electoral systems are not simple, but rather contain an "upper tier" of allocation (see Gallagher and Mitchell's chapter for definition) or other complicating features. Second, most of the literature in the field of comparative electoral systems analysis over recent decades has included a variable for upper tiers and, in addition, argued that "permissive" electoral systems are associated with high degrees of party fragmentation only in the presence of high demand emanating from social diversity.[28]

A central argument in the literature since Ordeshook and Shvetsova (1994) is that electoral systems and social diversity jointly affect the effective number of parties. Amorim Neto and Cox (1997) and Cox (1997) were the first to articulate that the effect was interactive; see

Moser et al. (this volume) for an extensive review and analysis. In the interactive formulation, "restrictive" electoral systems are associated with a low effective number of parties *even* when social diversity is high, whereas permissive systems are associated with a high effective number of parties *only* when social diversity is high. Absent demand from society, these authors claim, permissive systems do not result in increased number of parties. In these works, the degree of restrictiveness or permissiveness is measured by the mean district magnitude and the size of any upper tiers of allocation. Several subsequent works have rested their analysis on the same basic theoretical assumptions and variables but using different datasets and varying statistical estimating techniques or considering additional variables (Mozaffar et al. 2003; Clark and Golder 2006; Golder 2006; Hicken and Stoll 2011, 2012).

In the Seat Product Model the measure of permissiveness is the product of the mean[29] district magnitude and the assembly size. However, as detailed in the preceding sections of this chapter, this model originally applied only to simple electoral systems—those in which all seats are allocated within districts with some proportional formula (or FPTP) in one round of voting. The model thus does not take account of upper tiers, which are found in several complex proportional representation systems, including two-tier PR (as in Denmark or South Africa[30]) and mixed-member proportional (MMP) systems (as in Germany and New Zealand[31]).

The possibility of incorporating upper tiers into the Seat Product Model was first proposed and tested by Li and Shugart (2016); it was tested further and confirmed by Shugart and Taagepera (2017). The theory behind the extended model is that the mean district magnitude and the total number of seats in the *basic tier* only—that is, excluding upper-tier seats—affect the party system much the same as it would were it the entire system (i.e., were the system simple). Then the upper tier inflates the basic-tier effective number of parties, according to how much of the entire assembly is contained in this tier.[32] It is important to add that the theory assumes that the upper tier is compensatory; it is not expected to apply to noncompensatory allocation.[33] The extended SPM is

$$N_S = J^t \left( MS_B \right)^{1/6} \qquad \text{(Equation 9)}.$$

In this equation, $MS_B$ refers to the basic-tier seat product. The upper tier enters through the variable $t$, which is the "tier ratio," calculated as the number of upper-tier seats divided by the total assembly size. The term $J$, the base of the tier ratio, is determined empirically. For the full dataset employed by Shugart and Taagepera, $J = 2.5$, and given that this chapter is built on the same comprehensive dataset, we will use that here, yielding

$$N_S = 2.5^t \left( MS_B \right)^{1/6} \qquad \text{(Equation 10)}.$$

A more complete test also requires inclusion of a measure of social diversity. As we have no good operational way to measure social diversity, the much narrower notion of ethnic diversity is usually substituted. Most works in this field have used the effective number of ethnic groups ($N_E$), derived from Fearon (2003). Li and Shugart (2016) and Shugart and

Taagepera (2017) carry out a regression test that parallels the statistical strategy used by Clark and Golder (2006). The regression includes a term for the log of $N_E$, as well as a multiplicative interaction to test the combined effect of the electoral system and ethnic diversity.[34] The result shows a small but significant impact of $N_E$ when $MS_B$ is high (especially if there is also a large upper tier), thus offering some support for the notion of an interactive effect of electoral system permissiveness and social demand for additional parties.

Nonetheless, when individual countries' observed values are compared to both the regression estimates and the predictions of the institutions-only extended SPM, Shugart and Taagepera find that the inclusion of diversity improves the prediction for only a few cases. In Table 3.1 we summarize the results for each of the countries included in the statistical analysis of this chapter.

Table 3.1 breaks the cases into four categories: the first two include countries that have a below-median value of expected $N_S$ from the extended SPM (Equation 10), while the second two have above-median values of expected $N_S$. Within the groups of low and high expected $N_S$, a further division is between those with $N_E$ below or above the median. The table includes a column for the output of the regression that includes the interaction of electoral system permissiveness (i.e., the seat product and, where relevant, the tier ratio) with ethnic fragmentation. This is thus a "postdiction," because by the nature of a regression equation, it is telling us what the pattern is in the actual data on which it was run. Then there is a column for the output of the Seat Product Model; this is a prediction in the sense that it relies on institutional inputs only and is not a regression equation. The last two columns show the ratio of the system's observed mean $N_S$ to the regression postdiction and the SPM prediction.

If the interactive hypothesis is correct, we should see a tendency for the regression to perform substantially better when ethnic fragmentation is high, particularly when the seat product is also high. We can summarize the relative power of the two approaches by the medians indicated for the ratios in each group, as well as for the entire set at the bottom of the table. What we see is perhaps surprising: the institutions-only Seat Product Model performs better for the cases of high ethnic diversity despite the fact that ethnicity is not a parameter in the SPM! That is, the high seat product (and an upper tier, where present) appears to be sufficient to account for highly fragmented assembly party systems, on average.

A surprising finding is that the categories where the regression including $N_E$ performs its best are those with *low* ethnic fragmentation—especially the first category in the table, where we have both electoral system restrictiveness and low ethnic fragmentation. Such a finding is quite contrary to the standard interactive hypothesis, as the latter claims high $N_S$ is a joint effect of electoral system permissiveness and high $N_E$. Perhaps a more accurate claim would be that when the seat product is low, $N_S$ tends to be low, as expected from the SPM; the presence of low ethnic fragmentation tends to result in a still lower value of $N_S$.

It is worth considering a few specific countries that are *not* surprises from the standpoint of the SPM. Canada, which is often alleged to be exceptional from the perspective of the so-called Duverger's law, actually has a long-term mean $N_S$ that is ever so slightly *below* what we should expect, given its large assembly size (actual $N_S$ = 2.50 vs. expected

Table 3.1 Actual, Postdicted, and Predicted Effective Number of Seat-Winning Parties

| Country | System Type | Seat Product | Tier Ratio | Eff. No. of Ethnic Groups | Eff. No. of Seat-Winning Parties | Regression Postdiction | Seat Product Model (SPM) Prediction | Ratio of Actual to Regression Postdiction | Ratio of Actual to SPM Prediction |
|---|---|---|---|---|---|---|---|---|---|
| Below median on both seat product and ethnic diversity | | | | | | | | | |
| Jamaica | Simple | 57.8 | 0 | 1.20 | 1.67 | 1.77 | 1.97 | 0.945 | 0.850 |
| New Zealand (1945–1993) | Simple (FPTP) | 86.5 | 0 | 1.57 | 1.97 | 1.94 | 2.10 | 1.012 | 0.935 |
| Costa Rica | Simple | 440.7 | 0 | 1.31 | 2.66 | 2.53 | 2.76 | 1.053 | 0.965 |
| Cyprus | Two tier | 522.5 | 0 | 1.56 | 3.63 | 2.72 | 2.84 | 1.334 | 1.277 |
| United Kingdom | Simple | 639.4 | 0 | 1.48 | 2.16 | 2.78 | 2.94 | 0.777 | 0.737 |
| New Zealand (1996–2011) | Two tier | 68.7 | 0.43 | 1.57 | 3.29 | 3.18 | 3.01 | 1.033 | 1.091 |
| Honduras | Simple | 932.9 | 0 | 1.23 | 2.26 | 2.82 | 3.13 | 0.800 | 0.722 |
| Denmark | Two tier | 1,027.0 | 0.23 | 1.15 | 4.62 | 3.91 | 3.93 | 1.181 | 1.174 |
| Germany | Two tier | 270.3 | 0.49 | 1.10 | 3.38 | 3.69 | 4.00 | 0.917 | 0.846 |
| Median | | | | | | | | 1.022 | 0.950 |
| Below median on seat product, above median ethnic diversity | | | | | | | | | |
| Trinidad and Tobago | Simple (FPTP) | 36.8 | 0 | 2.83 | 1.79 | 1.69 | 1.82 | 1.063 | 0.984 |
| Ceylon (1960–1970) | Simple (FPTP) | 151 | 0 | 1.75 | 3.46 | 2.19 | 2.31 | 1.577 | 1.497 |
| Nepal (1991–1999) | Simple (FPTP) | 205 | 0 | 3.10 | 2.55 | 2.56 | 2.43 | 0.997 | 1.052 |
| Chile | Simple | 240 | 0 | 1.99 | 2.05 | 2.46 | 2.49 | 0.833 | 0.821 |

(continued)

**Table 3.1 Continued**

| Country | System Type | Seat Product | Tier Ratio | Eff. No. of Ethnic Groups | Eff. No. of Seat-Winning Parties | Regression Postdiction | Seat Product Model (SPM) Prediction | Ratio of Actual to Regression Postdiction | Ratio of Actual to SPM Prediction |
|---|---|---|---|---|---|---|---|---|---|
| Canada | Simple (FPTP) | 281.6 | 0 | 2.48 | 2.50 | 2.65 | 2.56 | 0.944 | 0.976 |
| United States | Simple (FPTP) | 435.1 | 0 | 1.96 | 1.94 | 2.77 | 2.75 | 0.701 | 0.705 |
| India | Simple (FPTP) | 536 | 0 | 5.29 | 3.77 | 3.69 | 2.85 | 1.022 | 1.322 |
| Dominican Rep | Simple | 641.0 | 0 | 1.63 | 2.42 | 2.86 | 2.94 | 0.848 | 0.825 |
| Peru | Simple | 884 | 0 | 2.76 | 3.38 | 3.53 | 3.10 | 0.957 | 1.090 |
| Venezuela | Two tier | 1,003.2 | 0.21 | 1.93 | 3.37 | 3.63 | 3.83 | 0.930 | 0.880 |
| Median | | | | | | | | **0.950** | **0.980** |
| Above median on seat product, below median ethnic diversity | | | | | | | | | |
| Norway (1949–1985) | Simple | 1,149.2 | 0 | 1.11 | 3.21 | 2.83 | 3.24 | 1.131 | 0.991 |
| Norway (1989–2009) | Two tier | 1,259.0 | 0.07 | 1.11 | 4.44 | 3.13 | 3.50 | 1.415 | 1.266 |
| Bulgaria | Two tier | 1,857.6 | 0 | 1.43 | 3.12 | 3.34 | 3.51 | 0.934 | 0.890 |
| Sweden (1948–1968) | Simple | 1,912.6 | 0 | 1.23 | 3.11 | 3.19 | 3.52 | 0.973 | 0.882 |
| Portugal | Simple | 2,628.3 | 0 | 1.04 | 2.85 | 3.16 | 3.71 | 0.902 | 0.768 |
| Finland | Simple | 2,660 | 0 | 1.15 | 5.11 | 3.29 | 372 | 1.554 | 1.373 |
| Czechia | Simple | 2,858 | 0 | 1.47 | 3.76 | 3.65 | 3.77 | 1.029 | 0.998 |
| Poland (2005–2011) | Simple | 5,161.2 | 0 | 1.05 | 3.36 | 3.52 | 4.16 | 0.955 | 0.808 |
| Poland (2001) | Two tier | 5,878.8 | 0 | 1.05 | 3.60 | 3.59 | 4.25 | 1.002 | 0.847 |

| | | | | | | | | | |
|---|---|---|---|---|---|---|---|---|---|
| Sweden (1970–2010) | Two tier | 3,395.5 | 0.11 | 1.23 | 3.74 | 4.04 | 4.30 | 0.927 | 0.871 |
| Austria | Two tier | 2,260.1 | 0.23 | 1.14 | 2.71 | 3.66 | 4.47 | 0.741 | 0.607 |
| Netherlands | Simple | 20,625 | 0 | 1.08 | 4.88 | 4.44 | 5.24 | 1.098 | 0.931 |
| Slovak Republic | Simple | 22,500 | 0 | 1.50 | 4.93 | 5.37 | 5.31 | 0.918 | 0.927 |
| Median | | | | | | | | **0.973** | **0.890** |
| Above median on both seat product and ethnic diversity | | | | | | | | | |
| Switzerland | Simple | 1,551.5 | 0 | 2.35 | 5.22 | 3.82 | 3.40 | 1.369 | 1.535 |
| Latvia | Simple | 2,000 | 0 | 2.41 | 5.37 | 4.07 | 3.55 | 1.321 | 1.514 |
| Croatia | Simple | 2,124.5 | 0 | 1.60 | 2.99 | 3.56 | 3.59 | 0.840 | 0.835 |
| Spain | Simple | 2,355.5 | 0 | 2.01 | 2.67 | 3.95 | 3.65 | 0.676 | 0.732 |
| Macedonia | Simple | 2,415 | 0 | 2.15 | 3.14 | 4.07 | 3.66 | 0.770 | 0.856 |
| Brazil | Simple | 9,677.9 | 0 | 2.22 | 8.70 | 5.55 | 4.62 | 1.568 | 1.884 |
| Israel | Simple | 14,400 | 0 | 2.11 | 5.15 | 5.89 | 4.93 | 0.875 | 1.044 |
| Median | | | | | | | | 0.875 | 1.044 |
| Median (overall) | | | | | | | | **1.023** | **1.009** |

*Notes:* Systems are sorted within categories by increasing SPM prediction.

Dates are indicated where the system is not a current one, or where there has been a change from simple to complex (or reverse).

Seat product refers to basic tier only, in case of a two–tier system.

If a system is indicated as two tier but no tier ratio is given, it is a remainder–pooling system (no fixed upper tier).

$N_S = 2.65$). The very high fragmentation in Israel, with its nationwide PR, has tended to average around the SPM expectation.[35] Strikingly, the only country that has an above-median $N_E$ and is explained substantially better by the regression that includes $N_E$ (and its interaction with the seat product) is India.[36]

When we compare the entire set of countries in Table 3.1, we see that the median ratio of actual $N_S$ to the SPM's prediction is 1.01. It is thus as good as the regression (1.02), despite the fact that the regression is almost guaranteed to be accurate, on average, because its parameters were estimated directly from these data. That is why we refer to the output of the regression as a *post*diction. The SPM, by contrast, is built on deductive logic. It is derived before going to the data, and is therefore genuinely a *pre*diction, based only on institutional parameters.

Extensions to votes and to disproportionality have been done (Shugart and Taagepera, 2017), but we leave the discussion here on seat fragmentation. It is, after all, through the seats in the assembly that legislation is passed and, if the executive is parliamentary, cabinets made and unmade. We have shown that two parameters of simple electoral systems, district magnitude and assembly size, can predict the average trend in the effective number of parties. The addition of the parameter of the share of seats in a compensatory upper tier can encompass a wider set of nonsimple systems. Moreover, Shugart and Taagepera (2017) show that even the systems in France (two-round majority plurality[37]) and Ireland (single transferable vote[38]) are broadly predictable, despite having electoral system features that are more complex.

# CONCLUSION

When $S$ is the number of seats in the assembly and $M$ is the number of seats in the average electoral district, four basic laws of party seats and votes emerge from our model and graphs (directly or indirectly):

1. Law of largest party seats: The most likely seat share of the largest party in an elected assembly is $s_1 = (MS)^{-1/8}$.
2. Law of number of assembly parties: The most likely effective number of parties in an elected assembly is $N_S = (MS)^{1/6}$.
3. Law of largest party votes: The most likely vote share of the largest party in assembly elections is $v_1 = [(MS)^{1/4} + 1]^{-1/2}$.
4. Law of number of electoral parties: The most likely effective number of parties in assembly elections is $N_V = [(MS)^{1/4} + 1]^{2/3}$.

In principle, they apply only to "simple" electoral systems and (with the adjustment term in Equation 10) to two-tier systems. Actually, even complex electoral systems (two rounds, legal thresholds, and single transferable vote) fit to a surprising degree. These laws also enable us to take the seat product of a given electoral system and from that estimate the deviation from PR and the effective number of presidential candidates—see Shugart and Taagepera (2017). Through the inverse square law of cabinet duration—$C = 42$ yrs / $N_S^2$ (Taagepera 2007, 165–175)—which we have not discussed here, the impact of electoral institutions reaches the workings of governments in parliamentary democracies.

But a big surprise awaits us when we try applying these laws in individual districts: They underestimate the effective number of parties. This is so because national politics boosts the number of local parties. In this sense, "all politics is national"! The nationwide impact on the district level is quite systematic, but we will bypass it here.[39]

The present overview lacks space to cover all this. Rather than skimming over too much new ground that goes beyond the four basic laws, we have focused on explaining the logic behind the four laws and presenting empirical evidence, in the form of graphs and statistical testing. Building on the so-called Duverger's law, fuzzy and quasi-quantitative as it is, the four laws raise the Duvergerian quest to a truly quantitative level, making specific prediction possible.

The permissiveness of electoral systems toward small parties has traditionally been measured mainly by district magnitude alone; *the product of district magnitude and assembly size now must replace this*. Indeed, 625 single-seat districts lead to as many parties as 25 districts of 25 seats each. This means there is little point in treating single-seat and multiseat systems as different species, for many purposes.

The reach of the seat product is powerful, doing away with the need for various other inputs. Presidential regimes fit in; indeed, Shugart and Taagepera (2017) show that the effective number of presidential candidates, rather than being a separate noninstitutional input factor, can be estimated from the seat product of the assembly. Social diversity, to the extent it can be reduced to mere ethnic diversity, finds its outlet in seat product, so that including the effective number of ethnic groups improves our predictive ability only when $MS$ is very low.

A hallmark of developed sciences is that they go beyond establishing quantitative connections among various factors: they furthermore establish connections among such connections. This is the level electoral studies have now reached, interconnecting institutional inputs such as district magnitude and assembly size, and political outputs such as number of seat-winning parties, effective number of parties, the largest seat and vote shares, and even cabinet duration through a network of equations, of which the equations in this chapter are samples.

When an individual election or country deviates from the expected value, this is an opportunity for further research into what it is about the politics that causes the deviation. Is it something in the history and culture of the country, a specific issue or party leader dominating the campaign of a specific election, or something else? If we lack a deductive baseline for what the outcome should be, given the institutional inputs, we are unable to ask these questions in a scientifically meaningful way. However, we now have a baseline, grounded in logic, and tested on a worldwide sample of elections. Having a baseline is not the endpoint. It is where the hard work begins—when seeking to understand the way context sometimes results in deviations from expectations, even the average of numerous elections across most countries conforms.[40] Few subfields of social sciences have reached such a degree of interconnected knowledge.

# AUTHOR NOTE

All figures are drawn by the authors specially for this chapter.

# NOTES

1. Or sometimes effective number of legislative parties (ENLP).
2. Moreover, ENP risks to be mistaken for multiplication of the quantities $E$, $N$, and $P$.
3. As with the effective number, so could $F$ be calculated on votes rather than seats.
4. Nor should it be called the "number of effective parties," as one sometimes sees. It is the number that is "effective"; judgment on whether the parties per se are effective might be beyond the scope of a mathematical index.
5. Caution needs to be taken if there is a substantial percentage of either votes or seats listed as "others"; these should not be treated as if they were one party, nor ignored when calculating effective $N$. See Taagepera (1997) for guidance; see also Gallagher and Mitchell (2005, 598–602).
6. For further detail on various indices of deviation from proportionality, see Taagepera (2007, 65–82) and Taagepera and Grofman (2003).
7. It even entered popular media discourse in Canada in late 2016, when a parliamentary committee charged with considering alternative electoral systems released its report. See "The Problem with Maryam Monsef's Contempt for Metrics," *McCleans's*, December 3, 2016, http://www.macleans.ca/politics/ottawa/the-problem-with-maryam-monsefs-contempt-for-metrics/ (accessed December 15, 2016).
8. For example, they might show graphs of "marginal effects" of the interaction of one variable with another, but not show an underlying bivariate relationship of theoretical interest through the plotting of actual election outcomes.
9. Even with many input (or "independent") variables, one could graph the regression-estimated outcome against the actual outcomes from elections (or country averages). Yet this is only infrequently done in political science.
10. See, for example, Table 3.2 in Clark and Golder (2006), in which the coefficient estimate on the log of magnitude ranges from –0.08 to 0.33, depending on what other variables are included and the precise sample. Even their interaction with ethnic fragmentation—testing their preferred hypothesis (discussed later in this chapter)—has a similarly wide range of coefficient values and is statistically significant in some specifications and insignificant in others.
11. In our larger work (Shugart and Taagepera, 2017), we plot and test regressions with data from individual elections. Here we report only the country averages.
12. Later we will discuss the impact of more complex systems.
13. For instance, D'Hondt, Ste.-Laguë, Hare, or Droop quota and largest remainders. See the introduction to this volume for definitions of common formulas.
14. On thirty-eight country means from simple systems, we obtain $\log(N_S) = 0.029 + 0.156\log(MS)$; the intercept is insignificant and the expected 0.167 lies firmly within the

95 percent confidence interval of the estimated coefficient on $\log(MS)$. $R^2 = 0.665$. Given that it must be that $N_S = 1$ (and thus $\log N_S = 0$) if we had any actual cases of assembly elections with $MS = 1$, we can re-estimate the regression with the constant term suppressed. If we do so, our coefficient on $\log MS$ is 0.1664. For general principles of avoiding regression results that yield absurdities, see Shugart and Taagepera (2017) and Taagepera (2008).

15. This means being high or low by a factor of four-thirds. In other words, $\log(3/4) = -0.125$ is the negative of $\log 1.33 = \log(4/3) = +0.125$.

16. While several presidential systems are on the low side of the line representing Equation 1, they are not to any degree outside the general data range for nonpresidential systems. See Shugart and Taagepera (2017) for a detailed discussion of why presidential systems need not be treated separately. See also Li and Shugart (2016).

17. Our three actual cases of $M = S$ (nationwide PR) are all, on average, very close to the line representing Equation 1. Note the three points closest to the right margin of the graph; these are Israel, the Netherlands, and Slovakia.

18. In this equation, we have dropped the prime mark from $N_{S0}$ because we are again referring to nationwide results.

19. For $M < S$, we have $M^{1/2}$ as the expectation for the mean district and $S^{1/2}$ as the mean for the assembly. The geometric average of these conditions leads directly to Equation 3: $N_{S0} = (M^{1/2} \times S^{1/2})^{1/2} = (MS)^{1/4}$.

20. The ordinary least squares (OLS) regression result is $\log N_{S0} = 0.0702 + 0.237 \log(MS)$. The constant is insignificant, and $R^2 = 0.670$. It is not surprising that the data plot shows some more outliers than does Figure 3.1, showing $N_S$. A few very small parties unexpectedly getting a seat or two—or, conversely, an expected party getting no seats—make a full integer jump in $N_{S0}$ for any given election. Yet such small deviations from the expected number have less consequence for $N_S$, due to its being a size-weighted count. The surprise is that the fit is so good, despite the bluntness of the actual number of parties ($N_{S0}$) as a measure.

21. The OLS regression result is $\log s_1 = -0.000518 - 0.4562(N_{S0})$. The constant is effectively zero, and $R^2 = 0.705$.

22. The OLS regression is $\log N_S = -0.0493 - 1.238 \log s_1$. The constant is actually significantly different from zero, at 95 percent confidence. However, it is logically impossible to have a constant in this equation that is different from zero, as it would imply a value of $N_S > 1$ when $s_1 = 1$, which is an absurdity. Given that the expected $-1.333$ is within the 95 percent confidence interval of the estimated coefficient, we can consider Equation 5 (which is based on deductive logic) to be confirmed.

23. As we noted earlier in this chapter, using the effective number in this manner can be somewhat misleading.

24. Cox (1997, 99) defines viable as "proof against strategic voting."

25. Cox goes on to suggest the answer is "economies of scale" that lead actors to "coordinate" around a smaller number of *party lists*.

26. We found that $N_{S0} = (MS)^{1/4}$ and $N_S = (MS)^{1/6}$; algebraically, then, we have to have $N_S = N_{S0}^{2/3}$.

27. Leaving out the Brazilian case would be justified, as the effective number of vote-earning parties at the national level is an overcount, due to the existence of multiparty alliances within the country's competing electoral lists. See Shugart and Taagepera (2017) for details. The same measurement problem affects seats, although less so. The regression without the Brazilian case is $\log N_V = 0.0141 + 0.682 \log[(MS)^{1/4} + 1]$; the constant is insignificant and $R^2 = 0.648$.

28. In addition, most standard regression treatments include variables found only in presidential systems: the effective number of presidential candidates ($N_P$) and how "proximate" the assembly election is to a presidential election. A key problem with these treatments is that it requires an unrealistic value of $N_P = 0$ for parliamentary systems for these cases to be in the same regression (with nonmissing values on $N_P$) with presidential systems. Yet the feasible minimum value of $N_P$ is 1.00. Moreover, it is untenable to assume, as these works implicitly do, that a parliamentary system is no different from a presidential system that has only midterm elections (like the Dominican Republic from 1998 to 2010); both situations incur a "proximity" value of zero in these models. For extended critique of such approaches, see Li and Shugart (2016) or Shugart and Taagepera (2017); see also Elgie et al. (2014).

29. Results are not different when median is used instead of mean. Moreover, Shugart and Taagepera (2017) do not find evidence that wide variation in magnitude affects the accuracy of the predictions from the SPM. This does not preclude the possibility that such variance may have other effects, for instance, favoring certain parties over others (Monroe and Rose 2002; Kedar et al. 2016).

30. On South Africa, see the chapter by Ferree in this volume. On Denmark and two-tier systems more generally, see Elklit and Roberts (1996).

31. See, respectively, the chapters by Zittel and Vowles in this volume.

32. Through disaggregation of two-tier systems into their district level and separately accounting for the impact of the upper tier, Shugart and Taagepera (2017) are able to confirm the logic proposed by Li and Shugart (2016).

33. Noncompensatory upper tiers are found, for example, in the mixed-member majoritarian systems (as in Japan—see Nemoto's chapter in the volume). The extended SPM also would not apply if the system used in the basic tier did not meet the criteria of "simple" (e.g., the two-round systems found in the basic tiers of Hungary and Lithuania).

34. The regression equation is $\log N_S = \alpha + \beta_1 \log(MS_B) + \beta_2 t + \beta_3 \log(N_E) + \beta_4 [\log(MS_B) * \log(N_E)]$. For details, see Li and Shugart (2016) or Shugart and Taagepera (2017).

35. In recent years it has been well above, balancing out past periods when it was below. It is worth noting that the country's recent surge in party fragmentation is also well above what is predicted when including its ethnic fragmentation in the regression. See Hazan et al. (this volume) for a detailed treatment. See also Stoll (2013).

36. India's recent period of very high party system fragmentation has seen most parties agglomerate into a smaller number of alliances that structure national-level competition and provide government and opposition organization of the assembly (see Ziegfeld, this volume). Shugart and Taagepera (2017) show that the effective number of alliances in India since 1999 closely matches the value predicted from the SPM. (The model itself is "agnostic" about whether the entities in question are called by different party names in different districts or are a nationwide entity; in most countries the entities at the district level and nationwide levels are the same, but not in India, in the era of alliances.)

37. See the chapter in this volume by Hoyo.

38. See the chapter in this volume by Marsh.

39. What is the adjusted formula for such "embedded" districts? For effective number of seat-winning parties in districts it is $N'_S = M^{2k/3}$, where (hold your breath!) $k = 0.5 + 0.2076\log(S/M) / M^{.25}$—most of it logically grounded. See proof and evidence in Shugart and Taagepera (2017).

40. Several chapters in this volume explore how specific electoral systems operate in their country contexts.

# REFERENCES

Amorim Neto, Octavio, and Gary W. Cox. "Electoral Institutions, Cleavage Structures, and the Number of Parties." *American Journal of Political Science* 44, no. 1 (1997): 149–174.

Bergman, Matthew E., Matthew S. Shugart, and Kevin A. Watt. "Patterns of Intraparty Competition in Open-List, and SNTV Systems." *Electoral Studies* 32, no. 2 (2013): 321–333.

Clark, William R., and Matt Golder. "Rehabilitating Duverger's Theory Testing the Mechanical and Strategic Modifying Effects of Electoral Laws." *Comparative Political Studies* 39, no. 6 (2006): 679–708.

Cox, Gary W. *Making Votes Count: Strategic Coordination in the World's Electoral Systems.* New York: Cambridge University Press, 1997.

Droop, Henry R. "On the Political and Social Effects of Different Methods of Electing Representatives", in *Electoral Systems*, Vol. III., edited by D. M. Farrell and M. S. Shugart. London: Sage, 2012 [1869].

Dunleavy, Patrick, and Françoise Boucek. "Constructing the Number of Parties." *Party Politics* 9 (2003): 291–315.

Duverger, Maurice. *Les partis politiques.* Paris: Armand Colin, 1951.

Duverger, Maurice. *Political Parties: Their Organization and Activity in the Modern State.* New York: John Wiley and Sons, 1954.

Elgie, Robert, Cristina Bucur, Bernard Dolez, and Annie Laurent. "Proximity, Candidates, and Presidential Power: How Directly Elected Presidents Shape the Legislative Party System." *Political Research Quarterly* 67, no. 3 (2014): 467–477.

Elklit, Jørgen, and Nigel S. Roberts. "A Category of Its Own? Four PR Two-Tier Compensatory Member Electoral Systems in 1994." *European Journal of Political Research* 30, no. 2 (1996): 217–240.

Fearon, James D. "Ethnic and Cultural Diversity by Country." *Journal of Economic Growth* 8, no. 2 (2003): 195–222.

Ferree, Karen E., Powell, G. Bingham, and Scheiner, Ethan. "How Context Shapes the Effects of Electoral Rules", *Political Science, Electoral Rules, and Democratic Governance*, ed. by M. Htun and G. B, Powell, Jr. Washington: American Political Science Association, 2013.

Gaines, Brian J., and Rein Taagepera. "How to Operationalize Two-Partyness." *Journal of Elections, Public Opinion, and Parties* 23, no. 4 (2013): 387–404.

Gallagher, Michael. "Proportionality, Disproportionality and Electoral Systems." *Electoral studies* 10, no. 1 (1991): 33–51.

Gallagher, Michael, and Paul Mitchell, eds. *The Politics of Electoral Systems.* Oxford: Oxford University Press, 2005.

Golder, Matt. "Presidential Coattails and Legislative Fragmentation." *American Journal of Political Science* 50, no. 1 (2006): 34–48.

Golosov, Grigorii V. "The Effective Number of Parties: A New Approach." *Party Politics* 16, no. 2 (2009): 171–192.

Hare, Thomas. *Treatise on the Election of Representatives, Parliamentary and Municipal.* London: Longman, Green, Reader, and Dyer, 1859.

Hicken, Allen, and Heather Stoll. "Presidents and Parties: How Presidential Elections Shape Coordination in Legislative Elections." *Comparative Political Studies* 44, no. 7 (2011): 854–883.

Hicken, Allen, and Heather Stoll. "Are All Presidents Created Equal? Presidential Powers and the Shadow of Presidential Elections." *Comparative Political Studies* 46, no. 13 (2012): 291–319.

Kedar, Orit, Liran Harsgor, and Raz A. Sheinerman. "Are Voters Equal under Proportional Representation?" *American Journal of Political Science* 60, no. 3 (2016): 679–691.

Laakso, Markku, and Rein Taagepera. "The 'Effective' Number of Parties: A Measure with Application to West Europe." *Comparative Political Studies* 12, no. 1 (1979): 3–27.

Li, Yuhui, and Matthew S. Shugart. "The Seat Product Model of the Effective Number of Parties: A Case for Applied Political Science." *Electoral Studies* 41, no. 1 (2016): 23–34.

Loosemore, John, and Victor J. Hanby. "The Theoretical Limits of Maximum Distortion: Some Analytic Expressions for Electoral Systems." *British Journal of Political Science* 1, no. 4 (1971): 467–477.

Molinar, Juan. "Counting the Number of Parties: An Alternative Index." *American Political Science Review* 85 (1991): 1357–1382.

Monroe, Burt L., and Amanda G. Rose. "Electoral Systems and Unimagined Consequences: Partisan Effects of Districted Proportional Representation." *American Journal of Political Science* 46, no. 1 (2002): 67–89.

Mozaffar, Shaheen, James R. Scarritt, and Glen Galaich. "Electoral Institutions, Ethnopolitical Cleavages and Party Systems in Africa's Emerging Democracies." *American Political Science Review* 97, no. 3 (2003): 379–390.

Ordeshook, Peter, and Olga Shvetsova. "Ethnic Heterogeneity, District Magnitude, and the Number of Parties." *American Journal of Political Science* 38 (1994): 100–123.

Rae, Douglas W. *The Political Consequences of Electoral Laws*. New Haven, CT: Yale University Press, 1967.

Reed, Steven R. "Structure and Behaviour: Extending Duverger's Law to the Japanese Case." *British Journal of Political Science* 20, no. 3 (1990): 335–356.

Reed, Steven R. "What Mechanism Causes the M+1 Rule? A Simple Simulation." *Japanese Journal of Political Science* 4, no. 1 (2003): 41–60.

Shugart, Matthew S., and Rein Taagepera. *Votes from Seats: Logical Models of Electoral Systems*. New York: Cambridge University Press, 2017.

Stoll, Heather. *Changing Societies, Changing Party Systems*. New York: Cambridge University Press, 2013.

Struthers, Cory L., Yuhui Li, and Matthew S. Shugart. "Introducing New Multilevel Datasets: Party Systems at the District and National Levels." *Research and Politics* 5, no. 4 (2018), https://doi.org/10.1177/2053168018813508.

Taagepera, Rein. "Effective Number of Parties for Incomplete Data." *Electoral Studies* 16, no. 2 (1997): 145–151.

Taagepera, Rein. "Supplementing the Effective Number of Parties." *Electoral Studies* 18, no. 4 (1999): 497–504.

Taagepera, Rein. *Predicting Party Sizes: The Logic of Simple Electoral Systems*. Oxford: Oxford University Press, 2007.

Taagepera, Rein. *Making Social Sciences More Scientific: The Need for Predictive Models*. Oxford: Oxford University Press, 2008.

Taagepera, Rein, and Bernard Grofman. "Mapping the Indices of Seats–Votes Disproportionality and Inter-Election Volatility." *Party Politics* 9, no. 6 (2003): 659–677.

Taagepera, Rein, and Matthew S. Shugart. "Predicting the Number of Parties: A Quantitative Model of Duverger's Mechanical Effect." *American Political Science Review* 87, no. 2 (1993): 455–464.

CHAPTER 4

......................................................................................................

# PARTY SYSTEM EFFECTS ON ELECTORAL SYSTEMS

......................................................................................................

## JOSEP M. COLOMER

## INTRODUCTION

......................................................................................................

POLITICAL parties and electoral systems have been analyzed both as a cause and as a consequence of each other. First, a long tradition of empirical studies focused on the consequences of electoral systems on party systems. Most prominently, Maurice Duverger postulated that "old" political parties were created internally in elected (and also in nonelected) assemblies and parliamentary groups (Duverger 1951). Empirical analyses of party systems, which typically focus on democratic regimes from the mid-twentieth century on, usually assume that political parties derive from given elections and electoral systems that can be taken as the independent variable in the explanatory framework.

A number of contributions have turned this relationship upside down by postulating that it is the parties that choose electoral systems and manipulate the rules of elections. The origins of the invention and adoption of different electoral rules and procedures, especially during the nineteenth and early twentieth centuries, can be found in the incentives created by political party competition. Further electoral reforms, as well as the choice of electoral systems in new democracies, can also be explained on the basis of political parties' relative strength, expectations, and strategic decisions. With this approach, it is the political parties that can be taken as given and work as the independent variable to explain the emergence of different electoral rules. It can also be hypothesized, nevertheless, that changes in the party system—which is the focus of this chapter—tend to have significant effects on the electoral systems in the long term, while changes in electoral rules may have short-term effects on political party competition.

This chapter reviews, first, the most remote origins of political parties and how they began to shape innovative electoral rules; second, how different political party configurations influence the choice, permanence, or change of electoral rules; and third, the tradeoffs that political parties consider between electoral systems and other institutional rules.

# ORIGINS OF PARTIES
# AND ELECTORAL SYSTEMS

To understand the origins of political parties and how they shaped innovative electoral rules, we must pay attention to the role of traditional elections in local settings. A very simple type of electoral system was used widely in local and national assemblies in pre-democratic or early democratic periods before and during the nineteenth century. The essential elements of this type of electoral system are multiseat districts, open ballot (permitting the voter to vote for a number of individual candidates equal or lower than the seats to be filled), and plurality or majority rule.

This combination of rules has been widely used, especially in relatively simple elections with rather homogeneous electorates, and particularly at the beginning of modern suffrage regulations and for small-size local governments. It is still a common type of procedure for local or municipal elections in many countries, as well as in many meetings and assemblies of modern housing condominiums, neighborhood associations, school and university boards and delegates, professional organizations, corporation boards, and students' and workers' unions. In these, as well as in many of the traditional communities just mentioned, individual representation is well suited to contexts of high economic and cultural homogeneity in which it is relatively easy to identify common interests and priority public goods to be provided by the elect.

This set of electoral rules appears indeed as almost "natural" and "spontaneous" to many communities when they have to choose a procedure for collective decision making based on votes, especially because it permits a consensual representation of the community. Such a simple electoral system is able to produce satisfactory and acceptable citizens' representation. But it also creates incentives for self-interested, would-be political leaders to coordinate on "factional" candidacies or voting coalitions—in a word, "parties." Under that system, forming or joining a "party" may increase the prospects of winning additional votes and seats. "Party" is thus defined here in a minimalist way that is not substantially different from traditional meanings of "faction" in early periods of voting and elections.

Under the previously identified set of rules, factions or parties tend to induce "voting in bloc" for a list of candidates, which may change election results radically. Once party candidacies are presented, it is not necessary that all or most voters follow the

advice of factional leaders to vote for all of and only the members of a list of candidates to attain a party sweep. It may be sufficient that a few people do it, since,
even if they are few, they can make a difference, especially under simple plurality rule
where no specific threshold of votes is required to win. Note that, in historical terms,
voting "in bloc" was not an institutionally induced behavior, but a party-strategy-
induced behavior.

In some crucial cases, it was largely as a consequence of this type of experience that
different political leaders, candidates, activists, and politically motivated scholars began
to search for alternative, less intuitive, or "spontaneous" electoral rules able to reduce
single-party sweeps and exclusionary victories. This new period began to develop by the
mid-nineteenth century. It can be held that from that moment on, it was the previously
existing political parties that chose, manipulated, and promoted the invention of new
electoral rules, including the Australian ballot, single-seat districts, limited ballot, and
proportional representation rules, rather than the other way around.

Virtually all the new electoral rules and procedures that were created since the nineteenth century can be understood as innovative variations of the previous, simple, "originating" system, which can be called "originating" precisely for this reason. The new
electoral systems can be classified in three groups, depending on whether they changed
the district magnitude, the ballot, or the rule.

The first group implied a change of the district magnitude from multiseat to single-
seat districts, keeping both individual-candidate voting and majoritarian rules. With
smaller single-seat districts, a candidate that would have been defeated by a party sweep
in a multiseat district with plurality rule may be elected. Thus, this system tends to produce more varied representation than multiseat districts with voting in bloc, although
less varied than multiseat districts with open ballot.

The second group of new electoral rules implied new forms of ballot favoring
individual-candidate voting despite the existence of party candidacies, while maintaining the other two essential elements of the traditional system: multiseat districts and
majoritarian rules. In particular, by limited vote, one party can sweep as many seats as
the voter has votes, but it is likely that the rest of the seats will be won by candidates of
different political affiliation.

Finally, the third group of new electoral rules implied the introduction of proportional representation formulas, which permit the maintenance of multimember districts and in some variants also open or individual-candidate ballot. Single-transferable
vote, double vote, preferential voting, and open ballots make individual-candidate voting compatible with proportional representation (Colomer 2007).

This discussion can clarify the conundrum of the relationship between party systems
and electoral systems, as if they were related like the chicken and the egg. Actually, biol-
ogists have an answer for the latter inquiry: in the beginning was an egg, but a very simple one, not a chicken's egg. Analogously, we can say that first, there were elections, but
with very simple rules, not party elections. Once the parties were formed, they delivered
more complex and varied "eggs," or electoral systems.

# The Parties' Strategic Choices
## of Electoral Systems

This early history can be expanded for the further period since the late nineteenth century. In contrast to the basic assumption in the old tradition of electoral studies referred to earlier, it is the number of parties that can explain the choice of new electoral systems, in particular regarding the introduction of proportional representation rules, rather than the other way around.

In fact, Maurice Duverger himself briefly noted that "the first effect of proportionality is to maintain an already existing multiplicity" (Duverger, 1950, 1951, 344). In a review of Duverger, John G. Grumm (1958, 375) held that "the generally-held conclusions regarding the causal relationships between electoral systems and party systems might well be revised . . . . It may be more accurate to conclude that proportional representation is a result rather than a cause of the party system in a given country." Leslie Lipson (1964, 343) developed a historical narrative from the premise that "chronologically, as well as logically, the party system is prior to the electoral system." Stein Rokkan noted:

> In most cases it makes little sense to treat electoral systems as independent variables and party systems as dependent. The party strategists will generally have decisive influence on electoral legislation and opt for the systems of aggregation most likely to consolidate their position, whether through increases in their representation, through the strengthening of the preferred alliances, or through safeguards against splinter movements.
>
> (Rokkan 1968; see also Lipset and Rokkan 1967)

Arend Lijphart and Bernard Grofman (1984) explored the factors for the "not highly probable, but possible" changes and choices in electoral systems. Rein Taagepera (2003, 5) more recently also suggested a "causality following in the reverse direction, from the number of parties towards electoral rules."

Some recent contributions in this approach compare not only different countries using different rules, as is customary in the previously cited works, but also every single country before and after the introduction of new electoral rules. By putting "the Duverger's laws upside down," Josep Colomer (2004, 2005) showed how previously existing political party configurations dominated by a few parties tend to establish majority-rule electoral systems, while multiparty systems already existed before the introduction of proportional representation.

The emphasis on this line of causality does not deny that existing electoral systems offer different positive and negative incentives for the creation and endurance of political parties. Precisely because electoral systems can have important consequences on shaping the party system, it can be supposed that they are chosen by already existing political actors in their own interest. Accordingly, it can be expected that, in general, electoral systems will crystallize, consolidate, or reinforce previously existing political party configurations, rather than (by themselves) generate new party systems.

We know that electoral systems based on the majority principle, which tend to produce a single, absolute winner and subsequent absolute losers, are riskier for nondominant actors than those using rules of proportional representation—a principle that was forged to create multiple partial winners and far fewer total losers than majority rules. In general, the "Micromega rule" can be postulated: the large will prefer the small and the small will prefer the large. A few large parties will prefer small assemblies, small district magnitudes (the smallest being one), and small quotas of votes for allocating seats (the smallest being simple plurality, which does not require any specific threshold), to exclude others from competition. Likewise, multiple small parties will prefer large assemblies, large district magnitudes, and large quotas (like those of proportional representation), which are able to include them within the legislature.

Changing electoral rules can be a rational strategy for likely losers or threatened winners if the expected advantages of alternative rules surpass those of playing by the existing rules minus the costs of change. In particular, an alteration of the electoral system can be more successfully promoted by parties with high decision, negotiation, or pressure power under the existing institutional framework. This makes incumbent rulers submitted to credible threats by new or growing opposition parties likely candidates to undertake processes of institutional change.

Thus, it can be expected that in situations in which a single party or two parties alternating or sharing power are institutionally dominant and expect to obtain or maintain most voters' support, restrictive rules based on majority requirements will be chosen or maintained. Since this type of electoral rule tends to produce a single absolute winner, it can give the larger parties more opportunities to remain as winners and retain control—as can happen, in particular, during long processes of gradually broadening suffrage rights and democratization, giving the incumbent rulers significant opportunities to define the rules of the game.

In contrast, it may be that no single group of voters and leaders, including the incumbent ruling party, is sufficiently sure about its support and the corresponding electoral prospects in future contests. In other words, there can be uncertainty regarding the different groups' relative strength or it can be clear that electoral support is going to be widely distributed among several small parties. Here changes in favor of less risky, more inclusive electoral rules, such as mixed-member or proportional representation electoral systems, are more likely to be promoted and established by the currently powerful actors in their own interest. This tends to be the development preferred by new or newly growing parties in opposition to traditional rulers, including, in particular, multiparty opposition movements against an authoritarian regime. But it can also be favored by threatened incumbent rulers to minimize their possible losses (Colomer 2004, 2005).

These analyses have been developed for the introduction of proportional formulas for the elections of parliaments. Analogous strategies have been observed more recently for the choice and change of rules to elect the president in separation-of-power regimes. In Latin America, it has been observed that while dominant and large parties are likely to choose plurality rule and concurrent elections, small parties are likely to choose nonconcurrent elections with majority rule with a second-round runoff, which permit multiparty competition. It has also argued that military rulers and military–civilian coalitions in processes of redemocratization, as they may feel threatened by newly emerging party configurations, tend to follow the logic of electoral choice of small parties (Negretto 2006).

When dealing with presidential elections, shifting partisan political fortunes have also been placed at the center of analysis. Changes in the rules of the electoral game tend to reflect the political self-interest of dominant political parties as defined in relation to mounting electoral uncertainty. The impact of electoral reforms on party system change, in contrast, appears to be less consistent with the expectations derived from the more traditional literature. In particular, party system change in Latin America has generated institutional change more predictably than vice versa (Remmer 2008).

Additional caveats can be introduced. If the incumbent rulers are still sufficiently powerful, they may prefer mixed-member systems, rather than openly proportional rules, in the aim of reducing political fragmentation and limiting the potential for new entrants to the party system (Shugart and Wattenberg 2003; Reilly 2007). Also, the incumbents' willingness to introduce electoral system change may derive not only from a serious threat to their dominance but also from their loss of control of the situation or some internal division of interests among its members. The rules for changing the rules also matter. If the incumbent government can change the electoral law without seeking a broader agreement, there is greater likelihood that partisan self-interest will dominate. On the other hand, change may be deterred by high barriers to change, such as the constitutionalization of the electoral system or the requirement of a parliamentary supermajority or a popular referendum for its change (Gallagher 2005; Katz 2005).

# ELECTORAL BEHAVIOR AND INSTITUTIONAL CHOICE

By reassuming the two approaches referred to previously, it can be postulated that self-interested parties competing in elections can develop two strategies at the same time: behavioral and institutional. In the behavioral field, the basic decision is to create or not create an electoral partisan candidacy. More specifically, to create a new partisan candidacy might imply either a new effort of collective action or splitting from a previously existing party, while not to create a new candidacy may mean entering a previously existing party, forming an electoral coalition, or merging with a rival party. In the institutional field, the decision is to promote or not a change in the electoral system, the two basic polar alternatives being either majoritarian or proportional representation rules.

Given the electoral system, the actors' relevant strategy lies mainly in the behavioral field. Under the "originating" system, there were incentives for self-interested actors to create new partisan candidacies. If there is a majoritarian electoral system, the rational strategy is not to create a party. Instead, it makes sense to coordinate efforts with other would-be leaders and groups to form only a few large parties or coalitions in the system (typically two), each of them able to compete for offices with a reasonable expectation of success. By contrast, if the existing electoral system is based on the principle of proportional representation and is inclusive enough to permit representation of small parties, rational actors may choose either coordination or running on their own candidacies, in the expectation that in both cases they will obtain the corresponding office rewards.

However, emerging parties may produce unwelcomed sweeps, coordination may fail, and, especially under majoritarian systems, lack of coordination may produce defeats and no representation for candidates, groups, and parties with some significant, real or potential, support among voters. In these cases, the alternative strategic field—the choice of electoral institutions—becomes relevant. Parties unable to coordinate themselves into a small number of large candidacies will tend to prefer electoral systems able to reduce the risks of competing by giving all participants higher opportunities to obtain or share power. Two-party configurations are likely to establish or maintain majoritarian electoral systems, while multiple-party configurations will tend to mean that political actors choose systems with proportional representation rules. Also, majoritarian electoral systems tend to restrict effective competition to two large parties, while proportional representation permits multiple parties to succeed.

This discussion brings together "institutional theories," which include those about the political consequences of electoral systems, and "theories of institutions," in this case regarding the choice and change of electoral systems. A "behavioral-institutional equilibrium" can be produced by actors with the ability both to choose behavioral strategies (such as a party, candidacy, or coalition formation deciding on electoral platforms or policy positions) and to choose institutions regulating and rewarding those behaviors.

In the long term, two polar behavioral-institutional equilibria can be conceived. In one, political actors coordinate into two electoral parties or candidacies under majoritarian electoral rules. In another, multiple parties compete separately under proportional representation electoral rules. Either of the two results can be relatively stable and durable, but there is no deterministic relationship able to predict which one is going to prevail (there are also other intermediate pairs of consistent behavioral and institutional alternatives, including imperfect two-party systems, mixed electoral systems, and so on).

In this approach the presumed line of causality is double. Two-party configurations tend to maintain or choose majoritarian rules, while multiparty systems tend to establish or confirm proportional representation rules. In turn, majoritarian rules induce the consolidation of two large parties, while proportional representation confirms the potential for the development of multiple parties.

A crucial point is that coordination failures can be relatively more frequent under majoritarian electoral systems than under proportional rules, especially for the costs of information transmission, bargaining, and implementation of agreements among previously separate organizations, as well as the cost of inducing strategic votes in favor of the larger candidacies. With coordination failures, people will waste significant amounts of votes, and voters' dissatisfaction with the real working of the electoral system may increase. Large numbers of losing politicians are also likely to use voters' dissatisfaction and their own exclusion, defeat, or underrepresentation to develop political pressures in favor of changing to more proportional electoral rules.

In contrast, coordination failures, properly speaking, should not exist under conditions of flawless proportional representation. Even if the number of candidacies increases, each of them can expect to obtain about the same proportion of seats that they would have obtained by forming part of more encompassing candidacies. In reality, coordination failures are relevant under proportional systems to the extent that they are not properly proportional, particularly when small assembly sizes and small district magnitudes are used.

An important implication is that, in the long term, we should expect that most electoral system changes should move away from majoritarian formulas and in favor of systems using rules of proportional representation. Reverse changes, from proportional toward more majoritarian rules, may be the bet of some potentially dominant, growing, or daring party. But they can imply high risks for a partial winner to be transformed into a total loser, if its optimistic electoral expectations are not confirmed. This occurrence may be more frequent when actors are risk prone or badly informed about electoral systems. In a historical perspective, there have been increasing numbers and proportions of electoral systems using proportional representation formulas rather than majoritarian rules.

## PARTY SYSTEM CONFIGURATIONS

Several discussions of specific political party configurations in which we should expect different types of electoral system change have been proposed. Stein Rokkan (1968) analyzed the origins of proportional representation by taking inspiration from Karl Braunias (1932), who distinguished two phases in the spread of proportional representation electoral rules: the "minority protection" phase, before World War I, and the "antisocialist" phase, in the years immediately after the armistice. This approach has been further developed with a focus on the turn of the twentieth century by Boix (1999); Blais, Dobrzynska, and Indridason (2005); and Cusack, Iversen, and Soskice (2007) regarding Europe, and by Calvo (2009), Wills-Otero (2009), and Gamboa and Morales (2015) for Latin America. Boix, in particular, analyzes the shift from the plurality/majority rule to proportional representation as a result of the entry of new voters (assumed to be left-wing voters) and a new party (socialist) at the turn of the twentieth century in the Western world.

Kenneth Benoit (2004, 2007) sketches a more general model of electoral system change at political parties' initiative. He assumes that the parties' objective is to maximize their share of seats. Benoit gives some real-life examples of electoral system change and discusses some empirical implications of his model. He predicts that the electoral rule will be changed when a coalition of parties, which have sufficient power to change the rule, exists such that each party in the coalition would gain more seats under the new rule.

In Colomer's (2005) analysis, parties will be interested in replacing majoritarian rules with more inclusive systems, typically proportional representation rules, if none of them can be sure of winning by a majority. In other words, electoral system change from majority rule to a more inclusive electoral system permitting representation of minorities can be a rational choice if no party has 50 percent of popular votes, which is the threshold guaranteeing representation under the former system. Configurations in which one party has more than 50 percent of votes have values for the effective number of parties of between 1 and 4, with an expected average at 2.5. Changes in favor of proportional representation will not take place with values of the effective number of parties below 2, for lack of powerful actors with an interest in such a change. Above four effective parties, maintaining or establishing a majority-rule electoral system would be highly risky for the incumbent largest party, and possibly not feasible either, due to pressures for an alternative system supported by a majority of votes.

We mentioned that the elections held immediately after the adoption of proportional rules tend to confirm, rather than increase, the previously existing multiparty configuration. However, the new rules transform the share of each party in votes into fairer party seat shares, thus making it more attractive for voters to give their support to new or emerging political parties. As a consequence, the effective number of parties tends to increase in the long term, thus creating further pressures in favor of maintaining proportional rules.

In further elaboration, Selim Ergun (2010) holds that for a change to occur, the government should be formed by a coalition. He finds that a change is more likely to occur when there is a larger number of parties and also when the spoils of office are shared equally among the members in the governing coalition. These results are extended to analyze partial reforms from a less proportional rule to a more proportional one.

Ergun finds that a change can also occur when the effective number of parties is between two and three. The crucial point is not necessarily the size of the largest party but the difference between the parties. In the case of three parties, the largest party is always against a change and the smallest party always in favor, and thus the electoral system will be changed depending on the size of the median-sized party. In a three-party configuration, the second party in size will successfully promote proportional representation if its size is sufficiently distant from the largest party size and, as a consequence, it cannot guarantee leading a majority coalition with the third party under majority rule.

Looking to the question from the other side, some authors have discussed the political party conditions for establishing majority rule. Eunju Chi (2014) examines how party competition led to electoral reforms in Taiwan. The two larger parties, driven by the goal of maximizing the number of seats, formed a coalition and passed reform bills to change the electoral system from a single nontransferable vote and multiseat district system to a first-past-the-post mixed-member system. Konstantinos Matakos and Dimitrios Xefteris (2015) identify more general, favorable conditions for introducing majority rule, such as the expected vote share of the smaller parties, the high rents from a single-party government, and sufficient uncertainty over the electoral outcome.

Further contributions include the examination of situations in which the party system is weakly institutionalized and high levels of electoral volatility can be observed. For relatively recent democracies, such as in Eastern Europe, these situations deter the stabilization of electoral systems and make relevant actors prone to engage in reforms (Bielasiak and Hulsey 2013). The role of actors other than parties, such as voters, academics, and reform activists, has also been highlighted in specific cases (e.g., Renwick 2010; Leyenaar and Hazan 2011).

# Institutional Tradeoffs

Political parties usually address the maintenance or change of electoral rules in the broader context of the institutional system, thus developing tradeoffs with changes of other institutional rules. The most significant rules to consider are the extension of suffrage rights, the size or number of seats of the assembly, and the number of territorial governments in a federal-like structure.

The extension of suffrage rights was usually perceived as a potential source of emergence of new political parties than can challenge the status quo. The dominant parties in the existing system were wary of expanding suffrage if no parallel institutional rules were introduced to reduce the risk of being defeated and becoming noncompetitive parties in the new system. That is why many successful processes of expansion of suffrage rights were accompanied by reforms in the electoral rules.

A case for reference is the United Kingdom, the oldest democracy still using plurality rule in single-seat districts. Major change of electoral rules was prevented by avoiding the sudden introduction of universal (male) suffrage and following a long process of gradual enlargements of suffrage rights in the nineteenth and early twentieth century. Requirements of wealth, property, income, or literacy for voting were safeguards against a possible turnabout of the political and party system by the sudden irruption of new mass voters. While the political system was dominated by alternations in government between the Conservative and the Liberal Parties, the electoral system (at the time still including a number of multimember districts by plurality rule) was not challenged.

It was the emergence of the new Labour Party, broadly supported by recently enfranchised workers, at the beginning of the twentieth century that introduced demands for proportional representation. Yet, when in the late 1920s the Labour leaders forecasted a possible party victory under the existing electoral rules they turned against their own former proposals for proportional representation. The new alternation between

Conservatives and Labourites since the end of the World War II had the effect of converting the Liberals, which were excluded then from government, into the heralds of electoral reform.

A different type of process could be observed in Germany and, even more clearly, in northern European countries such as Sweden, Norway, and Finland. In these countries, the sudden enfranchisement of a very large electorate was made compatible with appreciable degrees of political stability by the introduction "from above" by the incumbent rulers of new electoral systems favoring political pluralism. By the early twentieth century, proportional representation or similar institutional "safeguards" promoting multiparty politics were adopted. Governments were then able to rely on parliamentary coalitions in which centrist and moderate parties were expected to play a decisive role. In this way, the risk of instability and the threat of turnabouts were limited, and incumbent voters and leaders enjoyed continued opportunities of being included in government and maintaining a significant influence on the political process.

In these countries, suffrage rights were traded off with electoral rules. Proportional representation was adopted as an institutional safeguard in place of the traditional qualifications for voting rights. New electoral systems permitting multipartism were conceived to be protective devices. The Conservatives, the Liberals, or the Agrarians would become a minority, but they would not be expelled from the system as might be risked with a majoritarian rule. The incumbent rulers took the initiative of introducing universal suffrage "with guarantees" rather than witnessing their own defeat (Lewin 1989; Acemoglu and Robinson 2000; Colomer 2001; Ahmed 2013).

Another institutional rule that can be traded off with changes of electoral rules is the number of seats of the assembly. The total number of seats to be elected in a country may enlarge or restrict the number of viable parties and, more generally, the degree of inclusiveness of the political system. According to Rein Taagepera (2001, 2007), the number of parties in parliament, P, is related to the number of seats in the average electoral district, M, and the total number of seats in the assembly, S. In his notation

$$P = (MS)^{\frac{1}{4}}.$$

Taagepera's focus on predicting the number of parties may suggest that the number of parties is always a dependent variable of the basic elements of the electoral systems. But his formula accepts two-direction lines of causality. It can indeed be turned the other way around to present the electoral system as derived from the number of parties. Specifically, $M = P^4/S$.

This formula shows that the number of previously existing parties (which is raised to the fourth power) is more important than the size of the assembly to explain the choice of electoral system (as operationalized by M). As long as the size of the assembly is not manipulated, for a small country with a small assembly, just a few parties can be sufficient to produce a change of electoral system in favor of proportional representation.

In contrast, for a large country and a large assembly, many parties would be necessary to produce such a result—as reform activists in the United Kingdom, for instance, know very well.

But we can also deduct from the previous formula that, for a similar number of parties, P, the larger the country, and hence the larger the assembly, S, the smaller the expected district magnitude, M, can be. Very large countries, precisely because they have large assemblies, should be associated to small (single-seat) districts. For example, the institutional designers in large India are likely to choose single-seat districts, while the institutional designers in small Estonia are likely to choose multimember districts, typically associated with proportional representation rules. Thus, we should usually see large assemblies with small districts, and small assemblies with large districts.

The interest of this finding is that it is counterintuitive, since apparently small countries should have more "simple" party configurations, so that they could work with simple electoral systems with single-seat districts and majority rule in acceptable ways (actually this tends to happen in very small and micro-countries with only a few dozen thousand inhabitants in which only one or two significant parties emerge). But now we have an answer to the very intriguing question of why some very large countries, including the United States, in spite of the fact that large size is typically associated with high heterogeneity, keep small single-seat districts and have not adopted proportional representation. The answer may be that in large countries, such as Australia, Canada, France, India, the United Kingdom, and the United States, a large assembly can be sufficiently inclusive, even if it is elected in small, single-seat districts. By contrast, in small countries, including Belgium, Denmark, Estonia, Finland, the Netherlands, Norway, Switzerland, and so many others, the size of the assembly is small and, as a consequence, the development of multiple parties has favored more strongly the adoption of more inclusive, large multimember districts with proportional representation rules.

The large size of a country and its assembly is also usually associated with a federal structure. In fact, the electoral system can also be traded off with federalism, as a high number of decentralized territorial governments can play an inclusive role of the variety of the population in large countries and make proportional representation unnecessary, as discussed in Colomer (2010). As always, the tradeoff is operated through human collective action. If in a large country multiple territorial governments are established, much political action will focus on those local institutions and it will be less likely that multiple political parties will be formed at the countrywide level. As a consequence, there will be less pressure to adopt a federal large assembly and a federal electoral system of proportional representation. The United States, with a very high number of fifty states and extremely decentralized nationwide political parties, is a case in point.

In contrast, in a medium-sized country with a unitary territorial structure but with a variety of economic interests or cultural allegiances among the intertwined population, the formation of multiple political parties may push for a sufficiently inclusive assembly elected by proportional electoral rules, rather than for territorial governments (like, say, in the Netherlands).

This tradeoff between electoral system and federalism can also involve the size of the assembly. If the electoral system implies high levels of political party pluralism, the general assembly must be sufficiently large to capture that pluralism. If, in contrast, constitution makers privileged the representation of varied territories but were wary of the perils of multipartism when they chose the electoral institutions (or just imported them from the colonial metropolis before new rules of proportional representation had been invented), then the size of the federal assembly can remain relatively small. This is, in particular, the case of the United States, which has the largest number of territorial units and both the smallest single-seat electoral district magnitude and the smallest assembly in proportion to the population. For each country size there can be multiple equilibrium sets of institutions, but each of the sets involving different combinations of institutional alternatives will be in equilibrium if it is consistent with certain quantifiable tradeoffs between institutions.

A potentially fruitful exploration to investigate is the population density of the country (i.e., the quotient between population and area). Low density usually implies territorial dispersion of the population in several distant or separate groups. Even if the country's population as a whole is relatively homogeneous in economic and cultural terms, the costs of governance related to physical distance might make federalism an advisable formula for a durable democracy. Australia, for one, would be an example of this. If, in addition to being dispersed, the country's population taken as a whole is highly heterogeneous, it is likely that it will be concentrated into separated groups with relatively high degrees of internal homogeneity, as largely happens, for instance, in Canada. In any of the cases, nonideological territorial governments could be based on relatively homogeneous communities, which somehow would replace the representative and aggregative role of multiple political parties.

On the other side, high population density is likely to imply local heterogeneity, whether in economic terms, as high density is usually related to high degrees of urbanization and diversification of economic activity, or in cultural terms, which may be produced by recent migrations. With this type of structure, federalism may not be a suitable solution since the creation of small territorial governments would not reduce much the complexity of the communities, while multiple, nonterritorially based political parties able to represent different interests and values within a mixed population may require proportional representation electoral rules (related discussion about Africa appears in Mozaffar, Scarritt, and Galaich 2003 and Brambor, Clark, and Golder 2007). In fact, multiple parties successfully pressured for the adoption of proportional representation in the early twentieth century in a few medium-sized European countries, such as Belgium, Finland, Norway, and Sweden, soon followed by Austria, Denmark, Ireland, and Switzerland, and this has spread widely among new democracies in medium-sized countries across the world in recent decades.

In contrast, in large countries, federalism can be more effective for good governance and durable democracy than any variant of party systems or electoral rules. Large federal countries include, for instance, multiparty proportional Argentina, Brazil, Germany, and South Africa, as well as two-party majoritarian Australia, Canada, and the United States, while the extremely large size of India has forced both federalism and a multiparty system in spite of a single-seat electoral system (partly favored by significant territorial concentration of different ethnic groups in different states and electoral districts).

All in all, political parties tend to be the main actors in the choice of electoral rules, which they tend to develop in their own self-interest, although under the incentives and limits imposed by existing rules and procedures for institutional change. Broader sets of other political institutions, such as basic rules for democracy, voting rights, the representative assembly, or the territorial structure of the country, can also constrain the processes and outcomes of electoral system parties' choice.

## References

Acemoglu, Daron, and James A. Robinson. "Why Did the West Extend the Franchise? Democracy, Inequality, and Growth in Historical Perspective." *Quarterly Journal of Economics* 115, no. 4 (2000): 1167–1199.

Ahmed, Amel. *Democracy and the Politics of Electoral System Choice: Engineering Electoral Dominance.* Cambridge; New York: Cambridge University Press, 2013.

Benoit, Kenneth. "Models of Electoral System Change." *Electoral Studies* 23 (2004): 363–389.

Benoit, Kenneth. "Electoral Laws as Political Consequences: Explaining the Origins and Change of Electoral Institutions." *Annual Review of Political Science* 10 (2007): 363–390.

Bielasiak, Jack, and John W. Hulsey. "Party System Determinants of Electoral Reform in Post-Communist States." *Communist and Post-Communist Studies* 46, no. 1 (2013): 1–12.

Blais, Andre, Agnieska Dobrzynska, and Indridi H. Indridason. "To Adopt or Not to Adopt Proportional Representation: The Politics of Institutional Choice." *British Journal of Political Science* 35 (2005): 182–190.

Boix, Carles. "Setting the Rules of the Game: The Choice of Electoral Systems in Advanced Democracies." *American Political Science Review* 93 (1999): 609–624.

Brambor, Thomas, William R. Clark, and Matt Golder. "Are African Party Systems Different?" *Electoral Studies* 26, no. 2 (2007): 315–323.

Braunias, Karl. *Das parlamentarische Wahlrecht: Ein Handbuch über die Bildung der gesetzgebenden Körperschaften in Europa.* 2 vols. Berlin: Gruyter, 1932.

Calvo, Ernesto. "The Competitive Road to Proportional Representation: Partisan Biases and Electoral Regime Change under Increasing Party Competition." *World Politics* 61, no. 2 (2009): 254–295.

Chi, Eunju. "Two-Party Contests and the Politics of Electoral Reforms: The Case of Taiwan" *Government and Opposition* 49, no. 4 (2014): 657–680.

Colomer, Josep M. *Political Institutions.* New York: Oxford University Press, 2001.

Colomer, Josep M., ed. *Handbook of Electoral System Choice.* London, New York: Palgrave-Macmillan, 2004.

Colomer, Josep M. "It's the Parties That Choose Electoral Systems (or, Duverger's Laws Upside Down)." *Political Studies* 53 (2005): 1–21.

Colomer, Josep M. "On the Origins of Electoral Systems and Political Parties." *Electoral Studies* 26 (2007): 262–273.

Colomer, Josep M. "Equilibrium Institutions: The Federal-Proportional Trade-off." *Public Choice* 158, no. 3–4 (2010): 559–576.

Cusack, Thomas, Torben Iversen, and David Soskice. 2007. "Economic Interests and the Origins of Electoral Systems." *American Political Science Review* 101, no. 3 (2010): 337–391.

Duverger, Maurice. *L'influènce des systèmes électoraux sur la vie politique, Cahiers de la Fondation Nationale des Sciences Politiques, 16*. Paris: Armand Colin, 1950.

Duverger, Maurice. *Les partis politiques*. Paris: Seuil, 1951. (English translation: *Political Parties: Their Organization and Activity in the Modern State*. New York: Wiley, 1954)

Ergun, Selim J. "From Plurality Rule to Proportional Representation." *Economics of Governance* 11 (2010): 373–408.

Gallagher, Michael. "Conclusion." In *The Politics of Electoral Systems*, edited by Michael Gallagher and Paul Mitchell, 535–578. New York: Oxford University Press, 2005.

Gamboa, Ricardo, and Mauricio Morales. "Deciding on the Electoral System: Chile's Adoption of Proportional Representation in 1925." *Latin American Politics and Society* 57, no. 2 (2015): 41–58.

Grumm, John G. "Theories of Electoral Systems." *Midwest Journal of Political Science* 2, no. 4 (1958): 357–376.

Katz, Richard. 2005. "Why Are There So Many (or So Few) Electoral Reforms?" In *The Politics of Electoral Systems*, edited by Michael Gallagher and Paul Mitchell, chap. 3, 57–78. New York: Oxford University Press, 2005.

Leyenaar, Monique, and Reuven Y. Hazan. "Reconceptualising Electoral Reform." *West European Politics* 34, no. 3 (2011): 437–455.

Lewin, Leif. *Ideology and Strategy. A Century of Swedish Politics*. New York: Cambridge University Press, 1989.

Lijphart, Arend, and Bernard Grofman, eds. *Choosing an Electoral System: Issues and Alternatives*. New York: Praeger, 1984.

Lipset, Seymour, and Stein Rokkan, eds. *Party Systems and Voter Alignments: Cross National Perspectives*. New York: Free Press, 1967.

Lipson, Leslie. *The Democratic Civilization*. New York: Oxford University Press, 1964.

Matakos, Konstantinos, and Dimitrios Xefteris. "Strategic Electoral Rule Choice under Uncertainty." *Public Choice* 162 (2015): 329–350.

Mozaffar, Shaheen, James R. Scarritt, and Glen Galaich. "Electoral Institutions, Ethnopolitical Cleavages and Party Systems in Africa's Emerging Democracies." *American Political Science Review* 97 (2003): 379–390.

Negretto, Gabriel L. "Choosing How to Choose Presidents: Parties, Military Rulers, and Presidential Elections in Latin America." *Journal of Politics* 68, no. 2 (2006): 421–433.

Reilly, Benjamin. "Democratization and Electoral Reform in the Asia-Pacific Region: Is There an 'Asian Model' of Democracy?" *Comparative Political Studies* 40, no. 11 (2007): 1350–1371.

Remmer. Karen L. "The Politics of Institutional Change: Electoral Reform in Latin America, 1978-2002." *Party Politics* 14, no. 1 (2008): 5–30.

Renwick, Alan. *The Politics of Electoral Reform: Changing the Rules of Democracy*. Cambridge: Cambridge University Press, 2010.

Rokkan, Stein. "Electoral Systems." In *International Encyclopedia of the Social Sciences*. New York: Macmillan, 1968.

Shugart, Matthew S., and Martin P. Wattenberg. *Mixed-Member Electoral Systems: The Best of Both Worlds?* New York: Oxford University Press, 2003.

Taagepera, Rein. "Party Size Baselines Imposed by Institutional Constraints: Theory for Simple Electoral Systems." *Journal of Theoretical Politics* 13, no. 4 (2001): 331–354.

Taagepera, Rein. "Arend Lijphart's Dimensions of Democracy: Logical Connections and Institutional Design." *Political Studies* 51, no. 1 (2003): 1–19.

Taagepera, Rein. *Predicting Party Sizes. The Logic of Simple Electoral Systems.* New York, Oxford: Oxford University Press, 2007.

Wills-Otero, Laura. "Electoral Systems in Latin America: Explaining the Adoption of Proportional Representation Systems during the Twentieth Century." *Latin American Politics and Society* 51, no. 3 (2009): 33–58.

CHAPTER 5

....................................................................................

# ELECTORAL SYSTEM DESIGN IN NEW DEMOCRACIES

JOHN M. CAREY

....................................................................................

## New Democracies, Uncertainty, and Choice Sets

....................................................................................

THIS chapter starts with the premise that certain characteristics of elections are normatively desirable but far from certain to be established in new democracies. These include a tractable set of choices, competitiveness, and inclusiveness. I assume throughout that political parties are fundamental vehicles of representation.[1] A tractable choice refers to a set of viable parties large enough to afford voters meaningfully distinct options but not so large as to be cognitively overwhelming. Competitiveness means that no one party dominates all others in elections. Inclusiveness means that no one party seizes control of the state in a way that allows it to marginalize others before democratic institutions are well established. This chapter explores the ways in which electoral system design in new democracies can affect the choice sets offered to voters, as well as the competitiveness and inclusiveness of elections.

Electoral systems are rules for soliciting citizens' preferences over parties and candidates and for converting those votes into representation. One of the critical dimensions on which electoral systems can vary is the degree to which the rules reward size. That is, to what degree does a system confer representational bonuses and penalties as a function of how large a share of the votes a party wins? I focus on the returns to party size because both politicians and voters seek to convert votes into political representation as efficiently as possible—that is, to reap the biggest representational bang for the electoral "buck," each vote. How electoral rules distribute bonuses and penalties according to size shapes which electoral alliances politicians are inclined to form. This, in turn, shapes the tractability of the choice set and tendencies toward electoral competitiveness or dominance.

A key characteristic that distinguishes elections in new democracies from those in established ones is the level of certainty about who the viable electoral actors are. Certainty facilitates coordination—of elites into electoral alliances and of voters in casting ballots—and allows voters to understand the connection between how they vote and the representation they get (Cox 1997). In established democracies, experience—in the form of past electoral results—is the main source of such certainty. Elections in new democracies are often characterized by uncertainty over which parties are viable and which are not, diminishing the ability of political elites to present voters with tractable choice sets and the ability of voters to distinguish among the choices presented. I focus on countries that have experienced rapid and dramatic transitions from nondemocracy to democracy because I am particularly interested in the ability of new democracies to reduce the uncertainty surrounding the menu of party options and to establish competition over control of the government.

Consider a situation in which leaders of two would-be parties, A and B, are determining whether and how to compete in an upcoming election. The parties share some basic principles, but their leaders are rivals. Imagine they share the following expectations:

- Party A can command about 4 to 6 percent of the vote.
- Party B can command about 8 to 10 percent of the vote.
- It will be necessary to get about 10 percent of the vote to win any representation.

Party A is not close to the threshold for success, so a vote for Party A is, effectively, wasted, whereas the same vote cast instead for Party B might help it get over the hump and win representation. The leaders of Party B, moreover, are motivated to court the leaders and supporters of Party A, maybe parceling out list positions or policy concessions—even forming a coalition, call it AB—to minimize the risk that they come up empty. The motivation and the ability to coalesce depend on shared expectations about electoral viability, which in turn depend on knowledge about the levels of support across parties and about how support levels will translate into representation. In a new democracy, both sorts of knowledge may be in short supply, limiting coalitions. Where coalitions do not form, choice sets will be larger, and perhaps cognitively intractable.

In transitional democracies, the set of choices voters confront can be overwhelming. In their first post–Arab Spring election, Tunisian voters faced over 500 distinct party lists, but only 26 won any seats (and 15 of those won just one seat each). Egyptian and Libyan voters were presented with dozens of lists and with separate ballots that included dozens of candidates (Carey, Masoud, and Reynolds 2015). Afghan voters have regularly faced ballots with hundreds of individual candidates in parliamentary elections (Reynolds and Carey 2012).

Cognitive psychologists and behavioral economists have long recognized that the number of options among which people can make meaningful distinctions is limited (Iyengar 2010). Miller (1956) famously advanced the proposition that the "magical number" of options on a single dimension of choice among which humans can meaningfully discern is seven, or thereabouts. This line of reasoning suggests there may be a sweet spot in terms of the number of alternatives presented to voters—a range that combines variety with cognitive tractability—and that this perhaps also has downstream effects on governability and government accountability. This chapter suggests that electoral formulas can reward economies of moderate scale in party competition, and thus encourage choice sets for voters in the range of cognitive tractability.

All electoral formulas reward economies of scale in some manner, penalizing very small parties by denying representation below some minimum vote threshold, whether legally specified or not. Many systems deliver progressively larger bonuses to larger parties. The choice of electoral system is, in large part, a choice about how seat bonuses and penalties should be distributed. The prescriptive argument in this chapter is that, in new democracies, bonuses should be concentrated on parties as they reach the range of electoral viability to motivate potential allies to coalesce. Electoral engineers in new democracies should aim for economies of scale that peak in the lower end of the viable range.[2] Seat bonuses should be targeted to encourage groups below the threshold of viability to coalesce and rise above it. In these environments, bonuses for large parties are of relatively less value, and in new democracies, increasing returns to scale can threaten the establishment of inclusive democracy.

The rest of the chapter follows in three sections. The first assesses the problem of developing tractable partisan choice sets and competition in new democracies where uncertainty is high, presenting descriptive data from early elections after dramatic democratic transitions. I measure the fragmentation votes in parliamentary elections across parties and the gap between the first- and second-place parties, across countries and over time, to determine whether, and how quickly, the choice sets voters confront in new democracies converge in terms of their tractability, and whether competitiveness tends to increase or decrease over time after transitions. The next section zeroes in on the effect of one particular element of electoral system design, the choice of formula for translating votes to seats in proportional representation (PR) elections, and examines how formulas have affected choice sets, competition, and inclusiveness in Tunisia, Hong Kong, Peru, and Spain. The last section summarizes some principles of electoral system design for new democracies, drawing on the evidence the chapter presents, and speculates about how those principles might evolve as democracies endure.

# ELECTIONS AFTER BIG SWINGS TO DEMOCRACY

## The Polish Template?

Following the collapse of Central European communism in 1989, the first democratic election for Poland's parliament, the Sejm, took place in 1991.[3] In the absence of an established party system and firm expectations about which leaders and alliances would be viable, Poland adopted an inclusive electoral rule, with list proportional representation (PR), votes pooled at the national level, and no minimum threshold for representation, such that lists winning a fraction of a percent of the nationwide vote could gain representation. The top panel of figure 5.1 shows the highly dispersed distribution seats across the 30 lists that won seats in the 1991 election, the largest with 12 percent of the vote. Seven percent of the valid ballots were cast for the hundreds of lists that won less than 0.1 percent of the votes, and no seats. Another 6 percent of ballots were invalid.

During the next couple of years, Polish governments were highly unstable and susceptible to shifting coalitions. By 1993, the Sejm agreed to dissolve itself and call new elections, but under modified rules that adopted a 5 percent legal threshold for representation.[4] The 1993 election saw a continued dispersal of the vote, but the legal threshold restricted representation to the six parties that cleared the barrier, in turn conferring large winner bonuses to most of them given that 35 percent of votes were cast for parties that won no representation (panel B in figure 5.1). Coalition options were reduced, governments stabilized, and the new Sejm endured through its constitutional term. In the next election, in 1997, expectations about viability among both voters and elites strengthened, with fewer lists on the ballot, less than half as many votes thrown to parties below the threshold, and a resulting higher correlation between vote shares and seat shares. The pattern continued and stabilized in subsequent elections (panels C through F in figure 5.1) and has persisted to the present, with between four and six parties winning representation in each contest and less than 10 percent of votes wasted on parties winning no representation.

The Polish experience would appear to be an archetype for how electoral engineering can foster the formation of a tractable choice set following a dramatic swing to democracy. At the initial democratic founding, expectations about viability were ill-defined, and the choice set was bewildering. After the imposition of a rule establishing a clear benchmark for strategic alliances and voting, the set of viable choices narrowed, and actors updated expectations and behaviors accordingly.

## Cross-National Patterns

Research on the effects of institutional design on representation is plagued by the problem of imperfect identification. Electoral systems are not randomly assigned across societies. Political parties, which anticipate their own strengths and those of their rivals, generally have a hand in shaping the rules. In particular, where party systems and electoral systems codevelop over time, the relative degree to which rules shape the party system, as opposed to the reverse, is inherently hard to determine (Colomer 2005; Benoit 2007). The empirical exercise here does not pretend to resolve that problem but attempts to mitigate it by focusing on elections in new democracies where the transition from nondemocracy is rapid and dramatic. Where the electoral field of competitors most closely resembles a clean slate, and where expectations about relative strengths are weakest and alliances are least fixed, the degree to which electoral rules merely reflect existing

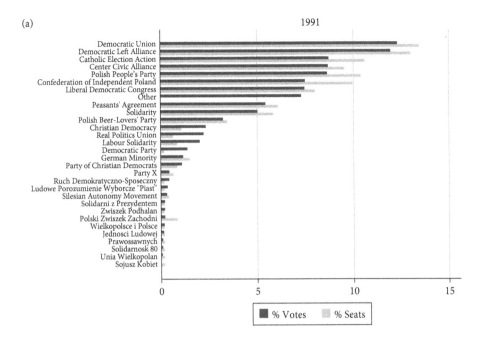

(a)                                              1991

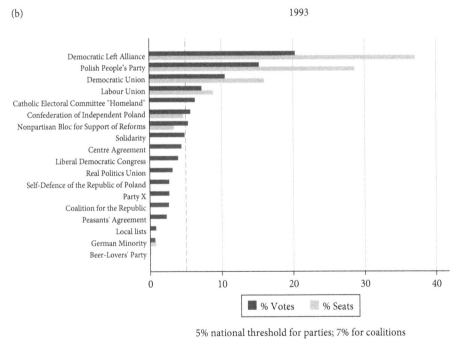

(b)                                              1993

5% national threshold for parties; 7% for coalitions

FIGURE 5.1. Vote shares and seat shares in Polish Sejm elections.

Data source: Nohlen and Stover (2010).

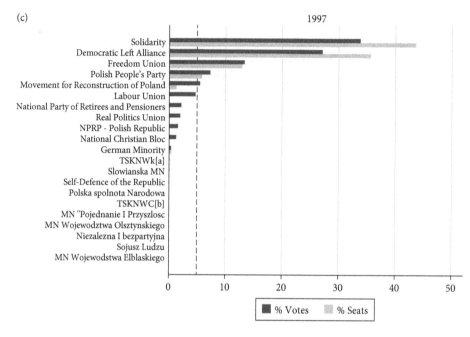

(c)                                                           1997

Solidarity
Democratic Left Alliance
Freedom Union
Polish People's Party
Movement for Reconstruction of Poland
Labour Union
National Party of Retirees and Pensioners
Real Politics Union
NPRP - Polish Republic
National Christian Bloc
German Minority
TSKNWk[a]
Slowianska MN
Self-Defence of the Republic
Polska spolnota Narodowa
TSKNWC[b]
MN "Pojednanie I Przyszlosc
MN Wojewodztwa Olsztynskiego
Niezalezna I bezpartyjna
Sojusz Ludzu
MN Wojewodstwa Elblaskiego

0     10     20     30     40     50

■ % Votes     ▨ % Seats

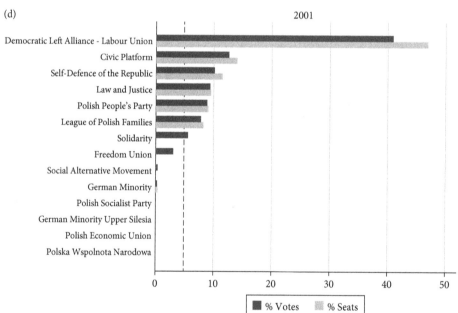

(d)                                                           2001

Democratic Left Alliance - Labour Union
Civic Platform
Self-Defence of the Republic
Law and Justice
Polish People's Party
League of Polish Families
Solidarity
Freedom Union
Social Alternative Movement
German Minority
Polish Socialist Party
German Minority Upper Silesia
Polish Economic Union
Polska Wspolnota Narodowa

0     10     20     30     40     50

■ % Votes     ▨ % Seats

FIGURE 5.1. Continued

(e)

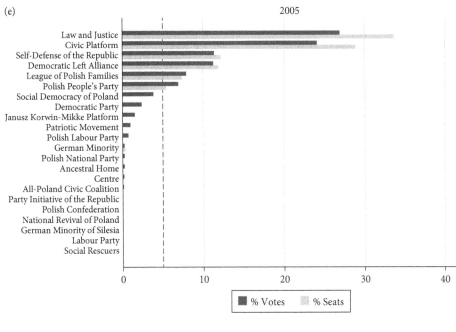

2005

Law and Justice
Civic Platform
Self-Defense of the Republic
Democratic Left Alliance
League of Polish Families
Polish People's Party
Social Democracy of Poland
Democratic Party
Janusz Korwin-Mikke Platform
Patriotic Movement
Polish Labour Party
German Minority
Polish National Party
Ancestral Home
Centre
All-Poland Civic Coalition
Party Initiative of the Republic
Polish Confederation
National Revival of Poland
German Minority of Silesia
Labour Party
Social Rescuers

■ % Votes     % Seats

(f)

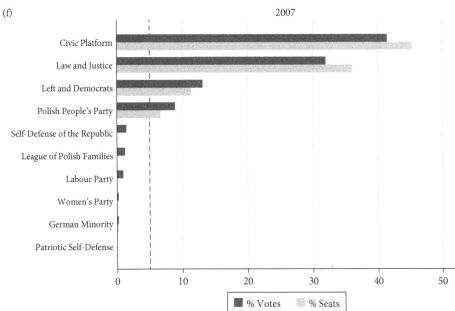

2007

Civic Platform
Law and Justice
Left and Democrats
Polish People's Party
Self-Defense of the Republic
League of Polish Families
Labour Party
Women's Party
German Minority
Patriotic Self-Defense

■ % Votes     % Seats

**FIGURE 5.1.** Continued

party structures should be minimized, and the impact of electoral system design should be the greatest and the most discernible. For this reason, I focus on founding elections that pronounced swings from nondemocracy to democracy.

I start with the Polity IV data, which provide a 21-point scale running from –10 (dictatorship) through 10 (fully democratic). Polity assigns values for 209 countries for every year from their origin (or 1800) up through 2015 (or the end of existence). Across all countries, all years, the mean score is –1, the standard deviation is 7.2, and the distribution is generally bimodal with concentrations at either extreme. I define a dramatic transition to democracy as any case where a country makes a positive swing of 7 or more points from one Polity score to the next, arriving at a score of 5 or greater.[5] Such big swings to democracy are rare events, with only 150 in the Polity data, making up less than 1 percent of country–year observations.[6] Of these, 42 occurred in countries that subsequently experienced both democratic backsliding and another big swing to democracy, whereas 108 represent the "last" big swing to democracy for that country. Of those 108, 75 (69 percent) of the countries have remained democratic (i.e., with Polity scores at 5 or above) in every year since their big swing. Sixty-seven of those big swings to stable democracy, listed in table 5.1, have occurred since 1945.

Of the countries that experienced big swings and remained democratic, I am particularly interested in patterns of party competition in the first five posttransition parliamentary elections, when expectations about party viability are taking shape. To examine patterns of competition and party system fragmentation, I merged the data on big swings to democracy with electoral data from Bormann and Golder (2013), as well as Teorell et al. (2016), supplementing those with electoral results I collected from various government and scholarly websites. Limiting our data to the first five (or fewer, if five have not occurred yet) parliamentary elections, the data include 211 elections from 57 of the 67 countries that experienced big swings and no democratic backsliding since 1945.

I rely on the Bormann and Golder (2013) data to classify electoral systems into six distinct categories: single-seat district plurality (or first-past-the-post (FPTP)), two-round systems (TRS), mixed systems, list PR using the D'Hondt divisors formula, list PR using the Hare quota and largest remainders (HQLR) formula, and list PR using formulas other than D'Hondt and HQLR for seat allocation. Many of these categories will be familiar to this volume's readers. The important thing to note is that mixed systems include elections in which parliamentary seats are awarded across distinct geographical tiers, whereas the cases coded as list PR are single-tier systems. Among those, I distinguish the two most frequently used formulas, D'Hondt and HQLR, from others, both because D'Hondt and HQLR are by far the most common PR formulas and because they represent polar extremes on the degree to which they distribute seat bonuses as a function of party size. I discuss the mechanics of D'Hondt and HQLR in detail later. Among the 211 post–big swing elections in new democracies noted in the previous paragraph, table 5.2 shows the distribution of electoral systems.

Now we can consider the question of whether the structure of party competition differs across elections in new democracies held under varying electoral rules. figure 5.2 shows linear fit estimates for party system fragmentation, measured as the effective

Table 5.1  Sixty–Seven Big Swings to Democracy since 1945 That Have Remained Democracies

| Country | Year | Country | Year | Country | Year |
|---|---|---|---|---|---|
| Austria | 1946 | Brazil | 1985 | Guyana | 1992 |
| France | 1946 | Uruguay | 1985 | Mali | 1992 |
| Israel | 1948 | Philippines | 1987 | Mongolia | 1992 |
| Italy | 1948 | South Korea | 1988 | Taiwan | 1993 |
| India | 1950 | Chile | 1989 | Czech Republic | 1993 |
| Japan | 1952 | Panama | 1989 | Slovak Republic | 1993 |
| Colombia | 1957 | Poland | 1989 | Mozambique | 1994 |
| Jamaica | 1959 | Bulgaria | 1990 | Armenia | 1998 |
| Cyprus | 1960 | Czechoslovakia* | 1990 | Indonesia | 1999 |
| Trinidad & Tobago | 1962 | Germany | 1990 | Croatia | 2000 |
| Botswana | 1966 | Hungary | 1990 | Senegal | 2000 |
| Mauritius | 1968 | Namibia | 1990 | Yugoslavia* | 2000 |
| Greece | 1975 | Nicaragua | 1990 | Peru | 2001 |
| Portugal | 1976 | Romania | 1990 | East Timor | 2002 |
| Dominican Republic | 1978 | Benin | 1991 | Kenya* | 2002 |
| Solomon Islands | 1978 | Cape Verde | 1991 | Congo Kinshasa* | 2006 |
| Spain | 1978 | Estonia | 1991 | Haiti* | 2006 |
| Ecuador | 1979 | Latvia | 1991 | Montenegro* | 2006 |
| Bolivia | 1982 | Lithuania | 1991 | Nepal* | 2006 |
| Honduras | 1982 | Macedonia | 1991 | Kosovo* | 2008 |
| Argentina | 1983 | Moldova | 1991 | Somalia* | 2012 |
| El Salvador | 1984 | Slovenia | 1991 | Tunisia* | 2014 |

*Data source:* Polity IV data.
* No data on post–big swing elections are included from these cases.

number of both vote-winning and seat-winning parties, across the first five post–big swing elections, according to the electoral system used.[7]

The conventional expectation that single-seat district (SSD) elections discourage party fragmentation receives modest support, with both vote and seat fragmentation

Table 5.2  Electoral Systems Used in New Democracies Following Big Swings

| Electoral System | Number | Percentage |
|---|---|---|
| First-past-the-post | 24 | 11 |
| Two-round system | 8 | 4 |
| Mixed system | 37 | 18 |
| List PR–D'Hondt divisors | 61 | 29 |
| List PR–Hare quota largest remainders | 43 | 20 |
| List PR–All other formulas | 38 | 18 |

*Data sources:* Bormann and Golder (2013); Polity IV (2013); Teorell et al. (2016).

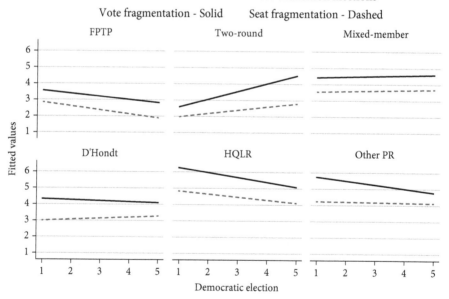

**Effective Number of Parties in Post-Transition Elections**

Vote fragmentation - Solid     Seat fragmentation - Dashed

FIGURE 5.2.  Fragmentation in the first five post–big swing elections.

Data sources: Bormann and Golder (2013); Polity IV (2013); Teorell et al. (2016).

lower than in other systems, and diminishing with successive elections (Duverger 1954). In two-round systems, both forms of fragmentation increase over time, although the number of two-round elections in new democracies is very low (see table 5.2). For mixed systems, measuring fragmentation based on the partisan vote distribution in the PR tier, we see higher, and stable, levels of fragmentation. Among the pure list PR formulas, fragmentation is lower under D'Hondt than under either HQLR or the other formulas (e.g., Droop quota, St. Lague divisor, or modified St. Lague), although under HQLR, both vote and seat fragmentation diminish gradually over time.

What about competitiveness? I measure competitiveness simply as the gap in percentage vote share between the first-place and second-place party. Figure 5.3 shows linear fit models, with 95 percent confidence intervals, for margin of victory across the first five post–big swing elections. In SSD systems, margins tend to be larger than in PR systems, and to rise over time, although the data are sufficiently dispersed that there is no pronounced pattern. That data on margins in two-round systems are sparse. Both in mixed systems and under HQLR, competitiveness increases and victory margins decline over time, from above 15 percent to around 5 percent, on average, between the founding and the fifth election.

What do these patterns tell us about electoral system design in new democracies? First, the standard caveats apply, that we are looking merely at correlations in observational data, and in a limited number of cases under highly unusual circumstances, so any conclusions are provisional. That said, the PR systems as a whole tend to produce closer competition between first- and second-place parties than do the single-seat district formats. Among the PR systems, D'Hondt constrains party fragmentation more than the other formulas, although where democracy survives to its fifth parliamentary election, the other PR formulas converge toward party systems with around five effective vote-winning parties and four effective seat-winning parties, only slightly above the D'Hondt averages.[8]

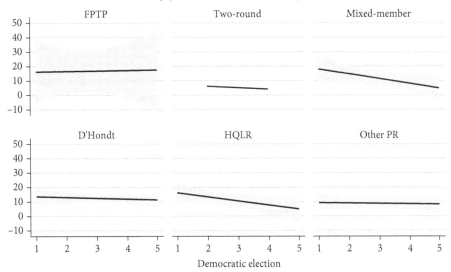

**Margin of Victory in Post-Transition Elections**

Percent gap between first and second place parties

FIGURE 5.3. Competitiveness in the first five post–big swing elections.

Data sources: Bormann and Golder (2013); Polity IV (2013); Teorell et al. (2016).

# ALTERNATIVE PROPORTIONAL REPRESENTATION FORMULAS AND THEIR EFFECTS

When we talk about the effects of electoral rules, we implicitly summon a counterfactual: how would the outcome of an election have differed had a different system been used? Cross-national comparisons allow for a counterfactual based on the idea that, had Spain, for example, employed Canada's electoral rules, perhaps party competition in Spain would look more like Canada's. But of course, Spain and Canada differ on countless dimensions beyond electoral rules so any such counterfactual is loose. A less crude counterfactual might simulate electoral outcomes within a given country, had alternative electoral rules been in place. A strong constraint on this kind of analysis is that votes are cast within geographical districts and the preferences voters can express are a function of ballot structure. So the most plausible simulations are limited to comparing outcomes under identical ballot structures, based on votes cast within the existing districts.

In this section, I compare results under HQLR versus D'Hondt formulas for vote distributions within the same district structure. Switching between these formulas would be, effectively, invisible to voters, with no impact on how ballots are formatted or marked. Politicians, by contrast, are attuned to how electoral formulas affect their competitive prospects, and as they gain experience with an electoral system, they adjust their behavior accordingly, as we shall see. Yet in the context of new democracies, when uncertainty prevails about the relative strengths of would-be parties and alliances, the distributional effects of electoral formulas might initially be opaque even to political elites. To the extent that strategic responses to electoral formulas are constrained in the context of new democracies, the simulations presented here shed light on how alternative electoral rules can drive representational outcomes. The results suggest that the choice of rules can profoundly affect who wins and by how much, encouraging or blocking the formation of legislative majorities, and shaping prospects for inclusiveness and the development of party systems that afford meaningful representation to the widest possible set of citizens.

## List Proportional Representation Formulas

There are two main "families" of PR formulas: quota-based methods and divisor methods. Within each family, there are various formulas, although Hare and D'Hondt are the clear "heads" of their respective families. They are the most common formulas employed in new democracies, as shown in table 5.2, and in modern democratic elections more generally (Bormann and Golder 2013).

## Hare Quota and Largest Remainders

The basic principle here is to set a "retail price," in the currency of votes, at which seats in each electoral district may be "purchased" by lists. That price, or quota, is determined by dividing the total number of valid votes cast in a district by some number—in the case of the HQLR, the district magnitude (DM), or the number of seats at stake in the district. Once votes are tallied, each list is awarded as many seats in the district as full quotas of votes it won. For each seat awarded in this manner, a quota of votes is subtracted from the list's district total. If not all seats in the district can be awarded on the basis of full quotas, any remaining seats are allocated, one per list, in descending order of the lists' remaining votes. These seats, then, are purchased for less than the retail price (or quota) for a seat. Lists that win seats on the basis of their remainders are, effectively, buying seats "wholesale."

Note that, under HQLR, it is virtually impossible for all seats in a district to be purchased at retail price—that is, unless the distribution of votes were such that every list won vote totals perfectly divisible by the district magnitude. Thus, the HQLR method almost guarantees that, within a given district, lists will pay different prices for seats they win. More specifically, it implies that, among lists that win seats at all, smaller competitors, who buy wholesale on the remainders market, will pay less per seat than larger competitors, who also buy seats retail, paying full quotas.

## D'Hondt

Rather than set a price in votes for the purchase of seats, divisors methods use the tallies of votes across lists to establish a matrix of quotients pertaining to lists, then allocate seats in descending order of quotients until all the seats in a given district are awarded. A hypothetical example illustrates. Imagine a district in which four lists—A, B, C, and D—compete and 1,000 votes are cast. The votes are distributed across lists as illustrated in the second row of table 5.3: 415, 325, 185, and 75, respectively. The D'Hondt method proceeds by calculating a matrix of quotients by dividing each list's tally by the sequence of integers 1, 2, 3, and so on. These quotients are shown in the successive rows of table 5.3. Once the matrix is constructed, seats are awarded in the descending order of quotients. In this district, for example, if DM = 5, then the distribution of seats would be A(2), B(2), C(1), D(0). By contrast, if DM = 10, the distribution would be A(5), B(3), C(2), D(0). The initial intuition behind divisors methods may be slightly less obvious than with quota-and-remainders methods, but an advantage is that all seats are awarded according to a uniform principle.

# Distributing Rewards According to Party Size

Either a quotas-based or a divisors-based approach can be modified from its simplest version to adjust the degree to which the formula rewards large versus small lists. HQLR is relatively friendly to small lists because the quota (retail price) it sets to purchase seats

Table 5.3 Illustration of the DHD Method in a Hypothetical District

| List  | A     | B     | C     | D    |
|-------|-------|-------|-------|------|
| Votes | 415   | 325   | 185   | 75   |
| 1st Q | 415.0 | 325.0 | 185.0 | 75.0 |
| 2nd Q | 207.5 | 162.5 | 92.5  | 37.5 |
| 3rd Q | 138.3 | 108.3 | 61.7  | 25.0 |
| 4th Q | 103.8 | 81.3  | 46.3  | 18.8 |
| 5th Q | 83.0  | 65.0  | 37.0  | 15.0 |
| 6th Q | 69.2  | 54.2  | 30.8  | 12.5 |

*Source:* Author's calculations.

is high. Lists that win enough votes to purchase seats at retail pay a steep price for doing so. By contrast, D'Hondt is relatively friendly to large lists because, in constructing the matrix of quotients by which seats will be awarded, its sequence of divisors erodes the tallies of large lists only gradually. Thus, the most common PR formulas have *opposite* effects with respect to rewards to size.

Note that many other features of electoral rules, besides formulas, shape the relative prospects for large versus small lists to win seats. DM is critical here (Taagepera and Shugart 1989; Cox 1997). Under any PR formula, lower DM favors larger lists, while higher DM reduces the vote share needed to win representation, opening the door to representation by smaller lists. As we saw in the Polish example earlier, legal thresholds that establish a minimum that vote share lists must win to be eligible to win seats also discourage smaller parties and alliances and favor larger ones.[9] In short, there are various ways to tilt the field of electoral competition in ways that affect the relative prospects for larger versus smaller lists.

## SIMULATING EFFECTS IN NEW DEMOCRACIES

To illustrate how the choice of rules can affect electoral outcomes, I consider four cases. First is from Tunisia's founding elections in the wake of the Arab Spring uprisings. Second, I examine Hong Kong's legislative elections following the transition of sovereignty over the region from Britain back to China in the late 1990s. Next is a recent election in Peru, which has experienced intervals of democracy and nondemocracy throughout its history, but where the party system has been consistently volatile. The final example is from the more established democracy, Spain.

# Tunisia

On October 23, 2011, Tunisians went to the polls to elect the first constituent assembly following from the first uprising of the Arab Spring (Brownlee, Masoud, and Reynolds 2015). The assembly had 217 members, elected by closed-list PR across 33 districts. Districts elected between 1 and 10 members, but most districts elected 5 or more. Across all 33 districts, 560 distinct groups registered lists to compete. The vast majority of these lists—over 400—were unique to a single district. Only four alliances—the Islamist Ennahda, the more secularist Congress for the republic, Ettakatol, and the Democratic Modernist Pole—managed to contest all 33 of the districts. Each voter cast a ballot for a closed list of candidates, and the distribution of seats within each district was determined by HQLR.

This set of electoral rules was brand new to Tunisia. During the long period of dictatorship under Zine el Abidine Ben-Ali (1986–2011), the country had held rigged elections under a mixed system that combined party bloc vote with list PR (Reynolds, Reilly, and Ellis 2005). The post–Arab Spring electoral rules were written and approved by a committee formed in the tumult after Ben-Ali fled and his regime crumbled. It included leaders from political parties, labor unions, and civil society organizations, but it was not elected and its membership was determined by improvisation (Brownlee, Masoud, and Reynolds 2015; Stepan 2012). In retrospect, three years after the Arab Spring uprisings, and after two successful parliamentary elections, some members of that committee described their decision to adopt list PR and the HQLR formula as motivated by a preference for an inclusive electoral rule in the context of upheaval and transition. Among those interviewed, however, recollections differed with respect to which political leaders supported which specific rules, when, and on what grounds (Carey, Masoud, and Reynolds 2015). At any rate, the superabundance of lists that registered for the 2011 election suggests great uncertainty among many political actors about their relative levels of electoral support.

To evaluate the impact of HQLR on Tunisia's founding election outcome, I collected district-level data on the distribution of votes across lists and replicated the distribution of seats according to HQLR, then used the same votes to simulate the seat distribution that *would have been* obtained under D'Hondt (Independent Higher Authority of the Election 2012). The results are summarized in table 5.4, which shows all the parties and alliances that won any seats under each rule, in descending order of their share of the vote nationwide.

The central question here is to what degree these formulas would have treated parties differently according to their size. The short answer is, dramatically. Note that the competitive field was unbalanced. The largest party, Ennahda, won 37 percent of the vote, more than four times the total of the next largest party. HQLR awarded Ennahda 89 seats (41 percent) in the assembly. By contrast, D'Hondt would have awarded Ennahda 150 seats (69 percent).

Tunisia's constitutional moment would likely have proceeded quite differently had elections been held under D'Hondt rather than HQLR. With an assembly supermajority, Ennahda might have been tempted to push through a constitution objectionable to its secularist opponents, and it would have had the votes to do so. By contrast, with only 41 percent in the assembly, which served as a parliament and a constituent assembly during its three-year tenure, Ennahda brought in coalition partners to form a working majority. The presidency of the assembly went to Ettakatol, and the interim presidency of Tunisia was held by a member of Congress for the republic. The process of drafting a constitution that could command coalition support extended past the initial target date of one year, but by January 2014, the assembly produced a charter that won approval from 93 percent of its membership (Stepan 2016).

Tunisia maintained the same electoral system for its second democratic parliamentary election, following the ratification of the Constitution of 2014. Again, the outcome would have differed dramatically had the D'Hondt formula been applied, although the beneficiaries of HQLR were reversed. Consistent with HQLR's economies of moderate scale, a number of the secular parties at the low end of the viability range from 2011, plus some that had fallen short of representation altogether, had coalesced behind a single party label, Nida Tunis, in 2014. Nida Tunis won a 38 percent plurality of votes, while Ennahda's national share fell to 28 percent. Overall levels of vote fragmentation dropped substantially, with the effective number of vote-winning parties falling from 6.3 in 2011 to 4.5 in 2014 (author's calculations). Nida Tunis's 38 percent of the vote converted to 40 percent of the assembly seats under HQLR, whereas a simulated outcome using D'Hondt would have afforded it 53 percent, enough to govern alone. Lacking a majority, Nida Tunis formed a coalition, bringing Ennahda into government along with three smaller parties (Stepan 2016). For a second time in Tunisia, by limiting the winner's bonus, HQLR encouraged inclusiveness in government and prevented a single party from seizing control of the state.

The difference between how the HQLR and D'Hondt formulas treat parties according to their size is illustrated by plotting each party's seat bonus or penalty—that is, its seat share minus its overall vote share—against its vote share. Figure 5.4 does this for both Tunisian elections. For the 2011 election, Panel A shows the actual outcome under HQLR and panel B the D'Hondt simulation. The most remarkable characteristic of the windfall of seat bonuses generated by HQLR is the extent to which it accrued to small alliances rather than Ennahda. Ennahda regularly paid full price for its seats, often winning more than one per district, but purchasing them with full quotas. Its smaller competitors, by contrast, rarely won more than one seat per district, almost always buying wholesale with remainder votes. As a result, the moderate-sized parties purchased votes more efficiently than Ennahda. HQLR delivered the greatest economies of scale to moderate parties rather than to the largest. D'Hondt, by contrast, confers sharply increasing economies to scale, and Ennahda would have captured far more seats and a vastly larger bonus. The 2014 election repeats this pattern, but with the winners reversed, as shown in panels C and D.

## Table 5.4 Tunisia 2011 National Constituent Assembly Election Results

| Rank | List | Votes | Percent | HQLR Seats | D'Hondt Seats |
|------|------|-------|---------|-----------|---------------|
| 1 | Ennahda | 1,501,774 | 37.09 | 89 | 150 |
| 2 | Congress for the Republic | 353,299 | 8.72 | 29 | 21 |
| 3 | Ettakatol | 285,460 | 7.05 | 20 | 14 |
| 4 | Popular Petition | 273,659 | 6.76 | 26 | 18 |
| 5 | Progressive Democratic Party | 160,471 | 3.96 | 16 | 2 |
| 6 | Initiative Party List | 129,131 | 3.19 | 5 | 8 |
| 7 | Democratic Modernist Pole | 113,022 | 2.79 | 5 | 1 |
| 8 | Prospects for Tunisia Party | 76,621 | 1.89 | 4 | 0 |
| 9 | Tunisian Worker's Party-RA | 60,565 | 1.5 | 3 | 0 |
| 10 | Free Patriotic Union | 51,671 | 1.28 | 1 | 1 |
| 12 | People's Movement | 30,497 | 0.75 | 2 | 0 |
| 15 | Movement of Socialist Democrats | 22,804 | 0.56 | 2 | 0 |
| 19 | Maghrebi Liberal Party | 19,219 | 0.47 | 1 | 0 |
| 21 | Independent Voice | 16,891 | 0.42 | 1 | 0 |
| 24 | National Social Democratic Party List | 15,569 | 0.38 | 1 | 0 |
| 26 | New Constitutional Party | 14,228 | 0.35 | 1 | 0 |
| 30 | Loyalty List | 12,607 | 0.31 | 1 | 0 |
| 31 | Independent List | 11,980 | 0.3 | 1 | 1 |
| 32 | List for Tunisian National Front | 11,396 | 0.28 | 1 | 0 |
| 33 | Hope List | 11,299 | 0.28 | 1 | 1 |
| 38 | Progressive Struggle Party | 9,322 | 0.23 | 1 | 0 |
| 45 | Social Struggle List | 7,823 | 0.19 | 1 | 0 |
| 47 | Justice and Equality Party | 7,621 | 0.19 | 1 | 0 |
| 52 | National Cultural Unionist Party | 5,581 | 0.14 | 1 | 0 |
| 63 | Independent Justice | 4,232 | 0.1 | 1 | 0 |
| 79 | Loyalty to the Martyrs List | 3,022 | 0.07 | 1 | 0 |

*Data source:* Independent Higher Authority of the Election (2012).

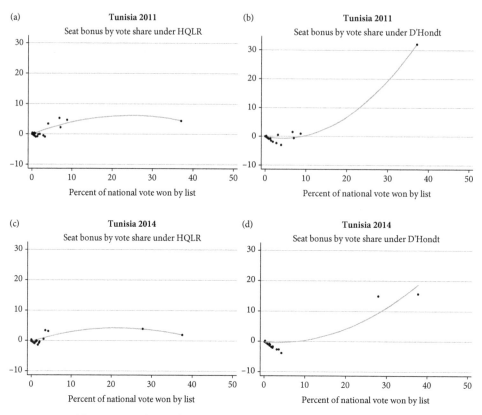

**FIGURE 5.4.** Tunisia—Seat bonus by vote share.

Data sources: Independent Higher Authority of the Election (2012 and 2014).

## Hong Kong

Hong Kong is neither a country nor a democracy; it is a "special administrative region" within the autocracy of China, but its experience with electoral system design in the past two decades is instructive nevertheless. Once an agreement had been established for the transfer of sovereignty over Hong Kong from the United Kingdom back to Beijing, the United Kingdom began to increase the prominence of Hong Kong's regional Legislative Council (LegCo) and expand the competitiveness of LegCo elections (Baum 2000). After the transfer in 1997, LegCo elections continued this trend, with the size of the assembly and the share of seats awarded via multiparty competition gradually increasing. Currently, half of the LegCo's seventy members are directly elected in five geographical constituencies from closed party lists using the HQLR formula.

Elections in Hong Kong are not fully open and free overall. Candidacies for the most important office, the chief executive, remain tightly controlled by Beijing and nearly half of LegCo seats are elected indirectly by groups stacked toward Beijing's interests (Pepper

2000). So the playing field is far from level. But for our purposes, the more interesting design feature was Beijing's insistence on HQLR for the election of the LegCos that are directly elected and freely contested.

Results from the last couple of elections held in Hong Kong under British rule had suggested a strong and growing bloc of pro-democracy voters who were motivated to protect Hong Kong's tradition of civil liberties and independent courts, and who could be expected to reject parties and candidates associated with Beijing and the Chinese Communist Party (Lam 1995; Fung 1996). Even according to those who worked inside the Chinese government committees that drafted the electoral law, the central motive of electoral system designers was to obstruct the formation of a party that could command a majority of the LegCo's directly elected seats, although even that would leave such a bloc far from controlling the region's government (Siu-kai 1999).

Beijing eventually settled on HQLR, and its choice has proved prescient. In each of Hong Kong's six LegCo elections since the system was adopted, lists from the broad pro-democracy camp have won majorities of the votes cast. These electoral successes have translated into majorities of the subset of LegCo seats that are directly elected (although not of the LegCo overall). But the use of HQLR has had two important effects beneficial to Beijing. First, as in Tunisia, HQLR constrains winners' bonuses, preventing the pro-democratic camp from translating its vote majorities into clean sweeps of the elected seats.

Second, HQLR encourages broad alliances to subdivide to convert seats to votes more efficiently. A list that wins more than one seat in a given district pays retail (i.e., a full quota) for at least one of those seats. A list that wins by remainders pays wholesale. Any list big enough to win a full quota might do better by splitting in two. Hong Kong politicians have responded strategically, dividing into ever more parties and splinter lists in elections between 1998 and 2012, even as the central divide in Hong Kong politics, between pro-democracy and pro-Beijing camps, has remained stable, with the pro-democracy side winning between 50 and 60 percent of votes (Ma and Choy 2003). In the first few open elections, about half of all the directly elected LegCo seats were won by lists that captured full quotas in their districts, but in more recent elections, as the two main camps adopted the strategy of fragmentation, that proportion dropped to about 10 percent, as shown in figure 5.5 (Carey 2017). Correspondingly, if we calculate vote fragmentation just *within* the pro-democracy camp (i.e., the effective number of vote-winning parties just within that camp), we see an increase from 2.0 effective parties in the 1998 election to 5.8 by 2016. The corresponding numbers within the pro-Beijing camp are 1.3 and 5.2 (author's calculations).

The effect of this fragmentation in the LegCo party system has been to hamper the formation of broad and stable legislative coalitions that could effectively advance platforms endorsed by the majority of Hong Kong voters, who have consistently supported greater autonomy of the region from Beijing and the protection of individual rights Choy 2013; Ma 2014; Chen 2015; Carey 2017).

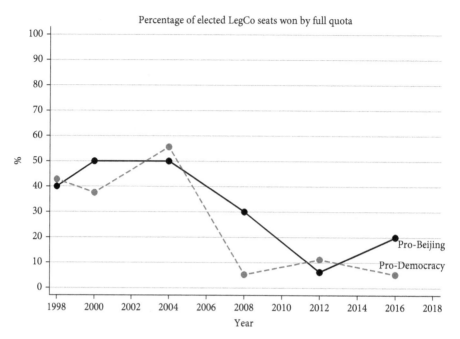

**FIGURE 5.5.** Hong Kong 1998–2016—Percentage of elected LegCo seats won by full quota.

Data source: Author's calculations.

## Peru

The potentially pivotal effects of the PR formula are not limited to brand new democracies, and with access to district-level returns that allow for replication and simulation of alternative outcomes, they are not difficult to find. For example, Peru uses the D'Hondt formula to elect its 130-member Congress. Most of Peru's twenty-six districts elect between two and five seats, and there is a nationwide 5 percent threshold. In the 2016 elections, the Popular Force party, headed by Keiko Fujimori, the daughter of disgraced former president Alberto Fujimori, won 36 percent of the vote but was awarded 56 percent of the seats. The enormous winner's bonus was due far more to the use of D'Hondt than to any penalties visited upon smaller parties by the legal threshold.[10]

Using the district-level votes from the Peruvian National Electoral Office (Oficina Nacional de Procesos Electorales 2016), I reproduced the election results under D'Hondt and also simulated results that would have been obtained under HQLR, both with and without the legal threshold. The threshold denied a total of six seats to two parties that would otherwise have won seats. Four of those seats were gained by Popular Force, but even without those, Popular Force would hold a 53 percent majority. Far more consequential was Peru's use of the D'Hondt formula. Under HQLR, Popular Force's 36 percent vote share would have translated into 41 percent of seats, even with the legal threshold shutting out smaller parties—and 40 percent without it. Here again, the contrast between D'Hondt and HQLR is clearest by contrasting seat bonuses as a function of vote share, as in figure 5.6. Bonuses increased sharply with size under D'Hondt, with Popular Force harvesting almost all of the representational penalties visited upon smaller parties. Bonuses would have increased far more gradually with size, and included more moderate-sized parties, under HQLR.

As in the other cases discussed, use of the alternative formula here could have substantial impact on how Peru is governed. Peru's congressional election was held concurrently with the first round of its presidential election. In the run-off that followed a month later, Pedro Pablo Kuczynski, who had finished second to Keiko Fujimori in first-round balloting, captured the presidency. Had Peru used any of the other PR formulas employed in other democracies around the world, with or without the legal threshold, Fujimori's Popular Force would not have won a congressional majority. Kuczynski would have faced the substantial challenge of piecing together coalitions in a fragmented Congress to govern. Instead, he will face a majority opposition party in Congress. At the time of this writing, it is too early to tell how that difference will affect governance in Peru.

## Spain

Finally, consider the case of Spain, which like Peru uses the D'Hondt formula in its fifty-two districts, which award between one and thirty-six seats. I replicated outcomes from Spain's 2011, 2015, and 2016 elections and simulated outcomes that would have prevailed under HQLR. In 2011, the Partido Popular won a 53 percent parliamentary majority based on a 45 percent vote share, and governed alone. Had HQLR been used, the same vote distribution would have yielded only a 47 percent seat share, and quite likely the need to govern in coalition. The next two elections, in December 2015 and June 2016, produced no majority—and at the time of this writing (July 2016) no governing coalition either. The patterns of bonuses by vote shares in Spain are consistent with all those

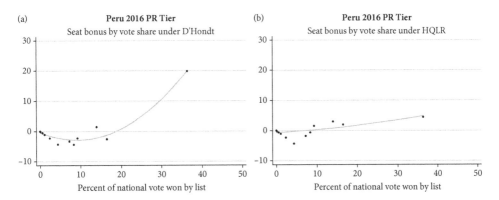

FIGURE 5.6. Peru 2016—Seat bonus by vote share.

Data source: Oficina Nacional de Procesos Electorales (2016).

(a)

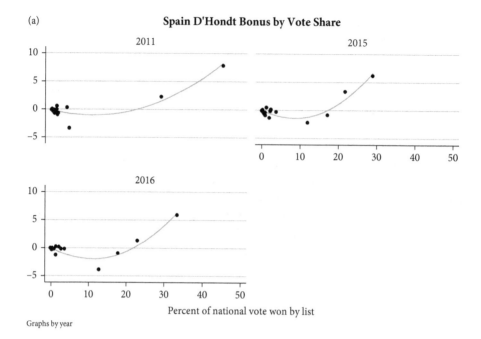

<!-- Spain D'Hondt Bonus by Vote Share -->

(b)

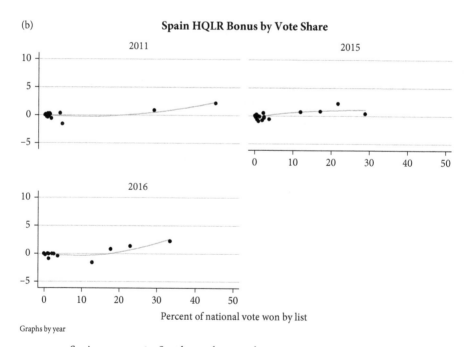

<!-- Spain HQLR Bonus by Vote Share -->

FIGURE 5.7.  Spain 2011–2016—Seat bonus by vote share.

Data source: Ministerio del Interior de la Republica de Espana (2016).

shown previously. In every election, D'Hondt produces sharply increasing returns to scale, whereas HQLR would have yielded returns that increase only gradually and that confer bonuses on smaller and moderate-sized parties commensurate with those for the largest competitors, as illustrated in figure 5.7.

# ELECTORAL SYSTEM DESIGN FOR NEW DEMOCRACIES AND BEYOND

The choice sets voters confront in transitional democracies can be vast, and the connection tenuous between a ballot cast and its effect on representation. A central challenge of electoral system design in these environments is to encourage the formation of a choice set that is large enough to reflect diverse societal interests but not so large that voters cannot distinguish among their options or parse how to channel their support to viable parties. Another challenge is to encourage partisan competition while limiting the likelihood that one party can parley an initial victory into a permanent electoral advantage by monopolizing the state apparatus. Electoral system design in new democracies should encourage the development of tractable partisan choice sets while fostering competition and inclusive governing coalitions.

Electoral rules can strike this balance by concentrating representational bonuses on parties at the low end of the viability range. Such economies of moderate scale reward alliance formation, and thus choice set tractability, in environments where high uncertainty can discourage electoral coordination. This design also insures against manufactured parliamentary majorities that would concentrate state authority.

The cross-national data presented early in this chapter show that, in new democracies, the most dramatic constraints on partisan choice sets are found in single-seat district elections. Mixed systems and list PR using the D'Hondt formula exhibit somewhat larger choice sets, and list PR using HQLR or other formulas constrains fragmentation least of all, at least initially. In those latter systems, however, vote fragmentation tends to decline over time such that, by the fifth posttransition election, choice sets resemble those under D'Hondt. Moreover, competitiveness tends to increase over time under HQLR.

The case studies visited in this chapter provide further insights. The Tunisian experience, as well as those of Peru and Spain, show that HQLR can act as insurance against manufactured majorities that would confer the authority to govern alone. Under D'Hondt, parties that fall far short of winning vote majorities can win large seat majorities, particularly when competition in unbalanced—that is, where the plurality party far outpaces others in a highly fragmented field, as in Tunisia's founding election or Peru's 2016 contest. In new democracies, the downside risk of such a result is particularly acute. Under these circumstances, the appeal of HQLR is most pronounced.

Yet the same mechanics of HQLR that make it attractive in environments of extreme fragmentation and uncertainty can produce liabilities. The Hong Kong case study shows that where the set of viable contenders is compact and their relative strengths are well known, HQLR's concentration of representational bonuses at the low end of the viability scale can discourage the formation of broad coalitions, even splintering natural alliances. The Hong Kong case is not unique. For example, Colombia used HQLR throughout the late twentieth century and witnessed a proliferation of lists even more pronounced than Hong Kong's, as parties would split into scores of factional lists to win seats by remainders.[11] The effect was widely regarded as corrosive to Colombian parties and an obstacle to the development of common policy platforms and effective governance. In 2004, Colombia passed a broad set of electoral reforms, among them replacing the HQLR formula with D'Hondt (Shugart, Moreno, and Fajardo 2007). Following the reform, the number of lists dropped and the correlation between the vote shares of the largest parties and their seat bonuses grew stronger as D'Hondt rewarded economies of larger scale and broader electoral alliances united under common banners (Pachon and Shugart 2010; Shugart, Moreno, and Fajardo 2007, tables 7.4 and 7.8).

The experiences of Hong Kong and Colombia—and, perhaps, of Spain—suggest that the principles of electoral system design in brand new democracies might differ slightly from those in more established ones. In new democracies, where uncertainty prevails about who is viable and who is not, and where the risks associated with one party capturing unfettered control of government are high, economies of moderate scale are the most attractive. Electoral rules that reward viability, but no more, can encourage the formation of tractable choice sets, competitiveness, and inclusiveness. Ideally, new democracies will develop party systems that deliver meaningfully distinct choices, but without overburdening the cognitive capacities, or will, of voters. Once a party system with those characteristics takes shape, however, and as expectations firm up around it, the premium on moderate scale should be less pronounced and the case for electoral economies of *increasing* scale—rules that confer the largest bonuses on the largest parties to foster governability and decisiveness—increases in appeal.

# Acknowledgments

Thanks to Guillermo Amaro Chacon for excellent research assistance.

# Notes

1. They may call themselves alliances, blocs, movements, fronts, or anything else, but I will use the term "party" to refer to a group of politicians who coordinate their actions to win elections as a team.
2. The location of the lower boundary is also shaped by electoral rules, but the threshold and the distribution of bonuses to parties above it are distinct issues. Scholarship on electoral systems has focused far more on the former issue than the latter. This chapter shifts that focus.
3. Poland held a partly competitive Sejm election in June 1989. Parties other than the Communists and their rural ally, the Peasant Party, were allowed to contest one-third of the seats. The landslide victory for the anti-communists triggered a mass defection of communist deputies, such that the Sejm then selected a noncommunist government. The first open elections, however, took place in 1991.

4. Two caveats were that a party representing German-speaking Poles was exempted from the threshold, and a 7 percent threshold applied for multiparty alliances. For a comprehensive account of adjustments (and manipulations) to Polish electoral law in the early 1990s, see Kaminski and Nalepa (2004).

5. Polity assigns placeholder scores off the 21-point scale (e.g., −66, −77, −88) for countries under foreign occupation or in the midst of regime transitions. In such cases, I identify swings based on the difference between the first standard value after such an interruption and the last prior standard value.

6. Of these, forty-four were cases in which countries had intervening Polity scores off the −10 to 10 scale, which indicate things like occupation (e.g., Japan, 1952) or civil war (El Salvador, 1984), or general political upheaval (e.g., Tunisia, 2014), and forty-six represent new countries that entered the Polity dataset with a score of 5 or above (e.g., Czech and Slovak Republics, 1993; Suriname, 1975; Kosovo, 2008).

7. Vote and seat fragmentation are measured using the method introduced by Laakso and Taagepera (1979).

8. It is worth keeping in mind that the effective number of parties understates the actual number of viable competitors. Except under the exceptional circumstance of every party winning equal vote (or seat) shares, the raw number of vote-winning (seat-winning) competitors is higher than the effective number. How much higher depends on the dispersal of vote shares across parties. So a system with five effective vote-winning parties likely includes seven to ten viable competitors—pushing against what Miller's (1956) results suggest is the upper boundary of citizens' cognitive capacity to make meaningful distinctions among their various options.

9. Legal thresholds may apply at the national level (e.g., Israeli parties must win 2 percent of the vote nationwide to be eligible for any representation) or the district level (e.g., lists in Costa Rica that do not win at least one-half a full quota in a given district are ineligible to be awarded seats by remainder in that district) or both (e.g., Argentine parties that win 3 percent nationwide are eligible to win seats in any district, but failing that, a list must win 8 percent of the votes in a given district to be eligible for seats in that district, regardless of its rank order in the D'Hondt quotient matrix).

10. This discussion of the Peruvian outcome is based on a blog post on *The Monkey Cage*, coauthored with Steven Levitsky, and published on the *Washington Post's* website on June 3, 2016. https://www.washingtonpost.com/news/monkey-cage/wp/2016/06/03/fujimoris-party-already-controls-perus-congress-heres-why-observers-are-worried/.

11. The practice came to be known as Operation Wasp (*Operacion Avispa*, in Spanish) because it was more effective to fight electoral battles as a swarm of tiny micro-lists than by uniting as a party under a single banner.

## REFERENCES

Baum, Richard. "Democracy Deformed: Hong Kong's1998 Legislative Elections—and Beyond." *China Quarterly* 162 (2000): 439–464.

Benoit, Kenneth. "Electoral Laws as Political Consequences: Explaining the Origins and Change of Electoral Institutions." *Annual Review of Political Science* 10 (2007): 363–390.

Bormann, Nils-Christian, and Matt Golder. "Democratic Electoral Systems around the World, 1946-2011." *Electoral Studies* (2013). http://mattgolder.com/elections.

Brownlee, Jason, Tarek Masoud, and Andrew Reynolds. *The Arab Spring: Pathways of Repression and Reform.* New York: Oxford University Press, 2015.

Carey, John M. "Electoral Formula and Fragmentation in Hong Kong." *Journal of East Asian Studies* (forthcoming 2017).

Carey, John M., Tarek Masoud, and Andrew Reynolds. "Institutions as Causes and Effects: North African Electoral Systems During the Arab Spring." American Political Science Association conference paper, 2015.

Chen, Weiyang. 2015. ("Empirical Analysis of the Electoral System's Effects on Directly Elected Representatives to the Hong Kong Legislative Council.") *Journal of Chongqing Institute of Socialism* 2 (2015): 38–42.

Choy Chi-keung. "比例代表制：早知今日，何必当初" ("Proportional Representation: Had We Known the Outcome, We Would Not Have Implemented This System.") *Ming Pao Daily News.* August 1, 2013.

Colomer, Josep M. "It's Parties That Choose Electoral Systems (or, Duverger's Laws Upside Down)." *Political Studies* 53, no. 1 (2005): 1–21.

Cox, Gary W. *Making Votes Count: Strategic Coordination in the World's Electoral Systems.* New York: Cambridge University Press, 1997.

Duverger, Maurice. *Political Parties.* New York: Wiley, 1954.

Fung, Wing K. "The Last Legislative Election of Hong Kong under British Rule, 1995." *Electoral Studies* 15, no. 1 (1996): 119–123.

Independent Higher Authority of the Election (ISIE). "District-Level Data from the 'District Records' (محاضر الهيئات الفرعية) Pages of the 'Results' Section of the ISIE site." 2012 and 2014. http://www.isie.tn/.

Iyengar, Sheena. *The Art of Choosing.* New York: Twelve, 2010.

Kaminski, Marek, and Monika A. Nalepa. 2004. "Poland: Learning to Manipulate Electoral Rules." In *Handbook of Electoral System Choice,* edited by Josep M. Colomer, 369–381. London: Palgrave, 2004.

Laakso, Marku, and Rein Taagepera. "Effective Number of Parties: A Measure with Application to West Europe." *Comparative Political Studies* 12, no. 1 (1979): 3–27.

Lam, Jermain T. M. "The Last Legislative Council Election in Hong Kong: Implications and Consequences." *Issues and Studies* 31, no. 1 (1995): 68–82.

Ma, Ngoc. "Increased Pluralization and Fragmentation: Party System and Electoral Politics and the 2012 Elections." In *New Trends of Political Participation in Hong Kong,* edited by Joseph Y. S. Cheng, 185–210. Hong Kong: University of Hong Kong Press, 2014.

Ma, Ngoc, and Chi-keung Choy. "The Impact of Electoral Rule Change on Party Campaign Strategy—Hong Kong as a Case Study." *Party Politics* 9, no. 3 (2003): 347–367.

Miller, George A. "The Magical Number Seven, Plus or Minus Two: Some Limits on Our Capacity for Processing Information." *Psychological Review* 63 (1956): 81–97.

Ministerio del Interior de la Republica de Espana. *Consulta de resultados electorales,* accessed June 28, 2016, http://www.infoelectoral.mir.es/min/.

Nohlen, Dieter, and Philip Stover. *Elections in Europe: A Data Handbook.* Baden-Baden: Nomos Verlagsgesellschaft, 2010.

Oficina Nacional de Procesos Electorales (ONPE). "Presentacion de resultados." 2016. http://resultadoselecciones2016.onpe.gob.pe/PRPCP2016/.

Pachon, Monica, and Matthew Soberg Shugart. "Electoral Reform and the Mirror Image of Inter-Party and Intra-Party Competition: The Adoption of Party Lists in Colombia." *Electoral Studies* 29, no. 4 (2010): 648–660.

Pepper, Suzanne. "Elections, Political Change and Basic Law Government: The Hong Kong System in Search of a Political Form." *China Quarterly* 163 (2000): 410–438.

Polity IV. 2013. Center for Systemic Peace data page. http://www.systemicpeace.org/polity/polity4.htm.

Reynolds, Andres, Ben Reilly, and Andrew Ellis. *Electoral System Design: The New International IDEA Handbook*. Stockholm, Sweden: International IDEA, 2005.

Reynolds, Andrew, and John M. Carey. *Fixing Afghanistan's Electoral System*. Kabul, Afghanistan: Afghan Research and Evaluation Unit, 2012.

Shugart, Matthew Soberg, Erika Moreno, and Luis E. Fajardo. "Deepening Democracy by Renovating Political Practices: The Struggle for Electoral Reform in Colombia." In *Peace, Democracy, and Human Rights in Colombia*, edited by Christopher Welna and Gustavo Gallon, 202–267. Notre Dame, IN: University of Notre Dame Press, 2007.

Siu-kai, Lau. "The Making of the Electoral System." In *Power Transfer & Electoral Politics: The First Legislative Election in the Hong Kong Special Administrative Region*, edited by Kuan Hsin-chi, Lau Siu-kai, Louie Kin-sheun, and Timothy Ka-ying Wong, 3–34. Hong Kong: Chinese University Press, 1999.

Stepan, Alfred. "Tunisia's Transition and the Twin Tolerations." *Journal of Democracy* 23, no. 2 (2012): 89–103.

Stepan, Alfred. "Multiple but Complementary, Not Conflictual, Leaderships: The Tunisian Democratic Transition in Comparative Perspective." *Daedalus* 145, no. 3 (2016): 95–108.

Taagepera, Rein, and Matthew S. Shugart. *Seats and Votes: The Effects and Determinants of Electoral Systems*. New Haven, CT: Yale University Press, 1989.

Teorell, Jan, Stefan Dahlberg, Sören Holmberg, Bo Rothstein, Anna Khomenko, and Richard Svensson. "The Quality of Government Standard Dataset, version Jan16." University of Gothenburg: The Quality of Government Institute, 2016. http://www.qog.pol.gu.se doi:10.18157/QoGStdJan16.

........................................................................................................

# CHAPTER 6

# ELECTORAL SYSTEM CHANGE

........................................................................................................

## ALAN RENWICK

THE study of electoral systems is acknowledged as among the most developed subfields of political science (Shugart 2005). By the early 1980s, Riker (1982) could already review over a century of work, which had generated considerable understanding of the effects of electoral systems on other aspects of politics. In contrast to such *effects*, however, the issue of how and why electoral systems *change* until recently received comparatively little attention: in 2005, Shugart could still characterize the subfield merely as "beginning to take greater note of the origins, or 'engineering' side, of the study of electoral systems" (Shugart 2005, 27). Today's situation is quite different from the one Shugart described little more than a decade ago. Many issues remain unresolved, but much work has emerged, from which we can draw important insights.

This chapter will seek answers to four questions. The first is a necessary conceptual precursor to all later questions: what do we actually mean by electoral system change? The second is descriptive: what electoral system changes happen? Or, to put it differently, what patterns can we observe in electoral system changes? The third and fourth questions are causal: what are the determinants of electoral system change, and what are its effects? Each of these questions has generated important debates that deserve our attention. Before getting to these questions, it will be useful to briefly survey the history of research into electoral system change.

## THE STUDY OF ELECTORAL SYSTEM CHANGE: A BRIEF HISTORY

..............................................................................................................................................

As just noted, a coherent body of research into electoral system change has only recently begun to emerge. Before the 1990s, only a few notable exceptions broke this pattern: Rokkan (1970) examined the switch from majoritarian to proportional systems in many European countries in the early twentieth century; Carstairs (1980) surveyed the history of electoral reforms across Western Europe; and detailed single-country studies included those of Butler (1963) on the United Kingdom, Campbell (1958) (later Cole and Campbell 1989) on France, Törnudd (1968) on Finland, and Ziegler (1958) on early developments in Germany.

The main reason for the dearth of interest in these early years was simple: major electoral system change in established democracies very rarely happened. In the 1960s and 1970s, not one long-standing democracy changed the basic principles of its electoral rules. Nohlen (1984, 217) argued, "Fundamental changes [to electoral systems] are rare and arise only in extraordinary historical situations." As Katz (1980, 123) put it, major electoral system change "seems likely only when, as in France after the Second World War or during the Algerian crisis, the nation seems on the verge of collapse."

New interest in electoral system change began to emerge in the 1990s. The main impetus was a wave of real-world reforms. France abandoned its two-round majoritarian system in favor of proportional representation for the election of 1986, only to revert back to majoritarianism in the election that followed. Of more lasting importance, in the mid-1990s, New Zealand moved from first past the post (FPTP) to a mixed-member form of proportional representation (MMP), Italy replaced a pure proportional system with a less proportional mixed-member system, and Japan adopted mixed-member rules in place of the system of single non-transferable vote. The first attempt to draw comparative lessons from these cases was a collection of studies edited by Norris (1995). At the same time, renewed interest spurred re-examination of earlier cases, such as the adoption of (West) Germany's postwar electoral system (Bawn 1993) and the wave of early twentieth-century reforms in Western Europe (Boix 1999).

The subfield has expanded enormously since the turn of the present century. Benoit (2004), Colomer (2005), Remmer (2008), and Calvo (2009), among others, offered rational choice theories of electoral system change, while Katz (2005) advocated a less parsimonious approach that acknowledged the variety and complexity of electoral reform processes. Edited volumes (Shugart and Wattenberg 2001a; Grofman and Lijphart 2002; Colomer 2004; Gallagher and Mitchell 2005; Blais 2008) provided both case studies and comparative analyses. Book-length monographs include my own (Renwick 2010; Renwick and Pilet 2016), as well as Ahmed (2013) and Pilon (2013). Surveys of the burgeoning literature are given by Benoit (2007) and Rahat (2011).

The lessons of this tide of work will be analyzed over the following sections. The first question to consider is that of what electoral system change actually is.

## What Is Electoral System Change?

Electoral system change is, simply, the process by which the rules of an election are altered. The concept is essentially identical to that of electoral reform (though it is free of the positive evaluative tone sometimes associated with the latter), and I will use these two terms interchangeably. Three principal questions can be asked of this definition.

First, does it include electoral system *origination,* as well as electoral system *alteration*? Second, which are the electoral rules that we have in mind? Third, how substantial does the change in these rules need to be before we count it?

The first of these questions is perhaps the least important, but clarity is needed. On the one hand, the concept of *change* would seem to imply the pre-existence of something to which that change is applied: an electoral system can be changed only if there is an electoral system already in place. On the other hand, this may be a rather academic distinction: existing rules are not necessarily used as a reference point in devising new rules, particularly during overarching regime change. A more common distinction separates changes in existing democratic contexts and changes during regime transitions. Processes in these two circumstances may be very different from each other: in the former, politicians elected through the old rules are almost certain to play a major role; in the latter, that may well not be the case. There is no single right answer to the question of whether this distinction is useful: it depends on our purposes. What matters is simply that we are clear about what we are referring to. For reasons of space, this chapter focuses on reforms in existing democracies.

The next question concerns which rules we have in mind. The concept of the electoral system can be understood broadly to encompass all the rules governing elections—including, for example, rules on who can vote or run for election, how candidates and their supporters can campaign, and how the election is administered. More commonly, however, the electoral system is defined narrowly to consist of two things: the nature of the votes that voters can cast; and the rules through which it is determined, on the basis of those votes, who is elected. In the FPTP system, for example, voters can cast a vote for a single candidate, whereas some other systems allow voters to rank candidates in order of preference, vote only for a party, or vote for a party and a candidate. In FPTP, the candidate who wins the most votes is elected; other systems specify a threshold that must be passed or allocate seats across parties in proportion to the votes cast. Given limited space, I will, in common with most studies, employ the narrow definition here. That is not remotely to suggest that other changes are unimportant. Notably, Celis, Krook, and Meier (2011, 515) are well justified in characterizing the increasing use of gender quotas as "among the widest-reaching electoral reforms of recent years" and in criticizing the excessively narrow focus of most electoral reform studies. I remain within those narrow bounds only to keep the scope of the chapter manageable.

Finally, we should think about the degree of change we have in mind. Those who see electoral system change as rare have in mind change from one type of system—such as first past the post or list proportional representation—to another. If, by contrast, we allow changes within these systems—such as changes to thresholds or to voters' ability to order the candidates on a party's list—then reforms look much more common. My own recent study, for example, found seventy-four reforms in European democracies between 1945 and 2009 (Renwick and Pilet 2016, 45–46). But how small can a reform be and still be counted? Do we count, say, a small change in the number of seats available in one electoral district? Lijphart (1994, 13) was the first to grapple in detail with this issue, proposing minima that a reform had to pass to count as significant. It was a revised version of this scheme that Jean-Benoit Pilet and I used to reach the reform count just cited. Jacobs and Leyenaar (2011) distinguish three categories of reform: major, minor, and technical. Again, there is no single correct definition of which reforms count. But precise criteria are always needed.

Bearing these conceptual considerations in mind, we can turn now to the question of what electoral system changes can actually be observed in the world.

## PATTERNS OF ELECTORAL SYSTEM CHANGE

The preceding paragraphs have already referred to one aspect of patterning in electoral system changes: namely, their frequency. As we have seen, how often we character-ize electoral systems as changing depends crucially on how we define electoral system change. Major shifts from one type of system to another are rare, but significant adjust-ments within those basic types are, in many countries, not unusual. In addition, changes to electoral systems are much more likely to happen during or immediately following democratic transitions than they are in long-established democracies (Renwick 2011, 470–471). Beyond the frequency of electoral system changes, we can examine two fur-ther patterns: first, the direction of change; second, its character.

Following Shugart (2001), the direction of change can be measured on two principal dimensions: interparty and intraparty. The interparty dimension relates to the degree of proportionality of the electoral system: the degree to which the system converges upon or diverges from the "ideal" in which each party's share of the seats is identical to its share of the votes. The intraparty dimension, meanwhile, refers to "personalization": the degree to which voters or parties can determine which individual candidates are elected.

The best-known finding on the interparty dimension is Colomer's conclusion (2005, 16–17) that the broad pattern of change has been toward more proportional systems. In 1874, there were, by his count, twenty electoral democracies in the world with popula-tions over one million, and all of those employed majoritarian electoral rules. By 1960, there were sixteen democracies with majoritarian systems and twenty-three with pro-portional rules. By 2002, there were still sixteen majoritarian systems, but the number of proportional democracies had risen to sixty-six. But this contrasts with the analysis of Núñez, Simón, and Pilet (2017, 385), drawing on the Electoral System Change in Europe database: looking at European democracies between 1945 and 2012, they find no clear direction of change: thirty-three reforms increased proportionality over that period, while twenty-nine reduced it.

These differing findings relate to the conceptual distinctions identified in the pre-vious section. The trend toward proportionality identified by Colomer has two com-ponents: first, in the early twentieth century, many European countries shifted from majoritarian to proportional rules (see also Boix 1999; Cusack, Iversen, and Soskice 2007; Kreuzer 2010; Ahmed 2013); second, the great majority of the countries that have democratized since World War II have adopted (wholly or partially) proportional systems (Bormann and Golder 2013). But that does not mean there is an inexorable trend toward proportionality everywhere. Some democracies—notably including the United States, United Kingdom, India, Canada, and Australia—have stuck with majoritarian systems, despite (in some cases) repeated waves of reform pressure (though the United Kingdom has shifted to new rules in both sub- and supranational elections— see Lundberg's chapter in this volume). As the data in Núñez et al. (2017) show, established European democracies manifest no general pattern of change. Among major changes of system type, New Zealand replaced FPTP with a proportional system (specifically, MMP) in 1993, but Italy moved partially in the opposite direction the same year. France briefly flirted with proportional representation in the 1980s but quickly restored majoritarianism.

The intraparty dimension of electoral system change has received much less attention: as Colomer put it in the title of his book on the subject, this is "the neglected dimension of electoral systems" (Colomer 2011). Karvonen (2010, 101) surveyed evidence from a range of cases and found no general pattern. By contrast, my own work with Jean-Benoit Pilet, drawing on detailed research into thirty-one European democracies, identified a clear trend: between 1945 and 2009, we found thirty-five reforms that increased personalization and only twelve that reduced it; for the period since 1989, that trend was overwhelming (Renwick and Pilet 2016, 45–46). In this case, the divergence of results appears to be due to the greater scope of the latter study and its use of a more fine-grained definition of personalization. There is no systematic study of electoral reforms affecting the intraparty dimension outside Europe, but changes have occurred in both directions. The adoption of mixed-member systems in Japan and New Zealand in the 1990s reduced personalization, as did the creation of a list PR system in Colombia a decade later (Pachón and Shugart 2010). By contrast, El Salvador (España-Nájera 2016) and Iraq (Younis 2011, 14) have both opened their previously closed lists.

Turning to the character of electoral system changes, one aspect that has received attention is the fact that electoral reforms tend not to be enacted in isolation; rather, they are often embedded within packages that include other changes (e.g., Bedock 2014, 371; Emmenegger and Petersen 2015, 8). This may matter to analysis of the origins of these reforms: many of those voting for them might not even want them but support them in return for agreement on other parts of the package. Equally, we should also remember that changes to the electoral system are not always the only possible means through which reformers might pursue their objectives: depending on what those objectives are, other options might also be available. This could again skew our analysis of causes.

Finally, electoral system change is a subset of the broader phenomenon of institutional change, and it is valuable to consider how the wider literature characterizes such change. One recent focus concerns the incremental nature of institutional change: because they face opposition from entrenched interests, reforms, when they occur, often preserve aspects of the status quo. Streeck and Thelen (2005, 19–31) argue that this can lead to a range of patterns, which they place under such headings as "displacement" (where subordinate elements in an institutional order rise in salience), "layering" (where aspects of the old are maintained as new arrangements are maintained), and "drift" (under which institutions change because they are not updated to reflect an evolving context).

As we will see in the following section, the pervasiveness of barriers to reform is recognized in work on electoral system change too (Rahat and Hazan 2011). That may help explain why most reforms retain the basic structure of the status quo. It may also explain one recent phenomenon: namely, a growth in the popularity of mixed-member electoral systems. While Shugart and Wattenberg (2001b, 24) suggest that such systems may be preferred because they are believed to offer "the best of both worlds," another interpretation is that they are manifestations of layering: while moving toward a new system, reforms are designed to preserve elements of the old.

# DETERMINANTS OF ELECTORAL SYSTEM CHANGE

The primary question asked by scholars of electoral system change is simple: what causes it? More particularly, we seek to understand why changes to electoral systems happen or do not happen and, where they happen, why they take the forms that they do. Approaches to answering these questions range from purely theoretical models (Benoit 2004), through statistical analyses (e.g., Boix 1999; Calvo and Micozzi 2005; Cusack et al. 2007; Bol 2016) and qualitative comparative studies (Sakamoto 1999; Katz 2005; Renwick 2010), to deep, sometimes interpretivist histories (Ahmed 2013; Pilon 2013). Cutting across these methodologies, most studies focus primarily on the microfoundations of reform processes, analyzing who is involved in those processes, what motivates them, and how they pursue their goals. But the broad political and social forces that shape the world in which these actors operate—shaping their interests and values, influencing their knowledge, and constituting the opportunities and constraints they face—are also crucial. In this section, I begin with microfoundations before moving out to the big picture. We can distinguish five main questions:

1. Who are the actors involved in electoral system change?
2. What are those actors' goals or purposes?
3. What do those actors know?
4. How are actors' preferences aggregated and translated into outcomes?
5. What broad political and social forces shape processes of electoral reform?

## Actors

The dominant actors of electoral system change are politicians: there is no case of significant electoral reform, at least in an established democracy, in which politicians have played no role (Renwick 2010, 16). That is so for two reasons: first, politicians typically control the mechanisms by which the rules can be changed; second, electoral reforms affect politicians more directly and more substantially than they affect anyone else. Many accounts of electoral system change focus exclusively on politicians, seeing decision making around the electoral system simply as an arena in which politicians seek to maximize their power (e.g., Benoit 2004; Colomer 2005; Calvo 2009).

But politicians are not always in sole charge, and the literature on electoral system change identifies four further sets of actors who can also be involved: judges, interest and pressure groups, the general public, and international actors. The last of these groups are often involved during democratic transitions (Reynolds 2011; Reilly 2013). But they are much less prominent in established democracies, so I will not consider them further here.

Decision making can be wrested furthest from the hands of politicians by judicial rulings. In 2013, for example, Italy's Constitutional Court determined that the electoral law passed in 2005 breached the constitution because it was insufficiently proportional and gave voters too little opportunity to vote for individual candidates (Baldini and Renwick 2015, 164–165). Four years later, the same court decided that key parts of a replacement law were also unconstitutional (see Passarelli in this volume). Other significant judicial interventions in the electoral system are discussed, for example, by Katz (2011), Williams (2005), and Zittel (this volume). Still, while court rulings have significantly changed aspects of the broad electoral system—notably in US Supreme Court decisions on the franchise, districting, and campaign finance (Hasen 2003)—major change via the courts in the electoral system narrowly defined remains rare.

More frequently important is the general public. Public influence is sometimes exerted through formal channels such as referendums (e.g., Donovan 1995; Vowles 1995; Curtice 2013) and citizens' assemblies (Fournier et al. 2011; LeDuc 2011). But more often it occurs informally, as public preferences shape politicians' agendas. Widespread public mobilization specifically around electoral reform is rare: voters are typically more concerned about matters that affect their daily lives than they are about the finer details of the representative system. But two more indirect mechanisms are more common (see Quintal 1970; Reed and Thies 2001, 153; Renwick 2011, 458). First, politicians might retreat from reforms that could bring them advantage if they fear voters would punish them for engaging in such self-interested maneuvering. Second, politicians might enact reforms they otherwise would not pursue if they believe voters will reward them for doing so. While cases of the first mechanism can be difficult to identify empirically, cases of the second are clearly widespread. My recent work on personalizing reforms in Europe, for example, suggests that many such reforms over the past quarter century have been influenced by politicians' desire to show they are responding to voters' disillusionment with the political status quo (Renwick and Pilet 2016, 210).

The role of interest and pressure groups in processes of electoral system change is perhaps the least researched. Democratic reform groups are common and can exert influence if the circumstances are right. Perhaps more interesting, however, is the potential that economic interests or other nonpolitical groups can have an important driving role.

Cusack et al. (2007), notably, present an interpretation of electoral system changes in the early twentieth century in which politicians are no more than the conduits for enacting the will of wider economic interest groups. Leeman and Mares (2014) offer a more nuanced model, in which deputies respond to electoral pressures in their districts, but these electoral pressures are shaped, in turn, by underlying economic patterns. Ahmed (2013), from a very different methodological perspective, similarly argues for the importance of class interests.

## Goals and Purposes

The preceding discussion of actors has begun also to open up the question of those actors' motivations. The dominant approach here sees participants in the electoral reform process as seeking to advance their own interests. Given that politicians are typically the principal actors, the assumption tends to be that those politicians are seeking to advance their (or their party's) power. The cleanest statement of this perspective is offered by Benoit (2004, 373–374):

> Electoral systems result from the collective choice of political parties linking institutional alternatives to electoral self-interest in the form of maximizing seat shares . . . . A change in electoral institutions will occur when a political party or coalition of political parties supports an alternative which will bring it more seats than the status quo electoral system, and also has the power to effect through fiat that institutional alternative.

There is no doubt that this captures a large part of the politics of electoral reform: it is the logic that underlies the fact that large parties (and the politicians within them) tend to prefer more majoritarian electoral systems, which favor large parties, while smaller parties (and their representatives) favor more proportional systems (e.g., Colomer 2005). It might also be reasonable to suppose a similar logic for voters: insofar as they think about electoral systems, they may prefer one that advances the electoral interests of their favored party.

On the other hand, two complications need to be considered before we have a rounded picture. First, pursuit of power can mean many things. Should we look at individual politicians' power interests or those of their parties? Do politicians look just at the next election or are their time horizons longer? Are they mainly interested in winning seats in the legislature or in exercising power in government (these are typically positively correlated, but are not always so)? Perhaps most important, building on the previous discussion of the role played by public opinion, do politicians look simply at the mechanical effects of different electoral systems on their electoral fortunes, or do they also look at whether the actions they take in regard to electoral reform will affect their popularity? This is the distinction, introduced by Reed and Thies (2001) and used also by Shugart (2008), between "outcome-contingent" and "act-contingent" motivations—between comparing the effects of the outcomes of reform processes (alternative electoral systems) and comparing the effects of one's actions in the course of the reform process (supporting or opposing reform). As suggested earlier, public opinion often has an important role in processes of electoral system change, and that is because politicians do look at options in an act-contingent as well as an outcome-contingent way. The first complication, thus, is that the pursuit of power can shape decision making around electoral systems in a wide variety of different ways.

The second complication is that, much as the pursuit of power clearly matters, it is not the only motivation that can influence how actors approach electoral system change. As Katz found, reviewing the papers in a symposium on electoral reform:

> the ideas that electoral reforms can be understood simply as stratagems of political parties to maximise their voting power, and that voting behaviour with regard to referendums concerning reform of the electoral system is driven simply by the desire for one's preferred candidate to win the present election, find little support in these papers. (Katz 2007, 308)

Similarly, I have argued that none of the three major electoral reforms of the 1990s—in Italy, New Zealand, and Japan—can be explained solely in terms of political interests (Renwick 2010, 167–238). Values matter too.

This point has now gained support from a range of empirical studies. Looking at electoral system changes in the early twentieth century, Blais, Dobrzynska, and Indridason (2005, 184) found that proportional systems were often adopted largely by consensus and that this reflected general acceptance of "the principle that each vote should count the same." Focusing on more recent times, Bowler, Donovan, and Karp (2006), drawing on surveys of politicians in four democracies between 1999 and 2002, found that their attitudes on electoral reform questions were shaped partly by their electoral interests, but partly also by their ideological commitments and democratic values. Bol (2016) surveys the positions of 115 parties in relation to twenty-two proposals for electoral reform across Organisation for Economic Cooperation and Development (OECD) countries between 1961 and 2011 and concludes that these positions were shaped by party ideologies as well as by party interests: "values appear to be as crucial as self-interests in explaining the overall electoral reform story" (Bol 2016, 102).

While the studies just cited concentrate on politicians, others look at the general public. Norris (2011) finds that high levels of popular "democratic aspiration," as measured through survey evidence, are associated with greater incidence of electoral reforms. Drawing on survey data from the 1993 electoral reform referendum in New Zealand, Lamare and Vowles (1996) found that a range of values, as well as party interests, correlated with voting patterns. Karp (2007) found similar patterns for a referendum in Colorado in 2004 on whether to allocate the state's nine votes in the presidential electoral college proportionally, as did Whiteley et al. (2012) regarding the United Kingdom's electoral reform referendum of 2011.

A full understanding of goals and purposes in relation to electoral system change thus requires us to engage both with the complexity of power interests and with the roles of a range of values. There is no doubt that many reforms do conform to the narrow rational choice model, in that they are dominated by the electoral interests of the politicians in power. But often those interests are shaped by act contingencies that depend on public opinion. And a growing body of work suggests that values are also central to the story of electoral reform.

## Knowledge

Our third question relates to what the actors know. Knowledge comes in two principal forms: what actors know about electoral systems and their effects; and what they know about their own positions—particularly, for politicians, about their popularity. It could be, for example, that a party's support among voters is falling and that it would therefore benefit from a more proportional system. If it does not know about proportional systems, however, or if it does not know about its falling support (or—more likely in a world of regular polling—it is uncertain of whether the decline is a short-term blip or a long-term trend), then it may fail to change its preferences.

The importance of knowledge about electoral systems is evident, for example, in the fact that proportional systems spread in the early twentieth century only once familiarity with them increased. We might expect variation in system knowledge to matter less in today's interconnected world than in the past. But knowledge can be about practical familiarity, as well as basic awareness: actors may be wary of options that they do not feel they understand or that they feel have little chance of catching on. Thus, for example, single transferable vote (STV) systems are widely used and advocated in the British Isles and, to varying degrees, other Anglophone democracies, but almost ignored elsewhere. Furthermore, knowledge about the effects of different electoral systems can be shaky: as we explore in the section below on the effects of change, reform supporters' claims (and probably often also their genuine beliefs) about the positive effects that electoral system change will bring are frequently exaggerated.

The key aspect of knowledge regarding future electoral prospects is often uncertainty. Andrews and Jackman (2005) offer evidence that the choices made in conditions of high uncertainty—particularly in the early stages of democratization—are often based on short-term calculations and turn out to harm the interests of their initial advocates. If actors are aware of uncertainty, this may, following the logic of the Rawlsian "veil of ignorance" (Rawls 1972, 136–142), lead them to prefer more proportional systems in which they essentially hedge their bets. Pilet and Bol (2011) show how perceptions of risk do indeed matter in electoral reform processes, and that they can vary across actors.

## Translating Preferences into Outcomes

Actors' goals and purposes combine with their knowledge to generate their *preferences* among the options that are available. But how do those preferences then translate into outcomes? If, as in Benoit's model (2004), there is a single, united party that has the power to decide the electoral system on its own, then this will be a simple business: the leadership of that party will enact whatever it thinks will best advance its purposes. If, on the other hand, parties contain a diversity of views or no one party has an overall majority, or public opinion is swayable, then the translation of preferences into outcomes will be far from straightforward.

Emmenegger and Petersen (2015) argue, indeed, that the complexity of this process means that large-n cross-sectional analyses of electoral reform processes will always struggle to find meaningful general patterns: processes of electoral system change are likely to involve "collective actors, such as political parties, social movements or governments," which "are likely to be characterized by internal factions, personal and ideological rivalry, charismatic leaders," such that their behavior will be "highly context-dependent and volatile" (Emmenegger and Petersen 2015, 2). Similarly, I have emphasized the importance of context-dependent processes of leadership and path dependence (Renwick 2010, 69–85). Some—notably, Browne and Hamm (1996), on an electoral system change in France in 1951—have sought to reconstruct particular instances of electoral reform using the techniques of social choice theory, but in doing so they simply illustrate the difficulties of generalizing beyond the single case.

Rahat and Hazan (2011) seek to systematize our understanding of some of the mechanisms through which preferences translate into outcomes by identifying seven "barriers" to reform. Some of these, such as political traditions and social structures, are in fact best seen as undergirding the formation of preferences. But others relate to aggregation of preferences into outcomes. The formal institutional structure is important for determining the number of veto points in the system and the degree to which power within any of these points is likely to lie in the hands of a single, unitary actor or multiple, complex actors. The nature of coalition politics and the degree to which different veto players have differing preferences are also crucial. Nunez and Jacobs (2016) draw a range of hypotheses from this work, which they test by combining statistical analysis of electoral system dynamics in sixteen countries from 1975 to 2005 and qualitative analysis of key cases. They find (perhaps unsurprisingly) that electoral system change is less likely in countries with more rigid constitutional structures. On the other hand, their expectation that strong judicial review will make reform harder is not supported; in fact, it appears that judicial review may be more likely to catalyze than to block electoral system change.

## Underlying Drivers

The preceding subsections demonstrate the importance of combining microfoundational analysis of actors with broader analysis of wide social and political forces: any study of actors requires engagement with the factors that shape those actors' interests, values, understandings, opportunities, and constraints. Many of the underlying drivers of processes of electoral system change have thus already been touched upon: democratic and other values frame the options that are considered legitimate; social structures influence class identities and interests; knowledge, values, and other ideas flow between people and places.

Some authors explore these same forces without paying much attention to the micro-foundational mechanisms through which they generate their effects. A literature on diffusion, for example, looks at the tendency for similar electoral rules to be adopted in particular time periods, regions, or colonial networks (Lundell 2010, 59–87). Pilon (2013) goes further, seeing electoral system change as a by-product of evolving struggles over the meaning of democracy: "the search for constant variables affecting choices over voting systems fails to capture what is really going on. The real battle is over what democracy will be, with voting systems and their reform taken up as one of many possible terrains" (Pilon 2013, 52). He tracks electoral system change in the twentieth century through four historical epochs; across these periods, it is above all the shifting character of the political Left that lies at the heart of his narratives.

The most developed non-microfoundational account of electoral system change is Shugart's theory of "systemic failure" (Shugart 2001, 2008). Shugart defines systemic failure of the electoral system as "the incapacity of the electoral system to deliver the normatively expected connection between the vote and the formation of executive authority" (Shugart 2008, 13). On one version, those expectations are shaped by the prevailing electoral system (Shugart 2008, 13); on another, any "extreme" system—one that is highly proportional, majoritarian, candidate-centric, or party-centric—is more likely to be seen as failing than a more balanced system (Shugart 2001, 28–29) The occurrence of such failure creates the circumstances in which a change in the system becomes more likely. Thus, the broad pattern of electoral reforms is determined at the systemic level, while the level of actors and their preferences just fills in the timing and detailed dynamics. Shugart does not argue that this systemic account of the drivers of electoral reform is sufficient to explain why reforms do or do not occur: he emphasizes that that requires an analysis also of the contingencies through which the failures feed into the key actors' rational calculations (Shugart 2008, 14–19). Still, his approach differs from many in highlighting the crucial role of the systemic level.

# EFFECTS OF ELECTORAL SYSTEM CHANGE

Our final question turns to the effects of electoral system change: once reform has happened, how does this affect wider political life? In part, this is a question simply about the effects of electoral systems as such: to understand the effects, for example, of a shift to a more proportional electoral system, we can consider, in part, the effects of electoral system proportionality in general. Indeed, it may seem that that is all we need to consider. Yet students of electoral reform have repeatedly found that the reality appears to be more complex: that changes to electoral systems do not necessarily deliver the effects that their advocates hoped for. For example, while there is general agreement in the literature on electoral systems that more proportional systems are associated with substantially higher electoral turnout (e.g., Endersby and Krieckhaus 2008), Vowles's detailed study concludes that the adoption of proportional rules in New Zealand in the 1990s had little or no effect on turnout (Vowles 2010). Similarly, Gambetta and Warner (1996) and Katz (2006) set out the expectations of electoral reform supporters in Italy in the 1990s and conclude that those expectations were frequently dashed. Concentrating on the Japanese reform at the same time, McKean and Scheiner (2000) found that it did not yield the shift toward more policy-oriented campaigning that was hoped for. My own recent work suggests that personalizing reforms, while often designed as a way of reconnecting voters with politics, have not discernibly produced any such effect (Renwick and Pilet 2016, 249–260). This recurring finding is summed up in the work of Bowler and Donovan (2013). Exploring a range of putative effects of a variety of reforms, they repeatedly find that effects are small or undetectable: "Our assessment demonstrates that expectations about the effects of electoral reforms are generally not met . . . . [F]or all the discussion of institutional engineering and manipulation and all the effort involved, institutional changes may not actually change very much" (Bowler and Donovan 2013, 5).

Still, this pattern should not be exaggerated. Electoral system changes do have effects on politics more broadly. Electoral reform in New Zealand, for example, has facilitated multiparty competition, contributed to a new normal of coalition governments, and helped open the system to greater gender and ethnic diversity (e.g., Vowles, Banducci, and Karp 2006). Reed (2001, 2002) offers a far rosier picture of the effects of the reforms in Italy and Japan than the aforementioned contributions suggest, and more recent assessments of the Japanese case confirm that it has stimulated a gradual shift toward more policy-based competition (e.g., Reed, Scheiner, and Thies 2012). Looking at data from fifty-nine countries between 1945 and 2010, Riera (2015) finds that reforms that open up the system to smaller parties do yield more proportional results (and vice versa), as would be expected. Fiva and Folke (2016) find that such effects have both mechanical and psychological elements.

Scheiner, reviewing this literature, points out that some of the desired effects of electoral reforms are more proximate to the electoral system itself than others (Scheiner 2008, 168–169). At one extreme, electoral systems have entirely mechanical effects on how votes are translated into seats. Their effects on the votes themselves, by contrast, are a step removed: they depend also on the responses of (potential) candidates, parties, and voters. And wider effects on modes of campaigning or satisfaction with democracy involve a still more complex causal chain. While purely mechanical effects flow inevitably from electoral system changes, more "distal" effects will be contingent upon other conditions.

Scheiner's account clearly provides some explanation for the mixed pattern of success and failure in the achievement of electoral reformers' goals. Several additional factors can also be taken into account. One is what Katz (2007, 312) calls "the pathological optimism of reformers": supporters of reform often believe (or at least claim to believe) that relatively limited institutional changes will have transformative effects on politics at large that no research in political science supports. Another is the fact that the reforms that are enacted are often more limited than those proposed by reform advocates: in both Italy and Japan in the 1990s, for example, campaigners pushed for pure majoritarian systems but had to compromise in the end on mixed-member systems that weakened the mechanisms that they hoped to introduce.

Such factors are not surprising. More intriguing is the possibility that electoral reforms may show the effects of electoral systems to be more subtle or complex than standard cross-sectional studies suggest. One possibility is that some effects of electoral systems may take multiple electoral cycles to emerge, as actors gradually update their expectations and their behavior. Studies conducted in the immediate wake of reforms—when interest is greatest—may therefore tend to underestimate ultimate effects. Another possibility is that the effects of electoral systems are contingent on other factors. For example, the effects of electoral systems on turnout may depend in part on modes of campaigning, which, once they have become entrenched in a country, may be difficult to change. A third possibility—and the most radical—is that some of the correlations between electoral systems and other aspects of politics may be (wholly or partly) spurious: causation may run the other way or unobserved third variables may intervene. Colomer (2005) is well known for arguing that party systems determine electoral systems, rather than the other way round. As the preceding section on the determinants of reform suggests, it may also be that a culture favorable to inclusive values favors the adoption of more inclusive electoral institutions. If such arguments are correct, then the insertion of particular electoral rules into an unsupportive environment may fail to yield the expected results.

Further research into the effects of electoral reforms will be needed to resolve these debates fully. What we can say is that electoral reforms do often have effects—on party systems, voting patterns, modes of competition, governing arrangements, and so on. But some of these effects are more predictable than others. And electoral reforms rarely deliver all that their advocates promise.

# Conclusion

Until the 1990s, the lack of much literature on electoral system change reflected widespread acceptance of what seemed like a simple truth: because the future of the electoral system is determined by those in power, who have typically entered power because they benefit from the prevailing rules, significant electoral reform is very rare. Since the 1990s, we have learned that, in fact, things are more complex. Significant electoral reforms do occur. They can come about via a variety of routes involving a range of actors, motivations, and contexts. Their effects range from the predictable to the highly uncertain.

Our task as political scientists is to find the order in this complexity. We can begin, as here, by systematically mapping the many possibilities. Beyond that, we want also to understand the most important recurring patterns. Benoit (2004) offered a crucial insight by crystallizing understanding of the central role of power-seeking behavior on the part of politicians. In my own work (Renwick 2010, 2011), I have argued for the value of locating electoral reform processes on a continuum from those that fit Benoit's model in being dominated by politicians to those in which politicians' approach is determined by their desire to curry public favor. Shugart (2001, 2008) and Pilon (2013), in very different ways, offer insights into the circumstances in which opposition to the status quo may be more likely to arise. Regarding the effects of reform, meanwhile, Scheiner (2008) highlights the need to consider the degree to which putative effects will arise only through interactions of the electoral system with other variables.

None of these attempts to draw out general patterns is set in stone: each can be contested or further refined, and other ideas may in the end prove more fruitful. Research into electoral system change has made much progress, but many opportunities for further work remain.

## References

Ahmed, Amel. *Democracy and the Politics of Electoral System Choice: Engineering Electoral Dominance.* Cambridge: Cambridge University Press, 2013.

Andrews, Josephine T., and Robert W. Jackman. "Strategic Fools: Electoral Rule Choice under Extreme Uncertainty." *Electoral Studies* 24, no. 1 (March 2005): 65–84.

Baldini, Gianfranco, and Alan Renwick. "Italy toward (Yet Another) Electoral Reform." In *Italian Politics: The Year of the Bulldozer,* edited by Chris Hanretty and Stefania Profeti, 160–178. New York: Berghahn, 2015.

Bawn, Kathleen. "The Logic of Institutional Preferences: German Electoral Law as a Social Choice Outcome." *American Journal of Political Science* 37, no. 4 (November 1993): 965–989.

Bedock, Camille. "Explaining the Determinants and Processes of Institutional Change." *French Politics* 12, no. 4 (December 2014): 357–374.

Benoit, Kenneth. "Models of Electoral System Change." *Electoral Studies* 23, no. 3 (September 2004): 363–389.

Benoit, Kenneth. "Electoral Laws as Political Consequences: Explaining the Origins and Change of Electoral Institutions." *Annual Review of Political Science* 10 (2007): 363–390.

Blais, André, ed. *To Keep or to Change First Past the Post? The Politics of Electoral Reform.* Oxford: Oxford University Press, 2008.

Blais, André, Agnieszka Dobrzynska, and Indridi H. Indridason. "To Adopt or Not to Adopt Proportional Representation: The Politics of Institutional Choice." *British Journal of Political Science* 35, no. 1 (January 2005): 182–190.

Boix, Carles. "Setting the Rules of the Game: The Choice of Electoral Systems in Advanced Democracies." *American Political Science Review* 93, no. 3 (September 1999): 609–624.

Bol, Damien. "Electoral Reform, Values, and Party Self-Interest." *Party Politics* 22, no. 1 (January 2016): 93–104.

Bormann, Nils-Christian, and Matt Golder. "Democratic Electoral Systems around the World, 1946–2011." *Electoral Studies* 32, no. 2 (June 2013): 360–369.

Bowler, Shaun, and Todd Donovan. *The Limits of Electoral Reform.* Oxford: Oxford University Press, 2013.

Bowler, Shaun, Todd Donovan, and Jeffrey A. Karp. "Why Politicians Like Electoral Institutions: Self-Interest, Values, or Ideology?" *Journal of Politics* 68, no. 2 (May 2006): 434–446.

Browne, Eric C., and Keith E. Hamm. "Legislative Politics and the Paradox of Voting: Electoral Reform in Fourth Republic France." *British Journal of Political Science* 26, no. 2 (April 1996): 165–198.

Butler, D. E. *The Electoral System in Britain since 1918.* 2nd ed. Oxford: Oxford University Press, 1963.

Calvo, Ernesto. "The Competitive Road to Proportional Representation: Partisan Biases and Electoral Regime Change under Increasing Party Competition." *World Politics* 61, no. 2 (April 2009): 254–295.

Calvo, Ernesto, and Juan Pablo Micozzi. "The Governor's Backyard: A Seat-Vote Model of Electoral Reform for Subnational Multiparty Races." *Journal of Politics* 67, no. 4 (November 2005): 1050–1074.

Campbell, Peter. *French Electoral Systems and Elections, 1789–1957.* London: Faber and Faber, 1958.

Carstairs, Andrew McLaren. *A Short History of Electoral Systems in Western Europe.* London: George Allen & Unwin, 1980.

Celis, Karen, Mona Lena Krook, and Petra Meier. "The Rise of Gender Quota Laws: Expanding the Spectrum of Determinants for Electoral Reform." *West European Politics* 34, no. 3 (May 2011): 514–530.

Cole, Alistair, and Peter Campbell. *French Electoral Systems and Elections since 1789.* Aldershot: Gower, 1989.

Colomer, Josep M., ed. *Handbook of Electoral System Choice.* Basingstoke: Palgrave Macmillan, 2004.

Colomer, Josep M. "It's Parties That Choose Electoral Systems (or, Duverger's Laws Upside Down." *Political Studies* 53, no. 1 (March 2005): 1–21.

Colomer, Josep M., ed. *Personal Representation: The Neglected Dimension of Electoral Systems.* Colchester: ECPR Press, 2011.

Curtice, John. "Politicians, Voters and Democracy: The 2011 UK Referendum on the Alternative Vote." *Electoral Studies* 32, no. 2 (June 2013): 215–223.

Cusack, Thomas, Torben Iversen, and David Soskice. "Economic Interests and the Origins of Electoral Systems." *American Political Science Review* 101, no. 3 (August 2007): 373–391.

Donovan, Mark. "The Politics of Electoral Reform in Italy." *International Political Science Review* 16, no. 1 (January 1995): 47–64.

Emmenegger, Patrick, and Klaus Petersen. "Taking History Seriously in Comparative Research: The Case of Electoral System Choice, 1890–1939." *Comparative European Politics* (2015).

Endersby, James W., and Jonathan T. Krieckhaus. "Turnout around the Globe: The Influence of Electoral Institutions on National Voter Participation, 1972–2000." *Electoral Studies* 27, no. 4 (December 2008): 601–610.

España-Nájera, Annabella. "The Legislative Elections in El Salvador, 2012 and 2015." *Electoral Studies* 42 (June 2016): 308–310.

Fiva, Jon H., and Olle Folke. "Mechanical and Psychological Effects of Electoral Reform." *British Journal of Political Science* 46, no. 2 (April 2016): 265–279.

Fournier, Patrick, Henk van der Kolk, R. Kenneth Carty, André Blais, and Jonathan Rose. *When Citizens Decide: Lessons from Citizens Assemblies on Electoral Reform*. Oxford: Oxford University Press, 2011.

Gallagher, Michael, and Paul Mitchell, eds. *The Politics of Electoral Systems*. Oxford: Oxford University Press, 2005.

Gambetta, Diego, and Steven Warner. "The Rhetoric of Reform Revealed (or: If You Bite the Ballot May Bite Back)." *Journal of Modern Italian Studies* 1, no. 3 (Summer 1996): 357–376.

Grofman, Bernard, and Arend Lijphart, eds. *The Evolution of Electoral and Party Systems in the Nordic Countries*. New York: Agathon, 2002.

Hasen, Richard L. *The Supreme Court and Election Law: Judging Equality from Baker v. Carr to Bush v. Gore*. New York: New York University Press, 2003.

Jacobs, Kristof, and Monique Leyenaar. "A Conceptual Framework for Major, Minor, and Technical Electoral Reform." *West European Politics* 34, no. 3 (May 2011): 495–513.

Karp, Jeffrey A. "Reforming the Electoral College and Support for Proportional Outcomes." *Representation* 43, no. 4 (2007): 239–250.

Karvonen, Lauri. *The Personalization of Politics: A Study of Parliamentary Democracies*. London: ECPR Press, 2010.

Katz, Richard S. *A Theory of Parties and Electoral Systems*. Baltimore, MD: Johns Hopkins University Press, 1980.

Katz, Richard S. "Why Are There So Many (or So Few) Electoral Reforms?" In *The Politics of Electoral Systems*, edited by Michael Gallagher and Paul Mitchell, 57–76. Oxford: Oxford University Press, 2005.

Katz, Richard S. "Electoral Reform in Italy: Expectations and Results." *Acta Politica* 41, no. 3 (September 2006): 285–299.

Katz, Richard S. "Comment." *Representation* 43, no. 4 (2007): 307–314.

Katz, Richard S. "Democracy as a Cause of Electoral Reform: Jurisprudence and Electoral Change in Canada." *West European Politics* 34, no. 3 (May 2011): 587–606.

Kreuzer, Marcus. "Historical Knowledge and Quantitative Analysis: The Case of the Origins of Proportional Representation." *American Political Science Review* 104, no. 2 (May 2010): 369–392.

Lamare, James W., and Jack Vowles. "Party Interests, Public Opinion and Institutional Preferences: Electoral System Change in New Zealand." *Australian Journal of Political Science* 31, no. 3 (November 1996): 321–345.

LeDuc, Lawrence. "Electoral Reform and Direct Democracy in Canada: When Citizens Become Involved." *West European Politics* 34, no. 3 (May 2011): 551–567.

Leeman, Lucas, and Isabela Mares. "The Adoption of Proportional Representation." *Journal of Politics* 76, no. 2 (April 2014): 461–478.

Lijphart, Arend. *Electoral Systems and Party Systems: A Study of Twenty-Seven Democracies, 1945–1990*. Oxford: Oxford University Press, 1994.

Lundell, Krister. *The Origin of Electoral Systems in the Post-War Era: A Worldwide Approach*. London: Routledge, 2010.

McKean, Margaret, and Ethan Scheiner. "Japan's New Electoral System: La plus ça change. ... " *Electoral Studies* 19, no. 4 (December 2000): 447–477.

Nohlen, Dieter. "Changes and Choices in Electoral Systems." In *Choosing an Electoral System: Issues and Alternatives*, edited by Arend Lijphart and Bernard Grofman, 217–224. Westport, CT: Praeger, 1984.

Norris, Pippa, ed. "The Politics of Electoral Reform." Special issue of *International Political Science Review* 16, no. 1 (January 1995).

Norris, Pippa. "Cultural Explanations of Electoral Reform: A Policy Cycle Model." *West European Politics* 34, no. 3 (May 2011): 531–550.

Nunez, Lidia, and Kristof T. E. Jacobs. "Catalysts and Barriers: Explaining Electoral Reform in Western Europe." *European Journal of Political Research* 55, no. 3 (August 2016): 454–473.

Núñez, Lidia, Pablo Simón, and Jean-Benoit Pilet. "Electoral Volatility and the Dynamics of Electoral Reform." *West European Politics* 40, no. 2 (2017): 378–401.

Pachón, Mónica, and Matthew S. Shugart. "Electoral Reform and the Mirror Image of Inter-Party and Intra-Party Competition: The Adoption of Party Lists in Colombia." *Electoral Studies* 29, no. 4 (December 2010): 648–660.

Pilet, Jean-Benoit, and Damien Bol. "Party Preferences and Electoral Reform: How Time in Government Affects the Likelihood of Supporting Electoral Change." *West European Politics* 34, no. 3 (May 2011): 568–586.

Pilon, Dennis. *Wrestling with Democracy: Voting Systems as Politics in the Twentieth-Century West*. Toronto: University of Toronto Press, 2013.

Quintal, David P. "The Theory of Electoral Systems." *Western Political Quarterly* 23, no. 4 (December 1970): 752–761.

Rahat, Gideon. "The Politics of Electoral Reform: The State of Research." *Journal of Elections, Public Opinion and Parties* 21, no. 4 (November 2011): 523–543.

Rahat, Gideon, and Reuven Y. Hazan. "The Barriers to Electoral System Reform: A Synthesis of Alternative Approaches." *West European Politics* 34, no. 3 (May 2011): 478–494.

Rawls, John. *A Theory of Justice*. Oxford: Oxford University Press, 1972.

Reed, Steven R. "Duverger's Law Is Working in Italy." *Comparative Political Studies* 34, no. 3 (April 2001): 312–327.

Reed, Steven R. "Evaluating Political Reform in Japan: A Midterm Report." *Japanese Journal of Political Science* 3, no. 2 (November 2002): 243–263.

Reed, Steven R., Ethan Scheiner, and Michael F. Thies. "The End of LDP Dominance and the Rise of Party-Oriented Politics in Japan." *Journal of Japanese Studies* 12, no. 2 (Summer 2012): 353–376.

Reed, Steven R., and Michael F. Thies. "The Causes of Electoral Reform in Japan." In *Mixed-Member Electoral Systems: The Best of Both Worlds?*, edited by Matthew Soberg Shugart and Martin P. Wattenberg, 152–172. Oxford: Oxford University Press, 2001.

Reilly, Benjamin. "Elections and Post-Conflict Political Development." In *Political Economy of Statebuilding: Power after Peace*, edited by Mats Berdal and Dominik Zaum, 33–47. London: Routledge, 2013.

Reynolds, Andrew. *Designing Democracy in a Dangerous World*. Oxford: Oxford University Press, 2011.

Remmer, Karen L. "The Politics of Institutional Change: Electoral Reform in Latin America, 1978–2002." *Party Politics* 14, no. 1 (January 2008): 5–30.

Renwick, Alan. *The Politics of Electoral Reform: Changing the Rules of Democracy*. Cambridge: Cambridge University Press, 2010.

Renwick, Alan. "Electoral Reform in Europe since 1945." *West European Politics* 34, no. 3 (May 2011): 456–477.

Renwick, Alan, and Jean-Benoit Pilet. *Faces on the Ballot: The Personalization of Electoral Systems in Europe*. Oxford: Oxford University Press, 2016.

Riera, Pedro. "Electoral systems and the Sheriff of Nottingham: Determinants of Disproportionality in New and Established Democracies." *Party Politics* 21, no. 2 (March 2015): 222–233.

Riker, William H. "The Two-Party System and Duverger's Law: An Essay on the History of Political Science." *American Political Science Review* 76, no. 4 (December 1982): 753–766.

Rokkan, Stein. "Electoral Systems." In *Citizens, Elections, Parties: Approaches to the Comparative Study of the Processes of Development*, edited by Stein Rokkan, with Angus Campbell, Per Torsvik, and Henry Valen, 147–168. Oslo: Universitetsforlaget, 1970. Revised from an article first published in David Sills, ed., *International Encyclopedia of the Social Sciences*, vol. 5 (Crowell Collier and Macmillan, 1968), 6–21.

Sakamoto, Takayuki. "Explaining Electoral Reform: Japan versus Italy and New Zealand." *Party Politics* 5, no. 4 (October 1999): 419–438.

Scheiner, Ethan. "Does Electoral System Reform Work? Electoral System Lessons from Reforms of the 1990s." *Annual Review of Political Science* 11 (2008): 161–181.

Shugart, Matthew Soberg. "'Extreme' Electoral Systems and the Appeal of the Mixed-Member Alternative." In *Mixed-Member Electoral Systems: The Best of Both Worlds?*, edited by Matthew Soberg Shugart and Martin P. Wattenberg, 25–51. Oxford: Oxford University Press, 2001.

Shugart, Matthew Søberg. "Comparative Electoral Systems Research: The Maturation of a Field and New Challenges Ahead." In *The Politics of Electoral Systems*, edited by Michael Gallagher and Paul Mitchell, 25–55. Oxford: Oxford University Press, 2005.

Shugart, Matthew Søberg. "Inherent and Contingent Factors in Reform Initiation in Plurality Systems." In *To Keep or to Change First Past the Post? The Politics of Electoral Reform*, edited by André Blais, 7–60. Oxford: Oxford University Press, 2008.

Shugart, Matthew Soberg, and Martin P. Wattenberg, eds. *Mixed-Member Electoral Systems: The Best of Both Worlds?* Oxford: Oxford University Press, 2001a.

Shugart, Matthew Soberg, and Martin P. Wattenberg. "Mixed-Member Electoral Systems: A Definition and Typology." In *Mixed-Member Electoral Systems: The Best of Both Worlds?*, edited by Matthew Soberg Shugart and Martin Wattenberg, 9–24. Oxford: Oxford University Press, 2001b.

Streeck, Wolfgang, and Kathleen Thelen. "Introduction: Institutional Change in Advanced Political Economies." In *Beyond Continuity: Institutional Change in Advanced Political Economies*, edited by Wolfgang Streeck and Kathleen Thelen, 1–39. Oxford: Oxford University Press, 2005.

Törnudd, Klaus. *The Electoral System of Finland*. London: Hugh Evelyn, 1968.

Vowles, Jack. "The Politics of Electoral Reform in New Zealand." *International Political Science Review* 16, no. 1 (January 1995): 95–115.

Vowles, Jack. "Electoral System Change, Generations, Competitiveness and Turnout in New Zealand, 1963–2005." *British Journal of Political Science* 40, no. 4 (October 2010): 875–895.

Vowles, Jack, Susan A. Banducci, and Jeffrey A. Karp. "Forecasting and Evaluating the Consequences of Electoral Change in New Zealand." *Acta Politica* 41, no. 3 (September 2006): 267–284.

Whiteley, Paul, Harold D. Clarke, David Sanders, and Marianne C. Stewart. "Britain Says NO: Voting in the AV Ballot Referendum." *Parliamentary Affairs* 65, no. 2 (April 2012): 301–322.

Williams, Kieran. "Judicial Review of Electoral Thresholds in Germany, Russia, and the Czech Republic." *Electoral Law Journal* 4, no. 3 (September 2005): 191–206.

Younis, Nussaibah. "Set Up to Fail: Consociational Political Structures in Post-War Iraq, 2003–2010." *Contemporary Arab Affairs* 4, no. 1 (2011): 1–18.

Ziegler, Donald J. *Prelude to Democracy: A Study of Proportional Representation and the Heritage of Weimar Germany, 1871–1920.* University of Nebraska Studies, New Series, no. 20. Lincoln: University of Nebraska, 1958.

# PART II

ISSUES AND
REPRESENTATION

CHAPTER 7

........................................................................................

# SOCIAL DIVERSITY, ELECTORAL SYSTEMS, AND THE PARTY SYSTEM

........................................................................................

ROBERT G. MOSER, ETHAN SCHEINER,
AND HEATHER STOLL

ONE of the fundamental features of democratic politics is the party system, and one of the most important aspects of a country's party system is the number of parties that comprise it. The number of parties shapes the type and range of alternatives offered to voters. As a result, it significantly affects governing coalitions and helps to determine the public policies that governments enact. Consequently, scholars have long sought to understand how different factors shape this all-important aspect of democratic political systems.

Scholars commonly argue that in democratic societies, the size or fragmentation of party systems—as well as other important features of party systems, such as their nationalization or aggregation—is a linear function of social heterogeneity, in interaction with political institutions such as the electoral system. This "interactive hypothesis" has generated a large body of clever and empirically grounded research, mostly in support of its fundamental claims.

Despite the prominence of this literature within the electoral system field, there is also a growing body of research that casts doubt on the interactive hypothesis. Ultimately, social diversity and the electoral system shape the national party system through a series of stages. In the all-important first stage, diversity and electoral rules shape the party system at the level of the electoral district—our primary focus in this chapter. However, as we argue, considerable work remains to be done to demonstrate convincingly the functioning of the interactive hypothesis in this first stage.

More specifically, we argue that to move the state of knowledge on the issue forward, future scholarship will do well to place greater priority on matching appropriate data to research questions addressing the first, district-level stage in the party system development process. That is, although societies exhibit a variety of different types of heterogeneity, from religious to socioeconomic diversity—which varies by subnational region—political scientists typically characterize countries' heterogeneity almost exclusively according to measures of *national-level ethnic diversity*. We draw attention to the importance of different types of heterogeneity and the level at which social heterogeneity is measured in ascertaining how social divisions and electoral institutions may or may not affect party fragmentation. As a preliminary and illustrative exercise, we use original census data for a number of advanced industrial and developing democracies to show just how misleading it can be to characterize heterogeneity solely according to nationwide ethnic diversity.

## SOCIAL DIVERSITY, ELECTORAL SYSTEMS, AND PARTY SYSTEMS: THE CORE LITERATURE

For more than half a century, scholars have looked to social diversity as the foundation of party system size—that is, the number of salient parties within a democratic polity. Although better known for his "law" about the effects of electoral systems on party systems, Maurice Duverger declared that political parties were a reflection of the "spiritual families" within society (as cited in Clark and Golder 2006, 682; see also Duverger 1954). Lipset and Rokkan's (1967) classic study further solidified the central role that social divisions, which emerged from fundamental societal transformations such as industrialization and nationalization, had on party systems. Not only did these divisions determine the size of party systems, but also they "froze" party systems in place until the next social upheaval created significant enough new social forces to create new parties (1967, 52). If social divisions are the raw material for political parties, producing what Cox (1997, 140) calls a society's "natural" number of parties, it stands to reason that more diverse societies would have more parties. As Clark and Golder (2006, 682) succinctly argue, "Duverger's theory implies that the number of parties should be an increasing function of the number of politically salient spiritual families in a polity."

One important point to clarify is that by "number of parties," we follow most of the literature in actually meaning the size of the party system, also known as "party system fragmentation." We use these terms interchangeably in what follows. The fragmentation of the party system takes into account both the number of political parties that enter the race and the distribution of votes across those parties: how fragmented or concentrated votes are, given the parties that choose to contest the election. Hence, we are not simply counting parties, but counting parties after taking into account their size, as reflected by their vote shares. The most common operationalization of party system fragmentation in the quantitative literature is N, the effective number of electoral (vote share weighted) parties (Laakso and Taagepera 1979).[1] The effective number can also be calculated using legislative seat shares instead of vote shares. The former is usually referred to as the effective number of electoral parties, and the latter as the effective number of parliamentary (or legislative) parties.

However, because our goal is to relate the size of the party system to the heterogeneity of society, it is also important to clarify that we mean the effective number of *electoral* parties (i.e., party system size with respect to votes, not seats) when we say "effective number" throughout. The rationale for this operationalization when social diversity is one of the explanatory variables is laid out cogently in Benoit (2002). In a nutshell, because the effective number of legislative parties is produced by the electoral system's translation of votes into seats, including explanatory variables other than the electoral system and the effective number of electoral parties risks biased and inefficient coefficient estimates.

Especially since the advent of the political science new institutionalism literature, most of the literature has suggested an interactive hypothesis, whereby the impact of social diversity on the number of parties is mediated by the electoral system. Duverger and Clark and Golder explain this logic most cogently: under "permissive" electoral systems (such as proportional representation formulae coupled with large district magnitudes and low legal thresholds of representation), there are few obstacles to the process of discrete social groups becoming manifest as individual political parties. In contrast, "restrictive" electoral systems (such as plurality formulae coupled with single-seat districts) create incentives for actors to coalesce behind only potentially competitive candidates and/or parties—particularly those capable of winning a plurality of votes. In restrictive systems, politically salient social groups who make up a small share of the district population are therefore discouraged from forming their own parties. The restrictive nature of the electoral system therefore acts as a brake on the impact of diversity on party system size. It is this fundamental logic that underpins Duverger's seminal theories: permissive systems such as proportional representation (PR) and two-round majority single-seat districts (SSDs) tend toward multiparty systems, whereas SSD/plurality systems, also known as first past the post (FPTP), tend toward two parties.[2] Considerable cross-national work (see especially Ordeshook and Shvetsova 1994; Amorim Neto and Cox 1997; Clark and Golder 2006; and Singer and Stephenson 2009) provides evidence for the interactive hypothesis in the form of a positive correlation between ethnic diversity and the number of parties under permissive rules, but no relationship under more restrictive ones.[3]

## Moving the Literature Forward

Despite a fair amount of empirical support for the interactive hypothesis, additional work is needed to lay out more convincingly the relationship between social diversity, electoral rules, and the number of parties. First, considerable literature, in particular work focused on the micro level, suggests that the constraining effect of restrictive rules (especially FPTP) may not be as great as posited by Duverger. Second, recent work has called into question the base assumption that the relationship between diversity and the party system is positive and linear. Third, and probably most important, part of the reason that additional work is needed on these first two points is the inadequacy of the data most commonly used to address the question of the relationship between social diversity, electoral rules, and the number of parties. More specifically, extant literature is often hampered by a disjuncture between theory and data: the use of nationally aggregated data that does not accurately represent realities within districts, where the first stage of the translation of social divisions into party systems actually occurs, and by the overwhelming use of data that uses only a narrow set of possible measures of social diversity. We discuss each of these issues in turn.

## Constraining Effect of Rules May Be Weaker Than Often Presumed

The literature's expectation that restrictive rules constrain the impact of social diversity on the party system is founded on the idea that such rules provide significant incentive for electoral actors to behave strategically. However, there is extensive evidence that many voters do not in fact cast strategic ballots. Most notably, Cox (1997) lays out a set of conditions necessary for such strategic behavior: (1) short-term instrumentally rational voters, (2) widespread knowledge of which candidates are "out of the running," (3) the absence of a widespread belief that one candidate is certain to win, and (4) relatively few voters who are so attached to their top choice that they are indifferent between the remaining options. However, as scholars such as Blais (2002) and Chhibber and Kollman (2004) highlight, there are many situations in which these preconditions do not hold. Indeed, Ferree, Powell, and Scheiner (2014) illustrate how these conditions can break down in a variety of contexts. Not surprisingly, therefore, many studies (see, e.g., Alvarez, Boehmke, and Nagler 2006; Cox 1997, 83–84) indicate that large numbers of voters do not cast strategic ballots—even when doing so might lead to a better electoral outcome (as measured by their preference for specific candidates in the race).

If many electoral actors do not behave strategically, the presumed "brake" effect of restrictive electoral systems will not work, in which case a relationship between social cleavages and party system size should exist under all types of electoral system.[4] Taagepera and Grofman (1985, 350) make perhaps the most forceful, if implicit, statement about the universality of the link between diversity and the number of parties, arguing that the effective number of parties can be successfully predicted by the number of issue dimensions plus one (N = I + 1) without taking electoral systems into account. We say "implicit" because their conception of issue dimensions (drawn from Lijphart 1984, 1999) refers to cleavages that divide actual parties, which is a related but distinct concept from social diversity. Nevertheless, if few issue dimensions are viewed as representing socially homogenous environments and many issue dimensions are viewed as representing socially diverse environments, the argument becomes relevant.

Specifically, they argue that the two-party configuration commonly associated with plurality elections only holds for political environments with one major issue dimension (i.e., socially homogenous environments). By way of contrast, when plurality elections operate in countries with multiple dimensions (i.e., in socially heterogeneous environments), they are not characterized by the expected Duvergerian outcome, instead producing between two and three parties (Taagepera and Grofman 1985, 347–348).[5]

This point is supported by a number of analyses that indicate that plurality elections often do not constrain district-level electoral competition to two parties (e.g., Grofman, Bowler, and Blais 2009; Gaines 1999; Chhibber and Kollman 2004; Johnston and Cutler 2009; Moser and Scheiner 2004; Diwakar 2007). Similarly, studies of presidential elections have generally found social diversity to have an effect on the fragmentation of the presidential candidate system, despite presidential elections all using relatively restrictive electoral systems (e.g., Cox 1997; Jones 1999; Golder 2006; Hicken and Stoll 2008; Stoll 2013).[6] Further, looking specifically at the link between social diversity and the number of parties in a legislative electoral setting, Ferree, Gibson, and Hoffman (n.d.) illustrate a link between racial diversity and candidate fragmentation in subnational FPTP elections in South Africa.[7] Moser and Scheiner (2012) demonstrate a similar relationship between ethnic diversity and the number of parties in the FPTP portion of mixed-member systems in New Zealand, Russia, Ukraine, and Wales. Milazzo, Moser, and Scheiner (in press) include analysis of district-level data from countries even beyond just new democracies and mixed-member systems to show that social diversity and party size are linked in pure plurality systems in Canada, Great Britain, India, and New Zealand.[8]

Despite these patterns running against the commonly held expectation of the interactive hypothesis, no new consensus holds regarding the interplay between social diversity and electoral rules in shaping party system size.

## Questions Remain about the Nature of the Relationship between Social Diversity and Party Fragmentation—Even under Permissive Electoral Rules

The most common approach to date has been to view the relationship between social heterogeneity and party system size as positive and monotonic—more groups should lead to more parties—but recent work raises a number of questions about just what the relationship is between diversity and party fragmentation.

One alternative—although consistent with most work on the subject—is that there is generally a positive relationship, but that there are diminishing returns at high levels of social heterogeneity, leaving further increases in diversity unlikely to produce more parties. We illustrate such a relationship between social heterogeneity and party system size in Figure 7.1. For example, Stoll (2013, 52–55) argues that even under permissive electoral systems, new social groups will often not be large enough for their parties to be politically

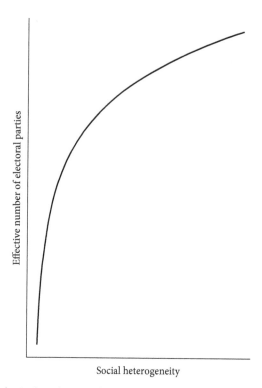

Effective number of electoral parties

Social heterogeneity

**FIGURE 7.1.** A hypothetical nonlinear relationship between social heterogeneity and party system size, where the relationship is generally positive but with diminishing returns.

influential when diversity is very high. This makes it unlikely that new parties will successfully emerge to represent most such groups. Consider, for example, the extreme case of a country where social heterogeneity increases over time until it becomes perfectly heterogeneous, with each citizen forming his or her own group. The conventional linear argument predicts that each citizen would form his or her own party. But no interest aggregation would then be taking place—a costly situation for all concerned. It is more realistic to posit a positive, but diminishing (nonlinear) relationship between social heterogeneity and party system size, where the number of parties will be less than the number of social groups, instead of a positive, constant (linear) one. A simple empirical strategy for modeling this type of relationship is to use logged measures of the key variables.

Another alternative, illustrated in Figure 7.2, is that at high levels of diversity, increases in the number of groups are actually associated with a decline in the number of parties. Stoll (2013) points out that in a fairly heterogeneous country, existing parties are likely to engage in a reactive consolidation to counterbalance a new party's entrance, particularly if the new group (and hence its party) is a large one. While much depends on the exact sizes of the new and existing groups, as well as on the extent of the reactive consolidation, the end result is that at high levels of diversity, the fragmentation of the party system might in fact *decrease* in response to an increase in social heterogeneity.[9] The result

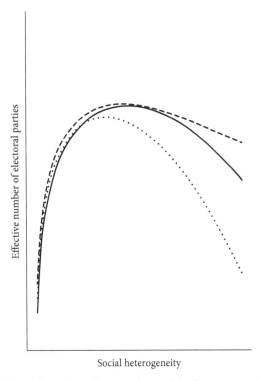

FIGURE 7.2. Several hypothetical nonlinear relationships between social heterogeneity and party system size, where at high levels of diversity, the relationship turns negative to varying degrees.

is some kind of upside-down "U"-shaped relationship between social diversity and the number of parties. Figure 7.2 shows several possible such relationships. Either nonlinear or polynomial linear regression models can be used to model this type of relationship.

Strikingly, scholars have recently found evidence for these nonlinear relationships under both permissive and restrictive rules, and using both nationally aggregated and district-focused measures of the key variables (e.g., Milazzo, Moser, and Scheiner., in press; Moser and Scheiner 2012; Stoll 2013; Raymond 2015). Specifically, using an analysis of presidential elections, Stoll (2013) finds a negative relationship between social heterogeneity and party system size beginning at the third quartile of her social heterogeneity index. Similarly, Milazzo, Moser, and Scheiner (in press) find that in a variety of countries that use FPTP in legislative elections, there is a positive correlation between diversity and party fragmentation in all but the most diverse districts within a given country, but within these most diverse districts the correlation is usually negative. Madrid (2005) also finds a curvilinear relationship between ethnic diversity and party system fractionalization in legislative elections using subnational census data for several Latin American countries.[10]

Another alternative still is found in studies such as that of Li and Shugart (2017), which question the degree to which ethnic diversity affects the effective number of parties at all once the impact of all relevant institutional factors is considered, such as the product of mean district magnitude and assembly size.[11] For example, when reanalyzing data from Clark and Golder for only established democracies with parliamentary systems, Li and Shugart's findings suggest that the relationship between social heterogeneity, district magnitude, and (national) party fractionalization is not interactive but additive—and, in fact, when dropping the outlying case of India, they find little relationship between ethnic diversity and party fragmentation (Li and Shugart 2017, 25). Indeed, based on analyses drawn from a broad range of institutional contexts such as presidential systems and complex electoral systems, Li and Shugart (2017, 30) argue that an approach "based only on institutions, predicts the effective number of seat-winning parties at least as accurately for the large majority of democracies as does the combination of institutions and a widely-used indicator of social diversity."[12] Shugart and Taagepera's (2017) more finely grained analysis reaches similar conclusions.[13] Although quite different from scholarship positing a curvilinear relationship between social diversity and party fragmentation, these studies also call into question the conventional narrative of the interactive hypothesis.

The diverse and even contradictory findings regarding the nature of the relationship between social heterogeneity and party fractionalization, and how it is or is not conditioned by electoral institutions,[14] further reinforces the need for continued study and greater attention to the use of appropriate data and research design.

## Electoral System Scholars Rarely Use District-Level Data on Social Heterogeneity

While the theoretical and empirical focus of many studies has rightly shifted to the level of the electoral district, measures of social heterogeneity have not usually followed suit.

As noted in numerous studies (e.g., Riker 1982, 1986; Cox 1997), the number of parties at the district level is a function of social forces *within the district* and the electoral rules used there. As the foundation for the number of parties in a district, the social heterogeneity variable is meaningful only insofar as it represents diversity within that district.

However, most empirical analyses of the interactive hypothesis have used nationally aggregated measures of the key variables (see especially Amorim Neto and Cox 1997; Clark and Golder 2006; Ordeshook and Shvetsova 1994). Even prominent studies conducted at the level of the electoral district such as Singer and Stephenson (2009) and Singer (2013) employ national-level measures of social heterogeneity. Given the lack of available district-level measures of diversity, the use of national measures, of course, makes great sense, but doing so forces the researcher to make the unrealistic assumption that all electoral districts are perfect mirrors of the nation as a whole.

To illustrate how much is lost by using nationally aggregated measures, we take a quick look at several countries using original data drawn from national censuses. Table 7.1 presents subnational data on racial or ethnic diversity for these countries for either

Table 7.1 Descriptive Statistics for the Effective Number of Racial/Ethnic Groups at Different Subnational Levels, Particularly the Level of the Electoral District

| Country and Census Year | Level and Number of Units | Corresponding Election Year(s) | Minimum | Median | Mean | Maximum | Standard Deviation |
|---|---|---|---|---|---|---|---|
| Bolivia (2001) | Department (9)* | 2009 | 1.4 | 1.9 | 1.9 | 3.0 | 0.47 |
| Bolivia (2002) | Municipality (314) | 2005 | 1.0 | 1.3 | 1.6 | 3.6 | 0.52 |
| Brazil (2009) | States (27)* | 2010 | 1.3 | 2.0 | 2.0 | 2.4 | 0.29 |
| Canada (2006) | Constituency (308)* | 2006 | 1.0 | 1.0 | 1.1 | 2.0 | 0.21 |
| Colombia (2005) | Department (33)* | 2014 | 1.0 | 1.3 | 1.5 | 2.6 | 0.44 |
| Costa Rica (2011) | Province (7)* | 2014 | 1.1 | 1.2 | 1.2 | 1.4 | 0.079 |
| Ireland (2006) | Constituency (43)* | 2007 | 1.1 | 1.2 | 1.2 | 1.6 | 0.12 |
| Ireland (2011) | Constituency (43)* | 2011 | 1.1 | 1.3 | 1.3 | 1.9 | 0.15 |
| Ireland (2011) | Constituency (40)[20]* | 2016 | 1.2 | 1.3 | 1.3 | 2.0 | 0.16 |
| Peru (2006) | Department (26*) | 2011 | 1.1 | 1.8 | 1.8 | 2.8 | 0.48 |
| Russia (2001) | Raion (62) | 2003 | 1.0 | 2.1 | 2.0 | 3.5 | 0.50 |
| Spain (2001) | Province (52)* | 2004, 2008 | 1.1 | 1.3 | 1.4 | 2.3 | 0.29 |
| Spain (2011) | Province (52)* | 2011 | 1.1 | 1.3 | 1.4 | 2.4 | 0.26 |
| Ukraine (2001) | Raion (1036) | 2002, 2012 | 1.2 | 1.6 | 1.8 | 3.5 | 0.51 |
| Ukraine (2010) | Constituency (225)* | 2012 | 1.0 | 1.2 | 1.4 | 2.0 | 0.32 |
| United States (2000) | Constituency (436)[21]* | 2006 (110th) | 1.0 | 1.3 | 1.4 | 2.8 | 0.36 |
| Uruguay (2011) | Department (19)* | 2009 | 1.1 | 1.1 | 1.2 | 1.4 | 0.11 |
| Wales (2003) | Constituency (40)* | 2003 | 1.2 | 1.4 | 1.5 | 2.0 | 0.25 |

* Subnational administrative units that additionally or solely serve as electoral districts.

Source for Bolivia 2002, Russia 1999, Ukraine 2002, and Wales 2003 is Moser and Scheiner (2012); all other sources are national censuses.

one or several election years, focusing on the electoral district (constituency) but also including a few other subnational units. The table indicates how greatly ethnic diversity levels vary within countries, thus highlighting the insufficiency of nationally aggregated measures of such diversity. With rare exceptions, such as Uruguay, ethnic diversity at the subnational level for these countries and census years typically ranges from the extremely homogenous (an effective number of ethnic groups approximating 1.0) to the fairly heterogeneous (usually an effective number of ethnic groups of at least 2.0, and often ranging into the 3.0s). Even more specifically, over all of the cases shown in Table 7.1, the effective number of ethnic groups in the subnational units on average deviates from the mean by almost 0.5—a nontrivial amount.

To illustrate further, we select three of these countries and election years for more intensive focus: the United States in 2006 (data from the 2000 census), Spain in 2011 (data from the 2011 census), and Ireland in 2016 (data from the 2011 census, using the constituencies as redrawn in 2013). Table 7.2 presents national (aggregate) data for racial or ethnic diversity, as well as for other measures of social diversity (discussed later), for these countries. Additionally, Figures 7.3, 7.4, and 7.5 present boxplots for all of the corresponding measures at the level of the electoral district. A number of differences between the national and district levels are apparent from the table and figures.

Take racial diversity in the United States, where we see substantial variation—wildly different from the national aggregate—in diversity across districts. Table 7.2 shows that the national effective number of racial groups is about 1.5—a fairly homogenous picture. However, Table 7.1 and Figure 7.3 together show that, strikingly, the effective number of racial groups at the district level varies widely from a perfectly homogenous 1.0 to a much more heterogeneous 2.8. In fact, on the heterogeneous end of the spectrum, almost 10 percent of US electoral districts have an effective number of racial groups that is greater than 2.0, and 27 percent (over one quarter) of districts have an effective number of racial groups that is greater than 1.6. On the homogenous end of the spectrum, 36 percent of districts have an effective number of ethnic groups that is less than 1.2. To further illustrate with respect to two specific ethnic or racial groups, Table 2 shows that Latinos and African Americans each make up about 13 percent of the US population as a whole. Yet in the districts, Latinos make up more than 30 percent of the population in 12 percent of all districts but, at the same time, compose less than 5 percent of the population in 50 percent of all districts. Similarly, African Americans make up less than 5 percent of the population in 45 percent of districts but, simultaneously, compose more than 30 percent of the population in 13 percent of districts. Our point here is not that greater party fragmentation is imminent in multiple districts in the United States. Rather, it is that nationally aggregated measures do not capture the substantial diversity that exists in many US districts—which might, indeed, be expected to promote more parties—and therefore may lead to inaccurate inferences about the reasons for the absence of greater fragmentation in the American party system.

In addition, on a less obvious point, while countries that are very homogenous nationally will also be very homogenous at the district level, countries that are heterogeneous at the national level may actually be homogenous at the district level. Canada is

**Table 7.2 National-Level Measures of Diversity for Several Important Social Divisions for Ireland (2011), Spain (2011), and the United States (2000)**

| | N, Age | % 65 and Over | N, Race/ Ethnicity | % Latino | % Black | N, Religion | N, Education | N, Occupation | N, Urban-Rural | % Primary Sector |
|---|---|---|---|---|---|---|---|---|---|---|
| Ireland | 2.1 | 12 | 1.3 | N/A | N/A | 1.3 | 4.0 | 3.1 | 1.1 | 5.0 |
| Spain | 2.1 | 17 | 9.9 | N/A | N/A | N/A | 2.7 | 2.7 | 1.1 | 2.9 |
| United States | 2.2 | 12 | 1.5 | 13 | 13 | N/A | 4.4 | 2.9 | 1.0 | 0.73 |

Note that the proportion of the population engaged in the primary sector includes occupations such as agriculture, forestry, fishing, and (where applicable) mining.

Sources are national censuses.

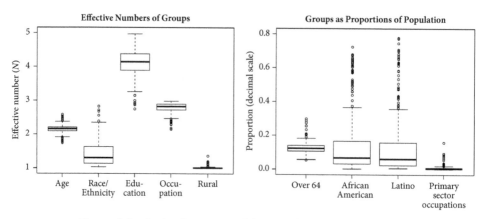

FIGURE 7.3. Electoral district-level measures of diversity for several important social divisions for the United States (2006 constituencies). Source is the 2000 national census. Proportions are measured on a decimal scale (0.0 to 1.0).

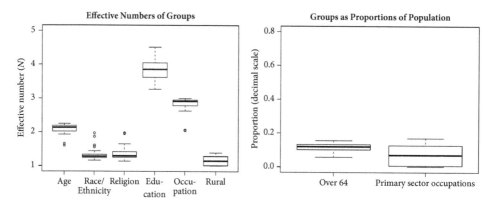

FIGURE 7.4. Electoral district-level measures of diversity for several important social divisions for Ireland (2016 constituencies). Source is the 2011 national census. Proportions are measured on a decimal scale (0.0 to 1.0).

a case in point here. In Table 7.1, census data from 2006 reveals that most electoral districts are ethnically (defined in linguistic terms in the Canadian case) homogenous: the effective number of groups ranges from 1.0 to 2.0, but the mean and the third quartile are both only 1.1, and the standard deviation is a mere 0.21. The corresponding national-level figure, however, while not shown in the table, is a much more heterogeneous 1.7. In this case, the difference between the more homogenous districts and the more hetero-geneous nation can be explained by the geographic segregation of English and French speakers, with French speakers concentrated in the province (and hence the districts) of Quebec.

This failure to match the measure to the mechanism, to paraphrase Posner (2004), seems to have consequences. As already discussed, studies using district-level mea-sures have come to markedly different conclusions from the standing wisdom—such

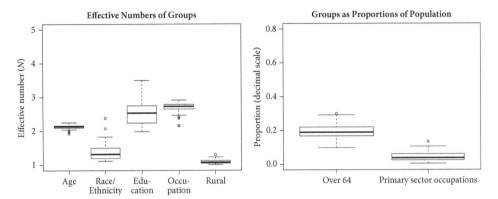

FIGURE 7.5. Electoral district-level measures of diversity for several important social divisions for Spain (2011 constituencies). Source is the 2011 national census. Proportions are measured on a decimal scale (0.0 to 1.0).

as finding nonlinear instead of linear relationships between social diversity and party system size, relationships that vary with the type of diversity considered, and relationships that exist even under restrictive electoral rules (e.g., Milazzo, Moser, and Scheiner, in press; Moser and Scheiner 2012; Stoll 2013).

Moreover, the use of national-level measures makes it impossible to determine how (or even if) subnational variation in social diversity shapes electoral coordination beyond the district-level stage of party system development that has been our focus up until this point. For example, Stoll (2008, 2013) suggests that diversity within districts might be expected to have a powerful effect on the size of the district-level party system, whereas diversity across districts and at the national level might be expected to powerfully shape the nationalization or aggregation of the party system. As Cox (1997, 181–202) argues, it is party system aggregation (which he calls "linkage") that is central to the projection of district-level party systems to the national level for the many countries with more than one electoral district, and hence to determining the size of the national party system.[15] National, cross-district diversity—and most notably differences in social diversity across districts—is likely to shape party aggregation in important ways. For example, the geographic concentration of social groups in specific regions provides incentives for the formation of regional parties, which is apt to reduce the aggregation of the party system and drive up the overall number of parties in a country (e.g., Brancati 2008; Ferree, Powell, and Scheiner 2014), even while maintaining a small number of district-level parties. Yet only a handful of studies, such as Cox and Knoll (2003) and Hicken and Stoll (2011, 2013), have studied how national-level ethnic diversity shapes party system aggregation. Potter's (2014) recent study is the first to empirically take up the issue of cross-district diversity, although he interestingly confines his focus to its effect on party system size in the districts (contrary to what was just suggested) and finds one. However, a comprehensive, multilevel analysis—which requires measures of diversity at all of these different levels—has yet to be conducted.

Some scholars have gotten around this data problem by examining presidential elections, which allow for the use of national-level data at the level of the electoral district because in almost all presidential elections, the electoral district is the country as a whole (e.g., Jones 1999, 2004; Stoll 2013; Golder 2006; Hicken and Stoll 2008; Dickson and Scheve 2010). However, there are reasons to expect that the relationship between social diversity and the number of presidential candidates does not generalize to legislative elections: among other things, the stakes involved in presidential elections are often so much greater that voters and elites may have stronger incentives to behave strategically in such races. Also, the greater availability of information regarding presidential contests—as well as the fact that presidential candidates tend to be more well known than candidates running for legislative office—makes it easier for voters to behave strategically. Indeed, Dickson and Scheve (2010, 365, fn. 20) express skepticism that their findings regarding ethnic diversity's effects on presidential party system size would extend to the legislative party system. Yet despite these points, studies of presidential elections generally find social diversity to shape the fragmentation of the presidential party (candidate) system, as discussed earlier. These findings run contrary to the expectations derived from the conventional interactive hypothesis—particularly in light of the greater incentives presidential elections provide for strategic behavior—but are consistent with recent findings of studies of legislative elections with restrictive electoral systems conducted at the district level.

At the legislative level, there are a few studies of party system size that use census data on district-level ethnic diversity, but each has important limits. Jones (1997) studies only a single state (Louisiana) in a single country (United States), while Moser and Scheiner's (2012) study is confined to a handful of countries that use single-seat districts within a mixed-member electoral system setting. Ferree et al. (n.d.) find a positive correlation between racial diversity and the number of parties in South African subnational elections. As noted earlier, Milazzo, Moser, and Scheiner (in press) find a nonlinear relationship between district-level measures of ethnic diversity and the number of parties across a range of FPTP cases. All of these studies focus on SSDs, thus confining their analyses to relatively restrictive electoral systems, and thereby again hindering their ability to draw judgments about the *interaction* between social diversity and electoral rules.

These studies are also hindered by their focus on ethnic diversity. For one, defining and measuring ethnic diversity is a difficult enterprise (e.g., Stoll 2008, 2013). For another, there are theoretical problems with allowing ethnic diversity to serve as a proxy for overall diversity. For example, Milazzo, Moser, and Scheiner (in press) speculate that the decline in the number of parties at high levels of ethnic diversity may be a result of minority ethnic groups concentrating their votes on a single large (ostensibly non-ethnic) party. As evidence for this speculation, they illustrate that in Great Britain and New Zealand, the Labour Party wins large vote shares in districts in which the effective number of groups score is greater than two. Given that the Labour Party in these examples is probably not campaigning simply on ethnic appeals, it is likely that a different type of appeal—for example, based on social or economic class—is actually the key driver of minority group support. Indeed, in an analysis of politics in India, Huber and Suryanarayan (2016) illustrate that there is likely to be a strong ethnic group base of support for political parties when there is substantial economic inequality between ethnic groups.[16] If this is the case, although an analysis founded on measures of ethnic diversity as a proxy for overall diversity is useful as a hard test of whether there is a relationship between social heterogeneity and party fragmentation, (1) it is more likely to miss many cases in which a relationship exists and (2) it is likely to miss the true nature of the link between social diversity and the party system, especially under restrictive electoral systems.

## Electoral System Scholars Rarely Use Data on Different Types of Social Heterogeneity

To elaborate on this last point, nearly all quantitative studies seeking to link social diversity to party system size in legislative elections focus solely on ethnic diversity, despite the (sometimes more qualitative) literature on party system development having long identified a number of consequential social divisions besides the ethnic one (e.g., Lipset and Rokkan 1967; Rae and Taylor 1970; Powell 1982; von Beyme 1985; Mainwaring and Scully 1995; Lijphart 1999; Caramani 2004). More specifically, most of the literature on the interactive impact that social diversity and electoral systems have on party systems focuses solely or primarily on ethnic heterogeneity to the exclusion of other social divisions (e.g., Amorim Neto and Cox 1997; Cox 1997; Jones 1997, 1999; Mozaffar, Scarritt, and Galaich 2003; Chhibber and Kollman 2004; Clark and Golder 2006; Golder 2006; Hicken and Stoll 2008; Singer and Stephenson 2009; Singer 2013).

There are some notable exceptions to the emphasis on *ethnic* diversity in most work on social heterogeneity, but, even still, most studies that use other (i.e., nonethnic) indices of diversity tend to look at a relatively narrow range of measures. For example, Powell (1982) includes measures of religious and urban–rural diversity; Ordeshook and Shvetsova (1994) use religious diversity; Jones (2004) studies ideological (left–right) diversity; and Moser and Scheiner (2012) examine urban–rural diversity. Stoll (2008, 2013) is the most prominent exception to date: in her most recent work, Stoll constructs measures of social diversity along six historically important divisions (ethnic, religious, urban–rural, socioeconomic, foreign policy, and postmaterialist), as well as measures of three historically prominent and exogenous sources of changes in a democracy's citizenry (changes in the franchise, changes in territory, and immigration). However, harkening back to our critique in the previous section on the lack of district-level indices, Stoll's measures are all at the national level.

Potter's (2014) survey-based measures of diversity are other recent exceptions that hold great promise.[17] In his district-level analysis, he finds a positive correlation (with the 95 percent confidence interval nearly entirely greater than zero) between social diversity and party fragmentation under all electoral system types in his base models, but drawbacks remain. Most important from our perspective, his measurement strategy, based on a novel and advanced statistical technique known as probabilistic topic modeling, returns only the size-weighted number of groups at the district and cross-district levels. As a result, it does not straightforwardly allow for the testing of hypotheses about the impact of different types of diversity. Moreover, it is not clear that the survey approach is a marked improvement over approaches using data from governmental sources, such as countries' national censuses; certainly, the longitudinal scope of survey-based approaches relative to census-based approaches is limited.

Of course, few would deny the powerful effect of ethnic divisions in many polities, but we have good reason to believe that other kinds of social diversity matter too. For example, Lipset and Rokkan's (1967) famous study identified a number of social divisions ("cleavages") related to the national and industrial revolutions, such as class and urban–rural differences, that have had a major impact on party system development. And once again, the preliminary evidence suggests that failing to match the measure to the mechanism has consequences—that different types of diversity do have different effects on the party system (e.g., Stoll 2008, 2013). Ultimately, the relative impact of different types of social divisions on party systems is an empirical question, one that deserves systematic examination based on the available data aggregated at the appropriate level of analysis.

A few examples highlight the importance of considering social diversity from multiple perspectives. Consider the urban–rural social division in the three countries listed in Table 7.2. In all three countries for the election year studied, Table 7.2 shows that the effective number of urban/rural groups at the national level is about 1.0—an essentially homogenous portrait.[18] However, the picture changes in important ways when we look at the district level. For example, Figures 7.3 to 7.5 show that the effective number in the districts ranges from a minimum of 1.0 (totally homogeneous) to a more heterogeneous maximum of 1.3 in Spain and 1.4 in both Ireland and the United States. The even more telling picture is painted by the shares of the district populations engaged in agriculture and other conventionally rural, primary sector occupations. As shown in Table 7.2, the national-level percentage of the population engaged in primary sector occupations ranges from a miniscule less than 1 percent in the United States, to 2.9 percent in Spain, to a larger but still small 5 percent in Ireland. On the other hand, at the district level, this measure ranges from a minimum of effectively 0 percent in some districts in all three countries, to a mean of 5 percent and a maximum of 13 percent in Spain; a mean of less than 1 percent and a maximum of 20 percent in the United States; and a mean of 7 percent and a maximum of 17 percent in Ireland. Some electoral districts, in other words, are substantially rural in character, in contrast to the portrait painted by the national-level data.

Consider, also, patterns of age groups. When thinking generally about types of sociodemographic diversity, age seems to be an important cleavage that is often understudied. Age is an important basis of party support in many advanced democracies like the United States. Moreover, there are parties that cater to older voters, such as 50PLUS, which won seats in the Netherlands in 2012 and 2017. Green parties, represented in several countries, tend to have a youthful electoral base (Burklin 1987; Vowles 2002). Table

7.2 shows that about 12 percent of the national population in Ireland and the United States is 65 or older, and about 17 percent in Spain. Yet Figures 7.3 to 7.5 show that at the level of the electoral district, some districts possess an age structure tilted toward the young, whereas in others, the age structure tilts toward the elderly. Of the more youthful districts, the minimal percentages of individuals aged 65 or older are 6 percent in Ireland, 5 percent in the United States, and 10 percent in Spain. Of the more elderly districts, the maximal percentages of individuals aged 65 or older are 16 percent in Ireland and a whopping 30 percent in both Spain and the United States. Hence, we again see that substantial variation exists at the level of the electoral district, as anyone who has visited the sunny American state of Florida would know.

Drilling more deeply into a single example, Ireland, provides perhaps even more insight into just why it is so important to develop more differentiated measures of diversity, and to do so at the district level. Nationally, with an effective number of ethnic groups equal to 1.3 in 2011 (Table 7.2), Ireland falls on the homogenous side of the ethnic spectrum for minimally democratic countries. And while Figure 7.4 shows that there is more ethnic heterogeneity at the level of the electoral district, Irish districts are still fairly homogenous: 75 percent of districts have an effective number of ethnic groups that ranges between 1.1 and 1.3, and the effective number of ethnic groups in 90 percent of districts is less than 1.5. This would lead us to predict a party system with a relatively small effective number of parties for Ireland. Yet over the entire postwar period, the average effective number of electoral parties has been almost 3.5 nationally and about 3 in the electoral districts, with numbers sometimes approaching 4 at both levels in more recent decades (such as in the 2011 election). While there are many countries with larger party systems, the Irish system clearly does not qualify as small. Accordingly, if social diversity is the demand-side explanation for the "natural" number of parties in a country (Cox 1997), and if one focuses solely upon ethnic diversity, one is left without an explanation for why Ireland has so many candidates and parties. Indeed, if anything, the "true" natural number of parties in Ireland is probably even higher, but is constrained by the Irish electoral system's relatively small district magnitude (an average magnitude of about 4 over the postwar period).

Two factors help us make sense of the large number of parties in Ireland. On one side, from a purely institutional perspective, Shugart and Taagepera's (2017) analysis suggests how Ireland's sizeable Seat Product helps permit a larger number of national parties. From a different perspective, in line with our analysis here, Ireland is quite diverse with respect to historically important social divisions, most notably socioeconomic ones (see Table 7.2 and Figure 7.4). For example, Table 7.2 shows that at the national level, the effective number of educational groups in Ireland is 4.0 and the effective number of occupational groups is 3.1.[19] Unlike the measures of ethnic diversity, these socioeconomic figures place Ireland on the heterogeneous side of the socioeconomic spectrum for the three countries in Table 7.2, with only the United States arguably edging it out. Moreover, Figure 7.4 shows that there is also great diversity with respect to occupation and, especially, education in the Irish electoral districts. Similarly, as already discussed, Ireland also exhibits more variation with respect to ruralness both at the national level and across its districts, with a significant minority of districts maintaining a fairly rural character. Turning to age, one of the most basic demographic fault lines, Ireland also looks more diverse at both the national and district levels. Finally, Ireland is largely homogeneous with respect to religion at the national level, but exhibits more diversity in many districts. Hence, a possible explanation for Ireland's relatively large number of parties is its significant diversity in areas other than ethnicity.

# CONCLUSION

Work on the relationship between social diversity, electoral rules, and the number of parties has developed markedly over the past decades as improved data sources have become available, but as we have highlighted in this chapter, the ability of the field to move forward on the central questions will depend on continued improvements in data, especially on social diversity. We argue that political scientists still tend to rely too heavily on measures of *national-level ethnic heterogeneity* as their sole estimate of social diversity. Specifically, we show how relying on a single, national-level indicator of diversity fails to capture the variance in diversity found *within* countries across politically salient subnational units such as federal regions or electoral districts. We also show how this misses the vast differences in the types of conflicts that divide societies. Countries may be similar on some dimensions (e.g., low levels of ethnic diversity) but differ wildly on others (e.g., their degree of religious or socioeconomic heterogeneity).

Key questions remain—and improved data will help significantly in answering these questions. Recent work challenges the interactive hypothesis that party system fractionalization is driven by the interaction between social divisions and the permissiveness of electoral systems, suggesting instead that the relationship between social diversity and party fragmentation holds even under restrictive electoral rules like first-past-the-post systems. This most likely is due to the existence of a large subset of voters who do not cast strategic ballots. The literature on the interaction between diversity and rules in shaping the party system will benefit from developing a clearer sense of why so many voters choose to behave sincerely even when they have electoral incentives not to do so. District-level data collection will help address such questions, as well as the question of why studies are increasingly finding a nonlinear relationship between diversity and the number of parties. Other political institutions besides the electoral system are also worthy of study as potential constraints on social heterogeneity.

To address these questions, as well as develop a clearer understanding of just how the process works, perhaps the most valuable direction for future work on the relationship between diversity and party fragmentation will be to track the mechanisms by which different societal divisions play out in the party system. For example, does the number of parties track more closely to district-level class division rather than the degree of ethnic diversity? In districts with multiple forms of diversity, how are political contestants' appeals structured around the core cleavages? In ethnically diverse districts, do candidates focus on ethnic appeals, class appeals, or both?

Moreover, developing improved data on social diversity measures is important for far more than simply learning about political parties. Social diversity has been one of the most utilized and important independent variables in all of social science. Scholars have examined the impact of various types of social diversity—from ethnic heterogeneity to income inequality—on a vast range of political and economic outcomes, including conflict, democratic electoral competition, party systems, collective goods provision, and regime stability and change (e.g., Fearon and Laitin 2003; Sambanis and Shayo 2013; Cox 1997; Clark and Golder 2006; Moser and Scheiner 2012; Stoll 2013; Easterly and Levine 1997; Alesina and Glaeser 2004; Crisp, Olivella, and Potter 2013; Horowitz 1985; Rabushka and Shepsle 2008). And while relatively recent initiatives have significantly upgraded our empirical measures of social diversity at the national level (e.g., Alesina et al. 2003; Fearon 2003; Posner 2004; Stoll 2013), available data lag far behind what is needed to address social science theories and hypotheses properly.

## NOTES

1. The precise formula is $N = 1/\sum v_i^2$, where $v_i$ is the $i$th party's vote share.
2. Josep Colomer's chapter in this volume challenges the causal direction of this relationship, suggesting that the makeup of party systems drives the choice of electoral rules.
3. Work by Powell (1982); Lijphart (1984); Ordeshook and Shvetsova (1994); Amorim Neto and Cox (1997); Cox (1997); Jones (1997, 2004); Mozaffar, Scarritt, and Galaich (2003); Clark and Golder (2006); Golder (2006); Stoll (2008, 2013); Singer and Stephenson (2009); Singer (2013); Moser and Scheiner (2012); and Potter (2014, in press), among others, firmly establishes the foundational influence of social divisions on the size of party systems, while also acknowledging the strong role that electoral systems play in mitigating the connection between social divisions and parties.
4. Dickson and Scheve (2010) suggest a way in which social diversity may affect party fragmentation under FPTP rules even if political actors behave strategically—but with increases in social diversity actually leading to a decline in the number of parties. Dickson and Scheve note that where the largest group in society has many more members than the second-largest group, the largest group could divide its vote between at least two candidates and still not lose to any candidates representing the other group. In short, substantial homogeneity can actually promote the presence of multiple candidates even under FPTP. However, as the size of the largest group relative to the second largest declines, the largest group becomes less capable of both dividing its vote and winning the election—thus providing the largest group with incentive to run no more than one candidate and overall there would only be two candidates in the race. In this way, increases in social diversity—moving from almost total homogeneity to two roughly equally sized groups—ought to be associated with a decline in the number of candidates under FPTP. Dickson and Scheve provide empirical support for this proposition using cross-national analysis of presidential elections, but also question whether their model will hold in lower-stakes district-level legislative elections. See Stoll (2013) for even more general arguments that while the

conventional interactive hypothesis assumes seat-maximizing strategic behavior, other types of policy-related strategic behavior such as portfolio maximizing and balancing may lead to different relationships between social heterogeneity and party system size than what is typically assumed. See also Bargsted and Kedar (2009).

5.  Taagepera and Grofman (1985: 350) argue further that perhaps the link between restrictive electoral systems and less party fractionalization lies in the tendency for countries with one-dimensional cleavage structures to adopt plurality systems while countries with multiple dimensions to adopt more permissive systems such as PR.

6.  Specifically, social diversity is usually found to have an effect in presidential elections that employ a run-off electoral formula, if not necessarily in presidential elections that employ simple plurality—although some studies even find an effect there.

7.  Similarly, Jones (1997) finds a relationship between racial diversity and the effective number of candidates in elections to the lower house of the Louisiana state legislature in the United States, where an only slightly less restrictive majority runoff electoral formula is used.

8.  More specifically, Milazzo, Moser, and Scheiner (in press) find that increases in social diversity in these countries lead to district-level effective number of electoral parties scores that are greater than two. In addition, they find a similar relationship between diversity and party fragmentation in the SSD races in the mixed-member systems in Russia, Scotland, and Ukraine as well. They also find a relationship between racial heterogeneity and party system size in the United States, but unlike the other cases the relationship in the United States is consistent with the Duvergerian expectation of no more than two contestants per district.

9.  Stoll additionally draws upon work by Dickson and Scheve (2010) to argue that increases in social heterogeneity may also lead to a decrease in the number of parties when the society is extremely homogenous (see her Figure 2.2, p. 55), for the reasons sketched out in footnote 4. She finds empirical evidence to this effect. Mozaffar, Scarritt, and Galaich (2003) make a similar argument when analyzing ethnic cleavages in African party systems.

10. However, rather than using weighted measures of ethnic fragmentation such as the effective number of ethnic groups, Madrid measures ethnic diversity with the size of the overall minority population within subnational units.

11. This is called the seat product, originally developed by Taagepera (2007).

12. See also Jones (2004) for somewhat similar findings in the context of presidential elections: that a purely institutional model is sometimes superior to and at least always the equal of an interactive model including social diversity.

13. Indeed, Shugart and Taagepera's analysis even addresses the case of India, where their institution-only model predicts the effective number of seat-winning parties precisely when alliances rather than parties are the object of study. At the same time, Shugart and Taagepera note that when using parties as the object of measure, including ethnic diversity helps improve the accuracy of the model.

14. It is also worth noting that Stoll (2013) argues that the electoral system is not the only political institution to condition the effect of social heterogeneity on party system size. She shows that, in the context of presidential elections, the size of the electoral prize—specifically, how powerful a directly elected president is—also acts as a conditioning factor.

15. However, recent work by Shugart and Taagepera (2017) argue this relationship is actually reversed—that national level forces shape district level results. See also work by Potter (2014) to this effect, which we discuss below.

16. Moreover, the analysis of Huber (2014: 987) further suggests that members of a specific ethnic group may be especially likely to vote as a unit under more restrictive systems, and do so in a way that may reduce the effective number of parties: "In majoritarian systems, small geographically dispersed groups can have strong incentives to vote cohesively for larger catch-all parties in efforts to be pivotal in elections. And in majoritarian systems with geographically concentrated groups, ethnically oriented parties can have strong chances to defeat larger catch-all parties."

17. See also Selway (2011) for another promising recent survey-based approach. Selway's focus is upon the cross-cuttingness of several cleavages (race, ethnicity, language, religion, income, and geography), but he reports information about the group structure as well.

18. We calculate this statistic by dividing the population into two occupational groups: those engaged in agriculture and other conventionally rural, primary sector occupations such as forestry (the rural population), and those engaged in all remaining occupations (the urban population).

19. Like age, educational level has been identified as an increasingly important social cleavage, especially in advanced democracies. Voters' education level has been found to significantly affect their political values, particularly along a libertarian-authoritarian dimension, which has created a growing fault line between more educated and less educated sectors of society that has important implications for the party system (Stubager 2010).

20. Data for the constituencies as redrawn in 2013, which were used for the recent 2016 elections.

21. Includes the Delegate District for the District of Columbia.

## References

Alesina, Alberto, Arnaud Devleeschauwer, William Easterly, Sergio Kurlat, and Romain Wacziarg. "Fractionalization." *Journal of Economic Growth* 8 (2003): 155–194.

Alesina, Alberto, and Edward L. Glaeser. *Fighting Poverty in the US and Europe: A World of Difference*. New York: Oxford University Press, 2004.

Alvarez, R. Michael, Frederick J. Boehmke, and Jonathan Nagler. "Strategic Voting in British Elections." *Election Studies* 25, no. 1 (2006): 1–19.

Amorim Neto, Octavio, and Gary Cox. "Electoral Institutions, Cleavage Structures, and the Number of Parties." *American Journal of Political Science* 41, no. 1 (1997): 149–174.

Bargsted, Matias A., and Orit Kedar. "Coalition-Targeted Duvergerian Voting: How Expectations Affect Voter Choice under Proportional Representation." *American Journal of Political Science* 53, no. 2 (2009): 307–323.

Benoit, Kenneth. "The Endogeneity Problem in Electoral Studies: A Critical Reexamination of Duverger's Mechanical Effect." *Electoral Studies* 21, no. 1 (2002).

Blais, Andre. "Why Is There So Little Strategic Voting in Canadian Plurality Rule Elections?" *Political Studies* 50 (2002): 445–454.

Brancati, Dawn. "The Origins and Strengths of Regional Parties." *British Journal of Political Science* 38, no. 1 (2008): 135–159.

Burklin, W. P. "Governing Left Parties Frustrating the Radical Non-Established Left: The Rise and Inevitable Decline of the Greens." *European Sociological Review* 3, no. 2 (1987): 109–126.

Caramani, Daniele. *The Nationalization of Politics: The Formation of National Electorates and Party Systems in Western Europe.* New York: Cambridge University Press, 2004.

Chhibber, Pradeep, and Ken Kollman. *The Formation of National Party Systems: Federalism and Party Competition in Canada, Great Britain, India, and the United States.* Princeton, NJ: Princeton University Press, 2004.

Clark, William, and Matt Golder. "Rehabilitating Duverger's Theory: Testing the Mechanical and Strategic Modifying Effects of Electoral Laws." *Comparative Political Studies* 39, no. 6 (2006): 679–708.

Cox, Gary W. *Making Votes Count: Strategic Coordination in the World's Electoral Systems.* New York: Cambridge University Press, 1997.

Cox, Gary W., and J. Knoll. "Ethnes, Fiscs and Electoral Rules: The Determinants of Party System Inflation." Paper presented at the annual meeting of the American Political Science Association, Philadelphia, PA, 2003.

Crisp, Brian F., Santiago Olivella, and Joshua D. Potter. "Party-System Nationalization and the Scope of Public Policy: The Importance of Cross-District Constituencies." *Comparative Political Studies* 46, no. 4 (2013): 431–456.

Dickson, Eric, and Kenneth Scheve. "Social Identity, Electoral Institutions, and the Number of Candidates." *British Journal of Political Science* 40, no. 2 (2010): 349–375.

Diwakar, Rekha. "Duverger's Law and the Size of Indian Party System: A District Level Analysis." *Party Politics* 13, no. 5 (2007): 539–561.

Duverger, Maurice. *Political Parties: Their Organization and Activity in the Modern State.* London: Methuen, 1954.

Easterly, William, and Ross Levine. "Africa's Growth Tragedy: Policies and Ethnic Divisions." *Quarterly Journal of Economics* 112, no. 4 (1997): 1203–1250.

Fearon, James. "Ethnic and Cultural Diversity by Country." *Journal of Economic Growth* 8, no. 2 (2003): 195–222.

Fearon, James, and David Laitin. "Ethnicity, Insurgency and Civil War." *American Political Science Review* 97, no. 1 (2003): 75–90.

Ferree, Karen, Clark Gibson, and Barak Hoffman. "Social Diversity Meets Electoral Institutions in Africa: Testing the Interactive Hypothesis at the Subnational Level in South Africa and Ghana." Working paper, UC San Diego, n.d.

Ferree, Karen E., G. Bingham Powell, and Ethan Scheiner. "Context, Electoral Rules, and Party Systems." *Annual Review of Political Science* 17 (2014): 421–439.

Gaines, Brian J. "Duverger's Law and the Meaning of Canadian Exceptionalism." *Comparative Political Studies* 32 (1999): 835–861.

Golder, Matt. "Presidential Coattails and Legislative Fragmentation." *American Journal of Political Science* 50, no. 1 (2006): 34–48.

Grofman, Bernard, Shaun Bowler, and Andre Blais. "Introduction: Evidence for Duverger's Law in Four Countries." In *Duverger's Law of Plurality Elections: The Logic of Party Competition in Canada, India, the United Kingdom, and the United States*, edited by B. Grofman, A. Blais, and S. Bowler, 1–12. New York: Springer, 2009.

Hicken, Allen, and Heather Stoll. "Electoral Rules and the Size of the Prize: How Political Institutions Shape Presidential Party Systems." *Journal of Politics* 70 (2008): 1109–1127.

Hicken, Allen, and Heather Stoll. "Presidents and Parties: How Presidential Elections Shape Coordination in Legislative Elections." *Comparative Political Studies* 44, no. 7 (2011): 854–883.

Hicken, Allen, and Heather Stoll. "Are All Presidents Created Equal? Presidential Powers and the Shadow of Presidential Elections." *Comparative Political Studies* 46, no. 3 (2013): 291–319.

Horowitz, Donald. 1985. *Ethnic Groups in Conflict.* Berkeley: University of California Press.

Huber, John. "Measuring Ethnic Voting: Do Proportional Electoral Laws Politicize Ethnicity?" *American Journal of Political Science* 56, no. 4 (2014): 986–1001.

Huber, John, and Pavithra Suryanarayan. "Ethnic Inequality and the Ethnification of Political Parties: Evidence from India." *World Politics* 68, no. 1 (2016): 149–188.

Johnston, Richard, and Fred Cutler. "Canada: The Puzzle of Local Three-Party Competition." In *Duverger's Law of Plurality Elections: The Logic of Party Competition in Canada, India, the United Kingdom, and the United States*, edited by B. Grofman, A. Blais, and S. Bowler, 83–96. New York: Springer, 2009.

Jones, Mark. "Racial Heterogeneity and the Effective Number of Candidates in Majority Runoff Elections: Evidence from Louisiana." *Electoral Studies* 16, no. 3 (1997): 349–358.

Jones, Mark. "Electoral Laws and the Effective Number of Presidential Candidates." *Journal of Politics* 61, no. 1 (1999): 171–184.

Jones, Mark. "Electoral Institutions, Social Cleavages, and Candidate Competition in Presidential Elections." *Electoral Studies* 23, no. 1 (2004): 73–106.

Laakso, Markku, and Rein Taagepera. "'Effective' Number of Parties: A Measure with Application to West Europe." *Comparative Political Studies* 12, no. 1 (1979): 3–27.

Li, Yuhui, and Matthew S. Shugart. "The Seat Product Model of the Effective Number of Parties: A Case for Applied Political Science." *Electoral Studies* 41, no. 4 (2017): 23–34.

Lijphart, Arend. *Democracies: Patterns of Majoritarian and Consensus Government in Twenty-one Countries.* New Haven, CT: Yale University Press, 1984.

Lijphart, Arend. *Patterns of Democracy.* New Haven, CT: Yale University Press, 1999.

Lipset, Seymour, and Stein Rokkan. "Cleavage Structures, Party Systems, and Voter Alignments." In *Party Systems and Voter Alignments: Cross-National Perspectives*, edited by S. Lipset and S. Rokkan, 1–64. New York: Free Press, 1967.

Madrid, Raul. "Indigenous Voters and Party System Fragmentation." *Electoral Studies* 25, no. 4 (2005): 689–707.

Mainwaring, Scott, and Timothy Scully. "Introduction: Party Systems in Latin America." In: *Building Democratic Institutions: Party Systems in Latin America*, edited by S. Mainwaring and T. Scully, 1–36. Stanford: Stanford University Press, 1995.

Milazzo, Caitlin, Robert G. Moser, and Ethan Scheiner. "Social Diversity Affects the Number of Parties Even under First-Past-the-Post Rules." *Comparative Political Studies.* In press.

Moser, Robert G., and Ethan Scheiner. "Mixed Electoral Systems and Electoral System Effects: Controlled Comparison and Cross-National Analysis." *Electoral Studies* 23, no. 4 (2004): 575–599.

Moser, Robert G., and Ethan Scheiner. *Electoral Systems and Political Context: How the Effects of Rules Vary across New and Established Democracies.* New York: Cambridge University Press, 2012.

Mozaffar, Shaheen, James Scarritt, and Glen Galaich. "Electoral Institutions, Ethnopolitical Cleavages, and Party Systems in Africa's Emerging Democracies." *American Political Science Review* 97, no. 3 (2003): 379–390.

Ordeshook, Peter, and Olga Shvetsova. "Ethnic Heterogeneity, District Magnitude, and the Number of Parties." *American Journal of Political Science* 38, no. 1 (1994): 100–123.

Posner, Daniel. "Measuring Ethnic Fractionalization in Africa." *American Journal of Political Science* 48, no. 4 (2004): 849–863.

Potter, Joshua D. "Demographic Diversity and District-Level Party Systems." *Comparative Political Studies* 7, no. 13 (2014): 1801–1829.

Potter, Joshua D. "Constituency Diversity, District Magnitude, and Voter Coordination." *British Journal of Political Science*. In press.

Powell, G. Bingham. *Comparative Democracies: Participation, Stability and Violence*. Cambridge, MA: Harvard University Press, 1982.

Rabushka, Alvin, and Kenneth Shepsle. *Politics in Plural Societies: A Theory of Democratic Instability*. New York: Pearson/Longman, 2008.

Rae, Douglas, and Michael Taylor. *The Analysis of Political Cleavages*. New Haven, CT: Yale University Press, 1970.

Raymond, Christopher D. "The Organizational Ecology of Ethnic Cleavages: The Nonlinear Effects of Ethnic Diversity on Party System Fragmentation." *Electoral Studies* 37 (2015): 109–119.

Riker, William. "The Two-Party System and Duverger's Law: An Essay on the History of Political Science." *American Political Science Review* 76, no. 4 (1982): 753–766.

Riker, William. "Duverger's Law Revisited." In *Electoral Laws and their Political Consequences*, edited by A. Lijphart and B. Grofman, 19–42. New York: Agathon Press, 1986.

Sambanis, Nicholas, and Moses Shayo. "Social Identification and Ethnic Conflict." *American Political Science Review* 107, no. 2 (2013): 294–325.

Selway, Joel. "The Measurement of Cross-Cutting Cleavages and Other Multidimensional Cleavage Structures." *Political Analysis* 19, no. 1 (2011): 48–65.

Shugart, Matthew S., and Rein Taagepera. *Votes from Seats: Logical Models of Electoral Systems*. New York: Cambridge University Press, 2017.

Singer Matthew M. "Was Duverger Correct? Single-Member District Election Outcomes in 53 Countries." *British Journal of Political Science* 43 (2013): 201–220.

Singer, Matthew, and Laura Stephenson. "The Political Context and Duverger's Theory: Evidence at the District Level." *Electoral Studies* 28, no. 3 (2009): 480–491.

Stoll, Heather. "Social Cleavages and the Number of Parties: How the Measures You Choose Affect the Answers You Get." *Comparative Political Studies* 41, no. 11 (2008): 1439–1465.

Stoll, Heather. *Changing Societies, Changing Party Systems*. New York: Cambridge University Press, 2013.

Stubager, Rune. "The Development of the Education Cleavage: Denmark as a Critical Case." *West European Politics* 33, no. 3 (2010): 505–533.

Taagepera, Rein. *Predicting Party Sizes: The Logic of Simple Electoral Systems*. Oxford: Oxford University Press, 2007.

Taagepera, Rein, and Bernard Grofman. "Rethinking Duverger's Law: Predicting the Effective Number of Parties in Plurality and PR Systems—Parties Minus Issues Equals One." *European Journal of Political Research* 13 (1985): 341–352.

von Beyme, Klaus. *Political Parties in Western Democracies*. New York: St. Martin's Press, 1985.

Vowles, Jack. "Offsetting the PR Effect? Party Mobilization and Turnout Decline in New Zealand, 1996–99." *Party Politics* 8, no. 5 (2002): 587–605.

...................................................................................................

# CHAPTER 8

# ELECTORAL SYSTEMS
# AND ETHNIC MINORITY
# REPRESENTATION

...................................................................................................

## DAVID LUBLIN AND SHAUN BOWLER

## WHICH GROUPS SHOULD BE REPRESENTED, AND WHY?

EVERY democratic process short of unanimity produces opinion minorities. Many ideas relating to the democratic process see nothing wrong with this provided that the end collective decision was arrived at fairly and participation was equal. This creation of opinion minorities and majorities is seen to be acceptable in part because today's minority could become tomorrow's majority (see, e.g., Coleman 2006; Bird, Saalfeld, and Wüst 2011; Segura and Rodrigues 2006). Though seen as problematic by the social choice literature, this instability or cycling is not only consistent but also often perceived as critical to the translation of the pluralist ideal into practical politics, as instability allows minorities to become majorities and vice versa (Miller 1983; McGann 2006).

There are, however, situations where that pluralist democratic ideal is not met in practice and opinion minorities become frozen, and that freezing becomes especially problematic in a broader sense when that opinion minority overlaps social and demographic traits so that certain groups of people are in a permanent minority (Peleg 2004). There may be situations in which the tie between opinion minority and demographic minority is quite loose and so, sometimes as a result, demographic minorities form part of the majority. In practice, however, there are times when this link between opinion and more solidly anchored demographic characteristics like language, religion, race, caste, or ethnicity is very tight and distinct social groups with distinct opinions are in a permanent or semipermanent minority. Democratic majority rule can therefore function as a system of exclusion of ascriptive minorities from influence over decision making even within well-established democracies. As Horowitz (1993, 29) writes: "In ethnically divided societies, majority rule is not a solution; it is a problem, because it permits domination, apparently in perpetuity."

Northern Ireland's parliament represented an archetypal case of ethnic minority exclusion even under well-established democratic rule. Northern Ireland held regular democratic elections for its own Home Rule legislature from 1921 to 1972. This parliament essentially ratified the political control of the Protestant, Unionist majority and the exclusion of the Catholic, Nationalist minority. The tight linkage between ethnic identification and political affiliation made the loss of Unionist control or the inclusion of Nationalists in the government all but unimaginable. The static political situation and systematic discrimination against the minority led to the Catholic civil rights movement and then to the Troubles, the common name for the long period of communally based violence prior to the Good Friday Agreement in 1998.

A series of normative arguments support political systems taking special measures to avoid this sort of perpetual exclusion and to ensure the representation of minorities within societies. Several scholars (Dovi 2012; Mansbridge 1999, 2003; Birch 1972), most prominently Pitkin (1967), have outlined normative arguments in support of why minorities should be represented.

These arguments rest on the inherent justice of including all groups in democratic decision making and the inadequacies of asking others to be the agents of those groups. There are important symbolic values in having minority representation in the legislature. That symbolism may, for example, have real effects in terms of encouraging minority citizens to support the legislative and electoral process more broadly (e.g., Mansbridge 1999; Gay 2002; Pantoja and Segura 2003; Preuhs 2006; Wängnerud 2009). But the real value of minority representation lies in substantive representation of minority interests. That is, minorities are likely better advocates of minority interests than members of the majority. After all, being in a minority is likely to bring with it not just a different set of policy preferences but a different perspective more broadly on how society should and does work. Furthermore, it is of value to democratic practice more broadly to include a diverse set of opinions and perspectives. Even when minority representatives hold similar views to a set of majority representatives, they may bring a greater intensity of interest based on experience to questions of particular interest to minority communities (Canon 1999). Scholars often see these arguments as justification for a range of specific institutional remedies designed to advance minority representation, such as multiseat districts, reserved seats, or party list quotas.

There is a practical justification for minority representation too, one that is not often highlighted in normative accounts. Chronic underrepresentation and exclusion challenges the legitimacy of the political system in general among the excluded. As in Northern Ireland, which, we should recall, had a long history of electoral democracy, civil disobedience and noncooperation may follow on the heels of exclusion to the detriment of the political system. Even more seriously, violence and civil war, as well as the overthrow of democracy, can result from ethnically based exclusion (Guelke 2004; Wimmer 2002).

Outside established democracies, these problems may become severe. Donald Horowitz (1985, 315–318) describes how Guyanese politics descended into increasingly bitter competition as the division between Indo- and Afro-Guyanese formed the central basis of the party system. Supported by the smaller Afro-Guyanese group, the governing party pursued first electoral manipulation and then authoritarianism to stay in power, as elections would have resulted in not just a loss of power but seemingly permanent exclusion by the more numerous Indo-Guyanese. Instances in the histories of Sri Lanka and Sudan provide other examples of ethnic exclusion, and Horowitz (1993, 21, 37) provides other examples of the kind of descent into ethnic conflict seen in Guyana: "Togo and the Congo Republic both have northern regimes (based, respectively, on the Kabrai and the Mbochi) that came to power after military coups reversed the ethnic results of elections." Similar tensions, albeit of varying intensity, have been seen across Africa (Sisk and Reynolds 1998; Osei-Hwedie 1998; Eifert, Miguel, and Posner 2010) and in India (Varshney 2003; see also Cederman, Gleditsch, and Hug 2013 and the chapter by Ziegfeld in this volume).

While our focus is on racial and ethnic minorities, it is worth noting that several of the techniques discussed in this chapter have been applied to improve the representation of women on similar grounds to those noted earlier. As a recent IDEA (2014, 15) report noted:

> Constituting half or more of any nation, women can hardly be conceptualized as a minority, but rather as a marginalized majority. Depending on the prevalence of patriarchal structures, women experience varying degrees of discrimination. The situation for women becomes even more precarious when they belong to a group that is considered a minority, as they are then exposed to double discrimination.

Whether we discuss the representation of women or racial and ethnic minorities, one response is to guarantee some form of minimal representation (Krook 2009; Reynolds 2006).[1] Some countries privilege certain minorities over others. For example, Slovenia guarantees seats in parliament to its tiny Italian and Hungarian minorities but does not do the same for larger groups from other ex-Yugoslav republics. This approach may be easier to implement in practice than in principle since it is not always clear a priori within the normative literature how one identifies which groups should be represented. Also unclear within the literature is the answer to the question of who makes the decision of which group to represent—a task made more difficult by the context-dependent nature of minority status. Dovi (2002) takes on these questions and outlines criteria by which we may think through the question of which citizens may need special protections via electoral rules or other political institutions. Part of the answer, for Dovi at least, should involve an assessment of how people are excluded from power.

The case of Asian Americans in the United States helps further illustrate the practical difficulties involved in defining which minorities are to be represented. Arguably, there is a similar rationale for addressing Asian American representation with African American representation. But in US practice, the term "Asian American" covers people whose national origins ranges from Pakistan to Japan. Dovi's work highlights the question of who decides on those categorizations. Whether people of different national origins can be combined into a single Asian American group is an open question, especially since surveys suggest that Asian Americans are more likely to identify with their national origin than as Asians more broadly (Pew Research Center 2013, 15).

Even leaving the problem of group designation aside, the mechanisms that help ensure representation of one group may not aid another. The intentional design of electoral districts with African American majorities has greatly expanded the ability of blacks to elect their preferred candidates (Lublin 1997; Davidson and Grofman 1994; Lublin et al. 2009). But the impossibility of drawing Asian American majority districts in many places renders districting an ill-suited tool for expanding Asian American representation.

The normative literature, then, speaks to a series of concerns about the exclusion of groups. Putting definitional difficulties to one side, the literature is clear that steps should be taken to ensure the representation of some excluded groups. But even if a society does address the symbolic or "descriptive" aspect of representing minority groups, it is not clear that guaranteed representation furthers the cause of "substantive" representation. If legislators are going to win the election more or less regardless of what they do, some contend that they will not work hard to reflect the views of minority citizens (Swain 1993). In other words, some institutional fixes are better than others, and all involve tradeoffs of various kinds.

Making the reflection of particular characteristics an institutionalized part of the electoral and legislative process may go some way toward institutionalizing them more broadly. The social divisions that guaranteed representation seeks to reflect may become permanently embedded in society. As law professors Rick Pildes (2008) and Sam Issacharoff (2004) note, institutionalization of community-based electoral rules may exacerbate these cleavages and still their replacement by nonethnic cleavages.

More broadly, guaranteed inclusion may conflict with some forms of democratic practice that involves community building. Setting up institutions may generate more demands for separation and distinction than a coming together as candidates and parties campaign to maintain those distinctions. In abstract, that possibility may not sound too bad, but in societies trying to build new nations and new states, enshrining division through minority representation may make building those new features harder (Bose 2002; Brancati 2006). India intended the reservation of parliamentary seats for Scheduled Tribes and Scheduled Castes as a temporary measure, but they have become enshrined as a permanent part of the Indian political scene (Lublin 2014, 149–153; McMillan 2005). Just as in reservations for government jobs and university places, other groups, such as Muslims (Ahmed 2008), have clamored for similar protections.

The French practice of not asking questions about race and ethnicity on the census is, in part, tied to a wish to maintain a sense of national identity. Put another way, in French law, the total equality of French citizens in a unitary republic remains paramount to the exclusion of consideration of these types of characteristics. In contrast, other states entrench minority representation through aid to minority political *parties* rather than group members—an approach that may hinder political integration and undermine state cohesion. Parties can still have a strong ethnic link even if countries do not recognize ethnic division. In Africa, bans on ethnic and regional parties are common, but they still persist in many countries under nonethnic names (Basedau et al. 2007; Lublin and Wright 2014; Moroff 2010).

While the questions of which communities to represent, and when, have uncertain answers, the question of *how* to represent groups has a set of much more well-defined answers. That is, the normative literature on electoral representation may not have as well-defined a sense of the problem as we might like, but the more empirical literature on electoral systems does have a well-defined sense of the set of potential solutions. We turn to discuss these in the next section.

# ELECTORAL SYSTEMS AND RACIAL AND ETHNIC MINORITIES

Electoral system design is one means by which societies can help manage questions of (un)fairness in societies with racial and ethnic diversity. Through electoral design, it is possible to ensure minority representation in a number of different ways.

## Boundary Delimitation

In districted systems, there may be overrepresentation of certain geographic areas. This is an especially appealing solution for districted systems where there is regional concentration of relevant populations.[2] In the United Kingdom, for example, there is a slight overrepresentation of Scotland and Wales in the House of Commons—each has 8.4 percent and 4.8 percent of the UK population but 9 percent and 6 percent of seats, respectively. Areas in Canada with large First Nations populations are slightly overrepresented in the Canadian House. Nunavut and the Northwest Territories benefit greatly from the guarantee of one seat to each territory, though they have less than one-tenth of 1 percent of Canada's population. First Nations also benefit from the routine underpopulation of vast, rural constituencies in the northern part of provinces relative to others in the same province (Lublin 2014, 184–188).

In more complex settings, states may arrange district boundaries to ensure representation of particular groups. In the United States, these are often known as majority-minority or minority-opportunity districts; that is, they are districts in which an underrepresented minority forms a sufficiently high share of voters and they can often choose the representative they wish. Among the 27 districts that contain an African American majority out of the total of 435 in the House, all but Tennessee's Ninth District elected African American members of Congress in 2014. African Americans gained election in 17 other districts in which African American voters do not make up over 50 percent of the vote. In many of these districts, African Americans and Latinos together compose a majority. African Americans often benefit in such districts because of comparatively low turnout among Latinos, partly due to lower citizenship rates.

Such solutions, at least in the US case, work fairly well to ensure descriptive representation so long as there is sufficient residential segregation and a relatively small number of group differences to accommodate. More complex demographics such as California's—with multiple groups and low residential segregation—pose problems for redistricting as a remedy for underrepresented groups like Asian Americans. The redistricting process may also cause tensions between such groups, as boundaries can aid the election of a member of one group rather than another. In part, some of these issues relate to conflicts between providing group representation and other desirable district properties, such as compactness and contiguity (see Kogan and McGhee 2012 for an account of California's redistricting).

## Proportionality

Both because districted systems do not always lend themselves to minority rights and because redistricting can lead to increasingly complex solutions, proportional systems seem to offer a simpler method of guaranteed minority representation. For that reason, a major building block in bridging ethnic differences is to rely on proportional electoral systems of some kind. This was the choice, for example, for post-Apartheid Namibia and South Africa,[3] where even highly marginal groups can gain a parliamentary seat.

Proportional systems of various kinds can help ensure the representation of any group, although implementation is critical to accessibility because high minimum vote thresholds can exclude groups. But a system such as list proportional representation (PR) could also provide an incentive to build coalitions, at least so far as government construction is concerned. On the other hand, at election time, the parties may not build bridges across ethnic divides so much as encourage appeals to one's ethnic community and facilitate division based on ethnic lines. Just as in majoritarian systems, there may be incentives for politicians to polarize the electorate around ethnic cleavages to encourage voters to support ethnically based parties. Indeed, parties may become increasingly aggressive group advocates and engage in ethnic outbidding, as identified by Horowitz (1993), to avoid challenges from parties presenting themselves as better or more authentic group advocates.

Preferential systems such as the alternative vote (AV) offer some incentives for parties and candidates to appeal across ethnic lines for lower-order preferences. However, AV is still ultimately majoritarian and can facilitate majority coalescence in constituencies and national dominance, even as it may spur some bridge building. In some ways the single transferable vote (STV) form of PR offers a compromise solution in that the proportionality of results generally implies coalitions and incentives to build coalitions postelection, while the preferential component will provide incentives to appeal across divisions at election time. That said, practice in Ireland suggests that STV rewards clientelism, which may help deepen ethnic divisions or, alternatively, strengthen the focus on candidates rather than parties.

Whichever mix of proportionality plus vote-gathering incentives may result from a particular electoral system, those results are often buttressed in practice by a mix of other electoral system rules and devices to help ensure minority representation. One such rule will be a minimum threshold of votes before obtaining representation. As with all questions in proportionality, this becomes a question of balance. On the one hand, a low threshold facilitates minority representation. But too low a threshold means that even fractional groups will gain representation and, possibly, have little need to develop cooperation or cooperative practices.

## Communal representation

Lebanon has multiseat districts in which seats are allocated according to strict quotas for each confessional group. All voters, regardless of their confession, may cast ballots for all candidates in these multiseat plurality elections. However, they may not vote for more candidates of a confession than the number of seats that confession has been allotted within the district (International Foundation for Electoral Systems 2009). Note that New Zealand has a communal roll combined with districting and they take a fluid approach by having the Maōri electoral option, which allows people to switch from a Maōri roll to a general roll from time to time.[4] Cyprus has had communal rolls too, and will almost certainly again if a settlement ends the division of the island.

The communal roll approach has largely been abandoned. This approach registers voters by particular community and restricts participation to members of the list. "[M]ost communal roll arrangements were abandoned after it became clear that communal electorates, while guaranteeing group representation, often had the perverse effect of undermining the path of accommodation between different groups, since there were no incentives for political intermixing between communities. The tasks of defining a member of a particular group and distributing seats fairly between them were also full of pitfalls" (Reynolds, Reilly, and Ellis 2005, 123).

That is, communal rolls do not allow for fluidity across dividing lines and so do not allow parties or candidates to build bridges across different communities. As a result, while protecting the representation of minority groups, it entrenches ethnic divisions and does not represent an appealing solution if the goal is to mitigate them. This solution would follow Bird's (2014) second "family" of ethnic quotas in which pan-ethnic parties are the vehicles for inclusion. Bird gives as examples Burundi, Djibouti, Jordan, Kazakhstan, Lebanon, Mauritius, Pakistan, and Singapore (Bird 2014, 19).

Mauritius applies a novel approach to communal representation. Candidates run in multiseat districts and must identify their membership in one of four recognized communities in advance of the election. Nevertheless, voters may cast votes for any candidates in these multiseat plurality elections, though they must cast all of their votes for their votes to be counted. This latter provision encourages voting for all members of a multiethnic party ticket. After the election, Mauritius applies its best-loser system to award an additional eight seats in a manner designed to render the House closely reflective of the country's ethnic composition without changing the balance between the parties (Mathur 1997).

## Reserved Seats

A more direct approach is simply to reserve a number of seats in the legislature for a particular minority to ensure representation regardless of vote share. Reynolds, Reilly, and Ellis (2005, 122) list twelve examples of countries with reserved seats: "Colombia ('black communities'), Croatia (the Hungarian, Italian, Czech, Slovak, Ruthenian, Ukrainian, German and Austrian minorities), India (the scheduled tribes and castes), Jordan (Christians and Circassians), Niger (Tuareg), New Zealand (Maori), Pakistan (non-Muslim minorities), Palestine (Christians and Samaritans), Samoa (non-indigenous minorities), Slovenia (Hungarians and Italians), and Taiwan (the aboriginal community)." Reynolds (2006, 16) identifies three more countries with seat reservations: Kiribati (Banabans), Romania (nineteen "small minorities"), and Venezuela (indigenous population). Additionally, Iraq reserves seats for Christians, Sabeans, Shabaks, and Yizidis.

The literature to date in discussing these solutions makes a number of points. First, there does not seem to be a one-size-fits-all solution and so paths to minority inclusion vary. Some—notably New Zealand—have adopted multiple approaches to the issue. Second, the geography of ethnic groups greatly influences what works and what does not. Districting solutions, whether the international drawing of districts as in the United States or the overrepresentation of minority regions as in the United Kingdom, depend heavily on residential segregation. Other countries, such as Denmark, Italy, and Poland, lower legal thresholds to make it easier for recognized minorities to gain representation under proportional electoral systems. But minorities must still be sizeable enough to win seats, and the German minority in Denmark failed to enter parliament after the support for its party fell too low (Lublin and Wright 2013).

Second, while it is clear that there is not a one-size-fits-all solution to ethnic representation, it is not always clear why some societies choose one solution rather than another. Critical issues that seem relevant to these choices are, first, that ethnic geography influences enormously what works, and, second, a key goal is often one that will allow for some form of minority inclusion, as well as representation, though this can occur in a number of ways (facilitating alternation in power as in Ghana, consociationalism as in Belgium, federalism as in Canada, encouraging multiethnic parties). We elaborate on this point later as we turn to address whether any or all of these approaches work to assist with ethnic conflict.

Before doing so, we will note our third point. For some societies, the impetus is to suppress ethnic or regional parties in the name of national unity, so these countries turn their focus in electoral engineering toward building national unity and undercutting ethnic or regionally based parties. After all, and as the work of Bratton, Bhavnani, and Chen (2012) and Elischer (2013) reminds us for the case of the highly fractionalized politics of Africa, voters are not always and everywhere "ethnic" voters. Issues such as government performance still matter to voters, and an overwhelming emphasis on ethnic representation may put questions of performance into the shade, to the detriment of all.

In terms, then, of suppressing ethnic conflict, societies have two basic kinds of electoral rules at their disposal.

## Ethnic/Regional Party Bans

Sometimes this is done in an effort to suppress minority parties (e.g., Bulgaria) or forestall regionalism (e.g., Brazil), but in many African countries, it stems from an effort to promote more national parties and to prevent pulling apart on ethnic lines (e.g., Kenya). Bans are not always effective but are more apt to work in more authoritarian contexts, likely because parties have greater legal recourse against them and governments are more reticent to apply them in free democracies (Lublin and Wright 2014; Becher and Basedau 2008).

Spatial Ballot Access Requirements can serve the same negative (e.g., preventing emergence of indigenous parties in Peru) or positive purposes (e.g., promoting national parties in Ghana). They operate by requiring parties to gain evidence of support, such as signatures, members, or votes, in more regions of the country than in which targeted groups inhabit or can create an effective party organization. More broadly, spatial ballot access requirements can forestall regionalism. They also have the distinct advantage of comparatively objective criteria in contrast to ethnic party bans. As a result, their application may appear fairer, at least in formal terms, though implementation also requires higher state capacity than ethnic party bans (Lublin and Wright 2014).

# ELECTORAL SYSTEMS AND ETHNIC CONFLICT: THE LIMITS OF ELECTORAL ENGINEERING?

For Bird (2014, 23), the variation among ethnic quota schemes appears to correspond more with regime type and the broader rules of the electoral system, and less with differences in ethnic demography. Generally speaking, the lesson from Lublin (2014) is that the various methods can be applied to stifle minority representation and, more specifically, ethnic parties. Ethnic parties do not appear where they cannot—not solely due to rules but because strategic political elites intent on power do not like to tilt at windmills. Electoral systems, then, do have an important role in the composition of the party system and, hence, in the descriptive representation of minorities.

Though electoral systems have consistent effects on the manifestation of ethnicity within the political system, the effect of a single electoral system is far from identical across countries. The great variation not just in the level but also in the geographic distribution of ethnic diversity can result in the same electoral system having quite different impacts. Moreover, they operate in conjunction with a variety of other rules and institutions, such as federalism and the presence of regional legislatures.

Nevertheless, scholars still debate fiercely the impact of electoral rules. While one of us contends that past studies have badly underestimated the effect of electoral rules (Lublin 2017), the other has argued that evidence for their impact is often limited, especially in comparison with the strongly theorized effects (Bowler and Donovan 2013). The key to resolving the debate appears to be consideration of the context in which the rules operate in terms of ethnic diversity, its distribution, and the presence of other institutions.

One important related but nonetheless not identical question, however, is whether or not these efforts do help reduce or avoid ethnic conflict. How to define and measure ethnic conflict is, of course, no easy matter. But putting those issues to one side to focus on managing such conflicts as they are generally understood, the literature to date does draw attention to a role for electoral system design, though studies often have inconsistent conclusions.

Saideman et al. (2002), for example, examine data on ethnic conflict and rebellion between 1985 and 1998 to show that proportional representation[5] helps to suppress ethnic conflict. The finding is consistent with Schneider and Wiesehomeier (2008), who examine 132 countries from 1950 to 2000, conducting some of their analyses on a subsample of 87 democracies, coding a majoritarian system as a dummy (0,1) measure and proportionality as another. Their findings, they argue, show that majoritarian electoral institutions promote conflict in divided societies, while more inclusive ones are beneficial (Schneider and Wiesehomeier 2008, 198). These findings are in line with the kinds of steps taken by divided societies in practice.

In some contrast, Selway and Templeman (2012) look at a somewhat longer period and bigger sample—1972 to 2003 and 106 regimes in 100 countries—and adopt a three-category definition of electoral systems, subsequently breaking this measure down and examining two dummy measures, one for proportional and one for majoritarian (Selway and Templeman 2012, 1554–1555). While some of the results from their modeling show patterns consistent with Saideman et al., they also show that—under some conditions— "PR is positively associated with political violence" (Selway and Templeman 2012, 1558). The conditions seem to be that PR works best in relatively homogenous societies (Selway and Templeman 2012, 1560).

To some extent, the difference in findings between these pieces is related both to different samples of cases and to differences in the modeling approach. But Selway and Templeman make the point that the effect of institutions is often conditional, rather than categorical. That is, and to underscore a point made earlier, electoral engineering solutions are not straightforward. There does not seem to be a way in which those hoping to deal with ethnic disputes can simply plug in an electoral arrangement and confidently expect a particular result. Rather, results vary, and often the variation is by context. Electoral engineering, then, is a harder task than we might think.

While the sense of the literature as a whole leans more toward PR as a conflict management tool, there are two important caveats to make. First, as Lublin (2014) notes, it is far easier to address issues of racial and ethnic division before society descends into ethnic violence. It is much easier to keep Humpty Dumpty on the wall than to put him back together again. Once there is a descent into the kinds of conditions examined by Horowitz, it is extremely hard to put the pieces back together again. The finding of Selway and Templeman (2012) is consistent with this broad theoretical point.

Second, and following on from that, it is hard to see that electoral institutions alone are enough to head off ethnic conflict. It is crucial to think about electoral institutions *in combination* with other institutions. There are several reasons for thinking that it is a combination of institutions that matters.

First, in general, constitutional engineers may sometimes miscalculate the effect of electoral systems. This would seem to be true, for example, where engineers are trying to balance fine differences, such as "over the thresholds" in PR systems. The Israeli experiment in direct election of the prime minister provides a good example.[6] Instead of resulting in party consolidation, it caused exactly the opposite. There was less of an incentive to vote for big parties so their leader could become prime minister even though the prime minister still needed a majority in the Knesset to survive. Mercifully, Israel abandoned the idea quickly.

But the example of Israel helps to illustrate two points about electoral system design in general. It is harder to engage in electoral system engineering than we might like. We know with varying degrees of certainty what the tie is between the electoral rule and the outcome we wish to see, and sometimes we get it wrong. Some examples are clear-cut. We know, for example, that we can guarantee minority representation by reserving 10 percent of seats for a given minority. But that kind of change essentially locks in the outcome we wish to see by mandate. It really does not leave much scope for the properties of choice or agency by voters and parties, properties that, in a democratic system, we may wish to preserve.

Moving to allow more choice and more agency means outcomes become less certain. We know with less certainty but with some fairly high probability that raising the threshold of representation in PR systems means that smaller parties (e.g., ones based on racial and ethnic divisions) are less likely to be represented in parliament. But where that threshold should be placed (4 percent? 6 percent?) depends on circumstances. Other changes, as in Israel's case with direct election of the prime minister, produce outcomes that were completely unanticipated.[7] In that regard, the work of both Bird (2014) and Lublin (2014) is especially important in reminding us that parties and elites will seek to game any given electoral arrangement.

When it comes to changes to the electoral system that depend on guessing about the strategic calculations of voters and parties, we may be wrong, or the outcome may be less certain than we would like. While the properties of choice (for voters) and agency (on the part of parties and candidates) may be desirable, they tend to make engineering harder. Over some range of electoral reforms, we move from electoral engineering to electoral art. Given that electoral engineers are likely to make mistakes, it seems reasonable to add in other institutions to reinforce the intended effect of dampening conflict in case the electoral incentives prove inadequate (or mistaken).

Second, the literature on ethnic conflict makes it clear that electoral institutions by themselves may be too slender a reed on which to build consensus across ethnic divisions. Those seeking to dampen conflict may need to rely on other institutions, whether highly formalized (decentralization, constitutional rights, rules on party commitment to democracy) or somewhat informal (consociationalism) to help buttress broader community building. Empirically, then, many issues of ethnic conflict are often examined in relation to other institutions, as is the case in the literature on institutions and ethnic conflict. Saideman et al. (2002), for example, discuss both parliamentarianism (which increased ethnic conflict—a finding somewhat at odds with the PR result) and federalism. Sometimes this literature casts doubt on some of the properties of institutions. Brancati (2006) examines thirty democracies from the period 1985 to 2000 and argues that decentralization is not an effective tool to help minimize conflict. If anything, for Brancati, decentralization produces regional parties that help to promote conflict.

The pattern of empirical findings as a whole is neatly captured by Schneider and Wiesehomeier (2008, 183), who succinctly state, "Constitutional engineers' advance various institutional arrangements, ranging from democracy in general to specific constitutional and electoral rules, as those mechanisms that help divided societies to resolve disputes peacefully. Political sociologists, by contrast, maintain that political institutions are largely an epiphenomenon." They go on to argue for a pattern that seeks a middle ground between the two kinds of approaches. But it is a middle ground that acknowledge the limitations of institutions in general and electoral systems in particular. Brancati (2006), in particular, has a keen sense of the selection process by which some institutions are created and introduced—a process not always modeled in some of the large-N cross-national works. Selway and Templeman's (2012) emphasis on conditionality of effects taps into some of those processes. More general still is Lublin's (2014) reminder that conflict management by electoral system is likely easier at relatively low levels of conflict.

# CONCLUSION

On one hand, this review of arrangements might well be seen as pessimistic: the effects of institutions are uncertain in their size and, more worryingly perhaps, in their direction. Moreover, in some ways the positive effects of institutions are at their greatest where they are needed least—in societies with relatively low levels of conflict.

That said, there are also grounds for optimism. One basis for optimism is that arriving at a more reasonable assessment of the role of institutions will allow for a clearer understanding of the problems at hand. If we cannot expect an institutional reform to provide solutions, then attention must turn to developing other—more efficacious—solutions to the conflicts and grievances, and we can stop designing ever more elaborate institutional schemes that waste time and effort. A more realistic understanding of institutional effects prevents false starts and false hopes.

A second basis for optimism is that institutions do have some effect. They are important in helping with the broader senses of representation and participation and, perhaps over time, may well build to a constructive solution. One of the limitations of the literature on electoral engineering is that we have few examples of what happens when divided societies do nothing and do not pursue electoral engineering (i.e., there is no counterfactual case). Furthermore, there seems to be an implicitly short time horizon: institutional fix-ups are supposed to take effect over a few elections. This is, perhaps, an unreasonable expectation. Therefore, giving institutions time to take effect may be a sensible approach. Of course, in the middle of particularly serious conflicts, there will not be the luxury of time. Still, institutional changes are concrete steps that, when taken in conjunction with other steps, can go some way toward helping some conflicts. That, in itself, is no mean achievement.

## NOTES

1. See the chapter by Krook in this volume.
2. See the chapter by Handley in this volume.
3. See the chapter by Ferree in this volume.
4. See the chapter by Vowles in this volume.
5. "[W]e code countries' electoral system in the following manner: representatives chosen by majority vote = 1, those chosen by a plurality system = 2, those selected using semiproportional representation systems = 3, and legislators chosen by true proportional representation = 4" (Saideman et al. 2002, 116). Coding taken from the 1997 edition of Reynolds, Reilly, and Ellis (2005). Saideman et al. acknowledge that this is a broad-brush definition and see possible scope for finer-grained effects (Saideman et al. 2002, 12).
6. See the chapter by Hazan et al. in this volume.
7. The effect was explained but ignored. The key point is that it is critical to think how actors will respond to the incentives, rather than how we would *like* them to respond.

## REFERENCES

Ahmed, Hilal. "Debating Muslim Political Representation." *India Seminar.* 2008. http://www.india-seminar.com/2008/586/586_hilal_ahmed.htm.

Basedau, Matthias, Matthijs Bogaards, Christof Hartmann, and P. Niesen. "Ethnic Party Bans in Africa." *German Law Journal* 8, no. 6 (2007): 617–634.

Becher, Anika, and Matthias Basedau. "Promoting Peace and Democracy through Party Regulation? Ethnic Party Bans in Africa." *German Institute of Global and Area Studies Working Papers*, no. 66 (January 2008).

Birch, Anthony H. *Representation.* New York: Praeger, 1972.

Bird, Karen. "Ethnic Quotas and Ethnic Representation Worldwide." *International Political Science Review* 35, no. 1 (2014): 12–26.

Bird, Karen, Thomas Saalfeld, and Andreas M. Wüst. "Ethnic Diversity, Political Participation and Representation." In *The Political Representation of Immigrants and Minorities: Voters, Parties and Parliaments in Liberal Democracies*. New York: Routledge 2011, 1–21.

Bose, Sumantra. *Bosnia after Dayton: Nationalist Partition and International Intervention*. New York: Oxford University Press, 2002.

Bowler, Shaun, and Todd Donovan, eds. *The Limits of Electoral Reform*. New York: Oxford University Press, 2013.

Brancati, Dawn. "Decentralization: Fueling the Fire or Dampening the Flames of Ethnic Conflict and Secessionism?" *International Organization* 60, no. 3 (2006): 651–685.

Bratton, Michael, Ravi Bhavnani, and Tse Hsin Chen. "Voting Intentions in Africa: Ethnic, Economic or Partisan?" *Commonwealth & Comparative Politics* 50, no. 1 (2012): 27–52.

Canon, David. *Race, Redistricting, and Representation: The Unintended Consequences of Black Majority Districts*. Chicago: University of Chicago Press, 1999.

Cederman, Lars-Erik, Kristian S. Gleditsch, and Simon Hug. "Elections and Ethnic Civil War." *Comparative Political Studies* 46, no. 3 (2013): 387–417.

Coleman, David. "Immigration and Ethnic Change in Low-Fertility Countries: A Third Demographic Transition." *Population and Development Review* 32, no. 3 (2006): 401–446.

Davidson, Chandler, and Bernard Grofman, eds. *Quiet Revolution in the South: The Impact of the Voting Rights Act, 1965-1990*. Princeton University Press, 1994.

Dovi, Suzanne. "Preferable Descriptive Representatives: Will Just Any Woman, Black, or Latino Do?" *American Political Science Review* 96, no. 4 (2002): 729–744.

Dovi, Suzanne. *The Good Representative*. Vol. 8. Chichester: John Wiley & Sons, 2012.

Eifert, Benn, Edward Miguel, and Daniel N. Posner. "Political Competition and Ethnic Identification in Africa." *American Journal of Political Science* 54, no. 2 (2010): 494–510.

Elischer, Sebastian. *Political Parties in Africa: Ethnicity and Party Formation*. New York: Cambridge University Press, 2013.

Gay, Claudine. "Spirals of Trust? The Effect of Descriptive Representation on the Relationship between Citizens and Their Government." *American Journal of Political Science* (2002): 717–732.

Guelke, Adrian. *Democracy and Ethnic Conflict: Advancing Peace in Deeply Divided Societies*. New York: Palgrave Macmillan, 2004.

Horowitz, Donald L. "Democracy in Divided Societies." *Journal of Democracy* 4, no. 4 (1993): 18–38.

Horowitz, Donald L. 1985. *Ethnic Groups in Conflict*. Berkeley: University of California Press, 1993.

International Foundation for Electoral Systems. "The Lebanese Electoral System." *IFES Lebanon Briefing Paper*. March 2009. https://www.ifes.org/sites/default/files/ifes_lebanon _esb_paper030209_0.pdf.

Issacharoff, Samuel. "Is Section 5 of the Voting Rights Act a Victim of Its Own Success?" *Columbia Law Review* 104, no. 6 (October 2004): 1710–1731.

Kogan, Vladimir, and Eric McGhee. "Redistricting California: An Evaluation of the Citizens Commission Final Plans." *California Journal of Politics and Policy* 4, no. 1 (2012): 1–22.

Krook, Mona L. *Quotas for Women in Politics: Gender and Candidate Selection Reform Worldwide*. New York: Oxford University Press, 2009.

Lublin, David. *The Paradox of Representation: Racial Gerrymandering and Minority Interests in Congress*. Princeton, NJ: Princeton University Press, 1997.

Lublin, David. *Minority Rules: Electoral Systems, Decentralization and Ethnoregional Party Success.* New York: Oxford University Press, 2014.

Lublin, David. "Electoral Systems, Ethnic Heterogeneity and Party System Fragmentation." *British Journal of Political Science* 47, no. 2 (April 2017): 373–389.

Lublin, David, Thomas Brunell, Bernard Grofman, and Lisa Handley. "Has the Voting Rights Act Outlived its Usefulness? In a Word 'No.'" *Legislative Studies Quarterly* 34, no. 4 (November 2009): 525–553.

Lublin, David, and Matthew Wright. "Engineering Inclusion: Assessing the Effects of Pro-Minority Representation Policies." *Electoral Studies* 32, no. 4 (December 2013): 746–755.

Lublin, David, and Matthew Wright. "Don't Start the Party: Assessing the Electoral Effect of Legal Provisions Impeding Ethnoregional Parties." *Election Law Journal* 13, no. 2 (2014): 277–287.

Mansbridge, Jane. "Should Blacks Represent Blacks and Women Represent Women? A Contingent 'Yes.'" *Journal of Politics* 61, no. 3 (1999): 628–657.

Mansbridge, Jane. "Rethinking Representation." *American Political Science Review* 97, no. 4 (2003): 515–528.

IDEA. "Marginalized Groups and Constitution Building." 2014. http://www.idea.int /publications/marginalized-groups-and-constitution-building/loader.cfm?csModule =security/getfile&pageID=67943.

Mathur, Raj. "Parliamentary Representation of Minority Communities: The Mauritian Experience." *Africa Today* 44, no. 1 (January–March 1997): 61–82.

McMillan, Alistair. *Standing at the Margins: Representation and Electoral Reservation in India.* New York: Oxford University Press, 2005.

McGann, Anthony J. *The Logic of Democracy: Reconciling Equality, Deliberation, and Minority Protection.* Ann Arbor: University of Michigan Press, 2006.

Miller, Nicholas R. "Pluralism and Social Choice." *American Political Science Review* 77, no. 3 (1983): 734–747.

Moroff, Anika. "Party Bans in Africa—An Empirical Overview." *Democratization* 17, no. 4 (August 2010): 618–641.

Osei-Hwedie, Bertha. "The Role of Ethnicity in Multi-Party Politics in Malawi and Zambia." *Journal of Contemporary African Studies* 16, no. 2 (1998): 227–247.

Pantoja, Adrian D., and Gary M. Segura. "Does Ethnicity Matter? Descriptive Representation in Legislatures and Political Alienation among Latinos." *Social Science Quarterly* 84, no. 2 (2003): 441–460.

Peleg, Ilan. "Transforming Ethnic Orders to Pluralist Regimes: Theoretical, Comparative and Historical Analysis." Chapter 2 In *Democracy and Ethnic Conflict: Advancing Peace in Deeply Divided Societies,* edited by Adrian Guelke. New York: Palgrave Macmillan, 2004, 7–25.

Pew Research Center. "The Rise of Asian Americans." Updated April 4, 2013. Washington, DC: Pew Research Center. http://www.pewsocialtrends.org/2012/06/19/the-rise-of-asian-americans/.

Pildes, Richard H. "Ethnic Identity and Democratic Institutions: A Dynamic Perspective." Chapter 6 In *Constitutional Design for Divided Societies: Integration or Accommodation?,* edited by Sujit Choudhry. New York: Oxford University Press, 2008, 173–203.

Pitkin, Hanna F. *The Concept of Representation.* Berkeley: University of California Press, 1967.

Preuhs, Robert R. "The Conditional Effects of Minority Descriptive Representation: Black Legislators and Policy Influence in the American States." *Journal of Politics* 68, no. 3 (2006): 585–599.

Reynolds, Andrew. "Electoral Systems and the Protection and Participation of Minorities." Report, Minority Rights Group International, 2006.

Reynolds, Andrew, Benjamin Reilly, and Andrew Ellis, eds. *Electoral System Design: The New International IDEA Handbook*. Stockholm: International Institute for Democracy and Electoral Assistance, 2005.

Saideman, Stephen M., David J. Lanoue, Michael Campenni, and Samuel Stanton. "Democratization, Political Institutions, and Ethnic Conflict A Pooled Time-Series Analysis, 1985-1998." *Comparative Political Studies* 35, no. 1 (2002): 103–129.

Schneider, Gerald, and Nina Wiesehomeier. "Rules That Matter: Political Institutions and the Diversity—Conflict Nexus." *Journal of Peace Research* 45, no. 2 (2008): 183–203.

Segura, Gary M., and Helena A. Rodrigues. "Comparative Ethnic Politics in the United States: Beyond Black and White." *Annual Review of Political Science* 9 (2006): 375–395.

Selway, Joel, and Kharis Templeman. "The Myth of Consociationalism? Conflict Reduction in Divided Societies." *Comparative Political Studies* 45, no. 12 (2012): 1542–1571.

Sisk, Timothy D., and Andrew Reynolds. *Elections and Conflict Management in Africa*. Vol. 31. Washington, DC: US Institute of Peace Press, 1998.

Swain, Carol. *Black Faces, Black Interests: The Representation of African Americans in Congress*. Cambridge, MA: Harvard University Press, 1993.

Varshney, Ashutosh. *Ethnic Conflict and Civic Life: Hindus and Muslims in India*. New Haven, CT: Yale University Press, 2003.

Wängnerud, Lena. "Women in Parliaments: Descriptive and Substantive Representation." *Annual Review of Political Science* 12 (2009): 51–69.

Wimmer, Andreas. *Nationalist Exclusion and Ethnic Conflict*. New York: Cambridge University Press, 2002.

..................................................................................................

# CHAPTER 9

# ELECTORAL SYSTEMS AND WOMEN'S REPRESENTATION

..................................................................................................

## MONA LENA KROOK

SCHOLARS have long recognized that electoral systems play a central role in shaping the dynamics of political representation, not only translating votes into seats but also influencing the number of parties, the strength of partisan ideological differences, and the incentives for elected officials to be responsive to their parties and their voters. Comparative research on gender similarly highlights electoral systems as an important—if not *the* most important—variable explaining cross-national differences in terms of women's access to elected positions. In recent years, this focus has evolved into a broader interest in electoral rules, in response to a doubling of the share of women in parliaments worldwide: while few countries have substituted one type of electoral system for another, many have reformed electoral laws to require that more women be selected and/or elected as candidates. These changes have sustained—and, indeed, widened—the gaps between electoral systems in terms of their effects on women.

Electoral systems are thus likely to remain a major focus of comparative gender and politics research into the future. Yet the rapidly expanding gender literature also merits closer attention from nongender scholars, offering important new empirical and theoretical contributions to the study of electoral systems. To this end, this chapter has a dual purpose: (1) to present an overview of how electoral systems have gendered effects and (2) to highlight some examples of how gender-focused studies of electoral systems provide new insights into political dynamics more generally. The first section provides a brief summary of women's representation globally, illustrating how these trends might be linked to electoral systems and electoral rules like gender quotas. The second section maps existing research on gender and electoral systems, focusing on the role of electoral formulas, district and party magnitude, and ballot structure in shaping women's opportunities to be elected. The third section identifies three areas within the gender literature that have foregrounded elements of electoral systems to generate new insights into the central dynamics of political life. The final section concludes by discussing several emerging areas of research related to gender, electoral systems, and political representation.

# WOMEN'S REPRESENTATION
# AND ELECTORAL FACTORS

In 2017, women achieved historic levels of representation, attaining 23.3 percent of parliamentary seats worldwide.[1] This reflects more than double the 11.7 percent share of seats held by women in 1997,[2] when the Inter-Parliamentary Union (IPU) first began to publish these global averages on its website. The IPU's most recent year-in-review report clearly links these gains to electoral factors. In countries where elections took place in 2016, women won 23.9 percent of the seats in chambers elected using proportional representation (PR); the figure is slightly higher if we add mixed-member electoral systems. In contrast, women gained only 15 percent of the seats in chambers elected through majoritarian (single-seat districts, or SSD) systems. Similarly, women won 25.6 percent of the seats in countries where gender quotas apply to parliamentary elections, compared to 16.1 percent in those where quotas are not applied (Inter-Parliamentary Union 2017, 1–2). Table 9.1, which lists the top ten countries in terms of women's parliamentary representation, confirms and starkly illustrates these patterns. Eight of these countries utilize list PR, and one has a mixed-member electoral system. Eight apply some form of gender quota, while the two remaining countries use informal quotas, which Krook, Lovenduski, and Squires (2009) term "soft quotas."

Comparative research offers several explanations as to why PR might result in the election of more women than in SSD systems (Krook and Schwindt-Bayer 2013). Some studies speculate that—in a context of possible voter bias against women—PR provides an advantage over SSD because lists, and not individual candidates, are the focus of voting. Party leaders seeking to get more women into office may thus be more confident putting women on their ballots, anticipating that few voters would change their support for this reason alone (Castles 1981; Rule 1987). Other scholars point out that PR systems have higher rates of legislative turnover than plurality systems (Matland and Studlar 2004), making it easier for women to run for and win office because they are not competing as newcomers against incumbents (Schwindt-Bayer 2005; Tremblay 2007). The most common account, however, focuses on the differences in district magnitudes across PR and SSD systems. In a majoritarian system, having only one seat per district creates a zero-sum game, requiring a man to be excluded if a woman is selected. In contrast, the availability of multiple seats in each district in PR systems permits—and, indeed, strongly compels—parties to "balance the ticket" by nominating candidates with a variety of profiles (Matland 1998; Stockemer 2008). The dynamics of party competition in PR systems further enhance the likelihood that women will become a focus

Table 9.1  Institutional Features of Top-Ranking Countries for Women's
Representation, March 2017

| Rank | Country | % Women | Electoral System | Gender Quotas |
| --- | --- | --- | --- | --- |
| 1 | Rwanda | 61.3% | List PR | Yes (RS) |
| 2 | Bolivia | 53.1% | List PR | Yes (LQ) |
| 3 | Cuba | 48.9% | Majority | No (Informal) |
| 4 | Iceland | 47.6% | List PR | Yes (PQ) |
| 5 | Nicaragua | 45.7% | List PR | Yes (LQ) |
| 6 | Sweden | 43.6% | List PR | Yes (PQ) |
| 7 | Senegal | 42.7% | List PR | Yes (LQ) |
| 8 | Mexico | 42.6% | MMP | Yes (LQ) |
| 9 | South Africa | 42.1% | List PR | Yes (PQ) |
| 10 | Finland | 42.0% | List PR | No (Informal) |

*Sources:* Inter-Parliamentary Union and International IDEA.

of political recruitment, as larger and more centrist parties respond to efforts by small leftist parties to promote women's election—pressures that are felt much less strongly in SSD systems (Matland and Studlar 1996).

Electoral gender quotas are a more recent phenomenon, growing out of increased recognition of the central role of electoral institutions and political parties in shaping women's opportunities to be selected as candidates. Quotas have now been introduced in more than 130 countries, the vast majority since the 1990s, largely in response to a combination of domestic mobilization by women's groups and growing international norms regarding gender-balanced decision making (Hughes, Krook, and Paxton 2015; Krook and True 2012; Towns 2012). These policies take three main forms: reserved seats, which set aside positions for women in political assemblies; party quotas, which involve commitments from political parties to nominate a minimum share of women; and legislative quotas, which require all parties to select a certain percentage of female candidates (Krook 2009). Quota measures vary in terms of where they appear, when they have been adopted, and how they attempt to alter candidate selection processes, but share a common goal: to increase the proportion of women nominated and elected to political office (Krook 2014). While varied in terms of their impact, comparative studies find that quotas are a key variable explaining why some countries have higher levels of female representation than others (Fallon, Swiss, and Viterna 2012; Paxton, Hughes, and Painter 2010; Tripp and Kang 2008), with quota policies generally becoming more, and not less, effective over time (Krook 2009; Paxton and Hughes 2015).

In addition to their separate effects, electoral systems and gender quotas also interact: quotas tend to be more successful in increasing the share of women elected when
implemented in PR systems with closed lists and high district magnitudes (Caul 1999;
Jones 2009). Some scholars, however, argue that variations across closed- and open-list
PR are due to institutional variables other than electoral systems per se, most notably
the use of placement mandates for quotas in closed-list systems that are not possible
when quotas are applied in open-list systems (Schmidt 2008). This perspective is consistent with work showing that quotas are most effective when they require at least
30 percent female candidates, include placement provisions ensuring that women are
placed in winnable list positions, and impose strong sanctions for noncompliance
(Schwindt-Bayer 2009; Rosen 2017). Given a plethora of case-study evidence indicating
strong resistance among many party elites to implementing quota provisions (Krook
2016), such mechanisms are crucial for translating quotas into practice, even in presumably favorable institutional contexts. At the same time, some quotas—notably reserved
seats—have been successful in increasing the share of women in parliament in countries
with SSD (Rosen 2017; Yoon 2008), suggesting that quotas can overcome some of the
barriers associated with electoral system design.

# ELECTORAL SYSTEMS
# AND GENDERED OUTCOMES

Scholars seeking to explain cross-national variations in women's parliamentary representation have investigated a series of potential explanations, including social, economic, cultural, and political factors that might favor or disadvantage women as political
candidates. Research focusing on Western countries notes correlations with women's
rates of education and labor force participation (Rosenbluth, Salmond, and Thies 2006;
Togeby 1994), whose positive effects are attributed to modernization processes that help
women move into higher social and economic roles, leading to greater influence in politics (Cherif 2015; Inglehart and Norris 2003). Cultural attitudes, measured by dominant religion (Rule 1987) and attitudes toward women in leadership roles (Paxton and
Kunovich 2003), also appear to play a role in shaping the election of women. Yet as studies have been expanded to include the non-Western world, many of these findings have
come under challenge, leading Matland (1998) to speculate that the dynamics explaining women's representation may operate distinctly across thresholds of development.
This intuition is confirmed by Rosen (2013), who finds that electoral systems and gender
quotas interact in crucial ways with levels of development to shape women's presence in
elected office.

Empirically, the turn to more global analyses has coincided with the widespread
introduction of gender quotas in countries with a wide range of social, economic, cultural, and political characteristics (Krook 2009). Notably, this new work consistently

shows that political factors have the most consistent impact on women's representation, regardless of the level of development (Kittilson 2006; Tremblay 2008; Tripp and Kang 2008). At the same time, more nuanced analyses of electoral systems also indicate that the advantage of PR over SSD is not absolute. While Yoon (2004) finds that Sub-Saharan African countries using PR elect more women than those with SSD or mixed-member electoral systems, Stockemer (2008) observes that the PR–SSD distinction holds in Europe but cannot account for variations across Latin America and the Caribbean. Addressing this mixed evidence, Krook and Schwindt-Bayer (2013) argue that, in fact, a closer look at the logic for why PR is supposedly superior to SSD relies closely on intervening variables—district magnitude, legislative turnover, party rules for candidate selection, and strategies employed by parties at election time—that are theoretically and empirically distinct from the electoral formula per se. While these factors may correlate with PR or SSD systems, they cannot be collapsed into a dichotomous classification of electoral formulas. Moser (2001) makes a similar case, pointing out that causal effects determining levels of women's representation appear to be linked more to other factors that vary widely within PR, SSD, and mixed-member electoral systems.

Two factors embedded within the design of individual electoral systems are district magnitude and ballot structure. District magnitude, shorthand for the number of positions available per electoral district, affects the incentives for parties to nominate women. In an SSD system, winning a legislative seat is a zero-sum game where a candidate from only one sex can win the election. The fact that men have traditionally been elected to these seats causes many parties to be conservative in their selection strategies, leading to male advantage as party elites view women as riskier to nominate (Valdini 2012). Interestingly, research on voter bias reveals this to be a poor electoral strategy, as citizens appear to be neutral toward, or to favor, women over men as political candidates (Golder et al. 2017; Murray, Krook, and Opello 2012). With PR, the availability of two or more seats per district reduces the pressures of this zero-sum game—and, indeed, as district magnitude increases, the nomination of women is often seen in positive-sum terms. Parties not only are able to make room for women without displacing men but also may view their nomination as a means to present a more "balanced" ticket. Studies show that in list systems, parties often seek candidates from a variety of backgrounds to appeal to different parts of the electorate (Reiser 2014), an opening that female party activists in many countries have exploited to argue in favoring of including women among these sectors (Kittilson 2006; Lovenduski and Norris 1993).

Comparative research confirms this pattern empirically (Tremblay 2008). In a pioneering study of twenty-three advanced industrial states, Rule (1987) finds that, among PR systems, those with larger district magnitudes have more women in office than those with smaller district magnitudes. The relationship also holds within countries: in Ireland, where district magnitude varies from three to five, Engstrom (1987) observes that more women get elected from the four- and five-seat districts than from the three-seat districts. Research on subnational politics reveals a similar tendency in the United States, where women are more likely to be elected in multiseat ("at large") districts than in single-seat ones (Matland and Brown 1992; Trounstine and Valdini

2008). Yet the effects of district magnitude are not necessarily linear. As Schwindt-Bayer (2005) points out, there appears to be a diminishing returns effect, whereby increases in district magnitude at lower levels (from one to two or three to four, for example) are likely to lead to larger increases in the election of women than increases in district magnitude at higher levels (from seventy-five to seventy-six, for instance), leading her to conclude that logging district magnitude offers a more appropriate specification of this variable in large-n cross-sectional statistical analyses.

Other studies, however, find little or no relationship between district magnitude and women's election to office (Kittilson 2006; Matland 1993; Schmidt 2008). To explain these mixed results, Matland and Taylor (1997) suggest that party magnitude may be a better predictor than district magnitude per se. As it is rare for one party to win every single seat, their logic goes, parties make calculations about whether to include women and where to put them on the ballot based on the number of seats they expect to win (party magnitude), rather than the total number of seats available (district magnitude). Empirical research taking party magnitude into account lends support to this line of reasoning (Jones 2004, 2009; Schmidt and Saunders 2004; Schwindt-Bayer, Malecki, and Crisp 2010). This variable also explains why quotas may lead to higher or lower numbers of women elected than stipulated by the quota. For example, the Tunisian parity law requiring that party lists alternate between men and women resulted in only 31.3 percent women in parliament in 2014. Further analysis reveals that, while all parties had conformed with the parity provision, most succeeded in electing only one member—and nearly all had placed men at the top of their lists (Krook 2016). Recognizing the role of party magnitude in shaping quota impact, presidential decrees in Argentina explicitly specify how quotas apply depending on how many seats a party expects to win in a given electoral district (Krook 2009).

Ballot structure, in turn, refers to whether party ballots are closed, open, or flexible. In systems with closed ballots, parties rank their candidates, who are elected in that order, depending on how many seats the party wins in the election. Where ballots are open, parties provide a list of candidates, often arranged alphabetically, and voters choose among these candidates, with those receiving the most votes being elected. Flexible lists are a variant of open lists: parties rank-order their candidates, but voters have the option of casting a vote either for the list as its stands or for individual candidates on that list—who, if they receive a certain threshold of votes, might move ahead of other more highly ranked candidates and gain election. Literature on gender and electoral systems posits two scenarios concerning the role of ballot structure. Closed lists may have a positive impact on women's representation in countries where party leaders are more supportive than the general public, as placing women highly on the lists can neutralize voter discrimination against female candidates. Yet, if parties are less supportive, open or flexible lists can provide an advantage for women, as citizens can help overcome party bias by casting preference votes for women (Golder et al. 2017).

Comparative studies that take ballot structure into account generally find that closed lists are correlated with higher numbers of women in office (Caul 1999; Jones 2009). The introduction of quotas has strengthened this association, with scholars emphasizing the benefits of closed lists for ensuring that quotas have their intended effects (Krook and Schwindt-Bayer 2013). This is largely because the closed-list structure, when combined with a placement mandate requiring that women be placed on winnable positions on party ballots, can contribute to a roughly similar share of women nominated and elected. When there is no such placement mandate, however, parties tend to place women in lower, and thus less electable, positions on party lists, undermining the full effects of gender quotas (Krook 2016; Rosen 2017; Schwindt-Bayer 2009). These patterns lead Schmidt (2008) to conclude that differences imputed to ballot structure—namely, the advantage of closed- versus open-list PR—is due to the presence of placement mandates for quotas in closed-list systems that are not possible in open-list PR.

Open-list systems are viewed as less favorable to women's representation due to the ability of voters to choose male over female candidates, even when more women appear on the list stemming from quota requirements (Jones 2009; Wauters, Weekers, and Maddens 2010). Research on Brazil, for example, attributes the low share of women in the Chamber of Deputies, despite the existence of a 30 percent quota law applying to these elections since 1997, to the use of open lists (Crocker, Schmidt, and Araujo 2017; Miguel 2008). Interestingly, experimental evidence uncovers a strong and consistent pro-female bias among Brazilian voters (Aguilar, Cunow, and Desposato 2015), suggesting that voters may not be the driving force behind this poor result—but, rather, other factors like the tendency among parties to channel the vast majority of campaign funds and resources to men (Sacchet and Speck 2012). Seeking to resolve these debates, Schwindt-Bayer et al. (2010) employ a comparative research design of open-list systems and conclude that the effect of ballot structure depends on citizen attitudes toward gender equality, with women winning more preference where voters hold more positive views. Valdini (2013) similarly finds that preference voting combined with cultural bias against women has negative consequences for women's representation. Taken together, literature on gender and electoral systems thus provides a more nuanced view of the distinction between PR and SSD systems, foregrounding the importance of additional electoral rules—gender quotas, district/party magnitude, and ballot structure—in shaping the opportunities for women to be elected.

# GENDERED ANALYSES OF ELECTORAL SYSTEMS

Applying a gender lens to electoral systems does not simply generate insights about women's representation, however. Such a focus can also provide fresh perspectives—and thus important new theoretical advances—in relation to central questions in political analysis. One such area is research on party competition, specifically "contagion." Rooted in classic contributions in the study of political parties (Duverger 1954; Epstein 1967; Kirchheimer 1966), contagion theory conceptualizes how the dynamics of party competition—whether initiated from the left or right of the ideological spectrum—lead to innovations in party platforms and organizational practices over time. Given that parties are generally conservative organizations, the sources of change are of intrinsic interest to both activists and scholars.

Although many of these intuitions were already present in gender and politics research in the 1980s and 1990s (Kolinsky 1991; Lovenduski and Norris 1993), Matland and Studlar (1996) were the first to use the word "contagion" in this context. They proposed that the dynamics of party competition drive changes in women's representation, noting that "as smaller but competitive parties, usually on the political fringe, start to promote women actively, larger parties will move to emulate them" (Matland and Studlar 1996, 712). In an advance over existing contagion theory, Matland and Studlar (1996) foreground the role of electoral systems in structuring party incentives, using district-level comparisons of PR in Norway and first past the post (FPTP) in Canada. They theorize, on this basis, that contagion is more likely to occur in countries governed by PR, where there are more opportunities for small parties to emerge, the political costs of responding are smaller, and the threat of losing voters is more serious. This theory is widely accepted as an account of how and why parties reorient themselves on the question of women's representation.

A more recent wave of studies has begun to revisit the concept of contagion, theorizing and testing logical extensions of the original formulation (Cowell-Meyers 2011; Davidson-Schmich 2010; Kenny and Mackay 2014; Thames and Williams 2013). Focusing on the case of Northern Ireland, Cowell-Meyers (2011) theorizes in a more expansive way the contextual conditions under which contagion may or may not occur, embedding the role of the electoral system within a wider range of factors that might facilitate or undermine innovation and imitation among parties, including historical moments and pressures from international actors. Studying Germany, Davidson-Schmich (2010) explores the degree to which gains in women's representation spill over across the two parts of the mixed-member electoral system. Her conclusions are largely negative: parties with quotas only minimally comply with these commitments, parties without quotas tend to lag behind those with these provisions, and parties of all types have stopped short of nominating large numbers of women to elections where quotas do not apply. These contributions provide new insights into the constraints and opportunities that electoral systems pose with regard to increasing women's representation. They also, however, nuance received explanations of party behavior and more deeply contextualize the determinants of electoral system effects.

A second area of research is electoral reform. Existing research tends to define "electoral reform" in narrow terms, focusing primarily on changes in electoral formulas (Lijphart 1994) and, in turn, the role of political parties and their motivations for supporting or opposing change. The result is "universal" and "single track" explanations, positing that reforms occur when and if parties in power have something to gain from moving to a new electoral formula. Recent work makes the case, however, for categorizing a much broader array of modifications to electoral rules as "electoral reform" (Hazan and Leyenaar 2012), while also recognizing that actors other than political parties might influence, or have a stake in, the shape of these regulations (Katz 2011; Renwick 2010). This approach opens up the possibility of multiple paths to electoral reform, driven by diverse and varied motives.

Celis, Krook, and Meier (2011) argue, in this context, that the adoption of gender quotas should be reconceptualized as instances of electoral reform. While quotas tend to be analyzed in relation to candidate selection, they also shape electoral outcomes in seeking to influence who may be nominated and elected. This is especially the case for quotas taking the form of reserved seats and legislative quotas, both of which entail altering the rules governing elections through changes to constitutions and/or electoral laws. The sheer number and range of countries adopting the measures—more than eighty democratic, semidemocratic, and nondemocratic states—make national-level quotas the widest-reaching electoral reforms of recent years. Approaching quotas from this perspective points to the need to revise prevailing frameworks to incorporate a wider range of actors, motivations, strategies, and paths to electoral reform (Celis, Krook, and Meier 2011).

First, research on quota adoption confers a more prominent role to "outsider" actors like social movements, whether operating at the national or transnational level (Kittilson 2006; Krook 2006). The expectation that parties are the principal actors driving electoral reform thus needs to be abandoned in favor of a more inductive approach. Second, with the move away from parties and elites as the primary actors, it is necessary to theorize motivations beyond simply seat maximization as a driving force behind electoral reform. Other possibilities suggested by the quota literature include principled motivations, empty gestures, and international pressures (Bush 2011; Krook 2009; Towns 2012). Third, quota scholars highlight the importance of discursive struggles as a strategy for electoral reform, presenting an opening for civil society actors to critique and redefine political values to gain support for quotas (Freidenvall 2005; Scott 2005). Fourth, taken together, cases of quota adoption point to a variety of pathways to reform, involving distinct configurations of actors, motivations, and strategies (Dahlerup and Freidenvall 2005; Krook 2009). The quota literature thus suggests that limiting research to political elites and their motivations and actions may lead scholars to overlook a wider array of explanatory forces and factors.

A third area of research is voter behavior, specifically manifestations of voter bias. In the case of gender, existing work is ambivalent as to the nature and effects of bias against female candidates (Black and Erickson 2003; Fulton 2012; Lawless 2004). A new wave of studies, however, has emerged in recent years, exploiting aspects of electoral system design to parse out causal effects. Employing a comparative research strategy, Valdini (2013) analyzes citizen attitudes about women as leaders in countries with the "personal vote"—open-list PR and SSD—and finds that when voter bias against women is high, personal voting has statistically significant and negative effects on women's election; when bias is low, the effect is neutral, not positive. Luhiste (2015) approaches this question from the perspective of party elites by comparing party rankings across closed-list and ordered open-list PR, finding that women enjoy more viable list rankings—that is, party bias against women is less—in more gender-equal societies. Yet, both of these studies only test one type of bias, leaving open the question of their roles relative to one another.

A growing literature on open-list PR—especially systems involving ordered lists—points out that these systems offer a unique opportunity to ascertain the role of voter versus party bias against women. In systems with pure open-list PR, the role of parties in shaping women's electoral successes and failures remains largely obscured, although new studies do attempt to nuance quantitative findings suggesting voter bias with more qualitative insights indicating party bias. In Brazil, for example, the introduction of a gender quota has led to a decline in women's electoral fortunes, suggesting voter bias against these women. Yet, upon closer inspection, these patterns can be attributed to parties nominating women who had no intention of actually competing for votes (Miguel 2008). Evidence from Finland lends nuance to arguments about voter bias by finding that 72 percent of men and 53 percent of women vote for candidates of their own sex (Giger et al. 2014; Holli and Wass 2010). In other words, women split their votes more or less evenly among male and female candidates, while men express strong preferences for male candidates. These studies treat the list itself as neutral in its effects, due to names being listed alphabetically. An analysis of Spanish Senate elections, however, suggests that even alphabetical listings can be engineered by parties to steer outcomes, with parties nominating female—but not male—candidates based on their surname to ensure that preferred male candidates are elected (Esteve-Volart and Bagues 2012).

Open-list systems with ordered lists, however, facilitate comparisons of the respective roles of voters and party elites. In these systems, parties rank-order their candidates, but voters can cast votes for individual candidates on these lists, with preference voting being mandatory or optional depending on the country. Candidates receiving a certain threshold of votes may move up the list and be elected ahead of candidates ranked more highly by the party. Taking advantage of this institutional design to compare the role of voters and elites, Kunovich (2012) finds that, in three consecutive elections in Poland, voters improved women's list placements through preference voting. This pattern held across all parties, but positive shifts were most notable in parties where women's presence and list placement were lower. Consequently, the number of women elected was higher than would have been expected based on parties' preferences. Data from Czech elections reaches a similar conclusion. Stegmaier, Tosun, and Vlachová (2014) note that women's representation increased dramatically between 2006 and 2010, despite a lower share of women nominated in 2010 and a similar number of women appearing in the top five positions on party lists. The authors attribute this change to new rules giving voters more power over which candidates won seats by expanding the number of preference votes and lowering the threshold of votes needed for candidates to move up the party lists. These within-case research designs, comparing party and voter preferences, provide innovative insights into enduring questions about voter behavior—and, in this case, further bolster the case for elite bias, and not voter bias, as the main factor responsible for women's underrepresentation.

# EMERGING DIRECTIONS OF RESEARCH

Gendered research on electoral systems has developed substantially over the last few decades, exploring how electoral arrangements affect women's representation and, increasingly, what gendered dynamics might reveal about political phenomena—like party competition, policy change, and voter behavior—more generally. While work on these questions is likely to continue, recent debates point to new areas of research further building on gendered electoral system analysis. One line of inquiry relates to the concept and centrality of "gender," which many view as the major analytical contribution of feminist research (Hawkesworth 2006). Yet new theoretical and empirical research on intersectionality seeks to draw attention to the ways in which multiple facets of identity interact to shape individual experiences and outcomes (Hancock 2007). At first glance, this focus appears to undermine studies of gender, making it impossible to speak of "women" as a group, much less generalize about gendered trends. As Weldon (2006) observes, however, systematic research on multiple identities together—like gender, race, and class, among others—can offer a better sense of each facet's effects by examining different instances of interactions with other identities.

Empirically, scholars have taken the lens of intersectionality to the study of electoral systems via a focus on quotas. More than a hundred countries have some type of gender quota, whether at the national or party level, while about forty countries guarantee the representation of minority groups—with "minority" encompassing a host of different identities, including race, ethnicity, language, religion, nationality, age, and disability (Krook and O'Brien 2010). Crucially, in most of these countries, only one group receives such guarantees. Yet by targeting one social category, preferential rules may undermine the election of the other historically marginalized groups. In a cross-national study of the representation of minority women in parliaments, Hughes (2011) confirms this expectation, finding that states with minority quotas tend to elect fewer women than countries without such measures. However, in cases where regulations are in place for both women and ethnic minorities ("tandem quotas"), minority women can benefit from this dual attention. Although Krook and Nugent (2016) also find some evidence for the effects of tandem quotas at the party level, Bird (2016) emphasizes that such an outcome is rare, as quotas for women and minorities are seldom "nested" but rather operate separately.

These questions connect to a second emerging line of research, comparing the mechanisms that facilitate the representation of women versus that of other marginalized groups. Although work on group representation has tended to treat exclusion on the basis of gender and race as posing similar challenges to democratic legitimacy (Mansbridge 1999; Phillips 1995), most scholars have attended to one of these groups and then generalized their findings to the other group. A growing body of comparative work on electoral systems, however, calls this tendency into question (in this volume, see Bowler and Lublin). Closed-list PR has long been viewed as being more favorable to the election of both women and minorities, as the "ticket balancing" incentives of PR can lead parties to be more willing to nominate "diversity" candidates (Norris 2004). While the disadvantages of single-seat districts are similar for female and minority candidates, there are important differences in the advantages of PR for each group (Krook and Moser 2013). For women, multiparty competition based on party lists can spur the adoption of gender quotas (Matland and Studlar 1996), which are also easier to implement in PR given the use of lists. For racial and ethnic minorities, in contrast, PR can foster the emergence of ethnic parties—which tend to elect members of their own group—due to the lower electoral thresholds necessary to gain representation (Norris 2004).

Yet new empirical evidence calls into question the robustness of these relationships. Some studies find, for example, that SSD systems may be more favorable to women than PR in certain circumstances, for example in postcommunist countries (Moser and Scheiner 2012). Others point out that SSD can in fact elect greater numbers of ethnic minorities than PR. This is because districts with a large geographic concentration of racial and ethnic minorities may prompt mainstream parties to nominate minority candidates, resulting in similar or even greater levels of minority election than in PR (Moser 2008; Reynolds 2011). At the same time, the logic of ethnic parties as the main avenue for minority representation in PR rests on the assumption of ethnic voting, which in reality varies across countries and groups, affecting incentives to form ethnic parties and for mainstream parties to nominate ethnic candidates (Moser 2008).

Research looking at both groups together provides additional nuance. In a study of ethnic parties and women's representation, Holmsten, Moser, and Slosar (2010) test the hypothesis that such parties will be less likely to elect women. They find that this is the case only in PR systems that do not involve gender quotas. In countries using SSD, in contrast, ethnic parties actually elect more women than nonethnic parties. Yet, analyzing data from twenty countries in the West from 2000 to 2010, Hughes (2015) observes that Muslim ethnic minority women are increasingly elected to parliament in countries with PR. In comparison, Muslim ethnic minority men are elected across a range of electoral systems. These findings point to the need for further research to unravel both the intersectional and comparative group dynamics leading to these different patterns of political representation.

A third emerging line of study involves examining the dynamics of representation after elections. Carey and Shugart (1995) argue that seat allocation formulas—related to the degree of party leadership control over access to and rank on ballots, the degree to which candidate are elected on individual votes, and whether voters cast party- or candidate-level votes—affect whether candidates will seek to cultivate a personal versus a party reputation. This work implies that how candidates are elected may affect how they behave in office and, moreover, how constituents might view their representational role and impact (see Crisp and Simoneau, this volume). Despite large literatures on women's legislative behavior, as well as women's impact on citizens' political attitudes and levels of engagement, research has only recently begun to investigate how electoral reforms like quotas might reinforce or change these existing patterns (Franceschet, Krook, and Piscopo 2012). Very little of this work to date links these findings to differences across electoral systems, although these may create distinct opportunities and incentives, as well as constraints, for elected women. Together with the other emerging areas of research outlined earlier, this suggests a rich agenda for future work on gender and electoral systems, even in light of rapidly expanding insights into existing research questions.

## NOTES

1. See the website of the Inter-Parliamentary Union, http://www.ipu.org/wmn-e/arc /world010317.htm.
2. See the website of the Inter-Parliamentary Union, http://www.ipu.org/wmn-e/arc /world010197.htm.

## REFERENCES

Aguilar, Rosario, Saul Cunow, and Scott Desposato. "Choice Sets, Gender, and Candidate Choice in Brazil." *Electoral Studies* 39 (2015): 230–242.

Bird, Karen. "Intersections of Exclusion: The Institutional Dynamics of Combined Gender and Ethnic Quota Systems." *Politics, Groups, and Identities* 4, no. 2 (2016): 284–306.

Black, Jerome H., and Lynda Erickson. "Women Candidates and Voter Bias: Do Women Politicians Need to Be Better?" *Electoral Studies* 22, no. 1 (2003): 81–100.

Bush, Sarah Sunn. "International Politics and the Spread of Quotas for Women in Legislatures." *International Organization* 65, no. 1 (2011): 103–137.

Carey, John M., and Matthew Soberg Shugart. "Incentives to Cultivate a Personal Vote: A Rank Ordering of Electoral Formulas." *Electoral Studies* 14, no. 4 (1995): 417–439.

Castles, Francis. "Female Legislative Representation and the Electoral System." *Politics* 1, no. 2 (1981): 21–27.

Caul, Miki. "Women's Representation in Parliament: The Role of Political Parties." *Party Politics* 5, no. 1 (1999): 79–98.

Celis, Karen, Mona Lena Krook, and Petra Meier. "The Rise of Gender Quota Laws: Expanding the Spectrum of Determinants for Electoral Reform." *West European Politics* 34, no. 3 (2011): 514–530.

Cherif, Feryal M. *Myths about Women's Rights: How, Where, and Why Rights Advance.* New York: Oxford University Press, 2015.

Cowell-Meyers, Kimberly. "A Collarette on a Donkey: The Northern Ireland Women's Coalition and the Limitations of Contagion Theory." *Political Studies* 59, no. 2 (2011): 411–431.

Crocker, Adriana, Gregory D. Schmidt, and Clara Araujo. *Gender Quotas in South America's Big Three: National and Subnational Impacts.* Lanham: Lexington Books, 2017.

Dahlerup, Drude, and Lenita Freidenvall. "Quotas as a Fast Track to Equal Representation for Women." *International Feminist Journal of Politics* 7, no. 1 (2005): 26–48.

Davidson-Schmich, Louise K. "Gender Quota Compliance and Contagion in the 2009 Bundestag Election." *German Politics and Society* 28, no. 3 (2010): 133–155.

Duverger, Maurice. *Political Parties: Their Organization and Activity in the Modern State.* London: Methuen, 1954.

Engstrom, Richard L. "District Magnitude and the Election of Women to the Irish Dail." *Electoral Studies* 6, no. 2 (1987): 123–132.

Epstein, Leon. *Political Parties in Western Democracies.* New York: Praeger, 1967.

Esteve-Volart, Berta, and Manuel Bagues. "Are Women Pawns in the Political Game? Evidence from Elections to the Spanish Senate." *Journal of Public Economics* 96, no. 3 (2012): 387–399.

Fallon, Kathleen M., Liam Swiss, and Jocelyn Viterna. "Resolving the Democracy Paradox: Democratization and Women's Legislative Representation in Developing Nations, 1975 to 2009." *American Sociological Review* 77, no. 3 (2012): 380–408.

Franceschet, Susan, Mona Lena Krook, and Jennifer M. Piscopo, eds. *The Impact of Gender Quotas.* New York: Oxford University Press, 2012.

Freidenvall, Lenita. "A Discursive Struggle: The Swedish National Federation of Social Democratic Women and Gender Quotas." *NORA* 13, no. 3 (2005): 175–186.

Fulton, Sarah A. "Running Backwards and in High Heels: The Gendered Quality Gap and Incumbent Electoral Success." *Political Research Quarterly* 65, no. 2 (2012): 303–314.

Giger, Nathalie, Anne Maria Holli, Zoe Lefkofridi, and Hanna Wass. "The Gender Gap in Same-Gender Voting: The Role of Context." *Electoral Studies* 35 (2014): 303–314.

Golder, Sona N., Laura B. Stephenson, Karine Van der Straeten, André Blais, Damien Bol, Philipp Harfst, and Jean-François Laslier. "Votes for Women: Electoral Systems and Support for Female Candidates." *Politics & Gender* 13, no. 1 (2017): 107–131.

Hancock, Ange-Marie. "When Multiplication Doesn't Equal Quick Addition: Examining Intersectionality as a Research Paradigm." *Perspectives on Politics* 5, no. 1 (2007): 63–79.

Hawkesworth, Mary E. *Feminist Inquiry: From Political Conviction to Methodological Innovation.* New Brunswick, NJ: Rutgers University Press, 2006.

Hazan, Reuven Y., and Monique Leyenaar, eds. *Understanding Electoral Reform.* New York: Routledge, 2012.

Holli, Anne M., and Hanna Wass. "Gender-Based Voting in the Parliamentary Elections of 2007 in Finland." *European Journal of Political Research* 49, no. 5 (2010): 598–630.

Holmsten, Stephanie, Robert G. Moser, and Mary Slosar. "Do Ethnic Parties Exclude Women?" *Comparative Political Studies* 43, no. 10 (2010): 1179–1201.

Hughes, Melanie M. "Intersectionality, Quotas, and Minority Women's Political Representation Worldwide." *American Political Science Review* 105, no. 3 (2011): 604–620.

Hughes, Melanie M. "Electoral Systems and the Legislative Representation of Muslim Ethnic Minority Women in the West, 2000–2010." *Parliamentary Affairs* 69, no. 3 (2015): 548–568.

Hughes, Melanie M., Mona Lena Krook, and Pamela Paxton. "Transnational Women's Activism and the Global Diffusion of Gender Quotas." *International Studies Quarterly* 59, no. 2 (2015): 357–372.

Inglehart, Ronald, and Pippa Norris. *Rising Tide: Gender Equality and Cultural Change around the World.* New York: Cambridge University Press, 2003.

Inter-Parliamentary Union. *Women in Parliament in 2016.* Geneva: Inter-Parliamentary Union, 2017.

Jones, Mark P. "Quota Legislation and the Election of Women: Learning from the Costa Rican Experience." *Journal of Politics* 66, no. 4 (2004): 1203–1223.

Jones, Mark P. "Gender Quotas, Electoral Laws, and the Election of Women: Evidence from the Latin American Vanguard." *Comparative Political Studies* 42, no. 1 (2009): 56–81.

Katz, Richard. "Understanding Democracy as a Cause of Electoral Reform: Jurisprudence and Electoral Reform." *West European Politics* 34, no. 3 (2011): 587–606.

Kenny, Meryl, and Fiona Mackay. "When Is Contagion Not Very Contagious? Dynamics of Women's Political Representation in Scotland." *Parliamentary Affairs* 67, no. 4 (2014): 866–886.

Kirchheimer, Otto. "The Transformation of Western European Party Systems." In *Political Parties and Political Development*, ed. Joseph LaPalombara and Myron Weiner. Princeton, NJ: Princeton University Press, 1966.

Kittilson, Miki Caul. *Challenging Parties, Changing Parliaments: Women and Elected Office in Contemporary Western Europe*. Columbus: Ohio State University Press, 2006.

Kolinsky, Eva. "Political Participation and Parliamentary Careers: Women's Quotas in West Germany." *West European Politics* 14, no. 1 (1991): 56–72.

Krook, Mona Lena. "Reforming Representation: The Diffusion of Candidate Gender Quotas Worldwide." *Politics & Gender* 2, no. 3 (2006): 303–327.

Krook, Mona Lena. *Quotas for Women in Politics: Gender and Candidate Selection Reform Worldwide*. New York: Oxford University Press, 2009.

Krook, Mona Lena. "Electoral Gender Quotas: Concepts and Comparative Analysis." *Comparative Political Studies* 47, no. 9 (2014): 1268–1293.

Krook, Mona Lena. "Contesting Gender Quotas: Dynamics of Resistance." *Politics, Groups, and Identities* 4, no. 2 (2016): 268–283.

Krook, Mona Lena, Joni Lovenduski, and Judith Squires. "Gender Quotas and Models of Political Citizenship." *British Journal of Political Science* 39, no. 4 (2009): 781–803.

Krook, Mona Lena, and Robert G. Moser. "Electoral Rules and Political Inclusion." *Perspectives on Politics* 11, no. 3 (2013): 814–818.

Krook, Mona Lena, and Mary Nugent. "Intersectional Institutions: Representing Women and Ethnic Minorities in the British Labour Party." *Party Politics* 22, no. 5 (2016): 620–630.

Krook, Mona Lena, and Diana Z. O'Brien. "The Politics of Group Representation: Quotas for Women and Minorities Worldwide." *Comparative Politics* 42, no. 3 (2010): 253–272.

Krook, Mona Lena, and Leslie Schwindt-Bayer. "Electoral Institutions." In *Oxford Handbook on Gender and Politics*, ed. Georgina Waylen, Karen Celis, Johanna Kantola, and S. Laurel Weldon, 554–578. New York: Oxford University Press, 2013.

Krook, Mona Lena, and Jacqui True. "Rethinking the Life Cycles of International Norms: The United Nations and the Global Promotion of Gender Equality." *European Journal of International Relations* 18, no. 1 (2012): 103–127.

Kunovich, Sheri. "Unexpected Winners: The Significance of an Open-List System on Women's Representation in Poland." *Politics & Gender* 8, no. 2 (2012): 153–177.

Lawless, Jennifer L. "Politics of Presence? Congresswomen and Symbolic Representation." *Political Research Quarterly* 57, no. 1 (2004): 81–99.

Lijphart, Arend. *Electoral Systems and Party Systems*. Oxford: Oxford University Press, 1994.

Lovenduski, Joni, and Pippa Norris, eds. *Gender and Party Politics*. London: Sage, 1993.

Luhiste, Maarja. "Party Gatekeepers' Support for Viable Female Candidacy in PR-List Systems." *Politics & Gender* 11, no. 1 (2015): 89–116.

Mansbridge, Jane. "Should Blacks Represent Blacks and Women Represent Women? A Contingent 'Yes.'" *Journal of Politics* 61, no. 3 (1999): 628–657.

Matland, Richard. "Institutional Variables Affecting Female Representation in National Legislatures: The Case of Norway." *Journal of Politics* 55, no. 3 (1993): 737–755.

Matland, Richard. "Women's Legislative Representation in National Legislatures: A Comparison of Democracies in Developed and Developing Countries." *Legislative Studies Quarterly* 28, no. 1 (1998): 109–125.

Matland, Richard E., and Deborah Dwight Brown. "District Magnitude's Effect on Female Representation in U.S. State Legislatures." *Legislative Studies Quarterly* 17, no. 4 (1992): 469–492.

Matland, Richard E., and Donley T. Studlar. "The Contagion of Women Candidates in Single-Member District and Proportional Representation Electoral Systems: Canada and Norway." *Journal of Politics* 58, no. 3 (1996): 707–733.

Matland, Richard E., and Donley T. Studlar. "Determinants of Legislative Turnover: A Cross-National Analysis." *British Journal of Political Science* 34, no. 1 (2004): 87–108.

Matland, Richard E., and Michelle M. Taylor. "Electoral System Effects on Women's Representation: Theoretical Arguments and Evidence from Costa Rica." *Comparative Political Studies* 30, no. 2 (1997): 186–210.

Miguel, Luis F. "Political Representation and Gender in Brazil." *Bulletin of Latin American Research* 27, no. 2 (2008): 197–214.

Moser, Robert G. "The Effects of Electoral Systems on Women's Representation in Post-Communist States." *Electoral Studies* 20, no. 3 (2001): 353–369.

Moser, Robert G. "Electoral Systems and the Representation of Ethnic Minorities: Evidence from Russia" *Comparative Politics* 40, no. 3 (2008): 273–292.

Moser, Robert G., and Ethan Scheiner. *Electoral Systems and Political Context.* New York: Cambridge University Press, 2012.

Murray, Rainbow, Mona Lena Krook, and Katherine A. R. Opello. "Why Are Gender Quotas Adopted? Parity and Party Pragmatism in France." *Political Research Quarterly* 65, no. 3 (2012): 529–543.

Norris, Pippa. *Electoral Engineering: Voting Rules and Political Behavior.* New York: Cambridge University Press, 2004.

Paxton, Pamela, and Melanie M. Hughes. "The Increasing Effectiveness of National Gender Quotas, 1990–2010." *Legislative Studies Quarterly* 40, no. 3 (2015): 331–362.

Paxton, Pamela, Melanie M. Hughes, and Matthew A. Painter. "Growth in Women's Political Representation: A Longitudinal Exploration of Democracy, Electoral Systems, and Gender Quotas." *European Journal of Political Research* 49, no. 1 (2010): 25–52.

Paxton, Pamela Marie, and Sheri Kunovich. "Women's Political Representation: The Importance of Ideology." *Social Forces* 82, no. 1 (2003): 87–113.

Phillips, Anne. *The Politics of Presence.* New York: Oxford University Press, 1995.

Reiser, Marion. "The Universe of Group Representation in Germany." *International Political Science Review* 3, no. 1 (2014): 55–66.

Renwick, Alan. *Changing the Rules of Democracy: The Politics of Electoral Reform.* Cambridge: Cambridge University Press, 2010.

Reynolds, Andrew. *Designing Democracy in a Dangerous World.* New York: Oxford University Press, 2011.

Rosen, Jennifer. "The Effects of Political Institutions on Women's Political Representation." *Political Research Quarterly* 66, no. 2 (2013): 306–321.

Rosen, Jennifer. "Gender Quotas for Women in National Politics." *Social Science Research* 66 (2017): 82–101.

Rosenbluth, Frances, Rob Salmond, and Michael F. Thies. "Welfare Works: Explaining Female Legislative Representation." *Politics & Gender* 2, no. 2 (2006): 165–192.

Rule, Wilma. "Electoral Systems, Contextual Factors, and Women's Opportunity for Election to Parliament in Twenty-Three Democracies." *Western Political Quarterly* 40, no. 3 (1987): 477–498.

Sacchet, Teresa, and Bruno Wilhelm Speck. "Financiamento eleitoral, representação política e gênero." *Opinião Pública* 18, no. 1 (2012): 177–197.

Schmidt, Gregory D. "The Election of Women in List PR systems: Testing the Conventional Wisdom." *Electoral Studies* 28, no. 2 (2008): 190–203.

Schmidt, Gregory D., and Kyle L. Saunders. "Effective Quotas, Relative Party Magnitude, and the Success of Female Candidates: Peruvian Municipal Elections in Comparative Perspective." *Comparative Political Studies* 37, no. 6 (2004): 704–734.

Schwindt-Bayer, Leslie A. "The Incumbency Disadvantage and Women's Election to Legislative Office." *Electoral Studies* 24, no. 2 (2005): 227–244.

Schwindt-Bayer, Leslie A. "Making Quotas Work: The Effect of Gender Quota Laws on the Election of Women." *Legislative Studies Quarterly* 34, no. 1 (2009): 5–28.

Schwindt-Bayer, Leslie A., Michael Malecki, and Brian F. Crisp. "Candidate Gender and Electoral Success in Single Transferable Vote Systems." *British Journal of Political Science* 40, no. 3 (2010): 693–709.

Scott, Joan Wallach. *Parite!: Sexual Equality and the Crisis of French Universalism.* Chicago: University of Chicago Press, 2005.

Stegmaier, Mary, Jale Tosun, and Klára Vlachová. "Women's Parliamentary Representation in the Czech Republic: Does Preference Voting Matter?" *East European Politics and Societies* 28, no. 1 (2014): 187–204.

Stockemer, Daniel. "Women's Representation: A Comparison between Europe and the Americas." *Politics* 28, no. 2 (2008): 65–73.

Thames, Frank C., and Margaret S. Williams. *Contagious Representation: Women's Political Representation in Democracies around the World.* New York: New York University Press, 2013.

Togeby, Lise. "Political Implications of Increasing Numbers of Women in the Labor Force." *Comparative Political Studies* 27, no. 2 (1994): 211–240.

Towns, Ann E. "Norms and Social Hierarchies: Understanding International Policy Diffusion 'From Below.'" *International Organization* 66, no. 2 (2012): 179–209.

Tremblay, Manon. "Democracy, Representation, and Women: A Comparative Analysis." *Democratization* 14, no. 4 (2007): 533–553.

Tremblay, Manon, ed. *Women and Legislative Representation: Electoral Systems, Political Parties, and Sex Quotas.* New York: Palgrave, 2008.

Tripp, Aili, and Alice Kang. "The Global Impact of Quotas: On the Fast Track to Increased Female Legislative Representation." *Comparative Political Studies* 41, no. 3 (2008): 338–361.

Trounstine, Jessica, and Melody E. Valdini. "The Context Matters: The Effects of Single-Member versus At-Large Districts on City Council Diversity." *American Journal of Political Science* 52, no. 3 (2008): 554–569.

Valdini, Melody Ellis. "A Deterrent to Diversity: The Conditional Effect of Electoral Rules on the Nomination of Women Candidates." *Electoral Studies* 31, no. 4 (2012): 740–749.

Valdini, Melody Ellis. "Electoral Institutions and the Manifestation of Bias: The Effect of the Personal Vote on the Representation of Women." *Politics & Gender* 9, no. 1 (2013): 76–92.

Wauters, Bram, Karolien Weekers, and Bart Maddens. "Explaining the Number of Preferential Votes for Women in an Open-List PR System." *Acta Politica* 45, no. 4 (2010): 468–490.

Weldon, S. Laurel. "The Structure of Intersectionality." *Politics & Gender* 2, no. 2 (2006): 235–248.

Yoon, Mi Yung. "Explaining Women's Legislative Representation in Sub-Saharan Africa." *Legislative Studies Quarterly* 29, no. 3 (2004): 447–468.

Yoon, Mi Yung. "Special Seats for Women in the National Legislature: The Case of Tanzania." *Africa Today* 55, no. 1 (2008): 61–86.

CHAPTER 10

........................................................................................

# ELECTORAL SYSTEMS AND VOTER TURNOUT

........................................................................................

DANIEL M. SMITH

## INTRODUCTION

........................................................................................

WHAT is the relationship between electoral systems and voter turnout? To answer this question, it is helpful to begin with the more general question of why voters turn out on Election Day at all. The pioneering rational choice work by Downs (1957), Tullock (1967), and Riker and Ordeshook (1968) argued that closely contested, competitive elections will increase the chance that a single voter might become "pivotal" in determining the outcome, and thus increase the incentives for voters who care about the outcome to turn out and vote. A problem is that such pivotal voter theories, if taken seriously, would predict increasingly lower turnout rates as the size of the electorate expands—even in competitive races—since the probability of any one voter becoming pivotal would get closer and closer to zero (Palfrey and Rosenthal 1985).[1] And yet citizens still turn out to vote.

To address this apparent paradox of voting, subsequent approaches shifted the focus from voters' personal calculations of pivotality to the mobilizational incentives and efforts of elites—including politicians, their parties, and various interest groups in society aligned with those parties (e.g., Morton 1987, 1991; Uhlaner 1989; Cox and Munger 1989; Shachar and Nalebuff 1999). The basic argument is that elite actors in close races might rationally invest in mobilizing voters (i.e., through increased campaign spending and get-out-the-vote activities), and those voters might rationally respond to such mobilization efforts by turning out to vote. There are two likely targets of mobilization: (1) individuals or groups who would likely be supportive but might not otherwise turn out if not contacted and (2) individuals or groups who would be most effective at *secondary* mobilization (e.g., Huckfeldt and Sprague 1992; Rosenstone and Hansen 1993). The former strategy might help explain the well-documented pattern of "friends and neighbors" voting around candidates' hometowns (e.g., Key 1949; Lewis-Beck and

Rice 1983; Rice and Macht 1987; Górecki and Marsh 2012; Fiva and Smith 2017). The latter means that politicians or parties will attempt to mobilize key activists or group leaders, and those individuals, in turn, will mobilize other members of their social groups. The micro-foundations behind the elite mobilization theories may thus be related to social pressure or influence within social networks (e.g., Cox, Rosenbluth, and Thies 1998; Bond et al. 2012; Cox 2015).

Even as the debate over the exact mechanisms behind voter turnout was very much unresolved, other scholars began to consider how turnout incentives might be conditioned by the electoral system, especially the degree of proportionality generated by the seat allocation rules (e.g., Powell 1980, 1986; Jackman 1987; Blais and Carty 1990). The early arguments about competitiveness and turnout by Downs and others were based on the assumption of electoral competition in single-seat district (SSD) races. However, Gosnell (1930) and Tingsten (1937) had long ago observed that turnout increased in Germany, Norway, and Switzerland following electoral system reforms in the early 1900s from a two-round runoff system with SSDs to a proportional representation (PR) system with multiseat districts (MSDs). Beginning with the seminal studies of Powell (1980, 1986) and Jackman (1987), a renewed interest in the relationship between electoral rules and turnout picked up speed. In a recent meta-analysis of 185 studies on the determinants of aggregate national and subnational turnout, Cancela and Geys (2016) count 51 studies since Powell (1980) that in some way or another test the relationship between the proportionality of the electoral rules and voter turnout (and their sample of studies is not exhaustive).

In this chapter, I first review the main theoretical arguments and empirical evidence of the relationship between electoral rules and turnout, as well as the puzzles that have emerged from that literature.[2] I then highlight some recent theoretical, methodological, and empirical advancements using subnational data that have refined our understanding about the interaction between electoral rules, competitiveness, and turnout—but have also opened up new and promising directions for future research.

# Proportionality and Turnout

The arguments for how proportionality might increase turnout rest on four basic—and related—mechanisms. The first explanation is that voters are likely to feel more "efficacious" in electoral systems that produce more proportional outcomes (e.g., Blais and Carty 1990; Lijphart 1997; Karp, Banducci, and Bowler 2008; Fisher et al. 2008). At higher levels of district magnitude (M), the translation of votes into seats will be less distorted (meaning there will be less disproportionality between vote shares and seat shares), thereby increasing voters' feelings that their votes actually count. Put differently, voters have less need to be concerned that their votes will be "wasted" on losing candidates or parties, and hence will be more likely to turn out to cast those votes. This explanation rests clearly on voter-driven incentives rather than elite-driven incentives as its mechanism, and is relatively underexplored in the literature.

A second explanation is that PR systems, owing to a larger M, are more permissive to the entry of a greater number of parties (Duverger 1954; Cox 1997). From the perspective of voter-based theories, this means that there may be less reason to abstain for a lack of party options matching voters' ideological preferences (e.g., Powell 1986; Jackman 1987; Ladner and Milner 1999). From the perspective of the elite mobilization theories, this explanation implies that there will be more parties that will make efforts at mobilizing different segments of the population. For example, niche or extreme left/right parties will mobilize voters on the edge of the political spectrum who might be indifferent to the mainstream parties, hence increasing the overall level of turnout.

A third explanation, which rests firmly in the camp of elite mobilization theories, is that PR systems may feature more powerful linkages between parties and groups in society, thereby facilitating mobilization (Powell 1980). For example, many of the early postwar parties of Western Europe, where PR systems have been prevalent, conformed to the "mass party" model of party organization (Duverger 1954; Neumann 1956), in which "the fundamental units of political life are pre-defined and well-defined social groups, membership in which is bound up in all aspects of the individual's life" (Katz and Mair 1995, 6). Given the close association with well-defined social groups—such as labor union organizations and religious movements—the mass party model facilitates mobilization, and especially secondary mobilization. Cox (2015) refers to this process as "subcontracting." Party elites need only get the assurance of support from leaders of such groups, who then mobilize their members on behalf of the party.

The fourth and final basic explanation is that PR elections tend to be more nationally competitive across districts than SSD elections (Jackman 1987). In SSD systems, some districts will be competitive "swing" districts, but many others will be "safe" districts, where one party is overwhelmingly expected to win the seat. Given the logic of either the pivotal voter theories or the elite mobilization theories, turnout will be much lower in these safe districts.[3] In PR systems, all districts are expected to be competitive, as each additional vote earned by a party can help increase the number of seats the party might win in parliament. Hence, parties have an incentive to campaign across all areas of the country, not just in the areas where such an effort might pay off. It follows from this logic that PR systems will also exhibit less variance in turnout across districts than SSD systems (Cox 1999).

More broadly, Cox (1999) postulates that elite incentives to mobilize voters will depend on three "translation" processes of a given system: (1) how effort translates into votes, (2) how votes translate into seats, and (3) how seats translate into portfolios (including executive offices, but also postelectoral legislative offices and judicial appointments).[4] The first speaks to the marginal costs and benefits of different technologies or strategies of voter mobilization. The second is determined by the electoral rules. The third can vary depending on higher-order conditions such as the dynamics of coalition formation or the separation of executive powers.

# Existing Empirical Evidence
# and Puzzles

Despite the compelling explanations for why turnout ought to be higher under proportional electoral rules, the existing empirical evidence paints a rather mixed picture. For the set of advanced industrialized democracies, there is broad and consistent evidence that mean turnout is higher under PR systems than under SSD systems (e.g., Powell 1980; Blais and Carty 1990; Jackman and Miller 1995; Franklin 1996; Blais and Dobrzynska 1998). The exceptions are Switzerland, where turnout is relatively low despite the use of PR, and New Zealand (prior to electoral reform in 1993), where turnout was high, despite the use of first-past-the-post (FPTP) plurality rule in SSDs.

However, when cross-national samples are expanded to include new and developing democracies in Latin America and Eastern Europe, the relationship between proportionality and turnout is much less consistent (e.g., Pérez-Liñán 2001; Kostadinova 2003; Fornos, Power, and Garand 2004; Blais and Aarts 2006; Endersby and Krieckhaus 2008; Gallego, Rico, and Anduiza 2012). The mixed empirical evidence from cross-national studies outside of the industrialized world leads Blais (2006, 111) to conclude that "the impact of institutional variables may be overstated." Others, such as Selb (2009), characterize the evidence for a positive relationship between proportionality and turnout as "overwhelming," with the main ambiguity in the literature being which of the four possible mechanisms is responsible for the effect.

In terms of voter feelings of efficacy, Banducci, Donovan, and Karp (1999) find an increase in perceptions of efficacy in the case of New Zealand after the 1993 electoral reform from FPTP to a mixed-member proportional (MMP) system. The effect they estimate is especially significant among political minorities and supporters of smaller parties. On the other hand, although aggregate turnout increased in the first election under MMP in 1996, it subsequently declined to levels that were lower than the pre-reform period (Vowles 2002, 2010), continuing a downward trend that began before the reform.

The evidence has also been mixed to poor in terms of the number of parties as a mechanism. Although many studies have found a relationship between PR and the number of parties entering competition (e.g., Cox 1997; Eggers 2015; Cox, Fiva, and Smith 2016), there is less evidence for a relationship between the number of parties and higher turnout (e.g., Brockington 2004; Blais and Aarts 2006). However, the mixed results apply mainly to increasing the number of parties *within* PR systems, beyond the initial difference between M = 1 and M > 1 (Grofman and Selb 2011). Within SSD systems, in contrast, there is strong evidence that increasing the number of parties or candidates does indeed increase turnout (e.g., Indridason 2008; Scheiner, Smith, and Thies 2016; Fiva and Smith 2017). The counterintuitive relationship between the number of parties and turnout may be because a greater number of party options in PR systems increases the decision costs facing voters (Downs 1957), or because more parties can lead to coalition governments and less clarity in voter choice (Jackman 1987).

In support of this latter explanation, Tillman (2015) finds evidence that pre-electoral coalitions help to mitigate the downward effect of multipartism on turnout. In terms of Cox's (1999) three translation processes, pre-electoral coalitions might be thought of as increasing certainty about the seats-to-portfolios translation insofar as they give voters and elites more information about which parties might form a government after the election. If the pre-electoral coalitions are formed across SSDs, they might also affect the votes-to-seats translation by removing the possibility that candidates from two or more ideologically proximate parties might split the vote and lose the district to a less ideologically compatible opponent.

Another possible explanation for the downward effect of multipartism on turnout is that when there are many parties, it might not always be clear that the additional vote gains from mobilization efforts targeted at specific groups of voters will accrue only to the party making those efforts. For example, if there are two parties on the left and an imperfect mapping of leftist voters into social groups that support those two parties, then any attempt to mobilize voters by one party might increase votes for its rival due to "mobilizational spillovers" (Cox 2015), reducing the incentives for either party to attempt to mobilize voters beyond its core supporters. The more parties there are in PR systems, the more likely it is that such scenarios will arise.

Only a handful of studies have attempted to directly measure differences in elite mobilization efforts across electoral systems. Using voter survey data from the Comparative Study of Electoral Systems (CSES) dataset, both Karp, Banducci, and Bowler (2008) and Rainey (2015) find that voters actually report *lower* levels of direct contact by parties in PR systems relative to SSD systems. This would seem to run counter to expectations about competitiveness and incentives to mobilize across districts under PR. However, the existence of subcontracting to affiliated groups as a mobilization strategy in PR systems may help to explain these results—if parties are working through secondary mobilization channels, they are less likely to need to engage in direct contact (Cox 2015). More generally, if PR districts tend to be larger in size and population than SSDs, then direct contact may be a less efficient mobilization strategy than other elite efforts, such as running television or newspaper ads that reach a large audience at once.

Overall, of the fifty-one aggregate-level studies included in the meta-analysis by Cancela and Geys (2016)—which collectively included 239 different tests (estimates) of the relationship between proportionality and turnout—only 61 percent of tests and just 53 percent of studies overall pointed in the expected (positive) direction. This contrasts with an earlier meta-analysis of fourteen studies (Geys 2006a), in which approximately 70 percent of tests and studies reported positive findings. A key difference in the study samples is the addition of many more studies using cases from outside the set of advanced industrialized democracies.[5] It would seem that the conventional wisdom regarding the effect of proportionality on turnout might be in need of rethinking.

However, one of the problems with any meta-analysis is that the aggregate pattern that emerges is only as good as the individual studies that go into the sample. One issue is measurement. About half of the studies included in the Cancela and Geys (2016) meta-analysis use a simple dummy variable to operationalize the entire electoral system as "majoritarian" or "proportional." The rest of the studies use either a measure of proportionality such as the Gallagher index (Gallagher 1991) or simply district magnitude. Most often, these variables are also measured at the aggregate (national) level as the mean across all districts and do not take into account how the level of competition, as well as the number of parties, varies at the subnational level across districts. The dynamics of mixed-member systems that combine SSD and PR in separate tiers also tend to be oversimplified—for example, treating MMP cases like New Zealand as "proportional" despite the potential variation in district-level competition across SSDs within the system.

The fact that most of the existing literature is based on cross-national comparisons of aggregate turnout data is itself another issue. As Herrera, Morelli, and Palfrey (2014, 132) point out, empirical investigations based on cross-national comparisons are likely to suffer from a number of confounding variables and measurement challenges, including "the measurement of competitiveness, properly controlling for social/cultural factors, endogeneity of the choice of electoral system, isolating the effects of district magnitude or multimember districts and taking into account institutional variations in government formation." This makes it harder to identify a causal effect of electoral rules on turnout.

Ironically, many of the studies that explore single-country variation are based on the well-known exceptions to the aggregate-level evidence, Switzerland and New Zealand. Nevertheless, when cross-national confounding variables are removed from the analysis, the state of the evidence appears to improve. Of the fifty-one studies surveyed by Cancela and Geys (2016), only ten use subnational variation to evaluate the relationship between proportionality and turnout; however, 70 percent of these subnational studies (and 76 percent of individual tests) produce positive findings. In contrast, the success rate for the subsample of forty-one studies using national-level data is just 51 percent (57 percent of tests). In other words, it would appear that subnational data do a better job at capturing the expected effects of electoral systems on turnout.

# MOVING BEYOND CROSS-NATIONAL COMPARISONS OF AGGREGATE-LEVEL DATA

The increased availability of district-level data, including newly digitized historical electoral data covering important periods of electoral system reform, has made subnational analyses of turnout possible for many democracies. For example, Selb (2009) uses district-level data from the CSES dataset to verify the hypothesis that variance in turnout across districts is lower in more proportional systems.[6] There have also been several methodological advancements in how to measure competitiveness across SSD and

MSD systems (e.g., Blais and Lago 2009; Grofman and Selb 2009; Folke 2014; Kayser and Lindstädt 2015). Using their "index of competition" measure, Grofman and Selb (2011) compare across districts of varying magnitude in Switzerland and Spain, two cases that feature both SSDs and MSDs. They find that once one moves beyond M = 2, subsequent increases in district magnitude do not appear to have a positive effect on either competitiveness or turnout.

A few subnational studies are also able to exploit quasi-experimental variation to provide better insight into the causal effect of electoral rules on turnout. A shortcoming is that such quasi-experimental settings are limited to the electoral systems in use, which are often not simple versions of FPTP or PR, making it harder to draw general inferences about the relationship between proportional representation and turnout. For example, Fauvelle-Aymar and Lewis-Beck (2008) compare simultaneous cantonal and regional elections in France that are held under two-round runoff (TR) and closed-list PR (CLPR) systems, respectively. In the regional CLPR elections, turnout is estimated to be 5 percentage points higher; however, they find no effect when the sample includes only first-round elections for the TR cantonal observations.

Eggers (2015) uses a population-based regression discontinuity (RD) design applied to municipal elections, also in France. There, a population threshold of 3,500 inhabitants triggers the use of CLPR with a 50 percent majoritarian bonus to the largest party, rather than a multiple nontransferable vote system in MSDs (MNTV). In the latter system, voters get M votes to cast in an M-sized district (average M = 25). They are allowed to engage in "plumping" (not using all M votes) and "panachage" (casting votes for candidates of different parties), but not "cumulation" (casting multiple votes for the same candidate) (Cox 1997, 42–43). Eggers (2015) finds a slight (1 percentage point) increase in mean turnout under the PR system and a lower level of variance in turnout across municipalities using PR, in line with the earlier cross-national, district-level analysis by Selb (2009).

Sanz (2017) uses the same RD approach to explore the case of Spain, where municipalities above 250 inhabitants use CLPR, those with fewer than 100 inhabitants only elect a local mayor through FPTP, and those with populations in between employ a system that is similar to the MNTV system in French elections studied by Eggers (2015), except that parties may nominate up to five candidates for five available seats, and voters are only allowed to cast up to four votes for candidates, within or across party lines.[7] Interestingly—in contrast to the results in Eggers (2015)—Sanz (2017) finds that turnout in the CLPR elections is 1 to 2 percentage points *lower* than turnout in the MNTV elections, a finding that he attributes to the fact that MNTV systems encourage competition not only between parties but also between candidates of the same party. In other words, Eggers (2017) interprets his findings from France to imply that greater proportionality under CLPR produces higher turnout than majoritarian systems; Sanz (2015) interprets the exact opposite findings to imply that open-list systems produce higher turnout than closed-list systems. A possible explanation for this apparent discrepancy is the 50 percent seat bonus given to the largest party in the French case. If elites' incentives to mobilize are conditioned by the translations of (1) effort to votes, (2) votes to seats, and (3) seats to portfolios, then the 50 percent bonus would have a larger impact on the votes-to-seats translation, and hence encourage more eager mobilization, than the conditions under more standard methods of seat allocation (i.e., D'Hondt or Sainte-Laguë).

Building on the variance hypothesis, Cox (1999, 399) conjectures that the differences in mean (aggregate) turnout between SSD and PR systems will ultimately depend on the distribution of the cross-district variance in competitiveness in the SSDs, a conjecture that has recently been formalized into a game-theoretic model by Herrera, Morelli, and Palfrey (2014). The basic logic of the model predicts that in highly competitive districts under FPTP, incentives to mobilize will actually be *higher* than under PR because the stakes are higher—with only one seat up for grabs and "winner take all" plurality rule. In SSDs where the result is a foregone conclusion, elites have fewer incentives to mobilize. In PR elections, incentives to mobilize, and hence turnout, will be somewhere between the two types of SSDs. Hence, moving from an SSD system to PR should produce a "contraction effect" in the variance of turnout (Cox, Fiva, and Smith 2016). Whether or not the aggregate level of turnout is higher under PR or SSD depends on how many competitive SSDs exist in a system.

Cox, Fiva, and Smith (2016) explore the historical case of electoral reform in Norway to provide empirical support for the "contraction effect" of PR on mobilization and turnout. In 1919, Norway switched from a TR system to CLPR. Using municipality-level data to construct stable subnational units across the two electoral system periods, they find that in the regions that were closely contested in the pre-reform period, competitiveness and turnout declined following the introduction of PR. In all other districts, competitiveness and turnout increased. Because there were more noncompetitive SSDs than competitive SSDs in the pre-reform period, the aggregate effect was an increase in turnout under PR. In the two elections immediately before and after the reform, mean turnout increased from 58 percent to 65 percent, and the standard deviation of turnout fell from 15 percentage points to 9 percentage points. The evidence from Norway thus provides compelling before-and-after evidence to corroborate the cross-sectional evidence of the variance hypothesis provided by Selb (2009) and Eggers (2015), and adds additional points to the scorecard of the cross-district competitiveness mechanism as an explanation for the proportionality–turnout nexus.[8]

# FUTURE DIRECTIONS

It should be clear from the previous sections that much work remains to be done. One promising direction for future research, building on the findings of Cox, Fiva, and Smith (2016), would be to explore additional cases of electoral reform using district-level data or municipality-level data aggregated to stable geographic units. Figure 10.1 makes a first attempt at this approach with box-and-whisker plots of the distribution of district-level turnout before and after major electoral reforms in the lower (or only) chambers of four countries: Norway, Italy, New Zealand, and Japan. The Norwegian case is the 1919 reform from TR to CLPR explored by Cox, Fiva, and Smith (2016), though here the data are the actual district-level returns to compare it to the other three cases. Italy used open-list PR (OLPR) for the Chamber of Deputies until 1993, when it switched to a mixed-member majoritarian (MMM) system. That system was in use for three elections before a second reform in 2005 to CLPR with a majoritarian bonus. As mentioned, New Zealand switched from FPTP to MMP in 1993. Japan changed its system for the House of Representatives from the single nontransferable vote (SNTV) system with MSDs (average $M = 4$) to its current MMM system in 1994. For the mixed systems, the data are only for the SSD tiers.

Even with turnout measured at the district level, the contraction effect on variance is clear for the Norwegian case. For the Italian case, there is also some evidence that the reverse logic of the contraction effect—that is, an "inflation effect" on variance—might hold when a country moves from a more proportional system to a less proportional system. Although turnout was already quite high under OLPR, some SSDs under the

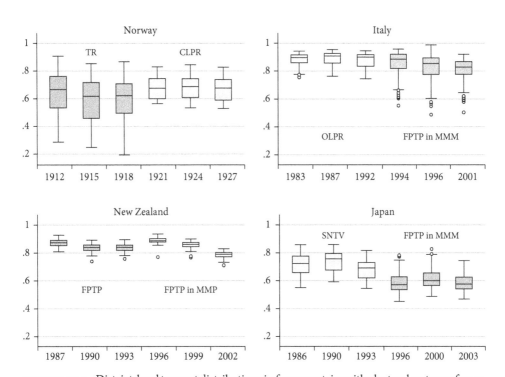

**FIGURE 10.1.** District-level turnout distributions in four countries with electoral system reforms.

Note: Norwegian data are from Cox, Fiva, and Smith (2016). Italian data are from the Italian Ministry of the Interior (http://elezionistorico.interno.it). Pre-reform data for New Zealand are from Jack Vowles (http://www.jackvowles.com /nzelect.html). Post-reform data are from the New Zealand Electoral Commission (http://www.electionresults.govt.nz). Japanese data are from the Reed-Smith Japanese House of Representatives Elections Dataset (Reed and Smith 2016). For all countries, the level of observation is the electoral district (SSD only for mixed-member cases; Māori districts excluded for New Zealand). For Norway's TR period, final-round turnout is used. Turnout is measured as (total votes cast/electorate), except in the case of Japan, where valid votes are used as the numerator.

MMM system had even higher turnout in the first two elections after the reform, even as many more experienced a drop in turnout.[9] In New Zealand, mean turnout initially increased in the first two elections under MMP and then decreased. However, the variance across districts appears to have contracted under MMP. The Japanese reform coincided with a drop in mean turnout, but the cross-district effect, if any, is less obvious. Future research should further explore these and other reforms with more fine-grained data. These reform cases, along with the disparate conclusions in much of the existing literature, also suggest the need to sharpen both predictions and measurement by moving beyond simplifications of electoral systems as "majoritarian versus proportional."

Mixed-member cases like Japan, New Zealand, and Italy provide some particularly interesting opportunities for further investigation. There are two common varieties of mixed-member systems: MMM and MMP (Shugart and Wattenberg 2001). Most are composed of two tiers—one SSD tier and one PR tier—though mixed systems can take other forms, such as in the Japanese House of Councillors (the upper chamber of parliament), which currently combines SNTV and OLPR. Under MMM, seat allocation in the two tiers occurs in parallel; under MMP, seat allocation is compensatory, meaning the PR vote determines the overall proportion of seats to which a party is entitled. Maeda (2016) argues that the patterns in competitiveness and turnout in MMM and MMP should be similar to the patterns in SSD and PR, respectively, as the SSD tier is most determinative of the final seat allocation outcome under MMM, while the PR tier matters most under MMP. Using district-level panel data from two MMM cases (Japan and South Korea) and two MMP cases (Germany and New Zealand), he finds that changes in competitiveness (measured by vote margin between the top two candidates) and changes in turnout are more strongly related in SSDs under MMM than under MMP.[10]

Although Maeda (2016) focuses his analysis on the change in competitiveness and turnout (i.e., the dynamic relationship), the static cross-sectional relationship is also revealing. Figure 10.2 plots the relationship between district-level turnout (y-axis) and the district-level vote share margin between the top two candidates (x-axis) for all elections held under the mixed-member systems in Japan and New Zealand between 1996 and 2014 (seven elections for each country). The figure shows a positive relationship between district-level competitiveness and turnout in both cases. However, it is also clear that there is more variance in competitiveness and turnout in Japan (MMM) than in New Zealand (MMP). Given that the variance in turnout was already low in New Zealand under FPTP, these differences are likely contextual. Nevertheless, such patterns are worth further exploration.

The fact that there is a positive relationship between competitiveness and turnout in SSD races in mixed-member systems suggests that elite effort is not uniform across districts despite the possibility that additional mobilization—even in less competitive SSDs—might impact a party's seat allocation outcome in the PR tier. In other words, individual effort by candidates in SSDs may still be important for mobilizing voters. Figure 10.3 illustrates the point with municipality-level vote returns in the SSD and PR tiers of Japan aggregated to the level of the SSD. Japan's MMM system combines 300

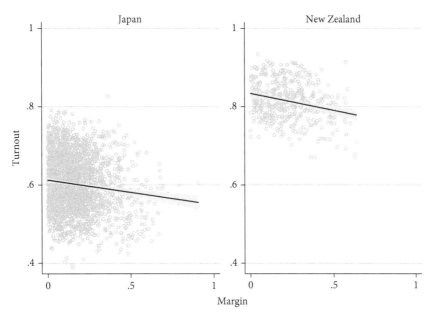

FIGURE 10.2.  District-level margin and turnout in Japan and New Zealand, 1996–2014.

Note: Level of observation is SSD. Data source for Japan is the Reed-Smith Japanese House of Representatives Elections Dataset (Reed and Smith 2016). Turnout is measured as (valid votes cast/electorate). Data source for New Zealand is the New Zealand Electoral Commission (http://www.electionresults.govt.nz). Māori districts are excluded. Turnout is measured as (total votes cast/electorate), so the measurement of turnout differs across the two cases.

SSDs (295 in 2014) and 180 (200 in 1996) seats allocated by CLPR in eleven regional districts. All of the SSDs "map into" the larger PR districts. The top-left panel of figure 10.3 plots the relationship between SSD-level turnout in the SSD tier on the y-axis and competitiveness in the SSD tier (measured using the Grofman-Selb index of competition for consistency of measurement across tiers) on the x-axis. The top-right panel plots the relationship between SSD-level turnout in the SSD tier and competitiveness in the PR tier (the clumping of points is because all SSDs located in the same PR district have the same value on the index of competition). The bottom-left panel plots the relationship between SSD-level turnout in the PR tier and competitiveness in the SSD tier, and the bottom-right panel plots the relationship between SSD-level turnout in the PR tier and competitiveness in the PR tier. The figure clearly shows that SSD-level turnout is positively related to competition in the SSDs, but *not* competition at the PR tier level. It also clearly shows the contraction effect in the measure of competitiveness (index of competition) across districts in the PR tier relative to the SSD tier.

The impact of individual-level effort on overall mobilization across different electoral rules is a third promising avenue for future research. Much of the existing research considers a general typology of "majoritarian" versus "proportional" families of electoral systems. However, subtler differences between types of electoral systems within these two broad families are also likely to play a role. For example, how do competitiveness and turnout differ between SNTV and single transferable vote (STV)

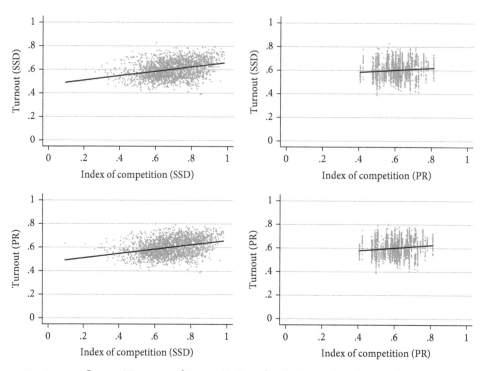

**FIGURE 10.3.** Competitiveness and turnout in Japan's mixed-member tiers, 1996–2014.

Note: Level of observation is SSD (PR votes within SSD boundaries). Data source is the Reed-Smith Japanese House of Representatives Elections Dataset (Reed and Smith 2016). Turnout is measured as (valid votes cast/electorate). The index of competition is calculated based on the method electorate described in Grofman and Selb (2009). Values closer to 1 represent more competitiveness.

systems? Or FPTP versus TR versus alternative vote (AV) variations in SSD systems?[11] Most obviously, among list PR systems, OLPR differs from CLPR in that it generates competition not only between parties but also between individual candidates on party lists. Such intraparty competition for preference votes can potentially increase mobilization and turnout—though the few existing studies to explore this hypothesis have produced mixed results (e.g., Karvonen 2004; Hix and Hagemann 2009; Robbins 2010; Nemoto and Shugart 2013; Sanz 2017). One challenge is the availability of quasi-experimental settings or subnational variation in electoral systems to get around the causal inference challenges posed by cross-national comparisons.

Much of the mobilizational effect of individual candidates, if it exists, may depend on how parties adapt nomination strategies under OLPR. Do they nominate candidates that represent different geographical regions in the district? Or different sectoral interests? Again, the case of Japan provides a useful example. Prior to 2001, the nationwide district tier of the mixed-member system for the House of Councillors used CLPR rather than OLPR.[12] After the switch to OLPR, Kōmeitō—a small religious party with a stable support base of voters—optimized its mobilization of supporters through an innovative strategy: the party leadership assigned its list candidates to specific geographic regions and instructed its followers on which candidates should earn their preference vote. The candidates, for their part, focused their mobilization efforts within their assigned territories. In the prefecture-based SNTV tier of the system, the party nominated a candidate in only a small number of districts in both 1998 (under CLPR) and 2001 (under OLPR). With the switch to OLPR, the vote share for Kōmeitō increased by several thousand more votes in the prefectures where the party did not run a prefectural-tier candidate in either election, but now had a dedicated "local" candidate on the party's nationwide list (Smith 2014).

Finally, it is important to keep in mind that the incentives for elites to mobilize voters in elections will ultimately depend on what is at stake, including the seats up for election, but also higher-order outcomes like which party or parties will be able to form a government. As Cox (1999) and Herrera, Morelli, and Nunnari (2016) argue, a complete assessment of how electoral rules affect turnout must take into account not only the votes-to-seats translation imposed by the electoral system but also the seats-to-portfolios translation in a given system, and interactions between them.

Does it make sense to believe that voters are simultaneously concerned with how their vote will be translated into the outcome of legislative seats, as well as how mundane higher-order rules will filter that choice into portfolio outcomes? Probably not. However, it may be reasonable to believe that individual elites are more likely to understand such structural incentives and target their mobilizational activity accordingly. For example, if cabinet promotion in a given system is decided on the basis of seniority rule, then an individual incumbent politician on the cusp of reaching the requisite seniority might invest a bit more effort in ensuring his or her party wins enough seats to enter government. This calculus, too, can be expected to differ under different electoral system rules. In systems such as PR or STV, where one individual's effort can help to elect his or her copartisans due to vote pooling or vote transfers, such effort will have a higher payoff. In SSD systems, the most important thing may be simply to win; winning by a larger margin through increasing turnout does not reap the same sort of additional payoffs. Research in this area is so far nonexistent, but efforts to explore such individual-level elite mobilization incentives will no doubt yield valuable insights into the overall relationship between electoral systems and turnout.

## Acknowledgments

I thank João Cancela and Benny Geys for kindly sharing detailed information about the studies included in their meta-analysis, Colleen Driscoll for assistance collecting additional literature, and Gary W. Cox, Jon H. Fiva, and Benny Geys for helpful feedback.

## Notes

1. For more detailed reviews of economic models of voting, see Aldrich (1993), Dhillon and Peralta (2002), and Geys (2006b).

2. Several recent articles have reviewed the broader empirical literature on turnout (e.g., Blais 2006; Geys 2006a; Cancela and Geys 2016), as well as the more specific theoretical and empirical literature on the relationship between electoral rules and turnout (Cox 1999; Blais and Aarts 2006; Herrera, Morelli, and Palfrey 2014; Cox 2015; Herrera, Morelli, and Nunnari 2016). These articles cover some of the literature that, for space reasons, is not included here, as well as the impact of other institutional variables, such as compulsory voting, presidentialism versus parliamentarism, concurrent elections, and bicameralism, all of which have inspired additional streams of research.

3. Multiple empirical studies on single-round SSD elections have confirmed that turnout is higher in close elections (e.g., Denver and Hands 1974; Dawson and Zinser 1976; Caldeira and Patterson 1982; Cox and Munger 1989; Denver, Hands, and MacAllister 2003). Studies on two-round SSD elections also find that close competition in the first round increases turnout in the second round (Indridason 2008; Fauvelle-Aymar and François 2006; Simonovits 2012; De Paola and Scoppa 2014; Garmann 2014; Fiva and Smith 2017).

4. Herrera, Morelli, and Nunnari (2016) make a related argument in more formal terms. For additional formal theories of electoral systems and turnout, see Kartal (2015) and Faravelli and Sanchez-Pages (2015).

5. In a separate meta-analysis of individual-level turnout studies (i.e., studies using voter survey data), Smets and van Ham (2013) identify only four journal articles published between 2000 and 2010; of these, only one single-test study found positive results for the relationship between proportional representation systems and voter turnout.

6. Another useful dataset is the Constituency-Level Elections Archive (CLEA) (Kollman et al. 2016).

7. Sanz (2017) refers to this system as "open-list, plurality-at-large." It is different from traditional open-list PR (OLPR) systems because vote pooling does not occur at the party level, and votes can be cast across party lines.

8. Cox (2015) notes that the variance hypothesis may not hold under three important conditions: upper tiers, concurrent executive elections, and compulsory voting.

9. For the 2001 election, the original Italian data source (the Italian Ministry of the Interior) gives turnout in the SSD tier as 100 percent in one district—Matera in Basilicata Province—with an abnormally large number of "invalid" votes. I estimate the "correct" turnout for Matera as 76.8 percent based on the recorded turnout in the PR tier for Matera voters.

10. An earlier study by Rich (2014) of cross-national aggregate-level turnout finds no differences between MMM and MMP but suffers from the measurement and causal inference problems already discussed.

11. Barone and de Blasio (2013) employ an RD design to study Italian mayoral elections, which use FPTP in municipalities with a population below 15,000 persons, but a TR system in larger municipalities (among some other variations in rules across municipalities with different population sizes). They find that turnout is higher by 1 percentage point in the latter.

12. The CLPR system was used from 1983 to 1998. Prior to 1983, SNTV was used to elect all members in the national tier. SNTV has always been used in the prefectural tier, though in some prefectures M = 1, making the system effectively FPTP.

# REFERENCES

Aldrich, John. "Rational Choice and Turnout." *American Journal of Political Science* 37, no. 1 (1993): 246–278.

Banducci, Susan A., Todd Donovan, and Jeffrey A. Karp. "Proportional Representation and Attitudes about Politics: Results from New Zealand." *Electoral Studies* 18, no. 4 (1999): 533–555.

Barone, Guglielmo, and Guido de Blasio. "Electoral Rules and Voter Turnout." *International Review of Law and Economics* 36 (2013): 25–35.

Blais, André. "What Affects Voter Turnout?" *Annual Review of Political Science* 9, no. 1 (2006): 111–125.

Blais, André, and Kees Aarts. "Electoral Systems and Turnout." *Acta Politica* 41, no. 2 (2006): 180–196.

Blais, André, and R. K. Carty. "Does Proportional Representation Foster Voter Turnout?" *European Journal of Political Research* 18, no. 2 (1990): 167–181.

Blais, André, and Agnieszka Dobrzynska. "Turnout in Electoral Democracies." *European Journal of Political Research* 33, no. 2 (1998): 239–261.

Blais, André, and Ignacio Lago. "A General Measure of District Competitiveness." *Electoral Studies* 28 (2009): 94–100.

Bond, Robert M., Christopher J. Fariss, Jason J. Jones, Adam D. I. Kramer, Cameron Marlow, Jaime E. Settle, and James H. Fowler. "A 61-Million-Person Experiment in Social Influence and Political Mobilization." *Nature* 489 (2012): 295–298.

Brockington, David. "The Paradox of Proportional Representation: The Effect of Party Systems and Coalitions on Individuals' Electoral Participation." *Political Studies* 52, no. 3 (2004): 469–490.

Caldeira, Gregory A., and Samuel C. Patterson. "Contextual Influences on Participation in U.S. State Legislative Elections." *Legislative Studies Quarterly* 7, no. 3 (1982): 359–381.

Cancela, João, and Benny Geys. "Explaining Voter Turnout: A Meta-Analysis of National and Subnational Elections." *Electoral Studies* 42 (2016): 264–275.

Cox, Gary W. *Making Votes Count: Strategic Coordination in the World's Electoral Systems.* New York: Cambridge University Press, 1997.

Cox, Gary W. "Electoral Rules and the Calculus of Mobilization." *Legislative Studies Quarterly* 24, no. 3 (1999): 387–419.

Cox, Gary W. "Electoral Rules, Mobilization, and Turnout." *Annual Review of Political Science* 18, no. 1 (2015): 49–68.

Cox, Gary W., Jon H. Fiva, and Daniel M. Smith. "The Contraction Effect: How Proportional Representation Affects Mobilization and Turnout." *Journal of Politics* 78, no. 4 (2016): 1249–1263.

Cox, Gary W., and Michael C. Munger. "Closeness, Expenditures, and Turnout in the 1982 U.S. House Elections." *American Political Science Review* 83, no. 1 (1989): 217–231.

Cox, Gary W., Frances M. Rosenbluth, and Michael F. Thies. "Mobilization, Social Networks, and Turnout." *World Politics* 50, no. 3 (1998): 447–474.

Dawson, Paul A., and James E. Zinser. "Political Finance and Participation in Congressional Elections." *Annals of the American Academy of Political and Social Science* 425 (1976): 59–73.

De Paola, Maria, and Vincenzo Scoppa. "The Impact of Closeness on Electoral Participation Exploiting the Italian Double Ballot System." *Public Choice* 160, no. 3–4 (2014): 467–479.

Denver, D. T., and H. T. G. Hands. "Marginality and Turnout in British General Elections." *British Journal of Political Science* 4, no. 1 (1974): 17–35.

Denver, David, Gordon Hands, and Iain MacAllister. "Constituency Marginality and Turnout in Britain Revisited." *British Elections and Parties Review* 13, no. 1 (2003): 174–194.

Dhillon, Amrita, and Susana Peralta. "Economic Theories of Voter Turnout." *Economic Journal* 112 (2002): 332–352.

Downs, Anthony. *An Economic Theory of Democracy*. New York: Harper and Row, 1957.

Duverger, Maurice. *Political Parties: Their Organization and Activity in the Modern State*. New York: John Wiley, 1954.

Eggers, Andrew C. "Proportionality and Turnout: Evidence from French Municipalities." *Comparative Political Studies* 48, no. 2 (2015): 135–167.

Endersby, James W., and Jonathan T. Krieckhaus. "Turnout around the Globe: The Influence of Electoral Institutions on National Voter Participation, 1972–2000." *Electoral Studies* 27 (2008): 601–610.

Faravelli, Marco, and Santiago Sanchez-Pages. "(Don't) Make My Vote Count." *Journal of Theoretical Politics* 27, no. 4 (2015): 544–569.

Fauvelle-Aymar, Christine, and Abel François. "The Impact of Closeness on Turnout: An Empirical Relation Based on a Study of a Two-Round Ballot." *Public Choice* 127, no. 3/4 (2006): 469–491.

Fauvelle-Aymar, Christine, and Michael S. Lewis-Beck. "TR versus PR: Effects of the French Double Ballot." *Electoral Studies* 27 (2008): 400–406.

Fisher, Stephen D., Laurence Lessard-Phillips, Sara B. Hobolt, and John Curtice. "Disengaging Voters: Do Plurality Systems Discourage the Less Knowledgeable from Voting?" *Electoral Studies* 27 (2008): 89–104.

Fiva, Jon H., and Daniel M. Smith. "Local Candidates and Voter Mobilization: Evidence from Historical Two-Round Elections in Norway." *Electoral Studies* 45 (2017): 130–140.

Folke, Olle. "Shades of Brown and Green: Party Effects in Proportional Election Systems." *Journal of the European Economic Association* 12, no. 5 (2014): 1361–1395.

Fornos, Carolina A., Timothy J. Power, and James C. Garand. "Explaining Voter Turnout in Latin America, 1980 to 2000." *Comparative Political Studies* 37, no. 8 (2004): 909–940.

Franklin, Mark. "Electoral Participation." In *Comparing Democracies: Elections and Voting in Global Perspective*, edited by L. LeDuc, R. G. Niemi, and P. Norris, 216–235. Thousand Oaks, CA: Sage, 1996.

Gallagher, Michael. "Proportionality, Disproportionality and Electoral Systems." *Electoral Studies* 10, no. 1 (1991): 33–51.

Gallego, Aina, Guillem Rico, and Eva Anduiza. "Disproportionality and Voter Turnout in New and Old Democracies." *Electoral Studies* 31, no. 1 (2012): 159–169.

Garmann, Sebastian. "A Note on Electoral Competition and Turnout in Run-off Electoral Systems: Taking into Account Both Endogeneity and Attenuation Bias." *Electoral Studies* 34 (2014): 261–265.

Geys, Benny. "Explaining Voter Turnout: A Review of Aggregate-Level Research." *Electoral Studies* 25, no. 4 (2006a): 637–663.

Geys, Benny. "Rational Theories of Voter Turnout: A Review." *Political Studies Review* 4 (2006b): 16–35.

Górecki, Maciej A., and Michael Marsh. "Not Just 'Friends and Neighbours': Canvassing, Geographic Proximity and Voter Choice." *European Journal of Political Research* 51, no. 5 (2012): 563–582.

Gosnell, Harold. *Why Europe Votes*. Chicago: University of Chicago Press, 1930.

Grofman, Bernard, and Peter Selb. "A Fully General Index of Political Competition." *Electoral Studies* 28, no. 2 (2009): 291–296.

Grofman, Bernard, and Peter Selb. "Turnout and the (Effective) Number of Parties at the National and District Levels: A Puzzle-Solving Approach." *Party Politics* 17, no. 1 (2011): 93–117.

Herrera, Helios, Massimo Morelli, and Salvatore Nunnari. "Turnout across Democracies." *American Journal of Political Science* 60, no. 3 (2016): 607–624.

Herrera, Helios, Massimo Morelli, and Thomas Palfrey. "Turnout and Power Sharing." *Economic Journal* 124, no. 574 (2014): F131–F162.

Hix, Simon, and Sara Hagemann. "Could Changing the Electoral Rules Fix European Parliament Elections?" *Politique européenne* 2, no. 28 (2009): 37–52.

Huckfeldt, Robert, and John Sprague. "Political Parties and Electoral Mobilization: Political Structure, Social Structure, and the Party Canvass." *American Political Science Review* 86 (1992): 70–86.

Indridason, Indridi H. "Competition & Turnout: The Majority Run-off as a Natural Experiment." *Electoral Studies* 27, no. 4 (2008): 699–710.

Jackman, Robert W. "Political Institutions and Voter Turnout in the Industrial Democracies." *American Political Science Review* 81, no. 2 (1987): 405–424.

Jackman, Robert W., and Ross A. Miller. "Voter Turnout in the Industrial Democracies during the 1980s." *Comparative Political Studies* 27, no. 4 (1995): 467–492.

Karp, Jeffrey A., Susan A. Banducci, and Shawn Bowler. "Getting Out the Vote: Party Mobilization in Comparative Perspective." *British Journal of Political Science* 38, no. 1 (2008): 91–112.

Kartal, Melis. "A Comparative Welfare Analysis of Electoral Systems with Endogenous Turnout." *Economic Journal* 125, no. 587 (2015): 1369–1392.

Karvonen, Lauri. "Preferential Voting: Incidence and Effects." *International Political Science Review* 25, no. 2 (2004): 203–226.

Katz, Richard S., and Peter Mair. "Changing Models of Party Organization and Party Democracy: The Emergence of the Cartel Party." *Party Politics* 1, no. 1 (1995): 5–28.

Kayser, Mark Andreas, and René Lindstädt. "A Cross-National Measure of Electoral Competitiveness." *Political Analysis* 23 (2015): 242–253.

Key, V. O., Jr. *Southern Politics in State and Nation*. New York: Alfred A. Knopf, 1949.

Kollman, Ken, Allen Hicken, Daniele Caramani, David Backer, and David Lublin. "Constituency-Level Elections Archive." Produced and distributed by Ann Arbor, MI: Center for Political Studies, University of Michigan, 2016.

Kostadinova, Tatiana. "Voter Turnout Dynamics in Post-Communist Europe." *European Journal of Political Research* 42, no. 6 (2003): 741–759.

Ladner, Andreas, and Henry Milner. "Do Voters Turn Out More under Proportional Than Majoritarian Systems? The Evidence from Swiss Communal Elections." *Electoral Studies* 18, no. 2 (1999): 235–250.

Lewis-Beck, Michael S., and Tom W. Rice. "Localism in Presidential Elections: The Home State Advantage." *American Journal of Political Science* 27, no. 3 (1983): 548–556.

Lijphart, Arend. "Unequal Participation: Democracy's Unresolved Dilemma." *American Political Science Review* 91, no. 1 (1997): 1–14.

Maeda, Ko. "Voter Turnout and District-Level Competitiveness in Mixed-Member Electoral Systems." *Journal of Elections, Public Opinion and Parties* 26, no. 4 (2016): 452–469.

Morton, Rebecca B. "A Group Majority Voting Model of Public Good Provision." *Social Choice and Welfare* 4, no. 2 (1987): 117–131.

Morton, Rebecca B. "Groups in Rational Turnout Models." *American Journal of Political Science* 35, no. 3 (1991): 758–776.

Nemoto, Kuniaki, and Matthew S. Shugart. "Localism and Coordination under Three Different Electoral Systems: The National District of the Japanese House of Councillors." *Electoral Studies* 32, no. 1 (2013): 1–12.

Neumann, Sigmund. "Towards a Comparative Study of Political Parties." In *Modern Political Parties*, edited by Sigmund Neumann, 395–421. Chicago: Chicago University Press, 1956.

Palfrey, Thomas R., and Howard Rosenthal. "Voter Participation and Strategic Uncertainty." *American Political Science Review* 79, no. 1 (1985): 62–78.

Pérez-Liñán, Aníbal. "Neoinstitutional Accounts of Voter Turnout: Moving Beyond Industrial Democracies." *Electoral Studies* 20, no. 2 (2001): 281–297.

Powell, G. Bingham. "Voting Turnout in Thirty Democracies: Partisan, Legal, and Socio-Economic Influences." In *Electoral Participation: A Comparative Analysis*, edited by Richard Rose, 396–412. Beverly Hills: Sage, 1980.

Powell, G. Bingham. "American Voter Turnout in Comparative Perspective." *American Political Science Review* 80, no. 1 (1986): 17–43.

Rainey, Carlisle. "Strategic Mobilization: Why Proportional Representation Decreases Voter Mobilization." *Electoral Studies* 37 (2015): 86–98.

Reed, Steven R., and Daniel M. Smith. "The Japanese House of Representatives Elections Data Set." 2016. https://sites.google.com/site/danielmarkhamsmith/data.

Rice, Tom W., and Alisa A. Macht. "The Hometown Advantage: Mobilization or Conversion?" *Political Behavior* 9, no. 3 (1987): 257–262.

Rich, Timothy S. "Institutional Influences on Turnout in Mixed Member Electoral Systems: An Exploratory Analysis." *Representation* 50, no. 2 (2014): 161–175.

Riker, William H., and Peter C. Ordeshook. "A Theory of the Calculus of Voting." *American Political Science Review* 62 (1968): 25–42.

Robbins, Joseph W. "The Personal Vote and Voter Turnout." *Electoral Studies* 29 (2010): 661–672.

Rosenstone, Steven J., and John Mark Hansen. *Mobilization, Participation, and Democracy in America*. New York: Macmillan, 1993.

Sanz, Carlos. "The Effect of Electoral Systems on Voter Turnout: Evidence from a Natural Experiment." *Political Science Research and Methods* 5, no. 4 (2017): 689–710.

Scheiner, Ethan, Daniel M. Smith, and Michael F. Thies. "The 2014 Japanese Election Results: The Opposition Cooperates, but Fails to Inspire." In *Japan Decides 2014: The Japanese General Election*, edited by Robert Pekkanen, Steven R. Reed, and Ethan Scheiner, 22–38. New York: Palgrave Macmillan, 2016.

Selb, Peter. "A Deeper Look at the Proportionality-Turnout Nexus." *Comparative Political Studies* 42, no. 4 (2009): 527–548.

Shachar, Ron, and Barry Nalebuff. "Follow the Leader: Theory and Evidence on Political Participation." *American Economic Review* 89, no. 3 (1999): 525–547.

Shugart, Matthew Soberg, and Martin P. Wattenberg. "Mixed-Member Electoral Systems: A Definition and Typology." In *Mixed-Member Electoral Systems: The Best of Both Worlds?*, edited by Matthew Soberg Shugart and Martin P. Wattenberg, 1–24. Oxford: Oxford University Press, 2001.

Simonovits, Gàbor. "Competition and Turnout Revisited: The Importance of Measuring Expected Closeness Accurately." *Electoral Studies* 31, no. 2 (2012): 364–371.

Smets, Kaat, and Carolien van Ham. "The Embarrassment of Riches? A Meta-Analysis of Individual-level Research on Voter Turnout." *Electoral Studies* 32, no. 2 (2013): 344–359.

Smith, Daniel M. "Party Ideals and Practical Constraints in Kōmeitō Candidate Nominations." In *Kōmeitō: Politics and Religion in Japan*, edited by George Ehrhardt, Axel Klein, Levi McLaughlin, and Steven R. Reed, 139–162. Berkeley, CA: Institute of East Asian Studies at the University of California, Berkeley, 2014.

Tillman, Erik R. "Pre-electoral Coalitions and Voter Turnout." *Party Politics* 21, no. 5 (2015): 726–737.

Tingsten, Herbert. *Political Behavior: Studies in Election Statistics*. London: P. S. King & Sons, 1937.

Tullock, G. *Toward a Mathematics of Politics*. Ann Arbor: University of Michigan Press, 1967.

Uhlaner, Carole J. "Rational Turnout: The Neglected Role of Groups." *American Journal of Political Science* 33, no. 2 (1989): 390–422.

Vowles, Jack. "Offsetting the PR Effect? Party Mobilization and Turnout Decline in New Zealand, 1996-99." *Party Politics* 8, no. 5 (2002): 587–605.

Vowles, Jack. "Electoral System Change, Generations, Competitiveness and Turnout in New Zealand, 1963–2005." *British Journal of Political Science* 40, no. 4 (2010): 875–895.

........................................................................................

# CHAPTER 11

# ELECTORAL SYSTEMS AND CITIZEN-ELITE IDEOLOGICAL CONGRUENCE

........................................................................................

## MATT GOLDER AND BENJAMIN FERLAND

How do electoral systems affect the degree of congruence between political elites and the ideological preferences of the people? For many, ideological congruence is the key to good representation. Electoral systems are an important determinant of ideological congruence because of the way they shape citizen preferences and the composition of party systems, legislatures, and governments. Representation occurs in stages. Citizen preferences are translated into votes, votes are translated into legislative seats, legislative seats are translated into governments, and government proposals are translated into policies. After some preliminaries, we examine how electoral rules influence ideological congruence at each of these stages in the representation process. We finish by briefly looking at how electoral systems can indirectly affect ideological congruence by influencing elite responsiveness and descriptive representation. In addition to summarizing the existing literature, we suggest new avenues for future research.

## SOME PRELIMINARIES

.......................................................................................................................................

We begin by situating studies of ideological congruence in the more general literature on political representation, distinguishing between ideological congruence and ideological responsiveness, and highlighting the different ways that scholars have conceptualized ideological congruence.

## Political Representation

Pitkin (1967) distinguishes between four different views of representation. Formalistic representation has to do with how representatives are authorized and held accountable. Symbolic representation addresses the symbolic ways in which representatives "stand for" and seek acceptance from the people. Descriptive representation focuses on the extent to which representatives resemble and hence "stand for" their constituents. Substantive representation emphasizes how representatives "act for" the people and promote their interests. A close correspondence between the people and their representatives is emphasized in both the descriptive and substantive views of representation. Descriptive representation calls for representatives who share the same characteristics, such as race, gender, religion, and class, as those they represent. Substantive representation calls for representatives to take actions in line with the substantive or ideological interests of those they represent. Many democratic theorists have argued that substantive representation is the most important form of representation as it focuses on what representatives do as opposed to who they are (Pitkin 1967). Empirical scholars have typically thought of substantive representation in terms of ideological congruence (Huber and Powell 1994) and responsiveness (Page and Shapiro 1983).

A central debate in the political representation literature has to do with whether representatives should be independent trustees or mandated delegates (Pitkin 1967). Trustees are generally understood as representatives who use their own independent judgment to promote the collective good. In contrast, delegates are typically viewed as representatives who are mandated to promote particular constituent-defined interests (Rehfeld 2009, 215). By equating "good representation" with a close correspondence between the actions of the representatives and the preferences of their constituents, empirical scholars of ideological congruence implicitly adopt a mandate or delegate view of representation (Rehfeld 2009, 216). In doing so, they ignore the possibility that good representation may require representatives to deviate from their constituents' preferences, perhaps because these preferences do "not conform to their [constituents'] true interests . . . or [because they] may be trumped by more important principles of justice" (Rehfeld 2009, 214). That said, even those adopting a trustee view of representation accept that deviations from constituent preferences should be infrequent and congruence the norm (Pitkin 1967, 209–210).

Several scholars have recently presented alternative views of representation that question the central importance of ideological congruence. Mansbridge (2003, 515), for example, discusses anticipatory, gyroscopic, and surrogate representation, each of which emphasizes the "deliberative rather than aggregative" function of representation. With anticipatory representation, representatives act on what they think the interests of their constituents will be at the next election. With gyroscopic representation, representatives act in line with their own beliefs and principles rather than those of their constituents. With surrogate representation, representatives act for constituents who did not elect them. The normative concern in all of these forms of representation has nothing to do with "whether representatives accurately reflect the current opinions or even the underlying interests of the members of their constituencies" (Mansbridge 2003, 524).

Saward (2006, 2014) goes so far as to suggest that substantive representation may not even be possible. He challenges the idea that there are exogenous and knowable constituent interests for representatives to represent. Rather than view representatives as passive conveyors of constituent interests, Saward argues that representatives play an active role in "creating" and "constructing" citizen interests through the types of representation claims they make. These representation claims, if accepted by the people, help to define the groups and interests that require representation, as well as the types of representatives that are considered good. In this framework, "representation is not a passive procedure of receiving clear signals from below; rather it is dynamic, performative, and constitutive" (Celis et al. 2008, 101–102). Among other things, the constructivist turn in representation studies emphasizes the role played by nonelectoral representatives in shaping representation (Saward 2009; Disch 2011; Näsström 2015; Kuyper 2016).

## Ideological Congruence and Responsiveness

Substantive representation has typically been studied in terms of either ideological congruence or responsiveness. Although ideological congruence and responsiveness are intimately connected, scholars who work in these two areas rarely talk to one another (Ferland 2015). Congruence tells us the extent to which the actions of the representative are in line with the interests of the represented at a fixed point in time, whereas responsiveness refers to how representatives change their behavior to become more congruent with the interests of the represented over time. In this respect, congruence and responsiveness represent static and dynamic forms of representation. Ideological congruence is the ultimate goal. Responsiveness is important because it leads to greater congruence at times when the actions of the representative and the interests of the people are not in complete alignment. This suggests that scholars of ideological congruence and responsiveness should not work in isolation but should instead adopt a unified theoretical framework.

Figure 11.1 highlights the conceptual distinction between congruence and responsiveness. Each of the five scenarios depicts a representative R and a citizen C in some policy space. In some scenarios, the citizen changes his preferences from C to C'. This is indicated by the solid black arrows. The dashed gray arrows indicate how a fully responsive representative would move in each of the different scenarios. Scenario (a) indicates a situation of perfect congruence, where the representative holds the same position as the citizen. In this scenario, the representative does not have to be responsive. In some sense, scenario (b) captures "ideal" representation. The representative starts off congruent. As the citizen changes his preferences, the representative moves to maintain her perfect congruence. The other scenarios capture instances of incongruence where the representative must move to establish congruence.

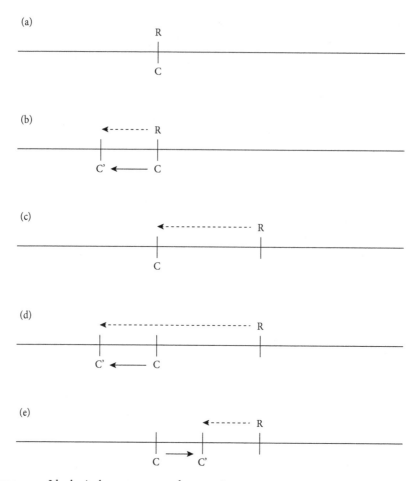

**FIGURE 11.1.** Ideological congruence and responsiveness.

Note: Figure 1 shows a representative R and a citizen C located in a policy space. C' indicates a new policy position adopted by the citizen C. The solid black arrow indicates the movement of the citizen in the policy space. The dashed gray arrow indicates the movement of a fully responsive representative. Ideological congruence occurs when the representative takes the same position as the citizen in the policy space.

Many scholars argue that representatives are responsive when they move in the same direction as the citizen (Adams et al. 2006; Adams, Haupt, and Stoll 2009; Kang and Powell 2010; McDonald and Budge 2005). In other words, they claim that a responsive representative moves left when the citizen moves left, and right when the citizen moves right. However, this claim is problematic. As scenario (e) indicates, there are cases in which a representative can achieve greater congruence, and hence be more responsive, by moving in the opposite direction to the citizen. Only if we start from a situation of perfect congruence will a responsive representative always move in the same direction as the citizen. If we start from a situation of incongruence, as will normally be the case, then whether a responsive representative will move in the same direction as the citizen depends on whether the citizen is located to his or her left or right (Ferland 2015).

As Figure 11.1 indicates, it is important to take account of ideological congruence when studying responsiveness.

Powell (2000) distinguishes between majoritarian and proportional visions of democracy. Both visions value responsiveness. However, they differ in terms of when responsiveness should occur. According to the majoritarian vision, representatives are mandated to implement the policies on which they campaigned. As a result, "majoritarian" representatives are expected to be responsive only at fixed points in time—when a new election is taking place. In contrast, "proportional" representatives are expected to continuously respond to changes in citizens' preferences. These normative standards have obvious implications for how we empirically evaluate the responsiveness of representatives in majoritarian and proportional systems.

## Conceptualizing Ideological Congruence

Empirical scholars conceptualize ideological congruence in different ways. One traditional way to conceptualize congruence is in terms of either dyadic or collective representation. Dyadic representation concerns the congruence between a single representative and his or her geographic constituency (Miller and Stokes 1963). Collective representation concerns the congruence between the representatives in a collective body, such as a legislature or government, and the citizens (Weissberg 1978). Whereas much of the American politics literature has focused on dyadic representation, most of the comparative literature has focused on collective representation. One reason for this is that comparative scholars have typically examined more party-centered elections in which parties are strong and individual legislators have limited independence. Electoral rules, such as party lists and district magnitude, influence the strength of parties and the extent to which representatives seek to generate a personal vote (Carey and Shugart 1995). As a result, they help to determine the appropriateness of adopting a dyadic or collective concept of representation.

Golder and Stramski (2010) argue that it is useful to distinguish between situations where there are many citizens and a single representative (a many-to-one relationship) and where there are many citizens and many representatives (a many-to-many relationship). Although we refer to a "single representative" in the many-to-one relationship, we can just as easily think of the single representative as being the government's policy position. Whereas American politics scholars typically ask how well a single legislator represents his or her constituents, comparative scholars typically ask how well a government represents its citizens. As Golder and Stramski (2010) highlight, there are many different ways to conceptualize many-to-one congruence. By far the most common way to conceptualize it is as the absolute distance between the representative's policy position and the citizenry's "most preferred" position. The position of the median citizen is typically taken as the citizenry's most preferred policy position, as this position minimizes the sum of absolute distances between the citizens (Huber and Powell 1994). This is referred to as *absolute median citizen congruence*.

One criticism of this conceptualization of many-to-one congruence is that it ignores the diversity of citizens' preferences. A way to incorporate information about the distribution of citizens' preferences is by conceptualizing congruence as the average absolute distance between *each* citizen and the representative, *absolute citizen congruence* (Achen 1978; Blais and Bodet 2006). A concern, though, is that representatives in homogeneous constituencies are automatically at an advantage when producing this type of congruence compared to representatives in more heterogeneous constituencies. This is problematic if one wants to compare the relative performance of representatives across constituencies. One way to address this issue is by conceptualizing congruence relative to the dispersion of citizen preferences, *relative citizen congruence*.

How one conceptualizes many-to-one congruence is important because it affects how one ranks a set of representatives in terms of their performance. As Golder and Stramski (2010, 95) point out, "the potential for these different rankings suggests that empirical claims regarding ideological congruence may depend critically on the particular conceptualization of congruence that is adopted." They propose that the concept of relative citizen congruence is often the most appropriate given the goals of empirical scholars.

Rather than focus on determining how congruent a single representative or government is with the preferences of the citizenry (a many-to-one relationship), one might also be interested in how well the collective body of representatives or legislature reflects the ideological positions of citizens (a many-to-many relationship). This conceptualization fits with a long line of democratic theorists who have emphasized the importance of having a representative body whose preferences accurately correspond to those of the country as a whole (Pitkin 1967). The few empirical scholars in this tradition usually compare the distance between the median legislator and the median citizen (Powell 2000; McDonald, Mendes, and Budge 2004; Golder and Lloyd 2014). However, this approach ignores the diversity of preferences among both the citizens and the representatives. Golder and Stramski (2010, 95–96) argue that many-to-many congruence is more appropriately conceptualized in terms of the extent to which the distribution of preferences among the representatives overlaps with the distribution of preferences among the citizenry.

## Stages of Ideological Congruence

Ideological congruence ultimately requires that policies be in line with citizen preferences. The translation of preferences into policies occurs in stages. Electoral rules are important because they influence the accuracy with which preferences are translated across the various links in the chain of representation.

# Citizen Preferences

The representation chain starts with citizen preferences. Ideological congruence scholars implicitly take citizen preferences as given and examine how well they are reflected in the actions of representative agents such as parties, legislatures, and governments. As previously mentioned, the fixed and exogenous nature of citizen preferences has been challenged by the "constructivist turn" among representation theorists (Disch 2011; Saward 2006, 2009). These theorists highlight how representatives are able to strategically manipulate and shape citizen preferences through a repeated claims-making process with the people.

That preferences are constructed is consistent with Downs's (1957, 124–125) suggestion that majoritarian electoral rules, by encouraging a two-party system in which parties converge in the policy space, may cause "voters' tastes . . . [to] become relatively homogenous in the long run; whereas the opposite may occur in a proportional representation structure." Downs suggests, in effect, that citizen preferences may be endogenous to electoral rules. Evidence for this comes from Golder and Stramski (2010, 101), who find that the dispersion of citizen preferences is smaller in majoritarian electoral systems than in proportional ones. As discussed earlier, this means that representatives in majoritarian systems will automatically find it easier than their counterparts in proportional systems to produce *absolute citizen congruence*. This is one reason scholars might want to conceptualize congruence relative to the dispersion of citizen preferences.

Electoral rules also shape citizen preferences because of their impact on political identity formation (Chandra 2004, 2006, 2012; Posner 2005). The standard story is that each country has a set of latent cleavages, such as language, ethnicity, religion, and class, that could be mobilized by political entrepreneurs. Political entrepreneurs, though, only mobilize those cleavages that provide the most usefully sized building blocks for constructing their "winning coalitions." Which differences become politicized and hence worthy of representation depends on the interaction between institutions like electoral rules and the distribution of latent social cleavages (Clark, Golder, and Golder 2017, 614–621). Electoral rules are important because they help to determine the necessary size of any winning coalition. Whereas proportional systems allow for the politicization of many "small" cleavages, majoritarian systems require larger winning coalitions and encourage the politicization of a small number of "large" cleavages. As an example, Posner (2004) employs this framework to explain why ethnicity is politicized in Malawi but not in Zambia.

# Party System Congruence

Citizen preferences are first represented in the party system. Party system congruence has been studied from two distinct perspectives. Whereas the first involves examining the congruence between individual parties and their voters, the second involves examining the congruence between the party system as a whole and the citizenry. Those who adopt the second perspective emphasize the importance of either having parties that are congruent with the "typical" citizen or having parties that are congruent with the diversity of citizen preferences. That a party system is unlikely to be able to produce both types of congruence illustrates the implicit conceptual and normative judgments underpinning analyses of ideological congruence.

A party system's size and ideological makeup strongly influence party system congruence. Electoral rules are important as they influence both the number of parties in the system and the location of these parties in the policy space. The dominant explanation for party system size is Duverger's (1963) theory. Duverger's theory argues that party system size is determined by the interaction of social diversity and electoral rules. Social diversity creates the "demand" for political parties. Demand is high when there are many cross-cutting cleavages. The extent to which demand is translated into parties depends on the permissiveness of the electoral system. Electoral rules matter because of their mechanical and strategic effects. The mechanical effect refers to how votes are translated into seats. The mechanical effect of disproportional systems hurts small parties and rewards large ones, as only large parties can win seats. This mechanical effect creates incentives for voters to engage in strategic voting and for elites to engage in strategic entry (Cox 1997). These strategic effects again hurt small parties and reward large parties. According to Duverger's theory, party system size will only be large when social diversity is high and electoral systems are proportional. Numerous empirical studies have supported Duverger's theory (Ordeshook and Shvetsova 1994; Amorim Neto and Cox 1997; Clark and Golder 2006).[1]

Electoral rules have a direct and indirect effect on where parties locate in the policy space. In terms of a direct effect, majoritarian systems reward large parties. To the extent that voter density is highest in the center of the policy space, majoritarian systems create incentives for parties to adopt centrist positions. In contrast, parties in proportional systems compete in a more permissive environment and can win legislative seats even if they hold noncentrist positions (Dow 2001, 2011). Matakos, Troumpounis, and Xefteris (2016) reach a similar conclusion based on a spatial model that directly incorporates electoral system disproportionality. The indirect effect of electoral rules occurs via party system size. The median voter theorem predicts that two parties competing along one policy dimension will converge on the median voter's position (Downs 1957). Cox (1990), as well as Merrill and Adams (2002), present spatial models showing that majoritarian systems with few parties create centripetal tendencies where parties adopt centrist positions, whereas proportional systems with many parties create centrifugal tendencies where parties disperse and carve out niche electorates. Agent-based models of multidimensional competition produce similar results. Kollman, Miller, and Page (1992, 1998) find that two parties competing on multiple dimensions adopt centrist, but distinct, positions. Focusing on a multiparty setting, Laver and Sergenti (2012) demonstrate that party system dispersion increases with the number of parties.

Significantly, the ideological makeup of party systems is not driven solely by electoral incentives. The electoral incentives for parties to disperse in proportional systems are tempered by *government formation* incentives to remain centrist to increase the chances of entering a coalition cabinet (Schofield 1993; Laver and Shepsle 1996; Martin and Stevenson 2001; Glasgow, Golder, and Golder 2011). Similarly, the electoral incentives for parties to adopt centrist positions in majoritarian systems are moderated by *valence* incentives that encourage low-valence parties to differentiate themselves in terms of policy (Schofield 2003; Schofield and Sened 2005). According to Calvo and Hellwig (2011), the centripetal tendencies in majoritarian systems only apply to large parties that can expect to benefit from disproportional vote–seat transfers.

Exactly how these incentives play out is an empirical question. Most empirical studies indicate that electoral rules have a direct (Dow 2011; Calvo and Hellwig 2011), an indirect (Andrews and Money 2009; Curini and Hino 2012), or both a direct and indirect (Matakos, Troumpounis, and Xefteris 2016) effect on party system dispersion. Specifically, they find that majoritarian electoral rules generally produce "compact" party systems where parties adopt centrist positions and that proportional electoral rules produce more ideologically diverse systems.[2] In line with the idea that the electoral incentives to disperse in proportional systems are tempered by government formation incentives to remain centrist, Curini and Hino (2012) find that the number of parties increases party system dispersion when coalition governments are rare but decreases it when coalition governments are common. These empirical results have obvious implications for the different types of party system congruence. On the one hand, party system congruence with the "typical" voter is usually greater in majoritarian systems. On the other hand, congruence between the party system as a whole and the diversity of citizens' preferences is typically greater in proportional systems.

Empirical scholars have yet to fully leverage theoretical developments related to multidimensional spatial competition (Laver 2005). Research on Voronoi diagrams shows that there is a maximum level of party system congruence that is possible for a given party system size and distribution of voter preferences (Laver and Sergenti 2012). A Voronoi diagram splits any policy space into Voronoi regions such that each region is associated with a unique party and all voters in a region are closer to the party "generating" that region than any other party. Party system congruence is maximized when each party is located at the centroid of its Voronoi region—the point that minimizes the sum of the squared distances between itself and all of the other points in the region (Du, Faber, and Gunzberger 1999). This situation is referred to as a centroidal Voronoi tesselation (CVT). If voters are more satisfied the closer their preferences are to the policy position of their closest party, then a CVT maximizes voter satisfaction (Laver and Sergenti 2012, 11). Empirical scholars might wish to use the CVT as a benchmark against which to examine the extent to which party system congruence is achieved in each country. Rather than evaluate congruence in some abstract sense, it may be better to evaluate it relative to what is possible.

The extent to which party system congruence is achieved may also depend on the types of parties in the system. In their agent-based model, Laver and Sergenti (2012) distinguish between three types of parties. "Stickers" are ideological parties that locate at their ideal point and do not move. "Hunters" are vote-seeking parties that repeat successful policy moves but try something different if their votes decline. "Aggregators" are "democratic" parties that adapt policy in line with the preferences of their current supporters. In their model, hunter parties adopt more centrist, but distinct, policy positions than other party types. More significant, though, is that a party system composed of aggregators converges to a CVT and therefore maximizes congruence with respect to citizen preferences. This is despite the fact that aggregators only seek to maximize the representation *of their own supporters* (Laver and Sergenti 2012). More research is required to determine whether electoral rules influence the propensity of these different party types to exist.

So far, we have focused on party system congruence as a whole. Many scholars, though, prefer to examine the congruence between individual parties and their voters. Much of this literature is descriptive and focuses on the extent to which congruence is achieved in different policy areas. Scholars generally find that parties are more congruent with their voters on the left-right and economic policy dimensions than they are on more social or cultural dimensions (Mattila and Raunio 2006; Costello, Thomassen, and Rosema 2012; Schmitt and Thomassen 1999; Klingemann and Fuchs 1995; Dalton, Farrell, and McAllister 2011). Only a few studies actually examine the factors that influence the congruence between parties and their voters (Dalton 1985, forthcoming; Belchior 2012; Boonen, Pedersen, and Hooghe 2014).

In terms of electoral systems most studies predict that party–voter congruence will be higher in proportional systems than in majoritarian ones. Drawing on the spatial models discussed earlier, scholars generally associate proportional systems with many parties that disperse throughout the policy space and majoritarian systems with two (or a few) parties that converge to the center of the voter distribution. Parties in majoritarian systems are expected to be large umbrella parties that represent a coalition of diverse voters, whereas parties in proportional systems are expected to be smaller parties that represent distinct constituencies and build coalitions only after elections have taken place.

There are reasons to believe, however, that the story is more complicated than this. It is important to recognize that most models of party competition assume that voters support the closest party in the policy space. Empirical evidence, though, suggests that many voters in countries with power-sharing institutions, such as proportional systems rules, engage in directional compensatory voting (Kedar 2009). With compensatory voting, individuals care less about having their preferences represented and more about the final policy outcome. A consequence is that many voters support parties whose policy positions differ from, and are often more extreme than, their own (Iversen 1994; Rabinowitz, McDonald, and Listhaug 1994). Thus, even if the average distance between voters and their closest party is smaller in proportional systems, this may not be true for voters and the parties they actually support. In terms of empirical studies, results have been mixed. Although some studies find a positive relationship between proportional systems and party–voter congruence (Dalton 1985), others do not (Belchior 2012; Dalton forthcoming).

# Legislative Congruence

The next stage in the representation process involves translating votes into seats. This brings us to legislative congruence. One way to think about this is in terms of the congruence between the median legislative party and the median citizen/voter. This type of congruence is considered important as the median legislative party, irrespective of its size, enjoys a pivotal position in one-dimensional bargaining models and in models of parliamentary government formation (Laver and Schofield 1990).

Theoretically, congruence between the median legislative party and median voter can be achieved under different electoral systems. Majoritarian systems should produce small party systems with centripetal incentives to adopt centrist positions relative to the electorate. Proportional systems should produce large party systems with centrifugal incentives to carve out niche electorates. By dispersing throughout the policy space, at least one of the parties in a proportional system is likely to be located close to the median voter (Budge et al. 2012; Powell 2009). Although this type of legislative congruence *can* be achieved under both types of electoral systems, many claim that the necessary conditions to achieve congruence in majoritarian systems are more demanding, and thus less likely to be met, than those to achieve congruence in proportional ones (Pinto-Duschinsky et al. 1999; Powell 2000, 2006, 2009; Grofman 2004). In line with this reasoning, Golder and Lloyd (2014) find that legislative congruence is not only lower in majoritarian systems but also more variable. Other studies have also shown that congruence between the median legislative party and median voter is lower in majoritarian systems (Powell and Vanberg 2000; McDonald, Mendes, and Budge 2004; McDonald and Budge 2005; Powell 2006).

Another potential reason legislative congruence is lower in majoritarian systems has to do with the way that electoral rules influence the partisan composition of legislatures. Rodden (2006, 2010) argues that the geographic distribution of voters brought about by the Industrial Revolution means that majoritarian electoral rules hurt the legislative representation of left-wing voters. Left-wing parties tend to draw their support from concentrated pockets of voters in urban industrial and mining areas. Under majoritarian rules, this geographic concentration of left-wing votes means that left-wing parties win their districts by a large margin, but with a high number of wasted votes. In effect, left-wing support is not efficiently translated into legislative representation in majoritarian systems. The geographic concentration of left-wing voters is less consequential in proportional systems, as votes are more accurately translated into seats. That said, Kedar, Harsgor, and Scheinerman (2016) show that proportional systems, to the extent that they have some constituencies with low district magnitudes, also overcompensate voters supporting right-wing parties. In effect, left-wing voters receive less legislative representation the more disproportional the electoral system is.

A second way to think about legislative congruence is in terms of the extent to which the distribution of legislative seats corresponds to the ideological distribution of preferences in a country. Many democratic theorists have emphasized the importance of having a collective body of representatives that accurately corresponds to, and hence advocates for, the diversity of citizens' preferences. Proportional electoral rules should produce higher levels of this type of legislative congruence as they encourage a more diverse party system and they more accurately translate votes into seats. Golder and Stramski (2010) find empirical evidence consistent with this claim.

A third way to examine legislative congruence is to look at how *individual* legislators represent citizens. On the whole, there is evidence of significant divergence between individual legislators and their district median voters (Gerber and Lewis 2004; Stadelmann, Portmann, and Eichenberger 2012).[3] Directly measuring congruence between individual legislators and voters can be difficult, as this requires identifying legislator and voter preferences with respect to particular policies. Some studies attempt to correlate legislator "ideology scores" with constituency characteristics such as district ideology (Erikson, Wright, and McIver 1993). This is problematic, though, as legislator and voter preferences are measured on different scales, and a positive correlation does not necessarily indicate evidence of legislative congruence (Achen 1977; Matsusaka 2001, 2010). Some of these difficulties can be avoided by looking at specific policy choices rather than broad ideological dimensions such as the left-right scale (Lax and Phillips 2009). If policy choices are dichotomous, scholars can examine congruence more directly by examining whether legislator roll-call votes are in line with the preferences of their district or national median voter.

Several recent studies have adopted this methodology to investigate how electoral rules affect legislator congruence. Portmann, Stadelmann, and Eichenberger (2012) and Stadelmann, Portmann, and Eichenberger (2013) match the voting record of Swiss members of parliament on legislative proposals with real referendum outcomes on the same issues. They argue that the centripetal incentives to align with the district median voter are strong when district magnitude is low. As political representation can be considered a public good, they also expect it to be underprovided as district magnitude increases. As predicted, they find that Swiss legislators are more likely to vote with their constituency (and national) median voter as district magnitude decreases.[4] Reanalyzing the data, Carey and Hix (2013) suggest that the relationship between district magnitude and legislative congruence is nonmonotonic. They claim that districts with four to eight legislative seats represent an "electoral sweet spot" (Carey and Hix 2011). This is because legislators in very small magnitude districts often fail to align with the district median voter due to "coordination failures" and because voters in very large magnitude districts with many representatives suffer from cognitive overload that makes it difficult for them to identify congruent representatives and monitor legislative behavior.

Stadelmann, Portmann, and Eichenberger (forthcoming) examine the interactive effect of electoral rules and party membership on legislator congruence. As multiparty systems create incentives for parties to disperse in the policy space, legislators in left- and right-wing parties should be less likely to vote with their district than legislators in centrist parties. Left- and right-wing legislators elected in "majoritarian" constituencies, though, have incentives to deviate from their party to attract their district median voter. An implication is that party affiliation is more likely to be a source of legislator incongruence in proportional systems than majoritarian ones. Leveraging the fact that members of the Swiss National Council are elected using proportional representation but that members of the Swiss Council of States are elected using majoritarian electoral rules, Stadelmann, Portmann, and Eichenberger show that left- and right-wing legislators are more incongruent with their districts in both legislative houses than centrist legislators. Importantly, they also show that left- and right-wing legislators in the majoritarian Council of States are significantly more congruent than their party counterparts in the proportional National Council.

## Government Congruence

The next stage in the representation process involves translating legislative seats into governments. In practice, government congruence is almost always conceptualized as the correspondence between the government's policy position and the preferences of the national median voter on the left-right dimension. However, one might also think of it as the correspondence between the government's policy position and the preferences of *its* supporters. Government congruence is especially important, as governments, rather than legislatures, typically play the dominant role in the policymaking process.

The government formation process takes a distribution of legislative seats as its input and produces a government (Golder, Golder, and Siegel 2012). The median legislative party has significant power in parliamentary democracies as governments must enjoy legislative majority support (Laver and Schofield 1998). According to Duverger's theory, majoritarian systems produce few parties. As a result, there is a good chance the median party will control a legislative majority and be able to form a single-party government. Spatial models indicate that majoritarian systems encourage parties to adopt centrist positions. This means that any single-party government is likely to be fairly congruent with the national median voter. According to this causal story where the median legislative party forms a single-party government, there will be no change in congruence with respect to the median voter as we move from the legislature to the government.

Coalition governments are more likely in proportional electoral systems, as these systems typically produce many parties, none of which are able to control a legislative majority. Although the median legislative party is likely to be in the government due to its pivotal position in the legislature, it will typically have to form a government with parties either to its left or right. This coalition-building process will often produce a government that is further from the median voter than the median legislative party is on its own (McDonald and Budge 2005). This causal story suggests that congruence will decline in proportional systems as we move from the legislature to the government. It also suggests that government congruence will be more variable in proportional systems as much depends on the size and ideological location of potential coalition partners. Empirical evidence in support of these claims comes from Golder and Lloyd (2014).

Whether government congruence will be better in an absolute sense under one electoral system or another is unclear. Government congruence results from a two-step causal process (Powell 2009). In the first step, party competition determines the size and ideological location of legislative parties. In the second step, these legislative parties form a government. As Cox (1997) notes, majoritarian systems are likely to experience coordination failures in the electoral stage—voters may not coordinate on the median legislative party and political elites may form too many parties. If this occurs, the median legislative party may not be the largest party and may not get to form the government. Such coordination failures help to explain why legislative congruence, as we have seen, tends to be lower in majoritarian systems than in proportional ones. Theory, though, suggests that this congruence advantage for proportional systems will decline, and may even disappear, during the government formation stage when parties form coalition governments.

Evidence that electoral rules influence the government's partisan composition further complicates the relationship between electoral systems and government congruence. Empirically, left-wing governments are more common than right-wing governments in proportional systems, whereas the opposite is true in majoritarian systems (Iversen and Soskice 2006; Döring and Manow 2017). One explanation for this, as previously discussed, is that proportional systems produce more left-wing legislatures due to the geographic distribution of left-wing support. Another explanation, though, is that differences in coalition bargaining across electoral systems also affect the government's partisan composition. Building on a model of redistribution, Iversen and Soskice (2006) argue that the middle class in the two-party systems produced by majoritarian electoral rules will vote for the right party, as the left party cannot credibly commit not to redistribute from both the rich and the middle class. In the multiparty systems produced by proportional electoral rules, though, the middle class will have its own centrist party, which will be the median legislative party. Given its pivotal position, the centrist party will be willing to form a coalition government with the left party to redistribute only from the rich. Empirically, Iversen and Soskice (2006) find not only that left-wing governments form more often and introduce more redistributive policies under proportional systems but also that right-wing governments, when they do form, also implement more redistributive policies than they would in majoritarian systems. These results hold even when the partisan composition of the government is measured relative to the median voter.

Numerous empirical studies have examined the effect of electoral rules on government congruence. Early studies indicated that government congruence was greater in proportional systems. This was the conclusion from scholars who used voter surveys to identify the position of the median voter and expert surveys to identify the ideological location of the government (Huber and Powell 1994; Lijphart 1999; Powell 2006; Powell and Vanberg 2000). It was also the conclusion from scholars who used data from the Comparative Manifesto Project to identify the positions of the median voter and the government (Budge and McDonald 2007; McDonald and Budge 2005; McDonald, Mendes, and Budge 2004).

More recent studies, though, have called these early findings into question. On measurement grounds, concerns have been raised about how scholars use the comparative manifesto data to identify the median voter's position (Warwick and Zakharova 2013). Concerns have also been raised about combining information from voter and expert surveys, as voters and experts do not seem to view the policy space in the same way (Golder and Stramski 2010). Using survey data from the Comparative Study of Electoral Systems (CSES) that sees voters place themselves and governments on the same left-right scale, Blais and Bodet (2006) and Golder and Stramski (2010) find no evidence that government congruence differs across majoritarian and proportional electoral systems. Powell (2009) suggests that these "null" results might be due to the more recent time period (post-1995) covered by the CSES data. However, using data that spans most of the postwar period, Golder and Lloyd (2014) and Ferland (2016) still find no evidence that government congruence differs across electoral systems. Significantly, this result holds whether one employs data from voter surveys or from the comparative manifesto project.

Most studies look at government congruence at a fixed point in time, typically after elections. However, one might also examine government congruence over time. According to Powell's (2000) visions of democracy, governments in majoritarian systems should not change their policy position between elections as they are "mandated" to implement the policies on which they campaigned. In contrast, governments in proportional systems are supposed to continually adapt their policy positions to reflect changes in voter preferences. It follows that any changes in the median voter's preferences should lead to incongruence over the course of a government's mandate in majoritarian systems but not in proportional ones. In a recent study, however, Ferland (2016) finds no evidence for this. Instead, he finds that congruence declines in both systems. Interestingly, he finds that congruence declines in majoritarian systems because governments move away from a "static" median voter and that congruence declines in proportional systems because the median voter moves away from a "static" government. His overall results show that there is no difference in government congruence across majoritarian and proportional electoral systems, either at the beginning or end of a government's term in office. Future research might wish to examine the robustness of these results.

To date, there has been almost no research on ideological congruence in presidential democracies. Scholars of government formation have historically focused on the parliamentary democracies of Western Europe. In recent years, though, there has been an upsurge of interest in how governments form in presidential democracies, especially in Latin America (Kellam 2015; Amorim Neto 2006; Amorim Neto and Samuels 2010; Samuels 2007; Cheibub, Przeworski, and Saiegh 2004).[5] This research offers an untapped resource for those interested in understanding government congruence in presidential democracies.

Most presidents are elected using an absolute majority electoral system (Bormann and Golder 2013). This electoral system creates centripetal incentives, at least in the second round, as candidates seek out the support of the median voter. The result is that presidential congruence should be fairly high. Research on government formation in presidential democracies suggests that the extent to which presidential congruence is reflected in the government and in policy will depend on the size of the presidential party and the power of the president. If the president's party has a legislative majority, then presidential congruence should be maintained when it comes to the government and policy. However, if the president's party does not control a legislative majority, much will depend on the power of the president. If the president is powerful, he or she is expected to eschew forming a coalition government and instead use decree powers to achieve his or her policy objectives. In this scenario, congruence can be maintained. In contrast, if the president is weak, he or she will need to form a coalition to achieve his or her policy objectives, likely diminishing congruence in the process. The negative effect of coalition formation on congruence in presidential democracies should not be as strong as in parliamentary democracies, though, as presidents are not as generous in the allocation of ministerial portfolios to their coalition partners as their counterparts in parliamentary democracies (Golder and Thomas 2014, Ariotti and Golder forthcoming). To our knowledge, these types of theoretical claims have not been tested.

## Policy Congruence

At the end of the representation chain is policy. Ultimately, ideological congruence requires that policies be in line with the preferences of the citizenry. Although scholars routinely examine party system congruence, legislative congruence, and government congruence, very few look at policy congruence. One reason for this is that it is difficult to get an overall measure of policy congruence. When looking at specific policies, it can be difficult to obtain citizen preferences, especially if the policy space is continuous. Even if one could obtain these preferences, it can be hard to place them on a common scale with the actual policy outcomes.

In the American context, scholars often seek to correlate policy outcomes with state ideology (Erikson, Wright, and McIver 1993). Are certain policies more likely to be adopted in conservative states than liberal ones? As Achen (1977) and Matsusaka (2001, 2010) point out, though, these studies do not actually address congruence. A strong positive correlation between policy adoption and state ideology says little about whether implemented policies are congruent with citizens' preferences because we do not know how broad measures of state ideology should be translated into preferences for actual policies.

Recently, some scholars have examined the extent to which dichotomous policies match up with majority opinion. Lax and Phillips (2012), for example, adopt this approach to examine policy congruence across a range of issues in the American states. They find that state governments translate majority opinion into policy only about half the time. To our knowledge, these types of studies have not examined the effect of electoral rules on policy congruence. What about continuous policies? Soroka and Wlezien (2010) suggest that one can examine continuous policies by looking at relative, as opposed to absolute, citizen preferences. Instead of asking citizens what the level of, say, education spending should be, we can ask them whether education spending should remain the same, be increased, or be decreased. We can then see whether policy moves in the direction desired by the citizens. As Soroka and Wlezien (2010) recognize, though, this approach speaks more to policy responsiveness than policy congruence.

Of potential relevance is the small literature that examines whether government parties fulfill the policy pledges in their manifestos. This literature is useful as it helps to indicate whether government congruence is a good proxy for policy congruence. In one recent study, Thomson et al. (2014) find that single-party governments fulfill more of their pledges than coalition governments. There are limitations to these types of studies, though. One is that they do not address whether the policy pledges are congruent with voter preferences. Another is that they say nothing about policies that do not appear in the manifestos.

# INDIRECT EFFECTS ON IDEOLOGICAL CONGRUENCE

So far we have looked at how electoral rules influence ideological congruence directly. However, electoral rules can indirectly influence ideological congruence by affecting elite responsiveness and levels of descriptive representation.

## Responsiveness

A responsive representative is one who changes his or her behavior to become more congruent with the preferences of those he or she represents. Two conditions are necessary for responsiveness (Soroka and Wlezien 2015; Ferland 2015). The representative must want to become more congruent *and* must be able to act on those desires. If there are weak incentives to be responsive, responsiveness will be low irrespective of whether or not the representative has the ability to respond. If there are strong incentives to be responsive but constraints on the ability to be responsive, responsiveness will also be low. Only if the representative has strong incentives and the ability to respond will responsiveness be high. This basic story is illustrated in Figure 11.2. To date, the existing literature has largely ignored the inherent interaction between demand-side (incentives) and supply-side (ability) factors affecting levels of responsiveness.

Scholars of ideological congruence generally share a common theoretical foundation built on spatial models of party competition and Duverger's theory of party system size (Powell 2009; Golder and Lloyd 2014). This is less the case with scholars of ideological responsiveness. Electoral rules are widely recognized as a key determinant of ideological congruence because of the way they create incentives for parties to converge or disperse in the policy space. These centripetal and centrifugal pressures determine elite incentives to be responsive to particular citizens, thereby influencing the level of

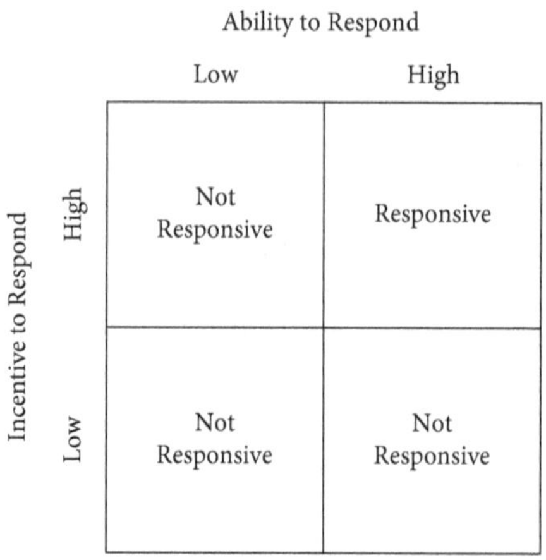

Ability to Respond

Low                          High

|  | Low | High |
| Incentive to Respond / High | Not Responsive | Responsive |
| Incentive to Respond / Low | Not Responsive | Not Responsive |

**FIGURE 11.2.** Conditions for responsiveness.

ideological congruence. Despite this, relatively few studies of ideological responsiveness address the impact of electoral rules, preferring instead to focus on things like issue salience (Page and Shapiro 1983; Burstein 2003), different policy domains (Miller and Stokes 1963; Jacobs and Page 2005), and unequal representation in the policymaking process (Bartels 2008; Gilens 2012; Wlezien and Soroka 2011). We believe that considerable progress can be made if scholars of congruence and responsiveness were to adopt a more unified theoretical framework.

Spatial models suggest that the incentives for governments to be responsive to the median voter's preferences will be higher in majoritarian electoral systems than proportional ones. Single-party governments, which typically form in majoritarian systems, have incentives to closely follow the preferences of the median voter.[6] Things are more complicated for the coalition governments that usually form in proportional systems. The centrifugal pressures created by proportional systems mean that not all government parties will want to be responsive to the median voter's preferences. In particular, those parties holding noncentrist positions are likely to be more responsive to the preferences of their own supporters. Studies of party responsiveness find that niche parties are more responsive to changes in the position of their supporters but that mainstream parties are more responsive to changes in the position of the median voter (Adams et al. 2006; Ezrow et al. 2010; Schumacher, De Vries, and Vis 2013). Although these studies do not directly address the impact of electoral rules, their results are in line with the idea that the parties in coalition governments face conflicting incentives about who they should be responsive to.

At least two other reasons have been proposed for why majoritarian systems create stronger incentives to be responsive than proportional ones. Some scholars argue that the greater vote–seat elasticity experienced in majoritarian systems encourages parties to respond more strongly to changes in public opinion (Wlezien and Soroka 2012; Soroka and Wlezien 2015). Others argue that the incentives to be responsive depend on the ability of voters to punish unresponsive elites (Ferland 2015). As coalition governments reduce clarity of responsibility (Powell and Whitten 1993; Fisher and Hobolt 2010), we should expect that single-party governments in majoritarian systems face stronger incentives to be responsive.

Although elites may have incentives to be responsive, institutions, such as electoral rules, can inhibit their ability to act on those incentives. Veto player theory, for example, indicates that the ability of elites to be responsive will be low if there is a large number of ideologically diverse veto players (Tsebelis 2002). By encouraging larger and more diverse party systems that result in coalition governments, proportional systems lower the ability of political elites to respond to changes in citizen preferences compared to their counterparts in majoritarian systems. Putting this all together suggests that responsiveness will be greater under majoritarian systems because both the incentives and ability to respond are higher under these systems.

On the whole, empirical results generally show that government responsiveness is higher in majoritarian systems. Although Hobolt and Klemmensen (2005, 2008) find that governments are more responsive in Denmark (proportional system) than in Britain (majoritarian system), most studies that examine a wider range of countries find the opposite (Coman 2015; Wlezien and Soroka 2012; Soroka and Wlezien 2015; Ferland 2015). In line with the idea that the ability to respond is important, Ferland (2015) and Coman (2015) find that government responsiveness declines with the number of parties in the cabinet. Similarly, Klüver and Spoon (2016) show that parties in coalition governments are less responsive to voters' issue priorities when the coalition is more ideologically divided. None of these empirical studies explicitly examine the inherent interaction between the incentives and ability to be responsive shown in Figure 11.2.

## Descriptive and Substantive Representation

There is a large literature that looks at descriptive and substantive representation with respect to gender and race. This literature has developed in almost complete isolation from the research on citizen-elite ideological congruence.[7] Significant gains can be made if scholars from these two literatures interact more often.

Descriptive representation is often viewed as inferior to substantive representation (Pitkin 1967). One reason for this is that representatives can only be held accountable for what they do, not who they are (Celis et al. 2008). Many scholars, though, have argued that descriptive representation is important, particularly when there is widespread mistrust or "uncrystallized interests" (Mansbridge 1999; Phillips 1998). Some claim that descriptive representation is important in its own right because it signals a politics of recognition and acceptance and enhances a sense of fairness and legitimacy. More significant for the current discussion, though, some claim that descriptive representation is also important because it promotes substantive representation. The underlying idea is that individuals who share similar descriptive characteristics are likely to have developed a sense of linked fate and shared experiences that generate a common set of perspectives and substantive interests (Dawson 1995; Phillips 1998; Tate 1994; Young 2002). By promoting descriptive representation, one can therefore promote substantive representation.

To the extent that this is true, electoral rules can influence substantive representation and ideological congruence by affecting levels of descriptive representation.[8] A common claim is that proportional representation with large district magnitudes produces greater descriptive representation of women than majoritarian systems (Krook, this volume; Matland and Studlar 1996; Paxton 1997; Caul 1999; Reynolds 1999; Tremblay 2008; Kittilson and Schwindt-Bayer 2010).[9] Several stories have been proposed to support this claim. One story is that the incumbency advantage is larger in majoritarian systems and that incumbents are typically men (Fréchette, Maniquet, and Morelli 2008). Another story is that majoritarian systems are more competitive and that parties think voters are less likely to support women candidates in these circumstances (Roberts, Seawright, and Cyr 2013). A third story builds on the idea that left-wing parties fare better under proportional representation. This is important, as women tend to hold more left-wing attitudes (Wängnerud 2009) and left-wing parties, especially of the new left variety (Kittilson 2006), have more women representatives.

Some studies have called into question the strength of the relationship between proportional representation and descriptive representation on methodological grounds (Salmond 2006; Roberts, Seawright, and Cyr 2013). Others have questioned the causal stories linking proportional representation to greater descriptive representation. It is not clear, for example, that women candidates always do worse in majoritarian systems and better in proportional ones (Lawless and Pearson 2008; Schwindt-Bayer, Malecki, and Crisp 2010; Fulton 2014), or that majoritarian systems are necessarily more competitive. Schmidt (2009) also notes that large district magnitudes tend to occur in wealthy urban areas where cultural attitudes are more amenable to women candidates irrespective of the electoral system.

With the apparent consensus that proportional representation promotes descriptive representation, many scholars have focused on whether open or closed list systems perform best (Jones and Navia 1999; Wauters, Weekers, and Maddens 2010; Thames and Williams 2010; Luhiste 2015; Golder et al. 2017). Empirical results are mixed. One reason for this is that scholars have generally ignored the interaction between demand-side and supply-side factors affecting descriptive representation (Dhima 2016).[10] Demand for descriptive representation can come from voters or elites. Whereas demand from elites is sufficient to produce high descriptive representation, demand from voters is neither necessary nor sufficient. If demand is low among both voters and elites, then descriptive representation will be low irrespective of the type of party list system. If demand is high among both voters and elites, then descriptive representation will be high irrespective of the list system. If demand from voters is low but high from elites, then elites can use closed lists with quotas and placement mandates to ensure a high level of descriptive representation. And if demand is high from voters but low from party elites, then party elites can use closed list systems to ensure that descriptive representation remains low.

In this framework, electoral rules and the level of descriptive representation are primarily determined by the preferences of party elites.

The claim that descriptive representation promotes substantive representation has been challenged on a number of grounds. One criticism is that scholars who make this claim are essentializing women, ignoring the diversity that exists among women, and failing to recognize that men can also act on behalf of women (Celis 2009; Childs and Krook 2006). One response to this criticism has been the increased focus on the representation of intersectional identities (Hughes 2011; Hancock 2007; Weldon 2006). A parallel development in the ideological congruence literature would be to focus on the diversity of citizen preferences rather than just those of the median voter. A second criticism is that too much attention is being paid to women's representation in formal political institutions such as legislatures rather than in other settings such as women's movements or policy agencies (Weldon 2002; Celis et al. 2008; Celis and Childs 2008). This is a criticism that can also be made of the ideological congruence literature, and harkens back to our earlier discussion of alternative views of representation. A third criticism is that scholars have taken a narrow and top-down approach to identifying women's substantive interests (Wängnerud 2009; Celis et al. 2008; Celis 2009). This often results in women's substantive interests being associated with a particular version of feminism and a failure to recognize the diverse and contested nature of women's interests.

The strength of the empirical evidence linking descriptive representation to substantive representation is also contested. For example, there is little compelling evidence for critical mass theory (Childs and Krook 2006), the idea that the substantive representation of women increases once the percentage of women representatives breaks some threshold (Kanter 1977; Dahlerup 1988). Htun (2016) refers to evidence of increased descriptive representation but low substantive representation as "inclusion without representation." The low substantive representation of women is often attributed to the fact that women representatives are constrained by their limited legislative experience, their party affiliations, institutional rules, and their limited access to powerful positions (Beckwith 2007; Celis et al. 2008; Celis 2009). Rather than simply focus on the number of women representatives for substantive representation, scholars have increasingly highlighted the important role that critical actors, both men and women, play in initiating women-friendly policy and encouraging others to take up particular causes (Celis et al. 2008; Childs and Krook 2006; Htun 2016).

We believe that the gender literature dealing with descriptive and substantive representation can benefit from incorporating ideas from the ideological congruence literature. Although congruence scholars focus on the ideological correspondence between representatives and voters, it would be easy to apply existing concepts, measures, theories, and methods to examine the representation of women voters. Doing so has the potential to address some of the criticisms made of existing studies of women's substantive representation.

# CONCLUSION

Electoral systems play an important role in determining citizen-elite ideological congruence. This is because they affect each stage of the representation process as we move from citizen preferences to policy outcomes. Indeed, electoral rules can shape the very preferences that citizens hold in the first place through the incentives they create for political entrepreneurs to politicize and mobilize some societal cleavages as opposed to others.

Whether majoritarian or proportional electoral systems produce greater citizen-elite ideological congruence depends on how we conceptualize congruence. As an example, consider ideological congruence in the party system. Majoritarian rules are associated with more compact party systems where parties tend to adopt centrist positions, whereas proportional rules are associated with more ideologically diverse party systems. A consequence is that majoritarian systems tend to produce greater party system congruence with the "typical" voter, whereas proportional systems tend to produce greater congruence with the preferences of the citizenry as a whole. A similar situation arises when we consider ideological congruence in the legislature. Proportional rules produce legislatures that are more reflective of the diversity of citizen preferences in society, but majoritarian rules encourage legislators to be more congruent with the preferences of the "typical" voter in their districts. Whether one prefers majoritarian or proportional electoral rules in these contexts is implicitly tied up with normative issues related to how we value different conceptualizations of ideological congruence and political representation more broadly.

Whether majoritarian or proportional electoral systems produce greater citizen-elite ideological congruence also depends on where we are in the representation process. Electoral rules and other institutions can cause deviations in citizen-elite ideological congruence to emerge and disappear as we move from citizen preferences to policy outcomes. As an example, proportional systems seem to have an empirical advantage over majoritarian systems when it comes to legislative congruence (the distance between the median legislative party and the median voter), but this advantage seems to disappear when it comes to government congruence (the distance between the government and the median voter). Thus, preferences for majoritarian or proportional electoral systems with respect to ideological congruence necessarily imply specifying which stage of the representation process is most important.

Electoral systems affect citizen-elite ideological congruence in both direct and indirect ways. Their direct effect is typically felt through their impact on party system size and the ideological location of parties in the policy space. Most existing studies have focused on these direct ways in which electoral rules influence ideological congruence. Importantly, though, electoral rules can also affect ideological congruence indirectly through their impact on elite responsiveness and descriptive representation. Elite responsiveness leads to improved congruence. Electoral rules are important here because they influence both the incentive and ability of elites to respond to citizen preferences. It is well known that electoral rules can have a strong impact on descriptive representation. To the extent that descriptive representation improves substantive representation, electoral rules will therefore have an indirect impact on citizen-elite ideological congruence.

Although research on citizen-elite ideological congruence is quite extensive, our review of the literature suggests that there are several lines of inquiry worth pursuing. We finish by highlighting just a few of them. Existing studies have focused primarily on the United States and the parliamentary democracies of Western Europe. Scholars might fruitfully examine ideological congruence in parliamentary and *presidential* regimes in other regions of the world. We believe that there are significant opportunities to be exploited by combining theoretical, empirical, and methodological insights from the ideological congruence literature and the descriptive and substantive representation literature as it relates to gender and race. For too long, these literatures have developed in relative isolation from each other even though they address the same fundamental issues. Similarly, we believe that much can be gained from a greater interaction between scholars interested in ideological congruence and those interested in ideological responsiveness.

## Acknowledgments

We thank Charles Crabtree, Kostanca Dhima, and Sona N. Golder for their helpful comments on this chapter.

## Notes

1. While Duverger's theory focuses on the effect of electoral rules on the size of the party system, it is worth recognizing that electoral system choice is often endogenous to the preferences of elites within the party system (Benoit 2007; Bawn 1993; Boix 1999; Colomer, this volume).

2. A few studies find no relationship between electoral rules and party system dispersion (Ezrow 2008; Dalton 2008; Budge and McDonald 2006). Ezrow (2011), though, later concurs with Dow (2011) that majoritarian electoral rules do, in fact, produce more compact party systems. Significantly, Dalton's (2008) analysis does not speak to questions of party system congruence per se as his measure of party system polarization is not calculated relative to voter preferences. The analysis conducted by Budge and McDonald (2006) is limited because it focuses only on the distance between the two most extreme parties in a system.

3. Much of the literature in this tradition focuses on the United States. Given the limited variation in electoral rules, Americanist scholars typically point to legislator ideology, party affiliation, interest groups, campaign contributions, party activists, and district-level heterogeneity to explain the ideological incongruence between legislators and their constituents (Gerber and Lewis 2004).

4. Stadelmann, Portmann, and Eichenberger (2014) note that although the probability that an *individual* Swiss legislator votes with his or her district median voter decreases with district magnitude, the law of large numbers, combined with the fact that legislators typically vote with their district more than half the time, means that the probability that a *majority* of a district's representatives vote with their district median voter actually *increases* with district magnitude.

5. A few studies have also begun to examine government formation in the presidential (and parliamentary) democracies of Africa (Arriola 2009; Arriola and Johnson 2014; Ariotti and Golder forthcoming).

6. There is some debate as to whether governments in majoritarian systems will respond to the national median voter or the median voter in the pivotal district (Hobolt and Klemmensen 2008).

7. For an exception, see Kernell (2012).

8. In what follows, we focus on the literature dealing with women's representation. Similar arguments, though, can be made with respect to the literature dealing with the representation of minority groups.

9. There is some evidence that cumulative voting can increase the descriptive representation of minority groups, as minorities can cumulate their vote on minority candidates (Gerber, Morton, and Rietz 1998). Golder et al. (2017) find that support for women candidates is also higher with cumulative voting, especially among women voters.

10. Although scholars have long recognized that demand-side factors, such as cultural attitudes, and supply-side factors, such as electoral rules, influence descriptive representation (Inglehart and Norris 2003; Paxton, Kunovich, and Hughes 2007), they almost always address these factors separately or include them only additively in their empirical analyses (Dhima 2016).

# REFERENCES

Achen, Christopher H. "Measuring Representation: Perils of the Correlation Coefficient." *American Journal of Political Science* 21, no. 4 (1977): 805–815.

Achen, Christopher H. "Measuring Representation." *American Journal of Political Science* 22, no. 3 (1978): 475–510.

Adams, James, Michael Clark, Lawrence Ezrow, and Garrett Glasgow. "Are Niche Parties Fundamentally Different from Mainstream Parties? The Causes and the Electoral Consequences of Western European Parties' Policy Shifts, 1976-1998." *American Journal of Political Science* 50, no. 3 (2006): 513–529.

Adams, James, Andrea B. Haupt, and Heather Stoll. "What Moves Parties? The Role of Public Opinion and Global Economic Conditions in Western Europe." *Comparative Political Studies* 42, no. 5 (2009): 611–639.

Amorim Neto, Octavio. "The Presidential Calculus: Executive Policy Making and Cabinet Formation in the Americas." *Comparative Political Studies* 39 (2006): 415–440.

Amorim Neto, Octavio, and Gary W. Cox. "Electoral Institutions, Cleavage Structures, and the Number of Parties." *American Journal of Political Science* 41, no. 1 (1997): 149–174.

Amorim Neto, Octavio, and David Samuels. "Democratic Regimes and Cabinet Politics: A Global Perspective." *Revista Ibero-Americana de Estudios Legislativos* 1 (2010): 10–23.

Andrews, Josephine T., and Jeanette Money. "The Spatial Structure of Party Competition." *British Journal of Political Science* 39, no. 4 (2009): 805–824.

Arriola, Leonardo R. "Patronage and Political Stability in Africa." *Comparative Political Studies* 42 (2009): 1339–1362.

Arriola, Leonardo R., and Martha C. Johnson. "Ethnic Politics and Women's Empowerment in Africa: Ministerial Appointments to Executive Cabinets." *American Journal of Political Science* 58 (2014): 495–510.

Ariotti, Margaret H., and Sona N. Golder. "Partisan Portfolio Allocation in African Democracies." *Comparative Political Studies*, forthcoming.

Bartels, Larry M. *Unequal Democracy: The Political Economy of the New Gilded Age*. Princeton, NJ: Princeton University Press, 2008.

Bawn, Kathleen. "The Logic of Institutional Preferences: German Electoral Law as a Social Choice Outcome." *American Journal of Political Science* 37, no. 4 (1993): 965–989.

Beckwith, Karen. "Numbers and Newness: The Descriptive and Substantive Representation of Women." *Canadian Journal of Political Science* 40, no. 1 (2007): 27–49.

Belchior, Ana Maria. "Explaining Left-Right Party Congruence across European Party Systems: A Test of Micro-, Meso-, and Macro-Level Models." *Comparative Political Studies* 46, no. 3 (2012): 352–386.

Benoit, Kenneth. "Electoral Laws as Political Consequences: Explaining the Origins and Change of Electoral Institutions." *Annual Review of Political Science* 10 (2007): 363–390.

Blais, André, and Marc-André Bodet. "Does Proportional Representation Foster Closer Congruence between Citizens and Policy Makers?" *Comparative Political Studies* 39, no. 10 (2006): 1243–1262.

Boix, Carles. "Setting the Rules of the Game: The Choice of Electoral Systems in Advanced Democracies." *American Political Science Review* 93, no. 3 (1999): 609–624.

Boonen, Joris, Eva Falk Pedersen, and Marc Hooghe. "The Influence of Political Sophistication and Party Identification on Party-Voter Congruence: A Comparative Analysis of 37 Countries." Paper presented at the 2014 Belgian Dutch Political Science Conference, Maastricht.

Bormann, Nils-Christian, and Matt Golder. "Democratic Electoral Systems around the World." *Electoral Studies* 32 (2013): 360–369.

Budge, Ian, and Michael D. McDonald. "Choices Parties Define: Policy Alternatives in Representation Elections, 17 Countries 1945-1998." *Party Politics* 12, no. 4 (2006): 451–466.

Budge, Ian, and Michael D. McDonald. "Election and Party System Effects on Policy Representation: Bringing Time into a Comparative Perspective." *Electoral Studies* 26 (2007): 168–179.

Budge, Ian, Michael McDonald, Paul Pennings, and Hans Keman. *Organizing Democratic Choice: Party Representation over Time*. New York: Oxford University Press, 2012.

Burstein, Paul. "The Impact of Public Opinion on Public Policy: A Review and an Agenda." *Political Research Quarterly* 56, no. 1 (2003): 29–40.

Calvo, Ernesto, and Timothy Hellwig. "Centripetal and Centrifugal Incentives under Different Electoral Systems." *American Journal of Political Science* 55, no. 1 (2011): 27–41.

Carey, John M., and Simon Hix. "The Electoral Sweet Spot: Low-Magnitude Proportional Electoral Systems." *American Journal of Political Science* 55, no. 2 (2011): 383–397.

Carey, John M., and Simon Hix. "District Magnitude and Representation of the Majority's Preferences: A Comment and Reinterpretation." *Public Choice* 154 (2013): 139–148.

Carey, John M., and Matthew Soberg Shugart. "Incentives to Cultivate a Personal Vote: A Rank Ordering of Electoral Formulas." *Electoral Studies* 14, no. 4 (1995): 417–439.

Caul, Miki. "Women's Representation in Parliament: The Role of Political Parties." *Party Politics* 5, no. 1 (1999): 79–98.

Celis, Karen. "Substantive Representation of Women (and Improving It): What It Is and Should Be About." *Comparative European Politics* 7 (2009): 95–113.

Celis, Karen, and Sarah Childs. "The Descriptive and Substantive Representation of Women: New Directions." *Parliamentary Affairs* 61, no. 3 (2008): 419–425.

Celis, Karen, Sarah Childs, Johanna Kantola, and Mona Lena Krook. "Rethinking Women's Substantive Representation." *Representation* 44, no. 2 (2008): 99–110.

Chandra, Kanchan. *Why Ethnic Parties Succeed.* Cambridge: Cambridge University Press, 2004.

Chandra, Kanchan. "What Is Ethnic Identity and Does It Matter?" *Annual Review of Political Science* 9 (2006): 397–424.

Chandra, Kanchan, ed. *Constructivist Theories of Ethnic Politics.* Oxford: Oxford University Press, 2012.

Cheibub, José, Adam Przeworski, and Sebastian Saiegh. "Government Coalitions and Legislative Success under Presidentialism and Parliamentarism." *British Journal of Political Science* 34 (2004): 565–587.

Childs, Sarah, and Mona Lena Krook. "Should Feminists Give Up on Critical Mass? A Contingent 'Yes.'" *Politics and Gender* 2, no. 4 (2006): 522–530.

Clark, William Roberts, and Matt Golder. "Rehabilitating Duverger's Theory—Testing the Mechanical and Strategic Modifying Effects of Electoral Laws." *Comparative Political Studies* 39, no. 6 (2006): 679–708.

Clark, William Roberts, Matt Golder, and Sona N. Golder. *Principles of Comparative Politics.* Washington, DC: CQ Press, 2017.

Coman, Emanuel Emil. "Electoral Proportionality, Multi-Party Cabinets and Policy Responsiveness." *Electoral Studies* 40 (2015): 200–209.

Costello, Rory, Jacques Thomassen, and Martin Rosema. "European Parliament Elections and Political Representation: Policy Congruence between Voters and Parties." *West European Politics* 35, no. 6 (2012): 1226–1248.

Cox, Gary. "Centripetal and Centrifugal Incentives in Electoral Systems." *American Journal of Political Science* 34 (1990): 903–935.

Cox, Gary W. *Making Votes Count—Strategic Coordination in the World's Electoral Systems.* Cambridge: Cambridge University Press, 1997.

Curini, Luigi, and Airo Hino. "Missing Links in Party-System Polarization: How Institutions and Voters Matter." *Journal of Politics* 74, no. 2 (2012): 460–473.

Dahlerup, Drude. "From a Small to a Large Minority: Women in Scandinavian Politics." *Scandinavian Political Studies* 4 (1988): 275–298.

Dalton, Russell. "The Quantity and the Quality of Party Systems." *Comparative Political Studies* 20, no. 10 (2008): 1–22.

Dalton, Russell J. "Political Parties and Political Representation: Party Supporters and Party Elites in Nine Nations." *Comparative Political Studies* 18, no. 3 (1985): 267–299.

Dalton, Russell J. "Party Representation across Multiple Issue Dimensions." *Party Politics*, forthcoming. https://doi.org/10.1177/1354068815614515

Dalton, Russell J., David M. Farrell, and Ian McAllister. *Political Parties and Democratic Linkage.* New York: Oxford University Press, 2011.

Dawson, Michael C. *Behind the Mule: Race and Class in African-American Politics*. Princeton, NJ: Princeton University Press, 1995.

Dhima, Kostanca. "Demand for Descriptive and Substantive Representation: A Voting Experiment." Paper presented at the 2016 Annual Meeting of the American Political Science Association.

Disch, Lisa. "Toward a Mobilization Conception of Democratic Representation." *American Political Science Review* 105, no. 1 (2011): 100–114.

Döring, Holger, and Philip Manow. "Is Proportional Representation More Favourable to the Left? Electoral Rules and Their Impact on Elections, Parliaments, and the Formation of Cabinets." *British Journal of Political Science* 47, no. 1 (2017): 149–164.

Dow, Jay K. "A Comparative Spatial Analysis of Majoritarian and Proportional Elections." *Electoral Studies* 20 (2001): 109–125.

Dow, Jay K. "Party-System Extremism in Majoritarian and Proportional Electoral Systems." *British Journal of Political Science* 41, no. 2 (2011): 341–361.

Downs, Anthony. *An Economic Theory of Democracy*. New York: Harper and Row, 1957.

Du, Qiang, Vance Faber, and Max Gunzberger. "Centroidal Voronoi Tesselations: Applications and Algorithms." *Society for Industrial and Applied Mathematics Review* 41, no. 4 (1999): 637–676.

Duverger, Maurice. *Political Parties: Their Organization and Activity in the Modern State*. New York: John Wiley, 1963.

Erikson, Robert S., Gerald C. Wright, and John P. McIver. *Statehouse Democracy—Public Opinion and Policy in the American States*. Cambridge: Cambridge University Press, 1993.

Ezrow, Lawrence. "Parties' Policy Programmes and the Dog That Didn't Bark: No Evidence That Proportional Systems Promote Extreme Party Positioning." *British Journal of Political Science* 38 (2008): 479–497.

Ezrow, Lawrence. "Reply to Dow: Party Positions, Votes and the Mediating Role of Electoral Systems?" *British Journal of Political Science* 41, no. 2 (2011): 448–452.

Ezrow, Lawrence, Catherine De Vries, Marco Steenbergen, and Erica Edwards. "Mean Voter Representation and Partisan Constituency Representation: Do Parties Respond to the Mean Voter Position or to Their Supporters?" *Party Politics* 17, no. 3 (2010): 275–301.

Ferland, Benjamin. "Electoral Systems, Veto Players, and Substantive Representation: When Majoritarian Electoral Systems Strengthen the Citizen-Policy Nexus." Ph.D. Dissertation, McGill University, 2015.

Ferland, Benjamin. "Revisiting the Ideological Congruence Controversy." *European Journal of Political Research* 55, no. 2 (2016): 358–373.

Fisher, Stephen D., and Sara B. Hobolt. "Coalition Government and Electoral Accountability." *Electoral Studies* 29 (2010): 358–369.

Fréchette, Guillaume R., François Maniquet, and Massimo Morelli. "Incumbents' Interests and Gender Quotas." *American Journal of Political Science* 52, no. 4 (2008): 891–909.

Fulton, Sarah. "When Gender Matters: Macro-Dynamics and Micro-Mechanisms." *Political Behavior* 36, no. 3 (2014): 605–630.

Gerber, Elisabeth R., and Jeffrey B. Lewis. "Beyond the Median: Voter Preferences, District Heterogeneity, and Political Representation." *Journal of Political Economy* 112, no. 6 (2004): 1364–1383.

Gerber, Elizabeth R., Rebecca B. Morton, and Thomas A. Rietz. "Minority Representation in Multimember Districts." *American Political Science Review* 92, no. 1 (1998): 127–144.

Gilens, Martin. *Affluence and Influence: Economic Inequality and Political Power in America*. Princeton, NJ: Princeton University Press, 2012.

Glasgow, Garrett, Matt Golder, and Sona N. Golder. "Who 'Wins'? Determining the Party of the Prime Minister." *American Journal of Political Science* 55, no. 4 (2011): 937–954.

Golder, Matt, Sona N. Golder, and David A. Siegel. "Modeling the Institutional Foundation of Parliamentary Government Formation." *Journal of Politics* 74, no. 2 (2012): 427–445.

Golder, Matt, and Gabriella Lloyd. "Re-Evaluating the Relationship between Electoral Rules and Ideological Congruence." *European Journal of Political Research* 53, no. 1 (2014): 200–212.

Golder, Sona N., Laura B. Stephenson, Karine Van der Straeten, André Blais, Damien Bol, Philipp Harfst, and Jean-François Laslier. "Votes for Women: Electoral Systems and Support for Female Candidates." *Politics and Gender* 13, no. 1 (2017): 107–131.

Golder, Matt, and Jacek Stramski. "Ideological Congruence and Electoral Institutions." *American Journal of Political Science* 54, no. 1 (2010): 90–106.

Golder, Sona N., and Jacquelyn A. Thomas. "Portfolio Allocation of the Vote of No Confidence." *British Journal of Political Science* 44, no. 1 (2014): 29–39.

Grofman, Bernard. "Downs and Two-Party Convergence." *Annual Review of Political Science* 7 (2004): 25–46.

Hancock, Ange-Marie. "Intersectionality as a Normative and Empirical Paradigm." *Politics and Gender* 3, no. 2 (2007): 248–254.

Hobolt, Sara Binzer, and Robert Klemmensen. "Responsive Government? Public Opinion and Government Policy Preferences in Britain and Denmark." *Political Studies* 53 (2005): 379–402.

Hobolt, Sara Binzer, and Robert Klemmensen. "Government Responsiveness and Political Competition in Comparative Perspective." *Comparative Political Studies* 41, no. 3 (2008): 309–337.

Htun, Mala. *Inclusion without Representation in Latin America: Gender Quotas and Ethnic Reservations*. New York: Cambridge University Press, 2016.

Huber, John D., and G. Bingham Powell. "Congruence between Citizens and Policymakers in Two Visions of Liberal Democracy." *World Politics* 46, no. 3 (1994): 291–326.

Hughes, Melanie. "Intersectionality, Quotas, and Minority Women's Political Representation Worldwide." *American Political Science Review* 105, no. 3 (2011): 604–620.

Inglehart, Ronald, and Pippa Norris. *Rising Tide: Gender Equality and Cultural Change Around the World*. New York: Cambridge University Press, 2003.

Iversen, Torben. "Political Leadership and Representation in West European Democracies: A Test of Three Models of Voting." *American Journal of Political Science* 38, no. 1 (1994): 45–74.

Iversen, Torben, and David Soskice. "Electoral Institutions and the Politics of Coalitions: Why Some Democracies Redistribute More Than Others." *American Political Science Review* 100, no. 2 (2006): 165–181.

Jacobs, Lawrence R., and Benjamin I. Page. "Who Influences U.S. Foreign Policy?" *American Political Science Review* 99, no. 1 (2005): 107–123.

Jones, Mark P., and Patricio Navia. "Assessing the Effectiveness of Gender Quotas in Open-List Proportional Representation Electoral Systems." *Social Science Quarterly* 80, no. 2 (1999): 341–355.

Kang, Shin-Goo, and G. Bingham Powell. "Representation and Policy Responsiveness: The Median Voter, Election Rules, and Redistributive Welfare Spending." *Journal of Politics* 72, no. 4 (2010): 1014–1028.

Kanter, Rosabeth Moss. "Some Effects of Proportions on Group Life." *American Journal of Sociology* 82, no. 5 (1977): 965–990.

Kedar, Orit. *Voting for Policy, Not Parties.* New York: Cambridge University Press, 2009.

Kedar, Orit, Liran Harsgor, and Raz A. Scheinerman. "Are Voters Equal under Proportional Representation?" *American Journal of Political Science* 60, no. 3 (2016): 676–691.

Kellam, Marisa. "Parties for Hire: How Particularistic Parties Influence Presidents' Governing Strategies." *Party Politics* 21 (2015): 515–526.

Kernell, Georgia. "Descriptive Representation of Women and Ideological Congruence in Political Parties." Working Paper 12-001, The Roberta Buffett Center for International and Comparative Studies at Northwestern University, 2012.

Kittilson, Miki Caul. *Challenging Parties, Changing Parliaments: Women and Elected Office in Contemporary Western Europe.* Columbus: Ohio State University Press, 2006.

Kittilson, Miki Caul, and Leslie Schwindt-Bayer. "Engaging Citizens: The Role of Power-Sharing Institutions." *Journal of Politics* 72, no. 4 (2010): 990–1002.

Klingemann, Hans-Dieter, and Dieter Fuchs. *Citizens and the State.* New York: Oxford University Press, 1995.

Klüver, Heike, and Jae-Jae Spoon. "Challenges to Multiparty Governments: How Governing in Coalitions Affects Coalition Parties' Responsiveness to Voters." *Party Politics* 2016. doi: 10.1177/1354068815627399

Kollman, Ken, John H. Miller, and Scott E. Page. "Political Parties and Electoral Landscapes." *British Journal of Political Science* 28, no. 1 (1998): 139–158.

Kollman, Kenneth, John Miller, and Scott E. Page. "Adaptive Parties in Spatial Elections." *American Political Science Review* 86 (December 1992): 929–937.

Kuyper, Jonathan W. "Systemic Representation: Democracy, Deliberation, and Nonelectoral Representatives." *American Political Science Review* 110, no. 2 (2016): 308–324.

Laver, Michael. "Policy and the Dynamics of Political Competition." *American Political Science Review* 99, no. 2 (2005): 263–281.

Laver, Michael, and Ernest Sergenti. *Party Competition: An Agent-Based Model.* Princeton, NJ: Princeton University Press, 2012.

Laver, Michael, and Norman Schofield. *The Politics of Coalition in Western Europe.* Oxford: Oxford University Press, 1990.

Laver, Michael, and Norman Schofield. *Multiparty Government: The Politics of Coalition in Europe.* Ann Arbor: University of Michigan Press, 1998.

Laver, Michael, and Kenneth A. Shepsle. *Making and Breaking Governments: Cabinets and Legislatures in Parliamentary Democracies.* New York: Cambridge University Press, 1996.

Lawless, Jennifer L., and Kathryn Pearson. "The Primary Reasons for Women's Underrepresentation? Reevaluating the Conventional Wisdom." *Journal of Politics* 70, no. 1 (2008): 67–82.

Lax, Jeffrey R., and Justin H. Phillips. "Gay Rights in the States: Public Opinion and Policy Responsiveness." *American Political Science Review* 103, no. 3 (2009): 367–386.

Lax, Jeffrey R., and Justin H. Phillips. "The Democratic Deficit in the States." *American Journal of Political Science* 56, no. 1 (2012): 148–166.

Lijphart, Arend. *Patterns of Democracy—Government Forms and Performance in Thirty-Six Countries.* New Haven, CT: Yale University Press, 1999.

Luhiste, Maarja. "Party Gatekeepers' Support for Viable Female Candidacy in PR-List Systems." *Politics and Gender* 11, no. 1 (2015): 89–116.

Mansbridge, Jane. "Should Blacks Represent Blacks and Women Represent Women? A Contingent 'Yes.'" *Journal of Politics* 61, no. 3 (1999): 628–657.

Mansbridge, Jane. "Rethinking Representation." *American Political Science Review* 97, no. 4 (2003): 515–528.

Martin, Lanny W., and Randolph T. Stevenson. "Government Formation in Parliamentary Democracies." *American Journal of Political Science* 45, no. 1 (2001): 33–50.

Matakos, Konstantinos, Orestis Troumpounis, and Dimitrios Xefteris. "Electoral Rule Disproportionality and Platform Polarization." *American Journal of Political Science* 60, no. 4 (2016): 1026–1043.

Matland, Richard E., and Donley T. Studlar. "The Contagion of Women Candidates in Single-Member District and Proportional Representation Electoral Systems: Canada and Norway." *Journal of Politics* 58, no. 3 (1996): 707–733.

Matsusaka, John G. "Problems with a Methodology Used to Evaluate the Voter Initiative." *Journal of Politics* 63, no. 4 (2001): 1250–1256.

Matsusaka, John G. "Popular Control of Public Policy: A Quantitative Approach." *Quarterly Journal of Political Science* 5 (2010): 133–167.

Mattila, Mikko, and Tapio Raunio. "Cautious Voters-Supportive Parties." *European Union Politics* 7, no. 4 (2006): 427–449.

McDonald, Michael D., and Ian Budge. *Elections, Parties, Democracy—Conferring the Median Mandate.* New York: Oxford University Press, 2005.

McDonald, Michael D., Silvia M. Mendes, and Ian Budge. "What Are Elections For? Conferring the Median Mandate." *British Journal of Political Science* 34, no. 1 (2004): 1–26.

Merrill, Samuel III, and James Adams. "Centrifugal Incentives in Multi-Candidate Elections." *Journal of Theoretical Politics* 14, no. 3 (2002): 275–300.

Miller, Warren E., and Donald E. Stokes. "Constituency Influence in Congress." *American Political Science Review* 57, no. 1 (1963): 45–56.

Näsström, Sofia. "Democratic Representation beyond Election." *Constellations* 22, no. 1 (2015): 1–12.

Ordeshook, Peter, and Olga Shvetsova. "Ethnic Heterogeneity, District Magnitude, and the Number of Parties." *American Journal of Political Science* 38 (1994): 100–123.

Page, Benjamin I., and Robert Y. Shapiro. "Effects of Public Opinion on Policy." *American Political Science Review* 77, no. 1 (1983): 175–190.

Paxton, Pamela. "Women in National Legislatures: A Cross-National Analysis." *Social Science Research* 26, no. 4 (1997): 442–464.

Paxton, Pamela, Sheri Kunovich, and Melanie M. Hughes. "Gender in Politics." *Annual Review of Sociology* 33 (2007): 263–284.

Phillips, Anne. *The Politics of Presence: The Political Representation of Gender, Ethnicity, and Race.* New York: Oxford University Press, 1998.

Pinto-Duschinsky, Michael, G. Bingham Powell, Arend Lijphart, Jack Vowles, and Matthew S. Shugart. "Send the Rascals Packing!" *Representation* 36 (1999): 117–155.

Pitkin, Hanna Fenichel. *The Concept of Representation.* Berkeley: University of California Press, 1967.

Portmann, Marco, David Stadelmann, and Reiner Eichenberger. "District Magnitude and Representation of the Majority's Preferences: Evidence from Popular and Parliamentary Votes." *Public Choice* 151 (2012): 585–610.

Posner, Daniel N. "The Political Salience of Cultural Difference: Why Chewas and Tumbukas Are Allies in Zambia and Adversaries in Malawi." *American Political Science Review* 98, no. 4 (2004): 529–545.

Posner, Daniel N. *Institutions and Ethnic Politics in Africa*. New York: Cambridge University Press, 2005.

Powell, G. Bingham. *Elections as Instruments of Democracy*. New Haven, CT: Yale University Press, 2000.

Powell, G. Bingham. "Election Laws and Representative Governments: Beyond Votes and Seats." *British Journal of Political Science* 36, no. 2 (2006): 291–315.

Powell, G. Bingham. "The Ideological Congruence Controversy: The Impact of Alternative Measures, Data, and Time Periods on the Effects of Electoral Rules." *Comparative Political Studies* 42, no. 12 (2009): 1475–1497.

Powell, G. Bingham, and Georg Vanberg. "Election Laws, Disproportionality and Median Correspondence: Implications for Two Visions of Democracy." *British Journal of Political Science* 30, no. 3 (2000): 383–411.

Powell, G. Bingham, and Guy D. Whitten. "A Cross-National Analysis of Economic Voting: Taking Account of the Political Context." *American Journal of Political Science* 37, no. 2 (1993): 391–414.

Rabinowitz, George, Stuart Elaine McDonald, and Ola Listhaug. "New Players in an Old Game: Party Strategy in Multiparty Systems." *Comparative Political Studies* 24, no. 2 (1994): 147–185.

Rehfeld, Andrew. "Representation Rethought: On Trustees, Delegates, and Gyroscopes in the Study of Political Representation and Democracy." *American Political Science Review* 103, no. 2 (2009): 214–230.

Reynolds, Andrew. "Women in the Legislatures and Executives of the World: Knocking at the Highest Glass Ceiling." *World Politics* 51, no. 4 (1999): 547–572.

Roberts, Andrew, Jason Seawright, and Jennifer Cyr. "Do Electoral Laws Affect Women's Representation." *Comparative Political Studies* 46, no. 12 (2013): 1555–1581.

Rodden, Jonathan A. *Hamilton's Paradox: The Promise and Peril of Fiscal Federalism*. New York: Cambridge University Press, 2006.

Rodden, Jonathan A. "The Geographic Distribution of Political Preferences." *Annual Review of Political Science* 13 (2010): 297–340.

Salmond, Rob. "Proportional Representation and Female Parliamentarians." *Legislative Studies Quarterly* 31, no. 2 (2006): 175–204.

Samuels, David. *Separation of Powers*. New York: Oxford University Press, 2007.

Saward, Michael. "The Representative Claim." *Contemporary Political Theory* 5, no. 3 (2006): 297–318.

Saward, Michael. "Authorisation and Authenticity: Representation and the Unelected." *Journal of Political Philosophy* 17, no. 1 (2009): 1–22.

Saward, Michael. "Shape-Shifting Representation." *American Political Science Review* 108, no. 4 (2014): 723–736.

Schmidt, Gregory D. "The Election of Women in List PR Systems: Testing the Conventional Wisdom." *Electoral Studies* 28, no. 2 (2009): 190–203.

Schmitt, Hermann, and Jacques Thomassen. *Political Representation and Legitimacy in the European Union*. Oxford: Oxford University Press, 1999.

Schofield, Norman. "Political Competition and Multiparty Coalition Governments." *European Journal of Political Research* 23 (1993): 1–33.

Schofield, Norman. "Valence Competition in the Spatial Stochastic Model." *Journal of Theoretical Politics* 15 (2003): 371–383.

Schofield, Norman, and Itai Sened. "Modeling the Interaction of Parties, Activists, and Voters: Why Is the Political Center So Empty?" *European Journal of Political Research* 44 (2005): 355–390.

Schumacher, Gijs, Catherine De Vries, and Barbara Vis. "Why Do Parties Change Position? Party Organization and Environmental Incentives." *Journal of Politics* 75, no. 2 (2013): 464–477.

Schwindt-Bayer, Leslie A., Michael Malecki, and Brian F. Crisp. "Candidate Gender and Electoral Success in Single Transferable Vote Systems." *British Journal of Political Science* 40, no. 3 (2010): 693–709.

Soroka, Stuart N., and Christopher Wlezien. *Degrees of Democracy—Politics, Public Opinion, and Policy*. New York: Cambridge University Press, 2010.

Soroka, Stuart N., and Christopher Wlezien. "The Majoritarian and Proportional Visions and Democratic Responsiveness." *Electoral Studies* 40 (2015): 539–547.

Stadelmann, David, Marco Portmann, and Reiner Eichenberger. "Evaluating the Median Voter Model's Explanatory Power." *Economics Letters* 114 (2012): 312–314.

Stadelmann, David, Marco Portmann, and Reiner Eichenberger. "Quantifying Parliamentary Representation of Constituents' Preferences with Quasi-Experimental Data." *Journal of Comparative Economics* 41 (2013): 170–180.

Stadelmann, David, Marco Portmann, and Reiner Eichenberger. "The Law of Large Districts: How District Magnitude Affects the Quality of Political Representation." *European Journal of Political Economy* 35 (2014): 128–140.

Stadelmann, David, Marco Portmann, and Reiner Eichenberger. "Preference Representation and the Influence of Political Parties in Majoritarian vs. Proportional Systems: An Empirical Test." *British Journal of Political Science,* forthcoming. https://doi.org/10.1017/S0007123416000399

Tate, Katherine. *From Protest to Politics: The New Black Voters in American Politics*. Cambridge, MA: Harvard University Press, 1994.

Thames, Frank C., and Margaret S. Williams. "Incentives for Personal Votes and Women's Representation in Legislatures." *Comparative Political Studies* 43, no. 12 (2010): 1575–1600.

Thomson, Robert, Terry Royed, Elin Naurin, Joaquin Artés, Rory Costello, Laurenz Ennser-Jedenastik, Mark Ferguson, Petia Kostadinova, Catherine Moury, François Pétry, and Katrin Praprotnik. "The Fulfillment of Election Pledges: A Comparative Study of the Impact of Government Institutions." Paper presented at the Annual Meeting of the American Political Science Association, 2014.

Tremblay, Manon. *Women and Legislative Representation: Electoral Systems, Political Parties and Sex Quotas*. New York: Palgrave Macmillan, 2008.

Tsebelis, George. *Veto Players—How Political Institutions Work*. Princeton, NJ: Princeton University Press, 2002.

Wängnerud, Lena. "Women in Parliaments: Descriptive and Substantive Representation." *Annual Review of Political Science* 12 (2009): 51–69.

Warwick, Paul V., and Maria Zakharova. "Measuring the Median: The Risks of Inferring Beliefs from Votes." *British Journal of Political Science* 43, no. 1 (2013): 157–175.

Wauters, Bram, Karolien Weekers, and Bart Maddens. "Explaining the Number of Preferential Votes for Women in an Open-List PR System: An Investigation of the 2003 Federal Elections in Flanders (Belgium)." *Acta Politica* 45, no. 4 (2010): 468–490.

Weissberg, Robert. "Collective vs. Dyadic Representation in Congress." *American Political Science Review* 72, no. 2 (1978): 535–547.

Weldon, S. Laurel. "Beyond Bodies: Institutional Sources of Representation for Women in Democratic Policymaking." *Journal of Politics* 64, no. 4 (2002): 1153–1174.

Weldon, S. Laurel. "The Structure of Intersectionality: A Comparative Politics of Gender." *Politics and Gender* 2, no. 2 (2006): 235–248.

Wlezien, Christopher, and Stuart N. Soroka. "Inequality in Policy Responsiveness?" In *Who Gets Represented?*, edited by Peter K. Enns and Christopher Wlezien, 285–310. New York: Russell Sage Foundation, 2011.

Wlezien, Christopher, and Stuart N. Soroka. "Political Institutions and the Opinion-Policy Link." *West European Politics* 35, no. 6 (2012): 1407–1432.

Young, Iris Marion. *Inclusion and Democracy*. New York: Oxford University Press, 2002.

CHAPTER 12

..................................................................................

# ELECTORAL
# SYSTEMS AND ISSUE
# POLARIZATION

..................................................................................

## JAMES F. ADAMS AND NATHAN J. REXFORD

THIS chapter reviews theoretical and empirical research pertaining to the question: How do electoral systems influence parties' programmatic incentives, that is, the policy positions party elites present to the public? More specifically, we discuss whether electoral systems influence the diversity of party policy positions, measured via the degree of *party system polarization*. We emphasize electoral laws' permissiveness or *proportionality*, defined in terms of the relationship between parties' national vote shares and their share of parliamentary seats.

The link between electoral systems and party system polarization matters because it pertains to the range of choices the party system provides to the electorate. When competing parties differentiate their issue positions from each other, voters confront diverse policy options, which enhance their abilities to direct government policy outputs via their votes (e.g., Powell 2000; McDonald and Budge 2005). Party system policy diversity has been linked to other features of mass-elite linkages including citizens' satisfaction with democracy (Ezrow and Xezonakis 2011), voters' abilities to hold governments accountable for national economic conditions (Hellwig 2012), and the degree to which voters punish parties for scandals and incompetence (Clark and Leiter 2014).

As we discuss later, empirical research on how electoral systems affect party system polarization has only emerged over the past fifteen years, primarily due to earlier limitations on cross-nationally comparable measures of parties' policy positions. Moreover, empirical studies on this topic typically analyze party system polarization in terms of a unidimensional left–right continuum associated with long-standing policy debates over social welfare programs, taxes, and government intervention in the economy. At the same time, theoretical arguments about how electoral systems affect party system polarization are more developed. Next we review these previous arguments (and propose some new arguments of our own), along with the empirical evidence reported in earlier studies. We conclude by discussing the implications of these findings and directions for future research.

# PARTY SYSTEM POLARIZATION AND ELECTORAL SYSTEMS: THEORETICAL ARGUMENTS

Theoretical and empirical studies analyze the factors that influence parties' programmatic incentives, including parties' policy responses to public opinion as a whole (e.g., Ward, Ezrow, and Dorussen 2011; Adams, Clark, Ezrow, and Glasgow 2004; Ezrow 2008); opinion among electoral subconstituencies including parties' core supporters, the politically sophisticated, and the affluent (Ezrow, De Vries, Steenbergen, and Edwards 2011; Schofield and Sened 2006; Gilens and Page 2014; Adams and Ezrow 2009); past election results (Budge 1994; Laver 2005; Somer-Topcu 2009); rival parties' policy positions (Han 2015; Spoon 2011; Williams 2015); parties' public images for competence and integrity (Adams and Merrill 2009; Clark 2014); parties' organizational characteristics (Schumacher, De Vries, and Vis 2013); and global economic conditions (e.g., Haupt 2009; Weschle forthcoming).[1] Later we review empirical studies on whether electoral systems influence party positions and, through these positions, party system polarization. First, however, we review the theoretical arguments pertaining to this issue. We consider the questions: Should we expect that electoral systems condition parties' strategic incentives to announce more radical or moderate policies, and to differentiate their policy positions from each other? And assuming the answer to this question is yes, should we expect these effects to be substantively significant, that is, that electoral system proportionality exerts a *major* influence on polarization? The first question is interesting because theoretical arguments point in conflicting directions. However, we believe the second question has a straightforward answer, namely, that we have strong theoretical reasons to expect electoral systems to exert at most modest effects on party system polarization.

## Why Electoral Proportionality Should Exert Only Modest Effects on Party Polarization

The fist reason to doubt that electoral systems strongly affect party system polarization is that polarization at times varies sharply over time within countries that do not change their electoral systems—which conflicts with the hypothesis that voting systems are the primary drivers of party system polarization. This pattern is seen in the United States and Britain, which have continuously employed the highly disproportional plurality (first-past-the-post) system, but where party system polarization has fluctuated sharply over time. In Britain, the post–World War II period initially featured highly consensual policy competition between the dominant Labour and Conservative Parties, which both endorsed the "postwar settlement" policies of higher taxes, extensive social welfare benefits, and Keynesian demand management (Garnett and Lynch 2016). Yet this postwar policy convergence was succeeded by dramatic party system polarization, with the Conservatives shifting sharply to the right under Margaret Thatcher beginning in the mid-1970s, while Labour shifted leftward in the early 1980s under the leadership of Michael Foot. This 1980s period of elite polarization was followed by a second period of party system convergence beginning when Tony Blair shifted "New Labour" toward the center ground starting in the mid-1990s, a moderation strategy the Conservatives subsequently pursued from 2006 onward under David Cameron (see Adams, Ezrow, and Somer-Topcu 2011).[2] The US party system displayed a dynamic similar to Britain's until the mid-1990s, in that the Democratic and Republican Parties converged programmatically on many issues from the end of World War II through the 1970s, prompting the American Political Science Association to publish a famous paper decrying the lack of meaningful policy alternatives on offer to American voters (American Political Science Association, Committee on Political Parties 1950). However, the parties have dramatically polarized over the past thirty-five years, with Republican elites shifting sharply rightward under the leadership of President Ronald Reagan and his successors, while the Democratic Party has shifted programmatically to the left (Carroll, Lewis, Lo, McCarty, Poole, and Rosenthal 2011). Finally, proportional representation (PR)-based systems at times exhibit similarly sharp over-time fluctuations in party system polarization. In the PR-based Dutch system, for instance, the two largest parties, the Christian Democratic Appeal (CDA) and the Labour Party (PvDA) were sharply polarized up to the mid-1980s, but then converged substantially across the next decade (Adams 2012; Ezrow and Xezonakis 2011), while in the PR-based German system the sharp left–right policy divide between the Social Democrats and the Christian Democrats narrowed substantially between 2005 and 2009 and again since 2013, when these parties cooperated in a national coalition government. If proportionality is the primary driver of polarization, how do we explain dramatic party polarization changes over time within countries that do not change their electoral laws?

The second reason to doubt that proportionality substantially affects party polarization is to note the long list of additional factors that have been shown to influence party policy positions. As discussed earlier, previous studies document that party positions respond to public opinion, past election results, parties' organizational characteristics, their images with respect to competence and integrity, and economic conditions. Intuitively, if electoral laws are at most one of many factors influencing party policy strategies, one might doubt that electoral laws by themselves substantially affect polarization.

We believe the considerations outlined earlier, that many factors besides electoral systems influence party policy positions, and that party system polarization at times fluctuates sharply within countries that have not changed their electoral systems, suggest that these systems do not strongly influence the degree of elite polarization.

## To the Extent Proportionality Matters, Should It Promote Party System Polarization or Convergence?

We next consider the question: To the extent that electoral systems influence system polarization, should we expect more proportional laws to enhance or depress polarization? This question is interesting because theoretical arguments point in conflicting directions. The argument that proportionality *increases* polarization is, first, that parties in plurality-based electoral systems (including the French majority-plurality system, described in Hoyo's chapter in this volume) plausibly experience greater pressure to maximize votes, since winning seats requires that a party's candidate finishes first in a district, whereas more proportional, multiseat district systems provide easier parliamentary access to smaller parties. And given survey-based evidence that the distribution of voter ideologies in most democratic publics is heavily concentrated near the center of the left–right scale (see, e.g., Powell 2000; Adams and Somer-Topcu 2009), there is an intuitive logic that parties maximize votes by offering moderate policies, all else equal. This logic might motivate the parties contesting plurality-based elections to present more moderate, vote-maximizing policies than do the parties contesting PR-based elections (Dow 2001).[3]

As a second, related, point, the fact that some voters strategically desert smaller parties' candidates under disproportional voting systems to avoid "wasting" their votes on smaller parties with no realistic chance of winning seats in the district (Cox 1997; Moser and Scheiner 2004) further enhances plurality-based parties' strategic incentives to promote moderate policy agendas that make them electorally competitive. Third, Kedar (2009) documents that voters in proportional electoral systems with multiparty coalition governments are more willing to vote for radical parties, recognizing that such parties cannot fully implement their radical policy promises in a governing coalition but may at least pull government policy outputs away from their moderate coalition partners, in the voter's preferred direction (see also Grofman 1985; Adams, Merrill, and Grofman 2005). To the extent that radical parties are more attractive to voters in proportional systems that feature more power sharing, the parties competing in PR systems have greater electoral leeway to promise radical policies. Finally, given that proportional electoral systems tend to increase the number of competitive political parties (see the chapter by Shugart and Taagepera in this volume), in particular that plurality-based systems are associated with two dominant parties, the Downsian logic of two-party convergence (Downs 1957) should apply more strongly to the smaller party systems in countries with disproportional voting systems.[4]

At the same time, alternative considerations suggest that electoral permissiveness *may not* increase party system polarization. First, to the extent that parties seek membership in the multiparty cabinets that typically govern under proportional representation, parties have strategic incentives to present nonradical policies that make them attractive coalition partners to the large, moderate, mainstream parties of the center-left and the center-right that are typically tasked with forming a government (Martin and Stevenson 2001). Thus, even if *seat-seeking* parties in PR-based systems can win parliamentary representation while espousing radical policies, *cabinet-seeking parties* (i.e., parties that aspire to join the government) may feel pressure to present more moderate positions. In this regard, Ezrow (2008) notes that centrist party positioning provides a greater number of potential coalition partners, so that moderate positions may prove attractive to small, cabinet-seeking parties in proportional systems.

Second, while the central argument that plurality-based systems prompt party policy convergence is that plurality systems enhance parties' incentives to present moderate, vote-maximizing positions, there are theoretical and empirical reasons to question whether moderate positioning actually enhances party support. Theoretically, spatial modeling studies advance reasons parties may maximize votes by presenting noncentrist—even radical—policies, including the consideration that such policies will prompt party activists, who trend to be ideologues, to contribute scarce campaign resources to the party (e.g., Schofield and Sened 2006; Moon 2005); the desire to maximize turnout among more radical party supporters who may abstain if they perceive the party abandoning its core principles (Adams et al. 2005, chap. 7–9); and the need to deter radical protest parties from entering the system and "outflanking" an established, moderate party (Calvert 1985). Empirically, cross-national studies reach conflicting conclusions about whether moderate policy positioning meaningfully enhances party support: Ezrow (2007) reports analyses that support this proposition; Adams and Somer-Topcu (2009) find little evidence that policy moderation systematically affects party support; and remarkable research by Karreth, Polk, and Allen (2013) documents that Social Democratic parties that pursued a "Third Way" policy moderation strategy increased their support in the short run but suffered longer-term reverses as their core supporters subsequently deserted the party. In this regard, the highly visible electoral successes enjoyed by sharply noncentrist elites such as the British Conservatives under Margaret Thatcher and the Republican candidate Ronald Reagan (and his Republican successors) also cast doubt on the maxim that the key to electoral success in plurality-based systems is to "occupy the center ground."

Finally, we note that extensive empirical research documents many non-policy-related considerations that influence voters' decisions including economic conditions (e.g., Powell and Whitten 1993), parties' images for competence and integrity (Clark 2009, and voters' long-term party identifications growing out of their early socialization experiences (e.g., Campbell 1960; Campbell, Converse, Miller, and Stokes 1960). And the "issue ownership" perspective on elections posits that voters are more easily moved by the issue areas that competing political parties emphasize than by the specific *positions* they stake out within these areas (e.g., Petrocik 1996; Green and Jennings

2012). This research casts doubt on whether parties' issue positions will substantially affect their support.[5]

In toto, the considerations outlined previously do not provide strong guidance about whether electoral system proportionality tends to increase party system polarization. Disproportional, plurality-based electoral systems may prompt parties to prioritize maximizing their electoral support, which may push parties toward the center of the voter distribution—provided elites believe that policy moderation is a vote-winning strategy. Yet we have outlined the reasons to doubt that "occupying the center ground" actually attracts many additional votes. Moreover, we have noted that even if seat-seeking parties feel more leeway to stake out radical positions in proportional electoral systems, parties seeking to enter the cabinet likely experience pressure to moderate to be an acceptable coalition partner. Hence, theoretical arguments about how electoral system proportionality affects party system polarization point in conflicting directions. However, we *do* see strong reasons to expect the net effect of proportionality on polarization—whether positive, negative, or neutral—to be modest.

# PARTY SYSTEM POLARIZATION AND ELECTORAL SYSTEMS: EMPIRICAL RESULTS

## An Empirical Focus on Parties' Left–Right Positions

With important exceptions discussed later, empirical studies of electoral systems and party polarization analyze party positions strictly in terms of the unidimensional left–right continuum, a focus motived by both theoretical and practical considerations. Theoretically, the left–right dimension—typically associated with long-standing debates over taxes, social welfare policy, and government intervention in the economy—is arguably the only dimension that travels across all Western democracies, thereby permitting meaningful cross-national comparisons of party positions. The related, more practical consideration is that until the recent releases of the codings of party manifestos provided by the Comparative Manifesto Project and of experts' cross-national party placements by the Chapel Hill Expert Survey team, there were no available cross-national measures of party positions along more specific dimensions that could be used to construct issue-specific measures of party system polarization.

## Measuring Party System Polarization and Electoral Law Proportionality

Empirical studies on whether proportionality affects elite polarization must first define and measure these concepts. With respect to polarization, some studies measure parties' left–right positions based on codings of parties' election manifestos (e.g., Budge and McDonald 2006; Matakos, Troumpounis, and Xefteris 2016), others analyze voter perceptions of party positions (Dow 2011), others employ factor analyses of voter election surveys (Dow 2001), and still others study political experts' party placements (Ezrow 2008). Moreover, studies differ on how to measure overall polarization, with some studies emphasizing a measurement analogous to the standard deviation of the party positions in the system (e.g., Ezrow 2008; Dow 2011)[6] and others emphasizing the distance between the two most extreme parties in the system (e.g., Budge and McDonald 2006; Andrews and Money 2009). However, as discussed later, empirical studies' conclusions on how electoral systems affect party polarization do not typically turn on these measurement issues, because alternative measures of party left–right positions (manifesto codings, expert surveys, voters' party placements, etc.) all correlate strongly with each other (Dalton and McAllister 2015), as do alternative measures of party system polarization (Best and Dow 2015).

Electoral system proportionality can be computed independently of specific election results, based on the average number of seats available per district (district magnitude),[7] while alternative, election-dependent measures use election results to measure proportionality, including Gallagher's (1991) disproportionality index, which aggregates the discrepancies between parties' national vote shares and their seat shares. A consistent finding from this literature is that systems of single-seat districts, such as those used in Britain, Canada, and France, are disproportional compared to PR systems with larger district magnitude, because smaller parties' candidates rarely finish first in a district, so that small parties' parliamentary seat shares under these systems typically fall well below their national vote shares (Shugart and Taagepera 2017).[8] Several of the empirical studies on electoral systems and party system polarization discussed later employ both proportionality measures and typically find that both measures support similar conclusions. The fact that substantive conclusions do not turn on issues pertaining to the measurement of party polarization and proportionality simplifies our task, and in our empirical literature review we will not discuss how different studies measure these concepts, except in the rare cases where this issue affects the authors' substantive conclusions.

## Overview of the Literature: No Consistent Findings on Whether Proportionality Affects Party Polarization

Empirical studies reach conflicting conclusions on whether proportionality increases party polarization. In the first cross-national study on this issue, Dow (2001) analyzes national election surveys from four countries, two with disproportional electoral systems (France and Canada) and two with highly proportional systems (Israel and the Netherlands), concluding that the major political parties were more polarized in the proportional systems.[9] In a follow-up study, Dow (2011) extends this research to thirty democracies between the mid-1990s and the mid-2000s and reaffirms the positive association between proportionality and left–right party polarization. Matakos et al. (2016) build on Dow's research by analyzing nearly fifty years of party manifestos from over twenty industrialized countries and substantiate Dow's conclusion.

At the same time, alternative empirical studies cast doubt on whether proportionality meaningfully increases party polarization. Dalton (2008), analyzing a dataset similar to that of Dow (2011), reports a detectable but substantively weak relationship between left–right proportionality and polarization, while Ezrow (2008) finds no relationship between these variables in analyses of party positions from fifteen party systems during the 1980s. Similarly, Andrews and Money (2009) find no relationship between proportionality and party polarization, on either social or economic policy dimensions, while Curini and Hino (2012) extend the voter surveys used in Dow (2011) to analyze thirty-three party systems and find no evidence that electoral proportionality directly increases left–right polarization.

Finally, scholars have analyzed whether proportionality influences party system polarization *indirectly* via the electoral system's effect on the number of competitive parties, based on the logic that the larger number of parties associated with proportional systems (see the Shugart and Taagepera chapter in this volume) may become more "crowded" near the center, pushing vote-seeking parties toward more radical policies (see Downs 1957; Cox 1990). Here too the literature reaches conflicting conclusions, with Dalton (2008), Ezrow (2008), and Dow (2011) finding no evidence that the number of competitive parties influences the degree of left–right party polarization, while Andrews and Money (2009) and Matakos et al. (2016) find some (inconsistent) evidence of a positive relationship between these variables.[10]

## What Substantive Conclusions Can We Draw from the Literature?

In toto, the literature on how electoral system proportionality influences party system polarization reaches inconsistent conclusions, in that Ezrow (2008) and Andrews and Money (2009) detect no relationship between these variables; Dalton (2008) and Curini and Hino (2012) estimate weak and inconsistent relationships; and Dow (2001, 2011) and Matakos et al. (2015) estimate that polarization systematically increases with proportionality. Moreover, these studies' conflicting conclusions do not stem from different approaches to measuring party positions or to defining either party polarization or proportionality.

At the same time, we believe that empirical studies, in combination with the arguments outlined earlier, support some tentative conclusions. First, both theory and empirics provide reasons to reject the hypothesis that proportionality actually depresses polarization; that is, *parties do not systematically take more **polarized** policy positions in more proportional electoral systems*. As discussed earlier, the results reported in empirical studies range from findings of no detectible relationship between proportionality and polarization to findings that party polarization systematically increases with proportionality. And the theoretical arguments suggest that any such effect will likely be modest, given the wide range of additional factors that influence party policy strategies (public opinion, past election results, economic conditions, etc.). This perspective is substantiated by the studies of Ezrow (2008) and Andrews and Money (2009) that report no detectible effects of proportionality on party polarization, and also by Dalton (2008) and Curini and Hino (2012), who report weak and inconsistent relationships. Moreover, even the two empirical studies that find that proportionality detectibly enhances left–right polarization estimate relatively modest effects. Matakos et al. (2016) estimate that a shift from the most majoritarian to the most proportional electoral systems in their sample increases the predicted distance between the two most extreme party platforms in the system by about 1.5 points on a 10-point scale. While the weighted party policy extremism measure discussed by Dow (2011) is harder to interpret, the magnitudes of the effects Dow estimates appear smaller than those estimated by Matakos et al. (2015).[11] We believe these estimates support the conclusions that (1) electoral proportionality exerts at most modest effects on party system polarization and (2) the effect of greater proportionality—if any effect exists—is to increase polarization.

Finally, we re-emphasize two constraints on studies of proportionality and party polarization. First, in cross-national comparisons linking proportionality to polarization, the number of cases is limited to the number of different democratic party systems in the world. Hence, unlike studies of political behavior that analyze survey responses from thousands of citizens, our unit of analysis is the party system and the country's electoral system; moreover, since democracies rarely enact substantial electoral system changes, empirical studies on this topic typically have fewer than thirty-five observations (and several studies have fewer than twenty observations).[12] These small samples hamper analysts' abilities to parse out how electoral system proportionality affects party system polarization. Given that the recent studies of Dow (2011), Curini and Hino (2012), and Matakos et al. (2015) already include most of the world's Western democracies, there is little more scholars can do to solve this small-N problem.

## CONCLUSION AND DISCUSSION

The extant theoretical and empirical literatures do not clearly answer the question: Does electoral system proportionality increase party system polarization? Some theoretical arguments suggest the answer is yes, yet other arguments cast doubt on this proposition; some empirical studies conclude that proportionality detectibly increases polarization, yet other studies report no detectible effects. This uncertainty notwithstanding, we see no theoretical or empirical reason to believe that proportionality actually *depresses* party polarization, that is, that greater proportionality promotes party policy convergence. The questions remain: Does proportionality actually increase polarization, and if so, how large are these effects? Our review of the relevant scholarship suggests that the answer to the first question is "maybe," while the answer to the second question is "any such effects are probably modest."

We close with some suggested directions for future research. First, given that most empirical studies on electoral laws and party policy positioning analyze the unidimensional left–right policy continuum, future studies might profitably develop *multidimensional* measures of party polarization. This approach seems feasible based on analyses of both parties' election manifestos and the issue-specific party position measures available through the widely used Chapel Hill Expert Survey (CHES) datasets. Indeed, Rexford's (2017) recent analyses of the CHES data uncover evidence that electoral permissiveness[13] modestly increases party system polarization with respect to more-specific issue dimensions. Rexford also demonstrates that electoral permissiveness enhances large parties' tendencies to "hedge their bets" by taking inconsistent stands across different policy dimensions.

Second, and related, it seems possible that electoral systems influence parties' incentives to develop distinctive *issue emphases* with respect to cross-cutting policy dimensions. In this regard, more proportional electoral systems may facilitate the emergence of "niche" parties such as green, radical right, agrarian, and ethno-territorial parties that emphasize specific policy dimensions (the environment, immigration, agriculture, and so on) that do not map onto long-term left–right economic policy debates. Rexford's (2017) research provides preliminary support for this hypothesis: he demonstrates that while smaller "limited issue" parties will be inclined to heavily emphasize their core issues (e.g., the Greens with the environment, nationalist parties with immigration, and so on) regardless of the electoral context, greater electoral permissiveness motivates larger parties to confront smaller parties on their core issues, so that large parties place more emphasis on smaller parties' core issues as electoral permissiveness increases.

Finally, an emerging strand of research analyzes the causes and consequences of party policy *ambiguity*, that is, the factors that motivate parties to present clear as opposed to ambiguous policy messages to the electorate (e.g., Kernell 2016; Somer-Topcu 2015). Here too, we might expect the nature of the electoral system to influence parties' strategic calculations about the clarity of their policies.

In this chapter we have analyzed the connection between electoral rules and the dispersion of rival parties' policy positions. The scholarship reviewed in this chapter does not conclusively establish the nature of this relationship, but it provides a positive basis for future research.

## NOTES

1. Additional research documents the conditional nature of these relationships, for instance, that the "openness" of the domestic economy mediates parties' responses to public opinion (Ward et al. 2011; Ezrow and Hellwig 2014), as do parties' organizational characteristics (Schumacher et al. 2013), along with party type, that is, niche versus mainstream parties

(Adams, Clark, Ezrow, and Glasgow 2006). See Adams (2012) for an overview of this literature.

2. We note that the post-2010 period in British politics has arguably seen the beginnings of renewed Labour–Conservative polarization, as the Conservatives in government (in coalition with their junior partner the Liberal Democrats between 2010 and 2015) have enacted more right-wing economic and social policies than was implied by the moderate policy rhetoric their leader David Cameron issued during the 2006–2010 period of opposition, while the Labour Party electorate selected the sharply left-wing leader Jeremy Corbyn in the 2015 leadership contest.

3. Dow (2001) also notes that given the well-known fact that plurality-based systems often "manufacture" a parliamentary majority for the largest party—that is, the largest party wins a majority in parliament with a national vote share below 50 percent—parties contesting plurality-based elections are more likely to believe that the only viable pathway to being in government and enacting desired policy change is to maximize their electoral support.

4. Eaton and Lipsey (1975), Cox (1990), and Merrill and Adams (2001) present spatial models of elections that predict that, all else equal, larger party systems motivate vote- and seat-seeking parties to promise more radical policies. McGann (2002) extends this spatial modeling logic to systems where parties are responsive to their activists.

5. This intuition is consistent with simulations on election survey data reported by Erikson and Romero (1990), Schofield and Sened (2006), and Adams et al. (2005), all of which conclude that parties' expected votes do not vary significantly with their policy images so long as the parties do not propose truly extreme positions.

6. Additional variations include whether to weight each party's position by its vote/seat share, and whether to standardize the dispersion of parties' ideologies against the dispersion of voter ideologies (see Ezrow 2008; Alvarez and Nagler 2004).

7. Typically, the logarithm of this measure is used to deal with the right-skewed distribution arising from single nationwide districts used by some countries (e.g. Slovakia, Israel).

8. The American plurality system is an exception to this generalization, because few votes are wasted on third-party candidates and thus most elected representatives win 50 percent of the vote, unlike in the other systems discussed here.

9. Dow's (2001) study, which reports factor analyses of citizens' survey responses, does not precisely specify which positional dimensions the parties contest, although Dow notes the strong reasons to believe that one of the dimensions denotes left–right issues in all of the countries.

10. Curini and Hino (2012) estimate that larger party systems are associated with more party polarization only when there is no expectation of a coalition government.

11. Dow's estimates imply that a shift across the entire range of proportionality values for the thirty democracies in his dataset will increase the average party's predicted left–right distance from the median party by roughly 0.5 units, along the zero-to-ten scale.

12. We note that some recent studies, notably Makatos et al. (2015), analyze multiple observations of party polarization within each country by including election-specific measures based on analyses of parties' election manifestos, which increase the number of observations. However, since these analyses necessarily cluster the data by country, incorporating multiple observations per country generates more reliable measures of the average degree of party polarization in each country, but without solving the small-N problem.

13. Rexford proxies "permissiveness" via the seat product (which is explained in the chapter in this volume by Shugart and Taagepera).

## References

Adams, James. "Causes and Electoral Consequences of Party Policy Shifts in Multiparty Elections: Theoretical Results and Empirical Evidence." *Annual Review of Political Science* 15 (2012): 401–419.

Adams, James, Michael Clark, Lawrence Ezrow, and Garrett Glasgow. "Understanding Change and Stability in Party Ideologies: Do Parties Respond to Public Opinion or to Past Election Results?" *British Journal of Political Science* 34, no. 4 (2004): 589–610.

Adams, James, Michael Clark, Lawrence Ezrow, and Garrett Glasgow. "Are Niche Parties Fundamentally Different from Mainstream Parties? The Causes and the Electoral Consequences of Western European Parties' Policy Shifts, 1976–1998." *American Journal of Political Science* 50, no. 3 (2006): 513–529.

Adams, James, and Lawrence Ezrow. "Who do European parties represent? How Western European parties represent the policy preferences of opinion leaders." *Journal of Politics* 71, no. 1 (2009): 206–223.

Adams, James, Lawrence Ezrow, and Zeynep Somer-Topcu. "Is Anybody Listening? Evidence That Voters Do Not Respond to European Parties' Policy Statements during Elections." *American Journal of Political Science* 55, no. 2 (2011): 370–382.

Adams, James, and Samuel Merrill III. "Policy-Seeking Parties in a Parliamentary Democracy with Proportional Representation: A Valence-Uncertainty Model." *British Journal of Political Science* 39, no. 3 (2009): 539–558.

Adams, James F., Samuel Merrill III, and Bernard Grofman. *A Unified Theory of Party Competition: A Cross-National Analysis Integrating Spatial and Behavioral Factors.* Cambridge: Cambridge University Press, 2005.

Adams, James, and Zeynep Somer-Topcu. "Policy Adjustment by Parties in Response to Rival Parties' Policy Shifts: Spatial Theory and the Dynamics of Party Competition in Twenty-Five Post-War Democracies." *British Journal of Political Science* 39, no. 4 (2009): 825–846.

Alvarez, R. Michael, and Jonathan Nagler. "Party System Compactness: Measurement and Consequences." *Political Analysis* 12, no. 1 (2004): 46–62.

American Political Science Association, Committee on Political Parties. *Toward a More Responsible Two-Party System: A Report.* Richmond, VA: University of Virginia, Johnson Reprint Company, 1950.

Andrews, Josephine T., and Jeannette Money. "The Spatial Structure of Party Competition: Party Dispersion within a Finite Policy Space." *British Journal of Political Science* 39, no. 4 (2009): 805–824.

Best, Robin, and Jay K Dow. "Party System Polarization: Measurement Strategies and Performance." Typescript.

Budge, Ian. "A New Spatial Theory of Party Competition: Uncertainty, Ideology and Policy Equilibria Viewed Comparatively and Temporally." *British Journal of Political Science* 24, no. 4 (1994): 443–467.

Budge, Ian, and Michael D. McDonald. "Choices Parties Define Policy Alternatives in Representative Elections, 17 Countries 1945–1998." *Party Politics* 12, no. 4 (2006): 451–466.

Calvert, Randall L. "Robustness of the Multidimensional Voting Model: Candidate Motivations, Uncertainty, and Convergence." *American Journal of Political Science* 29, no. 1 (1985): 69–95.

Campbell, Angus. "Surge and Decline: A Study of Electoral Change." *Public Opinion Quarterly* 24, no. 3 (1960): 397–418.

Campbell, Angus, Philip Converse, Warren Miller, and Donald Stokes. *The American voter.* New York: John Wiley & Sons, Inc., 1960.

Carroll, Royce, Jeff Lewis, James Lo, Nolan McCarty, Keith Poole, and Howard Rosenthal. "DW-NOMINATE Scores with Bootstrapped Standard Errors." 2011. http://voteview.com/dwnomin.htm.

Clark, Michael. "Valence and Electoral Outcomes in Western Europe, 1976–1998." *Electoral Studies* 28, no. 1 (2009): 111–122.

Clark, Michael. "Does Public Opinion Respond to Shifts in Party Valence? A Cross-National Analysis of Western Europe, 1976–2002." *West European Politics* 37, no. 1 (2014): 91–112.

Clark, Michael, and Debra Leiter. "Does the Ideological Dispersion of Parties Mediate the Electoral Impact of Valence? A Cross-National Study of Party Support in Nine Western European Democracies." *Comparative Political Studies* 47, no. 2 (2014): 171–202.

Cox, Gary W. "Centripetal and Centrifugal Incentives in Electoral Systems." *American Journal of Political Science* 34, no. 4 (1990): 903–935.

Cox, Gary W. *Making Votes Count: Strategic Coordination in the World's Electoral Systems.* Vol. 7. Cambridge: Cambridge University Press, 1997.

Curini, Luigi, and Airo Hino. "Missing Links in Party-System Polarization: How Institutions and Voters Matter." *Journal of Politics* 74, no. 2 (2012): 460–473.

Dalton, Russell J. "The Quantity and the Quality of Party Systems: Party System Polarization, Its Measurement, and Its Consequences." *Comparative Political Studies* 41, no. 7 (2008): 899–920.

Dalton, Russell J., and Ian McAllister. "Random Walk or Planned Excursion? Continuity and Change in the Left–Right Positions of Political Parties." *Comparative Political Studies* 48, no. 6 (2015): 759–787.

Dow, Jay K. "A Comparative Spatial Analysis of Majoritarian and Proportional Elections." *Electoral Studies* 20, no. 1 (2001): 109–125.

Dow, Jay K. "Party-System Extremism in Majoritarian and Proportional Electoral Systems." *British Journal of Political Science* 41, no. 2 (2011): 341–361.

Downs, Anthony. "An Economic Theory of Political Action in a Democracy." *Journal of Political Economy* 12, no. 1 (1957): 135–150.

Eaton, B. Curtis, and Richard G. Lipsey. "The Principle of Minimum Differentiation Reconsidered: Some New Developments in the Theory of Spatial Competition." *Review of Economic Studies* 42, no. 1 (1975): 27–49.

Erikson, Robert S., and David Romero. "Candidate Equilibrium and the Behavioral Model of the Vote." *American Political Science Review* 84, no. 4 (1990): 1103–1126.

Ezrow, Lawrence. "The Variance Matters: How Party Systems Represent the Preferences of Voters." *Journal of Politics* 69, no. 1 (2007): 182–192.

Ezrow, Lawrence. "Parties' Policy Programmes and the Dog That Didn't Bark: No Evidence That Proportional Systems Promote Extreme Party Positioning." *British Journal of Political Science* 38, no. 3 (2008): 479–497.

Ezrow, Lawrence, Catherine E. De Vries, Marco Steenbergen, and Erica E. Edwards. "Mean Voter Representation and Partisan Constituency Representation: Do Parties Respond to the Mean Voter Position or to their Supporters?" *Party Politics* 17, no. 3 (2011): 275–301.

Ezrow, Lawrence, and Timothy Hellwig. "Responding to Voters or Responding to Markets? Political Parties and Public Opinion in an Era of Globalization." *International Studies Quarterly* 58, no. 4 (2014): 816–827.

Ezrow, Lawrence, and Georgios Xezonakis. "Citizen Satisfaction with Democracy and Parties' Policy Offerings." *Comparative Political Studies* 44, no. 9 (2011): 1152–1178.

Gallagher, Michael. "Proportionality, Disproportionality, and Electoral Choice." *Electoral Studies* 10, no. 1 (1991): 33–51.

Garnett, Mark, and Philip Lynch. *Exploring British Politics*, 4th edition. Pierson, 2016.

Gilens, Martin, and Benjamin I. Page. "Testing Theories of American Politics: Elites, Interest Groups, and Average Citizens." *Perspectives on Politics* 12, no. 3 (2014): 564–581.

Green, Jane, and Will Jennings. "Valence as Macro-Competence: An Analysis of Mood in Party Competence Evaluations in Great Britain." *British Journal of Political Science* 42, no. 2 (2012): 311–343.

Grofman, Bernard. "The Neglected Role of the Status Quo in Models of Issue Voting." *Journal of Politics* 47, no. 1 (1985), 153–159.

Han, Kyung Joon. "The Impact of Radical Right-Wing Parties on the Positions of Mainstream Parties Regarding Multiculturalism." *West European Politics* 38, no. 3 (2015): 557–576.

Haupt, Andrea B. "Parties' Responses to Economic Globalization: What Is Left for the Left and Right for the Right?" *Party Politics* 16, no. 1 (2009): 5–27.

Hellwig, Timothy. "Constructing Accountability Party Position Taking and Economic Voting." *Comparative Political Studies* 45, no. 1 (2012): 91–118.

Karreth, Johannes, Jonathan T. Polk, and Christopher S. Allen. "Catchall or Catch and Release? The Electoral Consequences of Social Democratic Parties' March to the Middle in Western Europe." *Comparative Political Studies* 46, no. 7 (2013): 791–822.

Kedar, Orit. *Voting for Policy, Not Parties: How Voters Compensate for Power Sharing.* Cambridge University Press, 2009.

Kernell, Georgia. "Strategic Party Heterogeneity." *Journal of Theoretical Politics* 28, no. 3 (2016): 408–430.

Laver, Michael. "Policy and the Dynamics of Political Competition." *American Political Science Review* 99, no. 2 (2005): 263–281.

Martin, Lanny W., and Randolph T. Stevenson. "Government Formation in Parliamentary Democracies." *American Journal of Political Science* 45, no. 1 (2001): 33–50.

Matakos, Konstantinos, Orestis Troumpounis, and Dimitrios Xefteris. "Electoral Rule Disproportionality and Platform Polarization." *American Journal of Political Science* 60, no. 4 (2016): 1026–1043.

McDonald, Michael, and Ian, Budge. *Elections, Parties, Democracy: Conferring the Median Mandate.* Oxford: Oxford University Press, 2005.

McGann, Anthony. "The advantages of ideological cohesion: a model of constituency representation and electoral competition in multi-party democracies." *Journal of Theoretical Politics* 14, no. 1 (2002): 37–70.

Merrill, Samuel III, and James Adams. "Computing Nash Equilibria in Probabilistic, Multiparty Spatial Models with Nonpolicy Components." *Political Analysis* 9, no. 4 (2001): 347–361.

Moser, Robert G., and Ethan Scheiner. "Mixed Electoral Systems and Electoral System Effects: Controlled Comparison and Cross-National Analysis." *Electoral Studies* 23, no. 4 (2004): 575–599.

Petrocik, John R. "Issue Ownership in Presidential Elections, with a 1980 Case Study." *American Journal of Political Science* 40, no. 3 (1996): 825–850.

Powell, G. Bingham. *Elections as Instruments of Democracy: Majoritarian and Proportional Visions.* New Haven: Yale University Press, 2000.

Powell, G. Bingham, Jr. and Guy D. Whitten. "A Cross-National Analysis of Economic Voting: Taking Account of the Political Context." *American Journal of Political Science* 37, no. 2 (1993): 391–414.

Rexford, Nathan. 2017. *How Do "the Rules of the Game" Affect the Strategies of the Players?: Examining the Link between Electoral Permissiveness and Party Issue Positions in European Elections.* PhD diss., UC Davis.

Schofield, Norman, and Itai Sened. *Multiparty Democracy: Elections and Legislative Politics.* Cambridge: Cambridge University Press, 2006.

Schumacher, Gijs, Catherine E. De Vries, and Barbara Vis. "Why Do Parties Change Position? Party Organization and Environmental Incentives." *Journal of Politics* 75, no. 2 (2013): 464–477.

Somer-Topcu, Zeynep. "Timely Decisions: The Effects of Past National Elections on Party Policy Change." *Journal of Politics* 71, no. 1 (2009): 238–248.

Somer-Topcu, Zeynep. "Everything to Everyone: The Electoral Consequences of the Broad-Appeal Strategy in Europe." *American Journal of Political Science* 59, no. 4 (2015): 841–854.

Shugart, Matthew S., and Rein Taagepera. *Votes from Seats: Logical Models of Electoral Systems.* New York: Cambridge University Press, 2017.

Spoon, Jae-Jae. *Political Survival of Small Parties in Europe.* 2011. New Comparative Politics Series. Ann Arbor: University of Michigan Press, 2011.

Ward, Hugh, Lawrence Ezrow, and Han Dorussen. "Globalization, Party Positions, and the Median Voter." *World Politics* 63, no. 3 (2011): 509–547.

Weschle, Simon. "The Impact of Economic Crises on Political Representation in Public Communication: Evidence from the Eurozone." Forthcoming in the *British Journal of Political Science.*

Williams, Laron K. "It's All Relative: Spatial Positioning of Parties and Ideological Shifts." *European Journal of Political Research* 54, no. 1 (2015): 141–159.

# PART III

ELECTORAL
SYSTEMS AND
THE WIDER
POLITICAL
SYSTEM

CHAPTER 13

........................................................................................

# PORTFOLIO-MAXIMIZING STRATEGIC VOTING IN PARLIAMENTARY ELECTIONS

........................................................................................

GARY W. COX

THE notion that political actors anticipate how votes will translate into seats, adjusting their behaviors accordingly, is a staple in political science (Duverger 1955; Rae 1967; Taagepera and Shugart 1989; Cox 1997). Specific propositions, such as Duverger's law (Duverger 1955) and the M + 1 rule (Cox 1997), clarify how different electoral rules lead to different anticipatory strategies. These propositions concern what one might call "seat-maximizing strategic voting"—that is, voting to get the best possible allocation of seats.

Another branch of the literature imagines that political actors consider not just how votes translate into seats, but also how seats translate into ministerial portfolios. Actors in these models adjust their strategies mainly to win as many portfolios as possible. Thus, Cox (1997) speaks of "portfolio-maximizing strategic voting," while Meffert and Gschwend (2010) refer to "strategic coalition voting" and McCuen and Morton (2010) to "tactical coalition voting."

In this chapter, I review work that investigates portfolio-maximizing strategic voting in parliamentary systems.[1] I have three main goals. First, I offer a typology of strategies, sorting them into mutually exclusive and collectively exhaustive categories. This helps to organize the literature and identify possible gaps. Second, I consider the equilibrium levels of portfolio-maximizing voting. The extant literature has mostly taken a decision-theoretic approach, leaving it unclear exactly how much portfolio-maximizing voting of any particular kind might be expected in any given situation. Taking a game-theoretic perspective helps clarify how much strategic voting should be expected and also the interconnections between different varieties of strategic behavior. Third, I review the empirical evidence on the incidence of portfolio-maximizing voting. I conclude with some thoughts on fruitful ways forward for future research.

# A TYPOLOGY OF PORTFOLIO-MAXIMIZING
# VOTING STRATEGIES

In this section, I imagine that political actors think ahead to the government formation and policymaking games and act in elections to get the best possible outcome from
those games. I assume that government formation occurs in three stages, corresponding
roughly to the Baron and Ferejohn (1989) model:

(Stage 1)  A formateur is chosen by some process that depends on the seat shares won
by the various parties in the election.

(Stage 2)  The formateur proposes an allocation of portfolios.

(Stage 3)  If a majority of members of parliament (MPs) support the proposal, then
the government forms as proposed; otherwise, the incumbent formateur is dis-
charged and the game recommences with the selection of a new formateur.[2]

Finally, after ministerial portfolios have been distributed, the government may enact
some new policies. Actors' payoffs may hinge solely on the seats and portfolios they
hold, solely on the policies the government enacts, or on some combination of office-
holding and policymaking payoffs.

By specifying how the formateur is selected and how government policies are determined, one can generate various specific game forms. For example, Baron and Ferejohn
(1989) assume the formateur is selected stochastically and ignore policymaking (so
actors care only about the share of portfolios they receive).

Let the set of all possible government formation and policymaking game forms be
denoted by $\Omega$. Given a particular game form, $\Gamma \in \Omega$, portfolio-maximizing strategies
come in three basic types, depending on whether they seek to affect (1) who is chosen
as formateur, (2) who the formateur selects as partners, or (3) what policies the government implements (see table 13.1). Let's consider each possible goal in turn.

First, an individual or group can vote to get a better formateur. To elaborate, let the set
of all parties be $N = \{1, \ldots, n\}$. Every vector of seats awarded in the election, $S = (S_1, \ldots, S_n)$, implies a vector of probabilities that each party will be appointed as the initial for-
mateur, $F(S|\Gamma) = (F_1(S|\Gamma), \ldots, F_n(S|\Gamma))$. Parties may seek to change S to affect the par-
ties' respective chances of becoming formateur (i.e., $F(S|\Gamma)$). I call this kind of strategy
"formateur optimization." Any such strategy obviously depends on the rules governing
the selection of the formateur (hence on $\Gamma$). In the particular case where constitutional
rules or norms mandate that the largest party should be chosen as the first formateur,
the strategy is particularly simple (and discussed further later).

Second, an individual or group can vote to provide the formateur with a better set
of potential partners. Let the set of all minimal winning coalitions, given an electoral
outcome S, be MWC(S). The set of minimum winning coalitions with which formateur j
might govern is denoted $A_j(S) = \{C \subseteq N: j \in C \text{ and } C \in MWC(S)\}$. Pre-electoral alliances

Table 13.1  A Typology of Portfolio–Maximizing Voting

---

I. *Formateur optimization* (aka strategic sequencing): Voting to affect who becomes formateur

II. *Partner optimization*: Voting to affect who is available to the formateur as a governing partner (or how many seats he or she holds)

    A. Strategic threshold insurance

    B. Strategic manipulation of bargaining weights

III. *Policy balancing* (aka coalition-directed Duvergerian voting): Voting to affect the balance of power in the government most likely to form

    A. Strategic balancing by "out" voters

    B. Strategic balancing by "in" voters

---

(or bans) may render some of these numerically possible alliances politically infeasible. Let the *feasible set of coalitions* for formateur j, given S, be $A_j^*(S) \subseteq A_j(S)$. Parties may seek to change S to affect who can partner with whom—that is, $(A_1^*(S), ..., A_n^*(S))$—in which case I say they engage in "partner optimization." In some circumstances, the abstract notion of manipulating with whom the likely formateur(s) will be able to partner leads to simple strategic prescriptions (which I discuss further later).

Third, an individual or group can vote to alter the balance of power within a particular coalition government that the individual or group believes will form. I call such a strategy—which makes sense if government policies depend on a weighted average of the participating parties' preferences—"policy balancing" in table 13.1.

These basic types of strategic voting exhaust the possibilities. If an actor's votes do not change who will be the formateur, who will be available as partners to the possible formateur(s), or the balance of power within a likely government, then there is no sense in which those votes can count as portfolio maximizing.

In the remainder of this section, I provide examples and further discussion of each of the main species of portfolio-maximizing strategic voting. In the process, I discuss some of the subspecies.

## Formateur Optimization

Cox (1997, 194) called formateur optimization "strategic sequencing," defining it as "voting so as to affect which party gets the first opportunity to form a government." To illustrate, consider Hans, a supporter of Germany's Free Democratic Party (FDP). Hans goes to the polls believing the FDP is sure to clear the national threshold[3] but knowing that the party has left open its option to ally with either the Christian Democratic Union (CDU) or the Social Democratic Party (SPD) after the elections. If Hans prefers the CDU–FDP coalition, he may cast his list vote not for his most preferred party (the FDP) but instead for his most preferred coalition leader (the CDU). Voting for the CDU makes sense if Hans believes that whichever of the two large parties gets the first chance at forming a government will be able to reach an agreement with the FDP.

Of course, if "too many" people like Hans desert the FDP, then it may fall below the threshold. This suggests a limit on the equilibrium level of strategic sequencing, as I explain in the next section.

## Partner Optimization

Another strategy to affect which government forms is to alter the array of partners from which each formateur can choose. Cox (1997, 194) dubs one form of such voting "strategic threshold insurance," defining it as "voting so as to keep a prospective coalition partner's vote above some threshold mandated by the electoral code." To take the German case again, consider a year in which the FDP is clearly allied with the CDU but in which its ability to clear the national threshold is uncertain. In this case, CDU supporter Heidi may decide to vote for the FDP, to ensure its availability as a coalition partner. Slinko and White (2010) show that threshold insurance incentives exist generically in PR systems with thresholds.

There are other imaginable forms of partner optimization, in addition to threshold insurance. For example, consider a country in which the leftist bloc consists of three parties, A, B, and C. Voters consider it certain that party A will be the formateur but are uncertain whether an AB government will be able to form, or whether the only viable government will be ABC. Consider voters whose most preferred party is C. If some of these voters prefer an AB coalition to an ABC coalition, then they will have a strategic incentive to vote for B.[4] I dub this kind of behavior "strategic manipulation of bargaining weights" in table 13.1.

## Policy Balancing

Finally, suppose that which parties will form the government is a foregone conclusion. In this case, the only way to affect the allocation of portfolios is by altering the seat shares of those parties. I call this policy balancing. Bargsted and Kedar (2009) call it "coalition-targeted Duvergerian voting."

There are two main subtypes of such voting. First, suppose that a country has two blocs, one on the left and one on the right, each consisting of multiple parties. Suppose it is a foregone conclusion that a particular right-wing government will form. In this case, Bargsted and Kedar (2009) argue that leftist voters may desert their preferred party to support the most moderate party in the right-wing bloc. This makes sense if voters care about government policies and believe these will reflect a weighted average of the parties' preferences. I dub this "policy balancing by 'out' voters" in table 13.1.

Now consider a right-wing voter in the same country—again assuming that a particular right-wing government is sure to form. Anticipating that the coalition government's policies will reflect a weighted average of its members' preferences, such a voter may vote for a more extreme party, to pull the coalition's policies to the right. I dub this "policy balancing by 'in' voters" in table 13.1.

## The Preconditions of Strategic Voting

Figure 13.1 diagrams the conditions under which the three main forms of portfolio-maximizing voting are most likely to occur. The horizontal axis reflects how much uncertainty there is over who the initial formateur will be. The vertical axis reflects how much uncertainty there is concerning the partners with which each formateur can choose to ally.

If there is no uncertainty about either the formateur or the partners, then we are in the domain of policy balancing, located near the origin in figure 13.1. If there is substantial uncertainty about the formateur but little about the partners, then we are in the domain of formateur optimization, located far out on the horizontal axis in figure 13.1. Finally, if there is substantial uncertainty about who the partners might be but little about the formateur, then we are in the domain of partner optimization, located high on the vertical axis in figure 13.1.

It is possible to have high uncertainty about both the formateur and the available partners. For example, the CDU and SPD might be in a dead heat and the FDP hovering

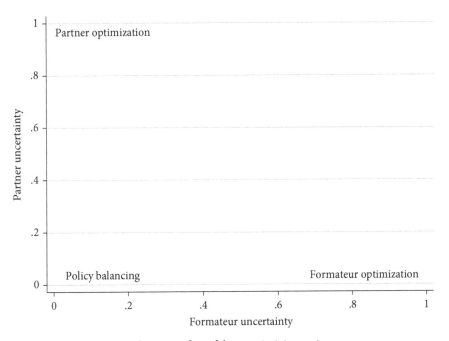

FIGURE 13.1. Diagramming the types of portfolio-maximizing voting.

right at the threshold. I do not consider these more complicated cases here but the basic approach outlined next could be extended to do so.

# EQUILIBRIUM CONSIDERATIONS

Papers in the current literature typically analyze one type of portfolio-maximizing strategy and use decision-theoretic methods. Relatively little has been written about the equilibrium levels of strategic portfolio-maximizing voting (although see Austen-Smith and Banks 1988; Baron and Diermeier 2001; Slinko and White 2010; Indridason 2011). Relatedly, little has been said about the interconnections between different types of strategy. In this section, I explore these issues.

Consider a hypothetical polity with the following characteristics. First, legislators are elected via list proportional representation (PR), with seats awarded only to lists that clear a nationwide threshold. For simplicity, I assume seats are allocated in perfect proportion to votes (unless a party falls below the threshold). Second, the largest party becomes the initial formateur. Third, the party system is a simplified version of West Germany's circa 1970. In particular, only three parties exist: the CDU on the right, the SPD on the left, and the FDP in the center. The CDU has $N_{CDU}$ supporters, the SPD has $N_{SPD}$ supporters, and the FDP has $N_{FDP}$, with $N_{CDU} \approx N_{SPD} >> N_{FDP}$. Fourth, government policy is determined by a weighted average of the participants' ideal points (as in Indridason 2011). Finally, I assume all voters vote. Thus, the total number of votes cast is $N = N_{CDU} + N_{SPD} + N_{FDP}$.

The actors in my analysis will be the two big parties (viewed as unitary actors) and two factions within the FDP (also viewed as unitary actors). Most of the literature focuses on individual voters. However, party and factional leaders should care deeply about portfolios and can encourage or discourage the casting of strategic votes by their followers. Thus, it makes sense to consider portfolio-maximizing strategies from an elite perspective.[5]

I assume elite actors care about three things: how many seats they win, how many portfolios they win, and the policies the government enacts. For specificity, imagine that if actor j wins a share $s_j$ of the seats and a share $p_j$ of the portfolios, and the government's policy is x, then j's payoff is $s_j + \gamma p_j + v_j(x)$.[6] One can think of this as a payoff denominated in seat-share equivalents, with $\gamma \geq 1$ indicating how much more valuable portfolios are than seats and the function $v_j$ giving j's policy payoff (also expressed in seat-share equivalents).

Note that, given the assumption of perfect proportionality, strategic voting always costs seats. Thus, an elite actor's incentive to orchestrate strategic voting depends on how much the resulting seat sacrifice buys in portfolios and policies.

As displayed in table 13.2, there are four possible scenarios that elite actors in our hypothetical country might face during a particular election. First, the FDP's sincere support can either put it above the threshold or below it. That is, either $N_{FDP} \geq T$ or $N_{FDP}$

## Table 13.2 Electoral Scenarios and Strategic Voting

|  | FDP in Winning Pre-Electoral Alliance with CDU (SPD, Respectively) | FDP Not in Pre-Electoral Alliance |
|---|---|---|
| FDP above threshold | Policy balancing by SPD (CDU, respectively) | Formateur optimization by FDP factions |
| FDP below threshold | Threshold insurance by CDU (SPD, respectively) | No portfolio-maximizing strategic voting |

< T, where T is the electoral threshold (expressed in raw votes).[7] Second, the FDP can either be allied with one of the big parties or not. Crossing these two dichotomous variables yields four scenarios. Under three of these scenarios, specific incentives to organize strategic voting exist, as I discuss in the following subsections.

# Above Threshold + No Alliance = Strategic Sequencing

In this section, I consider electoral scenarios in which the FDP is above the threshold and has kept its postelection coalitional options open (as in the top right cell in table 13.2). I shall assume that the FDP's two factions, denoted 1 and 2, have $N_{FDP_1}$ and $N_{FDP_2}$ members, respectively. Faction j assigns a value of $u_j(CDU)$ to a CDU-led coalition, a value of $u_j(SPD)$ to an SPD-led coalition, and a value of 0 to the event in which the FDP falls below the electoral threshold and thus gains no seats (and no portfolios). I assume that faction 1 prefers a CDU–FDP coalition to an SPD–FDP coalition (so $u_1(CDU) > u_1(SPD) > 0$). Meanwhile, faction 2 prefers an SPD–FDP coalition (so $u_2(SPD) > u_2(CDU) > 0$).

To illustrate the payoffs, suppose $N_{CDU} = N_{SPD} = .47N$ and $N_{FDP} = .06N$. In this case, a CDU–FDP alliance would give the FDP 6 percent of the seats in parliament and $.06/(.06 + .47) = 11.3$ percent of the government's portfolios. The government's policy would be $.887x_{CDU} + .113x_{FDP}$, where $x_{CDU}$ and $x_{FDP}$ denote the two parties' ideal points.

Each faction j chooses a number of its members, $\sigma_j \le N_{FDPj}$, that it instructs to vote strategically for the big party it wishes to become formateur. Assume, for the moment, that the two big parties instruct all their supporters to vote sincerely. Letting $\sigma = (\sigma_1, \sigma_2)$, the total votes received by the three parties' lists can be written as follows:

$$V_{CDU}(\sigma) = N_{CDU} + \sigma_1, \quad V_{SPD}(\sigma) = N_{SPD} + \sigma_2, \quad V_{FDP}(\sigma) = N_{FDP} - \sigma_1 - \sigma_2$$

$\sigma$ can be a Nash equilibrium in the subgame between the FDP's two factions only if it satisfies the following two conditions. First, the FDP must poll above the threshold: $V_{FDP}(\sigma) \ge T$. If this condition fails, then the FDP will be excluded from both parliament and the government. In this case, at least one faction can improve its payoff by unilaterally reducing its strategic voting enough to keep the FDP above the threshold.[8] Second, the FDP's "surplus" vote (how many votes it polls above the threshold) must not be too large: $V_{FDP}(\sigma) - T < |V_{CDU}(\sigma) - V_{SPD}(\sigma)|$. The second condition ensures that a losing faction[9] cannot cast enough strategic votes to change which of the large parties becomes formateur, while keeping the FDP above the threshold.

Now consider the case in which $N_{CDU} = N_{SPD}$ and $N_{FDP1} = N_{FDP2}$. Suppose one of the factions can announce its strategy first, with the other then given the opportunity to respond. What do the equilibria to this Stackleberg leadership game look like?

If faction 1 is the first-mover, then it will cast $\sigma_1 = g\left[\dfrac{N_{FDU} - T}{2}\right] + 1$ strategic votes for the CDU, where g[z] is the smallest integer greater than or equal to z. Faction 2's best response to this move is to vote sincerely.[10] If faction 2 is the first-mover, then the roles are reversed. Faction 2 casts $\sigma_2 = g\left[\dfrac{N_{FDU} - T}{2}\right] + 1$ strategic votes for the SPD and faction 1 casts $\sigma_1 = 0$ votes for the CDU. Thus, there are exactly two Stackleberg equilibria in this game.

In a simultaneous-move game, each faction's desire to outbid its intraparty rival—by casting more strategic votes—might drive the party over the cliff (i.e., push the party's vote total below the threshold). However, when one or the other can "move first," such disasters will be avoided.

If we call $N_{FDP} - T$ the FDP's "initial surplus," then the Stackleberg equilibrium amount of strategic sequencing is approximately 50 percent of the party's initial surplus. Even in simultaneous-move games, strategic sequencing will be limited by the risk of falling below the threshold (although there the precise equilibrium levels are more complicated to exposit).

Now reconsider the assumption that the two big parties will instruct their supporters to vote sincerely. Does this make sense? Neither big party can gain by telling its voters to vote for the other big party. If one of the big parties casts strategic votes for the FDP, this will cost the party seats, will reduce the party's chance of becoming the first formateur (from .5 to 0), and will not affect the set of feasible coalitions facing either formateur (since the FDP always clears the threshold in equilibrium). Thus, as assumed, each big party will instruct its supporters to vote sincerely.

## Below Threshold + Winning Alliance = Strategic Threshold Insurance

Now consider a scenario in which the FDP's sincere support falls short of the threshold and the party has entered a pre-electoral alliance with the CDU. Suppose, moreover, that the CDU will lose on its own but will win if the FDP clears the threshold: $N_{CDU} < N_{SPD} < N_{CDU} + N_{FDP}$.[11]

In this scenario, neither faction in the FDP can gain by strategic voting, so $\sigma_1 = \sigma_2 = 0$. To begin with, assume the SPD votes sincerely. The CDU's best response is to instruct $s_{CDU} = T - N_{FDP}$ of its supporters to vote for the FDP. In other words, the CDU should lend the FDP just enough votes to meet the threshold. Were the CDU to lend more votes, this could only lead to the FDP getting more portfolios at the CDU's expense.

When the CDU casts $T - N_{FDP}$ strategic votes for the FDP, what is the SPD's best response? If the SPD votes sincerely, the parties' seat shares will be $s_{CDU} = \left(N_{CDU} - T + N_{FDP}\right)/N$, $s_{SPD} = N_{SPD}/N$, and $s_{FDP} = T/N$. After the election, the CDU–FDP alliance will form the government and the parties' portfolio shares will be $P_{CDU} = \dfrac{S_{CDU}}{S_{CDU} + S_{FDP}}$, $P_{SPD} = 0$, and $P_{FDP} = 1 - P_{CDU}$. Finally, the coalition government's policy will be $p_{CDU} x_{CDU} + \left(1 - p_{CDU}\right) x_{FDP}$.

Now suppose the SPD casts just enough strategic votes to give the FDP just enough additional seats to award it one additional portfolio. The SPD will dislike losing seats to the FDP. However, the government's policy will improve, due to the FDP's additional portfolio. Thus, the SPD may choose to sacrifice some seats for better policies.

If, in fact, the SPD would cast coalition-targeted Duvergerian votes for the FDP, however, then the CDU would wish to reduce its own threshold insurance votes. Indeed, the CDU would reduce its threshold insurance votes by one for every one strategic vote cast by the SPD.

Were the CDU to retract any of its insurance votes, however, the SPD would prefer to retract all its Duvergerian votes—thereby driving the FDP below the threshold and winning all the portfolios for itself. These observations suffice to show that there is no pure-strategy equilibrium in the scenario under consideration in this section. They also suggest that the SPD's incentive to affect the balance of power in the impending coalition government will be reduced when the CDU engages in threshold insurance. To simplify the exposition, I shall henceforth assume that the SPD's best response (in this scenario) is to vote sincerely.

## Above Threshold + Alliance = Policy Balancing

Now consider a scenario in which the FDP's sincere support puts it above the threshold and the party has entered a pre-electoral alliance with the CDU. Again, assume that the CDU cannot get into government alone but can in alliance: $N_{CDU} < N_{SPD} < N_{CDU} + N_{FDP}$.

This scenario encourages coalition-targeted Duvergerian voting by the SPD. The party knows it will lose. It may, however, be able to give enough votes to the FDP to confer on it some additional seats, with those additional seats giving the FDP an additional portfolio and thereby improving the government's policies. In such a case, the SPD may find the price in seats it must pay for better government policies acceptable.

If, in fact, the SPD plans to vote strategically for the FDP, the CDU has no response.[12] However, the right-wing faction of the FDP might wish to vote strategically for the CDU.

## Table 13.3 Thresholds, Alliances, and Portfolio-Maximizing Voting

|  | FDP in Pre-Electoral Alliance with CDU and $N_{CDU} + N_{FDP} > N_{SPD}$ | FDP in Pre-Electoral Alliance with SPD and $N_{SPD} + N_{FDP} > N_{CDU}$ | FDP Not in any Pre-Electoral Alliance |
|---|---|---|---|
| FDP above threshold $(N_{FDP} \geq T)$ | SPD may cast coalition-targeted Duvergerian votes for FDP. | CDU may cast coalition-targeted Duvergerian votes for FDP. | FDP factions may cast strategic sequencing votes for their favored formateur parties. |
| FDP below threshold $(N_{FDP} < T)$ | CDU casts $T - N_{FDP}$ threshold insurance votes for FDP. | SPD casts $T - N_{FDP}$ threshold insurance votes for FDP. | There is no portfolio-maximizing voting. |

If all actors care only about portfolios (and not at all about seats), then the process of balancing and rebalancing the coalition would continue until the SPD received no votes. This sort of complete abandonment of parties that are out of contention for portfolios is formally derived by Indridason (2011).[13]

If parties and factions care about both seats and portfolios, then the SPD should never give away all its votes. The weight placed on the FDP's policy preferences is, eventually, concave increasing in its vote share. In addition, one might think the costs of sacrificing seats would be convex increasing. Thus, strategic voting should be subject to diminishing marginal returns and, eventually, negative marginal returns.

## Summary

Table 13.3 summarizes the conclusions of this section. The type of portfolio-maximizing voting should be a function of two variables: whether the FDP's own support puts it above or below the threshold, and whether the FDP has concluded a winning pre-electoral alliance with one of the larger parties. Given a particular scenario, the model makes predictions about which party (or faction) should encourage its followers to cast strategic votes for which of its competitors and why.

# EMPIRICAL FINDINGS

In this section, I review some of the empirical evidence regarding portfolio-maximizing voting. Among other things, I consider whether the three kinds of strategic vote displayed in table 13.3 arise in the expected scenarios, with the expected donor and recipient actors.

## Strategic Sequencing

Building on the previous discussion, strategic sequencing should arise only when two conditions are met. First, there must be uncertainty about who the formateur will be. Second, whoever becomes the first formateur must have a good chance of forming a government. The first condition is met when the largest party is likely to be chosen as the first formateur, and two or more large parties each has a significant chance of winning the most votes. The second condition is met when enough parties are willing to join a government headed by any of the likely formateurs that the first formateur has a good chance of success.

The willingness of nonformateur parties to join multiple formateurs in government is affected by whether they announce their intention to join with (or avoid) certain governing partners. As a general rule of thumb, strategic sequencing should play a bigger role as pre-electoral alliances become less comprehensive but should fade out as pre-electoral alliances (or bans) become more comprehensive.[14]

The number of studies focusing on strategic sequencing is small relative to the other categories of portfolio-maximizing voting. However, relevant studies do focus on contexts in which the two conditions listed previously are met. In particular, Israeli elections have generated both formateur uncertainty and a crop of parties willing to join either of the likely formateur parties in government. Several studies of Israel, including Felsenthal and Brichta (1985), Nixon et al. (1996), and Nachmias and Sened (1999), have offered evidence of strategic sequencing behavior.

## Threshold Insurance Voting

Threshold insurance voting should arise when a pre-electoral alliance exists and the smaller partner is in danger of falling below the threshold. Studies of German, Austrian, and Swedish elections meeting these conditions have been conducted. Cumulatively, the extant studies provide substantial evidence of threshold insurance voting in these cases.[15]

Investigations of threshold insurance in Germany have the longest pedigree. Early studies, such as Fisher (1973), Jesse (1988), Bawn (1993, 1999), and Cox (1997), compared the gap between a candidate's vote total and the votes cast for that candidate's party list in the same constituency. They found that small parties' candidates poll well below their respective lists. Most viewed the list vote as sincere and thus interpreted the fall-off as seat-maximizing strategic voting. However, as Cox (1997, 82) pointed out, some portion of the gap might reflect a sincere candidate vote coupled with a strategic threshold insurance vote. Thus, these early studies could be viewed as providing ambiguous evidence of threshold insurance.

More recent studies of German elections have utilized survey data and provided more compelling evidence. Pappi and Thurner (2002) showed that coalition preferences

induced certain kinds of split-ticket voting, while Gschwend (2007) showed more specifically that voter expectations regarding small parties' risks of falling below the threshold significantly increased their propensity to split their vote. Shikano, Hermann, and
Thurner (2009) also show that big-party voters who see their small-party ally as at risk
are more likely to vote for that ally.[16]

Sweden is not a mixed-member system like Germany. Thus, one cannot compare
list and candidate votes to infer levels of threshold insurance voting. However, Fredén
(2014, 473) exploits a series of specific survey questions to identify voters satisfying three
criteria: "the voter considers potential government outcomes, votes for a party at risk
of falling below an electoral threshold, and votes for another party than his or her most
preferred one." She finds that a considerable number of threshold insurance votes were
cast in 2010 for the Christian Democrats, a small member of the incumbent governing
coalition.

Meffert and Gschwend (2010) find similar evidence in the Austrian election of 2006.
In particular, they find that large-party supporters defected to a junior coalition partner in a district where the small party was at risk of falling below the district-specific
threshold.

Insurance voting should be something that the parties themselves might seek to
organize and manage. Certainly that is what the aforementioned models assume. In
addition, Roberts (1988) provides clear evidence that the major German parties do recognize and attempt to manage insurance voting. However, thus far the literature does
not contain a systematic study of how big parties approach the problem of threshold
insurance. This seems a good area for more research.

## Coalition-Targeted Duvergerian Voting

Research into coalition-targeted Duvergerian voting (aka policy balancing) has grown
substantially in the last decade. The most often articulated prediction is that *actors
should avoid voting for parties that have no chance of participating in government.*
Bargsted and Kedar (2009, 308), for example, put it this way: "When voters perceive
their favorite party as having little chance of participating in the governing coalition,
they often desert it and instead support the lesser of evils among those they perceive as
viable coalition partners." The theoretical reason voters abandon parties that have no
chance of winning portfolios is that (1) voters care mainly about the policy implemented
by the government, and (2) the government's policy is determined by the preferences of
the parties forming the government, weighted by their legislative seats (Schofield and
Laver 1985; Duch and Stevenson 2008; Indridason 2011). Given these two assumptions,
voters have no reason to vote for parties that do not get into government, because such
parties have no influence on the government's ultimate policy.

Another reason voters might abandon parties with no chance of joining government is that (1) voters care mainly about how the national budget—viewed as a divisible

pie—is carved up, (2) each governing party receives a share of the budgetary pie proportional to its share of portfolios, and (3) each governing party allocates its share of the pie to its supporters. Thus far, the literature has not considered this alternative.

Do voters in PR systems in fact avoid voting for parties unlikely to win portfolios? The literature offers several kinds of evidence pertinent to this question.

First, some studies show that voters in PR systems do not always vote sincerely. For example, Abramson et al. (2010) and Hobolt and Karp (2010), investigating surveys from six and thirty-two countries, respectively, show that about as many voters report voting insincerely in PR systems as in single-seat district systems. Such findings, however, do not speak directly to whether voters abandon their most preferred parties because they are not portfolio viable.[17]

Second, some papers show that voters in PR systems do know which coalitions are likely to form. Such coalition awareness exists even in systems with many parties, such as the Netherlands (Irwin and van Holsteyn 2012) or New Zealand (Bowler, Karp, and Donovan 2010). So voters do possess the knowledge needed to discriminate against portfolio-nonviable parties.

A third group of papers addresses Duvergerian incentives at the coalitional level more directly, providing substantial evidence that voters gravitate toward portfolio-viable parties. In New Zealand's 2002 elections, Bowler, Karp, and Donovan (2010) show that voters abandoned their most preferred parties as their perceived coalition prospects waned. In Austria's 2006 elections, Hermann (2008) finds a similar pattern. In Israel's 2006 election, Bargsted and Kedar (2009, 317) report as follows: "as voters on the left perceive a Kadima-Likud government a more likely outcome, they desert Labor and endorse Kadima. For voters on the right we observe a decline in support for Likud accompanied by increasing support for Kadima under the reverse circumstances."

But for whom should a voter vote, after abandoning a first choice with no chance of joining government? The literature offers two "balancing" answers, depending on whether the voter in question is in the bloc expected to anchor the government (an "in" voter) or not (an "out" voter). "In" voters anticipate the watering down of policy in a coalition government and counteract it by supporting the more extreme parties likely to get into government (cf. Kedar 2005; Hermann 2008). "Out" voters anticipate an extreme government policy and counteract it by supporting the more moderate government parties (cf. Bargsted and Kedar 2009; Hermann 2008).

How the competing preferences of "in" and "out" voters play out in equilibrium is not addressed in the empirical literature. However, Indridason (2011) develops a model within which this issue can be explored. He shows that, in equilibrium, all voters vote for a party that will participate in government. No one wastes his or her vote on a party that will not gain portfolios. Although there are no blocs in his model, one can interpret his main result as saying that all the "out" voters support the most moderate party in the prospective government, many of the "in" voters support the most extreme party in the prospective government, and ultimately the government's policy is near the median voter.

As with other forms of strategic voting, coalition-targeted Duvergerian voting supplies the defect of poor coordination at the entry stage. In particular, if parties merge or form strong pre-electoral alliances, leaving only two parties or two alliances, then none will be seat nonviable, nor will any be portfolio nonviable. Thus, voters will have no incentive to cast either seat- or portfolio-maximizing strategic votes.

## Other Results

The typology of strategic voting I have used in this chapter does not capture all types of "coalition-directed" voting explored in the literature. In particular, papers such as Blais et al. (2006) and Duch, May, and Armstrong (2010) do not have a strategic voting model per se. They assume that a voter's assessment of a particular party depends not just on that party's own positions, but also on the coalitions in which that party might participate.

Duch, May, and Armstrong (2010), for example, consider the expected distance between voter i's ideological position and the average position of the coalition governments in which party j might participate.[18] Thus, as they note (p. 700), their model does not capture the possibility that voters avoid parties that have slim chances of participating in government.

Analyses in which coalition preferences are entered as separate variables (as in Blais et al. 2006) or are derived (as in Duch, May, and Armstrong 2010) show clearly that voters do not behave according to a standard party-centered spatial model. However, such analyses do not tell us whether the departures from party-centered behavior are due to the specific kinds of portfolio-maximizing strategy typologized here.[19]

# Conclusion

In this review chapter, I have focused on how elite actors view the issue of strategic voting, and I have taken a game-theoretic, rather than decision-theoretic, approach. I have argued that certain electoral scenarios create incentives for party and factional leaders to encourage the casting of specific kinds of strategic portfolio-maximizing votes.

The scenarios are defined by two circumstances: whether or not a particular small party is in danger of falling below a defined voting threshold, and whether or not that party has concluded a pre-electoral alliance with a large party. Each of the four possible scenarios yields its own incentives. When the small party is below the threshold but in alliance, its larger ally should engage in threshold insurance voting. When the small party is below the threshold and not in alliance, none of the elite actors has any incentive to promote strategic voting. When the small party is above the threshold and has joined an alliance expected to form the government, nonallied parties may engage in strategic balancing. Finally, when the small party is above the threshold and not in alliance, then its factions may engage in strategic sequencing.

Most of the empirical papers in the literature focus on a particular country at a particular time. The scenario is thus held constant and the investigation concerns whether voters can be identified as having cast the expected strategic votes.

Another empirical approach would be to take the scenario as the main independent variable and look for responses to changing scenarios. For example, the theory of threshold insurance voting articulated earlier could be tested as follows. First, one would identify a subsample of cases in which threshold insurance voting should occur, because a party that had entered a pre-electoral alliance was in danger of falling below the threshold, and a subsample where such voting should not occur—say, systems with thresholds but with no alliances or no parties at risk of falling below the threshold. Second, one would compare the behavior of party leaders and voters in the two subsamples. Do party leaders actively encourage (or discourage) threshold-insurance votes? Do voters cast (or avoid) such votes?

## Notes

1. I do not deal with strategic entry here. See Cox (1997, 1999).
2. For simplicity, I ignore the possibility of minority governments. The main conclusions I reach do not appear to be sensitive to whether the model allows minority governments or not.
3. In Germany, if a party receives less than 5 percent of the nationwide vote, then it receives no seats.
4. If voters care only about government policy, which is a weighted average of the party positions, then it is possible for some C voters to prefer an AB coalition to an ABC coalition, if $x_A < x_C < x_B$. For example, suppose A expects to get 40 percent of the vote, B 40 percent, and C 20 percent. Normalize so that $x_A = 0$ and $x_B = 1$. In this case, an AB government's policy will be ½. Suppose C voters are distributed uniformly over the interval [.5,.7], with a mean (and party position) of .6. In this scenario, an AB government will be better for left-wing C voters—that is, those with ideal points to the left of .55.
5. When voters are the actors, even more opportunities for strategy and counterstrategy arise than are considered here.
6. I assume the two FDP factions share the FDP's seats and portfolios in proportion to their respective sizes.
7. We can write $T \equiv g[.05N]$, where $g[x]$ is the smallest integer greater than or equal to x, and the threshold is 5 percent of the total votes cast.
8. If $\sigma_1 > N_{FDP} - T$ and $\sigma_2 > N_{FDP} - T$, then neither faction can unilaterally reduce its strategic voting and put the FDP over the threshold. However, $\sigma_j > N_{FDP} - T$ is a dominated strategy for j = 1,2. Thus, assuming that players do not play dominated strategies, the result in the text follows.
9. For a given $\sigma = (\sigma_1, \sigma_2)$, faction 1 is losing if $V_{CDU}(\sigma) < V_{SPD}(\sigma)$, faction 2 is losing if $V_{CDU}(\sigma) > V_{SPD}(\sigma)$, and both are losing if there is a tie.

10. To see this, consider the three cases $\sigma_2 > \sigma_1$, $\sigma_2 = \sigma_1$, and $\sigma_2 < \sigma_1$. If faction 2 casts more strategic votes than faction 1 does ($\sigma_2 > \sigma_1$), then the party will fall below the threshold and receive zero seats and zero portfolios. The SPD will outpoll the CDU (because $\sigma_2 > \sigma_1$) and will thus form a single-party government, implementing its ideal policies. If faction 2 casts as many strategic votes as faction 1 ($\sigma_2 = \sigma_1$), then the party will again fall below the threshold and earn no seats and no portfolios. In this case, no government can command a majority and so we can imagine that new elections must be held. If faction 2 casts fewer strategic votes than does faction 1 ($\sigma_2 < \sigma_1$), then the FDP will clear the threshold and the CDU will be the formateur. Subject to these conditions, faction 2 wishes to cast as few strategic votes as possible, since reducing $\sigma_2$ increases the FDP's seat share, increases its portfolio share, and adjusts the government's policy favorably. Assuming that each faction prefers the FDP position to the SPD position, it can be shown that casting no strategic votes ($\sigma_2 = 0$) beats casting enough to put the FDP below the threshold ($\sigma_2 \geq \sigma_1$). Thus, faction 2's best response is to vote sincerely.

11. If $N_{CDU} + N_{FDP} < N_{SPD}$, then the CDU sets $s_{CDU} = 0$. That is, if the coalition parties together have fewer supporters than the SPD, then the CDU should maximize its own seats (lending no votes to its partner). This result of course would change with repeated play.

12. Unlike in the previous section, the CDU cannot counteract the SPD's strategy, since it is not casting any insurance votes to begin with.

13. His model envisions voters rather than parties as actors but the logic is similar.

14. This is similar to a rule of thumb about seat-maximizing strategic voting. Such voting becomes more likely to the extent that parties fail to coordinate candidacies. Here, portfolio-maximizing strategic voting becomes more likely to the extent that parties fail to coordinate their bids for portfolios.

15. In addition, McCuen and Morton (2010) provide experimental evidence of threshold insurance voting.

16. In a study of the German *Länder*, however, Meffert and Gschwend (2010) find little evidence of threshold insurance voting.

17. For example, if CDU supporters vote strategically for the FDP list (to keep it above the threshold), then this would count as an "insincere" vote but would not be motivated by worries about the CDU's viability.

18. To calculate the expected position of coalitions in which j might participate, one first calculates the position of each possible coalition in which j participates (given by the average of all participating parties' positions, weighted by their respective seat share in government) and then weights each coalition by its probability of appearing.

19. I have focused on parliamentary systems in this review. However, people may cast "portfolio-maximizing" votes in presidential and semipresidential systems too. That is, they may vote to affect the presidential contest and/or how the presidential victor will allocate ministerial positions. Some recent work that explores the many ways in which presidential contests influence electoral coordination include Engstrom and Kernell (2014; a case study of the nineteenth-century United States), Hicken and Stoll (2008; a comparative analysis of presidential party systems), and Batto et al. (2016; an edited volume explaining the differing responses of Japan and Taiwan to similar electoral reforms in terms of their differing executive structures).

# REFERENCES

Abramson, Paul, John H. Aldrich, André Blais, Matthew Diamond, Abraham Diskin, Indridi H. Indridason, Daniel J. Lee, and Renan Levine. "Comparing Strategic Voting under FPTP and PR." *Comparative Political Studies* 43, no. 1 (2010): 61–90.

Austen-Smith, David, and Jeffrey Banks. "Elections, Coalitions and Legislative Outcomes." *American Political Science Review* 82 (1988): 405–422.

Bargsted, Matias, and Orit Kedar. "Coalition-Targeted Duvergerian Voting: How Expectations Affect Voter Choice under Proportional Representation." *American Journal of Political Science* 53 (2009): 307–323.

Baron, D. P., and Daniel Diermeier. "Elections, Governments and Parliaments in Proportional Representation Systems." *Quarterly Journal of Economics* 116, no. 3 (2001): 933–967.

Baron, D. P., and John Ferejohn. "Bargaining in Legislatures." *American Political Science Review* 83, no. 4 (1989): 1181–1206.

Batto, Nathan, Chi Huang, Alexander Tan, and Gary W. Cox, eds. *Mixed-Member Electoral Systems in Constitutional Context: Taiwan, Japan, and Beyond.* Ann Arbor: University of Michigan Press, 2016.

Bawn, K. "The Logic of Institutional Preferences: German Electoral Law as a Social Choice Outcome." *American Journal of Political Science* 37 (1993): 965–989.

Bawn, K. "Voter Responses to Electoral Complexity: Ticket Splitting, Rational Voters and Representation in the Federal Republic of Germany." *British Journal of Political Science* 29 (1999): 487–505.

Blais, Andre, John H. Aldrich, Indridi H. Indridason, and Renan Levine. "Do Voters Vote for Government Coalitions? Testing Down's Pessimistic Conclusion." *Party Politics* 12 (2006): 691–705.

Bowler, Shaun, Jeffrey Karp, and Todd Donovan. "Strategic Coalition Voting: Evidence from New Zealand." *Electoral Studies* 29 (2010): 350–357.

Cox, Gary W. *Making Votes Count.* New York: Cambridge University Press, 1997.

Cox, Gary W. "Electoral Rules and Electoral Coordination." *Annual Review of Political Science* 2 (1999): 145–161.

Duch, Raymond, Jeff May, and David A. Armstrong II. "Coalition-Directed Voting in Multiparty Democracies." *American Political Science Review* 104, no. 4 (2010): 698–719.

Duch, Raymond, and Randy Stevenson. 2008. The Economic Vote: How Political and Economic Insitutions Condition Election Results. Cambridge: Cambridge University Press.

Duverger, Maurice. *Political Parties.* New York: Wiley, 1955.

Engstrom, Erik, and Samuel Kernell. *Party Ballots, Reform, and the Transformation of America's Electoral System.* Cambridge: Cambridge University Press, 2014.

Felsenthal, Dan S., and Avraham Brichta. "Sincere and Strategic Voters: An Israeli Study." *Political Behavior* 7 (1985): 311–323.

Fisher, S. L. "The Wasted Vote Thesis. West German Evidence." *Comparative Politics* 5 (1973): 293–299.

Fredén, Anika. "Threshold Insurance Voting in PR Systems: A Study of Voters' Strategic Behavior in the 2010 Swedish General Election." *Journal of Elections, Public Opinion and Parties* 24, no. 4 (2014): 473–492.

Gschwend, Thomas. "Ticket-Splitting and Strategic Voting under Mixed Electoral Rules: Evidence from Germany." *European Journal of Political Research* 46 (2007): 1–23.

Hermann, Michael. "Expectations about Coalitions and Strategic Voting under Proportional Representation." Unpublished typescript, University of Mannheim. SONDERFORSCHUNGSBEREICH 504, no. 08-28. 2008.

Hicken, Allen, and Heather Stoll. "Electoral Rules and the Size of the Prize: How Political Institutions Shape Presidential Party Systems." *Journal of Politics* 70, no. 4 (2008): 1109–1127.

Hobolt, Sara B., and Jeffrey A. Karp. "Voters and Coalition Governments." *Electoral Studies* 29 (2010): 299–307.

Indridason, Indridi. 2011. "Proportional Representation, Majoritarian Legislatures, and Coalitional Voting." *American Journal of Political Science* 55(4): 954–970.

Irwin, Galen, and J. J. M. van Holsteyn. "Strategic Electoral Considerations under Proportional Representation." *Electoral Studies* 31 (2012): 184–191.

Jesse, E. "Split-Voting in the Federal Republic of Germany: An Analysis of the Federal Elections from 1953 to 1987." *Electoral Studies* 7 (1988): 109–124.

Kedar, Orit. "When Moderate Voters Prefer Extreme Parties: Policy Balancing in Parliamentary Elections." *American Political Science Review* 99, no.2 (2005): 185–199.

McCuen, Brian, and Rebecca Morton. "Tactical Coalition Voting and Information in the Laboratory." *Electoral Studies* 29, no. 3 (2010): 316–328.

Meffert, Michael, and Thomas Gschwend. "Strategic Coalition Voting: Evidence from Austria." *Electoral Studies* 29 (2010): 339–349.

Nachmias, David, and Itai Sened. "The Bias of Pluralism: The Redistributive Effects of the New Electoral Law." In *The Elections in Israel*, edited by Asher Arian and Michal Shamir. Albany: State University of New York, 1999.

Nixon, David, Dganit Olomoki, Norman Schofield, and Itai Sened. "Multiparty Probabilistic Voting: An Application to the Knesset." *Political Economy Working Paper 186*. Washington University in St. Louis, 1996.

Pappi, Franz Urban, and Paul W. Thurner. "Electoral Behaviour in a Two-Vote System: Incentives for Ticket Splitting in German *Bundestag* Elections." *European Journal of Political Research* 41 (2002): 207–232.

Rae, D. W. *The Political Consequences of Electoral Laws*. New Haven, CT: Yale University Press, 1967.

Roberts, G. K. "The 'Second-Vote' Campaign Strategy of the West German Free Democratic Party." *European Journal of Political Research* 16 (1988): 317–337.

Schofield, Norman and Michael Laver. "Bargain Theory and Portfolio Payoffs in European Coalition Governments, 1945–83." *British Journal of Political Science* 15 (1985): 143–164.

Shikano, Susumu, Michael Hermann, and Paul W. Thurner. "Strategic Voting under Proportional Representation: Threshold Insurance in German Elections." *West European Politics* 32, no. 3 (2009): 634–656.

Slinko, Arkadii, and Shaun White. "Proportional Representation and Strategic Voters." *Journal of Theoretical Politics* 22, no. 3 (2010): 301–332.

Taagepera, Rein, and Matthew Shugart. *Seats and Votes*. New Haven, CT: Yale University Press, 1989.

......................................................................

# CHAPTER 14

# PRESIDENTIAL AND LEGISLATIVE ELECTIONS

......................................................................

## MARK P. JONES

THIS chapter examines presidential and legislative elections in political systems with popularly elected presidents. First, it analyzes the issue of how the nature and degree of democracy in a country affect how we view and examine the conduct of popular elections in different countries, and how the definition of democracy employed can affect the presidential and legislative elections chosen for different types of scholarly studies. Second, it explores the different types of political systems with popularly elected presidents, highlighting the principal differences between pure presidential and semi-presidential systems of government. Third, it details a set of key institutional rules governing the popular election of presidents and the consequences of those rules for partisan competition and party politics in a country. Fourth, it provides a similar discussion of a set of key institutional rules governing the election of national legislatures and the consequences of these rules. Fifth, it discusses the direct and indirect impact of presidential elections on legislative elections. Sixth, it focuses on the relationship between presidential and legislative elections and democratic governance in pure presidential systems.

## DEMOCRACY AND PRESIDENTIAL ELECTIONS

......................................................................

Presidents are popularly elected in more than one hundred countries across the globe. These elections, however, are held within a wide variety of political contexts, ranging from very democratic to very authoritarian/totalitarian, and everything in between.

This variance represents a potential issue of substantial import for scholars studying presidential (and legislative) elections, since depending on the specific line of inquiry, elections held within different contexts of democracy and authoritarianism are potentially not comparable, or only partially comparable. Where scholars draw the line between these two regime types hinges on a combination of the goals and topics of their particular study, as well as their broader beliefs regarding the measurement of democracy and the exact location of the blurry line that distinguishes a democracy from a dictatorship (Haggard and Kaufman 2016). For instance, there would exist unanimous agreement among serious scholars that former US president Barack Obama's 2012 election and Uruguayan president Tabaré Vazquez's 2015 election both occurred within a democratic context, and that Syrian president Bashar al-Assad's 2014 election and Belarusian president Alexander Lukashenko's 2015 election occurred within an authoritarian context. However, among these same scholars there would without question be dissent and disagreement over whether Nicaraguan president Daniel Ortega's 2016 election and Venezuelan president Nicolás Maduro's 2013 election occurred within a democratic or authoritarian context.

Numerous scholars have addressed this issue of where to draw the line in the study of democratic elections. Here I highlight two leading approaches that respectively are located near the maximalist and minimalist ends of the continuum of the democratic definitions employed in the scholarly community.

At the maximalist end of the spectrum is the work of Arend Lijphart, dating back to his seminal 1984 book, *Democracies* (Lijphart 1984). Lijphart's most recent version of this broader study of democracies (Lijphart 2012) includes those countries that were continuously democratic for at least twenty years, with democracy defined as being classified by Freedom House as "free."[1] Since 1973, Freedom House (2016) has annually rated countries as free, partly free, or not free based on expert review using a political rights and civil liberties checklist. In his 2012 book Lijphart coded the following eleven countries with popularly elected presidents as democracies, since as of the end of 2009 they had been continuously democratic for at least twenty years: Argentina, Austria, Costa Rica, Finland, France, Iceland, Ireland, Portugal, South Korea, the United States, and Uruguay.

At the minimalist end of the spectrum is the work of José Antonio Cheibub and his colleagues, dating back to an influential 1996 article (Alvarez et al. 1996), and most recently updated in Cheibub, Gandhi, and Vreeland (2010). This minimalist approach classifies as a democracy any country where the chief executive is selected via a popular election or a body (e.g., legislature, electoral college) that was popularly elected, the legislature is popularly elected, more than one party competes in the election, and there has been at least one alternation of power in the executive branch under the existing rules of the game (Cheibub et al. 2010). As of the end of 2008, this methodology classified sixty-one countries with popularly elected presidents as democracies: the eleven included by Lijphart along with fifty others.[2]

There is no "right" answer as to what constitutes a democracy, but the definition employed will (as demonstrated by the vastly different number of countries classified by Lijphart and Cheibub et al. as democratic for the purpose of their respective studies) influence the number and range of countries and elections included in any study, and therefore is potentially consequential for any inferences the study draws and any generalizations it might make (Svolik 2008). For example, a study interested in the manner in which electoral laws influence elite incentives and behavior may, other things being equal, find very different results if it focused on the sixty-one electoral democracies with popularly elected presidents identified by Cheibub et al. (2010) rather than the eleven consolidated democracies with popularly elected presidents identified by Lijphart (2012).

# REGIME TYPE AND PRESIDENTIAL ELECTIONS

Democratic regimes fall into three general categories: pure presidential, pure parliamentary, and semipresidential (Lijphart 2012). In pure presidential systems the chief executive is the president, who in turn is popularly elected for a fixed term and does not depend on the confidence of the legislature to remain in office. In pure parliamentary systems, the chief executive is the prime minister, is selected by the legislature, and depends on the legislature's confidence to remain in office. In presidential systems the president is endowed with significant constitutional power, with the same holding true for the prime minister in the parliamentary systems.

In between these two pure regime types are the mixed cases of semipresidentialism. In these systems the chief executive is the prime minister, but there is also a popularly elected president endowed with a varying degree of formal and informal constitutional and political power.[3] Semipresidential systems range from cases such as France and Senegal, where the president possesses some significant constitutional powers and enjoys substantial political authority, to Iceland and Ireland, where the president is for all intents and purposes a symbolic figurehead (Elgie 2016; Samuels and Shugart 2010; Shugart and Carey 1992).

The distinction between pure presidential systems and semipresidential systems, as well as that among the semipresidential systems in terms of the authority and power of the president, is important in terms of assessing the incentives, dynamics, and impact of presidential elections (Cheibub et al. 2010; Elgie 2016; Samuels and Shugart 2010). For example, in pure presidential democracies the president is the most powerful political actor and the presidential election is far and away the most important electoral contest. In contrast, in semipresidential systems the parliamentary election tends to be the most important electoral contest, with the relative degree of importance inversely proportional to the weight of the president's power and authority vis-à-vis that of the parliament.

# PRESIDENTIAL ELECTIONS: RULES OF THE GAME AND THEIR CONSEQUENCES

This section examines several of the key rules of the game for the popular election of presidents. These include the length of the president's term in office, the legislation that governs how the victor in the presidential election is determined, and a president's ability to seek re-election.

Presidential term lengths range from between four and seven years. Five years represents both the median and modal term length in democracies with popularly elected presidents.

With a few minor exceptions, the United States' indirect Electoral College method being the most noteworthy, the popular elections of the presidents in the world's democracies are today all direct. Within this population of direct popular elections there is, however, quite a bit of variance in the rules employed. The methods used to determine the winner in presidential elections can be subdivided into three general families: plurality formula, majority runoff formula, and double complement rule formula.

An important first distinction is between the one-round and two-round runoff systems. In the former systems (i.e., plurality formula/first past the post), the presidential candidate who receives the most votes in the first and only electoral contest is elected president.

All of the runoff systems have in common the requirement that a candidate surpass some type of threshold to avoid a second-round runoff. The most common form of runoff system is that which requires a candidate to win an absolute majority of the popular vote to avoid competing against the first runner-up in a second-round runoff. This absolute majority is normally calculated as the share of the valid vote, but the threshold is in some cases increased by including blank (e.g., Colombia) and/or spoiled votes in the denominator used to calculate the 50 percent + 1 threshold, or at an extreme requiring a candidate to win the support of an absolute majority of registered votes in the first round (e.g., Romania) or setting a threshold higher than 50 percent (e.g., 55 percent in Sierra Leone). While the Colombian, Romanian, and Sierra Leonean methods raise the effective valid vote threshold above 50 percent, it is also possible to adopt rules that have the opposite effect, such as by specifying a threshold below 50 percent that a candidate must cross to avoid a runoff. One example is Costa Rica, which possesses a 40 percent threshold, a bar that has been crossed in the first round in fourteen of the sixteen presidential elections in the country that have been held since the beginning of the current democratic period in 1949.

A small number of countries with salient ethnic cleavages combined with geographically concentrated ethnic communities have adopted an additional threshold requirement that is geography based, requiring a candidate to win a minimal level of support across the country's principal subnational territorial units to win in the first round (and thereby avoid a second-round runoff). Countries with this geographic requirement include Kenya and Nigeria. In Kenya, for instance, to avoid a second-round runoff, a candidate has to both win more than 50 percent of the vote nationwide and at the same time win at least 25 percent of the vote in a majority of the country's forty-seven counties.

In addition, an even smaller number of countries (Ireland, Sri Lanka) require the winning presidential candidate to win an absolute majority of the vote but accomplish this task via ranked-choice voting in the first and only round (i.e., the alternative vote or supplementary vote methods) rather than hold a second-round runoff.

The third principal family of presidential formulas was inspired by a 1994 article by Matthew Shugart and Rein Taagepera (Shugart and Taagepera 1994) proposing a new optimal method of presidential election that they coined as the "double complement rule." The most powerful critique of the plurality formula is that its lack of any type of threshold opens the door to a candidate winning with a relatively small share of the vote, raising the specter of a candidate who did not enjoy anywhere near a majority of popular support being elected president, quite possibly defeating a candidate preferred by a majority of the voting public over the winner. The most powerful critique of the majority runoff system is that it provides incentives for several viable candidates to compete in the presidential election, which in turn can lead to excessive fragmentation of the party system and ensuing small presidential legislative contingents and executive–legislative gridlock. The high level of fragmentation can also make the majority runoff systems more permeable to outsider candidates.

The double complement rule (DCR) was designed to ameliorate the principal defects of the plurality and majority runoff systems, to provide something akin to the "best of both worlds." Its innovation was in providing two distinct ways for a candidate to be elected in the first round: either via surpassing a specific threshold (e.g., 50 percent of the valid vote) or by crossing a lower threshold (e.g., 40 percent of the valid vote) while simultaneously besting the first runner-up by a substantial margin (e.g., 10 percent of the valid vote). Because of these innovations, the double complement rule incentivizes less fragmentation than majority runoff systems but also safeguards against an unpopular presidential candidate being elected with only a relatively small share of the popular vote.

The first country to adopt any variant of the double complement rule was Argentina. Informed by the 1992 Shugart and Taagepera article, as well as Shugart's related work on presidential elections (e.g., Shugart and Carey 1992), José Luis Manzano, a key adviser to then Argentine president Carlos Menem, introduced the option in Argentina during the country's 1994 constitutional reform process. In that year Argentina left the United States as the sole remaining democracy to indirectly elect its president via a popularly elected electoral college and adopted a modified version of Taagepera and Shugart's double complement rule. Under the Argentine variant of the method, a candidate can avoid a second-round runoff in one of two ways: by winning more than 45 percent of the valid vote in the first round or by winning at least 40 percent of the valid vote and defeating the first runner-up by at least 10 percent. Other countries that have subsequently adopted modified versions of the double complement rule for their presidential election are Bolivia, Ecuador, and Nicaragua.

Following Duverger's law (Cox 1997; Duverger 1954; Stoll 2013), use of the plurality formula tends to encourage two-candidate competition in presidential elections (see Table 14.1).[4] In contrast, use of the majority runoff formula tends to encourage multi-candidate competition (see Table 14.1), especially when an incumbent is not running for re-election (Jones 2004) and/or a country possesses more than one salient political cleavage (e.g., ideological and ethnic/racial; ideological and urban/rural; ideological and religious). The double complement rule tends to occupy a midpoint between the two poles represented by the plurality and majority runoff formulas, although generally leaning closer to the majority runoff formula in terms of incentives for two-candidate or multicandidate political competition. However, since the number of presidential elections held using the double complement rule still numbers in the low teens, any definitive conclusions regarding its impact on elite and mass political behavior must await substantially more empirical evidence resulting from additional countries adopting a form of the double complement rule and those countries that currently employ the method holding additional elections under it (which will obviously take time).

During the third wave of democracy, there has been a clear trend away from the use of the plurality formula toward the use of the majority runoff formula or hybrid methods like the double complement rule (Remmer 2008; Stoll 2013; Zovatto and Orozco Henríquez 2008). Today, there are fewer than a dozen presidential electoral democracies that continue to employ the plurality formula to elect their president, with the most prominent examples being Mexico, the Philippines, South Korea, and Taiwan.

Presidential systems also vary in regard to the limits they place on presidential re-election (Carey 2003; Payne et al. 2007). At one extreme are countries such as Guatemala, Mexico, and South Korea where the president may serve for only one term, with no possibility of ever seeking re-election, immediate or otherwise. At the other extreme are countries such as Belarus, Ecuador, and Iceland where no limits are placed on consecutive presidential re-election. The overwhelming majority of countries with popularly elected presidents are located between these two extremes, with the most common method being to allow the president to seek one immediate re-election, after

### Table 14.1  Effective Number of Presidential Candidates in Plurality and Majority Runoff Elections

| Effective Number of Candidates | Plurality Formula | Majority Runoff Formula |
| --- | --- | --- |
| Mean | 2.53 | 3.15 |
| Median | 2.25 | 3.00 |

The population for the analysis in Table 1 is restricted to elections held in countries identified by Bormann and Golder (2013) as democratic during the 1975–2011 period (i.e., the third wave of democracy) and includes pure presidential systems and semipresidential systems where the president's power is considered by Shugart and Taagepera (2017) to go beyond the merely ceremonial (e.g., France, Poland, Ukraine).

*Data sources:* Bormann and Golder (2013) and Li and Shugart (n.d.).

which he or she either may never seek re-election again or must wait one term before seeking election again. The next most common method prohibits immediate presidential re-election but allows a president to seek re-election after sitting out one term.

Historically many pure presidential systems prohibited immediate re-election, due primarily to the fear that once elected a president could use his or her control of the state and the resources provided by the state to remain in power indefinitely (Carey 2003). As a consequence, when Latin American countries transitioned from dictatorship to democracy during the third wave of democracy (Huntington 1991) in the 1970s, 1980s, and 1990s (or in the case of Costa Rica and Venezuela, maintained their democracies that had survived the second reverse wave of democratization), only one democracy (the Dominican Republic) allowed the president to seek immediate re-election. As time passed, however, ambitious and powerful presidents pushed through constitutional reforms to allow them to run for re-election (most commonly for only one term, but in some cases indefinitely), to the point where today almost half of the pure presidential systems in Latin America (Argentina, Bolivia, Brazil, Dominican Republic, Ecuador, Honduras, Nicaragua, Venezuela) allow presidents to run for immediate re-election either once or indefinitely.[5]

The rules regarding re-election are of considerable import in presidential elections since they affect the pattern of competition in these contests (Hicken 2009; Jones 1999). Incumbent presidents enjoy substantial built-in advantages, ranging from visibility and media access to control of state resources, the latter benefit especially salient in the more clientelist political systems (Kitschelt et al. 2010; Levitsky and Roberts 2011). Therefore, whether or not a president is eligible to run for re-election can have a profound impact on the pattern of competition in a presidential contest. For instance, when a president is eligible to run for re-election, his or her presence in the race can reduce fragmentation in the presidential field by simultaneously boosting support for the incumbent at the polls and providing incentives for the political opposition to unite behind a single candidate, especially when the incumbent is not considered to be a "sure winner" (Cox 1997). In this case, opposition to the incumbent's candidacy is often the glue the holds together an otherwise diverse and disparate group of opposition political parties and groups (a prominent example of this phenomenon is the past four presidential elections held in Venezuela).

Table 14.2 provides the effective number of presidential candidates by country in those systems where elections were held in which an incumbent president ran and did not run for re-election when the same electoral formula was used to determine the winner.[6] In the twelve countries that meet these criteria and utilize the majority runoff formula, there were on average a significantly smaller effective number of presidential candidates when an incumbent president was running for re-election than when there was no incumbent on the ballot. While the number of cases of countries that employ a modified version of the DCR is too small to make any statistical conclusions, it is noteworthy that in all three (Argentina, Ecuador, Nicaragua) of the DCR systems that meet the same criteria, the effective number of candidates was on average notably lower when an incumbent president was running than when an incumbent president was not running.

In contrast, the small number of similar cases for the plurality formula do not show a clear trend in either direction, potentially suggesting that the impact of an incumbent in the more restrictive plurality systems is not as powerful as that found in the more permissive runoff and modified DCR systems (Cox 1997).

At the dawn of the third wave of democracy in the mid-1970s, the use of popular (direct) primaries by political parties to select their presidential candidate was

**Table 14.2 Average Effective Number of Presidential Candidates When an Incumbent Is Running and Not Running for Re-Election**

| Country | Presidential Electoral Formula | No Incumbent Running (Average) | Incumbent Running (Average) |
|---|---|---|---|
| Armenia | Majority Runoff | 3.28 | **2.16** |
| Benin | Majority Runoff | 4.47 | **2.99** |
| Brazil | Majority Runoff | 3.57 | **2.47** |
| Colombia | Majority Runoff | 2.90 | **2.23** |
| Cyprus | Majority Runoff | 3.51 | **2.68** |
| Dominican Republic | Majority Runoff | 2.66 | **2.19** |
| France | Majority Runoff | **5.32** | 6.09 |
| Ghana | Majority Runoff | 2.12 | **2.11** |
| Poland | Majority Runoff | 3.52 | **3.43** |
| São Tomé and Príncipe | Majority Runoff | 3.35 | **2.43** |
| Sierra Leone | Majority Runoff | 3.70 | **1.84** |
| Ukraine | Majority Runoff | 4.47 | **2.92** |
| *12-Country Average* | *Majority Runoff* | *3.57* | *2.80* |
| Argentina | DCR | 3.90 | **2.84** |
| Ecuador | DCR | 5.43 | **2.74** |
| Nicaragua | DCR | 3.31 | **2.04** |
| *3-Country Average* | *DCR* | *4.28* | *2.54* |
| Dominican Republic | Plurality | **2.71** | 2.89 |
| Malawi | Plurality | 3.62 | **2.58** |
| Venezuela | Plurality | **2.62** | 2.63 |
| *3-Country Average* | *Plurality* | *2.98* | *2.70* |

*Note:* The lower value between a country's two values is in bold.

*Data sources:* Borman and Golder (2013) and Li and Shugart (n.d.).

extremely rare (outside of the United States). Today, a majority of the world's presidential candidates are still selected by party elites via either informal or formal (e.g., a party convention) methods. However, with each passing year more and more parties and coalitions choose their presidential nominee via popular primaries, open either to party members alone, to party members and independents, or to all voters (Carey and Polga-Hecimovich 2006; Freidenberg and Alcántara Sáez 2009). And, while in a majority of these countries the extant legislation allows the parties to determine how their presidential candidate will be selected, in others a popular primary is mandatory for all parties/coalitions.

## LEGISLATIVE ELECTIONS: RULES OF THE GAME AND THEIR CONSEQUENCES

The legislatures in countries with popularly elected presidents fall into three broad categories: bicameral legislatures with symmetric bicameralism (i.e., where the lower and upper houses are roughly equal in terms of power), bicameral legislatures with asymmetric bicameralism (i.e., where the lower house is significantly more powerful than the upper house), and unicameral legislatures (Lijphart 2012). Here the focus will be on the electoral systems used for all legislative elections except for those of the upper house in the asymmetric bicameral systems given the largely symbolic role played by the upper house in a majority of these countries.

The electoral systems employed for legislative elections in pure presidential and semipresidential systems can be placed into four broad families: majoritarian, semiproportional, proportional representation (PR), and mixed-member systems (Cox 1997; Lijphart 2012). The PR systems are far and away the most common, followed by the majoritarian systems and the different types of mixed-member systems, with semiproportional systems now virtually extinct in countries with popularly elected presidents.

The PR systems choose legislators at the multiseat district level, at the national level, or under an arrangement involving a mixture of multiseat districts and a national-level distribution (either a national district or a national distribution of residual votes). The multiseat districts are most commonly pre-existing subnational territorial units (e.g., departments, provinces, states) that in most cases vary in the number of legislators they elect in rough proportion to their share of the national population, with the more populous districts at times having ceilings on the number of legislators they receive and the least populous districts normally receiving a minimum number of legislators regardless of population.[7] Overall, the larger the average district magnitude in a system is, the more fragmented its legislative party system will be, although this positive impact of district magnitude on fragmentation can be attenuated by the use of district or national vote thresholds for parties to receive legislative seats or by using a less proportional allocation formula (e.g., D'Hondt) rather than a more proportional allocation formula (e.g., LR-Hare, pure Sainte-Lagüe). Empirically there is also a diminishing effect of district magnitude on fragmentation as district magnitude increases (Cox 1997).

The party lists in these PR systems can be closed or open. Under the closed-list framework, a political party presents a rank-ordered list of candidates in a district. If a party, for example, is allocated four seats based on its proportional share of the vote, then the first four candidates on the party list are elected. Under the open-list framework, a political party presents a list of candidates and voters cast preference votes for the candidate or candidates they prefer (some systems provide a voter with a single preference vote, while others provide the voter with a number of preference votes equal to the number of legislators being elected in the district, with remaining systems somewhere in between). If a party, for example, is allocated four seats based on its proportional share of the vote, then the four candidates with the highest number of preference votes are elected. Most open-list systems limit voters to casting preference votes within a single party, but a few presidential systems (e.g., Ecuador, El Salvador, Honduras) allow voters to distribute their preference votes across parties (i.e., *panachage*). All other things being equal, legislators in open-list systems will tend to be more independent and autonomous vis-à-vis party leaders than legislators in closed-list systems, which in pure presidential systems can mean that the presidential party's legislative delegation is expected to be more responsive to the president in closed-list systems than in open-list systems (Carey and Shugart 1995; Saiegh 2015; Scartascini et al. 2010).

Virtually all of the majoritarian systems in countries with popularly elected presidents employ a combination of single-seat districts with a plurality formula (i.e., first past the post). Under this system the candidate who wins the most votes in the district is elected. In a small number of other instances (e.g., France, congressional elections in the US state of Louisiana), a runoff is held if in the first round a candidate does not win an absolute majority of the vote in the single-seat district.[8] Following Duverger's law, the use of first past the post in concert with single-seat districts tends to result in less fragmented party systems (and, hence, larger presidential legislative contingents) than is the case under PR, especially PR in systems with medium to large average district magnitudes (i.e., relatively proportional PR systems).

Under the rubric of mixed-member systems fall two distinct types of arrangements: mixed-member majoritarian (MMM) and mixed-member proportional representation (MMP) (Ferrara et al. 2005; Shugart and Wattenberg 2003). Both arrangements have in common the use of first-past-the-post elections in single-seat districts combined with the use of PR (either via multiseat districts, a single national district, or some combination thereof). Where the two systems differ is in regard to the linkage between the single-seat and PR portions of the election. In the MMM (also known as parallel) systems the two elections are completely separate, while in the MMP systems the PR component is utilized to compensate for the disproportionality occasioned by the single-seat district first-past-the-post elections. As a result, the latter systems have a proportionality profile that is very similar to that of a PR system with characteristics (e.g., district magnitude, threshold) comparable to that of the MMP system. In contrast, the MMM systems tend to be much more majoritarian given the lack of any compensatory mechanism, with the degree dependent on the relative weight of the PR seats compared to the single-seat district seats.

In the world's presidential systems the legislative candidate selection process within the political parties ranges from cases where the presidential candidate and his or her close advisers effectively select most if not all of a party's legislative candidates to cases where the party's legislative candidates are elected in open primaries where all voters are eligible to participate (Freidenberg and Alcántara Sáez 2009; Hicken 2009; Siavelis and Morgenstern 2008). In between, though, lie the majority of the presidential democracies where local-level party elites determine who runs in their department/province/state in consultation with national party elites, primaries between candidates chosen by party elites determine who runs, and/or a mixture between open primaries and elite designation depending on the specific party and district determines who runs for legislative office under a party's banner. In terms of responsiveness to the president, as one moves away from designation by the national elite (in particular the presidential candidate) and toward open primaries with few if any elite filters, the responsiveness of the legislators belonging to the president's party or coalition to the directives of the president will, all other things being equal, decline (Crisp et al. 2004; Saiegh 2015; Scartascini et al. 2010).

# PRESIDENTIAL AND LEGISLATIVE ELECTIONS: DIRECT AND INDIRECT CONTAGION EFFECTS

The direct impact of presidential elections on legislative elections occurs when the presidential and legislative contests are held concurrently. The world's semipresidential democracies almost exclusively elect their president and the members of their national legislature at separate times, and hence in these systems there is no direct effect of the presidential election on the legislative election (or vice versa).

In a large majority of the pure presidential systems, the presidential and legislative contests are always held concurrently, with a handful of countries possessing a mixed format with, for example, concurrent presidential and legislative elections split by midterms where either all or a portion of the membership of the legislature is renewed. Only a minority of the pure presidential systems consistently hold their presidential and legislative elections on separate dates.

The direct impact of the presidential election in these concurrent elections comes primarily from the marquee status of the presidential race in pure presidential systems and the concomitant impact of this reality on elite and mass behavior. At the elite level, there is a tendency to coalesce behind a small number of viable presidential candidates either via party coalitions or individual agreements (Cox 1997; Hicken 2009; Stoll 2013). At the mass level, the most salient race is generally the presidential contest, with a person's vote for a presidential candidate frequently carrying over to support for the legislative lists/candidates of the party, parties (where fusion candidacies are permitted), or coalition backing the president (Golder 2006; Jones 1994; Shugart and Carey 1992; Stoll 2013). The strength of these presidential coattails is in turn influenced by ballot structure, voting mechanisms, and the nature of the party system. Fused ballots and, to a lesser extent, a straight-ticket voting mechanism enhance the robustness of presidential coattails, as does a nationalized (as opposed to a denationalized) political party system (Jones and Mainwaring 2003).

The indirect effect of presidential elections on legislative elections (and vice versa) occurs primarily through the manner in which these elections influence the composition and structure of a country's political party system (Guinjoan 2014; Samuels 2002; Samuels and Shugart 2010). This impact is primarily present in the pure presidential systems, where control of the executive branch via victory in the presidential election is far and away the most important electoral prize. As a result, in pure presidential systems the rules undergirding the election of the president structure the party system in a significant manner, for instance providing more incentives for parties to both consolidate and avoid splintering than is the case in parliamentary systems. Semipresidential systems occupy a broad range between these two extremes depending on the power and prestige of the office of president, with countries with weak, largely ceremonial presidents seeing little to no indirect impact of the presidential election on the broader party system, and countries with more powerful presidents seeing a more noteworthy indirect impact (albeit not approaching that seen in most pure presidential systems).

In addition to the direct and indirect effect of presidential elections on legislative elections, there also exists a reverse, albeit weaker, effect of legislative elections on the presidential contests (Jones West and Spoon 2013; Shugart and Taagepera 2017). Whether legislative electoral rules are more or less permissive can lead to a greater or smaller number of credible presidential candidates, independent of the laws governing the election of the president. For instance, the more permissive an electoral system is, the more likely a medium- to small-sized party is to present a candidate of its own in the presidential election (instead of, for example, supporting the candidate from a larger party), with the party's primary goal being to have its candidate provide modest coattails to allow the party to elect more legislators, not to actually achieve the election of their candidate as president.

# ELECTIONS AND DEMOCRATIC GOVERNANCE IN PURE PRESIDENTIAL SYSTEMS

In pure presidential systems, presidential effectiveness and governability are strongly affected by both the size and responsiveness of the president's legislative contingent in congress (i.e., legislators belonging to the president's party or coalition) (Alemán and

Calvo 2010; Calvo 2014; Saiegh 2015; Shugart and Mainwaring 1997). When the president's legislative contingent possesses an absolute majority of the seats in the legislature, and where that contingent tends to be responsive to the president, presidential power is (ceteris paribus) at its apex (with a corresponding weakness in the extent of legislative checks on the executive branch). In contrast, when the presidential legislative contingent is significantly less than a majority and also not especially responsive to the president, presidential power is (ceteris paribus) at its nadir.

While the impact of presidential elections and electoral rules on the size and responsiveness of the presidential legislative contingent are far from deterministic, several elements can work to either increase or decrease the probability of, for instance, the president's party/coalition possessing a majority of the seats in the legislature and the probability that members of the presidential legislative contingent will support or oppose legislation, appointments, and actions favored by the president.

Three institutional factors are pivotal for measuring the potential direct effect of presidential elections on presidential partisan power in the form of legislative support, both numeric and in terms of responsiveness: election timing, the presidential electoral formula, and the ability of a president to run for re-election. Also of relevance are societal factors (i.e., the number of salient political cleavages in the polity and the extent to which they are cross-cutting or cumulative).[9]

First, and most important, is the issue of election timing (Cox 1997; Jones 1994; Shugart and Carey 1992). The impact of the presidential election on the legislative contest is greatest when the elections are held concurrently, for two principal reasons. First, all other things being equal, a presidential election held concurrently with a legislative contest will in most circumstances result in a lower level of legislative fragmentation than is the case when the legislative contest is held on a different date. The source of this result is the ability of the more restrictive rules governing the presidential election to constrain the level of multipartism that would normally be expected from the legislative electoral systems, which, with a small number of exceptions, are more permissive (normally substantially more permissive) than the presidential electoral systems, which range from first past the post to majority runoff. The exceptions are the small number of countries that elect both their president and legislators using the plurality formula and an even rarer group that elect their president using the majority runoff formula and their legislators using first past the post.

Second is the formula utilized to elect the president when the elections are held concurrently: plurality, majority runoff, or double complement rule (Jones 1994; Shugart and Carey 1992; Stoll 2013). The plurality formula will on average result in a lower level of fragmentation than use of the majority runoff formula, with the double complement rule occupying a middle position between these two polar extremes.

As a result, legislative elections held concurrently with presidential elections are expected to experience a lower amount of fragmentation, with larger parties or coalitions (one of which is almost always aligned with the victorious presidential candidate) expected than when the presidential and legislative elections are held at separate times. The president's legislative contingent should therefore on average be larger in pure presidential systems with concurrent elections than in pure presidential systems with nonconcurrent presidential and legislative elections, with mixed systems (those featuring a mixture of concurrent and nonconcurrent elections) in the middle.[10]

In these concurrent elections, use of the plurality formula will, all other things being equal, tend to restrict the number of viable presidential candidates closer to two, while the majority runoff formula will tend to restrict the number of viable presidential candidates closer to three. This higher level of fragmentation generally carries over to the legislative contests where the majority runoff systems experience a higher level of partisan fragmentation than the plurality systems, and as a result smaller presidential legislative contingents given the smaller share of the seats held by the largest parties/coalitions (one of which is most commonly aligned with the president). In addition, another feature of the majority runoff system can lead to the candidate who finished at the top in the first round (but under 50 percent + 1) losing in the runoff to the candidate who finished second in the first round, and whose party more often than not also finished second (or, in a few instances, third or worse) in the legislative elections, therein leading to an even smaller legislative contingent for the president. For example, in the first round of the 2016 Peruvian presidential election, Keiko Fujimori (Popular Force) finished first with 40 percent of the vote, followed by Pedro Pablo Kuczynski (PPK) with 21 percent. Fujimori's Popular Force won 73 of the 130 seats in play in the concurrent elections for the country's unicameral congress, followed by the Broad Front for Justice, Life and Liberty with 20 seats, with PPK's Popular Force finishing third with 18 seats. PPK went on to narrowly defeat Fujimori in the runoff, assuming office with a miniscule legislative contingent.

Finally, the presence of an incumbent running for re-election reduces the number of viable candidates participating in the presidential contest and overall partisan fragmentation in the presidential and legislative elections (Hicken 2009; Jones 1999; Stoll 2013). The result is a tendency to have larger presidential legislative contingents emerge from elections where the president is eligible to run (and runs) for re-election in concurrent presidential and legislative elections than is the case when the president is not eligible to seek re-election.

When a president's party possesses a majority in the legislature, the president tends to enjoy substantial success in implementing his or her policy agenda, especially when his or her presidential legislative contingent is relatively responsive to presidential directives. When a president's party lacks a majority in the legislature, the president runs the risk of being ineffectual as the opposition blocks or substantially waters down his or her policy proposals (Stein et al. 2008). To avoid gridlock, presidents have in many countries formed either formal (e.g., with cabinet appointments) or informal coalitions with other parties to provide them with the legislative majority needed to pass priority legislation. In some countries these coalitions have been relatively stable, while in others they have been ephemeral, formed for specific bills and then rapidly abandoned.

Legislators belonging to the president's political party (or coalition) tend to be more responsive to the president and support his or her governance program when the following institutional conditions are present (Mainwaring and Shugart 1997): First, the presidential and legislative elections are held concurrently (as opposed to nonconcurrently), with the legislators who belong to the president's party or coalition in at least partial debt to the president's coattails for their election to legislative office. Second, multiseat PR districts with closed lists are employed for the legislative elections instead of either multiseat PR districts with open lists or single-seat plurality districts. In the latter systems, legislators tend to be elected more based on their personal characteristics and individual campaign efforts than in the case of the former system where legislators tend to be elected more based on their presence on their party's list rather than any personal attributes they might have or anything they did on the campaign trail. Third, the candidate selection process is a top-down system run by party elites (as opposed to a bottom-up system with open primaries), with a small group of individuals (often including the presidential candidate) largely determining who runs under the party label and, in closed-list systems, what position on the party list they occupy (ranging from "sure things" to "purely ornamental").

More than twenty years ago Juan Linz (1994) signaled the potential for presidents with modest legislative support as an Achilles' heel of pure presidential systems of government, since this scenario can easily lead to gridlock and, unlike the case in parliamentary systems, there is no vote of confidence that can force an ineffectual or problematic president out of office. Since the time of Linz's initial work, scholars have highlighted both the ability of minority presidents to thrive via the formation of coalitions and that presidential systems should remove presidents in cases of extreme gridlock via the route of impeachment (Amorim Neto 2006; Hagopian and Mainwaring 2005; Mezey 2013; Negretto 2006; Pérez-Líñan 2007; Pérez-Líñan and Mainwaring 2013; Shugart and Mainwaring 1997; Valenzuela 2004). That said, the literature is relatively clear that the nature of presidential government is often quite different when the president's party has a responsive legislative majority and when the president's party does not have a responsive legislative majority, making the impact of the electoral systems of profound importance for understanding the functioning of presidential systems of government.

## Notes

1. Lijphart (2012) included three borderline cases that at some point during the timeframe were briefly classified as "partly free" by Freedom House.
2. Had Lijphart's (2012) classification taken place simultaneously with that of Cheibub, Gandhi, and Vreeland (2010), there would have still been eleven countries (the same eleven) with popularly elected presidents coded as democratic.
3. While most scholars tend to include all of these mixed systems in a single category, others, most notably Shugart and Carey (1992), divide the semipresidential systems into two distinct categories: president parliamentary and premier presidential.
4. The effective number of presidential candidates is the standard measure used in political science to calculate the number of viable/relevant candidates in a presidential election (Bormann and Golder 2013; Cox 1997; Shugart and Taagepera 2017).

5. During this timeframe Colombia and Peru reformed their constitutions to allow for immediate presidential re-election but subsequently abolished that provision.
6. This subpopulation was drawn from the larger population employed for the analysis in Table 14.1.
7. All legislative electoral systems except those with only national-level districts have some level of malapportionment, with the degree of this malapportionment varying considerably, however, and especially prominent in the symmetric bicameral systems where every subnational territorial unit receives an equal number of senators regardless of population.
8. Two US states (California and Washington) utilize a top-two system for congressional elections where all candidates (often multiple candidates per party) compete in a first round and the two candidates receiving the most votes (regardless of whether or not a candidate wins an absolute majority) face off in a second round (Sinclair 2015).
9. This is, of course, in addition to the direct effect of the legislative rules on partisan fragmentation and responsiveness (Cox 1997; Golder 2006; Shugart and Taagepera 2017).
10. This description is based on the empirical data where nonconcurrent legislative elections are rarely held very early during the president's "honeymoon period," a time in which a nonconcurrent election could in theory boost the size of the presidential legislative contingent to a greater degree than when the presidential and legislative contests are held concurrently.

## References

Alemán, Eduardo, and Ernesto Calvo. "Unified Government, Bill Approval, and the Legislative Weight of the President." *Comparative Political Studies* 43 (2010): 511–534.
Alvarez, Michael, Jose Antonio Cheibub, Fernando Limongi, and Adam Przeworski. "Classifying Political Regimes." *Studies in Comparative International Development* 31, no. 2 (1996): 3–36.
Amorim Neto, Octavio. "The Presidential Calculus: Executive Policy Making and Cabinet Formation in the Americas." *Comparative Political Studies* 39 (2006): 415–440.
Bormann, Nils-Christian, and Matt Golder. "Democratic Electoral Systems around the World, 1946-2011." *Electoral Studies* 32 (2013): 360–369.
Calvo, Ernesto. *Legislative Success in Fragmented Congresses in Argentina: Plurality Cartels, Minority Presidents, and Lawmaking.* New York: Cambridge University Press, 2014.
Carey, John M. "The Reelection Debate in Latin America." *Latin American Politics and Society* 45 (2003): 119–133.
Carey, John M., and John Polga-Hecimovich. "Primary Elections and Candidate Strength in Latin America." *Journal of Politics* 68 (2006): 530–543.
Carey, John M., and Matthew S. Shugart. "Incentives to Cultivate a Personal Vote: A Rank-Ordering of Electoral Formulas." *Electoral Studies* 14 (1995): 417–439.
Cheibub, Jose Antonio, Jennifer Gandhi, and James R. Vreeland. "Democracy and Dictatorship Revisited." *Public Choice* 143 (2010): 67–101.
Cox, Gary W. *Making Votes Count: Strategic Coordination in the World's Electoral Systems.* New York: Cambridge University Press, 1997.

Crisp, Brian F., Maria C. Escobar-Lemmon, Bradford S. Jones, Mark P. Jones, and Michelle Taylor-Robinson. "Electoral Incentives and Representation in Six Presidential Democracies." *Journal of Politics* 66 (2004): 832–846.

Duverger, Maurice. *Political Parties: Their Organization and Activity in the Modern State.* New York: John Wiley, 1954.

Elgie, Robert. "Three Waves of Semi-Presidential Studies." *Democratization* 23 (2016): 49–70.

Ferrara, Federico, Erik Herron, and Misa Nishikawa. *Mixed Electoral Systems: Contamination and Its Consequences.* New York: Palgrave Macmillan, 2005.

Freidenberg, Flavia, and Manuel Alcántara Sáez, eds. *Selección de Candidatos, Política Partidista y Rendimiento Democrático.* Mexico City: Tribunal Electoral del Distrito Federal y Universidad Nacional Autónoma de México, 2009.

Freedom House. *Freedom in the World 2016.* New York: Freedom House, 2016.

Golder, Matthew. "Presidential Coattails and Legislative Fragmentation." *American Journal of Political Science* 50 (2006): 34–48.

Guinjoan, Marc. *Parties, Elections and Electoral Contests: Competition and Contamination Effects.* Burlington, VT: Ashgate, 2014.

Haggard, Stephan, and Robert R. Kaufman. "Democratization during the Third Wave." *Annual Review of Politics* 19 (2016): 125–144.

Hagopian, Frances, and Scott P. Mainwaring, eds. *The Third Wave of Democratization in Latin America: Advances and Setbacks.* New York: Cambridge University Press, 2005.

Hicken, Allen. *Building Party Systems in Developing Democracies.* New York: Cambridge University Press, 2009.

Huntington, Samuel P. *The Third Wave: Democratization in the Late Twentieth Century.* Norman, OK: University of Oklahoma Press, 1991.

Jones, Mark P. *Electoral Laws and the Survival of Presidential Democracies.* Notre Dame, IN: University of Notre Dame Press, 1994.

Jones, Mark P. "Electoral Laws and the Effective Number of Candidates in Presidential Elections." *Journal of Politics* 61 (1999): 171–184.

Jones, Mark P. "Electoral Laws, Social Cleavages, and Candidate Competition in Presidential Elections." *Electoral Studies* 23 (2004): 73–106.

Jones, Mark P., and Scott Mainwaring. "The Nationalization of Parties and Party Systems: An Empirical Measure and an Application to the Americas." *Party Politics* 9 (2003): 139–166.

Jones West, Karleen, and Jae-Jae Spoon. "Credibility versus Competition: The Impact of Party Size on Decisions to Enter Presidential Elections in South America and Europe." *Comparative Political Studies* 46 (2013): 513–539.

Kitschelt, Herbert, Kirk A. Hawkins, Juan Pablo Luna, Guillermo Rosas, and Elizabeth J. Zechmeister. *Latin American Party Systems.* New York: Cambridge University Press, 2010.

Levitsky, Steven, and Kenneth M. Roberts, eds. *The Resurgence of the Latin American Left.* Baltimore: Johns Hopkins University Press, 2011.

Li, Y., and Matthew Soberg Shugart. "National Level Party Systems Dataset." Unpublished, University of California, Davis, n.d.

Lijphart, Arend. *Patterns of Majoritarian and Consensus Government in Twenty-One Countries.* New Haven, CT: Yale University Press, 1984.

Lijphart, Arend. *Patterns of Democracy: Government Forms and Performance in Thirty-Six Countries.* 2nd ed. New Haven, CT: Yale University Press, 2012.

Linz, Juan J. "Presidential or Parliamentary Democracy: Does It Make A Difference?" In *The Failure of Presidential Democracy*, edited by Juan J. Linz and Arturo Valenzuela, 3–87. Baltimore: Johns Hopkins University Press, 1994.

Mainwaring, Scott, and Matthew Soberg Shugart. "Conclusion: Presidentialism and the Party System." In *Presidentialism and Democracy in Latin America*, edited by Scott Mainwaring and Matthew Soberg Shugart, 394–437. New York: Cambridge University Press, 1997.

Mezey, Michael. *Presidentialism: Power in Comparative Perspective*. Boulder, CO: Lynne Rienner Publishers, 2013.

Negretto, Gabriel. "Minority Presidents and Democratic Performance in Latin America." *Latin American Politics and Society* 48 (2006): 63–92.

Payne, J. Mark, Daniel Zovatto, and Mercedes Mateo Díaz. *Democracies in Development: Politics and Reform in Latin America*. Washington, DC: Inter-American Development Bank, 2007.

Pérez-Liñán, Aníbal. *Presidential Impeachment and the New Political Instability in Latin America*. New York: Cambridge University Press, 2007.

Pérez-Liñán, Aníbal, and Scott Mainwaring. *Democracies and Dictatorships in Latin America: Emergence, Survival, and Fall*. New York: Cambridge University Press, 2013.

Remmer, Karen. "The Politics of Institutional Change: Electoral Reform in Latin America, 1978-2002." *Party Politics* 14 (2008): 5–30.

Saiegh, Sebastián M. "Executive-Legislative Relations." In *Routledge Handbook of Comparative Political Institutions*, edited by Jennifer Gandhi and Rubén Ruiz-Rufiño. New York: Routledge, 2015.

Samuels, David J. "Presidentialized Parties: The Separation of Power and Party Organization and Behavior." *Comparative Political Studies* 35 (2002): 461–483.

Samuels, David J., and Mathew S. Shugart. *Presidents, Parties, and Prime Ministers: How the Separation of Powers Affects Party Organization*. New York: Cambridge University Press, 2010.

Scartascini, Carlos, Ernesto Stein, and Mariano Tommasi, eds. *How Democracy Works: Political Institutions, Actors, and Arenas in Latin American Policymaking*. Washington, DC: Inter-American Development Bank, 2010.

Shugart, Matthew S., and John M. Carey. *Presidents and Assemblies: Constitutional Design and Electoral Dynamics*. New York: Cambridge University Press, 1992.

Shugart, Matthew Soberg, and Scott Mainwaring. "Presidentialism and Democracy in Latin America: Rethinking the Terms of the Debate." In *Presidentialism and Democracy in Latin America*, edited by Scott Mainwaring and Matthew Soberg Shugart, 12–54. New York: Cambridge University Press, 1997.

Shugart, Matthew S., and Rein Taagepera. "Majority versus Plurality Election: A Proposal for a Double Complement Rule." *Comparative Political Studies* 27 (1994): 323–348.

Shugart, Matthew S., and Rein Taagepera. *Votes from Seats: Logical Models of Electoral Systems*. New York: Cambridge University Press, 2017.

Shugart, Matthew Soberg, and Martin P. Wattenberg, eds. *Mixed-Member Electoral Systems: The Best of Both Worlds?* New York: Oxford University Press, 2003.

Siavelis, Peter M., and Scott Morgenstern, eds. *Pathways to Power: Political Recruitment and Candidate Selection in Latin America*. University Park, PA: Pennsylvania State University Press, 2008.

Sinclair, Betsy. "Introduction: The California Top Two Primary." *California Journal of Politics and Policy* 7, no. 1 (2015): 1–7.

Stein, Ernesto, Mariano Tommasi, Carlos Scartascini, and Pablo Spiller, eds. *Policymaking in Latin America: How Politics Shapes Policies*. Washington, D.C.: Inter-American Development Bank, 2008.

Stoll, Heather. *Changing Societies, Changing Party Systems*. New York: Cambridge University Press, 2013.

Svolik, Milan. "Authoritarian Reversals and Democratic Consolidation." *American Political Science Review* 102 (2008): 153–168.

Valenzuela, Arturo. "Latin American Presidencies Interrupted." *Journal of Democracy* 15, no. 4 (2004): 5–19.

Zovatto, Daniel, and J. Jesús Orozco Henríquez, eds. *Reforma Política y Electoral en América Latina 1978-2007*. Mexico City: Universidad Nacional Autónoma de México—International IDEA, 2008.

CHAPTER 15

..................................................................................................

# ELECTORAL SYSTEMS AND LEGISLATIVE ORGANIZATION

..................................................................................................

## SHANE MARTIN

> [T]he organization of Congress meets remarkably well the electoral needs of its members. To put it another way, if a group of planners sat down and tried to design a pair of American national assemblies with the goal of serving members' electoral needs year in and year out, they would be hard pressed to improve on what exists.
>
> Mayhew (1974, 81–82)

LEGISLATURES are ubiquitous. They are often the foundation of democracy at the local, subnational, national, and even supra-national levels. In all democracies, legislatures play important roles in law making, executive oversight, and representation of citizens' interests and preferences. In parliamentary regimes, the executive comes from the legislature. Legislatures can even play significant roles in authoritarian regimes.

This chapter is concerned with legislative organization and in particular how electoral systems shape legislative organization. Alemán (2015, 145) helpfully defines legislative organization as "the set of procedures that regulate the legislative process and the related set of offices with internal authority." Legislatures vary significantly in how they are organized (Martin, Saalfeld, and Strøm 2014). Variation may occur over time in the same legislature, when we compare different legislatures, or when we compare different chambers in a multicameral legislature. Thus, the British Parliament is organized very differently from the US Congress, which is different in organization from many of the US state legislatures. The US House of Representatives is structurally very differently from the US Senate.

Virtually all legislatures update their organization at least occasionally. Scholars have been long intrigued by cross-sectional, intercameral, and intertemporal variation in the rules and procedures of legislatures (Zubek 2015; Sieberer et al. 2016). The structure and significance of committees has been a core focus for those interested in legislative organization (Martin 2014a).

One possible explanation of legislative organization is the electoral system used to select legislators. By deciding how votes in an election are translated into seats in the legislature, electoral systems shape what politicians must do to get elected and re-elected. Decades of research on various legislatures suggest that legislators are electorally oriented in their behavior (for overviews see Zittel and Uslaner 2009; André, Depauw, and Martin 2016a; and André and Depauw, this volume). Yet electoral considerations may well impact far more than behavior. As the quote from Mayhew at the beginning of this chapter illustrates, how a legislature chooses to organize itself may be directly impacted by members' electoral needs. If this is the case, we should be able to theoretically link variation in legislative organization to variation in electoral rules and support this supposition with some empirical evidence.

Theoretically, candidate-centered electoral systems ought to result in centrifugal legislatures with decentralized organizational structures. In contrast, party-centered electoral systems ought to produce centripetal legislatures with power concentrated in the chamber leadership or party leadership. In short, whether or not incumbents need to cultivate a personal vote or a party vote (Carey and Shugart 1995) defines incumbents' interests and, by extension, should shape legislative organization.

Understanding legislative organization is crucial because it allows uncovering the "black box" between electoral systems and public policy. While scholars have long postulated a relationship between electoral systems and public policy, we know very little about exactly how this happens (Rickard 2012). In other words, we may know the rationale for why electoral rules shape policy outcomes but not the foundational mechanism by which political elites are able to respond to incentives. Legislative organization may be the mechanism by which public policy is shaped in response to members' electoral incentives. Indeed, the link between electoral incentives and policy outputs may be fragmented by particular forms of legislative organization. Thus, legislative organization may serve to facilitate members' preferences, or, as I suggest in this chapter, it may condition (weaken) the effect of electoral incentives by taking powers and policy perquisites away from individual members.

The chapter is organized as follows: Next, I review theories of legislative organization that link centrifugal force in the US Congress to members' electoral goals. I then review how such theories have been applied to other legislative settings. Then I discuss the conditions under which legislative organization appears misaligned to members' electoral incentives. I conclude the chapter with suggestions for future research.

# THE ELECTORAL BASIS OF CONGRESSIONAL ORGANIZATION

Conventional wisdom suggests that members of the US Congress are influenced heavily by electoral considerations (Mayhew 1974; Fenno 1978). Because members of Congress need to build a personal reputation with constituents to aid re-election, district preferences drive representative behavior (Miller and Stokes 1963). In addition, incumbents take on constituency casework and other vote-winning activities in their district.

Yet, electoral incentives not only shape preferences but also play a role in shaping the organizational structure of Congress itself. Specific attention has focused on the reason for committees' popularity as a form of legislative organizations in the US Congress. Some of the most compelling arguments for a link between electoral systems and legislators' preferences over internal legislative structures, as distinct from behavior, are provided by scholars of the US Congress. These scholars have posited a relationship between the electoral system and the significance of committees in legislative structures within Congress. More specifically, strong committees within Congress are associated with the candidate-centered electoral environment and the related need for members of Congress to cultivate a personal vote to secure re-election. Katz and Sala (1996) suggest that with the emergence of the secret ballot and the resulting need for incumbent members to appeal directly to voters, legislators looked to committees as a means of creating policy changes (and distributive benefits) for which they could claim credit in their home districts. In explaining the strength of committees in Congress, Shepsle and Weingast (1987) explore the role of a strong committee system in meeting the electoral needs of members of Congress. They argue that strong committees exist because, in the parlance of electoral studies, committees serve to allow members to cultivate personal votes. Members choose to organize the legislature not around strong parties but around committees with strong property rights, which allows members to safeguard policy issues of most concern to their constituents and distribute particularistic spending projects to their districts.

This *distributive* theory gains its designation from the suggestion that legislatures are organized around strong committees to allow members to distribute particularistic benefits to their constituents. Such benefits could include specific policies favored by voters in the member's district or so-called *pork barrel* spending (fiscal legislative particularism), which refers to the practice of allocating for political reasons national tax revenues on economically inefficient, geographically targeted projects.

A number of assumptions underlie the distributive theory of legislative organizations. In particular, legislators' self-interest and motivations stemming from the goal of re-election require building personal reputations with constituents by providing vote-winning pork barrel projects and aligning policy concerns with voters' salient issues.

For example, rural voters may favor policies that promote agriculture and, in particular, assurance of continued flow of government subsidies to support rural communities. To be re-elected, incumbents must adopt policies most salient to their constituents, control public policy, and allocate scarce resources to the sector that enhances credentials with voters. Yet, in a plenary-centered legislature, where simple majorities can enact changes to policy, each legislator is equal in ability to influence all proposals. Thus, to continue our example, unless representatives from rural areas control a majority of the plenary, they cannot control and claim credit for agricultural policy. Complicating the situation is that the existence of multiple salient policy issues disallows the likelihood that any one interest can maintain a majority of the plenary. Social choice theory hypothesizes that political outcomes under such conditions, and assuming simple majority rules, are inherently unstable (Arrow 1951). The classic divide-the-dollar game illustrates the problem: In this game, three players must agree to divide a dollar. Under majority rules, any two can form a winning coalition to agree on the distribution of the 100 cents. Player A and player B may agree to divide the dollar equally between them, leaving player C with no money, thus "maximizing" the utility of A and B. However, player C may offer a counterproposal, perhaps by offering player A 51 cents and retaining 49 cents, thus denying player B any money and simultaneously improving player A's position (by 1 cent). And so the game continues. No obvious result is available and any counterdecision can easily negate a previous one.

The divide-the-dollar game applies, substantively, to any legislative setting that allocates scarce resources (Baron and Ferejohn 1989). Distribution of funding in pork barrel politics is a classic example—legislators must collectively agree on the amount each member receives, but in a majority setting, any decision has the potential for alteration by a counterproposal, just as in the divide-the-dollar game. However, cycling can occur in less obvious ways: For simplicity, consider a House of Representatives divided three ways based on members' and their constituents' preferences for policies. The focus of one group of incumbents is domestic manufacturing, the second agriculture, and the third urban environment, with all three interests aiming for spending-sensitive policy changes. This situation characterizes a sequential game, which requires a coalition of two groups to institute change. The domestic manufacturing and agricultural interests may coalesce with the agricultural group voting for the manufacturing group's interests with the agreement that the manufacturers will subsequently support agricultural interests at another time. But once the manufacturing bill gains approval, the manufacturers have no incentive not to renege on any promise made to their agricultural colleagues. Instead, the rational action for the manufacturers would be to seek to strike a new deal to secure an additional allocation of the remaining resources. Thus, cycling emerges, with always-changing coalitions and no credible ability to commit to logrolling—the sequential exchange of votes. The game, although simple, illustrates what social choice scholars typically refer to as the Condorcet cycle. In short, absent legislative organization, no decision is stable.

Shepsle and Weingast (1987) suggested that committees exist to break the chaos anticipated by cycling by allowing for credible commitment in logrolling, thus permitting members to secure vote-winning policies and spending for their constituents. If legislative chambers decide their internal organizations, the legislature can construct a system of committees to ensure that members with particular preferences for policies control those policy areas. Thus, representatives of agricultural interests seek establishment of an agricultural committee that has control of policies and allocation of resources that concern the industry—effectively removing decisions from the plenary and providing power to members who have the most to gain or lose in that policy area. Committees are a form of rules to prevent the breakdown of cooperation among groups with different priorities over policy and spending (Weingast and Marshall 1988).

Such parsimonious, but nonetheless powerful, explanations of committees' distributive origin require a committee system to have four characteristics: First, committees must have the ability to control the agenda and the outcome in the policy jurisdictions—commonly known as gatekeeping powers. The plenary, thus, must delegate significant authority to committees, making the relevant committee an agenda setter or veto player in the legislative process. Second, members must be able to self-select into preferred committees (Shepsle 1978). Third, and relatedly, committees are likely to be composed of "policy outliers" (Shepsle and Weingast 1987). In other words, committees should not be representative of the plenary (or the plenary median) but should include members with extreme preferences toward the committee's jurisdiction. Thus, to continue the example, an agricultural committee would consist of members strongly interested in, and committed to, that industry. As such, the committee would be "unrepresentative" of the chamber. Fourth, committee membership should associate with policy or financial rewards for a member's district.

The suggestion of committees as institutional solutions to drive geographically focused particularistic distribution, and thus incumbents' re-elections, has had a profound effect on the study of social choice theory and American political institutions. Yet, the idea that electoral incentives drive the organization of Congress is not without its critics. For example, Berry and Fowler (2016) question the causal link between committee assignments and pork barrel spending, instead finding that seats on key committees produce little additional spending. The proposition that committee membership fails to provide mechanisms for vote winning provides a fundamental challenge to the distributive theory of legislative organization.

The distributive perspective has also been questioned on theoretical grounds. The *informational* theory of legislative organization proposed by Gilligan and Krehbiel (1987) challenges the electoral-based distributive theory, suggesting instead that the legislature is structured to maximize members' acquisition and sharing of information (Gilligan and Krehbiel 1987, 1990; Krehbiel 1991). From this perspective, the organization of the legislature around strong committees allows member specialization. These gains from specialization facilitate informational advantages and tacit knowledge accumulation, resulting in better legislative activities of benefit to the entire chamber. In the distributive perspective, members' incentives revolve around delivering distributive benefits that aid re-election. In contrast, committees from the informational perspective provide a collective, but little individual, benefit.

Cox and McCubbins (1993) acknowledged that much of the observable work of Congress is undertaken within and between committees but suggested that political parties nevertheless play a crucial role in legislative organization. For Cox and McCubbins, the structuring of the system by political parties assists the party's leadership by cartelizing legislative power. The committee system, far from being the focal point of power, allows parties to control members. In this partisan cartel model of legislative organization, committees are not the dominant source of influence and authority that traditional accounts of congressional organization suggest.

Similar to the empirical investigation of earlier theories of legislative organization, Cox and McCubbins (1993) focus on the assignment (and reassignment) process—the rules by which members gain appointment to specific committees. The party leadership, Cox and McCubbins suggest, plays a far more significant role in the assignment process than previously acknowledged. The analysis of assignments to committees, between 1947 and 1988, undermines the assumption that committees consist of policy outliers. Evidence suggests that the party leaders cartelize the allocation of assignments and use the assignments strategically to reward loyal partisans and punish members who have defied the leadership during roll-call votes. A similar pattern of control emerges when exploring requests for switched assignments (reassignment of committee membership). In short, the suggestion is that the focus on committees as an important unit within Congress obscures the fact that party leaders control who sits on which committee. This control shapes not only the composition of committees, and by extension the nature of the committee, but also the power the party leadership wields to enforce the party discipline.

While the distributive theory of legislative organization focused on individual members' electoral interests, such electoral-origin theories of congressional organization are no longer taken for granted in the congressional literature. The centripetal force of the party leadership may serve to reduce the ability of members to use committees to win votes. At the same time, both the House of Representatives and the Senate likely enjoy some of the highest incumbency rates of any democratic legislature operating today—suggesting that the perquisites of congressional office, dispensed by legislative organization, greatly aid incumbents in holding their seats at election time.

## COMPARATIVE PERSPECTIVES

Given the inconclusive nature of the debate among congressional scholars on the link between electoral incentives and congressional organization, it is worth exploring the geographical generalizability of the distributive theory. Cross-national variation in electoral systems should provide an opportunity to test, comparatively, any connection between institutionally induced electoral incentives and legislative organization. A testable implication of the distributive theory of congressional organization is that candidate-centered electoral systems should result in legislatures with strong committees. Figure 15.1 depicts this view of the relationship between personal vote electoral systems and committee structures (Martin 2011). As the incentive to cultivate the personal vote increases, so too should the strength of committees in the legislature. The rationale is simple: In candidate-centered electoral systems, the legislature is organized in such a way as to privilege individual incumbent members to win votes via their legislative activity. These centrifugal pressures result in a strong committee system, allowing incumbents to control policy of most interest to their constituents and distribute particularistic benefits. Indeed, Powell (2000, 34) noted the empirical correlation between strong committees and proportionally representative electoral systems. In contrast, where members are dependent on their party for re-election, the legislature will also be party centered. For example, in a seminal contribution, Cox (1987) suggests that electoral reform in Britain resulted in procedural changes in the House of Commons. Specifically, less candidate-centered voting may associate with greater cabinet control of the legislative agenda and deterioration of parliamentary prerogatives and rights of individual members of parliament (MPs).

Despite the logic and pellucidity of the argument linking legislative organization to electoral politics, not all candidate-centered electoral systems produce legislatures with strong committees. Looking at fifty-five legislatures, Taylor (2006) finds some evidence that personal vote electoral systems associate with decentralized legislative procedures (procedures that give power to rank-and-file members rather than concentrate power in the leadership). Yet the best predictor of the legislative procedures is chamber size and bicameral power: legislative procedures are most decentralized in small chambers and the powerful chamber in bicameral systems (Taylor 2006), suggesting that electoral incentives may not be what drives legislative organization. Martin (2011) finds no relationship between a legislature's committee system and the incentive to cultivate personal votes generated by the electoral system.

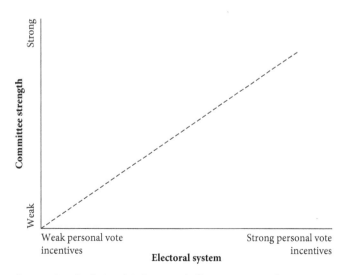

FIGURE 15.1. Conventional relationship between ballot structure and committee system.

Source: Martin (2011). Reproduced here by permission of John Wiley & Sons Inc.

While candidate-centered electioneering produces strong committees in the United States, other candidate-centered systems, with the same or even stronger incentives to cultivate a personal vote, produce weak legislative committees in other countries. For example, under the single transferable vote (STV) electoral system, Irish legislators face significant incentives to cultivate personal votes, not least because they must compete with copartisans for the same seats in parliament. Yet, the Irish parliament has a long tradition of weak committees (André, Depauw, and Martin 2016b). Arguments that this difference is due to the presidential nature of American government and the parliamentary nature of other regimes become less compelling when we observe strong committees operating within parliamentary regimes and more generally when significant variation in committee system structures across legislatures operating under parliamentarism is detected (Mattson and Strøm 1995; Martin 2011).

Because an analysis of appointments to committees forms the backbone of empirical research on congressional committees, scholars have also explored committee assignment patterns in other regimes to detect explanations of legislative organization. For example, Crisp et al. (2009) explore patterns of assignment to committees in Argentina, Costa Rica, and Venezuela. They find that procedures for selection of candidates and electoral rules contribute to explaining some but not most of the variation in patterns of assignments among national cases and individual careers. Raymond and Holt (2014) find that distributive and partisan models of legislative organization explain committee assignments in Canada. Research on the European Parliament noted that committee assignments tend to be proportionate to the party's plenary size, and parties thus influence and shape the composition of committees (Bowler and Farrell 1995; McElroy 2006)—suggesting evidence favoring the party-cartel perspective. In contrast, Whitaker (2001, 2011) noted that members are typically able to self-select assignments, based on members' own policy interests—suggesting evidence in favor of the informational perspective. Yordanova (2009) finds little evidence to support the partisan theory but noted that committees with distributive potential tend to consist of "high demanding" preferential outliers—suggesting evidence in favor of the distributive explanation. In contrast, committees with no distributive authority tend to attract members with relevant expertise but no special interests—suggesting evidence in favor of the informational perspective. As with the US Congress, research on committees in the European Parliament brings us no closer to agreeing on a theory of legislative organization linking electoral considerations to members' attitudes to committees (as measured through committee assignments). Ciftci, Forrest, and Tekin (2008) explore the Turkish case, finding evidence that policy interests and seniority are influential, interpreted as evidence for both distributive and informational theories. The Danish case suggests that assignment processes differ within the same chamber by party, leading Hansen (2010) to speculate that the entire process is potentially random (see also Hansen 2011 on the Irish case). Looking at the German case, Gschwend and Zittel (2016) find that legislators with local ties are more likely to be assigned to committees that deliver pork to please local constituents. But the mode of election (single-seat district vs. party list—Germany has a mixed-member electoral system) does not influence committee assignments.

We are left with something of a puzzle: In some cases, legislative organization can be traced to members' electoral incentives. In other instances, the link between legislative organization and the electoral system used to elect legislators is undetectable. Next I examine features of the political system that may condition or even break the relationship between electoral interests and legislative organization.

## CONDITIONING THE ELECTORAL EFFECT

To understand the relationship between electoral systems and legislative organization, it is necessary to recognize the consequences of what I call different *mechanisms to cultivate a personal vote* (MCPV). Legislators who need to cultivate personal votes have access to different MCPVs, with the exact nature of these vote-gathering mechanisms varying from polity to polity. Differences in how legislators cultivate votes ultimately determine legislators' preferences over internal legislative structures.

To understand how MCPV may differ from polity to polity, it is worth contrasting how legislators in the United States and the United Kingdom cultivate personal votes. In the United States, incumbents rely on a number of mechanisms: these include pork barrel projects, undertaking casework for individual constituents or groups within the district, and a range of other activities, such as arranging tours of federal buildings, nominating congressional interns, and attending public meetings and other events in their district. In the United Kingdom, parliamentarians do not typically secure or seek to secure pork barrel projects for their district. Instead, British MPs devote considerable time to extra-legislative constituency service, which, according to Norris (1997), has four components: dealing with constituency casework, holding meetings or "surgeries" with individual constituents, attending local party meetings, and attending other functions in their constituency. Notably absent from this list is work to secure pork spending projects for their district. Where the executive has budgetary authority and the sole right to introduce what are often referred to as money bills (bills with a spending element), it becomes impractical for individual legislators to cultivate personal votes by means of fiscal particularism. As others have demonstrated, British MPs, like legislators in many countries, have no or little opportunity to generate fiscal particularism for their districts (Cain, Ferejohn, and Fiorina 1987. As a result, British MPs rely on mostly extra-legislative mechanisms to enhance their reputation with constituents.

Existing research on electoral systems and legislative organization has tended to treat all personal vote-gathering strategies as being the same in terms of consequence. Here, not only do we draw attention to the obvious differences between legislative particularism and extra-legislative parochialism (service to a district or constituent that is not based on securing public spending projects), but we also highlight the need to explore the consequences of different MCPVs, particularly as they apply to members' preferences over internal legislative organization.

Legislators elected under candidate-centered ballot structures are obligated by virtue of the electoral system to focus on cultivating personal votes, but the vote-cultivating mechanism ultimately determines how the legislature will be organized. To clarify, let us think about two different legislative settings, the first where individual legislators can target spending to their geographical districts, and the second scenario where budgetary rules and the executive–legislative relationship make it impossible or unlikely that individual legislators will be able to impact spending plans. In the first, we would expect legislators to cultivate a personal vote by securing particularistic spending; in the second, we would expect the members to be focused on providing alternative, nonfiscal, benefits to constituents. Where individual legislators can target particularistic benefits to their constituents, there is every reason to expect the logic of the distributive theory of legislative organization to hold. Where committees provide opportunities for reputation building with constituents and the electoral system is candidate centered, legislators will have an incentive to participate in committee work. To ultimately ensure an incumbency advantage, legislators will organize a strong committee system where legislators' property and distributive rights can be used to ingratiate them with their geographical constituency. The key point here, à la Shepsle and Weingast (1987), is that the relationship between cultivating personal votes and strong committees holds because individual members can use committees to enhance their personal vote.

Absent the opportunity for gaining credit "back home" for legislative particularism, individual legislators will think more carefully about allocating their limited time and scarce resources to committee work, especially given that extra-legislative activities are more likely to enhance their opportunities for re-election. Focusing on constituency service leaves little time for legislators to perform nonparochial legislative roles such as active involvement in committee work. Frequently, legislative committees perform the role of assessing proposed legislation and holding the executive to account. In many legislative settings, committee work relates to issues of national policy, which provides little opportunity for individual legislators to differentiate themselves in terms of constituent interests and build personal reputations with constituents. A strong committee system may be electorally costly to a member who would be better served, in terms of enhancing their personal vote, focusing on local politics outside the legislature. In political systems where the MCPV is nonlegislative and therefore more reliant on brokerage or other forms of direct voter contact, members have little incentive to sit on committees. On the contrary, committee work could actively interfere with personal vote-gathering activities such as spending time in the constituency, meeting constituents, or undertaking constituency casework. Ultimately, where the design of committee systems is determined by the legislature itself, and where exogenous rules mandate that committees provide no avenue for particularistic spending credit-taking, we would not expect to see the emergence of strong committees.[1] Seeing no electoral benefit to committee work, members will shy away from having strong committees to which they would be expected to dedicate time, effort, and other scarce resources.

This conditional perspective on legislative organization is displayed in Figure 15.2 and can be contrasted with the conventional perspective, as shown in Figure 15.1. In Figure

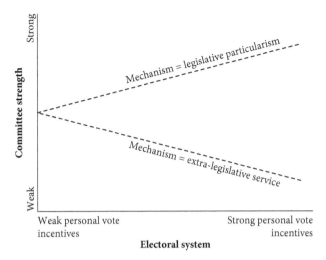

**FIGURE 15.2.** The interactive effect of mechanisms to cultivate a personal vote on the relationship between ballot structure and committee system.

Source: Martin (2011). Reproduced here by permission of John Wiley & Sons Inc.

15.2, the relationship between ballot structure and committee system is *conditional* on the MCPV. In essence, ballot structure interacts with MPCV to determine the shape of legislative structures. Where the MPCV is fiscal particularism, or where fiscal particularism is an important tool to cultivate personal votes, and the electoral system is candidate centered, we should expect to find strong committees. Indeed, as I have demonstrated elsewhere (Martin 2011), committee systems tend to be stronger the more significant the personal vote, but only if legislators can use committee assignments to further geographically targeted legislative particularism.

Other features of a political system may also break or weaken the link between members' electoral incentives and how the legislature is organized. For example, virtually all legislatures endow certain members with extra authority and responsibilities (Cox 2006; Smith and Martin 2017). Researchers have been largely silent on the impact of "chapter 2" (the allocation of mega-seats such as cabinet seats among legislators) on legislative behavior and organization. Allocation of mega-seats occurs by a variety of means. Party leader–centered allocation of mega-seats induces loyalty to the party leadership (as with party-centered electoral systems). In contrast, if the party leadership has no control over re-election (a candidate-centered electoral system) or over the allocation of mega-seats (a seniority-based system), individual legislators are free to act within the legislative arena without the need to act in accordance with the preferences of their party leaders. What happens when incentives to cultivate mega-seats diverge from incentives to cultivate personal votes? Figure 15.3 presents the likely consequences of this for one of the most observed and researched aspects of legislator behavior—the degree to which legislators from the same party vote the same way on floor votes. Two of the four typologies provide clean-cut predictions for the level of unified party voting: mega-seats filled

**Mega-Seat Allocation**

| | Party-centered | Other (e.g., seniority) |
|---|---|---|
| **Party-centered** | Strong discipline, unified party voting (example, Norway) | Level of voting unity reflects relative significance of seat to mega-seat (example, The European Parliament) |
| **Candidate-centered** | Level of voting unity reflects relative significance of seat to mega-seat (example, Ireland) | Little discipline, low levels of party voting unity (example, US Congress) |

(left axis label: **Electoral System**)

**FIGURE 15.3.** Complementary or competing impact of the electoral system and mega-seat allocation system on incentives for unified party voting.

Source: Martin (2014).

through seniority, or those more generally free of the involvement of party leaders, combined with a candidate-centered electoral system should result in relatively low levels of unified party voting in the plenary. Party voting unity should only occur when parties are ideologically cohesive—otherwise individual members will roll-call on the basis of their own preferences or the preferences of their constituents, with little regard for the wishes of the party leadership. The leadership can neither give nor remove much that the individual legislator values. Empirically, the US Congress perhaps approaches, or used to approach, most closely a reflection of this situation—the party leadership has little control over selection, election, and mega-seat allocation.

The example of the Irish case provides a hard test of the argument that mega-seats are of significance to how members behave within the legislative arena, and by extension their preferences over legislative organization. Irish legislators face competing principals: To gain re-election, incumbents must cultivate personal votes—the STV electoral system is considered the most candidate-centered electoral system used to elect a national legislature (André, Depauw, and Martin 2016a). Yet the Irish parliament is dominated by party leaders. Members have accepted highly centripetal legislative structures despite a personal vote electoral environment. What explains such centralized legislative structures in the presence of a highly candidate-centered electoral environment? A possible explanation is the ability of party leaders to control promotion opportunities from the backbenches to the frontbench (Martin 2014b). A real motivation for incumbents is promotion to ministerial office. Thus, promotional prospects may be more important for influencing legislators' interests than what goes on at the ballot box.

The Irish case arguably demonstrates that electoral interests do not necessarily translate into particular forms of legislative behavior or organization. Other political rules and institutions can condition this relationship. Thus, personal vote electoral systems do not always give rise to decentralized legislatures, as the US case would have us believe.

# CONCLUSION

Scholars have long been intrigued by the rules governing how legislators are elected. This is understandable, not least given the central role played by legislators and legislatures in most political systems. For similar reasons, scholars have expended considerable effort to explore how legislatures work and how they are organized. Indeed, intertemporal and cross-polity variation in how different legislative chambers organize themselves remains a central puzzle in legislative studies. In contrast, other organizations such as business firms tend to have far greater levels of similarity in how they organize, over time and across different countries.

Despite all that has been written about legislative organization, much remains to be done, not least in understanding better why some legislatures appear relatively better designed to meet the re-election needs of members. I conclude with some suggestions for future research.

As central as committee systems are to legislative organization, other rules and procedures greatly impact how a legislature operates. Scholars need to explore these other organizational attributes and whether electoral incentives explain organizational features other than committee systems. For example, are resources such as research and political staff within the legislature more likely to be employed by and for individual members in candidate-centered systems? In some legislatures, such resources are controlled and directed centrally; in other cases, staff associate with individual members. Similarly, are agenda setting and agenda control prerogatives more likely to be controlled by the party leadership in legislatures with party-centered electoral environments, as Cox (1987) hints? While scholars have long studied legislators' voting (roll-call) behavior (Carey 2009; Depauw and Martin 2009), do the rules that govern floor votes associate with the electoral system used to elect members? Hug, Wegmann, and Wüest (2015), for example, suggest that the transparency of the voting procedures is related to candidate selection rules. Thus, an entire world of legislative organization beyond committees remains to be explored in detail.

Second, and relatedly, the task of explaining legislative organization is complicated by lack of covariation in various parts of the legislative structure. While this chapter has talked of decentralized and centralized forms of legislative organization, different organizational features within the same legislature can pull power and influence in different ways within a legislature. For example, Cheibub, Martin, and Rasch (2015) find that legislatures tend to have a more significant formal role in selecting the executive (in parliamentary systems) when the executive enjoys stronger agenda control powers.

Thus, it may be inappropriate to look at any one feature of legislative organization and relate this to electoral politics. What is needed is a more nuanced measure of centralization and decentralization in legislative organization. Only then can we understand whether the electoral systems act as a centripetal or centrifugal force on legislative structures.

Third, we need to understand the historical foundations of legislative organization—in other words, how do legislative structures come about, and how do they change? Who are the actors designing legislative structures, and what are the actual processes by which legislatures are organized and reorganized? Existing research has tended to focus on the motivations for institutional design among incumbent legislators. The evolution of organization may involve more players than the legislators in that chamber—Sin (2014) finds that changes to the rules by the US House of Representatives reflect the bargaining context between the House, the Senate, and the president.

Finally, scholars should leverage change in electoral institutions and change in legislative organization to better identify the causal mechanisms underlying change. When a country changes its electoral system, do we see change to how the legislature is organized? If so, can we relate change in legislative organization to change in the electoral system? This may be a difficult task. For example, shifting to a more proportional system may be associated with a decentralization of power in the legislature, but this decentralization of power may arise from a change to the form of government rather than the electoral incentives of incumbents. André et al. (2016b) suggest that the shift from single-party cabinets to coalition cabinets motivated a strengthening of the committee systems in the Irish parliament. A more fragmented party system and resultant need to build a coalition, as distinct from single-party government, may be the real cause of legislative reorganization in the aftermath of electoral system change.

As this chapter has demonstrated, legislators' electoral motivations constitute just one explanation of legislative organization. Models suggesting the electoral basis of legislative institutions are, or at least were, a central tenet of research on American political institutions and political development. Members' electoral needs also appear to influence legislative organization in other settings. Candidate-centered electoral systems (such as open-list proportional representation) incentivize legislators to construct a legislature with decentralized organizational structures. This decentralization of power and influence permits incumbents to build personal reputations with constituents, which ultimately aids their re-election. In contrast, party-centered electoral environments (such as closed-list proportional representation) induce party-centered legislatures, with the party leadership controlling the legislative agenda and using legislative organization to shape the party label and party reputation in the electoral arena.

Yet, the empirical relationship between electoral incentives and legislative organization is not a perfect one. For one thing, some political systems have candidate-centered elections but party-dominated legislative structures (e.g., Ireland). Sieberer et al. (2016) find that changes to standing orders—the rules dictating legislative organization—are far more common than changes in electoral rules in Europe, suggesting that electoral rules alone can't explain legislative reorganization. As this chapter has discussed, the uncoupling of legislative organization from electoral institutions may be because other incentives trump members' electoral incentives. Thus, parties may be able to cartelize the allocation of prized offices to dull the effect of electoral rules on legislators' preferences. Moreover, rules governing executive–legislative relations may privilege the executive to the degree that decentralized legislative structures do not allow individual legislators to cultivate personal votes. For example, committee work absent the ability to use committees to buy votes may be of little interest to legislators, resulting in little incentive to delegate decision making away from the plenary.

## Note

1. Research on legislative rules and executive–legislative rules highlights the presence of a constitutional or higher-law provision stipulating exclusive executive authority over fiscal matters in many countries (Wehner 2010). Given the number of veto players needed to change constitutional/higher-law provisions, it seems fair to assume that, in most cases at least, individual legislators have little or no control over whether or not the political system permits legislative particularism.

## References

Alemán, Eduardo. "Legislative Organization and Outcomes." In *The Routledge Handbook of Comparative Political Institutions*, edited by J. Gandhi and R. Ruiz-Rufino, 145–161. Abingdon: Routledge, 2015.

André, Audrey, Sam Depauw, and Shane Martin. "The Classification of Electoral Systems: Bringing Legislators Back In." *Electoral Studies* 42 (2016a): 42–53.

André, Audrey, Sam Depauw, and Shane Martin. "'Trust Is Good, Control Is Better': Multiparty Government and Legislative Organization." *Political Research Quarterly* 69, no. 1 (2016b): 108–120.

Arrow, Kenneth J. *Social Choice and Individual Values*. New York: John Wiley & Sons, 1951.

Baron, David P., and John A. Ferejohn. "Bargaining in Legislatures." *American Political Science Review* 83, no. 4 (1989): 1181–1206.

Berry, Christopher R., and Anthony Fowler. "Cardinals or Clerics? Congressional Committees and the Distribution of Pork." *American Journal of Political Science* 60, no. 3 (2016): 692–708.

Bowler, Shaun, and David M. Farrell. "The Organizing of the European Parliament: Committees, Specialization and Co-ordination." *British Journal of Political Science* 25 (1995): 219–243.

Cain, Bruce, John Ferejohn, and Morris Fiorina. *The Personal Vote: Constituency Service and Electoral Independence*. Cambridge, MA: Harvard University Press, 1987.

Carey, John M. *Legislative Voting & Accountability*. Cambridge: Cambridge University Press, 2009.

Carey, John M., and Matthew Soberg Shugart. "Incentives to Cultivate a Personal Vote: A Rank Ordering of Electoral Formulas." *Electoral Studies* 14, no. 4 (1995): 417–439.

Cheibub, José Antonio, Shane Martin, and Bjørn Erik Rasch. "Government Selection and Executive Powers: Constitutional Design in Parliamentary Democracies." *West European Politics* 38, no. 5 (2015): 969–996.

Ciftci, Sabri, Walter Forrest, and Yusuf Tekin. "Committee Assignments in a Nascent Party System: The Case of the Turkish Grand National Assembly." *International Political Science Review* 29 (2008): 303–324.

Cox, Gary W. "The Organization of Democratic Legislatures." In *The Oxford Handbook of Political Economy*, edited by B. R. Weingast and D. A. Wittman. Oxford: Oxford University Press, 2006.

Cox, Gary W. *The Efficient Secret: The Cabinet and the Development of Political Parties in Victorian England.* Cambridge: Cambridge University Press, 1987.

Cox, Gary W., and Mathew D. McCubbins. *Legislative Leviathan.* Berkeley: University of California Press, 1993.

Crisp, Brian F., Maria C. Escobar-Lemmon, Bradford S. Jones, Mark P. Jones, and Michelle M. Taylor-Robinson. "The Electoral Connection and Legislative Committees." *Journal of Legislative Studies* 15 (2009): 35–52.

Depauw, Sam, and Shane Martin. "Legislative Party Discipline and Cohesion in Comparative Perspective." In *Intra-Party Politics and Coalition Governments in Parliamentary Democracies*, edited by Daniela Giannetti and Kenneth Benoit, 103–120. London: Routledge, 2009.

Fenno, Richard F. *Home Style: House Members in Their Districts.* Boston: Little, Brown, 1978.

Gilligan, Thomas W., and Keith Krehbiel. "Collective Decision-Making and Standing Committees: An Informational Rationale for Restrictive Amendment Procedures." *Journal of Law, Economics, and Organization* 3 (1987): 287–335.

Gilligan, Thomas W., and Keith Krehbiel. "Organization of Informative Committees by a Rational Legislature." *American Journal of Political Science* 34 (1990): 531–564.

Gschwend, Thomas, and Thomas Zittel. "Who Brings Home the pork? Parties and the Role of Localness in Committee Assignments in Mixed-Member Proportional Systems." *Party Politics* (2016). doi:10.1177/1354068816678884.

Hansen, Martin Ejnar. "Committee Assignment Politics in the Danish Folketing." *Scandinavian Political Studies* 33 (2010): 381–401.

Hansen, Martin Ejnar. "A Random Process? Committee Assignments in Dáil Éireann." *Irish Political Studies* 26 (2011): 345–360.

Hug, Simon, Simone Wegmann, and Reto Wüest. "Parliamentary Voting Procedures in Comparison." *West European Politics* 38, no. 5 (2015): 940–968.

Katz, Jonathan N., and Brian R. Sala. "Careerism, Committee Assignments, and the Electoral Connection." *American Political Science Review* 90 (1996): 21–33.

Krehbiel, Keith. *Information and Legislative Organization.* Ann Arbor: University of Michigan Press, 1991.

Martin, Shane. "Committees." In *The Oxford Handbook of Legislative Studies*, edited by S. Martin, T. Saalfeld, and K. W. Strøm, 352–370. Oxford: Oxford University Press, 2014a.

Martin, Shane. "Why Electoral Systems Don't Always Matter: The Impact of 'Mega-Seats' on Legislative Behaviour in Ireland." *Party Politics* 20, no. 3 (2014b): 467–479.

Martin, Shane. "Electoral Institutions, the Personal Vote, and Legislative Organization." *Legislative Studies Quarterly* 36, no. 3 (2011): 39–361.

Shane Martin, Thomas Saalfeld, and Kaare W. Strøm, eds. *The Oxford Handbook of Legislative Studies.* Oxford: Oxford University Press, 2014.

Mattson, Ingvar, and Kaare Strøm. "Parliamentary Committees." In *Parliaments and Majority Rule in Western Europe*, edited by H. Döring, 249–307. Frankfurt: Campus Verlag, 1995.

Mayhew, David. *The Electoral Connection.* New Haven, CT: Yale University Press, 1974.

McElroy, Gail. "Committee Representation in the European Parliament." *European Union Politics* 7 (2006): 5–29.

Miller, Wakken E., and Donald E. Stokes. "Constituency Influence in the Congress." *American Political Science Review* 57 (1963): 45–56.

Norris, Pippa. "The Puzzle of Constituency Service." *Journal of Legislative Studies* 3, no. 2 (1997): 29–49.

Powell, G. Bingham. *Elections as Instruments of Democracy: Majoritarian and Proportional Visions.* New Haven: Yale University Press; 2000.

Raymond, Christopher, and Jacob Holt. "Due North? Do American Theories of Legislative Committees Apply to Canada?" *Journal of Legislative Studies* 20, no. 2 (2014): 174–192.

Rickard, Stephanie J. "A Non-Tariff Protectionist Bias in Majoritarian Politics: Government Subsidies and Electoral Institutions." *International Studies Quarterly* 56, no. 4 (2012): 777–785.

Shepsle, Kenneth A. *The Giant Jigsaw Puzzle: Committee Assignments in the Modern House.* Chicago: University of Chicago Press, 1978.

Shepsle, Kenneth A., and Barry R. Weingast. "The Institutional Foundations of Committee Power." *American Political Science Review* 81 (1987): 85–104.

Sieberer, Ulrich, Peter Meißner, Julia F. Keh, and Wolfgang C. Müller. "Mapping and Explaining Parliamentary Rule Changes in Europe: A Research Program." *Legislative Studies Quarterly* 41, no. 1 (2016): 61–88.

Sin, Gisela. *Separation of Powers and Legislative Organization.* New York: Cambridge University Press, 2014.

Smith, Daniel M., and Shane Martin. "Political Dynasties and the Selection of Cabinet Ministers." *Legislative Studies Quarterly* 42, no. 1 (2017): 131–165.

Taylor, Andrew J. "Size, Power, and Electoral Systems: Exogenous Determinants of Legislative Procedural Choice." *Legislative Studies Quarterly* 31, no. 3 (2006): 323–345.

Wehner, Joachim. *Legislatures and the Budget Process: The Myth of Fiscal Control.* New York: Palgrave Macmillan, 2010.

Weingast, Barry R., and William J. Marshall. "The Industrial Organization of Congress; or, Why Legislatures, Like Firms, Are Not Organized as Markets." *Journal of Political Economy* 96, no. 1 (1988): 132–163.

Whitaker, Richard. "Party Control in a Committee-Based Legislature? The Case of the European Parliament." *Journal of Legislative Studies* 7 (2001): 63–88.

Whitaker, Richard. *The European Parliament's Committees: National Party Influence and Legislative Empowerment.* Abingdon: Routledge, 2011.

Yordanova, Nikoleta. "The rationale behind committee assignment in the European Parliament: Distributive, informational and partisan perspectives." *European Union Politics* 10, no. 2 (2009): 253–280.

Zittel, Thomas and Eric M. Uslaner. "Comparative Legislative Behavior." In *The Oxford Handbook of Political Science*, edited by R. E. Goodin, 392–408. Oxford: Oxford University Press, 2009.

Zubek, Radoslaw. "Legislative Organisation and Its Determinants in European Parliamentary Democracies." *West European Politics* 38, no. 5 (2015): 933–939.

# CHAPTER 16

# ELECTORAL SYSTEMS AND ROLES IN THE LEGISLATIVE ARENA

## AUDREY ANDRÉ AND SAM DEPAUW

Do electoral systems impact the roles that elected representatives play in the legislative arena? The simple answer, Bogdanor (1985, 299) concluded early on, is no: "The electoral system is not a fundamental cause of variations in the focus of representation." For the longest time, electoral systems did not feature very prominently in the scholarly inquiry into the sources of legislative roles. In spite of recent, neo-institutionalist efforts (Blomgren and Rozenberg 2012) to revive interest in whether electoral institutions bring about particular foci or styles of representation (to name the most influential operational definition of roles, see Wahlke et al. 1962), evidence today continues to be as "fragmentary and sometimes contradictory" (Jewell 1970, 483).

Still, the roles of parliamentarians are important because they are thought to underpin their behavior in the legislative arena and thereby policy outcomes. Elections, and specifically electoral systems, are instrumental in translating the public's preferences into the selection of representatives who, in turn, will set policy (Powell 2000). Many view the electoral system as the single most important lever to engineer democratic decision making (Norris 2004). Even though scholars' understanding of roles has varied over time (see later), the implicit reasoning in the literature, depicted in Figure 16.1, is that the electoral institutions generate incentives to cater to either broad or narrow constituencies to which parliamentarians' role orientations will strategically respond. Once in office, their role orientations will in turn inform their behavior in the legislative arena (see Mansbridge 2009).

Whereas a burgeoning literature demonstrates that policies as different as the redistribution of wealth, public goods spending, and protectionism vary systematically across different electoral systems (see André, Depauw, and Shugart 2014; Carey and Hix 2013; Persson and Tabellini 2003), evidence with regard to legislative roles is hard to come by. After detailing what are roles in the legislative arena and reviewing the state of the

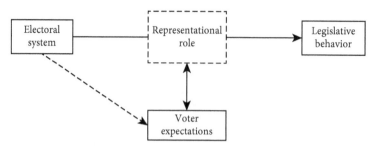

FIGURE 16.1. A conceptual model for studying representational roles.

literature, we explore three possible reasons. One is the perplexing dearth of comparative research in this field; another is that the causal mechanisms thought to underpin
observed correlations continue to be undertheorized. Finally, the very nature of electoral rules and the causal chain linking legislators' roles to them involves human discretion, allowing contextual factors to have a strong mediating impact. In this manner we
critically re-examine the utility of the role concept.

After approaching representational roles from the common perspective of the representatives, we turn to the perspective of their principals in the chain of delegation.
Only very recently has a literature on citizens' expectations regarding the representative
relationship started to develop, albeit in isolation. Given that popular democratic beliefs
hinge on the notion of responsiveness to the preferences of citizens, it is especially puzzling how little we know about voter expectations vis-à-vis the roles performed in the
legislative arena (see Figure 16.1). Nonetheless, insofar as variations in the gap between
voter expectations and their representatives' role orientations originate in the electoral
system, this knowledge may significantly further our understanding of growing popular
disenchantment with representative government and political disengagement.

# INSTITUTIONS AND ROLES IN THE
# LEGISLATIVE ARENA

What is a role—other than the means to relate individuals' behavior to the institution
they are part of? In the legislative arena, Wahlke et al. (1962, 8) argue, roles constitute
coherent sets of norms and expectations of behavior associated with being a legislator.
Together, they identify the behaviors "that make the legislature an institution" (Wahlke
et al. 1962, 20). Even though the interactionist tradition, by contrast, has emphasized
that individuals—complete with individual career goals and idiosyncratic motivations
(Searing 1994)—participate in defining their roles, they can hardly be expected to do so
in a vacuum (see Fenno 1978). This particular debate is largely settled (Searing 2012):[1]
that is, following the neo-institutionalist turn, most would agree that institutional

rules condition and constrain the role orientations adopted by legislators in their effort to satisfy their individual aims (see Strøm 1997; Blomgren and Rozenberg 2012; Andeweg 2014).

Despite the many misgivings about their meaning (see Blomgren and Rozenberg 2012), there is a recent neo-institutionalist revival in the scholarly interest to trace back to the electoral system the sources of legislators' role orientations. Most of the attention has concentrated on what legislators regard as their focus of representation and its counterpart, their style of representation (Wahlke et al. 1962). The focus of representation denotes whose opinions and interests legislators think to represent primarily, whereas their style of representation refers to the degree of leeway they feel they have in interpreting said interests. Both are thought to underpin, but ultimately to be distinct from, behavior in the legislative arena (Andeweg 2012).[2]

The style of representation separates *delegates*, who act upon their principals' instructions, from *trustees*, who act upon their own mature judgment to determine their principals' interest, to take the two extremes of the continuum. In their study of representation in France, Converse and Pierce (1986) added the distinction between district and party delegates, thereby conflating focus and style (Andeweg 2014), in an effort to better account for the political parties that throughout the world "make the constitutional chain of delegation and accountability work in practice" (Müller 2000, 309). Truly, in most—especially European—countries, the style of representation is biased toward party delegates. The 2014 Participation and Representation study (Deschouwer, Depauw, and André 2014), for instance, finds that while just under half of the legislators indicate to toe the party line in case of conflicting opinions, trustees tend to outnumber the constituency delegates almost three to one (see Table 16.1).

In addition, different foci of representation can be meaningfully described using two dimensions, Wessels (1999) argued (see Figure 16.2). Along the regional dimension, legislators may focus—adopting an ever wider view of their principal—on the people residing in the *constituency* (or district), in the *nation*, or even, in the particular case of Members of the European Parliament, in *Europe*. Across European democracies, legislators narrowly favor the district over the nation by about 10 percent (see Table 16.1, Deschouwer et al. 2014; but see Kielhorn 2001). MEPs, the 1996 European Representation Study (Wessels 1999) found, overwhelmingly adopt a national, rather than a European, outlook.

Along the group dimension, legislators may focus on representing a *specific functional group* defined by a common social, economic, or cultural interest (e.g., women, ethnic minorities, trade unions). Increasingly, interests may also extend, far beyond the electoral connection, to include the disenfranchised, or even animals and non-sentient nature (see Urbinati and Warren 2008). Alternatively, legislators may defer to the *party*, which typically combines and aggregates different group interests. Again, Deschouwer et al. (2014) found, the party electorate is the predominant focus across European democracies (see Table 16.1). Mirroring earlier surveys (see also Esaiasson 2000; Kielhorn 2001; Thomassen and Andeweg 2004), only a minority attributes great importance to representing a specific functional group.

# Table 16.1  Foci and Styles of Representation across Europe

| | Focus of Representation | | | | Style of Representation | | |
|---|---|---|---|---|---|---|---|
| | District | Party Voters | Functional Group | Country | District Delegate | Party Delegate | Trustee |
| **Closed-list PR** | | | | | | | |
| ISR | n/a | 73.7 | 62.2 | 85.7 | 19.4 | 45.2 | 35.5 |
| ITA | 55.6 | 46.7 | 16.7 | 47.7 | 21.4 | 23.8 | 54.8 |
| NOR | 52.2 | 82.6 | 13.0 | 65.2 | 9.5 | 83.3 | 7.1 |
| POR | 62.7 | 55.4 | 17.8 | 73.3 | 23.5 | 39.7 | 36.8 |
| SPA | 72.6 | 82.4 | 40.6 | 52.0 | 19.2 | 68.1 | 12.8 |
| *Mean* | *63.4* | *69.5* | *30.1* | *62.7* | *19.13* | *54.15* | *26.71* |
| **Flexible-list PR** | | | | | | | |
| AUT | 74.5 | 79.2 | 47.1 | 42.6 | 25.0 | 32.5 | 42.5 |
| BEL | 38.6 | 48.6 | 27.5 | 27.1 | 9.4 | 59.4 | 31.3 |
| NET | n/a | 76.9 | 46.8 | 46.0 | 7.5 | 80.0 | 12.5 |
| *Mean* | *53.0* | *66.7* | *38.9* | *37.8* | *13.19* | *57.64* | *29.17* |
| **Open-list PR** | | | | | | | |
| IRE | 61.8 | 45.5 | 14.7 | 48.5 | 10.0 | 80.0 | 10.0 |
| POL | 49.1 | 50.9 | 26.9 | 64.2 | 11.8 | 41.2 | 47.1 |
| SWI | 38.8 | 70.8 | 33.3 | 43.8 | 12.5 | 12.5 | 75.0 |
| *Mean* | *48.5* | *56.7* | *26.1* | *53.0* | *11.63* | *39.53* | *48.84* |
| **Mixed-member systems** | | | | | | | |
| GER | 65.9 | 65.7 | 29.0 | 44.6 | 7.9 | 41.2 | 50.9 |
| HUN | 59.0 | 69.1 | 44.1 | 46.9 | 19.5 | 51.2 | 29.3 |
| *Mean* | *63.0* | *67.1* | *35.3* | *45.6* | *12.76* | *45.41* | *41.84* |
| **Majoritarian systems** | | | | | | | |
| FRA | 57.5 | 21.3 | 15.9 | 75.0 | 2.1 | 35.4 | 62.5 |
| UK | 75.0 | 50.0 | 12.1 | 37.9 | 2.0 | 41.2 | 56.9 |
| *Mean* | *67.3* | *37.4* | *13.7* | *53.9* | *2.02* | *38.38* | *59.6* |

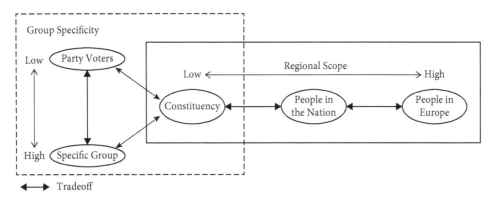

**FIGURE 16.2.** Disentangling the dimensions in legislators' focus of representation.

Source: Wessels (1999, 214).

# LITERATURE REVIEW: ELECTORAL SYSTEM EFFECTS ON ROLES FROM THE PERSPECTIVE OF THE REPRESENTATIVES

Despite roles' long pedigree in political science, evidence of electoral systems bringing about particular foci and styles of representation continues to be "fragmentary and sometimes contradictory" (see also Wessels 1999; Searing 1994; Jewell 1970). The observation is all the more startling given the role concept's intricate association with the institution wherein the roles are performed and the rules that govern it (see Wahlke et al. 1962). Table 16.2 maps recent efforts to unearth evidence of electoral system effects on the roles played in the legislative arena. Taken together, the summary in the table clearly demonstrates that (1) despite revived interest, truly comparative efforts are few; (2) the literature's propensity, moreover, to cherry-pick, reporting on only a small number of the possible foci and styles, has yielded at least as many "empty cells" as meaningful results; and (3) nonetheless, the number of reported nonfindings is considerable.

## Styles of Representation

Studies of electoral systems have concentrated on differences in electoral formula, ballot structure, and district magnitude, and role studies are no different. Solid evidence of such system effects is hard to come by, however. Theoretically, Wahlke et al. (1962; see also Rehfeld 2005) tied the existence of district delegates to the specific electoral incentive generated by the US first-past-the-post (FPTP) system, whereas the trustee orientation, they claim, is rooted in the heterogeneity of districts—which is also thought to vary across different electoral systems. Yet, scholars continue to disagree whether a legislator

Table 16.2 A Summary of the Literature Addressing Electoral System Effects on Legislators' Focus and Style of Representation

| | | Focus on Representation | | | | Style of Representation | | |
|---|---|---|---|---|---|---|---|---|
| | | District | Nation | Party | Group | District Delegate | Party Delegate | Trustee |
| **COMPARATIVE** | District magnitude | | | | | | | |
| | André et al. (2016a) | - | | + | | ns | ns | |
| | Dudzińska et al. (2014) | - | ns | ns | ns | - | ns | + |
| | Farrell and Scully (2010) | ns | | | | | | |
| | Pilet et al. (2012) | - | + | + | | | | |
| | Wessels (1999) | - | ns | + | ns | | | |
| | *Ballot structure:* Preferential system | | | | | | | |
| | André et al. (2016a) | ns | | ns | | ns | ns | |
| | Dudzińska et al. (2014) | - | ns | - | - | ns | - | + |
| | Farrell and Scully (2010) | ns | | | | | | |
| | Önnudóttir (2016) | | | | | ns | + | ns |
| | Pilet et al. (2012) | + | - | ns | | | | |
| | District magnitude* | | | | | | | |
| | André et al. (2015) | | | | | | ns | |
| | Preferential system | | | | | | | |
| | André et al. (2016b) | ns | ns | ns | | | ns | |
| | Farrell and Scully (2010) | ns | | | | | | |
| | Pilet et al. (2012) | ns | ns | ns | | | | |

| | | | | | | |
|---|---|---|---|---|---|---|
| *Electoral formula:* Majoritarian system | Cooper and Richardson (2006) | | | + | | – |
| | Dudzińska et al. (2014) | + | ns | ns | – | + |
| | Pilet et al. (2012) | + | ns | – | | |
| District vs. List Members | Chiru and Enyedi (2015) | + | ns | – | | |
| | Ilonszki (1998) | + | ns | – | | |
| | Klingemann and Wessels (2001) | + | | – | ns | + |
| | Lundberg (2007) | ns | | – | ns | ns |
| | Zittel (2012) | + | ns | ns | ns | ns |

**MIXED**

acts as a Burkean trustee because on most issues heterogeneous districts are unable to agree on clear instructions (Wahlke et al. 1962) or, alternatively, because he or she feels confident about knowing district opinion (Alpert 1979; see also Pitkin 1967). Trustees, it seems, are at least as good at assessing district opinion as delegates (Andeweg 2012; Erikson, Luttbeg, and Holloway 1975; Hedlund and Friesema 1972), calling into question the behavioral consequences of different styles (see also Jewell 1970).

Empirically, neither the electoral formula, nor the ballot structure, nor district magnitude is a major determinant of the degree of discretion a legislator sees in interpreting citizens' opinions (see Table 16.2). One exception is Cooper and Richardson (2006), who note that, among US state legislators, single-seat districts breed district delegates, whereas trustees are more numerous in multiseat districts. In the mixed-member system of Germany, Klingemann and Wessels (2001) also noted a clear mandate divide, district delegates being more numerous among the district members and trustees among those elected from the party list. Other studies either fail to find such system effects (André, Depauw, and Deschouwer 2016a; Lundberg 2007) or report findings that are at the least counterintuitive, if not contradictory (see Önnudóttir 2016; Dudzińska et al. 2014).

## Focus of Representation

The one consistent finding in the literature thus far is that, along the regional dimension, a strong district focus is closely associated with FPTP and two-round majoritarian systems (see Table 16.2). Yet scholars disagree whether the electoral formula or district magnitude is the relevant component driving the observed relation. Apparently, the ballot structure has neither a direct nor a mediating effect in this regard.

Some have found a legislator's district focus to be shaped by the binary distinction across different countries between single-seat and multiseat districts (Dudzińska et al. 2014; Pilet, Freire, and Costa 2012). Such evidence has also been found among Canadian city councillors—elected either by single-seat wards or at large (Koop and Kraemer 2016)—and in the context of mixed-member systems. Relative to the members elected by the party-list proportional representation (PR) tier, members elected in a single-seat district have a markedly stronger district focus (notwithstanding list members' efforts to shadow district members of competing parties, see Carman and Shephard 2007). The effect is consistent across different national cultures (in Germany: Klingemann and Wessels 2001; Zittel 2012; Hungary: Chiru and Enyedi 2015; Ilonszki 1998; and Romania: Chiru and Enyedi 2015) and in both mixed-member proportional and mixed-member majoritarian systems.

Others have reported a similar impact of district magnitude as a metric property. National legislators elected by single-seat districts favor a district focus, Wessels (1999) found; as district magnitude grows larger, by contrast, legislators tend to trade in their district focus. The 2014 Participation and Representation study provided further firm evidence, across over sixty national and regional legislatures, of district magnitude's negative effect on adopting a district focus (André et al. 2016a; Dudzińska et al. 2014). Wessels (1999) also found that the district focus becomes increasingly rare among MEPs, as district magnitude grows larger. Since then, however, the variation in district magnitude in European Parliament elections, and thereby its impact, is sharply reduced (Farrell and Scully 2010): following the 2002 change in EU legislation, the effect pertains more to districted versus at-large PR systems, as well as to the size of the country (Farrell and Scully 2005). Within countries, MEPs tend to put less emphasis on the district than the members of the national parliament—which is roughly in line with differences in district size (Wessels 1999).

However, these seemingly contrasting interpretations are easily reconciled. On the one hand, the contrast between single-seat and two-seat districts may well be greater than at any other district magnitude. Certainly, there are additional normative expectations of legislators being the sole defendant of the district associated with single-seat district systems (Mitchell 2000). Similar normative expectations are probably present in at-large systems, urging legislators to focus on representing the nation (Thomassen and Andeweg 2004). On the other hand, different modeling strategies (including both electoral formula and district magnitude as predictors, Dudzińska et al. 2014; or excluding single-seat districts as an additional robustness check, André et al. 2016a) strongly suggest that, even beyond the binary distinction, district magnitude continues to impact legislators' district focus.

What is less clear is which focus legislators trade in their district focus for as district magnitude increases. Along the regional dimension, one could argue legislators will increasingly adopt a national focus. But neither Wessels (1999) nor Dudzińska et al. (2014) found evidence supporting this contention. Nor is there consistent evidence of ballot structure effects in this regard. Only Pilet et al. (2012) found national orientations to be more important in the closed-list PR system of Portugal, compared to Belgium and France. Alternatively, legislators may put more emphasis on the group dimension as district magnitude grows. Certainly, there is some evidence that, as district magnitude increases, legislators trade in their district focus for a more partisan focus (André et al. 2016a; Pilet et al. 2012; Wessels 1999). In mixed-member systems as well, list members tend to have a stronger partisan orientation than district members, in line with theoretical expectations (in Germany and the United Kingdom: Lundberg 2007; Hungary: Chiru and Enyedi 2015; Ilonszki 1998; and Romania: Chiru and Enyedi 2015). But the effect has not been observable in all cases (see Table 16.2). Ballot structure, again, largely has no impact. As to legislators representing functional social groups, other individual and contextual factors pertaining to the interest group structure in the country are more relevant (Wessels 1999): only in mixed-member systems is there some indication that list members may be more likely to adopt a functional focus of representation (in Germany and the United Kingdom: Lundberg 2007; Hungary: Ilonszki 1998).

Finding a correlation between the electoral system in the country and a particular focus of representation is but the first condition, however. The causal mechanism underpinning the impact of electoral systems in this regard continues to be undertheorized.

The impact of district magnitude is a case in point. Three possible causal mechanisms for the negative effect have been put forward in this literature.[3]

One is the incentive generated by the electoral system to cultivate a personal vote. Legislators in small-magnitude districts are expected to favor a district focus *because* the smaller the district magnitude, the more personalized the electoral competition between candidates (Wessels 1999, 222) and the easier it is for voters to monitor and sanction their behavior (Bowler and Farrell 1993; Mitchell 2000).

The second mechanism hinges on legislators' uncertainty about district opinion. The relative homogeneity of small-magnitude districts will make it possible for legislators to discern and represent the district's opinion (Wessels 1999; Alpert 1979). Greater population size, by contrast, increases the heterogeneity of constituents' interests and preferences, and in an attempt to reduce uncertainty, legislators can be expected to trade in their district focus for a partisan focus.

The third causal argument pertains to the size of a legislator's re-election constituency (Grofman 2005): single-seat districts typically set a high threshold in this regard, necessitating a relatively large proportion of the vote to carry the district (see Lijphart 1994). Consequently, a legislator may be expected to focus on the entire district. Yet, as district magnitude increases, a legislator may be returned to parliament by winning a much smaller proportion of the vote (Myerson 1993), and he or she is not similarly constrained. He or she may well court sufficient support in a geographical, functional, or even partisan subpart of the district.

All three causal mechanisms can plausibly provide a theoretical explanation for the observed negative impact of district magnitude on legislators' district orientations, and therefore, as long as we cannot discriminate between them, our understanding of the consequences of electoral systems falls short. That research to date has been unsuccessful in demonstrating that district magnitude has a differential effect on legislators' focus of representation in open-list and closed-list systems might at least be taken as evidence against the plausibility of the "personal vote" mechanism.

# Why So Little Solid Evidence?

The poor performance of electoral systems as a source of legislative role orientations could be the result of three shortcomings. One stems from limited data availability, another results from the contested specification of the role concept, and the third is tied to the very nature of electoral systems and the endogeneity bias they present.

## Data Availability

One important reason is simply the dearth of widely comparative data: in recent years, there have only been a handful of projects surveying legislators across different countries on their roles (see Bailer 2014). They are further limited in geographical scope, concentrating on the European continent (see Andeweg 2014; Wessels 1999). Almost by design, by contrast, the single-country studies, which (continue to) predominate the literature on this topic, fail to consider the consequences of different electoral systems. Rarely do they take into account within-district variation in electoral incentives (for instance, in vulnerability). In addition, differences in the operational definition of roles raise serious doubts as to whether the shares of trustees and delegates, for instance, can be meaningfully compared across different legislatures (Jewell 1983). Yet, insofar as role orientations are distinct from the behavior they instigate, we have only surveys and interviews to unearth them.

## The Role Concept

From the perspective of electoral systems, the study of roles in the legislative arena presents an uneasy paradox. If roles are defined in terms of norms and expectations (in the structuralist tradition), we lack a convincing causal mechanism tying them to the electoral system. By contrast, if roles are taken to denote behavioral strategies in response to electoral incentives (in the neo-institutionalist tradition), we have no need for roles independent from these patterns of behavior (see also Andeweg 2012).

Additionally, the role concept, and its predominant operational definition, is contested primarily for three reasons (see Andeweg 2014). Theoretically, the mandate-independence controversy that underlies the trustee–delegate distinction cannot be resolved, for representation by definition entails both in equal measure (Pitkin 1967). Empirically, early on, the trustee–delegate distinction was heavily criticized for ignoring the central position of the party in the legislative arena (see Thomassen 1994; Converse and Pierce 1986). Trustee or delegate orientations, finally, bore little resemblance to the behavior, especially in roll-call voting, of elected representatives. The normative question wording, what *should* the representative do, may well have contributed to the gap separating norms and real-life behavior. The set of attitudes and motivations, Searing (1994) asserted, associated with a full-blown role can hardly be captured by a single survey item.

Regarding the focus of representation, moreover, the regional and group dimensions similarly fail to exhaust the many options open to politicians, thereby biasing our measurements. Evidence from fifteen countries, for instance, indicates that a sizeable number of legislators primarily represent some geographical subpart of the district—a possibility that is not captured by standard survey questions (André and Depauw 2016). Additionally, we cannot be sure thus far these foci constitute clear and distinct alternatives between which a legislator must choose: Is the opposite of a district orientation by necessity a national outlook? Is a functional group orientation by definition more national in focus? Clearly, the group in question may be concentrated geographically too. Can a partisan focus, furthermore, not be both district and nationally oriented?[4] Insofar as legislators in practice may combine different foci to build winning coalitions of supporters (see Bishin 2009), system effects will be diluted. Moreover, Andeweg (1997) argued that, just as actors play different parts in succession, legislators can adopt different foci and styles in different circumstances. Just as congress members' roll-calls are most responsive to the constituency on highly salient issues (see Kingdon 1977), legislators' focus may well vary across different policy areas.

## The Nature of Electoral Systems

Electoral systems are intricate configurations of the rules governing the act of voting and the translation of votes into seats. As such, they create an environment in which different behavioral strategies on the part of legislators likely become more, or less, successful at the polls. But electoral systems seldom force onto legislators a particular strategy (see Morgenstern and Vázquez-D'Elía 2007). Their strategic response entails human discretion, filtering the electoral incentives through their motivations and beliefs. Moreover, pushing beyond the simple notion that "it depends," we argue that, as noted before, a greater variety of role orientations are open to legislators especially in high-magnitude districts as just who their winning coalitions of supporters are is not forced by the electoral system.

Moreover, the argument that electoral systems bring about particular role orientations may well suffer from an endogeneity bias. Institutions matter, Przeworski (2004, 528) noted, only if they "prevent people from doing what they would otherwise have done or induce them to do what they otherwise would not have done." *Electoral* institutions are a case in point. We cannot comfortably think that legislators are assigned to different electoral systems by chance for two reasons. One is that particular electoral institutions emerge only in particular conditions; the other is that politicians self-sort into different systems in the sense that the electoral system is a consideration in their decision to stand for office in the first place.

Political parties choose electoral systems, Colomer (2005) observed.[5] PR systems emerge where multiple parties compete, rather than the electoral system generating a new party system (see also Benoit 2002). Where, taken together, niche parties poll significant support, they are likely instrumental in deciding on more proportional systems. It would probably overstate individual legislators' influence to argue that, because electoral systems are set by law, legislators with particular role orientations can decide on the rules that govern electoral competition. But, clearly, values—including values with regard to the relationship between elected representatives and constituents—enter the decision making on electoral system design and electoral reform (see Renwick and Pilet 2015).

Individuals may also self-select in another regard: there is a vast literature indicating that strategic considerations loom large in individuals' decision whether, and when, to run for public office (Maisel and Stone 1997; Maestas et al. 2006). Individuals enter races they think they can win. In conditions that put more emphasis on district representation, individuals lacking firm local roots and/or the appropriate focus of representation can be expected to withdraw. Of course, most elections also feature great numbers of candidates who have little to no hope of gaining election. But the (self-) selection may further be reinforced by voters' differential support for candidates advertising various role orientations (see Mansbridge 2009).

Nonetheless, despite recent misgivings about the endogeneity bias, one recent study found electoral system effects on legislators' district orientation to be strongest among trustees and weakest among those who are through their delegate role orientation already positively predisposed toward a strong district orientation, tentatively suggesting that electoral institutions may get them "to do what they otherwise would not have done" after all (André, Gallagher, and Sandri 2014, 180).

# LITERATURE REVIEW: ELECTORAL SYSTEMS AND PUBLIC EXPECTATIONS

The representational roles that legislators perform in the legislative arena have been studied almost exclusively from the perspective of how legislators themselves define their task (Blomgren and Rozenberg 2012, 9). Focusing on role orientations as they can be found in the minds of politicians, Searing (1994) argued, we are in the best position to explain their behavioral consequences. Yet, despite representational roles ultimately being about the manner in which politicians are responsive to the preferences of the public, relatively few efforts have been made to unearth citizens' preferences regarding their focus or style. Consequently, we have only a very patched understanding of what roles constituents expect their representatives to perform.

Individuals, Carman (2006, 2007) has demonstrated, have (latent) preferences for the style of representation their representative should adopt: some favor trustees who lead, while others want someone who listens and acts upon their instructions (see also André and Depauw 2016; Bengtsson and Wass 2010; Andeweg and Thomassen 2005; Converse and Pierce 1986). Their preferences have real consequences, moreover, for their voting behavior and incumbents' job approval (Barker and Carman 2012). Individuals also have meaningful preferences with regard to legislators' district versus national focus (André, Depauw and Andeweg 2017; Lapinski et al. 2016; Vivyan and Wagner 2016; Doherty 2013; Bengtsson and Wass 2011; Griffin and Flavin 2011; Grant and Rudolph 2004). Where there is a clear gap between citizen expectations and legislators' roles, the empirical evidence indicates, citizen satisfaction not just with individual legislators but with democracy suffers (André and Depauw 2017) and political disengagement ensues (André et al. 2017).

A natural conjecture, which thus far has not been studied, is that this gap varies across electoral systems. Just as levels of policy congruence are shaped by the institutional context (Curini, Jou, and Memoli 2012; Kim 2009), so too electoral systems likely affect the correspondence between individuals' expectations and legislators' role orientations. Yet, without exception, the extant studies have focused on a single country, and the variety, moreover, of survey question wordings and experimental designs used has further hampered the systematic comparison of voter expectations across institutional contexts. At least three competing expectations may be put forward for empirical testing.

The first expectation is simply that whereas politicians' roles mirror the incentives generated by the electoral system, citizens' expectations do not and may well reflect a general human tendency toward self-interest. This is what von Schoultz and Wass (2016) found with regard to district magnitude: in low-magnitude districts, politicians put a lot more emphasis on district representation than citizens do. Yet, as district magnitude increases, their district focus grows weaker—narrowing the gap with citizens' preferences that are more constant across districts.

Second, we might also expect ballot structure to have an impact, reducing the gap in strong preferential systems where voters can purposely select candidates with particular role orientations (see Mansbridge 2009) without having to change their partisan affiliation. In FPTP voters can similarly reward particular role orientations, but (possibly) only if they are prepared to vote for another party (Mitchell 2000). In closed-list systems, by contrast, because their vote for the party will benefit the candidates in the order they appear on the ballot, voters have no leverage toward the role orientations returned to parliament. As such, given the gap's negative impact on citizen satisfaction, this pattern may well underpin Farrell and McAllister's (2006) finding that preferential voting increases citizen satisfaction with democracy.

The third expectation builds on Shugart's (2001) notion of systems' electoral efficiency. Inefficiencies on the intraparty dimension come in two guises: deviations toward party centeredness leave politicians responsive to the party, not the electorate, whereas deviations toward candidate centeredness will squander public funds to narrow, local interests. In inefficient systems, citizens can be expected to stress in the survey setting the perceived flaws of the electoral system and have in such circumstances been known to actively pressure for electoral "reform from below" (see Norris 2011). As such, the gap is likely widest in inefficient systems of every ilk and smallest in efficient systems. Mixed-member systems, most notably, have been argued to effectively balance different role orientations, district members focusing on constituency interests and list members on representing citizens on the big national issues of the day (Shugart and Wattenberg 2001).

As such, as long as we ignore what voters want from their representatives and how their preferences vary across electoral systems, the "electoral sweet spot" (Carey and Hix 2011) will continue to elude us. Consequently, efforts to increase satisfaction with representative democracy through electoral engineering are very likely to miss their mark.

# Conclusion and Future Directions

The utility of the role concept is that it constitutes the linking pin between the institutions and behavior in the legislative arena (Andeweg 2014). But despite the concept's long pedigree in legislative studies, evidence of even the first step, a close association between the electoral institutions in the country and the role orientations adopted by legislators, is hard to come by. Large-scale comparative efforts inquiring into the sources of legislators' focus and style of representation are surprisingly few and far between: even a most thorough search failed to unearth more than a handful. Additionally, the extant studies demonstrate that general types of electoral systems are not particularly good predictors of role orientations.

In particular, the large within-country variation emerging from these studies should encourage us to explore operationalizations of the electoral incentives generated by electoral systems at a lower—district or even individual—level. While electoral systems may bring about particular role orientations among legislators in their effort to avoid defeat at the polls, to some defeat is a distinct possibility, whereas to others it is but a distant shadow. As such, individual electoral vulnerability has the ability to mediate, and thereby to baffle, the incentives generated by the electoral system: legislators who win by a narrow margin can be expected to be strongly constrained by the system's incentives, whereas legislators who rest on comfortable margins are not similarly constrained and are free to pursue other, even nonelectoral, interests (André, Depauw, and Martin 2015; Heitshusen, Young, and Wood 2005).

Additionally, electoral system effects have all too frequently been studied in isolation. The behavioral mechanisms underpinning electoral system effects necessitate human discretion—allowing context to exert a greater mediating impact and thereby to hamper our understanding of such system effects (Ferree, Powell, and Scheiner 2013). Contextual factors may include candidate selection procedures, electoral volatility, turnover, and devolution. Scholars have argued that inclusive candidate selection procedures may introduce incentives to cultivate a more personal support even in closed-list systems (Hazan and Rahat 2010; Atmor, Hazan, and Rahat 2011; Itzkovitch-Malka and Hazan 2017).

Moreover, a party's strategy to concentrate on mobilizing core supporters or chasing nonpartisans is shaped by country-, district-, and even party-level differences in electoral volatility (Rohrschneider and Whitefield 2012). High levels of electoral volatility may decidedly dampen a legislator's enthusiasm for a partisan role orientation (André, Depauw, and Beyens 2015): doing so would hardly ingratiate them with the growing scores of nonpartisans.

There are some indications that role orientations may change over the course of a legislator's career (Patzelt 1997; see also Fenno 1978). If so, aggregate-level differences in turnover between legislatures may affect observed role orientations, hiding from view possible electoral system effects.

Finally, insofar as role orientations differ by policy area (see earlier), the changing institutional architecture of politics in multilevel democracies may be expected to impact the roles played in the legislative arena (André, Bradbury, and Depauw 2014). If local economic policy is set by the regional authorities, not the federal, for instance, there are likely fewer federal legislators who embrace a strong district focus, or district delegate style, of representation. Insofar as context matters, therefore, we may well continue to wrongly underestimate the impact of electoral systems.

At the same time, conceptual and operational headaches continue to plague the role concept. As an intervening variable, it may provide the linking pin tying legislators' behavior to the electoral institutions governing their (re-)election. But, insofar as the role orientations as currently identified are neither exhaustive nor mutually distinct, what is the concept's added value? What's more, roles cannot be observed beyond individuals' internal attitudes and motivations. As such, using the same survey data to connect legislators' self-reported behavior to these attitudes and motivations may come perilously close to being tautological.

In this sense, the changing political landscape will increasingly challenge the notion that elected representatives can with any certainty delineate the groups of people whom they are representing and who in turn will see them returned to parliament. On the one hand, the growing trend toward individualization in society has dramatically undercut the presence of stable and homogenous social or ideological categories of citizens that underpin legislative roles (Andeweg 2003). The roots of political parties in society especially have withered, but not just those of political parties (Dalton 2004). Other social collectivities are similarly affected. On the other hand, the growing pace of social, economic, and technological change renders the public agenda unpredictable. Many new issues, particularly those involving identity such as gender, race, or ethnicity, that are nonterritorial clamor for inclusion on the political agenda (Urbinati and Warren 2008). To incorporate these new issues, political theorists have increasingly revived the notions of surrogate representation (Mansbridge 2003; Pitkin 1967) or even turned to representation by unelected private individuals (Saward 2009). By contrast, the manner in which roles are captured has been virtually unchanged for over fifty years! A critical re-examination and update of the content of roles, one that is not harking back to the social cleavages of the past, is certainly called for.

## NOTES

1. Saward (2010), for instance, states that any representative claim combines both an *aesthetic* (agency) and a *cultural* (structure) moment.
2. Insofar as role orientations include particular patterns of behavior—as both Searing (1994) and Strøm (1997) would seem to suggest, they are but a mere label or shorthand, not an explanation, of behavior.
3. A possible fourth, aggregate-level, mechanism may be discerned, rooted in the relative strength of mainstream and niche parties. District magnitude increases systems' proportionality and lowers the threshold for niche political parties to gain representation. But the

mechanism underpinning the association pertains more to the partisan culture than the electoral system per se. Even though there is some dispute among scholars as to the definition of niche parties (Ezrow 2010; Meguid 2010), most agree that party strategies differ by type: legislators representing niche parties can be expected to favor a partisan (or group) focus of representation that is not concentrated on the median voter within a particular geographical area (Ezrow et al. 2011; Adams et al. 2006).

4. Searing (1994, 486), for instance, defines the party as a disposition, not a role: "a disposition that functions like a decision rule and can be applied to MPs *in any role*." By contrast, others (Andeweg 1997; Scully and Farrell 2003) have defined the partisan as a full-blown role orientation.

5. Also see Colomer's chapter in this volume.

## References

Adams, James, Michael Clark, Lawrence Ezrow, and Garrett Glasgow. "Are Niche Parties Fundamentally Different from Mainstream Parties? The Causes and the Electoral Consequences of Western European Parties' Policy Shifts, 1976-1998." *American Journal of Political Science* 50, no. 3 (2006): 513–529. doi:10.1111/j.1540-5907.2006.00199.x.

Alpert, Eugene J. "A Reconceptualization of Representational Role Theory." *Legislative Studies Quarterly* 4, no. 4 (1979): 587–603.

Andeweg, Rudy B. "Role Specialisation or Role Switching? Dutch MPs between Electorate and Executive." *Journal of Legislative Studies* 3, no. 1 (1997): 110–127. doi:10.1080/13572339708420502.

Andeweg, Rudy B. "Beyond Representativeness? Trends in Political Representation." *European Review* 11, no. 2 (2003): 147–161. doi:10.1017/S1062798703000164.

Andeweg, Rudy B. "The Consequences of Representatives' Role Orientations: Attitudes, Behaviour, Perceptions." In *Parliamentary Roles in Modern Legislatures*, edited by Magnus Blomgren and Olivier Rozenberg, 66–84. Abingdon: Routledge, 2012.

Andeweg, Rudy B. "Roles in Legislatures." In *The Oxford Handbook of Legislative Studies*, edited by Shane Martin, Thomas Saalfeld, and Kaare W. Strøm, 267–285. Oxford: Oxford University Press, 2014. http://www.oxfordhandbooks.com/view/10.1093/oxfordhb/9780199653010.001.0001/oxfordhb-9780199653010-e-025.

Andeweg, Rudy B., and Jacques J. A. Thomassen. "Modes of Political Representation: Toward a New Typology." *Legislative Studies Quarterly* 30, no. 4 (2005): 507–528. doi:10.2307/3598548.

André, Audrey, Jonathan Bradbury, and Sam Depauw. "Constituency Service in Multi-Level Democracies." *Regional & Federal Studies* 24, no. 2 (2014): 129–150. doi:10.1080/13597566.2013.858708.

André, Audrey, and Sam Depauw. "Looking beyond the District: The Representation of Geographical Sub-Constituencies across Europe." *International Political Science Review* (2016). doi:10.1177/0192512116671527.

André, Audrey, and Sam Depauw. "The Quality of Representation and Satisfaction with Democracy: The Consequences of Citizen-Elite Policy and Process Congruence." *Political Behavior* 39, no. 2 (2017): 377–397. doi:10.1007/s11109-016-9360-x.

André, Audrey, Sam Depauw, and Rudy Andeweg. "Public and Politicians' Preferences on Priorities in Political Representation: The Consequences of an Unexplored Gap." In *Mind the Gap: Political Participation and Representation in Belgium*, edited by Kris Deschouwer. Colchester: ECPR Press, 2017.

André, Audrey, Sam Depauw, and Stefanie Beyens. "Party Loyalty and Electoral Dealignment." *Party Politics* 21, no. 6 (2015): 970–981. doi:10.1177/1354068813509521.

André, Audrey, Sam Depauw, and Kris Deschouwer. "State Structure and Political Representation: Comparing the Views of Statewide and Sub-State Legislators across 14 Countries." *European Journal of Political Research* 55, no. 4 (2016a): 866–884. doi:10.1111/1475-6765.12156.

André, Audrey, Sam Depauw, and Kris Deschouwer. "Institutional Constraints and Territorial Representation", 48–67. In *Political Representation: Roles, Representatives and the Represented*, edited by Mark Bühlmann and Jan Fivaz. London: Routledge, 2016b.

André, Audrey, Sam Depauw, and Shane Martin. "Electoral Systems and Legislators' Constituency Effort: The Mediating Effect of Electoral Vulnerability." *Comparative Political Studies* 48, no. 4 (2015): 464–496. doi:10.1177/0010414014545512.

André, Audrey, Sam Depauw, and Matthew S. Shugart. "The Effect of Electoral Institutions on Legislative Behavior." In *Oxford Handbook of Legislative Studies*, edited by Shane Martin, Thomas Saalfeld, and Kaare Strøm, 231–249. Oxford: Oxford University Press, 2014.

André, Audrey, Michael Gallagher, and Giulia Sandri. "Legislators' Constituency Orientation." In *Representing the People: A Survey among Members of Statewide and Substate Parliaments*, edited by Kris Deschouwer and Sam Depauw, 166–187. Oxford: Oxford University Press, 2014.

Atmor, Nir, Reuven Y. Hazan, and Gideon Rahat. "Candidate Selection." In *Personal Representation: The Neglected Dimension of Electoral Systems*, edited by Josep Maria Colomer, 21–35. ECPR—Studies in European Political Science. Colchester, UK: ECPR Press, 2011.

Bailer, Stefanie. "Interviews and Surveys in Legislative Research." In *Oxford Handbook of Legislative Studies*, edited by Shane Martin, Thomas Saalfeld, and Kaare Strøm, 167–193. Oxford: Oxford University Press, 2014.

Barker, David C., and Christopher J. Carman. *Representing Red and Blue: How the Culture Wars Change the Way Citizens Speak and Politicians Listen*. Series in Political Psychology. Oxford and New York: Oxford University Press, 2012.

Bengtsson, Åsa, and Hanna Wass. "Styles of Political Representation: What Do Voters Expect?" *Journal of Elections, Public Opinion and Parties* 20, no. 1 (2010): 55–81. doi:10.1080/17457280903450724.

Bengtsson, Åsa, and Hanna Wass. "The Representative Roles of MPs: A Citizen Perspective." *Scandinavian Political Studies* 34, no. 2 (2011): 143–167. doi:10.1111/j.1467-9477.2011.00267.x.

Benoit, Kenneth. "The Endogeneity Problem in Electoral Studies: A Critical Re-Examination of Duverger's Mechanical Effect." *Electoral Studies* 21, no. 1 (2002): 35–46. doi:10.1016/S0261-3794(00)00033-0.

Bishin, Benjamin G. *Tyranny of the Minority: The Subconstituency Politics Theory of Representation*. Philadelphia: Temple University Press, 2009.

Blomgren, Magnus, and Olivier Rozenberg, eds. *Parliamentary Roles in Modern Legislatures*. Oxford: Routledge, 2012.

Bogdanor, Vernon, ed. *Representatives of the People? Parliamentarians and Constituents in Western Democracies*. Aldershot: Gower, 1985.

Bowler, Shaun, and David M. Farrell. "Legislator Shirking and Voter Monitoring: Impacts of European Parliament Electoral Systems upon Legislator-Voter Relationships." *JCMS: Journal of Common Market Studies* 31, no. 1 (1993): 45–70. doi:10.1111/j.1468-5965.1993.tb00447.x.

Carey, John M., and Simon Hix. "The Electoral Sweet Spot: Low-Magnitude Proportional Electoral Systems." *American Journal of Political Science* 55, no. 2 (2011): 383–397. doi:10.1111/j.1540-5907.2010.00495.x.

Carey, John M., and Simon Hix. "Policy Consequences of Electoral Rules." In *Political Science, Electoral Rules, and Democratic Governance*, edited by Mala Htun and G. Bingham Powell, 46–55. Washington, DC: APSA Task Force, 2013.

Carman, Christopher Jan. "Public Preferences for Parliamentary Representation in the UK: An Overlooked Link?" *Political Studies* 54, no. 1 (2006): 103–122.

Carman, Christopher Jan. "Assessing Preferences for Political Representation in the US." *Journal of Elections, Public Opinion & Parties* 17, no. 1 (2007): 1–19. doi:10.1080/13689880601132497.

Carman, Christopher, and Mark Shephard. "Electoral Poachers? An Assessment of Shadowing Behaviour in the Scottish Parliament." *Journal of Legislative Studies* 13, no. 4 (2007): 483–496. doi:10.1080/13572330701663587.

Chiru, Mihail, and Zsolt Enyedi. "Choosing Your Own Boss: Variations of Representation Foci in Mixed Electoral Systems." *Journal of Legislative Studies* 21, no. 4 (2015): 495–514. doi:10.1080/13572334.2015.1077025.

Colomer, Josep M. "It's Parties That Choose Electoral Systems (or, Duverger's Laws Upside Down)." *Political Studies* 53, no. 1 (2005): 1–21. doi:10.1111/j.1467-9248.2005.00514.x.

Converse, Philip E., and Roy Pierce. *Political Representation in France*. Cambridge: Belknap Press of Harvard University Press, 1986.

Cooper, Christopher A., and Lilliard E. Richardson. "Institutions and Representational Roles in American State Legislatures." *State Politics & Policy Quarterly* 6, no. 2 (2006): 174–194. doi:10.1177/153244000600600203.

Curini, Luigi, Willy Jou, and Vincenzo Memoli. "Satisfaction with Democracy and the Winner/Loser Debate: The Role of Policy Preferences and Past Experience." *British Journal of Political Science* 42, no. 2 (2012): 241–261. doi:10.1017/S0007123411000275.

Dalton, Russell J. *Democratic Challenges, Democratic Choices: The Erosion of Political Support in Advanced Industrial Democracies*. Oxford: Oxford University Press, 2004.

Deschouwer, Kris, Sam Depauw, and Audrey André. "Representing the People in Parliaments." In *Representing the People: A Survey among Members of Statewide and Sub-State Parliaments*, edited by Kris Deschouwer and Sam Depauw, 1–18. Oxford: Oxford University Press, 2014.

Doherty, David. "To Whom Do People Think Representatives Should Respond: Their District or the Country?" *Public Opinion Quarterly* 77, no. 1 (2013): 237–255. doi:10.1093/poq/nfs052.

Dudzińska, Agnieszka, Corentin Poyet, Olivier Costa, and Bernhard Weßels. "Representational Roles." In *Representing the People*, edited by Kris Deschouwer and Sam Depauw, 19–38. Oxford: Oxford University Press, 2014. http://www.oxfordscholarship.com/view/10.1093/acprof:oso/9780199684533.001.0001/acprof-9780199684533-chapter-2.

Erikson, Robert S., Norman R. Luttbeg, and William V. Holloway. "Knowing One's District: How Legislators Predict Referendum Voting." *American Journal of Political Science* 19, no. 2 (1975): 231–246. doi:10.2307/2110434.

Esaiasson, Peter. "How MPs Define Their Task." In *Beyond Westminster and Congress: The Nordic Experience*, edited by Peter Esaiasson and Knut Heidar, 51–82. Parliaments and Legislatures Series. Columbus: Ohio State University Press, 2000.

Ezrow, Lawrence. *Linking Citizens and Parties: How Electoral Systems Matter for Political Representation*. Oxford: Oxford University Press, 2010.

Ezrow, Lawrence, Catherine De Vries, Marco Steenbergen, and Erica Edwards. "Mean Voter Representation and Partisan Constituency Representation: Do Parties Respond to the Mean Voter Position or to Their Supporters?" *Party Politics* 17, no. 3 (2011): 275–301. doi:10.1177/1354068810372100.

Farrell, David M., and Ian McAllister. "Voter Satisfaction and Electoral Systems: Does Preferential Voting in Candidate-Centred Systems Make a Difference?" *European Journal of Political Research* 45, no. 5 (2006): 723–749. doi:10.1111/j.1475-6765.2006.00633.x.

Farrell, David M., and Roger Scully. "Electing the European Parliament: How Uniform Are 'Uniform' Electoral Systems?" *JCMS: Journal of Common Market Studies* 43, no. 5 (2005): 969–984. doi:10.1111/j.1468-5965.2005.00604.x.

Farrell, David M., and Roger Scully. "The European Parliament: One Parliament, Several Modes of Political Representation on the Ground?" *Journal of European Public Policy* 17, no. 1 (2010): 36–54. doi:10.1080/13501760903465173.

Fenno, Richard F. *Home Style: House Members in Their Districts*. Boston: Longman, 1978.

Ferree, Karen E., G. Bingham Powell, and Ethan Scheiner. "How Context Shapes the Effects of Electoral Rules." In *Political Science, Electoral Rules, and Democratic Governance*, edited by Mala Htun and G. Bingham Powell, 14–30. Washington, DC: APSA Task Force, 2013.

Grant, J. Tobin, and Thomas J. Rudolph. "The Job of Representation in Congress: Public Expectations and Representative Approval." *Legislative Studies Quarterly* 29, no. 3 (2004): 431–445. doi:10.3162/036298004X201249.

Griffin, J. D., and P. Flavin. "How Citizens and Their Legislators Prioritize Spheres of Representation." *Political Research Quarterly* 64, no. 3 (2011): 520–533. doi:10.1177/1065912910373552.

Grofman, Bernard. "Comparisons among Electoral Systems: Distinguishing between Localism and Candidate-Centered Politics." *Electoral Studies* 24, no. 4 (2005): 735–740. doi:10.1016/j.electstud.2005.03.007.

Hazan, Reuven Y., and Gideon Rahat. *Democracy within Parties: Candidate Selection Methods and Their Political Consequences*. Oxford: Oxford University Press, 2010.

Hedlund, Ronald D., and H. Paul Friesema. "Representatives' Perceptions of Constituency Opinion." *Journal of Politics* 34, no. 3 (1972): 730–752. doi:10.2307/2129280.

Heitshusen, Valerie, Garry Young, and David M. Wood. "Electoral Context and MP Constituency Focus in Australia, Canada, Ireland, New Zealand, and the United Kingdom." *American Journal of Political Science* 49, no. 1 (2005): 32–45.

Ilonszki, Gabriella. "Representation Deficit in a New Democracy: Theoretical Considerations and the Hungarian Case." *Communist and Post-Communist Studies* 31, no. 2 (1998): 157–170. doi:10.1016/S0967-067X(98)00004-X.

Itzkovitch-Malka, Reut, and Reuven Y. Hazan. "Unpacking Party Unity: The Combined Effects of Electoral Systems and Candidate Selection Methods on Legislative Attitudes and Behavioural Norms." *Political Studies* 65, no. 2 (2017): 452–474. doi:10.1177/0032321716634094.

Jewell, Malcolm E. "Attitudinal Determinants of Legislative Behavior: The Utility of Role Analysis." In *Legislatures in Developmental Perspective*, edited by Allan Kornberg and Lloyd D. Musolf, 460–500. Durham, NC: Duke University Press, 1970.

Jewell, Malcolm E. "Legislator-Constituency Relations and the Representative Process." *Legislative Studies Quarterly* 8, no. 3 (1983): 303–337.

Kielhorn, Achim. *Rollenorientierungen von Abgeordneten in Europa*. Berlin: Freie Universität Berlin, 2001.

Kim, Myunghee. "Cross-National Analyses of Satisfaction with Democracy and Ideological Congruence." *Journal of Elections, Public Opinion and Parties* 19, no. 1 (2009): 49–72. doi:10.1080/17457280802568402.

Kingdon, John W. "Models of Legislative Voting." *Journal of Politics* 39, no. 3 (1977): 563–595. doi:10.2307/2129644.

Klingemann, Hans-Dieter, and Bernhard Wessels. "Political Consequences of Germany's Mixed-Member System: Personalization at the Grassroots?" In *Mixed-Member Electoral Systems the Best of Both Worlds?*, edited by Matthew Soberg Shugart and Martin P. Wattenberg, 279–296. Oxford: Oxford University Press, 2001. http://site.ebrary.com/id/10283339.

Koop, Royce, and John Kraemer. "Wards, At-Large Systems and the Focus of Representation in Canadian Cities." *Canadian Journal of Political Science* 49, no. 3 (2016): 433–448. doi:10.1017/S0008423916000512.

Lapinski, J., M. Levendusky, K. Winneg, and K. H. Jamieson. "What Do Citizens Want from Their Member of Congress?" *Political Research Quarterly* 69, no. 3 (2016): 535–545. doi:10.1177/1065912916652240.

Lijphart, Arend. *Electoral Systems and Party Systems: A Study of Twenty-Seven Democracies, 1945-1990.* Comparative European Politics. Oxford: Oxford University Press, 1994.

Lundberg, Thomas Carl. *Proportional Representation and the Constituency Role in Britain.* Basingstoke: Palgrave Macmillan, 2007.

Maestas, Cherie D., Sarah Fulton, L. Sandy Maisel, and Walter J. Stone. "When to Risk It? Institutions, Ambitions, and the Decision to Run for the U.S. House." *American Political Science Review* 100, no. 2 (2006): 195–208. doi:10.1017/S0003055406062101.

Maisel, L. Sandy, and Walter J. Stone. "Determinants of Candidate Emergence in U.S. House Elections: An Exploratory Study." *Legislative Studies Quarterly* 22, no. 1 (1997): 79–96.

Mansbridge, Jane. "Rethinking Representation." *American Political Science Review* 97, no. 4 (2003): 515–528. doi:10.1017/S0003055403000856.

Mansbridge, Jane. "A 'Selection Model' of Political Representation." *Journal of Political Philosophy* 17, no. 4 (2009): 369–398. doi:10.1111/j.1467-9760.2009.00337.x.

Meguid, Bonnie M. *Party Competition between Unequals: Strategies and Electoral Fortunes in Western Europe.* Cambridge: Cambridge University Press, 2010.

Mitchell, Paul. "Voters and Their Representatives: Electoral Institutions and Delegation in Parliamentary Democracies." *European Journal of Political Research* 37, no. 3 (2000): 335–351. doi:10.1023/A:1007025105144.

Morgenstern, Scott, and Javier Vázquez-D'Elía. "Electoral Laws, Parties, and Party Systems in Latin America." *Annual Review of Political Science* 10, no. 1 (2007): 143–168. doi:10.1146/annurev.polisci.10.081205.094050.

Müller, Wolfgang C. "Political Parties in Parliamentary Democracies: Making Delegation and Accountability Work." *European Journal of Political Research* 37, no. 3 (2000): 309–333. doi:10.1111/1475-6765.00515.

Myerson, Roger B. "Incentives to Cultivate Favored Minorities under Alternative Electoral Systems." *American Political Science Review* 87, no. 4 (1993): 856–869.

Norris, Pippa. *Electoral Engineering: Voting Rules and Political Behavior.* Cambridge: Cambridge University Press, 2004.

Norris, Pippa. "Cultural Explanations of Electoral Reform: A Policy Cycle Model." *West European Politics* 34, no. 3 (2011): 531–550. doi:10.1080/01402382.2011.555982.

Önnudóttir, Eva H. "Political Parties and Styles of Representation." *Party Politics*, 22, no. 6 (2016): 732–745. doi:10.1177/1354068814560934.

Patzelt, Werner J. "German MPs and Their Roles." *Journal of Legislative Studies* 3, no. 1 (1997): 55–78. doi:10.1080/13572339708420499.

Persson, Torsten, and Guido Enrico Tabellini. *The Economic Effects of Constitutions*. Munich Lectures in Economics. Cambridge, MA: MIT Press, 2003.

Pilet, Jean-Benoit, André Freire, and Olivier Costa. "Ballot Structure, District Magnitude and Constituency-Orientation of MPs in Proportional Representation and Majority Electoral Systems." *Representation* 48, no. 4 (2012): 359–372. doi:10.1080/00344893.2012.720880.

Pitkin, Hanna F. *The Concept of Representation*. Berkeley: University of California Press, 1967.

Powell, G. Bingham. *Elections as Instruments of Democracy: Majoritarian and Proportional Visions*. New Haven, CT: Yale University Press, 2000.

Przeworski, Adam. "Institutions Matter?" *Government and Opposition* 39, no. 4 (2004): 527–540. doi:10.1111/j.1477-7053.2004.00134.x.

Rehfeld, Andrew. *The Concept of Constituency: Political Representation, Democratic Legitimacy, and Institutional Design*. Cambridge and New York: Cambridge University Press, 2005.

Renwick, Alan, and Jean-Benoit Pilet. *Faces on the Ballot. The Personalization of Electoral Systems in Europe*. Oxford: Oxford University Press, 2015.

Rohrschneider, Robert, and Stephen Whitefield. "Institutional Context and Representational Strain in Party–Voter Agreement in Western and Eastern Europe." *West European Politics* 35, no. 6 (2012): 1320–1340. doi:10.1080/01402382.2012.713748.

Saward, Michael. "Authorisation and Authenticity: Representation and the Unelected." *Journal of Political Philosophy* 17, no. 1 (2009): 1–22. doi:10.1111/j.1467-9760.2008.00309.x.

Saward, Michael. *The Representative Claim*. Oxford: Oxford University Press, 2010.

Scully, Roger, and David M. Farrell. "MEPs as Representatives: Individual and Institutional Roles." *JCMS: Journal of Common Market Studies* 41, no. 2 (2003): 269–288. doi:10.1111/1468-5965.00422.

Searing, Donald. *Westminster's World: Understanding Political Roles*. Cambridge, MA: Harvard University Press, 1994.

Searing, Donald. "Foreword." In *Parliamentary Roles in Modern Legislatures*, edited by Magnus Blomgren and Olivier Rozenberg, xxi. Oxford: Routledge, 2012.

Shugart, Matthew Søberg. "Electoral 'Efficiency' and the Move to Mixed-Member Systems." *Electoral Studies* 20, no. 2 (2001): 173–193. doi:10.1016/S0261-3794(00)00007-X.

Shugart, Matthew Søberg, and Martin P Wattenberg, eds. *Mixed-Member Electoral Systems the Best of Both Worlds?* Oxford: Oxford University Press, 2001. http://site.ebrary.com/id/10283339.

Strøm, Kaare. "Rules, Reasons and Routines: Legislative Roles in Parliamentary Democracies." *Journal of Legislative Studies* 3, no. 1 (1997): 155–174. doi:10.1080/13572339708420504.

Thomassen, Jacques. "Empirical Research into Political Representation: Failing Democracy or Failing Models?" In *Elections at Home and Abroad: Essays in Honor of Warren E. Miller*, edited by Warren E. Miller, M. Kent Jennings, and Thomas E. Mann, 237–264. Ann Arbor: University of Michigan Press, 1994.

Thomassen, Jacques, and Rudy B. Andeweg. "Beyond Collective Representation: Individual Members of Parliament and Interest Representation in the Netherlands." *Journal of Legislative Studies* 10, no. 4 (2004): 47–69. doi:10.1080/1357233042000322463.

Urbinati, Nadia, and Mark E. Warren. "The Concept of Representation in Contemporary Democratic Theory." *Annual Review of Political Science* 11, no. 1 (2008): 387–412. doi:10.1146/annurev.polisci.11.053006.190533.

Vivyan, Nick, and Markus Wagner. "House or Home? Constituent Preferences over Legislator Effort Allocation." *European Journal of Political Research* 55, no. 1 (2016): 81–99. doi:10.1111/1475-6765.12119.

Von Schoultz, Åsa, and Hanna Wass. "Beating Issue Agreement: Congruence in the Representational Preferences of Candidates and Voters." *Parliamentary Affairs* 69, no. 1 (2016): 136–158. doi:10.1093/pa/gsv001.

Wahlke, John C., Heinz Eulau, William Buchanan, and LeRoy C. Ferguson. *The Legislative System: Explorations in Legislative Behavior*. New York: Wiley, 1962.

Wessels, Bernhard. "Whom to Represent? Role Orientations of Legislators in Europe." In *Political Representation and Legitimacy in the European Union*, edited by Hermann Schmitt and J. J. A. Thomassen, 209–234. Oxford: Oxford University Press, 1999.

Zittel, Thomas. "Legislators and Their Representational Roles: Strategic Choices or Habits of the Heart?" In *Parliamentary Roles in Modern Legislatures*, edited by Magnus Blomgren and Olivier Rozenberg, 101–120. Oxford: Routledge, 2012.

..............................................................................................

# CHAPTER 17

# ELECTORAL SYSTEMS AND CONSTITUENCY SERVICE

..............................................................................................

BRIAN F. CRISP AND WILLIAM M. SIMONEAU

## CONSTITUENCY SERVICE

..............................................................................................

CONSTITUENCY service by a member of the legislature involves activities addressing the nonpolicy grievances or looking out for the nonpolicy interests of citizens in the member's district.[1] Because the actions are not related to government or opposition programs, they are often, though not always, nonpartisan in nature as well. The term is used typically to describe private or club goods benefiting an individual or a relatively small group within the district. It is not clear if this last distinction is necessary by definition or if the provision of some public goods could also constitute constituency service.

Efforts to understand constituency service often involve references to other phenomena like home style, going home, pork barrel, and the personal vote. "Home style" refers to the way that a legislator behaves when in his or her district. While this may include engaging in constituency service, home style includes policy elements as well. A type of behavior central to the concept is the explanation of one's behavior on "the Hill," for example (Fenno 1978). The justification of one's policy positions falls outside the domain of constituency service. "Going home" is, self-evidently, travel back to one's district, and it is sometimes used to capture the level of commitment to constituency service (Fenno 1978). However, as with home style, members may frequently travel to their districts for reasons other than for engaging in constituency service. Aside from visiting loved ones, they may be raising campaign funds or giving policy-focused speeches, for example—neither of which constitutes constituency service. Particularized benefits— sometimes referred to as "pork barrel"—refer to the allocation of funds by the national government to projects for which a member of congress can credibly claim responsibility (Mayhew 1974, 52–59). To meet this last criterion in a single-seat district setting like the United States, these projects are typically given out to a specific individual, group, or geographic constituency, the scale of the recipient unit being such that a single congress-person can claim credit for the spending. In addition, the benefit must be given out in an ad hoc or discretionary fashion with the representative apparently having a hand in the allocation. These personal vote-earning attributes mean that pork barrel shares important characteristics with constituency service. Still, we would argue that particularized benefits might be considered distinct to the extent that they are not service, per se. What is more, pork barrel cannot be considered entirely a subset of constituency service if it cannot be delivered by the individual member or handful of members claiming credit for it. It may require a spending decision by the executive or be part of a legislative logroll—the trading of votes by one legislator or one group of legislators in support of an outcome preferred by others with the understanding that the legislator or legislators receiving support this time will return the favor in the future—requiring the cooperation of dozens if not hundreds of elected representatives. However, the increasing prevalence of "constituency development funds"—arrangements that channel spending from the central government directly to projects located in individual electoral districts, usually local infrastructure projects, chosen at the discretion of the legislator (Mezey 2014)—certainly seems to blur the line between constituency service and pork barrel spending.

"The personal vote" is the portion of a candidate's support that is earned due to individual attributes or activities (Cain, Ferejohn, and Fiorina 1987). Constituency service, given that it is delivered by an individual member of congress to recipients within his or her district, is often characterized as an effort to cultivate a personal vote. It is this connection between constituency service and the personal vote that brings constituency service into close contact with home style, going home, and pork barrel. The behaviors captured by all of these labels are often conceived of as sources of the personal vote. So, while constituency service and the personal vote are often associated with one another, theoretically and empirically, their relationship is not an exclusive one. Throughout this contribution to the handbook we will seek to elaborate on and clarify the relationship among all these concepts.

With some work on definitions out of the way, we will proceed as follows. In the next section we discuss the intimate connection between constituency service provision and *electoral system type* that seems to exist in the literature, showing that it is typically personal vote-seeking incentives embodied in electoral rules that are identified as the causal mechanism relating the two. Following that, we will simply catalog some of the activities that are identified in the existing literature as *examples of* constituency service. Where appropriate, we will comment on whether the form of constituency service measured in a particular study appears to be a function of electoral system type. Going beyond electoral system type, we will then discuss other *determinants of* the extent of constituency service carried out across legislatures and across members within a given legislature, highlighting representatives' contextual need for a vote-earning boost, on the one hand, and constituents' need for representation in the form of service on the other. We then turn briefly to the relatively less studied *consequences of* engaging in constituency service. As with determinants, we look for a pattern connecting the impact of constituency service with differences in electoral rules. We will conclude by offering some suggestions for future research.

## Constituency Service and Electoral Systems

Much of the existing literature proposes that the nature of constituency service makes it a prime strategy for enhancing a legislator's personal reputation. It is typically the case that a single member of congress (MC) or member of parliament (MP) can claim credit for the nonpolicy benefit delivered to an individual constituent or a small group of constituents within his or her district. As Mayhew (1974, 53) notes, members of the assembly "try to peel off pieces of governmental accomplishment for which [they] can generate a sense of responsibility." Not surprisingly, then, several works in the existing literature have cited and/or explored the personal vote-seeking incentives imposed by electoral rules (Carey and Shugart 1995) as determinants of the decision to engage in constituency service and as determinants of whether a meaningful number of votes can be awarded to the specific candidate or groups of candidates who provide it. Being able to claim credit for having provided constituency service is particularly valuable where personal vote-seeking incentives are high, and the votes such service garners may end up making the difference for an individual incumbent between winning re-election and being unseated.

The earliest works in the field focused exclusively on the United States, Britain, or a comparison of the two (Mayhew 1974; Fenno 1978; Cain et al. 1987; Searing 1994). As a result, electoral system incentives were identified as key to why representatives would provide constituency service and as key to how they might lead to re-election of those who best provided it. However, given that electoral rules were being held constant—single-seat district decided by plurality (or first past the post [FPTP])—any leverage over the variation in the provision and consequences of constituency service had to be gained from variables that actually varied given the research design, like the electoral vulnerability of the member or the member's need to focus on keeping a government in power in a parliamentary system.

Later studies also focused on the importance of electoral system incentives. As they branched out to cases other than the United States and Britain, scholars began to think about the relationship between other sets of electoral incentives and constituency service. In addition to examining additional individual systems (where a contrast with FPTP could be speculated about if not directly tested), some works included multiple national cases where electoral systems varied across those cases—and much less frequently, within cases (in the form of district magnitude). In conceptual terms, where access to the ballot or the nature of the ballot allows voters to signal a preference for one candidate in a party over other candidates from that same party, a personal vote is prized.

Likewise, where a vote cast at a level lower than the party does not pool to the level of the party for seat allocation purposes, again candidates are incentivized to develop a reputation distinct from that of the reputation of their parties.

With the exception of alternative vote rules—where voters rank candidates and votes are transferred until a single candidate has majority support—differences in electoral incentives, as compared to those in FPTP systems, include the use of multiseat districts. Where intraparty competition is ensconced, personal vote-seeking incentives may be multiplied as district magnitude increases, pitting more members of a party against one another.[2] The inverse may be true in systems without intraparty competition, with increasing magnitude obscuring the importance of individual candidates. One wrinkle when it comes to the connection between personal vote-seeking incentives and constituency service is whether multiseat districts complicate the connection. Does the fact that there are, by definition, multiple sitting representatives from a given district make it difficult for any one of them to claim credit for having provided constituency service? Or is the delivery of the service so intimate that attributing its arrival to a particular incumbent is not complicated?

Bowler and Farrell (1993), surveying members of the European Parliament (MEPs) from a dozen countries, concluded that electoral system effects were the biggest determinant of time spent on constituency service. More specifically, they found that where the ballot allows for "candidate-specific" voting, an MEP is more likely to receive requests for attention from individual constituents. They also used the term "magnitude" to refer to national list, regional list, and a "district-based" system, finding the latter to be regularly associated with time spent on individual voters' requests.

Based on interviews with junior parliamentarians in Britain and Ireland, Wood and Young (1997) concluded that constituency service provision was much greater in Ireland and that the Irish parliamentarians (or TDs) were much more likely to think that their re-election prospects were a function of the constituency service they provided. The single-transferrable vote (STV) system employed in Ireland, which entails intraparty competition in multiseat districts, has greater personal vote-seeking incentives than the FPTP system used in Britain. This would seem to indicate that TDs, despite the existence of other sitting incumbents in the district, felt that any rewards for the service they provided would be attributed to them individually.

In the US context, Harden (2013) coded for variation in district magnitude for electing legislators at the state level, hypothesizing that as the number of seats to be chosen increased, members may shirk on things like constituency service (apparently regardless of whether intraparty competition is permitted). He used an experiment sent to legislative offices via e-mail where the respondent assigned priority to a service request, an allocation request, or a policy request. He found that the priority given service requests declined with magnitude. Likewise, in a study focused primarily on legislator gender and constituency service (women do more, by the way), Freeman and Richardson Jr. (1996) found that the members across four American states elected in multiseat districts reported fewer requests for service than members in single-seat districts.

Surveying MPs across six chambers in five countries, Heitshusen, Young, and Wood (2005) concluded that district magnitude was negatively associated with a constituency focus where the lists were closed, meaning the ballot prevented voters from distinguishing copartisans from one another.[3] Conversely, surveying members of congress in Colombia, where voters could distinguish among candidates from the same party and votes pooled only to the subparty level (personal vote-seeking incentives were very high), Ingall and Crisp (2001) found that trips back home were associated with increasing district magnitude, referring to the number of seats to be handed out in a district. More specifically, they found that a drop from a district with the mean number of seats, forty, to the minimum number of two leads to approximately a 35 percent fall in the expected number of trips home. Again, this would seem to indicate that the existence of multiple incumbents within a district did nothing to dampen the sense that individual credit claiming was possible, instead, apparently, enhancing that sense.

It would stand to reason that if electoral rules are to influence legislator behavior in terms of constituency service, legislators must be able to seek and win re-election. Yet, Taylor (1992) found constituency service provision in a very inhospitable institutional environment—Costa Rica—where legislators are chosen by closed-list proportional representation (CLPR) and they are prohibited from re-election. She explained that they are induced by their party leaders to provide service to constituents because the leaders believe it reinforces support for the party in the district. Because legislators cannot run for re-election, party leaders control their futures if they wish to stay in politics, giving those leaders the leverage to insist upon service by representatives who will not be running again.

Finally, looking at regional and national MPs across twelve countries, André and Depauw (2013) were able to allow ballot type (open vs. closed) and district magnitude to vary, examining the interaction of the two. They concluded that MPs' time in the district, view that the interests of the local area is their single most important project, and weekly contacts with interest organizations all follow the patterns predicted previously. As Carey and Shugart (1995) suggested, these personal vote-earning activities increased with magnitude under open-list proportional representation (OLPR) systems and decreased with magnitude in CLPR systems.[4]

# CAPTURING FORMS OF CONSTITUENCY SERVICE

In his classic work on home style, Fenno (1978) divided constituency service into two forms that continue to be useful distinctions. Individual casework is the provision of a service that directly benefits an individual constituent. The second, project assistance, is the provision of benefits to constituents on a larger scale that achieves some collective goal. Both forms frequently involve the redress of grievances between constituents and other government offices (Cain et al. 1987; Searing 1994). In terms of individual casework, Cain et al. (1987) claimed that in the United States, the most frequent grievances were related to problems with social security and veterans' benefits. Less frequently, MCs addressed issues related to immigration, unemployment, disputes with the Internal Revenue Service, health care, and civil service issues. In Great Britain, MPs most frequently remedied grievances related to housing, education, planning permits, and public utilities. Similarly, the mediation of constituents' interactions with other levels of government, or the national bureaucracy, can also be categorized as project assistance. In an example, Searing (1994) related the case of a British MP who, in response to complaints from his constituents, persuaded the local council to spend 25,000 GBP to improve a local park.

Individual casework and project assistance are typically captured with elite-level survey questions regarding how the representative spends his or her time. Johannes (1983, 1984) asked members of the US House and Senate the amount of time they devoted to casework, the size of their casework staffs, the percentage of casework carried out in home offices, the degree to which the member solicited casework, and the propensity to use casework for electoral or public relations purposes. Regarding the latter, he found 92 percent of House offices and 77 percent of Senate offices reported using constituency service for electoral or publicity purposes, but, in general, he struggled to find an explanation for the variation reported across members on any of the indicators of constituency service. In Britain, Norris (1997) measured constituency service with a composite of the following questions: "Roughly how many hours do you think you usually devote to: dealing with constituency casework, holding constituency surgeries, attending local party meetings, and attending other functions in your constituency?" She found that British MPs spend about a third of their time (twenty-five hours) on constituency service. A substantial portion of that time is devoted to individual casework.

Beyond these studies of FPTP systems, at least one study posed a similar question in a CLPR system. In a study of Turkish MPs, Hazama (2005) asked MPs: "How much time do you annually spend in your constituency?" and "How much time do you annually spend meeting your constituents for their personal problems?" The study found that Turkish MPs spent relatively more time in the capital devoting themselves to policy work instead of in their district conducting constituency service. This finding supports the suspected relationship between personal vote-seeking incentives and constituency service. In fact, the study found that, though district magnitude (the number of seats to be awarded) ranges from only two to six in Turkey, increasing magnitude was negatively correlated with carrying out constituency service activities.

In Australia, which uses alternative vote (AV) rules (where voters rank candidates and votes are transferred until a single candidate has majority support), McAllister (2015) asked MPs: "We are interested in the amount of time you spent in your electorate and what you did there. Thinking back over the past year, about how many hours per month did you usually devote to the following activities within your electorate?" Activities included aiding with constituents' problems, attending local community functions, and speaking at public meetings. Similar to Norris's finding in the United

Kingdom, where the FPTP rules institutionalize somewhat lower personal vote-seeking incentives, McAllister's results showed that Australian MPs devoted most of their constituency service time to individual casework.

The Irish Dáil is elected using STV rules. The multiseat districts lead to intraparty competition, thus increasing personal vote-seeking incentives relative to FPTP and AV. Martin (2010) asked Irish parliamentarians: "What is the proportion of the working week that is spent attending to constituency related activities?," and O'Leary (2011) asked TDs whether the time they devoted to casework varied between days when they were in their Dáil offices and days when they were in their constituency offices. Social welfare and housing grievances were the most common constituency service requests for TDs (O'Leary 2011). In addition, 86 percent of Irish TDs surveyed claim to hold regular clinics with their constituents, and 40 percent of TDs stated they personally spend two to four hours a week on constituency work.

As part of a large, cross-national study of members of national and subnational parliaments in several European countries, André and Depauw (2013) asked representatives not only how much time they spent on constituency service but also whether they took explicit actions to seek out constituents' grievances. Their results find that 40 percent of legislators spent five hours or more per week on individual casework, and 61 percent of legislators solicit cases from their constituents. As we noted earlier, they also found support for the differential effect of district magnitude on personal vote-earning activities across OLPR and CLPR systems.

In a demand-side approach of how elected representatives spend their time, Bowler and Farrell (1993) asked MEPs the proportion of requests they received from individuals and community interest groups as opposed to national interest groups. The various electoral systems used to select MEPs allowed for a cross-national comparison of the demand for constituency service. They found that in systems with district-level constituencies, as compared to regional and national lists, MEPs receive a greater number of requests from individual constituents.

Similarly, but in an FPTP setting, Lapinski et al. (2016) used two nationally representative surveys of citizens in the United States to look for differences across individuals that would explain whether they thought members of Congress should work on constituency service or should represent them on broad policy issues. In both, about one-third of citizens said that constituency service mattered a great deal when selecting a representative.

Beyond specific questions about time spent on constituency service, several studies have asked broader questions about how the MP or MC perceives his or her role—with some form of "servicing the constituency" as one of the response options offered. Using the PARTIREP[5] study, André and Depauw (2013) identified an MP's priorities by asking: "What do you yourself consider the most important task you fulfill as a Member of Parliament?" Legislators who responded "looking after the social and economic needs of the local area" were considered constituency focused. Roughly 30 percent of respondents claimed to have the constituency as their primary focus. Heitshusen et al. (2005) asked legislators in Australia (AV), Canada (FPTP), Ireland (STV), New Zealand (mixed-member proportional [MMP]), and the United Kingdom (FPTP): "What are your priorities?" Legislators who responded "serving the constituency" were considered to have a constituency focus. As expected, legislators in single-seat districts had higher levels of constituency focus compared to their counterparts elected in districts using CLPR. Variations of the question "Who do you primarily represent?" or "How do you prioritize your relationship with your constituents?" were used to capture the linkage between legislator and constituent in Hungary's MMP system (Judge and Ilonszki 1995), Australia's AV system (Studlar and McAllister 1996), Canada's FPTP system (Clarke 1978), and Ireland's STV system (Martin 2010).

Although time spent in one's district can be used to engage in aspects of representation unrelated to constituency service, it is a common indicator of time spent on constituency service. André, Depauw, and Martin (2015) measure constituency effort in fourteen countries with the question "In a typical month, how many working hours would you say you spend in your constituency?" The results range from Spain and France, where legislators spend about thirty hours per week in their districts, down to Israel, where MPs spend on average two hours per week in their districts (given the nationwide district, defined as "area of residence"). The results for members of regional parliaments show a greater amount of time spent in one's district, with Spanish and Austrian regional legislators spending about thirty-six hours per week in their districts. Likewise, Ingall and Crisp (2001) used legislator self-reporting of trips home to talk generally about variation in Colombian MCs' "awareness of their constituents' wishes and . . . the importance that they attribute to district matters." Colombian MCs surveyed all returned to their districts at least once a month, and 67 percent returned every weekend. In a related way of getting at the same concept, MPs in Ireland and the United Kingdom were asked how many days per week they spent in their constituencies (Wood and Young 1997); MPs in New Zealand were asked whether they lived in their constituencies (Anagnoson 1983), and MCs and MPs in the United States and United Kingdom, respectively, were queried if they regularly (twice a month) visited their district (Cain et al. 1987).

Self-reporting through surveys is the primary identifier of constituency service. Exceptions include Martin (2011), who analyzed parliamentary questions in Ireland to identify constituency focus. TD Leo Varadkar, for example, asked the minister for education and science the government's position regarding the provision of a sports hall and extension for a school in Dublin 15. As another example, Edward O'Keeffe asked the minister for agriculture about the status of farm grant payments to an individual constituent in County Cork. Sozzi (2016) used a similar approach with parliamentary questions in the European Parliament as a measure of constituency focus by Italian and French MEPs.

In a field experiment extending the study of Butler and Broockman (2011) to local councils in South Africa, McClendon (2016) captured constituency service as the responsiveness of a lawmaker to e-mail requests. Digital indicators of constituency service, like Butler and Broockman's (2011) e-mail field experiment, seem to be more commonplace in the US context than elsewhere. In the nascent days of the Internet, Adler,

Gent, and Overmeyer (1998) measured the number of constituency components on the homepage of those members of Congress who had websites. Constituency components included constituency service information, contact information for congressional offices, contact information for district or Washington DC staff, and e-mail availability. In a study of the Texas state legislature, Dropp and Peskowitz (2012) sent six e-mails (three regarding a government program and three requests soliciting information on voter registration) to the personal e-mail addresses of each state legislator and counted the number of responses received per legislator.

Beyond digital indicators, observations of constituency service actually being conducted are quite rare. Sometimes the indicators chosen seem somewhat distant from the concept of interest. In a cross-state study, King (1991) used the entire legislature's operating budget as a measure of the resources available to incumbents for constituency service. Acknowledging the broad-brush nature of such an indicator, he noted that these were the funds that could have been used for constituency service, not those that were. Parker and Goodman (2009) used the amount of money spent on franked mail as a measure of constituency service. They argued that members of Congress have great flexibility in the mail that they are able to send, and that their mailings frequently contained news about successful constituency project assistance, upcoming local meetings, and solicitation of grievances. As additional measures of constituency service, Parker and Goodman (2009) captured an MC's attention to constituency service through dollars per mile for travel to the district and the level of expenditures carried out by the MC's office in his or her district. Again, though trips to one's constituents do not necessarily hone in on constituency service, Crisp and Desposato (2004) provided a test of how elected representatives target constituents with a set of travel records for members of the Colombian Senate.

In sum, the measurement of constituency service has primarily occurred through elite-level surveys. Systematic measures of the task actually being carried out are rare (with the few exceptions noted previously). Most studies of the concept have focused on single-country studies. Cain et al. (1987), Heitshusen et al. (2005), André and Depauw (2013), and André et al. (2015) have provided cross-national studies of constituency service, as well as methods for capturing constituency service across varied electoral and legislative settings. Although studies of constituency service involved a variety of electoral systems, measures employed in the existing literature for capturing constituency service do not appear to vary as a function of electoral rules.

# ELECTORAL CONCERNS AS DETERMINANTS OF CONSTITUENCY SERVICE

The extent to which legislators engage in constituency service is typically attributed to electoral concerns. Reviewing the existing literature, the electoral connection appears in at least two different, but related, guises: as electoral margins indicated by past performance and as constituents' need for or demand for representation in the form of service. After reviewing the literature in these terms, we will conclude by listing miscellaneous other factors beyond electoral concerns that have been cited as determinants of where and when elected representatives will most likely engage in constituency service.

Scholars have concluded that vulnerability leads to increased attention to constituency service. Talking to MPs in Great Britain, Buck and Cain (1990) came away with the strong impression that the competitiveness of the electoral district was a big determinant of whether the sitting MP was a faithful constituent servant. Specifically, they pointed out that the three most active members in their sample occupied seats that had been recently occupied by another party or demographically should have been. In the study of Colombian MCs mentioned earlier, Ingall and Crisp (2001) found that the electorally most vulnerable members had a predicted number of trips home that was nearly twice as frequent as their fellow incumbents who had won by the widest margin. Crisp and Desposato (2004) found a related outcome. With a unique dataset of flight destinations, they modeled where Colombian senators chose to visit each weekend with their government-provided airline tickets. They found that senators flew to destinations where they had won many votes but that the rate of increased visits slowed as the senators became less electorally vulnerable. As we noted previously, Dropp and Peskowitz (2012) sent e-mail requests to members of the Texas state legislature. Those in the most vulnerable or marginal districts responded more frequently. Note that in both FPTP systems, as in the United States, and in subparty list PR systems where most lists elect only a single member, as in Colombia, it is possible to conceive of margin of victory at the level of the individual candidate. These are zero-sum contests, with a drop below threshold not signaling one fewer of multiple seats, but instead signaling zero seats. Again, the individualistic nature of the service connection seems key.

That said, looking at local party organizations elected to city councils in Belgium, André et al. (2013) take a more collective approach. They concluded that parties are most likely to provide constituency service as they approach holding a majority on the council, but their likelihood of offering such services declines with majority status. In other words, it is not the individual candidate's vulnerability but the party's collective vulnerability that determines service provisions. From a different angle, perhaps majority status means a party can deliver on policy promises that its members could not provide when they were in the minority. In all of these single-country designs, the incentives imposed by electoral institutions were held constant, with personal vote-seeking incentives being relatively high. In these contexts, electoral vulnerability made constituency service an efficient choice.

Returning to the Heitshusen et al. (2005) study with data from Australia (AV), Canada (FPTP), Ireland (STV), Great Britain (FPTP), and New Zealand (MMP), electoral vulnerability led to very high levels of constituency focus when looking only at the MPs in their sample from single-seat districts. When members elected in multiseat districts were included, the relationship became much less pronounced. When they looked at respondents chosen in single-seat districts, they found that even safe legislators were predicted to devote high levels of attention to constituency focus with a probability of .23, while those in marginal seats had a .71 probability of high constituency focus. When they added respondents from multiseat districts into their dataset, the safe to vulnerable effect was attenuated, ranging from a .32 probability of high constituency focus for safe members to a probability of .54 for the most vulnerable. Finally, based on surveys of MPs across fourteen countries, André et al. (2015) find that the differential effect of district magnitude on personal vote-seeking incentives identified by Carey and Shugart (1995) is modulated by electoral vulnerability. In candidate-centered systems, the positive effect of district magnitude on constituency service increases with electoral vulnerability. In systems with party-vote-seeking incentives, in contrast, district magnitude's negative effect on constituency service is weaker among the most vulnerable.

The second way in which an electoral imperative is used to explain constituency service is through efforts to capture constituents' need for or expectation of this kind of representation. Norris (1997) used MP survey data from Great Britain where MPs were asked to record the number of hours spent on constituency service. She found that two indicators of demand, levels of urbanization and size of the minority population, had positive, substantively small but statistically discernible effects on hours dedicated to constituency service.[6] Urbanization is a proxy for the number of constituents dependent on welfare services, and intervention with welfare service agencies is often a major part of an MP's caseload. Conversely, based on interviews with MPs in Ghana, Lindberg (2010, 126) reports that "citizens, especially rural folk, feel that they have morally sanctioned claims to assistance of their MPs." In the US context, Griffin and Flavin (2011) use survey responses to show that the priority given to constituency service—as opposed to policy representation and federal allocations—decreases with household income. In the André et al. (2013) study of local party organizations in Belgium, the authors found that prosperity was negatively related to parties' efforts to provide constituency service and that population density was positively associated with it. Dropp and Peskowitz (2012) found that in Texas, citizen respondents' wealth and degree of partisanship was associated with their sense of whether members of Congress should primarily engage in acts of constituency service (as opposed to broad policy representation). The relatively wealthy and the highly partisan less frequently demanded constituency service.

Butler and Broockman (2011) conducted a field experiment by e-mailing state legislators in the United States asking for help with voter registration. They randomized whether the sender had a putatively black or white name and found that both white and black representatives were more likely to respond to members of their own race. McClendon (2016) basically replicated this research in South Africa and found that politicians—both black and white—were more responsive to same-race than other-race constituents. This is not demand for constituency service as it is conceived of in the works cited immediately earlier, but it does say something about which constituents (and constituencies?) might feel most empowered to place such requests.

There are a number of other factors for which authors control when seeking to explain constituency service, but none of them gets the attention that the theoretical lines of reasoning summarized previously has received. For example, several works account for the nature of the constituency in nonelectoral terms, including whether the district is far from the capital (Heitshusen et al. 2005), whether it is geographically challenging to access (Abdel-Samad 2009), whether it is devoid of beach resorts (Crisp and Desposato 2004), or whether the kidnapping rate for politicians is quite high there (Crisp and Desposato 2004). All of these are negatively associated with receiving constituency service. Other studies account for characteristics of the MPs in not-directly electoral terms—is he or she a senior member/frontbencher (Norris 1997; Heitshusen et al. 2005; Russo 2011) or does the member hold a cabinet portfolio (Heitshusen et al. 2005)? This kind of career status is expected to diminish the likelihood of providing constituent service. Butler, Karpowitz, and Pope (2012) suggest that constituency service might be more compatible with some parties' ideologies than others. Democrats were more likely to respond to requests for service than were Republicans. Finally, some scholars referred to role theory—the idea that it is the legislator's perception of his or her duties as a representative that drives the provision of constituency service. A sense of role is probably the single most widespread challenger to an electoral explanation of constituency service (Freeman and Richardson Jr. 1996; Searing 1994; Halligan et al. 1988; Clarke 1978; Clarke, Price, and Krause 1975; Norton and Wood 1993), but the theory seems to have faded in popularity.

# THE CONSEQUENCES OF CONSTITUENCY SERVICE

There is much less work done on assessing the consequences of constituency service than there is on attempting to identify its determinants. Given the identification of "electoral concerns" of one sort or another as the primary determinants of the effort by MPs and MCs put into constituency service, it is not surprising that scholars looking for its consequences frequently turn to vote totals or outcomes they claim should be associated with vote totals.

Looking directly at vote totals themselves, support for the idea that constituency service boosts a member's electoral prospects has been somewhat checkered. Looking at results for the US House in 1978, Johannes and McAdams (1981) found no statistically discernible relationship between hours reported as spent on casework and percentage of the vote received. However, in a response, Fiorina (1981) criticized their expectations and their methods. In a reanalysis of their data, he found that casework had a substantively significant impact on electoral outcomes. Contrary to a positive impact on votes or even a lack of an effect, examining members of Australia's lower house, which is elected by AV, Studlar and McAllister (1996) actually found that hours engaged in constituency service, as reported by members of the house, were associated with fewer first-preference votes in the subsequent election. They suggest that this might be a function of having less time to spend on being a good party MP as a result of having devoted time to constituency service. In contrast, Martin (2010), looking at representatives in Ireland, who are elected by STV, found that constituency service was positively associated with an array of important electoral outcomes—the prospect of winning re-election, the number of first-preference votes received, and the proportion of the electoral quota achieved. Again, as with determinants, both FPTP and STV allow scholars to look at vote total consequences at the level of the individual MP responsible for less or for more constituency service.

Rather than looking at vote totals themselves, some scholars have looked for an impact on reported vote choice. Serra and Cover (1992) uniquely captured constituency service by looking at the files of an individual member of the US House to identify all the citizens in the member's district who had benefited directly from constituency service. They then surveyed those citizens and citizens who had not benefited from constituency service. They found that having received constituency service positively impacted reported vote choice in the MC's favor. In a survey of the subscribers to the e-newsletters of two members of the British House of Commons, Jackson (2006), assuming that the newsletter is primarily used to inform readers of the MP's constituency service, found that about 10 percent of respondents said that receiving the newsletter caused them to change their vote in the MP's favor. Using twenty years of National Election Survey data from the United States, Roscoe (2003) found a correlation between assessments of casework and ticket splitting—claiming to have voted for a legislative candidate not from the party of one's choice for the presidency. Again, a common thread here is the choice to examine FPTP systems.

Some scholars have looked for the consequences of constituency in approval measured at both the individual member level and the level of the institution. Ilonszki and Papp (2012) report descriptive statistics showing an increase in the levels of constituency service provided by members of Hungary's national parliament. They conclude that in Hungary's MMP system, this outreach has not been reciprocated by citizens with increased rates of contact or with a more general sense of support for the institution.

Cain et al. (1987) found that engaging in constituency service enhanced the reputations of MCs in the United States and MPs in Britain, with the effect being substantively larger and more consistent in the United States. Using American National Election Studies (ANES) data, Parker and Goodman (2009) found that franking, office expenditures, and trips to the district, which they associate with "seeking to build a home style reputation for constituency service," were associated with positive assessments of the incumbent by respondents. In a later piece, they found that the situation was more complicated for senators, where office allowances could be used to enhance the sitting member's reputation for constituency service but only with copartisan respondents or in sparsely populated states where the media was less likely to shape the member's reputation (Parker and Goodman 2013).

Using a conjoint analysis design in a survey of British citizens, Vivyan and Wagner (2015) sought to determine what sort of balance respondents wanted their MPs to strike between national policy work and constituency service. They offered their respondents descriptions of MPs who spent one to four days working on constituency service while also varying other characteristics they theorized would support preference for a candidate. They found that describing a hypothetical MP who spent three days per week on constituency service had the biggest positive effect of that MP being preferred over the hypothetical MP with which he or she was paired. With the exception of Hungary, scholars have predominantly chosen to look for the consequences of constituency service in the form of citizen approval in contexts where FPTP rules were employed.

It has been argued that high personal vote-seeking incentives have resulted in a strong committee system in the national congress of the United States, giving the legislators for whom a policy area is important—because it is important to their constituents—credit-claiming ability. Martin (2011) argues that the connection between personal vote-seeking incentives and committee structures should be conditional on how exactly personal votes are earned. In a cross-national study of thirty-nine cases, he finds that strong committees exist where legislators use fiscal particularism to earn personal votes, but where constituency service is the most prevalent mechanism for earning a personal vote, legislative committees are weaker. His indicator of constituency service provision is the lack of budgetary powers to engage in fiscal particularism.

In sum, the only cross-chamber work on the consequences of constituency service of which we are aware is parts of Cain et al. (1987). Unfortunately, personal vote-seeking incentives as institutionalized by electoral rules do not vary across these cases. As we noted earlier, two studies of single-transferrable vote systems came to contradictory conclusions regarding the ability of constituency service to earn votes. So, we cannot offer any definitive conclusion about whether the consequences of constituency vary as a function of electoral rules.

## Future Work

There is a fundamental challenge to studying constituency service that the discipline needs to take up, and that is simply developing indicators of constituency service that will allow us to observe it in practice. Surveying members or their staffs about it is commonplace—and not entirely fulfilling for multiple reasons. We did not come across any study (those by one of the authors included) that gave much attention to the data-generating process when using such survey results. First, the survey instruments themselves (or interview protocols) are rarely discussed in detail, and any work that was done to ensure they were actually getting at the concept of interest was not shared. Some studies read as if a question has been "repurposed"—attempting to interpret it as reflecting on constituency service when it is not obvious that that was the original intent of the question.

Whether legislators or their office staff might have reason to prevaricate in response to questions about how they spend their time has not been taken seriously. If they all exaggerate, for example, equally, then the problem is limited. However, if self-reporting about one's efforts could be influenced by one's electoral circumstances, broadly conceived, then we have a serious problem. We do know from Norton and Wood (1993) that British MPs' claims regarding a variety of aspects of constituency service were very much at odds with the perceptions of well-placed respondents in their constituencies. This is troubling for the practice of simply taking responses to surveys at face value. We simply want to point out that there may be some issues related to the use of surveys that those contributing to the literature do not always give attention to.

This same fundamental challenge is probably responsible for the use of some other less-than-satisfying indicators. It is important not to conflate incumbency and constituency service. Presumably, only incumbents can have a record of having provided constituency service, but an incumbency advantage can stem from a much wider array of activities. Likewise, claiming that a legislative body's operating budget was a solid indicator of constituency service struck us as very poorly justified. Yes, perhaps it is a cap on the resources potentially available for service, but there are so many other lines in that budget that it is difficult to claim that we learn much from it. Again, as we noted repeatedly earlier, travel to one's district does not indicate that service is being carried out. Constituency service can be provided from a legislator's office in the capital, and a trip home can be used to do many things in addition to providing or claiming credit for constituency service.

In our review of the literature we noted the relative lack of cross-chamber work. Clearly, if we want to gain leverage on the impact of electoral incentives on the provision of constituency service, cross-system research programs are going to be necessary. We recognize that this compounds the challenge of finding good measures of the concept that can realistically be collected, but we think it is an effort worth making. One promising area identified by both Martin (2010) and Butler et al. (2012) is to focus on staffing in legislative offices—in terms of both job description and where staff are located, in the capital or in the district. If an MP or MC has staff in both locations, it is unlikely that those living in the district are primarily devoted to policy work. This type of information has the benefit of probably being available in a central location for every member of the legislature. It is also likely to be available online in an increasing number of systems.

We will conclude by suggesting that it makes sense to examine the provision of constituency service where personal vote-seeking incentives are low. We think that it is possible that the early scholarly attention to FPTP systems (the United States and United Kingdom) may have established a connection between electoral system incentives and constituency service that does not capture the whole picture. Electoral system incentives were fixed in these cases, yet they seem to have created a causal connection in many scholars' minds. Likewise, more recent work that identifies the carrying out of constituency service in other individual systems with high personal vote-seeking incentives reinforces the connection without directly testing it. That said, we did note a small number of multisystem studies, and a number of them did find support for a connection between variations in vote-seeking incentives and service. Still, we think that future multisystem studies should not shy away from what are assumed to be inhospitable environments. Low levels of development; the existence of multiple, strong levels of government (with which a citizen's interactions must be mediated by a representative); or the presence of large state bureaucracies may lead to the provision of constituency service where it is difficult for an individual representative to profit from it. As always, there is more work to be done!

## Notes

1. There is a great deal of work on constituency service in the United States. It was too copious to review here. Instead, we sampled from the US literature, focusing on works employing relatively unique indicators of constituency service being carried out—beyond the self-reporting that dominates the literature on other cases. We did not find many books focused in their entirety on constituency service. We know that some studies of legislative politics in a given country contain some discussion of constituency service, but we had no means to systematically track down those works. So, our review is dominated by refereed journal articles.
2. For a caveat in this regard, see Crisp et al. (2004).
3. In a formal theoretic piece, Ashworth and Mesquita (2006) reason that single-seat districts promote constituency service as the member of congress can credibly lay claim to any benefits delivered.
4. However, they found that time spent on casework and efforts to solicit additional casework do not follow this same pattern.
5. The PARTIREP cross-national study, hosted by the Vrije Universiteit Brussel, surveyed national and regional legislators in twelve European democracies.
6. She concluded that other measures of demand—council tenants, unskilled manual labor population, size of the pensioner population, and the level of unemployment—had no statistically discernible effects.

## References

Abdel- Samad, Mounah. "Exchanging Favours: The Predominance of Casework in Legislators' Behaviour in Jordan and Lebanon." *Journal of Legislative Studies* 15, no. 4 (2009): 420–438.

Adler, E. Scott., Chariti E. Gent, and Cary B. Overmeyer. "The Home Style Homepage: Legislator Use of the World Wide Web for Constituency Contact." *Legislative Studies Quarterly* 23, no. 4 (1998): 585–595.

Anagnoson, J. Theodore. "Home Style in New Zealand." *Legislative Studies Quarterly* 8, no. 2 (1983): 157–175.

André, Audrey, and Sam Depauw. "District Magnitude and Home Styles of Representation in European Democracies." *West European Politics* 36, no. 5 (2013): 986–1006.

André, A., Sam Depauw, and Shane Martin. "Electoral Systems and Legislators' Constituency Effort: The Mediating Effect of Electoral Vulnerability." *Comparative Political Studies* 48, no. 4 (2015): 464–496.

André, Audrey, Sam Depauw, and Giulia Sandri. "Belgian Affairs and Constituent Preferences for Good Constituency Members?" *Acta Politica* 48, no. 2 (2013): 167–191.

Ashworth, Scott, and Ethan Bueno de Mesquita. "Delivering the Goods: Legislative Particularism in Different Electoral and Institutional Settings." *Journal of Politics* 68, no. 1 (2006): 168–179.

Bowler, Shaun, and David M. Farrell. "Legislator Shirking and Voter Monitoring: Impacts of European Parliament Electoral Systems upon Legislator-Voter Relationships." *Journal of Common Market Studies* 31, no. 1 (1993): 45–70.

Buck, J. Vincent, and Bruce E. Cain. "British MPs in Their Constituencies." *Legislative Studies Quarterly* 15, no. 1 (1990): 127–143.

Butler, Daniel M., and David E. Broockman. "Do Politicians Racially Discriminate against Constituents: A Field Experiment on State Legislators." *American Journal of Political Science* 55, no. 3 (2011): 463–477.

Butler, Daniel M., Christopher F. Karpowitz, and Jeremy C. Pope. "A Field Experiment on Legislators' Home Styles: Service versus Policy." *Journal of Politics* 74, no. 2 (2012): 474–486.

Cain, Bruce, John Ferejohn, and Morris Fiorina. *The Personal Vote: Constituency Service and Electoral Independence.* Cambridge, MA: Harvard University Press, 1987.

Carey, John M., and Matthew Soberg Shugart. "Incentives to Cultivate a Personal Vote: A Rank Ordering of Electoral Formulas." *Electoral Studies* 14, no. 4 (1995): 417–439.

Clarke, Harold D. "Determinants of Provincial Constituency Service Behaviour: A Multivariate Analysis." *Legislative Studies Quarterly* 3, no. 4 (1978): 601–628.

Clarke, Harold D., Richard G. Price, and Robert Krause. "Constituency Service among Canadian Provincial Legislators: Basic Findings and a Test of Three Hypotheses." *Canadian Journal of Political Science* 8, no. 4 (1975): 520–542.

Crisp, Brian F. and Scott W. Desposato. "Constituency Building in Multimember Districts: Collusion or Conflict?" *Journal of Politics* 66, no. 1 (2004): 136–156.

Crisp, Brian F., Maria C. Escobar-Lemmon, Bradford S. Jones, Mark P. Jones, and Michelle M. Taylor-Robinson. "Vote-Seeking Incentives and Legislative Representation in Six Presidential Democracies." *Journal of Politics* 66, no. 3 (2004): 823–846.

Dropp, Kyle, and Zachary Peskowitz. "Electoral Security and the Provision of Constituency Service." *Journal of Politics* 74, no. 1 (2012): 220–234.

Fenno, Richard F. *Home Style: House Members in Their Districts.* New York, NY: HarperCollins, 1978.

Fiorina, M. P. "Some Problems in Studying the Effects of Resource Allocation in Congressional Elections." *American Journal of Political Science* (1981): 543–567.

Freeman, Patricia K., and Lilliard E. Richardson Jr. "Explaining Variation in Casework among State Legislators." *Legislative Studies Quarterly* 21, no. 1 (1996): 41–56.

Griffin, John D., and Patrick Flavin. "How Citizens and Their Legislators Prioritize Spheres of Representation." *Political Research Quarterly* 64, no. 3 (2011): 520–533.

Halligan, John, Robert Krause, Robert Williams, and Geoffrey Hawker. "Constituency Service among Sub-National Legislators in Australia and Canada." *Legislative Studies Quarterly* 13, no. 1 (1988): 49–63.

Harden, Jeffrey J. "Multidimensional Responsiveness: The Determinants of Legislators' Representational Priorities." *Legislative Studies Quarterly* 38, no. 2 (2013): 155–184.

Hazama, Yasushi. "Constituency Service in Turkey: A Survey on MPs." *European Journal of Turkish Studies. Social Sciences on Contemporary Turkey* 3 (2005).

Heitshusen, Valerie, Garry Young, and David M. Wood. "Electoral Context and MP Constituency Focus in Australia, Canada, Ireland, New Zealand, and the United Kingdom." *American Journal of Political Science* 49, no. 1 (2005): 32–45.

Ilonszki, Gabriella, and Zsófia Papp. "The Paradoxes of Parliament–Citizen Connections in Hungary: A Window on the Political System." *Journal of Legislative Studies* 18, no. 3–4 (2012): 334–350.

Ingall, Rachael E., and Brian F. Crisp. "Determinants of Home Style: The Many Incentives for Going Home in Colombia." *Legislative Studies Quarterly* 26, no. 3 (2001): 487–512.

Jackson, Nigel. "An MP's Role in the Internet Era–The Impact of e-Newsletters." *Journal of Legislative Studies* 12, no. 2 (2006): 223–242.

Johannes, John R. "Explaining Congressional Casework Styles." *American Journal of Political Science* 27, no. 3(1983): 530–547.

Johannes, John R. *To Serve the People: Congress and Constituency Service*. Lincoln, NE: University of Nebraska Press, 1984.

Johannes, John R., and John C. McAdams. "The Congressional Incumbency Effect: Is It Casework, Policy Compatibility, or Something Else? An Examination of the 1978 Election." *American Journal of Political Science* 25, no. 3 (1981): 512–542.

Judge, David, and Gabriella Ilonszki. "Member-Constituency Linkages in the Hungarian Parliament." *Legislative Studies Quarterly* 20, no. 2 (1995): 161–176.

King, Gary. "Constituency Service and Incumbency Advantage." *British Journal of Political Science* 21, no. 1 (1991): 119–128.

Lapinski, John, Matt Levendusky, Ken Winneg, and Kathleen H. Jamieson. "What Do Citizens Want from Their Member of Congress?" *Political Research Quarterly* 69, no. 3 (2016): 535–545.

Lindberg, Staffan I. "What Accountability Pressures Do MPs in Africa Face and How Do They Respond? Evidence from Ghana." *Journal of Modern African Studies* 48, no. 1 (2010): 117–142.

Martin, Shane. "Electoral Rewards for Personal Vote Cultivation under PR-STV." *West European Politics* 33, no. 2 (2010): 369–380.

Martin, Shane. "Using Parliamentary Questions to Measure Constituency Focus: An Application to the Irish Case." *Political Studies* 59, no. 2 (2011): 472–488.

Mayhew, David R. *Congress: The Electoral Connection*. New Haven, CT: Yale University Press, 1974.

McAllister, Ian. "The Personalization of Politics in Australia." *Party Politics* 21, no. 3 (2015): 337–345.

McClendon, Gwyneth H. "Race and Responsiveness: An Experiment with South African Politicians." *Journal of Experimental Political Science* 3, no. 1 (2016): 60–74.

Mezey, Michael L. "*Constituency Development Funds and the Role of the Representative*." Distributive Politics in Developing Countries: Almost Pork, 2014, 199.

Norris, Pippa. "The Puzzle of Constituency Service." *Journal of Legislative Studies* 3, no. 2 (1997): 29–49.

Norton, Philip, and David M. Wood. *Back from Westminster: British Members of Parliament and Their Constituents*. Cambridge University Press, 1993.

O'Leary, Eimar. "The Constituency Orientation of Modern TDs." *Irish Political Studies* 26, no. 3 (2011): 329–343.

Parker, David C., and Craig Goodman. "Making a Good Impression: Resource Allocation, Home Styles, and Washington Work." *Legislative Studies Quarterly* 34, no. 4 (2009): 493–524.

Parker, David C., and Craig Goodman. "Our State's Never Had Better Friends: Resource Allocation, Home Styles, and Dual Representation in the Senate." *Political Research Quarterly* 66, no. 2 (2013): 370–384.

Roscoe, Douglas D. "The Choosers or the Choices? Voter Characteristics and the Structure of Electoral Competition as Explanations for Ticket Splitting." *Journal of Politics* 65, no. 4 (2003): 1147–1164.

Russo, Federico. "The Constituency as a Focus of Representation: Studying the Italian Case through the Analysis of Parliamentary Questions." *Journal of Legislative Studies* 17, no. 3 (2011): 290–301.

Searing, Donald D. *Westminster's World: Understanding Political Roles.* Cambridge: Cambridge University Press, 1994.

Serra, George, and Albert D. Cover. "The Electoral Consequences of Perquisite Use: The Casework Case." *Legislative Studies Quarterly* 17, no. 2 (1992): 233–246.

Sozzi, Fabio. "Asking Territories: The Constituency Orientation of Italian and French Members of the European Parliament." *Italian Political Science Review/Rivista Italiana di Scienza Politica* 46, no. 2 (2016): 199–217.

Studlar, Donley T., and Ian McAllister. "Constituency Activity and Representational Roles among Australian Legislators." *Journal of Politics* 58, no. 1 (1996): 69–90.

Taylor, Michelle M. "Formal versus Informal Incentive Structures and Legislator Behavior: Evidence from Costa Rica." *Journal of Politics* 54, no. 4 (1992): 1055–1073.

Vivyan, Nick, and Markus Wagner. "What Do Voters Want from Their Local MP?" *Political Quarterly* 86, no. 1 (2015): 33–40.

Wood, David M., and Garry Young. "Comparing Constituency Activity by Junior Legislators in Great Britain and Ireland." *Legislative Studies Quarterly* 22, no. 2 (1997): 217–232.

CHAPTER 18

..............................................................................................................

# DIRECT DEMOCRACY
# AND REFERENDUMS

..............................................................................................................

MATT QVORTRUP

## INTRODUCTION

..............................................................................................................

ON December 3, 2015, at 9:03 AM, Ole Agger, a 46-year-old middle manager at Aalborg City Council in Denmark, updated his Facebook status. He told his friends the following:

> Polling day has arrived and we are going out to vote in the referendum. I have to admit that I have found it hard to arrive at a decision. So, instead of poring over complex legal prose and caveats, I have decided to concentrate on my work and on my family. So I opt for the uncommon approach and trust the politicians I normally follow. (https://www.facebook.com/ole.agger.5?fref=ts)

As many political scientists would be quick to tell you, Agger's was not the "uncommon approach" that he believed it to be. In fact, it has become almost a paradigm of referendum studies that voters make use of "cues" and "information shortcuts" as an alternative to the costly acquisition of encyclopaedic knowledge, and that this gives them sufficient knowledge to make reasoned decisions (Lupia 1994, 71). Agger's approach was the norm rather than the exception, and far from "uncommon." This Danish voter was an archetypical example of "the reasoning voter" (Popkin 1991, 7).

The study of referendums has progressed considerably since Arend Lijphart reached the depressing conclusion that referendums "fail to fit any clear universal pattern" (Lijphart 1984, 206). That voters can reach decisions consistent with their preferences even if they only have limited information is an important finding for democratic theory. It contrasts sharply with the negative conclusion reached by many politicians who have denounced direct democracy on the grounds that voters use "a referendum to answer a question that was not put to them" (EU Commissioner Margot Wallström quoted in *New Statesman,* June 13, 2005).

While such denunciations by politicians who have recently lost referendums can perhaps be dismissed as political rhetoric masking as analysis, there are many issues left unanswered by the reasoning voter paradigm: Why are issues submitted to referendums at all? What determines their outcome? And what are the policy implications of letting ordinary voters have the last word on complex issues?

The "reasoning voter" paradigm—its many merits notwithstanding—says little about these questions. This chapter will try to provide answers based on a combination of the state-of-the-art literature and original research. It will also trace the political history of the use of the referendum in democratic countries.

## DEFINITIONS

Broadly speaking, modern democracies know of two types of (semi)-direct democracy: the referendum and the initiative. Referendums are defined as "popular votes on laws before they become laws" and initiatives as "popular votes on laws proposed by the citizens" (Qvortrup 2014b). The word *plebiscite* is generally used about votes held in dictatorships.

Conceptually, using conventional political science terminology, a *referendum* can be regarded as a *veto player*, an institution that *can* prevent changes to the status quo, or a chance for the voters to hinder change (Tsebelis 2002). The *initiative*, by contrast, can be seen as an agenda setter (Tsebelis 1994). The former can potentially deal with politicians' sins of commission; the latter can address their sins of omission.

## HISTORY AND THEORY

There is something mildly paradoxical about the fact that the referendum was "invented" in Graubünden, the Swiss Canton that now plays host to plutocrats attending the World Economic Forum in Davos. In 1684, the *Bürger* (all male citizens over the age of 16) were given the right to cast their votes on the policy issues that were submitted to them *ad referendum* by the elected representatives (Pieth 1958, 146).

While the word *referendum* (from the Latin "to refer") was not used before the seventeenth century, the practice of letting the voters decide already had a long history in European politics. The Roman historian Tacitus famously described the use of proto-referendums among Germanic tribes where "on matters of minor importance only the chiefs debate; [but] on the major matters the whole community" (Tacitus 1970, 110). But it was not until the early sixteenth century that the institution was established in anything resembling the present-day referendum.

In 1527, King Francis I of France (1494–1547) held a vote in Burgundy on whether to transfer the area to the Spanish king and his son King Henry II of France (1519–1559), organized a plebiscite in 1552 in Verdun, Toul, and Metz before their annexation (Solière 1901, 26). But these referendums were the exception.

The emergence of referendums as a general mechanism of democratic decision making coincided with the American and French Revolutions. The referendums held on the ratification of the US Constitution and subsequent referendums on amendments to state constitutions provided the backdrop for the adoption of more radical forms of direct democracy in many American states toward the end of the nineteenth century. In an effort to bypass machine politics, so-called populists fought for the introduction of the initiative, the referendum, and the recall (the right to unseat elected representatives) in the first decade of the twentieth century (Qvortrup 2014b). At roughly the same time, the referendum (but *not* the initiative) became fashionable among British conservatives, who championed "the people's veto" in an attempt to block radical legislation proposed by Liberal and Labour Parties. A. V. Dicey, a conservative British constitutionalist, summed up the position by describing the referendum as "the one available check on party leaders [and the only institution that could] give formal acknowledgement of the doctrine which lies at the basis of English democracy that a law depends at bottom for its enactment on the consent of the nation as represented by its electors" (Dicey 1911, 189–190). But the proposals for more direct democracy came to naught. In the period after World War II, referendums were introduced in several constitutions in Europe and more and more votes were held. As of 2015, only four democratic countries have yet to hold nationwide referendums: Israel, India, Japan, and the United States.

# PROVISIONS FOR DIRECT DEMOCRACY AND THEIR USE

Provisions for direct democracy differ significantly. Roughly half of the US states have provisions for initiatives and referendums—though no such provisions exist at the federal level. In Switzerland, there are provisions for referendums at the cantonal and at the federal level (Kriesi 2005). In Europe, many of the constitutions in the former communist countries have provisions for initiatives (e.g., Croatia, Estonia, Hungary, Latvia, Lithuania, FYR Macedonia, Slovakia, Slovenia, and Ukraine). Conversely, such provisions are rare in Western Europe, where only Switzerland and the microstates of San Marino and Liechtenstein allow the voters to initiate legislation.[1] However, due to the high turnout requirement and special majority requirements, the use of initiatives in the former communist countries has never taken off and the total number of initiatives passed remains much lower than in Switzerland and many US states (Herrera and Mattozzi 2010).

All countries in Europe, as well as in Australia, Canada, and New Zealand, have some experiences with nationwide referendums. In some countries these are determined by strict constitutional requirements necessitating that all constitutional changes must be submitted to referendums (Ireland and Australia with, respectively, 34 and 44 referendums being classical examples). But in most other jurisdictions, ad hoc referendums have been held on all manner of issues. From World War I to 2012, there were 326 referendums in Western Europe, excluding Switzerland (Qvortrup 2014a, 45). Of these, 76 were constitutional referendums, 49 were initiatives, 95 were referendums initiated by citizens, and 144 were ad hoc referendums called by elected representatives or governments.

There are clearly different reasons these votes are initiated (Morel 2007). However, most of them (with the notable exception of constitutional referendums) follow a pattern of sorts and can be described as institutions that "substitute" representative democracies. To explain their occurrence in a theoretically grounded framework, it is useful to employ the metaphor of economic theory.

# The Occurrence of Referendums in Democracies

"Public Choice can be defined as the economic study of nonmarket decision making, or simply the application of economics to political science" (Mueller 2003, 1). If we analyze the democracies where the citizens or politicians can initiate referendums and initiatives, it is possible to analyze the strategy to opt for a popular vote in microeconomic terms, namely, as a "political commodity" that performs the role of a "substitution good."

Thus, if the "price" of representative democracy goes up (if, say, the contributions to election campaigns increase) and the return for this "investment" is low, then a political actor may have an incentive to shift to a cheaper political "good," such as the referendum or—if available—the initiative.

This argument can be formalized. Suppose an action A has a number of possible consequences $C_1 \ldots C_n$, each with the probability $p_1 \ldots p_n$ of occurring. Suppose further that the agent who brings about the action (A) has a utility function u, which assigns to each consequence a numerical utility value $u(C_i)$. Given this, the expected utility (EU) of the action A is given by:

$$EU(A) = p_1 u(C_1) + p_2 u(C_2) + \ldots + p_n u(C_n).$$    **Equation I**

A political actor has to determine which of two (or more) strategies will yield the best results. Formally, the dilemma facing the political actor can be described by the following equations:

$$EUp_{\text{Representative Democracy}} = p_1 u(I) + p_2 u(NI) \qquad \text{\textbf{Equation II}}$$

$$EUp_{\text{Direct Democracy}} = p_1 u(I) + p_2 u(NI), \qquad \text{\textbf{Equation III}}$$

with $EUp_{\text{RepresentativeDemocracy}}$ representing the expected utility of pursuing the actor's goals through pure representative institutions and $EUp_{\text{DirectDemocracy}}$ denoting the expected utility of pursuing the policy through organizing a referendum (or an initiative).

Hence, for a political group (or party) to pursue their goals through the channels of representative institutions, the expected utility must be greater than pursuing a strategy of organizing a referendum or an initiative. Stated formally:

$$EUp_{\text{Representative Democracy}} - EUp_{\text{Direct Democracy}} > 0.$$

But often this is not the case. Sometimes, activists reason that the representative process is too cumbersome and they resort to direct democracy. For example, in the mid-1970s, Howard Jarvis, an American antitax activist, unsuccessfully sought to be nominated as a Republican candidate for the US Senate but lost to the moderate Thomas Henry Kuchel (Smith 1999). Jarvis was not able to get his policies enacted through the mechanisms of representative democracy. In his case:

$$EUp_{\text{Representative Democracy}} - EUp_{\text{Direct Democracy}} < 0.$$

Jarvis consequently decided to use the provision in the Constitution of the State of California, which provides, in Art. 2 Section 8(b), that citizens may set "forth the text of the proposed statute or amendment to the Constitution [if the proposal has] been signed by electors equal in number to 8 percent . . . of the votes for all candidates for Governor at the last gubernatorial election." Jarvis easily managed to get the required number of signatures. And in the subsequent election in 1978, a total of 57 percent of California voters endorsed a drastic cut in property taxes (Magleby 1988).

The same logic applies in representative systems with no provisions for citizen-initiated votes. In these countries, politicians may substitute the pure representative processes and seek a referendum if they are unable to win a majority through the parliamentary channels.

For example, in Britain, in the 1970s, Labour backbenchers opposed to continued membership of the European Communities, the forerunner of the European Union, were unable to win support for a vote to leave the European Economic Community (EEC). So they shifted to a different strategy. As the utility of pursuing their policy through the channels of representative democracy was converging toward zero, they demanded a referendum as this was more likely to achieve their aim of taking Britain out of the European Communities. Put differently, the *cost* of convincing their fellow members of Parliament (MPs) to vote to leave was very high. Conversely, the *cost* of

convincing the electorate was perceived as smaller as opinion polls (at the time) indicated a clear majority in favor of leaving the EEC.[2] The same rationale, of course, could
be used in 2015, when Conservatives in favor of leaving the European Union forced
then–prime minister David Cameron to promise a referendum in the event that the
Tories won the general election that year. With this promise, there could be a referendum even though a majority of the members of Parliament were in favor of staying in
the European Union. As will be known by most readers, the consequent referendum on
June 23, 2016, resulted in a vote for leaving the European Union.

But Britain is not the only country in which the referendum has been used for tactical
reasons. The decision to shift to "substitute" representative democracy for a referendum
was also the hallmark of French President Charles de Gaulle's use of the referendum in
the early 1960s. Unable to win majority support for his policies in the French Parliament,
de Gaulle submitted issues to referendums on an unprecedented scale (Hayward 1969).

But a referendum—as noted in the preceding section—is not intended to make it easier to pass legislation. The referendum is usually a "veto" and an additional check on the
representatives. Once a decision has been made by a parliament, a referendum is usually
an additional requirement before a constitutional change is enacted. This situation can
also be analyzed using the terminology of microeconomics. Adding the requirement
that certain issues require the support both of a parliamentary majority and of the voters
(and sometimes even a super majority of the eligible voters—as in Denmark) effectively
pushes the indifference curve upward, hence increasing the price of the policy.

Notwithstanding these tactical considerations, there are some issues, which often—
but not always—are deemed to require the consent of the governed. One such issue is a
change of the electoral system. Reforms of the electoral system are seen as fundamental
constitutional changes—that is, changes that should not be undertaken lightly as the
dangers of gerrymandering are ever present.

For example, in the United Kingdom—it has almost become a convention of the constitution that electoral reforms and changes to the electoral system must be preceded
by a referendum. Yet statistically and comparatively speaking, the use of referendums
on electoral reform is the exception rather than the rule if we look at global trends since
1980. In fact, referendums on electoral reforms have only taken place in a small minority of cases. For example, the changes in the electoral system in France in the 1980s
were not submitted to a referendum (the Socialists introduced a proportional system
in 1985, which was changed back to the familiar two-round system after the bourgeois
parties won a majority in 1986). Thus, since 1980, there have been sixty-nine changes
or attempted changes to electoral systems at the state and federal level. In only twenty
of these cases were the changes submitted to the electorate for approval/rejection. The
voters have voted for electoral reform in eleven of the cases—though in one case (British
Columbia) the result failed to reach a majority requirement of 60 percent.

The reasons for this low propensity to hold referendums on electoral reform may be
that voting systems have frequently been changed in countries that have—at best—a
dubious democratic record—that is, countries with a low Freedom House Score, such
as Rwanda, Kyrgyzstan, Sudan, and, arguably, Venezuela. Given this, it is tempting to

## Table 18.1 Changes of Electoral Systems

| Country | Referendum | Success/Fail | Year | Proposed Electoral System |
|---|---|---|---|---|
| France | | Success | 1985 | List PR |
| France | | Success | 1986 | TRS |
| Bulgaria | | Success | 1991 | List PR |
| Andorra | Referendum | Not Enacted | 1992 | MMM |
| Canberra | Referendum | Success | 1992 | STV |
| New Zealand | Referendum | Success | 1992 | MMP |
| Albania | | Success | 1992 | MMP |
| Lithuania | | Success | 1992 | MMM |
| Macedonia | | Success | 1992 | MMM |
| Taiwan | | Success | 1992 | MMM |
| Italy | Referendum | Success | 1993 | MMP |
| New Zealand | Referendum | Success | 1993 | MMP |
| Russia | Referendum | Success | 1993 | MMM |
| Colombia | | Success | 1993 | List PR |
| Jordan | | Success | 1993 | SNTV |
| Latvia | | Success | 1993 | List PR |
| Venezuela | | Success | 1993 | MMP |
| Moldova | | Success | 1994 | List PR |
| South Africa | | Success | 1994 | List PR |
| Tunisia | | Success | 1994 | MMM |
| Armenia | | Success | 1995 | MMM |
| Slovenia | Referendum | Not Enacted | 1996 | TRS |
| Japan | | Success | 1996 | MMM |
| Sierra Leone | | Success | 1996 | List PR |
| Ecuador | Referendum | Success | 1997 | FPTP |
| Uruguay | Referendum | Success | 1997 | TRS |
| Algeria | | Success | 1997 | List PR |

*(continued)*

## Table 18.1 Continued

| Country | Referendum | Success/Fail | Year | Proposed Electoral System |
|---|---|---|---|---|
| Bolivia | | Success | 1997 | MMP |
| Liberia | | Success | 1997 | List PR |
| Ukraine | | Success | 1997 | MMM |
| Macedonia | | Success | 1998 | List PR |
| Philippines | | Success | 1998 | MMM |
| Italy | Referendum | Success | 1999 | SML |
| Fiji | | Success | 1999 | AV |
| Kazakhstan | | Success | 1999 | MMM |
| Kyrgyzstan | | Success | 1999 | MMM |
| Croatia | | Success | 2000 | List PR |
| Czech Republic | | Failure | 2000 | Revised List PR |
| Tajikistan | | Success | 2000 | MMM |
| Thailand | | Success | 2001 | MMM |
| Papua New Guinea | | Success | 2002 | MMM |
| Rwanda | | Success | 2003 | List PR |
| British Columbia | Referendum | Not Enacted | 2005 | STV |
| Iraq | Referendum | Success | 2005 | List PR |
| Prince Edward Island | Referendum | Not Enacted | 2005 | MMP |
| Afghanistan | | Success | 2005 | SNTV |
| Azerbaijan | | Success | 2005 | FPTP |
| Liberia | | Success | 2005 | FPTP |
| Cambodia | | Success | 2006 | List PR |
| Congo (Brazzaville) | | Success | 2006 | List PR |
| East Timor | | Success | 2006 | MMM |
| Kyrgyzstan | | Success | 2006 | TRS |
| Ukraine | | Success | 2006 | List PR |
| Ontario | Referendum | Not Enacted | 2007 | MMP |

## Table 18.1 Continued

| Country | Referendum | Success/Fail | Year | Proposed Electoral System |
|---|---|---|---|---|
| Romania | Referendum | Not Enacted | 2007 | TRS |
| Kyrgyzstan | | Success | 2007 | List PR |
| Russia | | Success | 2007 | List PR |
| Albania | | Success | 2008 | List PR |
| Mongolia | | Success | 2008 | Block |
| Nepal | | Success | 2008 | MMM |
| Serbia | | Success | 2008 | List PR |
| British Columbia | Referendum | Not Enacted | 2009 | STV |
| Italy | Referendum | Success | 2009 | Bonus |
| St Vincent and the Grenadines | Referendum | Not Enacted | 2009 | List PR |
| Bulgaria | | Success | 2009 | MMM |
| Sudan | | Success | 2010 | MMM |
| United Kingdom | Referendum | Not Enacted | 2011 | AV |
| New Zealand | Referendum | Not Enacted | 2011 | FPTP |
| Italy | | Success | 2015 | TRS |
| Bulgaria | | Not Enacted | 2016 | TRS |

TRS, two-round system; FPTP: first past the post; AV, alternative vote; MMP, mixed-member proportional system; STV, single transferable vote; SNTV, single nontransferable vote; MMM, mixed-member majoritarian.
*Sources:* IDEA and C2D.

conclude that referendums on electoral reform are more likely to take place in countries with more established democratic practices such as Canada, New Zealand, and Britain. However, electoral reforms have also been undertaken in countries like France and Japan *without* a referendum being held. Could there be a sort of path dependency involved?

A quick overview of the list of electoral reforms since 1980 seemingly suggests that referendums have been more likely to take place in polities in the commonwealth countries. For example, in Canada, a number of proposed (and in all cases unsuccessful) reforms were submitted to referendums: the introduction of the single transferable vote

(STV) in British Columbia in 2005 and 2009, the introduction of a mixed-member proportional (MMP) system in Ontario in 2007, and the introduction of MMP in Prince Edward Island in 2005. In Australia, a reform of the electoral system was submitted to the voters in the Australian Capital Territory in 1992 (a majority voted to introduce a variant of the STV). In New Zealand, voters voted to change from first past the post (FPTP) (1992) and in a separate referendum voted to introduce MMP in a multioption referendum in 1993. In Saint Vincent and the Grenadines, a 2009 constitutional reform including the introduction of proportional representation (PR) proposed by center-left Prime Minister Dr. Ralph Gonsalves was rejected by 56 percent of the voters—though his Unity Labour Party (ULP) was still able to win the general election shortly after.

The evidence suggests that commonwealth countries are more likely than other countries to hold referendums instead of electoral reforms. However, there have been referendums in countries that were not former British colonies: for example, in Romania, where President Băsescu's proposal to establish parliamentary elections in single-seat constituencies was rejected due to a low turnout in 2007; in Ecuador, where a proposal to modify the existing list PR system was approved by the voters in a referendum in 1997; and in Uruguay, where voters voted to replace the double-simultaneous vote with a two-round system for presidential elections in 1996. Further, in Italy, a referendum on a shift from list PR to supplementary vote was held in 1993, and a number of referendums on modifications have been held in 2000, 2005, and 2009. However, no referendum was held before the electoral system was changed in Italy in 2015. The latter suggests that the decision to hold a referendum in this country was due more to political opportunism than to a commitment to democratic legitimacy.

Referendums on electoral reform, like other referendums, seem to follow their own individual logic: a concern for party political expediency rather than a commitment to principles of fairness. So, much as politicians may like to see referendums as a principled mechanism for giving legitimacy to controversial decisions, their practical use in democracies has often had more to do with expediency than with concern for lofty principles.

But sometimes even dictators and autocrats allow the people to vote. Before looking at what determines the outcome of referendums, we need to briefly look at plebiscites in dictatorships.

# Plebiscites in Dictatorships

Letting the people decide is not just a characteristic of democratic regimes (Altman 2011, 88). Napoléon Bonaparte, his nephew Louis Napoléon, Adolf Hitler, Benito Mussolini, Ayatollah Khomeini, and Bashar al-Assad—rulers with dubious democratic credentials—are but some of the dictators who have felt compelled to submit issues to the voters in plebiscites. Others are the Romanian communist dictator Nicolae Ceauşescu, both Baby and Papa Doc Duvalier of Haiti, and more recently Nursultan Nazarbayev in Kazakhstan and Vladimir Putin in Crimea. If we limit ourselves to autocracies as defined by Polity IV, the use of plebiscites has increased in recent decades (see Figure 18.1).

While there has been remarkably little research about plebiscites in dictatorships by political scientists in recent years, earlier generations acknowledged the use of this

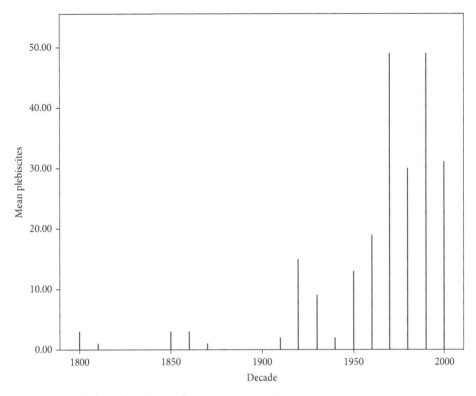

FIGURE 18.1. Referendums in nondemocratic states, 1800–2015.

Selection criteria: Before 1974, referendums held in single-party states. For cases after 1974, countries that scored six or seven on the Freedom House Index.

Source: C2D Database.

institution. Before World War II, Robert Michels warned that plebiscites ought to be avoided as "a *Führer* would lead the people astray through unclear questions, and would himself be solely entitled to interpret the result afterwards" (Michels 1925, 431, author's translation). Eric Voeglin likewise recognized that of the "screen devices" used by Hitler to gain legitimacy, "the most important ... [had] been the plebiscite" (Voeglin 1940, 193).

After World War II, the writings on plebiscites became sparser, though paradoxically the number of them increased. Friedrich and Brzezinski (1965) made passing reference to "rigged plebiscites" (p. 9) and mentioned "Hitler's *Volksbefragung* through plebiscites" (p. 13) but did little else.

In recent years, historians specializing in Nazi Germany and Fascist Italy have undertaken case study research into the use of plebiscites in these regimes. Beginning with Jung (1995), and more recently continued by Omland (2011), scholars have provided historical—thick description—accounts of the votes held under Hitler and Mussolini (Fimiani et al. 2010). According to the latter, the Italian plebiscites were "a symbolic fact, a *plastic* testimony of the link between the *new* power and popular consensus" (Fimiani 2011, 233, italics in the original). That the people are asked to decide in a dictatorship is obviously a paradox, which is yet to be solved. Although these autocratic regimes do allow dissent, there is still some suggestion that the votes may provide a legitimacy of sorts and that the outcome represents the preferences of the voters. A writer found that "the plebiscites staged in 1933, 1934, 1936 and 1938 [by Hitler] reflected genuine widespread approval" (Kershaw 1987, 258).

Whatever the level of support for the dictator, in practice, plebiscites held in repressive regimes have almost invariably been organized to show that "voting is not just a duty but an opportunity to express publicly, visibly and preferably joyously the identification with the regime" (Linz 2000, 92).

The single-country studies support this and show many examples of dictators who "exploited to the full the modern totalitarian plebiscite ... as a means of demonstrating ... [and] of indoctrinating the people and of testing ... [his] control over them" (Latey 1969, 145). The aim of the plebiscite is not primarily to win the backing of the people; rather, the "plebiscites in totalitarian systems," in the words of Juan Linz, "test the effectiveness of the party and its mass organizations in their success in getting out the vote" (Linz 2000, 92).

Seen in light of this, the paradox dissolves and the plebiscite becomes a straight, if ingenious, mechanism of repression and control. This aspect of the plebiscite explains some of the—at first sight—absurd examples of vote rigging and indoctrination often witnessed in connection with plebiscites. In a totalitarian regime, securing endorsement is a question of effective implementation, and steps are taken to secure maximum compliance, for example, by issuing instructions on how to fill out the ballot paper (as in Austria in 1938—see Illustration 1).

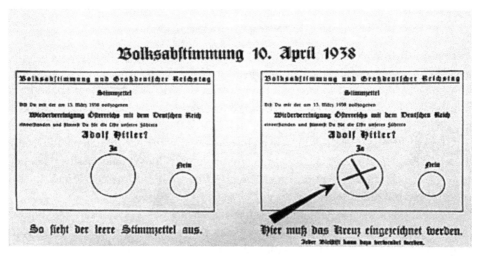

**ILLUSTRATION 1.** Instructions on how to fill out ballot paper in the Anschluss Plebiscite in Austria 1938. The specimen on the left shows an empty ballot paper. The specimen on the right shows where "you must put your cross." Note also that the box for "Ja" ("Yes") is considerably larger than the box for "Nein" ("No").

Source: *Dokumentationsarchiv des österreichischen Widerstandes.*

# The Outcome of Referendums

All referendums have a certain *sui generis* character. It is therefore difficult to make direct comparisons. Votes such as the Norwegian referendum on independence in 1905, the Canadian referendum on conscription in 1942, and the Swedish referendum on pensions in 1957, to name but three, have little in common. While there have been developed typologies of types of referendum campaigns (see Leduc 2002), political scientists specializing in referendums and initiatives have not (so far) been successful in predictive models akin to the VP functions developed for comparative election research (Lewis-Beck, Nadeau, and Elias 2008). But could similar models be developed for referendums? Could we find models that predict the outcome of referendums on the basis of macroeconomic data?

Given that referendums are about issues (some of which have nothing to do with economic matters, e.g., the Irish and Croatian referendums on same-sex marriage), it seems unlikely that a similar regularity should exist. However, some of the predictive models developed in studies of elections focus on factors other than macroeconomic performance (Lewis-Beck and Stegmaier 2013).

If we focus on a smaller subset of referendums on the same issue in different countries, we may find some recurrent patterns akin to those found by election specialists. Referendums on European integration (votes on membership of the European Union or further transfers of powers to the European Union) have been analyzed extensively (Atikcan 2015; Mendez and Mendez 2010) but rarely with the use of statistical models. Although not using econometric models, it has often been asserted that "yes" votes in EU referendums are correlated with higher levels of trust in the government (Franklin, Marsh, and Wlezien 1994). It has also been suggested that the wording of the question may sway the voters (Bishop, Oldendick, and Tuchfarber 1978) and that the number of years the government has been in office is inversely correlated with the percentage of voters supporting the proposition on the ballot (Qvortrup 2002).

As Figure 18.2 shows, not all these hypotheses are supported when analyzing the EU referendums since 1972. The wording of the question (here measured by a dummy variable for the presence of emotive words such as "agree" or "approve" in the referendum question) is a strong indicator of success.

Conversely, the hypothesized correlation between distrust and a high "no" vote—also known as the Franklin Thesis (Svensson 2002)—is not statistically significant. But there is a tendency that elite consensus is correlated with a high "yes" vote. There is also a tendency that a higher turnout is inversely correlated with a higher "yes" vote. Further, the hypothesized inverse relationship between longer government tenure and lower support for a "yes" vote is supported statistically.

Are any of these factors present in other referendums? If we look at all 183 of the referendums held in Europe since 1990, we find some of the same tendencies as in the narrower subgroup of EU referendums.

(a)

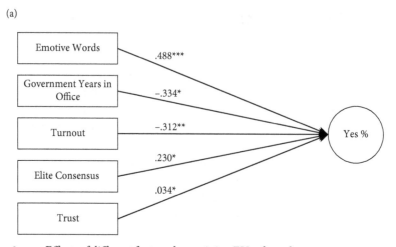

**FIGURE 18.2A.** Effects of different factors determining EU referendum outcomes, 1972–2015.

Notes: Entries are standardized beta-coefficients. *** Significant at 0.01, ** significant at 0.05, * significant at 0.10 (N: 44, R-squared: 0.50).

(b)

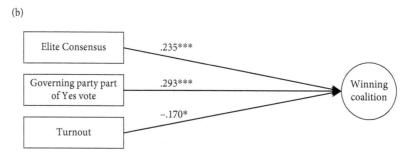

**FIGURE 18.2B.** Factors determining European referendum outcomes, 1990–2014.

Notes: ***Significant at 0.01 level, ** significant at 0.05 level, * significant at 0.10 level (R-squared: 0.10, N: 183).

Based on data from Vospernik (2014).

Elite consensus and turnout are statistically significant factors in both cases. However, the inverse relationship between a longer tenure and a lower support for a "yes" vote is not present when we use multiple-regression analysis with the "yes" percentage as the dependent variable.[3]

While analyses of referendums have yet to reach the same level of sophistication as the VP-functions in electoral research, the findings cannot be dismissed. The statistical study of when referendums are won is slowly becoming more grounded in quantitative data.

# POLICY EFFECT OF REFERENDUMS

Some scholars have suggested that the use of referendums is likely to lead to better government and higher levels of prosperity. One of the assumptions in the literature is that more use of direct democracy will lead to greater knowledge about politics (Smith and Tolbert 2004, 63). Yet others have suggested that "ballot initiatives in the United States do create an environment that encourages citizens to distrust their government" (Dyck 2009, 539).

When focusing on American initiatives and referendums, there is also a tendency that initiative and referendum states are more likely to allow the death penalty (Gerber 1999). This finding was corroborated by Hug (2004), who found that states with provisions for citizen initiatives "have a higher probability to have the death penalty on their books than states with no referendums" (p. 343). Further, it has been reported that initiatives and referendums in the United States have had an adverse effect on civil liberties and that "these [ballot propositions] experience extraordinary electoral success; voters have approved three-quarters of these" (Gamble 1997, 245).

Without challenging Gamble's finding in the United States, Frey and Goette (1998) found that "when the same type of civil rights issues [were] put to a vote at the Swiss federal level ... direct democracy protects civil rights" (p. 1343). One should be careful not to extrapolate these findings. Some may point out that while American initiatives and referendums regarding gay rights were roundly defeated in 2004, they won handsomely in the referendums held a decade later. The referendum may not be to blame. As Bochsler and Hug (2015) have shown recently:

> The political effect of referendums and initiatives [on gay rights] is not a genuinely positive or negative one, but rather, it depends on the preferences of the median voter. Namely, the possibility of using a referendum or an initiative in order to veto parliamentary legislation helps the median voter to realise a policy that is close to his preferences. In sum, policy outcomes in countries with direct democratic rights should be closer to the preferences of median voters than in countries with no referendums or initiatives. (p. 210)

In America, referendums supporting "pro-choice positions" have often been defeated (Bowler and Donovan 2004). The same pattern has been found elsewhere. For example, in the 1990s, the voters in Ireland followed the pattern identified in America and voted for tighter abortion laws. Yet, unlike the Americans, the Irish voted to abolish the death penalty in 2001 (O'Mahony 2001).

The fact that legal provisions for referendums and initiatives vary considerably makes direct comparisons difficult. Most of the studies regarding the policy effects of referendums have focused on countries where referendums and initiatives are central parts of the political system (such as California and Switzerland). Yet in most countries, referendums are used sparingly and generally only to resolve exceptional and controversial issues.

While referendums and initiatives generally have resulted in more conservative outcomes in America, the question is whether the opposite is true in states with fewer referendums. To determine this, Qvortrup (2014a) correlated the number of different occurrences of different types of referendums with policy indicators.

Table 18.2 reports Pearson's correlation coefficients between a number of policy outcomes and the total number of the different types of referendums and initiatives held. Overall, there is little support for the proposition that direct democracy mechanisms have an effect on policy outcomes. The most remarkable finding is perhaps the negative correlation between the number of referendums and inequality. When equality is measured by Gini coefficient (the greater the level of equality, the smaller the Gini coefficient), there is a statistically significant correlation between direct democracy and inequality (statistically significant at the 0.05 level). There is also a slight correlation between higher levels of general health and the number of citizens' initiated referendums.

Yet other factors are less encouraging for proponents of direct democracy; there is a negative correlation between the number of referendums held and the level of environmental protection. As a general rule, the environment suffers if environmental issues are submitted to the voters. Superficially speaking, it could be conjectured that the negative correlations could be a result of NIMBYism (Not-In-My-Back-Yard) and that referendums and initiatives provide an opportunity for politicians to pass the proverbial buck to the voters, and that this has detrimental effects on the environment (Ahlfeldt and Maennig 2012).

Moreover, there is a small tendency for provisions for citizens' initiatives to have a negative impact on the level of educational outputs. While a more detailed study would

**Table 18.2  Pearson's Correlations between Types of Referendums and Policy**

| Variable | Initiatives | Legislative Referendums | Citizen Referendums |
|---|---|---|---|
| Health | 1.07 | −0.18 | 0.30* |
| Education | −0.26* | −0.58 | 0.045 |
| Inequality | −0.685** | −0.483** | −0.79 |
| Environment | −0.66*** | −0.45** | −0.64 |
| *Human Development Index* | −0.205 | *0.15* | *0.070* |
| N | 49 | 83 | 95 |

*** Significant at 0.01 level
** Significant at 0.05 level
* Significant at 0.10 level
*Source:* Qvortrup (2014a)

be necessary to determine the precise arrows of causality, these findings go against the idea that provisions for referendums and initiatives improve policy outcomes (Matsusaka 2008). But often the number of referendums held is not the most important outcome. The referendum is very much a case of the proverbial "dog that didn't bark."

Being an institutional veto player, the referendum aims to encourage consensus, and in Europe, "the potential to call a referendum [paradoxically] is a strong stimulus for the majority to be heedful of minority views" (Lijphart 1999, 231). The possibility that the majority in parliament can force an issue to a referendum can create an incentive for them to negotiate, to avoid their policies being defeated in a referendum.

In line with institutionalist research, which emphasizes the effect of institutions on policy outcome, one could conjecture that referendums could have an effect on macroeconomic performance and social welfare in the same way that Lijphart has shown that majoritarian democracy characteristics impact policy outcomes (Lijphart 1999, 2012).

Using Lijphart's dataset,[4] we find that provisions for institutions of direct democracy have a considerable—and perhaps surprising—impact on policy outcomes (Table 18.3).

## Table 18.3  Peace, Welfare, and Direct Democracy

| Independent Variable | GDP per Capita | Human Development Index |
|---|---|---|
| Lijphart Majoritarian | −9,548.9** | −2.729 |
| | (3,610.6) | (1.78) |
| Immigration | 9.80 | 0.003 |
| | (10.7) | (0.05) |
| Population | −2,945.4 | 2.120 |
| | (3,919.2) | 1.932 |
| Provisions for Referendums[§] | 13,795.0* | 7.400** |
| | (7,357.3) | 3.620 |
| Constant | 48,850.2 | 70.04*** |
| | (28,462.7) | (14.03) |
| R-Squared | 0.40 | 0.21 |
| N | 36 | 36 |

[§] Constitutional provisions for constitutional referendums, citizen-initiated referendums, or referendums initiated by a minority of members of Parliament.

*** Significant at 0.01 level

** Significant at 0.05 level

* Significant at 0.1 level

The findings suggest that provisions for referendums are statistically correlated with higher levels of gross domestic product per capita and a higher score on the UNDP Human Development Index (HDI). Needless to say, the relationship between institutions and policy outcomes is a complex one, and it needs to be analyzed carefully before firm conclusions can be drawn; however, the findings outside Switzerland and the United States suggest that economic performance and higher levels of welfare are associated with provisions for direct democracy.

# CONCLUSION

In a deservedly celebrated study, William H. Riker (1964) lamented "that much of what passes as scientific investigation in our field is no more than elaboration of unique detail, e.g. the case study of a particular event" (p. xi). Riker was writing about federalism, not about direct democracy, but he could just as well have been writing about referendums. Until a generation ago, the empirical study of direct democracy was predominantly concerned with studies of "particular events" and single case studies. Like the institution studied by Riker, the referendum is a "precisely definable and an easily recognizable constitutional artifact that has been used in enough instances to admit generalization" (Riker 1964, xi).

With the development of "the reasoning voter" paradigm in the early 1990s, political scientists have started to move beyond narrow case studies. Yet much as this research program has given referendum research more rigor and enabled scholars to develop testable propositions, there is relatively little research on why referendums are held, on why they are won, and—in Europe at least—on the policy implications of the use of referendums.

The institutions of direct democracy are generally called to solve particular problems. In most cases the referendum (and its relative, the initiative) can be seen as a political "substitution" good, which is invoked when the "cost" of winning approval for a policy through the representative system gets too high. Thus, when politicians are unwilling to pass legislation, activists are likely to gather signatures for an initiative. And in systems without initiatives, politicians may call for a referendum if they are unable to win support for a policy through the representative channels but there is popular support for the policy.

This logic does not apply to plebiscites—public votes held in dictatorships. The holding of plebiscites is in many ways a paradox; why hold votes if you have total control? While the studies of plebiscites are few, and theorizing about them rarer still, there are indications from case studies that a plebiscite serves the function of communicating that the dictator is in total control.

Why referendums in democracies are won is a question that mainly has been studied through idiosyncratic case studies. Although referendum specialists have yet to develop models of the same elegance and sophistication as the VP functions, there is an emerging body of comparative findings that reveals recurrent trends and patterns. Thus, there is statistical evidence to suggest that referendums are won when there is an elite consensus, that high turnout rates are correlated with a high "no" vote, and that the presence of "emotive" words on the ballot statistically has swayed voters. Further, governments statistically tend to lose referendums if they have been in office for a long time.

Conversely, there is little statistical evidence that trust or distrust in the political class is statistically related to the success of referendums. It has often been hypothesized that referendums and direct democracy encourage more engagement and knowledge about politics. This hypothesis is consistent with findings from both Switzerland, California, and the two dozen US states where initiatives and referendums are used frequently. But there is also evidence that states with many initiatives have higher levels of distrust.

Regarding the policy implications of referendums, there have often been fears—among liberals—that greater use of referendums could lead to the reintroduction of the death penalty and more conservative policies on abortion. This concern is supported by empirical studies in the United States. However, the same has not been reported in Europe.

It is difficult and perhaps even methodologically illegitimate to compare Switzerland and California (where there are dozens of referendums every electoral cycle) with other democracies where referendums occur rarely (typically there is less than one referendum per parliamentary term in Europe, Oceania, and Canada). Given their rarity, it is perhaps not surprising that it is difficult to find evidence of direct policy effects of employing referendums. Yet there is a slight tendency for countries that hold more initiatives and legislative referendums to have lower levels of inequality. There is also a statistical tendency that more referendums are inversely correlated with environmental protection.

A referendum, observed President Woodrow Wilson, a convert to the institutions of direct democracy, is like a "gun behind the door—for use in an emergency, but a mighty good persuader, nevertheless" (Wilson, quoted in Smith and Tolbert 2004, 2). The efficacy of the referendum as a political tool is measured not only by its use but also by the effects that the threat of a referendum *could* have. Often a referendum can encourage politicians to seek a compromise for fear that the voters may veto legislation. For this reason, politicians in countries with provisions for referendums may be more careful to enact legislation that commands broad support. Whether this explains the strong correlations between provisions for referendums and, respectively, a high gross domestic product per capita and a high HDI cannot be determined with cast iron certainty. The referendum does not guarantee particular policy outcomes. In most cases referendums have few definite policy effects. To quote Theodore Roosevelt—another advocate—the referendum "is a device and nothing more; a means and not an end. The end is good government obtained through the people" (Roosevelt, quoted in Smith and Tolbert 2004, 168). Whether this implies that more referendums are desirable is for the reader to decide.

## NOTES

1. Italy's so-called *referendum abrogativo* is a special case as the voters can repeal any law on the statute book provided the required number of signatures are collected, but only if the turnout is higher than 50 percent in the referendum (Herrera and Mattozzi 2010).
2. In the actual referendum, those in favor of staying in won over 60 percent of the votes.
3. It should be noted that Vospernik found a slight correlation (R = .21, significant at the 0.05 level) between the government's period in office (measure in number of days) and a dummy variable for "government defeat" (Vospernik 2014, 681).
4. Lijphart (2012) analyzed countries that continuously have been democracies since 1986.

## REFERENCES

Ahlfeldt, Gabriel, and Wolfgang Maennig. 'Voting on a NIMBY' *Urban Affairs Review* 48, no. 2 (2012): 205–237.

Altman, David. *Direct Democracy Worldwide*. Cambridge, Cambridge University Press, 2011.

Atikcan, Ece Özlem. *Framing the European Union: The Power of Political Arguments in Shaping European Integration*. Cambridge: Cambridge University Press, 2015.

Bishop, George, Robert Oldendick, and Alfred Tuchfarber. "Effects of Question Wording and Format on Political Attitude Consistency." *Public Opinion Quarterly* 42, no. 1 (1978): 81–92.

Bochsler, Daniel, and Simon Hug. "How Minorities Fare under Referendums: A Cross-National Study." *Electoral Studies* 38 (2015): 206–216.

Bowler, Shaun, and Todd Donovan. "Measuring the Effect of Direct Democracy on State Policy: Not All Initiatives Are Created Equal." *State Politics & Policy Quarterly* 4, no. 3 (2004): 345–363.

Dicey, Albert V. *A Leap in the Dark*. London: John Murray, 1911.

Dyck, Joshua. "Initiated Distrust Direct Democracy and Trust in Government." *American Politics Research* 37, no. 4 (2009): 539–568.

Fimiani, Enzo. "Elections, Plebiscitary Elections and Plebiscites in Fascist Italy and Nazi-Germany: Comparative Perspectives." In *Voting for Hitler and Stalin: Elections under 20th Century Dictatorships*, edited by Ralph Jessen and Hedwig Richter, 231–253. Campus: Frankfurt aM, 2011.

Fimiani, Enzo, et al. *Vox Populi? Pratiche plebiscitarie in Francia, Italia, Germania*. Bologna: Clueb, 2010.

Franklin, Mark, Michael Marsh, and Christopher Wlezien. "Attitudes toward Europe and Referendum Votes: A Response to Siune and Svensson." *Electoral Studies* 13, no. 2 (1994): 117–121.

Frey, Bruno S., and Lorenz Goette. "Does the Popular Vote Destroy Civil Rights?" *American Journal of Political Science* 42, no. 4 (1998): 1343–1348.

Friedrich, Carl J., and Zbigniew K. Brzezinski. *Totalitarian Dictatorship*. Cambridge, MA: Harvard University Press, 1965.

Gamble, Barbara S. "Putting Civil Rights to a Popular Vote." *American Journal of Political Science* 41, no. 1 (1997): 245–269.

Gerber, Elizabeth R. *The Populist Paradox: Interest Group Influence and the Promise of Direct Legislation*. Princeton, NJ: Princeton University Press, 1999.

Hayward, Jack. "Presidential Suicide by Plebiscite: De Gaulle's Exit, April 1969." *Parliamentary Affairs* 22 (June 1969): 289–319.

Herrera, Helios and Andrea Mattozzi. "Quorum and Turnout in Referenda." *Journal of the European Economic Association* 8, no. 4 (2010): 838–871.

Hug, Simon. "Occurrence and Policy Consequences of Referendums: A Theoretical Model and Empirical Evidence." *Journal of Theoretical Politics* 16, no. 3 (2004): 321–356.

Jung, Otmar. *Plebiszit und Diktatur: Die Volksabstimmungen der Nationalsozialisten. Die Fälle, Austritt aus dem Völkerbund (1933), Staatsoberhaupt (1934) und Anschluss Österreichs (1938).* Tübingen: Mohr Siebeck, 1995.

Kershaw, Ian. *The "Hitler Myth": Image and Reality in the Third Reich,* Oxford: Oxford University Press, 1987.

Kriesi, Hanspeter. *Direct Democracy Choice: The Swiss Experience.* Lanham, MD: Lexington Books, 2005.

Latey, Maurice. *Tyranny: A Study in the Abuse of Power.* London: Macmillan, 1969.

Leduc, Lawrence. "Opinion Change and Voting Behaviour in Referendums." *European Journal of Political Research* 41, no. 6 (2002): 711–732.

Lewis-Beck, Michael S., Richard Nadeau, and Angelo Elias. "Economics, Party, and the Vote: Causality Issues and Panel Data." *American Journal of Political Science* 52, no. 1 (2008): 84–95.

Lewis-Beck, Michael S., and Mary Stegmaier. "The VP-Function Revisited: A Survey of the Literature on Vote and Popularity Functions after over 40 years." *Public Choice* 157, no. 3–4 (2013): 367–385.

Lijphart, Arend. *Democracies: Patterns of Majoritarian and Consensus Government in Twenty-One Countries.* New Haven, CT: Yale University Press, 1984.

Lijphart, Arend. *Patterns of Democracy: Government Forms and Performance in Thirty-Six Democracies.* New Haven, CT: Yale University Press, 1999.

Lijphart, Arend. *Patterns of Democracy: Government Forms and Performance in Thirty-Six Democracies.* 2nd ed. New Haven, CT: Yale University Press, 2012.

Linz, Juan J. *Totalitarian and Authoritarian Regimes.* Boulder, CO: Lynne Rienner Publishers, 2000.

Lupia, Arthur. "Shortcuts versus Encyclopedias: Information and Voting Behavior in California Insurance Reform Elections." *American Political Science Review* 88, no. 1 (1994): 63–76.

Magleby, David. "Taking the Initiative: Direct Legislation and Direct Democracy in the 1980s." *PS: Political Science & Politics* 21, no. 3 (1988): 600–611.

Matsusaka, John. *For the Many or the Few: The Initiative, Public Policy, and American Democracy.* Chicago: University of Chicago Press, 2008.

Mendez, Fernando, and Mario Mendez. "Referendums and European Integration: Beyond the Lisbon Vote." *Public Law* (2010): 223–230.

Michels, Robert. *Zur Soziologie des Parteiwesens in der modernen Demokratie: Untersuchungen über die oligarchischen Tendenzen des Gruppenlebens.* Leipzig: Alfred Kröner, 1925.

Morel, Laurence. "The Rise of 'Politically Obligatory' Referendums: The 2005 French Referendum in Comparative Perspective." *West European Politics* 30, no. 5 (2007): 1041–1067.

Mueller, Dennis C. *Public Choice III.* Cambridge: Cambridge University Press, 2003.

O'Mahony, Jane. "'Not So Nice': The Treaty of Nice, the International Criminal Court, the Abolition of the Death Penalty: The 2001 Referendum Experience." *Irish Political Studies* 16, no. 1 (2001): 201–213.

Omland, Frank. "Germany Totally National Socialist—Nationalist Socialist *Reichstag* Elections and Plebiscites, 1933-1938: The Example of Schleswig Holstein." In *Voting for Hitler and Stalin: Elections under 20th Century Dictatorships*, edited by Ralph Jessen and Hedwig Richter, 254–275. Frankfurt/New York, 2011.

Pieth, Friedrich. "Das altbündnerische Referendum." *Bündner Monatsblatt: Zeitschrift für Geschichte, Landes- und Volkskunde* 5 (May 1958): 137–153.

Popkin, Samuel L. *The Reasoning Voter*. Chicago: Chicago University Press, 1991.

Qvortrup, Matt. *A Comparative Study of Referendums: Government by the People*. Manchester and New York: Manchester University Press, 2002.

Qvortrup, Matt. *Referendums and Ethnic Conflict*. Philadelphia: University of Pennsylvania Press, 2014a.

Qvortrup, Matt. "Introduction: Theory, Practice and History." In *Referendums around the World: The Continued Growth of Direct Democracy*, edited by Matt Qvortrup. Basingstoke: Palgrave/Macmillan, 2014b, pp. 1–16.

Riker, William. *Federalism: Origin, Operation, Significance*. New York: Little, Brown & Company, 1964.

Smith, Daniel A. "Howard Jarvis, Populist Entrepreneur: Reevaluating the Causes of Proposition 13." *Social Science History* 23, no. 2 (1999): 173–210.

Smith, Daniel A., and Caroline Tolbert. *Educated by Initiative: The Effects of Direct Democracy on Citizens and Political Organizations in the American States*. Ann Arbor: University of Michigan Press, 2004.

Solière, Eugene. *Le Plébiscite dans l'annexion. Étude historique et critique de droit des gens*. Paris: L. Boyer, 1901.

Svensson, Palle. "Five Danish Referendums on the European Community and European Union: A Critical Assessment of the Franklin Thesis." *European Journal of Political Research* 41, no. 6 (2002): 733–750.

Tacitus, Publius C. *The Agricola and Germania*. London: Penguin, 1970.

Tsebelis, George. "The Power of the European Parliament as a Conditional Agenda Setter." *American Political Science Review* 88, no. 1 (1994): 128–142.

Tsebelis, George. *Veto Players: How Political Institutions Work*. Princeton, NJ: Princeton University Press, 2002.

Voeglin, Eric. "Extended Strategy: A New Technique of Dynamic Relations." *Journal of Politics* 2, no. 2 (1940): 189–200.

Vospernik, Stefan. *Modelle der direkten Demokratie*. Baden-Baden: Nomos Verlag, 2014.

....................................................

# CHAPTER 19

# ELECTORAL SYSTEMS
# IN AUTHORITARIAN
# STATES

....................................................

## JENNIFER GANDHI AND ABIGAIL L. HELLER

## INTRODUCTION

....................................................

MOST autocracies in the world today allow for multiparty national elections. The exceptions—such as China and Saudi Arabia—are very few. The rise of multiparty elections under authoritarianism became notable after the end of the Cold War as many single-party states in the developing world were forced to allow electoral openings (Levitsky and Way 2010). The increasing number of autocracies that hold elections has led to greater study of the phenomenon, and the reasons for elections in autocracies are the subject of a lively debate (for reviews, see Gandhi and Lust-Okar 2009; Hermet, Rose, and Rouquié 1978). Less closely examined are the rules under which these elections are held. Like elections in democracies, those in autocracies are held using a variety of electoral systems. In other words, there is a wide range of electoral rules, defined as laws that regulate "competition between and within parties" around elections (Cox 1997, 38). More specifically, electoral systems are the set of rules that regulate how citizens cast their votes and how these votes are translated into the seats for representatives (Gallagher and Mitchell 2005; Lijphart 1999). Thus, electoral systems include rules on the electoral formula (how votes are translated into seats), district magnitude (the number of seats per constituency), and electoral threshold (the minimum support necessary for representation), among others (Gallagher and Mitchell 2005; Lijphart 1994, 1999).

Given the proliferation of elections under autocracies, it seems natural that we should study the rules under which they are organized. We begin with some descriptive information about elections and electoral rules under authoritarianism, particularly from the post–World War II period, which provides the most systematic information. We then discuss two important aspects of electoral rules: the choice of rules and their effects in dictatorships. Regarding the choice of rules, the starting assumption in much of the literature is that dictators choose the rules that best suit their interests. While reasonable, it is worth highlighting that their choices are frequently made under constraints—in the form of other powerful actors and limits to their own knowledge. These constraints may account for why the choices of autocrats sometimes appear suboptimal. Regarding the effects of rules, the use of coercion and manipulation to win elections, along with the absence of sincere expressions of voting preferences through free media and polling, makes the problem of information especially acute in dictatorships. Without accurate information about voter preferences, it may be difficult for candidates, parties, and voters to coordinate, distorting the effect of rules on outcomes such as the size of the party system. These distortionary effects, in turn, make the problem of choice more difficult. These arguments stem from the small but growing literature on electoral rules in autocracies, but we also draw on studies of institutional choice in transitioning regimes and new democracies. In reviewing the literature, we also highlight areas for future research. The chapter closes with a brief conclusion.

## ELECTORAL SYSTEMS IN AUTOCRACIES

Elections to fill executive and legislative offices have been held in autocracies since at least the nineteenth century. By 1850, over thirty countries—none of which were democratic—held legislative elections (Przeworski 2009), and by 1880, over two-thirds of the countries in the world held them (Miller 2015). Data for the broader historical period show that prior to World War II, elections in autocracies generally experienced medium to high levels of contestation but maintained numerous restrictions on the franchise, limiting participatory opportunities (Miller 2015). Elites were willing to allow for some measure of competition among themselves as long as ordinary citizens could be kept out of the arena (either as voters or candidates). In contrast, elections in autocracies after World War II were increasingly characterized by low levels of contestation and high levels of participation. Newly independent countries in Sub-Saharan Africa and Asia guaranteed suffrage rights for all their citizens but were also responsible for the decline in electoral contestation. This notable lack of contestation, however, is primarily a Cold War phenomenon (Gandhi 2015). During the postwar period, while autocracies held almost as many legislative elections as democracies, the vast majority of these elections—until the 1990s—were noncompetitive (Barberá 2013). What makes multiparty elections in autocracies after the end of the Cold War distinct perhaps is the emergence of contestation in the context of full participation.

What we know empirically about electoral rules in autocracies comes from the post–World War II period. Majoritarian rules govern autocratic elections more frequently than democratic ones: 57 percent of legislative elections in dictatorships versus 29 percent in democracies (Barberá 2013). But variation in the rules still exists. The effective electoral threshold in dictatorships ranges from 0.27 to 37.5 (Higashijima and Chang

2016).[1] This means that autocracies run the gamut in their electoral systems—from very proportional systems with low electoral thresholds to pure single-seat district plurality (also known as first past the post, FPTP) systems with many forms of systems in between. Qualitative studies confirm this variation. Dictatorships, such as that under Hun Sen and the Cambodian People's Party, for example, have consistently maintained and dominated legislative elections held under proportional representation (PR). In Singapore, the People's Action Party wins overwhelming legislative majorities through a system with multi-seat "group representation constituencies": voters choose among competing party lists with the highest-polling party winning all the seats—between four and six—in the constituency (Reilly 2007).

Additionally, competitive elections were sometimes held even in the context of single-party rule. During single-party rule in Kenya and Tanzania, for example, the primary elections of the ruling party to fill legislative seats were competitive by design. Similarly, in Vietnam and China, where the Communist Party still has a monopoly on political power, elections for some National Assembly seats and for some local institutions (e.g., village committees and local congresses), respectively, see competition among candidates. Moreover, there is variation in electoral systems across these states. FPTP was used in Kenya under the Kenya African National Union (KANU) and in Tanzania under the Tanganyika African National Union (TANU) and its successor party, while Cuba uses a two-round majority system with single-seat districts, and Vietnam uses a system of multiple nontransferable vote in which voters have the same number of votes as there are seats in the district (Birch 2003; Malesky and Schuler 2010; Mozaffar 2004; Prevost 2015). In addition to differences in the electoral formula, there is also cross-national variation in the rules on candidate nomination, campaigning, and thresholds of participation for valid elections. For example, the Communist Party in the Soviet Union and TANU in Tanzania kept tight control of candidate nomination, Tanzania and Cuba both instituted strict rules regarding candidate campaigns, and the Soviet Union and Vietnam both instituted voter turnout thresholds below which the election would be void (Carson 1955; Hyden and Leys 1972; Inter-Parliamentary Union 2016; Prevost 2015; White, Rose, and McAllister 1997). Thus, while most contemporary efforts focus on electoral rules in postwar autocracies with multiparty elections, it may be worthwhile to consider broadening our scope.

The rules for translating votes into seats (electoral formulas) are important—as evinced by the frequency with which autocrats try to doctor them. Under the Institutional Revolutionary Party (PRI) between 1985 and 1997, Mexico used five different electoral systems for five legislative elections (Remmer 2008). Military rulers in Algeria switched from a two-round majority system to closed-list proportional representation in the late 1990s to prevent any repetition of an opposition victory—as occurred in the first round of the 1991 legislative elections (Bouandel 2005). Taiwan under the Kuomintang (KMT) adopted a new electoral system in 1992, and Cambodia under the Cambodian People's Party (CPP) changed their electoral formula between the 1993 and 1998 elections. In addition, authoritarian incumbents and opposition forces frequently clash over the rules. In Jordan, extra-parliamentary counsels have revised the electoral law a number of times—each of which has been met with serious opposition (Lust-Okar 2006). The change to reduce the number of votes per person from the number of seats in the district to a single vote was controversial enough to lead to an opposition boycott of elections in 1997. As Schedler (2002, 118) observes, elections under authoritarianism are "nested games" in which "the competition for votes and the struggle for electoral reform go hand in hand."

# AUTOCRATS' CHOICES OF RULES

One important area of research attempts to account for the variation in electoral rules under autocracy. Autocratic incumbents—like their democratic counterparts—want to stay in power. But there are multiple strategies that can be pursued to advance this goal. As a result, many of the predictions for the types of rules autocrats would choose are conditional on their regime type or underlying institutional structure. Moreover, a starting assumption seems to be that autocrats can unilaterally decide the rules under which elections are held. As a result, processes such as path dependence or diffusion—which sometimes are used to characterize rule choice in new democracies—are not important factors in this literature. While incumbents certainly are powerful and have preferences over rules, they often choose them under constraints—even in dictatorships.

For autocratic incumbents, the strategies for survival are many, and they are reflected in their consideration of different rules. If autocrats govern with a ruling party, they may tailor the electoral rules to increase the vote share of that party. Alternatively, incumbents may seek to write rules that explicitly disadvantage the opposition in a number of ways. But the time horizon of leaders matters greatly. Seat maximization for the dominant party and seat minimization for opposition parties take precedence when incumbents believe they are likely to remain in power. When they confront a regime transition or a high likelihood of losing power, then they may be more interested in providing themselves some insurance by securing a minimum of seats to make policy change less likely. However, even self-interest dominated by the logic of insurance can be thought of as seat maximization under the additional constraint of an expectation of loss.

Given the importance of self-interest in electoral rule choice, some have argued that different types of incumbents have divergent preferences for the distribution of power, leading to the selection of different electoral rules. Lust-Okar and Jamal (2002) argue that autocrats with dominant parties or single-party states likely already have well-developed organizations and thus prefer electoral systems that reinforce their dominance. They argue that in such regimes, autocrats will choose electoral rules with party lists, high national thresholds for representation, multi-seat districts, and electoral formulas that provide a bonus to the largest party. In the case of Mexico, Diaz-Cayeros and Magaloni (2001) demonstrate that the PRI chose electoral rules that would reinforce their existing dominance while dividing the opposition, in line with the theory presented by Lust-Okar and Jamal. The PRI shifted the electoral rules from a purely majoritarian system to a mixed-member system that included both FPTP and PR in multi-seat districts with a 1.5 to 2.5 percent threshold (the threshold was changed repeatedly between 1963 and 1999; Diaz-Cayeros and Magaloni 2001). Diaz-Cayeros and Magaloni argue that the multi-seat districts reduced the incentives for opposition parties to coordinate to dislodge the PRI, while the presence of plurality seats ensured the PRI could continue to win a disproportionately large share of seats. With a sufficiently divided opposition unable to mount a coordinated challenge, there was no need for high electoral thresholds to disadvantage small parties.

In contrast to the preferences of autocrats with established party organizations, Lust-Okar and Jamal (2002) argue that monarchs prefer to maintain their position by staying above the political fray. Monarchs prefer to act as a mediator between balanced competing forces because this role ensures their continued usefulness in the political system. This leads, according to Lust-Okar and Jamal, to monarchs selecting first past the post, small district magnitudes, and no electoral thresholds. These rules promote two-party systems (Cox 1997; Duverger 1954), or as Lust-Okar and Jamal argue, at least large blocs that are easier for the monarch to manage than many small parties.

While some argue that the choice of rules is dependent on the type of ruler, another section of the literature suggests that a ruler's expectations of winning the elections condition the choice of rules. By opening up the electoral arena to competition, a leader may expect to lose seats. In this case, the literature on electoral system choice and change in nineteenth- and twentieth-century Europe suggests that incumbents choose rules in an attempt to guarantee a minimum level of representation—to provide insurance for the future. This idea originated with Rokkan (1970, 157), who argued that incumbents threatened by the rising working class "demanded PR to protect their position against the new waves of mobilized voters created by universal suffrage." The theory was further refined and formalized by Boix (1999), who argued that incumbents alter the electoral system to increase proportionality when the electoral arena changes in such a way that is expected to significantly decrease their power and parliamentary seat share (see also Boix 2010; Kreuzer 2010). Specifically, Boix (1999) argues that when the coordinating capacity of the existing parties is low—when they secure roughly equal levels of support—there will be no focal party around which non-Socialist voters can rally and proportional representation will be adopted when a strong Socialist party enters the arena. Ahmed (2010, 2013) presents a slight variation of the insurance argument, recognizing that the starting point prior to reform in these countries was not FPTP but often a mixed-member system, and suggesting that both FPTP and proportional representation were reactions to the threat posed by Socialism. In contrast, Calvo's (2009) theory of electoral choice as insurance does not rely on the expansion of Socialism. He argues that majoritarian electoral rules combined with an increase in the number of parties exacerbate partisan biases (the extra seats a party secures beyond what is expected for other parties with the same vote share due to geographic concentration), which may not benefit incumbents, leading incumbents to pursue electoral system change.

The problem of choosing rules under conditions of loss appears to have been central for military rulers leaving power in Latin America as well. They confronted the choice between plurality and majority rules for the election of presidents. The latter typically requires candidates to win a majority of votes or else face a second-round runoff. Negretto (2006, 2009) argues that outgoing military rulers who knew they would have no partisan support or, at most, the support of small parties preferred majority runoff elections for the presidency. The two-round system encourages all parties to throw their hats into the electoral ring in the first round. The results of the first round help sort out who are the potential frontrunners around which other parties may coalesce for the second round. As such, the system is more inclusive in that small parties can influence who wins and, consequently, policy outcomes (see also Remmer 2008). Moreover, majority rule sets a threshold that is usually too high for any single party to achieve on its own, making it less likely that a single party—completely antagonistic to military interests— can win independently.

It is worth noting that expectations about losing and about regime change do not always coincide. In other words, the leaders of authoritarian regimes may facilitate a transition to democracy precisely because they expect that they will be able to win elections even under democracy (Slater and Wong 2013). Wright and Escribà-Folch (2012) find that in all dominant party regimes that democratized during the post–World War II period, the former ruling party remained electorally competitive after the transition, winning at least the second-largest share of seats in the legislature. In these cases, authoritarian incumbents may have few incentives to change the rules since they expect to use those same rules to win under democracy.

Major rules, such as PR versus FPTP, are obviously important since they have a large impact on outcomes, and hence are the object of study for much of the literature on electoral rules more generally. But it is important to note that even for autocrats trying to maximize their chances of retaining power and the number of seats for the ruling party, these major rules present tradeoffs. For rulers with dominant parties, FPTP may yield a seat bonus, but it also provides incentives for opposition candidates and voters to coordinate, potentially resulting in a stronger opposing force. PR, in turn, makes it more difficult for opposition forces to coordinate, but its proportionality potentially reduces the ruling party's dominance. Higashijima and Chang (2016), for example, examine the costs and tradeoffs associated with different rules. They argue that although single-seat district systems can give the ruling party a seat bonus that helps a dictator "co-opt ruling elites with institutionalized rent-seeking opportunities," they also "depress voter turnout and incentivize opposition parties to build a pre-electoral coalition" (Higashijima and Chang 2016, 3). Thus, a dictator may prefer to use PR to divide the opposition and increase turnout, which gives the regime an image of popularity and invincibility. Because the dictator faces a tradeoff between co-opting elites within the ruling coalition to ensure their continued support and dividing the opposition while also appeasing them by allowing them some representation, Higashijima and Chang argue that dictators with access to significant financial resources will use these resources to buy voter support and use PR to divide the opposition.

Because changes in major rules can have either contradictory effects or significant costs, autocratic rulers may turn their attention elsewhere to achieve victory. They often establish or alter smaller rules that structure competition, targeting the opposition without incurring the tradeoffs discussed previously. Autocrats, for example, may gerrymander to create protected constituencies for their parties and allies. They also may set high de facto vote thresholds that opposition candidates are unlikely to surmount. One common way of doing this is through distributional vote requirements. In Kenya, four months before the 1992 election, for example, the ruling party pushed through a constitutional amendment requiring successful presidential candidates to win at least 25 percent of the votes in no fewer than five out of eight provinces. The regulation was designed to diminish the electoral prospects of opposition candidates who often drew support from particular regions. If opposition parties attempt to surmount this problem by forming electoral coalitions, incumbents can deter this strategy as well. In Mexico, any parties seeking to form a pre-electoral coalition had to do so for both presidential and legislative elections, lowering the likelihood of an opposition coalition for any election. In Senegal, the Senegalese Democratic Party (PDS) banned coalitions to prevent opposition forces from mounting a credible electoral challenge against it. Because smaller rule changes enable incumbents to skirt the tradeoffs encountered in major rule changes, they should produce identifiable effects. Consequently, more attention should be paid to the full variety of electoral rules, including voter registration, candidate nomination, and campaign laws.

Recognizing and incorporating this variety into our theories is important because these rules may act as substitutes. In other words, while FPTP may present a variety of costs in terms of decreasing turnout and incentivizing opposition coordination (Higashijima and Chang 2016), a proportional system with high electoral thresholds, short campaign periods, and low district magnitudes may allow the dictator to alleviate these costs while also obtaining the benefit of a seat bonus similar to that under plurality. Thus, a better specification of the range of electoral rules will allow for a better understanding of how dictators balance the costs and tradeoffs discussed in the existing literature.

## SUBOPTIMAL CHOICES

Through their use of minor and major rule changes, it is tempting to assume that incumbents—especially autocratic ones—always achieve their goals. Yet country-level studies that simulate electoral results under various electoral rules frequently show that incumbents could have more effectively achieved their goals under a different choice of rules. Remington and Smith (1996) show that Yeltsin and his allies should have supported an all-FPTP system (rather than a mixed-member majoritarian one) in Russia if they wanted to advance the policy goals of reformers. Simulated electoral results show that Communists in both Hungary (Benoit and Schiemann 2001) and Poland

(Kaminski 2002) would have better maximized their seat shares if they had chosen pure PR. Instead, the former chose a mixed-member system with a relatively even division between PR and constituency seats, while the latter initially opted for majority runoff (for the lower houses).

Seemingly suboptimal choices by the incumbent may be the result of different factors. Incumbents may not be able to choose rules unilaterally so that their choices, in fact, are evidence of constrained optimization. Alternatively, incumbents may be making choices under conditions of high uncertainty, leading them to misestimate their level of support among the voters and to choose the "wrong" rules. Actors also may have limited information about the distributive effects of rules. We review these factors in turn.

## The Constraints of Opposition

While autocrats usually have great power to "structure the world so that they can win" (paraphrasing Riker 1986a, ix), they do not always make choices about electoral rules unilaterally. The threat of rebellion pushed incumbents to expand the franchise in Western Europe in the late nineteenth/early twentieth century. Further, some have suggested that this threat of rebellion is what led to the adoption of proportional representation. Alesina and Glaeser (2004, 8) argue that labor uprisings and strikes "effectively threatened the entire nation" in countries such as Belgium, Finland, the Netherlands, Sweden, and Switzerland. Since the strikers explicitly demanded proportional representation in many cases, electoral reform and the adoption of PR was a direct result of these threats. In a related argument, Ahmed (2013) suggests that the choice of PR was partly a function of the radicalization of the Socialist party. Ahmed argues that both FPTP and PR were reactions of the right parties to the electoral threat of Socialism. Where the Socialist party was moderate, their entrance triggered party realignment, but not proportional representation because the prospect of a Socialist electoral victory did not threaten the social order (Ahmed 2013). Conversely, where the Socialist party was more radical, they "not only posed an electoral threat, they posed a threat to the existing social order," making an outright Socialist victory under FPTP more problematic from the perspective of right parties and leading to the adoption of PR to prevent such a situation (Ahmed 2013, 24).

Brought to the bargaining table by the threat of unrest, autocrats may then be constrained by the actual bargaining protocol and the degree to which their opponents can mobilize against them. Hungarian Communists, for example, were forced to the bargaining table in 1989 by growing political opposition amid an economic crisis (Benoit and Schiemann 2001). Earlier in the year, they had tried to unilaterally impose their own preferences by proposing a mostly FPTP system, but opposition forces led massive demonstrations that ultimately terminated the effort. Once at the roundtable talks, the Communists had to negotiate with a united coalition of opposition parties that had agreed to make all their decisions unanimously before presenting a unified stance to their adversary.

While it is natural to focus on the political interactions characterized as "government versus opposition," it is critical to remember that opposition forces are not always united against authoritarian incumbents. In fact, there may be situations in which the ruling party colludes with certain opposition parties to diminish the electoral competitiveness of others. In Hungary, the Communists and some of the larger opposition parties argued for higher electoral thresholds to deter competition from smaller parties (Benoit and Schiemann 2001). In Mexico, in 1993, the ruling PRI and the largest opposition party, the National Action Party (PAN), both supported an electoral reform that required two parties wishing to cross-endorse, or nominate a single presidential candidate, to have common candidates in all other national legislative races (Diaz-Cayeros and Magaloni 2001). The PAN supported this because cross-endorsement of presidential candidates had previously benefited the Party of the Democratic Revolution (PRD), a smaller but rising opposition party. Additionally, the 1993 reform gave some other benefits to the PAN, including giving the power to certify election results to the Federal Electoral Institute and a new rule for choosing senators that ensured the fourth senator from every state would be a representative of the second-largest party, which would benefit the PAN more than the PRD (Diaz-Cayeros and Magaloni 2001).

## The Problem of Uncertainty

For autocrats choosing electoral rules for multiparty or multicandidate competition for the first time, it is difficult to imagine how there could not have been great uncertainty even if the incumbents themselves postured as if they were acting with certainty. In the initial electoral openings in Eastern Europe (1989–1990), leaders in Poland and other Communist countries were adamant about maintaining single-seat districts, believing that this electoral system would benefit them as the dominant party or as incumbent candidates with greater name recognition (Bielasiak 2002; Kaminski 2002). Yet their choice backfired on them. Similarly, in Algeria, the government first organized partisan elections at the local and regional levels in 1990. After a relatively new party, the Islamic Salvation Front (FIS), won control of more than half of the local assemblies, the government scrambled to change the electoral rules for elections to the national assembly to be held the following year (Bouandel 2005). It seems likely that in first elections or in later elections when new parties emerge, the distribution of support for the incumbent and challengers is relatively unclear. And since polling in authoritarian regimes is fraught with problems of "preference falsification" (Kuran 1991), it should not be surprising that parties make mistakes in calculating which rules would best serve their electoral interests.

In addition, there is clear evidence that autocrats sometimes suffer from lack of knowledge about how rules work and their effects. In choosing the PR formulas to be used in Hungary, both the Communist Party and the united opposition were "unsure about the distributive effects of alternative formulas" (Benoit and Schiemann 2001, 175). A similar account may explain what occurred in Chile where the military government and its civilian allies adopted an electoral system with two-seat districts in an attempt to reduce the party system fractionalization that characterized the pre-Pinochet period. While the binominal system has incentivized the emergence of two electoral blocs, it has neither reduced the number of parties (Siavelis 1997) nor guaranteed the stability of the electoral coalitions (Carey and Siavelis 2006).

# THE EFFECTS OF RULES

In democracies, electoral systems have been found to have effects on a variety of political and economic phenomena, but the strongest results about electoral systems lie in their effects on party systems. The well-known Duverger's law suggests that first past the post creates incentives for voters and candidates to coordinate, producing fewer parties at the constituency, and possibly national, level (Cox 1997; Duverger 1954, 1986; Rae 1971; Riker 1976, 1986b; Sartori 1986). Specifically, Duverger argues that FPTP tends to lead to two-party systems because of "mechanical" and "psychological" effects (Duverger 1954). The mechanical effect refers to the direct effect of the electoral formula—all but the two strongest parties are underrepresented in the legislature because other parties tend to be unable to win districts. The psychological effect reinforces the mechanical one—citizens realize that if they vote for third parties that are unable to win seats, they are wasting their vote, and will therefore vote instead for one of the two largest parties. In contrast, proportional electoral systems tend to produce multiparty systems (Cox 1997; Duverger 1954, 1986; Riker 1976, 1986b).

Do we observe the same effect in autocracies? The underlying question is whether there is something different about the authoritarian context that would alter or invalidate the mechanisms driving results consistent with Duverger's law. In autocracies, voters and candidates may have little information about the distribution of preferences across the electorate, creating uncertainty about around whom they should coordinate. With increasing experience with elections, they can learn the relevant information over time so that they may coordinate appropriately. (See Andrews and Jackman 2005 and Tavits and Annus 2006 about this in new democracies.)

Yet this process of learning is conditional on two factors: accurate information and the stability of rules. First, to some extent, strategic coordination among voters and candidates—the mechanism through which electoral rules influence party systems—works only to the extent that the fundamentals of democratic elections are respected. Voters and candidates need relatively accurate information about voters' preferences and the viability of candidates. This may be difficult to obtain in a context in which voters perceive the necessity of "preference falsification" (Kuran 1991), polls by independent organizations are rarely carried out and publicized, and media are not free to report on incumbents *and* challengers. In addition, to the extent that autocrats rely on fraudulent practices—such as ballot-box stuffing and manipulation of the vote aggregation process—they introduce significant amounts of noise to the vote totals. If voters are aware of the fraud (which they often are), then it creates even more doubt about the official electoral results as indicators of popular support for candidates and parties.

Second, when electoral rules change often within short spans of time, it may be difficult for voters and candidates to coordinate their behavior. This is a problem theoretically not only for autocracies but also for any regime that experiences frequent changes in rules and institutions.[2] Empirically, however, autocracies change their electoral rules much more frequently than democracies. Barberá (2013) reports that during the post–World War II period, 10 percent of autocracies made major rule changes, while 28 percent made minor ones (in comparison to 6 and 13 percent of democracies, respectively). These descriptive data confirm the relative ease with which authoritarian governments can change the rules. They also suggest that coordinating behavior may be difficult because of frequent rule changes.

Whether these problems are insurmountable is partly an empirical question. Examining over 100 elections in Sub-Saharan Africa, Mylonas and Roussias (2008) find that the interaction of electoral rules and ethnopolitical cleavages predicts the number of parties only in democracies, not autocracies. Barberá (2013), in contrast, investigates all postwar elections in autocracies and finds evidence of learning over time by voters and candidates: after changes to FPTP, the number of electoral opposition parties declines with each successive election, but after changes to PR, that number increases with each additional election. While the problems of information and rule instability initially may impede voter and candidate coordination, they may eventually resolve themselves as autocrats settle on rules that confer advantages and voters and candidates learn how to better operate under them. Consequently, electoral coordination, which ultimately influences the party system, may just occur more slowly under authoritarianism than under democracy.

It is critical to remember, however, that coordination within districts is different from—although related to—coordination across constituencies. FPTP generates incentives for two candidates to emerge within a constituency. Whether these effects scale up to a two-party system at the national level depends on a variety of other factors, including the distribution of power across levels of government (Chhibber and Kollman 1998, 2004), the number of legislative chambers, and the presence of policy or institutional domains controlled by unelected actors (e.g., appointed seats in the legislature; Hicken 2009). In fact, in authoritarian regimes with a nascent opposition, there is no guarantee that candidates will coordinate across districts to present a united challenge to the regime. So whether an autocrat ends up with a legislature divided between the ruling party and a united opposition party or one full of independents depends on the electoral system *and* other institutional rules. This discussion highlights one potentially fruitful avenue for future work on electoral systems in authoritarian regimes—considering the conditions (beyond simply the electoral system) under which opposition candidates are able to coordinate and when opposition parties nationalize. This will allow for better specification of the effects of different electoral rules.

Conditional on the current party system, changes in electoral rules may have short-term effects that are more immediately evident to decision-makers and researchers alike. Some types of changes immediately disadvantage opposition parties or augment the incumbency advantage. As discussed earlier, geographic requirements on the distribution of support for the winning candidate put the ruling party in a more favorable position to win. Restrictions on the length, content, or funding of campaigns often immediately disadvantage opposition candidates who struggle against the war chests and name recognition of incumbents (McElwain 2008).

Other rules may have short-term effects on the electoral strategies of incumbent and opposition actors. For example, electoral formulas affect what opposition parties have to lose by deciding to boycott. Under PR, even small parties have something to lose, and as a result, they are less likely to boycott. Under FPTP, small opposition parties have little hope of obtaining seats and so they may be more likely to boycott. Consistent with this argument, Schedler (2013) shows that opposition parties almost never withdraw from contesting legislative elections under PR or mixed-member systems, but they stage boycotts in about 40 percent of majoritarian elections. Electoral rules may also condition the use of violence in elections. Birch (2003) argues that two-round elections are destabilizing because they encourage the use of nonelectoral means to exercise power. The first round of the election provides electoral contestants with more information about the geographic distribution of support for themselves and their opponents. They can use this information to target voters with violence in the run-up to the second round, making victory more likely.

Distinguishing between the short- and long-term effects of electoral rules has obvious importance for studying the choice of electoral rules as well. In authoritarian regimes, the problems of information and rule instability may mean that the effects of some electoral rules either do not exist or are evident only in the long-term (e.g., PR vs. FPTP on size of the party system). This raises questions about what we can say about electoral choice. Incumbents and challengers have preferences over rules because they have expectations about how the rules work and the outcomes that they should produce. But if the effect of electoral rules is not evident within one or two election cycles, then what should vote- or seat-maximizing autocrats and opposition parties prefer and choose in terms of the electoral rules? The difficulty of determining the long-term effects of electoral rules makes the choice of these rules nonobvious. Smaller rules, such as laws on campaigning, may exhibit much more immediate and straightforward effects on electoral behavior and outcomes. In this case, the effects of rule manipulation are much clearer, encouraging those who have the power to tinker and tailor with them to do so.

# Conclusion

The literature on the choice and effects of electoral rules in autocracies tends to focus on the preferences of the dictator. In general, this is a sensible choice for at least two reasons. First, even the original literature on electoral rules in democracies recognizes that the power to alter the rules primarily rests with incumbents (Katz 2005). Second, dictators often face fewer constraints than their democratic counterparts and thus their preferences are likely the main determinant of the rules (Higashijima and Chang 2016; Lust-Okar and Jamal 2002).

Yet it is important to recognize that even the most powerful autocrats choose rules under constraints. The constraints may come in the form of opposition actors who can threaten to mobilize protests or deny the election's legitimacy through a boycott, if they are not allowed to compete under rules they deem acceptable. Additionally, the constraints may come in the form of the dictator's own limited information or knowledge about how the rules work and the distribution of preferences among the electorate. The uncertainty over voter preferences would seem to be a particularly acute problem for autocracies where the use of coercion, vote buying, and fraud in elections are rampant, and the expression of sincere preferences through media and electoral polls is limited. These tactics enable autocrats to win elections, but they also create more uncertainty about voter preferences and make coordination among voters and parties more difficult. The end result may be that the problem of electoral system choice is more difficult for autocrats even if they face fewer constraints than their democratic counterparts.

## Notes

1. The effective electoral threshold is "the proportion of votes that, for each electoral system, secures parliamentary representation to any party with a probability of at least 50" percent (Boix 1999, 614).
2. See, for example, Herron's chapter on Ukraine in this volume.

## References

Ahmed, Amel. "Reading History Forward: The Origins of Electoral Systems in European Democracies." *Comparative Political Studies* 43, no. 8/9 (2010): 1059–1088.

Ahmed, Amel. *Democracy and the Politics of Electoral System Choice: Engineering Electoral Dominance*. Cambridge: Cambridge University Press, 2013.

Alesina, Alberto, and Edward L. Glaeser. *Fighting Poverty in the US and Europe: A World of Difference*. Oxford: Oxford University Press, 2004.

Andrews, Josephine T., and Robert W. Jackman. "Strategic Fools: Electoral Rule Choice under Extreme Uncertainty." *Electoral Studies* 24, no. 1 (2005): 65–84.

Barberá, Pablo. "When Duverger Becomes Autocratic: Electoral Systems and Opposition Fragmentation in Non-Democratic Regimes." Manuscript, Department of Political Science, New York University, 2013.

Benoit, Kenneth, and John Schiemann. "Institutional Choice in New Democracies: Bargaining over Hungary's 1989 Electoral Law." *Journal of Theoretical Politics* 13, no. 2 (2001): 153–182.

Bielasiak, Jack. "The Institutionalization of Electoral and Party Systems in Postcommunist States." *Comparative Politics* 34, no. 2 (2002): 189–210.

Birch, Sarah. "Two-Round Electoral Systems and Democracy." *Comparative Political Studies* 36, no. 3 (2003): 319–344.

Boix, Carles. "Setting the Rules of the Game: The Choice of Electoral Systems in Advanced Democracies." *American Political Science Review* 93, no. 3 (1999): 609–624.

Boix, Carles. "Electoral Markets, Party Strategies, and Proportional Representation." *American Political Science Review* 104, no. 2 (2010): 404–413.

Bouandel, Youcef. "Reforming the Algerian Electoral System." *Journal of Modern African Studies* 43, no. 3 (2005): 393–415.

Calvo, Ernesto. "The Competitive Road to Proportional Representation: Partisan Biases and Electoral Regime Change under Increasing Party Competition." *World Politics* 61, no. 2 (2009): 254–295.

Carey, John, and Peter Siavelis. "Electoral Insurance and Coalition Survival: Formal and Informal Institutions in Chile." In *Informal Institutions and Democracy: Lessons from Latin America*, edited by Gretchen Helmke and Steven Levitsky, 160–177. Baltimore: Johns Hopkins University, 2006.

Carson, George Barr, Jr. *Electoral Practices in the U.S.S.R.* New York: Frederick A. Praeger, 1955.

Chhibber, Pradeep, and Ken Kollman. "Party Aggregation and the Number of Parties in India and the United States." *American Political Science Review* 92, no. 2 (1998): 329–342.

Chhibber, Pradeep, and Ken Kollman. *The Formation of National Party Systems: Federalism and Party Competition in Canada, Great Britain, India, and the United States*. Princeton, NJ: Princeton University Press, 2004.

Cox, Gary W. *Making Votes Count: Strategic Coordination in the World's Electoral Systems*. Cambridge: Cambridge University Press, 1997.

Diaz-Cayeros, Alberto, and Beatriz Magaloni. "Party Dominance and the Logic of Electoral Design in Mexico's Transition to Democracy." *Journal of Theoretical Politics* 13, no. 3 (2001): 271–293.

Duverger, Maurice. *Political Parties*. New York: Wiley, 1954.

Duverger, Maurice. "Duverger's Law: Forty Years Later." In *Electoral Laws and Their Political Consequences*, edited by Bernard Grofman and Arend Lijphart, 69–84. New York: Agathon Press, 1986.

Gallagher, Michael, and Paul Mitchell. "Introduction to Electoral Systems." In *The Politics of Electoral Systems*, edited by Michael Gallagher and Paul Mitchell, 3–23. Oxford: Oxford University Press, 2005.

Gandhi, Jennifer. "Elections and Political Regimes." *Government and Opposition* 50, no. 3 (2015): 446–468.

Gandhi, Jennifer, and Ellen Lust-Okar. "Elections under Authoritarianism." *Annual Review of Political Science* 12 (2009): 403–422.

Hermet, Guy, Richard Rose, and Alain Rouquié, eds. *Elections without Choice*. New York: Wiley, 1978.

Hicken, Allen. *Building Party Systems in Developing Democracies*. Cambridge: Cambridge University Press, 2009.

Higashijima, Masaaki, and Eric Chang. "The Choice of Electoral Systems in Dictatorships," Manuscript, Version 5.3, 2016.

Hyden, Goran, and Colin Leys. "Elections and Politics in Single-Party Systems: The Case of Kenya and Tanzania." *British Journal of Political Science* 2, no. 4 (1972): 389–420.

Inter-Parliamentary Union. "Vietnam: Quoc-Hoi (National Assembly)." 2016. http://www.ipu .org/parline-e/reports/2349_B.htm (accessed May 9, 2016).

Kaminski, Marek. "Do Parties Benefit from Electoral Manipulation? Electoral Laws and Heresthetics in Poland, 1989-93." *Journal of Theoretical Politics* 14, no. 3 (2002): 325-358.

Katz, Richard S. "Why Are There So Many (or So Few) Electoral Reforms?" In *The Politics of Electoral Systems,* edited by Michael Gallagher and Paul Mitchell, 57-76. Oxford: Oxford University Press, 2005.

Kreuzer, Marcus. "Historical Knowledge and Quantitative Analysis: The Case of the Origins of Proportional Representation." *American Political Science Review* 104, no. 2 (2010): 369-392.

Kuran, Timur. "Now Out of Never: The Element of Surprise in the East European Revolution of 1989." *World Politics* 44, no. 1 (1991): 7-48.

Levitsky, Steven, and Lucan Way. *Competitive Authoritarianism: Hybrid Regimes after the Cold War.* New York: Cambridge University Press, 2010.

Lijphart, Arend. *Electoral Systems and Party Systems: A Study of Twenty-Seven Democracies, 1945-1990.* Oxford: Oxford University Press, 1994.

Lijphart, Arend. *Patterns of Democracy: Government Forms and Performance in Thirty-Six Countries.* New Haven, CT: Yale University Press, 1999.

Lust-Okar, Ellen. "Elections under Authoritarianism: Preliminary Lessons from Jordan." *Democratization* 13, no. 3 (2006): 456–471.

Lust-Okar, Ellen, and Amaney Ahmad Jamal. "Rulers and Rules: Reassessing the Influence of Regime Type on Electoral Law Formation." *Comparative Political Studies* 35, no. 3 (2002): 337–366.

Malesky, Edmund, and Paul Schuler. "Nodding or Needling: Analyzing Delegate Responsiveness in an Authoritarian Parliament." *American Political Science Review* 104, no. 3 (2010): 482–502.

McElwain, Kenneth Mori. "Manipulating Electoral Rules to Manufacture Single-Party Dominance." *American Journal of Political Science* 52, no. 1 (2008): 32–47.

Miller, Michael. "Democratic Pieces: Autocratic Elections and Democratic Development since 1815." *British Journal of Political Science* 45, no. 3 (2015): 501–530.

Mozaffar, Shaheen. "Africa: Electoral Systems in Emerging Democracies." In *Handbook of Electoral System Choice,* edited by Josep M. Colomer, 419–435. Hampshire: Palgrave Macmillan, 2004.

Mylonas, Harris, and Nasos Roussias. "When Do Votes Count? Regime Type, Electoral Conduct, and Political Competition in Africa." *Comparative Political Studies* 41, no. 11 (2008): 1466–1491.

Negretto, Gabriel. "Choosing How to Choose Presidents: Parties, Military Rulers, and Presidential Elections in Latin America." *Journal of Politics* 68, no. 2 (2006): 421–433.

Negretto, Gabriel. "Political Parties and Institutional Design: Explaining Constitutional Choice in Latin America." *British Journal of Political Science* 39, no. 1 (2009): 117–139.

Prevost, Gary. "Cuba," In *Politics of Latin America: The Power Game,* 5th ed., edited by Harry E. Vanden and Gary Prevost, 515–537. Oxford: Oxford University Press, 2015.

Przeworski, Adam. "Constraints and Choices: Electoral Participation in Historical Perspective." *Comparative Political Studies* 42, no. 1 (2009): 4–30.

Rae, Douglas W. *The Political Consequences of Electoral Laws.* New Haven, CT: Yale University Press, 1971.

Reilly, Benjamin. "Democratization and Electoral Reform in the Asia-Pacific Region: Is There an 'Asian Model' of Democracy?" *Comparative Political Studies* 40, no. 11 (2007): 1350–1371.

Remington, Thomas F., and Steven S. Smith. "Political Goals, Institutional Context, and the Choice of an Electoral System: The Russian Parliamentary Election Law." *American Journal of Political Science* 40, no. 4 (1996): 1253–1279.

Remmer, Karen. "The Politics of Institutional Change: Electoral Reform in Latin America, 1978-2002." *Party Politics* 14, no. 1 (2008): 5–30.

Riker, William H. "The Number of Political Parties: A Reexamination of Duverger's Law." *Comparative Politics* 9, no. 1 (1976): 93–106.

Riker, William H. *The Art of Political Manipulation*. New Haven, CT: Yale University Press, 1986a.

Riker, William H. "Duverger's Law Revisited." In *Electoral Laws and Their Political Consequences*, edited by Bernard Grofman and Arend Lijphart, 19–42. New York: Agathon Press, 1986b.

Rokkan, Stein. *Citizens, Elections, Parties: Approaches to the Comparative Study of the Processes of Development*. New York: David McKay Company, 1970.

Sartori, Giovanni. "The Influence of Electoral Systems: Faulty Laws or Faulty Method?" In *Electoral Laws and Their Political Consequences*, edited by Bernard Grofman and Arend Lijphart, 43–68. New York: Agathon Press, 1986.

Schedler, Andreas. "The Nested Game of Democratization by Elections." *International Political Science Review* 23, no. 1 (2002): 103–122.

Schedler, Andreas. *The Politics of Uncertainty: Sustaining and Subverting Electoral Authoritarianism*. Oxford: Oxford University Press, 2013.

Siavelis, Peter. "Continuity and Change in the Chilean Party System: On the Transformational Effects of Electoral Reform." *Comparative Political Studies* 30, no. 6 (1997): 651–674.

Slater, Dan, and Joseph Wong. "The Strength to Concede: Ruling Parties and Democratization in Developmental Asia." *Perspectives on Politics* 11, no. 3 (2013): 717–733.

Tavits, Margit, and Taavi Annus. "Learning to Make Votes Count: The Role of Democratic Experience." *Electoral Studies* 25, no. 1 (2006): 72–90.

White, Stephen, Richard Rose, and Ian McAllister. *How Russia Votes*. Chatham: Chatham House Publishers, 1997.

Wright, Joseph, and Abel Escribà-Folch. "Authoritarian Institutions and Regime Survival: Transitions to Democracy and Subsequent Autocracy." *British Journal of Political Science* 42, no. 2 (2012): 283–309.

# PART IV

# ELECTORAL SYSTEMS AND RESEARCH DESIGN

# CHAPTER 20

# ELECTION DATA AND LEVELS OF ANALYSIS

KEN KOLLMAN

## INTRODUCTION

WELL-KNOWN areas of literature from political science demonstrate that researchers can draw different conclusions about domestic political processes depending on the level of analysis of the data used. What, for example, drives election outcomes? From survey data of individuals, we have learned that for many mature democracies, partisanship is the best predictor of how individuals will vote in national elections (e.g., Miller, 1976; Shively 1979; Green, Palmquist, and Schickler 2002; Brader and Tucker 2012). Yet, at the same time, nationally aggregated vote outcomes for parties change over time in response to macroeconomic outcomes (see Lewis-Beck and Paldam 2000; Duch 2007).

In the realm of public opinion, is the mass public rational? Public opinion measures when aggregated appear to be quite rational in response to new information, but individuals tend to show persistent biases and psychological inconsistencies in surveys, in experiments, and in the field (compare Page and Shapiro 1992 to Druckman 2004 and Chong and Druckman 2007).

Returning to elections: are national elections mostly about what happens within the countries themselves, or are there measurable spillover effects from other countries? Electoral politics within countries, namely, which parties rise and fall at election time, swing with the nature of the times and the idiosyncrasies of candidate personalities and exogenous events. Yet, using more aggregated election data, we observe strong correlations across countries in which kinds of parties tend to win elections. (See, for example, Caramani 2015.)

By *level of analysis*, we typically mean the level of data used to address a specific political phenomenon. Do we have individual-level survey data? Or aggregated data on election outcomes, such as at the state or county level? Put another way, what is a case in our data? A person? A candidate? A county? A party? A state? The notion of level of analysis seems straightforward. But in fact, it raises complicated issues in research and can be confusingly described and rendered in research literatures.

In this chapter I discuss the advantages, but also challenges, of having election data at various levels of analysis. I focus on the use of multiple levels of data to analyze various aspects of a given theoretical framework, using primarily the literature on Duverger's law as an example. The literature on Duverger's law, among other areas of research, has benefited from new sources of data and from research drawing upon those data at multiple levels of analysis.

Fortunately, election results across the world are being collected and organized into useable datasets at various levels of analysis, including voting machines, polling stations, precincts, villages, constituencies, provinces or states, regions, and countries. In some cases they are being matched to survey data (e.g., Comparative Study of Electoral Systems, or CSES). Some of these datasets described later in this chapter are organized in a manner that permits relatively easy aggregation and comparison across units to answer important questions about electoral systems and party systems.

## RELATED BUT DISTINCT USAGES

Confusion about levels of analysis stems from the fact that we blend together a variety of aspects of data collection, organization, and analysis that are related but distinct. First and foremost, *researchers make decisions about data when they have options.* A researcher decides which level of analysis to use to understand better a particular political phenomenon. Election results data, for instance, may be reported at the precinct, village, constituency, or national level. We might look for how the German Greens did in Bavarian areas, or how they did nationwide. Likewise, we might aggregate and summarize election results reported at the individual level with survey data. How did the Greens do among Catholic Bavarians? We might need individual-level survey data to divide out Catholics from Protestants and nonreligious people in Bavaria, and Bavarian respondents from the rest of German respondents. Different kinds of questions call for different kinds of data at various levels. This is matching the level of analysis to the research question.

Second, this crucial aspect of research design should not be confused with answering slightly different questions when the *objects of study are at different levels of aggregation.* One example is the difference between studying political parties and studying party systems. Another example from American politics is the literature on whether Americans trust Congress. The answer depends on what we want to understand. Measures of aggregate public opinion show that Americans as a whole dislike Congress and express mistrust in the institution, but these same polls show that most Americans like their own member of Congress and trust him or her (Cain, Ferejohn, and Fiorina 1990; King 1997; Weisberg 1979). The questions being asked are actually different. What is your attitude toward Congress? What is your attitude toward your representative? Here, the researcher may have chosen to study macro public opinion data (same level of analysis) but where the objects for which we are trying to understand attitudes are at two different levels of aggregation—individual member of Congress versus Congress as a whole.

Third, *researchers may have no choice but to use data at the "wrong" level of analysis*. We may have limited options over the level of analysis given the availability of data. Consider two kinds of aggregated data: Some data come in aggregated form and there is little or nothing that can be done to get data at lower levels of analysis. For instance, it may be the case that we can only get election results at the national level for some countries, or at the constituency level, but no lower. Perhaps we cannot find available precinct or polling station data. By the very nature of the data, it is aggregated at some level. We are relegated to analyzing the data, and something is lost by the aggregation. We can think of this as a negative form of aggregated data, because if we had the resources or the means, we would do better with data disaggregated.

Alternatively, data on elections can be aggregated intentionally, with theoretical motivation, leading to innovative research designs and new answers to questions. Consider, for instance, the aggregation of votes across parties into votes for party families, and then across the various countries' party families. The opportunities to combine data into larger units to look for broader patterns, while maintaining the data at smaller units, provide avenues for new, interesting insights. This is a positive form of data aggregation. In the case of research on party families, for example, Caramani (2015) can aggregate election results by party family, by party family within and across countries, and by decade, to tell a rich and important story about the Europeanization of party politics on that continent over the course of the twentieth century.

Researchers may not have options given available data, but often they do. Trite as it may be to state it this way, if a researcher has options over levels of analysis in answering questions about electoral politics, the correct level of analysis depends on the question. This (barely qualifying) pearl of wisdom is not as simplistic as it seems. Sometimes it is stated as such: ideally, if researchers have options, the focus of research attention, the phenomenon being studied, should match the level of data used to conduct empirical analysis. Theories about individual decision making would ideally have individual-level data. Theories about political parties would have data at the party level. And so on.

Yet, our fourth aspect is that sometimes it can be valuable to use *multiple levels of analysis to study the same phenomenon*. With a form of "triangulating," addressing research questions from multiple angles, researchers can make decisions to use data at multiple levels of analysis to study the empirical implications of a theory. We learn different, but often complementary and richer, things from coming at problems from various levels.

An example that I will expand upon later concerns Duverger's law. We can learn more about the law and its implications from multiple levels of analysis than we can from any one level of analysis, even if the phenomenon being studied is ultimately similar or the same. And as research on Duverger's law involves several actors and collections of actors—voters, candidates, parties, party systems—the research literature, when taken as a whole, offers insights into all of these.

Fifth and finally, we can have *data available at a similar level of analysis but not exactly the same*, greatly complicating efforts to create analyzable datasets. Consider, for instance, demographic or social data available at the US county level, with political data available at the congressional constituency level. It takes methodological skills, and sometimes careful, detailed statistical modeling, to extrapolate the county-level data into the congressional districts.

More concretely, suppose we had data on the number of welfare recipients at the county level, and we had election results for congressional elections at the constituency/district level. How do we get a measure of the number of welfare recipients at the congressional district level? We need to use methods to extrapolate, using geographic areal weights or population weights, or even to use a more complex kriging method (more details later), to provide estimated numbers at the congressional district level. These are common but knotty problems of geospatial mapping from the literature on geospatial statistics, and there is no escaping the fact that any method used to extrapolate data across most levels of analysis we would care about in political science requires a set of assumptions that can reasonably be considered arbitrary. The US case of counties and congressional districts is in the middle range in terms of how challenging it is to match up geographic units, a topic I return to later in this chapter.

The fifth and final thing discussed previously concerns mostly "horizontal" issues of levels of analysis—the units are roughly the same level but the boundaries of the units are not the same—whereas it is more common to have issues involving "vertical issues" of levels of analysis, with nested data that can, in principle, be aggregated to higher levels or disaggregated to lower levels. The horizontal situation mentioned, in which in the US county and congressional district boundaries overlap in haphazard ways, requires a very different set of tools to create useable datasets in comparison with the tools required in vertical situations. An example of a vertical situation would be where all counties lie within a given American state and if, given county-level data, one could aggregate up to state-level data.

The implications of researchers' decisions and their limited options due to data availability are shaped by what we know to be fundamentally true about aggregation and disaggregation properties of data in general, and political phenomena specifically. Micro-level data generation processes often do not aggregate to macro-level observables in straightforward ways that are easily understood and logically explained. More generally, political processes studied at lower levels of analysis can lead to different conclusions about politics compared to similar processes studied at higher levels of analysis (and, of course, vice versa). We often understand this to be the ecological inference fallacy, a large topic of research that I do not discuss in much depth at this point but address in a limited manner later (see Freedman 2002; King 1997).

As a classic example, from surveys of individuals we learn that voting participation is more strongly correlated with political interest and education than with mobilization efforts. But large-scale participation patterns have not changed over time in sync with increases in overall education attainment of populations, and variation across macro units in voter participation rates correlates with variation in mobilization efforts. Surveys help us understand individual motivations, but they are less helpful in understanding variation across space and time in voter participation patterns across, for instance, the US states. (See Rosenstone and Hansen 1993; Schlozman, Verba, and Brady 2012.)

# LOWEST LEVEL IS NOT ALWAYS BEST

In studying political behavior and political outcomes, one is tempted to state that it is always best to have data at the lowest level possible, even ideally at the individual level. This is certainly true for vertical situations. In principle, it makes sense because you can aggregate upward. If you have US presidential election results data at the precinct level and want to study election results at the county level, you can add up the precinct results to compile into county results. *Having* data at the lowest level possible makes sense, even if we do not always *analyze* data at that level because we wish to study a more aggregated phenomenon. The value of lower-level data is difficult to argue against.

One flaw, however, is not in the logic, but rather in the practice of gathering and organizing data. It is common for lower levels of data to be incomplete, with spotty areas of missing information. And missingness will likely be correlated with some factors of interest. Taking our example of precincts, it may be the case that precinct-level election results are available for some states and not others, or for some counties and not others, with the states or counties missing not for (assumed) random reasons but having to do with the quality of local government administration. True, with enough other kinds of data it may be possible to impute missing election data or model the missingness to account for it and correct for it, but this is not always possible.

Even more challenging, assuming one cares about comparing across counties or states, is when some precincts are missing election results information within counties or states. That is, for a given county, some precincts have reported results and others have not. One cannot, then, simply aggregate up from the precinct level to higher levels of aggregation. The higher levels of reported data will be unreliable, and the measurement error will likely be correlated with other factors of interest.

A tentative generalization is that the lower the level of data being reported, the less likely the election results will be completely, comprehensively reported. In the United States, it is easier to get state-level election results for all fifty (or fifty-one, counting the District of Columbia) states than it is to get precinct-level election results for the entire country. The missingness can be a function of where and how the election authorities who hold and distribute data devote their resources.

Related, our limitations can be simply the resources of researchers and the number of units of interest. We cannot learn how each voter in California voted in the previous election, and we often survey a sample of such voters. But we cannot sample enough people to estimate precinct-level election results from the survey itself.

While surely it is valuable to *have* lower-level data if possible, the value of *using* lower-level data at the analysis stage may not be so obvious. Elections entail aggregated individual decisions; they are typically contested among organizations. Other than the individual voter and candidate, the main elements to study in elections are aggregates, collections of individuals organized or corralled together taking action. Political parties, which are themselves aggregates, contest elections against each other. And they contest those elections, with the exception of certain presidential elections around the world, in piecewise geographic units that divide up the electorate into aggregates that rarely mirror the national electorate. In other words, the relevant component units in elections range from individuals (voters, candidates, funders), to organizations (parties, funding groups), to constituencies represented in government following those elections. Those constituencies, depending on the electoral system, typically mean targeted campaigning and targeted candidate choice, and often variation in which parties contest where and with what concerted effort.

In terms of connecting theoretical arguments and models to data analysis, lower levels of analysis are not always better. Our theories about politics often connect together ideas about individuals, organizations, institutions, governments, and even regions. We benefit from the testing of multiple implications of theories and, importantly, evolve those theories as new evidence stretches across multiple levels. An instructive example is in research over Duverger's law.

## Analyzing Different Layers of Duverger's Law

"It depends on the question" is not altogether satisfying as a general adage about choosing a level of analysis. And yes, it comes across (to me anyway) as trite but true when researchers have what they need. That is, the statement and use of "depends" suggests that researchers have options: they have the data they need at multiple levels and can competently match the questions they are asking to the data they are using.

There are notable examples, however, where the lack of available data has hindered the testing of theories at the appropriate level of analysis, yet researchers push on because it is the best they can do given the data. Put another way, there is a misfit between theory and data and it gets perpetuated throughout a literature.

As is the case for many complex books with huge scope, Duverger's famous *Political Parties*, first published in 1951, contains richness and many insights, but also inconsistent treatments of ideas and concepts. A close reading reveals that Duverger was adept throughout the book in moving among different levels of analysis when he was drawing from data on party organizations across various cases. A retrospective evaluation, however, cannot help but lead us to wonder why he did not attend more to the nuances of regional-level and constituency-level differences within countries.

Two phrases associated with Duverger have spawned a massive literature on political party systems and electoral systems. Commonly called the law, "the simple-majority single-ballot system favours the two-party system," Duverger ([1951] 1963, 217) wrote. A companion prediction was "the simple-majority system with second ballot and proportional representation favour multi-partism" (Duverger, [1951] 1963, 239). This original formulation from Duverger was clearly intended to refer to the number of political parties in a country.

And that is how Duverger's law was, and sometimes continues to be, written about and tested: at the national level. Various studies, beginning with Rae (1971) in his analysis of quantitative data on the number of parties across countries, compare how many parties received substantial votes with whether countries have plurality rule, majority rule, or some version of proportional representation (Lijphart 1994; Taagepera and Shugart 1989; Amorim and Cox 1997; Cox 1997, chap. 11; Ordeshook and Shvetsova 1994; Chhibber and Kollman 2004, chap. 8; Clark and Golder 2006). Across these studies, the samples of countries vary, the measurements of key variables are different, and the variables included in analyses vary.

The overall conclusions from this subliterature on national-level studies of Duverger's law have been mixed but generally center around the following: controlling for other aspects like social diversity and political centralization, the smaller the district magnitude is,[1] the fewer the number of competitive political parties in a country on average (Lijphart 1994; Taagepera 1997; Taagepera and Shugart 1989, 1993; Shugart and Carey 1992; Clark and Golder 2006). Even in proportional representation systems, lower district magnitude correlates with smaller numbers of parties.

Given the correlations between district magnitude and plurality rules, Duverger's law nevertheless earned a measure of predictability and theoretical credibility from these studies, with caveats. Qualitative studies (Riker 1982; Sartori 1986) likewise gave credence to the overall pattern. The caveats nagged at researchers, however. In all these studies, both quantitative and qualitative, outlier countries and temporal variation remained unexplained. Why did India have only one major party for so long? Why do Canada and the United Kingdom have strong third and fourth parties? And why would the number of parties change over time in plurality countries if the electoral system does not change over time?

Research in the 1990s and 2000s continued to test the basic ideas behind Duverger's law using national-level data on the number of parties. In widely cited findings, a trio of papers, using various measures and methods, interact social heterogeneity with district magnitude and detect conditional correlations (Amorim and Cox 1997; Ordeshook and Shvetsova 1994; and Clark and Golder 2006). Namely, more social heterogeneity in a country is associated with a greater number of parties competing, especially when electoral systems are "permissive."[2] Permissive usually means larger than average district magnitude or lower than average thresholds for minor parties to win seats. That is, permissiveness in the institutional factors (electoral system mostly) gives room for social heterogeneity to drive up the number of parties.

These were among the empirical findings from national-level analyses. Subsequent theoretical analyses of Duverger's law added considerable depth to our understanding of the mechanisms at work in reducing the number of political parties in first-past-the-post (FPTP) systems. In FPTP systems, as opposed to proportional systems, downward pressure on the number of parties occurs because of incentives by voters and by potential candidates not to waste their efforts. (See Riker 1982; Palfrey 1989; Feddersen 1992; Cox 1994, 1997.) A key move by Cox (1994, 1997) was to generalize the logic to any electoral system, including proportional ones. The electoral system causes a coordination of effort on the part of voters and candidates. But where does this coordination of effort occur? These theoretical accounts focus on isolating an election environment that looks like a single constituency. Why, then, were empirical tests being conducted on national-level data? The answer is that those were the data available until the late 1980s.[3] But it does not explain why national-level analyses continued to be conducted, and in fact continue to be conducted (see Lublin 2014).

National-level election outcomes are produced by complex mixtures of multiple layers of electoral competition, often multiple types of electoral systems within the same country. Many additional political and social factors affect national-level competition, including the existence of presidential elections in some places. Researchers quite early on understood that Duverger was too spare in describing the mechanisms driving the empirical patterns about the number of parties (Wildavsky 1959; see Bowler 2009 for a summary of the reception of Duverger's book). Duverger, and even Riker (1982), missed the importance of accounting for how the effects of electoral systems on the number of parties must occur mostly at the constituency level. Riker acknowledges that constituency-level tests of Duverger were critical, but then evaluates the law with national-level data.

Gaines (1997, 1999) and Cox (1997) made the important step of testing the core ideas behind the law at lower levels of analysis. Gaines (1997), for instance, analyzes Canadian, American, and British district-level results and determines, from tests of Duverger's law, that "the relative neglect of district-level data to date is counter-productive" (p. 56). He finds many exceptions to Duverger's predictions in constituency results in these three countries. Cox, meanwhile, was instrumental in putting together with Lijphart the Lijphart Elections Archive, which has constituency-level election results in 26 countries across 350 elections. (The archive, which was maintained until 2003, set the stage for similar efforts of larger scope later in the 2000s—discussed later). Using these data, Cox (1997) tests a broad set of ideas related to Duverger's law on constituency-level election results, concluding that there are patterns across a variety of electoral systems that voters and candidates act strategically in a manner consistent with the fundamental ideas of Duverger. Singer (2013) adds to this and provides a comprehensive analysis of constituency-level results across 53 countries, and finds mixed but moderate support for electoral system effects similar to those described by Duverger (and Cox).

Cox (1997) and Chhibber and Kollman (1998, 2004) take the further step of offering theoretical frameworks for understanding how electoral processes across geographic space operate to create patterns of election outcomes at higher, more systemic levels.

Cox refers to "electoral coordination" and "linkage," while Chhibber and Kollman refer to "party aggregation," as the knitting together of constituency-level election results into patterns of electoral conflict at the national, provincial, regional, or state levels. Those patterns can be driven by many factors. Cox focuses on the role of presidential elections in generally reducing the number of political parties in a country, while Chhibber and Kollman posit a correlation between political centralization and the number of national parties. Chhibber and Kollman (2004) analyze both constituency-level election results and national-level election results in four plurality, single-seat district countries. Their conclusion is that Duverger's law has its most potent impact at the constituency level, and that other factors in state, regional, or national levels matter in shaping national election outcomes as aggregations of local election outcomes. In both Cox (1997) and Chhibber and Kollman (1998, 2004), the obvious but often forgotten point motivates the analyses: electoral competition at subnational levels does not happen independently across time and space, and larger, systemic factors matter in shaping what happens at, for instance, constituency levels, but also at state and provincial levels.

That is, aggregation processes in elections are shaped by factors other than that identified by Duverger. These factors have been studied in depth in recent decades and are central to burgeoning literatures. The focus shifted in the literature, away from national-level tests of Duverger's law, to analyses of the differential ways party votes are aggregated across geographic space to create regionalized or nationalized party systems. This body of research on party systems nationalization has added considerable depth to our knowledge of the manner in which electoral systems combine with other political factors to create the electoral politics of a given country.

Several books and articles lay the theoretical and methodological groundwork for a surge in research on party systems and nationalization. Chhibber and Kollman (2004) link political centralization to the degree of party system nationalization. Caramani (2004) examines in great detail how the decline of religious intolerance and the rise of correlated economic interest across communities and across countries drove the nationalization of party systems in Europe.

Since these studies there have continued to be lively debates along several lines. The work is quite nuanced and rich, a consequence of the availability of new subnational data on election returns.

One line of research examines closely the meaning and measurement of party system nationalization (Jones and Mainwaring 2003; Lago-Peñas and Lago-Peñas 2009; Moenius and Kasuya 2004; Kasuya and Moenius 2008; Bochsler 2010; Morgenstern, Swindle, and Castagnola 2009; Morgenstern and Pothoff 2004; Schakel 2012). At last count there were a dozen measures of party system nationalization being proposed and used in the literature. Some of these measures apply to the party level and some to the party system level.

Many papers on nationalization use multiple measures to test for robustness. For our purposes here, there are two key things to note. First, the measures rely on constituency-level election returns to calculate measures at higher levels, and thus the availability of constituency-level results made this entire literature possible. Second, while the reference and the terminology are to nationalization, in fact the measures can be state level, regional level, or even, if aggregated across countries, party family level or continental level. The constituency-level election results data enables a multifaceted approach to the study of party systems, specific parties, candidate and government behavior, and many other elements of electoral politics.

Other lines of research examine the causes of party system nationalization (Hicken 2009; Brancati 2006, 2008; Caramani 2004; Chhibber and Kollman 2004; Ishiyama 2002; Jones and Mainwaring 2003; Morgenstern and Pothoff 2004; Morgenstern and Swindle 2005; Bochsler 2010; Morgenstern, Polga-Hecimovich, and Siavelis 2014; Lago-Peñas and Lago-Peñas 2011; Lublin 2014; Lublin and Wright 2013; Simon 2013). And finally, there is a growing literature on the consequences of party system nationalization (Crisp, Olivella, and Potter 2012; Castañeda-Angarita (2013); Lago-Peñas and Lago-Peñas 2009; Hicken, Kollman, and Simmons 2016; Simmons, Hicken, Kollman, and Nooruddin 2016).

I have focused on a multifaceted literature on Duverger's law that has developed and created new findings and insights based on analyses of election results data at multiple levels: from the national level down to the constituency level, with levels in between (e.g., state or province). There has also been some research into micro-level decision-making processes by voters as they decide in contexts that expose the incentives identified by Duverger and later theorists building on Duverger (e.g., Palfrey and Cox). Research in this literature has tended to be highly context specific, and my reading of this literature is that the findings point to context effects. Papers tend to focus on survey data or experimental data from one country. But even within country contexts, researchers have found temporal and geographic differences in the degree to which the Duvergerian downward pressures of the number of parties show up in systematic data. (See Blais and Carty 1991; Blais 2002; and Fujiwara 2011 for interesting micro-level studies.)

To summarize, in this central and valuable area of research in comparative politics on Duverger's law, the accumulation of knowledge took an interesting trajectory. It began with a mismatch between the core elements of a logical theory of electoral systems and party systems and the data used to test the hypotheses deriving from that theory. National-level data were being used to test a theory that at root was a theory about individual decision making and constituency-level election outcomes. Recognition of the mismatch occurred early on, but research continued in the same vein because of the availability of data (or lack thereof). In the area of election results, as more constituency-level data became available, it opened up new avenues for research and, more important, gave impetus for new theoretical constructs and theoretical development to link electoral politics across levels of analysis.

Constituency-level data enabled researchers to study more directly the implications of Duverger's law, and to do so better and more fittingly than previous research using national-level data. These constituency-level data could then be used to create measures of party strength at higher levels of aggregation, at the state or provincial level, at the regional level, and at the national level. Researchers have been able to validate some of the theoretical pieces of Duverger's law—for instance, the downward pressure on the number of parties, especially in FPTP systems. They have also been able to develop theories of how party systems at various levels of analysis form and refashion in response to various stimuli.

The literature on Duverger's law continues to be rich and illuminating, even though it has changed into a literature about nationalization of macro-party systems and a literature about micro-level psychological processes in voting decisions. The community of researchers has improved our understanding of electoral systems and party systems by answering questions using multiple kinds of data at different levels, centered on but moving far beyond the ideas behind Duverger's law.

# Meeting Election Data Challenges

Gathering and organizing datasets for the study of elections requires a commitment by many people to create public goods for researchers. It also requires funding. Two aspects of this are worth discussing and have already affected the study of elections: datasets of election returns and tools for linking data across disparate unit levels.

## Subnational Election Data

It is not difficult to find election data for most countries. National-level election results can be found from various sources, most often from websites of the electoral commissions for the given country. Even election results at lower levels—constituency or precinct or ward—are made available by many governments. Unofficial sources, such as Wikipedia or Adam Carr's Election Archives (nicknamed Psephos), provide data as well. The degree to which these sources have historical data older than a few years varies a great deal.

For researchers conducting comparative analysis of elections across countries or over time, or both, gathering and organizing election data across many countries can be time-consuming and sometimes prohibitive. Fortunately, over the past two decades, new sources of election data have been developed specifically with comparison as the primary motivation. Examples include Adam Carr's Election Archives (Psephos), Brancati's Global Elections Database (GED), Caramani's West European Database, Lublin's Election Passport, and CLEA (2014, directed by Kollman, Hicken, Caramani, Backer, and Lublin). Across these various databases, there are over 1,300 elections and 130 countries archived, and well over a million individual records of candidates or parties.

As one of the founders of CLEA, I take the opportunity here to remind readers of important considerations that researchers ought to abide by when they use such datasets. The development of a dataset oriented toward comparison of elections is itself an intellectual project. It is not straightforward to decide how to structure the data, create variables that make sense across diverse electoral systems and party systems, and exclude and include certain cases. Deciding what constitutes a case is also subject to debate. The process is one of classification, and as we know from other disciplines (like biology), classification requires an intellectual framework and having purposes in mind.

Fundamentally, creating a dataset of objects that are highly diverse but can be categorized into groupings so that researchers can analyze them is a theoretical enterprise. Theoretical enterprises entail making assumptions that are sometimes debatable. But the assumptions should always be transparent. Furthermore, the enterprise requires following the logic of those assumptions to their conclusions and being consistent in the applications of assumptions as appropriate.

One example is to consider what constitutes a political party. Many researchers use the CLEA data and the other datasets mentioned earlier to analyze political parties and to conduct party-level analyses. CLEA has party codes, which are unique numbers for each country attached to a given political party. For instance, the British Labour Party has the code "56" in the UK data, and that number should in principle be the same as long as the Labourites exist as a party in continuous time.

Parties come and go, and sometimes a party named X in one decade and another party named the same X in a later decade are in fact not the same party. There have been multiple Republican parties in the United States over history, although the one in existence now has been the same since 1856 (and has the same number in CLEA over all those elections since 1856). The earlier Republican parties in the early 1800s require different numbers.

At CLEA, we made the decision back in 2006 at the archive's founding to use the following numbering rule: if a given name for a party skips at least one national election (the party did not contest) when it comes back into the election process, even if it has the same name as before, we give it a new party code number. Why? Because we do not wish to imply that this is necessarily the same party as before; we cannot guarantee that it is the same party even though it might have the same name. It is up to researchers with knowledge of a given country to connect those two party labels and codes as in fact the same party. We understand at CLEA that this can create more work to combine the party codes if the facts require it, but we do not wish to aggregate data when we cannot be certain that the aggregation (i.e., giving the same party code to a label at two different points in time) is warranted.

A more general point needs emphasis. Some datasets, like CLEA, can act as archives because of the ambition to be comprehensive. But archiving data is not the only purpose, and archiving is not the same as creating datasets that will be useful for a relatively broad audience of researchers. Naturally, there is always the tradeoff between completeness of coverage and the depth of coverage for any dataset intended for research. But even assuming that completeness of coverage is a goal, the statements earlier—summarized in the claim that creating comparative datasets is an intellectual, theoretical enterprise—still stand. Most of us directly involved in creating CLEA were at the time of CLEA's origins writing about party system nationalization, and this has had implications. We developed CLEA to assist with our own research, but we always wished to gear it toward the needs of other researchers as well. This is typically true of anyone creating quality, comparative datasets.

## Geocoded Unit Boundaries

When we analyze election results in a broader context, we often try to find a common level of analysis for our data. This can be a challenge. The challenges for what I labeled earlier as horizontal issues are especially acute. These are sometimes referred to as the modifiable areal unit problem (MAUP) and ecological fallacy problem (Openshaw 1984; Arbia 1989; King 1997). It is really the linking of data from different sources and spatial supports, sometimes called the "change of support" problem (Gehlke and Biehl 1934).

The following discussion of three strategies for dealing with these problems assumes the existence of units that are already geocoded. This itself is a challenge for some countries. Fortunately, most administrative units around the world have been geocoded (see data made available from the Second Administrative Level Boundaries [SALB] project and the Global Administrative Unit Layers [GAUL] project). But only some electoral constituency boundaries have been geocoded. (CLEA has an archive of geocoded constituencies, though not for all countries contained in the archive.)

When we have geocoded electoral boundaries and mismatched administrative boundaries, with data at both levels, among the solutions are three strategies to mismatched data that are what we have called "horizontal" (i.e., not perfectly nested). We can do areal weighting, using information on the share of geographic area in one type of unit to assign weights to the share of the other unit's value. If we want to extrapolate to congressional district, suppose that 40 percent of that district was geographically contained in county Y and county Y had 100 traffic deaths, and 60 percent of that district was contained in county Z and county Z had 200 traffic deaths. We would assign 160 traffic deaths to that congressional district because $.4 * 100 + .6 * 200 = 160$. Another is to use weights by proportion of the population, and the logic is similar, except that weights are by the proportion of population in each respective county within the congressional district.

Kriging is a statistical approach interpolating values at one location based on the neighboring spatial data. In brief, researchers create a function of nearby values and statistically minimize prediction errors and provide weights according to a spatial covariance matrix (Oliver & Webster 1990). Measures of uncertainty for each predicted value can be used to create a standard error to use in later analyses. If appropriate, subunit areal estimates can be aggregated to a larger unit (Krivoruchko et al. 2011). There are techniques for constraining the data so that variable values when aggregated equal the value of the original support unit (Tobler 1979). Kriging methods exist for continuous and for count data.

The overall goal of these techniques is to create new datasets by combining information from disparate units. Preferably, researchers can create weighting tables and publish them so that future researchers can use the weights to combine their own data into the relevant units. For instance, if weights based on population and area were known between US counties and congressional districts, a lookup table with those weights could be used by anyone with data at those two levels who wanted to match up these data.

# THE FUTURE IS BRIGHT

Earlier in this chapter I mentioned research from the past using only cross-national election data, even though our theories and concepts spanned national and lower levels. Perhaps decades from now it will also seem quaint to conduct the kinds of research we are currently doing on elections.

One key to better data is convincing election authorities around the world to release data for local units, geocoded and archived for comparisons over time as elections happen in later periods. Perhaps the norm could spread among electoral commissions that transparency in elections requires the release of data at lower-level units, and ideally geocoded. Want to convince the world that your elections had integrity and were free from fraud and other forms of malfeasance? Release your data, and best would be to release data at lower levels, like at the polling station level. I would favor subtle (positive) incentives by nongovernmental organizations and by the governments of the world's wealthier democracies to induce all countries to release their election data as a demonstration of commitment to fair and meaningful democratic processes.

The frontier of data in the study of elections is beyond rectangular files of government- and election commission–produced data, and beyond survey data, as valuable as these are. The frontier has three features, sometimes combined and sometimes separate. They can be summarized by three words: amount, kind, and links. First, the massive volume of data potentially available from any given source (so-called Big Data) may require new methods for capturing, organizing, and analyzing information. In the realm of elections, for instance, researchers can track tweets, social media pages, emails, and ongoing survey responses from millions of people. Databases can (and in the future routinely will) include literally billions of cases.

Second, the different kinds of data available open up opportunities for new kinds of analysis. Social media information that can be captured, even in small quantities, reveals communications on politicians, parties, and issues, and can reveal public opinion trends in nuanced ways. There are new sources of information on lobbying, election results at various levels of analysis, mass media output, campaign finance, party evolution, and election platforms. Simply put, the variety of data on elections is changing rapidly.

Third, these various kinds of data, including some on a massive scale, can be linked across cases, levels of analysis, and time. Much of the innovations here have come from computer science in the form of novel methods of database structure and the building of meta-datasets. But also in the realm of any given research community (such as those who study democratic elections), the innovations also come simply from hard work using existing methods. It takes creativity, and often teamwork among people with different skill sets and substantive knowledge, to develop new datasets using various kinds of data. This is the most untapped of the three features, and I see tremendous potential for elections research as new data across multiple levels of analysis come forth.

The potential, in sum, is to understand better electoral processes using novel kinds of data linked across levels and units of analysis. Consider election forensics. How do we evaluate the integrity of election outcomes? This question can be urgent in places with fragile democratic institutions, but it also bears answering in established democracies. Detecting election fraud or other kinds of malfeasance in elections has typically required observers to be on-site, making personal observations of polling stations and ballot-counting procedures. In-person observations are still valuable and will remain valuable, but they cannot be comprehensive. It is common for election observation organizations to choose troublesome locations in a country based on past experiences. Observers watch what happens and record what they can in person, but they cannot, given their resources, blanket the entire country with personnel to watch election administration.

In some countries, or in subnational units in some countries, election results data are available at the polling machine level or at the polling station level. Data from voting machines or polling stations can be analyzed systematically over an entire country to detect evidence of human manipulation of election results using digital forensics techniques. Typically, a country's electoral commission (or the provincial or state-level government) reports vote totals for each candidate or party, the total number of votes cast, the total number of valid votes used in the election totals, and often the number of eligible voters for that polling station. Better yet, some countries can provide geocoded polling station locations, and researchers can map where electoral malfeasance has likely occurred, enabling the analysis of the spatial interdependence of specific forms of fraud or other kinds of anomalies in election results produced by human interventions. Obtaining election results at fine granularity (e.g., polling station level) opens up opportunities for analyses to provide, at a minimum, complementary analysis to in-person observation, and better yet, even more comprehensive and reliable answers to urgent questions about the integrity of election results.

Any research question should in principle be answered using the data necessary and sufficient, and there is power in simple data and straightforward, well-known methods answering important questions. I do not advocate for using sophisticated data and datasets merely for their own sake. We ought to be driven ultimately by substantive questions about politics. Nevertheless, I am not alone in believing that data science and new sources of data will continue to transform political science, including the study of elections—maybe especially the study of elections. New geocoded data at multiple and varied levels of analysis makes me conclude that the future is bright. The transformation has already begun.

## NOTES

1. District magnitude for a constituency is a measure of the number of parliamentary seats apportioned to that constituency; in the United States and Canada, district magnitude is one, for example.
2. See the chapter by Moser, Scheiner, and Stoll in this volume.
3. Some scholars, it should be noted, were specifically interested in national-level effects.

## REFERENCES

Amorim, Octavio Neto, and Gary Cox. "Electoral Institutions, Cleavage Structures, and the Number of Parties." *American Journal of Political Science* 41 (1997): 149–174.

Arbia, Giuseppe. "Statistical Effect of Data Transformations: A Proposed General Framework." In *The Accuracy of Spatial Data Bases*, edited by M. Goodchild and S. Gopal, 249–259. London: Taylor and Francis, 1989.

Blais, André. "Why Is There So Little Strategic Voting in Canadian Plurality Rule Elections?" *Political Studies* 50 (2002): 445–454.

Blais, André, and R. K. Carty. "The Psychological Impact of Electoral Laws: Measuring Duverger's Elusive Factor." *British Journal of Political Science* 21 (1991): 79–93.

Bochsler, Daniel. "Measuring Party Nationalisation: A New Gini-Based Indicator That Corrects for the Number of Units." *Electoral Studies* 29, no. 1 (2010): 155–168.

Bowler, Shaun. "Anglo-American Reaction to Maurice Duverger's *Political Parties*." Working paper. Department of Political Science, University of California, Riverside, 2009.

Brader, Ted, and Joshua A. Tucker. "Following the Party's Lead: Party Cues, Policy Opinion, and the Power of Partisanship in Three Multiparty Systems." *Comparative Politics* 44, no. 4 (2012): 403–420.

Brancati, Dawn. *Global Elections Database [computer file]*. New York: Global Elections Database. http://www.globalelectionsdatabase.com.

Brancati, Dawn. "Decentralization: Fueling the Fire or Dampening the Flames of Ethnic Conflict and Secessionism?" *International Organization* 60 (2006): 651–685.

Brancati, Dawn. "The Origins and Strength of Regional Parties." *British Journal of Political Science* 38, no. 1 (2008): 135–159.

Cain, Bruce, John Ferejohn, and Morris Fiorina. *The Personal Vote: Constituency Service and Electoral Independence*. Cambridge, MA: Harvard University Press, 1990.

Caramani, Daniele. *The Nationalization of Elections*. Cambridge: Cambridge University Press, 2004.

Caramani, Daniele. *The Europeanization of Politics*. New York: Cambridge University Press, 2015.

Castañeda-Angarita, Nestor. 2013. "Party System Nationalization, Presidential Coalitions, and Government Spending." *Electoral Studies* 32 (December): 783–794.

Chhibber, Pradeep, and Ken Kollman. "Party Aggregation and the Number of Parties in India and the United States." *American Political Science Review* 92 (1998): 329–342.

Chhibber, Pradeep, and Ken Kollman. *The Formation of National Party Systems*. Princeton, NJ: Princeton University Press, 2004.

Chong, Dennis, and James Druckman. "Framing Public Opinion in Competitive Democracies." *American Political Science Review* 101 (2007): 637–655.

Clark, William, and Matt Golder. "Rehabilitating Duverger's Theory Testing the Mechanical and Strategic Modifying Effects of Electoral Laws." *Comparative Political Studies* 39, no. 6 (August 2006): 679–708.

CLEA. Directed by Ken Kollman, Allen Hicken, Daniele Caramani, David Backer, and David Lublin. Constituency-Level Election Archive, 2014. http://www.electiondataarchive .org/.

Comparative Study of Electoral Systems (CSES). The Center for Political Studies and GESIS—Leibniz Institute for the Social Sciences, with support from the American National Science Foundation, GESIS, and the University of Michigan. http://www.cses.org. 2017.

Cox, Gary. "Strategic Voting Equilibria under the Single Nontransferable Vote." *American Political Science Review* 88 (1994): 608–621.

Cox, Gary. *Making Votes Count*. New York: Cambridge University Press, 1997.

Crisp, Brian, Santiago Olivella, and Joshua Potter. "Party-System Nationalization and the Scope of Public Policy: The Importance of Cross-District Constituency Similarity." *Comparative Political Studies* 46 (2012): 431–456.

Druckman, James. "Political Preference Formation: Competition, Deliberation, and the (Ir) relevance of Framing Effects." *American Political Science Review* 98 (2004): 671–686.

Duch, Raymond M. "Comparative Studies of the Economy and the Vote." In *The Oxford Handbook of Comparative Politics*, edited by Carles Boix and Susan C. Stokes, 805–844. Oxford: Oxford University Press, 2007.

Duverger, Maurice. *Political Parties: Their Organization and Activity in the Modern State (1951)*. Repr. New York: John Wiley and Sons, 1963.

Feddersen, Timothy. "A Voting Model Implying Duverger's Law and Positive Turnout." *American Journal of Political Science* 36 (November 1992): 938–962.

Freedman, David A. *The Ecological Fallacy*. Berkeley, CA: University of California, 2002.

Fujiwara, Thomas. "A Regression Discontinuity Test of Strategic Voting and Duverger's Law." *Quarterly Journal of Political Science* 6 (2011): 197–233.

Gaines, Brian. "Where to Count Parties." *Electoral Studies* 16 (March 1997): 49–58.

Gaines, Brian. "Duverger's Law and the Meaning of Canadian Exceptionalism." *Comparative Political Studies* 32 (1999): 835–861.

Gehlke, C. E., and Katherine Biehl. "Certain Effects of Grouping upon the Size of the Correlation Coefficient in Census Tract Material." *Journal of the American Statistical Association* 29 (1934): 169–170.

Hicken, Allen, Ken Kollman, and Joel Simmons. "Party System Nationalization and the Provision of Public Health Services." *Political Science Research and Methods* (July 2016): 1–22. doi:10.1017 psrm.2015.41.

Ishiyama, John. "Regionalism and the Nationalisation of the Legislative Vote in Post-Communist Russian Politics." *Communist and Post-Communist Studies* 35, no. 2 (2002): 155–168.

Jones, Mark P., and Scott Mainwaring. "The Nationalization of Parties and Party Systems." *Party Politics* 9, no. 2 (2003): 139–166.

Kasuya, Yuko, and Johannes Moenius. "The Nationalization of Party Systems: Conceptual Issues and Alternative District-Focused Measures." *Electoral Studies* 27 (2008): 126–135.

King, Gary. *A Solution to the Ecological Inference Problem: Reconstructing Individual Behavior from Aggregate Data*. Princeton, NJ: Princeton University Press, 1997.

Krivoruchko, K., Gribov, A., & Krause, E. 2011. Multivariate areal interpolation for continuous and count data. *Procedia Environmental Sciences* 3: 14–19.

Lago-Peñas, Ignacio, and Santiago Lago-Peñas. "Does the Nationalization of the Party Systems Affect the Composition of Public Spending?" *Economics of Governance* 10 (2009): 85–98.

Lago-Peñas, Ignacio, and Santiago Lago-Peñas. "Decentralization and the Nationalization of Party Systems." *Environment and Planning C-Government and Policy* 29 (2011): 244–263.

Lijphart, Arend. *Electoral Systems and Party Systems*. New York: Oxford University Press, 1994.

Lublin, David. *Minority Rules: Electoral Systems, Decentralization, and Ethnoregional Party Success*. New York: Oxford University Press, 2014.

Lublin, David, and Matthew Wright. "Engineering Inclusion: Assessing the Effects of Pro-Minority Representation Policies." *Electoral Studies* 32 (2013): 746–755.

Moenius, Johannes, and Yuko Kasuya. "Measuring Party Linkage Across Districts: Some Party System Inflation Indices and Their Properties." *Party Politics* 10, no. 5 (2004): 543–564.

Morgenstern, Scott, John Polga-Hecimovich, and Peter M. Siavelis. "Seven Imperatives for Improving the Measurement of Party Nationalization with Evidence from Chile." *Electoral Studies* 33 (2014): 186–199.

Morgenstern, Scott, and Richard Pothoff. "The Components of Elections: District Heterogeneity, District-Time Effects, and Volatility." *Electoral Studies* 24, no. 1 (2004): 17–40.

Morgenstern, Scott, and Steven Swindle. "Are Politics Local? An Analysis of Voting Patterns in 23 Democracies." *Comparative Political Studies* 38, no. 2 (2005): 143–170.

Morgenstern, Scott, Stephen M. Swindle, and Andrea Castagnola. "Party Nationalization and Institutions." *Journal of Politics* 71, no. 4 (2009): 1322–1341.

Oliver, M. A., and R. Webster. "Kriging: A Method of Interpolation for Geographical Information Systems." *International Journal of Geographical Information Systems* 4, no. 3 (1990): 313–332.

Openshaw, Stan. *The Modifiable Areal Unit Problem*. Norwich, UK: Geobooks, 1984.

Ordeshook, Peter, and Olga Shvetsova. "Ethnic Heterogeneity, District Magnitude, and the Number of Parties." *American Journal of Political Science* 38, no. 1 (1994): 100–123.

Page, Benjamin, and Robert Shapiro. *The Rational Public: Fifty Years of Trends in Americans' Policy Preferences*. Chicago: University of Chicago Press, 1992.

Palfrey, Thomas. "A Mathematical Proof of Duverger's Law." In *Models of Strategic Choice in Politics*, edited by Peter Ordeshook. Ann Arbor, MI: University of Michigan Press, 1989.

Rae, Douglas. 1971. *The Political Consequences of Electoral Laws*, 2nd ed. New Haven, CT: Yale University Press.

Riker, William. "The Two-Party System and Duverger's Law." *American Political Science Review* 76 (1982): 753–766.

Sartori, Giovanni—. 1986. "The Influence of Electoral Systems: Faulty Laws or Faulty Methods?" In Bernard Grofman and Arend Lijphart (eds.). *Electoral Laws and Their Political Consequences*, edited by Bernard Grofman and Arend Lijphart. New York: Agathon Press, 1986.

Schakel, Arjan. "Nationalisation of Multilevel Party Systems: A Conceptual and Empirical Analysis." *European Journal of Political Research* 52, no. 2 (2012): 212–236.

Schlozman, Kay Lehman, Sidney Verba, and Henry E. Brady. *The Unheavenly Chorus: Unequal Political Voice and the Broken Promise of American Democracy*. Princeton, NJ: Princeton University Press, 2012.

Shugart, Matthew, and John Carey. *Presidents and Assemblies: Constitutional Design and Electoral Dynamics*. New York: Cambridge University Press, 1992.

Simmons, Joel, Allen Hicken, Ken Kollman, and Irfan Nooruddin. "Party System Structure and Its Consequences for Foreign Direct Investment." *Party Politics* (April 2016). doi:10.1177/1354068816644762.

Simon, Pablo. "The Combined Impact of Decentralisation and Personalism on the Nationalisation of Party Systems." *Political Studies* 61, no. S1 (2013): 196–216.

Singer, Matthew. "Was Duverger Correct? Single Member District Election Outcomes in Fifty-Three Countries." *British Journal of Political Science* 43 (January 2013): 201–220.

Taagepera, Rein. "Effective Number of Parties for Incomplete Data." *Electoral Studies* 16 (June 1997): 145–151.

Taagepera, Rein, and Matthew Shugart. *Seats and Votes: The Effects and Determinants of Electoral Systems*. New Haven, CT: Yale University Press, 1989.

Taagepera, Rein, and Matthew Shugart. "Predicting the Number of Parties: A Quantitative Model of Duverger's Mechanical Effect." *American Political Science Review* 87 (June 1993): 455–464.

Tobler, Waldo R. "Smooth Pycnophylactic Interpolation for Geographical Regions." *Journal of the American Statistical Association* 74, no. 367 (1979): 519–530.

Weisberg, Robert. "Assessing Legislator-Constituency Policy Agreement." *Legislative Studies Quarterly* 4 (1979): 605–622.

Wildavsky, Aaron. 1959. "A Methodological Critique of Duverger's Political Parties." *Journal of Politics* 21(May): 303–318.

# CHAPTER 21

# EXPERIMENTAL RESEARCH DESIGN IN THE STUDY OF ELECTORAL SYSTEMS

## JOSHUA A. TUCKER AND DOMINIK DUELL

EXPERIMENTAL research has made broad inroads in the field of political science. The attractiveness of experimental research—by which we mean studies that utilize random assignment to treatment or attempt to find observational data that is in some way similar to random assignment—is clear: it allows scholars to more closely test causal arguments than many forms of observational analysis (Morton and Williams 2010; Gerber and Green 2012; Morton and Tucker 2014).

Electoral systems research, however, presents a paradoxical challenge to the rise of experimental research in political science. On the one hand, more than most topics we really *need* to know the causal impact of different electoral systems, because it is indeed possible to change electoral systems, and to do so quickly. If we, for example, believe that a certain electoral system is likely to reduce inequality, then politicians can act on our research and change the electoral rules in that manner, much more easily than, for example, research results showing that "the country needs a higher gross domestic product per capita" to achieve some political outcome or "the population should be better educated" to have a certain desirable result. Measuring the effect of education or wealth is of course important, but these are not factors that can be changed overnight; electoral rules, however, can be. Research on electoral systems can therefore have profoundly important policy consequences precisely because politicians can change electoral rules.

At the same time, the electoral rules in which we are most interested—*national* electoral rules—are practically impossible to ever randomly assign in an experiment, precisely because the effects of doing so would be too consequential. Indeed, some of the field's most prominent scholars seemed convinced that experimental research would play a small role in the field due to "practical and ethical impediments"

(Lijphart 1971, 684). As a result, most of the initial experimental work on electoral systems has been done in the lab. This in turn presents significant challenges to the development of the kind of research that can actually inform real-world reforms, but the developing literature in the field also suggests new opportunities for constructive developments.

In the remainder of this chapter, we have three objectives. First, we aim to situate experimental research in the broader framework of research design in the field of electoral systems, which, as an editor of this volume has noted, "can now be regarded as a mature field" (Shugart 2005, 25). We demonstrate that there is almost no experimental research in the landmark works on electoral systems, but that experimental research is appearing in more recent research at a greater frequency. Second, we summarize existing research in the study of electoral systems that employs an experimental framework, including lab, field, survey, and natural experiments. Finally, we conclude by outlining areas in which we believe the field can move forward in the future.

# RESEARCH DESIGN IN THE STUDY OF ELECTORAL SYSTEMS

Our first task is to demonstrate where experimental analysis fits within the universe of research designs employed in the study of electoral systems. By "research design," we refer to the overall research plan, which in turn helps others to evaluate the validity of the study, to understand where the research fits into the knowledge previously accumulated on the topic (here electoral systems), and to illustrate how to build on the study for future scholarship.[1] Our goal here is simply to get a sense of how prevalent experimental research is in the overall field of the study of electoral systems.

Given the size of the field, of course, this necessitated some form of sampling strategy. To be as transparent (and replicable) as possible in this task, our initial foray into the literature was essentially guided by two simple algorithms. First, we employed Google Scholar to find the "seminal works" in the field.[2] Then, to get at more recent developments in the field, we went through each issue of the *American Political Science Review*, the *American Journal of Political Science*, *World Politics*, *Comparative Political Studies*, and *Electoral Studies* published in 2014 and identified every article we could find that featured research on electoral systems. While we recognized that such a strategy was not necessarily going to give us a truly representative sample of the literature in the field, we did feel it would do a good job of highlighting both the history and current directions of the field and, hopefully, allow us to make some useful observations about the state of the literature with respect to the prevalence of experimental research as a form of research design. Nevertheless, in view of the shortcomings of this approach, we supplemented our review with other articles that caught our eye when reading the original set of papers and in the course of our own research.

## Seminal Papers

Our algorithm for finding "classic" works in the field was as follows. We began our inquiry with two seminal pieces in the study of electoral systems: Duverger's *Political Parties: Their Organization and Activity in the Modern State* and Lijphart's *Electoral Systems and Party Systems: A Study of Twenty-Seven Democracies, 1945-1990*. We then located every article that features electoral systems as either an independent or a dependent variable, has a citation count of at least two hundred on Google Scholar, and cites either one (or both) of these seminal works.

In this collection, we found scholars primarily exploring the correlation of electoral systems with institutions, behaviors, and attitudes—in other words, treating electoral systems as independent variables. Electoral systems are linked to various outcomes: among others, the number of parties in political competition (Neto and Cox 1997; Moser 1999; Mozaffar, Scarritt, and Galaich 2003; Van de Walle 2003); the coordination of voters on candidates with the potential to win elections (Cox 1990); the spread of parties' positions in the system (Cox 1990); the success of radical parties (Norris 2005); the proportionality of electoral outcomes (Lijphart 1994); the congruence of voters' preferences and policy outcomes (Powell 2000) or voters' preferences and party positions (Golder and Stramski 2010); public spending (Milesi-Ferretti, Perotti, and Rostagno 2002; Persson, Roland, and Tabellini 2007); corruption (Persson, Tabellini, and Trebbi 2003; Kunicova and Rose-Ackerman 2005); economic policy and performance in general (Persson and Tabellini 2005); frequency of divided government (Shugart 1995); legislators' defection from the party line (Hix 2004); the election of female candidates into public office (Jones 1998; Norris 2004; Schwindt-Bayer and Mishler 2005); and turnout and voting behavior in general (Norris 2004).

All eighteen studies mentioned in the previous paragraph model electoral systems as an independent variable related to some political or economic outcome of interest. None of the works attempts causal identification of the effect of interest by employing an experimental (or quasi-experimental) framework. In general, with the exception of one purely theoretical study (Cox 1990), these seminal papers all rely on observational data.[3]

## Papers Published in 2014

Next, we examine a population sample of publications in the *American Political Science Review,* the *American Journal of Political Science, World Politics, Comparative Political Studies*, and *Electoral Studies* in the year 2014, to gauge the prevalence of experimental research in the study of electoral systems more recently in top political science journals.

In the preceding section we argued that the modal research design in our collection of seminal papers in the field is an empirical study that tests theoretical implications with correlational evidence from observational studies, which is also the case in more recent research. Of all publications in the journals we reviewed, ninety-five explore electoral systems in some form: eighty-eight are quantitative studies and explicitly empirically operationalize electoral systems as either an independent variable (seventy-nine), as a dependent variable (Aytaç 2014; Cantú 2014; Curtice and Marsh 2014), or as both independent and dependent variables (Endersby and Towle 2014; Miller 2014), or do not explicitly operationalize electoral institutions but make comparisons across institutions (Adams, Ezrow, and Somer-Topcu 2014; Clark and Leiter 2014; Grossman and Woll 2014; Spoon and Klüver 2014).[4] Two studies are formal theoretical (Cho 2014; Gans-Morse, Mazzuca, and Nichter 2014) and one is normative (Murray 2014); four studies discuss measurement issues (Krook 2014; Otjes and Louwerse 2014; Wawro and Katznelson 2014; Wilson 2014).

Of the seventy-nine quantitative studies that explicitly model electoral systems, nineteen include country fixed effects to acknowledge the influence of electoral systems on their variable of interest while not modeling this variation across systems.[5] More generally, the modal research design, thirty-five out of ninety-two empirical studies, is still, as with the seminal papers described earlier, an empirical test of implications derived from either (formal or informal) theory or from the extant literature where conclusions are based on evidence delivered by conventional regression analysis. Another thirty-five studies implement refined statistical models, which account for some biases in the estimation of the relationship of interest and particular characteristics of the data: most frequently this means running a multilevel model (twenty out of thirty-five), but also modeling temporal correlations, other features of the error structure, or the survival-data nature of the inquiry. Among the refined models, one article conducts a regression discontinuity design (Harada and Smith 2014) and another employs propensity score matching (Kolev 2014).

However, eleven of the ninety-two empirical studies do employ some form of experimental design, insofar as they take advantage of a feature occurring in "nature" that induces randomness in the data generating process,[6] run simulations (Weschle 2014), conduct laboratory experiments (Corazzini et al. 2014; Blais et al. 2014a), or run survey experiments (González Ocantos, Jonge, and Nickerson 2014; Baujard et al. 2014). The remaining works are case studies (five), one paper using descriptive inference (one), and articles about research methodology (four).[7] Overall, therefore, experimental research design—although now part of the study of electoral systems—remains a relatively small portion of that field.

# EXPERIMENTAL RESEARCH IN THE STUDY OF ELECTORAL SYSTEMS

Given that (1) there is some experimental research in a field that (2) has in the past been dominated by more observational research and (3) largely remains so today, the next question to ask is what experimental research is contributing to the study of electoral systems. Here we break down our assessment of the state of the literature by different types of experimental research design.

## Laboratory Experiments

Investigations into the institutions and rules that govern politics and political attitudes and behaviors date back to the works of Condorcet in the eighteenth century, so it should come as no surprise that early experimental attempts in political science were concerned with testing implications of "ancient" formal theories (Kinder and Palfrey 1993) and their modern extensions. Since the 1960s, experimental work on decision-making procedures has been part of the research agenda in economics. In particular, Plott (1979) started a strand of literature that investigated experimentally how different rules (e.g., open or closed rules) affect committee outcomes.[8] In general, the richest set of literature studying electoral institutions presents "economics style," monetarily incentivized laboratory experiments. These studies usually build on clear-cut predictions derived from formal models. When institutional variation in electoral systems is modeled, it is usually a comparison at the most general level of distinguishing among electoral systems (i.e., majoritarian rule, plurality rule, Borda count, or approval voting). The most commonly asked question is about the degree of strategic voting under different electoral rules (Forsythe et al. 1996; Bassi 2015). Studies also explore turnout (Gschwend and Hooghe 2008), welfare implications (Bouton, Castanheira, and Llorente-Saguer 2016), the minority representation mechanism (Gerber, Morton, and Rietz 1998), or the ability of voters to make "correct"— that is, utility maximizing—choices (Blais et al. 2014a, 2014b) when the institutional framework is varied. Morton and Williams (1999) and Battaglini, Morton, and Palfrey (2007) derive and test predictions under different electoral institutions, institutions that do not fit the usual terminology of the study of electoral systems. In these articles, subjects' behavior under sequential or simultaneous elections are investigated and motivated by variation in the US primary election calendar over the years (Morton and Williams 1999) or the fact that in the same US state in one time zone election polls have already closed while in another time zone voting is still taking place (Battaglini et al. 2007).

With respect to results, a question often asked is whether subjects in the laboratory act according to expectations derived from Duverger's law under different electoral rules.[9] This part of the laboratory-experimental literature is therefore very much in conversation with the observational data literature discussed previously—Duverger is central—even though, interestingly, this relationship is not always reflected in cross-citations. Formal theory is well placed to spell out precise predictions about strategic behavior—which is the purpose of the language of game theory—and testing those predictions in the controlled environment of the laboratory is a logical follow-up. In other words, the (laboratory) experimental literature should be a welcomed addition to the "Duvergerian agenda."

One common criticism of laboratory experiments related to electoral systems is incongruences in the context in which decisions are made with those environments in real elections where voters are asked to cast their ballot. While one of the reasons for conducting laboratory experiments in the first place is precisely to "abstract away" from the context of real elections those elements that are theorized not to be important or confounding behavior to be observed, results from laboratory experiments nevertheless should be subjected to validation of obtained findings in different contexts, including other laboratory studies and studies conducted outside of the laboratory. For instance, Morton et al. (2015) exploit unique features of a particular electoral system, that is, the fact that polls in French overseas territories close their polls many hours before mainland France starts to vote, while Laslier and coauthors (Laslier and Van der Straeten 2008; Van der Straeten, Laslier, and Blais 2013) apply the same experimental design as used in the laboratory to broader samples of (online) participants. Combining the controlled setting in the laboratory with external context, Meffert and Gschwend (2011) study voting behavior by exposing subjects to polling information and coalition signals from concurrent electoral campaigns. This is a study of how polls and coalition signals affect the prevalence of strategic voting, holding the proportional electoral system constant, but nevertheless illustrates a tool for marrying lab experiments with external context.

It generally needs to be pointed out, though, that to test the precise claims derived from modeling the effect of electoral systems outside of the laboratory requires institutional variation unlikely to be found at the most general level of distinguishing electoral systems (e.g., proportional vs. majoritarian systems). The variation in incentives at this level is thus often best modeled in the laboratory. As we will show in the next sections on natural and field experiments, there can be, however, exploitable variation in electoral systems at lower levels of the institutional structure in many polities around the world; we show works that make clever use of this variation, but many more opportunities are available.[10]

## "Natural" Experiments and Close Relatives

Scholars studying electoral systems also have tried to utilize a research design around so-called natural (or quasi) experiments, which tend to take one of two forms. The first, and more common, is to exploit real-world variation in electoral systems that is caused by a random, exogenous shock. The second form is to utilize variation created by a randomization feature built into the electoral system.

With respect to the former, the common approach is to approximate a "natural" experiment in investigating political behavior before and after an electoral reform; studies have taken this approach following reforms in Italy and Japan (Giannetti and Grofman 2011), Israel (Andersen and Yaish 2003), and New Zealand (Vowles 1995).[11] To be clear, though, in contrast to what the label adopted for these studies suggests, neither the institutional reforms that took place in Italy and Japan in the early 1990s, nor the change from a single-ballot party list to a two-ballot system including a direct vote on the prime minister in Israel in 1996, nor the shift from a first-past-the-post system to a mixed-member proportional system in New Zealand in 1995 actually involved experimental manipulations. No exogenous shock in nature manipulated the institutional framework. Real-world legislators changed the electoral system, and they of course had particular reasons for doing so. In many cases, then, the variable of interest can turn out to be endogenous to the politically induced change, and therefore there may be an unobserved characteristic of these countries that implemented reform that made them susceptible to strive for changing their institution in the first place (which is an example of an identification problem rooted in selection). Alternatively, an expected voting pattern may have triggered interest among those in power to change the institutional framework (an example of an identification problem rooted in reverse causality).

In any case, while we should perhaps not call such a research design a "natural" experiment, the temporal dimension certainly allows for causal identification of some effects of institutional reform under less restrictive assumptions than findings backed by cross-country correlational evidence. However, interesting institutional variation may be found at lower levels of electoral systems, even when using this kind of a "natural experiment" requires "a rather large leap of faith" (Rodden 2009, 352) in the sense that why institutions assigned to "subjects" (i.e., citizens) should be random is often still a question of how persuaded the reader is by the researchers' argument.[12] Still, it is possible to get around these sorts of concerns if, for example, an electoral reform started as a political stunt seemingly unrelated to such an institutional rearrangement (Nagel 2004).

However, occasionally there are opportunities for researchers to exploit actual randomization processes that are part of the electoral systems and/or are carried out in collaboration with scholars specifically for the purpose of testing the effect of an electoral institution. A range of studies about minority quotas in India (e.g., Chattopadhyay and Duflo 2004; Bhavnani 2009) provides such robust identification, but for the specific context of the case at hand (see also Ziegfeld, this volume). Another branch of literature on US state and local elections facilitates the random assignment of candidate names to ballot positions to assess the impact of ballot structure on voters' choices (Koppell and Steen 2004; Ho and Imai 2006, 2008; Chen et al. 2014; Pasek et al. 2014).

Finally, Ferwerda (2014) leverages the fact that the repeal of compulsory voting in Austrian federal elections happened gradually. Within-country variation was created due to the fact that authority over electoral rules shifted between the state and national level several times and the abolishment of fees when failing to turn out spanned more than a decade to reach all constituencies. Of course, there may be some correlation between when the repeal happened and turnout in a given constituency, but the author argues that the complicated legal process leading to abolishment can be seen as approximating a random assignment of electoral rules.

Studies like the ones on electoral quotas for minorities in India, ballot name ordering, or repeal of compulsory voting epitomize the potential of exploiting variation that is locally concentrated and happens at lower levels of the electoral system. These are great opportunities to grasp—admittedly contextual—effects of electoral institutions on behavior. Nevertheless, generalizable statements about different kinds of electoral systems are more likely—over time—to come from a research agenda of studies exploiting institutional variations in many different contexts and not from a single, ideal experimental design.

## Field and Survey Experiments

Field experiments strive to test more context-specific hypotheses (Gerber and Green 2012); one could say they aim for ecological validity (Morton and Williams 2010, 264). A loss of control, relative to well-designed laboratory experiments, is accepted to observe behavior and elicit attitudes in a richer political environment. How context is created varies widely and includes such approaches as implementing an experiment while an election takes place, posing as a voter in communicating with politicians, or eliciting subjects' behavior in hypothetical elections.

Shineman (2016) and Bol et al. (2013) are good examples of how to analyze real voting and candidate behavior through variation in electoral systems. The former uses the occurrence of an actual election, while the latter initiates a response from candidates by posing as voters.

Shineman (2016) manipulates the existence of "negative" compulsory voting by randomly assigning a set of self-selected study participants to a treatment that rewards turnout with a gift card.[13] The author then checks whether the subject actually participates in the election via official vote registers before activating the gift card.[14] The experiment varies the degree of compulsory voting by rewarding turnout for the treatment group but not for the control group. Bol et al. (2013) vary incentives for a personal vote by priming parliamentarians to consider either their personal skills or their party's platform; these considerations are induced through an email from a fictitious voter who asks the candidate a question about either of the two characteristics. The experimental treatment tries to vary how much a candidate thinks about the single-seat district component of the German mixed-member proportional electoral system ("first vote") by priming the opportunity of a personal vote cast by the fictitious voter versus how much a candidate thinks about the party-list element ("second vote") by priming the possibility that the fictitious voter cares about the candidate's party's policies. The authors measure email response rates across treatments. In both examples, researchers observe actual behavior as their outcome variable but approximate different electoral systems with their randomly assigned experimental treatments. To be sure, some control is lost because candidates in the Bol et al. (2013) study may infer many different things from receiving such an email but not the intended, electoral system–related considerations, and voters in the Shineman (2016) experiment may see the gift card as something other than a negative fine for voting. Nevertheless, the influence of many unobservables that are inherent in the typical cross-country study of the effect of compulsory voting on turnout and electoral systems on candidates' behavior is muted.

Field experiments, however, require interference in reality often without the a priori knowledge of participants that they are part of an experiment; in the Bol et al. (2013) study, candidates do not know that the email they received is not from one of their actual constituents, but fictitious. This begs the question of how much scholars should interfere in an actual election for the purpose of generating scientific knowledge. The study of electoral systems in particular begs attention to this question, as the consequences of the experimental manipulation could in theory affect the outcome of an election. While such an intervention would have admirable scientific merit, in reality it will often be ethically questionable or legally infeasible.[15] The two studies described here, then, are also impressive with respect to ethics and feasibility: they manipulate individual-level behavior through a slight adjustment of the benefits of voting (Shineman 2016) or priming of candidates (Bol et al. 2013). In other words, both studies exert only a weak influence on the outcome of elections. Both studies still enable themselves to pick up treatment effects because of their direct measurement of the outcome variable (actual vote choice from vote register and email response rate).[16]

However, what happens when we want to broaden the scope of what we are able to say about electoral systems? Questions of feasibility and ethics will undoubtedly arise. With respect to feasibility, collaborations with various governmental and nongovernmental actors have proven valuable to gain access to the system or to finance larger experimental manipulations. A prominent example of exploiting a governmental program for research purposes is a design that uses the fact that for receiving development aid, a random selection of villages in Afghanistan were mandated to include women in political decision making (Beath, Christia, and Enikolopov 2013). In this way, suffrage extension is exogenously assigned to some villages but not others. In particular, within a larger development aid project, researchers were able to mandate 125 villages to make decisions based on a council elected in an at-large district, while another 125 villages were to elect council members in multiple districts (Beath et al. 2016). To be sure, a project of such scale needs a partner, in this case the government of Afghanistan and multiple nongovernmental organizations. The abundance of development programs in the world, however, provides many opportunities for such access. (For the interested reader, the Beath et al. study finds that at-large elections deliver higher average levels of education among council members than district elections with a bias toward locally targeted public goods)

In considering how to add an experimenter-induced manipulation to one's research design, access and funding are not the only concerns; ethical issues must be addressed as well. A gain in knowledge about the functioning of electoral systems must be balanced against the consequences of potentially changing electoral results. One way to think about this is that great care should be given in considering the potential scope of any induced effect. In many countries, research has to adhere to review boards that enforce standards, such as that no harm to subjects may arise from taking part in the study or that the privacy of subjects is to be protected (Morton and Williams 2010).[17]

However, there does not yet seem to be a clear consensus in the field as to how much interference into elections is too much. To illustrate, a recent attempt to study turning a nonpartisan electoral system into a partisan system by means of a field experiment received criticism, partly because of the scope of the manipulation. A quarter of the population of the US state of Montana received a leaflet advertising partisan leanings of candidates in a judicial election (Willis 2014). Due to the scope of the manipulation, there was a perception that the experiment could have changed the outcome of the election.[18] Explicitly addressing this issue of acceptable levels of impact in field experiments involving election would probably be of benefit to the field in the future.

While the list of survey experiments in political science, including studies that make comparisons across political systems and therefore across electoral systems, has grown to a respectable size, straightforward experimental manipulations of electoral systems are scarce. In those few studies, creating hypothetical elections and observing survey respondents' or experimental subjects' behavior is most common. As examples, Bol et al. (2016) present subjects with a hypothetical vote choice in the European Union parliament election on a hypothetical pan-European list of candidates; Baujard et al. (2014) ask self-selected subjects to vote on French presidential election candidates during the actual election according to either an approval voting system or an evaluative voting system and compare behavior under those rules to vote choices under the two-round system in place. These experiments are embedded in online surveys and illustrate a very typical operationalization of manipulating electoral systems: asking for behavior and attitudes under different hypothetical electoral systems.

## Other Types of Experimental Design

Finally, we conclude with an illustration of other, less common experimental designs aiming to model aspects of electoral systems. Among those are deliberation experiments in the run-up to a reform of British Columbia's electoral system (Warren and Pearse 2008) and before the 2009 European Parliament election (Isernia and Fishkin 2014). The Isernia and Fishkin (2014) study involves surveying a representative sample of the European Union population and inviting a random subsample to take part in deliberations about issues of the day with other citizens, politicians, and other experts. In a follow-up survey, the researchers elicit voting behavior in the election and political attitudes. In a sense, the election process is experimentally enriched with a deliberation phase to shape subjects' voting decisions. A different question regarding the influence of a deliberative system on voting behavior is pursued by Warren and Pearse (2008). They report on an initiative by the government of British Columbia that installed an assembly of randomly selected citizens to propose changes to the electoral system, which were then put to a vote in front of the general public. Even though no control group exists in this experiment, conveners of the assembly still manipulated the process of electoral reform by modeling variation in the legitimacy of the proposed changes (running from a random sample of citizens instead of a panel of experts or negotiations between political parties).

# CAUSALITY AND STATISTICAL METHODS

In political science writ large, experimental research may be the "gold standard" in causal inference, but in many cases an experimental research design may simply not be feasible. For example, no matter how much we might like to know how US elections would turn out under proportional representation rules, the likelihood that a set of states will be randomly assigned to switch to proportional representation for the 2018 US midterm elections seems unlikely at best. Cognizant of this fact, in recent years scholars have increasingly been using new forms of statistical analysis to attempt to get a better grasp of causal inference even outside of an experimental research design; such tools include matching, instrumental variables, or regression discontinuity design. These methodological innovations can also be found in the literature on electoral systems.

To give one example, scholars have used "matching" procedures not just in the standard sense of as a statistical estimator. Blais et al. (2011) exploit mixed-member electoral systems that typically give each voter a choice under majoritarian and under proportional rules, permitting scholars to assess the mechanical and psychological effects of electoral institutions on voters and parties (see also Herron, Nemoto, and Nishikawa, this volume). In a sense, this study matches each voter with him- or herself and compares behavior under each of the two electoral rules. Portmann, Stadelmann, and Eichenberger (2012) "match" representatives' legislative choices with voters' choices in referenda on the same proposals in Switzerland to estimate the effect of variation in district size on office holders' representativeness of citizens' preferences.

Persson and Tabellini (2005) use propensity score matching of countries as a statistical estimator to understand various economic outcomes associated with differences between majoritarian and proportional electoral rules. Calvo and Micozzi (2005) go down the route of a more sophisticated Bayesian estimator, which allows them to match electoral districts in Argentina with respect to partisan bias and majoritarian bias to capture the effects of electoral reforms.[19]

Persson and Tabellini (2005) aim to get at the causal effect of electoral rules on economic outcomes using the time of adoption of the country's constitution, the fraction of English-speaking or other European-language-speaking population, and latitude as instrumental variables. To make valid causal claims, a strong instrument should not have an effect on the outcome variable other than the impact through the endogenous regressors. Here, Acemoglu (2005) argues that the time of adoption of the constitution instrument is weak (i.e., only has a weak influence on the endogenous regressors) and that the language and latitude instruments cannot reasonably be assumed to be influencing institutional features on theoretical grounds.[20]

Funk and Gathmann (2011) use barriers to launching a referendum on constitutional change in Swiss cantons as an instrument to get at a causal estimate of the effect of referenda on public spending. In this study, the validity of the claim rests on the credibility of the assumption that barriers to launching a referenda affect the existence of the referenda themselves but not the outcome variable, which here is public spending. Finally, Gabel and Scheve (2007) study the effect of elite communication on public opinion instrumenting with institutional changes. Note that this is a different approach to including electoral systems in a study compared to most of those discussed previously in this chapter: electoral rules are included here not as an explanatory variable, but instead as a device to achieve identification.

Lastly, political science has recently developed a taste for regression discontinuity design. For instance, Dunning and Nilekani (2013) examine the effect of quotas on minority representation and welfare with a study that exploits how reserved districts are assigned. In several Indian states, whether an electoral district is a reserved district is determined by whether it surpasses a certain percentage of district residents being members of the scheduled caste. Dunning and Nilekani use the assumption that districts just above and just below that percentage are indistinguishable in all other characteristics; in this way causal inferences from the comparison of such districts about the effect of imposing quotas on political outcomes can be drawn.

Eggers (2015) takes advantage of the fact that municipal elections in France above certain population thresholds use proportional representation, while those below use a plurality rule (also see Hoyo, this volume). Comparing cities around that threshold allows the author to make causal claims about how electoral rules affect turnout. Gagliarducci, Nannicini, and Naticchionia (2011) look at Italy, where candidates can run for a seat in parliament in two tiers—a proportional and a majority electoral rule—but have to accept the latter should they win both. For causal claims, they make the assumption that in close elections, whether a candidate wins none, one, or both tiers is as-if random. What makes this design interesting is the fact that this peculiar electoral institution allows us to compare the behavior of representatives who won under proportional rule against those who picked up a seat under majority rule.

# Conclusion

Let us take it as a given that we want to learn whether electoral systems have a causal effect on some variable of interest. Experimental research provides a tool to do so. It is possible that in some instances we may simply be interested in describing a relationship between electoral systems and a particular variable of interest, in which case we can do without an experimental manipulation. But, mostly, researchers are interested in causal effects. Also, when we want to know whether a certain variable influences which electoral system emerges, a causality-driven research design is in order. For experimental research to work, researchers need variation—manipulable variation—at the institutional level. Unfortunately, it is unlikely that we will find studies where we can actually randomize the most general level of an electoral system, that is, whether the system is majoritarian or proportional. But there is constantly variation in other features of electoral systems waiting to be exploited. We argue that this is where field experimental research should move next while experimentalists in general should also continue to do careful, thorough, theory-driven laboratory studies.

Are all questions answerable by experiments? To be sure, the answer to that question is no. Many questions remain, however, that have not been studied experimentally yet address issues where the institutional variable of interest is open for exogenous manipulation. This could mean a carefully crafted experimental test of a formal model in the laboratory or using "naturally" occurring variation in already-existing institutions at a lower level of government.

To be clear, we are not recommending that observational data in the study of electoral systems be abandoned—far from it—but we do want to highlight the potential of experimental methods for the field. This is a call to use our broad knowledge about the different, multilayered features of electoral systems and start exploiting potentially exogenous variation at lower levels of electoral systems or create variation through experimental manipulation that is feasible at those lower levels.

That is not to say that treatment effects estimated from experimental data never face biases or always speak directly to the question at hand. The former concern is particularly relevant in natural and field experiments where context is specifically invited to play a role in the experiment but comes with confounding factors, such as selection bias, attrition, and so forth. The latter seems to apply more to laboratory experiments testing formal models—and there is certainly some truth to this—but experiments in general aim for abstraction that always has to be traded off against the scope of the claims one can make. A research agenda in any field—like the study of electoral systems and their consequences for political behavior and attitudes—needs balance in all different types of research design. It needs experimental research to enable causal claims but also deep descriptive knowledge of case studies and observational data to understand the scope of the precise treatment effect established. While experimental research may be much newer to the study of electoral systems than the observational research that is present in the classics in the field, we believe the studies described in this chapter are already making important contributions to moving the field forward and are likely to continue to do so in the future.

## NOTES

1. In general, we care about research design because it lays out the concepts we use associated with the object of our study; provides the theory about the mechanism behind the social phenomenon in which we are interested; answers questions regarding how to gather, measure, and analyze data about this phenomenon; and finally facilitates a dialogue between concepts, theory, and data by each individual researcher but also across the field; this definition of research design loosely follows Gschwend and Schimmelfennig (2007).
2. The exact algorithm we employed is described in more detail in the following section.
3. For those interested in more details regarding the operationalization of "electoral systems," eight of the seminal papers operationalize the electoral system as a comparison between proportional and majoritarian systems, two consider district magnitude, and three look at

the effect of downstream consequences of electoral systems on some other dependent variable of interest. The remainder test for the influence of multiple features of the electoral system at the same time.

4. These studies are looking at changes in vote share from one election to the other without acknowledging changes in electoral rules over time or do not model electoral rules at all.

5. This is a point worth emphasizing. Country fixed effects are often included in studies as a sophisticated acknowledgment that there are important differences between countries, including, but obviously not limited to, electoral systems. While such fixed effects can control for these differences, they do not tell us anything at all about the actual effects of electoral systems. Moreover, country fixed effects may not even control for variation due to electoral rules when countries switch electoral rules over the period of study. And depending on the level of the electoral system, such rules may change more frequently than is often realized.

6. A random separation of research units into "control" and "treatment" groups is induced orthogonally to the variable of interest through, for example, change in the composition of a school cohort (Dinas and Stoker 2014), gradual repeal of compulsory voting (Ferwerda 2014), variation in assignment of names to positions on ballots (Chen et al. 2014), assignment of nongovernmental organization field workers who then recommend decision-making rules to villagers (Grossman and Hanlon 2014), or alphabetical assignment of voters to polling stations by name (Cantú 2014); with a few more assumptions, the same can be said about comparing behavior across elections where in one election early voting rules were different (Finseraas and Vernby 2014).

7. Our sample of articles published in the year 2014 does not include publications in methods journals; the low number of methodology papers should be evaluated keeping this in mind.

8. See McKelvey and Ordeshook (1990) for an overview of this early research on experiments about decision rules within the framework of the spatial model of politics and Fiorina and Plott (1978) for yet another example of an experimental study of the functioning of majority rule in committee decisions.

9. That is, are proportional rules more likely to yield multiparty systems and majoritarian rules more likely to lead to two-party systems? See Duverger (1954) and Cox (1997) for more details.

10. By lower level we mean the features of the electoral system like the ballot structure, electoral thresholds, electoral formulae, or rules governing the electoral environment (i.e., candidate selection, campaign finances, polling center allocation, election oversight, appeals processes, ballot format, early voting, etc.), in contrast to the highest level of electoral system, that is, the distinction between majoritarian and proportional systems.

11. Also see chapters in this volume by Passarelli; Nemoto; Hazan, Itzkovich-Malka, and Rahat; and Vowles.

12. See the previous footnote for our definition of "lower levels" of electoral systems.

13. By "negative" compulsory voting, we refer to electoral rules that pay people for voting. This is, of course, from a certain perspective basically equivalent to fining people for not voting, insofar as both sets of rules leave the voter better off financially due to the decision to participate in the election. That being said, a wealth of research exists showing that people value gain and loss differently even when the monentary value is the same, so there is good reason to expect that the effects of "negative" compulsory voting might not generalize to more standard forms of "positive" compulsory voting.

14. In much of the United States, whether or not people have voted in an election is a matter of public record.

15. One could perhaps call this the "paradox of electoral system field experiments": the more consequential the result of the study is likely to be, the less likely it is to be legally or ethically feasible.

16. For full disclosure, one of the authors was a classmate of Shineman's when she worked on this project and the other was a dissertation adviser. Readers should take our praise of her work with appropriate caveats.

17. That being said, boards focused on protecting subjects may not be tasked with considering the downstream effect of experiments on nonsubjects, which can also raise important ethical considerations.

18. To be clear, there were other factors related to the experiment that also drew the ire of the residents of Montana; see Willis (2014) for additional details.

19. It is important to remember that making valid causal claims based on such a matching procedure requires scholars to make the strong assumption that no omitted variable bias exists, an assumption that is unlikely to be met in many cases.

20. Crisp et al. (2014) also take issue with regular cross-country studies and with the instrumental variables approach and implement a vector autoregressive model to capture the endogenous relationship between electoral volatility and legislative corruption; such an approach allows us to learn whether there is a feedback mechanism between the variables of interest but not what the mechanism looks like exactly. Crisp et al. claim to show that past perceptions of corruption increase electoral volatility but also that no reverse influence exists.

## References

Acemoglu, Daron. "Constitutions, Politics, and Economics: A Review Essay on Persson and Tabellini's The Economic Effects of Constitutions." *Journal of Economic Literature* 43, no. 4 (2005): 1025–1048.

Adams, James, Lawrence Ezrow, and Zeynep Somer-Topcu. "Do Voters Respond to Party Manifestos or to a Wider Information Environment? An Analysis of Mass-Elite Linkages on European Integration." *American Journal of Political Science* 58, no. 4 (2014): 967–978.

Andersen, Robert, and Meir Yaish. "Social Cleavages, Electoral Reform and Party Choice: Israel's 'Natural' Experiment." *Electoral Studies* 22, no. 3 (2003): 399–423.

Aytaç, S. Erdem. "Distributive Politics in a Multiparty System: The Conditional Cash Transfer Program in Turkey." *Comparative Political Studies* 47, no. 9 (2014): 1211–1237.

Bassi, Anna. "Voting Systems and Strategic Manipulation: An Experimental Study." *Journal of Theoretical Politics* 27, no. 1 (2015): 58–85.

Battaglini, Marco, Rebecca Morton, and Thomas Palfrey. "Efficiency, Equity, and Timing of Voting Mechanisms." *American Political Science Review* 101, no. 3 (2007): 409–424.

Baujard, Antoinette, Herrade Igersheim, Isabelle Lebon, Frédéric Gavrel, and Jean-François Laslier. "Who's Favored by Evaluative Voting? An Experiment Conducted during the 2012 French Presidential Election." *Electoral Studies* 34 (2014): 131–145.

Beath, Andrew, Fotini Christia, Georgy Egorov, and Ruben Enikolopov. "Electoral Rules and Political Selection: Theory and Evidence from a Field Experiment in Afghanistan." *Review of Economic Studies* 83, no. 3 (2016): 932–968.

Beath, Andrew, Fotini Christia, and Ruben Enikolopov. "Empowering Women through Development Aid: Evidence from a Field Experiment in Afghanistan." *American Political Science Review* 107, no. 3 (2013): 540–557.

Bhavnani, Rikhil R. "Do Electoral Quotas Work after They Are Withdrawn? Evidence from a Natural Experiment in India." *American Political Science Review* 103, no. 1 (2009): 23–35.

Blais, André, Romain Lachat, Airo Hino Pascal, and Doray-Demers. "The Mechanical and Psychological Effects of Electoral Systems a Quasi-Experimental Study." *Comparative Political Studies* 44, no. 12 (2011): 1599–1621.

Blais, André, Jean-Benoit Pilet, Karine Van der Straeten, Jean-François Laslier, and Maxime Héroux-Legault. "To Vote or to Abstain? An Experimental Test of Rational Calculus in First Past the Post and PR Elections." *Electoral Studies* 36 (2014a): 39–50.

Blais, André, Simon Labbé St-Vincent, Jean-Benoit Pilet, and Rafael Treibich. "Voting Correctly in Lab Elections with Monetary Incentives: The Impact of District Magnitude." *Party Politics* 22, no. 4 (2014b): 544–551.

Bol, Damien, Thomas Gschwend, Thomas Zittel, and Steffen Zittlau. "The Impact of the Electoral Context on Personal Vote Strategies: A Field Experiment on German Legislators." 2013.

Bol, Damien, Philipp Harfst, André Blais, Sona N. Golder, Jean-François Laslier, Laura B. Stephenson, and Karine Van der Straeten. "Addressing Europe's Democratic Deficit: An Experimental Evaluation of the Pan-European District Proposal." *European Union Politics* 17, no. 4 (2016): 525–545.

Bouton, Laurent, Micael Castanheira, and Aniol Llorente-Saguer. "Divided Majority and Information Aggregation: Theory and Experiment." *Journal of Public Economics* 134 (2016): 114–128.

Calvo, Ernesto, and Juan Pablo Micozzi. "The Governor's Backyard: A Seat-Vote Model of Electoral Reform for Subnational Multiparty Races." *Journal of Politics* 67, no. 4 (2005): 1050–1074.

Cantú, Francisco. "Identifying Irregularities in Mexican Local Elections." *American Journal of Political Science* 58, no. 4 (2014): 936–951.

Chattopadhyay, Raghabendra, and Esther Duflo. "Impact of Reservation in Panchayati Raj: Evidence from a Nationwide Randomised Experiment." *Economic and Political Weekly*, (2004): 979–986.

Chen, Eric, Gábor Simonovits, Jon A. Krosnick, and Josh Pasek. "The Impact of Candidate Name Order on Election Outcomes in North Dakota." *Electoral Studies* 35 (2014): 115–122.

Cho, Seok-Ju. "Voting Equilibria under Proportional Representation." *American Political Science Review* 108, no. 2 (2014): 281–296.

Clark, Michael, and Debra Leiter. "Does the Ideological Dispersion of Parties Mediate the Electoral Impact of Valence? A Cross-National Study of Party Support in Nine Western European Democracies." *Comparative Political Studies* 47, no. 2 (2014): 171–202.

Corazzini, Luca, Sebastian Kube, Michel André Maréchal, and Antonio Nicolo. "Elections and Deceptions: An Experimental Study on the Behavioral Effects of Democracy." *American Journal of Political Science* 58, no. 3 (2014): 579–592.

Cox, Gary. "Centripetal and Centrifugal Incentives in Electoral Systems." *American Journal of Political Science* 31 (1990): 905–935.

Cox, Gary. *Making Votes Count*. Cambridge: Cambridge University Press, 1997.

Curtice, John, and Michael Marsh. "Confused or Competent? How Voters use the STV Ballot Paper." *Electoral Studies* 34 (2014): 146–158.

Crisp, Brian F., Santiago Olivella, Joshua D. Potter, and William Mishler. "Elections as Instruments for Punishing Bad Representatives and Selecting Good Ones." *Electoral Studies* 34 (2014): 1–15.

Dinas, Elias, and Laura Stoker. "Age-Period-Cohort Analysis: A Design-Based Approach." *Electoral Studies* 33 (2014): 28–40.

Dunning, Thad, and Janhavi Nilekani. "Ethnic Quotas and Political Mobilization: Caste, Parties, and Distribution in Indian Village Councils." *American Political Science Review* 107, no. 1 (2013): 35–56.

Duverger, Maurice. *Political Parties: Their Organization and Activity in the Modern State.* London: Methuen, 1954.

Eggers, Andrew C. "Proportionality and Turnout Evidence from French Municipalities." *Comparative Political Studies* 48, no. 2 (2015): 135–167.

Endersby, James W., and Michael J. Towle. "Making Wasted Votes Count: Turnout, Transfers, and Preferential Voting in Practice." *Electoral Studies* 33 (2014): 144–152.

Ferwerda, Jeremy. "Electoral Consequences of Declining Participation: A Natural Experiment in Austria." *Electoral Studies* 35 (2014): 242–252.

Finseraas, Henning, and Kåre Vernby. "A Mixed Blessing for the Left? Early Voting, Turnout and Election Outcomes in Norway." *Electoral Studies* 33 (2014): 278–291.

Fiorina, Morris P., and Charles R. Plott. "Committee Decisions under Majority Rule: An Experimental Study." *American Political Science Review* 72, no. 2 (1978): 575–598.

Forsythe, Robert, Thomas Rietz, Roger Myerson, and Robert Weber. "An Experimental Study of Voting Rules and Polls in Three-Candidate Elections." *International Journal of Game Theory* 25, no. 3 (1996): 355–383.

Funk, Patricia, and Christina Gathmann. "Does Direct Democracy Reduce the Size of Government? New Evidence from Historical Data, 1890–2000." *Economic Journal* 121, no. 557 (2011): 1252–1280.

Gabel, Matthew, and Kenneth Scheve. "Estimating the Effect of Elite Communications on Public Opinion Using Instrumental Variables." *American Journal of Political Science* 51, no. 4 (2007): 1013–1028.

Gagliarducci, Stefano, Tommaso Nannicini, and Paolo Naticchionia. "Electoral Rules and Politicians' Behavior: A Micro Test." *American Economic Journal: Economic Policy* 3, no. 3 (2011): 144–174.

Gans-Morse, Jordan, Sebastian Mazzuca, and Simeon Nichter. "Varieties of Clientelism: Machine Politics during Elections." *American Journal of Political Science* 58, no. 2 (2014): 415–432.

Gerber, Alan S., and Donald P. Green. *Field Experiments: Design, Analysis, and Interpretation.* New York: W. W. Norton, 2012.

Gerber, Elisabeth R., Rebecca B. Morton, and Thomas A. Rietz. "Minority Representation in Multimember Districts." *American Political Science Review* 92, no. 1 (1998): 127–144.

Giannetti, Daniela, and Bernard Grofman. *A Natural Experiment on Electoral Law Reform: Evaluating the Long Run Consequences of 1990s Electoral Reform in Italy and Japan.* Vol. 24. New York: Springer Science & Business Media, 2011.

Golder, Matt, and Jacek Stramski. "Ideological Congruence and Electoral Institutions." *American Journal of Political Science* 54, no. 1 (2010): 90–106.

González Ocantos, Ezequiel, Chad Kiewiet Jonge, and David W. Nickerson. "The Conditionality of Vote-Buying Norms: Experimental Evidence from Latin America." *American Journal of Political Science* 58, no. 1 (2014): 197–211.

Grossman, Emiliano, and Cornelia Woll. "Saving the Banks: The Political Economy of Bailouts." *Comparative Political Studies* 47, no. 4 (2014): 574–600.

Grossman, Guy, and W. Walker Hanlon. "Do Better Monitoring Institutions Increase Leadership Quality in Community Organizations? Evidence from Uganda." *American Journal of Political Science* 58, no. 3 (2014): 669–686.

Gschwend, Thomas, and Marc Hooghe. "Should I Stay or Should I Go? An Experimental Study on Voter Responses to Pre-Electoral Coalitions." *European Journal of Political Research* 47, no. 5 (2008): 556–577.

Gschwend, Thomas, and Frank Schimmelfennig. *Research Design in Political Science*, 1–20. New York: Palgrave Macmillan, 2007.

Harada, Masataka, and Daniel M. Smith. "You Have to Pay to Play: Candidate and Party Responses to the High Cost of Elections in Japan." *Electoral Studies* 36 (2014): 51–64.

Hix, Simon. "Electoral Institutions and Legislative Behavior: Explaining Voting Defection in the European Parliament." *World Politics* 56, no. 2 (2004): 194–223.

Ho, Daniel E., and Kosuke Imai. "Randomization Inference with Natural Experiments: An Analysis of Ballot Effects in the 2003 California Recall Election." *Journal of the American Statistical Association* 101, no. 475 (2006): 888–900.

Ho, Daniel E., and Kosuke Imai. "Estimating Causal Effects of Ballot Order from a Randomized Natural Experiment: The California Alphabet Lottery, 1978–2002." *Public Opinion Quarterly* 72, no. 2 (2008): 216–240.

Isernia, Pierangelo, and James S. Fishkin. "The EuroPolis Deliberative Poll." *European Union Politics* 15, no. 3 (2014): 311–327.

Jones, Mark P. "Gender Quotas, Electoral Laws, and the Election of Women Lessons from the Argentine Provinces." *Comparative Political Studies* 31, no. 1 (1998): 3–21.

Kinder, Donald R., and Thomas R. Palfrey. *Experimental Foundations of Political Science*. Ann Arbor: University of Michigan Press, 1993.

Kolev, Kiril. "The Contingent Effect of Institutions: Electoral Formulas, Ethnic Polarization, and Election Quality." *Electoral Studies* 35 (2014): 200–214.

Koppell, Jonathan G. S., and Jennifer A. Steen. "The Effects of Ballot Position on Election Outcomes." *Journal of Politics* 66, no. 1 (2004): 267–281.

Krook, Mona Lena. "Electoral Gender Quotas: A Conceptual Analysis." *Comparative Political Studies* 47, no. 9 (2014): 1268–1293.

Kunicova, Jana, and Susan Rose-Ackerman. "Electoral Rules and Constitutional Structures as Constraints on Corruption." *British Journal of Political Science* 35, no. 4 (2005): 573–606.

Laslier, Jean-François, and Karine Van der Straeten. "A Live Experiment on Approval Voting." *Experimental Economics* 11, no. 1 (2008): 97–105.

Lijphart, Arend. "Comparative Politics and the Comparative Method." *American Political Science Review* 65, no. 3 (1971): 682–693.

Lijphart, Arend. "Democracies: Forms, Performance, and Constitutional Engineering." *European Journal of Political Research* 25, no. 1 (1994): 1–17.

McKelvey, Richard and Peter Ordeshook "A Decade of Experimental Research on Spatial Models of Elections and Committees." In *Advances in the Spatial Theory of Voting*, 99–144 edited by James Enelow and Melvin Hinich. New York: Cambridge University Press, 1990.

Meffert, Michael, and Thomas Gschwend. "Polls, Coalition Signals and Strategic Voting: An Experimental Investigation of Perceptions and Effects." *European Journal of Political Research* 50, no. 5 (2011): 636–667.

Milesi-Ferretti, Gian Maria, Roberto Perotti, and Massimo V. Rostagno. "Electoral Systems and Public Spending." *Quarterly Journal of Economics* 117, no. 2 (2002): 609–657.

Miller, Nicholas R. "The House Size Effect and the Referendum Paradox in US Presidential Elections." *Electoral Studies* 35 (2014): 265–271.

Morton, Rebecca B., Daniel Muller, Lionel Page, and Benno Torgler. "Exit Polls, Turnout, and Bandwagon Voting: Evidence from a Natural Experiment." *European Economic Review* 77 (2015): 65–81.

Morton, Rebecca B., and Joshua A. Tucker. "Welcome to JEPS." *Journal of Experimental Political Science* 1, no. 1 (2014): 1–3.

Morton, Rebecca, and Kenneth Williams. "Information Asymmetries and Simultaneous versus Sequential Voting." *American Journal of Political Science* 93, no. 1 (1999): 51–67.

Morton, Rebecca, and Kenneth Williams. *Experimental Political Science and the Study of Causality. From Nature to the Lab.* New York: Cambridge University Press, 2010.

Moser, Robert G. "Electoral Systems and the Number of Parties in Postcommunist States." *World Politics* 51 (1999): 359–384.

Mozaffar, Shaheen, James R. Scarritt, and Glen Galaich. "Electoral Institutions, Ethnopolitical Cleavages, and Party Systems in Africa's Emerging Democracies." *American Political Science Review* 97, no. 3 (2003): 379–390.

Murray, Rainbow. "Quotas for Men: Reframing Gender Quotas as a Means of Improving Representation for All." *American Political Science Review* 108, no. 3 (2014): 520–532.

Nagel, Jack H. "New Zealand: Reform by (Nearly) Immaculate Design." In *The Handbook of Electoral System Choice*, edited by Josep Colomer, 530–543. New York: Palgrave Macmillan, 2004.

Neto, Octavio Amorim, and Gary W. Cox. "Electoral Institutions, Cleavage Structures, and the Number of Parties." *American Journal of Political Science* 41, no. 1 (1997): 149–174.

Norris, Pippa. *Electoral Engineering: Voting Rules and Political Behavior.* Cambridge: Cambridge University Press, 2004.

Norris, Pippa. *Radical Right: Voters and Parties in the Electoral Market.* Cambridge: Cambridge University Press, 2005.

Otjes, Simon, and Tom Louwerse. "Spatial Models in Voting Advice Applications." *Electoral Studies* 36 (2014): 263–271.

Pasek, Josh, Daniel Schneider, Jon A. Krosnick, Alexander Tahk, Eyal Ophir, and Claire Milligan. "Prevalence and Moderators of the Candidate Name-Order Effect: Evidence from Statewide General Elections in California." *Public Opinion Quarterly* 78, no. 2 (2014): 416–439.

Persson, Torsten, Gerard Roland, Guido Tabellini. "Electoral Rules and Government Spending in Parliamentary Democracies." *Quarterly Journal of Political Science* 2, no. 2 (2007): 155–188.

Persson, Torsten, and Guido Enrico Tabellini. *The Economic Effects of Constitutions.* Cambridge: MIT Press, 2005.

Persson, Torsten, Guido Tabellini, and Francesco Trebbi. "Electoral Rules and Corruption." *Journal of the European Economic Association* 1, no. 4 (2003): 958–989.

Plott, Charles R. "The Application of Laboratory Experimental Methods to Public Choice." In *Collective Decision Making. Applications from Public Choice Theory*, edited by Clifford Russel, 137–159. Baltimore: John Hopkins University Press, 1979.

Portmann, Marco, David Stadelmann, and Reiner Eichenberger. "District Magnitude and Representation of the Majority's Preferences: Evidence from Popular and Parliamentary Votes." *Public Choice* 151, no. 3–4 (2012): 585–610.

Powell, G. Bingham. *Elections as Instruments of Democracy: Majoritarian and Proportional Visions*. New Haven: Yale University Press, 2000.

Rodden, Jonathan. "Endogenous Institutions and Comparative Politics." In *Comparative Politics: Rationality, Culture, and Structure*, edited by Mark Lichbach, and Alan Zuckerman, 333–357. New York: Cambridge University Press, 2009.

Schwindt-Bayer, Leslie A., and William Mishler. "An Integrated Model of Women's Representation." *Journal of Politics* 67, no. 2 (2005): 407–428.

Shineman, Victoria Anne. "If You Mobilize Them, They Will Become Informed: Experimental Evidence That Information Acquisition Is Endogenous to Costs and Incentives to Participate." *British Journal of Political Science* (2016): 1–23.

Shugart, Matthew S. "Comparative Electoral Systems Research: The Maturation of a Field and New Challenges Ahead." In *Politics of Electoral Systems*, edited by Michael Gallagher and Paul Mitchell, 5–56. Oxford: Oxford University Press, 2005.

Shugart, Matthew Soberg. "The Electoral Cycle and Institutional Sources of Divided Presidential Government." *American Political Science Review* 89, no. 2 (1995): 327–343.

Spoon, Jae-Jae, and Heike Klüver. "Do Parties Respond? How Electoral Context Influences Party Responsiveness." *Electoral Studies* 35 (2014): 48–60.

Van de Walle, Nicolas. "Presidentialism and Clientelism in Africa's Emerging Party Systems." *Journal of Modern African Studies* 41, no. 2 (2003): 297–321.

Van der Straeten, Karine, Jean-François Laslier, and André Blais. "Vote au Pluriel: How People Vote When Offered to Vote under Different Rules." *PS: Political Science & Politics* 46, no. 2 (2013): 324–328.

Vowles, Jack. "The Politics of Electoral Reform in New Zealand." *International Political Science Review* 16, no. 1 (1995): 95–115.

Warren, Mark E., and Hilary Pearse. *Designing Deliberative Democracy: The British Columbia Citizens' Assembly*. Cambridge: Cambridge University Press, 2008.

Wawro, Gregory J., and Ira Katznelson. "Designing Historical Social Scientific Inquiry: How Parameter Heterogeneity Can Bridge the Methodological Divide between Quantitative and Qualitative Approaches." *American Journal of Political Science* 58, no. 2 (2014): 526–546.

Weschle, Simon. "Two Types of Economic Voting: How Economic Conditions Jointly Affect Vote Choice and Turnout." *Electoral Studies* 34 (2014): 39–53.

Willis, Derek. "Professors' Research Project Stirs Political Outrage in Montana." 2014. http://www.nytimes.com/2014/10/29/upshot/professors-research-project-stirs-politicaloutrage-in-montana.html.

Wilson, Matthew C. "A Discreet Critique of Discrete Regime Type Data." *Comparative Political Studies* 47, no. 5 (2014): 689–714.

# CHAPTER 22

# RECONCILING APPROACHES IN THE STUDY OF MIXED-MEMBER ELECTORAL SYSTEMS

ERIK S. HERRON,[1] KUNIAKI NEMOTO, AND
MISA NISHIKAWA

THE incentives that electoral systems generate for voters and political actors are well established in the literature (e.g., Duverger 1954; Rae 1967; Riker 1982).[2] Foundational research emphasizes how the institutional rules of constituency-based systems, most notably first past the post (FPTP), as well as majority runoff and proportional representation (PR) systems, affect the structure of the party system. Over time, the literature has expanded to address the connection between election rules and different outcomes, and to consider the effects of variation in election rules on those outcomes.[3]

One form of institutional variation—the mixed-member electoral system—was present at the time this early literature was published but was not subjected to extensive empirical scrutiny as a distinct electoral system. The first long-standing mixed-member electoral system,[4] adopted in Germany after World War II, was at times categorized as a form of PR, or called semi-PR largely due to its proportional outcomes (e.g., Sartori 1994). Over the years, many countries and subnational units adopted mixed-member systems so that by the end of the 1990s, they were widespread (Ferrara, Herron, and Nishikawa 2005). While several societies that chose mixed-member systems during their extensive expansion in the 1990s subsequently abandoned them (e.g., Italy),[5] they are used in prominent established democracies (e.g., Germany, Japan, New Zealand),[6] in transitional societies and new democracies (e.g., Ukraine,[7] South Korea, and Taiwan), and in authoritarian states (e.g., Russia).[8] The diversity within mixed-member systems prompted seminal taxonomic assessments that established these electoral systems as a unique form (Massicotte and Blais 1999; Shugart and Wattenberg 2001).

The mixed-member system's combination of different formulas to simultaneously select members of legislative bodies spawned two seemingly distinct approaches. One approach, labeled "controlled comparison," focuses on how the use of different formulas in the same cultural, economic, and historical contexts and at the same time allows scholars to evaluate the effects of election rules. Another approach, labeled "contamination," focuses on how the interaction between the component parts of mixed-member systems may alter the incentives and undermine controlled comparisons. Scholars have investigated the effects of mixed-member systems from both perspectives but have not reached consensus on which explanation best accounts for outcomes. *In this chapter we argue that these two approaches are not mutually exclusive. Rather, they differ in degree, and the effects vary largely depending on whether or not electoral or legislative behavior is examined. We particularly argue that institutional arrangements of mixed-member systems influence political actors differently at the electoral and legislative levels.*

To support this argument, we survey the published literature on mixed-member electoral systems and their effects, categorizing the findings along a spectrum in which the evidence suggests that contamination plays an important role, where the evidence does not support a role, and where the evidence is inconclusive. We further discuss approaches that could advance knowledge about mixed-member systems by evaluating the logic of controlled comparison and contamination and/or extending empirical assessments to better understand how the systems function.

# WHAT IS A MIXED-MEMBER ELECTORAL SYSTEM?

The earliest comparative discussions of mixed-member electoral systems emphasize that they combine different electoral rules in an election for a single legislative body. Reynolds and Reilly (1997) identify mixed-member systems as those that combine PR list systems and constituency-based "winner takes all" systems. Massicotte and Blais (1999), Shugart and Wattenberg (2001), and Ferrara et al. (2005) widen the range of systems that are considered to be mixed. A minimalist definition encompasses any two-component system with PR list and nominal elections, such as FPTP, single transferable vote (STV), and single nontransferable vote (SNTV), overlaying one another in a geographic region.[9]

The challenge that all definitions of mixed-member systems confront is the wide variation in the institutional rules used to tally votes and allocate seats. Mixed-member systems may vary by the presence or absence of a formal linkage between the components, ballot structure, flexibility to contest in more than one component, and proportion of seats allocated to the different formulas. All of these features could affect incentives underlying contamination or affect the logic of controlled comparison.

Perhaps the most notable difference among mixed-member systems is the degree to which the two components are formally independent of one another for seat allocation. Mixed-member proportional (MMP) systems link the components in the seat allocation process, with the list component typically establishing the overall target distribution for seats. While the specific mechanisms to allot seats vary, parties typically receive all the seats that they win in the nominal component and garner additional seats in the list component. The target proportion of seats that the party receives overall is generally equivalent to the proportion "due" to that party as determined by the list component. Because MMP systems tend to generate proportional outcomes through the seat allocation mechanism up to the limit of district magnitude and thresholds, they have been characterized as a form of PR (Sartori 1994). Unlike a pure PR system, however, some seats are occupied by members of parliament who owe their success to local constituencies, and some are occupied by members of parliament who owe their success to the party's performance and their list placement.

Mixed-member majoritarian (MMM) systems, by contrast, formally treat both components independently. Parties receive all constituency seats that they win and a proportion of the PR allocation based solely on the PR results. Results in MMM systems tend to be less proportional[10] than those in MMP.

Ballot structure also differs among mixed-member systems. In some cases (e.g., Korea prior to 2000), voters' choices on the nominal and list components are formally tied via a fused ballot, with the party affiliation of the constituency candidate connected to the party list vote. Ballots may also be printed on the same sheet (e.g., Albania) or on separate sheets (e.g., Ukraine), affecting the order in which voters may cast votes for the different races. The amount of information provided to voters may also vary, with some ballots providing the identities of party list candidates or candidate biographical information.

Another important institutional feature in mixed-member systems is the opportunity for candidates to contest races in both components simultaneously. Dual candidacy is permitted in many mixed-member systems like Germany, Japan, and New Zealand, although others such as South Korea, Taiwan, and Ukraine forbid it. Dual candidacy systems can generate dually nominated list winners who lose in the nominal component but win seats via the list component.[11] From a strategic perspective, the possibility of candidates who lose in one component winning a seat in another could affect nomination and campaigning tactics.

The nominal and list components also differ across mixed-member systems in terms of the proportion of seats allocated to each component. In many cases, the balance is equal or nearly equal. But in some countries more seats are allocated by the nominal component (e.g., several East Asian countries[12]), and in others more seats are allocated by the list component (e.g., East Timor 2001 election, prereform Italy). The relative distribution of seats across formulas could change the power of incentives to influence behavior.

Mixed-member systems include a wide range of institutional features; no ideal form of mixed-member system exists. However, institutional variation among mixed-member systems is an important factor to explain differences in outcomes. The next section identifies these differences, discusses how scholars have treated mixed-member systems, and subsequently integrates the issue of institutional variation and theoretical expectations.

# Controlled Comparison and Contamination in Mixed-Member Systems

## Defining Controlled Comparison and Contamination

Although mixed-member systems were incorporated into the catalog of electoral systems, critical questions remained about how the incentives produced by mixed-member systems would influence the behavior of voters, candidates, parties, and elected legislators. Some scholars took advantage of the unique features of mixed-member systems to evaluate how institutional rules with competing incentives affect the behavior of actors. These scholars claimed that the independence of the nominal and list elections make "natural experiments" possible, since the two parts of the elections are conducted within the same country and any confounding factors, such as cultural, economic, or historical factors, are controlled. In effect, they treated the sections of mixed-member systems as functionally independent.

Figure 22.1 illustrates the basic argument of the "controlled comparison" approach. Under "controlled comparison," Duvergerian incentives predominate, with the nominal component moderating the number of political parties in competition in constituencies, and the list component encouraging multiparty competition. The selection of legislators using two distinct types of election rules encourages representatives who are chosen in the nominal component to advocate for constituency interests and encourages representatives who are chosen in the list component to advocate for national-level (party) interests. This approach does not deny the possibility of interaction across the components, but suggests that the effects are inconsequential. Contextual features, such as the level of party system institutionalization and experience with democratic practices, influence how election rules affect outcomes more, yielding different results cross-nationally when similar rules are applied (Moser and Scheiner 2012). The studies that follow the controlled comparison approach imply that mixed-member electoral systems can produce the "best of both worlds" by generating local and national representation, encouraging party formation in the list component, and mitigating the size of the party system through the nominal component. However, this outcome is not guaranteed,

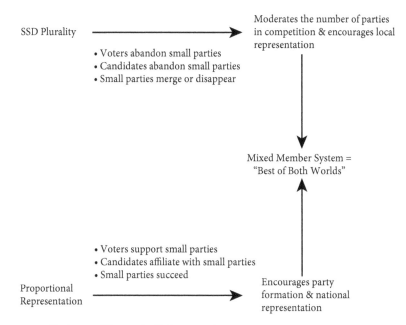

FIGURE 22.1. Features of the controlled comparison argument.

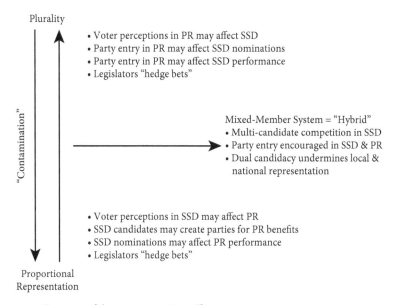

FIGURE 22.2. Features of the contamination effects argument.

as the question mark in the title of Shugart and Wattenberg's (2001) *The Best of Both Worlds?* suggests.

Other scholars challenged the notion of independence, claiming that the simultaneous use of different institutional rules would generate interaction, or "contamination," across the nominal and list components. The main consequence of contamination would be to alter the behaviors typically associated with "pure" versions of constituency-based or PR rules, illustrated in Figure 22.2. Instead of operating as functionally independent, the two components of the election system affect one another, generating a system with its own incentives. By the logic of contamination, voters, candidates, legislators, and party leaders take into account behavior in both components when making decisions about entry, voting, and advocacy. As a consequence, candidates may be "oversupplied" in the nominal component as parties that have decided to enter competition in the list component also nominate constituency candidates, even if they are not competitive. Pre-electoral coalitions may mitigate these effects, but the effective number of candidates should be higher than Duverger's law suggests at the district level for pure FPTP systems. Depending on the costs of party formation, ballot access, and especially the accommodativeness of the system (e.g., MMP with large district magnitude in the list component), candidates may be encouraged to form parties for the list component to take advantage of the resources they may gain, magnifying multipartism.

The logic of contamination is based on political actors' motivations, especially those associated with party leaders and candidates. Winning a *specific seat* is a primary goal for candidates; winning *as many seats as possible* is a primary goal for leaders. If party leaders believe that placing candidates in the nominal component is likely to increase the number of list votes the party receives, enhancing list seat acquisition, they should be motivated to place candidates in the nominal component even when those candidates have little chance of winning the particular seat. Party leaders also have multiple ways to entice candidates with resources available in government, the legislature, and the party (e.g., committee assignments, ranking in PR list, etc.), so that candidates can utilize resources to improve their electoral prospects and political careers (Pekkanen, Nyblade, and Krauss 2006).

In mixed-member electoral systems, candidates and leaders are expected to share the same incentives. Under any mixed-member systems—MMM or MMP—winning a constituency race guarantees a candidate a seat. Particularly for this reason, constituency seats may be perceived as more valuable prizes to acquire in the long term. For candidates with the goal of securing a nominal seat, contesting an election with the expectation that they can build a personal vote over more than one electoral cycle may mitigate concerns about short-term loss, especially if they are in a competitive party list position as well. If candidates adopt a longer time horizon, even candidates with little chance of winning may contest the nominal districts. The presence of these candidates may benefit the party as they may be especially motivated to campaign in their local districts, providing parties with electoral benefits.

A crucial mechanism for contamination is that the presence of such locally oriented candidates in the nominal component can make the party more visible in a given constituency. The visibility of the party is associated with contamination effects in two ways: first, supporters of locally oriented candidates are induced to cast list votes for the affiliated party, and second, party supporters cast straight tickets by voting for the candidates affiliated with the party regardless of competitiveness. Through either of the mechanisms (or both), the nominal component of the elections should witness some inflation in the number of candidates. In other words, party leaders' motivations combined with ambitious candidates' motivations promote contamination. We believe that this assumption is reasonable across mixed-member systems, although, as we explain later, the impact may be mitigated by a country's constitutional structure, a party's resources, and other factors.

Legislative behavior may also be contaminated like electoral behavior. Traditionally, the literature on electoral systems and parties has argued that candidates who are elected from pure FPTP systems are motivated to work for local interests, while candidates under PR work for broader interests (e.g., Katz 1980). Based on this intuition, a "stylized" version of controlled comparison in mixed-member systems would assume that nominal members are more likely than list members to defect from the party line, move from one party to another, and demand committee positions useful in providing parochial benefits.[13] This is because nominal members' principals (i.e., local constituents) may have conflicting interests with party leaders, who are interested in promoting their public policy platforms. In contrast, list members are more likely to work as loyal agents for party leaders because the power to rank candidates on the list gives leaders control.[14]

This "mandate divide" between nominal and list members may be ameliorated by the combined incentives.[15] In other words, if contamination influences legislative behavior, nominal and list members' theoretically expected behavioral differences should disappear. The specific hypotheses of contamination effects include expectations that nominal members may not be less loyal than list members in terms of roll-call voting or party switching, and that list members may act like nominal incumbents in committee assignments or constituency services. To put it differently, district incumbents act like list incumbents or list incumbents act like nominal incumbents in an effort to hedge bets. As discussed later, mixed-member systems' incentive structures per se may not promote legislative contamination. Rather, nuanced but important institutional differences within mixed-member systems seem to alter the motivations of legislators and activate contamination in legislative behavior. We explain the incentives of candidates and parties and their relationship to contamination effects at the electoral and legislative levels in more detail later.

While the controlled comparison and contamination approaches have been characterized as in direct opposition to one another in much of the literature, we treat them as differences in degree in this chapter. Both approaches acknowledge the likelihood of interaction between the components. The controlled comparison approach indicates that the interaction effects are likely to be small and are often eclipsed by other factors that affect behavior. The contamination effects approach recognizes that there are conditions in which the effects may be small or overwhelmed by other factors, but contamination effects depend on the institutional arrangements of mixed-member electoral systems and the effects differ at the electoral and legislative levels.

## Controlled Comparison and Contamination in the Literature

The late 1990s to early 2000s witnessed a substantial expansion in the discussion of mixed-member electoral systems[16] due in large part to the diffusion of these rules worldwide and the increased interest in studying their effects. While this early literature is generally characterized as constituting two defined schools of thought, they share important features. In this section, we evaluate published research about mixed-member electoral systems that speaks directly to the issues raised by the controlled comparison and contamination effects approaches.

To systematically identify relevant literature, we relied on the Web of Science and Google Scholar, searching several combinations of keywords: "mixed systems[17] and contamination," "mixed systems and interaction," and "mixed systems and controlled comparison." By focusing on these terms alone, our search may have omitted research that indirectly speaks to the differences between these two approaches but does not formally link the theoretical approach to the controlled comparison/contamination dichotomy. In addition, some scholarship acknowledges the debate about contamination and controlled comparison but does not pursue an empirical strategy designed to adjudicate between these approaches (e.g., Thames and Edwards 2006) and is not included in our assessment. We also include research conducted by the primary proponents of the two arguments, potentially overstating the volume of evidence supporting particular approaches. Finally, we emphasized journal articles rather than books, although books from both perspectives have been published (e.g., Ferrara et al. 2005; Moser and Scheiner 2012). In sum, while we rely on our collected literature to assess trends in research on mixed-member systems, we must be circumspect in our conclusions as the sample may be biased.

Table 22.1 classifies the publications we gathered in three ways. Articles that find evidence supporting principles of contamination are in the column labeled "contamination is more important." Articles that find no evidence supporting contamination, or evidence refuting it, are listed in the column labeled "contamination is less/not important." Articles that produce some findings leaning toward both approaches are labeled as "mixed." In addition to differentiating articles by their tendencies toward supporting the implications of contamination or controlled comparison, we separate research by the primary dependent variables, including the effective number of parties, list vote share, performance on nominal single-seat districts (SSDs), strategic/split-ticket voting, legislative behavior, and committee assignments. The table includes forty-six articles published between 2001 and 2016.

For most dependent variables, published research that we gathered in our search has not yielded a consensus on the controlled comparison/contamination debate. Twenty-four studies find evidence in support of the contamination approach. Even if we discount publications by the initial proponents of the argument, eighteen studies find evidence of contamination. Twelve studies find that contamination is not present or important to the outcomes, and nine find mixed evidence. This evidence is present in different national contexts, such as Italy, Russia, Japan, Korea, Spain, and Taiwan, as well

Table 22.1  Strength of Contamination Based on Different Dependent Variables

|  | Main Dependent Variable | Contamination Is More Important | Inconclusive Evidence | Contamination Is Less/Not Important |
|---|---|---|---|---|
| Electoral | Effective number of electoral parties | Herron and Nishikawa (2001); Golosov (2003); Nishikawa and Herron (2004); Ferrara and Herron (2005); Ferrara (2006); Lago and Martinez (2007); Lago and Montero (2009); Rich et al. (2014); Rich (2015) | Bochsler (2009) | Moser (2001); Moser and Scheiner (2004); Crisp, Potter, and Lee (2012) |
|  | List vote share | Ferrara (2004); Hainmueller and Kern (2008) | Karp (2009) | Maeda (2008) |
|  | SSD Performance | Krauss et al. (2012); Fortin-Rittberger and Eder (2013); Shin (2014) |  | Zittel and Gschwend (2008) |
|  | Strategic/split-ticket voting | Gschwend, Johnston, and Pattie (2003) | Kostadinova (2006) |  |
|  | Women's representation | Golosov (2014) | Fortin-Rittberger and Eder (2013) |  |
| Legislative | Legislative behavior | Herron (2002b); Heitshusen et al. (2005); Bernauer and Munzert (2014); Hennl (2014); Ohmura (2014); Rich (2014); Stoffel (2014); Corral et al. (2016) | Crisp (2007); Kerevel (2010); Rich (2012); Rich (2015) | Lundberg (2002); McLeay and Vowles (2007); Becher and Sieberer (2008); Sieberer (2010); Batto (2012); Olivella and Tavits (2014); Sieberer (2015) |
|  | Committee assignment | Pekkanen et al. (2006) | Centellas (2015) | Stratmann and Baur (2002) |

as wider cross-national samples. Scholars have found the influence of contamination on the effective number of parties (Herron and Nishikawa 2001; Golosov 2003; Nishikawa and Herron 2004; Ferrara and Herron 2005; Ferrara 2006; Lago and Martinez 2007; Lago and Montero 2009; Rich 2015), list vote share (Ferrara 2004; Hainmueller and Kern 2008), SSD performance (Krauss, Nemoto, and Pekkanen 2012; Fortin-Rittberger and Eder, 2013; Shin 2014; Zittel and Gschwend 2008), split-ticket voting (Gschwend, Johnston, and Pattie 2003), and women's representation (Fortin-Rittberger and Eder, 2013; Golosov 2014). Scholars have also found evidence of contamination in legislative behavior (Herron 2002b; Heitshusen, Young, and Wood, 2005; Bernauer and Munzert 2014; Hennl 2014; Ohmura 2014; Rich 2014; Stoffel 2014) and committee assignments (Pekkanen et al. 2006).

An almost equally diverse set of research finds limited or no evidence of contamination effects in electoral behavior. Using the effective number of parties as a dependent variable, scholars have found mixed (Bochsler, 2009) or no evidence that contamination provides leverage to explain variation in outcomes (Moser 2001; Moser and Scheiner 2004; Crisp, Potter, and Lee 2012). Similar findings are associated with other dependent variables like list vote share (Maeda 2008; Karp 2009) and split-ticket voting (Kostadinova 2006). Legislative dependent variables do not show solid support for the contamination argument, with mixed (Crisp 2007; Kerevel 2010; Rich 2012; Rich 2015) or limited effects in legislative behavior (Lundberg 2002; McLeay and Vowles 2007; Becher and Sieberer 2008; Sieberer 2010, 2015; Batto 2012; Olivella and Tavits 2014) and committee assignments (Stratmann and Baur 2002; Centellas 2015). These studies have not found contradictory results through replication, but rather have produced divergent interpretations by posing different questions, using different cases,[18] or configuring models with different explanatory variables. Scholars' varied approaches across the literature on mixed-member systems render a full adjudication infeasible.

Despite these challenges, our goal is to propose some potential mechanisms to develop scholarship that can better answer why we see such divergent results. One notable pattern on the table is the difference between studies emphasizing electoral dependent variables and those emphasizing legislative dependent variables. That is, contamination seems to find more robust support when it emphasizes electoral outcomes and less support when it emphasizes legislative outcomes. In our sample, five out of the nineteen studies in the electoral arena find no or unimportant effects of contamination. Contamination is more weakly associated with legislative outcomes; eight out of twenty-one studies in the legislative arena contend that contamination effects are unimportant. In the next section, we discuss how developing the research agenda on mixed-member systems may address these apparent discrepancies.

# ADVANCING THE RESEARCH AGENDA ON MIXED-MEMBER SYSTEMS

The divergent outcomes may be produced by faulty analysis, biased data, or some other mistake in the conduct of research. While error is certainly possible, it seems unlikely that such a wide range of scholars analyzing data from different countries and time periods would consistently get the wrong answer. Another possibility that has been hinted at in the literature on mixed-member systems is that the story of contamination or controlled comparison may be more nuanced than current research suggests. That is, the phenomenon may exist at measurable levels only under certain conditions that are sometimes—but not always—present in mixed-member systems. Institutional variation among mixed-member systems, along with other factors that differentiate how the incentives function, may contribute to the disparate research outcomes. We explore ways that scholars can confront the lack of consensus in findings and advance research on mixed-member systems to answer *how* and *under what circumstances* contamination may matter.

## Proximal and Distal Effects

The underlying logic of the contamination effects approach, noted earlier, is that voters, parties, and candidates pay close attention to both components when making strategic entry or voting decisions, disrupting the incentives that each component individually generates. But variation in the institutional features of mixed-member systems may influence these effects. If empirical results that both demonstrate contamination and challenge its presence accurately reflect the specific conditions scholars have identified (e.g., the particular array of institutional features and the social conditions of the societies under study), how can differences be reconciled?

One possibility is that the underlying theoretical accounts on both sides of the debate are underdeveloped. Later research from both approaches suggests that the argument should be more nuanced: institutional variation (Ferrara and Herron 2005) and social heterogeneity (Moser and Scheiner 2012) may be crucial intervening factors that condition the incentives and responses by political actors. In short, the mere presence of two simultaneous elections may not be enough to transform the incentives into contamination effects.

A potential avenue for further exploration comes from the controlled comparison literature. Scheiner (2008) (and earlier, Rae 1967) notes that electoral systems have proximal and distal effects. To influence outcomes, the proximal effects of electoral rules require few assumptions or limited causal chains, such as Duverger's mechanical effects. Distal effects, by contrast, involve multiple causal chains that go beyond the electoral system's mechanical effects.[19] Synthesizing this theoretical observation with the study of mixed-member systems requires scholars to more clearly articulate how institutional incentives are connected across the two types of elections and the conditions under which we would expect political actors to respond to these incentives. That is, what are the features of mixed-member systems that could "transmit" contamination?

If we extend this idea of electoral proximity to the logic of contamination, *electoral* effects are relatively proximal, while *legislative* effects are relatively distal. The basic requirements of contamination in models of electoral behavior require minimal assumptions, such as the presence of nominal component candidates affecting party visibility. Models of legislative behavior require additional conditions to alter legislative behavior. However, this observation does not specifically define characteristics unique to mixed-member systems that could enhance or mitigate contamination.

One approach to advancing research on mixed-member systems is to more clearly identify how specific features may influence interaction at the electoral and/or legislative levels and to develop empirical strategies to test these expectations. Such specific features include dual candidacy, one ballot systems, and a linkage between the two components (i.e., the MMM/MMP difference). We pay the greatest attention to dual candidacy since we believe it is particularly vital for transmission of contamination effects, but we also briefly discuss the other features.

## Dual Candidacy

Dual candidacy provisions that permit a candidate to simultaneously contest in the nominal and list components could be a powerful conduit for the incentives promoting contamination at both electoral and legislative levels. During an election, candidates are directly faced with the challenge of managing a campaign. If they are only contesting in a constituency or on the party list, their efforts can be directed toward efforts to best mobilize the vote to ensure their victory. If the candidate is contesting a constituency race, mobilization and policy appeals would be primarily focused on the district. If a candidate is contesting in PR, the candidate may campaign more widely to represent the party's national platform. That is, the principals of nominal candidates may be different from those of list candidates. Under such circumstances, two types of candidates under mixed-member systems are likely to possess distinctive incentives if they reach the legislature, making the mandate divide clear at the legislative level.

Once elected, a legislator must contemplate the possibility of running for re-election. The decision, and the rules under which the legislator will seek re-election, may be temporally distant. That is, if the next election is to be held four or five years in the future, many factors could affect how the legislator will contest that later election. Parties may permit legislators to promote local interests that challenge national party preferences during the term of office, but may also demand loyalty on certain key bills or when the election is approaching. In short, legislative behavior is more distal to electoral politics.

However, the potentially weaker distal effects should not automatically produce nonfindings in legislative behavior, since the way that dual candidacy affects decisions by parties and candidates in an election may make legislative behavior more directly connected to parties and legislators' decisions (years in advance of the next elections). Japan's MMM system used for the House of Representatives (HoR) provides an example. Candidates for the HoR are allowed to run on both the nominal and list components simultaneously. If they lose in the nominal election, they may gain a seat via the list component if they are ranked high enough. These dually nominated list winners are incentivized to serve local interests because their success as politicians depends more on their performance in the nominal component. Moreover, the MMM system used for Japan's HoR allows parties to "clump" dually nominated candidates at the same rank on the list component. Since clumped candidates' list rankings are determined by their vote margins in their nominal districts, this "best loser" provision is expected to intensify the effects of contamination.[20] Under MMM, winning a nominal seat enhances a party's seat acquisition, so a party leader also has the incentive to assign competitive candidates to local districts and have them work as nominal incumbents. Pekkanen et al. (2006), for instance, show that Japan's dually nominated list winners are more likely to assume positions useful for helping them win back SSD seats, suggesting that their legislative behavior becomes indistinguishable from nominal incumbents' behavior, leading to behavior consistent with the contamination logic at the legislative level.[21]

In contrast, the case of Japan's House of Councillors (HoC) illustrates what happens to legislators' characteristics if dual candidacy is prohibited. The Japanese HoC uses MMM, like the HoR, but candidates running for the HoC cannot be dually nominated. Candidates for the HoC's list component, which elects around fifty members on a single nationwide district, tend to be those with close connections to national interest groups, such as trade unions, agricultural cooperatives, and doctors' associations.[22] In contrast to the counterparts in the HoR, members elected on the HoC's list component are more likely to work as representatives for national policy interests instead of representatives for local constituents.

Barker and Levine's (1999) study also suggests evidence for legislative contamination under dual candidacy in New Zealand. It is usually the case that list incumbents are assigned "shadow" electorates where the party failed to win a seat (Barker and Levine 1999).

The effects of dual candidacy at the electoral level are more evident because of its proximity. In Japan, for instance, dually nominated list winners are allocated to the districts where they lose and are expected to mobilize local supporters. The presence of these pseudo-nominal incumbents lowers the costs of looking for additional candidates. Therefore, districts containing such incumbents are marked by a substantially larger number of candidates.[23] The list component can also exert contamination effects on the nominal component; a nominal candidate's ranking on the list component affects his or her performance on the nominal component (Krauss et al. 2012).[24]

## Mixed-Member Proportional and Mixed-Member Majoritarian Systems

We anticipate that MMP should promote contamination more than MMM at both the electoral and legislative levels. Because parties' seat shares are ultimately determined by their list votes under MMP, leaders' incentives to coordinate their candidates on the nominal component are expected to be weaker in MMP than MMM. Nominal component candidates themselves may also feel relatively free to remain uncoordinated in the districts under MMP, when compared to MMM. Since both party leaders and nominal component candidates are less motivated to coordinate in MMP than in MMM, the number of candidates is expected to be inflated more in MMP than MMM. Indeed, using fifty-three democracies between 1990 and 2001, Nishikawa and Herron (2004) empirically demonstrate that MMP produces a higher effective number of parties on average than MMM.

At the legislative level, nominal incumbents under MMP may act more like list incumbents than those under MMM. From a party leader's standpoint, nominal incumbents do not have to maintain their seats, because parties' seat shares are determined by list votes, not by the number of nominal seats they win, except for overhang seats. Thus, compared to their counterparts under MMM, party leaders' incentives to let nominal incumbents focus on parochial interests are weaker under MMP.[25] Similarly, nominal incumbents who were elected under MMP are also more motivated to work for broader interests, compared to those who are elected under MMM, since list elections influence their chance of re-election more than nominal elections. Without having local constituents as their principals, nominal and list candidates share the same incentives with party leaders under MMP, resulting in a blurred mandate divide between nominal and list incumbents.[26]

To be sure, the possibility of grabbing overhang seats may promote a clearer mandate divide. Party leaders would appreciate extra seats that they may receive beyond their party vote shares and would let nominal incumbents work for local interests. In addition, for nominal incumbents, winning nominal district seats necessarily allows them to maintain their incumbency.[27] As a result, nominal incumbents act more like nominal incumbents to cultivate local votes. However, the number of overhang seats is relatively small and is likely to be only relevant to a few candidates from the major parties who have benefited from the mechanical effect of the nominal elections with a high disproportionate seat and vote ratio.

MMP combined with dual candidacy may promote contamination further. By analyzing incumbents' utility calculations, Stoffel (2014) finds that most incumbents in Germany are motivated to serve broader party interests, since their likelihood of winning a seat is more likely to be determined by party vote shares than nominal vote shares (cf. Krauss et al. 2012). Stoffel suggests that list candidates with a safe slot on the party list and nominal candidates with secure nominal seats work for party interests, indicating the presence of legislative contamination.[28]

## Proportion of the Seats Allocated to Nominal and List Components

The proportion of the seats allocated to the nominal and list components should interact with the institutional features of mixed-member systems in influencing contamination effects. Ferrara and Herron (2005) argue that when seat allocation is more balanced, candidates and parties are likely to face incentives to hedge bets and promote contamination. This argument can be extended to the analysis of contamination at both electoral and legislative levels.

At the electoral level, the effects of contamination appear to become substantively unimportant when one of the components dominates the elections. When more seats are allocated by list components, party leaders are still motivated to place candidates in the constituency elections, since it will mobilize the local votes in those districts. Candidates who are placed in nominal districts are also motivated to win nominal seats, since it will guarantee them those seats that they win. As a result, the effective number of candidates in the nominal districts may be inflated, suggesting the presence of contamination. However, the overall substantive importance of contamination effects may be minimal, given the small number of nominal districts. That is, the number of list incumbents actually changing their strategy to act like nominal incumbents would be small.

When nominal elections dominate with more seats, party leaders may be more motivated to coordinate by forming alliances with other parties and reducing the number of candidates, especially if single-member district systems are used in MMM systems.[29] The number of seats that parties may be able to win by coordinating with other parties may yield more seats in the nominal component than placing candidates in nominal districts and gaining extra seats in the PR list component. Candidates are also pressured to exit. As a result, the number of candidates is reduced over time, minimizing the effects of contamination at the electoral level. The substantive importance of contamination should be at its peak when seats are distributed by the two components equally.

At the legislative level, the effects of contamination appear to vary depending on which component dominates. If more seats are allocated in the nominal component, contamination effects are expected to be weak. When the nominal component is dominant, nominal incumbents should serve local interests. An increased number of nominal seats is also associated with smaller-size districts that promote local interests further. In contrast, list candidates should serve broader interests to maximize the chance of winning future elections. However, list incumbents may also be motivated to serve local interests, since the chance of running for nominal seats in the next election may be high, because more seats are allocated by nominal elections. Under such circumstances, nominal and list candidates share similar interests, promoting legislative contamination. However, since the number of list candidates is small, the effects of contamination are substantively minimized. We will only observe a few list incumbents actually changing their behavior and acting like nominal incumbents. Overall, the incentives of "pure" nominal systems are promoted.

Similarly, if relatively more seats are allocated via a list component, nominal and list candidates would share similar interests with parties and are expected to serve broader interests. This similarity of incentives is also expected to blur the mandate divide between the two types of legislators, promoting legislative contamination. With fewer nominal seats contested, the nominal component becomes less important for party leaders in controlling electoral outcomes. Fewer seats also suggest that each district covers a larger region, which motivates nominal candidates to focus on broader interests. In turn, candidates are not strongly encouraged to serve local interests. The incentives of "pure" PR systems may be enhanced as the proportion of seats allocated by those mechanisms increases. However, since the number of nominal incumbents is small, few nominal incumbents actually change their strategy and act like list incumbents would. The substantive importance of contamination effects is minimized. Overall, the incentives of "pure" PR are promoted.

## Nomination Patterns Unique to Mixed-Member Systems

Nomination patterns unique to mixed-member systems may promote contamination at the electoral and legislative levels. In some contexts, a party leader may not be able to effectively control list members through nominations or list ranking, resulting in a blurred mandate divide. The norm in South Korea, for instance, is that list incumbents do not receive list component nominations for two consecutive terms; to seek re-election, candidates must win nominations on the nominal component through primary elections. To win primaries, South Korea's list members need to win support from local voters, creating incentives that may render list members indistinguishable from nominal members in terms of legislative behavior (Jun and Hix 2010) at the legislative level. This kind of arrangement does not occur outside of mixed-member systems.

This arrangement also increases the number of parties, promoting contamination at the electoral level. Since list incumbents, including minor party candidates, cultivate local votes, their incentives appear to inflate the number of parties when the next elections are held.

## Contextual Factors

The previous section argued that variation in features of mixed-member systems should influence the relative power of the incentives, with some variants of mixed-member systems more likely to yield evidence of contamination. However, variation in electoral rules does not fully explain observations from Table 22.1. Some studies find contamination to be unimportant even in the electoral arena (e.g., see Moser 2001; Moser and Scheiner 2004; Crisp et al. 2012). Other studies also find less contamination in the legislative arena, even in mixed-member systems with dual candidacy, including MMM in Japan (e.g., Maeda 2008) and MMP in Germany (Becher and Sieberer 2008; Fortin-Rittberger and Eder 2013; Sieberer 2010, 2015) and New Zealand (McLeay and Vowles 2007), although the seat distributions between the nominal and list components are quite even.

Additional context may be needed to understand these outcomes. For instance, legislative contamination requires additional assumptions about multiple principals that incumbents face (i.e., local constituents and party leaders) (Carey 2009; Maltzman 1997). The hypothesis that SSD incumbents act like list incumbents implies that nominal incumbents need to, or are forced to, prioritize party leaders over local constituents. As Herron (2002b) shows in Ukraine, nominal incumbents might want to demonstrate their loyalty to the party leadership when they are dually nominated in an unsafe rank on the list. Still, voting against local constituents' interests could backfire in later elections. Thus, for the hypothesis to hold, one would need to assume that nominal incumbents are relatively free from local constituents' constraints. To continue the example, it could be the case that under Ukraine's inchoate party system, the incumbency advantage was so weak that candidates would not need to cater to local demands. In other words, in addition to understanding the incentives introduced by institutional rules, the development of party organizations and level of party system institutionalization could influence the effects.

The previous discussion implies that institutional and contextual factors beyond the rules of mixed-member systems can dampen or accentuate contamination effects. The extant scholarship also suggests that factors such as constitutional structures, social homogeneity, candidate selection and campaign funding, and parties' linkage strategies could play important roles (Crisp 2007; Moser and Scheiner 2012).[30] In the remainder of this section, we describe how other institutional, social, and cultural features could explain variation in mixed-member systems' outcomes. Specifically, we address presidentialism, party organizations and resources, and cultural factors.

## Presidentialism

Some scholarship notes that presidentialism should pressure candidates and voters to coordinate in the electoral arena,[31] especially where the president is powerful and the presidential and legislative electoral cycles are concurrent (Hicken and Stoll 2011; Golder 2006).[32] Since there is only a single office, parties and candidates are motivated to coordinate because of the all-or-nothing nature of the elections.[33] As a result, small parties tend to align with electable presidential candidates, promoting two-party systems in legislative elections. Because of the alliances that parties form, the number of candidates in the nominal component of mixed-member systems may be suppressed. This feature dampens the parties' incentives to nominate hopeless candidates for the legislative elections and suppress contamination at the electoral level.

To be sure, presidential elections may generate two blocks of parties instead of two parties, and the number of parties may not be reduced. However, party leaders may see more opportunities to coordinate their candidates in legislative elections when their parties recognize an alliance. For instance, in semipresidential Taiwan, small parties (the Taiwan Solidarity Union and the New Party) tried to coordinate their legislative candidates with one of the two major parties (the Democratic Progressive Party and the Kuomintang), even though nominating hopeless candidates could help shore up list votes (Nemoto and Tsai 2016).

In contrast, the incentive to coordinate candidates in legislative elections should be weaker under parliamentary systems without the pressure of having presidential elections. Because achieving coordination takes time and energy, party leaders are less likely to create party blocks as they do in presidential systems. Moreover, winning as many parliamentary seats as possible improves the odds of joining the cabinet and eventually winning the post of prime minister.[34] Absent concurrent presidential elections that encourage coattail effects, parties also have stronger incentives to utilize the nominal component to influence list votes by populating constituencies with their candidates.

## Party-Level Factors

While mixed-member systems may produce incentives for political actors to create parties and for those parties to nominate candidates in district races, resource limitations may undermine contamination at the electoral level. Even if actors believe that, for example, nominating noncompetitive candidates in constituency races could improve their performance on the list component, they may lack the personnel, technical, or financial resources to find an appropriate candidate and gain ballot access. High-quality nominal candidates may produce more benefits to the party in the list component (Ferrara et al. 2005),[35] and conversely problematic candidates could counter those effects. In addition, parties must have adequate resources to register and effectively support candidates. Some political actors, even when they expect contamination, may choose to nominate fewer constituency candidates (Herron 2002a) or not seek ballot access for a party because of resource limitations.

The way that parties distribute resources may also affect candidate behavior and influence contamination effects at the legislative level. Depending on how parties are organized and function, campaign funding can concentrate power in the hands of party leaders.[36] If nominal candidates depend on a party for campaign funding and if campaigning is capital intensive, then the party becomes a more important principal controlling its members as agents. This condition implies that nominal candidates may act more like stylized list members. However, if nominal candidates depend more on party supporters for local canvassing than on funding from a party, then the mandate divide between nominal and list candidates could become sharper.

In addition to differences in resource management, parties may also adopt different strategies in approaching voters (Kitschelt 2000) that could affect contamination. With programmatic linkage strategies, parties access voters by developing ideologically cohesive sets of policy platforms. Under this model, candidates tend to become somewhat faceless conveying the party's policy message to voters. Meanwhile, with clientelistic linkage strategies, parties exchange electoral support for particularistic policy favors, especially in the form of pork barrel benefits. With this approach, a party becomes a franchise of locally oriented members seeking parochial benefits for their own personal supporters.

The Japanese case suggests that party leaders might have perceived, at least in the first few elections under MMM after the electoral reform, that clientelistic linkage strategies were still important in winning votes and seats. This could be partially explained by path dependency (Krauss and Pekkanen 2010; Scheiner 2008): the electoral system previously used in Japan was the SNTV, which necessarily created intraparty competition and therefore the incentive to cultivate personal votes (Carey and Shugart 1995). Thus, even though the Japanese ruling party's post allocation strategy described earlier (Pekkanen et al. 2006)—list incumbents assuming government and party positions useful in shoring up local votes—is compatible with the party incentive to maximize seats under MMM, the legacy from the past might have further blurred the mandate divide between nominal and list incumbents.[37]

## Social and Cultural Features

Moser and Scheiner (2012) point out several noninstitutional contextual factors that could affect mixed-member systems. Certain social characteristics, such as ethnicity, language, and religion, can serve as useful informational shortcuts for voters. Thus, in socially heterogeneous environments, ambitious politicians take advantage of such easy-to-understand heuristics to appeal to social minorities, resulting in party fragmentation (Amorim Neto and Cox 1997; Stoll 2013). In line with this argument, the presence of such useful heuristics under mixed-member systems might motivate party leaders to mobilize ethnic list votes by nominating as many nominal candidates as possible.[38]

Inherited traditions may also affect behaviors. For example, long experience with two-party systems and FPTP, as one finds in British colonial territories, could mitigate effects that we would expect from contamination (Crisp et al. 2012). Personalistic appeals, induced by decades of SNTV in Japan, may encourage list incumbents to work for local interests (Krauss and Pekkanen 2010; Nemoto, this volume; Crisp 2007).

A related factor that could affect behavior is the age of democracies. Party systems in fledgling democracies are often not institutionalized and may be accompanied by a large number of independents. For political actors to respond to incentives, they require consistent, systematic information to coordinate (e.g., withdraw candidates from nominal districts, engage in strategic voting to avoid wasting votes, or withdraw financial support from nonviable candidates). Adequate information may not be readily available among newly democratized countries. For example, Lesotho's mixed-member system produced an inflated number of parties, but parties and voters in Lesotho did not fully understand the mechanical effects of the mixed-member system, especially in the first two elections, and voters did not have appropriate information to determine candidate viability. Although Rich, Banerjee, and Recker (2014) state that the results from Lesotho are consistent with the contamination hypothesis, the deficiency of pre-election polling data could have caused the number of parties to increase.

# Conclusion

The expansion of mixed-member electoral systems at the end of the twentieth and beginning of the twenty-first centuries prompted extensive scholarly attention, particularly to the consequences of its diffusion. As we noted in this chapter, the scholarly debate about the effects of combining formulas in separate overlapping components for allocating seats into a single legislative election has not been conclusive. Some studies have found evidence of contamination effects in outcomes ranging from the number of political parties and women's representation to legislative voting behavior and committee assignments. These effects have been documented in democratic and nondemocratic regime types. At the same time, the controlled comparison approach has yielded important findings about the factors that mitigate effects of electoral rules, and some scholars have generated empirical evidence that challenges the expectations of the contamination effects approach. While the traditional interpretation of the controlled comparison and contamination approaches has been to treat them as diametrically opposed to one another, we argue that they are better viewed as differences in degree. Both approaches define conditions in which the components of mixed-member systems may behave more or less independently, and neither approach suggests that contamination is always—or never—present.

Advancing our understanding of the complex combination of electoral and nonelectoral factors that induce different incentives in mixed-member systems will enhance our understanding of these rules, and institutional rules more generally. Building upon scholarship from the last two decades, we envision several ways to advance the research agenda on mixed-member systems: formalizing theoretical expectations, adopting different research designs, and extending data collection to societies where limited work has been conducted.

Most of the work on mixed-member systems has not mathematically formalized theoretical expectations, relying instead on less rigorous expository logic. Developing formal models and testing hypotheses derived from these models is an important step to advance the discussion about mixed-member systems. Bawn and Thies (2003) and Hennl (2014) provide a model.

Experimental approaches could also be meaningfully incorporated into the study of mixed-member systems.[39] In the laboratory and potentially in the field,[40] treatments that induce participants to engage with one component or another (or to look across components) could advance our understanding of the microfoundations under which contamination matters or does not matter. Moreover, conducting experimental work in varied cultural settings could take into account contextual features that may influence behavior.

At the same time, digging deeper into specific cases would advance the study of mixed-member systems. Qualitative work that engages directly with political actors to better understand their motivations for making decisions during campaigns and in the legislature could reveal if they take into account the factors that the contamination effects scholarship implies. To assess if these effects are artifacts of the analytical approach, it would be valuable to discover if political actors are aware of the effects and adopt strategies to take advantage of them.

Extending research on mixed-member systems to incorporate additional country- and region-based cases is also crucial to understanding how context could influence their effects. While scholars have investigated mixed-member systems in a wide range of countries, some world regions have been less intensively explored. Mixed-member systems adopted in Sub-Saharan Africa (e.g., Cameroon, Lesotho, Senegal) are notable for limited scholarly attention, and research on subnational use of mixed-member rules would also extend our knowledge about their effects. In addition, single-country studies dominate the area of legislative contamination effects. To empirically analyze some of the theoretical predictions that this article proposed, scholars should construct comprehensive datasets covering roll-call voting, party switching, and committee assignments in a wide range of mixed-member systems.

As we emphasized in this chapter, a key to understanding the consequences of mixed-member systems may come from better articulating theoretical expectations. We advocate more exploration of ideas such as the implications of distal and proximal effects, more attention to institutional variation in mixed-member systems (e.g., dual candidacy), and additional work on ancillary factors that could enhance or attenuate contamination effects. Scholarship that extends what we know about mixed-member systems will advance research not only on electoral systems but also on the interaction among institutional rules in general.

## Notes

1. Names are in alphabetical order to reflect equal authorship.
2. Also see chapters in this volume by John Carey and Matthew S. Shugart and Rein Taagepera, as well as Shugart and Taagepera (2017).
3. But, as the chapter by Josep Colomer in this volume argues forcefully, scholars have generated a counterargument regarding the direction of causation between electoral and party systems.
4. Massicotte and Blais (1999) indicate that forms of mixed-member systems were adopted prior to the German variant but did not survive long.
5. See the chapter by Gianluca Passarelli in this volume.
6. See chapters in this volume by Thomas Zittel, Kuniaki Nemoto, and Jack Vowles.
7. See the chapter by Erik Herron in this volume.
8. Some countries, like Russia and Ukraine noted here, abandoned mixed-member systems and then readopted them (Lundberg 2009).
9. Scholars use different terms, such as "tiers" and "levels," for "components." In this chapter we use the term "components."
10. To illustrate the differences between MMP and MMM, imagine a hypothetical legislature with two hundred seats, one hundred allocated to the PR list component, and one hundred allocated to constituency races via FPTP in the nominal component. Party A receives 20 percent of the list vote and forty seats in the nominal component. In an MMP system, party A's total seat allocation should be 20 percent of the legislature, or forty seats. Since party A receives forty seats in the nominal constituency races, it would gain no additional list seats as MMP uses the list component to determine the overall allocation of seats in the legislature. In an MMM system, by contrast, party A would receive forty nominal constituency seats and twenty additional seats in the list component, for a total of sixty seats (30 percent of the legislature) because seats in the two components are allocated independently.
11. In the literature on Japan's mixed electoral system, dually nominated list winners are called "zombies" (Pekkanen et al. 2006). From a normative perspective, this term implies that one tier carries more legitimacy than another. We use "dually nominated list winners" to preserve neutrality.
12. For example, in Japan, the number of nominal seats exceeds list seats by 295 to 180; in South Korea the difference is 253 to 47; and in Taiwan the difference is 79 to 34.

13. Typically, the literature uses members' roll-call voting patterns, party switching records, and committee assignments to explore these theoretical predictions.

14. Assuming that the PR list is closed and that party rules privilege leaders in list construction.

15. The "mandate divide" describes the implication that behaviors vary based on the incentives of the two components and is consistent with a controlled comparison argument.

16. A Google N-gram assessment, focusing on the frequency of terms in books, shows an increase in the use of "mixed electoral system" and "mixed-member electoral system" beginning in the 1990s. However, the number of books the figure is based on is small. See http://bit.ly/2bgFXbY.

17. We use the term "mixed-member system" in the chapter, but we searched by "mixed system" to capture both labels.

18. Moser and Scheiner (2012) suggest that faulty case selection may drive contamination results.

19. According to Rae's (1967) original formulation, distal and proximal effects are primarily based on time: the former require more time to take place than proximal effects. Scheiner (2008) generalizes the idea, suggesting that the distal effects are the more indirect effects of electoral systems.

20. Parties can choose not to utilize this "best loser" provision and rank their favored candidates at the top. See Nemoto and Tsai (2016) and Nemoto's chapter in this volume for details.

21. Herron (2002b) uses the case of Ukraine to show that nominal incumbents' party loyalty is mediated by their safety on the party list. That is, members placed in unsafe positions on the list tend to toe the party line to appeal their loyalty to the leadership.

22. Since the open-list system was introduced in 2001, candidates with local political experience have been increasing (Nemoto and Shugart 2013).

23. See Nemoto's chapter in this volume.

24. One-ballot systems (fused ballot), used in countries such as Lesotho, should also promote contamination at the legislative and electoral levels. Rich, Banerjee, and Recker (2014) state that the introduction of the one-vote system in Lesotho encouraged parties to place noncompetitive nominal candidates in districts to win seats through party list competitions. Under such circumstances, as in dual candidacy, nominal candidates are motivated to serve broader party interests. In contrast, the introduction of two separate ballots (i.e., two votes) may be more likely to generate a clearer mandate divide between nominal and list members, ceteris paribus, although we cannot eliminate the possibility that two separate ballots actually promote contamination, since list candidates from minor parties may encourage split-ticket voting.

25. It is true that in New Zealand and elsewhere, nominal MPs provide constituency services to build up party supporters in local areas (Barker and Levine 1999). That said, however, our claim is that it should be relative in theory: such local orientations should be less pronounced under MMP than MMM. This is an empirical question that requires additional work, especially outside of New Zealand and Germany to evaluate how well the findings travel.

26. See Lancaster and Patterson (1990) and Stratmann and Baur (2002) for a different interpretation.

27. This assumes that their party satisfies other requirements, such as the minimum threshold. Under MMP in Germany, parties are required to receive 5 percent of the list votes or win three nominal seats.

28. Stoffel also suggests that those nominal candidates who are without such a secure seat are more motivated to work for local interests, potentially contributing to a clearer mandate divide. Although Stoffel's (2014) focus is more on the effects of dual candidacy than on MMP, they seem to speak equally to the effects of MMP.

29. This observation especially applies to MMM systems.

30. As we note later, to explore these factors, it is imperative to cross-sectionally compare different mixed-member systems under different contexts and institutions.

31. At the same time, fragmentation is observed in many presidential systems. The evidence about the effects of presidentialism on coordination is not conclusive.

32. See also Mark Jones's chapter in this volume.

33. The presidential office is also the most important political prize in presidential systems. For example, US presidents are considered to be relatively weaker than the counterparts in Latin America and Africa, but they possess the power to appoint cabinet members and other positions, exercise veto power, negotiate treaties, and sign executive orders.

34. Governing parties usually divide cabinet positions in proportion to their legislative seat shares.

35. See Chapter 5 in particular.

36. See the chapter by Joel Johnson in this volume for more on campaign finance.

37. Also see Nemoto in this volume.

38. See the chapter by Robert G. Moser, Ethan Scheiner, and Heather Stoll in this volume for more on social heterogeneity.

39. See the chapter by Tucker and Duell in this volume.

40. With full consideration of the ethical implications of fieldwork related to elections (Desposato 2016).

## References

Amorim Neto, Octavio, and Gary W. Cox. "Electoral Institutions, Cleavage Structures, and the Number of Parties." *American Journal of Political Science* 41, no. 1 (1997): 149–174.

Barker, Fiona, and Stephen Levine. "The Individual Parliamentary Member and Institutional Change: The Changing Role of the New Zealand Member of Parliament." *Journal of Legislative Studies* 5, no. 3/4 (1999): 105–130.

Batto, Nathan F. "Differing Mandates and Party Loyalty in Mixed-member Systems: Taiwan as a Baseline Case." *Electoral Studies* 31, no. 2 (2012): 384–392.

Bawn, Kathleen, and Michael Thies. "A Comparative Theory of Electoral Incentives: Representing the Unorganized Under PR, Plurality and Mixed-Member Electoral Systems." *Journal of Theoretical Politics* 15, no. 1 (2003): 5–32.

Becher, Michael, and Ulrich Sieberer. "Discipline, Electoral Rules and Defection in the Bundestag, 1983–94." *German Politics* 17, no. 3 (2008): 293–304.

Bernauer, Julian, and Simon Munzert. "Loyal to the Game? Strategic Policy Representation in Mixed Electoral Systems." *Representation* 50, no. 1 (2014): 83–97.

Bochsler, Daniel. "Are Mixed Electoral Systems the Best Choice for Central and Eastern Europe or the Reason for Defective Party Systems?" *Politics & Policy* 37, no. 4 (2009): 735–767.

Carey, John M. *Legislative Voting and Accountability*. Cambridge: Cambridge University Press, 2009.

Carey, John M., and Matthew Soberg Shugart. "Incentives to Cultivate a Personal Vote: A Rank Ordering of Electoral Formulas." *Electoral Studies* 14, no. 4 (1995): 417–439.

Centellas, Miguel. "Mixed-Member Election and Candidate Selection in Bolivia's 1993 and 1997 Elections." *Latin Americanist* 59, no. 1 (2015): 3–22.

Corral, Margarita, Francisco Sanchez, and Cristina Rivas Perez. "The Impact of Mixed-Member Districts on Legislators' Behavior: The Case of Bolivia." *Latin American Politics and Society* 58, no. 1 (2016): 29–48.

Crisp, Brian F. "Incentives in Mixed-Member Electoral Systems: General Election Laws, Candidate Selection Procedures, and Cameral Rules." *Comparative Political Studies* 40, no. 12 (2007): 1460–1485.

Crisp, Brian F., Joshua D. Potter, and John J. W. Lee. "Entry and Coordination in Mixed-Member Systems: A Controlled Comparison Testing the Contamination Hypothesis." *Journal of Politics* 74, no. 2 (2012): 571–583.

Desposato, Scott, ed. *Ethics and Experiments: Problems and Solutions for Social Scientists and Policy Professionals.* New York: Routledge, 2016.

Duverger, Maurice. *Political Parties, Their Organization and Activity in the Modern State.* London, New York: Methuen; Wiley, 1954.

Ferrara, Federico. "Electoral Coordination and the Strategic Desertion of Strong Parties in Compensatory Mixed Systems with Negative Vote Transfers." *Electoral Studies* 23, no. 3 (2004): 391–413.

Ferrara, Federico. "Two in One: Party Competition in the Italian Single Ballot Mixed System." *Electoral Studies* 25, no. 2 (2006): 329–350.

Ferrara, Federico, and Erik S. Herron. "Going It Alone? Strategic Entry under Mixed Electoral Rules." *American Journal of Political Science* 49, no. 1 (2005): 16–31.

Ferrara, Federico, Erik S. Herron, and Misa Nishikawa. *Mixed Electoral Systems: Contamination and Its Consequences.* New York: Palgrave Macmillan, 2005.

Fortin-Rittberger, Jessica, and Christina Eder. "Towards a Gender-Equal Bundestag? The Impact of Electoral Rules on Women's Representation." *West European Politics* 36, no. 5 (2013): 969–985.

Golder, Matt. "Presidential Coattails and Legislative Fragmentation." *American Journal of Political Science* 50 (2006): 34–48.

Golosov, Grigorii V. "Electoral Systems and Party Formation in Russia." *Comparative Political Studies* 36, no. 8 (2003): 912–935.

Golosov, Grigorii V. "Interdependence Effects in Mixed-Superposition Electoral Systems: An Empirical Test on Women's Participation in Sub-National Elections." *Journal of Elections, Public Opinion and Parties* 24, no. 4 (2014): 434–454.

Gschwend, Thomas, Ron Johnston, and Charles Pattie. "Split-Ticket Patterns in Mixed-Member Proportional Election Systems: Estimates and Analyses of Their Spatial Variation at the German Federal Election, 1998." *British Journal of Political Science* 33, no. 1 (2003): 109–127.

Hainmueller, Jens, and Holger Lutz Kern. "Incumbency as a Source of Spillover Effects in Mixed Electoral Systems: Evidence from a Regression-Discontinuity Design." 27 (2008): 213–227.

Heitshusen, Valerie, Garry Young, and David M. Wood. "Electoral Context and MP Constituency Focus in Australia, Canada, Ireland, New Zealand, and the United Kingdom." *American Journal of Political Science* 49, no. 1 (2005): 32–45.

Hennl, Annika. "Intra-Party Dynamics in Mixed-member Electoral Systems: How Strategies of Candidate Selection Impact Parliamentary Behaviour." *Journal of Theoretical Politics* 26, no. 1 (2014): 93–116.

Herron, Erik S. "Mixed Electoral Rules and Party Strategies: Responses to Incentives by Ukraine's Rukh and Russia's Yabloko." *Party Politics* 8 (November 2002a): 719–733.

Herron, Erik S. "Electoral Influences on Legislative Behavior in Mixed-Member Systems: Evidence from Ukraine's Verkhovna Rada." *Legislative Studies Quarterly* 27 (August 2002b): 361–382.

Herron, Erik S., and Misa Nishikawa. "Contamination Effects and the Number of Parties in Mixed-Superposition Electoral Systems." *Electoral Studies* 20, no. 1 (2001): 63–86.

Hicken, Allen, and Heather Stoll. "Presidents and Parties: How Presidential Elections Shape Coordination in Legislative Elections." *Comparative Political Studies* 44, no. 7 (2011): 854–883.

Jun, Hae-Won, and Simon Hix. "Electoral Systems, Political Career Paths and Legislative Behavior: Evidence from South Korea's Mixed-Member System." *Japanese Journal of Political Science* 11, no. 2 (2010): 153–171.

Karp, Jeffrey A. "Candidate Effects and Spill-Over in Mixed Systems: Evidence from New Zealand." *Electoral Studies* 28 (2009): 41–50.

Katz, Richard S. *A Theory of Parties and Electoral Systems*. Baltimore: Johns Hopkins University Press, 1980.

Kerevel, Yann. "The Legislative Consequences of Mexico's Mixed-Member Electoral System, 2000-2009." *Electoral Studies* 29, no. 4 (2010): 691–703.

Kitschelt, Herbert. "Linkages between Citizens and Politicians in Democratic Polities." *Comparative Political Studies* 33, no. 6/7 (2000): 845–879.

Kostadinova, Tatiana. "Party Strategies and Voter Behavior in the East European Mixed Election Systems." *Party Politics* 12, no. 1 (2006): 121–143.

Krauss, Ellis S., Kuniaki Nemoto, and Robert Pekkanen. "Reverse Contamination: Burning and Building Bridges in Mixed-Member Systems." *Comparative Political Studies* 45, no. 6 (2012): 747–773.

Krauss, Ellis S., and Robert Pekkanen. *The Rise and Fall of Japan's LDP*. Ithaca, NY: Cornell University Press, 2010.

Lago, Ignacio, and Ferran Martinez. "The Importance of Electoral Rules: Comparing the Number of Parties in Spain's Lower and Upper Houses." *Electoral Studies* 26 (2007): 381–391.

Lago, Ignacio, and José Ramón Montero. "Coordination between Electoral Arenas in Multilevel Countries." *European Journal of Political Research* 48, no. 2 (2009): 176–203.

Lancaster, Thomas D., and W. David Patterson. "Comparative Pork Barrel Politics: Perceptions from the West German Bundestag." *Comparative Political Studies* 22, no. 4 (1990): 458–477.

Lundberg, Thomas. "Putting a Human Face on Proportional Representation: Early Experiences in Scotland and Wales." *Representation* 38, no. 4 (2002): 271–283.

Lundberg, Thomas Carl. "Post-Communism and the Abandonment of Mixed-Member Electoral Systems." *Representation* 45, no. 1 (2009): 15–27.

Maeda, Ko. "Re-Examining the Contamination Effect of Japan's Mixed Electoral System Using the Treatment-Effects Model." *Electoral Studies* 27, no. 4 (2008): 723–731.

Maltzman, Forrest. *Competing Principals: Committees, Parties, and the Organization of Congress*. Ann Arbor: University of Michigan Press, 1997.

Massicotte, Louis, and Andre Blais. "Mixed Electoral Systems: A Conceptual and Empirical Survey." *Electoral Studies* 18 (1999): 344–366.

Mcleay, Elizabeth, and Jack Vowles. "Redefining Constituency Representation: The Roles of New Zealand MPs under MMP." *Regional and Federal Studies* 17, no. 1 (2007): 71–95.

Moser, Robert G. *Unexpected Outcomes: Electoral Systems, Political Parties, and Representation in Russia.* Pittsburgh, PA: Pittsburgh University Press, 2001.

Moser, Robert G., and Ethan Scheiner. "Mixed Electoral Systems and Electoral System Effects: Controlled Comparison and Cross-National Analysis." *Electoral Studies* 23 (2004): 575–599.

Moser, Robert G., and Ethan Scheiner. *Electoral Systems and Political Context: How the Effects of Rules Vary across New and Established Democracies.* Cambridge: Cambridge University Press, 2012.

Nemoto, Kuniaki, and Matthew S. Shugart. "Localism and Coordination under Three Different Electoral Systems: The National District of the Japanese House of Councillors." *Electoral Studies* 32, no. 1 (2013): 1–12.

Nemoto, Kuniaki, and Chia-hung Tsai. "Post Allocation, List Nominations, and Pre-Electoral Coalitions under MMM." In *Mixed-Member Electoral Systems in Constitutional Context: Taiwan, Japan, and Beyond*, edited by Nathan Batto, Gary Cox, Chi Huang, and Alex Tan, 165–193. Ann Arbor: University of Michigan Press, 2016.

Nishikawa, Misa, and Erik S. Herron. "Mixed Electoral Rules' Impact on Party Systems." *Electoral Studies* 23, no. 4 (2004): 753–768.

Ohmura, Tamaki. "When Your Name Is on the List, It Is Time to Party: The Candidacy Divide in a Mixed-Member Proportional System." *Representation* 50, no. 1 (2014): 69–82.

Olivella, Santiago, and Margit Tavits. "Legislative Effects of Electoral Mandates." *British Journal of Political Science* 44, no. 2 (2014): 301–321.

Pekkanen, Robert, Benjamin Nyblade, and Ellis S. Krauss. "Electoral Incentives in Mixed-Member Systems: Party, Posts, and Zombie Politicians in Japan." *American Political Science Review* 100, no. 2 (2006): 183–193.

Rae, Douglas. *The Political Consequences of Electoral Laws.* New Haven, CT: Yale University Press, 1967.

Reynolds, Andrew, and B. Reilly. *The International IDEA Handbook of Electoral System Design.* Stockholm, Sweden: International Institute for Democracy and Electoral Assistance, 1997.

Rich, Timothy S. "The Effects of Election Reform on Legislator Perceptions: The Case of Taiwan." *Japanese Journal of Political Science* 13, no. 3 (2012): 317–336.

Rich, Timothy S. "Party Voting Cohesion in Mixed Member Legislative Systems: Evidence from Korea and Taiwan." *Legislative Studies Quarterly* 39, no. 1 (2014): 113–135.

Rich, Timothy S. "Duverger's Law in Mixed Legislative Systems: The Impact of National Electoral Rules on District Competition." *European Journal of Political Research* 54 (2015): 182–196.

Rich, Timothy S., Vasabjit Banerjee, and Sterling Recker. "Identifying the Institutional Effects of Mixed Systems in New Democracies: The Case of Lesotho." *Journal of Asian and African Studies* 49, no. 6 (2014): 637–653.

Riker, William H. "The Two-Party System and Duverger's Law: An Essay on the History of Political Science." *American Political Science Review* 76 (1982): 753–766.

Sartori, Giovanni. *Comparative Constitutional Engineering.* London: Macmillan, 1994.

Scheiner, Ethan. "Does Electoral System Reform Work?: Electoral System Lessons from Reforms of the 1990s." *Annual Review of Political Science* 11 (2008): 161–181.

Shin, Ki-young. "Women's Sustainable Representation and the Spillover Effect of Electoral Gender Quotas in South Korea." *International Political Science Review* 35, no. 1 (2014): 80–92.

Shugart, Matthew S., and Rein Taagepera. *Votes from Seats*. Cambridge: Cambridge University Press, 2017.

Shugart, Matthew S., and Martin P. Wattenberg, eds. *Mixed-Member Electoral Systems: The Best of Both Worlds?* Oxford: Oxford University Press, 2001.

Sieberer, Ulrich. "Behavioral Consequences of Mixed Electoral Systems: Deviating Voting Behavior of District and List MPs in the German Bundestag." *Electoral Studies* 29, no. 3 (2010): 484–496.

Sieberer, Ulrich. "Using MP Statements to Explain Voting Behaviour in the German Bundestag: An Individual Level Test of the Competing Principals Theory." *Party Politics* 21, no. 2 (2015): 284–294.

Stoffel, Michael F. "MP Behavior in Mixed-Member Electoral Systems." *Electoral Studies* 35 (2014): 78–87.

Stoll, Heather. *Changing Societies, Changing Party Systems*. Cambridge: Cambridge University Press, 2013.

Stratmann, Thomas, and Martin Baur. "Plurality Rule, Proportional Representation, and the German Bundestag: How Incentives to Pork-Barrel Differ Across Electoral Systems." *American Journal of Political Science* 46, no. 3 (2002): 506–514.

Thames, Frank G., and Martin Edwards. "Differentiating Mixed-Member Electoral Systems: Mixed-Member Majoritarian and Mixed-Member Proportional Systems and Government Expenditures." *Comparative Political Studies* 39, no. 7 (2006): 905–927.

Zittel, Thomas, and Thomas Gschwend. "Individualised Constituency Campaigns in Mixed-Member Electoral Systems: Candidates in the 2005 German Elections." *West European Politics* 31, no. 5 (2008): 978–1003.

# PART V

## HOLDING ELECTIONS

# CHAPTER 23

...........................................................................................................

# ELECTION
# ADMINISTRATION

...........................................................................................................

## THAD E. HALL

ONE of the most complex tasks any nation does on a regular basis is run an election. The complexity is enhanced because elections occur at one moment in time, typically on a single day. Mozaffar and Schedler (2002, 6–7) describe an election as "the largest peacetime mobilization of the national population in a short time span." This mobilization of the population to vote is carried out largely by election poll workers who are trained to work on a single day and are tasked with coordinating an array of activities. The administration of elections is also highly sensitive to even small errors, be they errors in voting a ballot, with the quality of the voter registry, or in tabulating votes. For example, in an election with ten million registered voters, an error rate of just half of 1 percent in the voter registry will affect approximately fifty thousand individuals. Election administrators typically hope that their election results are not close and any election problems are random so that public confidence in the electoral process is not diminished.

James (2012, 3) provides a simple and clear definition of election administration: "the administrative procedure used for casting ballots and compiling the electoral register." Broadly construed, it is about making sure that there is procedural certainty—that the rules are understood clearly and implemented fairly throughout the electoral process. Across the globe, there is no one correct or best way to run an election; there are many ways to run an election with high levels of integrity (Massicotte, Blais, and Yoshinaka 2004). Most international election organizations view election administration as a cycle where any problems and issues related to procedural uncertainty that arise in one election are addressed before the next election. Given the complexity of election administration as a topic, the election cycle will be used to structure this discussion. The election cycle has three periods. First, there is a pre-election period, where voter registration occurs, election workers are trained, voter education occurs, and the election is planned. Second, there is the election period, where voting occurs, ballots are counted, and official results are announced. Finally, there is the postelection period, where the election is audited, the laws are changed, and new election boundaries are drawn (if necessary). The issues are discussed in chapters in this *Handbook* on redistricting, election integrity, and turnout and so are not considered here. Instead, the focus will be on the key administrative activities that determine whether an election is or is not successful.

One of the important things to remember in thinking about election administration is that context and history matter (Ewald 2009). Elites typically want to create rules of the game that advantage themselves (Grofman and Lijphart 1986; James 2012). The choices that are made regarding how elections are structured can have long-term effects on the political development of a country (e.g., Birch and Wallace 2003). In turn, the actions of political actors are shaped by elections. In elections, the rules of the game are typically set by strategic actors who want to create a playing field that benefits members of "their" team—their political party or political coalition—and these rules are often shaped by recent events.

As Mozaffar and Schedler (2002) note, elections involve rule making, rule application, and rule implementation. Election administration addresses all three areas. Although the population of people who can vote is often set and cannot be changed, how people vote, when people vote, and where people vote can often be manipulated in ways that can benefit certain segments of the population (e.g., Keyssar 2000; Schedler 2002). In this review of election administration, it is important to keep in mind how strategic changes to election administration can change either the outcome of the election or the confidence that citizens have in the outcome of the election.

As Norris (2013, 2014, 2015; Norris, Frank, and Martínez i Coma 2014) has argued, election administration is a difficult task and is challenged not only when overt acts of election fraud occur—vote buying, intimidation, and ballot-box stuffing—but also when election malpractice occurs. Such malpractice might include errors in voter registries, failures to follow appropriate standard operating procedures, or problems with counting ballots (e.g., the 2000 election in Florida). Claims of voter fraud and litigation over voter identification laws or voter registration issues can also fall into this category. Norris (2011, 2013, 2014) notes that citizens in well-established Western democracies have experiences with numerous elections and the legitimacy of the process is almost taken for granted. However, in countries with newer democracies, electoral malpractice can cause the same types of instability that would arise were there to be actual fraud in the election. As Birch (2011) notes, poor election administration can have dramatic consequences. It can reduce public evaluations of the quality of democracy, undermining confidence in the democratic process, and result in poor representation. Most problematic, under certain circumstances, violence and civil war can occur in the aftermath of electoral malpractice.

The reason malpractice can be so problematic is that it violates established norms for what constitutes electoral integrity, and these norms are broadly understood (Birch 2011; Lehoucq 2003; 2001; Norris 2013, 2014, 2015). Election norms have been established by various organizations, including the United Nations, and these norms are understood by both elites and members of the general public. Although the term "free and fair elections" is overused and can be interpreted in multiple ways, in general, the general public knows what constitutes an election that did not violate international norms because these norms are based on relatively simple concepts, such as universal suffrage. In authoritarian countries, elections lack this fairness because the choice of candidates or parties has been manipulated. Even with universal suffrage, voting is not democratic because there are not meaningful choices to be made at the polls (Herron 2009; Levitsky and Way 2002).

# ELECTION MANAGEMENT BODIES

For elections to have integrity, it is critical that they be well designed. In most countries, a central election management body (EMB) is the body that plans for the election and provides overall administrative support for all aspects of the election. The overall election structure in a country or state is established through lawmaking, but EMBs will typically interpret these laws, issue rules or guidance to election workers, and be responsible for implementing the election and resolving any election disputes. The activities of an EMB can be critical for setting the stage for how well elections are accepted.

López-Pintor (2000) summarizes the research on EMBs, noting that they are typically most effective when they are permanent and independent of the executive. Independent EMBs create a more stable political environment and are more cost effective than having a temporary body with little long-term institutional capacity. Across the world, there are five models for running elections: (1) an EMB that is "independent of the executive and has full responsibility for the direction and management of the election" (Lopez-Pintor 2000); (2) government management with oversight of a legal body; (3) government management; (4) two independent EMBs, with one handling administration and the other handling regulation; and (5) highly decentralized administration with little national supervision. Examples of countries falling into each category are (1) Canada, (2) France, (3) Belgium, (4) Chile, and (5) the United States.

Election management is also made more complex when there is a high level of decentralization in the electoral process. All but the smallest elections require decentralized administration. On Election Day, the workers in the polling place can be the only "election administrators" the voter encounters, and these workers can sometimes decide if a voter is able to cast a ballot (Alvarez and Hall 2004; Hall, Monson, and Patterson 2009). There is also complexity that can arise in federal systems caused by variations in election administration across subdivisions. For example, the United States is known for the variation it has in election administration across its fifty states and the subvariation that exists across the local election administration units (typically counties or municipalities) (Ewald 2009). Each of these national subdivisions often has its own election management body that is tasked with managing the electoral process, creating variation in administration that has the potential to undermine public confidence.

# Pre-Electoral Administration

The pre-electoral process is shaped by the laws that are in place at the time of the election, the recent history that shapes the environment of election planning, and current challenges that the jurisdiction faces. Election laws will determine things like the modes of voting that can be used in the election (e.g., early voting, absentee voting) and how many voting locations will be open for the election. Recent history will shape critical issues like security and election observation. In places where electoral violence or fraud occurred during the last election, the pre-election process will likely account for these issues in planning for the next election. There are two key activities in the pre-election process: voter registration and election staff training.

## Voter Registration

Voter registration is perhaps the most complex election administration task. Once a decision has been made as to who is eligible to vote—typically all citizens of a state who are aged 18 or older—efforts have to be made to ensure that only eligible individuals actually do vote and that they only vote once. Voter registries are used to ensure that only the eligible participate and participate only once. As the Administration and Cost of Elections (ACE) Project notes, there are three types of voter registries: (1) a periodic list, (2) a continuous list, or (3) a civil registry.[1] Periodic lists are typically used in countries with highly mobile populations, where people are concerned about having a permanent list, or where there is no infrastructure for this type of list. Civil registries are often in place in Europe, where all individuals register themselves at a residence. Continuous lists are maintained by the EMB, with individuals added or removed as their eligibility changes.

Voter registration systems have often been used for two purposes that are often in conflict. First, there is the desire to ensure that only individuals who are eligible to vote in an election do so. Basic eligibility is often limited to those individuals who are 18 years of age and citizens of the country in which they reside. In some countries, eligibility varies by election. For example, in Estonia, Estonian citizens can vote in all elections, but a citizen of another European Union member state can vote in local elections and European parliamentary elections.[2] Estonia needs to have a voter registry that can account for these differences in eligibility across its population. In the United States, several states have rules that limit the voting rights of individuals who have been convicted by a court of a felony crime.[3] Voter registries ensure that individuals who fall outside of the eligibility criteria are not allowed to vote.

Second, voter registration has been used historically to disenfranchise certain classes or groups of individuals. In the United States, prior to the passage of the Voting Rights Act and a constitutional amendment prohibiting the levying of poll taxes or other fees before a person could vote, voter registration was used to disenfranchise a variety of voters. For example, political parties that were in power in a state would sometimes change the voter registration rules in a way that would disenfranchise members of the other party (Keyssar 2000). In the southern United States, voter registration was a key tool for disenfranchising black and poor white citizens.[4] In New York State, literacy tests were used to disenfranchise immigrants who had become citizens but not completed the requisite amount of education.

The accuracy of voter registration can be more important in countries with single-seat districts compared to proportional representation because knowing a voter's exact place of residence is used to determine the district in which the member can vote. In countries like the United States, where voters make choices for many candidates in single-seat districts that do not have matching boundaries, the voter registration process has to be able to tie a voter's address to a specific ballot style. For example, in Los Angeles County, California, the election administrators have to account for at least eighteen US House districts, eight state Senate districts, fourteen state House districts, and five county supervisor districts. This variation in districts requires assigning each voter to a ballot that has the correct combination of races for that voter's address.

Election administration is much simpler in countries with proportional representation. If the voters only make a party choice in the election, the ballot may be the same across the entire country. If parties are required to list a slate of potential candidates who will be chosen from should the party gain enough votes, the ballot can be the same within large political subdivisions. Likewise, having fewer offices on a ballot, or offices that are the same statewide or nationwide, can ease the administrative burden as well.

## Electoral Staff Training

Elections are centrally organized but highly decentralized in administration. Although an EMB will plan out the election and be responsible for its overall conduct, it is the election staff in polling places who actually administer the election in a practical sense. The decisions that poll workers make can greatly influence the experience that voters have, the confidence they have in the process, and the legitimacy of the outcomes. In many respects, election workers are street-level bureaucrats, serving as servants of the state, providing a front-line service to citizens, and making decisions that can greatly affect the quality of the services they receive. Election officials are generally forced to delegate Election Day activities in the polls to poll workers, which creates many different opportunities for election-related problems, including poll workers substituting their own attitudes for what the law should be over what the actual law is (Alvarez and Hall 2006; Atkeson et al. 2010).

Election workers have been extensively studied in the American context. Election workers who provide effective services to voters and run a polling place relatively free of problems can greatly increase the likelihood that voters will feel confident that their ballot was counted accurately (e.g., Claassen et al. 2008; Hall, Monson, and Patterson

2009). Ensuring that election workers are trained well is important (Hall, Monson, and Patterson 2007) because well-trained election workers are able to avoid key problems running their polling place. However, there are other factors that are even more important, such as the attitudes of the election workers about following rules and their own educational attainment. Better-educated poll workers are more likely to put aside their own biases and implement election laws appropriately (Atkeson et al. 2014).

Even with the best training, election workers in authoritarian regimes may become involved, tacitly or explicitly, in perpetrating election fraud (e.g., Kornblith and Jawahar 2005; Way 2005). They may allow improprieties to occur under threat or because they have accepted payouts or favors from one party or another in the election. Authoritarian regimes can also fail to train workers effectively or provide necessary resources in certain polling places, which can result in a chaotic experience for voters. This can be done strategically—only the polls in certain regions are chaotic—or done throughout the country in an effort to undermine confidence in the entire election.

# VOTING PERIOD

The voting period is when the election as it is commonly understood occurs. People cast ballots and then they are counted once the voting period ends. However, the voting period often lasts longer than a single "Election Day"; with the advent of convenience voting methods—including voting by mail, voting over the Internet, or voting in person prior to Election Day—the voting period can last weeks (e.g., Gronke et al. 2008). In most of the world, voting is a civic duty but not a civic requirement. However, countries including Australia, Brazil, and Luxembourg have compulsory voting, where not voting can result in fines or other punishments (Birch 2013).

## Voting

Over the past two thousand years, the way in which individuals vote in elections has changed dramatically. Prior to the adoption of the Australian ballot—where all candidates from all parties are listed on the same ballot sheet, which is cast as a secret ballot—people typically voted using *viva voce* (voting out loud), raising hands, or using ballots printed by political parties (Evans 1917; Keyssar 2000). Evans (1917, 17) quotes an Englishman from the 1860s who states, "Before the [Australian] ballot was in operation our elections were exceedingly riotous . . . . I have been in the balcony of an hotel during one of the city elections, when the raging mobs down in the streets were so violent that I certainly would not have risked my life to have crossed the street."

Since then, elections around the world have changed dramatically. The United States has long been at the forefront of adopting new voting technologies. In the 1800s, mechanical voting machines, such as lever voting machines that allow individuals to cast a ballot by flipping a small lever next to their candidate choice, proliferated in an attempt to improve the voting process and limit voter fraud (Saltman 2006). Although there was a reform component to the adoption of many voting technologies, there were also political and administrative reasons for the adoption of these machines. As ballots in the United States became longer and longer, voting machines made ballot counting faster, so the results could be known quicker (Keyssar 2000; Saltman 2006). Although many Western countries still count ballots by hand, most ballots in the United States have been counted using computerized tabulators since the 1960s or early 1970s, and direct recording electronic voting machines—which often have touchscreens—have been used since the late 1980s.

The problems in the United States in the 2000 election and federal legislation passed in its aftermath facilitated the adoption of better paper-based scanning systems and the movement toward electronic voting in the United States. Electronic voting is viewed as being more user-friendly than paper ballots because electronic machines can be made accessible for individuals with disabilities and ballots can be rendered in multiple languages with relative ease (Alvarez and Hall 2008a; Saltman 2006). In countries like Brazil, electronic voting has been seen as a tool for both reducing electoral fraud and enfranchising individuals with limited literacy by allowing them to vote on a device that is easier to use and can be more graphical in display. Because of cost considerations and concerns about the security and auditability of electronic voting machines, the adoption of this technology in the United States has slowed in more recent years.

Since the mid-1990s, the idea of Internet voting has been proposed for making voting easier. With Internet voting, a person would be able to vote from anywhere, as long as he or she had access to a computer or smart device and to the Internet, but critics argue that the benefits of voting online are outweighed by concerns over Internet security and digital divides between the wealthy and well educated and those who are less so (Alvarez and Hall 2004, 2008a). These security concerns have led to the slow adoption of this reform, with three Swiss cantons using Internet voting in certain elections, and only Estonia having Internet voting as one channel for voting, along with in-person early voting and in-person Election Day voting, in all elections (Alvarez, Hall, and Trechsel 2009). Some countries, such as Norway, have experimented with Internet voting but have decided not to pursue the technology. The government there determined there was not broad political support for investing greater resources in additional Internet voting pilots.[5]

The adoption of new voting technologies, especially electronic voting technologies, has led to studies of whether the manner in which people vote (e.g., in person or absentee by mail) and the technology on which they vote (e.g., paper ballots or an electronic machine) affect their confidence that their vote is counted accurately.[6] Studies in the United States and internationally have found that voters are sensitive to both the manner in which they vote and the technology on which they vote (e.g., Atkeson and Saunders 2005; Alvarez, Hall, and Llewellyn 2008; Alvarez et al. 2009; Birch 2008; Katz et al. 2011; Reynolds and Steenbergen 2006). These perceptions, along with whether they voted for a winner or loser, can also affect a person's overall evaluation of the election (e.g., Bowler et al. 2015).

Part of the sensitivity people have regarding the manner and method in which they vote comes, in part, from the perceived level of usability associated with various voting technologies. Studies of paper-based and electronic voting systems in the United States and internationally have found that voting systems vary widely in their ease of use for voters (e.g., Bederson et al. 2003; Herrnson et al. 2009; Niemi and Herrnson 2003). Voting systems that provide voters with greater feedback tend to be perceived as easier compared to those where there is less feedback to the voter.[7] In addition, factors such as ballot length and whether a person can vote for candidates of a party on a "straight party" ballot can affect people's experience voting (Augenblick and Nicholson 2016; Bowler, Donovan, and Happ 1992; Calvo, Escolar, and Pomares 2009; Campbell and Byrne 2009).

## Election Observation

One of the biggest changes in elections over the past forty years has been the rise of third-party election observation. Organizations like the Carter Center, the United Nations, and the Organization for Security and Co-operation in Europe's (OSCE) Office for Democratic Institutions and Human Rights (ODHIR) conduct election observations around the world every year. The ODHIR's election observation handbook notes that election monitoring missions typically have four key components: a pre-election process review, Election Day observation, vote count and tabulation observation, and postelection observations.[8] The examination of the pre-election period includes a review of the country's legal framework and whether these laws have support from key stakeholder groups in the country. The legal framework includes election laws and laws related to citizenship, the media, and civil society organizations. This review also examines who implements the laws and whether implementing bodies are viewed as fair and impartial. Pre-election reviews also examine the rules for voter registration, the registration of candidates and political parties, the conduct of the political campaigns, and the freedom of the media to report. Election Day observations focus on the conduct of the election at the polls, including whether the election workers at the polls were impartial, the disabled were able to access the polling places, and there was any voter intimidation or unrest at the polls. The observers also monitor for any sorts of blatant fraud, such as ballot-box stuffing. Once the polls are closed, observers ensure that the tabulation and counting process is done correctly. Finally, election observers check to see that election complaints are adjudicated and official election results are produced in a timely manner. Election observation can be both active, with people observing in the polls, and passive, using webcams and similar technologies (Herron 2010).

Kelley (2008) notes that the evolution and spread of electoral monitoring can be seen as affected by changes in the normative environment and institutionalization of monitoring, coupled with timing—the end of the Cold War and the concomitant push by

Western countries for democracy around the world. Once monitoring became common, it created an incentive structure where honest governments invited election monitors and, therefore, not inviting monitors was seen as a sign of election fraud (Kelley 2012). The catch, as Hyde (2011a, 2011b) argues, is that the repeated use of election monitoring in various contexts also meant that election monitors became more and more effective over time in catching electoral fraud. This increased skill should have resulted in a decline in election observations in countries with subpar democracies. Instead, the norm of monitoring and the costs associated with not having election monitors became such that even more authoritarian regimes had an incentive to "fake" democratization.

The expansion of monitoring over time has also increased the numbers of monitoring organizations that operate around the world. Kelley (2009) argues that nondemocratic countries can use this increase in the number of monitors to their advantage.

> If governments are successful at engendering contradictions between monitors, then they can contrast contradictions to spin and manipulate their conclusions or quote only the assessment they prefer. The ability of governments to manipulate the election monitoring experience increases as the number of organizations available for monitoring grows . . . . The slate of invitations to the 2008 Russian presidential election, for example, carefully balanced the number of Western versus pro-Russian observers invited, almost as if strategically ensuring that the assessments would be split evenly. The ability of governments to exploit the diversity of monitors and engender contradictions is also higher in countries that are geopolitically important or experience violence during the election, because monitors may be willing to temper their criticisms to retain diplomatic goodwill or peace. (pp. 59, 60)

## Violence

One of the biggest problems that can arise during an election is violence and intimidation surrounding the election. Recent research by Hafner-Burton, Hyde, and Jablonski (2014) finds that election violence is most common when those in power in a country fear losing the election and have few institutional constraints that prevent the use of violence. However, using violence before elections can result in postelection protests, and such protests can be difficult to address and cause yet more violence. The use of violence in elections can also be exceedingly costly for regimes. There are international pressures against countries that use violence prior to an election. Also, violence is often a sign that there is an organized opposition party in the country that has the potential to be competitive in the long term. Using violence, therefore, can be seen as a sign of weakness, not of strength. Unfortunately, violence is difficult to predict.

Daxecker (2012, 2014) notes that election observation can have a direct effect on when electoral violence occurs. Studying African elections, she finds that election observers do not prevent violence but rather shift when violence occurs. Instead of violence and intimidation occurring on or just before Election Day, the presence of election observers results in a temporal shift in when violence occurs, with repression occurring earlier in the pre-election period. This reflects the concerns of regimes about the costs that might come from violence being too obvious when election observation missions are occurring. One question that is unanswered is whether more long-term election observation missions—which often begin several months before an election—would be able to deter such violence.

# POSTELECTION PERIOD

Different countries, and subjurisdictions within countries, have different rules governing what, if any, activities occur during the postelection process. In some cases, election officials are required to conduct recounts or audits after an election. In other cases, losing candidates have legal rights to challenge the outcome of an election in court.[9] In recent years, the recounts and audits have become more common in international elections. However, the laws and rules governing such activities are varied worldwide.

## Election Recounts and Audits

After elections end, winners and losers face a question of whether to accept the results of the election or to challenge the results (e.g., Anderson et al. 2005). Courts and electoral commissions can play critical roles in helping to ensure that there is compliance with election results in certain situations (Svolik and Chernykh 2015). Two key activities in election administration that electoral commissions engage in postelection are recounts and audits. However, as the International Foundation for Electoral Systems (IFES)/Democracy International (2015, 4) has noted, "there is no clearly accepted international model for how and when to conduct an electoral recount, and the process can vary widely from one country to another." Although recounts typically involve counting the ballots that were counted in the election, the manner in which the recount is conducted can vary in scope. For example, a recount might involve counting all of the ballots in a specific jurisdiction or just a sample of the ballots, or counting only the ballots cast in a specific subregion of the jurisdiction.

A second postelection activity is an audit.

An audit tends to be much less straightforward than a recount and entails a wider variety of activities. Whereas a recount is intended to confirm the accuracy of the tally, an audit is undertaken to investigate alleged fraud or malpractice. An audit may involve a full or partial recount, but it also includes other actions to evaluate whether the electoral process has been conducted according to the rules and regulations. Audit investigators may focus on whether or not certain voters were eligible to cast ballots, for example. Audits may focus on the mechanics of the vote or on broader issues such as the integrity of the voter list (IFES/Democracy International 2015, 5).

There are numerous issues associated with audits and with how election management bodies can engage in activities that are designed to ensure that the results of the election are legitimate and viewed as legitimate (Alvarez, Atkeson, and Hall 2012; Darnoff 2011; IFES/Democracy International 2015). Using Afghanistan as an example, IFES/ Democracy International (2015) identified an array of issues associated with conducting an election audit. These issues include determining who has standing to conduct the audit, the standards and practices for conducting the audit, the evidentiary standards that will be used for the audit,[10] the chain-of-custody rules and standard operating procedures used in the audit, and the transparency of the process.

Audits allow all parties in an election to know if standard operating procedures for the election were followed (Alvarez et al. 2012).[11] It is critical, however, that before an election a clear, regulatory framework for election audits is in place that includes standards and procedures for conducting the audit. If election officials conduct the audit correctly, transparency is increased and all key stakeholders understand the audit process.

# CONCLUSION

In any given country, an election is often viewed in isolation, as a single event. However, election administration is an ongoing activity, with the administration of one election shaping the policy and administration of subsequent elections. The electoral cycle of one election—and all of the events that are a part of an election—feeds into the legal and procedural reforms that follow the election and the election planning, logistics, and training that precede the next election. When maladministration occurs, election laws often change, procedures are updated, voter education may improve, and the planning for the next election accounts for the previous failures. Avoiding maladministration requires effective planning, well-developed standard operating procedures, and ongoing evaluation and auditing of the electoral process.

Even with effective election administration, election officials have to take proactive steps to ensure that the public continues to be confident in election outcomes. In more authoritarian states, voter confidence can be harmed because of electoral violence or intimidation, or because of more subtle efforts to disenfranchise minority populations or limit choices on the ballot by making it difficult for political parties to register candidates or gain ballot access. In well-established democracies, questions about election administration can cause the public to question the integrity of the voting process, lower voter confidence, and potentially reduce turnout. Throughout the world, the administration of elections is one of the most critical functions of government. The quality of the process can directly affect how the democratic process is perceived and who represents the public.

## Notes

1. http://aceproject.org/ace-en/topics/vr/vr10, accessed February 2, 2017.
2. http://www.vvk.ee/info-for-voters/, accessed February 2, 2017.
3. http://www.ncsl.org/research/elections-and-campaigns/felon-voting-rights.aspx, accessed February 2, 2017.
4. There is an extensive literature on the use of voter registration as a tool of disenfranchisement in the United States. See Keyssar 2000 and Highton 2004 for summaries of this literature.
5. https://www.regjeringen.no/en/aktuelt/Internet-voting-pilot-to-be-discontinued/id764300/, accessed February 2, 2017.
6. Kimball and Kropf (2005) examine the issues related to voting errors on paper ballots and provide a detailed summary of the literature related to residual votes in general.
7. For example, individuals who cast a ballot by mail have less information about whether their ballot was received by the election official and included in the final tabulation compared to a voter who casts a ballot in person at the polling place.
8. http://www.osce.org/odihr/elections/68439, accessed February 2, 2017.
9. See, for example, http://web1.millercenter.org/commissions/comm_2001_taskforce.pdf, chapter XII, accessed February 2, 2017.
10. IFES/Democracy International (2015, 9) note that "The collection and corroboration of substantiated facts and evidence goes to the very heart of an elections investigation and any subsequent adjudication process that leads to the invalidation of votes. Audit investigators should make every effort to substantiate facts and evidence without relying on hearsay, assumptions, or suppositions. An audit of election results based on claims of fraud must be managed according to the same basic evidentiary principles as other fraud investigations."
11. Standard operating procedures are critical in elections for many reasons, including their importance in the security of ballots and ensuring that all votes are treated equitably. See Alvarez and Hall 2008b for greater discussion.

## References

Alvarez, R. Michael, Lonna Rae Atkeson, and Thad E. Hall. Evaluating Elections: A Handbook of Methods and Standards. New York: Cambridge University Press, 2012.

Alvarez, R. Michael, and Thad E. Hall. *Point, Click, and Vote: The Future of Internet Voting.* Washington, DC: Brookings Institution Press, 2004.

Alvarez, R. Michael, and Thad E. Hall. "Controlling Democracy: The Principal–Agent Problems in Election Administration." *Policy Studies Journal* 34, no. 4 (2006): 491–510.

Alvarez, R. Michael, and Thad E. Hall. *Electronic Elections: The Perils and Promise of Digital Democracy.* Princeton: Princeton University Press, 2008a.

Alvarez, R. Michael, and Thad E. Hall. "Building Secure and Transparent Elections through Standard Operating Procedures." *Public Administration Review* 68, no. 5 (2008b): 828–838.

Alvarez, R. Michael, Thad E. Hall, and Morgan H. Llewellyn. "Are Americans Confident Their Ballots Are Counted?" *Journal of Politics* 70, no. 3 (2008): 754–766.

Alvarez, R. Michael, Thad E. Hall, and Alexander H. Trechsel. "Internet Voting in Comparative Perspective: The Case of Estonia." *PS: Political Science & Politics* 42, no. 3 (2009): 497–505.

Alvarez, R. Michael, Gabriel Katz, Ricardo Llamosa, and Hugo E. Martinez. "Assessing Voters' Attitudes towards Electronic Voting in Latin America: Evidence from Colombia's 2007 E-Voting Pilot." In *International Conference on E-Voting and Identity*, edited by Peter Ryan and Berry Schoenmakers, 75–91. Berlin: Springer, 2009.

Anderson, Christopher, Andre Blais, Shaun Bowler, Todd Donovan, and Ola Listhaug. *Losers' Consent: Elections and Democratic Legitimacy*. Oxford: Oxford University Press, 2005.

Atkeson, Lonna Rae, Lisa Ann Bryant, Thad E. Hall, Kyle Saunders, and Michael Alvarez. "A New Barrier to Participation: Heterogeneous Application of Voter Identification Policies." *Electoral Studies* 29, no. 1 (2010): 66–73.

Atkeson, Lonna Rae, Yann P. Kerevel, R. Michael Alvarez, and Thad E. Hall. "Who Asks for Voter Identification? Explaining Poll-Worker Discretion." *Journal of Politics* 76, no. 4 (2014): 944–957.

Atkeson, Lonna Rae, and Kyle L. Saunders. "The Effect of Election Administration on Voter Confidence: A Local Matter?" *PS: Political Science & Politics* 40, no. 4 (2005): 655–660.

Augenblick, Ned, and Scott Nicholson. "Ballot Position, Choice Fatigue, and Voter Behaviour." *Review of Economic Studies* 83, no. 2 (2016): 460–480.

Bederson, Benjamin B., Bongshin Lee, Robert M. Sherman, Paul S. Herrnson, and Richard G. Niemi. "Electronic Voting System Usability Issues." In *Proceedings of the SIGCHI Conference on Human Factors in Computing Systems*, edited by Gilbert Cockton and Panu Korhonen, 145–152. ACM, 2003.

Birch, Sarah. "Electoral Institutions and Popular Confidence in Electoral Processes: A Cross-National Analysis." *Electoral Studies* 27, no. 2 (2008): 305–320.

Birch, Sarah. *Electoral Malpractice*. Oxford University Press, 2011.

Birch, Sarah. *Full Participation: A Comparative Study of Compulsory Voting*. Manchester: Manchester University Press, 2013.

Birch, Sarah, and Helen Wallace. *Electoral Systems and Political Transformation in Post-Communist Europe*. Basingstoke: Palgrave Macmillan, 2003.

Bowler, Shaun, Thomas Brunell, Todd Donovan, and Paul Gronke. "Election Administration and Perceptions of Fair Elections." *Electoral Studies* 38 (2015): 1–9.

Bowler, Shaun, Todd Donovan, and Trudi Happ. "Ballot Propositions and Information Costs: Direct Democracy and the Fatigued Voter." *Western Political Quarterly* 45, 1992: 559–568.

Calvo, Ernesto, Marcelo Escolar, and Julia Pomares. "Ballot Design and Split Ticket Voting in Multiparty Systems: Experimental Evidence on Information Effects and Vote Choice." *Electoral Studies* 28, no. 2 (2009): 218–231.

Campbell, Bryan A., and Michael D. Byrne. "Straight-Party Voting: What Do Voters Think?" *IEEE Transactions on Information Forensics and Security* 4, no. 4 (2009): 718–728.

Claassen, Ryan L., David B. Magleby, J. Quin Monson, and Kelly D. Patterson. "'At Your Service' Voter Evaluations of Poll Worker Performance." *American Politics Research* 36, no. 4 (2008): 612–634.

Darnoff, Staffan. *Assessing Electoral Fraud in New Democracies: A New Strategic Approach.* IFES, 2011.

Daxecker, Ursula E. "The Cost of Exposing Cheating: International Election Monitoring, Fraud, and Post-Election Violence in Africa." *Journal of Peace Research* 49, no. 4 (2012): 503–516.

Daxecker, Ursula E. "All Quiet on Election Day? International Election Observation and Incentives for Pre-Election Violence in African Elections." *Electoral Studies* 34 (2014): 232–243.

Evans, Eldon Cobb. *A History of the Australian Ballot System in the United States.* Chicago: University of Chicago, 1917.

Ewald, Alec C. *The Way We Vote: The Local Dimension of American Suffrage.* Nashville: Vanderbilt University Press, 2009.

Grofman, Bernard, and Arend Lijphart. *Electoral Laws and Their Political Consequences.* Vol. 1. Algora Publishing, 1986.

Gronke, Paul, Eva Galanes-Rosenbaum, Peter A. Miller, and Daniel Toffey. "Convenience Voting." *Annual Review of Political Science* 11 (2008): 437–455.

Hafner-Burton, Emilie M., Susan D. Hyde, and Ryan S. Jablonski. "When Do Governments Resort to Election Violence?" *British Journal of Political Science* 44, no. 1 (2014): 149–179.

Hall, Thad, J. Quin Monson, and Kelly D. Patterson. "Poll Workers and the Vitality of Democracy: An Early Assessment." *PS: Political Science & Politics* 40, no. 4 (2007): 647–654.

Hall, Thad E., J. Quin Monson, and Kelly D. Patterson. "The Human Dimension of Elections: How Poll Workers Shape Public Confidence in Elections." *Political Research Quarterly* 62, no. 3 (2009): 507–522.

Herrnson, Paul S., Richard G. Niemi, Michael J. Hanmer, and Benjamin B. Bederson. *Voting Technology: The Not-So-Simple Act of Casting a Ballot.* Brookings Institution Press, 2009.

Herron, Erik. *Elections and Democracy after Communism?* New York: Springer, 2009.

Herron, Erik S. "The Effect of Passive Observation Methods on Azerbaijan's 2008 Presidential Election and 2009 Referendum." *Electoral Studies* 29, no. 3 (2010): 417–424.

Highton, Benjamin. "Voter Registration and Turnout in the United States." *Perspectives on Politics* 2, no. 3 (2004): 507–515.

Hyde, Susan D. "Catch Us if You Can: Election Monitoring and International Norm Diffusion." *American Journal of Political Science* 55, no. 2 (2011b): 356–369.

Hyde, Susan D. *The Pseudo-Democrat's Dilemma.* Cornell University Press, 2011a.

International Foundation for Electoral Systems (IFES)/Democracy International. *Election Audits: International Principles That Protect Election Integrity.* IFES/Democracy International, 2015.

James, Toby S. *Elite Statecraft and Election Administration: Bending the Rules of the Game?* Palgrave Macmillan, 2012.

Katz, Gabriel, R. Michael Alvarez, Ernesto Calvo, Marcelo Escolar, and Julia Pomares. "Assessing the Impact of Alternative Voting Technologies on Multi-Party Elections: Design Features, Heuristic Processing and Voter Choice." *Political Behavior* 33, no. 2 (2011): 247–270.

Kelley, Judith. "Assessing the Complex Evolution of Norms: The Rise of International Election Monitoring." *International Organization* 62, no. 2 (2008): 221–255.

Kelley, Judith. "The More the Merrier? The Effects of Having Multiple International Election Monitoring Organizations." *Perspectives on Politics* 7, no. 1 (2009): 59–64.

Kelley, Judith Green. *Monitoring Democracy: When International Election Observation Works, and Why It Often Fails.* Princeton University Press, 2012.

Keyssar, Alexander. *The Right to Vote: The Contested History of Democracy in the United States.* Basic Books, 2000.

Kimball, David C., and Martha Kropf. "Ballot Design and Unrecorded Votes on Paper-Based Ballots." *Public Opinion Quarterly* 69, no. 4 (2005): 508–529.

Kornblith, Miriam, and Vinay Jawahar. "Elections versus Democracy." *Journal of Democracy* 16, no. 1 (2005): 124–137.

Lehoucq, Fabrice. "Electoral Fraud: Causes, Types, and Consequences." *Annual Review of Political Science* 6, no. 1 (2003): 233–256.

Levitsky, Steven, and Lucan Way. "The Rise of Competitive Authoritarianism." *Journal of Democracy* 13, no. 2 (2002): 51–65.

López-Pintor, Rafael. *Management Bodies as Institutions of Governance.* UNDP, 2000.

Massicotte, Louis, André Blais, and Antoine Yoshinaka. *Establishing the Rules of the Game: Election Laws in Democracies.* Toronto: University of Toronto Press, 2004.

Mozaffar, Shaheen, and Andreas Schedler. "The Comparative Study of Electoral Governance—Introduction." *International Political Science Review* 23, no. 1 (2002): 5–27.

Niemi, Richard G., and Paul S. Herrnson. "Beyond the Butterfly: The Complexity of US Ballots." *Perspectives on Politics* 1, no. 2 (2003): 317–326.

Norris, Pippa. *Democratic Deficit: Critical Citizens Revisited.* Cambridge University Press, 2011.

Norris, Pippa. "Does the World Agree about Standards of Electoral Integrity? Evidence for the Diffusion of Global Norms." *Electoral Studies* 32, no. 4 (2013): 576–588.

Norris, Pippa. *Why Electoral Integrity Matters.* Cambridge University Press, 2014.

Norris, Pippa. *Why Elections Fail.* Cambridge University Press, 2015.

Norris, Pippa, Richard W. Frank, and Ferran Martínez i Coma, eds. *Advancing Electoral Integrity.* Oxford: Oxford University Press, 2014.

Reynolds, Andrew, and Marco Steenbergen. "How the World Votes: The Political Consequences of Ballot Design, Innovation and Manipulation." *Electoral Studies* 25, no. 3 (2006): 570–598.

Saltman, Roy. *The History and Politics of Voting Technology: In Quest of Integrity and Public Confidence.* Springer, 2006.

Schedler, Andreas. "The Menu of Manipulation." *Journal of Democracy* 13, no. 1 (2002): 36–50.

Svolik, Milan, and Svitlana Chernykh. "Third-Party Actors and the Success of Democracy: How Electoral Commissions, Courts, and Observers Shape Incentives for Election Manipulation and Post-Election Protest." *Journal of Politics* 77, no. 2 (2015): 407–420.

Way, Lucan. "Kuchma's Failed Authoritarianism." *Journal of Democracy* 16, no. 2 (2005): 131–145.

# CHAPTER 24

# ELECTORAL SYSTEMS AND ELECTORAL INTEGRITY

## PIPPA NORRIS

Do electoral systems determine how far contests meet international standards of electoral integrity? This question touches on some classic debates in the literature seeking to understand the reasons underlying electoral reforms and the effects of these changes. To examine these issues, the first part of this chapter develops the conceptual framework to unpack the meaning of electoral integrity. The second part builds upon this understanding and sets out several alternative theoretical arguments of why proportional representation (PR) electoral systems are generally believed to strengthen electoral integrity more effectively than majoritarian rules. This includes, on the positive side, the following: (1) PR generates checks upon the unconstrained power of the single-party executives and thus minimizes the potential danger that the largest party in government will be able to manipulate the electoral rules in their own favor in subsequent contests. (2) By maximizing the potential number of winners, PR elections are thought to build trust in the electoral process among all stakeholders, and thus reduce the temptation for losing parties to disrupt the electoral process and undermine the legitimacy of the outcome, such as by crying wolf, falsely alleging fraud, and/or engaging in electoral boycotts. (3) By increasing the incentive for parties to present balanced lists of candidates, PR contests are more inclusive for women and minority representatives. By contrast, on the negative side: (4) Plurality elections are believed to heighten the incentive for individual candidates to seek to win through illegal, fraudulent, or corrupt acts, especially in single-seat districts with wafer-thin majorities where even a few dozen votes could determine the winner. (5) The risks of partisan gerrymandering rise in single-seat districts, especially where constituency boundaries are drawn by the legislature or executive, compared with large multiseat regional districts in PR contests (see Handley, this volume). The third part explains the evidence and data, including how electoral integrity is measured worldwide through the rolling expert survey on

Perceptions of Electoral Integrity. The fourth part presents the results of the analysis, largely confirming most of the core propositions. The conclusion considers the findings and implications for strengthening electoral integrity and democracy around the globe.

## THE CONCEPT OF ELECTORAL INTEGRITY

Contests that meet international standards of electoral integrity can serve many essential functions. Elections can help to ensure the accountability of agents (elected representatives and political parties) to principals (citizens), generate periodic opportunities for mass deliberation and participation, confirm the mantle of popular legitimacy upon governments, strengthen political communications linking citizens and leaders, recruit representatives for assemblies, produce a peaceful and orderly leadership succession process, allocate government offices and patronage among elites, and determine policy priorities reflecting collective preferences (Powell 2000, 2014). In the absence of other effective political institutions, by themselves, multiparty elections meeting basic international standards are not sufficient mechanisms for delivering these functions, but they are the lynchpin and sine qua non of all modern procedural conceptions of representative democracy. In the classic words of Schumpeter (1942): "The democratic method is that institutional arrangement for arriving at political decisions in which individuals acquire the power to decide by means of a competitive struggle for the people's vote." Many other pathways can lead to power, from fratricidal bloodshed and hereditary inheritance to oligarchical control, theocratic anointment, and military coup d'état. To paraphrase Churchill, elections may be the worst form of leadership succession, but even flawed popular contests are better than all others.

Although multiparty contests have spread around the globe, unfortunately many suffer from multiple shortcomings. In recognition of these issues, the last decade has seen the emergence of a new research agenda focusing on challenges of electoral integrity. This approach can be used to re-examine what is known about a wide range of classic issues in the study of electoral systems within democratic, hybrid, and autocratic states (Birch 2011; Norris, Frank, and Martinez i Coma 2014; Norris, Martinez i Coma, and Groemping 2015; Flores and Noruddin 2016). Studies in this growing subfield are characterized by a perspective that is strongly normatively engaged, problem oriented, and policy relevant, bringing together practitioners from the world of international electoral assistance and scholars. It typically blends insights from a mélange of subfields, dissolving disciplinary boundaries, including studies of electoral systems and constitutional law, as well as public administration, international relations and conflict studies, normative theories of human rights, research on democratization and authoritarian regimes, political behavior, public policy, and comparative politics.

The concept of "electoral integrity" can be understood in several ways, whether framed negatively or positively (van Ham 2015). Concern about flawed and failed contests has generated a proliferating variety of elections-with-adjectives, with the danger of creating a conceptual Tower of Babel. Hence, studies have focused (negatively) on whether contests are "manipulated" (Schedler 2002; Simpser 2013), characterized by "malpractices" (Birch 2011), or "fraudulent" (Lehoucq 2003), and (positively) on whether they are "free and fair" (Bjornlund 2004; Bishop and Hoeffler 2014), "genuine and credible," "competitive" (Hyde and Marinov 2012), "clean,"[1] or "democratic" (Levitsky and Way 2010).

Each of these formulations has different pros and cons. In the news headlines, popular language commonly emphasizes fraudulent acts and illegal practices, such as vote buying, ballot stuffing, identify theft, and intimidation, which typically occur on polling day and its aftermath. In America, the Republican Party uses the rhetoric of fraud (meaning "voter impersonation") to justify revised state laws tightening voter identification requirements to gain access to the electoral register and ballot (Minnite 2010). Fraud is also often associated with intentional illegal acts, and this usage has also been adopted in several accounts (Lehoucq and Jiménez 2002). While powerful rhetorically, however, this approach reflects an incomplete, partial, and overly narrow understanding of the complex nature of problems of electoral integrity. Many electoral malpractices typically occur well before polling day—and these acts can reflect constitutional principles and domestic jurisprudence yet still be deeply ethically flawed. Moreover, laws violating the political rights and civil liberties of ordinary citizens, candidates, or parties, or constitutional revisions serving the self-interest of ruling parties, can embody many of the most important problems that need to be addressed. Problems like Florida's butterfly ballot in the 2000 US presidential election can arise from maladministration, without any intention to defraud. Other approaches seek to derive guidance from classical democratic theories, exemplified by attempts either to operationalize Schumpeter's minimalist definition (Przeworski et al. 2000) or to adopt Dahl's notion of polyarchy (Birch 2011). Nevertheless, general democratic theories, such as principles of contestation and participation, exist at such an abstract theoretical level that it remains difficult to draw unambiguous practical lessons useful for monitoring standards. Technical problems such as broken voting machines or inaccurate electoral registers may arise from shortcomings in governance and state capacity, not from lack of democracy per se. Moreover, notions of democratic elections remain essentially contested and open to the charge that these reflect American/Western liberal values that have not been universally endorsed within the international community.

A broader and more comprehensive perspective, employed in this chapter, recognizes that numerous types of flaws and failures can undermine the quality of elections at home and abroad, as documented by international monitoring reports published by agencies such as the Organization for Security and Cooperation in Europe (OSCE), the European Union (EU), the International Foundation for Electoral Systems (IFES), the Carter Center, and the Organization of American States (OAS); by public opinion surveys; and by expert indicators. Electoral authorities may be regarded as in the pockets of ruling elites. Parties may face legal bans and denied ballot access. Electoral registers may be incomplete and inaccurate. Minority voting rights can be suppressed. Women candidates face major barriers to elected office. Access to campaign money and media can be stacked in favor of the haves. The police and army may fail to protect citizens from coercion and threats. The count may contain fraudulent irregularities and cases of ballot stuffing. Delays in announcing the official results can heighten suspicion and trigger protests involving deadly violence. Authoritarian regimes typically display the most troubling repression of electoral rights. But malpractices are not confined to these types of states, by any means, and as Florida in the 2000 US presidential election shows, even countries with centuries of electoral experience, like the United States, are not immune from partisan bias and technical flaws in electoral procedures. Where electoral irregularities are believed to prevail, this can have critical consequences; survey evidence from the sixth wave of the World Values Survey across multiple societies suggests that citizens perceiving electoral malpractices are less likely to express trust and confidence in political parties, parliaments, and governments, as well as to be more unwilling to cast a ballot and to be more likely to engage in protest activism (Norris 2014). Within long-established democracies, public disquiet over specific flaws in technical electoral procedures in any particular contest can be expected to fade gradually over time due to deep-rooted civic cultures, repeated experience of the regular rotation of parties in office, and peaceful avenues of legal redress via the courts. Continuous and widespread systematic flaws, however, such as lack of effective regulations governing campaigns awash with cash, may prove more corrosive. And the consequences of even minor electoral problems can be expected to be prove more damaging, and even deadly, in fragile states such as Kenya, poorly consolidated regimes such as Thailand, and deeply divided societies such as Afghanistan, by eroding any consensus over the basic rules of the game, exacerbating instability, and heightening polarization.

What do all these diverse types of problems share in common, if anything? Should they be bundled together, to identify common features, or disaggregated, to avoid the dangers of concept stretching and imprecise (kitchen-sink) measurement? In general, a more comprehensive perspective is useful for identifying general causes and consequences, especially since many types of electoral malpractices are commonly interrelated, such as where techniques of bribery and intimidation are used interchangeably to gain support; where incumbent presidents seek to amend term limit requirements, thereby catalyzing opposition boycotts; or where technical delays in the ballot count trigger violent protests.

Therefore, from a human rights perspective, used in this chapter, the idea of "electoral integrity" can be understood as *referring to whether electoral procedures meet agreed-upon international conventions and global norms, applying universally to all countries worldwide through the election cycle, including during the pre-election period, the campaign, polling day, and its aftermath.* By contrast, the idea of "electoral malpractices" is used to indicate those that fail to meet these standards. The overarching concept of electoral integrity provides a new way of classifying, measuring, and analyzing problems in the quality of elections, adding to the traditional lexicon used to understand electoral systems, although one with centuries-old roots. The concept refers to whether electoral procedures fall short of certain authoritative principles, embodied in written declarations, conventions, treaties, protocols, case law, and guidelines issued by intergovernmental organizations of the international community and endorsed by member states worldwide. There are two main types of these instruments: declarations and conventions. Declarations are not legally binding, but they do have political and moral impact. Conventions are legally binding under international law.

As Article 21(3) of the 1948 Universal Declaration of Human Rights expressed these standards: "The will of the people shall be the basis of the authority of government: this will shall be expressed in periodic and genuine elections which shall be by universal and equal suffrage and shall be held by secret vote or by equivalent free voting procedures." Article 25 of the 1966 UN International Convention for Civil and Political Rights built upon this framework. Since then, a series of subsequent conventions endorsed by member states of the United Nations and by intergovernmental regional organizations like the OSCE and OAS have expanded further upon this foundation, providing the broadest guarantees for rights to political participation, including the rights to self-determination (Article 1) and the right for everyone to take part in the running of the public affairs of his or her country (Article 25), among others. International standards continued to evolve, including through International Convention on the Elimination of All Forms of Racial Discrimination (ICERD, 1966) and Discrimination against Women (CEDAW, 1979), the UN Convention against Corruption (UNCAC, 2003), and the Convention on the Rights of Persons with Disabilities (CRPD, 2006), as well as agreements secured at the 1990 Copenhagen Document of the Conference on Security and Cooperation in Europe (CSCE) and the 2002 Venice Commission's Code of Good Practice in Electoral Matters. These legally binding commitments and state ratifications have been collated by International Institute for Democracy and Electoral Assistance (IDEA) and codified in an integrated Elections Obligations and Standards (EOS) database maintained by the Carter Center (Tuccinardi 2014).[2]

# INSTITUTIONAL THEORIES OF ELECTORAL INTEGRITY

Given this conceptual framework, what accounts for problems of electoral integrity? Many drivers may affect whether contests fall short of international standards, including *structural constraints* like poverty and illiteracy, lack of state capacity, and pervasive cultures of corruption; *international forces* such as the role of globalization, electoral assistance, and diplomatic pressures; and *institutional arrangements*, including the role of electoral management bodies, electoral systems, and registration and balloting procedures (Norris 2015). Electoral institutions can be understood as the formal rules and the informal social norms structuring the workings of any contest, as authorized by law and enforceable by courts. Formal rules include the legislative framework governing the major features of electoral systems, as embodied in constitutions, official documents, and legal statutes, as well as more detailed electoral procedures specified in codes of conduct and administrative procedures. Institutions provide incentives and sanctions that constrain human behavior. It is neither necessary nor sufficient for rules to be embodied in the legal system to be effective; social norms, informal patterns of behavior, and social prohibitions also create shared mutual expectations among political actors that can exert a powerful influence on human behavior. Hence, for example, when regulating campaign finance, a pervasive culture of corruption can encourage an arms race of spending, trumping any number of legal deterrents (see chapter by Johnson, this volume). By contrast, pervasive social norms of integrity and trust may make laws largely redundant (Norris and van Es 2016). Nevertheless, this chapter focuses attention on the formal rules governing electoral systems and procedures as these represent the core instruments of public policy that are open to reform and amendment through legislation, executive order, constitutional revision, administrative decree, or judicial review (Carey 2000).

Ever since the seminal work by Maurice Duverger (1954) and by Douglas Rae (1971), a rich body of work has developed detailed typologies of electoral systems and sought to determine their mechanical and psychological consequences. The former refers to the strict application of laws, such as the way that statutory thresholds deprive parties falling below the specified threshold of gaining any seats. The latter refers to the ways that laws in turn shape the incentives and behaviors of governments, parties, and citizens, for example, where thresholds encourage strategic voting for supporters of minor parties judged unlikely to gain seats. The most common approach in the traditional literature has compared a range of democracies during the postwar period to identify the mechanical impact of electoral institutions upon seat and vote distributions, and thus patterns of party competition, as well as their consequences for the representation of women and ethnic minorities, issues of governability and political stability, types of constituency service and legislative behavior, patterns of ethnic conflict, and levels of voting turnout (Lijphart 1994; Cox 1997; Katz 1997; Powell 2000; Shugart and Wattenberg 2001; Norris 2004).[3] Building upon this literature, why might formal electoral rules be expected to influence patterns of electoral integrity and malpractices? At least five arguments can be offered, following the logic of electoral system design, generating several empirically testable propositions.

## Checks and Balances May Limit the Potential Abuse of Executive Power

The first argument builds upon traditional theories of "power sharing" constitutions, a perspective with a long and distinguished intellectual pedigree rooted in the theory of "consociational" and "consensus" democracy developed by Arend Lijphart (2012), updated more recently in veto-player theory by George Tsebelis (2002), among others (Norris 2008). Proportional representation electoral systems usually lower the threshold for minor parties to enter parliaments and deprive the largest party of an absolute parliamentary majority, thereby typically generating coalition governments. This arrangement produces institutional checks and balances, which maximize the number of institutional veto players in the policy process and thereby avoid the potential risks of electoral rules being manipulated in favor of any single party in government, especially ruling parties controlling the legislature and executive. Therefore, power-sharing arrangements are thought to limit the capacity of governing parties to rig the rules of the electoral game in future contests, such as by manipulating the procedures at any stage of the electoral cycle through gerrymandering and malapportionment of district boundaries, restrictions on ballot access, abuse of state resources, deployment of security forces to intimidate opposition supporters, appointing partisan sympathizers and acolytes to electoral commissions and courts, or, even more crudely, putting a thumb on the scales and stuffing the ballot count.

By contrast, the risks of majoritarian elections are particularly strong if used in autocratic states where the governing party holds an absolute majority in the legislature and in presidential republics where "rubber stamp" assemblies have weak legislative powers and autonomy, as opposition parties may then be unable to counterbalance and check any abuse of powers and manipulation of electoral rules by the executive. Malpractices may limit political competition to incumbent politicians, to established parliamentary parties (in a cartel arrangement), or to just the predominant party. By contrast, PR electoral systems typically produce coalition multiparty cabinets, which provide internal checks and balances on the power of any single party in government and thereby curb the capacity of the largest party to manipulate the electoral rules or to nominate and appoint partisan senior electoral commissioners in their pockets. Strong and independent legislatures with powers of oversight, where opposition parties can hold electoral authorities to account, provide an additional safeguard over the integrity of electoral laws and procedures, as well as over the appointment and nomination process of electoral authorities. This argument suggests the first proposition, namely, that *the type of PR, mixed-member, or majoritarian electoral system used for the lower house of the national parliament will be a significant predictor of general levels of electoral integrity in the legislative contest, with PR elections having the most positive effects*.

## PR Will Encourage Consensual Rather Than Contentious Outcomes

In addition to providing negative safeguards against abuse, advocates also argue that there may be several positive consequences of PR arrangements. In particular, proportional electoral systems maximize the number of "winners" elected to parliament and cabinet office. Through these mechanisms, inclusive power-sharing arrangements are thought to have a broader impact, even for election losers, by building feelings of political trust, social tolerance, and legitimacy, long regarded as the foundations for a civic culture and stable democratic states (Almond and Verba 1963). A series of studies have demonstrated that those voters who support the electoral "winners" are far more likely to trust democracy and have confidence in political institutions than those backing the losing side (Anderson et al. 2005). Compared with "losers," citizens who supported the winning party typically express far greater confidence and faith in the integrity of the electoral process (Norris 2014). Accordingly, PR electoral rules maximizing the number of party "winners" represented in parliamentary bodies or in coalition cabinets are likely to strengthen confidence in the political system and faith in the electoral process. Proportional representation electoral systems with large district magnitudes (including variants, such as mixed-member proportional systems) lower the effective threshold for translating votes into seats, facilitating the election of many smaller parliamentary parties and also usually producing multiparty government coalitions. By maximizing the number of "winners," political party elites with a stake in the legislature and executive are more likely to consent to the legitimacy of the electoral process, increasing trust in electoral procedures and rules among their supporters.

By contrast, majoritarian electoral systems concentrate the spoils of office in the hands of the winners, exaggerating the seat share for the largest party through a systematic "winner's bonus," while disproportionately penalizing geographically dispersed smaller parties through high vote–seat thresholds. As a result of majoritarian rules, party elites excluded from parliaments and cabinet office have a strong incentive to criticize the fairness of the electoral results, the rules of the game, and the electoral authorities, or to cry fraud following an election, thereby reducing confidence in the process among their members and voting supporters. Sustainable electoral rules and processes require that all actors with the power to challenge and disrupt the proceedings, whether incumbents who cling to office despite defeat or challengers deploying force, choose instead to respect and honor the rules and outcome.[4] By providing all parties with a stake in the process, PR elections are likely to maximize the legitimacy of the process and consensual outcomes.

In support of this argument, it is striking that party polarization over electoral administration and cries of fraud appear to have become most contentious in recent years in several countries with majoritarian elections. Debate about claims of voter suppression by Democrats and voter identify theft by Republicans have become more bitterly divided in the United States ever since an army of lawyers descended upon the Florida debacle in 2000 (Hasen 2012). Signs of a milder contagion of mistrust appear to be spreading to several other Anglo-American democracies as well, exemplified by passage of the Fair Votes Act by the Conservative government in Canada and contention in the United Kingdom following the government's introduction of the individual voter register, justified by ministers as a more secure system guarding against alleged voter fraud (UK Electoral Commission 2013; Pal 2014). There are some signs that this debate may have spread to Australia. By contrast, fewer controversies over the electoral process and voting procedures are evident in many Western European countries with PR rules, such as Sweden or Germany. These claims generate another testable proposition, namely, that *more contentious outcomes* (indicated by *party disputes about the results and more peaceful and violent protests) should be evident following contests in majoritarian electoral systems, compared with those held under PR rules.*

# PR Elections Strengthen Equal Opportunities for Women and Minorities

An extensive literature has long suggested that PR electoral systems with large district magnitudes usually offer more opportunities for the nomination and election of female candidates, and thereby generate more inclusive parliaments (Norris 1985). It is generally assumed that PR elections provide an incentive for vote-seeking parties to select a list of candidates that includes visible minorities, to maximize support and avoid discriminating explicitly against any substantial block of the electorate. By contrast, political parties in plurality and majoritarian electoral systems with single-seat districts generally recruit candidates locally within each district or constituency, so that parties face weaker collective penalties for lack of gender balance among nominated candidates. Moreover, gender quotas are easier to implement and monitor across collective party lists, compared with individual candidates selected in single-seat districts.

Arguments about gender equality may also hold parallel lessons for ethnic and national minority representation, although as Lublin highlights, the success of minority candidates and ethno-regionalist parties may also depend on many detailed and complex aspects of electoral rules, such as reserved seats, communal lists and low thresholds, and levels of decentralized governance, as well as the size and geographic dispersion of such groups within the electorate or region (Lublin 2014).[5] In plurality systems, vote-maximizing parties have an electoral incentive to select ethnic minority candidates within certain constituencies with high-density minority populations, such as within the United Kingdom in several seats in Bradford, Birmingham, and inner-city London, or in US minority-majority districts with a high density of African Americans. Nevertheless, PR is still generally more likely to call attention to the underrepresentation of visible minority candidates in collective lists of party nominees, especially for spatially dispersed minorities. The argument generates the proposition that, *compared with majoritarian systems, PR electoral systems are expected to strengthen equal opportunities for women and minority candidates.*

# Single-Member Districts May Heighten the Incentives for Ballot-Box Fraud

The power-sharing argument involves many constitutional arrangements, such as federal versus unitary states, and parliamentary versus presidential executives. But one aspect of the design of electoral systems, in particular, may be expected to prove negative for integrity. Majoritarian electoral rules may be expected to heighten the incentives for individual candidates to engage in several common malpractices; in particular, single-seat districts (SSDs) may exacerbate the risks of vote buying and ballot-box stuffing (Birch 2007). The reason is that in highly competitive marginal districts, in particular, under winner-take-all rules, even one vote may make the difference between victory and defeat. Hence, Lehoucq and Jiménez (2002) report that in the mixed-member electoral system operating in Costa Rica, in the same contest, plurality districts generated many more complaints about electoral fraud than multi-seat PR districts. Compared with representatives in closed-list multiseat PR districts, elected officials in SSDs—especially those with tight margins where even a few votes could tip the scales for the winner—may generate stronger incentive to engage in clientelism, patronage politics, rent seeking, and other corrupt acts, delivering pork to constituents (Persson, Tabellini, and Trebbi 2003; Kunicova and Rose-Ackerman 2005). PR electoral systems, especially those with large multiseat districts, are expected to guard against these dangers, since many more ballots would need to be manipulated to change the outcome for the winner. In closed-list PR systems, citizens cast a ballot for collective political party lists, not expressing preferences for individual candidates. For these reasons, Birch (2007) points out that individual candidates in SSD systems have more to gain from efforts to manipulate votes on polling day than is the case for equivalent candidates running in (closed-list) PR contests, and malfeasance is more efficient under SSD rules. At the same time, of course, this does not rule out the collective use of electoral malpractices or corruption by political parties that may happen during the earlier stages of the electoral cycle, for example, through packing membership in the EMB, restricting ballot access, or suppressing voter registration. This argument suggests the proposition that *PR elections should score higher in terms of both perceived electoral fraud and perceived fairness to minor parties compared with majoritarian systems.*

## Large Multiseat Districts May Reduce, or Even Eliminate, Gerrymandering

Moreover, single-seat districts may also be expected to raise the risks of partisan gerrymandering and malapportionment, where district boundaries are drawn to favor one party (usually incumbent office-holders) or a specific demographic group of the electorate, such as minority populations closely associated with one party (Handley and Grofman 2008).[6] The process of gerrymandering works by packing voters of one type into a single electoral district, thereby seeking to ensure a safe seat and reduce competition, diminishing the impact of this group elsewhere. In Singapore, for example, the ruling People's Action Party has been criticized for using this technique to secure its parliamentary majority (Tan 2013). In the 2013 Malaysian general election, the ruling coalition that has been in power since 1957, Barisan Nasional, won 47 percent of the vote but took 60 percent of the parliamentary seats. The opposition coalition, Pakatan Rakyat, won a majority of the popular vote (51 percent), but only 40 percent of the seats. The opposition ethnic-Chinese support is concentrated in densely populated urban seats, with far larger electorates, so that the opposition gets fewer members of parliament for every vote cast. The result of the malapportionment is to undermine the principle of equal votes. In the Perceptions of Electoral Integrity expert survey, experts rated Malaysia worst on the item "boundaries discriminate against some parties" among the eighty-six countries under comparison, although the United States, Zimbabwe, and Togo also came out poorly by this measure. Similar gerrymandering favoring the governing party has been observed in many other places, such as Cameroon (Albaugh 2011). Parties can thereby win a higher number of seats without increasing their share of the vote. These dangers are particularly common where elected politicians and the dominant party control the process of drawing constituency boundaries. They may diminish if the process is in the hands of nonpartisan officials, such as judges, independent commissions, or boards.

Handley (2008) notes that although almost all countries that do not delimit constituencies are list PR, some list PR electoral systems do delimit constituencies, although the boundaries often change infrequently in nations such as Belgium, Bulgaria, Poland, and Sweden. Large multiseat districts in PR systems thereby reduce, or sometimes even eliminate, the need for any redistricting, for example, where fixed district boundaries reflect the boundaries of administrative regions.[7] Worldwide, in around fifty countries, such as Norway, Portugal, and Russia, existing regional or provincial administrative boundaries are used to delimit election districts in the lower house of the national legislature.[8] Some empirical evidence supports the link between electoral systems and partisan gerrymandering; for example, when comparing varied electoral systems in two dozen post-Communist states, Birch (2007) found that electoral misconduct was associated with the proportion of SSD seats in a country. This argument suggests the final claim to be considered, namely, that *fewer malpractices in drawing electoral boundaries are expected to be found under PR elections compared with majoritarian systems*.

Despite all these plausible arguments, however, evidence from previous studies has not tested these claims systematically against evidence gathered across diverse types of systems, regimes, and contexts. Critics contend that both PR elections and power-sharing arrangements in general also have several potential *dis*advantages. The general benefits have long been strongly challenged by proponents of majoritarian arrangements: Donald Horowitz (1985, 1991, 2002) argues that PR rules and power-sharing constitutional arrangements may, in fact, unintentionally serve to heighten latent ethnic identities, strengthen party extremism and fragmentation, and freeze community boundaries, failing in the long term to generate the conditions of social tolerance and moderation where democracy flourishes. Moreover, even if an association is observed, it remains unclear from the previous literature whether formal electoral rules have the capacity to outweigh other factors typically associated with standards of electoral integrity, including conditions such as levels of development and the impact of other institutions, such as the role of the free press.

# Evidence

The debate concerning the claimed advantages of PR elections for strengthening electoral integrity deserves fresh examination against the available evidence for several reasons. In particular, there are many varieties of electoral systems within each of the major families and it remains unclear which aspects, if any, are most effective for different aspects of electoral integrity. Similarly, previous studies of these questions have used some simple indicators of the quality of elections, such as public perceptions of whether contests are seen as "free and fair" (Birch 2007), or they have been based on effects observed in a mixed-member electoral system within a single case study (Lehoucq and Jiménez 2002). As a result, scholars have been unable to measure the multidimensional concept of electoral integrity throughout the electoral cycle in a comprehensive and systematic fashion across multiple countries and contexts.

This chapter presents more thorough and comprehensive evidence measured in legislative elections for the lower house worldwide through the Electoral Integrity Project's expert rolling survey of Perceptions of Electoral Integrity (release PEI-3.5), with details described fully elsewhere (Norris, Martinez i Coma, and Frank 2013; Norris, Frank and Martinez i Coma 2014a, 2014b; Martinez i Coma and van Ham 2015). This dataset is used to test whether indicators of electoral integrity—including the summary one-hundred-point Perceptions of Electoral Integrity index and specific selected indices—are significantly more positive in countries with proportional representation electoral systems compared with mixed-member and majoritarian systems. Some of the survey items refer explicitly to electoral laws, but others make no direct reference to the electoral law per se. The PEI-3.5 expert survey evaluated all 153 national elections held around the globe from mid-2012 to mid-2015. The study covers almost three-quarters (125) of all independent nation-states, excluding a dozen microstates (with populations below 100,000), five states that do not hold direct elections for the lower house of parliament, and three states that have constitutional provisions for direct elections for the lower house but have never held such contests since independence or within the last thirty years. Excluding the presidential contests (which all use variants of plurality/majoritarian rules), this study analyzes PEI-3.5 scores under electoral systems used in ninety-five legislative contests in ninety-one sovereign countries. The contemporary type of electoral system used for the lower house of parliament (or the single house in unicameral systems) was classified for each election from the International IDEA database into three basic types: majoritarian/plurality (coded 1), mixed-member (coded 2), and proportional representation (coded 3).

Elections commonly have varied degrees of electoral competition, and thus the survey includes national elections in one-party states such as Cuba that ban all opposition parties; in states such as Bahrain and Swaziland where all political parties are banned; in countries where one specific type of party is restricted from ballot access, such as the

Freedom and Justice Party in Egypt; and in countries where candidates are restricted from standing, such as due to the vetting process in Iran.

The study selects a cross-section of electoral experts to participate in the survey, including both domestic and international respondents. The survey asks for around 40 electoral experts from each country, generating a mean response rate of around 28 percent across the survey with replies from 1,251 experts. The data has been found to display high degrees of external and internal validity, generating strong correlations when compared with equivalent independent indices. A dozen indicators were selected from the expert survey, matched to the propositions discussed earlier, as listed in Table 24.1. Responses to the specific indices were scaled on five points and recoded in a consistently positive direction so that higher scores reflect greater levels of perceived integrity.

# RESULTS AND ANALYSIS

To look at the results, the descriptive evidence can be examined for the observed association between the types of electoral system and the mean scores on the PEI index, the eleven stages in the electoral cycle, and the selected subindices.

Table 24.1 shows that, as expected by advocates of power-sharing arrangements, the mean perceptions of the one-hundred-point PEI index is indeed significantly more positive under proportional representation legislative elections, with a twelve-point gap over plurality/majority systems. Table 24.1 also confirms the significant advantage for PR systems across eight of the eleven selected specific indices under comparison. The main exception to this pattern concerns the measures reflecting indicators about the legitimacy of the results, through party challenges and peaceful and violent protests. This suggests that contentious outcomes cannot be prevented through electoral system design alone and alternative reasons need to be considered to account for electoral conflict and contentious elections, such as the role of deeply divided societies, structural conditions like deep-rooted poverty, the type of regime in power, and whether there are effective avenues for legal redress through the courts (Norris, Frank, and Martinez i Coma 2015). Overall, however, the descriptive evidence lends further support to the claims that PR elections generally have several benefits for electoral integrity over elections held under plurality and majoritarian systems, in terms of their overall levels of integrity, their lower vulnerability to fraud and bias, providing equal opportunities for women and minorities, and reducing the risks of gerrymandering district boundaries.

To explore further, since several institutional, international, and socioeconomic conditions have been found to shape the quality of elections, multivariate models need to see whether electoral systems persist as significant predictors of PEI after controlling for these factors (Norris 2015). Beyond electoral rules, independent reporting by the free

**Table 24.1  Selected Indices of Electoral Integrity by Type of Electoral System, All Regimes**

| Selected Indices | Mean Plural/ Maj | Mean Mixed | Mean PR | Eta/Sig | Sig |
|---|---|---|---|---|---|
| 1. OVERALL INTEGRITY | | | | | |
| 1   Perceptions of Electoral Integrity summary 100-pt index | 50.3 | 55.0 | 62.3 | .348 | *** |
| 2. LEGITIMACY AND PROTESTS | | | | | |
| 2   Parties/candidates (did not) challenge the results | 3.0 | 4.2 | 4.5 | .161 | N/s |
| 3   The election (did not) trigger violent protests | 4.3 | 3.4 | 3.8 | .197 | N/s |
| 4   The election (did not lead) to peaceful protests | 3.7 | 3.4 | 3.8 | .177 | N/s |
| 3. FRAUD AND BIAS | | | | | |
| 5   Some fraudulent votes were (not) cast | 2.6 | 2.8 | 3.3 | .289 | ** |
| 6   Electoral laws were (fair) to smaller parties | 2.7 | 3.1 | 3.2 | .226 | N/s |
| 7   Electoral laws (did not favor) the governing party or parties | 2.5 | 2.9 | 3.3 | .345 | *** |
| 4. EQUAL OPPORTUNITIES | | | | | |
| 8   Women had equal opportunities to run for office | 3.2 | 3.5 | 3.7 | .329 | *** |
| 9   Ethnic and national minorities had equal opportunities to run for office | 3.1 | 3.3 | 3.6 | .321 | *** |
| 5. GERRYMANDERING | | | | | |
| 10   Boundaries (did not) discriminate against some parties | 2.8 | 3.0 | 3.4 | .310 | ** |

## Table 24.1 Continued

|    | Selected Indices | Mean Plural/ Maj | Mean Mixed | Mean PR | Eta/Sig | Sig |
|----|------------------|------------------|------------|---------|---------|-----|
| 11 | Boundaries (did not) favor incumbents | 2.9 | 3.1 | 3.5 | .327 | *** |
| 12 | Boundaries were impartial | 2.8 | 2.9 | 3.5 | .365 | *** |
|    | # Countries | 28 | 20 | 43 | 91 | |

*Notes:* The significance of the mean difference was measured by ANOVA.

*** Significant at the 0.001 level (two-tailed).

** Significant at the 0.01 level (two-tailed).

* Significant at the 0.05 level (two-tailed). All the selected indices are measured on one-to-five-point scales. Responses were recoded so that all items were consistently pointing in a positive direction, so that a higher score represents greater integrity.

*Source:* Electoral Integrity Project. The Expert Survey of Perceptions of Electoral Integrity (PEI-3.5), 2015.

press and social media highlights cases of electoral abuse or attempts at fraud or ballot rigging, providing an important check on the potential abuse of powers by governing or opposition parties (Waisbord 2000). Hence, Birch (2011) reports that lack of press freedom was significantly linked with the problem of electoral administration and the manipulation of vote choice. In addition, other power-sharing institutions may also play a role; in particular, Fish (2006) suggests that a strong parliament is a powerful predictor of democratization and, by extension, this should also display a similar relationship with electoral integrity. Economic underdevelopment may also be a significant barrier to electoral integrity, especially in the world's poorest societies with high levels of illiteracy and with limited resources in the public sector for managing elections. To analyze these factors, ordinary least squares regression models (presented elsewhere) examined the effects of these and several other related variables on the PEI index. The results confirmed that the type of electoral system continued to predict the PEI score, even controlling for all these conditions.[9]

Of course, one reason for this observed correlation could be that the assumed causal direction needs to be reversed if democratic states are more likely to *adopt* proportional representation electoral systems, whereas authoritarian states may choose majoritarian or plurality arrangements. It is not possible to include standard measures of democratization by Freedom House or Polity IV in the multivariate models, in large part because these indices include many items of electoral integrity in their concepts and construction, generating spurious correlations with PEI. So instead, as an alternative strategy to see whether PR contests displayed more integrity in democratic states, Figure 24.1 limits the comparison to legislative elections in states classified as "free" by Freedom House,

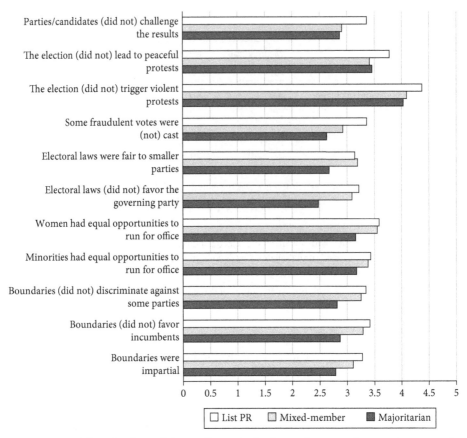

**FIGURE 24.1.** Selected indices of electoral integrity by electoral system, democratic states only.

Note: The mean scores for legislative elections for the lower house in forty-eight democratic states on the five-point Perceptions of Electoral Integrity selected indicators by type of electoral system, where a higher score represents greater integrity.

Source: Electoral Integrity Project. The Expert Survey of Perceptions of Electoral Integrity (PEI-4.5), 2015.

based on political rights and civil liberties. Figure 24.1 shows that *within the universe of democratic states, the type of electoral system still makes a difference across most of the indices, with PR elections consistently displaying fewer malpractices,* although the gaps across the items are commonly quite modest and varied in size.

Finally, the interpretation could be always biased by the particular indicators if these have been cherry-picked for comparison. After all, the idea that PR generates fairer outcomes is hardly in dispute, and proponents of majoritarian elections argue that this system has many other benefits, such as generating effective single-party governments capable of making tough decisions. To see whether the specific choice of items makes a difference, Figure 24.2 looks more broadly at all forty-nine indicators constructed from PEI to monitor eleven stages of the electoral cycle, from the electoral laws and procedures, determined early in the process, through campaign money and media, to Election Day and its aftermath. All the indicators are

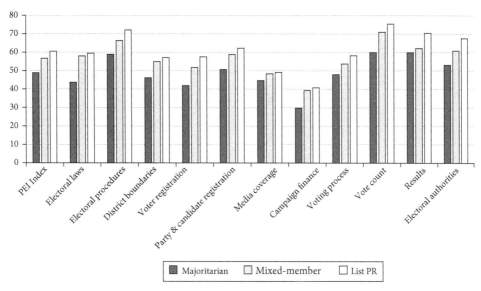

**FIGURE 24.2.** Stages of the electoral cycle and electoral systems.

Notes: The mean scores on the one-hundred-point Perceptions of Electoral Integrity index and its dimensions during the electoral cycle by type of electoral system, where a higher score represents greater integrity. The significance of the mean differences was estimated by ANOVA. Significance * .05, ** .01, *** .001.

Sources: Electoral Integrity Project. The Expert Survey of Perceptions of Electoral Integrity (PEI-4.5), 2015.

standardized to one hundred points and coded in a positive direction, to indicate that higher scores reflect better integrity, according to experts. Again, the evidence lends further confirmation to the patterns already reported: *PR scores consistently more highly in integrity than majoritarian electoral systems across all eleven stages of the electoral cycle.*

Therefore, on balance, PR does seem to clearly serve to strengthen the quality of elections for all the reasons discussed earlier. At the same time, however, several important qualifications should be noted about the evidence presented in this study. In particular, analysis draws upon observational cross-national data, since the expert survey of Perceptions of Electoral Integrity, which started in mid-2012, has only collected longitudinal data covering repeated elections in a few countries. Therefore, there are real limitations in seeking to make causal inferences on the basis of the correlational relationships. In general, social conditions such as levels of economic development can be treated as long-term or fixed factors that are likely to influence the quality of contemporary elections. The constitutional arrangements in any state are also expected to prove relatively stable and to shape the context of any particular electoral contest. Nevertheless, issues of endogeneity arise from the observed relationships, since the quality of elections is also plausibly linked to many major political institutions; for example, more competitive elections are likely to produce multiparty parliaments that can scrutinize the actions and policies of the executive, as well as protect against manipulation of the rules of the game and broader political and civil rights, such as freedom of the press. Therefore, ideally, time-series data needs to be examined to unpack the linkages, and this will become possible as the PEI expert survey is gradually extended over several years and a longer series of elections (Norris 2015).

# CONCLUSION

Theories drawing upon classical liberalism and consociational democracy emphasize that institutions dispersing powers and responsibilities for electoral governance vertically and horizontally among different branches, levels, and agencies of government provide checks and balances that help prevent potential abuses by any single actor (including incumbent power holders). By generating multiple stakeholders, PR elections are also believed to strengthen trust in the fairness, impartiality, and credibility of the electoral process, even among losing candidates and parties. By heightening the incentives and opportunities for gerrymandering and for ballot-box fraud, the risks of malpractices by parties and candidates are expected to be greater in single-seat district plurality and majoritarian electoral systems, where even one vote can make the difference between success and failure, compared with PR.

These are plausible arguments, although in previous research systematic cross-national evidence supporting these claims has been limited. At the same time, however, there is certainly room for debate, since general constitutional power-sharing arrangements may also have several potential general *dis*advantages for electoral governance, for example, where excessive party fragmentation hinders the implementation of effective procedural reforms needed for legislative effectiveness, where decentralization prevents clear channels of public accountability and timely responsiveness for any procedural problems that arise in administering elections, or where it undermines uniform and consistent standards for citizens across all localities.

The evidence presented in this chapter provides considerable support for arguments emphasizing the advantages of PR elections, which are the core institutions at the heart of any broader power-sharing constitutional arrangement. Across the several claims considered, compared with majoritarian systems, in many countries PR elections are found to be associated with more positive indices of electoral integrity. In particular, the evidence suggests that PR outperforms majoritarian systems in terms of the overall levels of electoral integrity, reducing the risks of fraud and gerrymandering, and expanding equal opportunities for women and minorities, while there were no significant advantages or disadvantages in terms of protests and contentious outcomes. Hence, proportional representation generally serves to safeguard the integrity of the electoral process and provide checks on manipulation and malfeasance at different stages of the electoral cycle. Elections are far from the sole mechanisms in this regard; institutions that also serve this function include strong parliaments and freedom of the press. For contests to work well, a host of detailed electoral procedures also need to be implemented, from the regulation of campaign finance to technical processes for registering and casting ballots.

Integrity is only one value and arguably there are many others that need to be carefully counterbalanced in the tradeoff choice of constitutional rules. Nevertheless, meeting international standards is a fundamental principle of human rights that the design of electoral rules should seek to observe.

The importance of these findings is that institutional changes, such as initiatives seeking to reform majoritarian electoral systems, like those strengthening the capacity and powers of legislators and independent media, are amenable to programmatic intervention by policymakers. In this regard, formal institutional reforms are far more policy relevant for strengthening the quality of elections and democracy, unlike fixed structural conditions, such as levels of societal modernization and economic development. The lessons are particularly important for the international community and for domestic stakeholders seeking to establish effective electoral systems in new or revised constitutional arrangements. Countries often choose electoral systems that reflect their past historical experiences, often under colonial rulers, or the legal rules that predominate among neighboring states and cultures in any world region. But in fact, the evidence in this study underlines the many advantages of PR for contests meeting international standards of electoral integrity. In the world's fragile states, emerging from decades of authoritarian rule and/or after years of deep-seated conflict, at a time of illiberal resurgence when there are serious doubts at home and abroad about the capacity of electoral assistance to promote effective and stable democratic governance, making fully informed choices about the basic electoral rules of the game could never be more important.

## Notes

1. The Variety of Democracy (V-Dem) project. See https://v-dem.net/.
2. Carter Center. *Elections Obligations and Standards Database.* http://electionstandards .cartercenter.org/tools/eos/.
3. Also see chapters in this volume by Herron, Pekkanen, and Shugart (Introduction); Krook (representation of women); Smith (turnout); Crisp (constituency service); and Strom and Tiwari (government stability).
4. This is similar to the notion of "self-enforcing democracy"; see Alberts, Warshaw, and Weingast 2011.
5. See also the chapter by Bowler and Lublin in this volume.
6. See also Handley's chapter in this volume.
7. As Handley notes in this volume.
8. AceProject.org. http://aceproject.org/epic-en/CDTable?question=BD001.
9. Ordinary least squares regression models, presented elsewhere, controlled for societal levels of economic development (measured by per capita gross domestic product [GDP] in purchasing power parity), natural resources (rents as a percentage of GDP), the index of political globalization, regional levels of electoral integrity (for neighborhood effects), press freedom (Freedom House), the independence of the judiciary, and the Fish-Kroenig Parliamentary Powers Index. All data was derived from the Quality of Government dataset, downloaded January 2015. For more details, see Norris 2015: chap. 5, Table 5.1.

## References

Albaugh, Ericka A. "An Autocrat's Toolkit: Adaptation and Manipulation in 'Democratic' Cameroon." *Democratization* 18, no. 2 (2011): 388–414.

Alberts, Susan, Chris Warshaw, and Barry R. Weingast. "Democratization and Counter-Majoritarian Institutions." In *Comparative Constitutional Design*, edited by Tom Ginsburg. New York: Cambridge University Press, 2011.

Almond, Gabriel, and Sidney Verba. *The Civic Culture*. Princeton: Princeton University Press, 1963.

Anderson, Christopher J., Andre Blais, Shaun Bowler, Todd Donovan, and Ola Listhaug. *Losers' Consent: Elections and Democratic Legitimacy*. New York: Oxford University Press, 2005.

Birch, Sarah. "Electoral Systems and Electoral Misconduct." *Comparative Political Studies* 40, no. 12 (2007): 1533–1556.

Birch, Sarah. *Electoral Malpractice*. Oxford: Oxford University Press, 2011.

Bishop, Sylvia, and Anke Hoeffler. "Free and Fair Elections: A New Database." Center for the Study of African Economies (CSAE) Working Paper WPS/2014-14. Oxford, 2014.

Bjornlund, Eric C. *Beyond Free and Fair: Monitoring Elections and Building Democracy*. Washington, DC: Woodrow Wilson Center Press, 2004.

Carey, John M. "Parchment, Equilibria, and Institutions." *Comparative Political Studies* 33, no. 6–7 (2000): 735–761.

Carter Center. Elections Obligations and Standards Database. http://electionstandards .cartercenter.org/tools/eos/.

Cox, Gary. *Making Votes Count*. New York and London: Cambridge University Press, 1997.

Duverger, Maurice. *Political Parties*. London: Methuen, 1964 [1954].

Fish, M. Steven. "Stronger Legislatures, Stronger Democracies." *Journal of Democracy* 17, no. 1 (2006): 5–20.

Flores, Thomas Edward, and Irfan Nooruddin. *Elections in Hard Times: Building Stronger Democracies in the 21st Century*. New York: Cambridge University Press, 2016.

Handley, Lisa. "A Comparative Survey of Structures and Criteria." In *Redistricting in Comparative Perspective*, edited by Lisa Handley and Bernie Grofman. New York: Oxford University Press, 2008.

Handley, Lisa, and Bernie Grofman, eds. *Redistricting in Comparative Perspective*. New York: Oxford University Press, 2008.

Hasen, Richard L. *The Voting Wars: From Florida 2000 to the Next Election Meltdown*. New Haven, CT: Yale University Press, 2012.

Horowitz, Donald L. *Ethnic Groups in Conflict*. Berkeley: University of California Press, 1985.

Horowitz, Donald L. *A Democratic South Africa? Constitutional Engineering in a Divided Society*. Berkeley: University of California Press, 1991.

Horowitz, Donald L. *The Deadly Ethnic Riot*. Berkeley: University of California Press, 2002.

Hyde, Susan D., and Nikolay Marinov. "Which Elections Can be Lost?" *Political Analysis* 20, no. 2 (2012): 191–210.

Katz, Richard S. *Democracy and Elections*. New York: Oxford University Press, 1997.

Kunicova, Jana, and Susan Rose-Ackerman. "Electoral Rules and Constitutional Structures as Constraints on Corruption." *British Journal of Political Science* 35, no. 4 (2005): 573–606.

Lehoucq, Fabrice Edouard. "Electoral Fraud: Causes, Types, and Consequences." *Annual Review of Political Science* 6 (2003): 233–256.

Lehoucq, Fabrice Edouard, and Iván Molina Jiménez. *Stuffing the Ballot Box: Fraud, Electoral Reform, and Democratization in Costa Rica*. New York: Cambridge University Press, 2002.

Levitsky, Steven, and Lucan Way. *Competitive Authoritarianism: Hybrid Regimes after the Cold War*. New York: Cambridge University Press, 2010.

Lijphart, Arend. *Electoral Systems and Party Systems: A Study of Twenty-Seven Democracies, 1945-1990*. Oxford: Oxford University Press, 1994.

Lijphart, Arend. *Patterns of Democracy*. 2nd ed. New Haven, CT: Yale University Press, 2012.

Lublin, David. *Minority Rules Electoral Systems, Decentralization, and Ethnoregional Party Success*. New York: Oxford University Press, 2014.

Martínez i Coma, Ferran, and Carolien van Ham. "Can Experts Judge Elections? Testing the Validity of Expert Judgments for Measuring Election Integrity." *European Journal of Political Research* 54 (2015): 305–325.

Minnite, Lorraine Carol. *The Myth of Voter Fraud*. Ithaca, NY: Cornell University Press, 2010.

Norris, Pippa. "Women in European Legislative Elites." *West European Politics* 8, no. 4 (1985): 90–101.

Norris, Pippa. *Electoral Engineering*. Cambridge: Cambridge University Press, 2004.

Norris, Pippa. *Driving Democracy*. New York: Cambridge University Press, 2008.

Norris, Pippa. *Why Electoral Integrity Matters*. New York: Cambridge University Press, 2014.

Norris, Pippa. *Why Elections Fail*. New York: Cambridge University Press, 2015.

Norris, Pippa, and Andrea Abel van Es. *Checkbook Elections*. New York: Oxford University Press, 2016.

Norris, Pippa, Ferran Martinez i Coma, and Richard W. Frank. "Assessing the Quality of Elections." *Journal of Democracy* 24, no. 4 (2013): 124–135.

Norris, Pippa, Richard W. Frank, and Ferran Martinez i Coma, eds. *Advancing Electoral Integrity*. New York: Oxford University Press, 2014a.

Norris, Pippa, Richard W. Frank, and Ferran Martinez i Coma. "Measuring Electoral Integrity: A New Dataset." *PS Politics and Political Science* 47, no. 4 (2014b): 789–798.

Norris, Pippa, Richard W. Frank, and Ferran Martinez i Coma, eds. *Contentious Elections*. New York: Routledge, 2015.

Norris, Pippa, Ferran Martinez i Coma, and Max Groemping. *The Year in Elections, 2014*. University of Sydney, Electoral Integrity Project, 2015.

Pal, Michael. "Canadian Election Administration on Trial: The 'Robocalls' Case and the Opitz Decision." Paper presented at EIP/MEDW workshop prior to the IPSA World Congress, Montreal, July 18, 2014.

Persson, Torsten, Guido Tabellini, and Francesco Trebbi. "Electoral Rules and Corruption." *Journal of the European Economic Association* 1, no. 4 (2003): 22–34.

Powell, G. Bingham. *Elections as Instruments of Democracy*. New Haven, CT: Yale University Press, 2000.

Powell, G. Bingham. "Why Elections Matter." In *Comparing Democracies 4*, edited by Lawrence LeDuc, Richard Niemi, and Pippa Norris. London: Sage, 2014.

Przeworski, Adam, Michael E. Alvarez, Jose Antonio Cheibub, and Fernando Limongi. *Democracy and Development: Political Institutions and Well-Being in the World, 1950-1990*. New York: Cambridge University Press, 2000.

Rae, Douglas. *The Political Consequences of Electoral Laws*. Rev. ed. New Haven, CT: Yale University Press, 1971.

Schedler, Andreas. "The Menu of Manipulation." *Journal of Democracy* 13, no. 2 (2002): 36–50.

Schumpeter, Joseph. *Capitalism, Socialism and Democracy.* New York: Taylor and Frances, 1942. Reprint 2003.

Shugart, Matthew S., and Martin P. Wattenberg, eds. *Mixed Member Electoral Systems: The Best of Both Worlds?* New York: Oxford University Press, 2001.

Simpser, Alberto. *Why Parties and Governments Manipulate Elections: Theory, Practice and Implications.* New York: Cambridge University Press, 2013.

Tan, Netina. "Electoral Engineering and Hegemonic Party Resilience in Singapore." *Electoral Studies* 32, no. 4 (2013): 632–643.

Tsebelis, George. *Veto Players: How Political Institutions Work.* Princeton, NJ: Princeton University Press, 2002.

Tuccinardi, Domenico, ed. *International Obligations for Elections: Guidelines for Legal Frameworks.* Stockholm: International IDEA, 2014.

UK Electoral Commission. *Electoral Fraud in the UK: Evidence and Issues Paper.* London: UK Electoral Commission, 2013. http://www.electoralcommission.org.uk.

van Ham, Carolien. "Getting Elections Right? Measuring Electoral Integrity." *Democratization* 22, no. 4 (2015): 714–737.

Waisbord, Silvio. *Watchdog Journalism in South America: News, Accountability, and Democracy.* New York: Columbia University Press, 2000.

CHAPTER 25

....................................................................................................

# ELECTORAL SYSTEMS
# AND REDISTRICTING

....................................................................................................

## LISA HANDLEY

REDISTRICTING refers to the redrawing of the boundaries of geographically based districts for electing representatives to legislative office. This process is known as redistricting in the United States; redistribution in the United Kingdom, Canada, Australia, and New Zealand; and delimitation in India and many other countries, especially in Asia and Africa.[1] Perceptions about the importance of redistricting vary dramatically—in most countries it is viewed as simply a technical exercise that rarely registers on the political radar. However, in other countries, particularly the United States, contentious partisan battles are fought over the district lines and the courts are often asked to intervene.

The impact that redistricting has on the election outcome depends on the type of electoral system in place. The configuration of electoral districts is important in systems that rely solely on single-seat or small multiseat districts, with no preference voting scheme to counterbalance any disproportionality of votes to seats. Redistricting is less important in proportional representation systems, including mixed-member systems with a district component.[2]

Even if the district boundaries have little impact on the outcome of an election, they still have consequences. Members and aspiring candidates for parliament, communities of interest, and individual voters are affected by the districts they are placed into, drawn out of, or divided by. How the lines are drawn will be determined by which authority is assigned the task of redistricting and the rules established to guide the process.

Redistricting matters not only because electoral district boundaries have consequences but also because a majority of the world's countries rely on districts to elect their representatives to the legislature. In a survey conducted by the author in 2005, sixty of the eighty-seven countries (69 percent) for which information was available reported delimiting electoral districts. The breakdown by region of the countries that delimit electoral districts is found in Table 25.1 (Handley 2008a).

While redistricting practices vary across the many countries that delimit electoral districts, these practices can be roughly divided into those designed to eliminate politics from the process and those that encourage political influence in the redistricting process. The discussion that follows describes the redistricting practices countries have

Table 25.1  Percentage of Countries, by Region, That Delimit Electoral Districts

| Region | Percent of Countries in Region That Delimit Electoral Districts | Number of Countries in Region for Which Information Was Available |
|---|---|---|
| Americas | 57% | 21 |
| Europe | 62% | 34 |
| Africa | 73% | 15 |
| Middle East | 100% | 2 |
| Asia | 91% | 11 |
| Australia and Pacific Islands | 100% | 4 |
| TOTAL | 69% | 87 |

adopted and considers the potential these practices have for excluding politics from the redistricting process.[3]

# ELECTORAL SYSTEMS AND REDISTRICTING

The redistricting of electoral boundaries is most commonly associated with plurality or majority electoral systems. Both of these systems rely heavily, if not exclusively, on single-seat electoral districts. These districts must be redrawn periodically to reflect shifts in the population; failure to redraw at regular intervals is likely to produce malapportioned districts.[4] The boundary configurations of single-seat districts in plurality and majority systems are particularly significant because the number of seats that a political party wins in the legislature depends not only on the proportion of the votes it receives but also on where those votes were cast.[5]

Plurality and majority systems, however, are not the only types of electoral systems that require the periodic redrawing of electoral districts; some proportional and semi-proportional systems also require redistricting. While electoral boundaries in party list proportional systems are rarely redrawn,[6] mixed-member electoral systems that employ both party list proportional representation and single-seat electoral districts must be regularly redistricted. The influence district configurations have on the outcome of the election depends on whether the party list seats in the mixed-member system correct for any distortions in the relationship between seats and votes produced by the single-seat districts. In countries with mixed-member proportional (MMP) systems, such as Germany and New Zealand, seats allocated under the party list system are used to compensate for any distortions in the seats-to-votes ratio produced at the electoral district level. However, in countries that use mixed-member majoritarian (MMM) rules, such as Russia, where party list seats are simply added to the seats won at the electoral district level, the partisan seats-to-votes ratio is likely to be distorted to some degree. In this type of mixed-member system, the redistricting process is more important because it can have a more pronounced effect on the partisan composition of the legislature.

There is another type of proportional representation system that requires regular redistricting: the single transferable vote (STV) system. Ireland and Malta, because they rely on small multiseat districts to rank candidates, must redraw electoral boundaries on a regular basis.[7] Other types of (semi- or nonproportional) electoral systems that require some delimitation of electoral districts include two-round, alternative, and multiple nontransferable vote (MNTV) systems.[8]

# Authority Responsible
# for Redistricting

Because the configuration of electoral boundaries can have an impact on the outcome of the election, at least in less-than-proportional electoral systems, it matters which authority is tasked with this responsibility. During the nineteenth century, in Europe and in self-governing European colonies around the world, redistricting was carried out by the legislature. Gerrymandering (drawing districts to intentionally favor one political party at the expense of others) and other electoral abuses were not uncommon.

These abuses led a number of countries to adopt reforms designed to remove political influences from the redistricting process. They established independent, nonpartisan commissions to redraw the electoral boundaries. Neutral (nonpolitical) criteria have been identified for the commissioners to take into account; these are often enshrined in the constitution or electoral law. The public also has been encouraged to participate in the process. If the legislature is granted any role at all in the reformed redistricting process, it is simply to approve the legislation incorporating the new boundaries.[9]

The United Kingdom, for example, adopted a nonpartisan approach to redistricting several generations ago, and many of the long-standing democracies that it once ruled have followed suit: Australia, New Zealand, and Canada, as well as many of the Caribbean countries (e.g., Bahamas, Barbados, Cayman Islands, St. Lucia, and St. Vincent and the Grenadines). In addition, several Anglophone African countries (e.g., Botswana, Namibia, and Zimbabwe) have also adopted boundary commissions for delimiting constituencies.

These independent boundary commissions are usually composed of nonpartisan civil servants and professionals with expertise in election administration, geography, demography, or statistics. In Australia, New Zealand, and the United Kingdom, for example, the commissions include election officers, as well as the Director of Ordnance Survey (United Kingdom) and the Surveyor-General (Australia and New Zealand). In Canada, academics knowledgeable about elections or geography are often asked to serve as commissioners. Judges play a prominent role on many boundary commissions: judges chair the commissions in Canada and New Zealand; judges serve as Deputy Chairs of the four boundary commissions in the United Kingdom (England, Scotland, Wales, and Northern Ireland); and, in India, two of the three members of the Delimitation Commission are required to be judges. It is noteworthy that members of parliament, state legislators, and representatives of political parties are usually specifically excluded (by law) from serving on these boundary commissions.[10]

The electoral law in many countries includes redistricting in the mandate of the national election commission, rather than convening a commission specifically for redrawing electoral boundaries. This assignment is typically accompanied by a list of criteria to take into account and instructions on how often redistricting is to be undertaken. In most countries, the election commission operates independently from the legislature, although legislative approval of the redrawn boundaries may be required. However, in some countries, electoral commissions are compromised by political ties to the executive.[11]

The United States is one of the very few consolidated democracies that has failed to reform its redistricting process. Once Congress apportions congressional seats to the states, each of the fifty states is responsible for drawing the allotted number of congressional districts within its own borders. Each state adopts its own redistricting procedures, and most states assign the task of congressional redistricting to the state legislature—legislators in 83.7 percent of states drew congressional districts after the 2010 census (Levitt 2015).[12] Because political actors are permitted to control the process, redistricting is usually an exercise in partisan gerrymandering, with the political party in charge of the redistricting process drawing electoral maps to its best advantage.[13]

## The Role of the Courts in Redistricting

After the electoral boundaries have been finalized and, if necessary, approved by the legislature, the redistricting process is complete in many countries. However, some countries permit legal challenges to the newly drawn electoral boundaries. Court intervention is a regular feature of the redistricting process in only one country, however—the United States.

There is a constitutional or statutory bar on court intervention in the delimitation process in some countries. Examples include India, Pakistan, and Nepal in Asia; Tanzania in Africa; Barbados and Trinidad and Tobago in the Caribbean; and Australia and New Zealand in the South Pacific. How far this hampers court consideration of the delimitation process and its outcome varies, however. In India, the Supreme Court has consistently expressed its reluctance to litigate issues related to delimitation. The courts in Pakistan, however, have been more ready to contemplate challenges related to constituency delimitation. In Australia, the courts have intervened on constitutional questions, mostly related to the question of population equality and how this is to be balanced with other redistricting requirements.[14]

The constitution and electoral law are silent on the role of the judiciary in the redistricting process in most countries. If there is a lack of litigation, it is either because of an absence of legal challenges (e.g., Fiji, Singapore, Cayman Islands, Mexico)[15] or a signal by the courts that such challenges will not be readily considered. The United Kingdom is an example of the latter.

Few legal challenges to the redistribution process and the resulting boundaries have been filed in the United Kingdom, and none has succeeded. The primary reason challenges have failed is a 1983 case in which the court imposed a very difficult burden of proof for claimants to meet before judicial review of the redistribution process or its resulting constituency plan would be granted. In *R. v. Boundary Commission for England* ex parte *Foot,* the court held that consideration of the recommendations of the Boundary Commission had to rely on the claim that the commission had clearly failed to follow the rules, and that its recommendations were such that no reasonable commission could possibly have made them.[16]

Delimitation plans can be challenged in court and have been, at least to a limited degree, in the African countries of Ghana, Nigeria, Sierra Leone, Uganda, and Kenya, as well as a number of Caribbean countries (e.g., St. Kitts and Nevis, Antigua and Barbuda, and Dominica). In Asia, the Japanese courts have faced questions regarding the delimitation of constituencies (Moriwaki 2008 and Hasebe 2007), as have courts in Malaysia (Grace 2006a).[17] The issue of delimitation has been considered on a number of occasions by the *Conseil constitutionnel* in France (Balinksi 2008), including its relatively recent decision upholding the validity of the 2010 redrawing of constituency boundaries.[18]

The Canadian Charter of Rights and Freedoms, enacted in 1982, provided Canadians with the first constitutional mechanism for challenging electoral boundaries. Since then, the courts have cautiously intervened in the redistribution process. The first case to consider the justiciability of a redistribution plan in light of the Charter was *Dixon v. Attorney General of British Columbia*.[19] The *Dixon* case, decided by the British Columbia Supreme Court in 1989, involved a challenge to the provincial constituencies in British Columbia, which varied in population from 86.8 percent below to 63.2 percent above the electoral quota. The Court found that the province's electoral districts violated the right to vote as set out in the *Charter* and ruled that a new set of constituencies be drawn.

The courts have not gone on to adopt the strict "one person, one vote" standard that US courts have embraced, however. The Supreme Court of Canada made it clear, in *Reference re Provision Electoral Boundaries (Saskatchewan)*, that the law did not guarantee absolute equality of votes, but rather "effective representation" and "[f]actors like geography, community history, community interests and minority representation may need to be taken into account to ensure that our legislative assemblies effectively represent the diversity of our social mosaic."[20]

Since this 1991 decision, Canadian courts have tended to defer to boundary commissions, although they have stepped in when they considered a constituency map particularly egregious.[21] For example, the Prince Edward Island Supreme Court declared Prince Edward Island provincial constituencies with significant population variations (the smallest district was 63 percent below the electoral quota and the largest was 115 percent above it) to be in violation of the *Charter* in *Mackinnon v. Prince Edward Island* in 1993.[22]

The United States is the major exception to limited judicial involvement in redistricting. Since the US Supreme Court ruled in 1962 that voters could challenge redistricting plans,[23] American courts have become active participants in the process and have, in the course of resolving disputes, established many of the rules that govern the redistricting process. In addition, the courts have been called upon to actually draw the electoral district boundaries when a state legislature is unable to agree on a redistricting plan or to produce a plan that satisfies legal requirements. For example, in the redistricting cycle that began after the release of the 2010 census, the courts were asked to intervene in forty-two of the fifty states (84 percent). According to Justin Levitt, "Courts reviewed congressional districts (or stepped in to correct legislative inaction) in 22 states, declared new districts unlawful in two states (Florida and Texas, later vacated), and actually drew the lines (or some of the lines) themselves in 9 states" (Levitt 2015).

The US Supreme Court's initial involvement with the redistricting process concerned the issue of equal population between districts. The court has also recognized the right of voters to challenge redistricting plans as dilutive of minority voting rights[24] or as unconstitutional partisan gerrymanders.[25] More recently, racial "gerrymanders" have been declared unconstitutional.[26] The result of these decisions has been that American courts play a very prominent role in the redistricting process—the courts have decreed not only how much population variation is too much but also what minority groups, political parties, and communities of interest might expect representation and under what circumstances.

# Redistricting Rules

Rules governing the redistricting process can have a decided effect on how the electoral districts are shaped. These rules include whether seats must first be allocated to territorial units within the country before drawing electoral districts and, if so, by what formula; how often redistricting must be undertaken; what criteria the boundary authority must take into account; and whether the public should have access to the process.

## Constituency Seat Allocation across States or Provinces

Many countries allocate parliamentary seats to territorial units on the basis of population before drawing constituency boundaries within these territorial units. This is especially true in federal systems such as the United States, Canada, and Australia. This allocation process has often produced malapportioned districts, especially when pro-visions are made to guarantee territorial units a specific number of seats regardless of population.

The US Constitution requires the apportionment of seats among the states by pop-ulation but guarantees every state at least one seat. This guarantee, along with a prede-termined number of seats (435), means that state population quotas vary widely from that of the national quota. For example, the range following the 2010 round of redis-tricting was from +39.9 percent (Montana, which is the largest state with only one seat) to −25.8 percent (Rhode Island, which is the smallest state granted more than one seat).

The formula for allocating constituencies to the provinces in Canada is based on a set electoral quota (established by law), but there are additional clauses that guarantee a minimum number of seats to certain provinces.[27] The implementation of these clauses generates a wide disparity in electoral quotas across the ten provinces and three territo-ries of Canada. The redistribution based on the 2011 census and completed in 2013, for example, produced a range in provincial deviations from the national quota of +9.0 per-cent (Alberta) to −64.3 percent (Prince Edward Island).[28]

Until recently, British law guaranteed a minimum number of seats to Scotland (71) and Wales (35), a minimum and maximum number of seats for Northern Ireland (16 to 18), and a total number of seats (613) to Great Britain (England, Wales, and Scotland combined). This meant that England has been underrepresented and Scotland, Wales, and Northern Ireland overrepresented in the House of Commons in the United Kingdom. However, the Scotland Act of 1998 reduced the number of parliamentary seats granted to Scotland, pegging the number of seats awarded to the electoral quota for England. This reduced the overrepresentation of Scotland, relative to England. In the Fifth Periodic Review (2000 to 2007)—the most recent to date—the four countries deviated from the UK electoral quota of 68,175 as follows: England +1.8 percent, Wales −18.4 percent, Scotland −0.7 percent, and Northern Ireland −10.6 percent.[29]

## Frequency of Redistricting

The majority of countries that delimit electoral districts have established some manda-tory time interval within which redistricting must occur. Although there is no standard time period, the range is not particularly large: from every three years (the Seychelles), to every twelve to fourteen years in France, to as much as every twenty years in Nepal.[30]

The most popular choice for periodic delimitation appears to be ten years: Botswana, Japan, Kenya, Lesotho, Malaysia, Mauritius, Mexico, Nigeria, Pakistan, Papua New Guinea, Tanzania, and Yemen all have electoral laws or constitutional provisions requir-ing delimitation at least every ten years (Handley 2008a).[31] The United States and Canada also require redistricting every ten years, following the release of the decennial census.

Bahamas, Fiji, New Zealand, Turkey, and Zimbabwe redraw their electoral districts every five years. Australia delimits at least every seven years. In the United Kingdom, the Parliamentary Constituencies Act of 1986 dictates that redistribution occur every eight to twelve years.[32] Ireland is required to delimit multiseat constituencies for its single transferable vote electoral system every twelve years (Coakley 2008).

The establishment of a mandatory time interval does not necessarily mean that redistricting will occur. Legislatures in a number of countries, including the United States and Canada, refused to redraw district boundaries to preserve their power at a time when the population balance was shifting from rural to urban areas. It required court intervention in the United States and law reform in Canada to prompt the redrawing of the district boundaries. More recently, although the Indian Constitution stipulates that delimitation should occur every ten years following the decennial census, the delimitations that should have occurred in 1981 and 1991 were suspended by a 1976 amendment to the constitution. Following the delimitation initiated after the 2001 census and finally approved by parliament in 2008, redistricting was again suspended, this time until the first census after 2026 (which will be in 2031) (Handley 2015).[33] As a consequence, the interval between the Fourth and Fifth delimitations (2001 to 2031), like the interval between the Third and the Fourth delimitation (1971 to 2001), will be thirty years.

The triggers for redistricting, other than a specified time period, include a national census, a change in the number of seats apportioned to an administrative region, changes in administrative boundaries, and reaching a prescribed level of malapportionment. For example, in Czechia, the prescribed level of malapportionment prompting redistricting is 15 percent; in Germany, the trigger is a 25 percent deviation from the population quota.[34]

## Redistricting Criteria

Countries often identify a set of criteria the boundary authority is obliged to consider when drawing electoral districts. These rules are usually listed in the constitution or electoral law, but they may be the result of court precedents (this is the case in the United States, for example). The rules very often specify that districts should be as equal in population as possible. Other common criteria typically include taking into account administrative and/or natural boundaries and other geographic features such as sparsely populated or isolated territory; respect for communities of interest; and, especially in developing countries, taking into account the means of transportation and/or communication.

### Equal Population

Most countries with single-seat districts that have established formal redistricting criteria require districts to be as equal in population as possible. The population data used to measure equality vary and include total resident population (as enumerated via a national census), the number of registered voters, and, in some European countries with a civil registry, citizen population. There are also variations in how far boundary authorities are permitted to deviate from population equality when constructing constituencies. Countries that have set specific limits to the permissible departure from the population quota have established limits that range from "virtually no deviation allowed" (the United States) to as high as a 30 percent tolerance limit (Singapore).

No other country requires deviations as small as the "one person, one vote" standard that has been imposed by US courts since the early 1960s. In the 1983 court case *Karcher v. Daggett*, the US Supreme Court held that there is no point at which population deviations in a congressional redistricting plan can be considered inconsequential and rejected a New Jersey congressional redistricting plan that had a total population deviation of only 0.7 percent.[35] Following this decision, most states interpreted *Karcher* as requiring the adoption of congressional redistricting plans with exact mathematical population equality. Although the courts later upheld the legality of some redistricting plans that had less than the minimum population variation possible, none of the plans upheld contained total deviations of even 1 percent.[36]

New Zealand and Yemen allow deviations of up to 5 percent from the population quota. Australia,[37] Belarus, Italy, and the Ukraine specify 10 percent as the maximum allowable deviation in the electoral law. Armenia, Germany, and Czechia allow population deviations of no more than 15 percent. Zimbabwe and Papua New Guinea have set the maximum allowable deviation at 20 percent.

In Canada, the independent commissions charged with creating federal electoral districts are allowed to deviate by up to 25 percent from the provincial quotas. But since 1986, commissions have been permitted to exceed the 25 percent limit under "extraordinary circumstances." This provision was used to create five seats in the Canadian House of Commons in 1987, and two seats in 1996, 2003, and 2013.[38]

Although the United Kingdom set a 25 percent limit on deviations from the electoral quota in 1944, this standard was repealed only two years later because the boundary commissions found it impossible to comply with this given the other criteria they were required to meet. In fact, the vast majority of constituencies fell within 25 percent of the electoral quota set for the four constituent countries in the Fifth Periodic Review (the last review to date). Three of the four constituencies that exceeded 25 percent were island communities (the Isle of Wight in England and the Western Isles and Orkney and Shetland in Scotland) that the Boundary Commissions of England and Scotland determined presented special circumstances.

*Geographic Factors*

Perhaps the most common geographic factor listed by countries is consideration for local administrative boundaries. For example, this as a criterion is considered in Bangladesh, Barbados, Botswana, Bulgaria, Cameroon, Canada, Croatia, Czechia, Fiji, France, Germany, India, Indonesia, Italy, Japan, Kenya, Lithuania, Malaysia, Mexico, Pakistan, Panama, Tanzania, Uganda, the United Kingdom, and Yemen (Handley 2008a). Geographic factors also might encompass such features as river valleys and islands, as well as natural barriers like mountain ranges and rivers. The remoteness of a territory and its population density are also sometimes mentioned as factors to consider when delimiting constituency boundaries (e.g., Botswana, Malaysia, Nepal, and the United Kingdom). In Malaysia, the Election Commission is required to weight sparsely populated rural constituencies in a manner to guarantee their overrepresentation in the legislature.

## Communities of Interest

The rationale for recognizing communities of interest in redistricting is the notion that electoral districts should be more than conglomerations of arbitrary, random groups of individuals—they should, as much as possible, be cohesive units with common interests related to representation. This makes a representative's job of articulating the interests of his or her constituency much easier. There are varying instructions to take into account communities of interest. German electoral law states that constituencies should form a "coherent" area. Nepal, Pakistan, and Papua New Guinea electoral laws instruct the boundary authority to consider "community and diversity of interest" or "homogeneity and heterogeneity of the community." Australian electoral law stipulates that the Redistribution Committee shall give due consideration to "community of interests within the proposed Electoral Division, including economic, social and regional interests." A handful of countries offer more explicit instructions as to which communities of interest are particularly pertinent when redistricting. In Hungary, for example, the boundary authority is to take account of ethnic, religious, historical, and other local characteristics when creating electoral districts. Panama and Ukraine also require consideration of minority populations: in Ukraine, the "density of national minority populations" is to be taken into account; in Panama, "concentrations of indigenous populations" must be considered. Without electoral law provisions specifically designed to promote minority representation, however, criteria requiring "due consideration" of the minority population are likely to have little impact on electing minority representatives.

## Minority Representation

In electoral systems that rely at least in part on single-seat districts to elect representatives, racial, ethnic, religious, linguistic, or other minorities are unlikely to be able to elect members of their group to legislative office if the minority population is not sufficiently large and geographically concentrated. However, if the electoral system includes seats that are elected via proportional representation, or nongeographically based seats are specifically reserved for minorities, minority groups may be well represented in the legislature. Drawing districts that will elect minorities is more complicated, but has been done by (1) requiring that candidate slates include minorities, (2) drawing districts that only minority candidates can compete in, or (3) drawing districts to encompass minority concentrations when possible.

In the MNTV vote systems of Singapore and Lebanon, candidate slates must include certain specified minorities. In Singapore, for example, most members of parliament are elected through a "Party Block Vote" in multiseat Group Representative Constituencies

(GRCs) and parties contesting a GRC must propose a slate that includes at least one member of an official minority (listed as Indian, Malay, Eurasian, or Other) (Grace 2006b).

In India, a certain number of parliamentary constituencies in each state are reserved for members of Scheduled Castes and Scheduled Tribes based on their proportion of the total state population. In reserved constituencies, only candidates from these communities can stand for election. Constituency reservations are reassigned after every delimitation.[39]

Fiji and Papua New Guinea, each with Alternative Vote systems, have separate sets of communal seats to guarantee representation of the major ethnic groups. In Fiji, for example, the seventy-one legislative constituencies are composed of forty-six "communal" constituencies (including separate constituencies for indigenous Fijians, Indo-Fijians, and Rotumans) and twenty-five "open" constituencies (where all eligible voters, regardless of race/ethnicity, cast votes), with the most members elected by indigenous Fijians.[40]

A unique feature of New Zealand's electoral system is a provision for representation of the descendants of New Zealand's aboriginal Maori population. In addition to sixty general legislative districts, the Representation Commission creates several Maori districts (five Maori districts were created in 1993, six in 1998, and seven from 2002 to date). These Maori districts are geographically defined and overlay the general electoral districts. To vote in a Maori district, rather than a general election district, a Maori voter must register on the Maori roll (McRobie 2006, 2008).[41] Maoris have been represented in the legislature roughly in proportion to their percentage of the population since this electoral feature was adopted.

The United States, because of its sizeable racial and ethnic minority population and its history of discrimination against certain minority groups, has had to address the issue of fairness to minorities in promulgating redistricting plans. The Voting Rights Act of 1965 and its amendments in 1982 have established that a redistricting plan that dilutes the voting strength of minority voters by dividing the minority community across different districts may be invalid. Protected minority groups (Blacks, Hispanics, Asians, and Native Americans) must meet three preconditions to qualify for protection: the group must be sufficiently large and geographically compact to form a majority in a single-seat district, it must be politically cohesive, and it must be able to demonstrate that the majority population votes as a bloc against the minority community's preferred candidates, who usually lose.[42] If a minority group is able to satisfy all three of these conditions, as well as some additional conditions (relating to the "totality of the circumstances"), a redistricting plan must be fashioned such that minority voters constitute a majority of voters in one or more districts. Because all three of these conditions must be satisfied, and because minority groups must have sufficient resources to sue in court if a jurisdiction fails to create minority districts when these conditions are met,[43] Blacks, Hispanics, Asians, and Native Americans are far from proportionally represented in the US Congress.

## Public Access to the Redistricting Process

Many countries that have reformed their redistricting process by adopting independent redistricting commissions and specifying a set of neutral criteria for redrawing have also incorporated public access provisions. For example, one of the aims of Canada's Electoral Boundaries Redistribution Act of 1964 was to increase the public's awareness of and involvement in the redistribution process. Once the commission has completed its redistricting proposal and published the map in the local newspapers, the general public is invited to present written briefs or oral representations at public hearings held by the commission. Commissions have received thousands of comments from a wide variety of sources including local jurisdictions, political parties, members of and candidates for parliament, political activists, and citizen groups. Redistribution plans have often been revised after these hearings (Courtney 2001).

In Australia, once provisional electoral boundaries have been drawn by the Redistribution Commission, the proposed plan is publicly released and a forty-two-day period commences in which objections and countercomments to the proposed map can be made. The Augmented Electoral Commission (which consists of the Redistribution Committee for the states,[44] plus the two members of the three-member Australian Electoral Commission who were not members of the Redistribution Committee) is then convened to consider these objections and make a final determination on the boundaries. If the Augmented Commission modifies the provisional redistribution plan such that it is "significantly different" from that proposed by the Redistribution Committee, further objections can be lodged, and another public inquiry must be held.

New Zealand has a similar approach to that of Australia. Provisional electoral boundaries are delimited by an independent Representation Commission, and once the plan is released, an inquiry is initiated for objections and counterobjections to be considered. At the conclusion of the public inquiry, the commission adopts a final electoral map. This map is not subject to legislative veto and cannot be challenged in a court of law.

In the United Kingdom, there is a statutory requirement for a public inquiry process if a sufficient number of objections have been received to the boundary commission's provisional recommendations. This local inquiry is chaired by a specially appointed assistant commissioner (almost always a senior lawyer), who invites those who have submitted objections to make oral submissions and answer any questions. The assistant commissioner then prepares a report recommending whether changes should be made to the provisional boundaries. If the boundary commission revises its boundaries, further local inquiries may be conducted, although this is rare.

In postconflict societies such as Liberia and Sierra Leone, extensive public hearings have played an important role in securing stakeholder (e.g., political party leaders and traditional tribal leaders) support for newly drawn or redrawn electoral districts.[45] The hearings helped ensure the credibility of the delimitation process and, ultimately, the legitimacy of the election and its outcome (Handley 2008b).

# CONCLUSION

The importance of the redistricting process varies, depending on the type of electoral system. Because plurality and majority systems rely on single-seat or small multiseat electoral districts, and because these systems produce election outcomes that are disproportional, the redistricting process is of particular importance. Electoral abuses such as malapportioned or gerrymandered districts can have a profound impact on the outcome of an election, and this can be compounded in a postconflict situation.[46]

Most democracies that rely on single-seat districts to elect their legislatures have reformed the redistricting process to remove politics from the process. Thus, even though districts drawn by independent boundary commissions have political consequences, the consequences are viewed by the public and stakeholders in the process as unintentional and therefore noncontroversial. The United States is the sole long-standing democracy that has failed to reform its redistricting process. The result is contentious partisan battles fought in the legislature, in the media, and, ultimately, in the courts.

## NOTES

1. I use the words *redistricting* and *delimitation* interchangeably in this chapter. My discussion of the redistribution process relies on Rossiter et al. (1999) and Johnston et al. (2006, 2008, 2011) for the United Kingdom; Courtney (2001, 2008) for Canada; Medew (2008), Maley (2006), and Maley et al. (1996) for Australia; and McRobie (2006, 2008) for New Zealand. My discussion on delimitation in India relies on McMillan (2008), as well as many of the chapters in Alam and Sivaramakrishnan (2015).
2. The importance of redistricting in mixed-member systems that do not include compensatory seats depends on the proportion of seats allocated to the nominal component—the higher the proportion of single-seat district seats to seats elected via proportional representation is, the more important the role of redistricting.
3. In this discussion of redistricting practices, I have relied heavily on some of my earlier work, including Handley (1998, 2006a, 2006b, 2008a, 2008b, 2015, 2016). In addition, I have been involved in election-related projects on behalf of the International Foundation for Electoral Systems (IFES) and the United Nations in dozens of countries and thus have firsthand knowledge of redistricting practices in such countries as Bangladesh, Botswana, Georgia, Ghana, Haiti, Kenya, Lebanon, Liberia, Malaysia, Myanmar, Nepal, Nigeria, Sierra Leone, Sudan, and Yemen.
4. Malapportioned districts are districts that vary substantially in population. This is usually measured as the deviation from the population or electoral quota. (The population quota is the average population of all of the electoral districts and is obtained by dividing the total population of the territory to be redistricted by the number of districts to be drawn. In the case of multiseat districts, it is the total population divided by the number of representatives to be elected.) Malapportionment does not have to be passive—it can be active or systemic. Passive malapportionment occurs when the electoral boundaries are simply

not redrawn for a long period of time. In the United States, for example, a number of states neglected to redraw legislative boundaries for decades prior to the 1960s because new district boundaries would shift power away from the rural areas to the rapidly growing urban areas. Active malapportionment occurs when the boundary authority makes a conscious effort to draw constituencies that vary substantially in population. In Malaysia, for example, the constitution decrees that rural constituencies be underpopulated and it falls to the election commission to determine whether a constituency is rural or urban and how much rural constituencies should be underpopulated and urban constituencies overpopulated. Because ethnic Malays predominate in the rural areas and nonethnic Malays reside primarily in the urban centers, this "rural weightage" has guaranteed Malay dominance of the political system (Grace 2006a). Systemic malapportionment exists when administrative units serve as single-seat electoral districts despite large differences in population. In the Republic of Georgia, for instance, *rayons* (administrative units) have been used as single-seat constituencies in the unicameral legislature despite dramatic variations in population (Handley 2006a).

5. Under plurality and majority systems, nonmajority political parties whose supporters are not geographically concentrated usually obtain fewer legislative seats than their proportion of the vote would suggest they are entitled to.

6. If electoral districts are used in a party list system, they are usually large multiseat districts whose boundaries tend to correspond to administrative divisions such as states or provinces. To accommodate shifts in population, the number of seats allocated to each of the multiseat districts is adjusted, rather than redrawing the district boundaries.

7. Ireland elects three to five members of parliament per constituency (Coakley 2008); Malta has five-seat constituencies.

8. Please see the chapter by Gallagher and Mitchell in this volume for further information.

9. In New Zealand, Australia, and India, for example, the plan produced by the boundary commission is final—no vote by parliament is required to enact or implement the new boundaries. In Canada, parliament can consider plans produced by the commissions (each province has its own boundary commission), but it has no vote on their implementation. In the United Kingdom, the final proposals of the four boundary commissions (England, Scotland, Wales, and Northern Ireland) take effect only after an affirmative vote by Parliament, but Parliament's power to accept or reject a plan is essentially a formality—it has almost always affirmed commission proposals.

10. New Zealand is an exception to the rule that politicians cannot serve on the boundary commission. Two political appointees, one representing the governing party and the other representing the opposition parties, serve on the seven-member Representation Commission tasked with redistricting the country. The rationale for including them on the commission is to ensure that any noticeable political bias in a proposed constituency boundary plan is recognized and rectified. Because the two political appointees form only a minority of the commission and cannot outvote the nonpolitical commissioners, the neutrality of the commission remains unquestioned (McRobie 2008).

11. Election observer and human rights reports cite a number of examples of election commissions that are not independent. See, for example, the following reports on Nigeria: European Election Observation Mission to Nigeria (2003), Third Preliminary Statement, Abuja, May 5, 2003, at http://ec.europa.eu/comm/external_relations/human_rights/eu_election _ass_observ/nigeria/3stat2.ht; and https://www.hrw.org/legacy/backgrounder/africa

/nigeria0407/nigeria0407web.pdf. For Pakistan, see, for example, https://www.hrw.org /news/2008/02/12/pakistan-election-commission-not-impartial.

12. Seven states have only one congressional district and therefore do not require the redraw-ing of congressional boundaries. Of the remaining forty-three states, thirty-six assigned the task of congressional redistricting to the state legislature).

13. Partisan gerrymandering has been a feature of redistricting in the United States since at least 1812, when the governor of Massachusetts, Elbridge Gerry, signed into law the salamander-shaped district designed to help his party that gave the "gerrymander" its name.

14. The Australian Commonwealth Electoral Act of 1918 stipulates that decisions made by any of the bodies responsible for constituency delimitation are final and are not subject to court consideration except on limited constitutional grounds.

15. Lujambio and Vives 2008 (Mexico), Frankel 2008 (Fiji), and Grace 2006b (Singapore).

16. *R v. Boundary Comm'n for Eng.* ex parte *Foot* (1983 W.L.R. 484) as discussed in Rossiter et al. (1999).

17. Also see *Malaysia's Many Scandals, New York Times*, August 20, 2015.

18. "*Le Conseil constitutionnel valide le redécoupage législatif*," *L'Express*, February 18, 2010, http://www.lexpress.fr/region/le-conseil-constitutionnel-valide-le-redecoupage-legislatif_849865.html.

19. *Dixon v. British Columbia (Att'y Gen.l)* Vancouver Registry No. A860246 [1986] B.C.J. No. 916 (Can.).

20. *Reference re Prov. Electoral Boundaries (Sask.)*, 1991 2 S.C.R. 158, http://scc-csc.lexum.com /scc-csc/scc-csc/en/item/766/index.do (Can.).

21. A redistribution plan drawn for electing representatives to the federal parliament was struck down for the first, and thus far only, time in 2004 in the province of New Brunswick. Prior to this, the only electoral maps rejected by the courts were maps for provincial legis-lative districts. To produce ridings (electoral districts) that were more equal in population, the New Brunswick Federal Electoral Boundaries Commission transferred portions of two French-speaking parishes into a majority English-speaking riding (electoral district). Residents of the French-speaking parishes that had been divided objected and filed suit, contending that the changes violated their interests as a community. The Federal Court of Canada, in *Raiche* v. *Canada (Attorney General)*, found for the plaintiffs, holding that they were being denied effective representation in their new riding. *Raiche v. Canada (Att'y Gen.)*, (F.C.), 2004 FC 679, [2005] 1 F.C.R. 93, (Can.).

22. *MacKinnon v Prince Edward Island*, 1993 101 D.L.R. (4th), 362, (Can.), http://www.gov .pe.ca/courts/supreme/reasons/ad725.pdf.

23. *Baker v. Carr*, 369 U.S. 186 (1962). Prior to this decision, US courts decreed that redistrict-ing was a political question best resolved by Congress and the state legislatures.

24. In *Thornburg v. Gingles*, 478 U.S. 30 (1986), the US Supreme Court was asked to consider the 1982 Amendments to the Voting Rights Act of 1965. (The Voting Rights Act of 1965 was designed to prevent the abridgement of the voting rights of minority voters and was amended in 1982 to make it clear that redistricting plans that had the effect of diluting minority voting strength were illegal.) The court ruled in *Gingles* that to succeed, minority voters have to satisfy three preconditions: the minority group must be sufficiently large and geographically compact to constitute a majority in a single-seat district, the minor-ity group must be politically cohesive, and the white majority must vote sufficiently as a bloc to defeat the minority group's preferred candidates. If plaintiffs can demonstrate

these factors, a district that provides minorities with an opportunity to elect candidates of choice must be drawn. This led to a substantial increase in the number of "majority-minority" districts and to an increase in the number of minority representatives elected to office. (See, e.g., Lublin et al. 2009.)

25. In *Davis v. Bandemer*, 478 U.S. 109 (1986), the US Supreme Court ruled that a redistricting plan that discriminates against an identifiable political group or party may violate the US Constitution. However, the court, recognizing the highly partisan nature of the American redistricting process, imposed a very difficult burden on voters who make such a claim. Despite a number of challenges, to date no congressional or state legislative redistricting plan has been rejected by the court on the grounds that it is an unconstitutional partisan gerrymander.

26. In *Shaw v. Reno*, 509 U.S. 630 (1993), the US Supreme Court ruled that voters could challenge "majority-minority" districts drawn on the basis of race. If voters can prove that race was the predominant motivating factor in the drawing of particular districts, the jurisdiction must show that the challenged districts were "narrowly tailored to further a compelling state interest." The immediate effect of *Shaw* and subsequent cases brought on these grounds has been to require the redrawing of a number of majority black and Hispanic districts.

27. For example, the "senatorial" clause guarantees that no province shall have fewer seats in the House of Commons than it does in the Senate, and the "grandfather" clause guarantees that no province shall have fewer seats in the House of Commons than it had in 1985.

28. These calculations are based on the provincial populations and seat allocations found at on the Elections Canada website: http://www.elections.ca/content.aspx?section=res&dir=cir/red/form&document=index&lang=e.

29. The sources for the electorate data for the four countries are as follows: Boundary Commission for England, *Fifth Periodic Report* (2007); Boundary Commission for Wales, *Fifth Periodic Report on Parliamentary Constituencies and First Report on National Assembly for Wales Electoral Regions* (2005); Boundary Commission for Scotland, *Fifth Periodic Report of the Boundary Commission of Scotland* (2004); and Boundary Commission for Northern Ireland, *Fifth Periodic Report on Parliamentary Constituencies* (2008). The electorates are not in fact directly comparable in time. The electoral quota is established using the electorate on the electoral roll at the commencement of the redistribution for each specific country, and these reviews do not begin simultaneously. The fifth periodic review began in England in February 2000 (and was approved in June 2007), in Scotland in June 2001 (approved February 2005), in Wales in December 2002 (approved April 2006), and in Northern Ireland in May 2003 (approved June 2008).

30. Constitution of Nepal 2015. Unofficial translation by Nepal Law Society, International IDEA and UNDP.

31. In the case of Botswana, the requirement is every five to ten years; in Kenya, the law dictates that delimitation occur every eight to ten years.

32. In 2011, legislation was passed in the United Kingdom (Fixed Term Parliament Act and the Parliamentary Voting System and Constituency Act) that established a new set of rules for redistribution, including a requirement to redraw constituencies every five years, rather than every eight to twelve years (Johnston et al. 2011). Redistribution under these new rules commenced in 2011 and provisional constituencies were completed for all four countries (England, Scotland, Wales, and Northern Ireland) by late 2012. However, in January 2013, Parliament amended the law and aborted the redistribution exercise until after the

2015 general election. As a consequence, the 2015 general election was conducted using constituencies drawn using electorate data that was as much as fifteen years old. The four boundary commissions recommenced the review process in 2016.

33. The 2008 delimitation was limited to equalizing the populations across constituencies within each state; there was no reallocation of parliamentary seats across states on the basis of population.

34. In Germany, proposed electoral districts cannot deviate by more than 15 percent, and districts that deviate by more than 25 percent must be redrawn (Schrott 2006).

35. *Karcher v. Daggett*, 462 U.S. 725 (1983).

36. The total population deviation is the percent deviation of the largest and smallest districts added together.

37. The population requirement in Australia is actually more complicated than a 10 percent tolerance limit: Australian election law also requires that electoral districts deviate by no more than 3.5 percent, three years and six months after the expected completion of the redistribution. This criterion was adopted to avoid wide discrepancies at the end of the seven-year redistribution cycle (Maley 2006). Australia's close attention to population equality is relatively recent. Thirty years ago, the practice of drawing rural districts that were much smaller in population than urban districts was very common.

38. This information is found on the following website: http://www.redecoupage-federal-redistribution.ca/content.asp?document=home.

39. The number of Scheduled Caste seats increased from 79 to 84 and the number of Scheduled Tribe seats increased from 41 to 47 (out a total of 545 seats) from the Third (1976) to the Fourth (2008) Delimitation (Handley 2015).

40. Frankel 2008.

41. Registration on the Maori roll is optional; Maoris can choose to register on the general roll instead.

42. *Thornburg v. Gingles,* 478 U.S. 30 (1986).

43. In addition, if the court is persuaded that race was the "predominate motivating factor" in the drawing of a district, the jurisdiction must show that the district boundaries were "narrowly tailored to further a compelling state interest." *Shaw v. Reno,* 509 U.S. 630 (1993). Although compliance with the Voting Rights Act may be a compelling state interest, what a narrowly tailored district might be is open to interpretation.

44. The four-member Redistribution Commission is composed of the Electoral Commission of the Australian Electoral Commission, as well as the Australian Electoral Officer, Surveyor-General, and Auditor-General of the state being redistricted.

45. The author provided technical assistance with redistricting on behalf of United Nations Development Programme (UNDP) in both of these countries: Liberia in 2005 and 2010 and Sierra Leone in 2005–2008 and again in 2016.

46. In conflict-ridden Nigeria, for example, a redistricting dispute led to the outbreak of violence in the town of Warri in the Niger Delta region in 2003. Two tribes, the Urhobos and Ijaws, contended that the local election constituencies unfairly favored another tribal group, the Iteskiri, at the expense of their own communities. Several people were killed and over 1,600 people were displaced in the skirmishes that followed. The army was deployed to the region and the Niger Delta governor had to promise to redistrict the area ahead of presidential and national elections to quell the conflict (Handley 2006b; *Violence in Nigeria Oil Delta Threatens to Disrupt Elections, Wall Street Journal*, April 1, 2003).

# REFERENCES

Alam, Mohd. Sanjeer, and K. C. Sivaramakrishnan, eds. *Fixing Electoral Boundaries in India*. New Delhi, India: Oxford University Press, 2015.

Balinksi, Michel. "Redistricting in France under Changing Electoral Rules." In *Redistricting in Comparative Perspective*, edited by Lisa Handley and Bernard Grofman, 173–190. Oxford, UK: Oxford University Press, 2008.

Coakley, John. "Electoral Districting in Ireland." in *Redistricting in Comparative Perspective*, edited by Lisa Handley and Bernard Grofman, 155–172. Oxford, UK: Oxford University Press, 2008.

Courtney, John. *Commissioned Ridings: Designing Canada's Electoral Districts*. Montreal: McGill-Queen's University Press, 2001.

Courtney, John. "From Gerrymandering to Independence: District Boundary Readjustments in Canada." In *Redistricting in Comparative Perspective*, edited by Lisa Handley and Bernard Grofman, 11–26. Oxford, UK: Oxford University Press, 2008.

Frankel, Jon. "The Design of Ethnically Mixed Constituencies in Fiji, 1970-2006." In *Redistricting in Comparative Perspective*, edited by Lisa Handley and Bernard Grofman, 123–139. Oxford, UK: Oxford University Press, 2008.

Grace, Jeremy. "Malaysia: Malapportioned Districts and Over-Representation of Rural Communities." In *Delimitation Equity Project: Resource Guide*, edited by Lisa Handley, 285–295. Washington, DC: IFES and USAID, 2006a.

Grace, Jeremy. "Singapore: Drawing Districts to Ensure Super-Majorities in Parliament." In *Delimitation Equity Project: Resource Guide*, edited by Lisa Handley, 319–333. Washington, DC: IFES and USAID, 2006b.

Handley, Lisa. "Boundary Delimitation." Topic area for the online ACE Electoral Knowledge Encyclopedia. UN, IFES, and International IDEA, 1998. http://aceproject.org/ace-en/topics/bd/default.

Handley, Lisa. "Constituency Delimitation in Georgia." In *Delimitation Equity Project: Resource Guide*, edited by Lisa Handley, 87–107. Washington, DC: IFES and USAID, 2006a.

Handley, Lisa. "Constituency Delimitation in Nigeria." In *Delimitation Equity Project: Resource Guide*, edited by Lisa Handley, 111–128. Washington, DC: IFES and USAID, 2006b.

Handley, Lisa. "A Comparative Survey of Structures and Criteria for Boundary Delimitation." In *Redistricting in Comparative Perspective*, edited by Lisa Handley and Bernard Grofman, 265–305. Oxford, UK: Oxford University Press, 2008a.

Handley, Lisa. "Delimiting Electoral Boundaries in Post-Conflict Settings." In *Redistricting in Comparative Perspective*, edited by Lisa Handley and Bernard Grofman, 191–202. Oxford, UK: Oxford University Press, 2008b.

Handley, Lisa. "One Person, One Vote, Different Values: Comparing Delimitation Practices in India, Canada, the United Kingdom and the United States." In *Fixing Electoral Boundaries in India*, edited by Mohd. Sanjeer Alam and K. C. Sivaramakrishnan, 88–111. New Delhi, India: Oxford University Press, 2015.

Handley, Lisa. "The Role of the Courts in Delimitation." In *International Election Remedies*, edited by John Hardin Young, 219–235. Chicago: American Bar Association Book Publishing, 2016.

Handley, Lisa, and Bernard Grofman, eds. *Redistricting in Comparative Perspective*. Oxford, UK: Oxford University Press, 2008.

Hasebe, Yasuo. "The Supreme Court of Japan: Its Adjudication on Electoral Systems and Economic Freedoms." *International Journal on Constitutional Law* 5 (2007): 2.

Johnston, Ron, Charles Pattie, and David Rossiter. "Electoral Distortion Despite Redistricting by Independent Commission: The British Case, 1950-2005." In *Redistricting in Comparative Perspective*, edited by Lisa Handley and Bernard Grofman, 205–224. Oxford, UK: Oxford University Press, 2008.

Johnston, Ron, David Rossiter, and Charles Pattie. "The United Kingdom Redistribution Process." In *Delimitation Equity Project: Resource Guide*, edited by Lisa Handley, 337–343. Washington, DC: IFES and USAID, 2006.

Johnston, Ron, David Rossiter, and Charles Pattie. "Boundary Delimitation Case Study: Redistribution in the United Kingdom." Online ACE Electoral Knowledge Encyclopedia. UN, IFES, and International IDEA, 2011. http://aceproject.org/ace-en/topics /bd/default.

Levitt, Justin. "All About Redistricting." 2015. http://redistricting.lls.edu/who.php.

Lublin, David, Thomas Brunell, Bernard Grofman, and Lisa Handley. "Has the Voting Rights Act Outlived Its Usefulness: In a Word, No." *Legislative Studies Quarterly* 35 (2009): 4.

Lujambio, Alonso, and Horacio Vives. "From Politics to Technicalities: Mexican Redistricting in Historical Perspective." In *Redistricting in Comparative Perspective*, edited by Lisa Handley and Bernard Grofman, 43–54. Oxford, UK: Oxford University Press, 2008.

Maley, Michael. "Australia: Using Projections to Equalize Electoral District Populations." In *Delimitation Equity Project: Resource Guide*, edited by Lisa Handley, 171–179. Washington, DC: IFES and USAID, 2006.

Maley, Michael, Trevor Morling, and Robin Bell. "Alternative Ways of Redistricting with Single-Member Seats: The Case in Australia." In *Fixing the Boundaries: Defining and Redefining Single-Member Electoral Districts*, edited by Iain McLean and David Butler, 119–145. Aldershot, UK: Dartmouth Publishing, 1996.

McMillan, Alistair. "Delimitation in India." In *Redistricting in Comparative Perspective*, edited by Lisa Handley and Bernard Grofman, 75–95. Oxford, UK: Oxford University Press, 2008.

McRobie, Alan. "Delimitation in New Zealand." In *Delimitation Equity Project: Resource Guide*, edited by Lisa Handley, 299–315. Washington, DC: IFES and USAID, 2006.

McRobie, Alan. "An Independent Commission with Political Input: New Zealand's Electoral Redistribution Practices." In *Redistricting in Comparative Perspective*, edited by Lisa Handley and Bernard Grofman, 27–42. Oxford, UK: Oxford University Press, 2008.

Medew, Rod. "Redistribution in Australia: The Importance of One Vote, One Value." In *Redistricting in Comparative Perspective*, edited by Lisa Handley and Bernard Grofman, 97–105. Oxford, UK: Oxford University Press, 2008.

Moriwaki, Toshimasha. "The Politics of Redistricting in Japan: A Contradiction between Equal Population and Respect for Local Government Boundaries." In *Redistricting in Comparative Perspective*, edited by Lisa Handley and Bernard Grofman, 107–112. Oxford, UK: Oxford University Press, 2008.

Rossiter, D. J., R. J. Johnston, and C. J. Pattie. *The Boundary Commissions: Redrawing the UK's map of Parliamentary Constituencies*. Manchester, UK: Manchester University Press, 1999.

Schrott, Peter. "Delimitation in Germany." In *Delimitation Equity Project: Resource Guide*, edited by Lisa Handley, 245–260. Washington, DC: IFES and USAID, 2006.

CHAPTER 26

....................................................................................

# ELECTORAL
# SYSTEMS AND
# CAMPAIGN FINANCE

....................................................................................

## JOEL W. JOHNSON

STUDIES that emphasize the importance of legislative electoral systems for campaign finance mostly fit into one of two groups. One literature focuses on how systems like open-list proportional representation (OLPR) and the single nontransferable vote (SNTV)—which fragment the vote at the subparty level and reward candidates who cultivate a personalized base of electoral support—increase the importance of money for electoral success and motivate heavy campaign spending (Cox and Thies 1998, 2000). To help satisfy legislators' demand for funds, the legislature may supply ample amounts of pork and particularistic policy (Cox and McCubbins 2001; Samuels 2002; Rosenbluth and Thies 2010). Also, the high demand for funds may fuel political corruption (Chang 2005; Pereira, Rennó, and Samuels 2011; Johnson 2015).

The second literature extends the debate among scholars of American politics about whether incumbents and challengers obtain significantly different "spending effects"—that is, vote-share gains per unit of expenditure. This literature focuses on electoral systems that, like OLPR and SNTV, use multiseat districts and allow a candidate-level vote (see Cox and Thies 2000, Samuels 2001b, Maddens et al. 2006, Benoit and Marsh 2010, and Johnson 2013, as well as Palda and Palda 1998 and Sudulich, Wall, and Farrell 2013). Spending effects have not been estimated for closed-list proportional representation (CLPR) systems because of data limitations. In countries that use CLPR, parties' campaign expenditures, *if* they are publicly disclosed, tend to be specified only at the national level.[1] That provides a small number of observations per election—too few to estimate spending effects.

Both literatures are populated mostly by single-country studies; however, nearly every study emphasizes its importance for system-level comparisons (i.e., across electoral systems). At the same time, both literatures pay some attention to how electoral systems affect campaign financing at the candidate or district level. For example, spending-effects studies consider the likelihood of the "Jacobson effect," which is a *negative* correlation between incumbents' spending and their vote shares.[2] It is widely believed that this occurs not because incumbents' spending hurts their standing with voters, but because incumbents spend reactively, in response to their perceived likelihood of defeat. Put differently, while some incumbents run in favorable districts and can win comfortably despite spending little, others spend heavily in an effort to fend off competitive challengers. And, although campaign spending helps in both cases, it does not turn competitive contests into blowout victories. Thus, the cross-incumbent correlation between spending and votes is negative, not positive.

A similar phenomenon may explain spending-votes relationships for challengers. In particular, a strongly positive relationship between spending and votes may reflect not the effectiveness of challengers' spending but rather a difference in fundraising ability between long-shot challengers, whose nonviability makes them poorly financed, and competitive challengers, whose viability allows them to attract money.

Spending-effects studies attend to these possibilities to properly estimate the effect of spending on votes. However, they still may be missing much about how campaign finance varies with individual prospects and district-level variables, including district magnitude (M). This chapter discusses two such topics. First, it considers the possibility of a campaign spending "M + 1 rule," which anticipates that campaign finance is (often) concentrated on only M + 1 competitors per district. Then, in section two, it examines how district magnitude may influence, via either demand-side or supply-side forces, patterns of incumbent spending and the likelihood of the Jacobson effect. Subsequently, sections three and four consider the consequences of intraparty competition, first at the candidate level and then at the system level. A final section concludes.

The literature on comparative political finance is much broader than what is reviewed here and includes analyses of campaign finance regulations, campaign finance reforms, and state subsidies for political parties (for an overview, see Scarrow 2007). On those topics there are a few works that emphasize electoral systems, such as Johnson's (2008) analysis of disclosure regulations and van Biezen's (2010) illustration that public funding for political parties is less common in countries with majoritarian electoral systems than in countries with proportional representation (PR). On the whole, however, those literatures pay little attention to legislative electoral systems. For that reason, they are not reviewed here.

# An M + 1 Rule?

It is well understood that electoral systems place a conditional upper bound on the number of viable competitors in a district (Reed 1990; Cox 1997). In particular, when parties fear nominating too many candidates and thus fragmenting their vote and losing winnable seats to their opponents, their collective efforts to coordinate entry often result in there being no more than M + 1 competitors in a district. And, when coordination fails and more than M + 1 competitors enter a race, coordination among voters (in the form of strategic abandonment of trailing candidates) may concentrate votes on only M + 1 competitors (Cox 1999, 160). As Cox (1997) explains, one of the key conditions for strategic voting is the existence of good, publicly available information about candidates' relative chances. If it is unclear which candidates are among the top M + 1, then strategic abandonment of trailing candidates will not occur—a situation that Cox called a "non-Duvergerian equilibrium." Cox found that "Duvergerian equilibria" (in which strategic voting concentrates votes on M + 1 competitors) are common in districts with magnitudes up to about five. In M > 5 districts, electoral coordination is challenged by the increasing difficulty of predicting which candidates are likely to be the top M + 1.

Expectations about candidates' relative prospects can also influence campaign fundraising and yield a mix of "Duvergerian" and "non-Duvergerian" spending patterns in low-magnitude districts, with the former consisting of a marked spending gap between the top M + 1 candidates and all other candidates. To explore this possibility, consider a simple three-period model of a plurality-rule election. First, an entry stage determines how many candidates contest the election and establishes expectations among elites about candidates' relative prospects. Second, a financing stage occurs in which suppliers of campaign donations, who seek to "make their money count," donate to viable candidates. To simplify matters, assume that all viable candidates are well funded and that no other candidates are funded such that (1) the number of funded candidates equals the number of viable candidates and (2) there is a stark financial difference between viable and nonviable candidates. The third stage is a campaigning period that ends with the election. During the campaign we allow expectations about candidates' relative prospects to change, but not dramatically. More specifically, none of the unfunded candidates can emerge as competitive, though to allow strategic voting some viable candidates may come to be seen as trailing the top M + 1 candidates. It follows that (hypothesis 1:) when spending is Duvergerian, votes will also be Duvergerian, and (hypothesis 2:) when spending is non-Duvergerian, votes may be either Duvergerian or non-Duvergerian, depending on whether strategic voting winnows the support for a candidate who was initially considered viable. Put differently, the distribution of spending mirrors the outcome of the entry coordination game, and votes are concentrated on the same or fewer candidates, depending on whether strategic voting occurs.

Of course, under more permissive assumptions many more patterns can emerge, and the connections between expectations, spending, and votes become muddled. For example, if election results can deviate more widely from initial expectations or if some long-shot candidates are able to raise and spend considerable sums of money— perhaps because challenger spending may occasionally have large positive "effects"— then spending patterns may bear little resemblance to electoral results and may rarely be Duvergerian.

With such considerations in mind, we turn to examine some data, first from Canada and then from Ireland.

## Evidence from a First-Past-the-Post System: Canada's 2011 and 2015 Elections

Figure 26.1 shows Cox's SF ratio and a similarly constructed "DS ratio" for "close" districts in Canada's federal election of 2011. Cox's SF ratio is the ratio of the *second* loser's vote to the *first* loser's vote, and a bimodal distribution of the ratio serves as aggregate evidence of the two strategic voting equilibria (see Cox 1997, chap. 4). The Duvergerian spending (DS) ratio is similar, except that candidates are ordered and compared according to their spending, not their votes. So, for an M = 1 district, the ratio is spending by the third-highest spender divided by spending by the second-highest spender. "Close" districts are those in which the winner's margin of victory was less than 10 percent of the vote.

Notice three main things about Figure 26.1:

1. The DS ratio has a bimodal distribution (see top-left histogram), which suggests two distinct tendencies. The Duvergerian pattern predominates—in more than 50 percent of close districts, the DS ratio is less than .25. This is striking given Canada's public financing system, which provides campaign-spending reimbursements to candidates who receive at least 10 percent of the vote.[3] Meanwhile, using DS greater than .70 as an indicator, we observe that 20 percent of close districts exhibit a non-Duvergerian spending pattern.
2. The SF ratio for districts with non-Duvergerian spending patterns is bimodal (top-right histogram), which is anticipated by hypothesis 2.
3. The SF ratio for districts with DS less than .70 (bottom-right histogram) provides mixed support for hypothesis 1. On the one hand, the distribution is much less bimodal than the histogram above it, as predicted. On the other hand, there is a nontrivial number of close three-way races that include a poorly funded candidate. (The frequency of low-DS/high-SF districts is related to the unprecedented success of the New Democratic Party in the 2011 elections. In nearly every low-DS/high-SF district, a poorly funded New Democratic Party candidate was among the top three vote winners.)

Figure 26.2 provides similar data for the 2015 elections. In three ways, the data are similar to 2011: (1) the DS ratio is bimodal; (2) districts that have Duvergerian spending patterns are more likely to have Duvergerian vote patterns, as anticipated; and (3) the bottom-right panel suggests that a nontrivial number of close three-way races included a poorly funded candidate, contra hypothesis 1. The main contrast with figure 1 is in the top-right histogram: in the 2015 data there is no pronounced SF bimodalism among districts with non-Duvergerian spending patterns. There are some reasons the 2015 elections might have exhibited below-normal levels of strategic voting. One is that polls predicted a close three-way race at the national level. A second was related to the Fair Representation Act of 2011, which added thirty seats to parliament and redistricted many other districts. In many districts, therefore, electoral outcomes might have been difficult to foresee.[4]

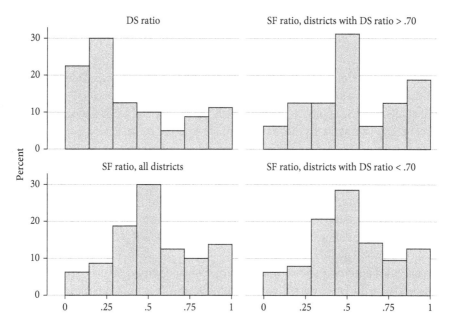

**FIGURE 26.1.** Distributions of SF ratios and DS ratios, close districts in Canada's 2011 federal elections.

Source: Author's calculations. Campaign finance data are from ElectionsCanada.org.

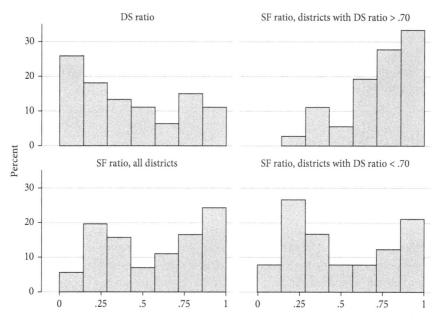

**FIGURE 26.2.** Distributions of SF ratios and DS ratios, close districts in Canada's 2015 federal elections.

Source: Author's calculations. Campaign finance data are from ElectionsCanada.org.

## District Magnitude Variation: Patterns in Irish Elections

Irish Dáil elections are worth examining in this context because district magnitudes vary from three to five. However, Dáil elections are not poised to produce Duvergerian patterns with either votes or spending. For one, the single-transferable vote (STV) electoral system challenges the ability to predict which candidates will be in the running for the last seat because it fragments the first preference vote and because results are contingent upon how votes will transfer among candidates during the count. Also, Ireland's system of public financing encourages likely losers to spend more than they otherwise might. The subsidy system provides a €8,700 reimbursement of campaign costs—equivalent to between one-third and one-quarter of candidates' legal limits on spending (which vary with M)—for any candidate who receives at least one-quarter of the district's vote quota at some stage of the count. Even candidates who rank as low as M + 3 by first-preference votes almost always qualify for the subsidy.

Regardless, figure 26.3 shows that Duvergerian spending patterns occur, that they are associated with Duvergerian voting patterns, and that both are more common in low-magnitude districts. The figure shows for each electoral district the SF ratio and campaign spending in excess of the subsidy by two candidates: those ranked M + 1 and M + 2 by spending (i.e., the two candidates used in the DS ratio). In this presentation, Duvergerian spending patterns are associated with large spending gaps, shown by long vertical lines. Notice the following about figure 26.3. First, Duvergerian spending patterns are associated with Duvergerian vote patterns. And, while it is rare for either candidate to spend less than the subsidy amount, the lower spender occasionally did so and those instances are associated with Duvergerian voting patterns. In other words, the data support hypothesis 1. Second, small spending gaps are accompanied by a wide range of SF ratios, as predicted by hypothesis 2. And third, both Duvergerian spending patterns and Duvergerian voting patterns dissipate with M.

## Implications and Next Steps

In short, Canadian and Irish elections provide evidence that (1) in small-magnitude districts campaign spending often concentrates on M + 1 candidates and (2) the within-district distributions of spending and votes are consistent with familiar models of strategic entry and strategic voting. That understanding of campaign financing suggests a strong relationship between candidates' expected performance and the amount of money that they spend on their campaigns. It also raises a question of how to conceptualize and model "spending effects" in a way that accounts for strategic voting, which has the effect of reducing the votes of trailing candidates and increasing votes for candidates in the top M + 1. This question is relevant because spending effects are normally understood as linear (i.e., each unit of expenditure buys the same number of votes) rather than contingent on whether conditions favor strategic voting or not.

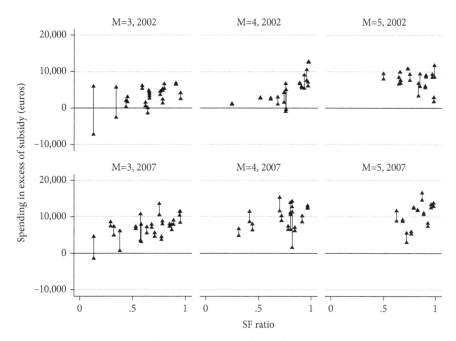

FIGURE 26.3. Campaign spending by M + 1-ranked spender and M + 2-ranked spender in Dáil elections, by SF ratio and district magnitude (2002 and 2007 elections).

Notes: The figure shows for each electoral district (1) SF ratio, (2) campaign spending in excess of the subsidy (€8700) by the M + 1-ranked spender, and (3) campaign spending in excess of the subsidy (€8700) by the M + 2-ranked spender. Same-district competitors are linked with vertical lines to highlight the spending differences.

Source: Author's calculation. Campaign finance data are from the Standards in Public Office Commission (http://www.sipo.gov.ie/).

The analysis offered here is merely a first step. Future analyses should seek to (1) identify how often spending and votes are concentrated on the *same* M + 1 competitors; (2) control for candidates' party affiliations; (3) investigate how often non-Duvergerian spending patterns are the result of coordination failures versus attempts to turn long-shot, nonviable competitors into "real" competitors; and (4) improve upon the expectations-driven model of campaign financing.

# MARGINALITY, SPENDING, AND THE JACOBSON EFFECT

While the M + 1 rule is a within-district pattern driven by supply, the Jacobson effect is an across-incumbent pattern driven by demand. However, the pattern is contingent on both demand and supply: it requires sufficient demand-side variation (i.e., a nontrivial number of electorally secure incumbents), and the supply of campaign finance must accommodate marginal incumbents' high demand. In other electoral systems these two conditions may exist infrequently.

## Running Scared in Multiseat Districts

In electoral systems that use multiseat districts, in which the vote is inevitably fragmented among many candidates, non-Jacobsonian patterns of incumbent spending may occur because too few incumbents feel secure in their re-election prospects. In their analysis of spending effects in Japan's SNTV system, which was used to fill the lower house of parliament from 1948 through 1993, Cox and Thies (2000) take this idea one step further to hypothesize that the probability of a Jacobson correlation diminishes with district magnitude as the vote becomes more fragmented and the outcome less predictable. Though Cox and Thies limit their attention to the Jacobson effect, their argument also implies that average incumbent spending will be greater in larger-magnitude districts, other things being equal.

Cox and Thies (2000, 41–42) find that Jacobson correlations are indeed less frequent in larger-magnitude SNTV districts, and table 26.1 suggests a similar tendency among major-party incumbents in recent Irish elections.[5] It is perhaps not surprising that there is a mixture of negative and positive spending-votes (SV) correlations among Dáil members. On the one hand, members are likely to perceive different levels of insecurity and spend reactively (cf. Benoit and Marsh 2010, 163). On the other hand, STV may breed widespread insecurity—especially in larger-magnitude districts—because of vote fragmentation and vote transfers.

Cox and Thies's hypothesis has not been investigated further, but to do so requires accounting for the fact that larger-magnitude districts tend to feature more incumbents per district-party. For example, in the data reported in table 1, one-third of the M = 5 districts have more than one Fine Gael incumbent, but the same occurs in only 6 percent

**Table 26.1  Spending–Vote Share Correlations for Major-Party Dáil Members, 2002 and 2007 Elections**

|  | 2002 | | | 2007 | | |
|---|---|---|---|---|---|---|
|  | Fianna Fáil | Fine Gael | Labour | Fianna Fáil | Fine Gael | Labour |
| M = 3 districts | −.06 (18) | .35 (13) | −.09 (7) | −.39 (29) | .65 (12) | −.12 (5) |
| M = 4 districts | .37 (20) | .25 (15) | −.25 (6) | .05 (19) | −.01 (8) | .25 (7) |
| M = 5 districts | .49 (29) | .26 (18) | .16 (6) | .05 (20) | −.33 (12) | −.14 (6) |

*Notes:* Cell entries are the Pearson correlations. The number of observations is in parentheses.

*Source:* Author's calculations. Campaign finance data are from the Standards in Public Office Commission (http://www.sipo.gov.ie/).

Table 26.2 Spending–Vote Share Correlations for Major–Party Dáil Members Who Ran without Same–Party Competitors, 2002 and 2007 Elections

|  | 2002 | | 2007 | |
| --- | --- | --- | --- | --- |
|  | Fine Gael | Labour | Fine Gael | Labour |
| M = 3 districts | .33 (3) | −.09 (7) | −.05 (5) | −.12 (5) |
| M = 4 districts | −1.00 (2) | −.17 (5) |  | .25 (7) |
| M = 5 districts |  | −.93 (3) |  | .06 (3) |

Notes: Cell entries are the Pearson correlations. The number of observations is in parentheses.

Source: Author's calculations. Campaign finance data are from the Standards in Public Office Commission (http://www.sipo.gov.ie/).

of the M = 3 districts. Thus, while the SV correlations for the M = 3 districts are predominantly across-district comparisons of solitary incumbents, the correlations for larger-magnitude districts have an added intradistrict dimension of comparison. That may make reactive spending difficult to detect if, say, strong incumbents do not resemble their weaker, more marginal running mates in terms of fundraising potential (see next subsection). Put differently, the tendency for SV correlations to become positive with district magnitude does not necessarily suggest the disappearance of electorally secure incumbents who spend less than they are able.

Evidence that this concern is warranted appears in table 26.2, which provides SV correlations for Dáil members who ran without any same-party competitors. (Fianna Fáil is not shown because all of its incumbents ran with at least one same-party competitor.) Note that the correlations are more consistently negative than those in table 26.1. They are also less favorable to the district magnitude hypothesis.

## Marginal Candidates and the Supply of Campaign Finance

As already suggested, non-Jacobsonian spending-votes patterns may be related not to demand homogenization but to the supply of campaign finance failing to accommodate marginal incumbents' demand. Four nonmutually exclusive reasons that marginal candidates may not have enough funds to outspend their more electorally secure running mates are (1) their fundraising potential is much less because they are less likely to hold positions of power in the party or legislature; (2) there are many marginal candidates per district, and a limited supply of funds leaves each only modestly funded; (3) where votes pool on party lists, partisan or ideologically motivated campaign contributions may privilege party leaders or popular candidates whose performance helps to "pull" their list; and (4) party-system fragmentation and intraparty competition may hinder fundraising by marginal candidates because they make their races not very relevant to the balance of power in the legislature or government.

The fourth possibility can probably be dismissed for Ireland and Japan since majority-party control of the parliament hangs in the balance of each election. However, it is the basis of Johnson's (2011) argument about spending-votes patterns in Chile. In concert with the country's party system and electoral geography, Chile's "binominal" electoral system, which uses D'Hondt to elect two members per district from open lists limited to two names each, makes it so that most vulnerable incumbents are only marginal vis-à-vis their own list mates, who are members of the same coalition.[6] That, Johnson argues, limits marginal incumbents' fundraising, puts them on a level playing field with their list mates, and prevents them from outspending the few incumbents in other districts who are more secure in their electoral prospects. Things might be different if Chile's executive-dominated budget-making and policymaking systems did not limit legislators' abilities to provide pork and particularistic policy. However, without those fundraising tools, and squaring up only against members of their own coalition, vulnerable incumbents face real fundraising limits.

Circumstances may be similar in other open-list systems. For example, vulnerable members of Finland's parliament—who are elected via OLPR in fourteen districts with magnitudes that range from six to thirty-four—face similar obstacles to fundraising, including intraparty competition, an inability to provide particularistic policy because policy authority is centralized in the government (Johnson 2015), and a weak connection between parties' electoral performance and the government's policy direction, which is due to the fact that multiparty government coalitions are formed after the elections and include parties of various sizes.[7] Also, spending-votes patterns for Eduskunta members are similar to those of Chilean deputies. In particular, while vote shares are positively correlated with campaign spending, they are negatively correlated with members' own spending. These patterns are shown in table 26.3. The first two columns provide the estimated sign on a regression estimate of the (within-district) relationship between vote shares and spending, and columns three and four provide estimates using only Eduskunta members' own spending. That more marginal incumbents tend to spend more of their own money on their campaigns suggests that they are not easily raising enough funds to satisfy their demand, and we should presume that that is at least part of the reason they do not outspend other, more dominant incumbents.

## Discussion

Research on how and why electoral systems influence patterns of campaign expenditure has only just begun, and much remains unknown. A better understanding of campaign finance markets and the relationships between electoral margins and spending will improve the estimation of spending effects, advance our understanding of the electoral value of incumbency, and refine our understanding of the relationship between

Table 26.3   Estimated Relationships between Vote Shares and Campaign Spending
for Major-Party Incumbents in the Eduskunta Elections of 2003
and 2007

|  | Total spending | | Own spending | |
|---|---|---|---|---|
|  | 2003 | 2007 | 2003 | 2007 |
| M = 6 | − | − | + | − |
| M = 7 | + | + | + | − |
| M = 9 | + | + | + | − |
| M = 10 | + | + | − | + |
| M = 12 | + | + | − | + |
| M = 14 | − | − | + | − |
| M = 17 | + | − | − | − |
| M = 18 | − | + | + | − |
| M = 21 | + | + | − | + |
| M = 33 | + | | − | |
| M = 34 | | + | | − |

*Notes:* Each cell reports the estimated sign (positive or negative) on a beta coefficient in an ordinary least squares regression of incumbents' total spending or own spending on their vote shares. Each regression includes party dummies to differentiate among the three major parties that are included in the analysis—the Social Democratic Party, the Center Party, and National Coalition Party (Kokoomus). (Other parties are excluded to ensure that the results are not driven by small parties that tend to win only in the largest districts.) If there is more than one district with the same magnitude, the data are pooled and the regression includes dummies for each district-party. The estimated coefficient on the vote share variable thus measures the *within-district-party* relationship between spending and vote shares.

*Source:* Author's calculations. The campaign finance data used in the regressions were compiled by Hyvärinen (2011) and Broberg (2004) and made available by the Finnish Social Science Data (FSD) Archive.

intraparty competition and campaign spending (see also the section "Intraparty Competition: Candidate-Level Effects on Spending).

# Extension: Margin-Driven Spending in Closed-List Systems?

To my knowledge, the connection between electoral marginality and campaign spending has not been investigated for parties in closed-list systems. The odds of such a relationship may be slim, given that *inter*party spending differences are so strongly related to parties' ideologies and their influence (or their expected postelectoral influence) over policy. Furthermore, any investigation into the question is hindered by two tendencies among CLPR-using countries: generous systems of state funding and financial disclosures that are annual rather than specific to the campaign period.

However, neither of these issues applies in the case of New Zealand, where parties that compete in the list tier of the mixed-member proportional (MMP) system are mostly privately financed and are required to report their campaign-related expenses.[8] There are two relevant thresholds for a party to be eligible for a proportional share of seats in the House of Representatives: it must receive at least 5 percent of the list-tier vote or win at least one seat in the nominal tier. Our question is: do parties near the 5 percent threshold—especially those that do not expect to win any constituency seats—spend relatively heavily?

Data from the 2011 and 2014 elections, presented in figure 26.4, suggest that the answer is yes. In the figure, parties are differentiated according to whether they won any nominal-tier seats and grouped according to their share of the list-tier vote. (Parties that won more than 12.5 percent of the vote are not shown.) The bar height indicates average "party spending," which includes both expenditures by the party organization and spending by its affiliated nominal-tier candidates and is presented as a percentage of the combined party/candidate spending limit, which is a function of how many candidates

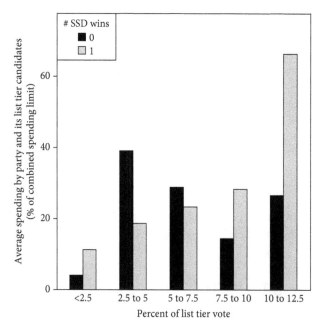

**FIGURE 26.4.** Average campaign spending by parties in New Zealand general elections (1996–2014), by parties' percent of the list vote.

Source: Author's calculation. Campaign finance data are from the Electoral Commission (http://www.elections.org.nz/).

run. Note that parties on the cusp of winning or losing representation—those that won no constituency seats and that were near the 5 percent threshold—spent relatively heavily, much more than parties that easily passed the 5 percent threshold or parties that were eligible for seats on account of winning at least one constituency seat. In other words, the data provide evidence that the phenomenon of margin-fueled spending is not exclusive to candidate-centered electoral systems.[9]

# Intraparty Competition: Candidate-Level Effects on Spending

The intraparty competition that occurs in many electoral systems has been linked to higher levels of spending both at the candidate level and at the system level. The candidate-level link is made by Cox and Thies (1998), who argue that spending per candidate increases with the number of same-party competitors because it means that the party's vote will be divided among more candidates, each of whom must compete more aggressively for a viable share. The argument mirrors Cox and Thies's (2000) argument about incumbent spending—that is, that incumbents are less likely to spend lightly in larger-magnitude districts (which have more competitors) because easy victories are less likely.

It may be difficult to measure the intraparty competition effect because there are other reasons that an additional same-party candidate may be associated with greater average spending. One is that both reflect greater *inter*party competition. For example, if a party attempts to win three seats in a district where it normally wins only two, it may funnel resources into that district to help it succeed. Another possibility is that the additional candidate frustrates electoral forecasting and thus reduces the likelihood that finance will concentrate on M + 1 candidates.[10] In other words, an increase in intraparty competition may increase spending through both demand-side effects and supply-side effects.

Yet, supply might be more relevant for the opposite reason: for limiting the (demand-driven) effect of intraparty competition. For spending to increase with the number of same-party competitors, supply must be sufficiently elastic; and yet the likelihood of that occurring may depend on several variables, including the baseline amount of intraparty competition or party-system fragmentation. For example, as the number of same-party competitors increases, we might suppose that supply will fall steadily behind the demand for funds because a supplier's expected benefit from a campaign contribution declines as the number of competitors per seat increases and each candidate's probability of winning declines. Thus, there may be a point at which additional intraparty competition would bring *less* spending per candidate. In other words, we might suppose that the effect of intraparty competition on spending will fade with the number of competitors per district-party (or with district magnitude)—potentially to a point where additional intraparty competition results in less spending per candidate.

Samuels (2001a, 93–94) makes an argument that is similar except that it is rooted in candidates' incentives to spend. Specifically, he argues that the intraparty competition effect fades with district magnitude because candidates reach a saturation point regarding their electoral uncertainty—that is, in large-magnitude districts, uncertainty is already very high and does not increase further if more same-party competitors decide to run. However, Samuels adds that candidates in large-magnitude districts may condition their spending on the "quality" of their same-party competitors: if more high-quality competitors run, a candidate will choose to spend more money.

The intraparty competition effect should also depend on whether the electoral system has vote pooling at the party level. Where there is vote pooling, as in open-list systems, per-candidate spending may not increase with the number of same-party competitors because parties have an incentive to pad lists with as many candidates as possible, including low-quality candidates who are unlikely to raise and spend much money. By contrast, in systems without vote pooling, like SNTV, parties have strong incentives to nominate only a select number of "quality" candidates because to do otherwise may result in costly "overnomination errors" (Cox and Niou 1994; Johnson and Hoyo 2012). That makes the intraparty competition effect much more likely.

# INTRAPARTY COMPETITION: SYSTEM-LEVEL EFFECTS

When contrasted with CLPR, OLPR is often touted for fostering intraparty democracy and making legislators more responsive to voters than to party leaders. The consequences for campaign spending mirror that additional layer of democracy: campaigns are more expensive under OLPR (and other systems with intraparty competition) because each party's vote is contested internally by a variety of personal campaigns. More interestingly, spending is greater in elections with intraparty competition because there it is *more effective* at building electoral support. The reason for this can be stated in general terms: the more candidate centered the election is, the greater the effect of spending on votes because candidates' success depends on building name recognition and a personal constituency, and for most candidates those are only established with considerable expense. By contrast, where elections focus on political parties and their leaders, persuasion-oriented campaign activities are very limited in their effectiveness because party platforms and the reputations of party leaders are already well known before the campaign and because voters have partisan and ideological preferences that are resistant to change. Going one step further, we may hypothesize that the spending-effects difference between open-list and closed-list systems is positively related to district magnitude. This is because as M increases, the electoral value of a personal reputation falls under CLPR and rises under OLPR (Carey and Shugart 1995).

The literatures on Brazilian, Italian, and Japanese elections are full of evidence that elections with intraparty competition are marked by high levels of spending. Especially noteworthy are the few studies of Japan's SNTV elections that make cross-system comparisons, like Carlson's (2006) illustration that the cost of campaigns in Japan declined following the shift from SNTV to a mixed-member electoral system, and Cox and Thies's (2000) comparison of spending effects in Japan and the United States.

However, there is still good cause for skepticism about the intraparty competition hypothesis. For one, there are CLPR-using countries that have very expensive elections, like Israel and Austria. Also, in his impressive and thorough attempt to compare spending across twenty-five democracies, Nassmacher (2009, 138–141) finds no relationship between intraparty competition and the cost of campaigns.[11] While this could be because he uses a measure of intraparty competition that is not explicitly linked to electoral formulas, it is also possible that the intraparty competition effect is swamped by other system-level factors, including electorates that vary in size, campaign periods that vary in length, whether legislative elections are concurrent with other elections, the presence or absence of free television time for parties and candidates, different levels of economic development, and different degrees of state regulation of the economy.

## From Demand to Supply

Legislatures elected by candidate-centered rules tend to allow members to secure pork and particularistic provisions in public policies, and legislators' interest in cultivating a personal vote is usually cited as the reason. However, pork, particularism, and the ability to individually influence policy are also useful for legislators who need their own cash to run their own re-election campaign (Ames 2002; Samuels 2002). The reasons are not mysterious: policymaking influence makes legislators naturally attractive to special interests, and policymakers can actively use their influence to solicit campaign contributions. It is possible, then, that legislative particularism is as much a function of legislators' interest in campaign finance as it is a function of their interest in using pork to win votes (see Cox and McCubbins 2001; Samuels 2002; Rosenbluth and Thies 2010). Either way, it is significant that candidate-centered elections tend to be accompanied by policymaking practices that allow individual members to make a mark on public policies and expenditures. It means that legislators who demand significant amounts of campaign contributions to finance their own campaigns tend to have means by which to secure them.

Although the connection between electoral rules and legislative particularism is strong, it is not a law of politics that policymaking practices must accommodate legislators' interests in particularism. Other factors also shape policymaking processes, and where particularism is stymied, legislators' campaign spending may be relatively light. For example, the constitution that Pinochet's dictatorship established for Chile includes a budget-making process that frustrates pork and particularism, and that in turn hinders legislators' fundraising. Particularistic incentives may also be frustrated if legislators have overriding incentives to centralize policymaking authority in the government, as they do in some parliamentary systems.[12] Consequently, system-level analyses of electoral systems and campaign spending may need to incorporate measures of policymaking particularism that are separate from electoral-system variables.

## Campaign Finance and Corruption

Many scholars argue that political corruption is more extensive in countries that use electoral systems that foster intraparty competition because of the high demand for campaign finance (Carey and Shugart 1995 433–434; Chang 2005; Chang and Golden 2007; Pereira, Rennó, and Samuels 2011).[13] The core of the argument is that politicians have a high demand for funds that is not easily satisfied through noncorrupt financing, and so they abuse their power in one way or another to get finance, say, by explicitly trading pork or influence for campaign funds or by concocting some more elaborate scheme that funnels public monies to their re-election campaigns. Here, again, the policymaking process is relevant, for if individual legislators have no ability to provide pork or otherwise influence policy, then their abilities to misuse power for campaign financing will be limited (Johnson 2015).[14]

Other theories that link electoral systems to corruption emphasize not campaign finance but either (1) the probability of electoral defeat for exposed corruption or (2) the incentives to engage in corruption monitoring. Myerson's (1993) theory is an example of the former. In his model, voters disapprove of corruption, so if a corruption scandal implicates their favorite party, they consider voting for another. Under PR they do so because there is at least one noncorrupt competitor who advocates similar policies, while under FPTP voters have no palatable alternatives for whom to vote because of bipartisanism. Therefore, PR systems are better at (electorally) penalizing corrupt politicians, and that leads to cleaner government.

Persson, Tabellini, and Trebbi (2003); Kunicová and Rose-Ackerman (2005); and Charron (2011) reach the opposite conclusion. Each essentially argues that PR systems allow more corruption than FPTP systems because of the free-rider problem regarding corruption monitoring in multiparty contexts. That is, no party wants to assume the costs of monitoring opponents for corruption when various other parties may also reap the electoral benefits of monitoring success. There is more monitoring and deterrence under FPTP because of the smaller number of competitors and the lack of the free-rider problem.

Among these theories, only Kunicová and Rose-Ackerman (2005) make a distinction among PR systems. Their argument about OLPR versus CLPR turns not on corruption monitoring but on electoral defeats. Specifically, they argue that CLPR harbors more corruption because party leaders are insulated from the electoral damage of corruption scandals by virtue of occupying the highest, safest spots on party lists. Put differently,

OLPR-elected legislators behave better because they are more worried about the possibility of electoral defeat.

Corruption-monitoring and electoral-defeat theories of legislative corruption have some disadvantages when compared to theories that focus on intraparty competition and campaign finance. One is that they ignore the possibility of interparty collusion, whereas the campaign finance–related theories allow legislators in all parties to misuse their policy influence for funds (to wage within-party contests). Also, there are reasons to think that the electoral-defeat theories overemphasize the expected costs of corruption. Politicians only engage in corruption when they think they will get away with it, and then to the extent that they worry about getting caught, they are likely to worry more about legal sanctions than the possibility that they might lose their re-election bids.

However, the debate about which electoral systems most motivate political corruption is unlikely to be settled with quantitative analyses of system-level corruption indices—at least not anytime soon. The empirical impediments are too numerous and severe. Corruption measures are inherently imprecise; existing measures do not focus on legislative corruption; there is a rather small number of consolidated democracies available for analysis; and many things besides electoral systems may contribute to political corruption at the system level, including dominant parties that are difficult to exclude from government and consociational power-sharing arrangements. Other research designs may provide more value.

# CONCLUSION

Comparative electoral systems is a mature field of study (Shugart 2005), except insofar as electoral systems matter for campaign finance. However, that gap is being filled. The literature has started to identify the importance of electoral systems for campaign finance, the effectiveness of campaign spending in elections, and political finance regimes.

Much of the early interest has been focused on either spending effects or the consequences of intraparty competition, and both literatures have important implications for the regulation of campaign finance and the quality of democratic governance. To advance both topics, however, we must have a better understanding of other ways that electoral systems shape patterns of expenditure within and across districts. Research on that topic is also poised to improve our understanding of electoral coordination and the supply side of campaign finance markets.

There is much work to be done at the system level too. However, there is already considerable evidence about one thing—that campaign financing is an important part of the link between electoral systems and public policies (e.g., Cox and McCubbins 2001; Rosenbluth and Thies 2010). And yet, much of the growing literature on the economic consequences of electoral systems (see Carey and Hix 2013 for a review) treats campaign finance as exogenous. That, then, is another area of electoral systems research that is poised to pay greater attention to campaign finance.

## Notes

1. See Johnson (2008). Also, for information about campaign finance disclosure regulations and practices, see International Institute for Democracy and Electoral Assistance (http://www.idea.int) and Money, Politics, and Transparency (http://moneypoliticstransparency.org/).
2. Gary Jacobson (1980, 1990) first found such a pattern among members of the US House.
3. Put differently, there might be more low DS ratios if not for the subsidy. The reimbursement covers 60 percent of campaign expenses and all of the candidate's personal expenses up to 60 percent of the legal limit on candidate spending. Although the system gives all candidates who are within reach of 10 percent of the votes added reason to spend, many candidates still spend close to nothing. For more, see Elections Canada, "Reimbursements to Candidates," http://www.elections.ca/content.aspx?section=fin&dir=can/rem&document=index&lang=e.
4. Another possibility is that voters who supported trailing candidates saw the two viable alternatives as equally bad. See Blais (2002).
5. The Irish campaign spending data reported herein include incumbents' reported use of office resources—on which, see Benoit and Marsh (2008).
6. Chile abandoned the binominal system in a 2015 reform.
7. That range of magnitudes was used in the 2003 and 2007 elections. The Eduskunta also includes a single member elected from the Åland Islands.
8. Parties that compete in the list tier are eligible for state-funded broadcasting, but their campaigns are otherwise financed privately.
9. Two notes. First, the pattern is nearly identical if we use dollar figures rather than percent of the spending limit. Second, there is also a Jacobson effect among nominal-tier incumbents (i.e., incumbents who run for re-election in the single-seat constituencies that they won in the previous election). In the 2011 elections the spending-votes correlation is $-.38$ ($N = 54$). In 2014 the correlation is $-.20$ ($N = 54$). The strength of the correlations is impressive given the country's limits on campaign spending, which if meaningful would bias SV correlations toward zero.
10. Another possibility extends the coordination idea within parties. Suppose that (1) there may be expectations that a party will win N seats, (2) there are also expectations that a particular N + 1 candidates will be the top N + 1 vote winners in the party, and (3) therefore, campaign finance concentrates on N + 1 candidates. In such cases, an additional same-party competitor might unravel expectations about candidates' prospects, in turn leading to greater average spending within the party slate.
11. In a simple bivariate analysis, Nassmacher (2009, 131) finds that spending *increases* with electoral proportionality. That implies that spending tends to be lower in FPTP systems than in PR systems.
12. See Johnson's (2014) discussion of Finland.
13. Chang and Golden (2007) also make a candidate-level argument that is linked to district magnitude.

14. Political corruption is also contingent on the effectiveness of anti-corruption institutions such as the judicial system and state auditors. That point is important because legislatures often control the resources that are available to state prosecutors, the legal penalties for corruption, and other resources that influence the effectiveness of the state's anticorruption institutions. For that reason, some scholars have argued that candidate-centered electoral systems facilitate the persistence of corruption in a way that goes beyond campaign financing: by making it relatively difficult to enact anti-corruption reforms (Taylor 2009; Johnson 2014).

## References

Ames, Barry. *The Deadlock of Democracy in Brazil.* University of Michigan Press, 2002.

Benoit, Kenneth, and Michael Marsh. "Incumbent and Challenger Campaign Spending Effects in Proportional Electoral Systems: The Irish Elections of 2002." *Political Research Quarterly* 63, no. 1 (2010): 159–173.

Benoit, Kenneth, and Michael Marsh. "The Campaign Value of Incumbency: A New Solution to the Puzzle of Less Effective Incumbent Spending." *American Journal of Political Science* 52, no. 4 (2008): 874–890.

Blais, André. "Why Is There So Little Strategic Voting in Canadian Plurality Rule Elections?" *Political Studies* 50, no. 3 (2002): 445–454.

Broberg, Jenny. "Election Funding of Finnish MPs 2003" [computer file]. FSD1360, version 1.0. Tampere: Finnish Social Science Data Archive [distributor], 2004.

Carey, John, and Simon Hix. "Consequences of Electoral Rules for Patterns of Redistribution and Regulation. Between Science and Engineering: Reflections on the APSA Presidential Task Force on Political Science, Electoral Rules, and Democratic Governance." *Perspectives on Politics* 11, no. 3 (2013): 820–824.

Carey, John M., and Matthew Soberg Shugart. "Incentives to Cultivate a Personal Vote: A Rank Ordering of Electoral Formulas." *Electoral Studies* 14, no. 4 (1995): 417–439.

Carlson, Matthew. "Electoral Reform and the Costs of Personal Support in Japan." *Journal of East Asian Studies* 6 (2006): 233–258.

Chang, Eric C. C. "Electoral Incentives for Political Corruption under Open-List Proportional Representation." *Journal of Politics* 67, no. 3 (2005): 716–730.

Chang, Eric C. C., and Miriam A. Golden. "Electoral Systems, District Magnitude and Corruption." *British Journal of Political Science* 37, no. 1 (2007): 115–137.

Charron, Nicholas. "Party Systems, Electoral Systems and Constraints on Corruption." *Electoral Studies* 30, no. 4 (2011): 595–606.

Cox, Gary W. *Making Votes Count: Strategic Coordination in the World's Electoral Systems.* Cambridge: Cambridge University Press, 1997.

Cox, Gary. "Electoral Rules and Electoral Coordination." *Annual Review of Political Science* 2, no. 1 (1999): 145–161.

Cox, Gary W., and Mathew D. McCubbins. "The Institutional Determinants of Economic Policy Outcomes." In *Presidents, Parliaments and Policy*, edited by S. Haggard & M. McCubbins, 21–63. Cambridge, UK: Cambridge University Press, 2001.

Cox, Gary W., and Emerson Niou. "Seat Bonuses under the Single Nontransferable Vote System: Evidence from Japan and Taiwan." *Comparative Politics* 26, no. 2 (1994): 221–236.

Cox, Gary W., and Michael F. Thies. "The Cost of Intraparty Competition: The Single, Nontransferable Vote and Money Politics in Japan." *Comparative Political Studies* 31, no. 3 (1998): 267–291.

Cox, Gary W., and Michael F. Thies. "How Much Does Money Matter? 'Buying' Votes in Japan, 1967-1990." *Comparative Political Studies* 33, no. 1 (2000): 37–57.

Hyvärinen, Varpu (University of Tampere. Department of Political Science and International Relations). "Election Funding of Finnish MPs 2007" [computer file]. FSD2412, version 1.1 (2011-03-01). Tampere: Finnish Social Science Data Archive [distributor], 2011.

Jacobson, Gary. C. "The Effects of Campaign Spending in House Elections: New Evidence for Old Arguments." *American Journal of Political Science* 34, no. 2 (1990): 334–362.

Jacobson, Gary C. *Money in Congressional Elections*. New Haven, CT: Yale University Press, 1980.

Johnson, Joel W. "Electoral Systems and Corruption." Unpublished manuscript. 2014. Available at SSRN, https://papers.ssrn.com/sol3/papers.cfm?abstract_id=2488834.

Johnson, Joel W. "Campaign Spending in Proportional Electoral Systems: Incumbents versus Challengers Revisited." *Comparative Political Studies* 46, no. 8 (2013): 968–993.

Johnson, Joel W., and Verónica Hoyo. "Beyond Personal Vote Incentives: Dividing the Vote in Preferential Electoral Systems." *Electoral Studies* 31, no. 1 (2012): 131–142.

Johnson, Joel W. "Incumbents without a Campaign Finance Advantage: Competition and Money in Chile's Congressional Elections." *Journal of Politics in Latin America* 3, no. 3 (2011): 3–33.

Johnson, Joel W. "Democracy and Disclosure: Electoral Systems and the Regulation of Political Finance." *Election Law Journal* 7, no. 4 (2008): 325–346.

Kunicova, Jana, and Susan Rose-Ackerman. "Electoral Rules and Constitutional Structures as Constraints on Corruption." *British Journal of Political Science* 35, no. 4 (2005): 573–606.

Maddens, Bart, Bram Wauters, Jo Noppe, and Stefaan Fiers. "Effects of Campaign Spending in an Open List PR System: The 2003 Legislative Elections in Flanders/Belgium." *West European Politics* 29, no. 1 (2006): 161–168.

Myerson, Roger B. "Effectiveness of Electoral Systems for Reducing Government Corruption: A Game-Theoretic Analysis." *Games and Economic Behavior* 5, no. 1 (1993): 118–132.

Nassmacher, Karl-Heinz. *The Funding of Party Competition*. Baden-Baden, Germany`: Nomos Verlagsgesellschaft, 2009.

Palda, Filip, and Kristian Palda. "The Impact of Campaign Expenditures on Political Competition in the French Legislative Elections of 1993." *Public Choice* 94, no. 1–2 (1998): 157–174.

Persson, Torsten, Guido Tabellini, and Francesco Trebbi. "Electoral Rules and Corruption." *Journal of the European Economic Association* 1, no. 4 (2003): 958–989.

Pereira, Carlos, Lucio Rennó, and David Samuels. "Corruption, Campaign Finance, and Reelection." In *Corruption and Democracy in Brazil: The Struggle for Accountability*, 80–99. Notre Dame, IN: University of Notre Dame Press, 2011.

Reed, Steven R. "Structure and Behaviour: Extending Duverger's Law to the Japanese Case." *British Journal of Political Science* 20, no. 3 (1990): 335–356.

Rosenbluth, Frances McCall, and Michael F. Thies. *Japan Transformed: Political Change and Economic Restructuring*. Princeton, NJ: Princeton University Press, 2010.

Samuels, David. "When Does Every Penny Count? Intra-Party Competition and Campaign Finance in Brazil." *Party Politics* 7, no. 1 (2001a): 89–102.

Samuels, David J. "Incumbents and Challengers on a Level Playing Field: Assessing the Impact of Campaign Finance in Brazil." *Journal of Politics* 63, no. 2 (2001b): 569–584.

Samuels, David J. "Pork Barreling Is Not Credit Claiming or advertising: Campaign Finance and the Sources of the Personal Vote in Brazil." *Journal of Politics* 64, no. 3 (2002): 845–863.

Scarrow, Susan E. "Political Finance in Comparative Perspective." *Annual Review of Political Science* 10 (2007): 193–210.

Shugart, Matthew S. "Comparative Electoral Systems Research: The Maturation of a Field and New Challenges Ahead." In *The Politics of Electoral Systems*, edited by Michael Gallagher and Paul Mitchell, 25–56. Oxford: Oxford University Press, 2005.

Sudulich, Maria Laura, Matthew Wall, and David M. Farrell. "Why Bother Campaigning? Campaign Effectiveness in the 2009 European Parliament Elections." *Electoral Studies* 32, no. 4 (2013): 768–778.

Taylor, Matthew. "Corruption, Accountability Reforms, and Democracy in Brazil." In *Corruption and Democracy in Latin America*, edited by Charles H. Blake & Steven D. Morris, 150–168. Pittsburgh, PA: University of Pittsburgh Press, 2009.

van Biezen, Ingrid. "Campaign and Party Finance." In *Comparing Democracies: Elections and Voting in Global Perspective*. 3rd ed., edited by Lawrence Le Duc, Richard G. Niemi and Pippa Norris, 65–97. London: Sage, 2010.

# PART VI

# ELECTORAL SYSTEMS IN CONTEXT

..................................................................

# CHAPTER 27

# ELECTORAL SYSTEMS
# IN CONTEXT

*The Netherlands*

..................................................................

KRISTOF JACOBS

THE Dutch electoral system is one of the most proportional in the world (Farrell 2011, 88), consisting of a 150-seat single nationwide electoral district with a very low legal threshold (one seat, or 1/150 of the total number of valid votes) and a proportional electoral formula. Because of its extreme proportionality, it is an ideal testing ground to examine some of the claims about the effects of electoral systems. After all, the Netherlands provides the most likely case to see effects such as high party system fragmentation, unstable governments, and long coalition negotiations (cf. Farrell 2011, 153–171). Additionally this chapter details the workings and consequences of the ballot structure dimension of the Dutch electoral system. While this dimension is often overlooked (Colomer 2011), it is worthwhile to examine as it influences how politicians behave in the parliament (Louwerse and Otjes 2016). The interplay between the interparty (proportionality) and the intraparty (ballot structure) dimension of the electoral system is especially noteworthy in the Dutch case. The Dutch ballot structure is rigid, but the electoral threshold is extremely low. Therefore, members of parliament (MPs) who disagree with the official party line have an incentive to break away and start a new party.

In this chapter I first discuss the Dutch political system. Afterward I outline the origins of the electoral system and show how it works in practice. I provide an example of how the seats are allocated to parties and an example of how seats are then allocated to candidates. The next section examines how the electoral system influences the party system, the parties, the parliament, and the government composition. In the section about electoral reform I discuss why electoral reform is always on the Dutch political agenda (and why these reform proposals almost always fail).

# POLITICAL BACKGROUND

Since 1848, the Dutch government has enjoyed the confidence of a parliamentary majority ("ministerial responsibility"). The main features of the political system are that the Netherlands has a constitutional monarchy, has a bicameral system, and features multilevel governance. Moreover, it is a "country of minorities," which is "without a doubt the single most important characteristic of Dutch politics" (Andeweg and Irwin 2014, 27). In line with this crucial sociological characteristic of the country, the parliament is elected through an extremely proportional electoral system accompanied by a multiparty system.

*Constitutional monarchy.* Even though the Netherlands is formally a monarchy, the power of the king is limited: the ministers are responsible for his every act. Up until 2012, the Dutch monarch could play an important role in government formation. Given that Dutch governments always consist of coalitions, a *formateur* needs to be appointed to explore potential viable coalitions. Previously the monarch appointed the formateur. Occasionally this led to criticism about the monarch being biased against certain parties (such as in 1994 and 2010), resulting in a change in which parliament now appoints the formateur (Andeweg and Irwin 2014, 142).

*Bicameralism.* The Dutch parliament consists of a directly elected lower house and an indirectly elected upper house.[1] The lower house is the more powerful of the two, but the role of the upper house should not be neglected. The upper house is elected by the members of the provincial legislatures (whose votes are weighted by the size of their province's population). Provincial elections do not automatically coincide with the general election. As a result, a government can be confronted by a hostile upper house during its government term, making these elections an important test of the popularity of the government (Elzinga, Kummeling, and Schipper-Spanninga 2012, 246). While the upper house is typically considered a forum for "reflection" and is supposed to focus mainly on the quality of the legislation, it can operate as a partisan vehicle as well. This is what happened, for instance, after the 2012 general elections. A coalition was formed between the Social Democrats and the conservative liberals. Together they commanded a comfortable lower house majority (79/150 seats) but lacked a majority in the upper house (30/75 seats). This in turn forced the government to broaden its support base and in many policy areas it effectively governed as a minority government.

*Multilevel governance.* The Dutch state is very centralized: it does not have regional governments (Andeweg 2008, 492). However, since 1982, the national government has decentralized significant competences to the provincial and local level (Andeweg and Irwin 2014, 212). The latest round of decentralizations transferred significant competences regarding health care and employment to the local governments. Nevertheless, many important decisions are still taken at the national level and therefore it is most appropriate to speak of multilevel governance.[2]

*Multipartism.* The Dutch have a long history of multipartism. Even before the intro-duction of proportional representation, multiple "parties" won seats. The religious minorities each had their own representatives. Next to the religious parties, a liberal party and, especially at the end of the nineteenth century, a labor party won seats. The religious and socioeconomic cleavages were the most dominant in the early days of the proportional electoral system (from 1917 onward). Yet this multipartism based on the two cleavages was "structured" (Andeweg and Irwin 2014, 117): Dutch society was "pillarized" and voting was structured along the lines of class and religion. Most voters voted faithfully for the party that represented their pillar. However, starting from the early 1960s, the pillars became less dominant and new parties started finding their way into the parliament.

Currently, most Dutch voters and MPs perceive the party system as fitted to a sim-ple left/right scale. However, undergirding this simple scale is a more complex system of three ideological dimensions (though there is overlap to some extent): religious, socioeconomic, and cultural (Andeweg and Irwin 2014, 76). The left/right distinction matters—if only because voters who identify themselves as left-wing seem unwilling to vote for perceived right-wing parties and vice versa (Van der Meer et al. 2012). Yet within these "blocks," considerable heterogeneity exists. Currently the Netherlands houses among others a social democratic, socialist, Christian democratic, left populist, populist radical right, progressive liberal, conservative liberal, and green party of con-siderable size. Multiple other (smaller) parties exist.

# ORIGINS OF THE ELECTORAL SYSTEM

The direct election of the lower house was introduced in 1848. Until 1917, a majority system was used. When no candidate reached a majority in the first round, a second round only including the two largest parties was organized. Most districts elected two representatives (Elzinga et al. 2012, 11), but they were rarely elected simultaneously as every two years half of the MPs were elected (Andeweg 2008, 492). Originally, the assembly size was explicitly linked to the size of the population—one seat per forty-five thousand inhabitants (cf. cube root law, Taagepera and Shugart 1989). However, in 1888, the number of MPs was fixed at one hundred (Elzinga et al. 2012, 11). At that time citizens had to pay a poll tax to be allowed to vote. The constitutional change of 1887 and the ensuing new electoral law of 1896 broadened the number and types of people who were allowed to vote. In 1896, all districts became single-member districts (Elzinga et al. 2012).

Universal (male) suffrage and the proportional electoral system were introduced in 1917.[3] As Andeweg (2008, 493) explains, the 1917 package deal was in essence a com-promise between the religious parties, the Labour Party, and the Liberals. The religious parties wanted (and got) full state financing of religious schools, while the Labour Party advocated universal suffrage (which would increase its influence greatly). Were universal suffrage to be coupled with the existing two-round electoral system, this would almost certainly have entailed the demise of the Liberal Party. To convince the Liberal Party, a system of proportional representation was included in the package deal. To ensure that all segments in society were represented as well as possible, compulsory voting was introduced, an element that reduced the uncertainty surrounding future elections and made sure that the parties were less likely to encounter unpleasant surprises due to low turnout (Elzinga et al. 2012, 8). Though officially the country was divided into eighteen (administrative) electoral districts, in practice the seat distribution functioned as if the country was one electoral district. Parties were to some extent allowed to field different candidates in different districts, but this only mattered for the allocation of seats to candidates. The vote totals of each of the lists were simply added up at the national level before the seat distribution was carried out.

From 1917 to 1951, the electoral legislation was changed several times. First, the original 1917 legislation included a legal electoral threshold: only lists that won 50 percent of the national (Hare) quota were included in the distribution of the remainder seats. However, the general election of 1918 saw no less than seven one-man factions win a seat. Hence, in 1921, the threshold was increased to 75 percent of the electoral quota. In 1935, the threshold was further increased to 100 percent of the electoral quota (at the time 1 percent of the valid votes). Second, in 1933, the electoral formula to calculate the distribution of the remainder seats was changed from the largest-remainders method (based on Hare quota) to the D'Hondt highest-averages method.[4] Both measures were introduced to reduce the party system fragmentation (Elzinga et al. 2012, 9). Third, the ballot structure changed from a purely open-list system to a flexible-list system in 1922.[5] The 1918 elections revealed that open-list systems led to "unwanted consequences": a substantial number of lower-ranked candidates with tiny numbers of preference votes were elected (Elzinga et al. 2012, 8, 203). To avoid such consequences a preference threshold of 50 percent of the electoral quota (calculated per party) was introduced.[6]

In 1951, a new electoral law replaced the 1917 law. It mainly introduced relatively small changes, but it also established an independent electoral management body (*Kiesraad*). Two major reforms of the law were implemented.[7] In 1956, the assembly size was increased from 100 to 150, and as a side effect the electoral threshold was lowered from 1 percent to 0.67 percent of the valid votes. In 1970, compulsory voting was abolished. According to Andeweg (2008, 493), this reform was mainly inspired by the advent of two new radical parties (the populist *Boerenpartij* and the progressive liberal *D66*). The parties believed that the new parties were successful because of protest voters, who mostly would have stayed home were it not for compulsory voting. One last significant (though not major) reform was implemented in 1973, when a system of apparentement was introduced whereby different (mostly smaller) parties could combine their lists for the distribution of the remainder seats, thereby increasing their chances to win remainder seats (De Jong 2015).

In 1989, another new electoral law was implemented. The changes were minimal, though the law made it slightly easier for candidates to get elected based on preference votes.[8] In 1997, the preference threshold was lowered from 50 percent to 25 percent of the electoral quota (for an analysis of the reform process, see Jacobs and Leyenaar 2011, 505–508).[9] Even though the electoral reform has constantly been on the political agenda ever since (see section "Electoral Reform"), no further changes were implemented.

# How the Electoral System Works

Dutch citizens over age 18 have the right to vote for the lower house. They are automatically registered. Two weeks before Election Day (at the latest), they receive a vote card that allows them to vote (*stempas*). Four days before the election (at the latest), they receive the list of candidates along with a list of addresses and opening hours of the polling station nearby.[10] To be allowed to cast their vote, voters need to show their vote card and ID in the polling station.[11]

Once they are in the polling station, voters receive a paper ballot (cf. Figure 27.1). The ballot shows all candidates sorted by party, which sometimes leads to fairly large ballot papers.[12] In each of the districts, parties can field up to fifty or even eighty candidates in any of the districts (Elzinga et al. 2012, 156).[13] They can register a name that is printed on top of that party's list (Andeweg 2008, 494), yet voters can only cast one vote and they cannot vote for a party: they are forced to cast a preference vote for one candidate (i.e., latent list system, Shugart 2008a, 43). The exact composition of the lists can vary per electoral district, allowing parties to include candidates who are well known in that given region or district. However, in practice, this is relatively rare. While technically there are twenty electoral districts nowadays, these effectively operate as one electoral district with a district magnitude of 150: the parties are allowed to pool the votes of lists in the individual districts. The electoral districts therefore primarily serve administrative purposes (Andeweg 2008, 497).

In practice, many voters who simply want to support the party and have no particular preference for a candidate vote for the first person on the list, the so-called list-puller. The overwhelming majority of the voters do so, and as a result most "preference votes" should actually be considered as votes for a party (Andeweg 2008, 494). In 2012, for instance, the list-pullers of the eleven parties elected to the parliament won between 65.54 percent (Christen Democratisch Appèl—CDA) and 93.32 percent (Partij voor de Vrijheid—PVV) of all the votes for candidates on their list.[14]

The initial distribution uses Hare quota, but the remainders are distributed using D'Hondt. Between 1977 and 2017, parties were allowed to form electoral alliances. Such alliances reduce the impact of the D'Hondt method on the disproportionality of the (remainder) seat distribution.[15]

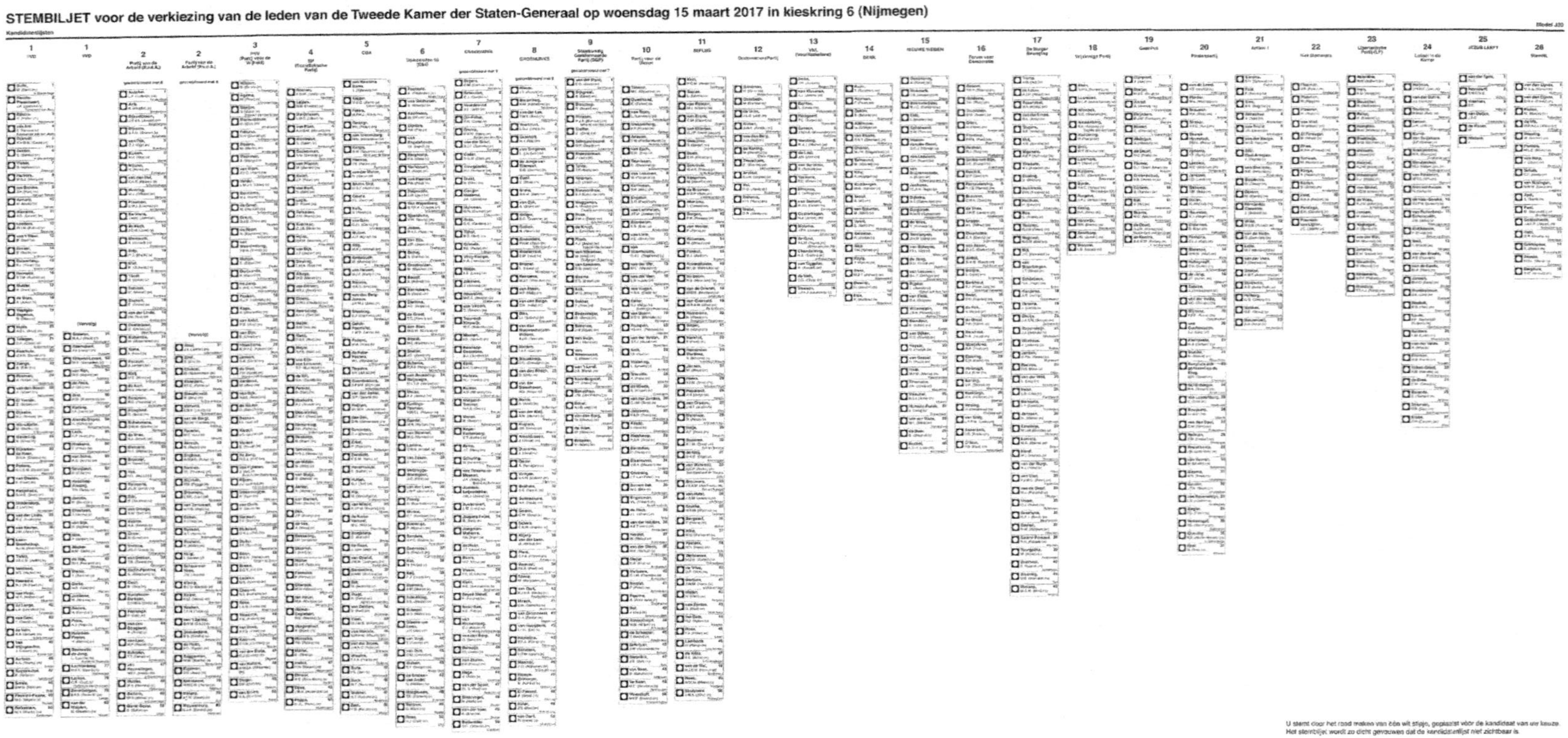
STEMBILJET voor de verkiezing van de leden van de Tweede Kamer der Staten-Generaal op woensdag 15 maart 2017 in kieskring 6 (Nijmegen)
U stemt door het rood maken van één wit stipje, geplaatst vóór de kandidaat van uw keuze.
Het stembiljet wordt zo dicht gevouwen dat de kandidatenlijst niet zichtbaar is.

**FIGURE 27.1.** Dutch ballot paper (1994).

Source: Ron De Jong (Kiesraad).

The (legal) electoral threshold is equal to the electoral quota. The threshold thus varies with the assembly size: it was lowered from 1 percent of the valid votes to 0.67 percent as a result of the expansion of the lower house from 100 to 150 in 1956. In the aftermath of the economic crisis, the First Rutte cabinet (2010–2012) wanted to lower the assembly size, but they did not introduce any bills to that end.

In what follows, I present a detailed step-by-step example of how the electoral system works in practice. The example uses data from the 2012 general election. I start by discussing how seats are allocated to parties (cf. Table 27.1). Afterward, a discussion of the allocation of seats to candidates is detailed. I also provide a practical example of the latter as most other studies of the Dutch electoral system do not include one.

## Seat Allocation to Parties

*Step 1.* The votes are counted and the party totals are calculated.[16] As each voter can only cast one vote and is obliged to vote for a candidate, the party totals are a simple sum of the votes for each of the candidates on that party list.

*Step 2.* The electoral quota is calculated by dividing the total number of valid votes by the total number of seats to be distributed. In 2012: 9,424,235 divided by 150, which yields an electoral quota of 62,828.23 votes.

*Step 3.* For each party, the total number of votes is divided by the electoral quota. In this phase, parties in an electoral alliance are counted as a single party.[17] Seats distributed in this phase are called full quota seats (*volle zetels*) and in practice never add up to 150. In 2012, the total number of full quota seats distributed to the parties and alliances was 144, leaving six remainder seats to be distributed.

*Step 4.* In this step the remainder seats are distributed. For each party the total number of votes is then divided by the number of full quota seats + 1 (cf. D'Hondt highest-averages method). The resulting averages are then ranked. The party having the highest average receives the first remainder seat. Afterward, that party's average is calculated based on its new number of seats (full quota seats + 1 remainder seat) + 1 and the averages are ranked again. This procedure is repeated until no remainder seats are left. It is important to note that parties in an electoral alliance are still counted as a single party. In 2012, the first and fifth remainder seats were distributed to the party Volkspartij voor Vrijheid en Democratie (VVD), and the second and sixth to the Partij van de Arbeid (PvdA) / Socialistische Partij (SP) / Groenlinks alliance. Remainder seat numbers three and four went to CDA and the ChristenUnie / Staatkundig Gereformeerde Partij (SGP) alliance, respectively. As can be seen from this example, the remainder seat distribution method slightly favors the bigger parties, but this advantage is to some extent offset by the possibility to form electoral alliances.

*Step 5.* The seats won by an electoral alliance are then distributed to the parties within that alliance (cf. Table 27.2). In 2012, two alliances won seats: PvdA/SP/Groenlinks (fifty-seven seats) and ChristenUnie/SGP (eight seats).

**Table 27.1  Calculation of Allocation Seats to Parties (2012 Dutch General Election)**

| Number of valid votes: | 9,424,235 |
|---|---|

| Electoral quota: | 62,828.23 (valid votes divided by total number of seats) |
|---|---|

| No. of competing parties: | 21 |
|---|---|

| Party Name | Votes | % Vote | "Full" Quota Seats | Remainder Seats | Total Seats | % Seats |
|---|---|---|---|---|---|---|
| VVD | 2,504,948 | 26.58% | 39 | 2 | 41 | 27.3% |
| *PvdA \| SP \| Groenlinks* | *3,470,499* | *36.82%* | *55* | *2* | *(57)* | |
| PvdA | 2,340,750 | 24.84% | | | 38 | 25.3% |
| SP | 909,853 | 9.65% | | | 15 | 10.0% |
| Groenlinks | 219,896 | 2.33% | | | 4 | 2.7% |
| PVV | 950,263 | 10.08% | 15 | 0 | 15 | 10.0% |
| CDA | 801,620 | 8.51% | 12 | 1 | 13 | 8.7% |
| D66 | 757,091 | 8.03% | 12 | 0 | 12 | 8.0% |
| *ChristenUnie \| SGP* | *491,366* | *5.22%* | *7* | *1* | *(8)* | |
| ChristenUnie | 294,586 | 3.13% | | | 5 | 3.3% |
| SGP | 196,780 | 2.09% | | | 3 | 2.0% |
| Partij voor de Dieren | 182,162 | 1.93% | 2 | 0 | 2 | 1.3% |
| 50PLUS | 177,631 | 1.88% | 2 | 0 | 2 | 1.3% |
| Others | 213,054 | 1.64% | - | | - | |

*Note:* Party alliances in italic. In the table I follow the template of Andeweg (2008, 498).

*Data source:* http://www.kiesraad.nl.

- To begin with, an intra-alliance electoral quota is calculated by dividing the total number of votes of the alliance by the number of seats won by that alliance. Regarding the PvdA/SP/Groenlinks alliance, that quota was equal to 60,885.95 votes. The ChristenUnie/SGP quota was 61,420.75.

Table 27.2  Example of Seat Distribution within an Electoral Alliance

| Alliance: PvdA | SP | Groenlinks | Votes | "Full" Seats | Remainder (of the Quota) | Remainder Seats |
|---|---|---|---|---|
| PvdA | 2,340,750 | 38 | 0.44 | 0 |
| SP | 909,853 | 14 | 0.94 | 1 |
| Groenlinks | 219,896 | 3 | 0.61 | 1 |

*Note:* Intra-alliance electoral quota: 60,885.95 and a total of 57 seats to distribute.

*Data source:* http://www.kiesraad.nl.

- Afterward, the total number of votes of each of the constituent parties is divided by the intra-alliance quota. In practice, some remainder seats then need to be allocated still.
- The remainder seats are then distributed according to a system of largest remainders (*not* the D'Hondt method).[18]

## Seat Allocation to Candidates

The distribution of the seats to candidates is divided into two phases.[19] First, the preference threshold is calculated by dividing the national electoral quota by four. In 2012, the threshold was 15,707 (62,828.23/4). Candidates who received more preference votes than the threshold are ranked and awarded a seat. Second, all remaining seats are distributed according to the list order. Table 27.3 provides an example where one candidate (Omtzigt) was elected despite his low list position.[20] Regardless of how the candidate obtained his or her seat (via preference votes or list position), the seat now is his or hers: when the candidate leaves the party, he or she can take the seat with him or her.

# POLITICAL CONSEQUENCES OF THE ELECTORAL SYSTEM

The Dutch electoral system is an "extreme" electoral system regarding its interparty dimension, but it is not regarding its intraparty dimension. One would thus expect its impact to be most visible on elements related to the interparty dimension. In this section I examine if this is the case.

**Table 27.3  Calculation of Allocation Seats to Candidates (2012 General Election, Party: CDA)**

| | Original List Position | | | Seat Allocation to Candidates | | |
|---|---|---|---|---|---|---|
| List Position | Name | Preference Votes | Seat No. | Name | Preference Votes | List Position |
| 1 | Van Haersma Buma | 517.397 | 1 | *Van Haersma Buma* | *517.397* | *1* |
| 2 | Keijzer | 127.446 | 2 | *Keijzer* | *127.446* | *2* |
| 3 | de Rouwe | 15.814 | 3 | *Omtzigt* | **36.750** | **39** |
| 4 | Knops | 8.466 | 4 | *de Rouwe* | *15.814* | *3* |
| 5 | Rog | 1.382 | 5 | Knops | 8.466 | 4 |
| 6 | van Hijum | 2.719 | 6 | Rog | 1.382 | 5 |
| 7 | Bruins Slot | 3.765 | 7 | van Hijum | 2.719 | 6 |
| 8 | Geurts | 5.648 | 8 | Bruins Slot | 3.765 | 7 |
| 9 | Mulder | 9.824 | 9 | Geurts | 5.648 | 8 |
| 10 | Oskam | 702 | 10 | Mulder | 9.824 | 9 |
| 11 | Heerma | 981 | 11 | Oskam | 702 | 10 |
| 12 | van Toorenburg | 3.558 | 12 | Heerma | 981 | 11 |
| 13 | Van Helvert | 13.952 | 13 | Van Toorenburg | 3.558 | 12 |
| 39 | Omtzigt | 36.750 | | | | |

Note: *Underlined and italic* signifies criterion of the seat distribution (based on preference votes or based on list position). Candidate elected despite low position on list in **bold**.

*Data source:* http://www.kiesraad.nl.

## Impact on the Party System

As one would expect from an extremely proportional electoral system, disproportionality is very low (Table 27.4). Furthermore, as expected, the proportional electoral
system correlates with a high number of political parties. The low electoral threshold,
proportional electoral formula, and high district magnitude all make the party system open and dynamic (cf. Farrell 2011, 158). At any given time the effective number
of parties has been high. Some, especially politicians from the largest parties, have
claimed that such party system fragmentation makes it difficult to govern and blame

the electoral system. As described earlier, such concerns led to a change of the electoral formula regarding the remainder seats in 1933 and the increase of the legal threshold in 1935, and have led to renewed calls for electoral reform to reduce fragmentation in the twenty-first century.

The electoral system and its low legal electoral threshold indeed make it easy for new parties to gain representation and sustain the high effective number of parties. As mentioned earlier, the high effective number of parties predates the introduction of the proportional electoral system and has its roots in the preferences of the electorate. Indeed, even before the change toward a proportional electoral system, the religious minorities (which were and still are relatively geographically concentrated) all had their own party and party system fragmentation was high. That said, new parties have entered the stage and older ones have disappeared.

Table 27.4 shows periods of increase and periods of decrease in the effective number of parties (mainly due to mergers). In the late 1960s and early 1970s, the party system expanded, but afterward the effective number of parties dropped due to several mergers, specifically the merger of the three main religious parties (CDA, 1977), of several left and progressive parties (GroenLinks, 1989), and of two Protestant parties (ChristenUnie, 2000). Especially since 2002, the effective number of parties once again increased.

As can be seen in the fifth column of Table 27.4, a high number of parties gained at least one seat in the lower house throughout the whole of the post–World War II period. To add to this, a significant number of MPs leave their party faction during the legislative term (cf. sixth column in Table 27.4). Typically, these breakaway MPs start a new party and compete in the next general election.

The electoral system allows voters to play a big role in shaping the party system. The high effective number of parties has to do not only with the number of small parties but also (and especially) with the size of the bigger parties. One of the reasons for the high number of parties is that the voters are divided over several medium-sized parties, and particularly so in the two periods of party system expansion (late 1960s–1970s and 2002–present). The impact of voters is also visible in the electoral elimination of breakaway MPs. Many of the MPs who break loose from their party start a new political party to try to win seats themselves. On paper, the electoral threshold is extremely low: merely sixty thousand to seventy thousand votes are needed to win one seat (depending on voter turnout). It should not be surprising, then, that many breakaway MPs think it is easy to gain representation by themselves. However, so far the voters have decided otherwise: in the 1946–2012 time period, only a measly two of these have been successful.[21]

In short, the extremely proportional nature of the Dutch electoral system makes the party system very sensitive to shifts in the preferences of the voters. As a result, substantial swings in the effective number of parties take place (ranging from as low as 3.75 in 1989 to 6.74 in 2010). While recent calls for electoral reform mostly focus on the low entry barrier of the electoral system, it is especially the high number of medium-sized parties that contributes to the high fragmentation.

## Table 27.4 The Dutch Party System (1946–2016)

| Election Year | Disproportionality | Effective Number of Parties (Votes) | Effective Number of Parties (Seats) | Parties Elected to the Parliament | Parliamentary Factions at the End of the Legislative Term |
|---|---|---|---|---|---|
| 1946 | 1.10 | 4.68 | 4.47 | 7 | 7 |
| 1948 | 1.27 | 4.98 | 4.68 | 8 | 8 |
| 1952 | 1.56 | 5.00 | 4.65 | 8 | 8 |
| 1956 | 0.98 | 4.26 | 4.07 | 7 | 7 |
| 1959 | 1.64 | 4.47 | 4.15 | 8 | 9 (+1) |
| 1963 | 1.30 | 4.80 | 4.51 | 10 | 11 (+1) |
| 1967 | 1.60 | 6.23 | 5.71 | 11 | 16 (+5) |
| 1971 | 1.73 | 7.09 | 6.40 | 14 | 15 (+1) |
| 1972 | 1.19 | 6.84 | 6.42 | 14 | 14 |
| 1977 | 1.52 | 3.96 | 3.70 | 11 | 13 (+2) |
| 1981 | 1.30 | 4.56 | 4.29 | 10 | 10 |
| 1982 | 1.16 | 4.24 | 4.01 | 12 | 15 (+3) |
| 1986 | 1.67 | 3.77 | 3.49 | 9 | 9 |
| 1989 | 0.90 | 3.90 | 3.75 | 9 | 10 (+1) |
| 1994 | 1.08 | 5.72 | 5.42 | 12 | 14 (+2) |
| 1998 | 1.28 | 5.15 | 4.81 | 9 | 9 |
| 2002 | 0.88 | 6.04 | 5.79 | 10 | 12 (+2) |
| 2003 | 1.05 | 4.99 | 4.74 | 9 | 13 (+4) |
| 2006 | 1.03 | 5.80 | 5.54 | 10 | 11 (+1) |
| 2010 | 0.81 | 6.97 | 6.74 | 10 | 13 (+3) |
| 2012 | 0.99 | 5.94 | 5.70 | 11 | 17 (+6) |

*Data source:* Disproportionality and effective number of parties: Gallagher (2016). Parties elected and parliamentary factions: own calculations based on http://www.parlement.com.

## Impact on the Parties

While the Dutch electoral system is mostly famous for its interparty dimension, its intraparty dimension should not be neglected. With the exception of a brief period when an open-list (or quasi-list) system was used, the Dutch ballot structure employs a flexible (or latent) list system. The preference threshold was high up until 1997: only three candidates got elected by preference votes before 1997. The 1989 and 1997 electoral reforms made it easier to get elected based on preference votes. Currently a candidate needs to win 25 percent of the electoral quota to get elected. Candidates have two options to get elected: either they convince their parties to put them high on the party list so they can get elected on the coattails of the party leader, or they wage a personal campaign to get elected based on preference votes. Of the two, the former is by far the most certain route to get elected.

From 1997 to 2012, merely nine candidates have gotten elected based solely on preference votes. In 2012, for example, the preference threshold was 15,707 votes (on a total of 9,424,235 valid votes), and twenty-eight candidates crossed that threshold. Yet twelve of these were so-called list-pullers—the first candidate on the list of a party.[22] Of the remaining sixteen, all but one (Pieter Omtzigt, CDA) would have been elected regardless as they were ranked high enough on the list.

There are at least three reasons for the low number of candidates elected based on preference votes. First are the mechanical effects of the electoral system. The preference threshold by itself is still fairly high: most candidates get between one hundred and ten thousand votes. On top of that, there is the interplay between the interparty and the intraparty dimension. Because the Netherlands effectively only has one electoral district, a lot of candidates get elected and very few well-known candidates need preference votes to get a seat. Second, the psychological motivations also play a role. Studies show that ballot position effects play an important role in the decisions of Dutch voters: given the large number of candidates on a list, most Dutch voters start at the top of the list and work their way down looking for a suitable candidate to vote for (Spierings and Jacobs 2014). Indeed, parties can submit up to fifty or eighty candidates per district (cf. footnote 12). Getting in-depth information on all these candidates is virtually impossible, and as a result few voters consider the lower-ranked candidates. Third, personal campaigns by individual candidates face substantial hurdles. To begin with, the parties devote most of their (limited) resources to the list-pullers. Individual candidates often do not have the means to organize a ground campaign. Furthermore, mass media still play a crucial role during campaigns. Most of the impact of these media is derived from the election debates and other types of "free publicity," for example, in news programs (Andeweg and Irwin 2014, 114). Such free publicity is heavily focused on the party leader, who functions as the spokesperson of the party (Boumans, Boomgaarden, and Vliegenthart 2013). Lower-ranked candidates stand little chance of getting mass media coverage and remain unknown to most of the electorate. This makes sense: the electoral system already allows for a lot of political parties. Opening up to allow multiple politicians for each party would complicate matters significantly and make matters even more unclear for journalists and viewers. Admittedly, this is not impossible, though in practice traditional media seem very reluctant to zoom in on lower-ranked candidates (Spierings and Jacobs 2014). Combined, these three elements make it very difficult for individual candidates to start a successful personal campaign and as a result they rely heavily on the party to get elected.

Candidates typically do not campaign against the leadership of their own party. If there is intraparty conflict, this occurs at the nomination stage when the party lists are crafted (Andeweg 2008, 501). When the parties craft the party lists, they often strive for a balance based on gender, ethnicity, policy expertise, and, depending on the party, age and region. Typically only party members get a say about the final composition of the list (Andeweg and Irwin 2014, 90).

The ballot structure dimension of the electoral system makes individual MPs highly dependent on their party. However, MPs retain their seat when they leave their party in between elections (even if they were elected solely based on their list position and not based on preference votes!). As a result, internal dissent within a party's parliamentary faction frequently leads to MPs leaving the party (cf. Table 27.4). Leaving the party and establishing a new one gives breakaway MPs a higher chance to get re-elected (given the low legal electoral threshold): they would simply not be included on the party ballot.[23] Again, this is an interesting example of how the interparty dimension of the electoral system interacts with the interparty dimension.

## Impact on Parliament

On November 17, 2015, the Dutch populist radical right politician Geert Wilders (PVV) called the Dutch parliament a "fake parliament" (NOS 2015), one that does not represent the people. At first sight, this is quite an unexpected statement: the proportional electoral system was introduced precisely to guarantee that the parliament is a microcosm of the Dutch society (Elzinga et al. 2012, 8). At the level of parties this is indeed the case: both disproportionality and the electoral threshold are low. Moreover, as Farrell (2011, 164) notes, in countries "where average district magnitude is large ... we should expect greater scope for parties to field more women candidates, allowing for a more balanced ticket, without fearing the upsetting of traditionalists." This argument can be extended to all sorts of minorities. Hence, one can expect the Dutch electoral system, which has one of the highest district magnitudes in the world, to correlate with a high degree of diversity.

Parties do try to craft a balanced list of candidates that they present to the voters (cf. section "Impact on the Parties"). To a certain extent, this indeed produces a diverse composition of the parliament. The Netherlands was the first to have an openly gay MP, Coos Huijsen in 1976 (LGBTQ Representation and Rights Research Initiative, 2016). As Table 27.5 shows, the number of female, foreign-born, and openly gay MPs has increased steadily. However, at the turn of the century the percentages seem to have stagnated (even though their respective share of the Dutch population is higher). On all three fronts some underrepresentation still exists, but the lower house is clearly fairly diverse.

The composition of the lower house is no microcosm of the Dutch society though. Indeed, another important change is the steady increase of the number of MPs who have a higher education (Bovens and Wille 2009, 48). Right after World War II, only slightly more than 50 percent had a higher education. In the twenty-first century, that

### Table 27.5  Composition of the Lower House

| Election Year | N Female MPs (%) | N Foreign-Born MPs[a] (%) | N LGBT MPs[b] (%) |
|---|---|---|---|
| 1946 | 4 (4%) | 0 | 0 |
| 1948 | 5 (5%) | 0 | 0 |
| 1952 | 7 (7%) | 0 | 0 |
| 1956 | 13 (8.7%) | 0 | 0 |
| 1959 | 13 (8.7%) | 0 | 0 |
| 1963 | 14 (9.3% | 0 | 0 |
| 1967 | 12 (8%) | 0 | 0 |
| 1971 | 13 (8.7%) | 0 | 0 |
| 1972 | 15 (10%) | 0 | 1 (0.7%) |
| 1977 | 18 (12%) | 0 | 0 |
| 1981 | 27 (18%) | 0 | 1 (0.7%) |
| 1982 | 29 (19.3%) | 0 | 3 (2%) |
| 1986 | 30 (20%) | 0 | 2 (1.3%) |
| 1989 | 38 (25.3%) | 0 | 2 (1.3%) |
| 1994 | 49 (32.7%) | 5 (3.3%) | 4 (2.7%) |
| 1998 | 54 (36%) | 6 (4%) | 5 (3.3%) |
| 2002 | 51 (34%) | 9 (6%) | 6 (4%) |
| 2003 | 55 (36.7%) | 13 (8.7%) | 7 (4.7%) |
| 2006 | 56 (37.3%) | 10 (6.7%) | 6 (4%) |
| 2010 | 64 (42.7%) | 5 (3.3%) | 8 (5.3%) |
| 2012 | 60 (40%) | 7 (4.7%) | 6 (4%) |

[a] MPs born outside the Netherlands.

[b] Only openly LGBT.

Data source: Female and ethnic minority MPs: http://www.parlement.com, complemented with own calculations for missing elections. LGBT MPs: https://lgbtqrepresentationandrights.org/data/.

percentage increased to more than 75 percent. To a certain extent this increase can be explained by politics becoming ever more complex. However, higher-educated citizens may well have policy preferences that differ from the average Dutch citizen. At the very least it makes the lower house vulnerable to the criticism that the legislative process is an elite affair. Even the extremely proportional electoral system could not prevent this discrepancy. In part, the ballot structure is to blame. Given how difficult it is to get elected based on preference votes, the composition of the lower house depends greatly on the list order (as determined by the selectorates of the parties). The ballot paper does not help either: it only shows the candidates' name, date of birth, gender, and place of residence (Van Driel and De Jong 2014, 79). The education level of the candidates is not listed explicitly, making it labor intensive for a voter to vote deliberately for a candidate who is not higher educated.

## Impact on Government Formation

Majoritarian electoral systems are said to produce stable, one-party governments, while proportional ones are expected to produce long coalition negotiations, multiparty coalitions, and unstable governments (Farrell 2011, 14). To a certain extent this is indeed the case in the Netherlands (cf. Table 27.6): coalition negotiations tend to take a long time, and while the lower house is elected for four years, 43 percent of the postwar cabinets formed after an election lasted less than three years. Before 1972, coalitions tended to consist of four or five parties, but since the merger of the three main religious parties, coalitions have become smaller and coalitions now typically consist of two or three parties.

One of the reasons coalition negotiations take so long is that parties do not form pre-election coalitions. This may seem strange given the possibility to form an electoral alliance for the remainder seats. However, in practice, such alliances are first and foremost symbolic and practical (Andeweg 2008, 504). Given the high number of parties and the relatively fragmented party system, it is often hard to predict in advance which parties will be able to form a majority cabinet. Center parties have a higher chance to be in government and have more options to choose from. As a result, it is extremely difficult for voters to remove them from government. Nevertheless, voters cannot predict the exact composition of the government as the electoral system makes the outcome sensitive to even relatively small vote swings. When a party declares a coalition preference, there is always the risk that the preferred coalition does not have a majority. This may make delicate coalition negotiations even more difficult. To avoid such a thorny situation, parties tend to be vague about their preferred partners and typically do not want to exclude anyone.

As a proxy, many voters currently vote to determine who will be the biggest party. Such "strategic voting" often occurs within a left- and right-wing block and means that some voters do not vote for their preferred party. The reason that being the biggest is so important is largely symbolic and does not directly stem from the electoral system: as an informal rule the biggest party is allowed to take the lead in exploring the coalition options. However, the biggest party does not automatically end up in the government, and strategic voting may lead to a horse race after which both of the biggest parties are forced into a coalition together (as happened in 2012).

**Table 27.6  Characteristics of the Dutch Governments (1946–2016)**

| Election Year | Government | Duration of Formation (Days)[a] | No. Parties in Coalition[b] | Days in Power[c] |
|---|---|---|---|---|
| 1946 | Beel I | 36 | 3 | 735 |
| 1948 | Drees I | 31[d] | 4 | 901[e] |
| 1952 | Drees III | 67 | 4 | 1,380 |
| 1956 | Drees IV | 119 | 4 | 789 |
| 1959 | De Quay | 65 | 4 | 1,457 |
| 1963 | Marijnen | 65 | 4 | 584 |
| 1967 | De Jong | 34 | 4 | 1,484 |
| 1971 | Biesheuvel I | 52 | 5 | 512 |
| 1972 | Den Uyl I | 157 | 5 | 1,411 |
| 1977 | Van Aght | 205 | 2 | 1,253 |
| 1981 | Van Aght II | 104[f] | 3 | 243 |
| 1982 | Lubbers I | 56 | 2 | 1,294 |
| 1986 | Lubbers II | 52 | 2 | 1,024 |
| 1989 | Lubbers III | 60 | 2 | 1,644 |
| 1994 | Kok I | 108 | 3 | 1,353 |
| 1998 | Kok II | 87 | 3 | 1,352 |
| 2002 | Balkenende I | 66 | 3 | 86 |
| 2003 | Balkenende II | 122 | 3 | 1,130 |
| 2006 | Balkenende IV | 89 | 3 | 1,097 |
| 2010 | Rutte I | 125 | 3[g] | 557 |
| 2012 | Rutte II | 47 | 2 | 1,593 |

*Notes:* Six caretaker governments are excluded, and two governments (Drees II, 1951–1952 and Cals, 1965–1966) are excluded because no elections were held prior to the coalition formation.

[a]  From day of appointment of formateur until administration of the oath. Note that this may slightly underestimate the duration as the period between Election Day and the appointment of formateur is excluded. For data calculated from the Election Day, see Andeweg and Irwin (2014, 147).

[b]  Excluding ministers/state secretaries without a partisan attachment.

[c]  From administration of the oath until the day the government is officially under resignation.

[d]  Data missing, therefore calculated from Election Day until administration of the oath.

[e]  Calculated by the author.

[f]  Corrected count, as http://www.parlement.com exhibits a calculation error.

[g]  Including PVV.

*Data source:* http://www.parlement.com.

# ELECTORAL REFORM

Since its introduction in 1989, the current electoral law has been amended forty-six times.[24] However, most changes were merely technical tweaks.[25] In 1997, the preference threshold was lowered from 50 to 25 percent of the electoral quota, but other than that no significant reform was implemented.[26] Yet since 1994, electoral reform has constantly been a salient topic on the political agenda. In the conclusion of the edited volume on electoral systems, Gallagher (2008, 565) lists the Netherlands as the only country exhibiting a high chance of major electoral reform. This was because of the attempts of the Balkenende II government to implement a mixed-member proportional system. However, like many before it, that reform process failed miserably and not even a minor electoral reform was implemented (Jacobs 2011). In this section I first sketch the major electoral reform debates in the postwar era.[27] Afterward, I discuss (1) why electoral reform is always on the Dutch political agenda and (2) why these discussions almost always fail.

## Brief Overview of Electoral Reform Debates since 1946

After World War II, reformers were mostly concerned with the link between voting and the composition of the government. To remedy the lack of influence of voters on government composition, proposals were made to reduce the district magnitude from 150 to 10 to 13 and to introduce the direct election of the formateur. Bills were introduced in 1971 and 1974 but failed (Andeweg 2008, 505).[28]

Afterward, reformers shifted their attention to reducing the (supposed) confidence gap between citizens and MPs. Specifically, they wanted to introduce an element of geographical representation and to strengthen the impact of voters on the allocation of seats to candidates. Regarding the former, attempts to implement a mixed-member proportional electoral system failed so far. Such an electoral system was first suggested in 1990 by a parliamentary committee of party leaders (Commission Deetman). However, a state commission (Commission De Koning) installed to follow up on the parliamentary committee rejected the idea in 1993. While the 1994 Kok I coalition agreement did include a paragraph about strengthening the connection between voters and the elected, no electoral reform toward a mixed-member system was introduced. Only a minor electoral reform was implemented: the preference threshold was reduced from 50 percent to 25 percent of the national electoral quota. The following government, Kok II, once again promised to make electoral system change a priority and promised to introduce legislation "quickly" (Jacobs 2011, 188). However, no bills were introduced as in 1999 it became clear that the government parties were divided on which alternative electoral system should be introduced. In 2005, the Balkenende II government once again tried (and failed) to introduce electoral reform because of disagreements within the parties and the government (Jacobs 2011, 189–190). Despite all these failures, electoral reform is still on the political agenda: a new state commission will once again examine whether, among others, the electoral system is appropriate. Two topics regularly popped up in recent discussions: (1) a substantial overhaul of the electoral system and (2) a more modest proposal, namely, increasing the legal electoral threshold:

1. *Changing the electoral system.* Some reform proposals have been discussed in recent times. These look familiar. For instance, the proposal that was defeated in 2005 still lingers on. Indeed, in the Netherlands, electoral reform proposals never seem to be completely off the table: path dependency pervades the reform discussions. The Christian Democrats (CDA) in particular still favor a mixed-member electoral system that allows for some form of geographical representation. Another proposal was put forward by the conservative liberal former mayor Paul Scholten (VVD) and suggests introducing a two-round system.[29] It is a variant of the system that some within the party advocated in 2005. However, as in 2005, the VVD is split on the issue (Jacobs 2011, 191). Few within the party want a major reform of the electoral system.

2. *Electoral threshold.* Party system fragmentation was already a matter of contention in the 1920s and 1930s, and the topic is once again on the agenda. For instance, in their 2017 electoral manifestos, several parties indicated that they wanted to reduce party system fragmentation by implementing an electoral threshold. The two center-right parties, CDA and VVD, and the party for the elderly, 50PLUS, were the most outspoken proponents. However, the proposals were relatively modest: CDA wanted to increase the threshold to three times the electoral quota (CDA 2016), while 50PLUS wanted an electoral threshold of 3 percent (50PLUS 2016).[30] Such low thresholds are unlikely to reduce the party system fragmentation. Why bother then? An interesting interplay between the inter- and intraparty dimension of the electoral system seems at the origin of these proposals. The proposed electoral thresholds seemed designed to deter MPs to break away and found their own party (psychological, preventive effect), rather than to reduce the number of existing parties (mechanical, repressive effect). Indeed, in their argumentation, the parties did not mention the elected number of parties, but the high number of *factions* in the parliament (e.g., CDA 2016, 8).

## Electoral Reform: A Sisyphean Task

Why is electoral reform always on the table, and why do so many reform proposals fail? The first question can be answered by looking at a combination of inherent and contingent factors (cf. Shugart 2008b). Inherent conditions make life hard for the bigger parties. Indeed, the Dutch electoral system is prone to a high party system fragmentation, and bigger parties are vulnerable to threats from new parties. Governments typically consist of a high number of parties and need to find broad compromises. Additionally, the low electoral threshold combined with the rigid ballot structure makes breakaway MPs and new parties a common feature. As Jacobs (2011, 212) notes, frustration with the high party system fragmentation and the need to forge compromises acts as a catalyst for electoral reform in the Netherlands.

It is no surprise that the bigger parties, who have most to win from electoral system change, are avid proponents of electoral reforms. The Christian democrats (CDA), who are strong in the regions, want an electoral system that increases the impact of a regional component. The conservative liberals (VVD) and Christian democrats (CDA) want an electoral threshold, which would again benefit them. In short, outcome-contingent motivations go a long way in explaining the position of the parties. Act-contingent motivations are less likely to play a role: citizens are not demanding a regional representation, and no majority favors a mixed-member system (Andeweg and Irwin 2014, 285).

One additional factor played a role in the past, and that is the progressive liberal party D66. Rational-choice theories and outcome-contingent motivations in particular can explain most of the parties' positions on electoral reform, but these explanations do not apply to D66. The party was founded to introduce electoral reform and has advocated it ever since. Most of the reforms it favored would have hurt the party (Jacobs 2011, 201). The party was an important driving force of reform discussions and put and kept the topic on the political agenda.

This brings us to the second question: why has the Dutch electoral system remained so remarkably stable? In a recent study, Nunez and Jacobs (2016) find that three factors in particular reduce the likelihood of a successful electoral reform: (1) the absence of a constitutional court, (2) the rigidity of the constitution, and (3) partial alternation. On all three factors the Netherlands scores high. First, in countries such as Germany, Italy, Belgium, the Czech Republic, and Japan, constitutional courts have triggered, demanded, or enabled electoral reforms. In the Netherlands, there is no court that can judge the compatibility of the electoral law with the constitution. Second, constitutional rigidity plays a role: the Dutch constitution is very hard to change. Both houses first have to approve the change by ordinary majority, but after elections they have to approve it again by a two-thirds majority. Several key parts of the electoral law are enshrined in the constitution: the assembly size, the duration of the legislative term, the voting age, and the principle of proportional representation. Several attempts at electoral reform have failed because of the constitutional rigidity, of which the 2005 failure is the most recent one (Nunez and Jacobs 2016, 468). Third, most Dutch governments consist of incumbents and parties that are new to the coalition. Both types of parties have different, and typically opposing, outcome-contingent motivations. While each party wants a change, they do not agree on which change they prefer. Such disagreements, for example, played a role in the attempts to introduce a mixed-member proportional electoral system in 1994 and 1999 (Nunez and Jacobs 2016, 469). In short, it seems that electoral reform is poised to be a Sisyphean task: there are constant pressures that keep electoral reform on the table, but the barriers are so high that the likelihood of succeeding is extremely low.

# Conclusion

The Dutch electoral system is extremely proportional: the electoral formula uses Hare quota, but the remainders are distributed using D'Hondt. Crucially, the district magnitude is very high (150) and the legal electoral threshold is low (one seat or 0.67 percent). The only element that slightly increases disproportionality is the electoral formula for the remainder seats (D'Hondt highest averages), but until 2017 this effect was partly offset by the option to form electoral alliances. The effects of the electoral system are visible in the high party fragmentation.[31] Dutch governments consist of coalitions, and these are formed after relatively long negotiations. Many governments fall early. The parliament is largely a microcosm of the Dutch society, and minorities have a lot of opportunities to get elected. However, the higher educated are overrepresented and, due to the ballot layout and composition, it is hard for Dutch voters to remedy this. Moreover, the ballot structure is relatively rigid, and few candidates get elected based on preference votes. Candidates who win a seat are allowed to keep that seat even if they leave the party. Given the low electoral threshold, intraparty conflicts often lead to breakaway MPs, who found their own new party. This is a nice illustration of how inter- and intraparty dimensions influence each other.

Given the party fragmentation because of both the proportionality and high number of breakaway MPs, electoral reform is always high on the political agenda. Several parties want to introduce an electoral threshold, not to eliminate small parties (repressive, mechanical effect), but rather to discourage MPs from leaving the party and founding a new one (preventive, psychological effect). However, given that the Dutch political system is rigid, the chances of a successful electoral reform are low. Electoral reform is thus a Sisyphean task: while there is constant pressure to reform, reform proposals are typically destined to fail.

## Notes

1. Somewhat confusingly, the Dutch label for the lower house is "Tweede Kamer" (Second Chamber), while the upper house is called "Eerste Kamer" (First Chamber). To avoid confusion I use the labels lower and upper house.
2. Obviously this does not take into account the competences that have been transferred to the European level.
3. Women obtained voting rights in 1919.
4. From 1925 to 1933, when fewer than fifteen remainder seats were to be distributed, the largest remainders method was used; otherwise, D'Hondt was used (Politiekcompendium 2016).
5. Or more precisely from a quasi-list to a latent list system, as voters were and are not allowed to cast a vote for a party (Shugart 2008a, 42).
6. Calculated as follows: the total number of votes for that party divided by the total number of seats won by that party. This threshold is virtually always higher than the official electoral quota. Moreover, until 1989, the candidates' votes were only added up when they

---

came from exactly the same lists. As the country was divided into eighteen separate districts, the parties often changed the candidates in the bottom positions to add regional candidates who had ties to that given district to attract more votes. Consequently, hardly any list was exactly the same, making it virtually impossible for individual candidates to cross the preference threshold.

7. "Major" according to the definition of Jacobs and Leyenaar (2011).
8. The requirement that lists were identical top to bottom (cf. footnote 6) was removed.
9. Before the reform (i.e., until 1997), just three candidates were elected based on preference votes, but since then thirteen have been elected this way (1998–2017).
10. In the past Dutch citizens residing abroad needed to register for each election. A law to abolish this requirement was approved in 2016.
11. Interestingly, the ID can be used even when it expired up to five years before the polling day.
12. Computer voting was possible since 1965. The municipal governments who organized the elections had the option to buy or rent voting machines that were approved by the ministry of the interior. After a fraud case, whereby the investigation was hindered by the fact that the voting machines left no paper trail, the nongovernmental organization "We Don't Trust Voting Computers" (*Wij vertrouwen stemcomputers niet*) succeeded in getting computer voting abolished in 2007 (Loeber 2008).
13. Only parties that won sixteen seats or more during the previous election are allowed to field eighty candidates. The other parties are only allowed to field a maximum of fifty candidates.
14. The average was 81.59 percent, the standard deviation 7.97.
15. Electoral alliances were abolished in 2017 (Tweede Kamer der Staten-Generaal 2017). The last election that electoral alliances were used was the 2017 election.
16. This section is based on the official guidelines provided by the electoral management body (http://www.kiesraad.nl) and the discussion of the Dutch seat allocation in Andeweg (2008, 498), Andeweg and Irwin (2014, 106–107), and Elzinga, Kummeling, and Schipper-Spanninga (2012, 198–203).
17. The votes of the constituent parties of that alliance are only added up when the constituent party would have crossed the legal electoral threshold independently. To calculate whether or not this was the case, the number of seats is calculated based on a hypothetical situation without *any* electoral alliances. Parties that received fewer votes than the electoral quota are removed from the alliance (Elzinga et al. 2012, 198).
18. Under the D'Hondt system, PvdA would have won a remainder seat, not Groenlinks. All in all, this means that the Dutch form of apparentement is, for example, different from the Israeli one (see chapter by Hazan et al., this volume). While both types of apparentement consider the electoral alliance as a single party at the stage of the allocation of remainder seats (using the D'Hondt system), the Dutch system is slightly more beneficial to smaller parties (who are more likely to be in an alliance). Specifically, (1) electoral alliances are also considered a single party in the initial seat allocation phase (while in Israel they are treated separately), and (2) the formula used to allocate seats within an electoral alliance does not favor bigger parties (while in Israel the D'Hondt system is used).
19. This section is based on the official guidelines provided by the electoral management body (http://www.kiesraad.nl).
20. At first Omtzigt was not listed on the ballot. After a series of complaints from provincial and local branches, the party decided to include him on the list, but only placed him at

a very low position. The same branches then successfully campaigned with Omtzigt to get him elected based on preference votes. He obtained most of his votes in the eastern provinces.

21. DS'70 in 1971 and PVV in 2006.
22. One candidate, Dirk Poot (Piratenpartij), was not elected because his party won no seat.
23. A low chance is still better than no chance.
24. Excluding the twenty-nine changes due to municipal mergers.
25. "Technical" according to the classification of Jacobs and Leyenaar (2011, 497).
26. The other main changes are making it easier for Dutch citizens residing abroad to vote and the abolition of computer voting in 2007, both of which would qualify as "technical" changes.
27. An excellent overview of past electoral reform debates is offered by Andeweg (2008, 504–509).
28. The bills were withdrawn because no majority supported the direct election of the formateur (Andeweg 2008, 505).
29. The proposal was fairly abstract and did not include many details about its specifics.
30. VVD did not mention a specific level of threshold.
31. Though multipartism was the norm even before introduction of the proportional electoral system in 1917.

## References

Andeweg, Rudi. "The Netherlands: The Sanctity of Proportionality." In *The Politics of Electoral Systems*, 2nd ed., edited by M. Gallagher and P. Mitchell, 491–510. Oxford: Oxford University Press, 2008.

Andeweg, Rudi, and Galen Irwin. *Governance and Politics of the Netherlands*. 4th ed. Houndmills: Palgrave MacMillan, 2014.

Bovens, Mark, and Anchrit Wille. *Diploma Democracy: On the Tensions between Meritocracy and Democracy*. Utrecht: Universiteit Utrecht, 2009.

Boumans, Jelle, Hajo Boomgaarden, and Rens Vliegenthart. "Media Personalisation in Context: A Cross-National Comparison Between the UK and the Netherlands, 1992–2007." *Political Studies* 61, no. S1 (2013): 198–216.

CDA. *Concept Verkiezingsprogramma 2017-2021. Keuzes voor een Beter Nederland*. 2016, 49p.

Colomer, Josep. *Personal Representation: The Neglected Dimension of Electoral Systems*. Colchester: ECPR Press, 2011.

De Jong, Ron. "De Lijstencombinatie. Een opmerkelijke figuur in ons kiesstelsel." *Tijdschrift voor Constitutioneel Recht* 4 (2015): 345–355.

Elzinga, Douwe, Henk Kummeling, and Hanneke Schipper-Spanninga. *Het Nederlandse Kiesrecht*. 3rd ed. Deventer: Kluwer, 2012.

Farrell, David. *Electoral Systems. A Comparative Introduction*. 2nd ed. Houndmills: Palgrave MacMillan, 2011.

Gallagher, Michael. "Conclusion." In *The Politics of Electoral Systems*, 2nd ed., edited by M. Gallagher and P. Mitchell, 535–578. Oxford: Oxford University Press, 2008.

Gallagher, Michael. *Election Indices*. 2016. http://www.tcd.ie/Political_Science/staff/michael_gallagher/ElSystems/Docts/ElectionIndices.pdf. (accessed October 25, 2016).

Jacobs, Kristof. "The Power or the People? Direct Democratic and Electoral Reforms in Austria, Belgium and the Netherlands." Unpublished dissertation, 2011.

Jacobs, Kristof, and Monique Leyenaar. "A Conceptual Framework for Major, Minor, and Technical Electoral Reform." *West European Politics* 34, no. 3 (2011): 495–513.

LGBTQ Representation & Rights Initiative. *Data.* 2016. https://lgbtqrepresentationandrights .org/data/ (accessed October 23, 2016).

Loeber, Leontine "E-Voting in the Netherlands; from General Acceptance to General Doubt in Two Years." Paper presented at the 3rd International Conference on E-Voting, Bregenz, Austria, 2008.

Louwerse, Tom, and Simon Otjes. "Personalised Parliamentary Behaviour without Electoral Incentives: The Case of the Netherlands." *West European Politics* 39, no. 4 (2016): 778–799.

NOS. *Wilders: Tweede Kamer is een Nepparlement.* 2015. http://nos.nl/artikel/2058288-wilders-tweede-kamer-is-een-nepparlement.html (accessed October 23, 2016).

Nunez, Lidia, and Kristof Jacobs. "Catalysts and Barriers: Explaining Electoral Reform in Western Europe." *European Journal of Political Research* 55, no. 3 (2016): 454–473.

Politiekcompendium. *Periode 1918-Heden.* 2016. https://www.politiekcompendium.nl /9353000/1/j9vvjvgivn417wd/vh4vajthpgzu (accessed October 23, 2016).

Shugart, Matthew. "Comparative Electoral System Research: The Maturation of a Field and New Challenges Ahead." In *The Politics of Electoral Systems*, 2nd ed., edited by Michael Gallagher and Paul Mitchell, 25–56. Oxford: Oxford University Press, 2008a.

Shugart, Matthew. "Inherent and Contingent Factors in Reform Initiation in Plurality Systems." In *To Keep or to Change First Past the Post? The Politics of Electoral Reform*, edited by André Blais, 7–60. Oxford: Oxford University Press, 2008b.

Spierings, Niels, and Kristof Jacobs. "Getting Personal? The Impact of Social Media on Preferential Voting." *Political Behavior* 36, no. 1 (2014): 215–234.

Taagepera, Rein, and Matthew Shugart. *Seats and Votes.* New Haven, CT: Yale University Press, 1989.

Tweede Kamer der Staten-Generaal. *Plenair verslag. Tweede Kamer, 49e vergadering, dinsdag 7 februari 2017.* 2017. https://www.tweedekamer.nl/kamerstukken/plenaire_verslagen /detail?vj=2016-2017&nr=49&version=2 (accessed February 12, 2017).

Van der Meer, Tom, Rozemarijn Lubbe, Erika Van Elsas, Martin Elff, and Wouter van der Brug. "Bounded Volatility in the Dutch Electoral Battlefield: A Panel Study on the Structure of Changing Vote Intentions in the Netherlands during 2006–2010." *Acta Politica* 47, no. 4 (2012): 333–355.

Van Driel, Niels, and Ron De Jong. *De Tweede Kamerverkiezingen in 50 stappen.* Amsterdam: Uitgeverij Boom, 2014.

# CHAPTER 28

......................................................................................................

# ELECTORAL SYSTEMS
# IN CONTEXT

*Israel*

......................................................................................................

## REUVEN Y. HAZAN, REUT ITZKOVITCH-MALKA,
## AND GIDEON RAHAT

ISRAEL was established in 1948 as a parliamentary democracy. It has a 120-member uni-cameral parliament called the Knesset, which is elected by a closed-list system of proportional representation with the entire country serving as one constituency. The Israeli electoral system holds many advantages. It is a system that is clear and simple to understand, and due to its high levels of proportionality, it reduces the number of wasted votes and grants voters considerable efficacy. Moreover, the system creates a highly representative legislature, reflecting the multiple social groups and sectors in Israeli society. The high level of proportionality of the electoral system in Israel brought Lijphart (1993) to conclude that the system fits the multicleavage character of Israeli society and helps contain social conflict within parliament rather than outside of it. In short, the Israeli electoral system fulfills two of the most important goals of an electoral system: it ensures a fair distribution of electoral power between the competing parties, and it enables the representation of different social groups, minorities, and interests.

Nevertheless, the system also has its disadvantages. For example, the combination of a proportional representation (PR) electoral formula with a relatively low legal threshold and a single nationwide electoral district creates a highly fragmented party system, which makes coalition maintenance difficult and often creates governance problems (Samuels and Shugart 2010). Furthermore, in the Israeli system the "electoral connection" (Mayhew 1974), which ties legislators' activity in parliament to their re-election aspirations, is largely absent. This has produced a rather puzzling expression in the last decades. The use of national PR with closed party lists, which should lead legislators to seek votes for the party rather than personal votes, has been coupled with reforms both "above" and "below" the parties, encouraging legislators to seek more personal support.

In other words, given that Israel is an extreme PR system with a low threshold, closed lists, and a single national district, we expect to see the lowest possible personalization; the results, however, are quite different.

This chapter, which focuses on the Israeli electoral system as a prototype of an extreme PR system, proceeds as follows. First, it uses the 2015 election results to analyze the properties of the electoral system and the nature of its outputs. It then reviews the three prominent features of the Israeli electoral system and their origins: its PR electoral formula, its nationwide electoral district, and its closed party lists. The third part of the chapter examines the developments that led to the consideration and implementation of reform initiatives. These can be seen as attempts to bypass an electoral system that was adopted as only a temporary mechanism but has largely stayed intact over the years. We conclude by assessing the political consequences of the system for parties and the party system, for government formation and durability, and for the legislature and legislative behavior.

# The 2015 Election Results as an Example of the Properties of the Electoral System and Its Outputs

The elections for the twentieth Knesset were held on March 17, 2015. The first and probably most evident impression is the extreme proportional outputs that the Israeli electoral system produces (Table 28.1). Vote and seat shares were quite similar, with a slight advantage given to the larger parties, as could be expected from the use of the D'Hondt formula for the allocation of the remainder seats.[1] The use of a proportional electoral formula is combined with a single nationwide electoral district for all 120 members of Knesset (MKs). The number of valid votes was high, with roughly only 1 percent of the votes deemed invalid. Additionally, fewer than 5 percent of the valid votes were cast for parties that did not pass the electoral threshold even though the 2015 elections were the first to use a 3.25 percent threshold. Voter turnout was 72.3 percent in 2015—higher than in the last four Knesset elections but lower than in the 1950s to 1990s—in a country where no early or absentee voting is allowed, but where no preregistration is required and Election Day (a Tuesday) is a national holiday.[2]

The second notable impression, which goes hand in hand with the extreme proportionality the system produces, is the fragmented multiparty system it creates. Indeed, the number of party lists elected to the Knesset in 2015 was lower than in previous elections as a result of the increase in the legal threshold; however, it was still extremely high, comparatively speaking—ten party lists (which represented sixteen registered parties) made it into the Knesset out of the twenty-six that ran. The decrease in the absolute

Table 28.1 Results of the Elections to the Twentieth Knesset (March 17, 2015)

| Eligible Voters | 5,881,696 | | | |
|---|---|---|---|---|
| Voters | 4,254,738 | (72.3%) | | |
| Valid votes | 4,210,884 | (98.9%) | | |
| Invalid votes | 43,854 | (1.1%) | | |
| List name | Votes | % Votes | # Seats | % Seats |
| Likud[a] | 985,408 | 23.4 | 30 | 25.0 |
| Zionist Camp[b] | 786,313 | 18.7 | 24 | 20.0 |
| Joint List | 446,583 | 10.6 | 13 | 10.8 |
| Yesh Atid | 371,602 | 8.8 | 11 | 9.2 |
| Kulanu[c] | 315,360 | 7.5 | 10 | 8.3 |
| Jewish Home[a] | 283,910 | 6.7 | 8 | 6.7 |
| Shas[d] | 241,613 | 5.7 | 7 | 5.8 |
| Yisrael Beitenu[c] | 214,906 | 5.1 | 6 | 5.0 |
| Yahadut HaTorah[d] | 210,143 | 4.9 | 6 | 5.0 |
| Meretz[b] | 165,529 | 3.9 | 5 | 4.2 |
| Others | 191,477 | 4.6 | 0 | – |

Letters next to list names indicate a "surplus agreement," the Israeli terminology for *apparentement* (see note 1).

*Source:* Israel Central Elections Committee, http://www.votes20.gov.il/ (last accessed January 1, 2017).

number of parties in the Knesset was not fully mirrored in the effective number of parties—which was still extremely high and stood at 6.94—due to the relative size of each party, a point we will address later.

The third impression, in line with the two previous points, has to do with government formation. In Israel, the law requires a vote of investiture within a specified time limit, and thus all governments formed have been majority coalitions. Given the extreme proportional character of the electoral system and the fragmentation of the party system, the number of parties needed to form a coalition and reach a parliamentary majority is rather high. In recent times, the party forming the coalition—the prime minister's party—more often than not lacks a majority within its own coalition. Benjamin Netanyahu's sixty-one-seat majority coalition formed after the 2015 elections included five parties; his party, Likud, held only thirty seats (49%) in his sixty-one-member coalition.

# THE ELECTORAL SYSTEM AND ITS
# BASIC FEATURES

The Israeli electoral system is based on three main characteristics: a proportional allocation formula, the exclusive use of a single nationwide district for seat allocation, and a rigid closed-party-list system (Rahat and Hazan 2005). The system, still in use today, was initially adopted in 1948 by the Provisional State Council, the legislative body that served from the May 1948 Declaration of Independence until the first elections in January 1949. In those days there was a clear preference for proportionality, a recognition that a nationwide district was a necessity justified by immediate circumstances, and little concern over the lack of any personal element. Furthermore, the system that was adopted was seen as a provisional mechanism that would have no bearing on the future, since the newly elected Constituent Assembly would formulate the electoral system within the framework of its constitution-making mission (Brichta 1988; Medding 1990). Nevertheless, almost seventy years after it was first implemented, the main features of the extremely proportional electoral system that was adopted in 1948 have been preserved, with only minor changes.

## A Proportional Electoral Formula with a Low Legal Threshold

When the electoral system was first engineered, it was rather clear that it would be based on a PR formula. Proportionality was perceived to be more democratic by the dominant political forces. It was part of the inclusive political legacy developed in the voluntary prestate institutions (Sager 1985), was compatible with the UN Partition Resolution, and fit the interests of small and medium-sized parties, which were the majority in those days (Doron and Maor 1989).

In addition to the proportional electoral formula, the election law adopted in 1948 introduced a single-seat quota (0.83 percent) as the legal threshold, calculated according to the Droop formula. Parties received a seat for every Droop quota, and the remaining seats were allocated using the D'Hondt formula. The fact that this formula gives an advantage to large parties seems to have passed unnoticed; it later became a contested issue, and in 1951 it was replaced by the largest remainder principle, using the Hare quota, which better served the interests of the small parties. That same year, the legal threshold was raised from 0.83 to 1 percent.[3] In 1973, the two large party alliances unilaterally returned to the D'Hondt formula for remainder allocation, while maintaining the Hare quota, and as a result slightly increased their representation at the expense of the smaller parties. The use of the Hare quota to allocate seats, with D'Hondt then applied to the parties' total votes for the allocation of remainder seats, is little more than a shortcut in the D'Hondt process—the results are identical. Prior to the 1992 elections, the legal threshold was slightly increased from 1 to 1.5 percent. In 2004, it was raised again to 2 percent, and in 2014 it was increased to 3.25 percent. The last change means that the Israeli electoral threshold can no longer be considered a comparatively low barrier but rather a moderate-level one.

The use of a PR formula with a relatively low (and more recently with a moderate) electoral threshold makes the Israeli electoral system highly inclusive, as the "payoff" per seat in the Knesset is relatively low. In other words, it was quite easy (and still is, to a high degree) for parties to win seats in the Knesset, which increases the diversity of the groups, sectors, and interests represented.

## A Single Nationwide Electoral District

The second distinctive characteristic of the Israeli electoral system is the lack of electoral districts, since the entire country serves as a single nationwide district, equal in magnitude to the size of the legislature (120 seats). Districts are used for the administration of elections but are irrelevant for the allocation of seats, which is based on the total number of valid votes in the entire country. The draft of the election law that the Constitution Committee submitted prior to the first elections in 1949 suggested the adoption of a single nationwide district (Rahat 2008a). This was partly based on the use of a single nationwide district during the prestate era, and partly because warfare complicated and even precluded the adoption and implementation of a system that would require a complicated division of the state into districts—during the war many recruits were far from their residence and were constantly transferred from one front to another, and even the borders of the country changed quite often.

During the 1950s, Israel's first prime minister, David Ben-Gurion, proposed the adoption of a plurality system, which required the adoption of single-member districts. Other parties suggested the introduction of small multimember districts, while maintaining the existing PR formula. In reaction to these suggestions, the smaller parties (some of them reformist in spirit) became zealous defenders of the existing electoral system. These initiatives—which threatened the existence of the smaller parties—led not to reform but rather to the entrenchment of the existing system. Thus, the use of a single nationwide district was transformed from a temporary necessity into a protected principle, becoming as sacred as proportionality and enshrined in the "Basic Law: The Knesset" of 1958 (part of Israel's constitution in the making; Rahat 2008a).

The use of a single nationwide district has meant that there is no geographical connection between the voters and their representatives, and this contributes to the centralized character of the system. Israeli MKs are not expected to demonstrate personal, geographically based responsiveness or accountability—even the term "electoral constituencies" is completely absent from Israeli political terminology. Likewise, Israeli voters have no specific representative to turn to with personal or local grievances.

## Closed Party Lists

The closed-list system, which does not allow the voters an opportunity to influence the ordering of the candidate lists, is the third prominent feature of the system. In the elections for the prestate legislative body, the Assembly of Representatives, voters could cross off the name of a particular candidate; those whose names were crossed off by at least one-half of the voters for their party list were transferred to the bottom of the list (which usually meant that they would not be elected). However, this element was rejected by the Provisional State Council, which made it harder for future reformers to promote any initiative aimed at introducing voter influence on the personal composition of the party lists, since they would first have to struggle for the acceptance of the very principle rather than focus on its enhancement (Rahat 2008a).

In the elections between 1949 and 1992, and since 2003, the Israeli voter could cast a ballot only for a party, or an alliance of parties that together presented a joint list of candidates.[4] There is one ballot paper for every list running, and the voter has to select his or her preferred paper from a choice of approximately thirty party lists that take part in the election. Voters have no discretion regarding the candidates on the parties' lists; they simply place one ballot paper in an envelope, drop it into the voting box, and by doing so accept the order of the candidate list produced by the party they voted for. Alongside the absence of electoral districts, this characteristic denies candidates and voters alike the possibility of establishing a personal, direct connection with one another, leaving the political parties as the sole mediators of the voter–representative connection. Given this kind of institutional design, the cultivation of a personal reputation and the demonstration of personal accountability to the voters cannot be expected (Carey 2009; Carey and Shugart 1995). Yet, as explained in the next section, while the party-centered electoral system has stayed in place, personalizing elements have been injected into the system.

# UNSUCCESSFUL REFORM INITIATIVES AND THE ADOPTION OF BYPASSES

The extreme nature of the electoral system, given its noticeable drawbacks and the fact that it was implemented as a provisional system, brought about many discussions regarding electoral reform. The prevalent reform initiatives of the 1970s and 1980s were relatively moderate in scope and included various versions of a two-tier system. These ranged from initiatives that would have substantially decreased proportionality—such as the adoption of a system in which eighty MKs would be elected in 20 four-member districts and the remaining forty in a national pool, with no compensation—to initiatives that preserved nationwide proportionality, suggesting a moderate increase of the legal threshold to about 3 to 4 percent. The moderate reform initiatives were supposed to fine-tune the system, decrease its extremely high level of proportionality, and add regional and personal elements. Several of these initiatives were successfully promoted in the early legislative stages, yet no initiative to reform the electoral system has ever reached the final legislative stages.

Most of the moderate reform initiatives demonstrated sensitivity to the needs of the smaller parties and allowed for their continued independent survival. Yet some of the small parties feared that even moderate reform might serve as a precedent, and thus put all of their political weight behind blocking any reform initiative. Even when the party system consolidated around two relatively large parties, who together held a majority of the seats and should have found common ground in advancing an electoral reform that would reduce proportionality and empower them both, their cooperation was stymied. The small parties succeeded in thwarting reform not only when they were crucial players in the minimal-winning coalitions but also when the two large parties ruled together in national unity governments.

While attempts to reform the electoral system failed, two reforms were adopted "above" and "below" the electoral system: the direct election of the prime minister and party primaries (Rahat 2008b).

## Bypass One:  Direct Election of the Prime Minister

In 1992, a major reform was adopted: the separate and direct election of the prime minister (Hazan 1996). This reform was grafted onto the existing electoral system for the Knesset, which remained unchanged. Given the repeated failure to enact electoral reform, the proponents of the direct election of the prime minister claimed this was the only viable cure for the malaise of Israeli politics. The advocates argued that by granting the choice of chief executive to the voters and taking it away from the small and extreme parties—which in itself held intrinsic democratic appeal—it would grant the prime minister both a mandate and legitimacy. They also argued that the direct election of the prime minister would solve the problems of coalition politics in the extreme multiparty party system that had been in place since 1977, by reducing the disproportionate political power held by the small parties. In short, the reformers promised that Israel would enjoy a more stable and efficient system of governance, and at the same time the representative nature of the Knesset—a central element of the inclusive political culture—would stay intact. However, the direct election of the prime minister produced outcomes that were mostly unanticipated by the proponents of the reform, while those that were expected never actually materialized. The unexpected ramifications were thus largely responsible for the subsequent abolition of direct elections in 2001 (Kenig, Rahat, and Hazan 2004).

The results of the only two instances of separate executive and legislative elections were dramatic. The availability of ballot splitting (electing the prime minister separately from a party running for the Knesset) decreased the incentives for compromise between

588    REUVEN Y. HAZAN, REUT ITZKOVITCH-MALKA, AND GIDEON RAHAT

social groups, as sectarian group identity became a major electoral asset. The 1996 and 1999 elections produced very high volatility rates (Table 28.2). Votes shifted from the large parties to the sectarian parties, as voters took advantage of the opportunity to split their vote. The largest party list in the Knesset fell to its lowest point ever; the two largest parties together held the lowest number of seats they had ever won; and the parties representing the three subcultural minorities in Israeli society together gained in 1999, for the first time, more seats than the two largest parties in the Israeli party system. The effective number of parties in parliament increased significantly in the 1996 elections from 4.39 to 5.61, and reached a peak of 8.69 in the 1999 elections.

The implications for governability, in light of the decline of the large parties and the concurrent upsurge in sectarian representation, were disastrous (Hazan 1997b). The erosion in the size of the major parties undermined the nucleus of support for the directly elected prime minister. Once the prime minister was separately elected, rather than being chosen in postelection party bargaining, coalition politics took on new behavioral characteristics; essentially, forming a coalition became much easier since only one formateur was possible, but the coalition became more difficult to maintain due to the increasing number of parties required and their diverging interests. During the coalition governments of 1996–2003, the prime minister's party was actually, for the first time, a minority within the coalition.[5] Confronting the increasingly difficult tasks of keeping the coalition intact and sustaining its legislative discipline became a full-time job. This pattern continued even after the abolition of the direct election, as part of its problematic heritage.

In 2001, the Knesset passed a bill that abolished the separate election of the prime minister and returned the country to a pure parliamentary form of government. This new-old system went into effect with the Knesset elections of 2003. The 2003 results already showed that the restoration of the old system reversed some of the trends brought about by the direct election, but only to a limited extent, as we will shortly see.

## Bypass Two: Democratization of Candidate Selection Methods

Although the closed-list electoral system continued to deny voters any influence on the composition and ordering of the candidate lists, the parties themselves took the initiative and democratized their candidate selection methods by opening up their selectorates. If in the 1950s and 1960s small nominating committees decided the composition and rank of the parties' candidate lists, by the 1970s and 1980s, candidate selection in most parties was transferred to the hands of selected party agencies (central committees, party congresses). This widening of the circle empowered the members of party agencies and opened a channel for the promotion of their private and group interests. Yet, the party as such, and especially its leadership, largely retained control of the list— and thus of its representatives.

Prior to the 1992 elections, Labor opened up its candidate selection method even further, giving all party members the opportunity to directly select both its leader and its list of candidates. In 1993, Likud started to select its leader through party primaries, and in 1996, it adopted party primaries for selecting its list of candidates. The third-largest party in the outgoing Knesset followed suit. In short, prior to the 1996 elections, candidates from the three largest parties, which together held over two-thirds of the seats in the outgoing Knesset, had to face intraparty elections by their members at large (Hazan 1997a).

While the democratization of party selectorates was largely carried out by internal party forces who saw the change of selectorates as serving their interests, the success of the reform initiatives within each separate party was due to the then-prevalent notion that the public would see these reforms as signifying a positive move toward the democratization of the system. In other words, while the main parties failed to reform the closed-list nationwide electoral system, they tried to compensate for this by means of an intraparty reform to their candidate selection methods, which would indirectly "personalize" the electoral process.

However, the unintended consequences of this reform also became apparent immediately. Parties, which until then had controlled the selection of candidates, were circumvented by politicians appealing directly to their selectorate. MKs became increasingly autonomous, unwilling to bend to party dictates and unable to vote against popular proposals. The result was a weakening of parties and party control, coupled with a hampering of the parties' abilities to aggregate positions and policies. The parties became less cohesive both in terms of their ideological image and in their ability to operate within the political process in general, and inside the legislature in particular.

The 1990s saw a dramatic increase in both the submission and the passage of private member bills, and growing instances of breaking party discipline. Much of this was due to the adoption of party primaries, which forced MKs to distinguish themselves as they individually confronted wider selectorates. It should, therefore, come as no surprise that the parties—unbound by legal restrictions—quickly overturned their experiments in internal democracy. Indeed, in 2006, there was a reverse trend away from intraparty democratization, with more than one-half of the MKs selected either by their party leaders or by nonelected party agencies. Today, Israeli parties are characterized by a dichotomy, using one of two extreme candidate selection methods: either highly exclusive methods, usually selection by the party leader, or highly inclusive methods, usually party primaries; intermediate methods are used by a small minority of the parties (Rahat 2010). As a result, about one-half of the MKs are disciplined soldiers under a single commander, while the other half tend to demonstrate individualized behavior and populist expression. Both types of MKs act within a single parliament, in a country where the electoral system and the parliamentary regime are expected to give the central role to political parties, not to single leaders or individual politicians.

# THE POLITICAL CONSEQUENCES OF
# THE ELECTORAL SYSTEM

One of the clearest, most evident consequences of the Israeli electoral system is the party system it produces and its nature. The highly proportional electoral system produces an extreme multiparty system, in terms of both the number of parties and the fragmentation of the party system.

## Impact on the Parties and the Party System

The dominance of one party for the first few decades—which consistently won the largest number of seats by a wide margin, held the pivotal position, and thus formed the core of all governing coalitions—was able to mask the system's drawbacks for almost one-quarter of a century (Medding 1990, 2000). Israel's dominant system ended in the 1970s, when elections began to result in two party alliances equal in size, though both were far from a majority (Figure 28.1).

The almost linear increase in the combined power of the two largest parties during the five elections beginning in the mid-1960s reached its peak in 1981, when together they held 95 of 120 seats. This development was largely a result of the amalgamation of parties, sometimes in electoral alliances and sometimes through unifications (Mendilow 2003). The system thus took on a bipolar structure, with elections becoming highly competitive and forcing the two major parties to woo the smaller ones to form a coalition (Hazan 1998). However, a two-party system did not develop, and since 1981 there has been a steady decrease in the combined power of the two largest party alliances. Until 1996, the two large party alliances together held significantly more than a majority of the seats in the Knesset.

The implementation of the direct election of the prime minister, designed to reverse this declining trend, actually exacerbated it, and the combined seat shares of the two largest alliances dipped below 50 percent for the first time. After the direct election of the prime minister was repealed and the original system was restored, the downward trend was stopped but not reversed. In fact, since 1999 and until today, the combined electoral power of the two largest party alliances has never risen above 50 percent of the total number of seats. Moreover, the seat share of the largest party has fluctuated at around thirty seats, making it a minority within the majority coalition formed after every election.

The trends in Figure 28.1 are reflected in Table 28.2, which presents the absolute number of parties elected to the Knesset, the effective number of political parties (Laakso and Taagepera 1979), and electoral volatility (Pedersen 1979) for each election year. The effective number of parties shows the trends in party system fragmentation.

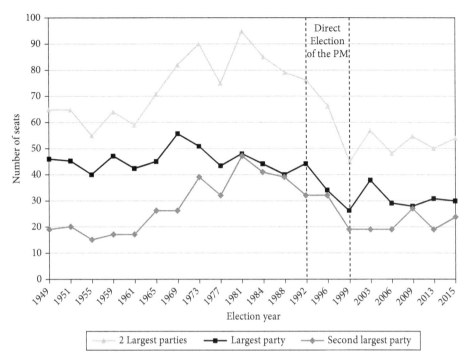

FIGURE 28.1. Party list seats in the Israeli Knesset, 1949–2015.

Source: Updated from Rahat and Hazan (2005, 340).

In the first decade it was rather high—as was electoral volatility—but from the mid-1960s onward, when the process of consolidation into two blocs took place, party fragmentation decreased and reached an all-time low of 3.13 in 1981. After an incremental increase in subsequent elections, the direct election of the prime minister brought about a sharp rise in fragmentation and volatility, even by international standards, due to split-ticket voting. The 1999 elections mark the all-time high in party fragmentation, when the largest party list won only twenty-six seats, electoral volatility was 25.7, and the effective number of parties peaked at 8.69. That is the highest score ever recorded in consolidated democracies since 1945 and until that year (Kenig et al. 2004). Since 2003, the level of party fragmentation has abated somewhat, though here too the situation was not entirely reversed after the abolition of the direct election of the prime minister. Between 2003 and 2015, the effective number of parties in the Israeli Knesset has ranged between 6.17 and 7.84—much higher than it was before the adoption of the direct election.

As a result of the increase in the legal threshold, the 2015 elections saw a decrease in the absolute number of parties elected to the Knesset. Only ten parties made it into the Knesset following these elections, out of twenty-six that ran. Comparatively this number is still high, and it is not mirrored in a substantial decrease in the effective number of parties due to the relative size of the parties elected.

**Table 28.2  Volatility, Number of Parties, and Effective Number of Parliamentary Parties in the Israeli Knesset, 1949–2015**

| Election | Number of Party Lists | Effective Number of Parliamentary Parties | Volatility* (%) |
|---|---|---|---|
| 1949 | 12 | 4.73 | — |
| 1951 | 15 | 5.05 | 15.6 |
| 1955 | 12 | 6.00 | 13.6 |
| 1959 | 12 | 4.89 | 9.3 |
| 1961 | 11 | 5.35 | 6.3 |
| 1965 | 13 | 4.71 | 6.3 |
| 1969 | 13 | 3.56 | 3.9 |
| 1973 | 10 | 3.35 | 11.1 |
| 1977 | 13 | 4.37 | 22.6 |
| 1981 | 10 | 3.13 | 21.3 |
| 1984 | 15 | 3.86 | 14.0 |
| 1988 | 15 | 4.38 | 13.3 |
| 1992 | 10 | 4.39 | 13.9 |
| 1996 | 11 | 5.61 | 20.4 |
| 1999 | 15 | 8.69 | 25.7 |
| 2003 | 13 | 6.17 | 26.8 |
| 2006[†] | 12 | 7.84 | 17.3 |
| 2009 | 12 | 6.77 | 15.6 |
| 2013 | 12 | 7.29 | 32.4 |
| 2015 | 10 | 6.94 | 16.4 |

*Source:* Authors' calculations based on data from the Knesset website—www.knesset.co.il (last accessed January 1, 2017).

* Pedersen (1979) index.

[†] In calculating volatility values for the 2006 elections, the Kadima Party, which split from Likud during the Knesset elected in 2003 and won the largest number of seats, is not treated as a new party. This conservative approach brings down the values for these elections. The alternative, treating Kadima as a new party, would increase the volatility value for these elections to 37.1.

# Impact on Government Formation and Durability

No party in Israel has ever won a majority, and several parties are needed to form a governing majority coalition (see Table 28.3). Despite the multiparty nature of Israeli coalitions, for the first several decades this was a relatively easy task because they usually included a dominant, relatively large formateur party. This changed in the 1970s, when dominance ended and a second large party appeared. The two major parties then competed fiercely for the support of the smaller parties, some of whom successfully played one major party against the other and not only demanded a high fee for their inclusion but also continuously threatened to bring down the government if their increasing demands were not met. Moreover, this bidding war took place in a parliament where the average number of parties represented was usually no less than a dozen. This constellation changed once again in the 1990s, when the direct election of the prime minister was first implemented. The effective number of parties in parliament substantially increased. In all but one of the governments formed between 1996 and 2015, the prime minister's party held a minority of seats within its own coalition. To create a governing majority, it has become necessary to include an ever-growing circle of partners. Under this state of affairs, the prime minister is forced to spend more time and effort than ever before on maintaining, rather than on heading, the government, while allocating more government ministries and more of the national budget to the coalition partners—thereby further constraining the ability to govern and to control the agenda of government (Nachmias and Sened 1999).

The constant need to sustain the coalition is fueled by recurrent coalition crises, which have triggered the premature collapse of most Israeli governments in recent decades, leaving only few Knessets to last their full, four-year term. This has brought about an ongoing debate on political stability, both in the political arena and in the public sphere, and a general feeling of government instability. However, when examining government stability in Israel using conventional measurements and definitions—such as the prime minister's length of term, the turnover in governing parties, government duration, or the government's term of office completion rate—it appears that Israel is not an outlier compared to other consensual democracies, even though over time instability has grown (Barnea, Driashpits, and Sharkansky 2013).

The pure proportionality of the electoral system, the existential issues facing a country constantly in a state of war, and the growing disaffection of the electorate from the two major parties all serve to make the contemporary Israeli party system highly fragmented. However, it appears that the feeling of government instability is not necessarily caused by their actual turnover, but rather by the constant threats they face and endure. Israeli governments are commonly perceived to be hanging by a thread, unable to enact important policies due to coalitional pressures because any important decision can bring down the government. As a result, most of the energies of the prime minister and his counterparts are devoted to their political survival, rather than to actual governing.

## Table 28.3 Israeli Coalition Governments, 1949–2015*

| Period | Knesset | Government | Prime Minister (Party) | No. of Parties | No. of Members | Size of Formateur's Party in Coalition (%) |
|---|---|---|---|---|---|---|
| 03/1949–11/1950 | 1st | 1st | David Ben-Gurion (Mapai) | 5 | 73 | 46 (63%) |
| 11/1950–10/1951 | | 2nd | David Ben-Gurion (Mapai) | 5 | 73 | 46 (63%) |
| 10/1951–12/1952 | 2nd | 3rd | David Ben-Gurion (Mapai) | 8 | 65 | 45 (69%) |
| 12/1952–10/1954 | | 4th | David Ben-Gurion (Mapai) | 9 | 89 | 45 (50%) |
| 10/1954–06/1955 | | 5th | Moshe Sharet (Mapai) | 9 | 91 | 45 (49%) |
| 06/1955–11/1955 | | 6th | Moshe Sharet (Mapai) | 6 | 68 | 45 (66%) |
| 11/1955–01/1958 | 3rd | 7th | David Ben-Gurion (Mapai) | 8 | 80 | 40 (50%) |
| 01/1958–12/1959 | | 8th | David Ben-Gurion (Mapai) | 8 | 80 | 40 (50%) |
| 12/1959–11/1961 | 4th | 9th | David Ben-Gurion (Mapai) | 9 | 92 | 47 (51%) |
| 11/1961–06/1963 | 5th | 10th | David Ben-Gurion (Mapai) | 6 | 68 | 42 (61%) |
| 06/1963–12/1964 | | 11th | Levi Eshkol (Mapai) | 6 | 68 | 42 (61%) |
| 12/1964–01/1966 | | 12th | Levi Eshkol (Mapai) | 6 | 67 | 42 (62%) |
| 01/1966–03/1969 | 6th | 13th | Levi Eshkol (Labor) | 7 | 75 | 45 (60%) |
| 03/1969–12/1969 | | 14th | Golda Meir (Labor) | 7 | 104 | 45 (43%) |
| 12/1969–03/1974 | 7th | 15th | Golda Meir (Labor) | 6 | 102 | 56 (55%) |

**Table 28.3 Continued**

| Period | Knesset | Government | Prime Minister (Party) | No. of Parties | No. of Members | Size of Formateur's Party in Coalition (%) |
|---|---|---|---|---|---|---|
| 03/1974–06/1974 | 8th | 16th | Golda Meir (Labor) | 3 | 68 | 51 (75%) |
| 06/1974–06/1977 | | 17th | Yitzhak Rabin (Labor) | 3 | 61 | 51 (83%) |
| 06/1977–08/1981 | 9th | 18th | Menachem Begin (Likud) | 5 | 62 | 43 (69%) |
| 08/1981–10/1983 | 10th | 19th | Menachem Begin (Likud) | 4 | 61 | 48 (78%) |
| 10/1983–09/1984 | | 20th | Yitzhak Shamir (Likud) | 6 | 62 | 48 (77%) |
| 09/1984–10/1986 | 11th | 21st | Shimon Peres (Labor) | 8 | 97 | 44 (45%) |
| 10/1986–12/1988 | | 22nd | Yitzhak Shamir (Likud) | 7 | 96 | 41 (42%) |
| 12/1988–06/1990 | 12th | 23rd | Yitzhak Shamir (Likud) | 6 | 97 | 40 (41%) |
| 06/1990–07/1992 | | 24th | Yitzhak Shamir (Likud) | 8 | 65 | 40 (61%) |
| 07/1992–11/1995 | 13th | 25th | Yitzhak Rabin (Labor) | 3 | 62 | 44 (70%) |
| 11/1995–06/1996 | | 26th | Shimon Peres (Labor) | 3 | 59 | 44 (74%) |
| 06/1996–07/1999 | 14th | 27th | Benjamin Netanyahu (Likud) | 6 | 66 | 32 (48%) |
| 07/1999–03/2001 | 15th | 28th | Ehud Barak (Labor) | 7 | 75 | 26 (34%) |
| 03/2001–02/2003 | | 29th | Ariel Sharon (Likud) | 7 | 80 | 19 (23%) |
| 02/2003–05/2006 | 16th | 30th | Ariel Sharon (Likud) | 5 | 68 | 38 (55%) |
| 05/2006–03/2009 | 17th | 31st | Ehud Olmert (Kadima) | 4 | 67 | 29 (43%) |
| 03/2009–03/2013 | 18th | 32nd | Benjamin Netanyahu (Likud) | 5 | 69 | 27 (39%) |

(continued)

**Table 28.3  Continued**

| Period | Knesset | Government | Prime Minister (Party) | No. of Parties | No. of Members | Size of Formateur's Party in Coalition (%) |
|---|---|---|---|---|---|---|
| 03/2013–05/2015 | 19th | 33rd | Benjamin Netanyahu (Likud) | 5 | 68 | 31 (45%) |
| 05/2015– | 20th | 34th | Benjamin Netanyahu (Likud) | 5 | 61 | 30 (49%) |

*Source:* Authors' calculations based on data from the Knesset website—www.knesset.co.il (last accessed January 1, 2017).* The table indicates the number of coalition parties and members on the day the government was sworn in; it does not address any changes made to the composition of the coalition during the government's term in office.

## Impact on the Legislature and on Legislative Behavior

The Israeli electoral system should create a party-based system, with little to no personal or geographical representation. Individual accountability, of any kind, should be absent in a system with no electoral districts and no preference vote (Farrell and Scully 2007). The combination of an extremely large district magnitude and closed party lists creates disincentives for personal representation of any kind, as legislators have no reason to cultivate a personal reputation (Carey and Shugart 1995). That is, legislative behavior in Israel should be party centered, at least in theory. This is, however, clearly not the case in the last two decades.

The behavior of MKs has changed over time. In the 1950s, MKs were first and foremost representatives of their parties. Levels of party discipline were very high and MKs hardly ever submitted private member bills. Over the years, there was an incremental decline in party cohesion and discipline, and an increase in the individual activity of MKs, not distinct from the changes seen in some other Western democracies. The last two decades, however, have seen a sharp increase in these attributes. Among the contributing factors were the introduction of the direct election for the prime minister, the growing personalization of politics, and the democratization of candidate selection methods (Balmas et al. 2014; Hazan and Rahat 2010; Rahat and Sheafer 2007; Rahat and Hazan 2005). The consequences of the first two factors are quite clear—an individual ballot for the prime minister, who had to win an absolute majority, meant a need to create a campaign distinct from the party (Hazan 1999b), and growing personalization brought the focus of politics to the individual at the expense of the party—but the third might not be apparent because few parliamentary systems have a nationwide closed-list electoral system and extensive intraparty democratization processes.

The combination of party primaries and a closed-list system proved to be an influential catalyst for the growth of personal politics. In a closed-list system, the reselection of most candidates is only tangentially related to their party's success in the general elections. That is, if a candidate is selected to a high position on the party list, he or she can safely assume that his or her re-election is secure. When the selectorate is composed of party leaders, or even a wider group of members such as a selected party agency, candidates must demonstrate their loyalty to the party. However, when the selection is dependent exclusively upon a wide, unstable, and uninformed selectorate of party members, the candidates no longer depend only on their party but also on nonpartisan moderators such as financial supporters, the mass media, and leaders of interest groups (Hazan and Rahat 2010). With the adoption of party primaries, personal political success became just as important as, and often disconnected with, that of the party.

Moreover, the introduction of party primaries added a geographical representation component in Israel. Most of the parties that adopted primaries established geographical selectoral districts, thus creating a new link between MKs and local interests, further circumventing the national party leadership (Hazan 1999a).

One prominent legislative consequence of the weakening of party cohesion was the increase in the number of private member bills that were submitted, and in the relative percentage of private member bills that were adopted. Since 2000, over 20,000 private member bills were submitted in the Israeli parliament. This is extremely high by any international standard. During the work of the nineteenth Knesset, which lasted less than two years (February 2013–December 2015), 3,100 private member bills were submitted. While only a small portion of private member bills were eventually enacted (roughly 5 to 6 percent), their percentage of the total legislation passed is extremely high: 50 percent of the bills enacted by the Israeli parliament between the years 1992 and 2015 originated as private member bills. Israeli legislators appear to use private legislation as a way to stand out among other MKs and to signal their responsiveness and accountability to their party selectorates.

# CONCLUSION: PERSONALIZATION IN THE ABSENCE OF A PERSONALIZED ELECTORAL SYSTEM

The Israeli electoral system is one of the most party-based electoral systems in the world. Two of its main features—its rigid closed party lists and its single nationwide electoral district—create the maximum distance between the voters and their elected representatives. Voters have no say as to the identity of the party candidates elected, nor do they have a geographically based connection to a specific representative. Under this kind of institutional design, the "electoral connection" (Mayhew 1974)—which explains members of parliament's personalized behavior in terms of the electoral incentives they face—is largely absent. The Israeli electoral system thus creates disincentives for personalization, and is therefore assumed to be an extreme form of a party-based electoral system.

However, as this chapter has shown, this is no longer the case. The behavior of both the voters and the MKs demonstrates the increasingly personalized nature of the Israeli system, in what appears to be a case of "personalization through the backdoor." In other words, the extreme, inflexible nature of the Israeli electoral system, along with the inability to reform the system moderately, has triggered "reform through bypass." This is true for the separate election of the prime minister, which grafted a direct method of electing the prime minister above the parties, and for party primaries, which created a direct connection between party members and MKs. In both cases, the results place Israeli politics between two contradictory poles: the largely intact electoral system since independence and the reforms adopted in the 1990s.

Despite the fact that the system of directly electing the prime minister was abolished in 2001, it continues to contribute to the increased personalization of Israeli politics for voters and politicians alike. Election campaigns are highly focused on the prime-ministerial candidates, leaving the party and its list of candidates mostly in the shadows. Israeli voters commonly state their intention to vote for individual party leaders, in spite of the fact that the Israeli electoral system allows them to cast a ballot only for a party. Moreover, the larger parties have adopted the practice of adding the name of the party leader to that of the party on the ballot, something that first appeared in anticipation of the direct election. Apparently, the electoral system appears quite different in the eyes of both the politicians and the voters in Israel compared to its actual institutional design.

It seems that the main characteristic of Israel's institutional design is extremism. While the electoral system is clearly extreme, the attempts to reform it—both from above and from below—have also been extreme, resulting in a political system pulling in opposite directions. In a paradoxical manner, a system that was unable to overhaul itself, despite wide support for moderate reform, instead adopted drastic reform measures. Israel is currently witnessing an ironic situation where the less personalized the electoral system de jure is, the more personalization exists de facto.

## Notes

1. Any two lists of candidates are allowed to sign a "surplus agreement," which is the Israeli terminology for *apparentement*, and applies only to the allocation of remainder seats. The agreement comes into effect only if both lists independently surpass the legal threshold. Israeli elections have sometimes resulted in an even sixty/sixty seat split between the two main parties and their potential coalition partners, or a close sixty-one/fifty-nine split, in which case surplus agreements can play an important role.

2. The election law does allow for a few exceptions of citizens who live outside Israel to vote from abroad, such as diplomats or other official state representatives.

3. It might seem surprising that the threshold was fixed and maintained at such a low level, since only the smallest parties would have a vested interest in it. However, the dominant Mapai party was also interested in a low threshold so that its preferred potential coalition partners, which were quite small, would be assured representation in the Knesset.

4. In the 1996 and 1999 elections, the voter had an additional ballot for the direct election of the prime minister. For the election of the prime minister, voters received a separate envelope and chose from a separate series of ballot slips on which the names of the candidates were printed. Both envelopes (each was colored differently) were then dropped into the voting box. In the 2001 special elections, voters cast a ballot only for the prime minister.

5. This does not include the deviant cases of national unity (grand) coalitions, where neither of the two major parties composed, by itself, a majority within the coalition.

## REFERENCES

Balmas, Meital, Gideon Rahat, Tamir Sheafer, and Shaul Shenhav. "Two Routes to Personalized Politics: Centralized and Decentralized Personalization." *Party Politics* 20, no. 1 (2014): 37–51.

Barnea, Shlomit, Shurik Driashpits, and Mattan Sharkansky. "Governments in a Catch: The Status of Israeli Governments—A Diagnosis." In *Reforming Israel's Political System,* edited by Gideon Rahat, Shlomit Barnea, Ofer Kenig, and Chen Friedberg, 291–310. Jerusalem: Am Oved and Israel Democracy Institute, 2013. [Hebrew]

Brichta, Avraham. "Forty Years of Struggle for Electoral Reform in Israel, 1948-88." *Middle East Review* 21, no. 1 (1988): 18–26.

Carey, John. *Legislative Voting and Accountability*. Cambridge: Cambridge University Press, 2009.

Carey, John, and Matthew S. Shugart. "Incentives to Cultivate a Personal Vote: A Rank Ordering of Electoral Formulas." *Electoral Studies* 14, no. 4 (1995): 417–439.

Doron, Gideon, and Moshe Maor. *Barriers to Entry into Israeli Politics*. Tel Aviv: Papyrus, 1989. [Hebrew]

Farrell, David M., and Roger Scully. *Representing Europe's Citizens? Electoral Institutions and the Failure of Parliamentary Representation*. Oxford: Oxford University Press, 2007.

Hazan, Reuven Y. "Presidential Parliamentarism: Direct Popular Election of the Prime Minister, Israel's New Electoral and Political System." *Electoral Studies* 15, no. 1 (1996): 21–37.

Hazan, Reuven Y. "The 1996 Intra-Party Elections in Israel: Adopting Party Primaries." *Electoral Studies* 16, no. 1 (1997a): 95–103.

Hazan, Reuven Y. "Executive-Legislative Relations in an Era of Accelerated Reform: Reshaping Government in Israel." *Legislative Studies Quarterly* 22, no. 3 (1997b): 239–250.

Hazan, Reuven Y. "Party System Change in Israel, 1948-1998: A Conceptual and Theoretical Border-Stretching of Europe?" In *Comparing Party System Change,* edited by Paul Pennings and Jan-Erik Lane, 151–166. London: Routledge, 1998.

Hazan, Reuven Y. "Constituency Interests without Constituencies: The Geographical Impact of Candidate Selection on Party Organization and Legislative Behavior in the 14th Israeli Knesset, 1996-99." *Political Geography* 18, no. 7 (1999a): 791–811.

Hazan, Reuven Y. "Yes, Institutions Matter: The Impact of Institutional Reform on Parliamentary Members and Leaders in Israel." *Journal of Legislative Studies* 5, no. 3–4 (1999b): 301–324.

Hazan, Reuven Y., and Gideon Rahat. *Democracy within Parties: Candidate Selection Methods and Their Political Consequences.* Oxford: Oxford University Press, 2010.

Kenig, Ofer, Gideon Rahat, and Reuven Y. Hazan. "The Political Consequences of the Introduction and the Repeal of the Direct Elections for the Prime Minister." In *The Elections in Israel 2003*, edited by Asher Arian and Michal Shamir, 33–62. New Brunswick, NJ: Transaction Publishers, 2004.

Laakso, Markku, and Rein Taagepera. "'Effective' Number of Parties: Measure with Application to West Europe." *Comparative Political Studies* 12, no. 1 (1979): 3–27.

Lijphart, Arend. "Israeli Democracy and Democratic Reform in Comparative Perspective." In *Israeli Democracy under Stress*, edited by Ehud Sprinzak and Larry Diamond, 107–123. Boulder, CO: Lynne Rienner, 1993.

Mayhew, David R. *Congress: The Electoral Connection.* New Haven, CT: Yale University Press, 1974.

Medding, Peter Y. *The Founding of Israeli Democracy 1948-1967.* Oxford: Oxford University Press, 1990.

Medding, Peter Y. "From Government by Party to Government Despite Party." In *Parties, Elections and Cleavages: Israel in Comparative and Theoretical Perspective*, edited by Reuven Y. Hazan and Moshe Maor, 172–208. London: Frank Cass, 2000.

Mendilow, Jonathan. *Ideology, Party Change and Electoral Campaigns in Israel, 1965-2001.* Albany: State University of New York Press, 2003.

Nachmias, David, and Itai Sened. "The Bias of Pluralism: The Redistributive Effects of the New Electoral Law in Israel's 1996 Election." In *The Elections in Israel 1996*, edited by Asher Arian and Michal Shamir, 269–294. Albany: State University of New York Press, 1999.

Pedersen, Mogens. "The Dynamics of European Party Systems: Changing Patterns of Electoral Volatility." *European Journal of Political Research* 7, no. 1 (1979): 1–26.

Rahat, Gideon. *The Politics of Regime Structure Reform in Democracies: Israel in Comparative and Theoretical Perspective.* Albany: State University of New York Press, 2008a.

Rahat, Gideon. "Trial and Error: Electoral Reform through Bypass and Its Repeal." *Israel Affairs* 14, no. 1 (2008b): 103–117.

Rahat, Gideon. "The Political Consequences of Candidate Selection to the 18th Knesset." In *The Elections in Israel 2009*, edited by Asher Arian and Michal Shamir, 195–224. New Brunswick, NJ: Transaction Publishers, 2010.

Rahat, Gideon, and Reuven Y. Hazan. "Israel: The Politics of an Extreme Electoral System." In *The Politics of Electoral Systems*, edited by Michael Gallagher and Paul Mitchell, 333–351. Oxford: Oxford University Press, 2005.

Rahat, Gideon, and Tamir Sheafer. "The Personalization(s) of Politics: Israel, 1949- 2003." *Political Communication* 24, no. 1 (2007): 65–80.

Sager, Samuel. *The Parliamentary System of Israel.* Syracuse, NY: Syracuse University Press, 1985.

Samuels, David J., and Matthew S. Shugart. *Presidents, Parties and Prime Ministers.* Cambridge: Cambridge University Press, 2010.

CHAPTER 29

........................................................................................

# ELECTORAL SYSTEMS IN CONTEXT

## *Finland*

........................................................................................

## ÅSA VON SCHOULTZ (*NÉE BENGTSSON*)

## PLACING THE ELECTORAL SYSTEM IN CONTEXT

........................................................................................

IN the family of proportional electoral systems, Finland makes a rare flower by combining a proportional formula and multiseat districts[1] with fully open lists and mandatory preferential voting. *Open-list proportional representation* (OLPR) provides the Finnish electoral system with two levels of competition. In line with Duverger's law (1954), the proportional formula applied in multiseat districts has generated a multiparty system, which in turn involves a high degree of *interparty* competition. Finnish elections, as elections in most Western European countries, are fought between parties (or alliances of parties), and the allocation of seats across parties determines how power is distributed and used in the parliament. The open lists and mandatory preferential voting features do, however, also provide the system with a high degree of *intraparty* competition. Alongside the constituency-based battle between parties, candidates within the same party compete over the seats that the party collectively will win.

This inherent duality has a multitude of effects on how elections are played out at different levels of the political system. It has consequences for the *nomination* of candidates, for how *campaigns* are fought and *elections* won, and for the behavior and attitudes of *voters, politicians,* and *parties,* just to name a few. The effects of this duality and in particular how the high degree of intraparty competition influences the logic of Finnish politics will be explored later on in this chapter after a thorough presentation of the basic features of the electoral system.

Apart from the two distinct dimensions characterizing the Finnish electoral system, another striking feature is the durability of the system. Many of the basic characteristics of the system date as far back as the Parliamentary Act of 1906 and were implemented at the first parliamentary election held with universal and equal suffrage in 1907. In 1906, when the system was introduced, it was considered far-reaching and radical. Finland— at the time an autonomous Grand Duchy of Russia—was the first European country to give women an equal right to vote (Karvonen 2014).[2] Other important features that date back to 1906 are the use of proportional representation with relatively large constituencies and the D'Hondt formula as the distributor of seats to parties (Raunio 2005, 474f).[3] The feature that makes the Finnish system particularly interesting in comparison to many other proportional systems—that is, the current use of fully open lists with mandatory preferential voting (of one candidate) in combination with the absence of party ranking of the candidates—was, however, not introduced until 1955 (Sundberg 2002, 76). Until 1955, fielded lists contained three internally ranked candidates. From 1906 to 1935, voters were given three options: to support the entire three-person list (the most common option), to alter the order of the candidates, or to alter the list by adding the names and addresses of (a maximum of three) eligible citizens not included on the list. The first candidate on the list was given one vote, the second half a vote, and the third one-third of a vote. In 1935, the number of candidates that a voter could cast a vote for decreased to two and the opportunity to alter the order of the candidates was abolished (Raunio 2005, 475; Sundberg 2002, 77).

Finland is a parliamentary democracy and a unitary state with no regional government,[4] but instead a relatively powerful local government (Karvonen 2014, 15). Up until the turn of the millennium, Finland was classified as a semipresidential system. Especially during the long presidency of Urho Kekkonen (1956–1981), the far-reaching constitutional powers of the presidency were used to control domestic politics and government formation to guarantee a stable foreign policy line and to avoid tension in the sensitive Finnish–Soviet relations that marked Finnish politics until the end of the Cold War (Karvonen 2014, 14). After the Kekkonen era a process of parliamentarization was initiated, culminating in the introduction of the new constitution of 2000, by which the powers of the presidency were substantially reduced and its former powers over cabinet formation were abolished (Paloheimo 2016, 57–66).

Historically, Finnish politics have been characterized by a high degree of party system polarization (Sartori 2005, 129) and government instability (Gallagher, Laver, and Mair 2001, 366), but these two tendencies have in the post-Kekkonen era been replaced by consensus (Mickelsson 2007) and government stability (Karvonen 2014, 73). Today, ideological differences are less pronounced and coalitions can be (and are) formed among virtually all parties (Karvonen 2016, 122). The most common type of government is that of a surplus majority coalition, representing twenty-six out of forty-three governments formed since 1945 (Bengtsson et al. 2014, 25).[5] Despite the candidate-centered electoral system, the Finnish parliament is characterized by a high level of intraparty voting cohesion, particularly among the government coalition parties (Pajala 2013, 44).[6] Finland is a corporatist country with extensive interest group consultations as an important feature of political decision making (Raunio 2005, 474). Party subsidies were introduced in 1967[7] (Sundberg 2002, 78) and since the 1970s they have accounted for the bulk of the financing of parliamentary party organizations (Karvonen 2014, 57f).

The Finnish multiparty system is one of the most fragmented in Western Europe (Bengtsson et al. 2014, 29f) with an average effective number of parties of 5.12 in the post–World War II era.[8] The core of the system is constituted by three medium-sized parties with a historical basis in two cleavages and three major poles of conflict: *labor/workers* (the Social Democratic party), *capital/business owners* (the National Coalition[9]), and *the rural periphery/farmers* (the Centre Party[10]) (Rokkan 1987, 81–95). In addition to these three parties, the modern Finnish party system contains several parties, generally gaining less than 10 percent of the vote: a left-wing party (the Left Alliance,[11] a former communist party), a party representing the Swedish-speaking minority (the Swedish Peoples Party), a social-conservative party (the Christian Democrats[12]), and a green party (the Green League[13]). In the 2011 election when the Finns Party, a populist right party, experienced a major breakthrough,[14] the traditional setup of the party system was disrupted and the fragmentation of the system further increased. This new configuration with four medium-sized parties and only one party exceeding 20 percent of voter support was continued in the 2015 election.

The following delving into the Finnish electoral system will revolve around elections to the National Parliament, the *Eduskunta* in Finnish, or *Riksdagen* in Swedish.[15] Finnish voters are, however, faced with relatively frequent elections since direct municipal, European, and presidential elections are not held concurrently. The electoral systems applied to all elections are similar (PR with the D'Hondt formula and mandatory preferential voting) for all elections except for the presidential elections, where a majoritarian two-round system has been applied since 1994.[16]

# The Electoral System and Its Peculiarities

Elections to the Finnish national parliament takes place on the third Sunday of April every fourth year with the Ministry of Justice as the highest election authority.[17] The electoral system used is classified as OLPR. The two hundred seats in the *Eduskunta* are, according to the constitution, to be distributed in twelve to eighteen constituencies using the D'Hondt highest average method. In the parliamentary election in 2015, the number of districts was thirteen,[18] including the single-seat district of the autonomous Åland Island,[19] and district magnitude ($M$) ranged from 6 to 35. The variation in $M$ across districts has increased over time, and no fixed electoral threshold or national tier is applied, the effects of which will be discussed further later.

Table 29.1  Election Result in the 2015 Parliamentary Election

|  | No. Votes | % Votes | No. Seats | % Seats | Diff. Votes–Seats |
|---|---|---|---|---|---|
| Centre Party | 626,218 | 21.1 | 49 | 24.5 | 3.5 |
| National Coalition | 540,212 | 18.2 | 37 | 18.5 | 0.3 |
| Finns Party | 524,054 | 17.7 | 38 | 19.0 | 1.3 |
| Social Democrats | 490,102 | 16.5 | 34 | 17.0 | 0.5 |
| Green League | 253,102 | 8.5 | 15 | 7.5 | −1.0 |
| Left Alliance | 211,702 | 7.1 | 12 | 6.0 | −1.1 |
| Swedish People's Party | 144,802 | 4.9 | 9 | 4.5 | −0.5 |
| Christian Democrats | 105,134 | 3.5 | 5 | 2.5 | −1.0 |
| Pirate Party | 25,086 | 0.8 | - | - | −0.8 |
| Independence Party | 13,638 | 0.5 | - | - | −0.5 |
| Others | 17,678 | 0.7 | - | - | - |
| Åland Islands | 22,222 | 0.5 | 1 | 0.5 | - |
| Total | 2,968,459 | 100 | 200 | 100 | |
| Gallagher LSq | 3.23 | | | | |
| Eff no. parliamentary parties | 5.84 | | | | |

Source: Statistics of Finland 2016, Ministry of Justice 2016.

## Interparty Competition: Parties as Central Actors

The Finnish OLPR combines the feature of open lists with a *pooling vote* (Cox 1997, 42), which makes the system highly competitive both between candidates (intraparty) and between parties (interparty). Parties[20] and constituency associations,[21] or an alliance of parties or constituency associations, present a single list of candidates at the district level, and all individual preference votes count for the list. The total amount of votes cast for candidates on each list determines how many seats the list is rewarded. The first seat is assigned to the party with the highest list total. In the following step the D'Hondt divisor (one, two, three, four, and so on) is used to calculate comparison figures for each list.

**Table 29.2 Allocation of Seats in the Constituency of Lapland in the 2015 Parliamentary Election**

| | % Won | Votes Won | First Divisor | | Second Divisor | | Third Divisor | | Fourth Divisor | | Fifth Divisor |
|---|---|---|---|---|---|---|---|---|---|---|---|
| | | | | | | | | | | | |
| Centre Party | 42.9 | 43,393 | 43,393.0 | (1) | 21,646.5 | (2) | 14,431.0 | (4) | 10,823.3 | (7) | 8,658.6 |
| Finns Party* | 16.5 | 16,621 | 17,733.0 | (3) | 8,866.5 | | | | | | |
| Left Alliance | 13.7 | 13,827 | 13,827.0 | (5) | 6,913.5 | | | | | | |
| Social Democratic Party | 10.8 | 10,943 | 10,943.0 | (6) | 5,471.5 | | | | | | |
| National Coalition | 10.1 | 10,155 | 10,155.0 | | | | | | | | |
| Green League | 2.6 | 2,643 | 2,642.0 | | | | | | | | |
| Christian Democrats* | 1.1 | 1,112 | – | | | | | | | | |
| Pirate Party | 0.8 | 818 | 818.0 | | | | | | | | |

The header "Comparison Figures" spans the divisor columns.

* The Finns Party and the Christian Democrats had formed an electoral alliance.

*Source:* Ministry of Justice 2016.

The comparison figures (or averages) determine the order in which the seats are distributed across the lists. See Table 29.2 for an example of how the seats were distributed in the Lapland district, a small-$M$ district in the far north of Finland, in the 2015 election.

The Finnish electoral system belongs in what Rein Taagepera (2007) labels a "simple" system, since it lacks a mechanism that links the share of votes a party receives at the national level with the distribution of seats at the district level. The single-tier system in combination with the D'Hondt highest average formula, which is one of the electoral formulas considered most advantageous for large parties (Gallagher 1991, 34), makes for a fairly disadvantageous system for parties with a lower and geographically equally distributed support. In the 2015 election (see Table 29.1), the national level of disproportionality was 3.13 using the Gallagher least squares index (LSq) (Gallagher 1991). This played out as a 3.5 percentage point overrepresentation for the Centre Party (corresponding to six seats) and an overrepresentation of the Finns Party by 1.1 percentage points (two seats), both gaining large shares of their voter support in small-$M$ constituencies. Three of the four minor parties (Left Alliance, Green League, and Christian Democrats[22]) were in turn underrepresented with about 1 percentage point each, corresponding to two seats per party in the *Eduskunta*. The level of disproportionality (LSq) has been relatively stable over time with an average of 3.02 between 1907 and 2015. However, it should be noted that the level of disproportionality at the district level is substantially higher but evened out at the national level (Sundberg 2002, 89f).

A strategy for small parties to deal with the occasionally relatively high effective electoral threshold is to form electoral alliances. Alliances are formed at the constituency level, most commonly in small-$M$ districts. Alliances are generally considered as purely strategic (Arter 2013, 105) and do not involve a joint political agenda or an effort to be consistent in terms of ideology or policy proposals. It should be noted, however, that votes only are pooled at the list level, and not over parties who decide to join forces in an alliance. A party can form alliances with different parties across constituencies or run independently in some districts while forming strategic alliances in others (Shugart and Taagepera 2017). The general pattern is that of smaller parties forming alliances with a larger party in small-$M$ constituencies where the minor party on its own would not receive enough votes to pass the effective threshold. Among the three parties traditionally dominating Finnish politics, the Centre Party has been more prone to form alliances, while the Social Democratic Party has been the most restrictive in this sense (Paloheimo and Sundberg 2009, 219). Smaller parties have generally been successful in their formed alliances, while larger parties have tended to come out on the losing side (Paloheimo and Sundberg 2009, 233).

The number of districts has been relatively stable over time. Since the first parliamentary election held in 1907, the number of districts has varied between thirteen and sixteen, and relatively few changes have been made over the years.[23] During a near-fifty-year period, from 1962 until 2011, the number and the configuration of districts was largely unchanged. While the period was characterized by stability in terms of the number of districts, the opposite can be said about the distribution of seats across districts. Due to a relatively strong wave of urbanization, there has been a steady redistribution

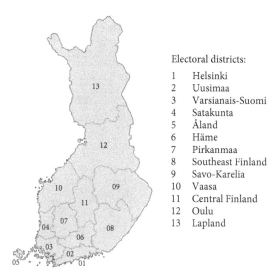

Electoral districts:

1   Helsinki
2   Uusimaa
3   Varsianais-Suomi
4   Satakunta
5   Åland
6   Häme
7   Pirkanmaa
8   Southeast Finland
9   Savo-Karelia
10  Vaasa
11  Central Finland
12  Oulu
13  Lapland

FIGURE 29.1.  Electoral districts in the 2015 parliamentary election.

of seats from the eastern and northern parts of the country toward the larger districts in the south, in particular to the large district of Uusimaa, surrounding the capital of Helsinki (see Figure 29.1).[24]

As has been acknowledged by Monroe and Rose (2002), the structure of districts is very important in determining the overall level of proportionality and the effective threshold in single-tier systems. This is evident from the development in Finnish district magnitude from 1962 to 2015 presented in Table 29.3. The difference in the effective threshold between districts has increased substantially over time and peaked in the 2011 parliamentary election, with the lowest threshold of 2.1 percent in Uusimaa, while the corresponding figure was as high as 10.7 in the two districts of North Karelia and South Savo in the eastern parts of the country.

This development has not gone unnoticed, and since the late 1990s there has been intense debate and several public commissions offering alternative solutions to increase the overall proportionality of the system, and in particular to decrease the variation in conditions across districts. The situation was heightened in the aftermath of the 2007 parliamentary election when the Green League failed to get their party leader elected in the district of North Karelia, despite the fact that she received the second highest number of personal votes in the constituency and the party's overall electoral support in the district reached 11.7 percent.[25] The government that formed after the election appointed a new commission, which proposed an introduction of a two-tier system with a national threshold of 3.5 percent (a local threshold of 12.5 percent) and a ban on electoral alliances, while keeping the existing district structure. However, the proposal failed to receive enough support,[26] and instead, it was decided to opt for a less radical solution with a merger of four districts in the eastern parts of Finland into two.[27] The change came into place in the 2015 election and contributed to a substantive decrease of the

**Table 29.3  District Magnitude and Effective Threshold: Development Over Time**

|  | 1962 | 1972 | 1983 | 1991 | 2003 | 2011 | 2016 | Change |
|---|---|---|---|---|---|---|---|---|
| Helsinki | 20 | 22 | 20 | 20 | 21 | 21 | 21 | 1 |
| Uusimaa | 17 | 21 | 27 | 30 | 33 | 35 | 35 | 18 |
| Varsinais-Suomi | 16 | 16 | 17 | 17 | 17 | 17 | 17 | 1 |
| Satakunta | 14 | 13 | 13 | 12 | 9 | 9 | 8 | –6 |
| Hämee | 14 | 15 | 15 | 13 | 14 | 14 | 14 | – |
| Pirkanmaa | 12 | 13 | 13 | 15 | 18 | 18 | 19 | 7 |
| Southeast Finland | (26) |  |  |  |  |  | 17 | –9 |
| Kymi | 15 | 15 | 14 | 13 | 12 | 12 | – |  |
| South Savo | 11 | 10 | 9 | 8 | 6 | 6 | – |  |
| Savo-Karelia | (22) |  |  |  |  |  | 16 | –6 |
| North Savo | 12 | 11 | 10 | 10 | 10 | 9 | – |  |
| North Karelia | 10 | 8 | 7 | 7 | 6 | 6 | – |  |
| Vaasa | 20 | 18 | 18 | 18 | 17 | 17 | 16 | –4 |
| Central Finland | 11 | 10 | 10 | 10 | 10 | 10 | 10 | – |
| Oulu | 18 | 18 | 18 | 18 | 18 | 18 | 18 | – |
| Lapland | 9 | 9 | 8 | 8 | 7 | 7 | 7 | –2 |
| Åland | 1 | 1 | 1 | 1 | 1 | 1 | 1 | – |
| Difference min-max | 11 | 14 | 20 | 23 | 27 | 28 | 28 | 17 |
| Min. effective threshold | 3.6 | 3.3 | 2.7 | 2.4 | 2.2 | 2.1 | 2.1 |  |
| Max effective threshold | 7.5 | 8.3 | 9.4 | 9.4 | 10.7 | 10.7 | 9.4 |  |
| Difference min-max | 3.9 | 5.0 | 6.7 | 7.0 | 8.5 | 8.6 | 7.3 | 3.4 |

Note: $T = 75\% / (M + 1)$. $T$ = effective threshold, $M$ = magnitude (Lijphart 1994, 4). This is often considered as the midway between the threshold of representation (min) and threshold of exclusion (max).

Source: Ministry of Justice 2016.

effective threshold in these districts, yet the problem with discrepancies in proportionality across districts still remains to a large extent.

## Intraparty Competition: Candidates as Central Actors

The aspect that makes the Finnish system stand out in comparison to most other PR systems is that the fully open-list system makes it is impossible for parties or constituency organizations to guarantee the election to parliament of any individual candidate. Preferential voting is mandatory: to cast a vote all voters are obliged to choose one candidate from a fairly large selection of aspirants, and they do so by writing the number of their preferred candidate on the ballot paper (see Figure 29.2). The sole criterion in determining the party internal ranking of candidates is the amount of preference votes each candidate receives (Reynolds, Reilly and Ellis 2005). Moreover, most parties refrain from ranking their nominated candidates.[28] By presenting candidates in alphabetical order on the lists, voters are left without indications of parties' preferred order of preference.[29]

Lists are allowed to contain a maximum of fourteen nominated candidates per constituency, or, if $M$ exceeds fourteen, as many candidates as there are seats to be distributed (Ministry of Justice 2016). If parties or constituency associations decide to join forces and form electoral alliances, the number of candidates nominated by an alliance (a joint list) may not exceed the maximum number of candidates for a single party. Within joint lists votes are not pooled; that is, the distribution of seats within the alliance follows the plurality principle and no account is taken of the relative vote shares for the partners within an alliance (Raunio 2005, 481). A candidate can only be nominated on one list (and hence in one district). The previously common strategy of parties to use popular and high-profile candidates as a means to increase the list total in several districts has been prohibited since 1969.

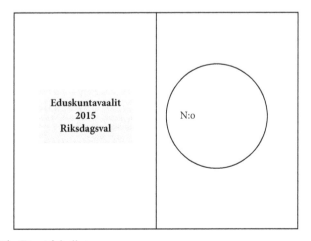

FIGURE 29.2. The Finnish ballot.

Up until the late 1960s, candidate nomination was fairly unregulated and in the hands of the central party organization (Karvonen 2014, 62). Today nomination of candidates is, as in most Nordic countries, a decentralized matter and takes place at the district level (Lundell 2004, 39). Since 1975,[30] parties are legally required to use membership primaries if the number of aspirants exceeds the maximum number of candidates that can be nominated (Kuitunen 2002, 69). The extents to which primaries are used vary across parties and districts, but the larger parties use them more frequently than the smaller ones. The difference in the practices is mainly due to the weaker recruitment basis of smaller parties and the fact that smaller parties more frequently enter into electoral alliances (Raunio 2005, 477). Parties can decide how to organize primaries, but most parties follow the regulation stipulated in the Election Act, according to which local party branches, or a group of at least fifteen members from the same branch, are entitled to nominate aspiring candidates. Party members resident in the district are entitled to vote in the primaries.

The party executive in the district does, however (since 1988), retain the right to replace up to one-fourth of the aspiring candidates that have been elected in the primaries.[31] List manipulation by the district party executive occurs frequently and rarely causes conflict within the district. Common motivations for replacements are candidate refusals and a need to create a more balanced list in terms of geography, gender, age, occupation, and ideology (Paloheimo 2007, 316). The decentralized nomination procedures make cross-constituency nominations rare (von Schoultz 2016, 182).[32] Most candidates are resident in the district where they are nominated, and many candidates receive the main share of support from their "home turf" (Arter 2013, 110), that is, the area in which they live and are politically active.

For parties, OLPR is considered as a relatively easy playground. Since all preference votes are pooled at the party level, a vote for any nominated candidate is always beneficial for the party and does not jeopardize the overall performance in terms of how many seats a party can win. This implies that parties need not care about the distribution of votes[33] and can apply a laissez-faire strategy when it comes to managing the internal competition within a party list, and also that they have an obvious incentive to nominate as many candidates as the system allows (Shugart and Taagepera 2017). The laissez-faire strategy cannot, by contrast, be applied when electoral alliances are formed, since no sublist pooling of votes within alliances is applied. The general pattern of alliance formation is that small alliance partners can only gather electoral power enough to win one seat, which in turn involves a need to concentrate their votes on one candidate.

Even under OLPR, where parties can have low incentives to manage intraparty competition, the nomination stage can be considered as strategically very important and parties apply different nomination strategies to try to maximize their vote shares (Arter 2013, 2014; Shugart and Taagepera 2017). The conventional nomination strategy used by Finnish parties is what David Arter labels *the balanced list strategy*. Fielding a balanced list can be described as a defensive strategy with the goal that no voter attracted by the party as a collective actor should be lost due to lack of a suitable candidate. Under this strategy, parties aim at attracting as many votes as possible by fielding a list, which resembles the composition of the potential electorate in the district in terms of age, gender, occupation, and locality. Among these aspects, a good regional distribution of candidates has been especially valued over time (Arter 2013, 104).

Another, more offensive nomination strategy is to engage in strategic nomination of candidates with high name recognition who can function as *vote magnets*. Here the primary goal of parties is to increase the anticipated vote total by targeting nonpartisan voters who emphasize the qualities of the candidate, or voters who are attracted by pure name recognition of a particular candidate. Vote magnets can come in different forms but are candidates that are able to attract a strong personal vote. They can be experienced politicians such as previous members of parliament (MPs), ministers, or candidates with prominent positions from public life. They can also come in the form of "celebrity candidates," politically inexperienced candidates with high name recognition from the world outside politics, such as media or sports (Arter 2014).

A third strategy identified by Arter is the *lead candidate strategy*,[34] a strategy associated with electoral alliances where vote management is vital to be successful. When entering an electoral alliance, parties—especially the smaller alliance partners—have similar incentives as parties under the single nontransferable vote (SNTV), where votes are not pooled at the party level. Vote concentration is necessary and parties try to convince voters to vote for a lead candidate, often by strategically nominating one experienced lead candidate (e.g., an incumbent) and a few candidates with far less vote-earning potential. It has, however, been noted that entering an alliance may be difficult for the local party branches across the district to accept if they are used to getting their own local aspirant nominated, which in turn might have an impact on the backing of the leading candidate (Almgren 1998, 65). From the perspective of voters, the lead candidate strategy applied within the framework of an alliance implies a limited intraparty choice and uncertainty in terms of outcome. Were the strategy to be unsuccessful, voters of the minor party within an alliance will have contributed to getting a candidate from another party elected to parliament.

After the nomination stage, which ends forty days before the election is held, the Electoral District Committee checks the eligibility of candidates. All with the right to vote who are not under guardianship or holding military office are eligible to stand for public office.[35] After candidates have been confirmed, the Electoral District Committee constructs the full candidate list, which is the record of all nominated candidates in the district. On this list all candidates are numbered consecutively but pooled so that all candidates running for the same list appear in sequence. The list starts with number two. The record is organized so that parties are ordered first, followed by joint lists and constituency organizations. A random draw determines the order of presentation within each of these groups of lists (Ministry of Justice 2016). The full candidate list is present at the polling stations and in the voting booth. Parties widely display and market their part of the list in the media, often with photographs of their candidates. The number given to each candidate is also extensively used in the individual campaigns run by candidates.

The common classification of the Finnish system is that of an open-list system. However, since Finnish voters are not given the opportunity to delegate the ranking of the candidates to other voters by merely casting a party vote, it has also been qualified as a subtype of the open-list PR called a *quasi list* (Shugart 2005, 42f). The system is hence only a list system in the sense that candidates are *pooled* at the party level when the number of seats is allocated among parties. The absence of a party vote ensures that all voters participate in the ranking of candidates and as such minimizes the risk of candidates winning a seat with a very low number of personal votes. If personal votes are optional, candidates can at least in theory be elected with very small personal networks, which in turn may lead to clientelistic relations (Shugart 2005, 44). The quasi list does not, however, fully avoid a situation where candidates are elected with a small amount of votes and the Finnish system does not stipulate a minimal vote share to gain representation. A list that fields a candidate with a very high number of supporters can by itself collect enough votes to guarantee that the list wins many seats. This in turn implies that the last candidates elected from that list will have won a marginal share of the list total. One such example is the Finns Party in the constituency of Uusimaa in the 2007 parliamentary election. The list total of 28,593 votes rewarded the party two parliamentary seats. Of the twenty-four candidates fielded, the party leader Timo Soini was ranked number one with 19,859 personal votes (69.5 percent of the list total). The second candidate on the list was Pirkko Rouhonen-Lerner with 1,058 personal votes (3.7 percent of the list total).[36]

## General Election Rules

In Finnish parliamentary elections, all Finnish citizens who have turned 18 no later than the day of the election are entitled to vote. As in most Western democracies (Bengtsson 2007), there has been a gradual decrease in the eligible voting age over time. The Election Act of 1906 stipulated 24 years of age, which was lowered to 21 in 1944, to 20 in 1969, and to the "age of 18 the year before the election" in 1972. The eligibility of 18 years or older on Election Day came into place in 1995 (Sundberg 2002, 79f). Since 1969, Finnish citizens living abroad are eligible to vote and do so at Finnish diplomatic missions or at Finnish ships abroad. Turnout within the group of around two hundred thousand expatriated Finns has increased slightly over time and was 10.1 percent in the 2015 parliamentary election (Statistics of Finland 2016). Turnout rates among eligible voters living in Finland (in 2015, it was 4,221,237) are substantially higher, although turnout has decreased since the 1980s and is considered low compared to the other Nordic countries (Bengtsson et al. 2014, 42). In the 2015 parliamentary election, 70.1 percent of the Finnish citizens resident in Finland cast their vote (Ministry of Justice 2016).

Voting can take place on Election Day, which since 1991 is on a Sunday, or in advance. Advance voting in Finland lasts for seven days. It begins on a Wednesday eleven days before the actual Election Day, and it ends on Tuesday five days prior to Election Day. Advance voting abroad starts on the same day as for domestic voters, but only lasts for four days. Despite the five-day period between the end of the advance voting period and

Election Day, voters who cast a vote in advance do not have the possibility to change their vote by casting a new one on Election Day. Despite this, the possibility to vote in advance is very popular in Finland, and since 1991 about 40 percent of all votes are cast in advance.

The register of eligible voters is compiled from the official population register fifty-one days before the election.[37] Voters living abroad are registered to vote in the munici-pality where they were resident prior to emigrating. All voters on the register receive a notice of their right to vote by mail including general information about the election, such as information about Election Day and the dates for advanced voting, the address and opening hours of the polling station on Election Day, and a list of advance polling stations within the electoral district. Advance voting can take place at any polling sta-tion, but voting on Election Day can only take place in the station noted in the voting register and on the voting card delivered by mail. The polling stations are open between 9 AM and 8 PM on the official Election Day. The municipality is responsible for arranging the polling stations (both on Election Day and for advance voting).[38] There should be at least one polling station in each municipality, but for practical reasons it is common to divide the municipality into several voting districts. On Election Day in 2015, there were about 2,200 polling stations in 317 municipalities (Ministry of Justice 2016).

After the polling stations close, ballots are counted and results are reported to the municipality's central election committee, which in turn reports the result to the Ministry of Justice. The constituency electoral committees count the advanced votes, and these results are made public after closing of the polling stations on the night of the election. A preliminary election result is published in the evening of Election Day. The electoral committee at the constituency level is responsible for the control count of casted votes. The official result is declared three days after the election and letters of appointment to the two hundred elected representatives are issued (Ministry of Justice 2016).

## Two Levels of Political Campaigning

After the introduction of the open-list system with mandatory preferential voting in 1955, Finnish election campaigning has experienced a shift from being party based to candidate centered (Helander 1997, 65; Paloheimo 2007, 93). Up until the 1960s par-ties were the main actors running the political campaigns. Today campaigns are clearly marked by the embedded duality of the system where both inter- and intraparty compe-tition is considered vital. Modern Finnish election campaigns involve two distinct levels of competition: a collective campaign organized by the party at the national and district levels and a multitude of individually run candidate campaigns (Karvonen 2010, 96f).

The collective campaign is run by the central party organization, revolves around the party leader, and generally involves relatively vague party slogans and platforms that are marketed nationwide. At the district level, local party branches in turn focus on marketing the district candidate list. The vagueness of party campaigns and the absence of explicit election pledges can be attributed to the Finnish culture of government formation, where no pre-electoral agreements on cabinet formation are made and bargaining on the composition and the program of the government takes place after the election. Parties strategically refrain from specifics during the campaign in order not to endanger their bargaining position in the face of upcoming negotiations on cabinet formation. Another equally important reason for the overall vagueness at the central level is that parties aim to attract votes from as many quarters as possible by allowing a great diversity among their nominated candidates (Karvonen 2014, 69).

Large shares of election campaigning are decentralized and run by the individual candidates independently of the party. These campaigns tend to be highly visible and to revolve around more specific issues. Most candidates gather support groups without formal organizational attachment to the party and most of the activities are organized without support from the party organization (Borg and Moring 2007, 48). In fact, many candidates stage joint campaign meetings with candidates from other parties rather than with copartisans (Arter 2013, 111). The average campaign team for the elected candidates and deputies in the 2011 election consisted of seventy people (Bengtsson 2011), and most teams combine traditional means of campaigning such as posters next to roads and newspaper ads with the use of social media channels (Mattila and Ruostetsaari 2002, 97; Strandberg 2013, 1330). Even though the level of intraparty competition is high and individual campaigns at the district level often are more targeted toward intraparty competitors, the system does not encourage negative (intraparty) campaigning since this could hurt the overall success of the party and in turn the relative chance for each candidate to become elected (Karvonen 2010, 96).

The public subsidies introduced in the 1960s contributed to an early professionalization of Finnish election campaigns compared to the other Nordic countries (Bengtsson et al. 2014, 103) and involved the use of opinion polls, focus groups, and comparatively large expenditures on television campaigning (Borg and Moring 2007). While the financial burden of election campaigns is divided between the central party organization and the individual candidates, the general trend is that it has been pushed toward candidates, who collectively spend a considerably larger amount on their individual campaigns than the parties do on their central campaigns (Moring et al. 2011). In the 2007 election the overall campaign spending was 35 to 38 million euros, of which two-thirds were used for individual campaigning and one-third for party campaigning (Mattila and Sundberg 2012, 233). The average campaign spending by elected MPs was 34,000 euros in the 2011 election (Mattila and Sundberg 2012, 234).[39] Many candidates receive some financial support from their party, but most of the money invested in the campaigns comes from donations and private resources (Arter 2009, 26). In the year 2000, the Act on a Candidate's Election Funding was introduced with the intention to regulate and increase transparency regarding campaign financing. The act required all elected MPs (and substitutes) to submit a report on their campaign budget to the Ministry of Justice after the election. The report was not actually made mandatory until 2009, after harsh critique from the Group of States against Corruption (GRECO) and extensive media attention directed toward several campaign finance scandals in the aftermath of the 2007 election.[40] Both party and candidate campaign financing have since become more regulated (Ministry of Justice 2016).

# The Dual Forces of the System: A Voter and Candidate Perspective

The Finnish open-list system, where parties have an incentive to (and generally do) field full lists, can be considered highly demanding for voters. In the largest-$M$ constituency of Uusimaa, the total number of fielded candidates in the 2015 election amounted to 395, of which Uusimaa voters were required to single out one candidate to cast their vote for. The extensive amount of candidates and the individualized style of campaigning mean that voters are overloaded with information to process, while receiving little guidance or shortcuts from parties as central actors (von Schoultz 2016, 167). Despite the challenge the system offers in terms of information processing, less than half of voters are positive toward introducing an option to cast a collective party vote: 35 and 43 percent in the Finnish National Election Studies of 2011 and 2015, respectively. The reluctance to introduce a party vote does not, however, imply that Finnish voters consider parties to be of low importance. On the contrary, most voters are highly aware of the inbuilt dual forces of the system, and many feel torn between the choice of a candidate and that of a party.[41]

When asked directly about the relative weight given to the choice of candidate and party respectively, about equal shares state that the choice of party was the most important for determining their vote (see Table 29.4). A slight increase in the emphasis given to parties is detectable in the period from 1983 to 2007, a period during which developments toward more candidate-centered campaigns have taken place. Since the 2011 election, however, the wind has turned and a clear majority of voters now emphasize the choice of party (Bengtsson 2012, 144). This is likely due to an increased party system polarization in terms of social-cultural issues generated by the growth of the Finns Party (Westinen, Kestilä-Kekkonen, and Tiihonen 2016).[42]

From the perspective of candidates running for election, the duality embedded in the electoral system provides them with binary campaign incentives: try to maximize the party vote total, as well as the personal share of the votes in the constituency. To be successful, therefore, they need to cultivate a "personal vote"—votes derived from their personal characteristics, experience, or record of constituency service (Cain, Ferejohn, and Fiorina 1987)—alongside a "party vote," which is considered as a collective good shared by all candidates running for the party (Cox and McCubbins 1993).

When asking candidates about which aspect they emphasized the most in their campaign, it becomes clear that they are highly aware of the importance of both aspects. On a scale from zero (attract as much attention to yourself as possible) to ten (attract as much attention to the party as possible), the average candidate scores 5.4 (Finnish Candidate

Table 29.4   "Which Was the Most Important to You When Casting Your
Vote, the Party or the Candidate?": Finnish Election Studies,
1983–2015 (%)

|            | 1983 | 1991  | 2003  | 2007  | 2011  | 2015  |
|------------|------|-------|-------|-------|-------|-------|
| Party      | 52   | 51    | 49    | 48    | 55    | 53    |
| Candidate  | 42   | 43    | 47    | 51    | 44    | 42    |
| Don't know | 6    | 6     | 4     | 1     | 1     | 5     |
| Total      | 100  | 100   | 100   | 100   | 100   | 100   |
| N          | 993  | 1,141 | 1,004 | 1,172 | 1,124 | 1,602 |

Sources: FSD1011, FSD1088, FSD1260, FSD2269, FSD2653, FSD3067.

Study 2011, n = 605).[43] About a third of the candidates have a distinct personal focus
while an equal share run party-centered campaigns, and successful candidates tended to
emphasize their personal reputation slightly more than candidates who fail to get elected
(4.7 compared to 5.5). Yet, there are substantial differences between candidates from different parties, where candidates from the National Coalition and the Centre Party are
more prone to be *individualizers* (Arter 2013, 104), while candidates standing for smaller
parties (with on average lower prospects of becoming elected) tend have a more party-
collective emphasis on their campaign.

# How to Get Elected under Open-List Proportional Representation

What contributes to individual-level electoral success under OLPR? The literature on
intraparty competition has emphasized the significance of personal vote-earning attributes (PVEAs) such as *political experience* (Erikson 1971; Ansolabehere, Snyder, and
Stewart 2000; Dahlgaard 2016), *name recognition* (Carey and Shugart 1995; Arter 2014),
and *local ties* (Shugart, Valdini, and Suominen 2005; Tavits 2010), expectations that are
largely confirmed by Finnish empirics (von Schoultz 2016, 176–184).

Incumbency is generally considered as the most valuable type of *political experience*,
though the incumbency generally is considered to be weaker in multiseat compared to
single-seat districts (Maddens, Wauters, Noppe and Fiers 2006). This is supported by
data from Finland, where the level of intrapartisan defeats has tended to be relatively
high (Villodres 2003, 64), while the level of interpartisan defeats has tended to be substantially lower (Arter 2009). Despite the tendency of Finnish voters to use intraparty
competition as an opportunity to assign accountability within, rather than across,

parties, the incumbency advantage is substantial. During the period 1962–2011, 85 percent of MPs ran for re-election, of which 76 percent were successful (Karvonen 2014, 67).[44] In an analysis of the candidates in the elections between 1999 and 2011, incumbency unsurprisingly stands out as the most powerful vote-earning attribute, while previous parliamentary experience and leading positions within the party at the national level were important but far less valuable attributes (von Schoultz 2016, 181).

While *name recognition* can be seen as vital to cultivate a personal vote, it can come in many forms. A distinct characteristic of Finnish politics has been that of celebrity candidates, that is, candidates who have gained a reputation from areas other than politics (Arter 2014).[45] Being a celebrity indeed significantly increases the chances of being elected (von Schoultz 2016, 181). The overall impact at the system level is, however, relatively minor considering that these types of candidates on average only constitute 1 percent of all elected MPs.[46]

Several aspects speak in favor of the importance of the local perspective in national politics. The geographical representativeness of the two hundred MPs in the *Eduskunta* is good. In the 2011 election, the two hundred elected MPs represent as many as 113 different municipalities (of a total of 336). Still, MPs from urban areas are overrepresented, since a voter-rich municipality provides an electoral advantage (Paloheimo 2007, 357; Put and Maddens 2014, 620). *Local ties* are generally considered a valuable proxy for "knowing the area and its interest" (Shugart et al. 2005). Among the MPs elected from 1999 to 2015, 60 percent were native to the district and close to 73 percent were elected to local office within their district.[47] Moreover, when asked about their views on representative roles and foci, Finnish voters, as well as their elected representatives, tend to downplay the role of parties and emphasize the importance of the local perspective (Bengtsson and Wass 2011; Esaiasson 2000).

While the open list without party ranking in theory provides candidates with an equal opportunity to become elected, it is important to note that far from all candidates enter the race with the goal or expectation of becoming elected. According to Paloheimo (2007, 333–334), candidates can be divided into four distinct categories: *incumbents* seeking re-election, *challengers* with an actual prospect of becoming elected, *career builders* who utilize the election campaign to enhance their reputation and increase recognition for future contests, and *top-up candidates* who are nominated to attract the support of specific subgroups of voters but without posing a threat to the "main" candidates (see also Carty, Eagles, and Sayers 2003, 64; Arter 2013, 103). Parties hence use the last category of top-up candidates to make sure that all potential voters can identify a suitable candidate on the list, mainly in terms of sociodemographic background or residence (see the *balanced list strategy* earlier).

A corresponding differentiation of candidates can be made based on their personal vote-earning attributes and clearly demonstrates the different electoral prospects by type of candidates (Table 29.5). Of the candidates in the period 1999–2011 (nominated on what turned out to be a successful list), close to 40 percent can be classified as "top-up" candidates, due to their lack of classic vote-earning attributes. Together with the group of candidates who (only) have local-level experience, they constitute the close to 80 percent of all candidates who in general attract a limited amount of (local) followers

Table 29.5  Candidates' Personal Vote-Earning Attributes and Electoral Success
(1999–2011)

|  | Success | Preference Votes | | | |
|---|---|---|---|---|---|
|  | % Elected | Average No. Preference Votes | Average % of Preference Votes/ List | % of All Candidates | (n) |
| Incumbent MP | 77.8 | 6,469 | 16.8 | 13 | (630) |
| Celebrity (only) | 29.9 | 3,155 | 7.1 | 1 | (67) |
| Quality candidate | 27.2 | 2,995 | 8.3 | 8 | (423) |
| Local-level incumbency (only) | 6.1 | 1,607 | 4.5 | 41 | (2,071) |
| No vote-earning attribute | 2.3 | 838 | 2.6 | 37 | (1,831) |
| Total | 15.8 | 2,074 | 5.7 | 100 | (5,022) |

*Note:* "Quality candidates" = not incumbents at the national level but at least one additional personal vote-earning attribute (leadership position within the party, previous MP, member of European Parliament, minister), to local-level incumbency. "Celebrities" = candidates who lack other attributes than name recognition from outside politics (media, sports, show business). Only candidates running for lists that were successful in winning a seat are included in the table.

*Source:* Database on Finnish candidates collected within framework of the project Intra-Party Dimension of Politics (Shugart and Bengtsson, 2012).

and have small prospects of getting elected. The probability of success increases substantially among the more qualified candidates (27 percent), among celebrity candidates (30 percent), and, as expected, among incumbent MPs (78 percent).

## CONCLUSION

The Finnish open-list PR electoral system is characterized by stability and simplicity. The single-tier system and the D'Hondt formula have been in place since the first election held in 1907 with universal and equal suffrage, and the preferential voting system since 1955. The transformation from votes to seats is considered transparent and is taught in elementary school. The system has survived development from semipresidentialism to parliamentarism in the post-Kekkonen era and recurrent attempts at reform to address the increasing differences in the effective threshold across electoral districts.

Despite the overall simplicity of the electoral system, it involves a peculiar combination of party and candidate centeredness with substantial effects on all levels. The decentralized nomination procedures empower the local and district level at the expense of the central party organizations, and the pooling of votes provides parties with incentives to field a diverse set of candidates at the expense of party cohesion. Candidates are in turn faced with the delicate balance of trying to maximize the collective party vote while simultaneously engaging in intraparty rivalry. And voters are overloaded with information and torn between political campaigns played out at two distinct levels, a party-centered campaign characterized by vagueness at the national level and a multitude of highly individualized candidate campaigns at the district level.

Against the backdrop of the modern Finnish political culture with oversized coalition governments, the high level of consensus, and the vagueness of national election campaigns, it seems fair to conclude that the Finnish OLPR system provides voters with a greater say over which candidates are to represent them in parliament but far less influence on the actual content of politics than voters in many other proportional electoral systems. The system does nevertheless enjoy a high level of legitimacy at all levels and is not likely to be changed in the near future.

## NOTES

1. The concepts of "district" and "constituency" are used interchangeably in the text.
2. The radical representation reform of 1906 is often seen as a response to the internal Russian turmoil after the country had been defeated by Japan in 1905 (Karvonen 2014, 12). It followed from a period of Russification, which can explain why the Finnish elite could reach unanimity on the far-reaching reforms (Raunio 2005, 475).
3. The radical representation reform caused the Finnish party system to emerge. The reform was not, however, matched by democratic executive institutions during the period from the first election held in 1907 up until independence in 1917. During the period cabinets were controlled by the czar, which effectively hindered major reforms (Karvonen 2014, 12).
4. The autonomous region of Åland Island in the southwest archipelago does, however, hold strong regional powers and elects a regional assembly every fourth year. Moreover, the government of Juha Sipilä (2015–) has far-reaching plans on introducing popularly elected regional parliaments with responsibility for health care—a model that resembles the system used in the neighboring countries of Sweden and Norway.
5. Due to the relatively high fragmentation of the party system, the absence of a dominating party, and the role of the Centre Party as a bridge builder, the system has been characterized by pragmatism and a willingness to form ideologically broad coalitions. Since 1977, all governments have interchangeably been formed around two of the three parties constituting the core of the party system (Paloheimo 2016, 66–70; Karvonen 2016, 95–110).
6. Intraparty voting cohesion has increased over time. Finland does, however, have lower cohesion compared to the other Nordic countries (Jensen 2000).
7. This was seen as a matter of justice from the Social Democratic Party, which had low chances of gaining funding from affluent donors. It was also considered a reduction of the risk of moneyed interests gaining undue influence over parties (Anckar 1974, 82–88).
8. The average number of parties during the period 1907–2015 is 4.42. The calculations are based on Sundberg (2002, 86) and updated by figures from the Statistics of Finland.

9. A traditional conservative party.

10. From 1907 to 1965 the Agrarian Union.

11. From 1945 to 1990 the Finnish People's Democratic Unit.

12. The Christian Democrats (from 1966 to 2002 the Finnish Christian League) gained representation in the Eduskunta for the first time in the 1970 election.

13. The Green League gained representation as a registered party in the Eduskunta in 1991 election. In the 1987 election (later) members of the party became elected as a part of a constituency association (Sundberg 2002, 78f).

14. A populist party has been present in Finnish politics since the late 1950s. The Small Farmers Party (characterized as an agrarian populist party) was formed in 1958 by Veikko Vennamo, a dissident of the Agrarian Union. The party—which changed name to the Finnish Rural Party (FrP) in 1966—received varying levels of electoral support with a peak in the early 1970s and the early 1980s. The Finns Party, founded in 1995, is seen as a successor party to the FrP and built upon the FrP both in terms of organization and the persons involved. The Finns Party (labeled the True Finns up until 2011) is generally classified as a member of the Radical Right Populist family (Jungar 2016, 113).

15. Finland is a bilingual country in which Finnish and Swedish are given the same status in the constitution. The mother tongue of the vast majority (88.7 percent) is, however, Finnish, while only 5.3 percent are registered as Swedish speakers (Statistics Finland 2016).

16. Legislation concerning all four elections is gathered in the Election Act of 1998 (Raunio 2005, 476; Ministry of Justice 2016).

17. Up until 1965, elections to the national parliament were traditionally held in July. In 1965, the Election Act was changed and elections were held on the third Sunday and the following Monday in March (Pesonen 1968, 11). Until 1991 the polling stations were open during two days (Raunio 2005, 478). Since 2011 the election has been held on the third Sunday of April (Ministry of Justice 2016).

18. In the 2015 election four districts were merged into two to increase proportionality and lower the effective electoral threshold (Ministry of Justice 2016).

19. The Åland Island is the only single-seat district in Finland. The electoral system is, however, the same as for the multiseat districts, meaning there are competing party slates containing more than one candidate. The winner then is defined as the candidate that receives the most votes within the party with the most votes. As such, the election in the Åland constituency is similar to former presidential elections in Uruguay (Shugart 2005, 40).

20. Parties allowed to nominate candidates are to be entered into the party register kept by the Ministry of Justice. A requirement to be entered into the register is the signed support of at least five thousand persons entitled to vote. Parties that fail to win a parliamentary seat in two consecutive elections will be deleted from the party register (Ministry of Justice 2016).

21. A constituency association may be established at the district level by the support of at least one hundred persons entitled to vote in the electoral district. Constituency associations have managed to win a seat in the parliament on two occasions. The first was in 1983 when a popular MP from the Communist Party was denied access to the party list due to an internal party conflict. The second was in 1987 when members of the (current) Green League managed to win four seats in parliament before having become a registered party (Sundberg 2002, 78f).

22. The Swedish People's Party fares better because their electoral support is concentrated in four constituencies (Helsinki, Uusimaa, Varsinais-Suomi, and Vaasa). The party has, however, in recent elections fielded candidates in constituencies outside their strongholds as a

means to prepare for a potential revision of the electoral system into a two-tier system. In 2011, they fielded candidates in six constituencies and in 2015 in eight constituencies.

23. The constitution (25§) stipulates that the number of constituencies on the mainland should vary between twelve and eighteen. In addition, one MP is elected in the district of Åland.

24. *M* is determined based on the number of Finnish citizens resident within each district six months prior to the election with the exception of the electoral district of Åland, which (since 1948) is a fixed single-seat constituency (Ministry of Justice 2016).

25. Tarja Cronberg, the party leader of the Green League, was, however, appointed as Minister of Labour in the government that was formed after the election.

26. Since the proposal would involve a change in the constitution, it was to be accepted in two stages by two different parliaments with an election in between (or in one stage by a two-thirds majority). The proposal was approved before the election in March 2011 but failed to receive enough support by the following parliament in 2011.

27. The electoral districts of Northern Savonia and North Karelia were merged into Savonia-Karelia, while the electoral districts of Kymi and Southern Savonia were merged into Southeastern Finland.

28. The Social Democratic Party generally deviates from this pattern by presenting their candidates according to their success in the primaries (Raunio 2005, 478).

29. According to studies by Helander (1997) and Villodres (2003), being placed high on the list due to a surname beginning with a letter that appears early in the alphabet does not provide an electoral advantage. In cases where candidates are ranked according to their success in primaries (a procedure at times used by the Social Democrats), high placement on the list does contribute to more preference votes (Villodres 2003).

30. Prior to the Electoral Act of 1969 and the Election Act of 1975, nomination was unregulated and more centralized and in the control of national party executives (Raunio 2005, 476).

31. In the Social Democratic Party the district party executive can replace one-fifth of the aspiring candidates (Kuitunen 2002, 69).

32. Among the MPs elected in 2011, only four were elected from a constituency where they were not resident. Moreover, all of these four cases were elected from the constituency of Uusimaa (Nyland), which surrounds the capital of Helsinki and is part of the same metropolitan area. The four MPs in question were all residents of Helsinki (constituting an electoral district of its own).

33. In comparison to single transferable vote (STV) and SNTV, parties run no risk of losing seats due to overnomination (Johnson and Hoyo 2012, 134).

34. Arter (2013, 109) also identifies a fourth strategy—the *level-playing-field strategy*—used by the Finns Party in the 2011 parliamentary election, where they had a very visible and popular party leader (only able to run in one constituency) and a strong tail wind in the national opinion polls (Borg 2012, 194), but lacked a pool of experienced candidates with personal followers to field in the thirteen mainland constituencies outside Uusimaa, where the party leader Timo Soini stood for election. This strategy involved running full lists of local candidates without extensive political experience or name recognition who were encouraged to engage in a high level of intraparty competition with fairly good prospects of becoming elected to parliament.

35. The following must resign from their office to serve as MPs: the chancellor of justice of the government, the parliamentary ombudsman, a justice of the supreme court, and the prosecutor-general (Constitution of Finland, section 27).

36. A similar example is from the same election and constituency but for the National Coalition Party, where the former party leader, Sauli Niinistö, the minister of finance who was to become elected as president in the year 2012, won 60,563 personal votes (45 percent out of the list total of 133,885), while the eleventh candidate on the list, and the last to become elected, Eero Lehti, only received 3,215 personal votes (2.4 percent of the list total) (Ministry of Justice 2016).

37. After this date moving across districts did not change where you are entitled to vote.

38. The Ministry of Foreign Affairs is responsible for organizing the advance vote abroad.

39. There are substantial differences in spending by elected MPs from different parties. Successful candidates from the National Coalition and the Centre Party in the 2011 election spent on average 49,000 and 41,000, respectively. Candidates from the Social Democratic Party had an average campaign budget of 30,000 euros, and candidates from the Finns Party had an average of 14,000 euros (Mattila and Sundberg 2012, 234).

40. For a detailed description of the process see Karvonen (2014, 56–60).

41. Confronted with the question of whether they would have voted for the same candidate would he or she have been nominated by another party, a majority of 56 percent said no in the 2011 election study. Only one out of ten gave an unconditional yes, while one-third stated that they would have voted for the same candidate if he or she had been nominated by "a party that was suitable to me" (Karvonen 2014, 131).

42. This political dimension is often described as the GAL (green-alternative-liberal)/TAN (traditional-authoritarian-nationalist) dimension (Hooghe, Marks, and Wilson 2002). This is played out as a new dimension with the Finns Party on the TAN side of the spectrum, and the Green League and the Swedish Peoples Party on the GAL side, cutting across the traditional left/right dimension.

43. Only including candidates nominated for a party that gained representation in the Eduskunta.

44. Updated figures from Paloheimo (2007, 334).

45. Another distinct feature of Finnish politics is that of *celebrity politicians*, that is, politicians who are incumbents frequently appearing in the media to boost name recognition and their political image (Arter 2014, 3; Karvonen 2014, 68).

46. This figure represents celebrity candidates without any other personal vote-earning attribute. The total share of celebrity candidates during the period 1999–2011 is 2 percent (von Schoultz 2016, 185).

47. "Double seats," that is, to hold elected office both at the national and local levels, is a popular strategy for MPs to maintain contacts with the local community and to increase the chances of becoming re-elected.

## References

Almgren, Esko. *Villenpoika*. Gummerus: Jyväskylä, 1998.

Anckar, Dag. *Analys av partiers beteende: en fallstudie i partistrategi*. Åbo: Åbo Akademi, 1974.

Ansolabehere, Stephen, James M. Snyder, and Charles Stewart. "Old Voters, New Voters, and the Personal Vote: Using Redistricting to Measure the Incumbency Advantage." *American Journal of Political Science* 44, no. 1 (2000): 17–34.

Arter, David. "Money and Votes: The Cost of Election for First-Time Finnish MPs." *Politiikka* 51, no. 1 (2009): 17–33.

Arter, David. "The 'Hows', Not the 'Whys' or the 'Wherefores': The Role of Intra-party Competition in the 2011 Breakthrough of the True Finns." *Scandinavian Political Studies* 36, no. 2 (2013): 99–120.

Arter, David. "Clowns, 'Alluring Ducks' and 'Miss Finland 2009': The Value of 'Celebrity Candidates' in an Open-List PR Voting System." *Representation* 50, no. 4 (2014): 453–470.

Bengtsson, Åsa. *Politiskt deltagande.* Lund: Studentlitteratur, 2007.

Bengtsson, Åsa. "Kandidatval och rörlighet." In *Muutosvaalit 2011. Reports and guidelines. 16/2012,* edited by Sami Borg. Ministry of Justice, 2012.

Bengtsson, Åsa, and Hanna Wass. "The Representative Roles of MPs: A Citizen Perspective." *Scandinavian Political Studies* 34, no. 2 (2011): 143–167.

Bengtsson, Åsa, Kasper M. Hansen, Olafur Hardarson, Hanne Marthe Narud, and Henrik Oscarsson. *The Nordic Voter. Myths of Exceptionalism.* Colchester: ECPR Press, 2014.

Borg, Sami, "Perussuomalaiset." In *Muutosvaalit 2011. Reports and guidelines. 16/2012,* edited by Sami Borg. Ministry of Justice, 2012.

Borg, Sami, and Tom Moring. "Vaalikampanja." In *Vaalit Yleisödemokratiassa. Eduskuntavaalitutkimus 2007,* edited by Sami Borg and Heikki Paloheimo. Tampere: Tampere University Press, 2007.

Cain, Bruce, John Ferejohn, and Morris P. Fiorina. *The Personal Vote: Constituency Service and Electoral Independence.* Cambridge, MA: Harvard University Press, 1987.

Carey, John M., and Matthew S. Shugart. "Incentives to Cultivate a Personal Vote." *Electoral Studies* 14, no. 4 (1995): 417–439.

Carty, Kenneth R., Munroe D. Eagles, and Anthony Sayers. "Candidates and Local Campaigns." *Party Politics* 9, no. 5 (2003): 619–636.

Cox Gary *Making Votes Count: Strategic Coordination in the World's Electoral Systems.* New York: Cambridge University Press, 1997.

Cox, Gary D., and Mathew D. McCubbins. *Legislative Leviathan: Party Government in the House.* Berkeley: University of California Press, 1993.

Dahlgaard, Jens O. "You Just Made It: Individual Incumbency Advantage under Proportional Representation." *Electoral Studies* 44 (2016): 319–328.

Duverger, Maurice. *Political Parties: Their Organization and Activity in the Modern State.* Translated by Barbara and Robert North. London: Methuen, 1954.

Erikson, Robert. "The Advantage of Incumbency in Congressional Elections." *American Political Science Review* 66 (1971): 1234–1255.

Esaiasson, Peter. "How Members of Parliament Define Their Task." In *Beyond Westminster and Congress. The Nordic Experience,* edited by Peter Esaiasson and Knut Heidar. Columbus: Ohio State University Press, 2000.

Gallagher, Michael. "Proportional Disproportionality, and Electoral Systems." *Electoral Studies* 10 (1991): 33–51.

Gallagher, Michael, M. Laver, and Peter Mair. *Representative Government in Modern Europe. Institutions, Parties, and Governments.* New York: McGraw-Hill, 2001.

Helander, Voitto. "Finland." In *Passages to Power: Legislative Recruitment in Advanced Democracies,* edited by Pippa Norris. Cambridge: Cambridge University Press, 1997.

Hooghe, Liesbet, Gary Marks, and Carol Wilson. "Does Left/Right Structure Party Position on European Integration?" *Comparative Political Studies* 35, no. 8 (2002): 965–989.

Jensen, Torben K. "Party Cohesion." In *Beyond Westminster and Congress. The Nordic Experience,* edited by Peter Esaiasson and Knut Heidar. Columbus: Ohio State University Press, 2000.

Johnson, Joel W., and Véronica Hoyo. "Beyond Personal Vote Incentives: Dividing the Vote in Preferential Electoral Systems." *Electoral Studies* 31, no. 1 (2012): 131–142.

Jungar, Ann-Cathrine. "From the Mainstream to the Margin? The Radicalisation of the True Finns." In *Radical Right-Wing Populist Parties in Western Europe. Into the Mainstream?*, edited by Tjitske Akkerman, Sarah de Lange, and Matthijs Rooduijn. New York: Routledge, 2016.

Karvonen, Lauri. *The Personalisation of Politics. A Study of Parliamentary Democracies.* Colchester: ECPR Press, 2010.

Karvonen, Lauri. *Parties, Governments and Voters in Finland. Politics under Fundamental Societal Transformation.* Colchester: ECPR Press, 2014.

Karvonen, Lauri. "No Definitive Decline. The Power of Political Parties in Finland: A Focused Analysis." In *The Changing Balance of Political Power in Finland*, edited by Tapio Raunio and Lauri Karvonen. Stockholm: Santerus Academic Press, 2016.

Kuitunen, Soile. "Finland: Formalized Procedures with Membership Predominance." In *Party Sovereignty and Citizen Control. Selecting Candidates for Parliamentary Elections in Denmark, Finland, Iceland and Norway*, edited by Hanne Marthe Narud, Mogens. N. Pedersen, and Henry Valen. Odense: University Press of Southern Denmark, 2002.

Lijphart, Arend, *Electoral Systems and Party Systems: A Study of Twenty-Seven Democracies 1945-1990.* New York: Oxford University Press, 1994.

Lundell, Krister. "Determinants of Candidate Selection: The Degree of Centralization in Comparative Perspective." *Party Politics* 10, no. 1 (2004): 25–47.

Maddens, Bart, Braum Wauters, Jo Noppe, and Stefaan Fiers. "Effects of Campaign Spending in an Open List PR System: The 2003 Legislative Election in Flanders/Belgium." *West European Politics* 29, no. 1 (2006): 161–168.

Mattila, Mikko, and Ilkka Ruostetsaari. "Candidate-Centred Campaigns and Their Effects in an Open List System: The Case of Finland." In *Do Campaigns Matter? Campaign Effects in Elections and Referendums*, edited by David M. Farrell and Rüdiger. Schmitt-Beck. London: Routledge, 2002.

Mattila, Mikko., and Jan Sundberg. "Vaalirahoitus ja vaalirahakohu." In *Muutosvaalit 2011. Reports and guidelines. 16/2012*, edited by Sami Borg. Ministry of Justice, 2012.

Mickelsson, Rauli. *Suomen puolueet: Historia, muutos ja nykypäivä.* Tampere: Vastapaino, 2007.

Monroe, Burt L., and Amanda G. Rose. "Electoral Systems and Unimagined Consequences: Partisan Effects of Districted Proportional Representation." *American Journal of Political Science* 46, no. 1 (2002): 67–89.

Moring, Tom, Juri Mykkänen, Lars Nord, and Marie Grusell. "Campaign Professionalization and Political Structures: A Comparative Study of Election Campaigning in Finland and Sweden in the 2009 EP Elections." In *Political Communication in European Parliamentary Elections*, edited by Michaela Maier, Jesper Strömbäck, and Lynda Lee Kaid. Farnham: Ashgate, 2011.

Pajala, Antti. "Government vs Opposition Voting in the Finnish Parliament Eduskunta since World War II." *European Journal of Government and Economics* 2, no. 1 (2013): 41–58.

Paloheimo, Heikki. "Eduskuntavaalit 1907-2003." In *Kansanedustajan työ ja arki. Suomen Eduskunta 100 vuotta 5*, edited by A. Ollila and Heikki Paloheimo. Helsinki: Edita, 2007.

Paloheimo, Heikki. "The Changing Balance of Power between President and Cabinet." In *The Changing Balance of Political Power in Finland*, edited by Tapio Raunio and Lauri Karvonen. Stockholm: Santerus Academic Press, 2016.

Paloheimo, Heikki, and Jan Sundberg. "Vaaliliitot eduskuntavaaleissa." In *Vaalit Yleisödemokratiassa: Eduskuntavaalitutkimus 2007*, edited by Sami Borg and Heikki Paloheimo. Tampere: Tampere University Press, 2009.

Pesonen, Pertti. *An Election in Finland. Party Activities and Voter Reactions*. New Haven, CT: Yale University Press, 1968.

Put, Gert-Jan., and Bart Maddens. "The Effect of Municipality Size and Local Office on the Electoral Success of Belgian/Flemish Election Candidates: A Multilevel Analysis." *Government and Opposition* 50, no. 4 (2014): 607–628.

Raunio, Tapio. "Finland: One Hundred Years of Quietude." In *The Politics of Electoral Systems*, edited by M. Gallagher and P. Mitchell. Oxford: Oxford University Press, 2005.

Reynolds, Andrew, Ben Reilly, Andrew Ellis. *Electoral System Design: The New International IDEA Handbook*. Stockholm: International Institute for Democracy and Electoral Assistance, 2005.

Rokkan, Stein. *Stat, nasjon, klasse*. Oslo: Universitetsforlaget, 1987.

Sartori, Giovanni. *Parties and Party Systems. A Framework for Analysis*. Colchester: ECPR Press, 2005 [1976].

von Schoultz, Åsa. "Passing through the Eye of the Needle—Individual Electoral Success in Finnish Parliamentary Elections." In *The Changing Balance of Political Power in Finland*, edited by Tapio Raunio and Larui Karvonen. Stockholm: Santerus Academic Press, 2016.

Shugart, Matthew S. "Comparative Electoral System Research." In *The Politics of Electoral Systems*, edited by Michael Gallagher and Paul Mitchell. Oxford: Oxford University Press, 2005.

Shugart, Matthew S., and Rein Taagepera. *Votes from Seats: Logical Models of Electoral Systems*. New York: Cambridge University Press, 2017.

Shugart, Matthew S., Melody E. Valdini, and Kati Suominen. "Looking for Locals: Voter Information Demands and Personal Vote-Earning Attributes of Legislators under Proportional Representation." *American Journal of Political Science* 49, no. 2 (2005): 437–449.

Strandberg, Kim. "A Social Media Revolution or Just a Case of History Repeating Itself?—The Use of Social Media in the 2011 Finnish Parliamentary Elections." *New Media & Society* 15, no. 8 (2013): 1329–1347.

Sundberg, Jan. "The Electoral System of Finland: Old and Working Well." In *The Evolution of Electoral and Party systems in the Nordic Countries*, edited by Bernard Grofman and Arend Lijphart. New York: Agathon Press, 2002.

Taagepera, Rein. *Predicting Party Sizes: The Logic of Simple Electoral Systems*. Oxford: Oxford University Press, 2007.

Tavits, Margit. "Effect of Local Ties on Electoral Success and Parliamentary Behaviour: The Case of Estonia." *Party Politics* 16, no. 2 (2010): 215–235.

Villodres, Carmen O. "Intra-Party Competition under Preferential List Systems: The Case of Finland." *Representation* 40, no. 1 (2003): 55–66.

Westinen, Jussi, Elina Kestilä-Kekkonen, and Aino Tiihonen. "Äänestäjät arvo- ja asenneulottuvuuksilla." In *Poliittisen Osallistumisen Eriytyminen: Eduskuntavaalitutkimus 2015. Reports and guidelines. 28/2016*, edited by Kimmo Grönlund and Hanna Wass. Ministry of Justice, 2016.

## Internet Sources

Ministry of Justice. 2016. www.vaalit.fi.
Statistics Finland. 2016, www.stat.fi.

## Databases

Bengtsson, Åsa. The Finnish Candidate Study 2011. Part of the project *The Comparative Candidate Survey*. 2011. www.comparativecandidates.org.

Borg, Sami, and Kimmo Grönlund. FSD2653 Eduskuntavaalitutkimus 2011.

Gallup Finland. FSD1011 Finnish Voter Barometer 1983.

Grönlund, Kimmo, and Elina Kestilä-Kekkonen. FSD3067 Eduskuntavaalitutkimus 2015.

Karvonen, Lauri, and Heikki Paloheimo. FSD1260 Eduskuntavaalitutkimus 2003.

Paloheimo, Heikki. FSD2269 Eduskuntavaalitutkimus 2007.

Shugart, Matthew S., and Åsa Bengtsson. Database on Finnish candidates collected within framework of the project Intra-Party Dimension of Politics. 2012.

Pesonen, Pertti, Risto Sänkiaho, and Sami Borg. FSD1088 Eduskuntavaalitutkimus 1991.

CHAPTER 30

..............................................................................................

# ELECTORAL SYSTEMS IN CONTEXT

## *United Kingdom*

..............................................................................................

THOMAS CARL LUNDBERG

## CONTINUITY AND CHANGE

..............................................................................................

THE United Kingdom is well known for what many political scientists call the single-member plurality electoral system.[1] More commonly, if colloquially, known as "first past the post" (FPTP)—a racing reference that highlights the winner-take-all nature of this majoritarian system—FPTP is used to elect the House of Commons, the lower house of Parliament. This system is used in many other countries, typically as a result of having some experience with British colonialism, and FPTP has been the subject of controversy in a number of the countries using it, not least the United Kingdom itself, where the system has been the subject of intense criticism and even a referendum.

While FPTP is strongly identified with its use in the United Kingdom, several other electoral systems have also been used for other bodies or positions in the United Kingdom, thanks to the process of decentralization (called "devolution") in the late 1990s. As a result of the transfer of power from Westminster to the constituent nations outside England (Scotland, Wales, and Northern Ireland), as well as to local and regional authorities within England, there were six different electoral systems operating in different parts of the United Kingdom by the year 2000. This chapter will examine all of these systems, not simply FPTP, whose historical developments from medieval times through the twentieth century have been explored in detail elsewhere (Bogdanor 1981; Carstairs 1980; Farrell 2011; Hart 1992; Mitchell 2005; Norris 1995). The main observation is that despite the presence of a multitude of different electoral systems and party systems in the United Kingdom since the expansion of multilevel governance, FPTP has persisted at Westminster, seemingly entrenched and immune to contagion from the other electoral systems in use in the United Kingdom.

Three of the United Kingdom's electoral systems in the early twenty-first century were majoritarian: FPTP; its predecessor, the multiple nontransferable vote (MNTV, much more commonly known in the United Kingdom as the block vote), used for council elections in some English and Welsh local authority areas; and the more modern supplementary vote (SV), used to elect the mayors of some English cities, as well as police and crime commissioners in England and Wales. The other three electoral systems were forms of proportional representation (PR): the single transferable vote (STV), used for most elections in Northern Ireland, as well as for local elections in Scotland; regional list PR, used for the election of Great Britain's members of the European Parliament (MEPs) when the United Kingdom was part of the European Union; and the mixed-member proportional (MMP) system (usually called the "additional member system" in the United Kingdom), used to elect the Scottish Parliament, the National Assembly for Wales, and the London Assembly.

This institutional diversity at the regional level has not led to electoral system change at Westminster, where a multiparty system has persisted despite the use of an electoral system better suited to a two-party system. While some observers, like Patrick Dunleavy, have correctly pointed out that the United Kingdom has made a transition from two-party politics to multiparty politics, with multiple party *systems* existing at the various levels of governance since devolution, the expectation that "some form of transition of representation at Westminster seems inevitable as existing multi-party politics develops further" (Dunleavy 2005, 505) had not been realized by the second decade of the twenty-first century. As international comparisons show, multiparty systems and FPTP can coexist, even at the electoral district level, in defiance of Duverger's "law" (Duverger 1954): Canada (Gaines 1999) and India (Diwakar 2007) feature prominently as examples of countries with FPTP systems resistant to reform. The case of the United Kingdom under multilevel governance reinforces this observation. Rather than a situation in which electoral rules at the various levels of governance in multilevel systems are the same or significantly influence one another, it appears that in the case of the United Kingdom, each level of governance constitutes its own political system, with only occasional influence on the other levels.

This chapter will explore the development of the six UK electoral systems, looking at the two waves of electoral reform attempts and their achievements. Examples of recent elections under the various systems will be provided to illustrate how these systems work in practice, as well as how proportional they are and what kind of party systems are associated with them. Issues and controversies associated with these systems will also be examined, including the importance of the constituency role of elected representatives in the United Kingdom. The story of the United Kingdom's electoral systems, it will be shown, is one of continuity and change.

# WAVES OF ELECTORAL REFORM

There were two waves of electoral reform attempts in British history (Norris 1995, 69). The first wave took place in the late nineteenth century, at the time British politics began to democratize. As demands for greater inclusion grew, the political parties gradually extended the franchise to more and more citizens, raising questions about how this process would affect the parties' fortunes. Contrary to popular belief, most constituencies (electoral districts) returned two members by the plurality method—MNTV, in which the winners were the two candidates with the most votes in contests where each voter had two votes—to the House of Commons throughout most of its existence (Hart 1992, 5). Therefore, the FPTP system is actually an electoral innovation away from MNTV and not an "ancient" feature of British political history, or at least not of English political history—Ireland, Scotland, and Wales did have, for the most part, single-seat constituencies, but these constituted a small portion of seats in the House of Commons (Carstairs 1980, 191).

The shift to a single-seat constituency norm came as the two major parties, the Conservatives and the Liberals, competed over the extension of the franchise and the redrawing of constituency boundaries at a time of great social and economic change in the United Kingdom. Part of the rationale for single-seat constituencies was the protection of minorities, especially the privileged minority that feared being swamped by the enfranchisement of more and more working-class men (Norris 1995, 69). With the 1867 Reform Act, there was a brief experiment in minority protection with the semiproportional "limited vote" system in which voters had one vote less than the number of members to be elected in a small number of three- and four-seat constituencies (Carstairs 1980, 192), but these were seen as failing to protect minorities and abolished with the introduction of a primarily single-seat constituency system in the 1885 Redistribution of Seats Act, with Prime Minister William Gladstone indicating that he was satisfied that minorities would be protected by the new system that would accompany the previous year's franchise extension (Hart 1992, 113–114). Eventually the Liberals came to support STV, but this shift came too late; as they went into decline, the Labour Party rose and ultimately replaced them as a major party. Both the Conservatives and Labour came to support FPTP.

The United Kingdom did, therefore, undertake electoral reform in the late nineteenth century, shifting from a mainly MNTV system to a mainly FPTP system, with a brief experiment with the limited vote system. Unlike most other European countries, however, the United Kingdom did not move to PR, though it was proposed during this era. John Stuart Mill and Thomas Hare advocated STV, a preferential system in which voters would rank candidates numerically, rather than a party list system, which came to predominate across the rest of Europe. STV failed to impress most of the political class, which saw the system as an overly complicated product of naïve, idealistic reformers who looked down on party politicians to such an extent that their system was designed to enhance the chances of independent candidates and allow voters to choose between candidates of the same party, something most party leaders would like to avoid (Hart 1992, 267–268). While STV's advocates were ultimately unsuccessful in the United Kingdom, they did help to lay the foundations of this system in Ireland. The president of Britain's Proportional Representation Society (now the Electoral Reform Society) recommended STV as a way to reassure the Protestant minority in the event of Home Rule when he visited in 1911, and this recommendation made its way into the 1922 constitution of the Irish Free State without controversy (Carstairs 1980, 203).

A second wave of attempts to reform the British electoral system began in the 1970s as the character of the British party system became more pluralistic, which was particularly apparent with the results of the two general elections of 1974. The two-party system of the mid-twentieth century was giving way to one in which the Liberals were gaining support after their replacement by a rising Labour Party in the earlier part of the century, and where Scottish and Welsh nationalists were competing more successfully in the "Celtic Fringe." The deteriorating political situation in Northern Ireland, whose FPTP-elected parliament had been suspended by Westminster, led to the introduction of STV for local council and European Parliament elections in an effort to reassure the minority community that it was going to be represented more equitably (Farrell 2011, 29). Discussions about the possibility of devolution for Scotland and Wales in the 1970s also facilitated interest in alternate electoral systems, but PR was opposed by the Conservatives and most in the Labour Party, though the latter party did show some interest in PR and even more interest in the majoritarian alternative vote (AV) system, which requires voters to rank candidates preferentially in single-seat constituencies. The Liberals and their successor party, the Liberal Democrats, supported STV, which has also been the preference of the Scottish National Party (SNP) and Plaid Cymru, the Party of Wales.

Nevertheless, the two major parties would normally benefit the most from FPTP, gaining seats as an increasing number of voters supported minor parties that failed to win seats. In the 1950s and 1960s, Conservative and Labour candidates won around 90 percent of the vote at general elections, but this dropped to about 75 percent in the 1970s and the following two decades, and hit 65 percent at the 2010 election, yet the two major parties still managed to win about 90 percent of the seats in the House of Commons (Clark 2012, 9–10). Labour's long spell in the political wilderness during Conservatives' eighteen continuous years in power (1979–1997) did lead to some questioning of the electoral system, with the party's Working Group on Electoral Systems, chaired by political philosophy professor Raymond Plant, recommending the majoritarian SV for the House of Commons, MMP for the Scottish Parliament, and regional list PR for elections to the European Parliament and a reformed House of Lords in its 1993 report (Plant 1995).

The Labour victory under Tony Blair in 1997 brought an end to Conservative rule for thirteen years and prompted a major increase in the number of electoral systems in the United Kingdom, which would double from three to six, with serious consideration given to changing the system used to elect the House of Commons. Roy Jenkins was charged with leading a commission that would investigate alternatives to FPTP and make a recommendation that Labour's 1997 manifesto said would be put to the voters in a referendum. Jenkins recommended what he called "AV Top-up," a largely AV-based system with a small compensatory tier of party list seats (15 to 20 percent of the total) to be allocated in small electoral regions, meaning that while the system would technically have been a form of MMP, its compensatory ability would have been so limited that it might have been better described as a diluted majoritarian system (Lundberg 2007a, 479). Ultimately the system was never put to a referendum.

Electoral reform came back onto the agenda after the 2010 election when the Conservatives formed a coalition government with the Liberal Democrats, a party that had advocated STV for decades. The Conservatives agreed to a referendum on the electoral system for the House of Commons, but the voters would be offered the non-proportional AV as the alternative, rather than STV or some other PR option. Labour had promised a referendum on AV in its manifesto, so the system was on the table, with the Liberal Democrats probably calculating that despite its majoritarian nature, AV was potentially better for the party than FPTP, provided that a lot of second prefer-ences could be won from the supporters of other parties (Curtice 2013, 217). Though the Conservatives agreed to the referendum and were presumably not worried about the potential impact of AV, they campaigned against change and seemed to reap the benefits of their own popularity while that of their smaller partner declined; ultimately, nearly 68 percent of those who voted in the 2011 referendum (on the low turnout of less than 42 percent) opposed AV (Curtice 2013, 220).

# THE SIX UK ELECTORAL SYSTEMS IN USE IN THE EARLY TWENTY-FIRST CENTURY

Despite the failure of the AV referendum, the United Kingdom was using six different electoral systems in the early twenty-first century (Table 30.1). One—the regional list PR system used to elect Great Britain's MEPs—would be eliminated as the United Kingdom left the European Union and its MEPs left the European Parliament. The remaining five would include three examples of the majoritarian family of electoral systems and two from the proportional family, though residents of England outside London would not use any form of PR voting once the United Kingdom left the European Union.

The following sections will describe the systems, noting their origins and providing examples of results with analysis, which will include voter turnout (which is calculated by the UK Electoral Commission as a proportion of the total electorate, not the voting age population), the number and percentage of women elected, the effective number of parliamentary parties calculated by the author according to Laakso and Taagepera (1979), and the Gallagher (1991) least squares index of disproportionality (the higher the number, the greater the disproportionality when translating votes into seats).[2]

632 THOMAS CARL LUNDBERG

Table 30.1  Electoral Systems in Use in the United Kingdom in the Early
           Twenty-First Century

| Majoritarian | Proportional |
| --- | --- |
| Single-seat plurality | Single transferable vote |
| Block vote | Regional list proportional representation |
| Supplementary vote | Mixed-member proportional representation |

# First Past the Post

FPTP for House of Commons elections accompanied mass enfranchisement in the late nineteenth century, as described earlier. The system has also been used for local council elections in England and Wales and was used for the House of Commons of the Parliament of Northern Ireland after it switched from STV in the late 1920s until it was suspended and then abolished by Westminster in the early 1970s. Scotland's local councils were elected by FPTP until 2007, when the Labour/Liberal Democrat coalition government in Scotland introduced STV.

When comparing votes and seats on a partisan basis, FPTP election results often display high levels of disproportionality, particularly in multiparty systems. This is the case in the two House of Commons election results displayed in Table 30.2, where the 2010 result (Table 30.2A) reveals a Gallagher disproportionality index of 14.9, with 15.0 for 2015 (Table 30.2B). The effective number of parliamentary parties is 2.6 in 2010 and 2.5 in 2015. A crucial difference between the two election outcomes is the "hung parliament" in 2010—the colloquial British term for the rare event at Westminster since World War II in which no party wins a majority of seats, leading to the first coalition government since that war. The Conservatives came close to a majority of seats on 36 percent of the vote, but rather than forming a minority government, they went into a formal coalition with the centrist Liberal Democrats. The Conservatives managed to win a small majority (on just under 37 percent of the vote) in 2015 after a big drop in support for their coalition partner. While Labour's support actually rose more than one percentage point, its seat share dropped four points.

Results in Table 30.2 show how the two major parties benefit from FPTP, winning a far larger share of seats than their vote share, while the medium-sized Liberal Democrats in 2010 manage to win less than 9 percent of the seats on their 23 percent of the vote (Table 30.2A). Smaller parties typically do even worse if their support is geographically diffuse, with the UK Independence Party winning only 1 of the 650 seats for its nearly 13 percent of the vote in 2015 (Table 30.2B), but territorially concentrated support in the same election gave the SNP a seat share that was nearly twice its vote share, with the party winning nearly all of Scotland's seats. Territorial concentration also helped the very small, regionally based parties from Wales and Northern

## Table 30.2  House of Commons Elections

### A. May 6, 2010

| Party | % Votes | Seats Won | % Seats |
|---|---|---|---|
| Conservative | 36.1 | 307 | 47.2 |
| Labour | 29.0 | 258 | 39.7 |
| Liberal Democrat | 23.0 | 57 | 8.8 |
| UK Independence | 3.1 | 0 | 0 |
| British National | 1.9 | 0 | 0 |
| Scottish National | 1.7 | 6 | 0.9 |
| Green | 1.0 | 1 | 0.2 |
| Sinn Fein | 0.6 | 5 | 0.8 |
| Democratic Unionist | 0.6 | 8 | 1.2 |
| Plaid Cymru | 0.6 | 3 | 0.5 |
| Social Democratic and Labour | 0.4 | 3 | 0.5 |
| Alliance | 0.1 | 1 | 0.2 |
| *Total (including speaker seeking re-election)* | | 650 | |

- Voter turnout: 65.1%
- Women elected: 143 (22.0%)
- Effective number of parliamentary parties: 2.6
- Index of disproportionality (Michael Gallagher's least squares): 14.9

### B. May 7, 2015

| Party | % Votes | Seats Won | % Seats |
|---|---|---|---|
| Conservative | 36.9 | 331 | 50.9 |
| Labour | 30.4 | 232 | 35.7 |
| UK Independence | 12.6 | 1 | 0.2 |
| Liberal Democrat | 7.9 | 8 | 1.2 |
| Scottish National | 4.7 | 56 | 8.6 |
| Green | 3.8 | 1 | 0.2 |
| Democratic Unionist | 0.6 | 8 | 1.2 |
| Plaid Cymru | 0.6 | 3 | 0.5 |
| Sinn Fein | 0.6 | 4 | 0.6 |

*(continued)*

**Table 30.2  Continued**

B. May 7, 2015

| Party | % Votes | Seats Won | % Seats |
|---|---|---|---|
| Ulster Unionist | 0.4 | 2 | 0.3 |
| Social Democratic and Labour | 0.3 | 3 | 0.5 |
| *Total (including speaker seeking re-election)* | | 650 | |

- Voter turnout: 66.1%
- Women elected: 191 (29.4%)
- Effective number of parliamentary parties: 2.5
- Index of disproportionality (Michael Gallagher's least squares): 15.0

*Sources:* BBC News (2010, 2015).

Ireland win a roughly proportional share of seats. Voter turnout was about the same at both elections, at 65 percent in 2010 and 66 percent in 2015, but there was a big increase in the proportion of women in the House of Commons—a rise from 22 percent in 2010 to 29 percent in 2015.

## Multiple Nontransferable Vote

In this variant of plurality voting, there are multiseat constituencies in which voters cast as many votes as there are candidates to be elected, with the winners being, for example, the top three candidates in a three-seat constituency. Votes cannot be cumulated upon a single candidate, so the multiseat nature of the system simply enhances the dispro-portionality typical of the FPTP system because voters tend to cast all of their votes as a block for candidates of the same party, who often take all the seats, meaning that the majoritarian effect of this system is magnified when compared to FPTP (Farrell 2011, 40). Voting for a "block" of candidates from the same party, as many voters do, has led to the colloquial name for MNTV in the United Kingdom block vote. The term MNTV is almost unheard of (Electoral Reform Society 2016).

While MNTV was used to elect two members from most English parliamentary constitu-encies from the medieval period to the nineteenth century, FPTP came to replace MNTV as the franchise was extended and became the predominant system for elections to the House of Commons after 1885. MNTV was retained for some local council elections in England and Wales, however, and is perhaps best known for its use in London borough elections, where most wards (constituencies) elect three members. Table 30.3 provides two examples of how MNTV worked in London in 2014. In the first example, one party—Labour—has won all of the council's seats on 69 percent of the vote (Barking and Dagenham 2014, Table 30.3A).

## Table 30.3  London Borough Elections, May 22, 2014

### A. Barking and Dagenham

| Party | % Votes | Seats Won | % Seats |
| --- | --- | --- | --- |
| Labour | 69.1 | 51 | 100.0 |
| UK Independence | 15.4 | 0 | 0 |
| Conservative | 9.9 | 0 | 0 |
| Liberal Democrat | 1.7 | 0 | 0 |
| *Total* | | *51* | |

- Voter turnout: 36.5%
- Women elected: 20 (39.2%)
- Effective number of parliamentary parties: 1.0
- Index of disproportionality (Michael Gallagher's least squares): 25.4

### B. Tower Hamlets

| Party | % Votes | Seats Won | % Seats |
| --- | --- | --- | --- |
| Labour | 38.6 | 22 | 48.9 |
| Tower Hamlets First | 34.9 | 18 | 40.0 |
| Conservative | 12.1 | 5 | 11.1 |
| Green | 6.3 | 0 | 0 |
| Liberal Democrat | 3.2 | 0 | 0 |
| UK Independence | 2.9 | 0 | 0 |
| Trade Unionist and Socialist Coalition | 1.2 | 0 | 0 |
| *Total* | | *45* | |

- Voter turnout: 47.2%
- Women elected: 11 (24.4%)
- Effective number of parliamentary parties: 2.4
- Index of disproportionality (Michael Gallagher's least squares): 9.8

*Sources:* Barking and Dagenham (2014); Tower Hamlets (2014).

In other cases, local elections can see independent candidates or local parties succeed in spite of the majoritarian nature of MNTV. This was the case for Tower Hamlets First in the borough of Tower Hamlets (Table 30.3B). In this example, Tower Hamlets First was the main challenger to Labour, coming in a close second, and while the Conservatives managed to win a nearly proportional share of seats, the smaller parties won none, so the level of disproportionality is rather high, at 9.8 on the Gallagher index, though not nearly as high as in Barking and Dagenham, at 25.4. Voter turnout was 36.5 percent in Barking and Dagenham and 47 percent in Tower Hamlets, while Barking and Dagenham saw a greater proportion of women elected (39 percent) than was the case in Tower Hamlets (24 percent).

## Supplementary Vote

This majoritarian system came to be used in the United Kingdom as a result of the Labour Party's Plant Report, which recommended it for House of Commons elections. A Labour member of Parliament, Dale Campbell Savours, claimed to have invented the system, though a very similar system (known as the contingent vote) was used in Queensland for state elections up to the mid-twentieth century and has been used to elect Sri Lanka's president since 1982 (Reilly 1997, 95). While this preferential, majoritarian system may superficially resemble Australia's AV, it does not allow the full expression of a voter's preferences, which can make very different outcomes possible (Reilly 1997, 100). Despite receiving significant criticism in the United Kingdom when it was proposed in the 1990s (Reilly 1997, 95), the system has been used for mayoral elections in English cities, boroughs and city regions, as well as for the election of police and crime commissioners in England and Wales.

With SV, voters may indicate up to two candidate preferences, so there are two columns on the ballot paper, allowing voters to put one cross (x) in the first column for their first choice and another cross in the second column for their second choice. If no candidate wins over 50 percent of the first preference vote, all candidates other than the top two are eliminated, with any second preference votes on their ballots for the remaining two candidates added to their totals. The candidate with the majority of votes, after the distribution of second preferences, wins. Direct elections for London mayor have taken place since 2000, and Table 30.4 shows how the system worked at the 2016 election, in which Sadiq Khan won easily on nearly 57 percent of the vote after the transfer of second preferences, with a voter turnout of 45 percent.

## Single Transferable Vote

Previously used for some of the university seats in the UK Parliament before the abolition of plural voting (giving university graduates more than one vote) in 1948, STV was used for elections to Northern Ireland's House of Commons after the Irish Free State became independent from the United Kingdom in the early 1920s. Not long afterward, the system was replaced by FPTP, and STV was not restored for use in Northern Ireland until the 1970s, when local elections were held under this proportional system to represent minorities more effectively than the FPTP and MNTV systems that the Unionist government had reinstated for local councils in 1922 after a brief use of

Table 30.4  London Mayor Election, May 5, 2016

| Candidate | Party | % First-Preference Vote | % Second-Preference Votes | % Vote after Second-Preference Distribution for Top Two Candidates |
|---|---|---|---|---|
| Sadiq Khan | Labour | 44.2 | 17.5 | 56.8 |
| Zac Goldsmith | Conservative | 35.0 | 11.3 | 43.2 |
| Sian Berry | Green | 5.8 | 21.2 | |
| Caroline Pidgeon | Liberal Democrat | 4.6 | 15.2 | |
| Peter Whittle | UK Independence | 3.6 | 10.1 | |
| Sophie Walker | Women's Equality | 2.0 | 9.0 | |
| George Galloway | Respect | 1.4 | 5.3 | |
| Paul Golding | Britain First | 1.2 | 3.3 | |

• Voter turnout: 45.3%

*Sources:* BBC News (2016a); London Elects (2016).

STV (Coakley 2008, 169). Eventually, the creation of the Northern Ireland Assembly by the Good Friday (Belfast) Agreement meant STV would be used for this body as well. STV was also used to elect Northern Ireland's three MEPs and was introduced to elect Scotland's local councils from 2007 as part of a coalition agreement between Labour and the Liberal Democrats in the early years of Scottish devolution.

The top choice of many British electoral reformers, particularly those affiliated with the Electoral Reform Society, and the preference of the Liberal Party and its successor, the Liberal Democrats, STV appeals not only because of its proportionality but also because of its preferential nature, allowing voters the freedom to rank any or all candidates in order of preference. This freedom can cause problems for parties that would prefer to get their top candidates into assemblies, for which a closed-list system would be preferable. Parties would probably also prefer a system that is less kind to independent candidates than STV.

This preferential PR system is strongly associated with its use in the Republic of Ireland—Malta is the only other country that uses the system for its lower or only national legislative chamber. In Ireland, STV has periodically been reviewed, with critics arguing that the system facilitates too much constituency service, distracting deputies from their other roles and potentially reducing party cohesion (All-Party Oireachtas Committee on the Constitution 2002, 20). Irish voters rank candidates in order of preference within parliamentary constituencies that elect three, four, or five deputies, and

Table 30.5 Northern Ireland Assembly Election, May 5, 2016

| Party | % First-Preference Vote | Seats Won | % Seats Won |
|---|---|---|---|
| Democratic Unionist | 29.2 | 38 | 35.2 |
| Sinn Fein | 24.0 | 28 | 25.9 |
| Ulster Unionist | 12.6 | 16 | 14.8 |
| Social Democratic and Labour | 12.0 | 12 | 11.1 |
| Alliance | 7.0 | 8 | 7.4 |
| Traditional Unionist Voice | 3.4 | 1 | 0.9 |
| Green | 2.7 | 2 | 1.9 |
| People Before Profit Alliance | 2.0 | 2 | 1.9 |
| *Total (including an independent)* | | *108* | |

- Voter turnout: 54.2%
- Women elected: 30 (27.5%)
- Effective number of parliamentary parties: 4.3
- Index of disproportionality (Michael Gallagher's least squares): 5.1

*Source:* BBC News (2016b).

because larger parties hope to win more than one of the available seats, they will normally nominate more than one candidate. Because candidates from the same party are competing, they must differentiate themselves on the basis of personal characteristics, rather than party policy, leading to the problems cited earlier. Defenders of STV argue that demands for constituency service are high around the world, regardless of electoral system (Gallagher and Komito 2005, 258–259), and that in Ireland, "it would be disingenuous to suppose that somehow this would dissipate if the electoral system were changed" (Farrell 2011, 147).

Table 30.5 shows how STV works in Northern Ireland Assembly elections, where eighteen 6-seat constituencies were used to elect the 108-member body until 2016; from 2017, the assembly's constituencies each returned 5 members. There was a multiparty system (effective number of parliamentary parties was 4.3 in 2016), and the largest party was somewhat overrepresented, but the others, including the smallest parties, won seat shares that were quite proportional to their vote shares. The index of disproportionality was 5.1 for the 2016 election, while the voter turnout was 54 percent. The proportion of women elected was 27.5 percent.

# Regional Party List Proportional Representation

The United Kingdom used FPTP to elect its MEPs coming from Great Britain—Northern Ireland's were elected via STV—until a regional list PR system was introduced for the 1999 European Parliament election. The Labour government elected in 1997 introduced PR because all other EU members used PR systems to elect their MEPs and the European Parliament was bound by treaty to have a "common electoral system," a fact pointed out in the 1993 Plant Report. Closed party lists were used, meaning that voters could not indicate any preference for a particular candidate. There had been support for opening up the lists to allow voters "to change the order of candidates on the lists" (Lamport 1995, 20), but the Labour government implemented a closed-list system, even though the House of Lords had amended the original legislation to allow voters to choose individual candidates on party lists, an amendment that Home Secretary Jack Straw somewhat misleadingly said gave voters less choice when he reversed it (BBC News 1998).

Table 30.6  European Parliament Members Elected from Great Britain, May 22, 2014

| Party | % Vote | Seats | % Seats |
|---|---|---|---|
| UK Independence | 27.5 | 24 | 34.3 |
| Labour | 25.4 | 20 | 28.6 |
| Conservative | 23.9 | 19 | 27.1 |
| Green | 7.9 | 3 | 4.3 |
| Liberal Democrat | 6.9 | 1 | 1.4 |
| Scottish National | 2.5 | 2 | 2.9 |
| English Democrat | 1.8 | 0 | 0 |
| An Independence from Europe | 1.4 | 0 | 0 |
| British National | 1.1 | 0 | 0 |
| Socialist Labour | 1.1 | 0 | 0 |
| No2EU | 1.0 | 0 | 0 |
| Plaid Cymru | 0.7 | 1 | 1.4 |
| *Total* | | *70* | |

- UK-wide voter turnout: 34.2%
- Women elected (Great Britain + Northern Ireland): 41%
- Effective number of parliamentary parties: 3.6
- Index of disproportionality (Michael Gallagher's least squares): 7.7

*Source:* BBC News (2014).

The results from the 2014 election in Table 30.6 are from Great Britain only; Northern Ireland's three STV-elected MEPs included one each from the Democratic Unionist Party, Sinn Fein, and the Ulster Unionist Party. A multiparty system was present (effective number of parliamentary parties is 3.6), with the populist, antipolitical establishment UK Independence Party (Abedi and Lundberg 2009)—whose main goal was to pull the United Kingdom out of the European Union—winning first place, beating the two major parties, with the pro-EU Liberal Democrats winning only one seat in this low-turnout (34 percent) election. The index of disproportionality was 7.7 in the context of small- and medium-sized electoral regions, while the proportion of women elected was relatively high, at 41 percent.

## Mixed-Member Proportional Representation

In most places using MMP, voters cast two votes—one for a constituency candidate and one for a party, so that representatives are elected in two different ways. The constituency candidates are typically elected by FPTP, while another tier of candidates is usually elected from regional or nationwide party lists. In an MMP system, the party list tier of representatives is elected in a compensatory way, so that the proportion of seats on a partisan basis in the region or nation overall—adding both constituency and list seats together—is roughly equivalent to the proportion of the list vote obtained by each party. Most mixed-member systems around the world are not PR systems because the two tiers of seats are either parallel—with the party list tier independent of and offering no compensation for the results of the constituency tier—or (much less often) very weakly compensatory. These systems are often called mixed-member majoritarian (MMM) and can be found worldwide, particularly in Asia (including Japan), Russia and other post-Soviet countries, and a number of African countries (Shugart and Wattenberg 2001).

In the United Kingdom, Labour chose MMP for elections to the Scottish Parliament (and eventually the National Assembly for Wales and the London Assembly) when developing its plans for Scottish devolution in the 1990s. In Scotland and Wales, several regions are used for the allocation of party list members, while London has only one citywide region. The Scottish Parliament consists of 129 members, with 73 elected in single-seat constituencies by FPTP and the remaining 56 elected via closed party lists (or, in rare instances, as independent candidates) in eight electoral regions, each containing an average of nine constituencies, while each region elects seven regional members. In Wales, the National Assembly consists of 60 members, with each of the five regions electing only four regional members, making it difficult to compensate for results from the average of eight constituencies in each region. The London Assembly is a far smaller body, with only 25 members elected from its fourteen constituencies and from Londonwide party lists; a 5 percent legal threshold applies in London, though no legal threshold exists for the other MMP-elected bodies.

Results from MMP elections in Scotland and Wales show that Scottish Parliament elections are typically more proportional in outcome than their Welsh counterparts. In

Scotland, there is a disproportionality index of 7.4 in 2011 and 5.5 in 2016 (Table 30.7), while the index is 10.4 in 2011 and 13.0 in 2016 in Wales (Table 30.8). Nevertheless, the SNP won a majority of seats in 2011 (Table 30.7A), while Labour has never quite managed this feat in Wales. The effective number of parties has been around three in both

## Table 30.7  Scottish Parliament Elections

A. May 5, 2011

| Party | % Regional Vote | Regional Seats | % Constituency Vote | Constituency Seats | Total Seats | % Seats |
|---|---|---|---|---|---|---|
| Scottish National | 44.0 | 16 | 45.4 | 53 | 69 | 53.5 |
| Labour | 26.3 | 22 | 31.7 | 15 | 37 | 28.7 |
| Conservative | 12.4 | 12 | 13.9 | 3 | 15 | 11.6 |
| Liberal Democrat | 5.2 | 3 | 7.9 | 2 | 5 | 3.9 |
| Greens | 4.4 | 2 | - | - | 2 | 1.6 |
| All Scotland Pensioners | 1.7 | 0 | 0.1 | 0 | 0 | 0 |
| *Total (including an independent)* | | *56* | | *73* | *129* | |

- Voter turnout: 51.1%
- Women elected: 45 (34.9%)
- Effective number of parliamentary parties: 2.6
- Index of disproportionality (Michael Gallagher's least squares): 7.4

B. May 5, 2016

| Party | % Regional Vote | Regional Seats | % Constituency Vote | Constituency Seats | Total Seats | % Seats |
|---|---|---|---|---|---|---|
| Scottish National | 41.7 | 4 | 46.5 | 59 | 63 | 48.8 |
| Conservative | 22.9 | 24 | 22.0 | 7 | 31 | 24.0 |
| Labour | 19.1 | 21 | 22.6 | 3 | 24 | 18.6 |
| Greens | 6.6 | 6 | 0.6 | 0 | 6 | 4.7 |
| Liberal Democrat | 5.2 | 1 | 7.8 | 4 | 5 | 3.9 |
| UK Independence | 2.0 | 0 | - | - | 0 | 0 |
| *Total* | | *56* | | *73* | *129* | |

- Voter turnout: 55.6%
- Women elected: 45 (34.9%)
- Effective number of parliamentary parties: 3.0
- Index of disproportionality (Michael Gallagher's least squares): 5.5

*Sources:* BBC News (2011a, 2016c).

## Table 30.8  National Assembly for Wales Elections

A. May 5, 2011

| Party | % Regional Vote | Regional Seats | % Constituency Vote | Constituency Seats | Total Seats | % Seats |
|---|---|---|---|---|---|---|
| Labour | 36.9 | 2 | 42.3 | 28 | 30 | 50.0 |
| Conservative | 22.5 | 8 | 25.0 | 6 | 14 | 23.3 |
| Plaid Cymru | 17.9 | 6 | 19.3 | 5 | 11 | 18.3 |
| Liberal Democrat | 8.0 | 4 | 10.6 | 1 | 5 | 8.3 |
| UK Independence | 4.6 | 0 | 1.8 | 0 | 0 | 0 |
| Greens | 3.4 | 0 | 0.2 | 0 | 0 | 0 |
| British National | 2.4 | 0 | 0.7 | 0 | 0 | 0 |
| Socialist Labour | 2.4 | 0 | - | 0 | 0 | |
| *Total* | | 20 | | 40 | 60 | |

- Voter turnout: 42.2%
- Women elected: 25 (41.7%)
- Effective number of parliamentary parties: 2.9
- Index of disproportionality (Michael Gallagher's least squares): 10.4

B. May 5, 2016

| Party | % Regional Vote | Regional Seats | % Constituency Vote | Constituency Seats | Total Seats | % Seats |
|---|---|---|---|---|---|---|
| Labour | 31.5 | 2 | 34.7 | 27 | 29 | 48.3 |
| Plaid Cymru | 20.8 | 6 | 20.5 | 6 | 12 | 20.0 |
| Conservative | 18.8 | 5 | 21.1 | 6 | 11 | 18.3 |
| UK Independence | 13.0 | 7 | 12.5 | 0 | 7 | 11.7 |
| Liberal Democrat | 6.5 | 0 | 7.7 | 1 | 1 | 1.7 |
| Abolish the Welsh Assembly | 4.4 | 0 | - | 0 | 0 | 0 |
| Greens | 3.0 | 0 | 2.5 | 0 | 0 | 0 |
| *Total* | | 20 | | 40 | 60 | |

- Voter turnout: 45.3%
- Women elected: 25 (41.7%)
- Effective number of parliamentary parties: 3.1
- Index of disproportionality (Michael Gallagher's least squares): 13.0

*Sources:* BBC News (2011b, 2016d).

nations' assemblies, though voter turnout has been somewhat higher in Scotland, at around 50 percent, while Welsh turnout has been closer to 40 percent. Both bodies have managed to elect a larger proportion of women than the House of Commons, with the Scottish Parliament over 30 percent and the National Assembly for Wales over 40 percent female in membership.

While MMP is based on the West German electoral system introduced in the late 1940s, it was New Zealand that coined the term "mixed-member proportional" for this system, which replaced the country's FPTP system in 1996 after two referendums on the subject. MMP is now the preferred name for this electoral system used by political scientists worldwide (Farrell 2011; Lijphart 2012; Reynolds, Reilly, and Ellis 2005; Shugart and Wattenberg 2001). In the United Kingdom, the Hansard Society used the term "additional member system" (AMS) back in the 1970s when it proposed an alternative to FPTP for the House of Commons based on the German system (Blake Commission 1976). This is unfortunate because the term MMP clearly distinguishes this mixed system from MMM, which is not a form of PR, while AMS could refer to either version and does not indicate that the version used for elections in Scotland, Wales, and London is actually a compensatory proportional one.

The term AMS is also problematic because it labels list-elected candidates as "additional members," implying that they are somehow a secondary by-product of the process by virtue of being added on after the election of constituency candidates to top up the numbers—indeed, the term "top-up members" is sometimes seen in the media and even in academic publications from British authors (Dunleavy and Margetts 2001). This kind of value-laden terminology can lead to a sense of inequality between constituency and regional members, a problem that was noted in a review of the Scottish MMP system, where the authors recommended that the term "mixed-member system" be used instead of AMS and that "additional" members be called "regional" members (Arbuthnott 2006, 4).

# EXPERIENCES WITH PROPORTIONAL REPRESENTATION ELECTORAL SYSTEMS IN THE UK

The United Kingdom's PR systems have led to results that are not highly proportional, though it would not be accurate to describe them as "semiproportional." Aside from getting categories confused—there are electoral formulas, such as MMM, that could fit into the semiproportional classification (Lijphart 2012, 133)—this label seems to assume that PR systems are perfectly proportional, which is not the case. MMP elections to the National Assembly for Wales struggle the most, with high disproportionality index values (10.4 and 13.0 for the elections in Table 30.8), thanks to the small number of regional members available to compensate for constituency results, but the Scottish Parliament's disproportionality index values of 7.4 and 5.5 (Table 30.7) under MMP are similar to those of list PR–using Spain (7.28), Uruguay (6.05), Norway (4.53), and Portugal (4.43), according to Lijphart's analysis of 1945–2010 election results (2012, 150). STV in Northern Ireland (5.1, Table 30.5) shows disproportionality similar to that of the Republic of Ireland (3.93 in Lijphart 2012, 150), while British European Parliament results with list PR display higher levels of disproportionality, at 7.7 in 2014 (Table 30.6).

Much of the United Kingdom's electoral system innovation took place with MMP. Despite its relatively rare worldwide occurrence, MMP has been found to be the experts' top choice, beating STV into second place (Bowler, Farrell, and Pettitt 2005). Although MMP may be popular among political scientists, there has been some controversy in the United Kingdom surrounding the competition between constituency and regional members over constituency service, with some constituency members of the Scottish Parliament (MSPs) and Welsh Assembly Members (AMs) complaining about being "shadowed" by regional members trying to enhance their name recognition among constituents to help with their efforts to stand as local constituency candidates at the next election. This competition over constituency service could be good for British constituents, reducing the safety of seats for constituency incumbents and improving the responsiveness of representative democracy (Lundberg 2006).

Tensions between constituency and regional representatives are far less common in Germany, where most people do not distinguish between the two different types of representatives (Burkett 1985, 130), largely because dual candidacy—the ability of candidates to stand in both constituencies and on party lists simultaneously—is common (Jesse 1988, 120; Massicotte 2004, 73). Candidates losing in constituency contests can be elected through party lists when they are high enough on their lists and then usually set up offices in constituencies where they were defeated, so shadowing of constituency-elected candidates is typical and constituents cannot tell who was "directly" elected in the constituency (Burkett 1985, 129–130). In New Zealand, which has used MMP since it replaced FPTP in 1996, dual candidacy has been more controversial, probably due to the long history of FPTP, but a 2012 review of MMP found that a majority of public submissions supported the retention of dual candidacy, which the New Zealand Electoral Commission recommended be retained (NZ Electoral Commission 2012, 37–38).

The different electoral routes for representatives elected under MMP have caused some concern in Britain, however, partially due to the public's familiarity with FPTP and the constituency role of representatives elected under it, and partially for partisan reasons. The issue of accountability—to constituents or to the party organizations that rank the closed party lists used in MMP—has been raised by some politicians and journalists who seem to believe that party list–elected members of the Scottish Parliament and National Assembly for Wales are "second-class" representatives (Lundberg 2007b, 3–4). There is also the broader question of what kind of constituency role should be played by regional members. Constituency service in Scotland and Wales has been explored by a number of studies (Bradbury and Mitchell 2007; Bradbury and Russell 2005; Carman and Shephard 2007; Cowley and Lochore 2000; Lundberg 2007b; McCabe and

McCormick 2000). Self-reported estimates of how time is allocated show that constituency MSPs and AMs spent more of their work time on constituency service than did their regional counterparts (Lundberg 2007b, 178–179). This difference could be due to rational electoral incentives, as research in Germany has shown (Klingemann and Wessels 2001; Lancaster and Patterson 1990), though personal reasons, such as simply the enjoyment of constituency service, could also be at work.

While MMP got caught up in bitter partisan competition between the SNP and Labour in Scotland (Lundberg 2014), the system also ran into controversy in Wales; dual candidacy became so unpopular with Labour that the National Assembly banned the practice in the 2007 and 2011 elections (though not for the Scottish Parliament or London Assembly). The Conservative/Liberal Democrat government at Westminster abolished it with the passage of the Wales Act of 2014. There was no ban initially, with Labour candidates standing as dual candidates in Wales before 2007, but Welsh Secretary Peter Hain claimed that candidates losing constituency races but winning via regional lists had been "rejected by the voters" and should not be allowed to enter the assembly (Lundberg 2007b, 164). The UK Electoral Commission found no evidence supporting Hain's assertion that the public disapproved of the dual candidacy and argued that the likely beneficiaries of the ban would be constituency (mainly Labour) incumbents because opposition parties would probably place their best candidates on the regional lists, leaving the constituency races to sacrificial lambs (UK Electoral Commission 2005, 5–6).

Labour's complaints about dual candidacy appeared to be based on partisan self-interest, according to the Conservative Welsh secretary and nearly everyone else outside the Labour Party who commented on the plans to rescind the ban (Roberts 2013), although Labour's ideology also lends itself to a zero-sum view of representation and a majoritarian view of democracy uneasy about political pluralism and incompatible with the positive-sum logic of PR (Lundberg 2007b, 164–165). Aside from Labour, no party opposed the UK Conservative/Liberal Democrat coalition government's abolition of the dual candidacy ban in the Wales Act of 2014, making the practice legal once again for National Assembly elections from 2016.

Labour should be given credit, however, for the large proportion of female members of the Scottish Parliament and National Assembly for Wales (relative to the female proportion of members of the House of Commons). This achievement was not so much a result of PR, but rather of Labour's "twinning" procedures used in the single-seat constituency component of MMP in which the party would match pairs of constituencies that seemed equally winnable, with one getting a female candidate (Russell, Mackay, and McAllister 2002, 56). Labour's success at winning constituency seats—a feature of the early years of devolution, particularly in Scotland—meant that many women were elected. For the 1999 elections, the SNP rejected formal use of a "zipping" procedure to alternate male and female candidates on regional party lists but did informally encourage the placing of female candidates higher up the lists so that nearly half of the party's elected regional members were women; Plaid used a similar approach in Wales with similar results (Russell et al. 2002, 60–62). Contentious as these efforts were for all parties—legal action was actually taken against Labour's efforts on grounds of sex discrimination—the result was a big increase in female representation.

## Conclusion: Continuity in the Face of Change

The United Kingdom had six different electoral systems operating at various levels of governance in the early twenty-first century. While the House of Commons resisted reform attempts in the late twentieth century, the new institutions and positions created by devolution allow for a study of the interaction of different electoral and party systems. Although there has been some interaction between the different levels of governance in the United Kingdom since devolution that has affected Westminster—most notably in the decline of Scottish Labour and the rise of the SNP, which won fifty-six of Scotland's fifty-nine seats in the House of Commons, replacing the Liberal Democrats as the United Kingdom's third-largest party in 2015—there has been little "bottom-up" impact.

Despite its use at several levels of UK governance, PR had not captured the British public's imagination, and the likelihood of a shift from FPTP to PR for the House of Commons appeared low (Renwick 2009), even though it is likely that FPTP "has lost the battle of ideas" (Blais and Shugart 2008, 206), with partisan interests overcoming most people's idea of electoral system fairness. While the Labour Party did introduce new electoral systems in the late twentieth century, the party failed to embrace the pluralism of party politics that accompanied these institutional reforms, perhaps being prevented from doing so by the majoritarian mentality permeating both major parties in the United Kingdom. With both the Conservatives and Labour apparently against change for the House of Commons, a third wave of electoral reform seemed unlikely.

## Author Note

Tables are compiled from news sources (usually the BBC) and have not appeared in this form elsewhere.

## Notes

1. Some do not like the term "single-member plurality"; for a discussion of terminology, see the blog post by Shugart (2014) and the chapter by Herron, Pekkanen, and Shugart in this volume. For the sake of consistent terminology, first past the post (FPTP) will be used here.

2. These are calculated by the author using data from all parties (and candidates in the London mayor election) winning at least 1 percent of the vote or one seat, with independent (nonparty) candidates not counted. In STV elections, the index of disproportionality calculation uses first-preference votes as the basis of party preference, while the same determination is made using the party vote in MMP elections, according to Lijphart (2012, 145).

## References

Abedi, Amir, and Thomas Carl Lundberg. "Doomed to Failure? UKIP and the Organisational Challenges Facing Right-Wing Anti-Political Establishment Parties." *Parliamentary Affairs* 62, no. 1 (2009): 72–87.

All-Party Oireachtas Committee on the Constitution. *Seventh Progress Report: Parliament.* Dublin: Stationery Office, 2002.

Arbuthnott, John. *Putting Citizens First: Boundaries, Voting and Representation in Scotland. Commission on Boundary Differences and Voting Systems.* Edinburgh: Stationery Office, 2006.

Barking and Dagenham. "Local Election—Thursday, 22 May 2014." 2014. http://moderngov .barking-dagenham.gov.uk/mgElectionResults.aspx?ID=1&RPID=5370771&TPID=5370774.

BBC News. "Government Reverses Lords Defeat." October 27, 1998. http://news.bbc.co.uk/1 /hi/uk_politics/202677.stm.

BBC News. "National Results after 650 of 650." 2010. http://news.bbc.co.uk/1/shared/election2010 /results/.

BBC News. "Scotland Elections." May 11, 2011a. http://www.bbc.co.uk/news/special/election2011 /overview/html/scotland.stm.

BBC News. "Wales Elections." May 11, 2011b. http://www.bbc.co.uk/news/special/election2011 /overview/html/wales.stm.

BBC News. "UK European Election Results." 2014. http://www.bbc.co.uk/news/events /vote2014/eu-uk-results.

BBC News. "UK Results." 2015. http://www.bbc.co.uk/news/election/2015/results.

BBC News. "London Mayor Results." 2016a. http://www.bbc.co.uk/news/election/2016 /london/results.

BBC News. "Northern Ireland Results." 2016b. http://www.bbc.co.uk/news/election/2016 /northern_ireland/results.

BBC News. "Scotland Results." 2016c. http://www.bbc.co.uk/news/election/2016/scotland /results.

BBC News. "Wales Results." 2016d. http://www.bbc.co.uk/news/election/2016/wales/results.

Blais, André, and Matthew Søberg Shugart. "Conclusion." In *To Keep or to Change First Past the Post? The Politics of Electoral Reform*, edited by André Blais, 184–207. Oxford: Oxford University Press, 2008.

Blake Commission. *The Report of the Hansard Society Commission on Electoral Reform.* London: Hansard Society, 1976.

Bogdanor, Vernon. *The People and the Party System: The Referendum and Electoral Reform in British Politics.* Cambridge: Cambridge University Press, 1981.

Bowler, Shaun, David M. Farrell, and Robin T. Pettitt. "Expert Opinion on Electoral Systems: So Which Electoral System Is Best?" *Journal of Elections, Public Opinion and Parties* 15, no. 1 (2005): 3–19.

Bradbury, Jonathan, and James Mitchell. "The Constituency Work of Members of the Scottish Parliament and National Assembly for Wales: Approaches, Relationships and Rules." *Regional and Federal Studies* 17, no. 1 (2007): 117–145.

Bradbury, Jonathan, and Meg Russell. "Learning to Live with Pluralism? Constituency and Regional Members and Local Representation in Scotland and Wales." *Devolution Briefings*, No. 28. Edinburgh: Economic and Social Research Council Devolution and Constitutional Change Programme, 2005.

Burkett, Tony. "The West German Deputy." In *Representatives of the People? Parliamentarians and Constituents in Western Democracies*, edited by Vernon Bogdanor, 117–131. Aldershot: Gower, 1985.

Carman, Christopher, and Mark Shephard. "Electoral Poachers? An Assessment of Shadowing Behaviour in the Scottish Parliament." *Journal of Legislative Studies* 13, no. 4 (2007): 483–496.

Carstairs, Andrew McLaren. *A Short History of Electoral Systems in Western Europe*. London: George Allen & Unwin, 1980.

Clark, Alistair. *Political Parties in the UK*. Basingstoke: Palgrave Macmillan, 2012.

Coakley, John. "Electoral Redistricting in Ireland." In *Redistricting in Comparative Perspective*, edited by Lisa Handley and Bernard Grofman, 155–172. Oxford: Oxford University Press, 2008.

Cowley, Philip, and Stephen Lochore. "AMS in a Cold Climate: The Scottish Parliament in Practice." *Representation* 37, no. 3/4 (2000): 175–185.

Curtice, John. "Politicians, Voters and Democracy: The 2011 UK Referendum on the Alternative Vote." *Electoral Studies* 32, no. 2 (2013): 215–223.

Diwakar, Rekha. "Duverger's Law and the Size of the Indian Party System." *Party Politics* 13, no. 5 (2007): 539–561.

Dunleavy, Patrick. "Facing Up to Multi-Party Politics: How Partisan Dealignment and PR Voting Have Fundamentally Changed Britain's Party Systems." *Parliamentary Affairs* 58, no. 3 (2005): 503–532.

Dunleavy, Patrick, and Helen Margetts. "From Majoritarian to Pluralist Democracy? Electoral Reform in Britain since 1997." *Journal of Theoretical Politics* 13, no. 3 (2001): 295–319.

Duverger, Maurice. *Political Parties: Their Organisation and Activity in the Modern State*. 2nd ed. London: Methuen, 1954.

Electoral Reform Society. "Block Vote." 2016. http://www.electoral-reform.org.uk/block-vote.

Farrell, David M. *Electoral Systems: A Comparative Introduction*. 2nd ed. Basingstoke: Palgrave, 2011.

Gaines, Brian J. "Duverger's Law and the Meaning of Canadian Exceptionalism." *Comparative Political Studies* 32, no. 7 (1999): 835–861.

Gallagher, Michael. "Proportionality, Disproportionality and Electoral Systems." *Electoral Studies* 10, no. 1 (1991): 33–51.

Gallagher, Michael, and Lee Komito. "The Constituency Role of Dáil Deputies." In *Politics in the Republic of Ireland*, 4th ed., edited by John Coakley and Michael Gallagher, 242–271. London: Routledge, 2005.

Hart, Jenifer. *Proportional Representation: Critics of the British Electoral System 1820-1945*. Oxford: Clarendon Press, 1992.

Jesse, Eckhard. "Split-Voting in the Federal Republic of Germany: An Analysis of the Federal Elections from 1953 to 1987." *Electoral Studies* 7, no. 2 (1988): 109–124.

Klingemann, Hans-Dieter, and Bernhard Wessels. "The Political Consequences of Germany's Mixed-Member System: Personalization at the Grass Roots?" In *Mixed-Member Electoral*

*Systems: The Best of Both Worlds?*, edited by Matthew S. Shugart and Martin P. Wattenberg, 279–296. Oxford: Oxford University Press, 2001.

Laakso, Markku, and Rein Taagepera. "'Effective' Number of Parties: A Measure with Application to West Europe." *Comparative Political Studies* 12, no. 1 (1979): 3–27.

Lamport, Tim. "The Plant Report Two Years on—Some Reflections." *Representation* 33, no. 2 (1995): 17–22.

Lancaster, Thomas D., and David Patterson. "Comparative Pork Barrel Politics: Perceptions from the West German Bundestag." *Comparative Political Studies* 22 (1990): 458–477.

Lijphart, Arend. *Patterns of Democracy: Government Forms and Performance in Thirty-Six Countries.* 2nd ed. New Haven, CT: Yale University Press, 2012.

London Elects. "2016 GLA Elections: Election of the London Mayor." 2016. https://www .londonelects.org.uk/sites/default/files/Mayor%20of%20London_0.pdf.

Lundberg, Thomas Carl. "Competition between Members of the Scottish Parliament and the Welsh Assembly: Problem or Virtue?" *Political Quarterly* 77, no. 1 (2006): 107–116.

Lundberg, Thomas Carl. "Electoral System Reviews in New Zealand, Britain and Canada: A Critical Comparison." *Government and Opposition* 42, no. 4 (2007a): 471–490.

Lundberg, Thomas Carl. *Proportional Representation and the Constituency Role in Britain.* Basingstoke: Palgrave Macmillan, 2007b.

Lundberg, Thomas Carl. "Tensions between Constituency and Regional Members of the Scottish Parliament under Mixed-Member Proportional Representation: A Failure of the New Politics." *Parliamentary Affairs* 67, no. 2 (2014): 351–370.

Massicotte, Louis. *Electoral System Reform: In Search of Compensatory Mixed Electoral System for Quebec.* Working document. Quebec City: Government of Quebec, 2004.

McCabe, Angela, and James McCormick. "Rethinking Representation: Some Evidence from the First Year." In *The New Scottish Politics: The First Year of the Scottish Parliament and Beyond*, edited by Gerry Hassan and Chris Warhurst, 40–47. Norwich: Stationery Office, 2000.

Mitchell, Paul. "The United Kingdom: Plurality Rule under Siege." In *The Politics of Electoral Systems,* edited by Michael Gallagher and Paul Mitchell, 157–184. Oxford: Oxford University Press, 2005.

NZ Electoral Commission. *Report of the Electoral Commission on the Review of the MMP Voting System.* Wellington: Electoral Commission, October 29, 2012.

Norris, Pippa. "The Politics of Electoral Reform in Britain." *International Political Science Review* 16, no. 1 (1995): 65–78.

Plant, Raymond. "The Plant Report: A Retrospective." *Representation* 33, no. 2 (1995): 5–16.

Reilly, Ben. "The Plant Report and the Supplementary Vote: Not So Unique After All." *Representation* 34, no. 2 (1997): 95–102.

Renwick, Alan. "How Likely Is Proportional Representation in the House of Commons? Lessons from International Experience." *Government and Opposition* 44, no. 4 (2009): 366–384.

Reynolds, Andrew, Ben Reilly, and Andrew Ellis. *Electoral System Design: The New International IDEA Handbook.* Stockholm: International Institute for Democracy and Electoral Assistance, 2005.

Roberts, Owain. *Proposed Changes to the Assembly's Electoral Arrangements.* Research paper. Cardiff: National Assembly for Wales, 2013.

Russell, Meg, Fiona Mackay, and Laura McAllister. "Women's Representation in the Scottish Parliament and the National Assembly for Wales: Party Dynamics for Achieving Critical Mass." *Journal of Legislative Studies* 8, no. 2 (2002): 49–76.

Shugart, Matthew S. "Plurality, FPTP, SMP. What's in a name?" February 24, 2014. https://fruitsandvotes.wordpress.com/2014/02/24/plurality-fptp-smp-whats-in-a-name/.

Shugart, Matthew S., and Martin P. Wattenberg. "Mixed-Member Electoral Systems: A Definition and a Typology." in *Mixed-Member Electoral Systems: The Best of Both Worlds?*, edited by Matthew S. Shugart and Martin P. Wattenberg, 9–24. Oxford: Oxford University Press, 2001.

Tower Hamlets. "Local Elections—Thursday, 22nd May, 2014." 2014. http://moderngov.towerhamlets.gov.uk/mgElectionResults.aspx?ID=22&RPID=8200541.

UK Electoral Commission. "White Paper: Better Governance for Wales. The Electoral Commission's Response." London: UK Electoral Commission, September 2005.

# CHAPTER 31

# ELECTORAL SYSTEMS
# IN CONTEXT
## *Ireland*

### MICHAEL MARSH

THE Republic of Ireland is almost alone in using the electoral system of the single transferable vote (STV) to select members of its national parliament. It operated from 1918 before separation from the United Kingdom and continued afterward, and its status was established firmly in the 1937 constitution.[1] Only Malta shares the same system for national elections to the lower house of parliament, although there are several places where it is used for subnational elections, notably in Scotland, Northern Ireland, Tasmania, and New Zealand. It has also been one of the systems under consideration in recent years for Canada, where it was once used for provincial elections in Alberta. This chapter focuses on the experience of the system in parliamentary elections in the Republic of Ireland. It starts by explaining how STV works and then explores its apparent impact on politics in Ireland. This is done by looking at how parties, candidates, and voters operate the system, and discusses how far some notable features of Irish politics can be seen to be a function of the electoral system.

## HOW SINGLE TRANSFERABLE VOTE WORKS

For the voters, the essential feature of STV is that they are asked to rank candidates in order of preference. As elsewhere, preferences are then used to distribute seats, but whereas most systems ask only for a first preference—the party or candidate the voter chooses first—under STV, second, third, and lower preferences may also be used in the allocation if the first preferences are not sufficient, beginning with first preference and then, as necessary, counting lower preferences. This is most easily understood when there is only one seat to be filled, such as in an election for a vacant seat in the lower house of parliament, the Dáil. We can take a very simple example where there are just three candidates. Voters are asked to rank these three candidates in preference order by placing a number, one, two, or three, on the ballot next to each candidate's name. The first preferences are then counted. If one candidate wins more votes than all the other candidates combined—an absolute majority—then that candidate is then declared elected. However, if no candidate exceeds that threshold, the candidate with the fewest votes is eliminated, and attention then turns to the ballots cast for that candidate. Votes are added to the first preferences won by the two candidates still in the race according to the second preference marked on those ballots. A candidate with an overall majority of all first-preference votes cast once again would be declared elected. But if no candidate has exceeded that threshold, the candidate of the two remaining who has now the most votes—first and second preferences combined—is declared as elected.

There are some important things to note here. First, a voter does not have to give a preference to all of the candidates. It is only necessary to express a first preference. However, a voter doing so can have no impact on who is elected if it is not his or her first choice. The second point to note is that lower preferences are examined only when a candidate is eliminated, and only the lower preferences expressed by voters (in the previous example) who chose that candidate first. Had there been four candidates and it had been necessary to eliminate another candidate, ballots for that second candidate would be transferred to one of the two remaining candidates according to which of them was preferred on that ballot. The system seeks to achieve the same outcome as a two-round system, such as used in France, where only two candidates contest the final vote. However, unlike those systems, STV achieves the same theoretical outcome—an elected candidate who commands an overall majority—without requiring the electors to come out to vote more than once.

The process is essentially no different when there are several seats to be filled, which is always the case in Irish general elections. The most important change is that the sufficient threshold for election changes. The formula for that threshold, known as the electoral quota (Q), is

$$Q = \left[ V / (M = 1) \right] + 1,$$

where V is the number of valid votes cast, M is the numbers of seats to be filled in a constituency (i.e., the district magnitude), and Q is the electoral quota sufficient for election.[2]

Where there is just one seat at stake, as in the previous example, Q will be half of the votes cast plus one, an absolute majority. Where there are two seats it will be a third of the votes cast plus one; where there are three seats it will be a quarter plus one; and so on. In all cases, whatever the threshold, when there is only one more candidate in the race than there are seats remaining to be filled, the candidates who simply have the most votes at that point will be declared elected.

The major complication in multiseat counts concerns the votes won by candidates once they are elected. Typically, a candidate is elected with more votes than the quota: they have what is termed a "surplus." These surplus votes are then redistributed. There are different ways of doing this, but in the case of Dáil elections, which involves a large number of votes counted by hand, there are essentially two methods. When a candidate achieves a surplus on the first count, a check is made of *all* the second preferences expressed by those for whom that candidate was the first choice, and an appropriate number of votes, corresponding to the size of the surplus and proportionate to the second preferences expressed, are then transferred to other candidates.[3] When a candidate achieves a surplus following a later count, surplus votes are simply taken from that candidate's pile and redistributed according to the highest preference marked for a candidate still in the race.

Parliamentary elections in Ireland take place in around forty constituencies of between three and five seats.[4] There were larger constituencies, with up to nine members, in the early years of the state. The range of district magnitudes is a political decision, conveyed to the independent boundary commission by successive governments since 1980. Before that, the whole process was effectively under government control, but there have been no constituencies larger than five in national elections since 1947 (although there have been in local elections). The main rationale for this is that constituencies would be too large, making it more difficult for the voter to make an informed choice. The median constituency has had four seats since 1980, but between 1935 and 1980 it was typically just three.

The ballot provides a list of candidates. Figure 31.1 shows a sample ballot from 2016. The candidates and parties are fictitious and in this instance there is no more than one candidate from any party. Instructions to the voter are shown in Irish and English. In the 2016 election, such lists contained as few as six names in one constituency and as many as twenty in another, with an average of fourteen, up from eleven in 2007 and thirteen in 2011. As indicated, the voter is provided with some additional information for each candidate: a party label (if any), a home address, occupation (as supplied by the candidate), and a portrait photograph; all information (other than party) is as supplied by the candidate. Until 1965, names and addresses were given but there was no party label. Arguably, the voters knew party affiliations, but these were added under the 1963 Electoral Act to make it easier for voters to identify the candidates they wanted to support. Photographs have been added since 1999. The reason given was that it would help those with poor reading skills. The ballots are organized alphabetically by candidate name, just like the ballots used under the first-past-the-post system prior to independence. There has been little effort made to change this, but arguably this format gives an advantage to candidates whose name gives them a high place on the ballot (Ortega and de la Peurta 2004; Curtice and Marsh 2014). Some candidates have indeed changed their names to give them a higher place.

1. Scríobh an figiúr 1 sa bhosca le hais an chéad iarrthóra is rogha leat, scríob an figiúr 2 sa bhosca le hais an dara hiarrthóir is rogha leat, agus mar sin de.
2. Fill an páipéar ionas nach bhfeicfear do vóta. Taispeáin cúl an pháipéir don oifigeach ceannais, agus cuir sa bhosca ballóide é.

## INSTRUCTIONS
1. Write 1 in the box beside the candidate of your first choice, write 2 in the box beside the candidate of your second choice, and so on.
2. Fold the paper to conceal your vote. Show the back of the paper to the presiding officer and put it in the ballot box.

**DOYLE – LIBERAL SOCIALISTS**
MARY DOYLE, of 10 High Street, Knockmore, Nurse.

**LYNCH – URBAN PARTY**
JANE ELLEN LYNCH, of 12 Main Street, Ardstown, Shopkeeper.

**MURPHY**
PATRICK MURPHY, of 12 Main Street, Ballyduff, Carpenter.

**Ó BRIAIN — CUMANN NA SAORÁNACH**
SÉAMUS Ó BRIAIN, as 10 An tSráid Ard, Carn Mór, Oide Scoile.

**O'BRIEN — NON-PARTY**
EAMON O'BRIEN, of 22 Wellclose Place, Knockbeg, Barrister.

**O'BRIEN – THE INDEPENDENT PARTY**
ORLA O'BRIEN, of 103 Eaton Brae, Cahermore, Solicitor.

**O'CONNOR — NATIONAL LEAGUE**
CAROLINE O'CONNOR, of 7 Green Street, Carnmore, Engineer.

**THOMPSON — RURAL PARTY**
WILLIAM H. THOMPSON, of Dereen, Ballyglass, Farmer.

FIGURE 31.1. Sample Irish ballot from 2016.

Source: Supplied by the Department of Housing, Planning, Community, and Local Government. http://www.housing.gov .ie/local-government/voting/dáil-elections/sample-ballot-paper-general-election-2016.

# The Parties: Fragmentation and Proportionality

The first few elections fought under this system in the Irish Free State involved two large parties that each reflected a different side of the struggle for independence and subsequent civil war, as well as a number of other groups, including a small Labour Party whose formation predated the conflict. Within a dozen years the system had simplified into something close to the "two and a half" party system described by Brian Farrell thirty years later (Farrell 1970). There were challenges to that system, but by the early 1980s, fragmentation seemed to be a thing of the past as the three main parties won more than 90 percent of the vote, and the two largest 85 percent. This was to be a high point of consolidation as many new small parties entered the system, followed by an increase in nonparty candidates. The two elections since the financial crisis in 2008 showed further fragmentation, most clearly in 2016 when the three old parties won just 56 percent of the vote between them. This fragmentation, measured by the effective number of parties (Laakso and Taagepera 1979), was above 6 in terms of first-preference votes and almost 5 in terms of seats allocated (Gallagher 2016, 126). The average since the foundation of the state has been just 3.5 (votes) and 3.1 (seats), but fragmentation has always been higher than this since 1987.

Figure 31.2 shows fragmentation and proportionality, as measured by the Gallagher (1991) index of disproportionality. The value of this index has generally fluctuated

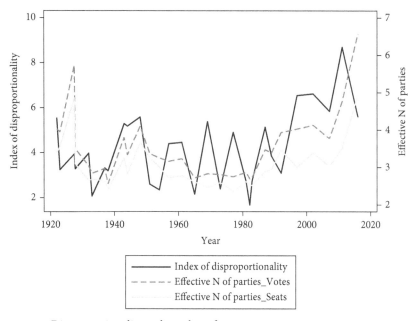

**FIGURE 31.2.** Disproportionality and number of parties since 1922.

Source: Data from Gallagher (2017).

around a level well below its long-term average of 4.2 but, like fragmentation, it has been trending upward since the late 1980s and has been around 6 over the last few elections, although it exceeded 8 in 2011. While this is a high figure in comparison with some proportional representation (PR) systems, it is on par with many of the middle-ranking European countries on this measure (Gallagher 2016).

Since the electoral system remained unchanged through consolidation and fragmentation, it is hard to attribute any simple causal role to the electoral system. What the system did provide was sufficient proportionality to allow some new groups to enter parliament, but (sometimes) also a big enough seat bonus to help the bigger parties form governments. The bonus helped Fianna Fáil to govern between 1957 and 1973, providing it twice with an overall majority and once with just half of the seats, as well as pushing the party to within three seats of an overall majority on another occasion. In 2002, a massive bonus pushed the party to within four seats of a majority with just 41.5 percent of the first-preference votes.

To win a seat, a candidate only has to obtain a quota, or close to a quota, of votes. This is currently something less than fifteen thousand votes, less than 0.7 percent of the vote nationally, although the fifteen thousand votes do have to be concentrated in a single constituency. And these votes include both first and lower preferences. This is not to say getting elected is easy, but the threshold for success is certainly not a high one.

Looking at past elections, it is possible to calculate the chances of a party winning a seat with a given share of the vote. Figure 31.3 shows the patterns in three-, four-, and

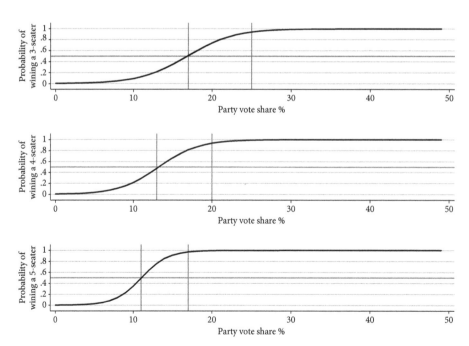

FIGURE 31.3. Probability of winning a seat in a three-, four-, and five-seater by share of vote, 1997–2016.

five-seat constituencies in elections since 1997. The electoral quota is marked with a line meeting the x-axis: 16.7 in a five-seater to 25.0 in a three-seater. The point at which the chances of winning a seat are better than fifty/fifty is also marked: at 11 percent in a five-seater, 13 percent in a four-seater, and 17 percent in a three-seater. This is a smaller range than the difference in the quotas. When we look at disproportionality across constituencies, magnitude indeed matters. Over the last few elections, back to 1997, the average difference between share of the seats and the votes by party[5] has been 7.9 percent in three-seaters, 6.9 percent in four-seater, and 5.7 percent in five-seaters. However, smaller parties have won seats regardless of district magnitude. The combined Fine Gael and Fianna Fail haul has been much the same regardless of magnitude: 68 percent of the seats in three-seaters, 67 percent in four-seaters, and 70 percent in five-seaters. Independents have been rather more likely to take seats in three-seaters, as have Labour candidates. Sinn Féin's record is much the same everywhere, but the success of other small parties has been less in three-seaters than in four- and five-seat constituencies. This is certainly not to say that were constituencies to increase in magnitude to six, seven, and eight seats it would not have any effect on who is elected and on overall proportionality, but merely that the range currently used seems to make little difference in practice.

To look more closely at who wins and who loses, we can look at proportionality since 1980, covering the period when constituency boundaries were drawn independently and district magnitude was between three and five. This also takes us from the election with the most to those with the least proportional outcomes. Figure 31.4 shows the

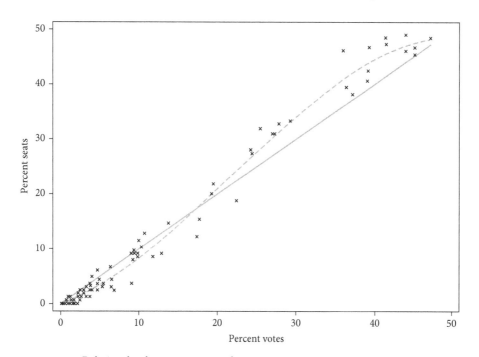

FIGURE 31.4. Relationship between votes and seats, 1981–2016.

Note: Points are parties and party groups, the curved line shows the best fit, and the straight line indicates proportionality.

national percentage of seats won by each party (or grouping) by the national percentage of votes won. The diagonal line indicates the expected share of seats given perfect proportionality. The curved line best describes reality, the line of best fit based on a polynomial transformation of votes. The first point to note is that parties winning over 20 percent tend to win more seats than we would expect under pure proportionality, while those obtaining less than 20 percent win a smaller share. There are some obvious exceptions. One is Fine Gael, which in 2002 won 22 percent of the vote and obtained less than 20 percent of the seats. Fianna Fáil did even worse in 2011, but its vote was below 20 percent. There are also several cases where a party won 10 to 15 percent of the vote and yet won a similar proportion of seats. These cases are largely those of the Labour Party, which has typically won what might be expected under pure proportionality, and so has done better than our best-fitting line. In addition, several of the worst-performing "parties" below the line are "Others," essentially independents and so not strictly comparable with the parties. More will be said about those later.

Of course, any measure of disproportionality that relies just on shares of first-preference votes can be unfair to the principle of the system, which is to pick the winner(s) that a majority would favor in a run-off. Lower preferences matter, and they are supposed to. Fianna Fáil did very poorly in attracting lower-preference votes in 2011 when it was held accountable for the economic crisis, and this contributed to its failure to turn its first-preference votes into seats. The relatively extreme Sinn Féin party has also done poorly in this respect and has consistently won several seats less than might have been expected from its vote share.

# Voters and Their Preferences

When we look at proportionality, we are focusing on parties, but there is no necessity for voters to prioritize party or to confine themselves to the candidates of a single party. Indeed, many express a preference for candidates from several parties and frequently do so to the disadvantage of the party of their first-choice candidate. There are two sorts of evidence for this. The first is the evidence from the published counts. These show the patterns of transfers, the movement of votes from one candidate to others when a candidate is elected or eliminated. From this data, it is possible to establish to whom voters with a higher preference for a candidate from, for instance, Fine Gael give a lower preference. The counts give us evidence about which other parties get the support of Fine Gael voters and the extent to which Fine Gael voters tend to vote on party lines. The second set of evidence comes from surveys using mock ballots, in which voters are given something like a facsimile of a ballot and asked to indicate how they voted. Such surveys have been conducted for the Irish National Election Study (INES) after the last four elections, but there are some earlier surveys (Bowler and Farrell 1991). There is also evidence from the short-lived experiment with electronic voting used in three constituencies in 2002 (Laver 2004), and this largely validated the evidence from the mock ballot used in the INES that same year.

If we take the counts first, which cover a much longer period, it is evident that voters are not constrained by party labels. Where a party runs more than one candidate in a constituency, it is evident that not all of the support for any one of them transfers to another when the first is elected or eliminated. Looking at elections between 1948 and 2011, Sinnott and McBride (2011, Figure 9.1) show that even at its peak, what they term "loyalty" among voters for the two largest parties did not exceed 80 percent, a level Fianna Fáil and Fine Gael were at in the early 1980s. That is now at a level closer to 60 percent. There are difficulties in this exercise, as Sinnott and McBride detail (2011, 206–207), but what is clear is that loyalty is declining. Using a similar methodology, Gallagher (2016) indicates that loyalty—he uses the term "intraparty solidarity"—in these two parties was below 60 percent for the first time in 2016. While Fianna Fáil and Fine Gael have tended to run more than one candidate in most constituencies until very recently, the smaller Labour Party has more often run just one, but there are enough cases to explore the level of intraparty transfers in that party as well. It has tended to be lower than that within the two larger parties, but it also has shown a downward trend from the 1970s. Sinn Féin provides an exception to all this, as in the nine areas where it ran two candidates in 2016, over three-quarters of support stayed within the party, a level far exceeding solidarity shown in any other party since the last century.

This leakage is, however, often offset by support from elsewhere. A candidate may not pick up all of the votes from an eliminated running mate, but will win votes from candidates of other parties. Indeed, the larger parties will usually compile more support at the end of the process of counting than they have at the start. So too will most successful candidates. This support may be due to party labels. The most obvious case here is where two parties run in alliance, promising to form a coalition with one another if possible. In such a case, they will each tend to ask supporters to give lower preferences to the other's candidates (see Marsh 2010 for an extended discussion). In 2016, the incumbent Fine Gael and Labour parties campaigned to continue their governing coalition. The count data suggests that coalition voters did tend to go on to give support to candidates from the other party (Gallagher 2016, 147–148). These two parties have typically exchanged votes (Sinnott and McBride 2011, 211–213) and governed together on several occasions, aided by the additional seats attributable to the mutual support.

The survey evidence has some advantages over the count data, the key one being that it provides a full set of expressed preferences. The counts give us a series of snapshots, showing aggregated subsets of preferences from which we try to construct a more complete image of how people actually voted. In many respects, both tell a similar story, but there are differences. The most important concerns what has been loyalty or intraparty solidarity. Survey data might be expected to provide estimates of loyalty that exceed those given by the counts because we can look just at those who voted first for a candidate from party A and see how many voted for another candidate from that party with the second preference. (We could see an almost equally clear picture from the distribution of first-count surpluses, except for the fact that this ignores ballots with no second preference.) There is no contamination arising from the fact that some of the support for a candidate at a later count may have given a first preference for someone else. But it is also possible to look at loyalty not just across two candidates but across more than two: how many of those voting for party A with a first preference give a second and a third to the same party where it runs three candidates? Analyses run on INES data suggest loyalty is rather lower than the count data suggest (Bowler and Farrell 1991; Marsh et al. 2008; Marsh and Plescia 2016). (This is also the conclusion from analyses of the electronic count data: Laver 2004; Sinnott and McBride 2011.) Table 31.1 shows the loyalty of Fine Gael and Fianna Fáil voters in 2016. The estimates of loyalty here are not dissimilar from those calculated by Gallagher (2016) from the count data. However, what is striking is that less than half of each party's voters are willing to vote one, two, and three for their party. Yet they may be willing to remember the party in lower preferences even if the "ticket" they vote is not strictly "straight": some voters will give a third if not a second preference to "their" party even when they give the second to a candidate from elsewhere.

The survey data also give us a better idea of how much of the ballot voters tend to mark, and how many parties they tend to support. Almost all, 94 percent, do give a second preference, 76 percent give a third, but only a minority, 40 percent, give a fourth. The average number of preferences is 3.7, with only Green voters (4.6) much above this and Sinn Féin (3.2) much below. There is some reason to be cautious about these figures as the electronic data for 2002 suggested the average was about one preference more. There is no reason to think that the electronic ballot itself encouraged more preferences. The differences are more likely to be because, while people would vote the full ballot in reality, few were willing to do so when polled in the street. Even so, these figures are very comparable to those found in INES surveys from 2002 to 2011. The similarity across parties means that those voters whose first-choice party runs only one candidate are likely to vote for a wider range of parties than those whose first choice has running mates. In fact, the average voter spread support across three parties in 2016, and a significant minority gave a vote to more.

### Table 31.1  Party Loyalty in 2016

| | Second Preference for Same Party: 2 Candidates | Second Preference for Same Party: 3 Candidates | Second and Third Preference for Same Party: 3 Candidates | Second or Third Preference for Same Party: 2 Candidates |
|---|---|---|---|---|
| Those giving their first preference to: | % | % | % | % |
| Fianna Fáil | 61 | 67 | 44 | 66 |
| Fine Gael | 63 | 62 | 39 | 70 |

*Source:* Author's calculations from INES/RTE exit poll 2016.

The best explanation for this behavior lies in the strength of support for parties. Partisanship and the extent to which voters are attracted by candidates rather than parties are important determinants of party loyalty; there is little evidence that either behavior is a consequence of the amount of interest in or information about politics. A second source, and this appears to be more powerful, lies in what people are asked to do in the ballot box, and in factors connected with the choices that confront them. A voter given just two candidates from his or her party, perhaps in a small constituency, and with both being incumbents, is much more likely to manifest party loyalty than the voter faced with three nonincumbents spread out across a long ballot (Marsh and Plescia 2016; see also Curtice and Marsh 2014 for Irish/Scottish comparisons).

One question all this must raise is, how important is the party label to voters? If a first preference is cast for a Fine Gael candidate but not the second or third, it is arguable that the voter is thinking about the candidate rather than the party. As we have seen, when a party runs more than one candidate, a sizeable portion of its voters do not support all of them, and certainly not all of them before any other. Party may be a primary factor in vote choice, but it is clearly not the only one structuring preferences, and it would appear that other characteristics of the candidates are also very important for some voters. These are typically referred to as "candidate" as opposed to "party" factors. So, what is it about a candidate that is more important than party?

# WHAT MAKES A GOOD CANDIDATE?

There is a lot of evidence to indicate that voters want a representative who is as "local" as possible. Surveys carried out since the 1970s have recorded between 40 and 50 percent of voters as saying the main criterion for them was getting a good local representative to look after the constituency (Sinnott 1995, 170–172). Over 40 percent of voters in the INES/Raidió Teilifís Éirean (RTE) exit poll chose that option in 2016. Candidates do have a strong constituency base. Almost all successful candidates outside the large urban areas live in their constituency, and many would have always done so. "Local" here can also indicate placement within the constituency. Parties picking multiple candidates will generally have an eye to pick candidates from across the district, and where a constituency brings together two counties—a very significant focus of identity for many voters—they will normally try to represent both of them. There is good evidence from voting records that candidates tend to gather support from their own local area. Official voting records exist only for a constituency as a whole, but the parties try to record support in a much more detailed fashion by making tallies of votes for candidates at the level of the local polling station.[6] This data has sometimes been used by academics to describe geographical support patterns of first preferences (Johnson 1989; Parker 1982, 1984, 1986; Sacks 1976). Impressionistic evidence from count data shows that transfers are often explicable in terms of geography, as the candidates whose bases are closer to a source of transfers often do much better than those farther away, although it can be difficult to estimate effects more systematically (Marsh 1981; see also O'Kelly 2016). Survey data also show that those supporting a party tend to vote for the candidate who lives closer to them before a running mate who lives farther away (Gorecki and Marsh 2012). This tends to help parties who want to ensure their vote is spread evenly across their several candidates to maximize their chances of winning several seats (for more discussion on this, see "Nomination Strategies"). They usually to do this by advising their voters in one area to support candidate A and then B, and those in another to support candidate B and then A. They also try to get candidates to focus their campaigns on "their" areas. This is not always easy, as candidates will often see their running mate as their main rival rather than their best friend. Intraparty conflict is endemic and frequently bitter, and not just during the campaign. Incumbents in many elections have lost seats more often to someone in their own party than to someone from another party.

Another factor is incumbency. Incumbents are well known and tend to have a more recognizable profile across the constituency; they will probably spend more money and so will be better placed to obtain lower preferences, including those from across party lines. This has not been studied systematically, although the evidence makes it clear that incumbents do win more votes than nonincumbents. This is true in terms of first preferences but is equally true in terms of lower preferences. In 2016, the average preference given to an incumbent in the INES/RTE exit poll was 2.6 versus 3.4 for a nonincumbent, and this sort of difference holds across all parties and groups.

There has also been speculation that a candidate's gender could be important. One reason for the paucity of women in the Dáil has been the lack of women candidates, and it was suggested that voters would not support them to the extent that they would a male candidate. In fact, the evidence is very strong that gender is not significant for voters and that women can get elected once they are nominated (McElroy and Marsh 2010, 2011). Parties have been encouraged to nominate more women or face funding penalties, and this pushed up the number of women candidates significantly in 2016. However, new candidates will still find it hard to outrun incumbents, and it is likely to take some time before incumbents are not disproportionately male (Buckley, Galligan, and McGing 2016).

Whatever the factors that go into making a good candidate, voters do consistently respond to surveys to say that candidates matter. Since 2002, INES surveys have asked voters whether it was the candidate or the party that was most important for them, and followed this up by asking if they would still have voted (first) for the same candidate had that candidate had a different party label. Putting these two measures together indicates that while some voters think firmly in terms of either party or candidate, a very sizeable minority is more ambivalent: their candidate focus would not survive a candidate's move to another party, while some firm "party" voters say they would follow a candidate who moved. In 2016, 28 percent could be said to prioritize party and 29 percent the candidate, with 43 percent giving a mixed or uncertain response. These figures have not changed much since 2002, although fewer now say they prioritize party and more give a mixed response (Marsh et al. 2008: 148). Candidate factors were less important in the crisis election of 2011 (Marsh and Schwirz 2016; Thomson and Suiter 2016).

Some validity is given to this measure of candidate versus party focus by looking at how loyal each type of voter was, as measured by his or her set of candidate preferences. Among Fine Gael voters, 76 percent of "party" voters voted first and second Fine Gael, as opposed to just 42 percent of "candidate" voters. The equivalent figures for Fianna Fáil are 83 and 51 percent. Of course, this indicates that even (reportedly) candidate-centered voters can still behave like party loyalists, but it does underline that parties build support by trying to give voters the "best" candidates. And even if only one of them is really good, that may be sufficient to encourage voters to support a running mate.

Over the last few elections more and more voters have been rejecting all parties and opting for a nonparty candidate (Weeks 2016). Independents won 23 seats (of 158) in 2016, 15 (of 166) in 2011, and 13 (of 166) in 2002, but had a quieter election in 2007, when they won just 5. This development is facilitated by a ballot paper that gives all candidates from each party equal prominence, subject only to possible benefits that come from alphabetical ordering. It also fits with the fact that electoral competition is driven by both candidates and parties. And as we have seen, there now seems to be less loyalty to parties. Conventional survey measures of attachment suggest that less than one-third of voters are "identifiers" in the US sense (Marsh et al. 2008; Thomson 2017). In 2016, some of these incumbent independents mimicked parties to a degree by banding together to run under a label: Independents4Change. Some others formed an Independents Alliance, and most of those went on to support the government in exchange for policy agreements and some ministerial posts. The two candidate–party survey measures described earlier were not asked of independent voters in 2011 or 2016. Instead, such voters were asked whether the candidate him- or herself or the fact that the candidate was independent was the most important factor in their decision and whether or not they would stay with the same candidate if he or she moved to a party. The results suggested a lot of ambivalence as just under half, 44 percent, were committed clearly to the candidate and only 10 percent to that candidate's independence. Interestingly, of those who voted for an independent or independent grouping in 2016, 28 percent voted independent with their second preference. Of those committed to an independent, 60 percent voted independent first and second, as opposed to just 26 percent of the candidate-centered independents.

# NOMINATION STRATEGIES

Against this background where party loyalty among voters is not to be relied on and voters are swayed by candidate characteristics, nomination strategies are very important if a party is to maximize its potential to win seats. One of the worst failures in recent years was Fianna Fáil's haul of just 20 seats (out of 166) from its 17 percent of the vote. Figure 31.2 suggests that it should have won 28 seats. Its failure to do this was in part a reflection of its inability to attract lower preferences in that election. Gallagher (2011) estimated that this could have cost the party 10 seats, but this was combined with poor nomination strategies, with too many candidates looking for too few votes. Parties can lose out by not nominating enough candidates. Labour did this in 1992, missing out on seats in several places where a second candidate would have been almost sure to win an extra seat for the party. But parties can also fail to win one seat when its two candidates fall well down the rankings and the transfer between them is inadequate to bring the stronger one up.

In 2011, Fianna Fáil's nomination strategy was made difficult by the fact that it had one or two incumbents in every constituency and found it hard to believe its vote would match its historically low poll ratings. The consequence was that it failed to win a seat in thirteen constituencies where it ran two candidates; had it run just one, it would probably have done rather better. Figure 31.5 shows the probability of a party winning a seat according to whether it runs one or more than one candidate, other things being equal. The analysis here is limited to three-seat districts. This is for ease of presentation and because the big parties rarely run just one candidate in the larger districts. The graph shows the probability of winning a seat with a given share of the quota. With one candidate, the chance exceeds 50 percent with 62 percent of the quota, but where it runs two candidates, the threshold is much higher at 82 percent. A second candidate could bring in more first-preference votes, but the risk is that if this advantage is not substantial, the gains will be insufficient to make up for a lower first-preference vote for either candidate and a subsequent disadvantage in the count. While the threshold will vary for

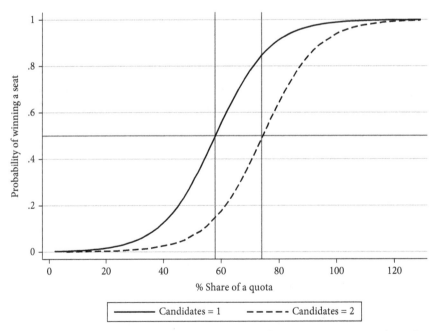

FIGURE 31.5. Probability of a party winning a seat in a three-seat constituency depending on share of the quota and whether it nominates one or two candidates. Estimation based on 1997 –2016 results. Independents excluded.

larger-magnitude districts and will be different for different parties—because the ability to attract transfers varies—the basic pattern is the same in three-, four-, and five-seaters: overnomination risks losing seats that could have been won. This, of course, is because of the fact that party loyalty is relatively weak. If almost all votes transferred within the party, there would be no real cost to nominating many more candidates.[7]

# MAJOR CRITICISMS AND SUGGESTIONS FOR REFORM

There have been criticisms of the system and some attempts to change or reform it. Fianna Fáil made two efforts to replace STV with a first-past-the-post (FPTP, or plurality) system. Because the electoral system is specified in the 1937 constitution, a referendum was required. Both times, in 1959 and 1968, the change was rejected. The basis for making the change was essentially that Fianna Fáil saw itself as the main beneficiary if Ireland was to move to the UK system, but Fianna Fáil argued that the current system encourages a multiplicity of parties and provokes government instability, the classic arguments against PR. Ironically, these referendums were both held at a time when fragmentation was relatively low and governments were very stable.

In later years, the system was criticized as encouraging a focus on so-called clientelist politics—a system in which representatives see their role as providing selective benefits to constituents at the expense of a focus on national affairs and the national interest. Rather than a concern with the proportional representation of parties, this places the emphasis on the personal element of the electoral system, which arises from the preferential vote. Most of the Irish academic literature rejects the popular term "clientelism" on the basis that Teachtaí Dálas (TDs) cannot and do not provide material advantages to constituents (see Komito 1984; a good summary is Gallagher and Komito 2010). Rather, politicians act as brokers, interceding between state agencies and citizens to ensure that citizens know their rights and obtain what is due to them, as well as ensuring that constituency views are heard as appropriate.[8] Some of this is exactly what local representatives are supposed to do, and some is perhaps what citizens' advice bureaus could do. Certainly, TDs are for the most part extremely active, holding "clinics" across the constituency and dealing increasingly with emails.

A special report on the electoral system by the nonpartisan Constitution Review Group (1996) opened up the debate and suggested the merits of a mixed-member system. This system would keep the proportionality aspect and maintain, to a degree, a link between small constituencies and the Dáil, but it would (arguably) do away with the intraparty rivalries that are thought to be at the basis of TDs' constituency activities. Change was rejected by the all-party parliamentary committee that investigated the report (All-Party Oireachtas Committee 2002). One related change introduced made a formal break between national and local government by preventing sitting deputies from also being local councilors, arguably relieving them of local duties and permitting them to spend more time on national ones. However, the wider issue of electoral reform remains topical. The idea of scrapping the electoral system gets a regular airing in the media, and in late 2009 the Oireachtas Committee on the Constitution initiated another lot of hearings on electoral reform, which again failed to generate widespread support for change. Discussion continued following the 2011 election. The economic crisis led to questions about most aspects of Irish democracy. A citizens' assembly was established by the government to deliberate and issue recommendations on a number of political reforms, including the electoral system, but it voted decisively against recommending any change. Indeed, asked immediately after the 2011 elections about support for a number of reforms, public opinion did not favor change and in fact saw the constituency focus as a strength of the system. Moreover, the same study found that voters saw something like a sixty/forty breakdown in TDs' workload between national and constituency business and thought it should be nearer to fifty/fifty.[9]

Other criticisms have been directed at improving the way STV works in practice and making it more proportional, but they have not had anything like the coverage given to "clientelism." Constituencies are most important here. The Dáil debates on the 2012 report of the Boundary Commission established to determine electoral boundaries for the 2016 election saw many deputies complaining about proposed changes in their areas, and in particular the lack of integration of constituency and county boundaries—counties being the major unit for local government but also a focus on local identity. However, one Sinn Féin deputy did make a more general point that greater district magnitude would avoid so many breaches in county boundaries: "The terms of reference given to the Constituency Commission were too narrow. Crucially, they were constrained by the undemocratic legislation which restricts the number of TDs per constituency to a maximum of five."[10] The party has generally argued for slightly larger district magnitude from which it, as a smaller party, might hope to benefit, although as we have seen this is not necessarily the case. The same point has been made at various times by politicians from other parties, but no government has yet opted to allow even six-seaters. Any very significant increase is unlikely, largely because it would make decisions more difficult for voters and certainly add to the intense and chronic competition between deputies and would-be deputies, which is the object of so much criticism. But larger constituencies—in terms of both district magnitude and population—could be the key to ending the frequent need for boundary changes and secure the primacy of counties (Coakley 2007).

Of more abstruse concern is the process of transferring surpluses. Because it would be time-consuming, the normal practice has been to explore only a small number of the votes to determine where the surplus should go. In the smaller-scale elections to the Seanad (upper house) all votes are examined and transferred at an appropriate weighting of their value, a system known as the "Gregory method" (see Gallagher and Unwin 1986), which is employed in STV elections in Northern Ireland. The justification for the current method is that the Gregory alternative is time-consuming, and also unnecessary inasmuch as all ballots are mixed together before the counting starts and so are effectively randomized. As some studies have pointed out, however, even random samples might not be representative, and it could well be that sometimes the "wrong" person is elected (Coakley and O'Neill 1984; Gallagher and Unwin 1986). There are no wider concerns about this. Indeed, even when electronic voting was about to be implemented, there was no move to change the method of counting to avoid these problems. Criticisms are also made of STV that chance plays too great a role in who gets elected (Nurmi 1997). This arises because lower preferences are only explored when a candidate is eliminated or elected. Some voters might get their ballots looked at several times, while others only once. The order of elimination can sometimes matter, and that too is often the result of tiny margins, or a handful of votes (a rare real-world example is given by Gallagher [1999, 145–146], who dismisses the criticism on the basis that these are unpredictable, and so voters cannot behave tactically to bring them about).

## Summary and Reflections

Ireland has now experienced almost one hundred years of elections under what is still termed as PR. During that period the party system has fragmented, coalesced, and then fragmented again. Proportionality has varied, but at worst it has been on par with list systems in many countries and better than most FPTP systems. Relatively small district magnitude has been the norm, but new parties, independents, and minor parties generally have all shown they can win in three-seaters and five-seaters. We may see some increase in district magnitude at some point in the future, but there seems little chance of seeing any repeat of the eight- or nine-seaters used in the past.

One of the most striking trends over the past few decades has been the change in the manner in which voters structure their preference votes. While once those opting for a Fianna Fáil or Fine Gael candidate would normally have gone on to support the other candidates of that party, such loyalty is characteristic of around two-thirds of voters for those parties, and only a minority seem to support three candidates from the same party with their first three preferences. This raises the question of the extent to which voters do opt for a party rather than a candidate. The dichotomy is almost certainly a false one, as for most voters there seems to be no conflict: the best party has the best candidate, and the best candidate comes from the best party. Yet this match can be down to the influence of the party or the candidate. What is clear is that a significant number of people say they prioritize the candidate, and the preferences people expressed are not structured clearly along party lines. Candidates are fully aware of this, and indeed probably contribute to its continuation by their campaigning styles. They highlight their own abilities and achievements, as well as their party label, and if they have no label that is sometimes seen as a bonus. The weakness of party is perhaps most evident in the fact that a party needs more votes to win a seat when it runs two candidates than when it runs just one.

Change in the system over the years has been minimal. The change in average district magnitude and the introduction of party labels onto the ballot paper are the most notable. Partisan advantage was the driving force behind the two proposals to swap PR-STV for a FPTP system in the mid-twentieth century. Complaints about the nature and work of the average Dáil deputy have promoted discussions of change to a mixed-member system in more recent years, but politicians themselves are divided on the issue, and the public as a whole seems reluctant to surrender the control it has under STV to select a local TD.

# CONCLUSION

How much of what we see as normal in Irish politics comes down to the electoral system? This is hard to answer without some comparisons with other countries. Comparisons are difficult given the fact that only Malta used STV for national elections, and where STV is used subnationally, the nature of politics is still likely to be driven by what works on the national stage. However, it is possible to compare aspects of the Irish electoral system with aspects of other ones. A key feature in Ireland is the constituency, and although there may be several deputies elected for an area, they do see their role— as do the voters—as local representatives. The same is no less true in countries using FPTP systems. Deputies in the United Kingdom and Canada, for instance, would recognize the need to balance local and national duties, as would those in the United States, although congress people might be aghast at the relative lack of resources. Indeed, the time spent by TDs on constituency work is not excessive compared to what is done by deputies under a range of different systems (Gallagher and Komito 2010, 244–245), so it is hard to attribute this focus to the electoral system. And there are other explanations, such as the nature of state bureaucracy, which is not "consumer friendly" (e.g., Roche 1982), although the same point could surely be made about state agencies elsewhere. It is likely that the nature of the TDs' role does have a part to play in recruitment. It has certainly been argued that the demands for constituency service might dissuade able young people interested in policy from becoming politicians (and a similar point has been made with respect to the lack of female candidates). There is probably less truth in this now than a generation ago, as the deputies with university degrees and a professional background are now in a majority, but family connections remain an important element in recruitment as almost one in five deputies in 2016 were closely related to former TDs (Gallagher 2016, 153).

In FPTP systems there is of course no freedom for the voter to choose between candidates of the same party, but in many proportional systems that use a preference vote there is the opportunity to do so, and in many cases voting means selecting one or more candidates. Where there is preference voting, politics do not necessarily display the characteristics noted in Ireland. In Finland, for instance, where voters choose one candidate from a list, there is no equivalent to "constituency service" (Arter 2011), but candidates do need to distinguish themselves from rivals by reference to things like social group attachments or locality, and there is ample room for candidates to matter (see the chapter by von Schoultz in this volume). Preferential voting in such small constituencies, however, is rare.

The weakness—and growing weakness—of parties is also certainly not unique to Ireland. The same system used to see high levels of loyalty, so it is hardly responsible for the decline, but it does allow that decline to manifest itself in different ways. The electoral system allows weaker partisanship to manifest itself in the way people vote, both by supporting new parties (and independents) and by showing less party solidarity in preference orderings. Irish parties have been unusual until very recently in a comparative context because of the absence of clear social or ideological underpinnings to support. Arguably this has contributed to the nature of electoral competition between candidates, but even in the newer, more ideologically extreme parties such as Sinn Féin, candidates are no less active in serving the constituency and its voters still say that the "candidate" is what attracts their vote.

A wider problem raised by the way in which elections in Ireland operate under STV is the nature of representation. In light of Schattschneider's comment that democracy is unthinkable without political parties, the Irish case might give us some insights into what the problems are. If voters are ambivalent about parties and do give priority to local concerns and the need for a good local representative, this certainly makes it hard to see elections as being effective in terms of providing a coherent mandate for the incoming government. Discussions on the formation of the 2016 government saw constant references to party manifestos and promises that could not be broken, as well as references to each party's mandate and that of the Independent Alliance, all of which assume that voters were motivated by these things. Parties are quite good at implementing formal election promises (Costello, O'Neill, and Thomson 2016), but there is little evidence that voters know what they are or make them the basis of their vote. However, this is hardly unique to Ireland. Whatever voters say about their motivations, and however weak their tendency is to vote on party lines, the electorate has been seen to hold government to account. This was most notable in 2011, when a Fianna Fáil–led coalition that presided over a severe economic downturn that necessitated a bailout from the European Union and International Monetary Fund suffered historically large losses, as its incumbents were swept away almost regardless of local strengths. There are big shifts in some elections, explicable only in terms of people voting for, or against, particular parties.

## Notes

1. Clause 1.5: The members [of Dáil Éireann] shall be elected on the system of proportional representation by means of the single transferable vote.
2. As noted in the introductory chapter, this is equivalent to what is known as the Droop quota.

3. Ballots where no second preference is marked are ignored in this calculation. However, in later counts nontransferable ballots are recorded as such and no adjustment is made for them.

4. The constitution prescribes that a deputy should represent between twenty thousand and thirty thousand inhabitants and that the variation in this figure across constituencies should be as small as practicable but does not prescribe the number of representatives per constituency. The courts later indicated limitations on the variation that they would permit.

5. Independents are classified as a single group here. Smaller parties and Labour and Sinn Féin include the Greens, the Progressive Democrats, the United Left Alliance, and Anti Austerity Alliance/People Before Profit. The rest are subsumed into "Others."

6. This is done by "tallymen," who watch as ballots are emptied out of the boxes in which they are brought from each polling station to the count center and keep a record.

7. This is the norm in Malta where loyalty is very high: see Hirczy de Miño and Lane (2000).

8. An exception is those TDs who are ministers and who are often able to ensure that their constituency gets more than its fair share of the department budget (Suiter and O'Malley 2014a, 2014b).

9. Asked to agree/disagree with the statement that "Our PR-STV (Single Transferable Vote) electoral system should be replaced," 42 percent disagreed, 27 percent agreed, and the rest were uncertain. This might be thought to be a somewhat lukewarm endorsement, but the public was in favor of the other six reforms suggested. Fifty-two percent agreed that the assumption that TDs should provide a local service is a strength of the Irish political system (24 percent disagreed). See Marsh et al. (2017, appendix); Gallagher and Suiter (2017) provide a more extensive exploration of what voters expect of their representatives.

10. Electoral (Amendment) (Dáil Constituencies) Bill 2012: Second Stage (Resumed) Thursday, January 17, 2013.

## References

Arter, David. "The Michael Marsh Question: How Do Finns Do Constituency Service?" *Parliamentary Affairs* 64, no. 1 (2011): 129–152.

Bowler, Shaun, and David M. Farrell. "Voter Behaviour under STV-PR: Solving the Puzzle of the Irish Party System." *Political Behavior* 13 (1991): 303–320.

Buckley, Fiona, Yvonne Galligan, and Claire McGing. "Women and the Election: Assessing the Impact of Gender Quotas." In *How Ireland Voted 2016: The Election That Nobody Won*, ed. Michael Gallagher and Michael Marsh, 185–206. London: Palgrave Macmillan, 2016.

Coakley, John. "Revising Constituency Boundaries: Ireland in Comparative Perspective." *Administration* 55, no. 3 (2007): 1–29.

Coakley, John, and Gerald O Neill. "Chance in a Preferential Voting System: An Unacceptable Element in Irish Electoral Law." *Economic and Social Review* 16, no. 1 (1984): 1–18.

Costello, Rory, Paul O'Neill, and Robert Thomson. "The Fulfilment of Elections Pledges by the Outgoing Government." In *How Ireland Voted 2016: The Election That Nobody Won*, ed. Michael Gallagher and Michael Marsh, 27–46. London: Palgrave Macmillan, 2016.

Curtice, John, and Michael Marsh. "Confused or Competent? How Voters Use the STV Ballot Paper." *Electoral Studies* 34 (2014): 146–158.

Farrell, Brian. "Labour and the Irish Political Party System: A Suggested Approach to Analysis." *Economic and Social Review* 1, no. 4 (1970): 477–502.

Gallagher, Michael. "Proportionality, Disproportionality and Electoral Systems." *Electoral Studies* 10 (1991): 33–51.

Gallagher, Michael. "The Results Analysed." In *How Ireland Voted 1997*, ed. Michael Marsh and Paul Mitchell, 121–150. Boulder, CO: Westview Press, 1999.

Gallagher, Michael. "Ireland's Earthquake Election: Analysis of the Results." In *How Ireland Voted 2011: The Full story of Ireland's Earthquake Election*, ed. Michael Gallagher and Michael Marsh, 139–171. London: Palgrave Macmillan, 2011.

Gallagher, Michael. "The Results Analysed: The Aftershocks Continue." In *How Ireland Voted 2016: The Election That Nobody Won*, ed. Michael Gallagher and Michael Marsh, 125–158. London: Palgrave Macmillan, 2016.

Gallagher, Michael. "Election Indices Dataset." 2017. http://www.tcd.ie/Political_Science/staff/michael_gallagher/ElSystems/index.php (accessed February 21, 2017).

Gallagher, Michael, and Lee Komito. "The Constituency Role of Dáil Deputies." In *Politics in the Republic of Ireland*, ed. J. Coakley and M. Gallagher, 230–262. London: Routledge, 2010.

Gallagher, Michael, and Jane Suiter. "Pathological Parochialism or a Valuable Service? Attitudes to the Constituency Role of Irish Parliamentarians." 2017. pp. 143–171 in Marsh et al.

Gallagher, Michael, and Anthony, Unwin. "Electoral Distortion under STV Random Sampling Procedures." *British Journal of Political Science* 16, no. 2 (1986): 243–253.

Górecki, Maciej, and Michael Marsh. "Not Just 'Friends and Neighbours': The Effects of Canvassing on Vote Choice in Ireland." *European Journal of Political Research* 51, no. 5 (2012): 563–582.

Hirczy de Miño, Wolfgang, and John C. Lane. "Malta: STV in a Two–Party System." In *Elections in Australia, Ireland and Malta under the Single Transferable Vote*, ed. S. Bowler and B. Grofman, 178–204. Ann Arbor: University of Michigan Press, 2000.

Johnson, Nuala C. "An Analysis of the 'Friends and Neighbours' Effect in an Irish Urban Constituency." *Irish Geography* 22, no. 2 (1989): 93–105.

Komito, Lee. "Irish Clientelism: A Reappraisal." *Economic and Social Review* 15, no. 3 (1984): 173–194.

Laakso, Markku and Rein Taagepera. "'Effective' Number of Parties: A Measure with Application to West Europe." *Comparative Political Studies* 12, no. 1 (1979): 3–27.

Laver, Michael. "Analysing Structures of Party Preference in Electronic Voting Data." *Party Politics* 10 (2004): 521–541.

Marsh, Michael. "Localism, Candidate Selection and Electoral Preference in Ireland." *Economic and Social Review* 12 (1981): 167–186.

Marsh, Michael. "Voting for Government Coalitions in Ireland under Single Transferable Vote." *Electoral Studies* 29 (2010): 329–338.

Marsh, Michael, Gail McElroy, and David M. Farrell, eds. *A Conservative Revolution.* Oxford: Oxford University Press, 2017.

Marsh, Michael, and Carolina Plescia. "Split-Ticket Voting in an STV System: Choice in a Non-Strategic Context." *Irish Political Studies* 31, no. 2 (2016): 163–181.

Marsh, Michael, and Schwirz, Laura M. "Exploring the Non-Alignment of Party and Candidate Assessments in Ireland: Do Voters Really Follow Candidates?" In *The Act of Voting: Identities, Institutions and Locale*, ed. David Farrell and Johan Elkink, 178–192. London: Routledge, 2016.

Marsh, Michael, Richard Sinnott, John Garry, and Fiachra Kennedy. *The Irish Voter: The Nature of Electoral Competition in the Republic of Ireland.* Manchester: Manchester University Press, 2008.

McElroy, Gail, and Michael Marsh. "Candidate Gender and Voter Choice: Analysis from a Multi-Member Preferential Voting System." *Political Research Quarterly* 63, no. 4 (2010): 822–833.

McElroy, Gail, and Michael Marsh. "Electing Women to the Dáil: Gender Cues and the Irish Voter." *Irish Political Studies* 26, no. 4 (2011): 521–534.

Nurmi, Hanno. "It Is Not Just the Lack of Monotonicity." *Representation* 34, no. 1 (1997): 48–52.

O'Kelly, Michael. "Locality in Irish Voter Preferences." In *The Act of Voting: Identities, Institutions and Locale*, ed. David Farrell and Johan Elkink, 137–160. London: Routledge, 2016.

Ortega Villodres, Carmen, and Belen Morata Garcia de la Puerta. "Position Effects under STV: Ireland and Malta." *Representation* 41 (2004): 3–14.

Parker, Alan J. "The 'Friends and Neighbours' Voting Effect in the Galway West Constituency." *Political Geography Quarterly* 3, no. 3 (1982): 243–262.

Parker, Alan J. "An Ecological Analysis of Voting Patterns in Galway West, 1977." *Irish Geography* 17, no. 1 (1984): 42–64.

Parker, Alan J. "Geography and the Irish Electoral System." *Irish Geography* 19, no. 1 (1986): 1–50.

Roche, Richard. "The High Cost of Complaining Irish Style." *IBAR—Journal of Irish Business and Administrative Research* 4, no. 2 (1982): 98–108.

Sacks, Paul M. *The Donegal Mafia: An Irish Political Machine*. New Haven, CT: Yale University Press, 1976.

Sinnott, Richard. *Irish Voters Decide: Voting Behaviour in Elections and Referendums since 1918*. Manchester: Manchester University Press, 1995.

Sinnott, Richard, and James McBride. "Preference Voting under PR-STV 1948-2011." In *How Ireland Voted 2011: The Full Story of Ireland's Earthquake Election*, ed. Michael Gallagher and Michael Marsh, 205–221. London: Palgrave Macmillan, 2011.

Suiter, Jane, and Eoin O'Malley. "Chieftains Delivering: Testing Different Measures of 'Pork' on an Irish Data Set of Discretionary Sports Grants." *Journal of Elections, Public Opinion and Parties* 24, no. 1 (2014a): 115–124.

Suiter, Jane, and Eoin O'Malley. "Yes, Minister: The Impact of Decision-Making Rules on Geographically Targeted Particularistic Spending." *Parliamentary Affairs* 67, no. 4 (2014b): 935–954.

Thomson, Robert. "The Malleable Nature of Party Identification." In *A Conservative Revolution*, ed. Michael Marsh, Gail McElroy, and David Farrell, 123–142. Oxford: Oxford University Press, 2017.

Weeks, Liam. "Independents and the Election: The Party Crashers." In *How Ireland Voted 2016: The Election That Nobody Won*, ed. Michael Gallagher and Michael Marsh, 207–226. London: Palgrave Macmillan, 2016.

# CHAPTER 32

························································································

# ELECTORAL SYSTEMS
# IN CONTEXT

*France*

························································································

## VERÓNICA HOYO

THE current French electoral system dates back to the founding of the Fifth Republic in 1958. Originally created to respond to a political crisis due to the military *putsch* in Algeria, the establishment of the French Fifth Republic was an extraordinary event. It sought not only to avoid a civil war but also to create a completely new distribution of power, centered on strengthening the powers of government and preventing the instability and party polarization of the *régimes d'Assemblée* that had characterized and eventually led to the demise of the Third and Fourth Republic (Sowerwine 2009). Historically, France had consistently alternated between periods of extreme concentration of power (single-man autocracies) and ineffective and unstable parliamentary regimes; De Gaulle's constitution was designed to break away from what seemed to be "innate" conditions.[1]

This chapter analyzes the current French electoral system by focusing on the actual operation of these rules in the larger political context: including the interaction between the rules, the party system, and the main political actors that compete in them. Electoral systems are mechanisms by which power is allocated. But like all rules, they do not exist in a vacuum. Their realm of action is dependent on and constrained by the choices made by the individuals (citizens and candidates) and the parties that apply them. Although the electoral system of the French Fifth Republic was de jure devised to incentivize the creation of assembly majorities that would guarantee the regime's survival, de facto the task may not be so easily accomplished, or rather, its design does not preclude the possibility of political actors adapting and manipulating these rules to best serve their interests.

The chapter is organized into four sections: it starts with a description of the "rules of the game" and then moves into the discussion of the principal changes that have impacted them. The second section focuses on the consequences of the French electoral system and the larger structural context in which the system operates. The third section contains the analysis of recent "first order" elections (the 2012 national contests) and a brief mention to what happens at the local ballots (the "second order"). Before concluding, there is a general discussion on some of the major party system changes observed in the 2017 presidential and legislative ballots focusing on their relation and their impact on the prevalent electoral system.

> *Il vaut mieux avoir une méthode mauvaise plutôt que de n'en avoir aucune.*
> Charles De Gaulle, *Le fil de l'épée*[2]

Having experimented with a large number of electoral systems since 1789, the French have learned that different rules produce different results and that each particular option may be the deciding factor in the struggle between competing political camps vying for control of the state (Campbell 1965). Yet the French Fifth Republic stands out for the remarkable stability of its two-round (TR) majority-plurality electoral system. This is a system of single-seat districts in which, if no absolute majority was obtained at the first round, there may be more than two candidates qualifying for the second round, at which point a plurality suffices. This system has operated continuously since 1988 (Elgie 2005).[3]

The electoral system is not inscribed in the constitution and thus is potentially subject to tampering by strongly motivated political actors. One example was the 1986 legislative election, which was conducted under a department-list proportional representation (PR) system in an attempt by President Mitterrand to mitigate his party's almost-assured losses and to split his contenders' vote. Nonetheless, there are certain important regularities worth noting. Overall, elections take place in a two-round system (with the exception of the European elections) and most chosen rules promote majoritarian principles, although each different electoral arena has its own particular procedures. Table 32.1 summarizes the different rules that coexist in France's current electoral system.

All democratic electoral systems presuppose a major analytical decision, a tradeoff between two contrasting principles: either to favor majoritarianism and its subsequent increased capacity to govern or to maximize access and representation, opting instead for pluralism and consensus-building mechanisms (Lijphart 1994, 1999). The French Fifth Republic was conceived as an institutional response to the chaos and inaction brought about by a very powerful legislature that coexisted with a "party dictatorship" (commonly thought to have been produced by the PR rules of the Fourth Republic), and as such it was designed to assert the supremacy of the executive office and to favor "effective" governance (Safran 1998; Perraudeau 2001). The choice of a two-round system was not, however, a novelty. Both the Second Empire (1852–1870) and the Third Republic (1870–1940) had already used it given the freedom of choice it gave to the electors, but its potential failings, due to the loose qualifications for the second round that prevailed then, had also been pointed out (Campbell 1965). The Fifth Republic's more stringent rules, in conjunction with the new regime type, gave rise to an entirely different electoral arena.

## Table 32.1  The French Electoral System of the French Fifth

| Type of Election | District Magnitude (M)/Total Seats | Electoral Rule | Threshold | Term Length |
|---|---|---|---|---|
| Presidential | 1 | Direct, universal suffrage, two-round (TR) majority | Only top two vote getters access second round | 5 years with re-election |
| Legislative elections: lower chamber (*Assemblée Nationale*) | 1/577 | Direct, universal suffrage, TR majority-plurality | 12.5% of registered voters | 5 years with re-election |
| Upper chamber: Senate (*Sénat*) | Varies per each of the 101 territorial constituencies (*départements*)/348 | Indirect, universal, and compulsory suffrage for members of Electoral College* The electoral rule changes depending on M. In those departments where 3 or less are elected, TR majority-plurality vote applies. For 4 or more, proportional representation (PR) highest-average, list-based, no *panachage* or preferential vote is used. | | 6 years with re-election Since 2011, half of Senate is renewable every 3 years |
| Municipal | Range depending on commune size. For example, M = 7 for communes with fewer than 100 inhabitants, and M = 69 for those with more than 300,000 inhabitants/ 36,681 communes (2014) | Direct, universal suffrage. Rules depend on size of community. <1,000 people: TR-majority plurality >1,000 people: TR, PR, list based† | To avoid second round, absolute majority and one-quarter of registered voters needed For list-based: only those lists with at least 10% access second round. These lists can be modified and candidates having obtained at least 5% of vote in first round can be included (if their list did not make it to second round) | 6 years |

(*continued*)

**Table 32.1 Continued**

| Type of Election | District Magnitude (M)/Total Seats | Electoral Rule | Threshold | Term Length |
|---|---|---|---|---|
| Regional | M varies by department size/ 96 metropolitan departments, 18 regions in France (2016) but 18 regional presidencies, 1,757 regional councilors, and 157 territorial councilors (2015) | Direct, universal suffrage, TR, PR list based with majority bonus (prime majoritaire) | 10% of vote to qualify to second round. Lists with 5% or less may join together to gain access. Lists must respect gender parity rules | 6 years |
| European | 8 interregional constituencies[†] with varying M ranging from 3 to 15/74 seats (2014) | Direct, universal suffrage, PR, closed party list | Lists obtaining less than 5% of vote are not included in the seat distribution | 5 years |

Table composed with information from the Interior Ministry and the public information website *Vie publique*. This is not, however, a comprehensive list of all electoral processes that take place in France; cantonal elections (which happen at the same time as municipals) and other ballots (i.e., referendum) are omitted for the sake of space.

* The Senate's Electoral College is composed of approximately 145,000 people including *députés*, regional councilors elected at the department level, department councilors, and delegates from the municipal councils.

† Paris, Marseille, and Lyon are treated as special cases of the rules applied to communes larger than 1,000 inhabitants. For Paris and Lyon, each *arrondisement* forms its own sector. Marseille is divided into eight sectors with two *arrondisements* each. The number of councilor seats for each of these city councils depends on the results obtained by sector.

† The eight interregional constituencies are Nord-Ouest, Ouest, Est, Sud-Ouest, Sud-Est, Massif central-Centre, Ile de France, and Outre-Mer.

Constitutionally, France is a semipresidential regime (Duverger 1980; Shugart 2005; Elgie 2009). By design, the French state is meant to be a hybrid: to exert presidential dominance when both the president and the legislative majority come from the same political party or, contrastingly, if the majorities do not coincide (called *cohabitation* and discussed later in the chapter), to strengthen the dual executive constitutional logic, thus depriving the president of cabinet influence (Samuels and Shugart 2010). There is much debate on whether the French president is, constitutionally speaking, a powerful actor (Elgie and Machin 1991; Siaroff 2003). Although the extent of presidential or prime ministerial leadership has varied across time, depending on the particular individuals in each of these offices, in practice, the alleged balancing act between the executive and the legislative powers in the French setting is tilted in favor of the executive (*la primauté présidentielle*), once the regime type combines with the electoral system.

Today, French presidential elections occur under direct universal suffrage under the majority runoff rule (Elgie 2005). A runoff occurs if no absolute majority is achieved in the first round (which no one has obtained since 1962); only the top two vote getters may participate in the second round. To be a candidate, a presidential hopeful must submit and have confirmed by the Constitutional Council at least 500 endorsements (*parrainages*). Such endorsements must come from elected officials (a total of 14,296 valid endorsements in 2017) and should be nationally representative. The president is commander in chief, has the power to call a referendum and ratify treaties, and appoints and may, implicitly and if he has a supporting legislative majority, dismiss the prime minister (PM) after prior dissolution of the government (articles 5, 8, 11–12, 15–16, and 52 of the constitution). De Gaulle sought to make the president a sort of "father figure," free from dealing with the day-to-day activities of governance that ought to be the realm of operation of the prime minister. In particular, through articles 20 and 21, the French PM was given very real power as head of government: in charge of the government's actions and responsible for national defense, for the implementation of legislation, and for proposing a list of ministers and cabinet members to the president. The PM is accountable to Parliament and has the right to initiate legislation. It is the presence or absence of a legislative majority and the president's relationship with that majority that explains who will be the determinant agent in this dual executive hybrid system.

France is the only advanced democracy to conduct elections to its legislative body, the Assemblée Nationale (AN), using a two-round system (Blais and Loewen 2009). The ballot for the members of Parliament (MPs) (*deputés*) happens under direct universal suffrage in single-seat district (577 constituencies), majority-plurality runoff rules. To make it to the second round, candidates must meet the threshold of 12.5 percent of registered voters, which means there may be more than two, at times three ("triangular," thirty-four in 2012, one in 2017), or rarely four candidates ("quadrangular," last one in 1973) in the second ballot of the legislative races. Given the predominant mistrust of legislatures due to their past two republican experiences and the hybrid nature of the regime, the AN has often been deemed an "emasculated legislature." Yet recent research has challenged the "decline of Parliament thesis" by documenting punctuated increases in the legislature's oversight activities (Lazardeux 2009). In short, the AN is indeed an essential actor in French politics, a "real part of the legislative process" (Kerrouche 2006, 361).

Besides the methods of vote-seat allocation, it is important to mention briefly certain other important aspects of the electoral system. In particular, to be eligible to vote, an individual must be a French national, 18 years old at least, in full possession of civil and political rights at the time of the vote, and registered in the electoral rolls. To be eligible to stand for office in France, a person must be eligible to vote, be of French nationality, and comply with the specific requirements of the particular election in which the individual wants to be a candidate. For all local elections (municipal, cantonal, and regional), as well as for the legislative vote, the minimum age requirement is 18, while for senatorial candidates it is 24. The nationality requirement is "enlarged" for both European and municipal elections, whereby nationals of any other European Union (EU) member state are eligible to vote (prior registration in "complementary electoral lists") and may also present their candidacies.

Despite the stronger majoritarian undertones in the French electoral system, addressed later, "elections are clumsy instruments" and distortions may, and often do, occur (Powell 2000, 6). The key issue is, then, not to focus exclusively on institutional design, but rather on how key actors interpret and manipulate the rules of the game to advance their interests.

# CHANGES TO THE ELECTORAL SYSTEM OF THE FRENCH FIFTH REPUBLIC

There have been few major constitutional amendments, namely, the introduction of direct suffrage for presidential elections in 1962, the 1974 reform of access to the Constitutional Council, successive reforms of the AN to increase its oversight capacities, and the reduction of the presidential mandate to a five-year term (*le Quinquennat*) in 2000 (Grossman and Sauger 2009).

Until 1962, the election of the president under the Fifth Republic was indirect, through the vote of an electoral college composed of about eighty thousand notables (members of the AN, senators, assembly members from overseas territories, and municipal councilors). Only a single president was elected under these rules: Charles de Gaulle in 1958 (who garnered 78.5 percent of the votes). Together with direct elections, presidential endorsements were established in an effort to prevent irrelevant candidacies, to avoid a potential return to "party rule," and to protect the unifying spirit of the executive (Grosieux 2004).[4] It was precisely at this time that the semipresidential regime was consolidated. Just then did de Gaulle really fulfill his dream of "doing away" with the remnants of parliamentary government and a true-hybrid system came into existence.

However, the direct election of the president also increased the likelihood of shared government or cohabitation. Cohabitation happens when two conditions are met: first, the president and prime minister are from opposing parties, and second, the president's party is not represented in the cabinet (Elgie 2007, 2009; Samuels and Shugart 2010). Despite the hybrid nature of the regime, cohabitation has actually been less frequent and less paralyzing (or, rather, more successful) than originally expected. In its fifty-nine years of existence, there have been a total of three periods of cohabitation in the Fifth Republic, all of which have come and gone without breaking France's semipresidentialism. The first instance happened under the socialist presidency of François Mitterrand and the premiership of Jacques Chirac (Rassemblement pour la France [RPR]—Gaullist moderate Right) in 1986–1988. The second cohabitation was during the second Mitterrand presidency and with the more centrist Edouard Balladur as PM in 1993–1995, and the most recent one was during the presidency of Jacques Chirac and the socialist premiership of Lionel Jospin from 1997 to 2002 (Poulard 1990). The first two instances of cohabitation were considered transitory stages due to very particular electoral contexts. Namely, the first cohabitation took place at the end of the legislative term during the final two years of Mitterrand's first presidency and was produced by quite close results in the 1986 elections (held under PR, as noted earlier). The second one occurred also at the end of the legislative term, but in the final two years of the presidency of an increasingly frail and elderly Mitterrand, and this time it happened after a decidedly clear victory for the Right in the 1993 election. The third cohabitation was a more serious test on the institutionalization of the hybrid regime. Not only was it longer but also, contrastingly, it was brought about by President Chirac's strategic choice to dissolve the AN early. It was precisely the fear of more cohabitation that became one of the motivating forces to reduce the length of the presidential term.

The reduction of the presidential mandate from seven to five years was first discussed in the 1970s during Pompidou's presidency, but it finally came back up in 2000 under the leadership of former president Valery Giscard d'Estaing. Lionel Jospin, then socialist PM, soon joined the rank of sponsors, as well as a number of constitutional scholars who deemed the initiative necessary to combat cohabitation and strengthen the institution of the presidency. President Chirac, who at the beginning was opposed to the idea, eventually rallied behind it given its popular appeal. In its core, the reduction of the term was another mechanism to restore the "Gaullist operation" of the Fifth Republic (Grunberg 2003).

There have been other "minor" changes that have influenced how the electoral system works: notably, the adjustment of the electoral calendar and the introduction of party primaries as means for candidate selection for the major establishment parties.

In 2002, in a strategic move, Lionel Jospin, then socialist PM, in cohabitation with the Union pour un Mouvement Populaire's (UMP's) President Jacques Chirac, decided to stack the deck in his favor for the upcoming presidential race of that same year. He did so by passing a law to reverse the electoral calendar so that presidential elections, which now matched in term the legislative (due to the new five-year mandate), would come four weeks ahead of the parliamentary elections (Jerome, Jerome-Speziari, and Lewis-Beck 2003). Although Jospin did not make it to the presidency (or even to the second round!), his actions initiated a new era of sequenced national elections—legislative following presidential elections—that has unequivocally impacted the functioning of the entire system.

Party primaries began to be used as mechanisms for candidate selection only recently. In 2006, the Socialist Party (PS) decided to open the selection of their future nominee to their party members, a decision that provoked great interest in voters and that eventually, with the help of the media and opinion polls, made this closed party primary into a national political event. Soon after Ségolène Royal's defeat, the PS decided to open the primary to the larger citizenry, thus deemed a "citizen's primary," as a democratizing solution to the party's internal scandals (Grunberg 2015). The success of the PS's open primary (which yielded François Hollande as winner after two rounds and with 56.6 percent of the vote) inspired the UMP to emulate the practice for their 2017 candidacy.

Taken together, all these changes have had three important outcomes. First, there has been an increased "presidentialization" of the French regime whereby the vote for the president now inaugurates the process of power allocation, dominates the electoral campaign, and impacts the legislative race; political parties have become electoral vehicles for the presidential aspirations of their leaders, and regardless of the absence of a constitutional mandate to do so, presidents frequently remove and replace prime ministers (Machin 1989; Samuels and Shugart 2010). *Ceteris paribus*, the balancing act of the hybrid semipresidential regime is clearly leaning to the president's side. Second, the importance of candidates and their image have contributed to an increase in personalization of the electoral arena. The use of primaries for candidate selection, the introduction of candidate debates as part of the campaigns (and, starting in 2017, even in between rounds of the primary race), and the emphasis on candidates' personal qualities and charisma and less on their ideological stances are examples of this phenomenon.

Finally, the timing of elections has become ever more relevant (Dupoirier and Sauger 2010). Since the reduction of the presidential term and the reversal of the election calendar, cohabitation has been rendered less likely both because of effects of presidential coattails and because the same mandate length and sequencing of elections have reduced the opportunity for "midterm elections" to serve as sanctioning mechanisms to the president (Elgie 2009, 259). Yet just like the electoral system, these changes are not written in stone—or in the constitution—and, under exceptional circumstances, namely, death or resignation of the president, the two terms (i.e., presidential and legislative) may become misaligned once again, giving French citizens renewed opportunity to use their vote to divide the government and activate the parliamentary component of the regime.[5] Though not theoretically impossible, cohabitation is extremely unlikely.

## Intended and Unintended Consequences of Electoral Rules in France

Electoral systems may be studied in a two-pronged manner: by focusing on the *psychological* impact of electoral rules (i.e., how they affect the voters and the candidates that apply them) and by analyzing their *mechanical* effect (i.e., how votes translate into seats).

Maurice Duverger was the first to identify that a two-round majority system, like PR, would tend to produce multipartism (Duverger 1951), the reason being that parties have limited incentives to coalesce during the first round. Instead, they can wait and hold off on any deal making and simply "stand and be counted" (Elgie 2005). However, more recent research on the consequences of electoral rules suggests that there is a lot more room for strategic behavior than Duverger originally thought of. Namely, in a majority runoff system, where only the top two candidates advance to the second round, there are in fact two winners from round one. Applying the M + 1 rule, a total number of three viable candidates exist as strategic voting will kick in from the first round (Shugart and Taagepera 1994; Cox 1997, 1999). Yet strategic voting, *vote utile*, is definitely more complicated under a two-round (TR) system. On one hand, supporters of a first-place candidate may be willing to strategically desert their preferred choice for a weaker, less desired one if they believe that their first choice is surely getting to the next round and the race for second place is close and they have incentives to sway the balance of the second-place race in a particular direction.[6] On the other hand, voters require more information under these particular rules and engaging in strategic behavior entails greater risks (i.e., miscalculation of your preferred candidate's actual support à la Jospin in 2002, of the closeness of each of the races, etc.). See Table 32.2 for an illustration of these risks.

Lastly, there are certain particular types of electors that would prevent the TR rules from reducing the number of viable candidates, namely, noninstrumental voters who care about other things beyond winning that particular election (i.e., signaling their discontent to establishment parties, increasing the potential bargaining power of their ideal candidate even if he or she is nonviable, etc.). Although the drafters of the French Fifth Republic sought to create electoral mechanisms that would produce majorities and reduce fragmentation, it is not always a given that the two-round rules will readily facilitate such conditions.

Another important aspect of the psychological effect of the electoral system on party elites pertains to the choice to enter a race (or not) and to the building and timing of alliances. The TR, majority-plurality system makes pre-electoral alliances a common phenomenon. Research has shown that in every election since 1962, a coalition has been present (Blais and Loewen 2009). A study of twenty-two countries from 1946 to 1988 revealed that two-party pre-electoral alliances formed in 5.3 percent of the cases, while the frequency for France was 22.5 percent (Golder 2006). In fact, the typical pattern of competition—deemed bipolar multipartism (Duverger 1986) with two dominant parties—has been to have two distinct ideological blocs (the Left and the Right) with intrabloc competition for the first round and exclusively interbloc contests in the runoff. Since the first round is quite permissive (many candidates enter and receive significant vote shares) and the second round is restrictive (i.e., thresholds), no party can assume that a first-round victory is large enough to guarantee a second-round one (Schlesinger and Schlesinger 2000). So parties that trailed their alliance partners usually stand down, leaving a top-two runoff. However, pre-electoral agreements themselves are more intricate. First, parties do not field candidates in every district; coalition pacts often involve "gentlemen's agreements," whereby formal or informal specification of the candidate who will compete in the second round and the designation of the party to which the seat will be assigned are stipulated. Despite all this bargaining, members of the same party may still defy the pact and run against each other in the same district, usually with one candidate being officially endorsed by the national party and the other one perhaps with the implicit support of the local party (Sauger and Grofman 2016). Although both

**Table 32.2  2002 Presidential Election First- and Second-Round Votes**

| Candidate | Political Party | Total of First-Round Votes | Percentage of First-Round Votes | Total of Second-Round Votes | Percentage of Second-Round Votes |
|---|---|---|---|---|---|
| Bruno Mégret | National Republican Movement (MNR) | 667,043 | 2.34% | | |
| Corinne Lepage | Citizenship, Action, Participation for the 21st Century (CAP21) | 535,875 | 1.88% | | |
| Daniel Gluckstein | Workers Party (PT) | 132,696 | 0.47% | | |
| François Bayrou | Union for French Democracy (UDF) | 1,949,219 | 6.84% | | |
| *Jacques Chirac* | *Rally for the Republic (RPR)* | *5,666,021* | *19.88%* | *25,537,894* | *82.21%* |
| *Jean-Marie Le Pen* | *National Front (FN)* | *4,804,772* | *16.86%* | *5,525,034* | *17.79%* |
| Christiane Taubira | Radical Party of the Left (PRG) | 660,515 | 2.32% | | |
| Jean Saint-Josse | Hunting, Fishing, Nature, Traditions (CPNT) | 1,204,801 | 4.23% | | |
| Noel Mamère | The Greens (les Verts) | 1,495,774 | 5.25% | | |
| Lionel Jospin | Socialist Party (PS) | 4,610,267 | 16.18% | | |
| Christine Boutin | Forum of Social Republicans (FRS) | 339,157 | 1.19% | | |
| Robert Hue | French Communist Party (PCF) | 960,548 | 3.37% | | |
| Jean-Pierre Chevènement | Citizens' Movement (MDC) | 1,518,568 | 5.33% | | |

## Table 32.2 Continued

| Candidate | Political Party | Total of First-Round Votes | Percentage of First-Round Votes | Total of Second-Round Votes | Percentage of Second-Round Votes |
|---|---|---|---|---|---|
| Alain Madelin | Liberal Democracy (DL) | 1,113,551 | 3.91% | | |
| Arlette Laguiller | Workers' Struggle (LO) | 1,630,118 | 5.72% | | |
| Olivier Besançenot | Revolutionary Communist League (LCR) | 1,210,562 | 4.25% | | |
| Abstentions | | 11,700,076 | 28.40% | 8,359,440 | 20.29% |
| Blank or null vote | | 998,401 | 3.38% | 1,769,904 | 5.39% |
| Valid votes | | 28,499,487 | 69.18% | 31,062,928 | 75.41% |
| Total registered voters | | 41,197,964 | 96.62%* | 41,192,272 | 94.61%* |
| Turnout | | 29,497,888 | 71.60% | 32,832,832 | 79.71% |

Table composed with information from the French Interior Ministry. In italics, the second-round contenders; the winner of the race is also bolded.

* Total percentage of valid votes given turnout.

first-round agreements and stand-down pacts matter in France, the latter are the main feature of the system.

Turning to the mechanical effect of electoral rules, Table 32.3 shows that the two-round rules have, indeed, fostered multipartism and penalized smaller parties. On average, the effective number of vote-earning parties has been 5.26, while it has been substantially less for seat-winning parties, at 3.23. The number is reduced due to the coalition-building aspects of the system. The mean effective number of presidential candidates has been 4.55. In terms of disproportionality (the measure of correspondence of votes to seats), Blais and Loewen (2009) have shown that smaller parties are underrepresented and large parties systematically overrepresented, in a similar manner to what happens in first-past-the-post (FPTP) systems, a feature that is to be expected of the TR ballot given its majoritarian principles.

A final example of agent adaptation to two-ballot rules is the rise of differential, party-based strategies to gain power (or party specialization) (Schlesinger and Schlesinger 2000). There are two main approaches to the French electoral system: either pursue vote maximization or work toward the "Goldilocks" "just right" number of votes. Both of them can take two variants given the number of rounds and the role of the given

**Table 32.3** Effective Number of Vote–Earning and Seat–Winning Parties, Effective Number of Presidential Candidates, and Disproportionality Index for the French Fifth Republic

| Election Year | Least Squares Index (LSq) | Effective Number of Vote-Earning Parties ($N_v$) | Effective Number of Seat-Winning Parties ($N_s$) | Effective Number of Presidential Candidates ($N_p$) |
|---|---|---|---|---|
| 1958 | 21.22 | 6.09 | 3.45 | 1.56 |
| 1962 | 14.99 | 4.93 | 3.43 | |
| 1965 | | | | 3.06 |
| 1967 | 10.03 | 4.56 | 3.76 | |
| 1968 | 19.21 | 4.31 | 2.49 | |
| 1969 | | | | 3.32 |
| 1973 | 11.01 | 5.68 | 4.52 | |
| 1974 | | | | 3.14 |
| 1978 | 6.57 | 5.08 | 4.20 | |
| 1981 | 16.04 | 4.13 | 2.68 | 4.85 |
| 1986* | 7.23 | 4.65 | 3.90 | |
| 1988 | 11.84 | 4.40 | 3.07 | 4.74 |
| 1993 | 25.25 | 6.89 | 2.86 | |
| 1995 | | | | 5.94 |
| 1997 | 17.69 | 6.56 | 3.54 | |
| 2002 | 21.95 | 5.22 | 2.26 | 8.66 |
| 2007 | 13.58 | 4.32 | 2.49 | 4.70 |
| 2012 | 17.66 | 5.27 | 2.83 | 4.77 |
| 2017 | 21.12 | 6.82 | 3.00 | 5.32 |
| Mean: | 15.69 | 5.26 | 3.23 | 4.55 |

Table compiled with information from Michael Gallagher, 2017. Election indices dataset at http://www.tcd.ie/Political_Science/staff/michael_gallagher/ElSystems/index.php, accessed February 15, 2017. Except for $N_p$, which was based on Blais and Loewen (2009) and complemented with my own calculations for the 1958 and 2012 elections. Averages are calculated on first-round votes and, as Gallagher points out, the numbers are probably slight underestimations given the usual practice of official sources to lump together independents and very minor parties under larger groups labeled "*Divers droite*" or "*Divers Gauche*," which I translated in Tables 32.5 and 32.7 as "Other Right/Left."

* 1986 election occurred under a different electoral system, namely, department-list PR.

political party that applies it in the larger party system. First-round vote maximization was, historically, the preferred strategy of the Gaullist party, the RPR, and continues to be used by the largest right-wing force today, the Republicans (Les Républicans [LR]).[7] Second-round vote maximization (or the "party as umbrella") has been the Socialists' favorite electoral maneuver, especially since it allowed them to gain the presidency in 1981; the "Goldilocks" or doing well enough on both rounds has been the choice of the Union for French Democracy (UDF) and other centrist parties, and finally, doing well enough on either round is the classic "fringe party" option, most often portrayed by the Communist Party (PCF) but perhaps more adeptly lately by the National Front (FN) (Schlesinger and Schlesinger 1990).[8]

The French electoral system of the Fifth Republic has performed its primary function of stabilizing the party system; alternating majorities have been the norm and not the exception. And yet, the actual names/labels and even the identities of the major parties in France have changed over time as their electoral fortunes have fluctuated. Following Duverger, the French party system has been characterized as bipolar multipartism, a dualism of forces split over ideological lines with two dominant parties. Starting from the *quadrille bipolaire* in the 1960s (which contrasted two left-wing forces, the PS [main party] and the PCF on one side to the right-wing forces of the Gaullists [RPR, main party] and the centrists [UDF]), these four main parties have continuously dominated the political scene. The 1980s brought along two new actors to the party scene: the Greens on the left side of the spectrum and the FN on the extreme right. Gradually, these two latecomers have carved out a niche for themselves in the electoral and party arenas, to the point that the Greens have now replaced the PCF as the major coalition partner of the Socialists and the FN have become, perhaps now more than ever, a serious contender for the title of "third major party" in the system.

There are a series of structural changes—such as social change, loosening of bonds among former homogeneous groups, decline of party identification, value change, rise of new issue dimensions, greater permeability of the insider/outsider divide, and crisis of the "traditional" political party—that have impacted all electoral arenas in contemporary democracies (Mair, Müller, and Plasser 2004). France has been fertile ground for all of them. Globalization and value change, a reconfiguration of the economic structures (new emphasis on service sector in detriment of the traditional sectors), an aging population, and increased diversity of incoming immigrant flows (from South and East European to African and Asian populations) have all had an impact on the political attitudes of French citizens. Although the classic explanatory variables (class, religion, etc.) of the vote continue to tell part of the story, they are no longer necessary and sufficient conditions to explain why French voters are currently reporting across all major national and European surveys increased dissatisfaction with representative democracy, decreased interest in politics, and a lack of identification with left and right political cleavage (Lewis-Beck 1998; Mayer 2003).

To evaluate the impact of institutional design on the actual operation of the French electoral system, let's look at the most recent elections across different levels of aggregation: first-order elections (presidential and legislative of 2012) and second-order elections (regional of 2014 and municipal of 2015) (Reif and Schmitt 1980).

# Two Examples of "First Order" Processes: The 2012 National Elections

Both electoral processes took place in a context of continued economic crisis that was not unexpected: every French election since 1981 has been impacted by economic and social crises. Traditional economic and social concerns were at the top of voters' minds, namely, unemployment, increasing purchasing power, stimulating growth, security, and immigration and refugees. Perhaps the only new issue was the irruption of Europe and the European Union in the national discourse, as a result of the European sovereign crisis (Goodliffe and Brizzi 2015, 4–5).

## Presidential Elections of 2012

François Hollande ran a campaign focused on a "return to normalcy," which was perfectly in tune with the citizens' need to put behind them the "excesses" and boisterous nature of the government of Nicolas Sarkozy, who, having failed on his promises to prosperity, was denied a second mandate. Table 32.4 shows that, despite the alternation, the Socialist victory was far from a landslide; the National Front had reappeared in full force (17.90 percent), while Bayrou's MoDem almost disappeared (9.13 percent). For the first time since 1981, a candidate supported by the PCF (Mélenchon of the Left Front) managed to garner double-digit results and to outperform the remaining radical left candidates (Arthau and Poutou). In fact, the successes of the FN and the Left Front (FG) explain why the combined vote of the establishment parties (PS, Greens, MoDem, and UMP) eroded by over 8 percentage points from the 2007 level (75.6 percent to 67.25 percent). The Greens performed particularly poorly in the presidential race (only 2.31 percent of the vote), but their fate, as will be seen later in the chapter, was not sealed because of their ability to strike legislative deals with the PS. Despite being the first incumbent to trail on the first round, Sarkozy's campaigning style and charisma contributed to tightening the race, and his decision to keep his campaign focused on the same issues that got him to power in 2007 (i.e., immigration, security, and national identity) also allowed him to keep the shape of his voter coalition almost intact (Gougou and Labouret 2013).

## Legislative Elections of 2012

The 2012 election to the AN was another "honeymoon election" (Shugart 1995). The Socialists managed to obtain an absolute majority of seats, see Table 32.5, due to the

## Table 32.4  2012 Presidential Election Results First and Second Round

| Candidate | Political Party | Total of First-Round Votes | Percentage of First-Round Votes | Total of Second-Round Votes | Percentage of Second-Round Votes |
|---|---|---|---|---|---|
| Eva Joly | Europe-Ecology–the Greens (EELV) | 828,345 | 2.31% | | |
| Marine Le Pen | National Front (FN) | 6,421,426 | 17.90% | | |
| *Nicolas Sarkozy* | *Union for a Popular Movement (UMP)* | *9,753,629* | *27.18%* | *16,860,685* | *48.36%* |
| Jean-Luc Mélenchon | Left Front (FG) | 3,984,822 | 11.10% | | |
| Philippe Poutou | New Anticapitalist Party (NPA) | 411,160 | 1.15% | | |
| Nathalie Arthaud | Workers' Struggle (LO) | 202,548 | 0.56% | | |
| Jacques Cheminade | Solidarity and Progress (SP) | 89,545 | 0.25% | | |
| François Bayrou | Democratic Movement (MoDem) | 3,275,122 | 9.13% | | |
| Nicolas Dupont-Aignan | Republic Arise (DLR) | 643,907 | 1.79% | | |
| ***François Hollande*** | ***Socialist Party (PS)*** | ***10,272,705*** | ***28.63%*** | ***18,000,668*** | ***51.64%*** |
| Abstentions | | 9,444,143 | 20.52% | 9,049,998 | 19.65% |
| Blank or null vote | | 701,190 | 1.52% | 2,154,956 | 4.68% |
| Valid votes | | 35,883,209 | 77.96% | 34,861,353 | 75.68% |
| Total registered voters | | 46,028,542 | 98.08%* | 46,066,307 | 94.18%* |
| Turnout | | 36,584,399 | 79.48% | 37,016,309 | 80,35% |

Table composed with information from the French Interior Ministry. In italics, the second-round contenders; the winner of the race is also bolded.

* Total percentage of valid votes given turnout.

## Table 32.5  2012 Legislative Election Results First and Second Round

| Political Party | Votes First Round | % Valid Votes First Round | Elected First Round | Votes Second Round | % Valid Votes Second Round | Elected Second Round |
|---|---|---|---|---|---|---|
| Extreme Left (EXG) | 253,386 | 0.98 | | | | |
| Left Front (FG) | 1,793,192 | 6.91 | | 249,498 | 1.08 | 10 |
| *Socialists (PS)* | *7,618,326* | *29.35* | *22* | *9,420,889* | *40.91* | *258* |
| Left Radicals (RDG) | 428,898 | 1.65 | 1 | 538,331 | 2.34 | 11 |
| Other Left (DVG) | 881,555 | 3.40 | 1 | 709,395 | 3.08 | 21 |
| Europe-Ecology–the Greens (VEC) | 1,418,264 | 5.46 | 1 | 829,036 | 3.60 | 16 |
| Regionalists (REG) | 145,809 | 0.56 | | 135,312 | 0.59 | 2 |
| Ecologiste (ECO) | 249,068 | 0.96 | | | | |
| Autres (AUT) | 133,752 | 0.52 | | | | |
| Centre pour la France (CEN) | 458,098 | 1.77 | | 113,196 | 0.49 | 2 |
| Centrist Alliance (ALLI) | 156,026 | 0.60 | | 123,132 | 0.53 | 2 |
| Radical Party (PRV) | 321,124 | 1.24 | | 311,199 | 1.35 | 6 |
| New Centre (NCE) | 569,897 | 2.20 | 1 | 568,319 | 2.47 | 11 |
| Union for a Popular Movement (UMP) | 7,037,268 | 27.12 | 9 | 8,740,628 | 37.95 | 185 |
| Other Right (DVD) | 910,034 | 3.51 | 1 | 417,940 | 1.81 | 14 |
| National Front (FN) | 3,528,663 | 13.60 | | 842,695 | 3.66 | 2 |
| Extreme Right (EXD) | 49,499 | 0.19 | | 29,738 | 0.13 | 1 |
| Abstentions | 19,712,978 | 42.78 | | 19,281,162 | 44.60 | |
| Blank or null vote | 416,267 | 0.90 | | 923,178 | 2.14 | |
| Valid votes | 25,952,859 | 56.32 | | 23,029,308 | 53.27 | |
| Total registered voters | 46,082,104 | 98.42* | | 23,952,486 | 96.15* | |
| Turnout | 57.22% | | | 55.40% | | 577 Deputés |

Table composed with information from the French Interior Ministry. In italics and bolded, winning party.

* Total percentage of valid votes given turnout.

combination of voters' reluctance to go back to cohabitation and the momentum built by Hollande's victory four weeks earlier.

The legislative arena has never been an auspicious realm of competition for minor parties. To do well in them, political parties must possess a well-anchored local power base and a series of *notables* who can mobilize supporters and can eventually become instrumental in facilitating alliances (Evans and Ivaldi 2005). As discussed previously, the logic of coalition building is further complicated by the strategy specialization of the different parties. Smaller parties did not have it any easier in 2012, despite their strong showing in the previous national elections. Although survey data showed that UMP sympathizers were now favorable to engaging in alliances with the FN, none was reached. So, after a relatively strong showing (13.60 percent of the vote), the FN only obtained two seats and Marine Le Pen narrowly missed her chance to become an MP. Contrastingly, due to a pre-election coalition pact with a major party, the Greens managed to elect sixteen deputies, gain two ministerial posts, and, for the first time, have their very own parliamentary group given a series of good results obtained in second-order elections.[9] The successful performance of Mélenchon in the presidential race was clouded by a poor showing in the legislative realm, where only ten MPs were elected for his Left Front and he himself was defeated in Marine Le Pen's constituency. MoDem's demise (under the new name Center for France, CEN) was reconfirmed in the legislative results as it failed to reach a meager 2 percent of the vote; despite fielding four hundred candidates in the first round, only seven made it to the second where only two MPs got elected, and Bayrou himself lost his seat in Pau (Gougou and Labouret 2013). The varying fates of these four parties (Greens, MoDem, FN, and FG) highlight the impact of the electoral system on which parties get represented and which do not: the moral of the story is that pre-electoral coalitions are essential.

# "Second Order" Elections: Local Elections in France

Second-order elections are, by definition, secondary or less relevant than their first-order counterparts. Since they elicit less interest in the general population and also in the news cycle, they are ideal battlegrounds for minor political actors looking to break in and leave a mark, or use as leverage in coalition-building negotiations. Second-order elections are also seen as protest mechanisms since citizens will use them to cast sanction votes toward incumbent governments. The 2014–15 second-order results illustrate quite well this latter usage but perhaps more generally toward the establishment parties.

Local elections in France are difficult to interpret as a whole because different tracks often happen simultaneously (municipal and cantonal, for instance) and the electoral rules applied often change (see Table 32.1) depending on population size at the electoral constituency level (Grunberg 2001). The 2014 municipal and 2015 regional elections resulted in a very clear sanction vote toward the government. In the wake of the municipal ballot, the Left lost 196 municipalities of more 9,000 inhabitants (where 60 had a population larger than 30,000) and the UMP and its new allies (namely, Union of the Right) had a net gain of 163 municipalities (Foucault 2014).

In addition, local elections have demonstrated the increased electoral capacity of some minor parties—at least on the first round and most notably the National Front—even though, in the end, the majoritarian and coalition-building aspects of the two-round ballot denied them what would have been extraordinary successes.[10] Historically, local elections have been the hardest for the FN and its least successful electoral realm (gathering only about 10 percent of the vote). Yet since 2011, Marine Le Pen has sought a policy of "local implantation." The 2015 results, a tripling of the FN's score on the first round in the regional ballot (28 percent), show that the FN's strategy may be paying off and that if they are not yet in position to become a "*local* Front," they are well situated to become kingmakers in the near future (Perrineau 2014).

# Party System Changes and Confirmed Trends in the 2017 Presidential and Legislative Elections

The 2017 campaign cycle marked a set of firsts: the first time that three political parties used primary elections as means to select their presidential candidates (namely, the PS, the Greens, and the Republicans). For both traditional dominant parties, the Republicans (LR) and the Socialists (PS), the primaries backfired and exposed their weaknesses and internal factionalism by selecting more extreme candidates—François Fillon and Benoît Hamon, respectively. Overall, it was a tumultuous campaign plagued by corruption scandals (Fillon on nepotism, Le Pen on misuse of EU funds), accusations of cyber-attacks (against Macron) and of foreign interventions (Russia), and even a terrorist attack three days before the first ballot. Similarly, the presidential election also set several new records. Two unconventional candidates—Marine Le Pen for the National Front and Emmanuel Macron from the one-year-old En Marche—made it to the second round.[11] It was also the first race in which the incumbent president did not stand for re-election. As Table 32.6 illustrates, this election had the largest second-round abstention rate (25.4 percent) and marked the first time that participation failed to increase between the two rounds since 1969, as well as a record-breaking rise in the blank or spoiled vote rate, surpassing four million voters (11.52 percent). Certain other party system trends were confirmed in the final results, namely, the unpopularity of the last two presidents given their inability to respond to societal demands and stimulate economic growth; the increasing popular disenchantment with political elites evidenced not only in the preponderance of an antisystem rhetoric in all presidential candidacies but also in the decrease of vote share for traditional parties at the hands of more radical options

### Table 32.6  2017 Presidential Election Results First and Second Round

| Candidate | Political Party | Total of First-Round Votes | Percentage of First-Round Votes | Total of Second-Round Votes | Percentage of Second-Round Votes |
|---|---|---|---|---|---|
| Benoît Hamon | Socialist Party (PS) | 2,291,565 | 6.36% | | |
| *Marine Le Pen* | *National Front (FN)* | *7,679,493* | *21.30%* | *10,638,475* | *33.90%* |
| François Fillon | The Republicans (LR) | 7,213,797 | 20.01% | | |
| Jean-Luc Mélenchon | Unsubmissive France (FI) | 7,060,885 | 19.58% | | |
| Philippe Poutou | New Anticapitalist Party (NPA) | 394,582 | 1.09% | | |
| Nathalie Arthaud | Workers' Struggle (LO) | 232,428 | 0.64% | | |
| Jacques Cheminade | Solidarity and Progress (SP) | 65,598 | 0.18% | | |
| Jean Lassalle | Democratic Movement (MoDem) | 435,365 | 1.21% | | |
| Nicolas Dupont-Aignan | Republic Arise (DLR) | 1,695,186 | 4.70% | | |
| ***Emmanuel Macron*** | ***Socialist Party (PS)*** | ***8,657,326*** | ***24.01 %*** | ***20,743,128*** | ***66.10%*** |
| François Asselineau | Popular Republican Union (UPR) | 332,588 | 0.92% | | |
| Abstentions | | 10,577,572 | 22.23% | 12,101,366 | 25.44 % |
| Blank vote | | 659,302 | 1.39% | 3,021,499 | 8.52% |
| Null vote | | 285,431 | 0.60% | 1,064,225 | 2.24% |
| Valid votes | | 36,058,813 | 75.78% | 31,381,603 | 65.97 % |
| Total registered voters | | 47,581,118 | 97.45%* | 47,568,693 | 88.48%* |
| Turnout | | 37,003,546 | 77.77 % | 35,467,327 | 74.56 % |

Table composed with information from the French Interior Ministry. In italics, the second-round contenders; the winner of the race is also bolded.

* Total percentage of valid votes given turnout.

(Mélenchon's FI[12] got almost 20 percent); and above all, the "electoral breakthrough" of the FN, which obtained a little under 34 percent (almost 11 million votes!) in the second round. But the single most important party system change was the transformation of the FN from a fringe, pariah party into a mainstream one. The former *cordon sanitaire* that prevented mainstream parties from even considering much less forming alliances with the FN was broken this time around (by a former Gaullist, Nicolas Dupont-Aignan, after the first-round ballot).

The 2017 presidential results further reinforced the actual operation of the TR, majority-runoff system that allowed Emmanuel Macron, a newcomer, to win the presidency given not only first-round fragmentation (eleven candidates) and the obliteration of the candidates from both main parties (the moderate Left and Right) but also the creation of an informal "Republican front" in the second round—weaker than the 2002 version and with the notable self-exclusion of the radical forces—which barred Marine Le Pen, still devoid of significant allies, from having a real shot at victory.[13]

Similarly, the 2017 legislative ballot showed the resilience of the French electoral system by putting it to a harsher test in a set of unique circumstances: a leading centrist party (Macron's newly formed La République En Marche, or REM) flanked by severely weakened traditional parties on either side of the ideological spectrum (PS and LR). Despite the fact that the REM is a new creation and that it fielded political novices in about two hundred constituencies, the honeymoon cycle in conjunction with the majority-plurality rule awarded the president's party an overwhelming majority of seats (308 out of 577 as shown in Table 32.7). It is thus a powerful example of "presidential-ization" (Samuels and Shugart 2010), whereby a popular president dominates the party system, in this case with a party formed specifically to back Macron.

Such a large majority is remarkable, given that the REM obtained only around 28 percent of the votes in the first round. This figure was already greater than Macron himself obtained in his own first round, consistent with the boost offered by honeymoon elections; the percentage rises to the low thirties when small first-round allies are included. In the second round, the REM obtained 43 percent of the votes. With these figures, we see a profound demonstration of how two-round majority works, turning a relatively small initial voting plurality into a larger one after withdrawals of trailing candidates and finally into a clear majority of seats.[14] Thus, the 2017 result dramatically demonstrates the disproportionality and expected majoritarian propensities of the system. In the aftermath of the 2017 elections, France finds itself in an unprecedented situation of a single dominant center party in government and no solid opposition on either side because of the collapse of the Socialist Left and the decline of the traditional Right.

# Conclusion

The French electoral system of the Fifth Republic has been remarkably stable. For many decades now scholars have been stressing the system's permanence and ability to survive, in spite of the challenges, due to the fact that the main political actors "have mastered the two-round rules" (Schlesinger and Schlesinger 2000). This continues to be true today, but it differs in subtle ways in the 2017 outcome compared to most elections of the Fifth Republic. Since the adoption of direct election of the president and the

## Table 32.7 2017 Legislative Election Results First and Second Round

| Political Party | Votes First Round | % Valid Votes First Round | Elected First Round | Votes Second Round | % Valid Votes Second Round | Elected Second Round |
|---|---|---|---|---|---|---|
| Extreme Left (EXG) | 175,214 | 0.77% | | | | |
| Communist Party (COM) | 615,487 | 2.72% | | 217,833 | 1.20% | 10 |
| Unsubmissive France (FI) | 2,497,622 | 11.03% | | 883,573 | 4.86% | 17 |
| Socialists (SOC) | 1,685,677 | 7.44% | | 1,032,842 | 5.68% | 30 |
| Left Radicals (RDG) | 106,311 | 0.47% | | 64,860 | 0.36% | 3 |
| Other Left (DVG) | 362,281 | 1.60% | 1 | 263,488 | 1.45% | 12 |
| Ecologists (ECO) | 973,527 | 4.30% | | 23,197 | 0.13% | 1 |
| Others (DIV) | 500,309 | 2.21% | | 100,574 | 0.55% | 3 |
| Regionalists (REG) | 204,049 | 0.90% | | 137,490 | 0.76% | 5 |
| *The Republic Onwards (REM)* | *6,391,269* | *28.21%* | *2* | *7,826,245* | *43.06%* | *308* |
| Democratic Movement (MDM) | 932,227 | 4.12% | | 1,100,656 | 6.06% | 42 |
| Union for Democrats and Independents (UDI) | 687,225 | 3.03% | 1 | 551,784 | 3.04% | 18 |
| The Republicans (LR) | 3,573,427 | 15.77% | | 4,040,203 | 22.23% | 112 |
| Other right (DVD) | 625,345 | 2.76% | | 306,074 | 1.68% | 6 |
| France Arise (DLF) | 265,420 | 1.17% | | 17,344 | 0.10% | 1 |
| National Front (FN) | 2,990,454 | 13.20% | | 1,590,869 | 8.75% | 8 |
| Extreme right (EXD) | 68,320 | 0.30% | | 19,034 | 0.10% | 1 |
| Abstentions | 24,403,480 | 51.30% | | 27,128,488 | 57.36% | |
| Blank vote | 357,018 | 0.75% | | 1,409,784 | 2.98% | |
| Null vote | 156,326 | 0.33% | | 578,765 | 1.22% | |
| Valid votes | 22,654,164 | 47.62% | | 18,176,066 | 38.43% | |
| Total registered voters | 47,570,988 | 97.78[*] | | 47,293,103 | 90.14[*] | |
| Turnout | 23,167,508 | 48.70% | | 20,164,615 | 42.64% | 577 Deputés |

Table composed with information from the French Interior Ministry. In italics and bolded, majority party.

[*] Total percentage of valid votes given turnout.

two-round majority-plurality election of the National Assembly, France had developed a "textbook" case of bipolar multipartism. That is, just as Duverger (1986) claimed in his retrospective on the "law" that bears his name, the majoritarian nature of the two-round system in single-seat districts had encouraged two major blocs, but each bloc had various distinct parties jockeying for strength in the first-round contests. The 2017 election result continues to show the majoritarian element as a strong feature of the electoral system but reminds us that the precise alignment of the party system can shift with political context. The majority supporting Macron is of the ideological center, and thus there is no single main opposition bloc. Instead, Macron's REM party faced in the run-offs a candidate of the traditional Right in some districts, of the Socialists in others, and of Mélenchon's Far Left or Le Pen's National Front in still others.[15] In the absence of a coherent second bloc opposed to the winner, the system's impact was even more majoritarian, and the newly elected president ended up with a single-party majority despite the fact that his party literally recruited many of its candidates only after his own election a month earlier.

The current French electoral system has seen the consolidation of De Gaulle's original vision for France: a strong presidency, increased governing capacity, and a peaceful transition of power between left and right political forces. The French Fifth Republic has witnessed and survived through erstwhile unimaginable scenarios (the rise of the PCF as relevant actor, three Socialist presidencies, the qualification to the second round of a fringe political actor in 2002 and 2017) and has come out of these challenges stronger (Grunberg 2007). Nonetheless, there have been certain allegedly minor institutional changes that have taken place in the course of time and that have, through a blend of intended institutional design and agent adaptation to those changes, seriously impacted the functioning of the system such as term reduction, the institution of party primaries, and the reversal of the electoral calendar.

It would be risky to claim that the current electoral rules are here to stay,[16] especially since they are not inscribed in the constitution. And yet, most research on electoral reform states that changes to the electoral system happen only when two main conditions are met, namely, that the electoral arena has itself undergone transformations (i.e., potentially new actors/political cleavages have arisen) and the main/traditional political actors, fearful of losing their benefits and access to power, have enough incentives and, still, the necessary political capital to go through the reform process (Boix 1999). Although the first condition is closer to having been met, the second one is much less clear given that all major players seem to have adapted to and mastered the current rules of the game and that even the most recent newcomer to the political scene, Emmanuel Macron, has already benefited from the prevalent electoral system.

## NOTES

1. Since 1789, five of France's eleven political systems have been republics. The remaining six were three monarchies, two empires, and one fascist puppet state. See (Safran 2009).

2. "It is better to have a bad method than none at all": Charles de Gaulle, *The Edge of the Sword* (my translation).
3. Campbell's historical review set the record of the longest-lasting electoral system in France since 1789 in thirty consecutive years (1889–1919, during the Third Republic), followed by eighteen years (1831–1848 and 1852–1870). For the "remaining 103 years, no system has been used for as long as twelve years before being considerably changed or completely discarded," p. 17. By my count, the new runner-up would be the French Fifth's latest stretch of twenty-nine consecutive years under the same electoral system (1988–2017), followed closely by twenty-four consecutive years (1962–1986). Important to note is that these counts focus on the rules used for presidential and legislative elections only. The year 1988 marked the return to two-round majority-plurality rule at the National Assembly elections after a two-year experiment with PR (see later).
4. Originally, the number of presidential endorsements was set low (one hundred endorsements per presidential candidate), but according to the Conseil Constitutionnel, the first three direct presidential elections (1965, 1969, and 1974) revealed the organizational problems of elections with a multiplicity of candidates (six in 1965, seven in 1969, and twelve in 1974), and soon after, a reform to the organic law was introduced (1976) with the current requirement of five hundred signatures from at least thirty different departments or overseas territories (with a maximum of fifty signatures per department and only a tenth possible from overseas).
5. Granted, a new president in such conditions could dissolve the assembly and re-establish the honeymoon pattern in the hopes of achieving a more auspicious legislature.
6. Most likely to further guarantee the victory of their most preferred candidate in the second round. See (Cox 1997), 129–130.
7. RPR: Rassemblement pour la France was the name used by the Gaullist party since 1976. In 2002, the UMP (Union pour un Mouvement Populaire) substituted it. Since 2015, they have been called Les Républicains (LR).
8. The Schlesingers came up with a typology of parties given these specialized strategies to compete in a two-ballot system: namely, primary party (first-round vote maximization), secondary party (second-round vote maximization), dual electoral party (just enough in both rounds), and marginal party (just enough in either round).
9. PS and the Greens signed a pre-electoral agreement (*contrat de mandature*) in November of 2011 that, besides joint programmatic commitments (in terms of immigration, globalization, economic model, and environmental issues, among other topics), included the written ad hoc compromise for the legislative elections involving sixty electoral districts where they would endorse one another in an effort to guarantee a parliamentary group for the Greens. See http://www.lemonde.fr/politique/article/2011/11/16/lesprincipauxpoints-delaccordpseelv_1604266_823448.html.
10. http://www.lemonde.fr/elections-regionales-2015/article/2015/12/14/le-front-national-bute-une-fois-de-plus-sur-l-obstacle-du-second-tour_4831226_4640869.html.
11. Marine Le Pen has had a long career in politics; she was first elected as a regional councilor in 1998, has been an MEP (Member of the European Parliament) since 2004, and has been president of her party since 2011 (a member since 1986). On the other hand, Emmanuel Macron was a member of the PS from 2006 to 2009, had a senior role in Hollande's staff from 2012 to 2014, and became minister of economy, industry, and finance during Vall's second cabinet (Valls II) in 2014.
12. La France Insoumise (Unsubmissive France).

13. http://www.liberation.fr/politiques/2017/04/23/second-tour-qui-soutient-qui_1564799.
14. By comparison, in the 2012 National Assembly election the PS obtained 29.35 percent of the vote in the first round. For the second round, it went on to garner 40.91 percent of the vote and 258 seats. Unlike with Macron, its assembly majority depended on its alliance partners (295 seats for the "Socialist, Republican, and Citizen" coalition). If we consider allies for Macron, his legislative majority increases to 350 seats (with the 42 seats of MoDem). See http://www.huffingtonpost.fr/2015/01/26/ps-majorite-absolue-assemblee-deux-ans-demi _n_6545608.html and https://www.washingtonpost.com/news/monkey-cage/wp/2017 /06/20/emmanuel-macron-just-won-a-majority-in-frances-national-assembly-here-is- why-it-matters/?utm_term=.45f942fa15e9.
15. In 2017, there were 110 FN candidates in the second round, versus only 61 in 2012.
16. During his first speech to Congress in July, at Versailles, President Macron claimed that he will seek to introduce "some element of proportionality" to the legislative ballot so that "all political sensibilities may be represented" in the larger context of major institutional reforms that he is committed to undertake to transform France. See http://www .lemonde.fr/politique/article/2017/07/03/proportionnelle-discours-annuel-levee- de-l-etat-d-urgence-les-annonces-d-emmanuel-macron-devant-le-congres_5154976 _823448.html.

## REFERENCES

Blais, André, and Peter John Loewen. "The French Electoral System and its Effects." *West European Politics* 32, no. 2 (2009): 345–359.
Boix, Carles. "Setting the Rules of the Game: The Choice of Electoral Systems in Advanced Democracies." *American Political Science Review* 93, no. 3 (1999): 609–624.
Campbell, Peter. *French Electoral Systems since 1789*. Hamden, CT: Archon Books, 1965.
Cox, Gary. "Electoral Rules and Electoral Coordination." *Annual Review of Political Science* 2 (1999): 16.
Cox, Gary W. *Making Votes Count*. Cambridge: Cambridge University Press, 1997.
Dupoirier, Elisabeth, and Nicolas Sauger. "Four Rounds in a Row: The Impact of Presidential Election Outcomes on Legislative Elections in France." *French Politics* 8 (2010): 21–41.
Duverger, Maurice. *Les Partis Politiques*. Paris: Librarie Armand Colin, 1951.
Duverger, Maurice. "A New Political System Model: Semi-Presidential Government." *European Journal of Political Research* 8 (1980): 165–187.
Duverger, Maurice. "Duverger's Law: Forty Years Later." In *Electoral Laws and Their Political Consequences*, edited by B. Grofman, and A. Lijphart. New York: Agathon Press, 1986, 69–84.
Elgie, Robert. "France: Stacking the Deck." In *The Politics of Electoral Systems*, edited by M. Gallagher and P. Mitchell, 119–136. Oxford: Oxford University Press, 2005.
Elgie, Robert. "Varieties of Semi-Presidentialism and Their Impact on Nascent Democracies." *Taiwan Journal of Democracy* 3, no. 2 (2007): 53–71.
Elgie, Robert. "Duverger, Semi-Presidentialism and the Supposed French Archetype." *West European Politics* 32, no. 2 (2009): 248–267.
Elgie, Robert, and Howard Machin. "France: The Limits of Prime-Ministerial Government in a Semi-Presidential System." *West European Politics* 14, no. 2 (1991): 17.

Evans, Jocelyn, and Gilles Ivaldi. "An Extremist Autarky: The Systemic Separation of the French Extreme Right." *South European Society & Politics* 10, no. 2 (2005): 351–366.

Foucault, Martial. "Bilan des elections municipales francaises de 2014 dans les villes de plus de 9000 habitants." *Les enjeux*, 6. Centre de la Vie Politique Francaise (CEVIPOF), 2014.

Golder, Sona. "Pre-Electoral Coalition Formation in Parliamentary Democracies." *British Journal of Political Science* 36, no. 2 (2006): 193–212.

Goodliffe, Gabriel, and Riccardo Brizzi, eds. *France after 2012*. New York: Berghahn, 2015.

Gougou, Florent, and Simon Labouret. "Elections in France: Electoral Disorder in a Realignment Era." In *Developments in French Politics*, edited by Alistair Cole, Sophie Meunier, and Vincent Tiberj, 153–169. Basingstoke, Hampshire: Palgrave MacMillan, 2013.

Grosieux, Patrick. "Le 'parrainage' des pretendants a l'election presidentielle: simple formalite juridique?" *Revue Francaise de Droit Constitutionnel* 3, no. 59 (2004): 567–594.

Grossman, Emiliano, and Nicolas Sauger. "The Institutions of the French Republic at 50." *West European Politics* 32, no. 2 (2009): 243–247.

Grunberg, Gérard. "Les élections locales françaises de mars 2001: un échec pour la majorité." *French Politics* 19, no. 3 (2001): 17–31.

Grunberg, Gérard. "Le système politique français après les élections de 2002 en France." *French Politics* 21, no. 3 (2003): 91–106.

Grunberg, Gérard. "Les élections françaises de 2007." *French Politics* 25, no. 3 (2007): 62–73.

Grunberg, Gérard. "The Year of the Rose: The Socialist Victory of 2012." In *France after 2012*, edited by Gabriel Goodliffe and Riccardo Brizzi, 74–87. New York: Berghahn Books, 2015.

Jérôme, Bruno, Véronique Jérôme-Speziari, and Michael S. Lewis-Beck. "Reordering the French Election Calendar." *European Journal of Political Research* 42 (2003): 425–440.

Kerrouche, Eric. "The French Assemblee Nationale: The Case of a Weak Legislature?" *Journal of Legislative Studies* 12, no. 3–4 (2006): 336–365.

Lazardeux, Sebastien G. "The French National Assembly's Oversight of the Executive: Changing Role, Partisanship and Intra-Majority Conflict." *West European Politics* 32, no. 2 (2009): 287–309.

Lewis-Beck, Michael. "Class, Religion and the French Voter: A 'Stalled' Electorate?" *French Politics* 16, no. 2 (1998): 8.

Lijphart, Arend. *Electoral Systems and Party Systems: A Study of Twenty Seven Democracies 1945-1990*. Oxford: Oxford University Press, 1994.

Lijphart, Arend. *Patterns of Democracy*. New Haven, CT: Yale University Press, 1999.

Machin, Howard. "Stages and Dynamics in the Evolution of the French Party System." *West European Politics* 12, no. 4 (1989): 59–81.

Mair, Peter, Wolfgang C. Müller, and Fritz Plasser, eds. *Political Parties and Electoral Change: Party Responses to Electoral Markets*. London: SAGE Publications, 2004.

Mayer, Nonna. "Que reste-t-il du vote de classe? Le cas francais." *Lien social et Politiques* 49 (2003): 101–111.

Perraudeau, Eric. "Le système des partis sous la Ve République." *Pouvoirs* 4, no. 99 (2001): 101–115.

Perrineau, Pascal. "La présence pertubatrice du Front National aux élections municipales." *Les enjeux*, 4. Centre de la Vie Politique Française, 2014.

Poulard, Jean V. "The French Double Executive and the Experience of Cohabitation." *Political Science Quarterly* 105, no. 2 (1990): 243–267.

Powell, G. Bingham, Jr. *Elections as Instruments of Democracy*. New Haven, CT: Yale University Press, 2000.

Reif, Karl, and Hermann Schmitt. "Nine Second Order National Elections: A Conceptual Framework for the Analysis of European Election Results." *European Journal of Political Research* 8, no. 1 (1980): 3–44.

Safran, William. *The French Polity*. New York: Longman, 1998.

Samuels, David J., and Matthew S. Shugart. *Presidents, Parties and Prime Ministers: How the Separation of Powers Affects Party Organization and Behavior*. Cambridge: Cambridge University Press, 2010.

Sauger, Nicolas, and Bernard Grofman. "Partisan Bias and Redistricting in France." *Electoral Studies* 44 (2016): 388–396.

Schlesinger, Joseph A., and Mildred Schlesinger. "The Reaffirmation of a Multiparty system in France." *American Political Science Review* 84, no. 4 (1990): 1077–1101.

Schlesinger, Joseph A., and Mildred S. Schlesinger. "The Stability of the French Party System: The Enduring Impact of the Two-Ballot Electoral Rules." In *How France Votes*, edited by M. S. Lewis-Beck, 130–152. New York: Chatham House, 2000.

Shugart, Matthew, and Rein Taagepera. "Plurality versus Majority Election of Presidents: A Proposal for a 'Double Complement Rule.'" *Comparative Political Studies* 27, no. 3 (1994): 323–348.

Shugart, Matthew S. "The Electoral Cycle and Institutional Sources of Divided Presidential Government." *American Political Science Review* 89, no. 2 (1995): 327–342.

Shugart, Matthew S. "Semi-Presidential Systems: Dual Executive and Mixed Authority Patterns." *French Politics* 3 (2005): 27.

Siaroff, Alan. "Comparative Presidencies: The Inadequacy of the Presidential, Semi-Presidential and Parliamentary Distinction." *European Journal of Political Research* 42 (2003): 287–312.

Sowerwine, Charles. "The Fall of the Fourth Republic, 1958." In *France since 1870: Culture, Politics and Society*, 296–306. New York: Palgrave Macmillan, 2009.

CHAPTER 33

..................................................................................................................

# ELECTORAL SYSTEMS
# IN CONTEXT
*India*

..................................................................................................................

ADAM ZIEGFELD

SINCE India won its independence from the United Kingdom in 1947, its electoral rules have remained fairly constant. Like many former British colonies, India adopted first-past-the-post (FPTP) electoral rules, which remain in place to this day. FPTP rules are relatively common throughout the world, but India's experience with this electoral system stands out in three ways: how India has (and has not) addressed large disparities in the populations of its electoral constituencies;[1] how India ensures representation for historically underrepresented groups; and, finally, how Indian political parties respond to FPTP rules by forming pre-election alliances.[2]

First, India's electoral constituencies exhibit considerable malapportionment; that is, the number of eligible voters varies markedly across constituencies. The recent revision of electoral boundaries—known as "delimitation"—in 2008 only partially addressed this problem, remedying malapportionment *within* states but not *between* them. Second, to mandate representation for marginalized groups, India "reserves" certain constituencies for members of historically underrepresented groups, permitting only candidates from members of specified groups to compete for these seats. This system of quotas therefore guarantees that these "reserved" constituencies elect representatives from quota beneficiary groups. Third, as a strategy for working around the FPTP electoral system—which typically benefits the largest vote winner and disadvantages smaller parties—Indian political parties frequently form pre-election alliances in which multiple parties agree not to field candidates against one another, instead fielding a common candidate in each constituency. Today, India's two main national parties—the Indian National Congress (INC or Congress) and the Bharatiya Janata Party (BJP)—each head their own election alliance, the United Progressive Alliance (founded in 2004 by Congress) and the National Democratic Alliance (founded in 1998 by the BJP). Before addressing each of these three topics in turn, the chapter first describes India's electoral rules in greater detail.

# INDIA'S ELECTORAL SYSTEM

India is a parliamentary democracy with a bicameral legislature. An appointed nonpartisan body, the Election Commission of India (ECI), oversees national and state elections. Voters directly elect 543 members to the first legislative chamber, the Lok Sabha (House of the People), from single-seat constituencies using FPTP rules. The president of India can (and usually does) appoint two additional members to the Lok Sabha who are Anglo-Indian—of mixed British and Indian origin—if he or she believes that the community is not adequately represented in the Lok Sabha. In the first two national elections, held in 1951–1952 and 1957, a sizeable minority of legislators (35 percent in 1951–1952 and 38 percent in 1957) came from two-seat constituencies.[3] The two-seat constituencies guaranteed representation for the Scheduled Castes (SCs) and Scheduled Tribes (STs), historically marginalized groups in India. In 1961, legislation abolished all two-seat constituencies in favor of an alternative method for guaranteeing the election of SC and ST legislators.

India's second chamber, the Rajya Sabha (Council of States), has 233 indirectly elected members, whose terms are fixed at six years and staggered such that one-third of the chamber's seats are elected every two years. The president also appoints twelve members who have distinguished themselves either through their contributions to fields such as the arts, literature, or science or through their service to society as a whole. Rajya Sabha members are indirectly elected by India's state legislatures using the single transferable vote (STV) system. Because parties' legislative strengths in state legislatures are common knowledge and parties therefore know how many Rajya Sabha members their legislative delegations can elect, parties often nominate only as many candidates as their state legislators can elect. Consequently, many Rajya Sabha elections are uncontested. For the most part, scholars of electoral politics have paid little attention to the Rajya Sabha, meaning that we know very little about how the STV rules function in practice or how they affect outcomes of Rajya Sabha elections.

Electoral rules in subnational elections closely resemble those used in national elections. As of 2017, India has twenty-nine states and seven Union territories (UTs). UTs have far less autonomy than states, depend on the central government for a greater share of their financial resources, and tend to be relatively small, in terms of both population and geographic area. Each state, as well as two UTs (Delhi and Puducherry), has its own legislature.[4] Most state legislatures are unicameral, though several are bicameral. The first or sole chamber is known as the Vidhan Sabha (State Assembly), and all its members are elected using FPTP rules.[5] Just as with the Lok Sabha, prior to 1961, some members of the Vidhan Sabhas were elected in two-seat constituencies.

After many decades in which few states held local elections, the Seventy-Third and Seventy-Fourth Amendments to the Indian constitution mandated in 1992 that states hold local elections both in rural areas (Seventy-Third Amendment) and urban areas (Seventy-Fourth Amendment).[6] Each state has its own State Election Commission

(SEC) to oversee local elections. The Seventy-Third and Seventy-Fourth Amendments provide general guidelines about how states should conduct local elections but leave many of the specific decisions to the states. Although the constitution does not preclude the possibility of states using multiseat constituencies in local elections, all states use FPTP rules. However, in many other regards, local elections vary considerably from state to state. For example, states can decide whether local bodies have directly or indirectly elected chairpersons. To illustrate, the elected members of the Brihanmumbai (Greater Mumbai) Municipal Corporation choose the corporation chairperson, or mayor, from within their ranks, typically from the party with the most seats. Meanwhile, from 1996 through 2016, the mayor of the Greater Chennai Corporation was directly elected for a fixed term.[7] Additionally, the states determine whether rural elections are partisan or nonpartisan, though parties are widely believed to play an important role even in officially nonpartisan elections (Dunning and Nilekani 2013). Finally, the states decide how to constitute the upper levels of rural local government. The Seventy-Third Amendment requires there to be three levels of rural local government. The lowest is the *gram panchayat* (village council) and the highest is the district *panchayat*. There is also an intermediate level between the levels of the village and the administrative district (which is somewhat akin to an American county). States have discretion in determining the extent to which these upper levels include directly elected members, members indirectly elected by lower levels of local government, or *ex officio* members who hold other posts. How and to what extent differences in the structure and conduct of local elections matter—whether for election results or for a whole host of other nonelectoral outcomes—remains largely unexplored.

# Mandated Representation
# for Underrepresented Groups

Since independence, national and state elections have guaranteed representation for two historically marginalized groups, the Scheduled Castes (SCs or Dalits) and Scheduled Tribes (STs or Adivasis). Both groups are collections of various *jatis*, which are endogamous social groups variously referred to as either castes or subcastes. The SCs comprise those *jatis* that historically suffered from the practice of untouchability, which prohibited many types of social interactions between "untouchable" castes and others, relegated members of these *jatis* to low-status occupations, and precluded them from access to many public spaces and amenities such as wells or temples. Though untouchability originated with the Hindu caste system, other religious groups have also practiced untouchability, which has since been outlawed by India's postindependence constitution. The STs' defining features are their economic deprivation and historic isolation from mainstream society, usually in mountainous or heavily forested areas.

Until 1961, India guaranteed the representation of SCs and STs in the Lok Sabha and the various Vidhan Sabhas through a system of two-seat constituencies. Each of these two-seat constituencies was reserved for either SCs or STs. Additionally, some single-seat constituencies were reserved for STs, because STs often constitute a majority of the constituency's population. In the two-seat constituencies, voters could vote for two different candidates. The SC or ST candidate with the highest number of votes was elected, as was the remaining candidate with the highest number of votes. If the two candidates with the most votes were both SC or ST, then two SC or ST candidates could win. However, because one of the seats had to go to an SC or ST, the two winning candidates were not necessarily the two with the most votes. If, for example, the SC candidate with the most votes placed third in an SC-reserved constituency, then the first- and third-place candidates would be elected. In 1961, India abandoned this system, dividing two-seat constituencies into two single-seat constituencies, one reserved and one unreserved.

Under the new system of reservation—so called because certain seats are reserved for members of a particular group—all voters in a reserved constituency can vote, but only candidates from the reserved group (whether SC or ST) may contest. The number of seats reserved for SCs and STs reflects their proportion of the overall population. Seats reserved for SCs are generally those where SCs are comparatively numerous; however, the procedures used to reserve SC seats ensure that these constituencies are dispersed throughout each state.[8] In contrast, because STs are typically geographically concentrated, ST-reserved seats are usually those with the highest shares of STs. In addition to mandating the formation of local governments, the Seventy-Third and Seventy-Fourth Amendments also required reservation for SCs and STs at the local level. Furthermore, these amendments required, for the first time, reservation for women. At least one-third of all local-level seats are reserved for women, though some states reserve a greater share. Some states have also extended reservation to Other Backward Classes (OBCs)—a collection of *jatis* that are neither upper caste nor SC or ST.

India's system of reservation has elicited considerable interest from scholars in both political science and economics, but a consensus on the efficacy of reservation has proven elusive. With respect to reservation's economic and distributive benefits to quota beneficiary groups (i.e., SCs, STs, and women), findings have been mixed. Whereas some have found that the groups targeted by reservation benefit in terms of public goods provision (Pande 2003; Besley et al. 2004), others have found little evidence that officials elected from reserved seats disproportionately distribute to members of their own group (Dunning and Nilekani 2013) or that quota beneficiary groups see advances on other development indicators (Jensenius 2015). Still others have found that reservations help some beneficiary groups but not others (Bardhan, Mookherjee, and Torrado 2010; Chin and Prakash 2011). There is further disagreement as to whether elected officials from reserved seats make decisions about public goods that are consistent with the preferences of their fellow group members (Chattopadhyay and Duflo 2004) or if they behave similarly to politicians from unreserved seats (Ban and Rao 2008).

Apart from potential economic benefit, reservation could also benefit target groups by changing attitudes toward these groups among others in society. In this regard, there is some room for optimism. Thanks to reservation, perceptions of social and legal norms involving SCs have changed among non-SCs (Chauchard 2014), and some measure of caste bias and discrimination has eroded (Jensenius 2017). That being said, the news is not all good. Citizens' evaluations of politicians elected through reservation tend to be worse, even when there is no evidence of poorer performance (Duflo and Topalova 2004; Deininger et al. 2015), and reservation does not ameliorate pernicious caste stereotypes (Chauchard 2014). Finally, reservation could help members of targeted groups get elected even after the withdrawal of quotas by habituating voters to having elected officials from underrepresented groups. Evidence suggests that this is, indeed, the case for women in India (Beaman et al. 2009; Bhavnani 2009) but not for SCs (Bhavnani 2017).

Taken together, this research presents a nuanced picture of the ways in which reservation does and does not help beneficiary groups. Despite having received much scholarly attention, reservations merit continued study as scholars do not necessarily understand why reservations seem to have different effects in different parts of the country, at different electoral levels (local vs. state or national), and for different economic and social outcomes. Furthermore, much remains to be learned about why reservations seem to function differently for different beneficiary groups.

# MALAPPORTIONMENT

Whereas not all countries mandate representation for otherwise underrepresented groups, all FPTP countries must draw electoral boundaries. In India, this task falls to the ECI. The Indian constitution originally mandated a delimitation (or redistricting) following every decennial census to both determine the number of seats allocated to each state and redraw constituency boundaries. After India's first elections in 1951 and 1952, the ECI redrew constituency boundaries in accordance with the 1951 census. Legislation in 1962 and 1972 prompted subsequent delimitations after the 1961 and 1971 censuses, respectively. However, in 1976, the Forty-Second Amendment to the constitution froze electoral boundaries until after the first post-2000 census. The Forty-Second Amendment was promulgated during the nineteen-month period from 1975 to 1977 known as the Emergency—a quasi-authoritarian interlude during which the Congress-led national government postponed elections and imprisoned many political opponents. The Emergency was also well known for the government's draconian efforts at family planning, which included large numbers of forced sterilizations. As part of its population control campaign, the national government postponed delimitation so that state governments could embrace population control efforts without worrying that successful implementation would result in them losing parliamentary seats to states that had less zealously pursued the government's initiative. Thanks to the Forty-Second

Amendment, India used the same state- and national-level constituency boundaries from 1977 through March 2008.

The 2008 delimitation involved two major changes. The first was the redrawing of national and state electoral constituencies to ensure that constituencies *within the same state* had roughly equal populations. By the early 2000s, malapportionment was a major problem, particularly in formerly rural areas that had become the suburbs of rapidly growing cities. For example, in the state of Maharashtra, the state-level constituencies of Opera House and Belapur had similar populations in 1978: approximately 109,000 eligible voters in Opera House and 119,000 in Belapur. Opera House was located in the heart of the city of Mumbai, and Belapur was, at the time, largely rural. By 2004, Opera House had only about 92,000 eligible voters, while Belapur—now located in a major Mumbai suburb—had more than 1.2 million voters. A second major change was in the reservation of constituencies. For thirty years, the same constituencies had been reserved for SCs and STs. With the change in constituency boundaries, the ECI also decided anew which seats were reserved for SCs and STs.

Importantly, what did not change with the 2008 delimitation was the number of seats allocated to each state. The Eighty-Fourth Amendment to the constitution, passed in 2002, froze the size of each state's delegation to the Lok Sabha and the sizes of the state legislatures until after 2026, ostensibly for the same reasons that boundaries had been frozen in the first place: to avoid rewarding states that had failed to curb population growth (McMillan 2000). Consequently, the most recent delimitation did nothing to address malapportionment *between* states. Figure 33.1 illustrates the delimitation's

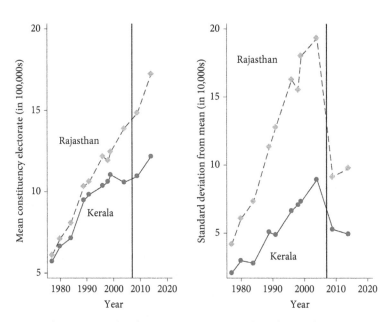

**FIGURE 33.1.** Delimitation and malapportionment in Kerala and Rajasthan.

Source: Election Commission of India and author calculation.

impact (or lack thereof) on malapportionment by contrasting two states: Kerala in southern India and Rajasthan in northern India. According to the 1971 census, Kerala and Rajasthan had relatively similar populations, about twenty-one million and twenty-six million people, respectively. Between 1971 and 2011, Kerala's population increased by about 56 percent to approximately thirty-three million people, while Rajasthan's increased by 166 percent to more than sixty-eight million.

The left panel in Figure 33.1 emphasizes how the delimitation failed to address malapportionment *between* states. The panel plots the average population of eligible voters in Lok Sabha constituencies in the two states (in 100,000s). In 1977, shortly after constituency boundaries were frozen, the mean constituency populations in Kerala and Rajasthan were similar. Over time, as Rajasthan's population grew much faster than Kerala's, those means diverged. The vertical line represents the 2008 delimitation. As the data points for the 2009 and 2014 elections indicate, delimitation did not close the gap between the two states.

In contrast, the right panel shows that delimitation had a major impact on malapportionment *within* states. This panel presents the standard deviation from the mean population of eligible voters in national-level constituencies (in 10,000s). In other words, this figure indicates how variable the constituencies' populations are over time. When the standard deviation is low, constituencies have similar populations; when the standard deviation is high, constituencies vary greatly in their populations. In both states, the standard deviations rose noticeably during the period of frozen boundaries as populations shifted within the states. Following the 2008 delimitation, these standard deviations dropped precipitously because the delimitation successfully redrew boundaries to make constituency populations more uniform within each state. A similar story applies to state legislatures. Within states, constituency populations are far more uniform after the 2008 delimitation than they were before. However, because the sizes of the state legislatures have remained constant, legislators in states with faster-growing populations represent more populous constituencies than those in states with slower-growing populations.

Although there is little evidence of intentional efforts at gerrymandering in the 2008 delimitation (Iyer and Reddy 2013), malapportionment affects India's political parties very differently. Apart from the BJP and Congress, most parties in India are regional parties whose supporters are concentrated mainly in one or two states. Naturally, regional parties in states that are currently overrepresented (i.e., those whose populations have grown more slowly since 1971) benefit from malapportionment as compared to regional parties in states that are underrepresented (i.e., those whose populations have grown more quickly). For instance, parties such as the Bahujan Samaj Party (BSP) or Samajwadi Party (SP) that are based primarily in India's most underrepresented state, Uttar Pradesh, suffer from the current malapportionment. Their voters are concentrated in a smaller number of more populous seats, meaning that their electoral support potentially translates into a smaller share of seats in the Lok Sabha than it would if won in an overrepresented state.

For the two national parties, the benefits of malapportionment depend on the distribution of their supporters across the country. Over the last several elections,

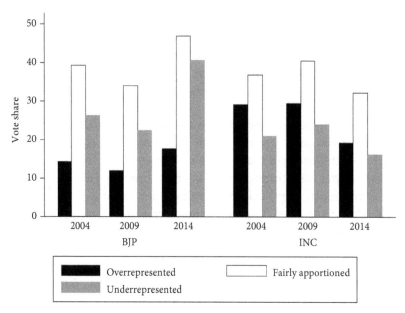

**FIGURE 33.2.** BJP and Congress electoral strength and malapportionment.

Source: Election Commission of India and author calculation.

malapportionment has appeared to favor Congress more than the BJP because Congress has tended to draw more of its support from overrepresented states than the BJP. Figure 33.2 presents the vote shares won by the BJP and Congress in the 2004, 2009, and 2014 national elections, broken down by states that are overrepresented (black bars), fairly apportioned (white bars), or underrepresented (gray).

To calculate the vote shares in Figure 33.2, I determined how many seats each state should elect based on its population from the 2011 census. (The calculations are nearly identical based on the 2001 census.) In doing so, I ensured that even the smallest states received at least one representative. Eight states accounting for more than 40 percent of the population are currently underrepresented. Fifteen states are overrepresented, and the remaining twelve—most of which are very small states and UTs—are fairly apportioned. As the left side of Figure 33.2 illustrates, the BJP is fairly weak in overrepresented states, relative to both its performance in the rest of India and Congress's performance in these states. Meanwhile, the BJP's electoral support in underrepresented states is much greater than in overrepresented states and is generally somewhat higher than Congress's vote share in underrepresented states. The right side of Figure 33.2 indicates that Congress has fared better in overrepresented states than in underrepresented ones. Both parties do best in fairly apportioned states, but these states only account for about 7 percent of India's total population.

The extent to which malapportionment has actually helped Congress win more seats than it otherwise would have or deprived the BJP of seats that it should have won in a more fairly apportioned system is difficult to estimate. Because reapportioning seats in an FPTP system also requires redrawing constituency boundaries, it is hard to know whether a fairer apportionment of seats across states would have actually changed the parties' seat shares in 2004, 2009, or 2014. However, so long as the patterns of electoral support evident in Figure 33.2 continue, Congress is more likely to benefit from the current malapportionment than the BJP.

# PRE-ELECTION ALLIANCES

Political competition in countries using FPTP rules typically exhibits several features. First, competition at both the constituency and national levels revolves around a relatively small number of parties. Second, the largest party (in terms of votes won) almost always wins a disproportionate share of legislative seats. Third, if very small parties exist, they seldom win legislative representation. Despite employing an FPTP electoral system, India does not, as a rule, exhibit these characteristics. First, although competition at the constituency level usually revolves around a few main candidates, state and national party systems feature a much larger number of parties, many more than are frequently found in FPTP countries. Second, though the largest vote winner usually wins the most seats, in a surprising number of cases smaller parties actually come away with more seats. Third, a sizeable number of very small parties win seats.

These unusual characteristics all stem at least in part from the prevalence of pre-election alliances, which occur, in the Indian context, when two or more parties agree not to compete against one another.[9] Prior to the election, they decide where each party will field candidates, so that only one candidate from among the allied parties competes in each seat. Pre-election alliances of this kind are especially common in India, where they profoundly influence how many seats each party wins and who ultimately comes to power after an election. This section first outlines several of the key features of pre-election alliances in India before detailing several ways in which election alliances differ from one another. Finally, the section explains how pre-election alliances are responsible for several aspects of political competition in India that are unusual for an FPTP country.

## Common Features

Election alliances in India have three features that are almost universal across the country and over time. First, pre-election alliances are brokered at the state level, even in national elections. Ahead of the 1998 election, the BJP established an election alliance called the National Democratic Alliance (NDA). Later, after the 2004 election, Congress established the United Progressive Alliance (UPA). The BJP and Congress formed these alliances largely for the purposes of governing at the national level after elections. Actual agreements not to compete with other parties in the run-up to elections, whether national- or state-level, are nonetheless made on a state-by-state basis. Nearly all NDA and UPA members—apart from the BJP and Congress—are regional parties whose support bases are limited to one or two states. Therefore, negotiations over pre-election alliances must, in effect, take place on a state-by-state basis since the relevant actors in each state vary tremendously.

The state-by-state nature of alliance formation is largely an artifact of India's highly successful regional parties, particularly in recent decades. However, even when there have been opportunities for the same parties to form alliances across multiple states— as was more often the case before the regionalization of the Indian party system in the 1990s—parties have rarely brokered the same alliances across multiple, let alone all, states. For example, in the 1971 election, Congress's main national-party opponents— Bharatiya Jana Sangh, Congress (O), Samyukta Socialist Party, and Swatantra Party— formed an electoral front. But the extent to which this "nationwide" alliance produced effective coordination on common candidates varied considerably. In two of India's most populous states, Bihar and Uttar Pradesh, a number of seats featured contestants from more than one alliance partner.[10] Similarly, in the 1970s, the Communist Party of India (CPI) allied with Congress as a matter of national policy. Nevertheless, ahead of the 1977 election, the party's Central Executive Committee "directed the state units of the Party to make an electoral alliance with the Congress Party 'wherever it is desirable and possible'" (Varkey 1979, 892). This weak directive resulted in Congress–CPI alliances in some states but not others. More recently, the Nationalist Congress Party (NCP), founded by Congress dissidents in 1999, was allied with Congress for most of the 2000s in the state of Maharashtra but was part of the main alliance opposing Congress in the state of Kerala.

The second feature common to most alliances is that the parties in alliance retain their own party labels and symbols when competing in elections, even when the alliance formally adopts a name. Election ballots in India do not feature party names; rather, they feature party symbols along with the candidates' names. India uses party symbols for the benefit of illiterate voters. Parties that meet certain criteria in terms of votes or seats won in prior elections are entitled to use the same symbol in all constituencies in a state. For parties that fail to meet these criteria or for independent candidates, there are a number of "free symbols" that are allocated on a constituency-by-constituency basis shortly before an election.

When parties ally, they appear on ballots with their own symbols, not a new symbol unique to the alliance. In other words, ballots provide no indication of when parties are competing in alliance. In some places, parties agree on a name for the alliance, which may be used in campaigning, but these names are never associated with an election symbol, nor do they appear on ballots. For example, in the state of Kerala, Congress heads an election alliance called the United Democratic Front (UDF). Although campaign posters mention the UDF, members of the alliance retain their own party symbols. Indeed, the ECI makes no provisions for the registration of election alliances. In theory, parties in an alliance could register as a new political party in advance of an election, with full intention of parting ways afterward. Or they could field candidates officially as independents and try to secure the same symbol in each constituency. Both of these strategies have major drawbacks. Registering as a new party comes with significant logistical hurdles, and there is no guarantee that an alliance fielding its candidates as independents will necessarily get the same symbol in all constituencies. Moreover, because party symbols are integral parts of parties' brands and identities, they are reluctant to give up use of those symbols. Consequently, nearly all parties compete on their own party symbols and retain all the trappings associated with independent parties, even if they are part of long-standing alliances. The only exceptions occur when very small parties—typically not entitled to use their own symbol throughout a state and sometimes not even registered with the ECI—compete on the symbol of a much larger party. Such instances are, however, relatively rare and usually involve only very tiny parties.

The third feature of nearly all pre-election alliances in India is that parties in an alliance have no say over their allies' candidates. When forming a pre-election alliance, parties negotiate how many seats each party will contest and in which specific seats each party will compete. Sometimes parties arrive at these decisions simultaneously, but often bargaining first involves decisions about the number of seats and then moves to the allocation of seats. However, at no point do the parties negotiate over which candidates each party will nominate. Alliance candidates should not therefore be viewed as consensus candidates who meet the approval of all alliance partners. Frequently, alliances that are otherwise successful in ensuring that allied parties do not compete against one another fail to fully agree on where each party should field candidates. As a result, they may engage in "friendly fights" in a handful of seats where more than one party will field candidates despite otherwise avoiding competing with one another. Friendly fights typically occur in places where multiple parties believe they have a good chance of winning, either because they have sizable support bases or because they have high-quality candidates from the constituency or powerful party members wishing to compete from that seat.

## Differences

Though pre-election alliances in India exhibit several common features, they vary considerably on two related dimensions. First, alliances vary tremendously in their durability. Some alliances are stable and long lasting. One such example is the Shiv Sena–BJP alliance in the western state of Maharashtra, which endured at both the state and national levels from 1989 through the spring 2014 national election, ending just ahead of the Maharashtra Vidhan Sabha election in October 2014. Other alliances are intermittent but consistently involve the same parties. For instance, in the northern state of Punjab, the BJP and its predecessor, the Bharatiya Jana Sangh, have been on-and-off allies with the Akali Dal, a regional party, since the 1960s. Though not all elections feature an Akali Dal–BJP (or Jana Sangh) alliance, on occasions when the parties form an alliance, it is usually with one another. Finally, in many other cases, alliances last just a single election.

India's two national-level alliances, the UPA and NDA, are durable only in the sense that the leading party in each alliance has remained the same and the alliance names have persisted, but membership in these alliances has changed over time. Some parties have moved in and out of the same alliance but never switched alliances. The Telugu Desam Party, for example, has been an intermittent member of the NDA, while the Rashtriya Janata Dal has similarly been part of the UPA for much, but not all, of its existence. At no point has either party joined the rival alliance. In contrast, other parties have switched from the UPA to the NDA or vice versa. Examples include the Pattali Makkal Katchi in Tamil Nadu, Trinamool Congress in West Bengal, and Lok Jan Shakti Party in Bihar.

The second, and related, way in which alliances differ from one another is in the extent to which they are purely election-time agreements. Some alliances, including the NDA and UPA, openly function on the assumption that the alliance will endure after the election, into the subsequent governing period, and then into future elections. The members of such alliances often create institutions, such as coordinating committees, that function outside of election time. Some also formulate policy documents prior to elections—often known as common minimum programs. The most notable state-level examples of highly institutionalized alliances are the Left Front in West Bengal and the Left Democratic Front and United Democratic Front in Kerala. Not only do these alliances have names—signals of their intended durability—but also they have had relatively stable memberships, at least in terms of their key players.[11]

At the other end of the spectrum, some pre-election alliances are intended purely as election-time agreements that involve only decisions about how many and which seats each party will contest in the coming election. For instance, the Communist Party of India (Marxist) in West Bengal insisted that its 2016 alliance with Congress was purely for the purposes of the upcoming election. In some cases, victorious pre-election alliances do not even translate into postelection coalitions. In the southern state of Tamil Nadu, the Dravida Munnetra Kazhagam (DMK) and Congress formed a pre-election alliance in the 2006 state election. The DMK won a plurality of seats but not a majority. Instead of including Congress as a coalition partner, the DMK formed a minority government with outside support from Congress. In the next state election, in 2011, the All India Anna Dravida Munnetra Kazhagam (AIADMK) won a single-party majority and refused to include its pre-election allies in the government. More generally, parties often expect that an alliance will not endure over the course of subsequent elections or constitute the basis for broader political cooperation. Consequently, they take few steps to institutionalize the alliance. Many alliances—perhaps most—take shape in the absence of postelection policy goals and common policy platforms during the election campaign. Decisions about the postelection allocation of ministerial berths virtually always take place only after the election, once the distribution of legislative strength among parties is known.

## Impact

The impact of pre-election alliances on political competition in India is profound, resulting in patterns of competition that are relatively unusual in FPTP countries. The first and most direct consequence of pre-election alliances in India is the reduction in the number of major competitors at the constituency level without necessarily diminishing levels of party system fragmentation at the state or national levels. Duverger (1954) suggested that FPTP rules tend to produce two-party competition at the constituency level. If the same parties compete in all constituencies, then this constituency-level two-party system should aggregate up to a two-party system nationally (Cox 1997). Though many countries with FPTP rules fail to meet the Duvergerian expectation of only two major parties, many FPTP countries have national party systems with relatively few parties (e.g., Canada, Jamaica, the United Kingdom, the United States), and constituency-level competition in FPTP countries typically features fewer major parties than in countries with higher district magnitudes and proportional representation rules (Singer 2013).

What is remarkable about India is the extent to which constituency-level competition revolves around a fairly small number of parties even as the state- and national-level party systems feature many parties. To measure party system fragmentation at the constituency level, the solid black line in Figure 33.3 presents the average effective number of electoral parties ($N_V$) across constituencies in national elections from 1962 through 2014. This line excludes India's first two elections because of their use of two-seat constituencies.[12] The horizontal dashed line indicates an $N_V$ of 2.5, which is sometimes used as a threshold distinguishing two-party from multiparty competition (Gaines 1999; Chhibber and Kollman 2004, chap. 2). Although there is some variation in the average constituency-level $N_V$ over time, it has remained between 2.4 and 3.1 in all elections but 1977. The average for all constituencies across all elections is 2.7. Put another way, of the 7,466 constituency-level races in national elections from 1962 through 2014, almost

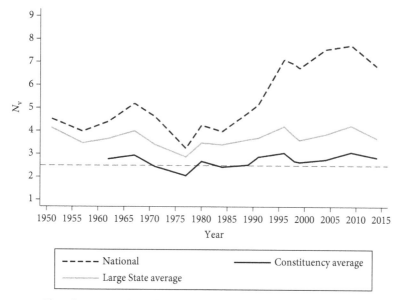

**FIGURE 33.3.** The effective number of parties in Indian national elections.

Source: Election Commission of India and author calculation.

92 percent had three or fewer candidates that each won more than 10 percent of the constituency-level vote.[13]

Meanwhile, India has always had a highly fragmented multiparty system at the national level, first during the period of Congress dominance (1947–1989) and then, later, during the more competitive period (1989–present).[14] The dashed black line in Figure 33.3 presents the nationwide $N_V$ in Lok Sabha elections. For most of India's first forty years after independence, the $N_V$ was routinely between four and five. During this time, Congress, which had spearheaded the country's independence movement, dominated national politics, winning single-party majorities in the Lok Sabha in eight of India's first nine elections. Although Congress never won a nationwide majority of votes cast in any of India's national elections, it nevertheless won sizeable legislative majorities in most elections prior to 1989 because it was far and away the largest party and faced a fragmented opposition consisting of a handful of medium-sized national parties and a host of smaller regional parties. Later, during the competitive multiparty period, India's $N_V$ rose considerably, to between six and eight, as Congress's vote share declined sharply and tiny regional parties proliferated.

Of course, some of the disjuncture between the number of parties at the constituency level and at the national level is a function of the country's regionalized party system (Ziegfeld 2016). Different parties compete in different parts of the country, so even if there are dozens of parties represented in the Lok Sabha, very few of these parties are competitive in any particular region of India. Nevertheless, the regionalized party system alone cannot account for the small number of major parties found in most constituencies because many constituencies are located in states where four or five parties enjoy considerable support, as illustrated by the gray line in Figure 33.3, which plots the average state-level $N_V$ in national elections. The gray line excludes states that elect three or fewer members of parliament (MPs), since these state-level party systems are little different from constituency-level ones. As Figure 33.3 demonstrates, there is a persistent difference between the (greater) number of major parties successfully competing in most states and the (smaller) number of major parties successfully competing in most constituencies. Why, then, do most constituencies feature noticeably fewer major parties than are successful at the state level? Pre-election alliances are a large part of the answer.

In multiparty settings where many sizeable parties might otherwise field candidates, pre-election alliances essentially force voters to converge on a smaller number of viable candidates because some parties opt not to field candidates and instead support another party's candidates. In this way, the multiparty nature of the party system can persist even as competition at the constituency level converges on a few main candidates. To illustrate, consider elections in the state of Tamil Nadu. The solid gray line in Figure 33.4 plots the state-level $N_V$ in Tamil Nadu's state elections from 1962 through 2016. Throughout most of the state's history, but particularly since 2000, Tamil Nadu has had a highly fragmented multiparty system. The solid black line depicts the average constituency-level $N_V$ in the state, which is much lower. In most elections, the average constituency-level

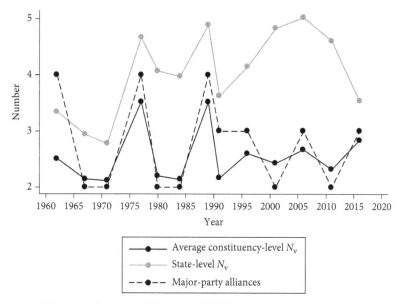

FIGURE 33.4. Election alliances and $N_V$ in Tamil Nadu state elections.

Source: Election Commission of India and author calculation.

$N_V$ is between 2 and 2.5, compared to between 4 and 5 at the state level. Not surprisingly, the solid gray and solid black lines typically move in concert, though not always.

However, the line that more closely tracks the average constituency-level $N_V$ is the dashed black line, which is the number of major-party election alliances. This dashed black line indicates the number of alliances competing in the election, counting only alliances in which the largest party in the alliance won at least 5 percent of the vote. These two black lines—the dashed and solid—are much closer together and virtually always rise and fall together. Compare, for example, the 1977 and 1980 elections. From one election to the next, the state-level $N_V$ declined slightly from about 4.5 to about 4, but the average constituency-level $N_V$ plummeted from about 4 to about 2. What happened? In 1977, there were four main parties, none of which competed in alliance with one another. By 1980, one of those parties had essentially collapsed, leaving three parties. But two of these parties, the DMK and Congress, contested in alliance against the AIADMK. Both the DMK- and AIADMK-led alliances also included smaller parties, ensuring that nearly every party competing in the election was part of one of the two alliances. As a consequence, though the party system as a whole remained fairly fragmented, most constituency-level races featured only two major competitors. Later, in the 2000s, the party system fragmented further, but thanks to pre-election alliances, competition remained centered on only a few candidates in each constituency. Importantly, Tamil Nadu is not alone; several other states in India have multiparty systems yet routinely see constituency-level competition confined to a much smaller number of parties.

A second major consequence of pre-election alliances in India is that the party winning the most votes sometimes "loses" an election, an outcome that runs counter to most expectations. Conventional wisdom suggests that FPTP elections should favor the party winning the most votes, awarding it seat shares that are disproportionately large relative to its vote share. Indeed, many Indian elections—particularly those where pre-election alliances are absent—conform to this conventional wisdom. For example, in the 2007 state election in the state of Uttar Pradesh, the BSP captured just over 30 percent of the vote, making it the largest vote winner in the state. With less than a third of the vote, the party nevertheless won more than 50 percent of the state's legislative seats. Because the non-BSP vote was divided among several other parties, the party's candidates narrowly edged out competitors in many seats, turning its narrow advantage in vote share into a significant advantage in legislative seats.

Pre-election alliances can, however, undermine the advantages usually associated with the largest party under FPTP rules (Ziegfeld and Tudor 2017). They do so by consolidating the votes of smaller parties behind a single candidate in each electoral constituency, ensuring a more efficient translation of votes into seats for these parties. For instance, in the eastern state of Odisha, Congress was the largest vote winner in national elections in 1998, 1999, and 2004 and in state elections in 2000 and 2004. Yet, in all five elections, Congress failed to win the most seats. In all of these elections, the Biju Janata Dal (BJD), a regional party, and BJP formed an alliance, and the BJD won the most seats even though it won fewer votes than Congress. In fact, in four of these five elections, the BJP won more seats than Congress despite being only the third-largest vote winner. By amassing the supporters of both the BJD and BJP behind a single candidate in each constituency and ensuring that Congress faced only one major opponent instead of two, the smaller parties—not the largest party—benefited from the disproportionality in the translation of votes to seats associated with FPTP systems.

During the period from 1962 through 2015, India's largest states held 197 state-level elections.[15] Of these, the party winning the most votes failed to win the most seats in 27 elections (or about 14 percent of cases). Of these 27 elections, 24 were instances in which the largest vote winner faced a pre-election alliance.[16] In some cases the largest vote winner sometimes "won" by a considerable margin in terms of vote share but still came away with fewer seats. But in a context of frequent pre-election alliances and FPTP rules, winning elections does not necessarily require winning the largest number of votes.

The third and final consequence of pre-election alliances is that very small parties often win substantial legislative representation. The expectation from FPTP electoral rules is that small parties face considerable hurdles in winning legislative representation because the "effective" threshold for winning seats is very high: a party must garner a large share of the vote in a seat to win. Scholars have noted, however, that when small parties have support bases that are geographically concentrated, FPTP electoral systems do not necessarily disadvantage small parties (Calvo 2009; Ziegfeld 2013). Such parties with narrow but deep support bases can win seats in low-magnitude electoral districts about as well as they can under higher-magnitude electoral districts. Pre-election alliances allow very small parties to win legislative representation by, in effect, creating narrow but deep pockets of support for these parties where they would not have otherwise existed. Typically, very small parties that are members of an election alliance compete in a relatively small number of constituencies. In those seats, candidates from small parties benefit from the votes of larger allied parties, helping the small parties' candidates to win sizeable vote shares in the modest number of constituencies where they contest.

Elections in the state of Kerala illustrate just how important pre-election alliances can be for the fortunes of very small parties. In Kerala's 2006 state election, fifteen parties won seats in the 140-member legislature. Of these, eleven won less than 5 percent of the vote. Table 33.1 presents the results from this election, including all parties that

## Table 33.1  Results of Kerala's 2006 State Election

| Left Democratic Front | Vote Share | Seats Contested | Seats Won |
|---|---|---|---|
| Communist Party of India (Marxist) | 30% | 85 | 61 |
| Communist Party of India | 8% | 24 | 17 |
| Janata Dal (Secular) | 2% | 8 | 5 |
| Kerala Congress | 2% | 6 | 4 |
| Revolutionary Socialist Party | 1% | 4 | 3 |
| Indian National League | 1% | 3 | 1 |
| Nationalist Congress Party | 1% | 2 | 1 |
| Kerala Congress Secular | <1% | 1 | 1 |
| Congress (Secular) | <1% | 1 | 1 |
| *Total* | *47%* | *134* | *94* |
| United Democratic Front | Vote Share | Seats Contested | Seats Won |
| Indian National Congress | 24% | 77 | 24 |
| Muslim League | 7% | 21 | 7 |
| Democratic Indira Congress (Karunakaran) | 4% | 17 | 1 |
| Kerala Congress (M) | 3% | 11 | 7 |
| Janadhipathya Samrakshana Samithi | 2% | 5 | 1 |
| Communist Marxist Party Kerala State Committee | 1% | 3 | 0 |
| Kerala Congress (B) | 1% | 2 | 1 |
| *Total* | *42%* | *136* | *41* |
| Other Parties | Vote Share | Seats Contested | Seats Won |
| Bharatiya Janata Party | 5% | 136 | 0 |
| Bahujan Samaj Party | 1% | 107 | 0 |
| All India Anna Dravida Munnetra Kazhagam | <1% | 29 | 0 |

*Source:* Election Commission of India.

either won 0.1 percent or more of the vote or were part of one of the two main alliances, the Left Democratic Front (LDF) and United Democratic Front (UDF).[17] The LDF won the election, and all members of the alliance won seats, no matter how small their vote share. Parties like the Kerala Congress Secular and Congress (Secular) were allocated just one seat as part of the LDF. But because their candidates won votes from supporters of the other LDF parties, these parties won large vote shares in the seats in which they contested—far larger than they could have won on their own. Meanwhile, the BJP failed to win legislative representation even though it won a greater vote share than all but four other parties. The BJP did not contest as part of an alliance; therefore, its votes were spread evenly and inefficiently across constituencies, and it suffered the fate most often expected of small parties in FPTP electoral systems.

All told, pre-election alliances profoundly influence electoral politics in India. They enable constituency-level competition to revolve around a few major candidates while preserving the multiparty character of politics in many states; they provide smaller parties with an effective strategy for defeating the party likely to win the most votes; and they allow very small parties to avoid electoral oblivion and, instead, consistently win legislative representation.

# Conclusion

This chapter has described some of the more noteworthy topics surrounding India's use of FPTP electoral rules: malapportionment, reservation, and pre-election alliances. Although the persistence of malapportioned constituencies, the widespread use of reservation, and the frequency of pre-election alliances are hardly secrets to scholars of India, much is still unknown.

First, the study of India's malapportionment remains understudied. Although some work has explained the political origins of malapportionment (McMillan 2000; Sivaramakrishnan 2000; Bhavnani n.d.), few studies have examined the implications of malapportionment. Two recent studies by Bhavnani constitute important exceptions. In the first study, Bhavnani (n.d.) shows that malapportionment affects cabinet composition in India's states; legislators from less populous constituencies are more likely to become members of the cabinet because, he argues, large parties focus on winning constituencies with smaller populations. In the second study, Bhavnani (2016) highlights some of the economic implications of malapportionment, demonstrating that constituencies with greater representation (i.e., those that are overrepresented) exhibit greater light output at night, a proxy for economic development. Bhavnani's work constitutes a promising beginning to this area of research, but we still know relatively little about how malapportionment may have affected election outcomes in the past or how it may have affected public policy by granting greater representation to certain types of parties or interests over others.

Second, though reservation has received much scholarly attention, far more studies examine reservations for SCs and women than reservations for STs. Because ST populations are geographically concentrated in ways quite unlike SCs and women, ST reservations may operate differently in practice and are therefore worth additional study. Furthermore, a major focus in the literature has been on the economic and distributive implications of reservation with comparatively little attention to the political effects. Recent work by Jensenius (2017), who shows how reservation created a new class of SC politicians, as well as by Auerbach and Ziegfeld (2016), who demonstrate that the nature of political competition in reserved constituencies differs from unreserved constituencies, highlights the importance of better understanding how reservation shapes electoral and party politics.

Third and finally, though pre-election alliances are common in India and widely reported on by the news media prior to elections, they are poorly understood. During the period of Congress dominance, pre-election alliances usually took the form of a single front uniting most or all opposition parties. Following the end of Congress dominance, many states now frequently witness competition between two or more rival alliances, suggesting that the formation of pre-election alliances has become more common over time. Yet, we know little about the conditions under which pre-election alliances take shape, how parties choose alliance partners, how election alliances shape voting behavior, or whether alliances have downstream effects on policy or distributive outcomes. In short, in spite of India's consistent use of one of the world's most common electoral systems, the country remains fertile territory for those interested in understanding the operation and consequences of electoral rules.

## ACKNOWLEDGMENTS

I thank Asgar Syed for his excellent research assistance.

## NOTES

1. In India, electoral districts are called "constituencies." Throughout, I use the term "constituency" to refer to electoral districts.
2. Much of the scholarly literature in comparative politics uses the term pre-election "coalitions" instead of "alliances." I use the term "alliance" because it is more commonly used in India.
3. National elections in India are often staggered across multiple polling dates. The first election took place in late 1951 and early 1952; it also featured one three-seat constituency.
4. I use the terms "state" and "state legislature" to refer to both states and any relevant UTs.
5. The second chamber in bicameral states is the Vidhan Parishad (Legislative Council).
6. Several areas of India—whose combined population is very small—are exempt from the Seventy-Third and Seventy-Fourth Amendments.

7. In mid-2016, the Tamil Nadu Vidhan Sabha passed legislation abolishing directly elected mayors.
8. See McMillan (2005) and Jensenius (2017) for more details on reservation, particularly for SCs.
9. Pre-election alliances in other countries and under other electoral rules often take other forms.
10. In Bihar, twenty-seven of fifty-three seats featured more than one candidate from the alliance, while twenty-two of eighty-five constituencies in Uttar Pradesh featured multiple candidates from the alliance.
11. Smaller members of the LDF and UDF have frequently changed. However, the two largest parties in each alliance have remained stable since the 1980s. The Left Front's four main members have been allies since the early 1980s.
12. Beginning in 2013, the ECI began offering voters the option of "None of the Above" on all ballots. For comparability with previous elections, votes cast for "None of the Above" are excluded from all calculations.
13. More specifically, 33 races (0.4 percent) had only one candidate winning more than 10 percent of the constituency-level vote; 4,070 (54.5 percent) had two such candidates; 2,754 (36.9 percent) had three; 559 (7.5 percent) had four; and 50 (0.7 percent) had five.
14. See Rudolph and Rudolph (2008) on why 1989 marks the transition from a dominant-party system to a competitive multiparty system.
15. This number includes only states with legislatures of more than seventy members and excludes the Jammu and Kashmir legislature prior to 1977, when many seats were uncontested or major parties were banned.
16. In the other three cases, the margin separating the vote shares for the largest and second-largest parties was less than 1 percent, making it less surprising that the largest vote winner did not win the most seats.
17. Table 33.1 does not include independent candidates backed by the LDF or UDF, who won five seats.

## References

Auerbach, Adam, and Adam Ziegfeld. "How Do Electoral Quotas Influence Political Competition? Evidence from Municipal, State, and National Elections in India." Presented at the annual meeting of the American Political Science Association, Philadelphia, 2016.

Ban, Radu, and Vijayendra Rao. "Tokenism or Agency? The Impact of Women's Reservation on Village Democracies on South India." *Economic Development and Cultural Change* 56, no. 3 (2008): 501–530.

Bardhan, Pranab K., Dilip Mookherjee, and Monica Parra Torrado. "Impact of Political Reservations in West Bengal Local Governments on Anti-Poverty Targeting." *Journal of Globalization and Development* 1, no. 1 (2010): 1–34.

Beaman, Lori, Raghabendra Chattopadhyay, Esther Duflo, Rohini Pande, and Petia Topalova. "Powerful Women: Does Exposure Reduce Prejudice?" *Quarterly Journal of Economics* 124, no. 4 (2009): 1497–1540.

Besley, Timothy, Rohini Pande, Lupin Rahman, and Vijayendra Rao. "The Politics of Public Good Provision: Evidence from Indian Local Governments." *Journal of the European Economic Association* 2, no. 2–3 (2004): 416–426.

Bhavnani, Rikhil R. "The Effects of Malapportionment on Cabinet Inclusion: Subnational Evidence from India." *British Journal of Political Science*. n.d.

Bhavnani, Rikhil R. "Do Electoral Quotas Work after They Are Withdrawn? Evidence from a Natural Experiment in India." *American Political Science Review* 103, no. 1 (2009): 23–35.

Bhavnani, Rikhil R. "The Effects of Malapportionment on Economic Development: Evidence from India's 2008 Redistricting." University of Wisconsin-Madison, Typescript, 2016.

Bhavnani, Rikhil R. "Do the Effects of Temporary Ethnic Group Quotas Persist? Evidence from India." *American Economic Journal: Applied Economics* 9, no. 3 (2017): 105–123.

Calvo, Ernesto. "The Competitive Road to Proportional Representation: Partisan Biases and Electoral Regime Change under Increasing Party Competition." *World Politics* 61, no. 2 (2009): 254–295.

Chattopadhyay, Raghabendra, and Esther Duflo. "Women as Policy Makers: Evidence from a Randomized Policy Experiment in India." *Econometrica* 72, no. 5 (2004): 1409–1443.

Chauchard, Simon. "Can Descriptive Representation Change Beliefs about a Stigmatized Group? Evidence from Rural India." *American Political Science Review* 108, no. 2 (2014): 403–422.

Chhibber, Pradeep K., and Ken Kollman. *The Formation of National Party Systems: Federalism and Party Competition in Canada, Great Britain, India, and the United States.* Princeton, NJ: Princeton University Press, 2004.

Chin, Aimee, and Nishith Prakash. "The Redistributive Effects of Political Reservation for Minorities: Evidence from India." *Journal of Development Economics* 96, no. 2 (2011): 265–277.

Cox, Gary W. *Making Votes Count: Strategic Coordination in the World's Electoral Systems.* Cambridge: Cambridge University Press, 1997.

Deininger, Klaus, Songqing Jin, Hari K Nagarajan, and Fang Xia. "Does Female Reservation Affect Long-Term Political Outcomes? Evidence from Rural India." *Journal of Development Studies* 51, no. 1 (2015): 32–49.

Duflo, Esther, and Petia Topalova. "Unappreciated Service: Performance, Perceptions, and Women Leaders in India." Massachusetts Institute of Technology, Typescript, 2004.

Dunning, Thad, and Janhavi Nilekani. "Ethnic Quotas and Political Mobilization: Caste, Parties, and Distribution in Indian Village Councils." *American Political Science Review* 107, no. 1 (2013): 35–56.

Duverger, Maurice. *Political Parties: Their Organization and Activity in the Modern State.* London: Methuen, 1954.

Gaines, Brian J. "Duverger's Law and the Meaning of Canadian Exceptionalism." *Comparative Political Studies* 32, no. 7 (1999): 835–861.

Iyer, Lakshmi, and Maya Reddy. "Redrawing the Lines: Did Political Incumbents Influence Electoral Redistricting in the World's Largest Democracy?" Harvard Business School Working Paper 14-051, 2013.

Jensenius, Francesca Refsum. "Development from Representation? A Study of Quotas for the Scheduled Castes in India." *American Economic Journal: Applied Economics* 7, no. 3 (2015): 196–220.

Jensenius, Francesca R. *Social Justice through Inclusion: The Consequences of Electoral Quotas in India.* Oxford: Oxford University Press, 2017.

McMillan, Alistair. "Delimitation, Democracy and the End of the Constitutional Freeze." *Economic and Political Weekly* 35, no. 15 (2000): 1271–1276.

McMillan, Alistair. *Standing at the Margins: Representation and Electoral Reservation in India.* New Delhi: Oxford University Press, 2005.

Pande, Rohini. "Can Mandated Political Representation Increase Policy Influence for Disadvantaged Minorities? Theory and Evidence from India." *American Economic Review* 93, no. 4 (2003): 1132–1151.

Rudolph, Susanne Hoeber, and Lloyd I. Rudolph. "Congress Learns to Lose: From a One-Party Dominant to a Multiparty System in India." In *Political Transitions in Dominant Party Systems*, edited by Edward Friedman and Joseph Wong, 15–41. Abingdon, UK: Routledge, 2008.

Singer, Matthew M. "Was Duverger Correct? Single-Member District Election Outcomes in Fifty-Three Countries." *British Journal of Political Science* 43, no. 1 (2013): 201–220.

Sivaramakrishnan, K. C. "North-South Divide and Delimitation Blues." *Economic and Political Weekly* 35, no. 35/36 (2000): 3093–3096.

Varkey, Ouseph. "The CPI-Congress Alliance in India." *Asian Survey* 19, no. 9 (1979): 881–895.

Ziegfeld, Adam. "Are Higher-Magnitude Electoral Districts Always Better for Small Parties?" *Electoral Studies* 32, no. 1 (2013): 63–77.

Ziegfeld, Adam. *Why Regional Parties? Clientelism, Elites, and the Indian Party System.* New York: Cambridge University Press, 2016.

Ziegfeld, Adam, and Tudor, Maya. "How Opposition Parties Sustain Single-Party Dominance: Lessons from India." *Party Politics* 23, no. 3 (2017): 262–273.

CHAPTER 34

..................................................................................

# ELECTORAL SYSTEMS
# IN CONTEXT

*United States*

..................................................................................

STEVEN L. TAYLOR

THE United States of America has one of the longest continually operating electoral systems in the world. While the system has evolved since the late 1780s, the basic dynamic of that system is based fundamentally on plurality winners in single-seat district elections for the national (and state) legislatures. This feature has dominated the development of the party system, which is one of the most rigid two-party systems in the world. This is not to say that third parties do not exist, but rather that they are almost always unsuccessful in their quest to win office.

Despite the seeming simplicity of the US electoral process, there are two unique features of the US system that are especially noteworthy and that add a good deal of complexity to the overall system: the usage of primary elections to nominate the candidates of the two major parties, and the Electoral College used to elect the president. It is true that while it is possible to find numerous examples of experimentation with electoral rules at the local level, the basic system demonstrates the power of path dependency on an institutional framework constructed well before the universe of institutional options for electoral systems was understood.

The United States has a federal system, so it is necessary to consider both the national system and state and local processes, although the main focus here is the election of the national government. The federal nature of the United States is also important for understanding various aspects of the electoral system, including laws on how voters vote (including voter identification requirements), districting, and general voting procedures (including ballot format). It is especially noteworthy that US electoral administration is decentralized and the exact voting experience (such as ballot format and voting technology) can vary from state to state (and even within states). There is no central authority for gathering and counting votes. All of those processes are handled by individual states.

In short, understanding the electoral system of the United States requires paying attention not just to the main electoral institutions, which range from the very simple (electing members of Congress) to the complex (electing the president), but also to the role played by historical origins and the candidate nomination process (i.e., primaries).

# BASIC ORIGINS, THE EVOLUTION OF VOTING RIGHTS, AND DISTRICTING

While this chapter is focused on the rules that have dominated from roughly the mid-twentieth century to the present, it is worth highlighting the basic origin of the current constitutional system, which dates to 1789.[1] It is central to understand that the institutional design of that era, which persists in large part to the present period, was born of a political compromise that featured (and arguably created) federalism and presidentialism, with the commensurate task of trying to figure out how to wed those institutional forms to what was a very early foray into representative government. The point here is that the US system is the result of early experimentation without many examples from which lessons could be gleaned while, at the same time, it was tasked with placating numerous interests.[2] So we see a system in which various political compromises shaped the nature of representation in the national legislature, most notably the equality of representation by state in the second chamber, as well as creating a unique process for electing the national executive. It should also be noted that the process to amend the US Constitution is quite cumbersome, making deviations for its institutional pathways all the more unlikely, at least as pertains to any changes that would require changing constitutional language.

While one can credibly argue that the right to vote in the United States was, in terms of global comparison at the time, extensive in 1780s, the fact remains that by contemporary democratic standards it was quite limited. It is noteworthy that there is no explicit, blanket declaration of the right to vote in the original US Constitution, but rather this issue was left to the states. Hence, voting rights were originally limited in various ways to free males, and typically to those with property. Constitutionally, universal male suffrage came via the Fifteenth Amendment (1870), which barred denial of the right to vote based on "race, color, or previous condition of servitude," although practically it would take roughly a century (until the Voting Rights Act of 1965) before the spirit of that amendment would have full legal force. The right for women to vote was extended by the Nineteenth Amendment (1920).

The issue of voting rights as linked to federalism continues in the current period due to various attempts at applying voter identification procedures in numerous states. While this is proffered by local officials as a means to combat voter fraud, the reality is that this process has the effect of making it difficult for certain voters (e.g., the poor, the elderly, and minorities) to exercise their right to vote.[3] There is no universal identification card or process in the United States, and no universal voter registration mechanism. These are all handled at the state level.

Another aspect of the electoral system that is governed on the state level, and that has evolved over time, has been that of setting the boundaries of electoral districts. This is relevant for US House districts (save in states with only one representative) and for internal state districts (e.g., state legislative districts and so forth).[4] Over time the United States has evolved to a system of one district per House seat, but prior to the 1960s many states used at-large districts (and did not redraw districts on a decennial basis to adjust for population shifts, as is the current practice).[5]

Many offices in the United States are linked to single-seat districts. This is true of the House and the Senate, and it is the dominant format for state legislatures.[6] There is a mix of single-seat and multiseat elections for county- and city-level legislative bodies. A large number of other locally elected offices, often including judges and other functionaries, are typically elected by plurality, but with some variation across the country. Given the importance of districts in most of these cases, the issue of who draws districts is of huge political significance. The concept of gerrymandering, or purposefully drawing a district in a way to purposefully favor a given candidate, party, or group, was named, in fact, for an American politician from an 1812 political cartoon.[7]

The exact role of gerrymandering is currently under debate both in the popular press and in academic circles. Some authors argue, for example, that a major factor explaining US electoral outcomes, including much of the lack of competition we see in these contests (especially for Congress[8]), is the result of geographic sorting. Specifically, adherents to the Democratic Party tend to disproportionately cluster in urban areas. This dilutes their influence at the ballot box in a system dominated by single-seat districts.[9] Others argue that gerrymandering, especially in recent years, has had a significant effect on competitiveness.[10] Further, as McCarty, Poole, and Rosenthal (2009) have shown, party polarization exists distinctly from the issue of how districts themselves are drawn. Regardless, the very existence of districts, and the need to periodically redraw those lines, shapes electoral outcomes in the United States.

Three other generic aspects of the American electoral system that should be noted are the electoral calendar, the length of the ballot, and turnout. The United States has national elections every two years (owing to the short length of House terms). Apart from those elections, held by statute on the second Tuesday following the first Monday in November, many states hold their state-level elections during the midterm elections to avoid presidential contests, and a handful in odd-numbered years to avoid national elections entirely. Note that due to the essentially universal usage of primaries (discussed later), each general election has a primary (and perhaps a runoff) associated with it. As such, to be elected to a given office in some states might require three (or more) trips to the polls, that is, primary, primary runoff, and general election (and in rare cases for a general election runoff). Additionally, local elections are often held on an independent calendar. American voters, therefore, often face a large number of potential trips to the polls. And most elections in the United States are held during the workweek and are not days off from work. Not only do Americans have numerous opportunities to go to the polls, but also they have ballots that are typically multiple pages in length, owing to the large number of national, state, and local offices open to election (not to mention that many states and localities have ballot initiatives and referenda).

The United States also has low voter turnout, both in absolute terms and comparatively.[11] From 1972 to 2016, the average turnout of citizens of voting age for presidential elections was 56.46 percent, and turnout for congressional midterm elections from 1974 to 2014 was 38.86 percent.[12] And while systematic data for local elections is more difficult to obtain, one recent study of 114 larger cities in 2011 placed turnout in those elections at 20.9 percent.[13] Turnout for primaries is frequently even lower (especially for local elections).

## The US Party System

The party system of the United States is stable, integrated from the national to the local levels, and consists of nonhierarchical parties heavily influenced by the presidential nature of the system. They have become increasingly polarized in recent decades.[14]

The United States has long had one of the most rigid two-party systems in the world, and its parties are among the oldest. The current system is dominated by the Democrats and Republicans, and that basic configuration dates back to the late 1850s. The Democratic Party traces its history to the founding era and Thomas Jefferson (although the mass party as we understand it is more directly linked to Andrew Jackson). The Republican Party cites Abraham Lincoln as a founder, although its origins slightly predate his presidency. As such, we are talking here about a system that has been in recognizable operation since the mid-nineteenth century, even if the parties themselves have evolved over that span. Indeed, the longevity of these two parties is a testament to the degree to which new party formation is not fostered by the institutional order in the United States.

There is a long-term history of bipartism, as even prior to the current system, electoral competition tended to operate at the two-party level for the most part, even in its early proto-party period of conflict between Federalists and Anti-Federalists. Indeed, many will cite historical precedents as a main reason for the durability of bipartism in American politics, although, as will be discussed, numerous institutional factors provide far more convincing reasons.

A key historical element of the party system that springs from its Civil War–era origins is that from the Reconstruction period (1870s) until the 1990s, the Republican Party was highly unsuccessful in the Southern states that formed the Confederacy. Specifically, we find that most of the South voted solidly Democratic, especially in congressional, state, and local elections, until a shift occurred in the 1990s.[15] From the advent of the New Deal era in 1933 until the "Republican Revolution" of 1994, the Democrats controlled the House of Representatives for all but four years (the Eightieth Congress in 1947, and the Eighty-Third in 1953). Republicans fared slightly better in the Senate during this period, controlling that chamber for a total of ten years. That 1933–1994 period was one of less polarized parties, with a Democratic Party that had both a liberal and a moderate (if not a conservative) faction and a Republican Party with both moderate and conservative factions. This made deal making in the US Congress easier. The 1994 electoral victory by the Republicans was made possible by a realignment in Southern states, which shifted away from one-party Democratic dominance to a mix of two-party competition/Republican dominance. Over the course of the late 1990s and early 2000s, a clear ideological shifting of the parties was taking place, so that the two parties were both more ideologically homogenous. During this period the parties became increasingly polarized.

A cursory look at the US party and electoral systems would suggest that they represent clear-cut proof of Duverger's law, the notion that single-seat plurality elections tend to create two-party systems. However, given that the presence of first-past-the-post systems do not create such outcomes in Canada, India, or the United Kingdom, such rules do not typically create the type of rigidity that we see in the United States (Riker 1976, 1982). While we can throw into the mix presidentialism, another factor Duverger thought would contribute to bipartism, we still find that those institutional features do not account for the two-party dominance that we see in the United States.

Table 34.1 compares the United States to four other single-seat, plurality-winning systems for electing the first chamber of the legislature. All three columns underscore how the United States conforms far closer to the expectations of Duverger's law than do the other cases in terms of both the effective number of electoral parties ($N_V$) and the effective number of parliamentary parties ($N_S$), with some convergence with New Zealand.[16] The effective number of electoral parties indicates a low incidence of third-party competition, and the effective number of parliamentary parties demonstrates the nearly nonexistent number of winning third-party candidates. The disproportionality score is low despite the electoral rules, as voters cast very few votes for third parties, unlike similar systems (most notably the United Kingdom). Indeed, Taylor et al. (2014, 145) show that in comparison to other major democracies, US disproportionality clusters more

Table 34.1  First Chamber Elections, First–Past–the–Post, Single–Seat District Cases

|  | $N_V$ | $N_S$ | LSq |
|---|---|---|---|
| Canada (1945–2015) | 3.28 | 2.51 | 11.63 |
| India (1990–2015) | 6.63 | 5.14 | 7.56 |
| New Zealand (1946–1993) | 2.53 | 1.96 | 11.10 |
| United Kingdom (1945–2015) | 2.94 | 2.18 | 11.87 |
| United States (1946–2014) | 2.07 | 1.94 | 4.73 |

*Source:* Gallagher (n.d.) and author's calculations.

with proportional representation systems than it does with other plurality cases, such as the United Kingdom. The United States lacks regional parties, and in any given district the likelihood is that the two-party vote share is exceptionally high.

The US party system well reflects what Samuels and Shugart (2010) call the presidentialization of the party system—the presidency heavily shapes the party system, in that the presidency is the focal point of the electoral system in terms of the preeminent electoral prize, and because presidential candidates become the leaders of their party. While the former confederate states were locked into a partisan pattern that favored the Democratic Party, initial cracks in partisan preferences were seen at the presidential level well before there were shifts at the senatorial, congressional, and local levels. The president, as the de facto head of the party, shapes the party far more than the nominal chair of the party's national committee or congressional leadership.

Parties in the United States are exceptionally integrated party systems in terms of all levels of office (federal, state, and local) where partisan elections are held. There is a low incidence of successful local parties. That is, the Republicans and Democrats compete across the country and at all levels of government. Further, US parties lack hierarchy. The lack of central control is the result of multiple factors, with the most significant being a lack of control over party label, that is, the nomination process (as discussed later).

# A Unique, and Central, Institutional Feature: Primary Elections

A key component of the US electoral process is the primary election, used almost universally[17] for nominating major party candidates in partisan elections (some local elections are nonpartisan).[18] Often nomination processes are not thought of as a central feature of a national electoral system, if anything because such systems either are party specific or vary so much across parties, cases, and elections that they cannot be easily addressed systematically. Hence, some might wish to relegate primaries to the category of internal party activity, since they are about candidate selection, but in truth, between form (they are conducted via state mechanisms in a manner essentially identical to a general election) and function (they heavily shape the party system, and therefore who gets elected to office), they should be considered an integral part of the US electoral system.[19] Any understanding of electoral outcomes in the United States, therefore, requires understanding this institutional feature. Since primaries are relevant to electing both the national legislature and the national executive (as well as relevant to state and some local elections), it is best to outline the basics here for application in the relevant sections that follow.

The prominence of the primary is especially key in understanding US elections in a comparative context given that no other country uses this mechanism in the same fashion and certainly not to the same systematic degree. That is, in other countries that use primaries, they are not a central feature and are instead used on a party-by-party or election-by-election basis. Moreover, none of those applications come anywhere near to the comprehensive significance of primaries to US elections.

The basic purpose of primaries is to select the major party candidates who will run in the general election (although they are sometimes also used by third parties). The two main effects of this process are to (1) create nonhierarchical parties and (2) disincentivize new party formation. Lack of hierarchy is clear, as in this system party elites have limited to no influence on who uses the party's label. New party formation is discouraged because it is actually easier to seek and win the nomination of one of the major parties than it is to form a new party and then achieve an electoral victory over the two existing parties.

Let's consider that the easiest way to make it to the general election ballot is to be nominated by one of the major parties. As such, a new entrant into the political process has two basic choices: seek the nomination of a major party or try an alternative route. Since politicians do not need the acquiescence of party elites to utilize the party label, but rather rely on primary voters to bestow that privilege, they are not beholden to those elites. Further, state election laws essentially guarantee a ballot slot for major party nominees in the United States, but not for smaller third parties (most especially not new ones). So it makes far more strategic sense for power seekers to pursue nominations of either the Democrats or Republicans than it does to take the more precarious pathway of a third-party candidacy. A key example of this can be seen via the behavior of the Tea Party faction of the Republican Party in the 2010 and 2012 electoral cycles (and the commensurate behavior of the Tea Party caucus in the House, and its successor, the Freedom caucus).[20] Specifically, the Republican Speaker of the House had a difficult time controlling his party caucus during several confrontations over the debt ceiling and the federal budget as a result of factionalism made possible by the nonhierarchical nature of the parties. Indeed, one could argue it was this mechanism that allowed the Southern Democrats to eschew the Republican Party for over a century after Reconstruction: they simply competed within the Democratic primaries.

The two major parties (and occasionally third parties) have used primary elections as their main method for nominating candidates for national legislative and most state-level races since the early twentieth century. They have existed as part of the presidential selection process for roughly as long, but have only been pivotal since the 1972 McGovern-Fraser Commission. The specific roles played by primaries in filling specific offices will be discussed later, but some general parameters need to be discussed in advance of those sections.

A primary election is an example of the combination of partisan activity and state mechanisms. The basic rules and parameters of the process are set, in part, by party preferences, but the controlling authority is the state, which also conducts primary elections. These contests can be open (voters choose their party affiliation on the day of the event) or closed (voters register in advance of the events and are bound by their preference). There are variations in some states wherein same-day registration is allowed or where unaffiliated voters can choose a primary even if they have not registered as a member of a given party.[21] In some cases primaries assign winners based on plurality and in other cases they require runoffs. Presidential primaries have their own idiosyncrasies, which will be discussed later.

California and Washington employ a "top two" system in which the candidates in the general election are the top two vote getters in the first round, irrespective of party or of the margin of difference between candidates in the first round. This frequently leads to general election contests that feature candidates of only one party. Fundamentally, this system is not really a nomination process, and hence not a primary, as the candidates all self-nominate and multiple candidates from the same party can compete. The top-two model was built on the (flawed) assumption that it would generate more moderate candidates who would have an incentive to appeal to the more numerous moderate voters in a given district. However, there is often an assumption of Downsian districts (i.e., a normal distribution of voters with most being moderate and the extremes being limited), which is not warranted as districts tend to be skewed in favor of one party or the other.

Indeed, it is sometimes argued that properly configured primaries can moderate the ideological perspective of nominees, but the evidence does not suggest this is the case. Also, the debate in American politics about primaries is often about the degree to which primaries do, or do not, produce ideologically more extreme candidates than would otherwise be selected by other methods.[22] As noted earlier, and as will be discussed further later, most districts are skewed heavily in favor of one party, meaning the real contest to determine the office holder is the primary election (i.e., if a given district consists of 80 percent likely Democratic voters, the winner of the Republican primary is a foregone general election loser). It is also worth noting that voter turnout in primary elections is typically quite low.

Louisiana also employs a two-round process to elect members of Congress, wherein multiple candidates from the same party can compete in the "primary" (the first round, held on the general election day), and if anyone wins an absolute majority of votes, then the candidate is elected. Really, the only differences between the Louisiana system and that of California and Washington are timing and the fact that a second round is not automatic.

## ELECTING THE NATIONAL LEGISLATURE

The US Constitution does not stipulate the methods by which Congress is elected, but rather dictates in Article I, Section 4 that "The Times, Places and Manner of holding Elections for Senators and Representatives, shall be prescribed in each State by the Legislature thereof; but the Congress may at any time by Law make or alter such Regulations." Initially states elected their members to the House via single-seat districts, or at large for the whole state. Congress passed a law in 1842 requiring single-seat districts, although some states continued to elect their House slates at large even after the passage of that law. Currently, all members of the Congress of the United States are elected in single-seat districts, and the overwhelming majority of them are elected by plurality (with the exception of California, Louisiana, Washington, and Georgia, which require an absolute majority and hold runoffs if necessary).[23] Additionally, the state of Maine voted in 2016, via Question 5, to start using instant runoff voting (a.k.a., the alternative vote) for congressional elections (as well as for some state-level elections).

The Congress of the United States consists of two chambers, the House of Representatives and the Senate. The House consists of 435 seats, as set by federal law. Each of the fifty states is guaranteed one seat and the allocation of the remaining seats is based on the population of the states, with the number of seats allocated to each state being adjusted every ten years to accommodate population shifts. The 100 seats in the Senate are allocated on the basis of two seats per state, but are elected for staggered terms, so each contest is a single-seat election (even in the rare case of both seats being vacant at the same time). The federal district and the various territories of the United States are not afforded full representation in Congress. Puerto Rico has a resident commissioner that serves a four-year term, and the remaining five localities, American Samoa, the District of Columbia, Guam, the Northern Mariana Islands, and the US Virgin Islands, have delegates who serve two-year terms. These actors can participate in committee activity and introduce legislation but cannot vote on the floor of the chamber.

While the only way to change the size of the US Senate is by adding states,[24] the size of the House is set by law, and has been the same since 1912.[25] At that time, the US population was roughly 92 million, and each congressional district held 210,328 residents. As of the most recent census (in 2010), the population was over 324 million, and each district contained an average of 710,767 persons. In comparative terms, the US first chamber is small relative to population.[26]

If we apply the cube root law of assembly size to the US case, it suggests an assembly size for the House of 687.[27] Interestingly, that method would have suggested an assembly size of 452 in 1912, not far off from what was established by law, but that has not changed despite an over threefold increase in population. This issue matters because it influences a number of factors in the electoral system, such as how well a given legislator can represent such a large number of persons. Additionally, in a system of single-seat districts, it makes gerrymandering easier.

The linkage of districts to population requires the need to redraw districts on a decennial basis and also introduces the issue of gerrymandering into the process. In most states the districts for congressional (and other) offices are drawn by state legislatures, although in some cases this is done by commissions. Beyond gerrymandering, there is the fundamental issue of the way in which geographic sorting influences competitiveness, as was discussed earlier.

An important aspect of single-seat districts and the geographical sorting issue is that it can create a situation in which a spurious majority is possible. In 1914, 1942, 1952, 1996, and 2012, the party that won the most votes nationally did not win the most seats in the House.[28] This issue is interesting from the perspective of democratic theory insofar as it raises questions about the quality of representation in the system. It is worth noting, however, that since there is no formal/legal process for counting the national vote, this is rarely an issue for public discussion. The clerk of the US House does eventually compile this information after every electoral cycle, however.[29]

Third-party representation in the US Congress is all but nonexistent. An excellent illustration of this fact is that Bernie Sanders served as an "independent" in the House from 1991 to 2007, and in the Senate from 2007 to the present. During most of this time he was the only nonmajor party member of the chambers in question, and he always caucused with the Democratic Party. More significantly, he was a competitor for the Democratic Party's nomination for the presidency in 2016, competing in the primary process. This choice underscores that even actors who nominally operate outside the major parties often find it necessary to work within their institutional constraints. Sanders's choice to run for the Democratic nomination was an acknowledgment that (1) the primary allows even party outsiders a chance and (2) that having a legitimate shot at the US presidency requires working within the two-party system.

## Electing the National Executive

The United States arguably has the most complicated process in the world for choosing its chief executive. The United States has a separation-of-powers system and the executive is chosen separately from the legislature for a fixed term, and the president does not have to maintain the confidence of a majority of the legislature to remain in power. The only constitutional exit from power, apart from the end of a fixed term in office, is via impeachment, which is an extraordinary action linked to malfeasance in office, not policy impasse. Terms are four years with a two-term limit. This system also means that the president is the preeminent elected official in the United States and is the nominal head of the party.

To the casual observer, it likely appears as if the system is one of two major parties competing for the plurality of the popular vote. However, while the basic results of the process tend to reflect that general reality, the specifics are far more involved. To fully understand the selection of the president, it is necessary to think of the process as having two major steps, nomination and election, with each of those being divided into two substeps, for a total of four distinct steps. These processes and subprocesses are a mixture of partisan, statutory, and constitutional parameters. It should be noted that this discussion of the nomination process focuses predominantly on the two major political parties. This is not to ignore third parties, but is a recognition that for all practical purposes, the mechanism described is, de facto, the only route to the presidency.

The four steps are as follows. Nomination by either party requires (1) competing in state-level contests to try to win a majority of party delegates who (2) assemble in the summer of election years to nominate the major party candidates. Once nominated, (3) voters register their preferences for the candidate of their choice (but are really voting for slates of electors) in November at the state level to win claim to each state's electoral votes (plus the District of Columbia). This leads to (4) the electors assembling in their state capitals in December to cast the official vote for the presidency (which are counted in Congress in January). Each step is further unpacked and analyzed later.

The pathway to the presidency takes over a year to successfully traverse, with the nomination stage taking the most time. Starting well over a year before the formal election process, numerous candidates of the Democratic and Republican Parties announce their intentions to pursue the nomination of their respective parties. This is essentially a self-nomination process with relatively low barriers for entry (e.g., fees). Each group of partisan candidates competes in intraparty contests at the state and territory levels called caucuses or primaries. Caucuses are collections of local partisan meetings in which candidate preferences are registered by participants,[30] while primary elections are more standard processes wherein voters who identify with a given party go to the polls to vote their preferences on ballots in a manner similar to a standard election. The first caucus takes place in the state of Iowa, typically in January, followed soon thereafter by the first primary in New Hampshire, with the remaining states and territories conducting their contests into June of election year. This system has its origins in the 1972 McGovern-Fraser Commission within the Democratic Party and has evolved since that time. Historically, the usage of primaries to select some delegates dates to 1912, although prior to the 1972 reforms the convention was a far more party-elite-driven institution.

The goal of each of these contests is to win access to delegate slots assigned to each state by the rules of the two major parties. To win the nomination of the two major parties requires the ability to acquire an absolute majority of the available delegates who attend the nominating convention for each party. The allocation rules for delegate acquisition vary by state and by party.[31] Hence, in some cases, the candidates will win delegates on the basis of winning the plurality of votes in a given state, while in other cases delegates are assigned by winning individual congressional districts, or in some cases semiproportionally or proportionally.

The Democratic Party has relatively uniform rules across its nominating processes. Candidates can win delegates at large in the state as a whole and in districts. Delegates are awarded proportionally in these contests for candidates who meet a 15 percent threshold. For example, the 2016 Democratic primaries produced an outcome in which Hillary Clinton won, across contests, 55.23 percent of the votes cast and 54.43 percent of the contested delegates and Bernie Sanders won 43.13 percent of the votes cast and 45.57 percent of the contested delegates. This does not count the so-called superdelegates (see later).

Republicans also allocate delegates at large at the state and district levels, but with more variation on a state-to-state basis and with rules that favor early plurality winners. To illustrate: in 2016, Donald Trump won 44.95 percent of the votes cast in the 2016 primaries, but won 58.29 percent of the delegates as a result.

Upon completion of the delegate-gathering process, the Republican and Democratic Parties have national conventions late in the summer. Going into those events, it is known whether or not there is an absolute majority of delegates to nominate a candidate.

Theoretically, a given convention could be "contested"—that is, if no candidate could claim an absolute majority of delegates, the various factions would have to negotiate to construct a majority coalition of delegates to select a candidate. Since the advent of this system, no such negotiation has been necessary (despite frequent speculation of the possibility in the popular press). In truth, the process tends to encourage candidates to drop out quickly (the length and cost of the process mean that if candidates cannot score wins in the first several contests, they exit). Further, both parties have construed their rules in a way that makes it very difficult for the delegate distribution to end up in a way that would lead to a brokered convention. The Republicans' rules over time have tended to reward plurality winners in their contests (meaning an early front-runner has an advantage). The Democrats, whose delegate distribution is more proportional than that employed by the Republicans, give seats to numerous elected officials to act as uncommitted delegates to the convention (often called "superdelegates") who could (if needed) help push a plurality winner over the top to nomination without negotiations. This system was instituted after the Hunt Commission of 1981 recommended the mechanism following conflicts in the 1980 convention.

Once two candidates are nominated (along with various processes to nominate third-party and independent candidates), the general election campaign officially runs from the end of the conventions until the first Tuesday following the first Monday in November (as dictated by federal law). At that time, the citizens vote in their states for preselected slates of electors (each candidate on the ballot has such a slate). These are multiseat districts with plurality winners (save Maine and Nebraska).[32] Each state is assigned, by the Constitution, electors equal to the number of House seats (based on population) and the number of Senate seats (two per state) that each state has. By constitutional amendment, the District of Columbia has the same number of electors as the least populated state (which is currently three). This sums to a grand total of 538 electors, the only votes that count toward electing the president of the United States. Each elector casts one ballot for president and a separate one for vice president.[33] It is required that the president receive an absolute majority of those votes, meaning at least 270. If no candidate receives 270 electoral votes, the top three electoral vote getters become the candidates for the House of Representatives to consider. In such a scenario, each state delegation is given one vote, and an absolute majority of state delegations is needed to elect the president. The top two vote getters for the vice presidency go to the Senate, where each senator gets one vote. This has happened only twice in history: 1800 and 1824. It was assumed early on that the House would frequently choose the president,[34] but the institution has helped contribute, instead, to strong bipartism.

The Electoral College is an excellent example of how political compromise shapes institutional choices, as well as the way in which sequencing and path dependency have influenced the evolution of US electoral and party politics. In regards to compromise, like much of the original federal bargain, the process to elect the president required a system that would allow for constitutional ratification. The inclusion of this institution was deemed necessary to convince Southern states to ratify the document.

Table 34.2  2016 Presidential Election

|  | Electoral Votes | Percentage EV | Popular Vote | Percentage PV |
|---|---|---|---|---|
| Donald J. Trump | 304 | 56.51% | 62,984,825 | 46.09% |
| Hillary R. Clinton | 227 | 42.19% | 65,853,516 | 48.18% |
| John Kasich | 1 | 0.19% |  |  |
| Bernie Sanders | 1 | 0.19% |  |  |
| Colin L. Powell | 3 | 0.56% |  |  |
| Ron Paul | 1 | 0.19% |  |  |
| Faith Spotted Eagle | 1 | 0.19% |  |  |
| Other candidates |  |  | 7,830,896 | 5.73% |
| Totals | 538 | 100.00% | 136,669,237 | 100.00% |

*Source:* FEC (http://www.fec.gov/pubrec/fe2016/2016presgeresults.pdf)

The democratic deficiencies of this system start with the fact that there is a constitutional gap between the citizen and the election of the president insofar as the electors of the Electoral College are the only persons imbued with the constitutional power to cast a vote for the presidency. This is well reflected by the fact that the system can produce an inversion between the winner of the national popular vote and the electoral vote. This has happened in 1876, 1888, 2000, and 2016. Also, since the Constitution only gives the right to vote for president to the electors, it is theoretically possible for "faithless" electors to cast their votes contrary to the will of the voters. No election has ever hinged on such faithlessness, as electors are selected in a partisan process that essentially guarantees that electors will remain faithful. There are, however, the occasional protest votes cast as a result of this constitutional opening. The 2016 electoral cycle saw an unusual number of faithless electors, with seven (two Republicans and five Democrats).[35] Table 34.2 details the 2016 election, in terms of both the electoral and popular vote.

## STATE AND LOCAL ELECTIONS

The fifty states have electoral systems (and governmental structures) quite similar to the federal government. Each state has an elected chief executive (a governor), and in many cases other executive officers are also elected. All but one state (Nebraska) has a bicameral state legislature. Many states also elect their judicial branch. Beyond the three main branches of government, numerous bodies (such as school boards, county commissions, and other special district entities) are elected, as well as city governments.

Additionally, many states and localities allow either ballot initiatives or referenda, which increases the number of choices citizens may have. Ultimately, the proliferation of elected offices at the state and local levels contribute heavily to the aforementioned long ballot (typically multiple pages). One study noted that the average ballot in 2010 contained seventeen offices and five ballot questions.[36] On balance, these are done by plurality election and via single-seat districts, although there is some amount of variation and experimentation at the local level. It is not unusual for municipal elections to be elected not via single-seat district, but rather using an at-large format, for example. Some cities have a mixture of both. A 2003 study surveyed 649 municipalities of various sizes and found 45.0 percent used the at-large method, 28.8 percent used the district method, and 26.2 percent used a mixture (Svara 2003, 13). Larger cities are far more likely to use districts, while smaller and medium cities are more likely to use the at-large system. Municipal elections in the United States are also often nonpartisan (i.e., candidates are not identified on the ballot adhering to a specific party). According to the National League of Cities, roughly 75 percent of municipalities hold nonpartisan elections.[37]

Beyond the usage of districts, there is some experimentation with electoral rules at the local level. For example, there are a handful of cities across the country that use instant runoff voting (IRV) to elect their mayors (with the most prominent examples being the Bay area of California [Berkley, Oakland, and San Francisco] and Minneapolis, Minnesota). An example of this experimentation is the aforementioned passage of Question 5 in Maine, which will result in not only congressional elections being decided by IRV but also the governor and members of the state legislature. Some experimentation over time has also seen the use of the single-transferable vote (which is still used in Cambridge, Massachusetts, for its city council and school board), the limited vote, cumulative voting, and ranked choice voting (Amy 2000, 181–182; Donovan and Smith 1994; Santucci 2016).

An oddity of state and local elections in the United States is that in many jurisdictions, the judicial branch is elected (often in partisan elections). There are a larger number of types of judicial positions and methods to select for them to be fully catalogued here. However, looking at state supreme courts will help provide a basic idea. We find that twenty-one of the fifty states directly elect members of their supreme courts, with fifteen of those being in nonpartisan elections and six via partisan contests. An additional seventeen states employ systems wherein judges are initially appointed but can retain office via a yes/no choice submitted to the voters upon expiration of their initial term. As such, thirty-eight of fifty states allow for some linkage between voters and the bench.[38]

# Conclusion

The electoral system of the United States is one that appears quite simple at an initial glance, but one that contains a substantial amount of complexity just under the surface.

While very straightforward plurality rules dominate basic decisions from the national to the local level, various factors shape its outcomes. Specifically, two unique features,[39] primaries and the Electoral College, are of great importance. The near ubiquity of the primary election as a means of selecting the two major party candidates makes it an essential aspect of the electoral system, since it means the route to elected office usually requires a candidate to win two (if not three) elections. The combination of this system with single-seat districts that tend not to be competitive means that more often than not, the process that is supposed to solely exist for nomination ends up being the real election (i.e., if a district is heavily Democratic, the winner of the primary will likely be the winner in the general). The fact that single-seat districts dominate the system also contributes to lack of competition and representativeness due to gerrymandering and geographic sorting. All of these factors help to explain the prevalence of long-term, rigid bipartism in the United States.

The process to elect the executive, the Electoral College, also contributes to the structure of party competition. The system is one in which the electoral rules make it easier to pursue a major party nomination via the primary/caucus system than it is to compete as a third-party competitor. The Electoral College further creates potential difficulties for representativeness, given that the system can elect a president who fails to win a national plurality of the vote (as has happened twice in the last five cycles). Such outcomes are especially significant given the important role played by presidents vis-à-vis their parties (as opposed to the way that parties can influence prime ministers in parliamentary systems).

The United States is a case where early adoption of basic institutional parameters illustrates how path dependency can shape a system over a long period of time. The United States was an early adopter of these processes and decisions were made to find a way, to borrow a phrase from Stepan (2004), to "bring together" the original thirteen states into one political union. This act of political will required placation of smaller states that feared losing political clout to larger ones, as well as states with slave-dependent economies fearful of losing political ground to those that were not (and these cleavages were, in some cases, self-reinforcing). As a result, three key institutional choices were made that continue to heavily influence electoral outcomes: parity of state representation in the Senate, the Electoral College to elect the national executive, and a very difficult constitutional amendment process. These all work together to make systemic change unlikely. The US electoral system is likely to persist as a bit of an anachronistic amalgam of institutional choices made at its founding.

## NOTES

1. This is using Elkins, Ginsburg, and Melton's 2009 approach. Even the US Civil War did not put this system on hold, although it was not enforced in the seceding states during the war.
2. There were very few examples of representative institutions from which to model the new constitution. Further, it was necessary to assuage political concerns of large and small states, as well as those whose economies were dependent on slavery. See Taylor et al. (2014).

3. For a substantial set of resources on this topic, see the Brennan Center for Justice's online repository "Research on Voter ID": http://www.brennancenter.org/analysis/research-and-publications-voter-id (accessed February 25, 2017).

4. Note that this includes state-level offices, municipalities, and numerous special districts. In 2012, the US Census Bureau counted some 89,055 governmental districts, almost all of which have some sort of elected governance.

5. There were two key Supreme Court cases that influenced this shift. The first was *Baker v. Carr* (1962), which opened the door for the courts to become involved in districting, treating it as a legal, not political, question given the substantial, increasing malapportionment between urban and rural districts. The second was *Gray v. Sanders* (1963), which explicitly asserted the notion of "one person, one vote" as it pertained specifically to the drawing of legislative districts.

6. There are some prominent deviations, such as New Hampshire, which elects is first chamber of 400 members from 204 districts.

7. For a discussion, not just of gerrymandering, but of the politics of districting in the United States, see Cox and Katz (2002) and the chapter by Handley in this volume.

8. For example, the *Cook Political Report* rated 379 of House seats as "solid" (i.e., safe for the incumbent party), with 31 as "likely" for a given partisan outcome and only 25 as toss-ups. Seven Senate seats were in the "toss-up" category for that election. Online at http://cookpolitical.com/house/charts/race-ratings/10160 and http://cookpolitical.com/senate/charts/race-ratings/10166 (accessed March 4, 2017).

9. See Chen and Redden (2013) and also Nate Silver (2010).

10. See Keena et al. (2016). For a briefer run of the book's argument, see Michael Latner (2016).

11. In a study comparing the United States to thirty other democracies during the 1990–2010 period, Taylor et al. (2014, 136) found that the median turnout for those cases was 74.72 percent, while the United States stood well below that at 57.28 percent (looking only at presidential elections). Only three other cases in that study (Canada, Colombia, and Switzerland) had lower turnout.

12. The voting age was lowered to 18 by the Twenty-Sixth Amendment in 1971, hence the date ranges. Data from the International Institute for Democracy and Electoral Assistance Voter Turnout Database, http://www.idea.int/data-tools/data/voter-turnout (accessed on February 26, 2017).

13. See Maciag (2014).

14. For an extensive exploration of the polarization issue, visit the Voteview site (https://voteview.polisci.ucla.edu/) that includes extensive information on the DW-NOMINATE measure of ideological position as developed by Keith T. Poole and Howard Rosenthal.

15. Indeed, early cracks in this dynamic started in some limited cases earlier. However, the watershed moment in terms of national politics was the unexpected capturing of the House by Republicans in the 1994 elections. It would take another several years, at least in some cases, for the Republican Party to assume full dominance in the region even down to the state and local levels.

16. For a detailed explanation of these indices of party system fragmentation, see Shugart and Taagepera (this volume).

17. A few states have mechanisms that are called primaries but really aren't (e.g., California and Louisiana). These are explored later in the chapter.

18. Occasionally state party organizations will use a convention as the nomination mechanism. For example, the Virginia Republican Party has used conventions instead of primaries numerous times in recent years.

19. See the chapter about Israel by Hazan, Itzkovitch-Malka, and Rahat in this volume.

20. We can look back and see other examples, such as the rise of the evangelical wing of the Republican Party in the 1970s/1980s, and the New Democrats in the 1980s/1990s.

21. For a rundown of types, as well as a categorization of all the states, see Fair Vote, "Primaries," http://www.fairvote.org/primaries#open_and_closed_primaries.

22. See McCarty, Poole, and Rosenthal (2009) and McGhee et al., (2014).

23. Of course, the top two states (California and Washington) require a second round regardless of the results of the first round, and Georgia combines a two-round system with a standard primary.

24. The matter of two senators per state is one of the most deeply entrenched elements of the US constitutional order, given that in Article V, which described the amendment process, it is stated that "no State, without its Consent, shall be deprived of its equal Suffrage in the Senate." This would suggest, at a minimum, that any attempt to change the allocation of seats to the states in the Senate would require unanimous consent of the states (or, at least, an amendment first of Article V). Nonetheless, the deeply institutionalized nature of state representation in the second chamber was very much part of the initial constitutional bargain and shapes the legislature, and nature of representation, in the US national legislature to this day.

25. Save for a brief bump to 436 from 1959 to 1961 and 437 from 1961 to 1963 to accommodate the additions of Alaska and Hawaii as states.

26. A few examples: The United Kingdom's House of Commons is 650 seats, the German Bundestag is 622 seats, and Mexico's Chamber of Representatives is 500 seats. For a study of the size of the House, see Frederick (2010).

27. The cube root law suggests that the appropriate size of a legislature can be determined by the formula $S = P^{1/3}$ (where S is assembly size and P is national population). For a discussion of the cube root law, as well as references to a broader literature on the significance of assembly size, see Taagepera (1972; 2007, 187–190).

28. For more on this see Shugart (2012).

29. This can be found online at http://clerk.house.gov/member_info/electionInfo/ (accessed March 4, 2017).

30. In the most famous of the caucuses, Iowa, caucuses are local meetings wherein participants meet and hear short speeches in support of the candidates. In the Republican process, participants mark their preferences on paper, while for the Democrats, they vote by standing in one corner of a room—a process that can include some last-minute negotiations, especially if a given candidate fails to meet a viability threshold (15 percent), and supporters of nonviable candidates can then shift their support before the final tally is taken.

31. For an excellent reference to the variations to these rules, see *The Green Papers* available online at http://www.thegreenpapers.com/.

32. These states award two electors for the winner of the statewide plurality and allocate remaining electoral votes to the plurality winners of their House districts.

33. Originally the ballots were not separate and the top electoral vote getter (if an absolute majority) was the president and the runner-up was vice president. This system was exposed as flawed in the election of 1800 as Thomas Jefferson and his running mate, Aaron

Burr, each received the same number of electoral votes. This flaw was rectified by the Twelfth Amendment.

34. At least that is what Alexander Hamilton suggested in *Federalist 66*.

35. The two faithless Republican electors were from the state of Texas, and they voted for Ron Paul and John Kasich. Faithless Democrats came from Hawaii (one) and the state of Washington (four), voting for Bernie Sanders, Colin L. Powell (thrice), and Faith Spotted Eagle, respectively.

36. See Wheaton (2013).

37. See National League of Cities (n.d.).

38. See Brennan Center for Justice (n.d.).

39. It is worth noting that both Argentina and Finland did have Electoral Colleges, which they both abandoned in 1994. See Shugart and Carey (1992: 210–213) for further discussion of those examples and how they compare to the US case.

## References

Amy, Douglas J. *Behind the Ballot Box: A Citizen's Guide to Voting Systems*. Westport, CT: Praeger, 2000.

Brennan Center for Justice. "Judicial Selection: An Interactive Map," n.d. http://judicialselectionmap.brennancenter.org/?court=Supreme&state=VT (accessed February 26, 2017).

Chen, Jowei, and Jonathan Redden. "Unintentional Gerrymandering: Political Geography and Electoral Bias in Legislatures." *Quarterly Journal of Political Science* 8 (2013): 239–269.

Cox, Gary W., and Jonathan N. Katz. *Elbridge Gerry's Salamander: The Electoral Consequences of the Reapportionment Revolution*. Cambridge: Cambridge University Press, 2002.

Donovan, Todd, and Heather Smith. "Proportional Representation in Local Elections: A Review." Washington State Institute for Public Policy. 1994. http://www.wsipp.wa.gov /ReportFile/1181/Wsipp_Proportional-Representation-in-Local-Elections-A-Review_Full-Report.pdf (accessed March 4, 2017).

Elkins, Zachary, Tom Ginsburg, and James Melton. *The Endurance of National Constitutions*. Cambridge: Cambridge University Press, 2009.

Frederick, Brian. *Congressional Representation & Constituents: The Case for Increasing the U.S. House of Representatives*. New York: Routledge, 2010.

Gallagher, Michael. "Election Indices." n.d. http://www.tcd.ie/Political_Science/staff/michael _gallagher/ElSystems/Docts/ElectionIndices.pdf (accessed April 30, 2017).

Keena, Alex, Anthony J. McGann, Charles A. Smith, and Michael Latner. *Gerrymandering in America: The House of Representatives, the Supreme Court, and the Future of Popular Sovereignty*. Cambridge: Cambridge University Press, 2016.

Latner, Michael. "Republicans Will Likely Keep Their House Majority—Even if Clinton Wins by a Landslide—and It's Because of Gerrymandering," *Fruits and Votes*. (September 27, 2016). https://fruitsandvotes.wordpress.com/2016/09/27/republicans-will-likely-keep-their-house-majority-even-if-clinton-wins-by-a-landslide-and-its-because-of-gerrymandering/ (accessed February 25, 2017).

Maciag, Mike. "Voter Turnout Plummeting in Local Elections," *Governing*. (October 2014). http://www.governing.com/topics/politics/gov-voter-turnout-municipal-elections.html (accessed on February 26, 2017).

McCarty, Nolan, Keith T. Poole, and Howard Rosenthal. "Does Gerrymandering Cause Polarization?" *American Journal of Political Science* 53, no. 3 (2009): 666–680.

McGhee, E., S. Masket, B. Shor, S. Rogers, and N. McCarty. "A Primary Cause of Partisanship? Nomination Systems and Legislator Ideology." *American Journal of Political Science* 58, no. 2 (2014): 337–351.

National League of Cities. "Cities 101—Partisan and Non-Partisan Elections," n.d. http://www .nlc.org/resource/cities-101-partisan-and-non-partisan-election (accessed on February 26, 2017).

Riker, William. "The Number of Political Parties: A Reexamination of Duverger's Law." *Comparative Politics* 9, no. 1 (October 1976): 93–106.

Riker, William. "The Two-Party System and Duverger's Law: An Essay on the History of Political Science." *American Political Science Review* 76, no. 4 (December 1982): 753–766.

Samuels, David J., and Matthew S. Shugart. *Presidents, Parties, and Prime Ministers: How the Separation of Powers Affects Party Organization and Behavior.* Cambridge: Cambridge University Press, 2010.

Santucci, Jack. M. "Exit from Proportional Representation and Implications for Ranked-Choice Voting in American Government." Working Paper, 2016. http://www.jacksantucci .com/docs/papers/repeal_dec2016.pdf (accessed March 4, 2107).

Shugart, Matthew. "Spurious Majorities in the US House in Comparative Perspective," *Fruits and Votes,* (November 14, 2012). https://fruitsandvotes.wordpress.com/2012/11/14/spurious-majorities-in-the-us-house-in-comparative-perspective/ (accessed on February 26, 2017).

Shugart, Matthew Soberg, and John M. Carey. *Presidents and Assemblies: Constitutional Design and Electoral Dynamics.* Cambridge: Cambridge University Press, 1992.

Silver, Nate. "Exburban Growth Should Bolster G.O.P. in Congressional Redistricting," *FiveThirtyEight.* (December 21, 2010) https://fivethirtyeight.blogs.nytimes.com/2010/12/21 /exurban-growth-should-bolster-g-o-p-in-congressional-redistricting/ (accessed February 25, 2017).

Stepan, Alfred. "Toward a New Comparative Politics of Federalism, Multinationalism, and Democracy: Beyond Rikerian Federalism." In *Federalism and Democracy in Latin America,* edited by Edward L. Gibson. Baltimore: Johns Hopkins University Press, 2004.

Svara, James H. *Two Decades of Continuity and Change in American City Councils.* Washington, DC: National League of Cities, 2003. http://www.skidmore.edu/~bturner/Svara%20city-councilrpt.pdf (accessed February 26, 2017).

Taagepera, Rein. "The Size of National Assemblies." *Social Science Research* 1 (1972): 385–401.

Taagepera, Rein. *Predicting Party Sizes: The Logic of Simple Electoral Systems.* Oxford: Oxford University Press, 2007.

Taylor, Steven L., Matthew S. Shugart, Arend Lijphart, and Bernard Grofman. *A Different Democracy: American Government in a Thirty-One-Country Perspective.* New Haven, CT: Yale University Press, 2014.

Wheaton, Sarah. "Comparing Ballot Lengths around the Country," *The Caucus.* (February 6, 2013). https://thecaucus.blogs.nytimes.com/2013/02/06/comparing-ballot-lengths-around-the-country/?_r=1 (accessed February 12, 2017).

CHAPTER 35

......................................................................................................

# ELECTORAL SYSTEMS IN CONTEXT

## *Canada*

......................................................................................................

## LOUIS MASSICOTTE

THIS chapter offers a summary of the evolution of the electoral system in Canada, where the predominance of first past the post did not prevent lively debates on alternative voting, the number of seats in each constituency, proportional representation, or the very process by which such reforms might be introduced. Canada's political system has been strongly influenced by Britain and the United States, and when it comes to electing legislators, it shares with these two countries a predilection for the plurality rule. In recent decades, uneasiness has been expressed about the appropriateness of this rule, and attempts have been made to reform the electoral system to make it more proportional. All have been unsuccessful so far, including the latest one, launched in 2015–2016.[1]

## HISTORICAL BACKGROUND

Canadian electoral history began well before the existing federation was created. Early New France had no representative institutions, though *syndics* and *marguilliers* were elected à *la pluralité des suffrages*. Nova Scotia was the first British colony on Canadian soil to elect a representative assembly, in 1758. Two other jurisdictions carved from Nova Scotia, Prince Edward Island and New Brunswick, later followed suit, in 1773 and 1785, respectively. In 1791, the Constitutional Act created the provinces of Lower Canada (now Québec) and Upper Canada (Ontario), which held their first elections the next year. In 1840, both jurisdictions were forcibly merged into a single entity known as the Province of Canada. Starting in 1832, Newfoundlanders held elections to their House of Assembly.

The country today is a federation of ten provinces and three self-governing territories, and began in 1867, under the British North America Act (now the Constitution

Act), with the creation of a bicameral federal Parliament including a directly elected House of Commons. Ontario and Québec, hitherto merged into a single jurisdiction, were re-established as distinct provinces with their own legislatures and were federated with the Atlantic colonies of New Brunswick and Nova Scotia. In 1871, British Columbia was admitted into the federation as a province, followed by Prince Edward Island two years later. New provinces were carved from the Northwest Territories by the federal Parliament in 1870 (Manitoba) and 1905 (Alberta and Saskatchewan) and immediately acquired representative institutions,[2] while Newfoundland was admitted only in 1949 following a referendum. Table 35.1 provides basic relevant data on each jurisdiction.

Most legislatures in Canada included an appointed upper chamber upon their creation, but such bodies were reduced to near impotence following the advent of responsible government in 1848, and were later abolished one by one, leaving the appointed federal Senate as the only unelected legislative chamber in the country today. However, a few years before Confederation, two attempts were made to rejuvenate, through direct election, some of the existing legislative councils. In the Province of Canada, the Legislative Council became elective in 1856 but gave way to an appointed Senate when Confederation occurred eleven years later. In Prince Edward Island, the Legislative Council was also transformed into a directly elected body in 1862, until it was merged with the lower house in 1893. Prime Minister Harper's plans to transform the federal Senate into a directly elected body came to nothing in 2014 when they were declared unconstitutional by the Supreme Court of Canada. Like the two previous upper chambers cited, Harper's Senate would have been elected by plurality.

Summing up, first past the post (FPTP) now the standard way Canadians elect their federal and provincial legislators. That the plurality rule was initially adopted should not come as a surprise, for the original assemblies were established in a colonial context where the institutions of the mother country were seen as the model to be emulated. That it still prevails indicates that successive generations of politicians, subject to a few exceptions, found it to their liking. Referendums that were held in three provinces throughout the 2000s on the issue suggest that most Canadians felt the same way. However, whether constituencies should elect a single member or more remained an issue for a long time, as, indeed, in the United States (Klain 1955).[3]

## SINGLE-SEAT OR MULTISEAT CONSTITUENCIES?

Constituencies are officially known in Canada as "electoral districts" (in French: *circonscriptions électorales*),[4] though they are informally referred to as ridings in English and *comtés* in French. Whether they should elect one legislator or more remained an issue in some provinces until late in the twentieth century. The pre-1885 British standard arrangement for returning "two knights from every shire and two burgesses from every

## Table 35.1 Electoral Systems in Force in Canada (May 2017)

| Jurisdiction | Legislative Body | Number of seats | Year MMDs abolished | Latest Election | Electoral System | Population Census 2016 |
|---|---|---|---|---|---|---|
| Canada | House of Commons | 338 | 1968 | 2015 | FPTP | 35,151,728 |
| Newfoundland & Labrador | House of Assembly | 48 | 1975 | 2015 | FPTP | 519.716 |
| Prince Edward Island | Legislative Assembly | 27 | 1996 | 2015 | FPTP | 142.907 |
| Nova Scotia | House of Assembly | 51 | 1981 | 2013 | FPTP | 923.598 |
| New Brunswick | Legislative Assembly | 49 | 1974 | 2014 | FPTP | 747.101 |
| Québec | Assemblée Nationale | 125 | 1861 | 2014 | FPTP | 8,164,361 |
| Ontario | Legislative Assembly | 107 | 1926 | 2014 | FPTP | 13,448,494 |
| Manitoba | Legislative Assembly | 57 | 1958 | 2016 | FPTP | 1,278,365 |
| Saskatchewan | Legislative Assembly | 61 | 1967 | 2016 | FPTP | 1,098,352 |
| Alberta | Legislative Assembly | 87 | 1959 | 2015 | FPTP | 4,067,175 |
| British Columbia | Legislative Assembly | 87 | 1991 | 2017 | FPTP | 4,648,055 |
| Northwest Territories | Legislative Assembly | 19 | 1894 | 2015 | FPTP | 41.786 |
| Yukon | Legislative Assembly | 19 | 1920 | 2016 | FPTP | 35.874 |
| Nunavut | Legislative Assembly | 22 | Never had | 2017* | FPTP | 35.944 |

*Sources:* Websites of assemblies, Canadian Census 2016.

* Scheduled for October 2017.

borough" (i.e., two-seat or "dual-member" constituencies) was not always emulated on this side of the Atlantic, and the presumed virtues of single-seat districts seem to have been largely ignored by the politicians who delimited older constituencies. As a result, every Canadian jurisdiction but the Nunavut territory had experience at some time with multiseat districts.

From 1792 to the late 1830s, Lower Canada (now Québec) had mostly two-seat districts, while in Upper Canada (now Ontario) single-seat districts prevailed until 1820, when two-seat districts came to predominate. The decision to switch to single-seat districts for both units, under the Union Act of 1840—forty-five years before the United Kingdom made the same move—came from above. The British Parliament decided that the number of incumbent legislators in the two provinces to be merged, at 152, was too high, and that 84 was a more appropriate figure. As a result, most of the existing two-seat constituencies lost a seat. The Legislative Assembly of the United Canadas (1840–1867) had only a handful of two- or three-seat districts, which disappeared in 1861, thus establishing a pattern that survives to this day.

The vast majority of members of the Canadian House of Commons have always been returned from single-seat districts, but for a long time there were two-seat districts as well. The first House included a single one, but there were seven following the 1872 redistribution, ten in 1874, seven in 1896, three in 1904, five in 1917, and four in 1925. From 1935, there were only two such districts, which disappeared in 1968.

From their ancient origins up to the twentieth century, constituencies for the Atlantic provincial legislative assemblies tended to coincide with existing administrative boundaries, either counties or townships, with each being granted a variable number of seats, depending on their respective population. As a result, the number of legislators returned by each constituency generally ranged between two and as many as five. Multiseat districts remained the rule in New Brunswick until 1974, and in Prince Edward Island until 1996. Nova Scotia's transition was less clear-cut, as multiseat districts predominated until 1933, and disappeared only in 1981. We find the same pattern in Newfoundland (not a part of Canada before 1949), where single-seat districts became prevalent in 1928, though the last two-seat district was abolished in 1975. In all four provinces, each voter in former multiseat districts cast as many votes as there were members to be returned, and all members now sit for single-seat districts.

Prince Edward Island offered for a long time the following original arrangement. Each two-seat constituency returned one assemblyman and one councillor. However, while the right to vote for the former was universal, voting for the latter was subject to a CDN $325 property franchise, which in addition could be exercised in every constituency where this requirement was fulfilled. This was a remnant of the pre-1893 era when the franchise for the Assembly was wider than for the Legislative Council. In 1963, the property franchise was eliminated, and all electors were allowed to vote for both seats at stake. In deference to tradition, legislators continued to be respectively styled councillors and assemblymen until two-seat districts were eliminated in 1996.

In the sparsely populated prairie provinces, single-member districts always predominated. However, a few multiseat districts were established, with boundaries coinciding with those of major cities like Winnipeg, Regina, Saskatoon, Calgary, and Edmonton. They were broken into single-seat districts in Manitoba (1958), Alberta (1959), and Saskatchewan (1967).

British Columbia stands out among western provinces for its long-time attachment to multiseat districts. Starting in 1894, multiseat districts became the exception instead of the rule, but the last ones survived until 1991. As late as in 1986, close to one half of Members of the Legislative Assembly (MLAs) were returned from two-seat districts.

In theory, the existence of multiseat districts might have facilitated the introduction of proportional representation, or of majoritarian systems providing for minority representation, like the limited vote or cumulative voting. The multiseat constituencies that existed in Winnipeg (Manitoba) from 1920 to 1958 and in Calgary and Edmonton (Alberta) between 1926 and 1959 elected their provincial legislators using the single transferable vote (STV) system of proportional representation. Ontario had a brief experience with the limited vote when Toronto was a three-seat constituency for the 1886 and 1890 elections.

However, in all other multiseat constituencies that ever existed in Canada, electors cast a number of votes equal to the number of members to be elected (multiple non-transferable vote [MNTV], also called the block vote). The most common practice was for each elector to be offered a single ballot paper where all candidates were listed and to mark the spots corresponding to their preferred candidates, up to the number of votes they had, a practice that allowed for ballot splitting. Ballots marked for more candidates than there were members to be elected were rejected. A second arrangement was to letter each of the seats at stake (seat "A," seat "B") and to provide electors with one ballot paper (often identified by different colors) for each, thus creating two distinct competitions. The distinction, within every Prince Edward Island two-seat constituency, between the councillor seat and the assemblyman seat had the same effect. Finally, a unique arrangement existed in New Brunswick until 1967, whereby there was no official ballot paper. Electors voted instead by inserting in the ballot box an envelope including either a ballot paper supplied by their preferred party and bearing only the names of the candidates sponsored by this party, an arrangement that encouraged straight party voting, or a blank ballot paper on which they had written the names of their preferred candidates (Campbell 2007, 289). Whichever formula was in force, most of the time the leading party within the constituency carried all seats, and the minority party was obliterated, provided that enough supporters of the former cast a straight party vote (Ward 1967).

Multiseat districts were advocated for various reasons. By following municipal boundaries in urban areas, they were said to avoid charges of gerrymander. They increased the likelihood for a district to end up with a cabinet minister. Different electoral formulas, like STV or the limited vote, necessitated multiseat districts to operate.[5]

MNTV is usually detrimental to political minorities, on the assumption that the latter might otherwise prevail within at least one of the smaller single-seat districts. However, it appears that in the Atlantic provinces, both traditional parties sometimes agreed among themselves to sponsor a bidenominational slate of candidates (one Roman Catholic and one Protestant), thereby ensuring minority representation on religious grounds, a practice that was at times extended to the language minority group in the constituency (Dyck 1986, 94, 126, 165). Gender might be seen as an appropriate ground for splitting the representation. Two-seat districts, with one seat for male candidates and one for females, were indeed proposed for the territory of Nunavut in 1997, but were rejected at a referendum.[6]

# DELIMITING CONSTITUENCIES

For a long time, the delimitation of constituencies was a privilege of legislators, and redistribution bills passed by legislatures were either prepared by the government or by a multiparty committee of the legislature (Ward 1963). Allegations of outrageous gerrymanders have been less frequent than south of the border (Engstrom 2016, 200–202), in part because delimitations tended to follow existing county boundaries. However, legislative malapportionment, with the weight of rural areas being inflated, was rampant until it came under critical scrutiny in the 1960s (Qualter 1970, 84–93; Pasis 1990; Massicotte and Bernard 1985).

Manitoba was the first province, in 1957, to entrust redistribution to an independent boundary commission. The House of Commons followed in 1964, and all jurisdictions but Ontario now provide for boundary commissions working on the basis of criteria ensuring what the Supreme Court of Canada called "effective representation," that is, constituencies being roughly equal in population, though rural and especially northern constituencies have lower population figures.[7] Since the adoption of the Canadian Charter of Human Rights and Freedoms in 1982, the judiciary has been invited to intervene in redistribution issues, notably in British Columbia, Prince Edward Island, and Saskatchewan.[8]

Representation in the federal Parliament offers a supplementary challenge, as seats must first be apportioned *among* provinces before boundaries can be delimited *within* provinces. The existing apportionment rules were revised for the last time in 2011. They guarantee that no province will have fewer seats in the House than senators, a rule that allows New Brunswick and Prince Edward Island to have more seats than their population would warrant, while the faster-growing provinces of Ontario, Alberta, and British Columbia now have representation closer to their population figures than before. The three territories have one seat each, with smaller-than-average populations scattered in jurisdictions that may cover areas twice as large as France.

Following each decennial census, under the Electoral Boundaries Readjustment Act, ten redistribution commissions (one for each province) must be appointed. Each one is chaired by a judge designated by the chief justice of the province and includes two other members appointed by the Speaker of the House of Commons, who in Canada is expected to behave in a nonpartisan way. Each commission prepares a detailed proposal, which is published in newspapers. The criteria for delimitation include population, communities of identity and interest, historical patterns of an electoral district, and geographic size of electoral districts. Constituencies must have a population as close as practicable to the provincial average, and deviations may not exceed plus or minus 25 percent of the provincial quota. However, since 1986, commissions are authorized to exceed this limit "in circumstances viewed by the commission as being extraordinary," a provision that has been invoked very rarely. Public hearings on this proposal must be held throughout the province, allowing the general public, members of the House, and party officials to air their respective views. This is followed by the reports of the boundary commissions, on which MPs have the privilege of offering their objections before the commissions issue their final reports, which will be enacted through a representation order that will not be debated in Parliament. The whole process is now spread over twenty months. In the past, Parliament has repeatedly interrupted the process before its conclusion to alter the rules for allocating seats to provinces, so that, for example, the redistribution that followed the census of 1971 came into force only in 1979. However, the two most recent redistributions came into force on schedule, in 2004 and 2015, respectively.[9]

# EXPERIENCES WITH OTHER ELECTORAL SYSTEMS

For those who revel in electoral system change, Canada is quite boring a country indeed. Though other former parts of the British Empire, like Australia and New Zealand, offer a more varied electoral system history at the national level, Canada sticks to first past the post at all levels of government. As in Britain, experimentation has been confined at the subnational level (Pilon 1999, 2007).

The short experience of Ontario with the limited vote at the end of the nineteenth century has been cited earlier (Bélanger and Stephenson 2014, 118 n. 3). A more far-reaching move was made in 1920 when the city of Winnipeg was made a ten-member district using STV for the election of its representatives in the Manitoba legislature. In 1924, alternative voting (AV) was substituted for plurality (FPTP) in the other forty-five single-seat districts. In 1949, Winnipeg was divided into three 4-seat districts and neighboring St. Boniface became a two-seat district, all using STV. The outcome was a mixed system based on the coexistence of a majoritarian system in rural areas and of proportional representation in Winnipeg. Also in 1924, Alberta introduced on a single stroke the same kind of hybrid, with STV governing the election of the members from Calgary and Edmonton, and AV the election of all other members.[10]

This kind of arrangement made sense from a territorial point of view. The physical dispersion of the rural population in these two western provinces could be plausibly seen as a strong obstacle to creating large multiseat districts, while the same objection lost salience in urban areas. Still today, such a mix has some supporters. Yet, both hybrids were discarded in the mid-1950s and were replaced by plurality in single-seat districts. Revealingly, neither province emulated other Canadian jurisdictions by seizing the opportunity, in the early 2000s, to re-examine the issue.

British Columbia is the only Canadian province where FPTP was ever discarded province-wide and replaced by another system. In 1951, an amendment to the Provincial Elections Act introduced alternative voting. Most constituencies were single seat, but the same system was also used in the existing multiseat constituencies, with each seat being a distinct competition. AV was used for the 1952 and 1953 elections, and jettisoned immediately after, when FPTP was re-established.

It is also worth mentioning that STV was introduced in fourteen cities and towns located in the western provinces between 1916 and 1928 and had been repealed everywhere by 1930, except in Calgary and Winnipeg, where abolition came in the early 1970s (Johnston and Koene 2000). In 1921, the voters of Montreal, then the largest city in Canada, rejected at a referendum the introduction of STV for municipal elections.

A few general remarks can be offered on these experiences, the only ones so far that were successful in Canadian history. First, all were followed in due course by a return to the status quo ante, which suggests at a minimum that none of the systems introduced gained enough general acceptance to become unchallenged.

Second, actual experience with proportional representation in Canada has been confined to only two western provinces, and to *urban* areas within these provinces. In both, STV-elected legislators never accounted for more than one quarter of the total. This means that they never were in a position to alter substantially the general outcome. Wherever it was in force, STV generated more proportional outcomes and allowed smaller parties to obtain representation.

Third, the variant of AV that was introduced in the three provinces, known in Australia as "optional preferential voting," was actually the one that is the closest to FPTP, because ballots simply marked "1" with no indication of further preferences, or even with an "X," were accepted as valid. This feature is not unimportant, because it encourages voters accustomed to a straight choice to perpetuate their past voting habits and reduces the impact of subsequent preferences. The other variant, known as "compulsory preferential voting," obliges the voters, on pain of ballot invalidation, to number each and every candidate by order of preference, thereby increasing the impact of subsequent preferences, but it was never implemented in Canada. There are strong indications that many voters did not embrace the spirit of AV and instead chose to cast a ballot, known as "plumper," marked for a single candidate (Jansen 2004).

Fourth, as a result of this, the actual impact of subsequent preferences on electoral outcomes under AV was minimal. It was of course nonexistent whenever a candidate had a majority of first preferences (for in such cases, subsequent preferences were never counted) or when a candidate was acclaimed. When preferences had to be counted and transferred, they mostly confirmed the victory of the candidate leading after the first count, and therefore did not change anything, apart from delaying the proclamation of the final outcome.

Fifth, some of these electoral system changes were controversial. British Columbia's experiment with AV still stands today as one of the worst examples of the electoral system being manipulated for blatantly partisan purposes. The narrative is well known. In a province where the labor unions–supported Cooperative Commonwealth Federation (CCF) party had become a strong contender for power, fear of socialism led the Liberal and Conservative parties in 1941 to join hands in a coalition government and afterward to agree on a single candidate in all ridings to guarantee the defeat of the socialists, a tactic that worked brilliantly in the 1945 and 1949 elections. By 1951, however, relations between both coalition partners had soured, and the popularity of the coalition government had faded away—hence the introduction of a system that would allow the supporters of each traditional party to direct their second preferences to the other traditional party, thus ensuring the defeat of CCF candidates whenever the latter were short of a majority. Actually, voters solved the dilemma by supporting a new free-enterprise party, William Bennett's Social Credit, who walked away with the prize, while the incumbent premier was defeated in his own riding due to the preferences generated by the very system he had engineered (Harrison 2008; Elkins 1976).

None of the hybrids introduced in Manitoba and Alberta seems to have been the outcome of such obvious party considerations or to have generated as much controversy. In particular, adopting proportional representation in Winnipeg, in the aftermath of a bitter general strike that had left many scars in the community, may be viewed as a device allowing each of the contenders to get some representation, much as the United Nations tends to recommend today for divided polities. Yet the retention of a majoritarian rule in the rural areas, coupled with the introduction of proportional representation (PR) in urban areas, may be viewed as somewhat Machiavellian when it is appreciated that the United Farmers of Alberta (UFA), who introduced this mix in the province, happened to be predominant in the former and in a minority position in the latter.

While the return to plurality in Manitoba does not appear to have been inspired to the same extent by considerations of party advantage, the same cannot be said of the same move in Alberta and in British Columbia. In the former, there is documented archival evidence that the change resulted from hidden partisan motives (Hesketh 1987). In both cases, it was alleged that the defeat, at the latest election, of ruling party stars due to the impact of subsequent preferences led to the change.

# THE IMPACT OF THE SYSTEM

Any analysis of the implications of FPTP is fraught with dangers, insofar as what can be hailed as a virtue by some can easily be reviled by others as shameful. Hence, we will proceed by distinguishing between the virtues claimed by the supporters of plurality and the vices pointed out by its detractors.

## Virtues Claimed by Supporters of First Past the Post

The chief political consequence of the plurality rule at all levels of government has been to foster and to maintain a pattern of strong and stable governance based on single-party majority governments, despite the continuing presence of what Canadians (revealingly) call "third parties." Such governments typically hold a majority of seats and can expect their policies to be endorsed by the legislature, because party discipline, since the second half of the nineteenth century, has become an accepted norm of behavior within the government party, as well as within opposition parties.[11] As a result, Canadian governments tend to be long-lasting. Within the ruling party, the position of the prime minister (or the premier, in provinces and territories) is very strong. The overthrow of a ruling party leader, and therefore the unseating of the head of a government, was historically very rare, though there have been quite a few in this millennium.[12] Canadian executives are strong. Short-lived governments tend to be led by a successor appointed following the resignation, a few months before an election, of an unpopular prime minister, and who had tried in vain to overcome the legacy of his or her predecessor.[13]

Third parties emerged following World War I. Since then, as a consequence, securing a majority *of the popular vote* in federal elections is a feat that few governments have achieved.[14] Despite this, most governments during the same period had a majority in the House of Commons because their plurality in the popular vote was translated into a parliamentary majority. A single-party majority government emerged from eighteen of the twenty-nine elections (62 percent) held from 1921 to 2015 inclusive. In the provinces, the occurrence of a parliamentary majority for the same period was even higher (about 89 percent), though there are regional variations. Legislatures with no majority, colloquially referred to as "hung parliaments" in Westminster countries, have been extremely rare in the Atlantic provinces, but more common west of the Ottawa river (except in Alberta). Québec, where minority governments were unknown before 2007, has since moved in the latter direction.

At times in recent decades, the ruling party's share of the popular vote has been quite low. Both Stephen Harper (in 2011) and Justin Trudeau (in 2015) secured a comfortable majority of seats with about 39.5 percent of the vote, because they led their closest challenger by, respectively, 9 and 7.6 points. Jean Chrétien won a majority in 1997 with 38.5 percent of the vote, largely because he was facing a split opposition and was leading his main challenger by almost twenty points. Since 1993, none of Canada's federal governments has been supported by more than 41 percent of the voters. Indeed, in 2010, this author was invited to write an article exploring the issue whether minority government had become, in Ottawa, the new normalcy, in view of the increasing fragmentation of the electorate and the election of three minority parliaments in a row. So far, the outcome of the two general elections that followed suggests that the negative answer I then gave remains appropriate (Massicotte 2009). Electoral fragmentation is lower in provinces. In the ten most recent provincial elections, support for the winning party ranged from 38.6 percent in Ontario (2014) to 62.6 percent in Saskatchewan (2016). While the latter was one of the three where the 50 percent benchmark was crossed, all these elections resulted into majority governments.

When facing minority parliaments, Canadian prime ministers and premiers, with rare exceptions, have preferred to lead single-party minority governments, to such extent that both notions are now understood as synonymous in public parlance. Creating a parliamentary majority through a multiparty coalition remains theoretically possible but has rarely occurred in Canadian history. Coalitions were tried a long time ago in British Columbia, Saskatchewan, Manitoba, and Ontario, and the resulting administrations typically lasted for the full duration of one or more legislative terms, but nowadays coalitions tend to be denounced as inappropriate or even downright immoral. The most recent attempt at building one at the federal level, in December 2008, generated outrage because the proposed coalition would have depended on the support of the separatist Bloc Québécois, and it failed (Topp 2010).

The life of minority governments may be described as nasty, if not brutish, and short (Gervais 2012). They typically try to govern on an ad hoc basis rather than building a stable parliamentary alliance with one of the third parties, to swallow defeats on secondary issues, and to rely on the threat of dissolution to win endorsement on touchy issues. The average life of a minority parliament hovers around eighteen months, during which the government muddles through while waiting for the best moment to call a snap election and hopefully win a majority, unless the opposition parties join hands to defeat the government should they expect, all of them, to do better at the election that will follow. In Ontario (1985) and British Columbia (2017), minority governments emerged from negotiations between two parties, based on a specific policy agenda, and designed to last respectively for two years, or for the duration of the legislature.

The plurality system, while admittedly failing to deliver majority governments each and every time, arguably encourages political leaders to deal with hung parliaments through single-party minority governments rather than multiparty coalitions. The latter might prove longer-lasting, but would require political power to be shared among two parties, something that goes against the instincts of most politicians, who prefer to hold on to their monopoly of executive power for a while, and to rely on the workings of the plurality system to provide them with a majority at the ensuing election. This is a plausible assumption, though it tends to be more successful for newly appointed government parties (like John Diefenbaker's in 1958) than for incumbent administrations that try to cling to office despite losing their majority. Lester Pearson in the 1960s and Stephen Harper in the 2000s had to lead two minority administrations in a row before their party at long last won a majority.[15] Under a proportional system, securing a majority through a snap election would become far less likely, and parties would be arguably forced to share power on a routine basis through government coalitions.

In addition to fostering a strong and stable government, FPTP is alleged to create a closer connection between legislators and their constituents. Within the ideal territorial framework of a smaller constituency, members of Parliament reign supreme, meeting constituents on a regular basis conducting what the British call "constituency surgeries," attending local social events, and keeping themselves busy with constituency matters rather than focusing exclusively on their legislative work, where their individual impact, while sometimes real, remains much smaller than normative theories of legislatures tend to assume. In Ottawa, the schedule of House sittings now allows MPs to spend a full week in their constituencies during each month the House is sitting. Constituency activities tend to be overlooked both by academic works and by national media (though not by local media), but conversations with MPs routinely confirm how important such activities are in their eyes, even if the consensus is that they ultimately do not make much of a difference at the polls (Irvine 1982). Electoral landslides (as in 1993 and 2015) tend to sweep even the most hardworking MPs who happen to be sitting for swing ridings.

## Criticism Raised by Opponents of First Past the Post

To a greater extent than PR in the European countries where it exists, the plurality rule has been, and still is, criticized on many grounds, some of them existing in all countries with a plurality system, but some others that are uniquely Canadian. Plurality is a disproportional system insofar as it does not guarantee in any way that the number of seats won by each party will be proportional to the number of votes obtained, or that each member will be supported by more than half of the votes cast.[16] A federal general election in Canada is actually a collection of 338 individual contests, fortunately held on the same day, and the number of votes won by each party is sometimes dismissed as an interesting statistic, though federal party subsidies were allotted on that basis when they existed.

The Gallagher index is a standard instrument for measuring the extent to which the apportionment of legislative seats fails to match the distribution of the popular vote (Gallagher 1991). Among 36 Western democratic countries, Canada, at 11.72, ranked 29th for the years 1945 to 1996 (Lijphart 1999, 162). This figure compared with 4.90 for the US House of Representatives, 9.26 for the Australian House of Representatives (elected by AV), 10.33 for the United Kingdom, and 11.11 for pre–mixed-member proportional (MMP) New Zealand. Small FPTP-elected legislatures in Caribbean countries exhibited higher figures.

Distortions in Canadian provincial legislative assemblies were even higher over the same period of time, ranging from 12.32 in Manitoba, to 16.58 in New Brunswick, to 16.61 in Newfoundland, to 16.66 in British Columbia, to 17.46 in Ontario, to 18.74 in Québec, to 18.92 in Nova Scotia, to 19.92 in Saskatchewan, to 20.47 in Prince Edward Island, up to a whopping 24.47 in Alberta.[17] That provinces are smaller and more homogeneous jurisdictions, with smaller assemblies, helps to understand why distortions are much higher there than in Canada as a whole. This is in keeping with the finding that majority governments are much more frequent in provinces than for the House of Commons.

The leading party in terms of popular vote is typically overrepresented in the legislature, to the detriment of the other parties, especially the smaller ones. Some outcomes have been particularly puzzling. That federal Liberals won 60 percent of the vote with 41 percent of the seats in 1993 was not surprising, but the two right-wing parties, with about the same level of support, fared very unevenly. With less than 19 percent of the vote, the Reform Party won fifty-two seats, while the Progressive Conservatives were reduced to two seats despite winning 16 percent. Most intriguingly, the Bloc Québécois, with fifty-four seats, won official opposition status while ranking fourth, with 13.5 percent of the popular vote. A closer look at the map helps to understand such distortions. The Bloc had sponsored only 75 candidates, all in Québec, a normal attitude for a party committed to the independence of the province, and its support there amounted to a whopping 49 percent of the total, enough to win many seats against divided opponents. The Progressive Conservatives had fielded candidates nationwide, but their vote was not territorially concentrated and therefore they lost almost everywhere, while the Reform Party had only 220 candidates (none in Québec) and the votes they won were concentrated in the western provinces.

Despite all these oddities, it can be pointed out that at least, in this case, a legislative majority went to the party *leading in the popular vote*. However, there have been plenty of instances of "wrong winner elections," where the party that came *second in the popular vote* actually emerged with a plurality or even a majority of seats. This occurred in the federal elections of 1957 and 1979, while in the provinces the latest instances on record are New Brunswick (2006), Saskatchewan (1999), Québec (1998), British Columbia (1996), and Newfoundland (1989). This kind of outcome usually arises only when the gap between the two leading parties is narrow. It may result from legislative malapportionment, whenever the leading party does much better in larger constituencies than in smaller ones. But even if constituencies are of equal size, the leading party may nevertheless lose the election if its electoral support is overly concentrated in some districts (the "overkill factor"), winning huge pluralities that amount to wasted votes. When both factors are combined, as in Québec in 1966, as much as a seven-point plurality in the popular vote may be reversed.

Skeletal, or even skinny, representation for the official opposition was never a problem in the federal Parliament, where the government party never won more than three quarters of the seats, but lopsided government majorities are not rare in smaller provincial assemblies. In British Columbia, the Liberals won all but two of the 79 seats at stake in 2001. Quebec Liberals won 102 of the 110 seats in 1973, leaving only 6 to the official opposition. Some extreme cases are almost embarrassing to quote: in both New Brunswick (1987) and Prince Edward Island (1935), the government party won *all* seats in the legislature (there were only 30 seats in the latter, but 58 in the former). In Alberta, the numerous opposition parties have traditionally been reduced to shambles on a routine basis since the 1920s, a feature that may help to understand why only four parties ruled the province in succession during its first 110 years of existence.[18]

The reformers' slogan, "Make every vote count," strikes a chord among supporters of smaller parties, especially if their support is not territorially concentrated. They may be denied any representation or secure much fewer seats than their popular support would warrant. Emerging political parties typically loath the plurality formula, which they tend to see as an existential threat, for fear that in the future their supporters will vote strategically so as to have some impact on the outcome.

The record does not support the view that FPTP prevents the emergence of new parties but confirms that it treats them harshly as long as they remain small. In federal elections, the New Democratic Party (known until 1961 as the CCF) has been represented uninterruptedly in the House of Commons since its first try. Except in 2011, it has been unable to break the two-party mold, though in six provinces so far, the party was successful in becoming a major contender and actually won elections. The Parti Québécois in Québec provincial elections is another fine example. In 1970, they fared poorly under the plurality system, coming second with 23 percent of the popular vote, but ending fourth in the Assembly with only 7 seats out of 108. Their supporters mounted an unsuccessful campaign to move toward a more proportional system. Yet, six and a half years later, this party formed a majority government, and the premier was unable to convince his caucus to support a reform of the electoral system. Social Credit started from scratch and always languished on the opposition benches in the federal Parliament before disappearing, but in both Alberta and British Columbia, it won office and remained in power for decades. The plurality system may curb the ascent of new political forces, but it cannot block the emergence of those that reflect deep-seated and widespread popular frustrations. The same system also tends to work in a merciless way against established parties that fall to third or fourth place, and who get the same treatment as the smaller parties they formerly towered over.

Another criticism against the plurality rule is that it tends to depress electoral turnout, because the outcome depends on a few swing (battleground) ridings where parties tend to focus their resources, while respective party strongholds are taken for granted. In Québec provincial elections, no Parti Québécois candidate was ever successful in ridings dominated by the English-speaking community, which are routinely won by huge margins by their Liberal opponents. Incentives for turning out in these ridings are lower than elsewhere, both for Parti Québécois and Liberal supporters. In 2008, the lowest turnout in the province (36.8 percent) occurred in the heavily non-French-speaking district of Westmount-Saint-Louis.

Electoral turnout in Canada has always been below the average among established democratic countries, though the country fares better compared with all countries that hold elections. A study of electoral turnout covering 169 countries between 1945 and 2001 found Canada's average turnout to be 26th or 83rd highest, whether turnout was computed as a percentage of the voting age population or of registered voters (López Pintor, Gratschew, and Sullivan 2012). While the electoral system is only one among the many determinants of turnout, foreign experience suggests that turnout might be higher by a few points under a more proportional formula. There are no reasons to assume that the latter would prevent turnouts from declining further, as they have in most mature democracies over the last two decades, whichever electoral system is used.

The argument that single-member constituencies hinder women's representation in legislatures has also been raised in Canada. Though women were enfranchised following World War I, the presence of women in Canadian legislatures was rather skeletal until the 1980s, and the country remains well below the percentage of women found in PR-elected legislatures. Following the 2015 election, the House of Commons included eighty-eight women, which accounted for 26 percent of the total. The latter figure put Canada 62nd among the 193 countries covered by the study. The percentage of women legislators in Canadian provinces and territories currently ranges from 9 percent in Nunavut to 37.6 percent in British Columbia.[19] Here again, single-seat districts hinder, but do not block, the increase in female representation. Some jurisdictions have dealt with the issue by putting many women in cabinet positions. Justin Trudeau's cabinet in November 2015 included fifteen women out of thirty-one members, a move the new prime minister defended by saying "because it's 2015." In June 2015, women cabinet ministers were 36.4 percent in British Columbia, 35.5 percent in Ontario, and 34.8 percent in Alberta. Tremblay (2012) confirms that the presence of women was stronger in cabinets than in legislatures.

Criticisms based on disproportional outcomes, low turnout, and lower female representation are routinely raised in all countries that elect their legislators by plurality or majority. In Canada, they are supplemented by another issue that is typically Canadian. In a huge federal country where regionalism is a salient feature of its politics, support for federal parties has varied at times widely among regions. The efforts of prime ministers to make their cabinets regionally representative have been hindered by the dearth of MPs from some regions within the government caucus. The chief argument is that the plurality system, while admittedly not *creating* regional electoral cleavages, exacerbates them by providing scant representation for major national parties in some regions. In 1979, for example, the Progressive Conservative caucus included only two MPs from Québec (out of a possible seventy-five), and the paucity of cabinet material from a province that was scheduled to hold a referendum on sovereignty within the year to come proved to be a daunting challenge for Prime Minister Joe Clark. In due course, the Liberals were confronted with the same problem in reverse after having won the 1980 election, with a whopping seventy-four MPs from Québec but only two (out of a possible seventy-seven) in the western provinces. A change of party leaders occurred prior to the 1984 election with the Progressive Conservatives selecting a leader from Québec and the Liberals an English-speaking leader with roots in the West and in Ontario. Brian Mulroney, for the first time in Canadian electoral history, then won both a plurality of votes and a majority of seats within *each and every* province and territory. This had the effect of defusing the issue, but it re-emerged during the 1990s when the Reform Party and the Bloc Québécois became dominant within two major regions. Stephen Harper's Conservatives lacked strong support from Québec throughout their successive terms in office. Justin Trudeau, however, has been blessed so far, leading in every province but Alberta and Saskatchewan.

Instead of moving toward electoral system change, successive Canadian prime ministers have dealt with this problem by opting for a panoply of less far-reaching measures. Senators from the underrepresented regions were at times appointed to the cabinet; opposition MPs from these regions switched sides and were rewarded with cabinet appointments; smaller cabinets (Justin Trudeau's has thirty-one) reduced the necessity of finding people for filling the formerly standard forty-minister contingent; and more attention has been paid to avoiding measures that were deemed provocative in specific regions, like the National Energy Policy of 1980.

# ATTEMPTS AT REFORM IN RECENT YEARS

The academic debate on electoral system reform was ignited during the 1960s by Alan Cairns's seminal contribution, which led to rebuttals from supporters of plurality.[20] In view of the then-ongoing regional electoral polarization, electoral system reform was the talk of the town in Ottawa in 1979–1980. To no avail, the Pépin-Robarts Task Force on Canadian Unity proposed in January 1979 that the House of Commons be expanded by sixty seats to be apportioned proportionately among federal parties.[21] Unable to convince the ruling party caucus, the government opted for an Australian-style PR-elected Senate, but the parliamentary committee appointed to inquire on the issue opted instead for a plurality-elected Senate. In Quebec, there were two unsuccessful attempts to implement a list system of proportional representation in 1978–1979 and 1982–1984. The possibility of a Charter challenge to the existing electoral system has been explored (Knight 1999; Beatty 2001), but the single judicial decision on that issue has been negative.[22]

The years 2000–2007 were quite active in the field, with reform efforts in Ottawa and in five provinces. Through a federal government agency (the Law Commission of Canada), royal commissions (New Brunswick and Prince Edward Island), or the government itself (Québec), the issue was explored at length, and detailed proposals were made (Law Commission of Canada 2004; British Columbia Citizens Assembly on Electoral Reform 2004; Ontario Citizens Assembly on Electoral Reform 2007; Massicotte 2004; New Brunswick Commission on Legislative Democracy 2004; Prince Edward Island Electoral Reform Commission 2003). British Columbia pioneered the use of a "Citizens Assembly" composed of randomly selected interested individuals, excluding politicians, an approach that was emulated by Ontario. Immediate catalysts seem to have been either wrong-winner or lopsided-majority recent elections, though wider concerns were invoked as well. British Columbia stood out by proposing STV, while all others opted for a New Zealand–inspired MMP system. Yet, in the end, it came to nothing. STV was endorsed by 58 percent of British Columbia voters at a referendum in 2005, short of the 60 percent threshold the legislature had imposed right from the start, while in a second referendum held four years later, the same formula won only 39 percent against 61 percent for FPTP. Ontario held a referendum on MMP in 2007, subject to the same threshold as British Columbia, and FPTP won over MMP by 63 percent to 37 percent. Prince Edward Island's referendum on MMP was held under no fixed threshold of victory, but the premier made it clear during the campaign that he would feel bound to adopt MMP only if the latter was endorsed by more than 60 percent of the voters. In the end, support was only 36 percent, on a turnout of about 33 percent, as this referendum, unlike the three previous ones, was not held simultaneously with a general election. A referendum on the New Brunswick proposal was scheduled for May 2008, but the incumbent government was defeated in 2006 and the issue was shelved. Québec's proposal was killed by the government caucus.

The debate was reignited by Liberal leader Justin Trudeau's commitment that the 2015 federal election would be the last one held under FPTP. Two options were envisaged, either AV, which Trudeau preferred, or some form of proportional representation. The promise was made at a moment when a minority parliament with the Liberals in third place seemed the most likely outcome, but Trudeau defied the odds and emerged instead as the leader of a majority government. The Conservatives made it clear that such a change would necessitate a referendum, a position that met with much sympathy in opinion polls. During the summer of 2016, a special committee of the House heard academic experts, both Canadian and foreign, as well as the general public. The government had accepted that the representation of parties within the committee mirrors the distribution of the popular vote instead of party strength in the House. In December 2016, all opposition parties agreed to recommend that a national referendum be held on two options, one being FPTP, and the other a proportional formula the government was invited to devise.[23] As the ruling party members within the committee dissented from this recommendation, claiming that Canadians were not sufficiently engaged on the issue, and with the government criticizing the majority report, prospects for reform became poor. Failure became official in February 2017, when electoral system reform was eliminated from the mandate of the newly appointed minister for electoral reform. The most common interpretation is that many Liberals found AV attractive in a political context where New Democrat (NDP) voters were expected to give their second preferences to Liberal rather than Conservatives candidates. However, AV fared poorly among supporters of electoral system reform, while MMP emerged as the strongest alternative to FPTP. As the prime minister was strongly opposed to PR, the status quo prevailed.[24]

In Prince Edward Island, a "Plebiscite on democratic renewal," actually a nonbinding referendum inviting the electorate to express sequential preferences for five reform options, was held in October and November 2016. After first preferences were counted, first past the post led with 31.2 percent, followed by MMP (29 percent), proportional representation with 2-seat districts (21.4 percent), preferential voting (10.6 percent), and "first-past-the-post leaders" (7.6 percent). The elimination of the least favored options and the transfer of preferences produced a narrow victory for MMP with 52 percent of the votes. However, the premier expressed doubts that the result constituted a clear expression of the public will, as turnout reached only 36.5 percent, and expressed his intention to hold another referendum to be held simultaneously with the next election and with only two options. In New Brunswick, an independent commission on electoral reform proposed that AV be adopted in time for the next election, scheduled for September 2018.[25] Premier Gallant decided instead that a referendum on this proposal would be held simultaneously with the next municipal elections, scheduled for 2020, should of course his government be re-elected in between. It is interesting to point out that in November 2016, voters in the neighboring American state of Maine approved a reform to the same effect (locally known as ranked-choice voting) for state and federal elections. On May 2, 2017, the city of London, Ontario, decided that future municipal elections will be held using the "ranked ballot," as alternative voting has come to be called by some in recent years. Following the inconclusive outcome of the British

Columbia election in May 2017, the Greens accepted to support a minority NDP administration. The accord between both parties states that both are committed to proportional representation and will campaign together in support thereof, at a referendum to be held in the fall of 2018. The outcome of the mail-in referendum was disclosed in December 2018. Keeping FPTP was the choice of 61.3 percent of voters. Among the three variants of PR offered in addition to this question, MMP was the most popular, but this did not carry any legal effect in view of the answer to the first question. Prince Edward Island put MMP to another referendum in April 2019, the same day as a general election, and it was rejected, 51.7 percent to 48.3 percent. In Quebec in September 2019, the newly elected Coalition Avenir Québec (CAQ) government presented a bill establishing an MMP system. However, Premier Legault made it clear that this bill would be passed only if the two opposition parties that advocated electoral reform concur, and the adoption of the bill will simply trigger the holding of a referendum on this bill, to be held simultaneously with the next election, scheduled for 2022.

# CONCLUSION

As this chapter makes clear, the preponderance of first-past-the-post in Canada did not preclude interesting debates in the twentieths century on the number of members to be elected by each constituency, or on the introduction of proportional representation during the new millennium. The virtues and defects of both the existing system and of various reform options have been explored at length in the literature and in public consultations, with the public remaining divided so far. The chief obstacles to electoral system reform in Canada remain the aversion of most politicians to power sharing through government coalitions and the reluctance of MPs to share constituency representation. In view of the failure of all attempts so far, it remains doubtful whether these obstacles can be overcome.

## NOTES

1. This chapter expands on another contribution from the author (Massicotte 2005).
2. Between 1898 and 1905, an elected legislative assembly in the Northwest Territories allowed the people living in what is now Alberta and Saskatchewan to acquire experience in representative institutions before these two provinces were formally created.
3. Ten US states still have multiseat constituencies for electing state legislators, down from thirty-nine in the 1950s (Kurtz 2011).
4. Electoral districts are officially called "constituencies" in Saskatchewan and Nunavut. The expression "electoral divisions" is used in Manitoba and Alberta, as well as in the English version of Quebec Statutes, together with the French *circonscriptions*.
5. For a summary of the arguments, see Qualter (1970, 118 and 122).
6. Voters split 43 percent to 57 percent, on a 39 percent turnout (Steele and Tremblay 2005).

7. There is no boundary commission for Ontario because in 1996, the province decided that in the future provincial legislators would be returned by the same districts delimited by an independent commission for federal elections. Subject to a few adjustments, this arrangement has prevailed since then.

8. The most important decision was made by the Supreme Court of Canada: *Reference Re Provincial Electoral Boundaries (Sask.)*, [1991] 2 S.C.R. 158.

9. Courtney (2001, 2004); Courtney, MacKinnon, and Smith (1992); Carty (1985). The last three redistributions are summarized in Massicotte (1997, 2006, 2016a).

10. In Ontario, the United Farmers government of Premier Drury tried to introduce a similar system in the dying days of the legislature in 1923 but was forced to withdraw it because of Conservative opposition. In 1933, the Legislative Assembly of Saskatchewan passed a motion supporting in principle an AV–STV hybrid, but the vote (twenty-six to twenty-one) revealed profound divisions within the ruling coalition and the issue went no further. See *Journals of the Legislative Assembly of Saskatchewan*, March 9, 1933, 72–73.

11. However, a consensual form of governance excluding political parties exists in the Northwest Territories and in Nunavut.

12. Prime Minister Jean Chrétien was forced in August 2002 to announce that he would retire by late 2003 after clear indications emerged that he would lose a vote of confidence at the next party convention. In recent years, the following provincial premiers were forced out of office: Kathy Dunderdale in Newfoundland and Labrador, and Alison Redford in Alberta, both in 2014. In Manitoba, Premier Greg Selinger withstood strong pressures within his own caucus to resign the same year and narrowly won the ensuing party convention. Earlier examples are the resignation of Prime Minister Mackenzie Bowell in 1896 and of Premiers Parent in Québec (1905) and Greenfield in Alberta (1926).

13. Standard examples are John Turner (1984) and Kim Campbell (1993).

14. Only Mackenzie King in 1940, John Diefenbaker in 1958, and Brian Mulroney in 1984 won more than 50 percent of the popular vote. In 1949 and 1953, Louis St-Laurent came very close to that figure.

15. Pearson's Liberals had to select a new leader after five years in office before winning such a majority.

16. One candidate at a provincial election (Québec, 1944) was elected with 21 percent of the votes, apparently a Canadian record. In the 2015 federal election, 28.5 percent was enough to elect an MP.

17. Computations made by Angelo Elias for the author.

18. When the NDP became the fifth party to reach office in Alberta in 2015, they terminated the existence of a 44-year-old Progressive Conservative dynasty, itself preceded by a 36-year-old Social Credit dynasty.

19. For exact figures, see https://en.wikipedia.org/wiki/Women_in_Canadian_provincial _and_territorial_legislatures.

20. Three useful readers include the most significant academic contributions: Johnston and Pasis (1990, 313–384); Milner (1999); and Howe, Johnston, and Blais (2005). See also Weaver (1997); Blais (2008); Massicotte (2016b); and the special issues of *Policy Options* 22, no. 6 (July–August 2001); *Policy* 4, no. 1 (January–February 2016); and *Policy Options*, June 2016, available at http://policyoptions.irpp.org/magazines/june-2016 /electoral-reform/.

21. Canada, Task Force on Canadian Unity (1979); Irvine (1979).

22. *Brian Gibb* et al. v. *A.G. Québec*, Québec Superior Court, [2009] QCCS 1699. In September 2011, the Québec Court of Appeal rejected an appeal from this decision in [2011] QCCA 1634. In April 2012, the Supreme Court of Canada refused to hear an appeal from the decision of the Court of Appeal.

23. Canada, Special Committee of the House of Commons on Electoral Reform, *Report. Strengthening Democracy in Canada. Principles, Process, and Public Engagement for Electoral Reform*, Ottawa, December 2016. http://s3.documentcloud.org/documents /3229059/ERRE-ElectoralReform-9466525-Final-E.pdf.

24. For a detailed analysis, based on insider accounts, of the considerations that led to the shelving of the reform, see Althia Raj, "Fears of Alt-Right, Divisive Referendum behind Liberal Electoral Reform Reversal: Insiders." *Huffington Post*, February 4, 2017, http://www.huffingtonpost.ca/2017/02/03/liberals-electoral-reform-alt-right-fears_n _14603884.html.

25. New Brunswick Commission on Electoral Reform, *A Pathway to an Inclusive Democracy*, Fredericton, March 2017. http://www2.gnb.ca/content/dam/gnb/Departments/eco-bce /Consultations/PDF/PathwayToAnInclusiveDemocracy.pdf.

## References

Beatty, David. "Making Democracy Constitutional." *Policy Options* 22, no. 6 (2001): 50–54.

Bélanger, Éric, and Laura B. Stephenson. "The Comparative Study of Canadian Voting Behaviour." In *Comparing Canada: Methods and Perspectives in Canadian Politics*, edited by Luc Turgeon, Martin Papillon, Jennifer Wallner, and Stephen White, 118 n. 3. Vancouver: UBC Press, 2014.

Blais, André, ed. *To Keep or to Change First-Past-the-Post?* Oxford: Oxford University Press, 2008.

British Columbia Citizens Assembly on Electoral Reform. *Making Every Vote Count. Final Report*. Vancouver, December 2004.

Campbell, Gail. "Defining and Redefining Democracy: The History of Electoral Reform in New Brunswick." In *Democratic Reform in New Brunswick*, edited by William Cross, 273–299. Toronto: Canadian Scholars' Press, 2007.

Canada, Task Force on Canadian Unity. *A Future Together: Observations and Recommendations*. Ottawa: Ministry of Supply and Services, 1979.

Carty, R. Kenneth. "The Electoral Boundary Revolution in Canada." *American Review of Canadian Studies* 15, no. 3 (1985): 273–287.

Courtney, John C. *Commissioned Ridings. Designing Canada's Electoral Districts*. Montreal and Ithaca, NY: McGill-Queen's University Press, 2001.

Courtney, John C. *Elections*. Vancouver: UBC Press, 2004.

Courtney, John C., Peter MacKinnon, and David E. Smith, eds. *Drawing Boundaries: Legislatures, Courts, and Electoral Values*. Saskatoon: Fifth House Publishers, 1992.

Dyck, Rand. *Provincial Politics in Canada*. Scarborough: Prentice-Hall Canada, 1986.

Elkins, David J. "Politics Make Strange Bedfellows: The B.C. Party System in the 1952 and 1953 Provincial Elections." *BC Studies*, no. 30 (Summer 1976): 3–26.

Engstrom, Erik J., *Partisan Gerrymandering and the Construction of American Democracy*. Ann Arbor: University of Michigan Press, 2016.

Gallagher, Michael. "Proportionality, Disproportionality and Electoral Systems." *Electoral Studies* 10, no. 1 (1991): 33–51.

Gervais, Marc. *Challenges of Minority Government in Canada*. Ottawa: Invenire Books, 2012.

Harrison, Stephen. *The Alternative Vote in British Columbia: Values Debates and Party Politics.* MA thesis, University of Victoria, 2008.

Hesketh, Bob. "The Abolition of Preferential Voting in Alberta." *Prairie Forum* 12 (1987): 123–143.

Howe, Paul, Richard Johnston, and André Blais, eds. *Strengthening Canadian Democracy*. Montreal: Institute for Research on Public Policy, 2005.

Irvine, William. *Does Canada Need a New Electoral System?* Kingston: Queen's Studies on the Future of the Canadian Communities, Monograph No. 1, 1979.

Irvine, William P. "Does the Candidate Make a Difference? The Macro-Politics and Micro-Politics of Getting Elected." *Canadian Journal of Political Science* 15, no. 4 (1982): 755–782.

Jansen, Harold J. "The Political Consequences of the Alternative Vote: Lessons from Western Canada." *Canadian Journal of Political Science* 37, no. 3 (2004): 647–669.

Johnston, J. Paul, and Miriam Koene. "Learning History's Lessons Anew: The Use of STV in Canadian Municipal Elections." In *Elections in Australia, Ireland, and Malta under the Single Transferable Vote. Reflections on an Embedded Institution*, edited by Shaun Bowler and Bernard Grofman, 205–247. Ann Arbor: University of Michigan Press, 2000.

Johnston, J. Paul, and Harvey Pasis, eds. *Representation and Electoral Systems. Canadian Perspectives*. Scarborough: Prentice-Hall Canada, 1990.

Klain, Maurice. "A New Look at Constituencies: The Need for a Recount and a Reappraisal." *American Political Science Review* 49, no. 4 (1955): 1105–1119.

Knight, Trevor. "Unconstitutional Democracy? A Charter Challenge to Canada's Electoral System." *University of Toronto Faculty of Law Review* 57, no. 1 (1999): 1–42.

Kurtz, Karl. "Declining Use of Multi-Member Districts." July 13, 2011. http://ncsl.typepad.com /the_thicket/2011/07/the-decline-in-multi-member-districts.html.

Law Commission of Canada. *Voting Counts. Electoral Reform in Canada*. Ottawa: Law Commission of Canada, 2004.

Lijphart, Arend. *Patterns of Democracy. Government Forms and Performance in Thirty-Six Countries*. New Haven, CT, and London: Yale University Press, 1999.

López Pintor, Rafael, Maria Gratschew, and Kate Sullivan. "Voter Turnout Rates from a Comparative Perspective." In *Voter Turnout since 1945: A Global Report*, edited by Jamal Adimi, Maria Gratschew, and Rafael López Pintor, 75–116. Stockholm: International Democracy and Electoral Assistance (IDEA), 2012. http://www.idea.int/publications/vt /upload/Voter%20turnout.pdf.

Massicotte, Louis. "Electoral Reform in the Charter Era." In *The Canadian General Election of 1997*, edited by Alan Frizzell and Jon H. Pammett, 167–191. Toronto: Dundurn, 1997.

Massicotte, Louis. *In Search of a Compensatory Mixed Electoral System for Quebec. Working Document*. Québec: Secrétariat à la réforme des institutions démocratiques, 2004.

Massicotte, Louis. "Canada. Sticking to First-Past-the-Post, for the Time Being." In *The Politics of Electoral Systems*, edited by Michael Gallagher and Paul Mitchell, 199–218. Oxford: Oxford University Press, 2005.

Massicotte, Louis. "Electoral Legislation since 1977: Parliament Regains the Initiative." In *The Canadian General Election of 2006*, edited by Jon H. Pammett and Christopher Dornan, 196–219. Toronto: Dundurn, 2006.

Massicotte, Louis. "Les gouvernements minoritaires sont-ils devenus la nouvelle norme?" *Policy Options Politiques* 30, no. 10 (November 2009): 60–62.

Massicotte, Louis. "Roll Back! The Conservatives Rewrite Election Laws, 2006-2015." In *The Canadian General Election of 2015*, edited by Jon H. Pammett and Christopher Dornan, 163–194. Toronto: Dundurn, 2016a.

Massicotte, Louis. "Canadians to Debate Electoral Reform Again—but at This Stage, Success Seems Unlikely." *Constitution Unit*, May 2016b. https://constitution-unit.com/tag/louis-massicotte/.

Massicotte, Louis, and André Bernard. *Le Scrutin au Québec. Un Miroir déformant*, Montréal: Hurtubise HMH, 1985.

Milner, Henry, ed. *Making Every Vote Count. Reassessing Canada's Electoral System*, Toronto: Broadview Press, 1999.

New Brunswick Commission on Legislative Democracy. *Final Report and Recommendations*. Fredericton, December 2004.

Ontario Citizens Assembly on Electoral Reform. *One Ballot, Two Votes. A New Way to Vote in Ontario*. Toronto, May 2007.

Pasis, Harvey E. "Electoral Distribution in the Canadian Provincial Legislatures." In *Representation and Electoral Systems. Canadian Perspectives*, edited by J. Paul Johnston and Harvey E. Pasis, 251–253. Scarborough: Prentice-Hall Canada, 1990.

Pilon, Dennis. "The History of Voting System Reform in Canada." In *Making Every Vote Count: Reassessing Canada's Electoral System*, edited by Henry Milner, 111–121. Peterborough: Broadview Press, 1999.

Pilon, Dennis. *The Politics of Voting, Reforming Canada's Electoral System*. Toronto: Edward Montgomery, 2007.

Prince Edward Island Electoral Reform Commission. *Report*. Charlottetown, December 2003.

Qualter, Terence H. *The Election Process in Canada*. Toronto: McGraw-Hill, 1970.

Steele, Jackie, and Manon Tremblay. "Paradise Lost? The Gender Parity Plebiscite in Nunavut." *Canadian Parliamentary Review* 28, no. 1 (2005): 34–39.

Topp, Brian. *How We Almost Gave Tories the Boot: The Inside Story behind the Coalition*. Toronto: Lorimer, 2010.

Tremblay, Manon. "Women's Access to Cabinets in Canada: Assessing the Role of Some Institutional Variables." *Canadian Political Science Review* 6, no. 2–3 (2012): 159–170.

Ward, Norman. *The Canadian House of Commons. Representation*. 2nd ed. Toronto: University of Toronto Press, 1963.

Ward, Norman. "Voting in Canadian Dual-Member Constituencies." In *Voting in Canada*, edited by John C. Courtney, 125–129. Scarborough: Prentice-Hall Canada, 1967.

Weaver, R. Kent. "Improving Representation in the Canadian House of Commons." *Canadian Journal of Political Science* 30, no. 3 (1997): 473–512.

CHAPTER 36

....................................................................................

# ELECTORAL SYSTEMS
# IN CONTEXT
*Australia*

....................................................................................

## IAN MCALLISTER AND TONI MAKKAI

For more than a century, Australia has experimented widely with the design of its electoral institutions.[1] Writing in 1952, the distinguished American political scientist Louise Overacker commented that "no modern democracy has shown greater readiness to experiment with various electoral methods than Australia" (Overacker 1952, 15). This experimentation had taken place among the six states and two territories that constitute the federation, as well as at the federal level itself, and between the upper and lower houses. The net result is that Australia has a wide range of electoral systems operating at local, state, and national levels, all with different rules and procedures and all conducted under a system of compulsory voting. It is hardly an exaggeration to say that to navigate this complex and often changing system, the Australian voter has become one of the most sophisticated in the world.

Electoral experimentation began in the colonies in the mid-nineteenth century, prior to the formation of the Commonwealth in 1901. A range of political reforms were introduced that were far ahead of those of any other country in the world, with the possible exception of New Zealand. By 1859, all but two of the colonies had introduced universal manhood suffrage, and votes for women were part of the first Commonwealth elections in 1902.[2] The principle of payment for elected representatives was established early—in 1870 in Victoria, with most of the remaining colonies following by 1890. Perhaps the most internationally conspicuous innovation was the secret ballot—what is still called "the Australian ballot" in many countries. In 1856, Victoria became the first jurisdiction in the world to adopt a secret ballot in elections, with the last, Western Australia, adopting it in 1877. By any standards, nineteenth-century Australia was a world leader in democratic reform.

This propensity toward electoral experimentation is explained by three factors that converged in the nineteenth and early twentieth centuries. One was the international debates that were taking place about electoral reform, most notably those in Britain (Hancock 1947; Reeves 1902). This was the period when Britain was considering the adoption of proportional representation (PR), and the debates over the merits of the single transferable vote influenced Australia's early electoral reformers. There is also evidence that Belgium, the first country to adopt PR, was also closely studied by these reformers (Graham 1968).[3] Second, there was already a great deal of electoral experimentation among the colonies that came together to form the Commonwealth in 1901. This meant that legislators had a diversity of systems and experiences to draw on when considering any change. The final factor was a small group of influential actors who were staunch advocates of preferential voting systems and well connected with the legislators of the day.[4]

Internationally, this electoral diversity makes Australia an important case study to examine the operation and consequences of different types of electoral systems. While the alternative vote method of preferential voting has been used outside Australia only in several subnational elections and in small Pacific nations (Reilly 2004), it has been widely discussed and considered, and was the reform offered (and rejected) in the 2011 British referendum on electoral reform. Compulsory voting has also been widely discussed as a possible solution to declining turnout in the voluntary voting systems. It was raised in 2015 by President Obama, who argued that applying the Australian system to the United States would be "transformative."[5] And while Australia lagged behind Ireland and Malta in its adoption of the single transferable vote (STV), the way in which it has been continuously adapted for Senate elections has been extensively studied (Farrell and Katz 2014; Weeks 2014).

This chapter examines the evolution of the electoral system in Australia at the national level and its consequences for voters and parties.[6] The first section outlines the development of the House of Representatives electoral system, while the second section examines the more complex design of the Senate system, which has been subject to continuous change since 1949. The third section focuses on the implementation of compulsory voting in the 1920s and its consequences, arguably the most internationally distinctive feature of the Australian electoral system. How the design of the system has shaped the development of the party system and voter behavior is the subject of the fourth section, while the final section draws some general conclusions about the electoral system and places it within a comparative context.

# The House of Representatives Electoral System

A variety of influences have shaped the evolution of Australia's varied electoral systems, most notably electoral practice in Britain, where first-past-the-post voting has applied since democratization in the late nineteenth century. Prior to federation, four of the six colonial parliaments used first-past-the-post voting. The exceptions were Queensland, which in 1892 adopted optional preferential voting, and Tasmania, which in 1896 adopted proportional representation or, as it is known locally, "Hare-Clark." This term combines the names of Thomas Hare, the British electoral reformer who had first proposed the system in 1859, and Andrew Inglis Clark, Tasmania's attorney-general from 1887 to 1892 and again from 1894 to 1897, who implemented the system in the then colony (Farrell and McAllister 2005, 27ff).

As a consequence of these differing colonial electoral arrangements, the methods of voting and counting used for the first federal election in 1901 were determined by the colonies. These systems are outlined in Table 36.1. In 1902, a draft bill was presented to parliament to introduce a preferential system for the House of Representatives and a proportional system for the Senate. The system for the lower house stipulated single-seat constituencies and optional preferences and was essentially majoritarian. The bill failed to be passed because of shifting party priorities, conflicts between electoral specialists over what was seen as the best system, and a crowded legislative agenda. Following this failed attempt to introduce preferential voting for both houses, first past the post was used uniformly for the six Commonwealth elections conducted between 1903 and 1917.

In 1918, preferential voting was finally adopted for the House of Representatives, the one major change from the 1902 proposal being the use of exhaustive preferences. This change was consistent with the practice being used by the states that had already adopted preferential voting. Another reason for the change was that an election was imminent and the parties wished to see the new electoral system settled. One particular event that hastened the adoption of preferential voting was a by-election in May 1918 in the Victorian electorate of Flinders. In what became known as "the Flinders deal," the two non-Labor groups agreed that one of them would withdraw their candidate in return for the other tabling legislation to introduce preferential voting. The pressing

## Table 36.1  The House of Representatives Electoral System

| Period | State | Electoral System |
|---|---|---|
| 1901 | NSW, Victoria, W Australia | First past the post, single-seat constituencies |
| | Queensland | Contingent voting, single-seat constituencies |
| | S Australia | First past the post, block voting |
| | Tasmania | Hare-Clark |
| 1903–1918 | All states | First past the post, single-seat constituencies |
| 1918– | All states | Preferential, single-seat constituencies |

*Source:* Farrell and McAllister (2005, 23).

need to prevent non-Labor parties losing because of triangular contests was therefore a major incentive for the introduction of preferential voting.

Preferential voting in the House of Representatives has remained largely unchanged since 1918, with only minor changes. One change in 1940 provided that a vote would not be made "informal" (the Australian term for invalid) by one blank square and the absence of a number would be deemed to indicate a last preference. In 1984, three changes were made. First, candidate order on the ballot was chosen by lottery rather than alphabetical order. This was introduced to reduce the incidence of the "donkey vote," which is a vote where the voter has simply numbered the candidates in lower house elections in rank order.[7] Second, the names of the political parties were included on the ballot paper for the first time. Third, as a result of the introduction of new criteria for the formality of ballot papers, votes could become exhausted in the course of a distribution of preferences.

# THE SENATE ELECTORAL SYSTEM

In contrast to the House of Representatives, there have been many changes to the electoral system used in the Senate; these are outlined in Table 36.2. Between 1901 and 1917, six senators were elected by each state (or three at half Senate elections) using the first-past-the-post system, with the exception of Tasmania, which used Hare-Clark in 1901. In 1919, Senate voting became preferential as it was believed there would be confusion if electors had to vote with crosses on their Senate voting paper and with numbers on their House of Representatives paper. In 1927, a royal commission was established that recommended the introduction of proportional representation in the Senate. After numerous delays, this recommendation was finally implemented in 1948.

Table 36.2  The Senate Electoral System

| Period | Electoral System |
| --- | --- |
| 1901–1917 | First past the post (except Tasmania in 1901) |
| 1919–1931 | Preferential block majority/optional preferences |
| 1934–1946 | Preferential block majority/compulsory preferences |
| 1949–1983 | Proportional representation/compulsory preferences |
| 1984– | Proportional representation/ticket preferences |
| 2016– | Proportional representation/preferential party preferences |

*Source:* Farrell and McAllister (2005, 23) and updates.

A variety of other less contentious changes have been made to Senate elections. In 1922, a provision was made whereby candidates of the same party could be grouped together, the most favorably placed group being the one with the highest alphabetical average. In 1934, voters were required to indicate a preference between all the candidates; otherwise, the vote is counted as informal. As the number of candidates grew, the combination of compulsory voting and the requirement that electors number all of the squares produced both a high informal vote and a high "donkey vote." As the information burden on voters increased from election to election, it became clear that a change to the electoral system would be required to ensure the system's integrity.

In response to these concerns, the method of voting was changed in 1984 so that voters had the option of casting their ballot by means of the system popularly known as "pick a box." The elector had the choice of either adopting the party's voting ticket, which required simply ticking one box, or selecting particular candidates consecutively in order of preference. In practice, the Senate electoral system became a de facto closed-party-list system, since the parties could choose where to place their candidates within their own list, and thereby effectively decide who would be elected and who would not. Not unnaturally, the parties regarded this as an improvement on the previous system, and while claiming that it was implemented to assist voters, they began using the system to elect their favored candidates.

Since their introduction in 1984, group voting tickets have been widely used by voters, and the proportion increased through the late 1980s and early 1990s. In 1984, for example, 85.3 percent of Senate votes were cast in this way, rather than voters ordering all of the candidates on the ballot paper; in 2013, the figure was even higher at 96.5 percent. This increase was caused by the increasing numbers of candidates and group tickets on the ballot paper, demanding ever more time and knowledge from voters to lodge a valid vote. In this context, casting a group ticket vote reduced the information burden on the voter. Until 2016, lodging a valid vote below the line required the voter to number all of the candidates in order of preference. In the 2013 New South Wales Senate election, for example, this would have required the voter to number no less than 110 boxes. To avoid this, 97.9 percent of New South Wales Senate voters in the election voted for a group ticket.

The Senate electoral system was changed yet again in 2016. Instead of ticket preferences, which allowed voters to cast one vote above the line for a single party, voters were required to list in order of preference at least six parties above the line, or at least twelve candidates below the line. In practice, then, group tickets were abolished and instead voters could order parties (or candidates) preferentially. However, the system remained effectively a de facto closed-party-list system since the parties retained control over the order of their candidates within the list.

This further change to the Senate system in 2016 was motivated by two factors. First, there was an unprecedented surge in support for minor parties in the 2010 and 2013 elections. In the first election conducted under STV, in 1949, the major parties attracted 95.4 percent of the first preference vote and won all of the available seats. Figure 36.2 shows that support for minor parties and independent candidates in Senate elections has been gradually eroding the major party vote ever since, and consistently exceeding

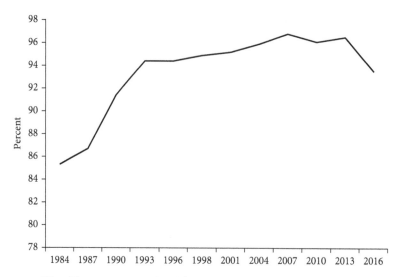

**FIGURE 36.1.** Use of Senate group voting tickets, 1984–2016.

Note: Figures are the percentage of voters who voted using a group voting ticket ("above the line") in the Senate election.

Source: Australian Electoral Commission.

the minor party vote in House of Representatives elections. There was a very significant increase in 2013, when almost one in three Senate votes was cast for a minor party. That trend continued in the 2016 Senate election.

The second factor that caused the change to Senate voting in 2016 was the minor parties' use of the vote transfer arrangements. The evolution of the Senate electoral system into a de facto closed-party-list system has provided multiple opportunities for parties to "game" the system through the direction of preferences, particularly since the late 1990s. This was an effective tactic because—as Figure 36.1 has illustrated—the vast majority of voters opted for a party ticket. Their unused votes were then directed by the parties in a complex scheme of alliances. While preference arrangements had to be registered with the Australian Electoral Commission and are available on their website and in polling stations, in practice the vast majority of voters had no knowledge of where their vote would ultimately go. In turn, voters had little option other than to vote for a party ticket because of the complexity and size of the ballot paper.

The potential for "harvesting" vote transfers between large numbers of minor parties was not lost on an election consultant, Glenn Druery, who became known as the "preference whisperer." From the late 1990s, Druery had been providing advice to minor parties about how to maximize their Senate vote. He first came to prominence in the 1999 New South Wales state election when he registered twenty-four minor parties, resulting in one of the largest ballot papers ever seen in Australia and one of the largest in the world.[8] The purpose of these parties, "relying on nothing more than attractive names to gain votes" (Smith 2006, 136), was to direct preferences to Druery's own party.[9] In the 2013 Senate election two minor party candidates were elected having initially attracted

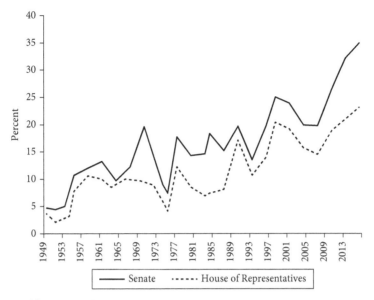

FIGURE 36.2. The non–major party vote, 1949–2016.

Sources: Barber (2011); Australian Electoral Commission.

just 0.23 percent and 0.51 percent of the first preference vote in their respective states, but ultimately winning a quota through the direction of preferences.[10]

The success of what became known as the "micro parties" in the 2013 Senate election attracted widespread criticism, based on the small first preference vote many of them received, and on the opaque way in which votes were transferred between them. To stop these parties from "gaming" the system, optional preferential voting above and below the line was implemented in the 2016 election. This change has had the effect of allowing voters who vote above the line to determine the order of preferences, rather than following a party-determined order. In the 2016 election, the use of "above the line" voting on the Senate ballot paper was 93.5 percent, a decrease of 3 percentage points compared to the previous 2013 election. Voters were required to number at least six boxes above the line, and in 2016, 81.2 percent did so.[11]

The 2016 change to the Senate electoral system had the desired effect of largely eliminating the micro parties. Of the forty-seven parties that contested the Senate, just eight attracted a national vote of 1 percent or more. Five of the eight parties gained at least one seat, and one party (Pauline Hanson's One Nation) won four seats. Two candidates who received less than 1 percent of the national vote did win election, but their votes were concentrated in their home states, and one candidate (Jacqui Lambie in Tasmania) attracted a full quota on the first count, while the other candidate (Derryn Hinch in Victoria) polled just under a full quota on the first count and gained election after transfers. In practice, then, while the change to the electoral system proved to be a barrier for the micro parties, it did not prevent the election of minor party candidates and popular state-based independents.

# COMPULSORY VOTING

The operation of an effective system of compulsory voting for almost a century makes Australia internationally distinctive. This distinctiveness is for a good reason: compulsory voting is rare among democracies, but countries that enforce it are rarer still. In this latter category, only two countries—Australia and Belgium—are reasonably sized, stable democracies.[12] The origins of compulsory voting can be traced to the system of compulsory enrollment that was introduced for Commonwealth elections in 1911. This change was intended to reduce the administrative resources required to maintain an up-to-date electoral roll. Once implemented, the change established the principle of compulsion and effectively opened the door to compulsory voting, which was introduced for Commonwealth elections in 1924.[13]

The move to introduce compulsory voting attracted bipartisan support at all levels of government. The new system suited the convenience of all parties who could reduce the time and effort required to mobilize the vote and instead commit their resources to converting voters. Among the states, the legislation to introduce compulsion was normally introduced by a private member, enabling the major parties to allow an important shift in the system to occur without the risk that any party machine would be blamed if it proved to be unpopular. In the case of the Commonwealth, the entire 1924 debate in both houses took just one hour and twenty-six minutes in the Senate, and fifty-two minutes in the House of Representatives. The effect on turnout was dramatic: the last House of Representatives election under voluntary voting took place in 1922 and recorded a turnout of 59.4 percent; in the first election under compulsory voting, in 1925, turnout increased to 91.4 percent. Over the thirty-six Commonwealth elections held since 1925, turnout has averaged 94.9 percent.[14]

Compulsory voting operates effectively because it is popular among voters. When the question was first asked in a 1943 opinion poll, 60 percent of the respondents supported the system. In the late 1960s, around three-quarters of voters supported it (Figure 36.3), dropping to 64 percent in 1987, and increasing again to peak at 77 percent in 2007. Consistently strong support for compulsory voting reflects, first, the fact that by the 1960s, most voters had known no other system, and second, the absence of any political debate concerning its advantages or disadvantages. Consequently, voters support the system because they see no other practical alternative. Surveys that permit the respondents to register the strength of their opinion for or against the system indicate that voters who favor compulsory voting have stronger views than those who oppose it.[15]

Since 1996, the Australian Election Study has asked the survey respondents if they would still vote if turnout was voluntary. Figure 36.3 shows that between 79 and 88 percent have said that they would "definitely" or "probably" vote if it was voluntary, with most saying they would "definitely" vote. In 2016, for example, 62 percent said they would "definitely" vote, and a further 18 percent said that they would "probably" vote.

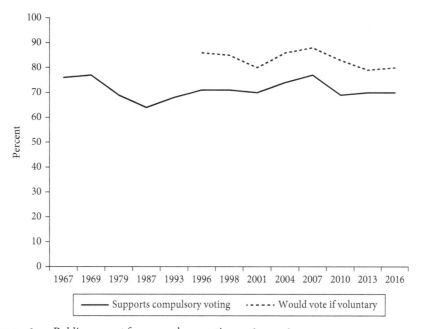

FIGURE 36.3.  Public support for compulsory voting, 1967–2016.

Note: For supports compulsory voting, estimates are (1967–1979) "compulsory better"; (1987–2013) "favor compulsory voting" and "strongly favor compulsory voting." For would vote if voluntary, estimates combine "definitely would have voted" and "probably would have voted."

Source: Cameron and McAllister (2016).

These figures are close to the experience of other countries that have abolished compulsory voting. In the Netherlands, for example, turnout was 92.1 percent in 1967, the last election before compulsory voting was abolished. Turnout declined to an average of 84.1 percent over the six voluntary voting elections immediately following 1967 (Irwin 1974). The estimate that turnout in Australia would drop to around eight out of every ten voters in a voluntary voting election is therefore comparable.

Compulsory voting works in Australia for three reasons. First, as already noted, it attracts widespread public support. Citizens view it as a logical way of ensuring that all citizens are adequately represented in government and that public policy is designed to cater for as large a group as possible (Hill 2002). Second, despite the complexities of the electoral system and the element of compulsion, the Australian Electoral Commission makes registration and voting as user-friendly as possible. There are multiple opportunities to cast an early vote in person or by post, and there are numerous polling booths on Election Day. Moreover, the authorities go out of their way to avoid fining anyone for not voting.[16] Third, the prevailing utilitarian political culture supports compulsion in other areas of public life as a means to achieving "the greatest happiness of the greatest number." Consequently, there are few arguments against compulsory voting based on individual rights and liberty, as would be the case in rights-based political cultures, such as Britain or the United States.

# ELECTORAL SYSTEM DESIGN AND
# ITS CONSEQUENCES

The design of an electoral system—or in the case of Australia, multiple electoral systems—has significant consequences for voters and parties, and for the political system as a whole. Some of these consequences are directly related to how the system operates; this is the case, for example, with the proportion of invalid votes cast in an election. Other consequences are indirect, such as patterns of legislative recruitment. This section examines three specific examples of the consequences of the Australian electoral system. The first example, split-ticket voting, comes about because the system permits voters to cast two votes at each federal election, which the voter can then use tactically. Second, the high proportion of invalid votes cast at each election can be traced to the interaction between complex electoral rules, compulsory voting, and a large proportion of immigrants in the electorate. Third, the existence of strong, highly disciplined political parties has its origins in frequent elections held under compulsory voting.

*Split-ticket voting.* The design of the electoral system provides the opportunity for voters to behave tactically, and to cast a ballot for one party in the lower house and for a different party in the upper house. Split-ticket voting reflects a desire to ensure that the government of the day does not control the upper house and therefore cannot enact its legislative agenda without proper scrutiny. The potential of tactical voting to moderate government policy has its origins in the 1955 election when the election of a single Democratic Labor Party senator gave a minor party the balance of power in the Senate for the first time since federation.[17] Figure 36.4 shows that split-ticket voting began to increase significantly in the late 1990s, peaking at 22 percent in 2013, and falling back to 19 percent in 2016 with the change in the Senate ballot paper.[18]

As in the United States and other countries, split-ticket voting appears to be a relatively recent phenomenon and at least partly a symptom of declining popular trust in parties (Bowler and Denemark 1993; Fiorina 1992). However, in a comparison of Australia and the United States, Bean and Wattenberg (1998) show that Australian split-ticket voters are largely motivated by a desire to see power shared between the parties, a factor that plays no role in shaping the phenomenon in the United States. More recent studies endorse this view and show that split-ticket voters are less likely to want the government to control both houses, and view casting a tactical vote as an important means of forcing a government to compromise on unpopular policies (see, e.g., McAllister 2011, 15–17).

*Informal voting.* Australia has one of the highest rates of informal voting among the established democracies. While compulsory voting systems in general have higher levels of informal voting than is found in voluntary systems—Belgium and Luxembourg, for example, both have levels of informal voting that are on par with Australia—two

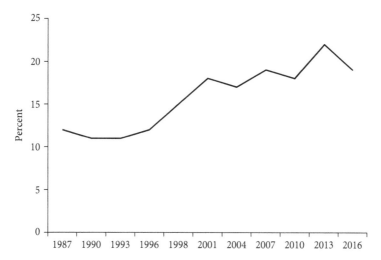

**FIGURE 36.4.** Split-ticket voting, 1987–2016.

Note: The Liberal and National Parties are treated as a single party.

Source: 1987–2016 Australian Election Studies.

additional factors in Australia interact with compulsory voting to increase the informal vote. First, there are a large number of non-English-speaking immigrants in the electorate, many from countries lacking democratic traditions who are unfamiliar with the process of democratic participation. The Australian Electoral Commission goes to considerable lengths to make the system user-friendly for immigrants and prints ballot papers and leaflets in a range of languages. Polling booth data matched to the census show that the highest levels of informal votes are found in areas with large numbers of immigrants from non-English-speaking backgrounds (McAllister and Makkai 1993).

A second factor that leads to high levels of informal voting is the heavy information burden that the electoral system places on voters, both in the frequency of elections and in the complexity of their procedures. In practice, voters must attend the polls about once every eighteen months at either a state or a federal election, with different systems being used between federal and state elections, and between the upper and lower houses. In addition, the increasing tendency to hold House of Representatives elections in conjunction with Senate elections and constitutional referendums, all of which have different rules for completing the ballot paper, creates considerable potential for voter confusion. The net effect of these three factors—compulsory voting, large proportions of voters from immigrant backgrounds, and the information burden the various electoral systems place on voters—accounts for the internationally high levels of informal voting.

Until the 1984 change in Senate voting described earlier, the proportion of informal votes in the Senate was sometimes higher than one in ten of all votes cast, while informal votes in the lower house averaged just 2.1 percent (Figure 36.5). In permitting citizens

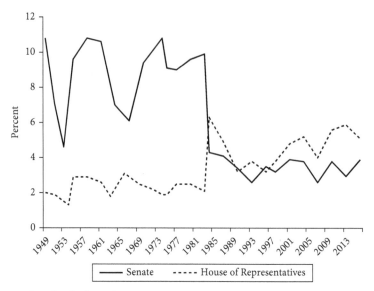

**FIGURE 36.5.** Levels of informal voting, 1949–2016.

Sources: Barber (2011); Australian Electoral Commission.

to cast a single vote "above the line," the 1984 change had the effect of bringing about a substantial reduction in the Senate informal vote, as it was designed to do. However, it unexpectedly increased the informal vote for the House of Representatives, with many electors confusing the two ballot papers. Figure 36.5 shows the impact of this change on informal voting. In both the 1984 and 1987 elections, following the change, for the first time in Australian electoral history informal voting in Senate elections was less than that for the House of Representatives. Since 1998, informal voting in the House of Representatives has gradually edged higher than in the Senate, peaking at 5.9 percent in 2013, compared to 3.0 percent in the Senate.

*Strong political parties.* One of the consequences of compulsory voting combined with frequent elections is a high level of party identification (Singh and Thornton 2013). As the vast majority of voters attend the polls on a regular basis, party loyalty acts as an important informational shortcut to arriving at an electoral decision. The evidence in Figure 36.6[19] from US and Australian elections from the mid-1960s onward does suggest that nonpartisans are a significantly larger proportion of the electorate in the United States than in Australia. Moreover, there has been little change in the gap between the two countries, with nonpartisans averaging almost 25 percentage points less in Australia than in the United States. The most obvious reason for this gap is the differing electoral systems.

Strong political parties mean that voters use partisan loyalties to guide their vote. But it also gives political parties a significant role in how they use the electoral system to direct later preferences toward other parties. As Carey and Shugart (1995, 427) have noted, a preferential system such as Australia's that permits "vote pooling across candidates" provides considerable scope for parties to negotiate transfer arrangements with

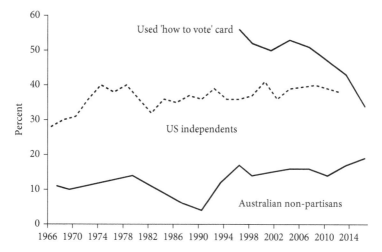

**FIGURE 36.6.** Partisanship and use of voter prompts, 1966–2016.

Note: See note 18 for exact question wordings.

Sources: American National Election Study, 1966–2012; 1967–1979 Australian National Political Attitudes Surveys; 1987–2016 Australian Election Studies.

other parties to maximize their vote. To direct preferences, party supporters hand out "how to vote" (HTV) cards to their potential voters outside polling booths, and voters use them as a guide when completing the lower house ballot paper, ordering candidates according to what the cards stipulate. Figure 36.6 shows that in 1996, just over half of the respondents in the Australian Election Study (AES) said that they followed an HTV card in completing their ballot paper. The proportion has declined since then, to an all-time low of 34 percent in the 2016 election.[20]

Prior to an election, there is considerable negotiation and maneuvering between the parties to reach vote transfer agreements. In most cases these involve parties directing preferences to a party in a seat that they expect to lose, in return for that party reciprocating in a seat that they expect to win. The major parties are always eager to secure transfers from minor parties that have little chance of success. On rare occasions, the major parties can agree to direct preferences away from a particular candidate to ensure that he or she is not elected. Such an example occurred when the One Nation leader Pauline Hanson contested the seat of Blair in the 1998 election. Both the Labor and Liberal parties used HTV cards to place Hanson last on the ballot. While Hanson topped the first preference vote with 36 percent, she ultimately lost the election because she received very few vote transfers from other candidates (Reilly 2004, 261).

The existence of strong, highly disciplined political parties, reinforced by the electoral system, also has consequences for legislative recruitment. Among the major Australian parties, legislative recruitment normally takes place from inside the party's own ranks, rather than from outside. This is because party loyalty is considered to be a primary criterion for candidate selection, with the result that current and former party employees often dominate shortlists. Surveys show that the proportion of election candidates who had been employed in a local member's office increased from 20 percent in 1996 to 29 percent in 2013 (McAllister 2014a, 342). In the Senate, where the electoral system has operated as a de facto closed-party-list system since 1984, the proportion of former employees is even higher, at 41 percent in 2013. The operation of the electoral system therefore has a strong indirect influence on patterns of legislative recruitment.

# CONCLUSION

Writing in the nineteenth century, the close observer of colonial politics, James Bryce, called Australia and New Zealand "laboratories of democracy." He saw both countries as "trying experiments which only countries favoured by nature could possibly venture to try."[21] Since Bryce wrote those words, Australia has continued its democratic experimentation, adopting a range of electoral innovations that has turned it into one of the most electorally complex—and its voters some of the most sophisticated—among the established democracies. Compulsory voting has operated effectively for more than a century, overseen by one of the first electoral management bodies to be established anywhere in the world. A preferential voting system has operated for the lower house, while the single transferable vote system that was introduced for the upper house in the middle of the twentieth century had become a de facto closed-party-list system by century's end. As the previous section demonstrated, this constant experimentation has had specific consequences for voters and parties, and for the political system more generally.

This chapter has outlined some of these distinctive characteristics and examined their origins, operation, and political consequences. What are the challenges for the electoral system in the twenty-first century? First, the three-year cycle for national elections increases the electoral burden on voters. All of the states and territories now have four-year terms; indeed, Australia is one of only a handful of countries that have less than four-year legislative terms.[22] The three-year electoral cycle means that, in practice, a government has little more than one year to implement its legislative agenda before it is has to prepare for the next election. In addition to the negative impact on voters, this constant electoral cycle arguably undermines responsible party government since governments have insufficient time to implement an agenda on which to be judged by voters. A referendum held in 1988 on four-year parliamentary terms was defeated decisively, largely because the major parties could not agree on the proposal and therefore sent confusing messages to their supporters.[23]

A second challenge is the design of the Senate electoral system. In bicameral systems with strong upper houses, who gains election to the upper house is obviously crucial to the success of the government's legislative program. Australia ranks as one of a small number of advanced democracies in which an upper house can exercise any significant legislative authority. In practice, the Senate acts as an institutional veto player and its composition can have major implications for governance. In this context, the method of election to the upper house takes on a greater significance than is the case in other democracies. What began as a candidate-centered proportional representation system in 1949 had by the 1990s become a de facto party list system, substantially undermining the original purpose of the Senate as a guardian of the states' interests. Either the electoral system needs to be changed to return to the Senate's original purpose or the Senate's powers must be significantly reduced.

There are, of course, other challenges for the electoral system. Revitalizing young people's interest in elections has to be a primary goal, as it is in almost all of the other established democracies. While the debate about lowering the voting age to 16 is not as advanced in Australia as in other countries, it is likely to become more salient in the medium term (McAllister 2014b). As Australia's immigrant population increases, changing the franchise so that enrollment is based on permanent residency rather than on citizenship, as is the case in New Zealand, will become more pressing. And not least, simplifying and harmonizing the diverse electoral systems to reduce the informational burden on voters must have a high priority. Voters' interests, rather than the requirements of political parties, need to be placed at the forefront of electoral reform.

# AUTHOR NOTE

Statement: The tables and figures included in the chapter have not appeared elsewhere.

## NOTES

1. For general discussions of the history and development of the electoral system, see Farrell and McAllister (2005), Sawer (2001), and Uhr (1999, 2000). Parts of this chapter draw on Farrell and McAllister (2005).
2. This compares with 1879 for its introduction in New Zealand, 1870 in the United States, and 1918 in Britain. New Zealand led the world in granting votes for women, in 1893, with most of the Australian colonies following shortly after. In the United States, women had to wait for the passage of the Nineteenth Amendment in 1920 to gain the right to vote.
3. Hancock (1947) suggests that while Australia has experimented widely with different electoral methods, most of the ideas for reform "have come from outside" (p. 81). Reeves (1902, 181) makes a similar point.
4. These were Catherine Helen Spence, an electoral reform campaigner; Inglis Clark, a legislator; and Edward Nanson, a theorist. For accounts of these individuals and their influence, see Haward and Warden (1995), Magarey (1985), McLean (1996), Reid and Forrest (1989), and Uhr (2002).
5. https://www.theguardian.com/us-news/2016/apr/10/barack-obama-praises-australias-mandatory-voting-rules (accessed June 20, 2016).
6. The chapter examines only national elections. State elections represent another level of complexity and are beyond the scope of the current exercise.
7. The most famous example of the donkey vote in Australia was Labor's nomination of the "four As"—Amour, Ashley, Armstrong, and Arthur—as candidates in the 1937 New South Wales upper house election. All four were elected.

8. The ballot paper measured 70 cm by 100 cm, the size of a small tablecloth. *Sydney Morning Herald*, September 10, 2013.

9. In the event, Druery failed to win election, but a surprised candidate from the Outdoor Recreation Party did win a seat with just 0.2 percent of the first preference vote. His victory came about thanks to preferences from no less than twenty-two mostly unknown micro parties, most of which had been recently registered.

10. The Australian Sports Party candidate received 0.01 of a quota in Western Australia and the Australian Motoring Enthusiast Party candidate received 0.04 of a quota in Victoria. In total, the 2013 Senate election resulted in the election of eleven minor party and independent candidates, composed of seven minor party and independent candidates from six separate groupings, plus four Green Party candidates.

11. The changes and their implications are discussed in detail in Antony Green's elections blog at http://blogs.abc.net.au/antonygreen/2016/10/how-voters-reacted-to-the-senates-new-electoral-system.html#more and in Muller (2016).

12. The other countries are Cyprus, Fiji (not currently a democracy), Luxembourg, Nauru, Singapore, Switzerland (parts of), and Uruguay. See Pintor and Gratschew (2002). Using different criteria, Sarah Birch (2009) identifies twenty-nine countries that operate some form of compulsory voting.

13. Queensland was also the first state to introduce compulsory voting, in 1915, followed by the Commonwealth in 1924, Victoria (1926), New South Wales and Tasmania (both 1928), Western Australia (1936), and South Australia (1941). There was no agreement on the introduction of compulsion for local government elections and currently it applies in half of the states, with South Australia, Western Australia, and Tasmania operating voluntary voting.

14. Turnout is much lower if we use voting age population rather than enrolled electorate. In the 2016 election, for example, voting age population turnout was 78.0 percent. See http://www.idea.int.

15. In the 2016 AES, for example, of the 70 percent of voters who supported compulsory voting, 47 percent held their view strongly, and of the 30 percent who opposed the system, just 12 percent held a strong view.

16. The fine is relatively small—$A20—but the Australian Electoral Commission will normally accept most reasons for not voting. In the 2004 election, for example, there were 685,937 apparent nonvoters, of whom only 52,796 were fined (Bennett 2005, 27–28).

17. Sharman (1999, 358) sees this as a turning point: "once a minor party had been elected to the Senate and had held the balance of power, a clarion call was sent to parties and voters that PR in the Senate could be used by a minor party with great effect to influence government policy."

18. While comparisons using survey estimates prior to 1987 are less accurate, the evidence suggests that there were lower levels of split-ticket voting in the 1960s and 1970s. For example, when asked in a 1979 survey about their voting intention, only 9 percent of the respondents said that they would split their vote between the House of Representatives and the Senate.

19. The questions were: "In voting for the House of Representatives, did you follow a 'how to vote' card or did you decide your own preferences?"; (United States) "Generally speaking, do you usually think of yourself as a Republican, a Democrat, an Independent or what?"; (Australia) (1967–1969) "Generally speaking, do you think of yourself as Liberal, Labor, Country Party or DLP?"; (1979) "Generally speaking, do you think of yourself as Liberal, Labor, National Country Party or Australian Democrat?"; (1987–2013) "Generally speaking, do you think of yourself as Liberal, Labor, National or what?"

20. These estimates are the same as the Victorian Electoral Commission's estimate that around 39 percent of voters in the 2010 state election cast ballots that were in conformity with the HTV card of the candidate they supported (Victorian Electoral Commission 2010, 72).

21. See http://paperspast.natlib.govt.nz/cgi-bin/paperspast?a=d&d=THD19131229.2.13 (accessed June 21, 2016).

22. The other countries are the United States, New Zealand, the Philippines, and Mexico.

23. The proposal was defeated by 67.1 percent to 32.9 percent. Three other proposals put forward at the same time were also defeated.

## REFERENCES

Barber, Stephen. *Federal Election Results, 1901-2010*. Canberra: Parliamentary Library Research Paper No. 6, 2011-12, 2011. http://www.aph.gov.au/About_Parliament/Parliamentary _Departments/Parliamentary_Library/pubs/rp/rp1112/12rp06 (accessed May 1, 2015).

Bean, Clive, and Martin P. Wattenberg. "Attitudes towards Divided Government and Ticket-Splitting in Australia and the United States." *Australian Journal of Political Science* 33 (1998): 25–36.

Bennett, Scott. *Compulsory Voting in Australian National Elections*. Canberra: Parliamentary Library Research Brief No. 6, 2005.

Birch, Sarah. *Full Participation: A Comparative Study of Compulsory Voting*. New York: United Nations University Press, 2009.

Bowler, Shaun, and David Denemark. "Split Ticket Voting in Australia: Dealignment and Inconsistent Votes Reconsidered." *Australian Journal of Political Science* 28 (1993): 19–37.

Cameron, Sarah, and Ian McAllister. *Trends in Australian Political Opinion: Results from the Australian Election Study, 1987-2016*. Canberra: ANU, 2016.

Carey, John M., and Matthew S. Shugart. "Incentives to Cultivate a Personal Vote." *Electoral Studies* 14 (1995): 417–439.

Farrell, David M., and Richard S. Katz. "Assessing the Proportionality of the Single Transferable Vote." *Representation* 50 (2014): 13–26.

Farrell, David M., and Ian McAllister. *The Australian Electoral System: Origins, Variations and Consequences*. Sydney: UNSW Press, 2005.

Fiorina, Morris P. *Divided Government*. New York: Macmillan, 1992.

Graham, Bruce D. "The Choice of Voting Methods in Federal Politics, 1902–1918." In *Readings in Australian Government*, edited by Colin Hughes, 139–161. St. Lucia, Queensland: University of Queensland Press, 1968.

Hancock, W. Keith. *Politics in Pitcairn: And Other Essays*. London: Macmillan, 1947.

Haward, Marcus, and James Warden, eds. *An Australian Democrat: The Life, Work, and Consequences of Andrew Inglis Clark*. Hobart: Centre for Tasmanian Studies, 1995.

Hill, Lisa. "On the Reasonableness of Compelling Citizens to 'Vote': The Australian Case." *Political Studies* 60 (2002): 306–320.

Irwin, Galen. "Compulsory Voting Legislation: Impact on Voter Turnout in the Netherlands." *Comparative Political Studies* 7 (1974): 292–316.

Magarey, Susan. *Unbridling the Tongues of Women: A Biography of Catherine Helen Spence*. Sydney: Hale & Iremonger, 1985.

McAllister, Ian. *The Australian Voter: Fifty Years of Change*. Sydney: UNSW Press, 2011.

McAllister, Ian. "The Personalization of Politics in Australia." *Party Politics* 21 (2014a): 337–345.

McAllister, Ian. "The Politics of Lowering the Voting Age in Australia: Evaluating the Evidence." *Australian Journal of Political Science* 49 (2014b): 68–83.

McAllister, Ian, and Toni Makkai. "Institutions, Society or Protest? Explaining Invalid Votes in Australian Elections." *Electoral Studies* 12 (1993): 23–40.

McLean, Iain. "E. J. Nanson: Social Choice and Electoral Reform." *Australian Journal of Political Science* 31 (1996): 369–385.

Muller, Damon. *Senate Voting Reform and the 2016 Senate Election.* Canberra: Parliamentary Library, 2016. http://www.aph.gov.au/About_Parliament/Parliamentary_Departments /Parliamentary_Library/pubs/BriefingBook45p/SenateVotingReform.

Overacker, Louise. *The Australian Party System.* New Haven, CT: Yale University Press, 1952.

Pintor, Rafael López, and Maria Gratschew. *Voter Turnout since 1945: A Global Report.* Stockholm: International IDEA, 2002.

Reeves, William Pemper. *State Experiments in Australia and New Zealand.* London: Alexander Moring, 1902.

Reid, Gordon S., and Martyn Forrest. *Australia's Commonwealth Parliament, 1901-1988: Ten Perspectives.* Carlton, Victoria: Melbourne University Press, 1989.

Reilly, Ben. "The Global Spread of Preferential Voting: Australian Institutional Imperialism?" *Australian Journal of Political Science* 39 (2004): 253–266.

Sawer, Marian, ed. *Elections—Full, Free and Fair.* Sydney: Federation Press, 2001.

Sharman, Campbell. "The Representation of Small Parties and Independents in the Senate." *Australian Journal of Political Science* 34 (1999): 353–361.

Singh, Shane, and Judd Thornton. "Compulsory Voting and the Dynamics of Party Identification." *European Journal of Political Research* 52 (2013): 188–211.

Smith, Rodney K. *Against the Machines: Minor Parties and Independents in New South Wales.* Sydney: Federation Press, 2006.

Uhr, John. "Why We Chose Proportional Representation." In *Representation and Institutional Chance: 50 Years of Proportional Representation in the Senate*, edited by Marian Sawer and Sarah Miskin, 13–40. Canberra: Department of the Senate, 1999.

Uhr, John. *Rules for Representation: Parliament and the Design of the Australian Electoral System.* Canberra: Parliamentary Library Research Paper No. 29, 2000.

Uhr, John. *Catherine Helen Spence and Australian Electoral Reform.* Canberra: Australian Political Studies Association Jubilee Conference, 2002.

Victorian Electoral Commission. *Report to Parliament on the 2010 Victorian State Election.* 2010. https://www.vec.vic.gov.au/Publications/StateElectionReports.html.

Weeks, Liam. Crashing the Party: Does STV Help Independents? *Party Politics* 11 (2014): 604–616.

CHAPTER 37

......................................................................................................

# ELECTORAL SYSTEMS IN CONTEXT
## *Germany*

......................................................................................................

THOMAS ZITTEL

## THE SIGNIFICANCE OF THE GERMAN ELECTORAL SYSTEM

......................................................................................................

MIXED-MEMBER electoral systems enjoy widespread popularity among practitioners and academics (Bowler, Donovan, and Karp 2006). This results from their assumed electoral efficiency. They are considered to be best able to reconcile conflicting goals in electoral system choice at the intra- and interparty levels of analysis (Lijphart 1994; Shugart and Wattenberg 2001b). At the interparty level, mixed systems are expected to strike a balance between representation (proportionality of votes–seats) and accountability (party system concentration). At the intraparty level, they are assumed to balance candidates and parties as main agents of representation (Shugart 2001a, 2001b; Cox 1997; Powell 2004).

This chapter stresses the embeddedness of electoral systems (Bowler and Grofman 2000) whose political feasibility, workings, and performance to some degree depend on context. It particularly provides a discussion on the structure, origins, and performance of the German mixed system. The German case merits attention for historical reasons since it represents the archetype (Saalfeld 2005) or mother (Carey 2009) of mixed-member systems. It came to birth with the founding of the Federal Republic in 1949, for decades remained a unique type of electoral system (Pollack 1952), but then became the blueprint for an increasing number of countries that started to emulate it. Most important, the German case merits attention for systematic reasons since it is widely seen as a successful electoral system that was instrumental in securing the stability of the second

German democracy by striking a balance between representation and accountability (Capoccia 2002). The German case thus allows one to explore the conditions under which mixed-member systems might result in electoral efficiency and thus contribute to stable democratic governance.

The chapter at hand pursues its main goal in three distinct steps. In a first step, it explores the main structural properties of the German electoral system and the extent to which it differs from other mixed-member systems, and also how much it has changed since the first elections in the Federal Republic in 1949. In a second step, the chapter sketches the historical and political context that affected the introduction and the development of the German system. In a third step, it focuses on system performance. It first explores the performance of the German mixed-member system at the interparty level and the extent to which it is able to strike a balance between representation (proportionality) and accountability (party system concentration). The chapter then focuses on the intraparty level and the extent and the way in which individual candidates matter vis-à-vis their parties.

# THE BASIC STRUCTURAL FEATURES OF THE GERMAN MIXED-MEMBER SYSTEM

The German electoral system falls into the category of a mixed-member proportional (MMP) system. It provides a candidate and a party vote to voters and combines a plurality formula at the candidate tier with a proportional (PR) one at the party tier to elect candidates to public office. However, it compensates for disproportionalities that result from the plurality tier by ensuring that parties' shares of seats match closely their shares of the party vote (Massicotte and Blais 1999; Shugart and Wattenberg 2001a). The following paragraphs further elaborate on the proportional nature of the present German system, discuss features that nevertheless aim at counteracting party fragmentation, and also sketch the development of the German electoral system since the first elections to the German Bundestag in 1949 (excellent references are Farrell 1997, 87–100; Farrell 2011, 93–118; Nohlen 2000, 304–330).

The compensation mechanism that links the candidate (plurality) and the party (PR) tier is a key component to the proportional nature of the German electoral system. It presupposes two different steps in the process of seat allocation. In a first step, seats in the Bundestag are proportionally allocated to vote shares on the basis of the party vote. With this vote, voters elect closed party lists in sixteen multimember districts that coincide with the sixteen German states. In a second step, the seats of each party that result from the candidate tier are deducted from the seats won at the party tier. This compensates for any disproportionality that results from the candidate tier and renders the German system a de facto proportional system (for an excellent book-length treatment see Behnke 2007a).

The compensation mechanism, however, is not the only feature that stresses the proportional nature of the German mixed system. It is enhanced by three additional components that point in a similar direction. This first concerns the de facto pooling of state-level votes to one national district to determine the vote shares of the party vote. This increases district size at the second tier and thus allows for, but does not determine, greater proportionality. The second component concerns the compensation of possible surplus mandates to adjust for disproportional outcomes. The first (candidate) vote gives voters a say in the selection of the political personnel and introduces an element of individual accountability in the system. With this vote, voters nominally elect a candidate in a single-seat district (SSD) in a one-round plurality contest. If parties manage to win nominal seats in excess of the number of seats they received on the basis of the second (party) vote, they win so-called surplus mandates that increase the size of the Bundestag. However, possible disturbances to proportionality are corrected by compensation seats for all other parties, which further increases the size of the Bundestag. A third feature that stresses the proportional nature of the German system concerns the ratio of seats that are allocated at each tier of election. The share of the seats that are allocated on the basis of the second (party) vote is 50 percent, easily large enough to compensate for any disproportionality at the candidate tier.

The German system aims to balance proportionality by means of a legal threshold of 5 percent, which means that only parties that manage to win 5 percent of the vote are able to win mandates. This measure de facto aims to contradict party fragmentation that might result from the system's proportional nature and to facilitate governmental majorities. It does not, however, prevent small parties with geographically concentrated vote bases from winning seats, even if they fail to surpass the 5 percent threshold. Parties that win at least three nominal seats are allowed to keep the seats won and receive a share of seats proportional to their party vote independent of the legal threshold (*Grundmandatsklausel*). Parties with fewer than three nominal seats keep these mandate(s) without receiving additional seats in proportion to their vote shares.

The basic features of Germany's electoral system underwent changes between 1949 and 2013 that are summarized in Table 37.1 and that to a great extent aimed at reconciling the conflicting goals of proportionality and party system concentration in changing social and political contexts (for an excellent overview see Jesse 1985, 1987). This process advanced from the first (provisional) electoral law that governed the elections on August 14, 1949, and that substantially differed from the present framework. Most important, it provided voters with only one (nominal) vote to elect a candidate in a single-seat district (SSD). The parties' vote shares were calculated by pooling their SSD vote shares for each of the then nine German states. The actual seat shares were then awarded to parties proportional to their vote shares in these virtual state-level districts. The number of candidates elected from these state-level district lists was determined after deducting a party's SSD seats from its overall seat total; 40 percent of all seats in the first Bundestag were allocated in that way, and 60 percent were allocated to district winners. The first elections also were conducted on the basis of a weak legal threshold since parties only needed to surpass 5 percent in one of the states or win one nominal seat to win seats

**Table 37.1  Main Developments in German Electoral Law, 1949–2013**

| | First Election Law (1949) | Second Election Law (1953) | Third Election Law (1956) | Major Amendments |
|---|---|---|---|---|
| Number of votes | 1 | 2 | 2 | None |
| Electoral formula | Proportional | Proportional | Proportional | None |
| Share of compensatory seats in % | 40 | 50 | 50 | None |
| Level of seat allocation | State | State | Federal | None |
| Method of seat allocation | D'Hondt | D'Hondt | D'Hondt | Hare/Niemeyer (since 1985) St. Lague (since 2008) |
| Surplus seats | Yes, not compensated | Yes, not compensated | Yes, not compensated | Yes, compensated since 2013 |
| Threshold in % | 5 | 5 | 5 | None |
| Scope of threshold | State | Federal | Federal | Special rule in 1990, federal east–federal west |
| Nominal votes needed to surpass threshold | 1 | 1 | 3 | None |

proportional to their vote shares. This resulted in the relatively high absolute number of eleven seat-winning parties (effective number Ps 4.65) in the first German Bundestag, including the regionalist Bavarian Christlich-Soziale Union (CSU) that forms a parliamentary party group with the Christlich Demokratische Union (CDU), and including the Südschleswigsche Wählerververband (SSW), which is a Danish minority party that only fielded candidates in the state of Schleswig-Holstein, where it managed to surpass the 5 percent threshold.

The 1953 law brought one important change by introducing the current two-vote system. To some degree, this strengthened the candidate-centeredness of the system. Hypothetically, voters now would be better able to distinguish between party and nominal votes and to even split tickets if they valued a specific candidate independent of his or her party (Kitzinger 1960, 62). However, the introduction of the second vote also provided greater leverage for parties to control recruitment processes at the party list tier and to balance tickets. The sole recruitment via a nominal tier, in contrast, multiplies recruitment arenas, renders central control more difficult, and thus empowers local party chapters and also candidate-centered networks as recruitment agents (Kreuzer 2000, 55–56).

The second and third (final) electoral laws that governed the elections of 1953 and 1957 at face value can be read as a reaction to party system fragmentation in the first

Bundestag. This is because their outcome was a stepwise increase of entry barriers. The 1953 law first applied the 5 percent legal threshold from the state to the federal level, which meant that parties now had to win 5 percent of the nationwide vote to win seats. The 1956 law that governed the 1957 federal elections introduced a second change by increasing the number of nominal victories needed to be granted an exemption from the 5 percent legal threshold and to win representation. Since the 1957 elections, parties need to win three nominal seats to gain representation proportional to their party vote share.

The increase of entry barriers, however, was balanced by two crucial changes that strengthened vote–seat proportionality for those parties able to surpass the threshold requirement. The first change took place in the 1956 law and allowed parties to nationally pool their state-level vote shares. District magnitude thus de facto increased to one national district of the size of the Bundestag (Shugart and Wattenberg 2001a, 19). The second important adjustment to improve proportionality in changing contexts was introduced prior to the 2013 elections and concerned the way surplus seats are treated. It marked an important step in readjusting the system after increasing levels of disproportionality during the 1990s. Prior to the 2013 elections, surplus seats for parties were not compensated for. Between 1949 and 1987, this hardly mattered because the number of surplus seats never rose beyond five (Behnke 2010, 533). However, this changed with the elections in 1990, when the number of surplus seats rose to six, and since the 2002 elections it further accelerated up to the record number of twenty-four surplus seats in 2009. This development resulted in levels of disproportionality that caused significant concern in the political and academic realm. It eventually led to the current scheme where surplus seats are compensated for by additional seats for all other parties to readjust for overall proportionality (Behnke 2007b; Grotz 2010).

# Origins and Politics of the German Mixed-Member System

The first electoral law (*Wahlgesetz*) of the Federal Republic of Germany originated from a complex process that ranged from early 1946 to May 24, 1949, when Germany's postwar constitution (*Grundgesetz*) went into effect. This process involved all levels of government since the reconstruction of local and state governments preceded the founding of the Federal Republic. Due to time constraints, the first electoral law was considered a provisional measure. Two revisions in 1953 and 1956 significantly reconfigured some of its initial choices and resulted in a final framework that first governed the 1957 elections. This framework experienced a larger number of minor and some major changes in subsequent years.

Early German electoral politics resulted from the choices of a unique set of protagonists that wavered between strategic behavior and enlightened constitutional engineering in a unique historical context. The Western military governments, the newly licensed political parties, the newly reconstructed state governments, the constitutional convention (*Verfassungsrat*), and later the German constitutional court (*Bundesverfassungsgericht*) were the most important actors in this regard. Their interactions constituted exceptional electoral politics that led to a novel type of electoral system.

History loomed large in early German electoral politics. Historical experiences with the breakdown of the first short-lived German democracy, the Weimar Republic, provided reasons to engage in enlightened constitutional engineering to make electoral democracy work in Germany. The "shadow of Weimar" was invoked in public debates by vocal German social scientists, especially Ferdinand Hermens (1936, 1940, 1949) and Dolf Sternberger (1964), who specifically identified Weimar's proportional closed-list system as a decisive factor that contributed to party fragmentation and political instability. Furthermore, in abstract ways, practitioners within all parties were partial to this narrative since they liked the idea of failed institutions better than envisioning Germans as genuinely authoritarian personalities unfit for democracy (see, e.g., Kreuzer 2001, 133–156, 163–169).

The "Weimar shadow" thus provided good reasons to seriously consider majoritarian rules as an option for a new German electoral system. The fact that majoritarian electoral rules were no stranger to German authorities provided additional support for expectations in this regard. Federal elections in the German empire (1871–1918) were held in absolute majority two-round contests in single-seat districts.

However, when local and state officials drafted the first election laws, a complex set of preferences resulted in the striking fact that the cure did not reflect historical reasoning. Despite the blame that was put on PR, all evolving systems at the local and state levels did not deviate much from it. The preferences of the Soviet military government for proportional voting systems, the pragmatism of the Western military governments that aimed at including all social groups to make postwar social life work again, the less-than-convincing experiences in the German empire when majoritarian electoral rules nevertheless produced a fair amount of party fragmentation, the lower stakes at the local and regional levels, and the institutional legacies of Weimar all contributed to reinstall a tried-and-true electoral formula.

Historical references nevertheless were not entirely lost in postwar German electoral politics. They resulted in the aim to make PR safe for democracy by better reconciling the perceived tensions between proportional electoral rules and a stable democratic government. One approach was to check "excessive proportionality" via legal thresholds (Lange 1975) and by mixing electoral formulas in two-tier systems that sometimes adopted compensatory mechanisms and sometimes did not. A second approach focused on mixing ballots in a two-tier design to personalize candidate choice and to decentralize candidate recruitment (Lange 1975, 62; Scarrow 2001). This second approach aimed to forge a closer relationship between local constituents and candidates to facilitate intraparty democracy and accountable party leadership.

The local and state-level experiences were of crucial importance when it came to choosing an electoral system for the new federal state. The preferences of state governments were partly shared and emulated by an emerging partisan coalition in the constitutional assembly and partly reinforced and imposed by the Western military governments. This three-level game significantly characterizes the early stages in German electoral politics.

The CDU and CSU delegates to the constitutional convention were the only ones that supported majoritarian elements on the basis of historical reasoning and vote-seeking motivations (Lange 1975, 143–144). With twenty-seven seats, the CDU/CSU was an equal partner with the Sozialdemokratische Partei Deutschlands (SPD) in the constitutional assembly, potentially the biggest party in the new German state, and thus could expect to benefit from a majoritarian system. Consequently, the party proposed to elect members of parliament (MPs) in three hundred SSDs under plurality rules and to recycle wasted SSD seats at a second tier through fifty compensatory list seats allocated on the basis of a proportional formula.

The constitutional assembly in its final draft bill opted for a solution that was very different from the CDU/CSU preference and from related historical reasoning. It subscribed to a fifty/fifty mix of electoral formulae but decided on a mechanism to compensate for any disturbance to proportionality that would result from the plurality tier. It thus designed a de facto proportional system. Furthermore, the constitutional assembly also rejected a legal threshold and thus any constraint to party entry. The reasons for this outcome can be found in a complex partisan bargain in the constitutional convention. The SPD as the second big party in the constitutional assembly never seriously considered coalescing with the CDU/CSU on majoritarianism for party organizational and strategic reasons. The party traditionally supported list PR as a means to provide fair representation for its urban blue-collar constituency. This position had been part of its official agenda since 1891, when it was introduced in the Erfurt Program (Scarrow 2001, 58). Furthermore, the SPD feared that the threatened elimination of smaller, bourgeois parties by a majoritarian electoral system could provide additional center-right votes for the CDU/CSU and thus tip the balance (Bawn 1993, 987).

To push for a proportional system, the SPD successfully coalesced with the four small parties represented in the constitutional assembly that had little to gain from majoritarian rules (the national conservative German Party with two seats, the liberal Free Democrats with five seats, the Catholic Center Party with two seats, and the Communists with two seats). The SPD's opening position in the constitutional assembly proposed a purely proportional preference voting system in which voters would be able to cast multiple candidate votes in multiseat districts (MSDs) with six seats each, candidates with the highest votes would be directly elected, and the unused remaining votes would be recycled through federal adjustment seats (Lange 1975). However, to mobilize a majority in the constitutional assembly, the SPD supported the preference of the Freie Demokratische Partei (FDP) for a two-tier solution that would include candidate votes in SSDs (50 percent of all MPs) and a recycling of unused votes at a second tier that would determine the rest of the MPs. The SPD also agreed to oppose any legal threshold requirement to win support from the Communist Party (KPD).

At this point in the constitutional process, the military government was much less passive than some observers have argued (e.g., Merkl 1963). It literally imposed the state governments' preferences for a legal threshold and a strengthened candidate (plurality) component. To everyone's surprise, the military government declared the electoral system a matter of state competency, *after* the constitutional assembly had handed over a final draft bill. Once the states declared their preference for a national solution that would include a legal threshold and that would increase the share of SSD seats to 60 percent, the military government simply inserted the states' preferences into the final draft bill and then imposed this version as the electoral law that was designed to govern the first elections to the German Bundestag in 1949 (Golay 1958, 141–142).

The first electoral law was meant to serve as a provisional measure that would govern the 1949 elections and then be replaced by a permanent law. It, however, was succeeded by a second provisional law that governed the 1953 elections, and only afterward by a 1956 law that was permanent; in subsequent decades this permanent law was frequently amended, mostly in smaller ways. With increasing historical distance to Weimar, with decreasing constraints resulting from the military governments, and with the stabilization of the German electorate, debates on electoral reform became increasingly strategic and specific. In essence, they aimed to improve proportionality for established midsized to large parties while raising obstacles for the entry of very small and new parties.

In the debates leading up to the 1956 permanent law, the CDU/CSU continued to push for majoritarian rules, now by proposing to remove any compensatory link between SSD and MSD seats; 50 percent of seats were to be directly elected from SSDs and 50 percent from state lists. However, similar to previous debates, for electoral and ideological reasons, this move continued to lack wider partisan support. Most important, the FDP, who governed with the CDU/CSU in the second and third Bundestag and who had nothing to gain electorally from strengthening majoritarian elements, effectively blocked this move during this period of time. The first grand coalition that governed between 1965 and 1969 provided a window of opportunity for proponents of majoritarian rules and marked a final effort in this regard. However, at this time, the Weimar shadow only lurked from a distant past, the student protest movement pushed for more political pluralism and participation rather than majoritarian measures, and, most important, due to party culture and tradition, the SPD continued to feel ill at ease with majoritarian rules and thus in the end refrained from supporting them.

Strategic considerations and partisan bargains also affected developments with regard to entry barriers and ballot structure. After the 1949 elections, for reasons of electoral and coalition politics, the CDU/CSU and the FDP both supported strengthening the existing entry barrier by introducing a 5 percent national threshold (1953) and by raising the one nominal seat requirement to a three nominal seat requirement to exempt parties from the threshold quota (1956). The CDU/CSU increasingly trusted in its ability to attract the center-right share of an increasingly stable German electorate that would become available once voters wished not to waste their votes for small parties. The FDP as the biggest of the small parties supported this position since it expected to electorally benefit from a decreasing number of small competitors and, most important, from assuming a pivotal strategic position in future coalition politics.

The introduction of the second list vote in 1953 resulted from strong support provided by the SPD and the FDP, on the one hand, and from a political compromise between the CDU/CSU that supported higher barriers for party entry and the SPD demanding to lower them to 3 percent on the other. The SPD and the FDP pushed for the second list vote since they hoped that the CDU would no longer benefit from SPD- or FDP-leaning voters who preferred and hence voted for incumbent CDU/CSU candidates. The second vote reduced this risk by permitting voters to express their party and candidate preferences separately. The CDU/CSU was willing to compromise on the two-vote ballot once the SPD was willing to agree to the national 5 percent threshold in return.

The highly strategic considerations surrounding the debates on the second vote are stressed by the fact that the SPD in the deliberations on the 1956 law reversed its 1953 position and preferred again a single vote. The party entertained the somewhat hypothetical example that the FDP might withdraw all SSD candidates in all states, thus favoring CDU/CSU candidates, in return for the CDU/CSU not fielding a party list. This fear proved exaggerated since in 1953 the CDU/CSU had only forty-two withdrawal agreements with other bourgeois parties (Bawn 1993). Most important, the CDU/CSU and the FDP did not support this revision in the systems' ballot structure.

The previous paragraphs stress that the German electoral system emerged from an interplay between partisan strategic bargaining and efforts to learn from history in a unique political context. Judicial politics contributed to this process in special ways. It reinforced historical reasoning in early stages but later also helped to adapt the German electoral system to changing political contexts. The German Supreme Court first sustained legal thresholds in a number of rulings between 1950 and 1979 by arguing for the need to contradict party fragmentation and to facilitate stable majorities (Becht 1990). In these rulings, the court invoked the Weimar shadow and called on lawmakers to draw the right conclusions. In more recent rulings, however, the court took an opposite position and argued for the need to improve electoral equality by striking down the 5 percent threshold for the European elections in 2011 and by ruling the increasing disproportionality of federal elections due to an increasing number of surplus seats as unconstitutional (Krumm 2013). With the elections in 2013, surplus seats were compensated for by additional seats for the other parties to correct disturbances to vote–seat proportionality.

# THE PERFORMANCE OF THE GERMAN MIXED-MEMBER SYSTEM

The main structural properties of the German electoral system and its historical origins raise three distinct questions with regard to its performance. First, how successful is the German system in securing vote–seat proportionality, and to what extent does it result from the electoral formula? Second, did the legal threshold help to prevent party fragmentation and secure stable majorities? Third, did the candidate vote help to strengthen the role of individual legislators vis-à-vis their parties? These are the three questions this section will focus on.

## Proportionality

The German electoral system has been designed to sustain the proportional nature of the Weimar system and at the same time prevent party fragmentation. With regard to the former goal, the performance of the German system is widely considered more than satisfactory. Generally, comparative research suggests that compared to pure PR systems, disproportionality in mixed-member systems is higher if we include all of its types (Bochsler 2009). However, mixed-member systems differ in this regard, and the German system falling into the MMP category on average is found to fare exceedingly well, compared to pure PR systems (Farrell 2011, 102f; Lijphart 2012, 150). Gallagher's least squares index measures a mean of 2.67 for all German elections between 1949 and 2010. This is lower than the mean of 3.76 for the list of European PR systems that is compiled by Lijphart (2012, 150).

The satisfactory performance of the German system with regard to proportionality must be considered a result of a distinct configuration of the following three factors. First is the distribution of seats across both tiers that affects the mechanical relationship between votes and seats. According to Moser and Scheiner (2005, 580), with 50 percent of compensatory seats, "the result is a distribution of seats almost fully controlled by the PR vote," whereas lower shares of compensatory seats are likely to decrease this effect. Second, a high magnitude at the list tier allows (but does not cause) a greater proliferation of parties and produces less disproportionality (Taagepera and Shugart 1989). Since in Germany votes are de facto transferred into seats in a national "virtual district," district size equals the number of seats in parliaments and thus facilitates proportional outcomes. The third factor results from the highly institutionalized German party system. This makes behavioral incentives resulting from the list tier project to the nominal tier rather than the other way round (Cox 1997). Party institutionalization renders (partisan) voters less likely to vote for independent candidates at the SSD tier or to split tickets, which both would potentially increase vote–seat disproportionality. Party institutionalization, at the elite level, renders independent candidates less likely to run at the SSD level (Moser and Scheiner 2004) and makes parties less likely to enter into alliances or to strategically circumvent the compensation mechanism by urging voters to split their vote, by withdrawing from the nominal contest, or by not fielding candidates at the nominal tier (Bochsler 2012). Organizationally strong and ideologically cohesive parties are less likely to engage in these activities because under these circumstances, the human faces of SSD candidates function as vote-earning mechanisms to boost the PR vote. This creates centrifugal tendencies, in contrast to a Duvergerian gravity, which would result in electoral coordination and in pulling down the number of parties at the plurality tier (Cox and Schoppa 2002, 1028).

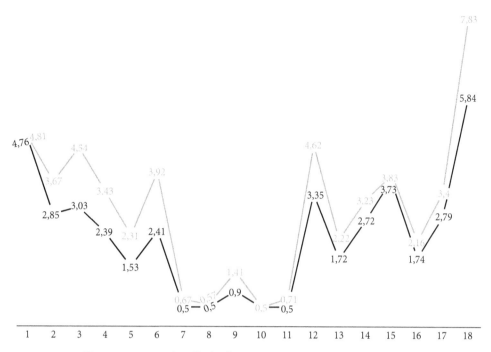

**FIGURE 37.1.** Vote–seat proportionality in Germany, 1949–2013.

Note: The figure shows proportionality scores computed on the basis of Gallagher's least squares index. The dark line denotes the scores computed only on the basis of the votes for seat-winning parties; the lighter line denotes scores computed on the basis of all valid votes for all parties.

Source: Author's calculation based on results provided by the Federal Returning Office.

The cross-national perspective obscures interesting longitudinal developments that we turn to in the remainder of this section and that are visualized in Figure 37.1. Figure 37.1 shows a U-shaped curve demonstrating that disproportionality significantly declined between the first and the seventh Bundestag, then remained solid at an extremely low level until the eleventh Bundestag, and is on the rise since the early 1990s. This increase has been seen as an effect of an increasing number of surplus seats that resulted from increased disproportionality at the nominal tier (Manow 2011, 2015). After 1990, more parties entered the nominal tier competition, and vote shares necessary to win a nominal mandate declined. This led to a constellation, in which a party with a relatively low percentage of candidate votes still won many districts, and in which consequently the percentage of list votes and the percentage of district mandates won in a state diverged, leading to surplus mandates (Behnke 2003) The German Bundestag corrected this cause of increased disproportionality by a change of the electoral law prior to the 2013 elections. Since the 2013 elections, surplus mandates are compensated, as explained earlier.

Figure 37.1, however, demonstrates that surplus mandates are not the only source of disproportionality. It shows single peaks that are striking and that reflect the effects of the 5 percent threshold. All peaks reflect situations in which parties narrowly failed to surpass the threshold and in which large number of votes thus got wasted. In 1969 (elections to sixth Bundestag), this concerned the right-wing Nationaldemokratische Partei Deutschlands (NPD); in the postunification elections of 1990 (elections to the twelfth Bundestag), the West German Greens failed to surpass the threshold that in this election counted separately for the western and the eastern parts of the country; and in 2013 (elections to the eighteenth Bundestag), the right-wing populist Alternative für Deutschland (AfD) and the liberal mainstream FDP both narrowly missed the threshold. Consequently, the German system, as a result of the 5 percent threshold, from a longitudinal perspective produces incidents of significantly above-average disproportionality. The extent to which this affects party concentration is a question that we turn to in the following section.

## Party System Concentration

The architects of the German electoral system succeeded for many decades in "squaring the circle" by simultaneously securing proportional outcomes and party system concentration. Standard measures such as the widely used effective number of parties index[1] developed by Laakso and Taagepera (1979) are able to empirically demonstrate this success. The $N_s$ index based on seats scores at a mean value of 3.39 for all eighteen German elections between 1949 and 2013. It declined from 4.65 in 1949 to an all-time low of 2.71 in 1969, then remained for two decades in the narrow range between 2.79 (1972) and 3.17 (1990) with a singular peak in 1987 (3.47). Since 1990, however, the index value shows greater fluctuation and even rose in 2009 to an all-time high of 4.81. Clearly, in recent years, party system fragmentation is on the rise in German politics (Gallagher 2015). Figure 37.2 demonstrates developments in party system concentration in German politics.

The 5 percent legal threshold has been widely portrayed as a major guarantee for securing party system concentration and thus for successfully fighting the Weimar shadow (Nohlen 2000, 316). This factor admittedly resulted in psychological effects preventing German voters from wasting their votes. The fact that small parties are generally more likely to receive fewer nominal votes compared to list votes has been interpreted that way (Fisher 1973). It furthermore had visible mechanical effects in German politics. This concerns not only the electoral fate of very small parties but also the fate of temporarily surging parties. The 1969 elections provide a first example in this regard, when the extreme right-wing NPD was on the verge of winning representation in the Bundestag but narrowly missed the 5 percent threshold and subsequently disappeared from the scene (Antoni 1980; Krumm 2013). However, as already indicated in the previous section, this incident remained by no means a singular event in German electoral politics. In the most recent federal elections in 2013, the surging populist right-wing AfD, with 4.7 percent of the party vote, narrowly missed the threshold. It remains to be seen whether this put an end to this party or whether the 5 percent threshold only delayed its

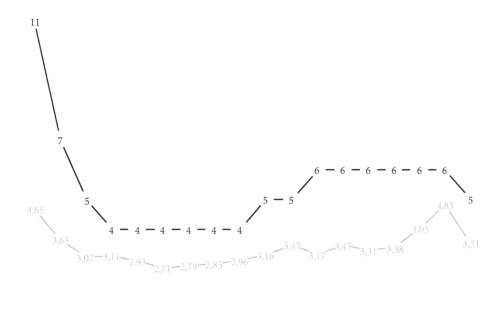

**FIGURE 37.2.** Party system concentration in Germany, 1949–2013.

Note: The figure shows scores for the absolute number of seat-winning parties (dark line) and for the effective number of seat-winning parties (N_s) denoted by the lighter line and computed on the basis of Laakso and Taagepera (1979). Note that in this analysis the regionalist CSU that only competed in Bavaria but that forms a party group with the CDU in the Bundestag is treated as an independent party.

Source: Author's calculation based on results provided by the Federal Returning Office.

entry and thus was a next step in the process of a further fragmentation of the German party system after unification.

The entry of the Green Party in the Bundestag in 1983 and later the entry of the Left Party after unification demonstrate that the legal threshold is by no means a magic bullet to facilitate party system concentration. In both cases, social and political change driven by the rise of postmaterialism and by political unification restructured the German electorate and brought about voter coalitions that were large enough to contradict its mechanical effects. Moreover, the social and ideological cohesiveness of these voter coalitions also were able to contradict the psychological effects of the legal threshold and thus strategic considerations to not risk wasting one's vote. Clearly, the legal threshold facilitated party system concentration after the Federal Republic came into existence, but it did not determine it independently of social and political context. In light of this, the 2013 federal elections might have slowed down the process of party system fragmentation in German politics only temporarily. (Indeed, the AfD and FDP both cleared the threshold in the 2017 election.)

## The Behavioral Effects of the Nominal Vote

The question of the effects of the candidate-centered tier of the German electoral system has represented a contested issue since its early beginnings. While some answers to it stress the partisan nature of the nominal vote, others envision a greater level of personalization that is related to it. This debate involves two levels of analysis that need to be kept distinct: the issue of personalized choices at the voter level and the issue of personal vote seeking at the elite level. The following paragraphs first focus on the former and then advance to the latter level of analysis.

Skeptical accounts on the distinct behavioral effects of the candidate vote on vote choices contradict that German voters might discriminate between the two tiers of election and that they might vote for a party at the second tier while taking a deliberate and independent candidate choice at the first tier. They rather envision voters to cast a party vote at both tiers (Nohlen 2000, 318). This argument flows from two particular voter-level explanations that are empirically contested, however. The first explanation emphasizes the complexity of the German mixed-member system and resulting cognitive effects. From this perspective, voters are not able to personalize their vote since they don't understand the difference between the two tiers and thus the behavioral opportunities available to them (Jesse 1988; Kaase 1984; Schmitt-Beck 1993). However, this does not equally hold for all voters at all points in time; the likelihood that voters recall candidates, for example, is said to increase as a result of campaign efforts (Klingemann 1969, 189f). Furthermore, a survey conducted prior to the 2009 elections found that 55 percent of voters were able to recall the name of at least one candidate in their districts and that 30 percent were able to recall more than one candidate (Gschwend and Zittel 2011, 378). This suggests that a significant majority of German voters does discriminate between the different tiers of election. Compared to older analyses on this issue that report lower numbers in this regard, this also suggests that German voters are increasingly able to distinguish between the candidate and the party vote (for related data on the 1998 elections see Behnke 2007a, 221).

The second voter-level explanation argues that voters do not wish to take advantage of available opportunities to personalize their vote choices because of their distinct and strong partisan loyalties (Pappi 1973; Müller 1999; Wessels 2000; Falter, Schoen, and Caballero 2000; Moser and Scheiner 2005). This assumed spillover effect from the list to the nominal tier, however, has been challenged in several ways. Cox and Schoppa (2002) stressed that voters under Germany's MMP rules will be most effectively mobilized by the human faces of district candidates. This argument is difficult to test since all parties field district candidates and we thus lack counterfactuals. Survey evidence, however, suggests that candidates do exert a mobilization effect on voters of their own party contingent upon campaign effort (Gschwend and Zittel 2015). Furthermore, there is some evidence that candidates' campaign efforts, district work, and incumbency status are able to mobilize extra nominal votes and to increase the gap between nominal and party votes (Hainmueller and Kern 2008; Bawn 1999; Klingemann and Wessels 2001). Survey-based evidence finally suggests that contingent upon candidates' campaign efforts, the nominal vote might even make some partisan voters cast a truly personal vote independent of party identification (Gschwend and Zittel 2015, 347).

The direct effects of candidate-centered ballots on the behaviors of German legislators are another contested issue among students of German politics. Theoretically, Germany's nominal tier provides incentives to district winners to represent local individuals and groups in ways that list members would not (Bawn 1999, 490). In contrast to list members, nominally elected legislators are personally accountable to geographic constituents in most visible ways. Empirically, this assumption of a mandate divide received some support in the literature with analyses that show systematic differences between district and list members with regard to committee assignments (Stratmann and Baur 2002), efforts to secure particularistic policies (Lancaster and Patterson 1990), constituency communication (Klingemann and Wessels 2001), and roll call behavior (Sieberer 2010). However, critics have argued that neither of the two tiers functions in independent ways due to a number of mechanisms that result in contamination effects and related complex behavioral incentives (Herron and Nishikawa 2001; Ferrara, Herron, and Nishikawa 2005). Dual candidacies and party control over candidate nominations and campaign resources are said to constitute major sources of contamination and thus complexity.[2]

Dual candidacies are a widespread phenomenon in contemporary elections to the Bundestag. A large majority of more than 80 percent of all members of the Bundestag run as dual candidates (Manow 2013, 289), and almost 50 percent of all candidates do so (Zittel and Gschwend 2008, 988). This results in a great number of legislators who identify with a single-seat district and who are expected to do so by their party, independent of their modes of election, due to their modes of candidacy (Saalfeld 2005; Gschwend and Zittel forthcoming). This finding does not envision that nominally elected legislators do not care for their district. It only suggests that list MPs might do so to equal degree contingent upon their mode of candidacy. This widely shared rejection of a mandate divide in German legislative politics (see, e.g., Jesse 1988, 120; Schweitzer 1979, 12; Patzelt 2007, 83) is challenged by observations that stress the anticipated mode of election as a major source of personal vote-seeking behavior in German politics. Members that are likely to win a nominal vote in future elections—either previous winners or previous narrow losers—are found to be more likely to pay attention to geographic constituents (Zittel and Gschwend 2008).

German parties are organizationally still strong and able to control ballot access and campaign resources and to thus constrain the behaviors of legislators, independent of electoral incentives. The nomination for nominal candidates in Germany is either taken by a membership or a delegate vote in the local chapters (Schüttemeyer and Sturm 2005). In established German parties, both processes are controlled by an informal seniority rule, relevant sociological groups, and local party leadership. This results in uncontested nominations as long as incumbents seek renomination and no major conflict with party leadership and relevant sociological groups arises. In case of vacant seats, nomination requires the support of major partisan groups in a usually open but party-centered process of coalition building. This functional role of party organizational chapters provides constraints on personal vote-seeking behavior and suggests to legislators that they should represent geographic constituencies without disturbing party unity. This might involve, for example, minor signaling behavior to local constituents via parliamentary questions compared to pushing local interests in collective choice situations such as roll call votes (Martin 2011; Zittel 2017).

The German parliamentary system functions as a further important contextual factor that constrains the effects of the candidate-centered tier in the German electoral system. It allows for a vote of no confidence and thus provides incentives for members of the majority to not risk their seats and to support the government. It further provides incentives for vote-seeking members of the opposition to collectively challenge the government in the most effective and disciplined ways to win next time (Diermeier and Feddersen 1998). From a comparative perspective, this device constrains German legislators in special ways since it requires them to elect a new government to unseat the old one (constructive vote of no confidence). From this perspective, the size of governing coalitions is a crucial variable that affects the leeway of potential nominally elected mavericks to seek personal votes or not. Minimal winning coalitions that require perfect unity to sustain the government contradict electoral incentives to cultivate a personal vote. They further emphasize that electoral systems are embedded institutions whose behavioral effects are contingent upon contextual factors.

# Conclusion

This chapter explored the mixed-member type of electoral systems in the German context. In its first part, it highlights the particular construction of the German mixed-member system that aims to facilitate vote–seat proportionality and personalization. This is achieved by allowing for a fifty/fifty distribution of nominal and party seats, by compensating disproportionality that flows from its nominal (plurality) tier via party votes at its second tier, and by a de facto national multimember district that allows the most accurate allocation of vote shares into seat shares. Increasing disproportionality as a result of increasing numbers of surplus seats after unification in 1990 furthermore was countervailed by compensating surplus seats in proportion to the party vote since the 2013 elections. In contrast, the German constitutional convention aimed to facilitate the goal of party system concentration solely on the basis of a relatively high 5 percent national threshold.

In its second part, this chapter explores the unique postwar politics that led to the design of this novel electoral system. It shows that historically informed demands for greater party system concentration and for countervailing "excessive proportionality," which was said to explain the downfall of the Weimar Republic, were contradicted by the strategic preferences of vote-seeking political parties and by the long-standing support of the SPD for proportional representation. It also shows, however, that the guardianship of the Western military governments, and later the German Supreme Court, in combination with the strategic considerations of the liberal FDP resulted in support for a relatively high national threshold as a means to reconcile the conflicting goals of party system concentration and vote–seat proportionality. For established midsized parties such as the liberal FDP, the 5 percent threshold for a long time represented a convenient instrument to keep competitors at bay while at the same time showing support for stabilizing the country's party system.

The third and closing part of the chapter focuses on the performance of the German mixed-member system. It stresses the fact that from a cross-national perspective, and also with regard to most stages in postwar political history, the system successfully secured high levels of proportionality and party system concentration at the same time. It also stresses, however, increasing tensions in that regard and rising levels of disproportionality and party system fragmentation since unification in 1990. In recent years, the German party system has experienced significant levels of fragmentation and disproportionality, which signals a declining ability of the country's mixed-member system to sustain the best of both worlds amid political and social change. However, recent findings also demonstrate increasing behavioral effects of the nominal vote at the voter and elite levels and thus a reinforcement of the system's abilities to reconcile candidate- and party-centered politics.

## Notes

1. $N_v$ denotes the effective number of electoral parties and $N_s$ denotes the effective number of legislative parties. (See the chapter in this volume by Shugart and Taagepera.)
2. See the chapter by Herron, Nemoto, and Nishikawa in this volume for further discussion of this issue.

## References

Antoni, Michael. "Grundgesetz und Sperrklausel: 30 Jahre 5 Prozent-Quorum: Lehre aus Weimar?" *Zeitschrift für Parlamentsfragen* 11, no. 1 (1980): 93–109.

Bawn, Kathleen. "The Logic of Institutional Preferences: German Electoral Law as a Social Choice Outcome." *American Journal of Political Science* 37, no. 4 (1993): 965–989.

Bawn, Kathleen. "Voter Responses to Electoral Complexity: Ticket Splitting, Rational Voters and Representation in the Federal Republic of Germany." *British Journal of Political Science* 28, no. 3 (1999): 487–505.

Becht, Ernst. *Die 5 %-Klausel im Wahlrecht. Garant für ein funktionierendes parlamentarisches Regierungssystem?* Stuttgart: Richard Boorberg, 1990.

Behnke, Joachim. "Ein integrales Modell der Ursachen von Überhangmandaten." *Politische Vierteljahresschrift* 44, no. 1 (2003): 41–65.

Behnke, Joachim. *Das Wahlsystem der Bundesrepublik Deutschland. Logik, Technik und Praxis der Verhältniswahl.* Baden-Baden: Nomos, 2007a.

Behnke, Joachim. "The Strange Phenomenon of Surplus Seats in the German Electoral System." *German Politics* 16, no. 4 (2007b): 496–517.

Behnke, Joachim. "Überhangmandate bei der Bundestagswahl 2009—das ewige Menetekel." *Politische Vierteljahresschrift* 51, no. 3 (2010): 531–552.

Bochsler, Daniel. "Are Mixed Electoral Systems the Best Choice for Central and Eastern Europe or the Reason for Defective Party Systems?" *Politics & Policy* 37, no. 4 (2009): 735–767.

Bochsler, Daniel. "A Quasi-Proportional Electoral System 'Only for Honest Men'? The Hidden Potential for Manipulating Mixed Compensatory Electoral Systems." *International Political Science Review* 33, no. 4 (2012): 401–420.

Bowler, Shaun, Todd Donovan, and Jeffrey A. Karp. "Why Politicians Like Electoral Institutions: Self-Interest, Values, or Ideology?" *Journal of Politics* 68, no. 2 (2006): 434–446.

Bowler, Shaun, and Bernhard Grofman. *Elections in Australia, Ireland, and Malta under the Single Transferable Vote: Reflections on an Embedded Institution.* Ann Arbor: University of Michigan Press, 2000.

Capoccia, Giovanni. "The Political Consequences of Electoral Laws: The German System at Fifty." *West European Politics* 25, no. 3 (2002): 171–202.

Carey, John M. *Legislative Voting and Accountability.* Cambridge: Cambridge University Press, 2009.

Cox, Gary. *Making Votes Count. Strategic Coordination in the World's Electoral Systems.* Cambridge: Cambridge University Press, 1997.

Cox, Karen E., and Leonard J. Schoppa. "Interaction Effects in Mixed-Member Electoral Systems: Theory and Evidence from Germany, Japan, and Italy." *Comparative Political Studies* 35, no. 9 (2002): 1027–1053.

Diermeier, Daniel, and Timothy J. Feddersen. "Cohesion in Legislatures and the Vote of Confidence Procedure." *American Political Science Review* 92, no. 3 (1998): 611–621.

Falter, Jürgern W., Harald Schoen, and Claudio Caballero. "Dreißig Jahre danach: Zur Validierung des Konzepts 'Parteiidentifikation' in der Bundesrepublik." In *50 Jahre Empirische Wahlforschung in Deutschland*, edited by Markus Klein, Wolfgang Jagodzinski, Ekkehard Mochmann, and Dieter Ohr, 235–271. Wiesbaden: Westdeutscher Verlag, 2000.

Farrell, David. *Electoral Systems. A Comparative Introduction.* Houndmills: Palgrave Macmillan, 2011.

Farrell, David M. *Comparing Electoral Systems.* London: Prentice Hall, 1997.

Ferrara, Federico, Erik S. Herron, and Misa Nishikawa. *Mixed Electoral Systems. Contamination and Its Consequences.* New York: Palgrave Macmillan, 2005.

Fisher, Stephen L. "The Wasted Vote Thesis. West German Evidence." *Comparative Politics* 5, no. 2 (1973): 293–299.

Gallagher, Michael. "Election Indices." 2015. https://www.tcd.ie/Political_Science/staff/michael_gallagher/ElSystems/Docts/ElectionIndices.pdf.

Golay, John Ford. *The Founding of the Federal Republic of Germany.* Chicago: University of Chicago Press, 1958.

Grotz, Florian. "Die personalisierte Verhältniswahl unter den Bedingungen des gesamtdeutschen Parteiensystems. Eine Analyse der Entstehungsursachen von Überhangmandaten seit der Wiedervereinigung." *Politische Vierteljahresschrift* 41, no. 4 (2010): 707–729.

Gschwend, Thomas, and Thomas Zittel. "Machen Kandidaten im Wahlkreis einen Unterschied? Die Persönlichkeitswahl als interaktiver Prozess." *Politische Vierteljahresschrift* 45 (Special issue "Wählen in Deutschland," edited by Rüdiger Schmitt-Beck) (2011): 371–392.

Gschwend, Thomas, and Thomas Zittel. "Do Constituency Candidates Matter in German Federal Elections? The Personal Vote as an Interactive Process." *Electoral Studies* 39 (2015): 338–349.

Gschwend, Thomas, and Thomas Zittel. "Who Brings Home the Pork? Committee Assignments under Germany's Mixed System." *Party Politics*, forthcoming.

Hainmueller, Jens, and Holger Lutz Kern. "Incumbency as a Source of Spillover Effects in Mixed Electoral Systems: Evidence from a Regression-Discontinuity Design." *Electoral Studies* 27, no. 2 (2008): 1–15.

Hermens, Ferdinand A. "Proportional Representation and the Breakdown of German Democracy." *Social Research* 3, no. 1 (1936): 411.

Hermens, Ferdinand A. *Democracy and Proportional Representation*. Chicago: University of Chicago Press, 1940.

Hermens, Ferdinand A. *Mehrheitswahlrecht oder Verhältniswahlrecht*. Berlin: Duncker & Humblot, 1949.

Herron, Erik S., and Misa Nishikawa. "Contamination Effects and the Number of Parties in Mixed-Superposition Electoral Systems." *Electoral Studies* 20, no. 1 (2001): 63–86.

Jesse, Eckhard. *Wahlrecht zwischen Kontinuität und Reform. Eine Analyse der Wahlsystemdiskussion und der Wahlrechtsänderungen in der Bundesrepublik Deutschland 1949-1983*. Düsseldorf: Droste Verlag, 1985.

Jesse, Eckhard. "The West German Electoral System: The Case for Reform, 1949-87." *West European Politics* 10, no. 3 (1987): 434–448.

Jesse, Eckhard. "Split-Voting in the Federal Republic of Germany: An Analysis of the Federal Elections from 1953 to 1987." *Electoral Studies* 7, no. 2 (1988): 109–124.

Kaase, Max. "Personalized Proportional Representation: The 'Model' of the West German Electoral System." In *Choosing an Electoral System*, edited by Arend Lijphart and Bernhard Grofman, 155–164. New York: Praeger, 1984.

Kitzinger, Uwe W. *German Electoral Politics: A Study of the 1957 Campaign*. Oxford: Clarendon Press, 1960.

Klingemann, Hans-Dieter. *Bestimmungsgründe der Wahlentscheidung: Eine Regionale Wahlanalyse*. Meisenheim: Hain, 1969.

Klingemann, Hans-Dieter, and Bernhard Wessels. "The Political Consequences of Germany's Mixed-Member System: Personalization at the Grass Roots." In *Mixed-Member Electoral Systems. The Best of both Worlds?*, edited by Matthew S. Shugart and Martin P. Wattenberg, 279–296. Oxford: Oxford University Press, 2001.

Kreuzer, Marcus. "Electoral Mechanisms and Electioneering Incentives—Vote-Getting Strategies of Japanese, French, British, German and Austrian Conservatives." *Party Politics* 6, no. 4 (2000): 487–504.

Kreuzer, Marcus. *Institutions and Innovation: Voters, Parties, and Interest Groups in the Consolidation of Democracy: France and Germany*. Ann Arbor: University of Michigan Press, 2001.

Krumm, Thomas. "Wie wirksam sperren Sperrklauseln? Die Auswirkung von Prozenthürden auf die Parteienzahl im Bundestag und im internationalen Vergleich." *Zeitschrift für Politikwissenschaft* 23, no. 3 (2013): 393–424.

Laakso, Markku, and Rein Taagepera. "'Effective' Number of Parties: A Measure with Application to West Europe." *Comparative Political Studies* 12, no. 1 (1979): 3–27.

Lancaster, Thomas D., and W. David Patterson. "Comparative Pork Barrel Politics. Perceptions from the West German Bundestag." *Comparative Political Studies* 22, no. 4 (1990): 458–477.

Lange, Erhard. *Wahlrecht und Innenpolitik*. Meisenheim: Anton Hain, 1975.

Lijphart, Arend. *Electoral Systems and Party Systems*. Oxford: Oxford University Press, 1994.

Lijphart, Arend. *Patterns of Democracy. Government Forms and Performance in Thirty-Six Countries.* 2nd ed. New Haven, CT: Yale University Press, 2012.

Manow, Philip. "The Cube Rule in a Mixed Electoral System: Disproportionality in German Bundestag Elections." *West European Politics* 34, no. 4 (2011): 773–794.

Manow, Philip. "Mixed Rules, Different Roles? An Analysis of the Typical Pathways into the Bundestag and of MPs' Parliamentary Behaviour." *Journal of Legislative Studies* 19, no. 3 (2013): 287–308.

Manow, Philip. *Mixed Rules, Mixed Strategies. Candidates and Parties in Germany's Electoral System.* Colchester: ECPR Press, 2015.

Martin, Shane. "Using Parliamentary Questions to Measure Constituency Focus: An Application to the Irish Case." *Political Studies* 59, no. 2 (2011): 259–270.

Massicotte, Louis, and André Blais. "Mixed Electoral Systems: A Conceptual and Empirical Survey." *Electoral Studies* 18, no. 3 (1999): 341–366.

Merkl, Peter. *The Origins of the West German Republic.* New York: Oxford University Press, 1963.

Moser, Robert G., and Ethan Scheiner. "Mixed Electoral Systems and Electoral System Effects: Controlled Comparison and Crossnational Analysis." *Electoral Studies* 23 (2004): 575–599.

Moser, Robert G., and Ethan Scheiner. "Strategic Ticket Splitting and the Personal Vote in Mixed-Member Electoral Systems." *Legislative Studies Quarterly* 30, no. 2 (2005): 259–276.

Müller, Walter. "Class Cleavages in Party Preferences in Germany—Old and New." In *The End of Class Politics?*, edited by Geoffrey Evans, 137–180. Oxford: Oxford University Press, 1999.

Nohlen, Dieter. *Wahlrecht und Parteiensystem.* 3rd ed. Opladen: Leske & Budrich, 2000.

Pappi, Franz Urban. "Parteiensystem und Sozialstruktur in der Bundesrepublik Deutschland." *Politische Vierteljahresschrift* 14, no. 1 (1973): 191–313.

Patzelt, Werner J. "The Constituency Roles of MPs at the Federal and Lander Levels in Germany." *Regional and Federal Studies* 17 (2007): 47–70.

Pollack, James K. "The Electoral System of the Federal Republic of Germany." *American Political Science Review* 46, no. 4 (1952): 1056.

Powell, G. Bingham. "Political Representation in Comparative Politics." *Annual Review of Political Science* 7, no. 1 (2004): 273–296.

Saalfeld, Thomas. "Germany: Stability and Strategy in a Mixed-Member Proportional System." In *The Politics of Electoral Systems*, edited by Gallagher Michael and Paul Mitchel, 209–231. Oxford: Oxford University Press, 2005.

Scarrow, Susan. "Germany: The Mixed Member System as a Political Compromise." In *Mixed Electoral Systems. The Best of Both Worlds?*, edited by Matthew and Martin Wattenberg Shugart, 55–70. Oxford: Oxford University Press, 2001.

Schmitt-Beck, Rüdiger. "Denn sie wissen nicht was sie tun . . . Zum Verständnis des Verfahrens der Bundestagswahl bei westdeutschen und ostdeutschen Wählern." *Zeitschrift für Parlamentsfragen* 24, no. 3 (1993): 393–415.

Schüttemeyer, Suzanne S., and Roland Sturm. "The Candidate—The (Almost) Unknown Creature: Findings and Considerations on the Nomination of Candidates for the German Bundestag." *Zeitschrift fur Parlamentsfragen* 36, no. 3 (2005): 539–553.

Schweitzer, Carl Christoph. *Der Abgeordnete im Parlamentarischen Regierungssystem der BRD.* Opladen: Leske & Budrich, 1979.

Shugart, Matthew S. "Electoral 'efficiency' and the move to mixed-member systems." *Electoral Studies* 20, no. 2 (2001a): 173–193.

Shugart, Matthew S. "'Extreme' Electoral Systems and the Appeal of the Mixed-Member Alternative." In *Mixed-Member Electoral Systems. The Best of Both Worlds?*, edited by M. S. Shugart and Martin P. Wattenberg, 25–51. Oxford: Oxford University Press, 2001b.

Shugart, Matthew S., and Martin P. Wattenberg. "Mixed-Member Electoral Systems: A Definition and Typology." In *Mixed-Member Electoral Systems. The Best of Both Worlds?*, edited by Matthew Soberg Shugart and Martin P. Wattenberg, 9–25. Oxford: Oxford University Press, 2001a.

Shugart, Matthew S., and Martin P. Wattenberg, eds. *Mixed-Member Electoral Systems: The Best of Both Worlds?* Oxford: Oxford University Press, 2001b.

Sieberer, Ulrich. "Behavioral Consequences of Mixed Electoral Systems: Deviating Voting Behavior of District and List MPs in the German Bundestag." *Electoral Studies* 29, no. 3 (2010): 484–496.

Sternberger, Dolf. *Die große Wahlreform: Zeugnisse einer Bemühung.* Köln: Westdeutscher Verlag, 1964.

Stratmann, Thomas, and Martin Baur. "Plurality Rule, Proportional Representation, and the German Bundestag: How Incentives to Pork-Barrel Differ across Electoral Systems." *American Journal of Political Science* 46, no. 3 (2002): 506–514.

Taagepera, Rein, and Matthew S. Shugart. *Seats and Votes: The Effects and Determinants of Electoral Systems.* New Haven, CT: Yale University Press, 1989.

Wessels, Bernhard. "Gruppenbindung und Wahlverhalten: 50 Jahre Wahlen in der Bundesrepublik." In *50 Jahre Empirische Wahlforschung in Deutschland*, edited by Markus Klein, Wolfgang Jagodzinski, Ekkehard Mochmann, and Dieter Ohr, 129–158. Wiesbaden: Westdeutscher Verlag, 2000.

Zittel, Thomas. "The Personal Vote." In *The Sage Handbook of Electoral Behavior*, edited by Kai Arzheimer, Jocelyn Evans, and Michael Lewis-Beck. Thousand Oaks, CA: Sage, 2017.

Zittel, Thomas, and Thomas Gschwend. "Individualised Constituency Campaigns in Mixed-Member Electoral Systems: Candidates in the 2005 German Elections." *West European Politics* 31, no. 5 (2008): 978–1003.

PART VII

## ELECTORAL SYSTEMS IN THE CONTEXT OF REFORM

# CHAPTER 38

# ELECTORAL SYSTEMS IN CONTEXT

## *New Zealand*

### JACK VOWLES

NEW ZEALAND provides one of the few cases of a major electoral system change in an "old" democracy: from a first-past-the-post (FPTP) to a mixed-member proportional (MMP) system (Renwick 2011; Jackson and McRobie 1998). After seven New Zealand general elections using the MMP system between 1996 and 2014, it is time to move on to an analysis of electoral system consolidation. Concurrent with its 2011 general election, New Zealand held a referendum on whether or not the MMP system would be retained. The margin to retain MMP at 58 to 42 percent was greater than at the referendum in 1993 that gave the system its mandate (Arseneau and Roberts 2012). Despite electoral system experts' scepticism about "the limits of electoral reform" (Bowler and Donovan 2013), New Zealanders have increased their support for the MMP system. It has become institutionally embedded. The only significant debates that remain concern reform on the margins.

This chapter has three sections: the first examines whether the change to MMP has achieved the goals of electoral reformers or confirmed the fears of its opponents; the second assesses the fit between the MMP system and the cleavage structure of New Zealand's electoral politics and its party system; and the third provides some evidence from individual-level opinion and behavior since 1996.

## EXPECTATIONS OF CHANGE

A recent review of the New Zealand case finds "only limited evidence that the 'new' electoral system lived up to expectations and arguments made by pro-reform advocates" (Bowler and Donovan 2013, 78). But it is equally important to consider negative consequences predicted by MMP opponents. The weights of various expectations also need to be compared: some are more important than others. One needs to distinguish between expectations generated by experts and campaigners and those that matter among the mass public.[1]

First, one should consider the reformers. A core principle of MMP is, of course, proportional representation (PR), proportionality of parliamentary seats to votes. As designed by the Royal Commission on the Electoral System (RCES) that recommended it in 1986, New Zealand's system of MMP has two votes, one for a candidate for a district or constituency (in New Zealand discourse, an electorate) and one for a party (see RCES 1986). Using the Sainte-Laguë formula, the count of the party vote allocates the total number of seats for each registered political party's standing candidates. There were 71 electorates for the 2014 election, in a parliament that has a normal total of 120 seats. The total can be slightly higher where a party wins more electorate seats than are allocated by the party vote, a so-called overhang. After the electorate seats are distributed, the 50 seats remaining are assigned from closed party lists, topping up from each party's electorate seats to the total number of members of parliament (MPs) determined by the party vote. A representation threshold applies at 5 percent of the party vote. It may also be crossed where a party wins an electorate seat or seats with less than the 5 percent party vote. This may sometimes lead to an overhang.

List-based PR systems are often advocated because they are said to enhance the representation of women and ethnic minorities. Women's representation in the New Zealand House of Parliament was increasing prior to the introduction of MMP. At the last FPTP election in 1993, it stood at just over 21 percent. At the first MMP election, women's representation did increase steeply and has subsequently stayed around 30 percent. Women tend to take more list seats, up to 44 and 45 percent in 1996 and 2005, respectively, but only once, in 2014, have women been successfully returned in more than 30 percent of the electorates.[2] Because there are fewer list seats than electorate seats, list effectiveness is limited. Parties on the left tend to elect more women than those on the right (Curtin 2012, 2014).

The subject of ethnic minorities is more complex. Immigration and demographic changes over the past twenty years have increased New Zealand's cultural diversity. In 2013, 75 percent of the population of 4.5 million identified within the category of "European," 12 percent as "Asian," 8 percent as from one or another island in the Pacific Ocean, and 16 percent as indigenous Māori. These numbers add up to more than the total: 11 percent report more than one ethnic identification (Statistics New Zealand 2016a). Pacific peoples' representation lagged behind their population until 2014, when it reached just under 6 percent. Most MPs of Pacific origin have been returned from electorate seats, reflecting the spatial concentration of their ethnic group in low-income Auckland suburbs. Asian MPs lagged badly until 2008, and in 2014 were still only 4 percent of the house: in 2014 their ratio of list to electorate MPs was about two to one. The recent arrival of most Asians living in New Zealand partly explains their low representation.

Indigenous Māori representation has benefited most from the MMP system. Māori often joke that MMP stands for "more Māori in parliament." Since 1867, New Zealand has maintained a system of separate Māori representation. Persons of Maori ancestry have the choice to enroll in a Māori or a general electorate. Prior to 1996 there were four Māori electorates, the number of which did not recognize a significant increase in the Māori population. The RCES recommended the abolition of the Māori electorates assuming that Māori would be better represented under PR. However, after consultation with Māori, it was decided that the MMP system would continue to include Māori seats with the number dependent on the number of Māori who enroll in them. There are currently seven. People of Māori descent are now often elected as MPs for general electorates, and Māori are even better represented on the lists. In 2014, Māori MPs were just over 20 percent of the house. MMP has enabled recent Māori social and political development to be carried through smoothly into political representation.

Advocates of MMP cited findings in the electoral system literature reporting higher electoral turnout under PR than under majoritarian systems. There are good reasons to expect a PR system to encourage turnout more than a majoritarian system (Selb 2009; Cox, Fiva, and Smith 2015). In New Zealand, a long-term trend of decreasing turnout prior to the establishment of MMP has continued afterward, except for a small immediate upward shift (Karp and Banducci 1999). The balance of age cohorts who vote more against those who vote less is still changing in favor of the latter. Most of this habitual behavior was primed prior to electoral system change. Those entering voting after the introduction of MMP could generate a reversal of the trend, but research findings about the turnout behavior of this group run into data quality issues (Vowles 2010, 2014a, 2015a). In the 2011 referendum the young were more likely to vote for MMP than the old (Karp 2014).

A shift to PR changes the incentives shaping parties' mobilization strategies. Parties should shift resources to the national level, which can increase overall turnout. On-the-ground efforts should also be more effective in parties' areas of concentrated support (Denemark 1998). However, comparative research shows that there is relatively low "on the ground" activity in closed-list PR systems (Karp, Banducci, and Bowler 2008), and lower party memberships than in the past reduce the capacity for voter mobilization in many countries. "On the ground" party contact declined over the first few MMP elections in New Zealand, only recovering after 2005 (Vowles 2014b, 68). Mixed-member systems also complicate the incentives shaping party strategies. Electorate candidates may still wish to expend resources to win competitive districts even if such resources could be better placed to encourage turnout elsewhere. While turnout has increased at some post-MMP elections, notably in 2005 and 2014, the general trend remains downward and the failure to reverse it is a disappointment for reformers. But turnout is unlikely to have been a significant concern to members of the mass public.

The principal goal of electoral system change was to increase proportionality of votes to seats. As Figure 38.1 shows, there is no doubt that the New Zealand MMP system works well to generate high levels of proportionality. Yet the dual threshold can generate discrepancies. At two elections in particular, a party has failed to win any seats despite gaining over 4 percent of the party vote: the Christian Coalition in 1996 and the New Zealand First Party in 2008. On the other hand, several parties have been able to win multiple seats despite having party votes lower than 4 percent, because they have won a single electorate seat and crossed the threshold.[3]

The RCES had recommended a 4 percent threshold, but the Electoral Act of 1993 designates 5 percent (RCES 1986). The electorate seat threshold was intended to encourage the representation of minority parties representing spatially concentrated ethnic groups. Experience has not borne out that expectation: instead, parties have exploited the electorate seat threshold strategically, to help potential coalition partners into the house. Two of the members of the RCES have advocated the removal of the electorate seat threshold (Wallace 2002; Mulgan 1999). An Electoral Commission review of the system after the 2011 referendum also recommended the abolition of the electorate threshold, the abolition of overhang seats, and the lowering of the party vote threshold to 4 percent (Electoral Commission 2012). However, the center-right National-led government decided not to implement those reforms.

This issue aside, as Figure 38.1 shows, the MMP system has facilitated a high level of proportionality. The most significant political consequence has been the failure of any single party to gain a parliamentary majority since 1996. This is the expectation of the new system that should be given the greatest weight, particularly in the realm of public opinion. Virtually all narratives about the process of electoral system change emphasize New Zealanders' dissatisfaction with the three governments that governed the country after 1975. All three were able to use New Zealand's lack of fundamental constitutional law combined with concentrated cabinet power in a relatively small single-chamber parliament to practice "electoral dictatorship," taking advantage of their "unbridled power" (Palmer 1987; Vowles 1995; Renwick 2011; Jackson and McRobie 1998).

Those governments were responsible for extreme policies, many unanticipated. The Muldoon National government from 1975 to 1984 embarked on controversial policies despite strong opposition. It made big investments in the energy sector, imposing high levels of risk on the taxpayer. Seeking to stabilize the economy, in the early 1980s the

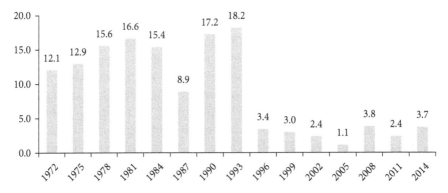

**FIGURE 38.1.** Disproportionality of votes to seats in New Zealand elections 1972–2014.

Note: Disproportionality is estimated by Gallagher's least squares index (Gallagher 2015).

government took tight control of wages, prices, and interest rates. It took a highly adversarial stance against its critics, narrowly winning the 1978 and 1981 elections only in terms of seats, not votes. To retain its support in conservative provincial areas, it allowed a national sporting team from apartheid South Africa to tour the country despite opposition from a well-organized antiracist movement, which led to unprecedented social disorder (Richards 1999).

Between 1984 and 1990, a Labour government embraced economic liberalization, much of it overdue. But neoliberals captured the process and their reform proposals, many of which were implemented, were widely criticized as going too far and too fast. The next National government from 1990 onward campaigned on re-establishing a "decent society" but once elected extended reform into social policy and the labor market, two policy domains where Labour had resisted the neoliberal surge. The two MMP referendums followed in 1992 and 1993. Reacting against the experience of the previous three governments, those campaigning, and most of those who voted for MMP, wanted to prevent single-party governments coming to power with only plurality support in the mass electorate. Reformers wished to establish the conditions for broadly based coalitions based on majorities that would be obliged to consult more widely about proposals for change (Nagel 1994; Katz 1997, 302–308; Nagel 2000, 2012; Lamare and Vowles 1996).

Table 38.1 lists New Zealand's post-MMP governments. The first was a majority coalition of the National and New Zealand First Parties. National had been in government prior to the election, and New Zealand First had campaigned as an antigovernment party, with a nationalist policy stance slightly to the right of center. After the election, New Zealand First engaged in concurrent negotiations with both the National and Labour Parties, but after two months opted for National, confounding many expectations.[4] Together National and New Zealand First could command a parliamentary majority: a Labour-led government would have required the Alliance Party to Labour's left. The Alliance had ruled out a formal coalition with Labour without a pre-election agreement, to which Labour would not concede, and New Zealand First had ruled out any pre- or postelection arrangement with the Alliance (Miller 1998). Tensions soon emerged within the coalition. Prime Minister Jim Bolger was forced from his leadership of the party and replaced by Jenny Shipley, who took a more combative approach with New Zealand First and its leader, former National MP Winston Peters. Peters withdrew his party from the coalition in 1998. New Zealand First then split, sufficient of its MPs leaving New Zealand First and remaining with the government for it to retain office (Vowles 1999).

This paved the way for a Labour-led coalition with the Alliance Party that took office in 1999. Based on election night results, the two parties would have been able to command a slim majority, but the final count put the Green Party over the 5 percent threshold and the number of Labour and Alliance seats fell into a minority. Formerly part of the Alliance, and also to the left of Labour, the Green Party agreed to support the government on matters of confidence and supply, and was given promises of consultation on environmental matters (Miller 2002). From 1999 onward, all New Zealand government cabinets have had minority status.

## Table 38.1 Types of Government and Support Arrangements, 1996–2014

| Year | Coalition or Single-Party Government | Core Party | In Cabinet | Confidence and Supply in Ministry | Confidence and Supply only | Majority or Minority Government |
|---|---|---|---|---|---|---|
| 1996 | Coalition | National | NZ First | | | Majority |
| 1998 | Coalition | National | Government independents | | | Majority |
| 1999 | Coalition | Labour | Alliance | | Green | Minority |
| 2002 | Coalition | Labour | Progressive coalition | | United, Green | Minority |
| 2005 | Coalition | Labour | Progressive coalition | United NZ First | Green* | Minority |
| 2008 | Single-party cabinet | National | | United, ACT, Māori | | Minority |
| 2011 | Single-party cabinet | National | | United, ACT, Māori | | Minority |
| 2014 | Single-party cabinet | National | | United, ACT, Māori | | Minority |

* Cooperation agreement to abstain only.

The 2002 election was held early because of a split in the Alliance between left and right factions. Differences were also emerging between the government and the Green Party (Vowles 2003). The Alliance Party's leader was Jim Anderton, a former Labour MP who had left the Labour Party in 1989 to oppose its neoliberal turn. His New Labour Party had become part of the Alliance. In 2002, taking most of its MPs, Anderton set up the Progressive Party based in the Alliance's right-leaning faction, leaving the Alliance to retain its left, based in the party organization. The left-wing remainder of the Alliance failed to win any seats in 2002. Anderton retained his electorate seat, was able to bring in one Progressive list MP, and continued in coalition with Labour. A historically low vote for the Opposition National Party and a surge in the vote for the centrist United Future Party gave Labour two options for government partnership. Differences between Labour and the Green Party on the regulation of genetic modification of plants and animals led Prime Minister Helen Clark to look for support to the center and to rule out Green Party cabinet participation. Confidence and supply arrangements were negotiated with both the Green Party and United Future (Vowles 2003).

At the next election held in 2005, the Labour Party beat National to a narrow plurality win. Again, Prime Minister Helen Clark looked to the center, this time bringing New Zealand First Party leader Winston Peters into the ministry, but not into the cabinet. United Future Party leader Peter Dunne took on another ministerial position outside the cabinet. The Green Party remained on the margins of the government, only agreeing to abstain on confidence and supply, with some concessions for consultation (Vowles 2006). The surviving single Progressive MP Jim Anderton made the minority Labour-led government technically a coalition until 2008. But in all but party name he had been reabsorbed into Labour. A minority single-party model of government has continued under the National governments from 2008 onward: a single-party cabinet, with ministers outside the cabinet from other parties, signed up for collective responsibility only in the areas covered by their portfolios, while providing support on confidence and supply (Malone 2008, 54–56; Boston 2009).

This development is a result of elite learning. Coalition cabinets can be difficult to manage, and tensions can be disruptive within all parties concerned. Both New Zealand First and the Alliance split under those conditions, and in 1998 National ousted an able and experienced leader only to lose the following election. Growing voter disenchantment in an incumbent tends to most adversely affect the smaller coalition partner (Miller and Curtin 2011). Lower junior partner exposure and responsibility coupled with tightly defined policy influence works better (Lundberg 2013, 619). But even these arrangements are not risk-free. New Zealand First's supply and confidence arrangement with Labour from 2005 to 2008 gave Winston Peters the high-profile role of minister of foreign affairs outside cabinet. Allegations of his failure to disclose a campaign donation did much damage both to New Zealand First and to the government as a whole, and New Zealand First failed to cross the threshold for parliamentary representation after the 2008 election (Vowles 2009). Opponents of the MMP system claimed that a small party in government would be "the tail that wagged the dog." While a single-party minority cabinet must make some concessions to small parties, the concessions have tended to be token and marginal, as often adding good or popular ideas for policy development as providing grounds for criticism. Winston Peters's tenure as minister of foreign affairs is a good example of the token concession. The role was prestigious, but the extent of Peters's influence on the direction of the government's foreign policy was virtually zero.

The 2005 election pitted a center-hugging incumbent Labour-led government against a National Party that had taken another neoliberal turn, coupled with a stance that apparently aspired to bring an end to affirmative action to improve the lot of Māori. Even more controversially, National Party leader Don Brash appeared to deny Māori their status as an indigenous people with treaty rights, a principle now widely accepted as part of New Zealand's unwritten constitution (Palmer 2008). The latter approach struck a chord in conservative public opinion: National Party polling support shot up from its low ebb at the 2002 election. Had the Don Brash–led National Party won in 2005, New Zealand politics would have headed rapidly toward a level of polarization and confrontation not seen since the 1980s. Two percentage points separated the Labour and National Party votes in 2005. Had the election been run under the previous FPTP rules, the National Party could well have won more seats than Labour. The spatial distribution of district-based voting in New Zealand tends to favor the National Party (Vowles 2008b).

Instead, election of a National-led government was postponed until 2008 after leader Don Brash had been replaced by the moderate John Key. Much as previous Labour prime minister Helen Clark had hugged the center from a position slightly to its left, Key adopted the same strategy from the right, continuing the broad thrust of Labour's social policy initiatives, including income support for those working on low and low-to-middle incomes (Aimer 2014). New Zealanders adopted MMP as a reaction to extreme and unpopular government policies. The experience of center-oriented politics since the introduction of the MMP system supports the claims of those who advocated reform to bring New Zealand politics back toward moderation (also see Vowles, Banducci, and Karp 2006). The party of the median voter was unrepresented in the New Zealand governments between 1978 and 1993: since 1996, that party has been the main party of government except for 2008, when the party in question, United Future, was a government support partner (Nagel 2012, 6).

Meanwhile, the fears of opponents of the MMP system have not been strongly borne out by the evidence. Governments have not been formed by party backroom bargaining that fails to take account of the vote distribution. Every government since 1996 has been led by the plurality winner. Coalition and government support agreements have been transparent post facto. The National–New Zealand First coalition in 1996 was unexpected, but National led Labour by several points in the party vote and it was the only viable arrangement possible containing only two parties that were ideologically proximate. Government formation has at times been difficult but when resolved has been stable, except for the National–New Zealand First breakdown and the very final months of the Labour–Alliance coalition: even in that latter case, the government could have continued to the end of its term as both Alliance factions had agreed to support its continuation. So far there are no grounds to justify the fear that governments under MMP would be unable to handle an external shock or crisis. The Labour-led government took effective measures to respond to the global financial crisis, provided a bank deposit guarantee, and came up with a successful countercyclical economic strategy that was continued by the following National-led government after the 2008 election.

# The Party System

The consolidation of MMP has been more successful than many might have expected. Disruptions have occurred: in particular, the coalition breakdown of 1998 and the temporary electoral collapse of the National Party in 2002. But after such disruptions the system has reset and the dust has settled. The two major parties have remained the main players, and the party system has not changed dramatically. With the exception of core supporters of the Alliance, most of those seeking electoral reform did not necessarily want to displace the two major parties or realign the party system toward significantly higher levels of vote fragmentation.

The work of Maurice Duverger (1954) has often been interpreted to imply that PR systems inevitably proliferate the number of parties. FPTP is a "strong" electoral system that can have the effect of suppressing tendencies toward multiparty politics. By contrast, PR systems are "feeble" (Sartori 1994). However, examination of voting patterns in New Zealand before MMP pours cold water on a strong interpretation of Duverger. The idea of the wasted vote lies behind Duverger's "psychological effect" of FPTP systems. Rational and well-informed people whose preferences are for a party unable to effectively compete in their district will have an incentive to transfer their votes to a more competitive party, but they tend to be a minority among those who have an incentive to do so (Kiewiet 2013, 104). As the literature on electoral behavior reports, the majority have far from complete information; are driven by a mixture of past habits, loyalties, emotions, and cues;[5] and therefore cast their vote regardless of electoral system incentives: they either do not know or do not care that their votes are "wasted." Party politics can develop outside the two main players under electoral rules that should discourage such behavior.

Pure two-party politics has been the exception rather than the rule in New Zealand's political history, only occupying the years between 1938 and 1954. Data from the beginning of effective party competition in New Zealand up to the present shows that between 1972 and 1984, the effective number of elective parties (Laakso and Taagepera 1979) rose from two and a half to three. Between 1984 and 2002, there followed a period of high volatility both in the number of parties and in party choices being made at the individual level. This is a period that combines the "shock" from two related experiences: New Zealand's neoliberal era and its aftermath, and the change to MMP. In 2005, the effective number of elective parties returned to three, and then rose only very slightly at each following election (Vowles 2014b, 34–35; Gallagher 2015). The party system has restabilized with an effective number of elective parties very similar to the number before the "shock" period of 1984 to 2002.

The psychological effect applies among party elites more strongly than among voters. Even so, in an FPTP system elites still form parties that cannot win. Aspiring elites are more likely to form new parties under a permissive PR electoral system. But they can only be successful if those new parties can gain votes. The number of genuinely "new" parties that have achieved even marginal success under New Zealand's MMP system is only two, and even those have historical precedents.[6] Outside of National and Labour, the more successful competing parties under MMP predated the system: the Alliance, formed as a coalition of small parties to become more viable under the FPTP system; the Green Party, part of the Alliance for a few years but with its own origins dating back to the 1970s in the form of the Values Party; and New Zealand First, formed by Winston Peters after his departure from the National Party in 1992, in yet another rebellion against neoliberalism. The Māori Party, formed in 2004, had its precursor in the form of Mana Motuhake, a Maori self-determination party formed in 1980, and more recently Mana Māori, a party with an even stronger position on such matters.

The two "new" parties were the Association of Consumers and Taxpayers (ACT) and the United (later the United Future) Party. Refugees from the National and Labour

Parties formed the ACT in 1994 to continue the promotion of neoliberalism. Its precedent, an earlier right-wing liberal party, had been formed in the 1930s but became incorporated in the National Party in 1936. A group of National and Labour MPs from the 1993–1996 parliament formed the United Party. It was intended to be a centrist liberal party, holding the balance of power and therefore entering coalition governments with either the left or right, playing a moderating role. But even the "new" United Party had a historical precedent: the party's name was taken from a party in the 1920s, the original name of which was the Liberal Party.

Neither ACT nor United achieved their goals. The ACT vote tends to go up as the National vote goes down. It appeals to the ideological right that is most closely associated with the National Party. Its very small electoral success since 2008 has been conditional on National encouraging its voters to transfer their electorate support to an ACT candidate in the Auckland electorate of Epsom to make sure the party crosses the threshold. The only person to win a seat for the United Party in 1996 was former Labour MP Peter Dunne. In 1996 and 1999, Dunne held it with the aid of the National Party, which did not run a candidate against him. Dunne himself conforms to the model of a centrist liberal, but his party has had very limited traction except for a temporary upsurge in 2002. Dunne sought to recruit members and resources by opening his party to several others: one of conservative Christians, another representing hunters and fishers, and two representing ethnic minorities.[7] In 2014, after having held ministerial positions in both National- and Labour-led governments, he continued to retain his seat. In the previous year, United Future briefly lost its status as a registered party as its records could not confirm that it had the necessary five hundred members (Trevett 2013).

The pivotal party in New Zealand politics has never been a traditional liberal party: it has been a populist liberal party, "liberal" in the interventionist sense of the "new liberalism" of the early twentieth century (Freeden 1978), and consistent with the general understanding of liberalism in the United States. Applying a broad interpretative brush, one can describe the dominant New Zealand political tradition as "popular liberalism" (Vowles 1987). This tradition is characterized by egalitarian social policies and strong leaders with a common touch: its leadership archetype is Richard Seddon, New Zealand's longest-serving prime minister, in New Zealand's first party government, formed by the liberals between 1891 and 1912. The party continued under the "United" name into the 1920s and merged into the National Party in 1936. The Labour Party, purged of most of its early socialist policies, took over much of populist liberal mantle in the 1930s and 1940s, establishing a welfare state. As Labour support retreated, the Social Credit Party emerged from the 1954 election onward, primarily drawing on a small business constituency that placed hopes for prosperity in financial reform, assuming the pivotal position in the system occupied by United in the 1920s.

Social Credit went on to claim over 20 percent of the votes cast in 1981. With two seats in the house it misjudged its pivotal position, providing support for the National government in legislation to enable the construction of an unpopular High Dam on the river Clyde. Social Credit support collapsed. Further to the right, the New Zealand Party in 1984 briefly occupied the populist pivotal slot, before a brief and temporary reversion to two-party voting at the 1987 election. By the early 1990s, the position of populist pivot was open for the New Zealand First Party, centrist and sometimes left-leaning on economic policy, and socially conservative on moral and cultural issues.

Another significant player is the Māori Party. The Labour Party had developed strong support among Māori in the 1930s and 1940s. From the 1970s onward, demands generated by a Māori cultural and political renaissance put increasing strain on the relationship. The first Māori split from Labour was Mana Motukahe. It failed to win seats until 1993 as part of the Alliance. In 1996, all the Māori seats moved from Labour to New Zealand First. That party had selected strong candidates in the Māori seats: the party's leader, Winston Peters, is also Māori. In the fallout from the split in New Zealand First, many Māori moved back to Labour in 1999. But in 2004, Labour passed a law to confirm New Zealand's foreshore and seabed as public property, to forestall Māori legal claims for customary indigenous rights over some parts of the coast and seabed. While only one of Labour's MPs left the party on the issue, she formed the Māori Party and it won five out of the seven Māori seats at the 2005 election. The Maori Party returned two MPs in 2014 and continued in support of the National-led government first negotiated in 2008.

The remaining corner of the party system is that occupied by the Green Party. Its forerunner was the Values Party that first contested the 1972 election: the first national Green Party to be established anywhere in the world. In 1975, it gained just over 5 percent of the votes. Like most of its counterparts elsewhere, the Green Party draws predominantly on environmental values and is a party of the left. Its place in the party system emerged as increasing levels of education provided the conditions for development of its social base. Discouraged by the FPTP system, the Values Party had few votes or members from 1978 onward, and Labour was the beneficiary of those who might otherwise have voted Values. In 1990, the Green Party was established as Values' successor, gained 5 percent at that year's election, joined the Alliance in 1992, and re-established its independence in 1997 after the first MMP election. The Green Party received a 10 percent vote share at both the 2011 and 2014 elections.

To sum up, the New Zealand party system has four parties that have proved their viability under the MMP system: National, Labour, the Green Party, and New Zealand First, a four-party system with an effective number of elective parties near three. The conditions for this party system have existed since the 1970s and 1980s. As Clark and Golder (2006) argue, a PR system allows the structural foundations of a party system to be reflected more clearly in representation. A change of electoral system may realign a legislature, but not necessarily an elective party system. By allowing votes to translate more clearly into seats, the change to PR does provide the foundation for a more stable elective party system. Smaller parties that do well will no longer tend to subside in frustration when the electoral system fails to deliver seats consistent with their votes.

Other players could make greater headway in future. A 4 percent threshold would have kept New Zealand First in parliament after the 2008 election, but also might prove a foundation for a Christian Conservative Party, a force represented by the Christian Coalition in 1996 and the Conservative Party in 2011 and 2014. The Māori Party may continue to be a pivotal player, but its base remains in the Māori electorates. The ACT party will continue so long as National supports it, but United Future was left with no seats in 2017 after Peter Dunne abruptly withdrew his candidacy.

# EFFICACY AND ELECTORAL SYSTEM OPINION

Finally, this analysis of the consolidation of the MMP electoral system in New Zealand moves to the individual and behavioral level, exploring public attitudes about the system. The first comprehensive survey research on New Zealand voting behavior was conducted in 1963. It showed very high levels of social trust and political efficacy. Similar questions were not asked again until 1993, at the time of the referendum on MMP. Levels of trust had collapsed. In 1963, 77 percent had agreed "you can trust the government in most things rather than having to watch them closely" (Vowles 1998, 106). In 1993, only 31 percent agreed with the statement "you can trust the government to do what is right most of the time."

Figures 38.2 and 38.3 indicate a significant recovery in political efficacy since the adoption of the MMP system, indicating high correlations with the simple passage of time, although the scatter of points indicates this linear trend is something of an approximation. Some qualifications are therefore in order. Trust in MPs stabilized from 2005 onward, and trust in government from 2001. Most subsequent changes are within confidence intervals. New Zealand Election Survey (NZES) response rates have declined, potentially biasing the series, but progressively, not sharply at those points. NZES contains a panel. Movements within the panel are consistent with the cross-sectional changes. Both estimates of political efficacy record a significant collapse of political efficacy in 1998, when a midterm sample survey captured the effects of the collapse of the first MMP coalition government (Karp and Bowler 2001). Prior to the global financial crisis, one could argue that the recovery in efficacy paralleled more robust economic growth from about 2000 onward. But the efficacy recovery was robust to recession in 2007–2008, and there has been relatively low growth from that period onward.

These changes parallel shifts in New Zealanders' attitudes to coalition versus single-party governments. A preference for coalition rather than single-party government was one of the biggest predictors of MMP support in 1993 (Lamare and Vowles 1996). Despite the vote for MMP, a majority of New Zealanders still favored single-party government in 1996. The balance tipped in 1999: the Labour–Alliance coalition had agreed and announced its intentions before the election. Since 1993, the NZES has asked respondents whether single-party or coalition governments are better or the same for four aspects of government performance: providing stability, making tough decisions, keeping promises, and "doing what the people want." Despite majority preferences for single-party government as late as 1996, in 1993 and 1996, New Zealanders had quite high expectations of the performance of coalition governments. These soon fell back to more realistic levels. Nonetheless, post-MMP coalitions have been consistently perceived to be

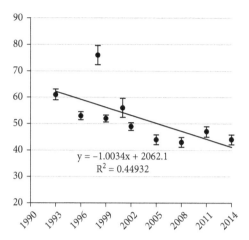

**FIGURE 38.2.** Trust in members of parliament, 1993–2014.

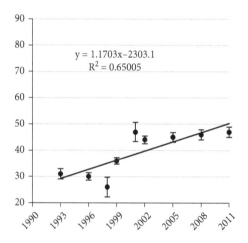

**FIGURE 38.3.** Trust in government, 1993–2011.

Note: The questions were "Most members of Parliament are out of touch with the rest of the country" and "You can trust the government to do what is right most of the time." Five-point agree/disagree scales, percentages strongly agreeing/agreeing.

Source: New Zealand Election Study (NZES) 1990–2014.

better than single-party governments at "keeping promises" and "doing what the people want." These perceptions remain stable up to the present (Vowles 2011, 132–134). In technical terms New Zealand has had single-party minority governments since 2008 and the nearest thing to a single-party minority government since 2002. But in New Zealand, the language of coalition continues to be understood in public discourse to refer to and describe the phenomena of minority governments accompanied by confidence, and supply agreements that often include ministerial appointments outside the cabinet.

The importance of public perceptions came to the fore in the 2011 referendum. Table 38.2 displays the distributions of responses to questions tapping into the most

### Table 38.2  MMP Campaign Statements, 2011 Referendum

| Favoring MMP | Agree | Neutral or Don't Know | Disagree | N |
|---|---|---|---|---|
| A good electoral system ensures everyone's vote counts equally wherever they live | 85 | 13 | 2 | 2,381 |
| A good electoral system ensures the party with the most votes gets the most MPs | 81 | 17 | 2 | 2,374 |
| MMP encourages politicians with different views to seek common ground | 60 | 33 | 8 | 2,366 |
| MMP prevents a party with a minority of votes being able to dominate Parliament | 46 | 34 | 21 | 2,368 |
| MMP is the fairest electoral system we have been given to choose between | 42 | 32 | 26 | 2,377 |
| MMP makes Parliament look and feel like New Zealand | 31 | 47 | 22 | 2,369 |
| **Against MMP** | | | | |
| List MPs should be reduced or eliminated* | 46 | 20 | 25 | 2,378 |
| Another system would be better than MMP in creating security for business | 29 | 53 | 18 | 2,354 |
| MMP gives party bosses too much power over MPs | 20 | 60 | 20 | 2,369 |
| **Relatively Neutral** | | | | |
| A good electoral system should make it easy to vote MPs out | 69 | 27 | 4 | 2,373 |
| A good electoral system should give voters certainty | 84 | 15 | 1 | 2,374 |

*Note:* Five-point agree/disagree scales, percentages strongly agreeing and agreeing, disagreeing and strongly disagreeing, neutral and don't know combined, except for *.

* While keeping the number of MPs at 120, do you think the number of list MPs should be increased, kept as at present, be reduced, or eliminated entirely? (Those responding reduced or eliminated; increased or kept at present; don't know.).

*Source:* 2011 New Zealand Election Study (NZES).

central campaign claims. Strong agreement with two pro-MMP claims stands out: votes counting equally wherever one lives and a preference for seats–votes proportionality. But agreement with these statements is wide, including many MMP opponents. Strong agreement with politicians seeking common ground plays into claims that an MMP system encourages consensus in government. More doubt and opposition emerge on governments with minorities of votes, fairness, and descriptive representation, but MMP still has the edge. Anti-MMP statements have less leverage. Opposition to list MPs has been the most effective, and has been a theme in criticism of MMP since 1993. Because their election is less direct than that of electorate MPs, some critics identify a legitimacy deficit or at least assign list MPs a lower status (Ward 1998). Dual candidacy for electorate and list seats was the subject of criticism. The 2012 MMP review recommended that candidates should continue to be able to run both for an electorate seat and on the list.

Power to "party bosses" had virtually no leverage. Security for business had some force, but those neutral or lacking knowledge on this matter were by far the biggest response group. "Easy to vote MPs out" had strong agreement, but New Zealand's experience of the MMP system has seen the regular replacement of governments consistent with majority preferences, and more circulation of individual MPs by way of defeats and retirements, as was the case under the old FPTP system (Vowles 2015b). Strong agreement for "certainty" disadvantaged MMP, but with the exception of the 1996 and 2005 elections, it was very clear almost immediately after the votes had been counted which major party would form the government.

A regression model of these campaign statements, MMP-related sentiments, and preferences for and against coalitions against referendum voting choice identifies which of these claims structured choice. All questions from Table 38.2 were entered in an initial model, and those with insignificant results excluded for the version are reported in Table 38.3. "Fairness" was the strongest MMP appeal, followed by favoring descriptive representation and preference for coalition governments. Being against the interests of business, opposition to list MPs, and uncertainty of election results were the most effective arguments against MMP.

### Table 38.3  Vote for or against Retaining the MMP System

| Logistic Regression<br>For = 1, Against = No | Coeff | | Robust Standard Error | Min-Max Probability Shift |
|---|---|---|---|---|
| Against list MPs | −0.72 | ** | 0.14 | −0.20 |
| MMP fair | 1.90 | ** | 0.14 | 0.83 |
| MMP bad for business | −1.26 | ** | 0.17 | −0.48 |
| MMP descriptive | 0.86 | ** | 0.13 | 0.34 |
| MMP uncertainty | −0.29 | * | 0.14 | −0.10 |
| Prefer coalitions | 1.19 | ** | 0.41 | 0.11 |
| Constant | −0.70 | | 0.69 | |
| $R^2$ (N) | 0.59 | | (2,486) | |

Notes: All but one of the predictor variables are five-point scales, with "don't know responses" recoded to the neutral midpoint. Opposition to list MPs is based on the five categories explained in the notes to Table 2 earlier. Preference for coalitions is a nine-point scale made up of responses to questions whether single-party or coalition governments are better at four different aspects of government performance: providing stability, making tough decisions, keeping promises, and "doing what the people want"; the three possible responses were "more than one party," "one party," and "both the same." Don't knows were coded to "both the same."

Source: 2011 New Zealand Election Study (NZES).

# CONCLUSION

The most important expectations of New Zealand's electoral reformers have been met. The MMP system is proportional, with some imperfections. It has delivered a higher level of descriptive representation than before. And, most important, no single party has so far been able to gain a majority in parliament. While ACT to the right and the Green Party to the left are widely separated ideologically, mainstream political discourse has moderated and since 1999 there has been a high level of policy continuity. While the back and forth of day-to-day political conflict is not quite consistent with the idea of "consensus," behind the scenes under MMP there has been less ideological polarization in New Zealand politics than in the 1970s and 1980s. Admittedly, at the 2014 election, the National Party appeared to have achieved a narrow one-seat majority on election night: it was lost after the further count of special votes. With its close ally the ACT Party the government could still command a majority, but it lost a further seat to New Zealand First the following year at a by-election. As a result, the government was forced to compromise on a controversial law reform that would have prioritized economic growth over environmental protection.

The change of electoral system has not fundamentally changed the party system. It has allowed its structural foundations to be translated into seats and votes, and over the last four elections the pattern has stabilized. Of course, one cannot be sure that this will continue. The next change of government is likely to require a formal coalition between the Labour and Green Parties. Those two parties coordinated their campaigns in 2017 formed a governing arrangement (along with New Zealand First) following the election. The National Party continued to be the plurality winner in 2017, thus presenting a challenge to legitimacy from those who continue to think in plurality terms. New Zealand First continues to seek to play off center-left against center-right. Changes to the threshold would be likely under a Labour–Green government. Those who see an advantage in encouraging small party allies will oppose the ending of the electorate seat threshold. It is ironic that without its electorate seat deal with ACT at the 2014 election, the National Party would have secured a single-party majority (Farrar 2014).

The result of the 2011 referendum has institutionalized the MMP system. Attitudes to proportional representation and MMP do fluctuate, and opinion can turn negative under an unpopular government and under conditions of uncertainty, such as a protracted government formation process (Vowles 2008a). But at the 2011 referendum, there was no active campaign to return to the FPTP system, even though FPTP remained the most popular alternative. Instead, opponents of MMP chose to promote a supplementary member system that would have continued to elect list MPs while largely abandoning proportionality. It failed to gain traction. Sometimes advertised as "the best of both worlds" (Shugart and Wattenberg 2003), New Zealand's MMP system is perhaps more accurately summed up as "better than the alternatives, but could be improved."

## NOTES

1. For summaries of expectations see Vowles et al. 2002, 188–189; Vowles, Aimer, Banducci and Karp 1998 Vowles, Banducci and Karp 2006.
2. See Parliamentary Library 2014. This Report on the 2014 Election provides data on elections and representation both before and after the advent of the MMP system.
3. Detailed results for the elections in question can be found at the New Zealand Electoral Commission's election results website at URL: http://www.electionresults.org.nz/
4. New Zealand's government formation process has been criticised as lacking a "formateur," leaving the political parties to negotiate among themselves (Boston 1998). However, since 1996 the process has been handled more successfully.
5. See Achen and Bartels 2016 for a particularly pessimistic reading of this evidence.
6. For a general introduction to political parties and elections in New Zealand see Miller 2005.
7. Parties that have merged into United Future are the Asia-Pacific United Party, the Ethnic Minority Party, Future New Zealand (two different parties under the same name), and the New Zealand Conservative Party (1994-1996). The Outdoor Recreation Party was affiliated in 2005, although later broke away and disbanded in 2007. At the 2014 election United Future received 0.2 percent of the party vote.

## REFERENCES

Achen, Christopher, and Larry Bartels. *Democracy for Realists: Why Elections Do Not Produce Responsive Government.* Princeton, NJ: Princeton University Press, 2016.

Aimer, Peter. "New Zealand's Electoral Tides in the 21st Century." In *The New Electoral Politics in New Zealand: the Significance of the 2011 Election*, edited by J. Vowles, 9–26. Wellington: Institute for Governance and Policy Studies, 2014.

Arseneau, Therese, and Nigel S. Roberts. "'Kicking the Tyres' on MMP: The Results of the Referendum Reviewed." In *Kicking the Tyres: The New Zealand General Election and Referendum of 2011*, edited by Jon Johansson and Stephen Levine, 325–346. Wellington: Victoria University of Wellington Press, 2012.

Boston, Jonathan. *Governing Under Proportional Representation: Lessons from Europe.* Wellington: Institute of Policy Studies, 1998.

Boston, Jonathan. "Innovative Political Management: Multi-Party Governance in New Zealand." *Policy Quarterly* 5, no. 2 (2009): 52–59.

Bowler, Shaun, and Todd Donovan. *The Limits of Electoral Reform.* Oxford: Oxford University Press, 2013.

Clark, William R., and Matt Golder. "Rehabilitating Duverger's Theory: Testing the Mechanical and Strategic Effects of Electoral Laws." *Comparative Political Studies* 39, no. 6 (2006): 679–708.

Cox, Gary W., Jon H. Fiva, and Daniel M. Smith. "The Contraction Effect: How Proportional Representation Affects Mobilization and Turnout." Working Paper, September 8, 2015. http://www.jon.fiva.no/docs/CoxFivaSmith.pdf.

Curtin, Jennifer. "New Zealand: Gendering Parliamentary Representation, a Mixed System Producing Mixed Results." In *Women and Legislative Representation: Electoral Systems, Political Parties, and Sex Quotas*, edited by Manon Tremblay, 197–210. New York: Palgrave MacMillan, 2012.

Curtin, Jennifer. "From Presence to Absence: Where Were the Women in 2011." In *The New Electoral Politics in New Zealand: the Significance of the 2011 Election*, edited by Jack Vowles, 125–139. Wellington: Institute for Governance and Policy Studies, 2014.

Denemark, David. "Campaign Activities and Marginality: The Transition to MMP Campaigns." In *Voters' Victory? New Zealand's First Election under Proportional Representation*, edited by Jack Vowles, Peter Aimer, Susan Banducci, and Jeffrey Karp, 81–100. Auckland: Auckland University Press, 1998.

Duverger, Maurice. *Political Parties: Their Organization and Activity in the Modern State* London: Methuen, 1954.

Electoral Commission. *Report of the Electoral Commission on the Review of the MMP Voting System*. Wellington: New Zealand Electoral Commission, 2012. http://www.elections .org.nz/sites/default/files/bulk-upload/documents/Final_Report_2012_Review_of _MMP.pdf.

Farrar, David. "What If." 2014. Kiwiblog. http://www.kiwiblog.co.nz/2014/10/what_if.html.

Freeden, Michael. *The New Liberalism: An Ideology of Social Reform*. Oxford: Oxford University Press, 1978.

Gallagher, Michael. "Election Indices." 2015. Electoral systems. https://www.tcd.ie/Political _Science/staff/michael_gallagher/ElSystems/Docts/ElectionIndices.pdf.

Jackson, William Keith, and Alan McRobie. *New Zealand Adopts Proportional Representation*. Aldershot: Ashgate, 1998.

Karp, Jeffrey A., and Susan Banducci. "The Impact of Proportional Representation on Turnout: Evidence from New Zealand." *Australian Journal of Political Science* 34 (1999): 363–377.

Karp, Jeffrey A., and Shaun Bowler. "Coalition Politics and Satisfaction with Democracy: Explaining New Zealand's Reaction to Proportional Representation." *European Journal of Political Research* 40 (2001): 57–79.

Karp, Jeffrey A. "Generations and the Referendum on MMP." in *The New Electoral Politics in New Zealand: The Significance of the 2011 Election*, edited by Jack Vowles, 187–198. Wellington: Institute for Governance and Policy Studies, 2014.

Karp, Jeffrey A., Susan Banducci, and Shaun Bowler. "Getting Out the Vote: Party Mobilization in a Comparative Perspective." *British Journal of Political Science* 38 (2008): 91–112.

Katz, Richard S. *Democracy and Elections*. New York: Oxford University Press, 1997.

Kiewiet, D. Roderick. "The Ecology of Tactical Voting in Britain." *Journal of Elections, Public Opinion and Parties* 23 (2013): 86–110.

Laakso, Markku, and Rein Taagepera. "'Effective' Number of Political Parties: A Measure with Application to Western Europe." *Comparative Political Studies* 12, no. 1 (1979): 3–27.

Lamare, James W., and Jack Vowles. "Party Interests, Public Opinion, and Institutional Preferences: Electoral System Change in New Zealand." *Australian Journal of Political Science* 31, no. 3 (1996): 321–346.

Lundberg, Thomas. "Politics Is Still an Adversarial Business: Minority Government and Mixed-Member Proportional Representation in Scotland and in New Zealand." *British Journal of Politics and International Relations* 15 (2013): 609–625.

Malone, Ryan. *Rebalancing the Constitution: The Challenge of Government Law-Making Under MMP*. Wellington: Institute of Policy Studies, 2008.

Malone, Ryan. "Coalition Government: The Peoples' Choice?" In *Voters' Victory? New Zealand's First Election under Proportional Representation*, edited by Jack Vowles, Peter Aimer, Susan Banducci, and Jeffrey Karp, 120–134. Auckland: Auckland University Press, 1998.

Miller, Raymond. "Coalition Government: The Labour-Alliance Pact." In *Proportional Representation on Trial: The 1999 Election in New Zealand and the Fate of MMP*, edited by Jack Vowles, Peter Aimer, Jeffrey Karp, Susan Banducci, Raymond Miller, and Ann Sullivan, 114–129. Auckland: Auckland University Press, 2002.

Miller, Raymond. *Party Politics in New Zealand.* Melbourne: Oxford University Press, 2005.

Miller, Richard, and Jennifer Curtin. "Counting the Costs of Coalition: The Case of New Zealand's Small Parties." *Political Science* 63, no. 1 (2011): 106–125.

Mulgan, Richard. "Have New Zealand's Political Experiments Increased Public Accountability?" Australian National University Discussion Paper No. 59, 1999. https://digitalcollections.anu.edu.au/bitstream/1885/41948/1/dp_59.html.

Nagel, Jack H. "What Political Scientists Can Learn from the 1993 Electoral Reform in New Zealand." *PS: Political Science and Politics* XXVII (1994): 525–529.

Nagel, Jack H. "Expanding the Spectrum of Democracies: Reflections on Proportional Representation in New Zealand." In *Democracy and Institutions: The Life Work of Arend Lijphart,* 113–128. edited by Markus M. L. Crepaz, Thomas A. Koehle, and David Wilsford. Ann Arbor: University of Michigan Press, 2000.

Nagel, Jack H. "Evaluating Democracy in New Zealand under MMP." *Policy Quarterly* 8, no. 2 (2012): 3–11.

New Zealand Election Study 1990-2014. http://www.nzes.org/.

Parliamentary Library. *The 2014 New Zealand General Election: Final Results and Voting Statistics.* Wellington: Parliamentary Library, 2014. https://www.parliament.nz/en/pb/research-papers/document/00PLLawRP2015011/final-results-2014-general-election#RelatedAnchor.

Palmer, Geoffrey. *Unbridled Power.* Auckland: Oxford University Press, 1987.

Palmer, Matthew. *The Treaty of Waitangi in New Zealand's Law and Constitution.* Wellington: Victoria University Press, 2008.

Renwick, Alan. *The Politics of Electoral Reform: Changing the Rules of Democracy.* Cambridge: Cambridge University Press, 2011.

Richards, Trevor. *Dancing on Our Bones: New Zealand, South Africa, Rugby and Racism.* Wellington: Bridget Williams Books, 1999.

Royal Commission on the Electoral System. *Report of the Royal Commission on the Electoral System: Towards a Better Democracy?* Wellington: Government Printer, 1986.

Sartori, Giovanni. *Comparative Constitutional Engineering: An Inquiry in the Structures, Incentives, and Outcomes.* Houndmills: MacMillan, 1994.

Selb, Peter. "A Deeper Look at the Proportionality–Turnout Nexus." *Comparative Political Studies* 42 (2009): 527–548.

Shugart, Matthew S., and Martin Wattenberg. *Mixed-Member Electoral Systems: The Best of Both Worlds?* Oxford: Oxford University Press, 2003.

Statistics New Zealand. "2016a Estimated Resident Population (ERP), National Population by Ethnic Group, Age, and Sex, 30 June 1996, 2001, 2006, and 2013." http://nzdotstat.stats.govt.nz/wbos/Index.aspx?DataSetCode=TABLECODE7511.

Trevett, Claire. "United Future Party Registration Cancelled." *New Zealand Herald,* May 31, 2013. http://www.nzherald.co.nz/nz/news/article.cfm?c_id=1&objectid=10887711.

Vowles, Jack. "Liberal Democracy: Pakeha Political Ideology." *New Zealand Journal of History* 21, no. 2 (1987): 215–227.

Vowles, Jack. "The Politics of Electoral Reform in New Zealand." *International Political Science Review* 16, no. 1 (1995): 95–115.

Vowles, Jack. "Aspects of Electoral Studies, Present and Past: New Zealand Voters and 'the System', 1949-1996." *Political Science* 49, no. 1, Special Anniversary Issue (1998): 90–110.

Vowles, Jack. "New Zealand." *European Journal of Political Research* 36, no. 3/4 Political Data Yearbook issue (1999): 473–481.

Vowles, Jack. "New Zealand." *European Journal of Political Research* 44, no. 3/4 Political Data Yearbook issue (2003): 1037–1047.

Vowles, Jack. "New Zealand." in *European Journal of Political Research* 45, no. 3/4 Political Data Yearbook issue (2006): 1055–1068.

Vowles, Jack. "The Genie in the Bottle: Is New Zealand's MMP System Here to Stay." In *In the Public Interest: Essays in Honour of Professor Keith Jackson, edited by* Mark Frances and Jim Tully, 105–125. Christchurch: University of Canterbury Press, 2008a.

Vowles, Jack. "Systemic Failure, Coordination, and Contingencies: Understanding Electoral System Change in New Zealand." In *To Keep or Change First Past the Post: The Politics of Electoral Reform*, edited by Andre Blais, 163–183. Oxford: Oxford University Press, 2008b.

Vowles, Jack. "The 2008 Election in New Zealand." *Electoral Studies* 28, no. 3 (2009): 507–510.

Vowles, Jack. "Electoral System Change, Generations, Competitiveness and Turnout in New Zealand, 1963-2005." *British Journal of Political Science* 40, no. 4 (2010): 875–895.

Vowles, Jack. "Why Voters Prefer Coalitions: Rationality or Norms." *Political Science* 63 (2011): 126–145.

Vowles, Jack. "Down, Down, Down: Turnout from 1946 to 2011." In *The New Electoral Politics in New Zealand: The Significance of the 2011 Election*, edited by J. Vowles, 53–73. Wellington: Institute for Governance and Policy Studies, 2014a.

Vowles, Jack. "Putting the 2011 Election in Its Place." In *The New Electoral Politics in New Zealand: the Significance of the 2011 Election*, edited by J. Vowles, 27–52. Wellington: Institute for Governance and Policy Studies, 2014b.

Vowles, Jack. "Voter Turnout." In *New Zealand Government and Politics,* 6th ed., edited by Janine Hayward, 287–299. Melbourne: Oxford University Press, 2015a.

Vowles, Jack. "Legislative Accountability in a Mixed System." *Australian Journal of Political Science* 50, no. 2 (2015b): 279–296.

Vowles, Jack, Peter Aimer, Susan Banducci, and Jeffrey Karp. *Voters' Victory? New Zealand's First Election under Proportional Representation.* Auckland: Auckland University Press, 1998.

Vowles, Jack, Peter Aimer, Jeffrey Karp, S. Banducci, R. Miller, and A. Sullivan. *Proportional Representation on Trial: The 1999 Election in New Zealand and the Fate of MMP.* Auckland: Auckland University Press, 2002.

Vowles, Jack, Susan A. Banducci, and Jeffrey A. Karp. "Forecasting and Evaluating the Consequences of Electoral Change in New Zealand." *Acta Politica* 41 (2006): 267–284.

Wallace, John. "Reflections on Constitutional and Other Issues Concerning Our Electoral System: The Past and the Future." *Political Science* 54, no. 1 (2002): 47–65.

Ward, Leigh J. "'Second-Class MPs'? New Zealand's Adaptation to Mixed-Member Parliamentary Representation." *Political Science* 49 (1998): 125–152.

# CHAPTER 39

# ELECTORAL SYSTEMS IN CONTEXT

## *Japan*

### KUNIAKI NEMOTO

JAPAN uses several different electoral systems at different levels of government. At the local level, every municipality (cities, towns, villages, and special wards in Tokyo) selects its council members usually in one single district with single nontransferable voting (SNTV). District magnitude for municipal council elections ranges from one to more than fifty.[1] Prefectural assembly elections also feature SNTV, although a prefecture is divided into several districts and district magnitude is slightly smaller, ranging from one to less than twenty. Municipal mayors and prefectural governors are elected under first past the post (FPTP).

For the purpose of this volume, the electoral systems used at the national level should be of more interest. Japan's National Diet (*Kokkai*) features fairly symmetric bicameralism, whereby any bill except the budget, treaty ratification, and the vote of investiture requires approval from both of the chambers. The upper house, the House of Councillors (*Sangiin*, or HoC), now has 242 members with a fixed term of six years, with half of its members elected every three years. The system is mixed-member majoritarian (MMM), with the nominal component's forty-five districts electing 1 to 6 members through SNTV. The nationwide list component now elects 48 members with open-list proportional representation, where a voter can choose to vote for a party list or a candidate.[2]

This chapter focuses on the lower house, the House of Representatives (*Shugiin*, or HoR), because it attracts more attention from scholars and ordinary citizens in Japan for a couple of reasons. First, the HoR is seen as more powerful and important in lawmaking and forming and maintaining a government. The HoR can override the upper house's decision over a bill with a two-thirds majority. In the cases of the budget, treaty ratification, and the vote of investiture, when the two chambers' decisions differ, the HoR's decisions prevail. The prime minister can dissolve the HoR anytime but not the HoC, while only the HoR can submit a nonconfidence motion against the prime minister.

Second, perhaps more important, the system used for the HoR was changed in the mid-1990s from hyperpersonalistic SNTV to MMM. To put it very simply, the reform was expected to bring about two immediate consequences (Shugart 2001): on the interparty dimension, the introduction of first past the post (FPTP) on the nominal component would favor two large blocs of parties; on the intraparty dimension, candidate-centered campaigning would be replaced by emphasis on party label. These combined would further transform party organizations, as party-centered competition would call for a strong leader and a centralized party. Thus, the case of Japan, along with the countries that experienced electoral reform (e.g., Italy and New Zealand), offers the opportunity for researchers to conduct comparative analysis between the pre- and postreform periods controlling for other factors.[3]

As shown in subsequent sections, the main topics of research on Japan's electoral system and its consequences have been widely ranging from candidate entry, Duvergerian convergence, and campaigning strategies to party and legislative organizations. The review that follows reveals that in general, evidence supports the theoretically expected consequences of the electoral reform: a move toward two-party competition, party-centered campaigning, and party centralization. Meanwhile, the review also reveals that the reform did not completely transform Japanese party politics as expected (Scheiner 2008). Some of the institutions and practices considered peculiar to the old electoral system, such as personal support networks and factions, were not wiped away by the reform. Other rules considered minor, such as dual candidacy,[4] surprisingly had a major impact on incumbency advantage and Duvergerian convergence. These suggest that Japan's electoral reform opens the way for new comparative research on the effects of electoral systems.

This chapter is divided into five sections. Following this introduction is a section describing the old and new systems and a section detailing expectations about how the electoral reform would transform the party system, campaigning patterns, and party organizations. The third section reviews in depth the impact of the reform on electoral competition in terms of the interparty and intraparty dimensions. The fourth section in turn focuses on the reform's impact on party and legislative organization. The concluding section discusses the literature's findings so far and the research agenda going forward.[5]

# ELECTORAL REFORM

Japan's HoR used single nontransferable voting from 1947 to 1993. Under SNTV, a voter casts only one vote for a candidate. A vote is nontransferable, so even if a candidate wins a seat with a huge margin or loses, his or her votes cannot be transferred to or pooled with another candidate. Each district elects multiple top vote winners depending on district magnitude (M). When SNTV was put in place in Japan, most of the districts elected three to five members, with the median M being four. Reapportionment over the postwar period shrank M in some rural districts and expanded it in others, usually in cities. In the 1993 HoR election, for example, the country was divided into 129 districts with M ranging from two to six, inclusive.

The effects of SNTV can be understood in terms of interparty and intraparty dimensions. On the interparty dimension, party competition at the district level was, if not perfectly, marked by the "M + 1 rule": that is, the number of viable candidates should converge on M + 1 (Cox 1994; Reed 1990). Between 1955 and 1993, where M was three, four, and five, the average effective numbers of candidates were 4.65, 5.89, and 6.96, respectively.[6] At the national level, SNTV's "superproportional" feature allowed several small parties to secure seats (Cox 1996; Taagepera and Shugart 1989), because candidates were able to win seats with even 10 to 15 percent of the votes. During the long period of the Liberal Democratic Party's (LDP) rule under SNTV (1955–1993), several opposition parties survived.[7] Thus, the number of parties was five to seven, although the LDP's one-party dominance pushed down the effective number of legislative parties at the national level to around 2.5 and 3.3, as shown in Figure 39.1.[8]

SNTV's equally or more interesting consequence manifested on the intraparty dimension. Due to its nature, the SNTV system forces a majority-seeking party to nominate multiple candidates in the same district. As votes are not pooled by candidates

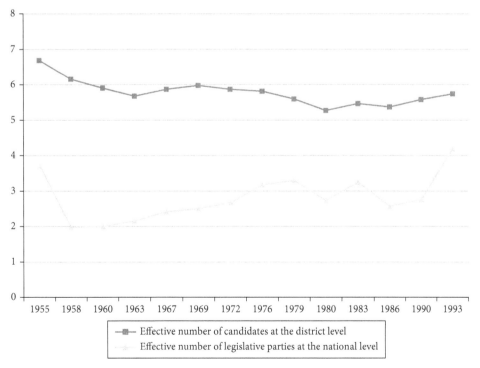

**FIGURE 39.1.** The effective number of candidates at the district level and the effective number of legislative parties at the national level, 1955–1993.

Source: The author's own calculations.

even from the same party, copartisan candidates engage in zero-sum competition over the same vote. As candidates from the same party share similar policy positions, they have to distinguish themselves from the other candidates, using their personal appeals (Carey and Shugart 1995; Grofman 1999).

Thus, Japanese candidates under the SNTV system, especially those from the LDP, extensively utilized constituency services and even illicit activities in mobilizing votes. Candidates facing more competitors from the same party tended to spend more (Cox and Thies 1998, 2000) and even engage in vote buying (Nyblade and Reed 2008). Between elections, they tried to expand their personal supporters through apolitical networks called *koenkai* (Bouissou 1999). Because launching and maintaining *koenkai* was very costly, hereditary candidates—those second-generation politicians, usually the sons or sons-in-law of retiring politicians, who inherit *koenkai* from their predecessors—became pervasive (Ishibashi and Reed 1992).

Personalism also affected the ruling party's internal structure in two ways: intraparty factions and the policymaking process. During the SNTV period, factions had mainly three functions for their members: money, nominations, and posts (Watanabe 1958). First, since SNTV made the party label inadequate in seeking votes, candidates relied on intraparty factions for campaigning funds. Second, nominations were given to new candidates based on bargaining between factions. Third, posts in the government and the party were allocated in accordance with Gamson's law, that is, in proportion to the size of factions.[9] In return for these benefits, members supported their factional bosses in the LDP's leadership elections (Cox and Rosenbluth 1993, 1996; Kohno 1992; Leiserson 1968; Nemoto, Pekkanen, and Krauss 2014; Ono 2012; Ramseyer and Rosenbluth 1993; Thies 2001).

Second, the LDP administration under SNTV featured a decentralized policymaking process through its Policy Affairs Research Council (PARC). Because under SNTV candidates would be able to win seats by focusing on only small segments of the electorate, LDP members tended to specialize in one or two particularistic policy areas, such as agriculture and construction. The PARC was divided into seventeen subdivisions corresponding to policy areas, such that LDP members could effectively coordinate with each to divide the conservative vote in the same districts. Since every bill submitted by the cabinet to the Diet needed prior approval from the PARC, in which consensus was the norm, each LDP member was able to access governmental resources for their parochial benefits (Campbell 1977; Cowhey 1993; George-Mulgan 2000; Hayao 1993; McCubbins and Rosenbluth 1995; Ramseyer and Rosenbluth 1993; Schoppa 1991).

By the early 1990s, this "hyperpersonalistic" system's problems became apparent (Shugart 2001). Incumbents focused on their ability to deliver parochial benefits to their local districts in campaigning, while sidelining nation-in-scope programmatic policy issues. The leadership's and the prime minister's power was significantly curtailed by factions and the PARC's policymaking process. As money scandals hit LDP heavyweights in the late 1980s and early 1990s, the public called for political reform, but the LDP's reform plan failed in the midst of factional feuds. As some groups of members defected from the perennial ruling party to join the opposition's no-confidence motion, the 1993 HoR election was called, resulting in a government turnover for the first time in nearly forty years. A non-LDP coalition government thus formed after the election and enacted electoral reform.[10]

The new system adopted was MMM.[11] Now under this system, each voter has two votes: a vote for a nominal-component candidate and a vote for a party list. As of 2016, the nominal component elects more than 60 percent of the total HoR members: 295 members are elected with FPTP, while the closed-list proportional representation component elects 180 with the D'Hondt method.[12] The two components are not linked, such that list seats are allocated "in parallel," no matter how many seats a party wins on the nominal component.

It should be important to note here some institutional details on the list component. Although there is no linkage between the two components in terms of seat allocation, candidates can be dually listed on both components.[13] With very few exceptions like the Communists, now parties choose to dually nominate most of their candidates: in 2012, for instance, 97.2 percent of the 914 nominal-component candidates from the eight parties that won at least one SMD seat were dually listed. These dually nominated candidates can lose on their SMDs but still win seats on the list component. Such dually nominated list winners (DNLWs)—or "zombies" (Pekkanen et al. 2006)—have been increasing on the list component: 42.0 percent in 1996 to 67.2 percent in 2014. They behave as if they are district members of parliament (MPs) or "shadow MPs" as in New Zealand (Barker and Levine 1999) providing constituency services through their offices located within their districts. Some districts can contain two or even three incumbents: 33.7 percent of the 2,095 SMDs elected at least one DNLW between 1996 and 2014. The presence of these DNLWs can make district winners vulnerable in the next elections, as reviewed later.

Given these institutional changes, theoretically, the following predictions can be made:

*Interparty Prediction*: As M on the nominal component was reduced from four on average to one, the effective number of candidates at the district level should converge on two. As members elected in single-seat districts (SSDs) account for more than 60 percent of the House, two major parties should be dominant at the national level, although several smaller parties should survive thanks to the list component.

*Intraparty Prediction*: As there is no intraparty competition, candidates do not have to differentiate themselves from other copartisans with their personal appeals. Instead, candidates and parties should utilize more cost-efficient campaigning methods, by focusing on nationwide programmatic policy and party label.

*Party Organization Prediction*: Now that two major parties compete over nationwide programmatic policy and party label, they need to have cohesive organizations. Decision making as to selecting candidates, monitoring incumbents, and developing policy platforms should be centralized into the leadership.[14]

As reviewed in detail later, these predictions are generally confirmed with empirical evidence. However, some of the institutions and practices that the literature predicted would die out—such as personal vote mobilization and intraparty factions—have been weakened but survived. Let us now turn to how the reform transformed electoral competition (or not).

# Electoral Competition

To repeat, the *Interparty Prediction* says that as M is reduced to one, district-level competition should favor two major camps. Data suggest that since the reform, Japan has been shifting "haltingly towards a two-party system" (Reed 2005), at least up to 2009. As shown in Figure 39.2, although parties were a little slow in adapting to the Duvergerian force in the first few elections, the effective number of district-level candidates and national-level parties gradually declined. Most of the districts featured competition between two major camps (the LDP–Komeito coalition and the Democratic Party of Japan [DPJ][15]) by the 2009 election. Nonpartisan floating voters' swing to the DPJ, together with this rise of two-way competition across the country, contributed to a landslide government turnover in 2009.

The flip side of this is that smaller parties now have to survive on the list component. All parties fare better on the list component except the LDP and the DPJ, even though more seats are allocated to the nominal component.[16] The result is fragmentation of the list component, with the effective number of legislative parties on the list component hovering around three to five. This fragmentation also partly contributed to the inflation of the number of national-level legislative parties in 2012 and 2014, as shown in Figure 39.2.

Despite the trend toward two-party competition, the number of national-level legislative parties in the 2012 and 2014 elections increased. It is yet to be seen whether the surge will be temporary. The surge was largely caused by the rise of some third parties (Reed 2013).[17] Although these parties were not very competitive on the nominal component, many of their candidates created three- or even four-way competition in many districts, which indirectly contributed to the LDP's landslide.[18] Some of these third parties were consolidated before and after the 2014 election (Pekkanen and Reed 2015).[19] As of July 2016, the national-level effective number of parties stands at 2.34. Let us review this trend toward a two-party system and whether the 2012 and 2014 elections will really be anomalies or not.

## Strategic Voting and Candidate Coordination

Whether or not the surge in the effective number of parties in 2012 and 2014 will be only temporary, the introduction of MMM appears to have created the Duvergerian force at least up to 2009. It works in two ways: strategic voting and candidate coordination. First, strategic voting takes place because voters do not want to waste their votes by

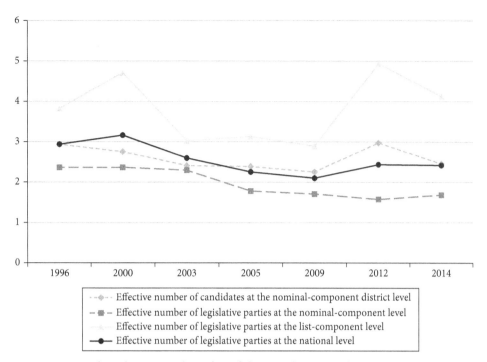

**FIGURE 39.2.** The effective number of candidates at the nominal-component district level and the effective number of legislative parties at the nominal-component, list-component, and national levels, 1996–2014.

Source: The author's own calculations.

supporting losing candidates. Therefore, in single-member plurality systems, two major parties tend to earn more votes than smaller parties.

This argument is more readily tested under mixed-member systems, where voters have two votes. Assuming that list votes reflect voters' true party preferences, researchers typically infer that a large party's receiving more nominal-component votes than list votes should mean the presence of strategic voters in a given district. Kohno (1997) uses the 1996 election results to find that the Japanese Communist Party tended to receive fewer nominal-component votes, while the LDP attracted more nominal votes than list votes. Reed (1999) similarly finds that candidates with a higher probability of victory—measured as their ex post electoral margins or ex ante estimates—tend to have larger nominal-component votes than list votes.

The Duvergerian force can also encourage parties to coordinate their candidates, with hopeless candidates withdrawing from the race to support more competitive ones. For instance, in the 2009 election, partial (but not really complete) withdrawal by the Communists and other small parties contributed somewhat to the DPJ's victory (Maeda 2010). Learning from coordination failures and the devastating outcome of the 2012 election, opposition parties stepped up efforts to coordinate their candidate entry on the nominal component in the 2014 election (Scheiner, Smith, and Thies 2015; Smith 2015).

As one of the DPJ leaders put it, "The LDP played both ends against the middle since too many opposition candidates competed in a district" (*Asahi Shimbun,* December 3, 2014, 4).

The 2012 and 2014 elections suggest that a couple of factors might have prevented these mechanisms from working. The first is personal votes: voters personally supporting certain candidates do not care about strategic calculations. Empirical evidence by Moser and Scheiner (2005) on five countries using mixed-member systems suggests that Japanese voters' split-ticket voting patterns are more consistent with personal voting than strategic voting. Although the importance of personal votes has been declining in Japan, personal votes are not incompatible with single-seat districts in theory. Japanese candidates still appear to consider personal networks useful, as reviewed later (Krauss and Pekkanen 2004). As long as third-party candidates can expect some personal votes, they try to run, taking advantage of the dual candidacy provision as discussed later.

Another factor that could make Duvergerian convergence difficult in Japan is the presence of the list component. According to the literature on the contamination effects, a party has the incentive to run even hopeless candidates on the nominal component, because such candidates can increase voter awareness and potentially gain more list votes (Cox and Schoppa 2002; Herron and Nishikawa 2001).[20] This is in fact the strategy adopted by the Japanese Communist Party: it usually nominates candidates in almost all of the districts in every election, to shore up list votes (*Asahi Shimbun,* December 17, 2012, 3).[21] A further complication is that such hopeless candidates from small parties could win seats through the list component if they are dually nominated. As we have seen, such DNLWs can stay in the Diet for a while as if they are district incumbents. Because a Diet member can have three government-funded secretaries and a limitless free travel pass from Tokyo to the local district, DNLWs can expand their personal supporters in the districts and challenge SMD seats in the subsequent elections.

The increased number of candidates in the 2012 and 2014 elections was partially caused by these combined factors. In 2012, the three new small parties nominated 327 candidates on the nominal component. Where they nominated candidates, their average list vote share stood at 15.6 percent, compared to 9.0 percent where their candidates were not present.[22] Only 20 of the 327 candidates won SMDs, while 52 survived through the list component. In 2014, 48 of these 52 DNLWs from the small parties ran again. These DNLWs fared better this time, as 18 of them (37.5 percent) successfully came back to the Diet, compared to 72 out of 327 (22.0 percent) in the 2012 election. The district-level effective number of candidates was 2.85 where the 48 DNLWs were present. This was higher than 2.39 in the districts where there was no such small-party DNLW incumbent.

All in all, it might be the case that when parties have a clear focal point for an alternative to the LDP–Komeito coalition, they can relatively easily coordinate their candidates as they did up to 2009. Meanwhile, when they lack such a focal point, they may rather exploit the list component and especially the dual candidacy provision, resulting in upward shifts in the number of candidates. These expectations could be theoretically refined and empirically tested with systematic data going forward.

## From Particularism to Programmatism

According to the *Intraparty Prediction* presented earlier, the move to MMM should make electoral competition more focused on party label and policy. Rosenbluth and Thies (2010) argue that the elimination of intraparty competition and the introduction of the single-member district system promoted broader policy appeals to the median voter.[23] Reed, Scheiner, and Thies (2012, 355) state that "[b]eginning with the 2005 election, campaigns in Japan shifted from focusing principally on the personal attributes of individual candidates toward nationalized contests based on candidates' partisan affiliations and policy manifestos." Winkler (2014) analyzes the LDP's election platforms from 1956 through 2013 to find that the party's policy pledges started shifting away from clientelistic to programmatic appeals in the 1990s. Parties' increasing use of media was a parallel development (Koellner 2009).

Changing parties' campaigning should also affect policy outputs. Scholars generally agree that policy outputs have become more programmatic and less particularistic since the reform. In issue areas like agriculture, banking, pollution, and welfare, the literature points to the shift of policy focus from particularism to programmatism (Davis and Oh 2007; Estevez-Abe 2008; Horiuchi and Saito 2010; Rosenbluth and Thies 2010; Rosenbluth and Thies 2001, 2002; Sasada 2008). Noble (2010, 262–263) observes that "the role of particularistic expenditures on roads, bridges, rural airports, agricultural land reclamation, and the like declined sharply," while "[p]rogrammatic spending, in contrast, increased across a wide range of areas, from public order and social welfare to research and development."

This change in campaigning focus also should be observed at the candidate level. As candidates now need to capture a plurality of the votes, they need to adjust their policy pledges to appeal to the median voter in a district. Catalinac (2016a, 2016b) uses individual candidates' campaigning pledges (*senkyo koho*) to find that LDP candidates' emphasis on particularism significantly declined after the reform. Meanwhile, candidates emphasize more of national security and other types of programmatic public goods in their pledges after the reform. Geographical vote mobilization patterns should also change. In contrast to the prereform period, when candidates needed to appeal to only a segment of the electorate around their hometowns, now candidates need to mobilize votes more or less evenly within their districts (Hirano 2006).

As campaigning becomes increasingly focused on national issues and local issues are sidelined, candidates face nationalized partisan swings. Seniority, past electoral performance, and other personal traits become less important in insulating incumbents from swings (McElwain 2012). Reed et al. (2012) demonstrate that the electoral importance of a candidate's personal quality declined after 2005.[24] In the 2000 and 2003 elections, a high-quality candidate from the LDP or the DPJ was more likely to win an open seat than a low-quality candidate. However, in the 2005 and 2009 elections, the statistically significant difference between high- and low-quality candidates disappeared, meaning that candidates' party affiliations now largely control their electoral fortune.

That partisan swings matter more than personal traits in the recent elections implies that an incumbency advantage should be eroding. Combined with this increasing nationalization of partisan swings, the presence of DNLWs as shadow district incumbents should also make incumbents' scare-off effects less relevant.[25] Using regression discontinuity design, Ariga et al. (2016) show that an LDP candidate winning a seat on the nominal component does not significantly improve his or her electoral chance in the next election.

Parties' candidate selection strategies appear to be changing as well. Now they need to present a fresh image to the electorate with an attractable set of candidates. Therefore, parties increasingly utilize the open recruitment process (*kobo*) in selecting candidates (Smith, Pekkanen, and Krauss 2013; Yu, Yu, and Shoji 2014). In addition, given that the Japanese public does not necessarily have a good impression with second-generation candidates and that now parties may not have to eagerly seek for candidates with strong personal support, the proportion of the LDP's second-generation candidates has been declining since the reform. In the 2012 election, for instance, less than 10 percent of the LDP's new candidates had family connections to former politicians, compared to more than 50 percent in 1990 (Smith 2013).

This declining emphasis of particularistic and personalistic campaigning, however, does not mean that it has completely disappeared. Even though the average number of *koenkai* that candidates possess has been declining (Carlson 2006), candidates still rely on them (Krauss and Pekkanen 2004, 2010). As discussed earlier, the patterns of split-ticket voting in Japan are more consistent with personal voting than strategic voting (Moser and Scheiner 2005). According to Koellner (2009, 138), "national party-centered election campaigns of the manifesto or the media-spin type have not simply replaced localized and personalized election campaigns in Japan."

In explaining why *koenkai* still continue to exist, scholars point to institutional complementarities and contextual path dependency. First, Japan maintains one of the world's most stringent restrictions on candidates' campaigning activities (Bouissou 1999; Krauss and Pekkanen 2004; McElwain 2008). The Public Officials Election Act provides that election campaigning is permitted only during the twelve-day election period.[26] Any activity meant to mobilize votes before that is illegal as "pre-election campaigning" (*jizen senkyo undo*). Candidates and activists are prohibited from canvassing voters door to door, collecting signatures, and buying ads on TV. They are allowed to distribute only up to 70,000 handbills, while 353,387 voters resided in the average district at the time of the 2014 election. Candidates and activists can hand in handbills directly to only those who show up at campaigning rallies, virtually prohibiting candidates from distributing handbills to random voters through snail mail. Posters can be put up only on designated official boards. The ban on campaigning on the Internet was only removed in 2013 (Williams and Miller 2015), but candidates still cannot send out emails to random voters. Thus, candidates' access to voters during the campaigning period is very much limited. All they can do is deliver speeches where random passersby gather (usually in front of train stations) and repeat their names through sound trucks equipped with loudspeakers (Klein 2011). This is why expanding a personal support base between elections—*without explicitly soliciting votes*—is still considered important.

Second, as Krauss and Pekkanen (2010) argue, politicians continue to use *koenkai*, simply because they are just there. Under SNTV and the very strict campaigning regulations, *koenkai* were found to be useful in mobilizing personal votes. It is true that the move to MMM weakened the incentive to mobilize personal votes, but personal votes are useful even under FPTP systems, as in the United Kingdom or the United States (Cain, Ferejohn, and Fiorina 1987). Thus, to the extent that "running in an election is risky business and politicians tend to want to acquire all the victory insurance they can" (Krauss and Pekkanen 2010, 98), candidates use *koenkai*. On top of this, except for a couple of very hierarchical parties like the Communists and the Komeito, Japanese parties' local organizations are very weak and unreliable as voting blocs: for instance, the LDP has 890,000 party members as of 2015 (*Asahi Shimbun,* November 30, 2015, 2).[27] This means that the average district has slightly more than 3,000 LDP members, 3.2 percent of the 93,000 votes the average SMD winner won in 2014.

In sum, the literature suggests that the move from particularism to programmatism is generally supported by empirical evidence. Parties and candidates care about the median voter now more than ever. Incumbency and other personal profiles cannot sufficiently insulate candidates from national partisan swings. Parties try to recruit attractive candidates through the open process. However, one caveat is that personalistic campaigning and *koenkai* still exist. Even though their importance has been declining, candidates still have to rely on them in approaching voters. This implies that, in analyzing candidate–voter linkage strategies, scholars should look beyond the mechanical features of electoral systems (Kitschelt 2000).

## PARTY AND LEGISLATIVE ORGANIZATION

Some scholars argue that, since the introduction of MMM, Japan's electoral and party politics has been shifting toward a Westminster system (Estevez-Abe 2006; Shinoda 2006): two major parties compete over programmatic policy platforms, single-party majority cabinets form based on parliamentary confidence, and responsible party governments control the legislative agenda. The descriptions earlier about Japan's new party system and campaigning after the reform generally support this idea.

As in Victorian England (Cox 1987), parties and politicians should also adapt their organizations and behavior to this new environment. As electoral competition becomes more party oriented, members belonging to the same party now need to work as the same team. They need to develop and adhere to consistent policy platforms so that they can cohesively fight the elections under the same banner. Parties can solve the collective action dilemma by delegating decision-making authority to the leadership, screening candidates through the nomination process, or monitoring incumbents through party whips. Ultimately, political powers will be centralized into the leadership as long as it is held accountable to party members (Samuels and Shugart 2010).

These expectations should be particularly interesting in the context of Japan. Before the electoral reform, scholarly attention was paid to the "uncommon" nature of Japan's one-party dominant regime (Pempel 1990). In particular, as reviewed earlier, the existing literature on the SNTV period focuses on the LDP's organizations such as intraparty factions and the decentralized policymaking process in the PARC (Campbell 1977; Cowhey 1993; Cox and Rosenbluth 1993, 1996; George-Mulgan 2000; Hayao 1993; Kohno 1992; Leiserson 1968; McCubbins and Rosenbluth 1995; Nemoto, Pekkanen, and Krauss 2014; Ono 2012; Ramseyer and Rosenbluth 1993; Schoppa 1991; Thies 2001). These organizations helped the LDP maintain its dominance by effectively limiting the leadership's roles in personnel management, candidate selection, and policymaking.

## Factions and Leadership

Let us look at factions first. Factions emerged because the LDP's party leaders were elected through a majority run-off system, whereby each LDP member in the Diet had one vote as a delegate. Factional bosses provided money, nominations, and posts in return for votes in the LDP's leadership elections (Nemoto et al. 2014). Therefore, to mobilize as many loyal headcounts as possible, factional bosses needed to amass huge amounts of money. Partly as a result, large-scale corruption scandals ensued. A good example is Kakuei Tanaka, the winner of the 1972 leadership election, who stepped down as the prime minister in 1974 amid a money scandal and got arrested two years later on charges of receiving bribes from Lockheed (Johnson 1986). In the 1972 leadership election, the media reported that Tanaka and other candidates used approximately 5 to 10 billion yen in total ($40,000 to $80,000 per delegate) (Tsurutani 1980).

This leadership selection system was very compatible with SNTV. Winning a factional endorsement was almost a necessary condition to win a seat, because party label was not reliable in differentiating from other copartisan candidates: between 1960 and 1990, of the LDP's 442 new members of the House of Representatives, 29 (6.6 percent) did not belong to any faction. Candidates needed to have monetary backing from factions, because of the very expensive koenkai. LDP members did not need to have a more transparent system to select a leader popular among the mass public, because the party's image had only a marginal impact on their electoral fortune.[28] Therefore, despite the public's complaints about this leadership selection process, it stayed almost completely intact until the mid-1990s (Nemoto et al. 2014).

Since the electoral reform, however, for candidates to win seats, receiving endorsements and financial support from factions has become much less important. Instead, a candidate's affiliation with a popular party and having a leader who can improve the party's image is much more important now. Therefore, the LDP's party leader elections are now focused on selecting popular leaders, rather than on collecting headcounts and distributing money. Jun'ichiro Koizumi won the LDP presidency in 2001 not because he was supported by large factions or able to buy off votes, but because younger incumbents and rank-and-file members needed a strong party leader that could build a popular party image to appeal to the mass public (Kabashima and Steel 2007; Lin 2009).

Factional lines becoming less relevant in the LDP's party leader elections means that factions lose the incentive to maintain members' loyalty. Thus, factions now provide less of the three major benefits: money, nominations, and posts. In turn, the party headquarters now provides more of these benefits to backbenchers, as it can concentrate its scarce resources to its only one candidate in a given single-seat district. First, the money a faction gives out to its members has been significantly reduced from tens of million yen to a couple of million yen (*Nihon Keizai Shimbun,* August 30, 2015, 14). In contrast, in the 2014 election, the LDP headquarters provided 10 to 14.5 million yen to each of its candidates, depending on their marginality (*Asahi Shimbun,* November 28, 2015, 5).

Second, now more candidates get LDP nominations without factional endorsements. For instance, in 2005, out of the eighty-three LDP members who newly won their seats, sixty-seven (80.7 percent) did not join any faction prior to the election (Krauss and Pekkanen 2010, chap. 5).[29] The candidates selected through the open recruitment system by the party headquarters are more centrist and cohesive than the candidates recruited through the other methods (Smith and Tsutsumi 2016). These imply that the party headquarters handpicked and nominated most of the new non-incumbent candidates based on their policy and ideological stances, while ignoring recommendations from factions.

Third, after the reform, being in a large faction does not necessarily improve the chance of assuming positions in the government (Pekkanen, Nyblade, and Krauss 2014). To repeat, prior to the electoral reform, cabinet portfolios were fairly proportionally allocated to factions in accordance with their size. As the various indexes show in Figure 39.3, disproportionality between factions' seats in the LDP and their shares in the cabinet started increasing after the first Murayama cabinet, the first cabinet that the LDP joined after the electoral reform.[30] This suggests that the leadership now has more leeway than in the past in appointing ministers, as explored in detail later.[31]

Despite these changes, however, factions have not completely disappeared. As of 2015, still nearly two-thirds (193 out of 292, or 66.1 percent) of the LDP members belong to factions, and factions never stop recruiting new candidates. In September 2015, a new faction was launched by Shigeru Ishiba, a former defense minister and the former secretary-general of the LDP, in preparation for the next party leader election after Abe (*Nihon Keizai Shimbun,* September 29, 2015, 4). Why weakened factions still exist in the LDP and a future leader launches a new faction is an open empirical and theoretical question. As Park (2001) argues, factions may serve roles other than money, nominations, and posts—members may still benefit from factions for sharing information and communicating with colleagues in a huge organization like a political party, for instance (*Nihon Keizai Shimbun,* August 30, 2015, 14).

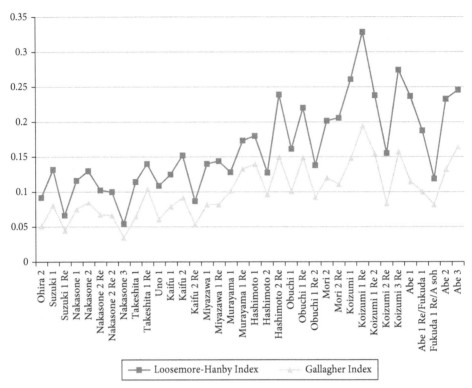

FIGURE 39.3. Disproportionality between factions' shares in the Liberal Democratic Party and factions' shares in the cabinet.

Source: The author's own calculations.

## Policymaking and Leadership

Let us turn to the electoral reform's impact on the policymaking process. To repeat, the decentralized policymaking process in the PARC was compatible with SNTV. Under SNTV, specializing in one or two particularistic policy areas and bringing pork barrel benefits to their home districts was the key for electoral success. The LDP made sure that its members would have institutional access to governmental resources in two ways: bills and the budget required prior approval from the PARC before submission to the Diet, and unanimity was the norm in each of the seventeen subdivisions of the PARC to allow for the logrolling of parochial interests. Under this system, it was difficult for leaders to discuss and promote their policy agenda (Hayao 1993).

Postreform prime ministers, particularly Jun'ichiro Koizumi, stepped up efforts to make the policymaking process more compatible with the new electoral system. First, high-profile cabinet-level councils, most notably the Council on Economic and Fiscal Policy, were newly established within the cabinet office directly under the prime minister. Chaired by the prime minister and attended by key ministers and private-sector advisors, they are designed to lead debates over policy reform programs and ultimately bypass the PARC's entrenched decision-making process. As these councils' discussion minutes, reports, and decisions are all made openly and publicly available online, they attract substantial media and public attention, while making it increasingly difficult for backbenchers to have policy input behind the scenes (Estevez-Abe 2006; Mishima 2007).

Second, prime ministers now take advantage of their exclusive personnel management powers for party and governmental posts to promote their policy agenda and build up the party's policymaking reputations. Evidence by Pekkanen et al. (2014) indicates that relatively young policy experts are more likely to assume cabinet positions than in the prereform period. Nemoto (2013) also shows that backbenchers' promotion appears to be correlated with their active participation in parliamentary activities, such as asking policy questions against the government and proposing private members' bills. Backbenchers with greater electoral security tend to assume high-policy positions, or become ministers and committee chairs in policy issues pertaining to national security, finance, and the like (Pekkanen, Nyblade, and Krauss 2006). Combined with the empirical analysis earlier suggesting that prime ministers are now more independent from factional constraints in appointing ministers, these imply that able backbenchers are promoted to help lead the leadership's policy agenda and contribute to the party's policy image.

These changes met opposition from inside the LDP. Nearly fifty LDP backbenchers in the HoR defected from the party line on the vote for Koizumi's pet policy project, the postal privatization bill, in 2005. Nemoto et al. (2008) show that members defected for different reasons. Some senior factional bosses voted against the government bill because they had grievances with Koizumi's cabinet appointment. Other midcareer members specializing in the postal policy issue defected because Koizumi imposed his own bill in a top-down manner without consultations with them. Joined by members with different motives, the defection was ultimately an attempt to oust the Koizumi cabinet and restore the powers of factions and the old policymaking process.

What happened after the defection is more interesting. After the bill managed to clear the HoR, the LDP's anti-Koizumi group in the House of Councillors defected and the bill was killed. Koizumi dissolved the HoR—the house that passed the bill—to call a snap election. While twelve HoR members who abstained from voting had to sign written pledges promising to support the Koizumi bill to get nominations, the thirty-seven defectors were denied LDP nominations and would have to face LDP candidates in their districts. A couple of them gave up running, while most of them ran as independents or launched their own new parties. In the 2005 election, Koizumi's LDP won a sound majority of 296 seats, successfully purifying his own party with supporters of his pet policy.

To conclude this section, the LDP has been transforming its organizations since the reform in line with the incentives created by the new electoral system. Factions become less important in allocating money, nominations, and posts, while the party headquarters fulfills these functions. The policymaking process is centralized to the extent that backbenchers now have a hard time exerting influence over the leadership's programmatic policy agenda. However, this organizational restructuring process has not been automatic. Factions have weakened but survived, and on one occasion they revolted against the prime minister's centralization drive.

# CONCLUSION

As we have seen, empirical evidence is generally supportive of the three theoretical predictions presented. First, Japan has been moving toward a two-party system at least up to 2009, with the effective numbers of district-level candidates and national-level legislative parties both declining. Second, the elimination of intraparty competition resulted in the change of campaigning focus from particularism to programmatism. Parties and candidates now offer nation-in-scope policy platforms to attract the median voter. Third, parties are centralized. Now the party leadership plays the roles that factions traditionally played: money, nominations, and posts. It also promotes its policy agenda by utilizing its nomination and post allocation powers.

But the electoral reform did not completely bring about the theoretically expected changes: the Duvergerian force does not necessarily drive small parties to completely coordinate candidate entry, and the elimination of intraparty competition does not result in the extinction of *koenkai* and factions. The discussions in this chapter suggest that, in understanding why the electoral reform looks unfinished, researchers should consider some factors beyond electoral systems' mechanical features.[32]

It is important to bear in mind that electoral systems do not shape parties' and candidates' strategies in a vacuum. Rather, their effects are mediated by their surrounding institutions. For instance, the literature on the contamination effects reminds us that small parties' nomination strategies on the nominal component are not solely affected by how the nominal component works. They would rather run even hopeless candidates and therefore disturb the Duvergerian convergence, because the presence of such candidates is considered to help to mobilize list votes. If such hopeless candidates are dually nominated and win seats through the list component, they could work as virtual district incumbents to further complicate parties' candidate entry coordination in the following elections.

In line with this logic, other potentially important but previously neglected institutions include the House of Councillors. As briefly mentioned in the introductory section, the HoC is much more accommodative than the HoR, as the nationwide list component elects nearly fifty members with open-list proportional representation and no threshold. This means that slightly more than 2 percent of the votes nationwide should guarantee a party one seat in the HoC. To the extent that tiny parties' survival hinges on this very accommodative chamber, they may utilize the HoR race in the hope of raising their national visibility, giving additional upward boost to the effective number of parties.[33] While there is a dearth of literature on the impact of intercameral contamination effects with some exceptions like Lago and Martínez (2007), Japan's highly symmetric bicameralism offers research opportunities going forward.

Japan also can be a good starting point for an underexplored comparative study of campaigning regulations.[34] To repeat, Japan's campaigning regulations are arguably the world's most restrictive, in that they impose unconditional bans on most of the voter contact methods any candidate can think of: pre-election campaigning before the twelve-day election period, door-to-door canvassing, advertisements on TV, and mail advertising targeted at many and unspecified voters. Therefore, one of the consequences of having such restrictive regulations is the continued reliance on *koenkai*, despite the decreasing effectiveness of personal votes (Bouissou 1999; Krauss and Pekkanen 2004; McElwain 2008). The other consequences of campaigning regulations can include incumbency advantage and legislative turnover, because banning candidates from accessing random voters should make candidate entry barriers high. Therefore, these understudied but still potentially important aspects of electoral systems can expand future research frontiers.

## Acknowledgments

The helpful comments of Robert Pekkanen, Steven Reed, Ethan Scheiner, Matthew Shugart, and Dan Smith are greatly acknowledged. I also wish to thank Dong Myung Kim who provided research assistance. The remaining errors are mine.

## Notes

1. So where M is one, the system is simply plurality.
2. Between 1947 and 1980, the nationwide district used SNTV. It switched to a closed-list system in 1983. The current open-list proportional representation (OLPR) system was put in place in 2001. Due to space constraints, this chapter cannot discuss the HoC's electoral system and its consequences fully, but there is emerging literature on it, taking advantage of these institutional features (Fukumoto and Matsuo 2015; Nemoto and Shugart 2013).
3. See also the country chapters by Vowles on New Zealand and Passarelli on Italy.
4. Dual candidacy allows candidates to be dually nominated on both of the nominal and list components. Although the provision is widely seen in mixed-member systems, including Germany and New Zealand, the unique way of using it in Japan appears to affect the way candidates and parties compete, as discussed later. See also the chapter by Herron, Nemoto, and Nishikawa in this volume.
5. For reasons of space, this chapter has to omit some important research areas such as voting behavior, interest groups, malapportionment, bicameralism, coalition governments, and legislative behavior.
6. The effective number of parties, proposed by Laakso and Taagepera (1979), is not without problems as a measure of how well M + 1 is being met (e.g., Niemi and Hsieh 2002), but it is the most widely used index.

7. They include the short-lived conservative New Liberal Club splinter group from the LDP; the centrist Democratic Socialists; the Socialist Democratic Federation; the Komeito party, which sprang from a lay Buddhist religious movement; the Japanese Communist Party; and the leading opposition party, the Japan Socialist Party.

8. The effective number of candidates is calculated at the district level, while the effective number of legislative parties is calculated with parties' aggregate seat shares in the HoR.

9. Gamson's law refers to Gamson's (1961) claim that each party in a coalition should get payoffs, such as ministerial positions, in proportion to its share in the coalition.

10. On the process of the reform in Japan, see Reed and Thies (2001). See also Renwick's and Colomer's chapters in this volume on electoral reform.

11. On the details of the new system, see McKean and Scheiner (2000), among many others.

12. The country is divided into eleven regional proportional representation blocs, each of which is to elect six (Shikoku) to twenty-nine (Kinki) according to the population size. The number of total seats on the list component was originally set at 200 but later reduced to 180 in 2000. There were 300 single-seat districts on the nominal component but the number was reduced to 295 in 2013.

13. A party can choose to assign discrete ranks or the same ranks to candidates on the list. As for candidates ranked at the same ranks, their final ranks are to be determined according to a best loser provision (*sekihai ritsu*) or their performance on the nominal component (McKean and Scheiner 2000). Parties, especially the two major parties, now tend to avoid giving out discrete ranks to encourage candidates to maximize their performance on the nominal component (Nemoto and Tsai 2016).

14. Party organization can be arguably part of the intraparty dimension. But for editorial purposes this chapter differentiates them.

15. The DPJ was renamed as the Democratic Party in 2016 when it merged with the Japan Innovation Party. This chapter uses its conventional name, DPJ.

16. The LDP always won more seats on the nominal component than on the list component. The DPJ won more nominal-component seats in 2003, 2009, and 2014.

17. They include the Your Party, the Japan Restoration Party, and the Tomorrow Party of Japan. The latter two were born just before the 2012 election.

18. Therefore, even though the district-level effective number of candidates was moderately high (2.98 in 2012 and 2.46 in 2014), the LDP's sweeping victory on the nominal component resulted in the effective number of legislative parties on the nominal component being well below two (1.57 and 1.69).

19. The Your Party disbanded before the 2014 election. The Japan Restoration Party disbanded in 2014, when most of its members merged with a splinter of the Your Party called the Unity Party and together formed the Japan Innovation Party. Meanwhile, several ex-JRP members formed the Party of Future Generations, which further changed its name to the Party for Japanese Kokoro in 2015, as all of its HoR members switched to the LDP after the 2014 election. The JIP merged in 2016 with the DPJ to become the Democratic Party. A group of the JIP members mainly from Osaka did not join the new DP and instead formed their own party, the Initiatives from Osaka. The Tomorrow Party of Japan was renamed as the People's Life Party in 2012 and further as the People's Life Party and Taro Yamamoto and Friends when it was joined by a leftist actor-turned-politician Taro Yamamoto in 2014.

20. Maeda (2008) counterargues that a party only nominates candidates in districts where it is strong and popular. His empirical evidence controlling for this endogeneity suggests

there is no contamination effect. See the chapter by Herron, Nemoto, and Nishikawa in this volume for more discussion on these issues.

21. But in the 2016 House of Councillors election, the JCP and the other opposition parties formed a pre-electoral coalition for thirty-two single-seat districts.

22. It is true that their decisions to send candidates might have been endogenous. But even when excluding the Japan Restoration Party's regional stronghold in the Kinki region, still this contamination effect exists: the party's list share increased by 4.5 percent where it stood candidates.

23. The Downsian median-voter theorem also predicts that the platforms advocated by two major parties would become indistinguishable, to the extent that voters would have to rely on valence considerations, such as the party image as a reformer (Scheiner 2013).

24. They define high-quality candidates as former House of Councillors members, local politicians, bureaucrats, TV personalities, and second-generation candidates.

25. This logic—an incumbency advantage decreases as the number of district incumbents increases—could be extended to SNTV. Ariga (2015) shows that an LDP candidate's probability of returning to the race and winning a seat does not significantly improve even if he or she won the race in the previous election.

26. The election period is seventeen days for the House of Councillors elections.

27. The DPJ had 230,000 party members and supporters as of 2015 (*Asahi Shimbun*, March 6, 2015, 2).

28. After the Lockheed scandal in 1976, the LDP introduced a new leadership selection system whereby the mass membership could participate. However, the result was that factional bosses used their supporters' *koenkai* to expand grassroots followings (Krauss and Pekkanen 2010; Tsurutani 1980).

29. After 2005, the ratio of such nonfaction new members decreased, but not to the prereform level. In 2012, 65 (54.6 percent) out of the LDP's 119 newcomers were nonfaction. In 2014, it was 9 (60.0 percent) out of 15.

30. The Loosemore-Hanby index was originally developed as a seat–vote disproportionality measure, defined as $\frac{1}{2}\Sigma|V_i - S_i|$, where $V_i$ and $S_i$ denote party *i*'s vote percentage and seat percentage, respectively. As this index approaches zero, votes are more proportionally translated into seats. Gallagher proposed another measure, defined as $\sqrt{\frac{1}{2}\Sigma(V_i - S_i)^2}$. See Gallagher (1991) and Taagepera and Grofman (2003) for the advantages and disadvantages of these and other measures.

31. Ono (2012) suggests that this does not necessarily imply that the leadership allocates more positions to its factional followers after the reform, when he finds that there is no significant difference between the pre- and postreform periods in terms of the leadership's portfolio share.

32. See the chapter by Moser, Scheiner, and Stoll on how contexts shape party systems.

33. As of July 2016, there were three parties that have seats in the HoC but no seat in the HoR. Since 2009, it has been always the case that one or two HoC-only parties enter the HoR race.

34. There is no comparative research on election campaigning regulations except Kreuzer (2000).

# REFERENCES

Ariga, Kenichi. "Incumbency Disadvantage under Electoral Rules with Intraparty Competition: Evidence from Japan." *Journal of Politics* 77, no. 3 (2015): 874–887.

Ariga, Kenichi, Yusaku Horiuchi, Roland Mansilla, and Michio Umeda. "No Sorting, No Advantage: Regression Discontinuity Estimates of Incumbency Advantage in Japan." *Electoral Studies* 43 (2016): 21–31.

Barker, Fiona, and Stephen Levine. "The Individual Parliamentary Member and Institutional Change: The Changing Role of the New Zealand Member of Parliament." *Journal of Legislative Studies* 5, no. 3/4 (1999): 105–130.

Bouissou, Jean-Marie. "Organizing One's Support Base under the SNTV: The Case of Japanese Koenkai." In *Elections in Japan, Korea, and Taiwan under the Single Non-Transferable Vote: The Comparative Study of an Embedded Institution*, edited by Bernard Grofman, Sung-Chull Lee, Edwin A. Winckler, and Brian Woodall, 87–120. Ann Arbor: University of Michigan Press, 1999.

Cain, Bruce E., John A. Ferejohn, and Morris P. Fiorina. *The Personal Vote: Constituency Service and Electoral Independence*. Cambridge, MA: Harvard University Press, 1987.

Campbell, John Creighton. *Contemporary Japanese Budget Politics* Berkeley: University of California Press, 1977.

Carey, John M., and Matthew Soberg Shugart. "Incentives to Cultivate a Personal Vote: A Rank Ordering of Electoral Formulas." *Electoral Studies* 14, no. 4 (1995): 417–439.

Carlson, Matthew M. "Electoral Reform and the Costs of Personal Support in Japan." *Journal of East Asian Studies* 6, no. 2 (2006): 233–258.

Catalinac, Amy. *Electoral Reform and National Security in Japan: From Pork to Foreign Policy*. Cambridge: Cambridge University Press, 2016a.

Catalinac, Amy. "From Pork to Policy: The Rise of Programmatic Campaigning in Japanese Elections." *Journal of Politics* 78, no. 1 (2016b): 1–18.

Cowhey, Peter F. "Domestic Institutions and the Credibility of International Commitments: Japan and the United States." *International Organization* 47, no. 2 (1993): 299–326.

Cox, Gary W. *Efficient Secret*. Cambridge: Cambridge University Press, 1987.

Cox, Gary W. "Strategic Voting Equilibria under the Single Nontransferable Vote" *American Political Science Review* 88, no. 3 (1994): 608–621.

Cox, Gary W. "Is the Single Nontransferable Vote Superproportional? Evidence from Japan and Taiwan." *American Journal of Political Science* 40, no. 3 (1996): 740–755.

Cox, Gary W., and Frances Rosenbluth. "The Electoral Fortunes of Legislative Factions in Japan." *American Political Science Review* 87, no. 3 (1993): 577–589.

Cox, Gary W., and Frances Rosenbluth. "Factional Competition for the Party Endorsement: The Case of Japan's Liberal Democratic Party." *British Journal of Political Science* 26, no. 2 (1996): 259–269.

Cox, Gary W., and Michael F. Thies. "The Cost of Intraparty Competition: The Single, Nontransferable Vote and Money Politics in Japan." *Comparative Political Studies* 31, no. 3 (1998): 267–291.

Cox, Gary W., and Michael F. Thies. "How Much Does Money Matter?: 'Buying' Votes in Japan, 1967-1990." *Comparative Political Studies* 33, no. 1 (2000): 37–57.

Cox, Karen E., and Leonard J. Schoppa. "Interaction Effects in Mixed-Member Electoral Systems: Theory and Evidence from Germany, Japan, and Italy." *Comparative Political Studies* 35, no. 9 (2002): 1027–1053.

Davis, Christina, and Jennifer Oh. "Repeal of the Rice Laws in Japan: The Role of International Pressure to Overcome Vested Interests." *Comparative Politics* 40, no. 1 (2007): 21–40.

Estevez-Abe, Margarita. "Japan's Shift toward a Westminster System: A Structural Analysis of the 2005 Lower House Election and Its Aftermath." *Asian Survey* 46, no. 4 (2006): 632–651.

Estevez-Abe, Margarita. *Welfare and Capitalism in Postwar Japan.* Cambridge: Cambridge University Press, 2008.

Fukumoto, Kentaro, and Akitaka Matsuo. "The Effects of Election Proximity on Participatory Shirking: The Staggered-Term Chamber as a Laboratory." *Legislative Studies Quarterly* 40, no. 4 (2015): 599–625.

Gallagher, Michael. "Proportionality, Disproportionality and Electoral Systems." *Electoral Studies* 10, 1 (1991): 33–51.

Gamson, William A. "A Theory of Coalition Formation." *American Sociological Review* 26, no. 3 (1961): 373–382.

George-Mulgan, Aurelia. "Japan's Political Leadership Deficit." *Australian Journal of Political Science* 35, no. 2 (2000): 183–202.

Grofman, Bernard. "SNTV: An Inventory of Theoretically Derived Propositions and a Brief Review of the Evidence from Japan, Korea, Taiwan, and Alabama." In *Election in Japan, Korea, and Taiwan under the Single Non-Transferable Vote: The Comparative Study of an Embedded Institution*, edited by Bernard Grofman, Brian Woodall, Sung-Chull Lee, and Edwin Winckler, 375–416. Ann Arbor: University of Michigan Press, 1999.

Hayao, Kenji. *The Japanese Prime Minister and Public Policy.* Pittsburgh: University of Pittsburgh Press, 1993.

Herron, Erik S., and Misa Nishikawa. "Contamination Effects and the Number of Parties in Mixed-Superposition Electoral Systems." *Electoral Studies* 20, no. 1 (2001): 63–86.

Hirano, Shigeo. "Electoral Institutions, Hometowns, and Favored Minorities: Evidence from Japan's Electoral Reforms." *World Politics* 58, no. 1 (2006): 51–82.

Horiuchi, Yusaku, and Jun Saito. "Cultivating Rice and Votes: The Institutional Origins of Agricultural Protectionism in Japan." *Journal of East Asian Studies* 10, no. 3 (2010): 425–452.

Ishibashi, Michihiro, and Steven R. Reed. "Second-Generation Diet Members and Democracy in Japan: Hereditary Seats." *Asian Survey* 32, no. 4 (1992): 366–379.

Johnson, Chalmers. "Tanaka Kakuei, Structural Corruption, and the Advent of Machine Politics in Japan." *Journal of Japanese Studies* 12, no. 1 (1986): 1–28.

Kabashima, Ikuo, and Gill Steel. "How Junichiro Koizumi Seized the Leadership of Japan's Liberal Democratic Party." *Japanese Journal of Political Science* 8, no. 1 (2007): 95–114.

Kitschelt, Herbert. "Linkages between Citizens and Politicians in Democratic Polities." *Comparative Political Studies* 33, no. 6/7 (2000): 845–879.

Klein, Axel. "The Puzzle of Ineffective Election Campaigning in Japan." *Japanese Journal of Political Science* 12, no. 1 (2011): 57–74.

Koellner, Patrick. "Japanese Lower House Campaigns in Transition: Manifest Changes or Fleeting Fads?" *Journal of East Asian Studies* 9, no. 1 (2009): 121–149.

Kohno, Masaru. "Rational Foundations for the Organization of the Liberal Democratic Party in Japan." *World Politics* 44, no. 3 (1992): 369–397.

Kohno, Masaru. "Voter Turnout and Strategic Ticket-Splitting under Japan's New Electoral Rules." *Asian Survey* 37, no. 4 (1997): 429–440.

Krauss, Ellis S., and Robert Pekkanen. "Explaining Party Adaptation to Electoral Reform: The Discreet Charm of the LDP?" *Journal of Japanese Studies* 30, no. 1 (2004): 1–34.

Krauss, Ellis S., and Robert Pekkanen. *The Rise and Fall of Japan's LDP*. Ithaca, NY: Cornell University Press, 2010.

Kreuzer, Marcus. "Electoral Mechanisms and Electioneering Incentives: Vote-Getting Strategies of Japanese, French, British, German and Austrian Conservatives." *Party Politics* 6, no. 4 (2000): 487–504.

Laakso, Markku, and Rein Taagepera. "'Effective' Number of Parties: A Measure with Application to West Europe." *Comparative Political Studies* 12, no. 1 (1979): 3–27.

Lago, Ignacio, and Ferran Martínez. "The Importance of Electoral Rules: Comparing the Number of Parties in Spain's Lower and Upper Houses." *Electoral Studies* 26, no. 2 (2007): 381–391.

Leiserson, Michael. "Factions and Coalitions in One-Party Japan: An Interpretation Based on the Theory of Games." *American Political Science Review* 62, no. 3 (1968): 770–787.

Lin, Chao-chi. "How Koizumi Won." In *Political Change in Japan: Electoral Behavior, Party Realignment, and the Koizumi Reforms*, edited by Steven R. Reed, Kenneth Mori McElwain, and Kay Shimizu, 109–132. Palo Alto, CA: Walter H. Shorenstein Asia-Pacific Research Center, 2009.

Maeda, Ko. "Re-Examining the Contamination Effect of Japan's Mixed Electoral System Using the Treatment-Effects Model." *Electoral Studies* 27, no. 4 (2008): 723–731.

Maeda, Ko. "Factors behind the Historic Defeat of Japan's Liberal Democratic Party in 2009." *Asian Survey* 50, no. 5 (2010): 888–907.

McCubbins, Mathew D., and Frances M. Rosenbluth. "Party Provision for Personal Politics: Dividing the Vote in Japan." In *Structure and Policy in Japan and the United States*, edited by Peter F. Cowhey and Mathew D. McCubbins, 35–55. Cambridge: Cambridge University Press, 1995.

McElwain, Kenneth Mori. "Manipulating Electoral Rules to Manufacture Single-Party Dominance." *American Journal of Political Science* 52, no. 1 (2008): 32–47.

McElwain, Kenneth Mori. "The Nationalization of Japanese Elections." *Journal of East Asian Studies* 12, no. 3 (2012): 323–350.

McKean, Margaret, and Ethan Scheiner. "Japan's New Electoral System: La plus ca change . . . ." *Electoral Studies* 19, no. 4 (2000): 447–477.

Mishima, Ko. "Grading Japanese Prime Minister Koizumi's Revolution: How Far Has the LDP's Policymaking Changed?" *Asian Survey* 47, no. 5 (2007): 727–748.

Moser, Robert G., and Ethan Scheiner. "Strategic Ticket Splitting and the Personal Vote in Mixed-Member Electoral Systems." *Legislative Studies Quarterly* 30, no. 2 (2005): 259–276.

Nemoto, Kuniaki. "New Inter-Election Campaigning Tools." In *Japan Decides 2012*, edited by Robert Pekkanen, Steven R. Reed, and Ethan Scheiner, 123–138. New York: Palgrave, 2013.

Nemoto, Kuniaki, Ellis S. Krauss, and Robert Pekkanen. "Policy Dissension and Party Discipline: The July 2005 Vote on Postal Privatization in Japan." *British Journal of Political Science* 38, no. 3 (2008): 499–525.

Nemoto, Kuniaki, Robert Pekkanen, and Ellis Krauss. "Over-Nominating Candidates, Undermining the Party: The Collective Action Problem under SNTV in Japan." *Party Politics* 20, no. 5 (2014): 740–750.

Nemoto, Kuniaki, and Matthew S. Shugart. "Localism and Coordination under Three Different Electoral Systems: The National District of the Japanese House of Councillors." *Electoral Studies* 32, no. 1 (2013): 1–12.

Nemoto, Kuniaki, and Chia-Hung Tsai. "Post Allocation, List Nominations, and Preelectoral Coalitions under MMM." In *Mixed-member Electoral Systems in Constitutional Context:*

*Taiwan, Japan, and Beyond*, edited by Nathan F. Batto, Chi Huang, Alexander C. Tan, and Gary W. Cox, 165–193. Ann Arbor: University of Michigan Press, 2016.

Niemi, Richard G., and John Fuh-sheng Hsieh. "Counting Candidates: An Alternative to the Effective N (With an Application to the M + 1 Rule in Japan)." *Party Politics* 8, no. 1 (2002): 75–99.

Noble, Gregory W. "The Decline of Particularism in Japanese Politics." *Journal of East Asian Studies* 10, no. 2 (2010): 239–273.

Nyblade, Benjamin, and Steven R. Reed. "Who Cheats? Who Loots? Political Competition and Corruption in Japan, 1947-1993." *American Journal of Political Science* 52, no. 4 (2008): 926–941.

Ono, Yoshikuni. "Portfolio Allocation as Leadership Strategy: Intraparty Bargaining in Japan." *American Journal of Political Science* 56, no. 3 (2012): 553–567.

Park, Cheol Hee. "Factional Dynamics in Japan's LDP since Political Reform: Continuity and Change." *Asian Survey* 41, no. 3 (2001): 428–461.

Pekkanen, Robert, Benjamin Nyblade, and Ellis S. Krauss. "Electoral Incentives in Mixed-Member Systems: Party, Posts, and Zombie Politicians in Japan." *American Political Science Review* 100, no. 2 (2006): 183–193.

Pekkanen, Robert J., Benjamin Nyblade, and Ellis S. Krauss. "The Logic of Ministerial Selection: Electoral System and Cabinet Appointments in Japan." *Social Science Japan Journal* 17, no. 1 (2014): 3–22.

Pekkanen, Robert J., and Steven R. Reed. "From Third Force to Third Party: Duverger's Revenge?" In *Japan Decides 2014*, edited by Robert J. Pekkanen, Steven R. Reed, and Ethan Scheiner, 62–71. New York: Palgrave, 2015.

Pempel, T. J., ed. *Uncommon Democracies: The One-Party Dominant Regimes*. Ithaca, NY: Cornell University Press, 1990.

Ramseyer, J. Mark, and Frances McCall Rosenbluth. *Japan's Political Marketplace*. Cambridge, MA: Harvard University Press, 1993.

Reed, Steven R. "Structure and Behavior: Extending Duverger's Law to the Japanese Case." *British Journal of Political Science* 20, no. 3 (1990): 335–356.

Reed, Steven R. "Strategic Voting in the 1996 Japanese General Election." *Comparative Political Studies* 32, no. 2 (1999): 257–270.

Reed, Steven R. "Japan: Haltingly Towards a Two-Party System." In *The Politics of Electoral Systems*, edited by Michael Gallagher and Paul Mitchell, 277–293. Oxford: Oxford University Press, 2005.

Reed, Steven R. "Challenging the Two-Party System: Third Force Parties in the 2012 Election." In *Japan Decides 2012*, edited by Robert Pekkanen, Steven R. Reed, and Ethan Scheiner, 72–83. New York: Palgrave, 2013.

Reed, Steven R., Ethan Scheiner, and Michael F. Thies. "The End of LDP Dominance and the Rise of Party-Oriented Politics in Japan." *Journal of Japanese Studies* 38, no. 2 (2012): 353–376.

Reed, Steven R., and Michael F. Thies. "The Causes of Electoral Reform in Japan." In *Mixed-Member Electoral Systems: The Best of Both Worlds?*, edited by Matthew Soberg Shugart and Martin P. Wattenberg, 152–172. Oxford: Oxford University Press, 2001.

Rosenbluth, Frances, and Michael F. Thies. "The Electoral Foundations of Japan's Banking Regulation." *Policy Studies Journal* 29, no. 1 (2001): 23–37.

Rosenbluth, Frances, and Michael F. Thies. "The Political Economy of Japanese Pollution Regulation." *American Asian Review* 20, no. 1 (2002): 1–32.

Rosenbluth, Frances, and Michael Thies. *Japan Transformed: Political Change and Economic Restructuring*. Princeton, NJ: Princeton University Press, 2010.

Samuels, David J., and Matthew Søberg Shugart. *Presidents, Parties, and Prime Ministers: How the Separation of Powers Affects Party Organization and Behavior*. Cambridge: Cambridge University Press, 2010.

Sasada, Hironori. "Japan's New Agricultural Trade Policy and Electoral Reform: 'Agricultural Policy in an Offensive Posture [seme no nosei].'" *Japanese Journal of Political Science* 9, no. 2 (2008): 121–144.

Scheiner, Ethan. "Does Electoral System Reform Work?: Electoral System Lessons from Reforms of the 1990s." *Annual Review of Political Science* 11 (2008): 161–181.

Scheiner, Ethan. "The Electoral System and Japan's Partial Transformation: Party System Consolidation without Policy Realignment." In *Japan under the DPJ: The Politics of Transition and Governance*, edited by Kenji E. Kushida and Phillip Y. Lipscy, 73–102. Stanford: Walter H. Shorenstein Asia-Pacific Research Center, 2013.

Scheiner, Ethan, Daniel M. Smith, and Michael F. Thies. "The 2014 Japanese Election Results: The Opposition Cooperates but Fails to Inspire." In *Japan Decides 2014*, edited by Robert J. Pekkanen, Steven R. Reed, and Ethan Scheiner, 22–38. New York: Palgrave, 2015.

Schoppa, Leonard J. "Zoku Power and LDP Power: A Case Study of the Zoku Role in Education Policy." *Journal of Japanese Studies* 17, no. 1 (1991): 79–106.

Shinoda, Tomohito. "Japan's Top-Down Policy Process to Dispatch the SDF to Iraq." *Japanese Journal of Political Science* 7, no. 1 (2006): 71–91.

Shugart, Matthew Soberg. "Electoral 'Efficiency' and the Move to Mixed-Member Systems." *Electoral Studies* 20, no. 2 (2001): 173–193.

Smith, Daniel M. "Candidate Recruitment for the 2012 Election: New Parties, New Methods … Same Old Pool of Candidates?" In *Japan Decides 2012*, edited by Robert Pekkanen, Steven R. Reed, and Ethan Scheiner, 101–122. New York: Palgrave, 2013.

Smith, Daniel M. "Candidates in the 2014 Election: Better Coordination and Higher Candidate Quality." In *Japan Decides 2014*, edited by Robert J. Pekkanen, Steven R. Reed, and Ethan Scheiner, 118–133. New York: Palgrave, 2015.

Smith, Daniel M., Robert J. Pekkanen, and Ellis S. Krauss. "Building a Party: Candidate Recruitment in the Democratic Party of Japan, 1996-2012." In *Japan under the DPJ: The Politics of Transition and Governance*, edited by Kenji E. Kushida and Phillip Y. Lipscy, 157–190. Washington, DC: Brookings Institution Press, 2013.

Smith, Daniel M., and Hidenori Tsutsumi. "Candidate Selection Methods and Policy Cohesion in Parties: The Impact of Open Recruitment in Japan." *Party Politics* 22, no. 3 (2016): 339–353.

Taagepera, Rein, and Bernard Grofman. "Mapping the Indices of Seats–Votes Disproportionality and Inter-Election Volatility." *Party Politics* 9, no. 6 (2003): 659–677.

Taagepera, Rein, and Matthew Soberg Shugart. *Seats and Votes*. New Haven, CT: Yale University Press, 1989.

Thies, Michael F. "Keeping Tabs on Partners: The Logic of Delegation in Coalition Governments." *American Journal of Political Science* 45, no. 3 (2001): 580–598.

Tsurutani, Taketsugu. "The LDP in Transition? Mass Membership Participation in Party Leadership Selection." *Asian Survey* 20, no. 8 (1980): 844–859.

Watanabe, Tsuneo. *Habatsu: Hoshuto no Kaibo*. [Factions: Analyzing the Conservative Party]. Tokyo: Kobundo, 1958. [Japanese]

Williams, Joshua A., and Douglas M. Miller. "Netizens Decide 2014?: A Look at Party Campaigning Online." In *Japan Decides 2014*, edited by Robert J. Pekkanen, Steven R. Reed, and Ethan Scheiner, 144–152. New York: Palgrave, 2015.

Winkler, Christian G. "Between Pork and People: An Analysis of the Policy Balance in the LDP's Election Platforms." *Journal of East Asian Studies* 14, no. 3 (2014): 405–428.

Yu, Ching-Hsin, Chen-Hua Eric Yu, and Kaori Shoji. "Innovations of Candidate Selection Methods: Polling Primary and Kobo under the New Electoral Rules in Taiwan and Japan." *Japanese Journal of Political Science* 15, no. 4 (2014): 635–659.

CHAPTER 40

......................................................................................................

# ELECTORAL SYSTEMS IN CONTEXT

*Italy*

......................................................................................................

## GIANLUCA PASSARELLI

ITALY stands out among established democracies because of multiple reforms of its electoral system. Established democracies generally tend to retain their electoral systems (Katz 2005), and the total number of electoral reforms over the last seventy years in established democracies stands at approximately twenty. Among the worldwide reforms, Italy is remarkably well represented, with three main electoral system changes during its democratic experience (and a fourth[1] reform has now come into operation, as we shall see). After the end of fascism and the dictatorship, a new democratic regime was established and a parliamentary republic initiated in 1948. Since that time, Italy's electoral law has been amended several times, and many other attempts to reform it were repelled. What were the triggers of such reforms? In Italy, the "causes" for electoral reforms were a mix of conjunctures: leadership initiative, judicial action, mass pressure, and international change and constraints. Moreover, if triggers of reform are "unlikely to be predictable from systemic characteristics" (Katz 2005, 74), in Italy it is not easy to generalize about the causes of reform. Thus, in the presence of such a mix of variables, it is necessary to analyze both the characteristics of each electoral reform in Italy and the context in which it is generated.

A diachronic study of the Italian case is opportune both for an in-depth analysis and for a general test of theory. As we know, electoral systems matter: they "may make a big difference to the shape of the party system, to the nature of government (coalition or single-party), to the kind of choices facing voters at elections, to the ability of voters to hold their representative(s) personally accountable, to the behavior of parliamentarians" (Gallagher and Mitchell 2005, 4). The next sections detail each of these systems and the reasons for their adoption, before turning to an assessment of the consequences.

# ITALY'S ELECTORAL SYSTEMS: PROVISIONS AND ORIGINS

Italy has formally had four different electoral systems between 1948 and 2015, not counting the proportional representation (PR) system used to elect the Constituent Assembly in 1946. The provisions of each law to be discussed in this section are summarized in detail in Table 40.1.

## The PR Electoral System of the Italian First Republic (1948–1992)

For the first democratic parliamentary election in 1948, a PR formula (Imperiali quota with largest remainders)[2] with preference voting was adopted. The system of proportional representation was introduced before the approval of the constitution,[3] and was never included in it, so that reforming the rules does not require a constitutional amendment. The system combined comparatively high proportionality with intraparty competition. From 1946 to 1992, Italy had thirty-two electoral districts.[4] It was a two-tier "remainder pooling" system (for a general definition, see Gallagher and Mitchell's chapter) in which remainder seats were allocated in an upper tier. The number of seats allocated in the upper tier depended on the number of votes not used by parties to elect members of parliament (MPs) in the districts (typically about 10 percent of the total). Nevertheless, to participate in the allocation of seats by remainders, parties had to satisfy two requirements: to have obtained at least three hundred thousand votes at the national level *and* to have succeeded in electing at least one candidate in one district, which meant having a geographically concentrated electoral support of about sixty thousand to seventy thousand voters.[5]

The PR open-list system emphasized intraparty competition among candidates (Carey and Shugart 1995) and also generated—or at the very least did not impede—party factionalism. Between 1946 and 1991, voters were allowed to cast up to four preference votes depending on district magnitude (Passarelli 2017).[6] Therefore, the way in which candidates were elected from a list was completely determined by the individual preference votes cast by the party's voters in a given district.[7] During that period, the only reforms of the electoral system involved changes in the denominator used in calculating the quota (Passarelli 2014).[8]

Although it never actually came into operation, the *legge truffa* (swindle law) of 1953 could be counted among Italy's electoral reforms. This system aimed to ensure a parliamentary majority.[9] The Christian Democrats (DC) won an absolute majority of seats (53.1 percent in 1948) with 48.5 percent of votes. This was the only election in which a single party obtained a parliamentary majority. Nevertheless, the DC's decline in local

**Table 40.1 Electoral Systems in Italy (1946–2017) (Chamber of Deputies)**

| Electoral law number and date of approval | Election | Electoral system | Formula and Quota | Threshold | Preference voting | Bonus | Number of Districts | Assembly Size |
|---|---|---|---|---|---|---|---|---|
| 1946, n. 74, March 10 | 1946 | Open-list PR (OLPR) | LR-quota (+1 or +2, depending on district magnitude) | – | up to 2-3[1] | no | 31 | 556 |
| 1948, n. 6, January 20 1948, n. 26, February 5 | 1948 | OLPR | LR-Imperiali (+3) | 1 seat[8] | up to 3-4[2] | no | 31 | 574 |
| 1953, n. 148, March 31 | 1953[7] (did not come into operation) | OLPR with bonus | LR-Imperiali (+3) | 1 seat | up to 3-4 | 380 seats to winning party or coalition > 50%[5] | 31 | 590 |
| | 1958 | OLPR | LR-Imperiali (+2) | 1 seat and 300.000 votes | up to 3-4 | no | 32 | 596 |
| | 1963 | | | | | | | 630 |
| 1954, n. 615, July 31 | 1968 | | | | | | | 630 |
| 1956, n. 493, May 16 | 1972 | | | | | | | 630 |
| 1957, n. 361, March 30 | 1976 | | | | | | | 630 |
| | 1979 | | | | | | | 630 |
| | 1983 | | | | | | | 630 |
| | 1987 | | | | | | | 630 |
| 1991, n. 200, July 3 | 1992 | OLPR | LR-Imperiali (+2) | 1 seat and 300.000 votes | up to 1 | no | 32 | 630 |
| 1993, n. 277, August 4 | 1994 | MMM | Plurality (475) + LR-Hare (155) | 4% national | no | no | 475 SSD + 1 national | 630 |
| | 1996 | | | | no | no | | 630 |
| | 2001 | | | | | | | |

*(continued)*

# Table 40.1 Continued

| Electoral law number and date of approval | Election | Electoral system | Formula and Quota | Threshold | Preference voting | Bonus | Number of Districts | Assembly Size |
|---|---|---|---|---|---|---|---|---|
| 2005, n. 270, December 21 | 2006 | PR with bonus (closed lists) | LR–Hare | 4% party; 10% coalition; 2% party in coalition | no | 340 seats to the winning party or coalition | 26 | 630[4] |
| | 2008 | | | | | | | |
| | 2013 | | | | | | | |
| 2015, n. 52, May 6 | none | PR with bonus (open lists with protection for list-heads) | LR–Hare | 3% national | up to 2[3] | 340 seats to party with > 40%[6] | 100 | 630[4] |

*Source:* Author's own elaboration on Italian Minister of Interior data.

[1] In 1946 voters could cast three preferences votes in constituencies returning to up 16 members, and four preferences votes in larger constituencies.

[2] Voters could cast three preferences votes in constituencies returning to up 15 members, and four preferences votes in larger constituencies.

[3] If voters cast their first preference to choose a woman, the second vote must go to select a man, and vice versa. Otherwise, the second preference will be considered void.

[4] 12 seats attributed to representatives of Italians living abroad, and one seat for the Aosta Valley region.

[5] 380 of 590 seats in the Chamber of deputies would be given to any alliance of parties that won at least 50 per cent of the votes plus one vote. It must be underlined that two different quotas were indicated. First, if the bonus would be assigned, then the quota will be calculated on two different bases: votes / 380 seats for the winning party(ies), and votes / 209 for the loosing parties. Vice versa, if no party had obtained the 50% plus one vote, then the 1948 system would have worked with a quota plus 3.

[6] On January 25, 2017 the Constitutional Court dropped the second–ballot to allocate the majority bonus for the Chamber of Deputies in order to make "more similar" the two electoral systems for the two Houses, albeit the Senate would still have a regional allocation of seats. However, the supreme judges kept the provision of a majority bonus allocated to the party with 40% of votes.

[7] The total score for the coalition parties was 49.2% with the DC being the pivotal party (40.1%).

[8] The allocation of seat by large remainders method with Hare quota was allowed to parties able to obtain at least one seat (entire quota) in one of the districts. Since 1957, in addition parties had to obtain also at the least 300,000 votes nationally.

elections and the fear of a neo-fascist resurgence induced the ruling party to seek a system that would secure a stable majority. Eventually approved over the vehement opposition of the Communist and Socialist parties, the law stated that after the elections, 380 of 590 seats in the Chamber of Deputies would be given to any alliance of parties that won over 50 percent of the votes (Katz 2001, 59; Renwick 2010). The coalition was composed of four parties: the DC, the Social Democrats (PSDI), the Liberals (PLI), and the Republicans (PRI). The total score for the coalition parties was 49.2 percent, with the DC being the dominant party (40.1 percent). However, this good performance was not sufficient for them to reach their goal. In fact, although they lacked only 204,742 votes to reach a majority and consequently the bonus of seats, the *legge truffa* did not come into operation. The law was repealed in 1954, restoring the 1948 system until the 1990s.[10]

## Electoral Reform of 1993 from Proportional Representation to Mixed-Member Majoritarian: Mani Pulite, Tangentopoli, and Scorporo

The major change to the Italian electoral system that was introduced in the 1990s started with a citizens-initiated referendum held on June 9, 1991. This measure modified one critical component of the electoral law, although only partially. Voters were asked whether the clause relating to the law on the number of preference votes available to the voter should be reduced to just one. The result was 95.6 percent in favor, with a turnout of 65.1 percent. The catalyst for this change was the government's refusal to introduce a new electoral law to accompany the local government reform introduced in 1990. The referendum of 1991 represented the first step on the path away from proportional representation in the Italian system, although only partially, as we shall see.

In the early 1990s, Italy's established political system collapsed amid dramatic changes in the international political system with the end of the Cold War, judicial activism and investigations, and a widespread popular disaffection, culminating in several referendums. The judiciary, especially in Milan, laid bare the widespread links between politicians and illegal activities. The so-called *mani pulite* (clean hands) investigations targeted many MPs and party secretaries such as those of the DC and the PSI. The *Tangentopoli* (bribe city) scandal finally discredited the Italian ruling class among a public fed up with rampant corruption.

Among other consequences, these events led to the adoption in 1993 of a new electoral law. Although a referendum (based on the citizens' initiative) on the Italian constitution does not allow the initiation of new laws—it merely allows the abrogation of a bill or part of it—the referendum of April 1993 clearly represented a breakthrough in the political system and the electoral framework. The overwhelming result undoubtedly paved the way for the successive complete reform of the electoral law. The parliament could not ignore the "popular will," namely, the demand for a significant and real change that would especially emphasize the role of voters in determining the formation of the government and the choice of its leader. The long-standing phenomenon of prime ministers chosen via a bargaining process among the party leaders was an established ritual that was particularly disliked by voters. More than eight voters in ten (82.7 percent, on 77.1 percent turnout) decided to answer yes to the question posed by the referendum on the desire to modify the rules for the election of the Senate, in particular by eliminating the proportional part of the seat distribution.[11]

The consequences of the referendum were significant institutionally and politically. The result was a Senate in which 75 percent of seats were allocated by plurality in single-seat districts (SSDs), and the rest by PR. Had the new system been applied to the following general elections, it would have meant there was a real chance of having a "divided" government between the two chambers. Such division would be a particular problem because the chambers have equal power to confer or withdraw their confidence in the government. Although popularly discredited, the parliament was thus forced to legislate electoral reform before eventually going to early elections (which are called by the president of the republic).

The new electoral law introduced a mixed-member majoritarian (MMM) system (Shugart 2001; Shugart and Wattenberg 2001) in which three-quarters of the Chamber seats (475) were allocated in SSDs via plurality, and the remaining one-quarter (155) via party lists through proportional representation. The PR seat allocation formula was changed to Hare quota and largest remainders (LR) with a nationwide threshold of 4 percent, now with closed lists instead of the open lists that had prevailed in the preceding PR period (see Table 40.1). The MMM system was in operation between 1993 and 2005.[12]

The plurality and PR tiers were linked through a complex mechanism of "negative vote transfers (*scorporo*)" (D'Alimonte 2005, 257). The aim of this mechanism was to reduce the disproportionality typical of plurality elections by deducting votes from those parties that win SSDs. In the assignment of PR seats, the first step is the calculation of the "effective vote" for each list in each constituency. This is done by subtracting, from a list's total vote, a number one greater than the votes received by the second-placed candidates in all the SSDs where candidates affiliated with that list have won seats. The "effective vote" then becomes the tally used for determining the number of PR seats that go to each list. Once this calculation has been made, the second step is to determine which lists have received more than 4 percent of PR votes at the national level (regardless of the *scorporo*). These lists will get seats on the basis of their "effective vote" according to the LR-Hare method (D'Alimonte 2005, 257).

The biggest parties were more likely to win in the districts and thus would tend to suffer *scorporo* transfers. As a result, these parties sidestepped the negative vote transfer rule. They created "fake lists" that no voter knew about, and the surplus votes were subtracted from that list, avoiding the penalty to the real list.[13] The result of the *scorporo* was to render the system only partially compensatory, which is why it is properly considered a type of MMM system, rather than mixed-member proportional (Shugart and Wattenberg 2001).

The system hardly differed for the two houses: as noted earlier, for the Chamber of Deputies, the proportional seats could go only to those parties that had received on a separate ballot at least 4 percent of the national vote. Such a nationwide threshold was not introduced for the Senate, where the PR seats were allocated on a regional basis. In addition, the Senate system allowed the best losers in regional constituencies to join the parliament. However, the *scorporo* negative vote transfer also operated in the Senate, albeit with a significant difference from the Chamber of Deputies: subtracting *all* the votes gathered by the winner in each district, and not just the vote difference between the winner and the first loser. This greatly limited the majoritarianism in the system, relative to that of the Chamber.

## The Electoral Reform of 2005: Back to Proportional Representation but with a Majority Bonus

Another electoral reform took place in 2005. In this case, the system was changed as a defensive mechanism in response to anticipated potential electoral losses by the governing center-right coalition, headed by Silvio Berlusconi and his Forza Italia party. The new law scrapped the mixed-member system and was touted as a possible "simplification" of the party system structure. The law stipulated a proportional system with closed lists that allocates a sizable seat "majority bonus"—guaranteeing 55 percent of seats—to whichever pre-electoral *coalition* of parties obtained the highest number of votes. The new law introduced a defined rule for these coalitions, obligating lists to adhere formally to them by specifying the name of the political leader of the coalition from the outset. *It thus introduced a strongly majoritarian element, by prioritizing pre-electoral coalitions that could obtain a plurality*. The proportional element came in only after the majority bonus was applied, allocating seats among the component parties of the winning and other coalitions.

Berlusconi's government changed the electoral rules in advance of elections scheduled a year later (Massetti 2006; Benoit 2007). The leading advocates for changing the law were the smaller parties of the center-right coalition, such as the Union of the Centre (UDC) and the National Alliance, with strong support by the Northern League, whose leader was the principal rapporteur and author Roberto Calderoli. The law was approved only a few months before the 2006 election (Law 270, December 21, 2005) (Bardi 2007; Pasquino 2007). The center-right coalition explicitly wanted to reintroduce a PR system given its better electoral performance in that tier vis-à-vis the SSDs in the past electoral system. However, the often-evoked implicit goal of the law to attempt to impede the likely success of the center-left resided in three aspects: (1) the nationalization of electoral competition, which was thought to be advantageous to Forza Italia, because of the gap between the appeal of its candidates and that of its party leader; (2) the way that the majority bonus was conferred (see next paragraph) and the geographic concentration of center-right support in two large districts in the north; and (3) differentiating the basis of allocation of seats in the two chambers.

To elaborate on the last point, the likelihood of different coalitions winning each chamber would be increased through the differentiation of their rules for allocating seats, combined with the different geographical pattern of the electoral strength of the parties. In other words, Berlusconi's goal was, in part, to engineer divisions among his opponents, as well as enhance his own party's prospects of seat maximization.

The peculiarity of the 2005 electoral reform is the way the majority bonus was attributed in the Senate: the majority bonus was allocated region by region. Therefore, each electoral plurality in each region obtained 55 percent of seats attributed to that specific region. Consequently, winning in the most populous regions with the largest district magnitude would increase the possibility of obtaining a majority of seats in the Senate.[14] Given the different parties' electoral strongholds, the possibility of having a "divided government" was very likely. The consequence is that this mechanism does not guarantee a clear majority for any block in the Senate, unlike the national majority-bonus provision in the Chamber of Deputies. Thus, the result of the Senate became a sort of lottery. In fact, the center-left obtained a sizable majority of seats in the Chamber, but not in the Senate, where it was in the majority by only two seats.

Together with the majority bonus to the winning coalition and closed-list PR, the new electoral law introduced a complex set of thresholds for seat allocations: 617 out of 630[15] Chamber seats were allocated among the parties that passed thresholds of the total vote on a *national* basis. The thresholds were as follows: (1) 10 percent for a coalition, (provided that at least one list within the pre-electoral coalition got 2 percent);[16] (2) 4 percent for single parties; and (3) 2 percent for any party in a coalition, except for the first party below 2 percent in the coalition. For the Senate, the thresholds were the following, on a *regional* basis: (1) 20 percent for a coalition (provided that at least one list got 3 percent); (2) 8 percent for any party not in a coalition; and (3) 3 percent for any party in a coalition (there is no exception for the first party in a coalition below this threshold, unlike the Chamber).[17] These systems were in place for three elections, 2006, 2008, and 2013.

In 2014, the Constitutional Court entered the electoral-reform fray when it declared unconstitutional the previous electoral law of 2005. In particular, the Constitutional Court ruled inapplicable the majority bonus, and specified that the voter must be allowed to cast a preference vote (Constitutional Law n. 1/2014). The court thus reintroduced the electoral system in operation between 1991 and 1993, but also modified the law by also introducing preference voting for the Senate (Ceccanti 2016). In response, parliament approved a new electoral system in 2015.[18]

## The Electoral System Reform of 2015 and the Italicum

The new electoral law came into force in July 2016 (D'Alimonte 2015; Chiaramonte 2015; Pasquino 2015). However, it was not used in any general election, due to a ruling by the Constitutional Court and subsequent changes in 2017 (detailed in the chapter postscript). The main political actors involved in the process were the Democratic Party and its leader, Prime Minister Matteo Renzi. Basically all other parties were against the reform, except Forza Italia, which had voted in favor initially and then later withdrew its support. At first glance, the 2015 system showed similarities with the 2005 laws. Both had bonus provisions. However, the new bonus adjustment mechanism—the so-called *Italicum*—differed in that the majority bonus was to be allocated to the most voted list, unlike in the 2005 system where it was allocated to a coalition of parties. The list receiving the plurality of votes was to be allocated 340 out of 618 deputies, provided that it reached 40 percent[19] of the valid votes at the national level. If no list earned this many votes, the law provided that a runoff would be held two weeks later between the two most voted lists.[20] This is highly unusual, as there are few examples of runoffs in list systems for national assemblies.[21] As it happened, the Constitutional Court invalidated the runoff provision in a ruling in 2017. A further peculiarity of the *Italicum* was that it was intended to function only for the Chamber. For the Senate, the electoral law remained PR without a majority bonus, which was the 2005 law after the changes introduced by the Constitutional Court in 2014.

The *Italicum* foresaw only one legal threshold to enable access to the distribution of seats. Such access was allowed solely for those lists that reach at least 3 percent of valid votes nationwide. Once the majority bonus was assigned (in this sense the system was *majority assuring*, whatever the result of the first round), the rest of seats were to be allocated via PR (Hare quota and largest remainders) to the lists that met the national threshold.

The new electoral law promised a reintroduction of the open list, but with features protecting list heads and encouraging gender balance. However, the law finally enacted in 2017 retains the closed list, as summarized in the postscript to this chapter.

# CONSEQUENCES OF ELECTORAL
# SYSTEMS IN ITALY

Having now reviewed Italy's electoral systems of the postwar period, we turn to their consequences. For almost fifty years the political system had featured highly unstable governments in part due to the fragmentation of the party system, albeit with stability in political and governmental personnel (Cotta and Verzichelli 2009). This was a consequence of a *pure* proportional electoral system, which offered several chances to small parties to be represented (Ignazi 2002). Neither of the two biggest parties was able to govern alone, and the Christian Democrats were prone to forming oversized coalitions (Newell and Bull 1997). Dissatisfaction with the performance of the PR system led to the first major electoral reform, that of 1993. This section will consider several indicators of electoral system impacts on the party system, for each of Italy's electoral systems over time.

## Electoral Reform and Governmental Stability

As a result of the introduction of a polarizing political actor—Silvio Berlusconi—the party system and electoral competition moved toward a bipolar framework. Beginning with the 1994 general elections, there were three power turnovers between center-right and center-left coalitions. However, the fragmentation of the coalitions and the weakness and heterogeneous nature of the parties affected governmental stability and ability to implement programs and policies. In essence, Giuseppe Di Palma's (1977) words from more than forty years ago still rang true, in that Italian parties continued to survive without governing. Moreover, a new party, the Five Star Movement (M5S), which won the highest percentage of the vote for any individual party in the 2013 elections (albeit with only 25.6 percent), may be generating a tripolar party system as an unexpected outcome of electoral reform.

The electoral law first adopted in the general election of 1994 did not produce governmental stability. The paradox is that it generated identifiability without stability (durability of governments). In the space of less than twenty years, Italy experienced twelve governments (two of which were technocratic), six different prime ministers, two oversized coalitions, and two changes of parliamentary majorities during the same legislature. The first Berlusconi government collapsed—due to the defection of the Lega Nord (*Northern League*)—after just over half a year in office (Cento Bull and Gilbert 2001; Passarelli and Tuorto 2012; Passarelli 2013b). The early dissolution of parliament, the change of prime ministers, the lack of support by a parliamentary majority, and the ensuing instability and party fragmentation have remained the main characteristics of the Italian political system despite the 1994 and 2005 reforms.[22] Such tendencies were detectable in the political and institutional dynamics, which are exemplified by both the 1994–2001 and 2006–2008 periods, lasting through both "majoritarian" and a "proportional" electoral law, respectively (Capano 1997; Bull and Pasquino 2007; Donovan 1995; Hine 1996; Gilbert 1998).

## The Party System and the Electoral Reforms

Italy's electoral reforms also offer an opportunity to explore the effect of the electoral system on the party system. Table 40.2 shows several indicators of the party system, by election and by period means, representing Italy's different electoral systems. For the effective number of seat-winning parties ($N_S$) (Laakso and Taagepera 1979; see also the chapter in this volume by Shugart and Taagepera), we can observe the following: during the First Republic (1948–1992), the average was 3.71, while during the majoritarian electoral system for the Second Republic, the average was 6.35. For the majority-bonus PR system, 2006–2013, it was 3.87. Thus, surprisingly, $N_S$ was at its highest during the period of the MMM electoral system. We see the same pattern with $N_V$, the effective number of vote-earning parties.

The reason for the seeming anomaly of party system fragmentation peaking under MMM lies in a peculiar complexity of the system identified earlier—the establishment of fake lists to benefit from the *scorporo* process of partial compensation. While many new parties thus entered and won votes and seats, these parties were grouped into alliances, which were coordinated in the SSDs of this system, and generated "fake lists" to minimize their negative vote transfers from the SSDs to the PR component. In fact, when we consider the actual number of parties that won at least one seat, we find that number declined in the MMM period, but—strikingly—it was greater in the SSDs (8.3, on average) than in the list component (6.7). This is due to the alliances being represented by different parties in different districts, and also to ethno-regionalist parties being able to win (very few) seats in their strongholds.[23] The number of seat-winning parties was higher in the pure-list periods (1948–1992 and 2006–2013), as we might expect. However, many of these parties were very small, as revealed by the lower effective numbers during that period.

As reported in Table 40.2, in 2008, there was a significant reduction in the number of parties winning seats, compared to 2005, the first election under the majority-bonus list PR system. However, that was due to the birth of two new parties, each resulting from the merging of two existing parties. The merger between Forza Italia and the National Alliance created the People of Freedom led by Berlusconi, while the Democrats of the Left and the Daisy formed the basis of the Democratic Party on the center-left. These parties obtained approximately 75 percent of votes and as many seats, the highest top-2 percentage since 1976. Nevertheless, the power acquired by the two parties eroded, not least due to their joint participation in the unity government "rainbow coalition" they formed after Berlusconi's resignation due to judicial and financial troubles.

Regarding the proportionality of the system, we can use the Gallagher (1991) index of disproportionality (see also the chapter by Shugart and Taagepera) to compare across electoral systems. The lowest index value was recorded in 1987 and 1992 (2.5), when the purely PR system was in place. The average during the initial PR period was 2.87, whereas the two "majoritarian" periods have had high values, as we would expect from either MMM (average 8.31) or the majority-bonus system (8.89). The election of 2013, when the party system fragmented again due to the arrival of the Five Star Movement, saw an extraordinarily high value for a "PR" system, 17.3. This resulted from the bonus provision awarding nearly half the seats to a party with barely a quarter of the votes—the Democratic Party—as the main partner in the alliance that won the plurality.

# Electoral Reform and Voters: Accountability and Volatility

Although we might detect a general shift toward a bipolar structure since 1994, and a quasi-two-party system in 2008, Italy has also seen substantial electoral

**Table 40.2   The Effects of Electoral Systems on Political and Electoral Outcomes (1948–2013)**

| Electoral system | Legislature year | Two biggest parties votes | Two biggest parties seats | Gallagher index | Eff *Nv* | Eff *Ns* | Parties with seats | Electoral Volatility | Index of nationalization |
|---|---|---|---|---|---|---|---|---|---|
| OLPR (up to 4 votes) | 1948 | 79.5 | 77.5 | 3.64 | 2.95 | 2.57 | 10 | – | 0.833 |
| | 1953 | 62.7 | 64.4 | 3.68 | 4.18 | 3.54 | 9 | 14.1 | 0.836 |
| | 1958 | 65.0 | 65.6 | 2.74 | 3.87 | 3.45 | 12 | 5.2 | 0.856 |
| | 1963 | 63.5 | 67.6 | 2.58 | 4.16 | 3.74 | 10 | 8.5 | 0.864 |
| | 1968 | 66.0 | 70.3 | 2.66 | 3.94 | 3.53 | 9 | 7.8 | 0.870 |
| | 1972 | 65.8 | 70.6 | 3.25 | 4.08 | 3.55 | 9 | 5.3 | 0.866 |
| | 1976 | 73.1 | 77.8 | 2.75 | 3.53 | 3.16 | 11 | 9.1 | 0.888 |
| | 1979 | 68.7 | 73.5 | 2.69 | 3.91 | 3.47 | 12 | 5.3 | 0.874 |
| | 1983 | 62.8 | 67.1 | 2.57 | 4.52 | 4.02 | 13 | 8.3 | 0.861 |
| | 1987 | 60.9 | 65.2 | 2.52 | 4.62 | 4.07 | 14 | 9.1 | 0.859 |
| OLPR (1 vote) | 1992 | 45.8 | 49.7 | 2.51 | 6.63 | 5.71 | 16 | 19 | 0.785 |
| MMM | 1994* | 41.4 | 35.2 | 7.81 | 7.58 | 7.67 | 7 (9) | 36.7 | 0.749 |
| | 1996* | 41.6 | 46.8 | 6.91 | 7.17 | 6.09 | 8(10) | 13.0 | 0.798 |
| | 2001* | 46.0 | 52.4 | 10.22 | 6.32 | 5.3 | 5 (6) | 22.4 | 0.830 |
| Majority-bonus PR | 2006 | 41.5 | 41.7 | 3.61 | 5.69 | 5.06 | 13 | 9.5 | 0.865 |
| | 2008 | 70.6 | 76.7 | 5.73 | 3.82 | 3.07 | 7 | 9.7 | 0.836 |
| | 2013 | 51.0 | 63.5 | 17.34 | 5.33 | 3.47 | 10 | 39.1 | 0.836 |
| period means | 1948–2013 | 59.2 | 62.7 | 4.89 | 4.84 | 4.20 | 10.3 | 13.9 | 0.841 |
| | 1948–1992 | 64.9 | 68.1 | 2.87 | 4.22 | 3.71 | 11.4 | 9.2 | 0.854 |
| | 1994–2001 | 43.0 | 44.8 | 8.31 | 7.02 | 6.35 | 6.7 (8.3) | 24.0 | 0.792 |
| | 2006–2013 | 54.4 | 60.6 | 8.89 | 4.95 | 3.87 | 10.0 | 19.4 | 0.845 |

*Sources*: Author's calculations from data from the Italian Ministry of the Interior; Passarelli (2014).

* For the MMM period, data refer to the PR component except the numbers in parentheses for parties with seats, which refer to SSDs.

volatility. This includes the eruption of new parties such as the populist Five Star Movement. In part, this comes as an unintended consequence of electoral reform, as discussed next.

Especially with the 2006–2013 period and the presence of a majority-bonus proportional system, without preference voting (closed list), the party (in central office) greatly strengthened its power in recruiting party personnel. This increased the voters' disaffection due to the diminishing ability to affect the choice of candidates and, to some extent, to determine social representation (especially in terms of gender, expertise, and generation). The frustration felt by citizens was, in the end, one of the main factors favoring abstentions, the rise of populist parties such as the Northern League, the flourishing of new (and significant) parties such as the Five Star Movement, and so on. Most interestingly, if we consider electoral volatility, it is possible to observe that the 1994–2001 elections registered a different score: they obtained the highest period average in terms of volatility (24.0, as shown in Table 40.2). In the 2013 election volatility was even higher (39.1), mostly due to the extraordinary success of the Five Star Movement, as well as from retrospective voting on ruling parties' performances (ITANES 2013).

Votes for a particular candidate were possible under the 1948–1993 electoral system, because of the open lists. However, given the SSDs of the 1993 electoral reform, voters started to attach more importance to the characteristics of candidates than previously (ITANES 2001, 2006, 2008, 2013; Bellucci and Segatti 2011). Moreover, voters have generally become increasingly accustomed to bipolar competition and the expectation of having a government that is a reflection of electoral results, and not, as in the past, based on parliamentary bargaining. The collapse of the pre-1989 party system further opened the door to different electoral behavior, in tandem with new parties that were not linked to historical political traditions. The success of the M5S in 2013, attractive to younger voters (about 44 percent according to ITANES 2013), and the Northern League since 1992–1994 highlights the need for parties to focus on a few regions where the number of seats allocated to the Senate was greater, as in Lombardy, Campania, or Veneto. This was particularly true for the Senate and especially after the 2005 electoral reform.

This brings us to a brief examination of electoral nationalization, shown in Table 40.2. There exists the possibility that electoral laws can affect the ratio between what parties obtain at a regional level and the numbers they achieve throughout the entire territory. The index of nationalization, which varies between 0 and 1—the lower the index, the higher the parties' concentration of votes in a few areas, and the higher the index, the higher the nationalization of the vote (Caramani 2004; Bochsler 2010; Passarelli 2013a)—has been quite homogenous during the entire period. The lowest level was registered in 1994 (0.749), and the highest in 1976 (0.888). In terms of the effects of electoral systems, we can observe a lower nationalization during the mixed-member period (0.79), when the SSDs meant that parties with regional base were privileged, vis-à-vis quite similar higher values in the other two periods (about 0.85).

# CONCLUSIONS

Italy has experienced three major electoral reforms in the last twenty-five years and multiple elections under quite different systems: PR, MMM, and majority-bonus PR. The chapter's review of the main political results in the Italian context and electoral reforms has partially confirmed our knowledge of the effects that electoral systems have produced (Gallagher 1975, 1992; Shugart 2005). However, not all the political expectations were realized. For example, the effects of the 1993 reform on both parties and voters were important, even if it did not achieve the political goals of strengthening parliamentary majorities, prolonging governments, and increasing accountability. In particular, the absence of big, cohesive national parties has mitigated the effects of electoral reforms, especially in the case of the mixed-member majoritarian system (1994–2001), as the decline of the percentages of votes and seats allocated to the two biggest parties has confirmed. Beyond the electoral laws' technicalities and details, the important lessons from the Italian case is that so much system change compared to other countries is mostly explained by party system fragmentation and governmental instability. From a theoretical perspective, then, the Italian case perfectly fits with the research question on the effects of electoral systems. The case has empirically demonstrated that the electoral system alone cannot change the *political system* if the electoral reforms are not coupled with other features. Consistent with an observation made over forty years ago by Sartori (1976; see also Renwick 2010; Baldini 2011), the most important contextual reason that electoral reform in Italy has disappointed its advocates is the absence of strong national parties.

# POSTSCRIPT: DEVELOPMENTS IN 2017

Following the outcome of a referendum and a ruling of the Constitutional Court, the electoral system of Italy underwent further changes. This postscript will review developments since the passage of the electoral reform of 2015 including the adoption of a new electoral system in 2017. Beyond the technicalities and arguments for and against the 2015 reform, its taking effect was conditional on a constitutional reform regarding the role of the Senate, which voters rejected in December, 2016. The referendum result led to Prime Minister Renzi's resignation and, a week later, a new government headed by Paolo Gentiloni, former minister of foreign affairs under Renzi. Because of the referendum's failure, the country was left for several months in a situation of potential stalemate.

This was the third referendum of its kind in Italy, with the other two having been held in 2001 and 2006. The two options presented to voters in 2016 were related to the approval or rejection of the reform promoted by Renzi's government and his center-left parliamentary majority.[24] The result of the referendum was both clear and decisive.

Approximately 60 percent of voters cast a "no" vote in opposition to the proposed reforms. Perhaps the most striking result was voter turnout. Nearly 70 percent of eligible voters cast a vote, a percentage that is similar to that reached in general elections in Italy (e.g., 75 percent in 2013). This figure also confirms that Italy continues to have one of the highest electoral participation rates in the world. Despite this high turnout figure, one of the most notable features of the referendum is the persistent north–south divide in terms of turnout and the level of rejection of the reform. Rejection of the referendum was particularly high in southern regions, with peaks in Sicily, Sardinia, and Campania. Support for the referendum was limited and prevailed in only two regions (i.e., Tuscany and Emilia-Romagna), as well as in the province of Bolzano.

The elimination of Italy's "perfect" or symmetrical bicameralism was central to the reform. Such bicameralism is unique among contemporary parliamentary democracies and is a subject of much debate by politicians and scholars alike. It has contributed to political instability, especially after 1994, as the risk of different majorities in the two chambers has increased due to differences in who selects deputies and how.[25] These different electorates have divergent electoral behaviors that are further accentuated by the regional allocation of seats for the Senate versus the national allocation for the Chamber.

The law approved in 2015 did not change the Senate's electoral law, because the reform's supporters thought the referendum would pass. The possibility of having two very different electoral laws for the two Chambers in a context of symmetric bicameralism may generate uncertainty and political weakness. A first clarification came from the Constitutional Court decision on January 25, 2017. The court intervened by invalidating parts of the law. In particular, the decision dropped the second round to allocate the majority bonus for the Chamber of Deputies to make "more similar" the two electoral systems for the two Houses, although the Senate would still have a regional allocation of seats. However, the Court kept the provision of a majority bonus allocated to the party with 40 percent of votes. After the 2016 referendum, *another* (!) electoral law has been approved, even beyond the changes the Constitutional Court made.

In October, 2017, the Italian Parliament approved a new electoral law (n. 165/2017). The MMM system (with no differences for the two chambers) features 37% SSD seats and 61% elected by closed-list PR (LR-Hare) with a maximum district magnitude of 7 or 8, and no linkage between the tiers. Additionally, 12 seats in the Chamber of Deputies and 6 in Senate are to be elected by Italians abroad. A nationwide threshold is set at 3% for a party or 10% for a coalition, with a lower threshold for lists representing linguistic minorities. Votes for the lists receiving less than 1% in coalitions are wasted (votes for parties between 1% and 3% are conferred to allies). The law indicates that PR lists should alternate candidates by gender; moreover, parties can nominate no more than 60% (SSD candidates and PR list-heads) from the same gender. The ballot is unique: voters can cast a vote for a PR list and in that case the vote is also attributed to the candidate in the SSD. However, a voter can vote separately for the SSD candidate and a list linked to that candidate. In cases of votes only for an SSD candidate nominated by a coalition of parties, votes for the candidate are proportionally distributed to the linked party lists according to their proportions of the intra-coalition vote. The ballot thus does not permit splitting the vote between the SSD candidate's party or coalition and a party outside the coalition.

## Notes

1. Renwick (2010, 111) reports five reforms, including the first electoral law introduced in 1946 after the end of fascism, and the 1954 law that reintroduced that of 1948 after the 1953 change. See also Clementi (2015). In fact, Italy had five electoral laws: 1948, 1953, 1993, 2005, and 2015, to which we could add the electoral law—albeit never applied—generated by the 2014 constitutional judgment that abolished the 2005 law.

2. The calculation of the quota is as follows: $V / (M + n)$, where $V$ is valid votes, $M$ is the district magnitude, and $n$ varies with the specific provision of the system. In the 1946 law, the provision was for $n = 1$ (equivalent to Hagenbach-Bischoff or Droop) in districts of $M \leq 20$ seats, and $n = 2$ in higher-magnitude districts. As explained later, and in Table 40.1, the definition of the quota was changed in subsequent laws of this period.

3. A constitutional referendum was held on June 2, 1946, and the Constituent Assembly was elected at the same time: the choice was between the republic or the monarchy, which was the existing Italian form of state. The republic obtained 54.3 percent of votes, whereas the monarchy obtained 45.7 percent. The law allowed for only one preference vote in 1946. The proportional system was used by the DC to divide the left field, especially the PSI from the PCI. In that way, the hegemonic role of the DC was not in danger, as it was guaranteed by the Cold war system (Clementi 2015).

4. Specifically, thirty-one multiseat constituencies and one single-seat constituency for the Valle d'Aosta.

5. The thresholds applied to the remainder seats only. Parties could thus gain access to the parliament through district seats, as in the cases of regionalist parties such as Union valdôtaine or the Svp (Südtiroler Volkspartei), which won their seats in a district but do not have access to the distribution of the remainder seats.

6. According to Article 59 of the presidential decree (n. 361/1957), voters could cast up to three preferences in a district with a magnitude equal to or less than fifteen. In bigger districts, four preference votes were allowed.

7. The steps to assign the remaining seats were as follows: (1) all votes not used to win a seat were collected together at the national district (*collegio unico nazionale*); (2) at this level the number of seats to each party was calculated; (3) to decide *where* those seats would be allocated, a rank among the districts was made—therefore, party X would have won its seats in the districts with the highest remainders in percentage (e.g., if party X obtained a 50 percent remainder out of the quorum, then the first seats will be allocated, etc.); and (4) finally, in terms of *which* candidate will be elected, that with the highest number of preferences will be considered first.

8. In 1948, the definition of the quota was changed to $V / (M + 3)$, and in 1956 back to $V / (M + 2)$. The 1948–1953 formula generated an extraordinarily low quota, which would benefit the larger parties (Gallagher and Mitchell 2005, 587; Shugart and Taagepera 2017, 36–39). See Table 40.1 for a summary of these changes.

9. A similar proposal was adopted during the fascist era, in 1924. The Acerbo law gave the party that won the most votes two-thirds of the seats. However, the bonus was possible only if the party got at least 25 percent of the votes.

10. A minor change was approved in 1956: it slightly increased the proportionality of the system without changing its identity (Renwick 2010, 119). The value +2 in the Imperiali quota formula was introduced at the district level together with the provision of obtaining at the least three hundred thousand votes.

11. The choice to call the referendum was motivated by the fact that the Senate had a dual formula. It would function as an SSD system wherever a candidate obtained 65 percent of votes; seats not filled in SSDs were instead allocated at the regional level via the D'Hondt method. In fact, few seats were filled as SSDs: on average, only 3.6 senators per election (out of 315) were elected this way. Therefore, the referendum calling for the abrogation of the 65 percent clause implied shifting the Senate to a plurality system. In contrast, the Chamber had a strictly PR system.

12. For the election of the Italian Chamber of Deputies, in 1993, Italy was divided into twenty-seven districts (*circoscrizioni*). However, given that the distribution of the PR seats was calculated at the national level, as in the PR system previously adopted, districts served only to choose individual candidates inside the party lists. In contrast, for the Senate, each region is a separate district and votes are not pooled nationally. The meaning of "the Senate is elected on a regional basis" provision (Article 57) remains subject to debate by scholars.

13. For example, if the "RED" candidate won an SSD with 45,000 votes and the runner-up got 42,100 votes, as a consequence, the vote to the PR list linked to the "RED" candidate was reduced by 2,901. The logic was to "drop" the vote surplus used to win the SSD. Moreover, if a party was connected to more than one list, then the "excess votes" (2,901 in our example) were partitioned among the affiliated list on the basis of the PR vote of each list.

14. In 2006 and 2008: Lombardy (forty-seven seats; forty-nine in 2013), Campania (thirty seats; twenty-nine in 2013), Lazio (twenty-seven seats; twenty-eight in 2013), Sicily (twenty-six seats; twenty-five in 2013), Veneto (twenty-four seats), Piedmont (twenty-two seats), Emilia-Romagna (twenty-one seats; twenty-two in 2013), Tuscany (eighteen seats), Apulia (eighteen seats; twenty in 2013), Calabria (ten seats), Sardinia (nine seats; eight in 2013), Liguria (eight seats), Marches (eight seats), Umbria (seven seats), Basilicata (seven seats), Abruzzo (seven seats), Trentino Alto Adige (seven seats), Friuli Venezia Giulia (seven seats), and Molise (two seats).

15. Additionally, one MP is elected from the Aosta Valley (SSD) and twelve are elected by a constituency consisting of Italians living abroad.

16. Among coalitions that do not satisfy this requirement, the list that passes 4 percent on a national basis has access to the seat distribution. The same provision applies to the coalition running for the Senate, where the threshold is equal to 8 percent for single list in the coalition.

17. The law also allowed multiple candidacies in different districts, thus placing a supplementary power in the hands of the central party in choosing candidates.

18. Together with parliamentary reforms, one must also consider the series of popular attempts to change the electoral system. Coherently with the tradition of 1991 and 1993, two referenda were called: in 1999 and in 2000. Although both obtained more "yes" votes than "no" votes, meaning that voters supported the changes (basically dropping the proportional part of the 25 percent of seats as established by the 1993 law), both referendums failed because they did not clear the required threshold of voter turnout of 50 percent +1 of voters (in part because the voter list was outdated).

19. Different proposals were presented during the parliamentary debate: in particular, at the beginning the threshold was placed at 35 percent and then at 37 percent.

20. No formal alliances (the so-called *apparentamento*) are allowed for the runoff between lists that competed in the first round.
21. See the chapter on France by Hoyo for examples of runoffs among lists at the subnational level.
22. The average government tenure was eleven months during the First Republic (1948–1992).
23. For another prominent example of multiparty alliances coordinating on nominations in SSDs, see the chapter in this volume by Ziegfeld on India.
24. The reform was approved earlier by an absolute majority in both houses of parliament, but the proposed changes required a two-thirds majority in parliament to be implemented without a referendum according to the Italian constitution (Article 138.3). Since this threshold was not met in parliament, the referendum was called (by the government) by collecting the required number of voter signatures, as stated by Article 138.2, while the opponents to the reform were not able to get the minimum number of required signatures (five hundred thousand).
25. Chamber: minimum voter age is 18 years old. Senate: minimum voter age is 25 years old.

## References

Baldini, Gianfranco. "The Different Trajectories of Italian Electoral Reforms." *West European Politics* 34, no. 3 (2011): 644–663.

Bardi, Luciano. "Electoral Change and Its Impact on the Party System in Italy." *West European Politics* 30, no. 4 (2007): 711–732.

Bellucci, Paolo, and Paolo. Segatti, eds. *Votare in Italia: 1968-2008. Dall'appartenenza alla scelta.* Bologna: Il Mulino, 2011.

Benoit, Kenneth. "Electoral Laws as Political Consequences: Explaining the Origins and Change of Electoral Institutions." *Annual Review of Political Science* 10 (2007): 363–390.

Bochsler, Daniel. "Measuring Party Nationalisation: A New Gini-Based Indicator That Corrects for the Number of Units." *Electoral Studies* 29 (2010): 155–168.

Bull, Martin, and Gianfranco Pasquino. "A Long Quest in Vain: Institutional Reforms in Italy." *West European Politics* 30, no. 4 (2007): 670–691.

Capano, Giliberto. "1992-94, The Roots of Ambiguous Transition: Yearbooks and Journals on Italy." *South European Society and Politics* 2, no. 1 (1997): 166–172.

Caramani, Daniele. *The Nationalization of Politics.* Cambridge: Cambridge University Press, 2004.

Carey, John, and Matthew Soberg Shugart. "Incentives to Cultivate a Personal Vote: A Rank Ordering of Electoral Formulas." *Electoral Studies* 14, no. 4 (1995): 417–439.

Ceccanti, Stefano. *La transizione è (quasi) finite. Come risolvere nel 2016 i problemi aperti 70 anni prima.* Torino, Giappichelli, 2016.

Cento Bull, Anna, and Mark Gilbert. *The Lega Nord and the Northern Question in Italian Politics.* Basingstoke: Palgrave, 2001.

Chiaramonte, Alessandro. "The Unfinished Story of Electoral Reforms in Italy." *Contemporary Italian Politics* 7, no. 1 (2015): 10–26.

Clementi, Francesco. "Vent'anni di legislazione elettorale (1993-2013): tra il già e il non ancora." *Rivista trimestrale di diritto pubblico* 2 (2015): 557–610.

Cotta, Maurizio, and Luca Verzichelli. "Ministers in Italy: Notables, Party Men, Technocrats and Media Men." *South European Society and Politics* 7, no. 2 (2009): 117–152.

D'Alimonte, Roberto. "Italy: A Case of Fragmented Bipolarism." In *The Politics of Electoral Systems*, edited by M. Gallagher and P. Mitchell, 253–276. Oxford: Oxford University Press, 2005.

D'Alimonte, Roberto. "The New Italian Electoral System: Majority-Assuring but Minority-Friendly." *Contemporary Italian Politics* 7, no. 3 (2015): 286–292.

Di Palma, Giuseppe. *Surviving Without Governing. The Italian Parties in Parliament.* Berkeley: University of California Press, 1977.

Donovan, Mark. "The Politics of Electoral Reform in Italy". *International Political Science review* 16, no. 1 (1995): 47–64.

Gallagher, Michael. "Disproportionality in a Proportional Representation System: The Irish Experience." *Political Studies* 23, no. 4 (1975): 501–513.

Gallagher, Michael. "Proportionality, Disproportionality and Electoral Systems." *Electoral Studies* 10, no. 1 (1991): 33–51.

Gallagher, Michael. "Comparing Proportional Representation Electoral Systems: Quotas, Thresholds, Paradoxes and Majorities." *British Journal of Political Science* 22 (1992): 469–496.

Gallagher, Michael, and Paul Mitchell, eds. *The Politics of Electoral Systems.* Oxford: Oxford University Press, 2005.

Gilbert, Mark. "Transforming Italy's Institutions: The Bicameral Committee on Constitutional Reform." *Modern Italy* 4, no. 3 (1998): 49–66.

Hine, David. "Italian Political Reform in Comparative Perspective." In *The New Italian Republic. From the Fall of the Berlin Wall to Berlusconi*, edited by S. Gundle and S. Parker, 311–325. London and New York: Routledge, 1996.

Ignazi, Piero. *Il potere dei partiti.* Roma-Bari: Laterza, 2002.

Italian National Election Studies (ITANES). *Perché ha vinto il centro-destra.* Bologna: Il Mulino, 2001.

Italian National Election Studies (ITANES). *Dov'è la vittoria? Il voto del 2006 raccontato dagli italiani.* Bologna: Il Mulino, 2006.

Italian National Election Studies (ITANES). *Il ritorno di Berlusconi. Vincitori e vinti nelle elezioni del 2008.* Bologna: Il Mulino, 2008.

Italian National Election Studies (ITANES). *Voto amaro. Disincanto e crisi economica nelle elezioni del 2013.* Bologna: Il Mulino, 2013.

Katz, Richard. "Reforming the Italian Electoral Law, 1993." In *Mixed-Member Electoral Systems: The Best of Both Worlds?*, edited by M. S. Shugart and M. P. Wattenberg, 96–122. Oxford: Oxford University Press, 2001.

Katz, Richard. "Why Are There So Many (or So Few) Electoral Reforms?" In *The Politics of Electoral Systems*, edited by P. Gallagher and M. Gallagher, 57–78. Oxford: Oxford University Press, 2005.

Laakso, Markku, and Rein Taagepera. "The 'Effective' Number of Parties: A Measure with Application to West Europe." *Comparative Political Studies* 12, no. 1 (1979): 3–27.

Massetti, Emanuele. "Electoral Reform in Italy: From PR to Mixed System and (Almost) Back Again." *Representation* 42, no. 3 (2006): 261–269.

Newell, James L., and Martin J. Bull. "Party Organisations and Alliances in Italy in the 1990s: A Revolution of Sorts." In *Crisis and Transition in Italian Politics*, edited by M. Bull and M. Rhodes, 81–109. London: Frank Cass & Co., 1997.

Pasquino, Gianfranco. "Tricks and Treats: The 2005 Italian Electoral Law and Its Consequences." *South European Society and Politics* 12, no. 1 (2007): 79–93.

Pasquino, Gianfranco. "Italy Has Yet Another Electoral Law." *Contemporary Italian Politics* 7, no. 3 (2015): 293–300.

Passarelli, Gianluca. "National and Regional Elections between Homogeneity and Differentiation: The Case of Italy." *Modern Italy* 18, no. 3 (2013a): 285–301.

Passarelli, Gianluca. "Extreme Right Parties in Western Europe: The Case of the Italian Northern League." *Journal of Modern Italian Studies* 18, no. 1 (2013b): 53–71.

Passarelli, Gianluca. "Electoral Law(s) and Elections in the Italian Second Republic. The 2013 Landmark (?)." *Polis* 28, no. 1 (2014): 107–124.

Passarelli, Gianluca. (2017) "Determinants of Preferential Voting in Italy. General Lessons from a Crucial Case". *Representation* (on line first, 20 July 2017) doi: 10.1080/00344893.2017.1354910.

Passarelli, Gianluca, and Dario Tuorto. *Lega & Padania. Storie e luoghi delle camicie verdi.* Bologna: Il Mulino, 2012.

Renwick, Alan. *The Politics of Electoral Reform: Changing the Rules of Democracy.* Cambridge: Cambridge University Press, 2010.

Sartori, Giovanni. *Parties and Party Systems. A Framework for Analysis.* Cambridge: Cambridge University Press, 1976.

Shugart, Matthew Soberg. "Electoral 'Efficiency' and the Move to Mixed-Member Systems." *Electoral Studies* 20, no. 2 (2001): 173–193.

Shugart, Matthew Soberg. "Comparative Electoral Systems Research: The Maturation of a Field and New Challenges Ahead." In *The Politics of Electoral Systems*, edited by M. Gallagher and P. Mitchell, 24–55. Oxford: Oxford University Press, 2005.

Shugart, Matthew Soberg, and Martin P. Wattenberg. "Mixed-Member Electoral Systems: A Definition and Typology." In *Mixed-Member Electoral Systems: The Best of Both Worlds?*, edited by Matthew S. Shugart and Martin P. Wattenberg, 9–24. Oxford: Oxford University Press, 2001.

Shugart, Matthew Soberg and Rein Taagepera. *Votes from Seats: Logical Models of Electoral Systems.* Cambridge: Cambridge University Press, 2017.

CHAPTER 41

..................................................................................................

# ELECTORAL SYSTEMS
# IN CONTEXT
## *Colombia*

..................................................................................................

STEVEN L. TAYLOR AND
MATTHEW S. SHUGART

DESPITE its struggles with political and criminal violence, Colombia has had one of the longest sustained experiences with electoral processes in all of Latin America. This lengthy experience coupled with several instances of institutional reform over the decades provides an excellent case for illustrating the ways in which power-seeking political actors adapt to changes in electoral systems over time. Specifically, Colombia affords the chance to observe various electoral systems and party adaptation to system changes over a multi-decade timeframe. This case includes a change from one common proportional representation (PR) formula to another, with constant district magnitudes across the systems—one of the few such reforms in recent times in a purely districted PR system. The prior system was Hare (or simple) quota with largest remainders (LR-Hare), while the reformed system uses D'Hondt divisors.[1] An unusual—probably unique—feature of the Colombian PR system is that parties have the option of presenting either closed or open lists.[2] As we detail later in this chapter, the former LR-Hare system had evolved, through the adaptive behavior of political elites, into a de facto version of single nontransferable vote (SNTV), making it among the few cases of this rare system (see also the chapter on Japan by Nemoto in this volume). Earlier, Colombia's electoral system had undergone a major change in 1991 with the move to a nationwide district for the election of its Senate and the adoption of set-aside legislative seats for various minority groups. All of these electoral-system changes make the case a veritable laboratory for electoral system experimentation.

Regarding the wider political context, in addition to the aforementioned violence, the Colombian political system demonstrates how power-seeking actors use party labels as a means of political differentiation. Colombia was a latecomer to the use of official state-provided ballots[3] and until quite recently featured parties that lacked control over their own labels; as we discuss later, this lack of label control was one of the features that

**FIGURE 41.1.** Privately published ballot as part of an advertisement in Medellín, Colombia, in the newspaper *El Colombiano* (February 25, 1978).

resulted in the LR-Hare system turning into what we shall term a quasi-SNTV system. Figure 41.1 illustrates a privately produced ballot published in a Colombian newspaper reflecting one of four Conservative sets of lists in the department of Antioquia for that election. The list explicitly states which local party leaders support this particular set of candidates (Jaime R. Echavarría and his additional linkage to key party leader Belasario Betancur Cuartas). Note that voters could cut out the ballot to use on Election Day.[4]

For much of Colombian political history, office-seekers needed to belong, at least nominally, to one of the two "great" political parties. Thus, different factions within the major parties, Liberal and Conservative, tended to present separate lists to compete with one another in an electoral district, but using the valuable label of either of these big parties. This had the further effect of curtailing new party development, even though the proportional electoral system should have encouraged multipartism. However, as rules changed, so too did the behavior of parties and candidates, demonstrating clearly how rules can matter for party systems.

# RELEVANT POLITICAL HISTORY AND INSTITUTIONAL CONTEXT

Colombia is a unitary state divided into thirty-two administrative departments that also serve as electoral districts for the Chamber (see Figure 41.2). The governing institutions are composed of a separation of powers system with an elected president and a bicameral legislature. There are also elected officials at the departmental and municipal level. The basic electoral system is one of proportional representation with almost identical electoral rules from the national to the local levels (with some variations).[5]

As measured by Polity IV, Colombia became democratic in 1958, the year in which a short-lived military government was replaced by a power-sharing arrangement known as the National Front. This arrangement ended in 1974, and thus we will make only brief reference to earlier times. Despite the country having qualified as democratic for nearly sixty years, indices of democracy reveal limitations since the mid-1990s.[6] During the 1974–2014 period, Colombia's Civil Liberties score on the Freedom House index averages a 3.55, putting it in the "partly free" classification for that metric. Its Political Rights score is slightly better, averaging 2.83, placing it on the border of "free" and "partly free." Like Polity IV, Freedom House downgraded Colombia in 1995 and the decade of 1995–2005 was one of Colombia being scored a 4 (or "partly free") in both categories. While still problematic, the period since 2005 has been marked by improvement. And indeed, on a number of metrics, such as kidnappings, displacements, and the homicide rate, there has been marked improvement (Taylor 2016); however, coca production has been on the rise (UNODC 2016) and continues to fuel criminality.

While the current democratic period can be said to have begun in 1958, Colombia's history of elections dates back much further. The country's experience with at least

**FIGURE 41.2.** Colombia departments and district magnitude for Chamber of Representatives (1991–2014).

limited suffrage elections started in the nineteenth century, and unlike many of its regional neighbors it has rarely been ruled by unelected autocrats. Still, the first truly democratic election (i.e., one with universal suffrage) was the December 1957 plebiscite to adopt a power-sharing agreement to re-establish civilian rule under the National Front. Ironically it was a military dictator, General Gustavo Rojas Pinilla (in power from 1953 to 1957), who extended the franchise to women, although he never provided a chance to use said right.

The National Front was a pact between the Liberal Party and the Conservative Party designed to resolve a civil war between forces of these parties. The two pillars of the agreement were parity and alternation. Parity meant that all elected and appointed positions in the Colombian government would be split fifty/fifty between the Liberals and the Conservatives. This meant that all electoral competition for legislative bodies was intraparty. This led to the factionalizing of the two parties or, more accurately, encouraged existing factions to more aggressively assert themselves and for new ones to emerge.[7] This feature also meant the deepening of the quasi-SNTV aspects of this system as factions of both parties presented separate lists that competed with others for the seats allocated to the party (Liberal or Conservative). This point will be expanded upon in the section on electing the national legislature. Alternation meant that the presidency would shift between the two parties every four years, making each electoral cycle an internal contest.[8]

The post-1974 period on which this chapter focuses is marked by two important institutional changes. The first is the promulgation of a new constitution on July 4, 1991, to replace a constitution that had been in use since 1886. The new constitution replaced plurality election of the president with a two-round majority system and shifted to nationwide election of the Senate.[9] The second significant reform occurred in 2003, which ended the LR-Hare/quasi-SNTV system for all legislative bodies, replacing it with D'Hondt. The exact nature and implications of these changes are discussed later.

Voter turnout in Colombia is low in comparison to other democratic systems, whether regionally or globally. This fact is well illustrated that in Colombia itself citizens speak of the "abstention rate" rather than speaking of "voter turnout." Table 41.1 compares turnout in presidential elections across the region for select cases during the 1974–2014 period. Colombia's average is well under 50 percent. This proclivity for low participation rates can be illustrated by pointing to two additional major elections that nonetheless drew low levels of participation. In December of 1990 the country held a plebiscite alongside an election for a constituent assembly to write a new constitution should the plebiscite pass. Turnout of the voting-aged population was 26.06 percent. A September 2016 vote on a peace accord with the rebel movement, the Revolutionary Armed Forces of Colombia (FARC), had a turnout of 37.43 percent.

Table 41.1  Selected Voter Turnout in Western Hemispheric Democracies (Presidential Elections)

| Country | Election Years | Voter Turnout |
|---|---|---|
| Uruguay | 1989–2014 | 94.77% |
| Brazil | 1989–2014 | 78.86% |
| Argentina | 1983–2011 | 78.00% |
| Peru | 1980–2016 | 75.26% |
| Chile | 1989–2013 | 68.09% |
| Bolivia | 1985–2014 | 67.08% |
| Mexico | 2000–2012 | 62.63% |
| United States | 1976–2016 | 56.05% |
| Colombia* | 1974–2014 | 44.27% |

* Final round data used for 1994-2014.

Source: IDEA (http://www.idea.int/es/data-tools/data/voter-turnout), Registraduría Nacional del Estado Civil, and authors' calculations.

# THE COLOMBIAN PARTY SYSTEM: CONGRESSIONAL ELECTIONS

In this section, we offer an overview of the Colombian party system, with a focus on congressional elections. Later sections review executive elections. All seats in both houses of the bicameral Congress are up for election simultaneously, every four years. The Chamber of Representatives and the Senate are symmetrical in legislative power. Congressional elections take place typically in March, about two months before the presidential contest.[10] Colombia thus represents a relatively rare case of a "counterhoneymoon" electoral cycle (Shugart and Carey 1992; Shugart and Taagepera 2017), in which the election of legislators shortly precedes a presidential election. Under such a cycle, the congressional election may provide information about the relative standings of various parties or intraparty factions, thereby potentially shaping the upcoming presidential election. Colombia's counterhoneymoon election cycle thus implies presidential candidates' "coattails" have little effect on the balance of forces in the Congress, in contrast to countries where legislative elections are concurrent or early in a presidential term.

The elections in 2014 to the two chambers of the Colombian Congress were the third under the current electoral system of D'Hondt PR. In the Chamber of Representatives, depicted in Table 41.2,[11] there are 166 seats elected predominantly from districts corresponding to the country's major regional subdivisions, the Departments (see

Figure 41.2). There are also 5 seats set aside for minority representation. In Table 41.2 we also see the results of the 2014 Senate election. The Senate's 102 seats are elected principally in one nationwide district of 100 seats; the other two seats are elected in a special constituency for indigenous Colombians. Note that Colombian voters have the option to vote *en blanco* (literally "white" or blank). These are valid votes for calculating quotas.[12]

The Colombian party system as we see it in the 2014 contests is a marked contrast from what it was for most of the country's history, which saw dominance of Conservatives and Liberals, both with roots in the country's early struggles over state formation. While these parties persist to the present period, their centrality clearly has diminished, owing largely to electoral reform and new pathways for partisan expression in the system.

Table 41.3 details the effective number of seat-winning parties ($N_S$) in the Colombian Congress in the post-1974 period.[13] Horizontal lines in the table indicate specific institutional eras, as described in the previous section. The numbers clearly show that over time the system has become more overtly fragmented in response to changes to the rules.

The low values of $N_S$ seen in Table 41.4 in elections from 1974 to 1990 result from the dominance of the Conservatives and Liberals. During this time, the Liberal Party always had majorities in both chambers and the only time the Conservatives won the presidency was 1982 when a splinter party, New Liberalism, ran a candidate and split the Liberal vote.[14] The low values of $N_S$, of course, mask the great intraparty fragmentation of this period, a point to which we shall return. Starting in 1991, under the new constitution, there was increased intraparty fragmentation, leading to the emergence of new parties. This was especially prominent on the Conservative side.[15] The Liberals, though internally fractionalized, initially held the line on breakaway parties due to their electoral dominance in presidential elections and their ability to command majorities in the legislature. However, as their lock on the presidency evaporated starting in 1998 and their legislative prowess started to erode, more breakaway parties formed from Liberal factions. Other new partisan entrants during this period included ex-guerrillas, evangelicals, and regional actors.

The watershed election was 2002, which saw a surge in the number of micro parties. This extreme fragmentation helped lead to the 2003 reforms (Shugart, Moreno, and Fajardo 2007). While the system has remained fragmented since 2006, it now consists of several midsized to small parties, rather than a plethora of micro parties. For comparison's sake, in 2002 there were fifty-six unique labels associated with members of the Chamber and forty-seven in the Senate.[16] In 2014 there were fifteen in the Chamber and ten in the Senate (see Table 41.2).

The stark changes in the party system are illustrated by the decline in the vote percentages obtained by the traditional parties for president (Figure 41.3) and Senate (Figure 41.4). The decline of both parties is quite evident, especially for the Conservatives. Indeed, for the presidency they disappear between 1990 and 2010, where there were no official Conservative candidates. In 1994 and 1998, a prominent member of a Conservative family, Andrés Pastrana, ran as an independent (after a stint in the Senate with his own party, the New Democratic Force).[17] He would lose in 1994 to Liberal Ernesto Samper (the last Liberal president to date) and would win in 1998; Pastrana was

## Table 41.2 Colombian Congressional Elections, 2014

| | Chamber | | | | Senate | | | |
| --- | --- | --- | --- | --- | --- | --- | --- | --- |
| | Seats | % Seats | Votes* | % Votes | Seats | % Seats | Votes† | % Votes |
| Liberal Party | 39 | 23.49% | 2,022,093 | 16.75% | 17 | 16.67% | 1,768,825 | 14.52% |
| PSUN (La U) | 37 | 22.29% | 2,297,786 | 19.04% | 21 | 20.59% | 2,268,911 | 18.62% |
| Conservative Party | 27 | 16.27% | 1,884,706 | 15.62% | 18 | 17.65% | 1,973,009 | 16.19% |
| Democratic Center | 19 | 11.45% | 1,355,700 | 11.23% | 20 | 19.61% | 2,113,347 | 17.35% |
| Radical Change | 16 | 9.64% | 1,108,502 | 9.18% | 9 | 8.82% | 1,006,260 | 8.26% |
| Green Alliance | 6 | 3.61% | 479,521 | 3.97% | 5 | 4.90% | 567,102 | 4.65% |
| Citizen's Option | 6 | 3.61% | 467,728 | 3.88% | 5 | 4.90% | 534,250 | 4.39% |
| PDA | 3 | 1.81% | 414,346 | 3.43% | | | | |
| MIRA | 3 | 1.81% | 411,800 | 3.41% | | | | |
| 100% for Colombia | 3 | 1.81% | 157,621 | 1.31% | 5 | 4.90% | 540,709 | 4.44% |
| AICO | 2 | 1.20% | 94,248 | 0.78% | | | | |
| FUNECO | 2 | 1.20% | 58,965 | 0.49% | | | | |
| For a Better Huila | 1 | 0.60% | 73,573 | 0.61% | | | | |
| ASI | 1 | 0.60% | 46,789 | 0.39% | 1 | 0.98% | 35,906 | 0.29% |
| Regional Integration | 1 | 0.60% | 4,440 | 0.04% | | | | |
| MAIS | | | | | 1 | 0.98% | 48,928 | 0.40% |
| Other | | | 100,507 | 0.83% | | | 334,836 | 2.75% |
| Other (Special) | | | 151,397 | 1.25% | | | 93,296 | 0.77% |
| Blancos | | | 824,956 | 6.83% | | | 757,907 | 6.22% |
| Blancos (Special) | | | 115,039 | 0.95% | | | 139,547 | 1.15% |
| | 166 | | 12,069,717 | 100% | 102 | | 12,182,833 | 100% |

* *Source:* Bulletin 42 http://elecciones.registraduria.gov.co:81/congreso2014/preconteo/99CA/DCA9999999_L1.htm.

† CNE Resolution 3006 of 2014.

Table 41.3 Absolute and Effective Number of Seat-Winning Parties ($N_S$), Colombian Congress, 1974–2014

|  | Chamber | | Senate | |
|---|---|---|---|---|
|  | Absolute | $N_S$ | Absolute | $N_S$ |
| 1974 | 4 | 2.28 | 4 | 2.17 |
| 1978 | 4 | 2.06 | 3 | 2.01 |
| 1982 | 4 | 1.98 | 4 | 2.04 |
| 1986 | 13 | 2.46 | 9 | 2.47 |
| 1990 | 18 | 2.20 | 11 | 2.24 |
| 1991 | 19 | 3.03 | 18 | 3.10 |
| 1994 | 25 | 2.82 | 21 | 2.90 |
| 1998 | 42 | 3.27 | 27 | 3.56 |
| 2002 | 56 | 7.39 | 47 | 9.19 |
| 2006 | 23 | 7.60 | 12 | 7.10 |
| 2010 | 16 | 5.12 | 10 | 5.77 |
| 2014 | 15 | 6.34 | 10 | 6.45 |

*Source:* Registraduría Nacional del Estado Civil and authors' calculations.

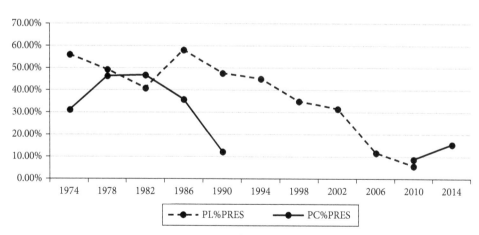

FIGURE 41.3. Liberal and Conservative vote shares, presidential elections 1974–2014.

Source: Registraduría National del Estado Civil and authors' calculations.

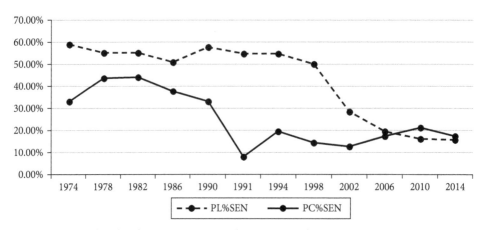

**FIGURE 41.4.** Liberal and Conservative vote shares, Senate elections, 1974–2014.

Source: Registraduría National del Estado Civil and authors' calculations.

a key promoter of reform of the electoral system, even if it would not be enacted until the presidency of his successor, in 2002. In that year a former Liberal, Álvaro Uribe Velez, ran and won as an independent.[18] He decisively won re-election in 2006 (after a constitutional amendment allowed him to run again; see discussion later). The success of Uribe clearly affected the Liberals (who plummeted in vote share as shown in Figure 41.3) and caused the Conservatives to not even run candidates in those cycles. By 2010 both traditional parties were winning less than 20 percent of the vote in the first round of presidential elections. It was this context of fragmentation of the party system that spurred the electoral-system reform of 2003, as the traditional parties now shared with many of the newer parties a desire for a system that would give more prominence to party labels and their collective identity (Shugart et al. 2007).

The party system observed in the 2014 election (see Table 41.2) has a number of moderate-sized parties that have emerged mostly since the 2003 electoral reform. In addition to the traditional parties, there are several parties that have been created by existing political elites who calculated that unique party identities would be in their political interests. The most important of these are Radical Change and the Party of National Social Unity. Radical Change was formed by dissident Liberals in 1998, but did not become significant until it became part of the pro-Uribe coalition in 2002. The Party of National Social Unity, known colloquially as "the Party of the U" or "La U," was formed rather explicitly to support Uribe in the 2006 elections, with its main founding members all being defectors from the Liberals. The most prominent of these was Juan Manuel Santos, whose granduncle had been a Liberal president of Colombia in the 1930s. Santos would go on to be defense minister in the Uribe administration, and later president (elected in 2010 and re-elected in 2014). Additional parties of note include the center-left Green Alliance and the most prominent party of the left, the Alternative Democratic Pole. A number of additional smaller parties are also electorally active.

The newest party in this constellation is the Democratic Center, which was formed by Uribe in 2014 as a vehicle for his return to electoral politics as the head of a list for the Senate. Interestingly, despite the origins of La U and Santos's service in Uribe's government, the Democratic Center has been an opposition party to the Santos administration, and an electoral competitor.

A concluding note on the party system is needed in regards to the problem of violence in Colombian parties. First, the peace process with the FARC will lead to the formation of a new party for the ex-guerrillas. It is worth noting that a party linked to the FARC was founded back in 1985 as the result of peace talks at the time. The Patriotic Union (UP) would go on to win seats in Congress, as well as a handful of mayoralties. However, they would suffer a great deal from political violence. Between 3,500 and 4,000 UP members and associates would be murdered by paramilitary groups between 1988 and 2004.[19] The Patriotic Union still exists, and it ran as part of a coalition of the Left in the 2014 presidential elections (see Table 41.8).

In addition to the gruesome history of the UP, there have been ties between Colombian political parties and paramilitary groups in recent years. For example, in 2006–2010, the National Integration Party (PIN) was formed by relatives and associates of several parties that had been linked to paramilitary groups whose members were either indicted or sentenced to prison. This party was also disbanded in the wake of the "parapolítica" scandal that sent several members of Congress to prison in the early 2000s. Some remnants of political actors affiliated with the PIN continue to run (and win) seats in Congress under the label Citizen's Option.

These two bits of recent history underscore that party politics in Colombia remain placed in a context of violence that cannot be forgotten and that is central to remember as the country works to integrate the FARC into civilian life (as it also hopes to do with the National Liberation Army, i.e., the ELN).

# THE ELECTORAL SYSTEM AND ITS REFORMS IN 1991 AND 2003

In this section, we go into deeper detail on the electoral systems, following the division of periods established in the prior section: (1) 1974–1990 under quasi-SNTV (LR-Hare with multiple lists per party); (2) 1991–2002 with the same formula but changes in districting, particularly the adoption of the nationwide Senate district; and (3) the post-2003 adoption of D'Hondt divisors with party option to present either an open or closed list.

District magnitude and assembly size, the two critical defining features of an electoral system aside from the seat allocation formula (Shugart and Taagepera, this volume), change only with the constitutional reform of 1991. These changes are summarized in Table 41.4. The 1991 reform reduced the size of the Chamber of Representatives, from

Table 41.4  Assembly Size (*S*) and District Magnitude (*M*), Colombian Congress (Excluding Special Seats)

| | *S* (Chamber) | *S* (Senate) | Average *M* (Chamber) | Average *M* (Senate) |
|---|---|---|---|---|
| 1974–1990 | 199 | 112 (1974–1978) | 7.24 | 5.09 (1974–1978) |
| | | 114 (1982–1990) | | 4.96 (1982–1990) |
| 1991–2014 | 161 | 100 | 4.88 | 100 |

*Source:* Registraduría Nacional del Estado Civil and authors' calculations.

199 to 161 (not counting special minority seats, which we will discuss separately), and substantially reduced the average district magnitude. This reduction in the number of representatives left Colombia with one of the most undersized first chambers, relative to population, of any long-term democracy (Taylor et al. 2014, 212), yet the more significant change was to the Senate. Prior to 1991, like the Chamber, it was elected in departmental districts. Since then it has been elected in a one-hundred-seat nationwide district. This reform did not change the electoral formula, thus giving Colombia several years under what is by far the largest district ever used with a (quasi-)SNTV formula. The changes summarized in Table 41.4 make Colombia an unusual case in which it is the second chamber (Senate) that represents the population, via the nationwide district, while the first chamber represents regions.[20]

Colombia's history of proportional representation dates to 1929, when LR-Hare was established by law.[21] Lists were always closed until the 2003 reform gave parties the option of presenting open lists, which, as we shall see, has been the prevalent choice. However, it would be highly misleading to refer to the pre-2003 system as closed-list PR, or as list PR at all, because of the tendency of parties to offer numerous lists per district. There was intense intraparty competition as a result of multiple factions of the Liberals and Conservatives, reflecting allegiances to different regional or national leaders. As time progressed, party leaders, especially in the Liberal Party, understood that running more lists gave them an electoral advantage.[22] As the behavior of parties evolved over time, the LR-Hare system became one of "personal lists" in that it was rare, especially in the Chamber, for any list to have sufficient votes to elect more than its top candidate. This is what made the system essentially SNTV rather than list PR (Cox and Shugart 1995).

SNTV is a top-*M* system, meaning that the candidates with the *M* highest vote shares win the seats, regardless of party affiliation. In Colombia, these winners were technically the heads of lists, which would include other nominees aside from the list head, but given that few lists could win, or would have expected to win, more than one seat, the system was hardly different from SNTV. In practice, a party typically would win only as many seats as it had personal lists that finished with the top

$M$ vote totals in a district. As with "pure" SNTV, the system rewarded a party that could equalize the votes among its candidates (or an electable subset of its candidates if it has more running than the party can possibly elect). This phenomenon is well known from the experience of strictly SNTV systems in Japan and Taiwan (e.g., Batto 2008; Cox and Niou 1994; Grofman et al. 1999; Reed 2009; Shugart and Taagepera 2017). Colombian parties, particularly the major ones, typically had numerous lists running in each district.

The system was not pure SNTV, insofar as some lists did win multiple seats, although the vast majority of lists won only one seat. In addition, prior to 1991, if a member left office before the end of the term, he or she had a *suplente* (substitute) on the list who would assume the seat (see Figure 41.1). From 1991, the *suplente* list was eliminated, and a vacancy was filled by the next available candidate. Lists electing more than one member became less common over time. For example, in 1991 nine Senate lists won multiple seats (accounting for 34 of 102 seats). That number would dwindle to three lists in the elections prior to the shift to D'Hondt, accounting for only six seats in 1994 and 1998, and seven in 2002 (Taylor 2009, 121). Between 1991 and 2002, the incidence of multi-seat-winning lists was even rarer in the Chamber; four lists won multiple seats in 1991 and two lists won multiple seats in 1998 (and there were no multiseat winners in 1994 and 2002).[23] Table 41.5 illustrates the Liberals' and Conservatives' substantial degree of overnomination prior to the 2003 reforms. Figure 41.5, which is the Chamber ballot for the department of Sucre in 1991, illustrates this tendency quite clearly. Even though this is a district with a small $M$ (three), there are seventeen lists (each number represents a list, not just a single candidate) and the Liberals offered six lists and the Conservatives three. The ballot also illustrates that voters had

Table 41.5  Number of Liberal and Conservative Electoral List for the Senate, 1974–2002

|  | Number of Territorial Districts | Number of Liberal Lists | Number of Conservative Lists |
|---|---|---|---|
| 1974 | 22 | 67 | 54 |
| 1978 | 22 | 92 | 61 |
| 1982 | 23 | 104 | 72 |
| 1986 | 23 | 73 | 67 |
| 1990 | 23 | 107 | 57 |
| 1991 | 1 | 90 | 25 |
| 1994 | 1 | 134 | 35 |
| 1998 | 1 | 147 | 25 |
| 2002 | 1 | 148 | 30 |

*Source:* Registraduría Nacional del Estado Civil and authors' calculations.

FIGURE 41.5. 1991 Chamber ballot, Department of Sucre.

the choice to vote in either the departmental district or the national election for Afro-Colombians (discussed later).

The phenomenon of multiple lists was due to the fact that there was never, until 2003, any legal requirement for parties to limit the number of lists per district. In fact, until 1994 parties lacked a legal mechanism to control their labels. As a result, multiple

Table 41.6 Quota versus Largest-Remainder Winners, Colombian Congress, 1974–2002

| | Percentage Quota Winners | Percentage Largest-Remainder Winners |
|---|---|---|
| Chamber | | |
| 1974–1990 | 34.37% | 65.63% |
| 1991–2002 | 4.62% | 95.38% |
| Senate | | |
| 1974–1990 | 30.44% | 69.56% |
| 1991–2001 | 18.63% | 81.37% |

Source: Taylor (2009, 114).

factions of the traditional parties would offer lists in a given district, taking advantage of the cheaper "wholesale price" of seats via remainders, as Carey (this volume) terms it (as illustrated in Table 41.6). Because remainder seats cost less, in terms of votes, than do quota seats, the system is supposed to work in such a way that large parties mostly pay full price (i.e., a full quota) for most of their seats, while small parties could win a bargain-price largest-remainder seat here and there.[24] However, with multiple lists per party, Colombia's version of LR-Hare allowed the big parties to have their size and bargain shop too. If small parties overnominated, they risked diluting their votes, leading to fewer seats than they would have won had they made better strategic choices.[25] Despite the large number of lists under this system, the Liberal and Conservative Parties became adept at managing their votes such that their rate of commission of "errors" (failing to elect the number of candidates that they had collective votes to elect, due to divisions) declined over time (Cox and Shugart 1995).

# THE ELECTORAL REFORM OF 2003

In 2003, the electoral rules were reformed to shift the system to allocate seats via D'Hondt divisors, with parties given the option for their lists to be open or closed (see Figure 41.6). Interest in changing the electoral system was driven by discontent over the impact of the 1991 constitutional reforms. Fragmentation had only increased in the interim. As shown, the new post-1991 acceleration of fragmentation included a proliferation of new party labels, yet at the same time continuing intraparty fragmentation through the presentation of multiple competing lists within the parties, in particular the Liberal Party. Summing up the need to change the electoral system, then-president Andrés Pastrana said, in 1998, "Our political system . . . is marked by a crisis of representation wherein citizens do not recognize their elected officials as the spokesmen

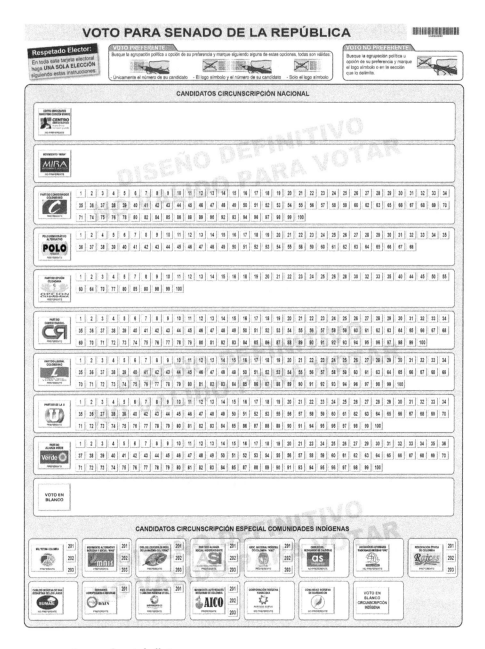

**FIGURE 41.6.** 2014 Senate ballot.

of collective interests. Instead, these officials are generally identified as the purveyors of local favors and nothing else" (República de Colombia 1998). With this statement, Pastrana was indicating that political parties, and their labels, were weak under the extant Colombian electoral system. The advocates of reform thus correctly identified the quasi-SNTV features of the system as a key cause for the lack of collective account-ability in the legislative party system. Accordingly, they promoted adoption of the *cifra repartidora*, otherwise known as the D'Hondt divisor formula. The new law restricted parties to one list per district, although in fact the use of D'Hondt renders the restric-tion moot. Unlike with LR-Hare, in which a party can gain by splintering as long as it can manage its votes across its multiple lists, under D'Hondt splintering can cost a party seats (see Carey, this volume).

A particularly contentious aspect of the reform debate was the *type* of list—open, closed, or some hybrid (Shugart et al. 2007). In the end, the two chambers of Congress agreed on a compromise measure that allowed each party the option of presenting either an open or closed list. (A party is free to vary its list type across different dis-tricts, even in the same election.) In an open list, any seats a party wins (based on application of D'Hondt to all parties' vote totals in the district) are awarded to can-didates in the order determined by their preference votes. In the version adopted in Colombia, the preference vote is optional—a voter may simply indicate a party vote even if the list the party has presented is open. Crucially, however, party-label votes on an open list have no bearing on the order of election. That is, a voter who casts a label vote is essentially delegating to the party's other voters the choices of which candidates will take any seats the party wins. Only if the party has opted to present a closed list is there a pre-established party ranking of the candidates to determine which ones are elected.

As shown by Pachón and Shugart (2010), the immediate effect of the reform was to reduce, at the district level, the effective number of vote-earning parties ($N_V$) in larger-magnitude districts, but to increase it in the smaller districts. This pattern shows the twin effects of the change from what was essentially an SNTV system to D'Hondt. Under the former system, much competition was intraparty, and thus in low-magnitude dis-tricts often both winners (if M = 2) or two winners (if M = 3, for example) were sepa-rate lists bearing the label of the same party. On the other hand, in higher-magnitude districts, the LR-Hare (quasi-SNTV) system meant that the last winners could be lists either from a major party or from a small party that had concentrated its votes. Because a seat could be won on an exceedingly small share of the district votes, large-magnitude districts—especially the one-hundred-seat Senate—could see many very small parties with representation. Given the change to D'Hondt, parties with small vote shares could no longer be so sure of winning a seat, and so the new system encouraged consolidation of party labels.

The consolidation of the party system is apparent in the effective number of *seat*-winning parties ($N_S$) for the Senate in Table 41.3 by comparing the values for 2002 and 2006. In the Senate, with its one-hundred-seat district, $N_S$ dropped from 9.19 to 7.10, still a high figure, but a big drop for a single election.[26] The proliferation of small seat-winning parties was further reduced by the adoption of a legal threshold, initially 2 per-cent of the national vote, raised to 3 percent in 2014. The increase in $N_S$ for the Chamber in 2006 results mainly from variation across districts in the new parties that entered lists under the new system. (This figure also dropped in the 2010 election and remained below the 2002 value in 2014.)

In Table 41.7 we offer an example from one district showing how parties and individual politicians adapted to the changed incentives of the new system, comparing the results in the Cauca district in 2002 and 2006. This district has a magnitude of four, making it just under the Chamber mean (see Table 41.4). Winning candidates in each election are shown in bold. In 2002, the party names are indicated in a separate column after the name of the candidate who headed his or her own list, and we indicate the votes for each "personal" list. No list came close to winning a quota seat, and hence all seats were won via largest remainders. Thus, the candidates with the top four vote totals each won a seat, regardless of party.

The 2002 result is a classic "SNTV" outcome, in that the fourth seat was won cheaply, with only about 60 percent of the votes of the first winner. These candidates, García (22,593 votes) and Negret (37,708), were both from the Liberal Party. The Liberal Party did an excellent job of equalizing the votes of its third and fourth candidates, suggesting it was aiming to manage its votes so as to elect three in the district. However, unfortunately for the party, Orozco's 22,383 made him narrowly the first loser. Given the SNTV-like features of the system, the party could not transfer any surplus from its "too popular" candidate, Negret, nor from its "hopeless" candidate, López De Joaquin, whose votes were about half that of Orozco's. Thus, of the four seats in the district, two were won by Liberals, and each of the others by candidates bearing separate labels. The Liberals wasted a lot of votes from having too many lists (overnomination) and from the failed equalization of votes on their most viable lists.

Now compare the 2006 result. Here we see candidate votes indicated again, but now we have grouped them by party, reflecting how the electoral system aggregates votes and how the ballot organizes the voting process. Voters must select a party; then they may select a candidate, if their party has presented an open list. We see that some candidates have changed labels between the two elections, reflecting the realignment of the party system that resulted from a new electoral system that put more emphasis on parties as collective actors. One of our losing Liberals from 2002, López De Joaquin, has won a seat on the Liberal list. When her votes and those of other candidates (and votes solely for the label) are summed and compared to the votes of other parties in the district, she is joined in the Chamber delegation from Cauca by another Liberal candidate. The imbalance of their votes no longer matters, because seats are allocated first to lists, and only then to candidates.

We also see that one of the winners from 2002, Piamba, wins a seat on the Conservative Party list. He had won on a distinct label in 2002 (Movimiento Unionista) but linked up with other Conservatives in 2006. Importantly, his own 22,093 votes (not too different from what he won with in 2002) would have been insufficient to win in 2006 were it not for the pooling of other Conservative votes on one list. Yet another of the winners from 2002 shifted to another list, that of Radical Change (which also had a candidate who had run as a Conservative in 2002), and

**Table 41.7 District-Level Results in 2002 (Quasi-SNTV) and 2006 (D'Hondt List-PR): Cauca**

| 2002 | | | 2006 | | | |
|---|---|---|---|---|---|---|
| Candidate (List Head) | Party | Votes | Party and Candidate | Candidate Votes | Party Votes | Seats by Party |
| **Cesar Negret** | **Liberal** | **37,708** | Liberal | | 60,966 | 2 |
| **José Piamba** | **Unionist Mov.** | **27,884** | (votes for list) | 5,990 | | |
| Luís Velasco | Liberal Opening | 24,452 | **Gema López De Joaquin** | **29,204** | | |
| **Jesus García** | **Liberal** | **22,593** | **Crisanto Pizo** | **9,652** | | |
| Felipe Orozco | Liberal | 22,383 | Emith Montilla | 8,729 | | |
| Diego Llanos | Conservative | 14,673 | Orlan Vergara | 7,391 | | |
| Carlos Solarte | Social Indígena | 14,673 | Conservative | | 35,745 | 1 |
| Gema López De Joaquin | Liberal | 12,022 | (votes for list) | 2,235 | | |
| María Elena Ramírez | ANAPO | 8,236 | **José Piamba** | **22,093** | | |
| María Del Carmen Florez | Radical Change | 5,538 | José Silva | 4,383 | | |
| Edgar Guaza | Radical Change | 4,841 | (two others combined) | 7,034 | | |
| (8 others combined) | | 21,615 | Radical Change | | 27,140 | 1 |
| | | | (votes for list) | 2,439 | | |
| | | | **Felipe Orozco** | **10,773** | | |
| | | | Diego Llanos | 9,766 | | |
| | | | (two others combined) | 4,162 | | |
| | | | (10 other parties combined) | | 70,751 | 0 |

Winners in **bold**.

Quota in 2002: 54,026.

*Source:* Registraduría Nacional del Estado Civil.

won a seat, despite a sharp decline in his own votes. In this way we see the priority that the D'Hondt system of 2006 (and subsequent elections) places on collective vote shares for candidates running under common labels that pool votes.[27] The number of parties that won in this district stayed the same between the two elections, but the way in which they won seats was no longer by how many candidates (technically, personal lists) they placed in the top four vote totals, but how their pooled votes translated into seats under the rule of D'Hondt divisors.

Table 41.8 offers a second example of the impact of the change at the district level. In this case, we consider one of Colombia's smallest districts, electing just two members. As we noted previously, in these districts, the tendency under the old system was often for

Table 41.8  District-Level Results in 2002 (Quasi-SNTV) and 2006 (D'Hondt List-PR): Chocó

| 2002 | | | 2006 | | | |
|---|---|---|---|---|---|---|
| Candidate (list head) | Party | Votes | Party and Candidate | Candidate votes | Party votes | Seats by party |
| **Darío Córdoba** | Liberal | **18,977** | Partido Social de Unidad Nacional | | 15,618 | 1 |
| **Edgar Eulices Torres** | Liberal | **17,893** | (votes for list) | 3,001 | | |
| (name missing) | Liberal | 16,066 | **Odin Sanchez** | **10,834** | | |
| Esteban Caicedo | Conservative | 2,986 | Ismael De Jesus Aladana | 1,783 | | |
| Yesíd Perea | Popular Participation | 1,215 | Radical Change | | 13,670 | 1 |
| Jorge Iván Salgado | MOIR | 513 | (votes for list) | 13,670 | | |
| Ramiro Botero | Christian Union | 329 | **Edgar Eulices Torres** | (closed list) | | |
| (no other candidates) | | | Liberal | | 9,023 | 0 |
| | | | (votes for list) | 9,023 | | |
| | | | Francisco Córdoba López | (closed list) | | |
| | | | (other parties not shown) | | | 0 |

Winners in **bold.**

*Source:* Registraduría Nacional del Estado Civil.

both seats to be won by separate lists of one party, but in the new system often the seats have gone to separate parties. Under D'Hondt, the leading party wins the second seat only if it has double the votes of the runner-up party. In Chocó in 2002, the top three lists were headed by Liberals, and no candidate of any other party was competitive.[28] The three candidates have approximately equal votes, with the third one having nearly 85 percent of the votes of the leader. In other words, competition was entirely intraparty, with three candidates competing for two seats—conforming nicely to the "$M + 1$ rule" noticed by Reed (1990) for SNTV in Japan.

We see that a Liberal list head who was elected in 2002, Torres, ran in 2006 with Radical Change. This list was closed, with Torres ranked in the first position and thereby assured of election (as long as the list qualified for a seat, which it did easily). The Liberal Party also presented a closed list (but did not win).[29] Meanwhile, the Party of National Social Unity presented an open list, but one candidate dominated the preference votes within this list. Effectively, then, competition changed from purely intraparty in 2002 (with three roughly even Liberal vote winners vying for the two seats) to purely interparty in 2006—in one list because most votes were cast for one of the candidates, and in the others because of a list format prohibiting competition between the list's candidates.

The example of two of the three main parties in Chocó in 2006 presenting closed lists conforms to a pattern observed by Pachón and Shugart (2010) and Achury, Ramírez, and Cantú (2017). Closed lists are more common in low-magnitude districts, where a party expects to elect only one candidate anyway. The closed list then effectively signals that this is the list of whichever candidate the party is putting forward as its proposed representative. The second candidate is effectively not competing for votes and would win only in the unlikely event the list doubled the votes of its closest competitor. Closed lists also tend to be presented by parties that are strongly identified by a single leader. For instance, when ex-president Álvaro Uribe formed his own party, Democratic Center in 2014, he was the head of a closed list for the Senate. Other examples have included various parties formed by politicians based on the capital, Bogotá, who presented closed lists in Chamber districts around the country. In this way they downplay the identities of their individual candidates and can focus the campaign around the nationwide reputation of the party leader.

In this sense, and perhaps ironically, the closed lists are often the choice of the most personalistic parties, by which we mean those that are vehicles for the ambitions of a single leader. By contrast, open lists tend to be presented by parties that have several local candidates with personal vote-mobilizing organizations (e.g., the Liberal Party in many of the larger-magnitude districts) or—again, perhaps ironically—those that have a strong party label and want to motivate their candidates to work to get out the vote (e.g., the Democratic Pole; see Achury et al., 2017). In practice, a large majority of representatives and senators have been elected on open lists,[30] but the Colombian electoral law has the unusual feature of giving parties the option of averting competition for votes among their candidates.

# SPECIAL CONSTITUENCIES FOR MINORITIES

Colombia is one of several countries to have special constituencies to represent designated minorities (see the chapter by Lublin and Bowler in this volume for a comparison of such cases). These provisions were first established in the constitution of 1991, which provided for two Senate seats to represent the indigenous population. The 1991 constitution allowed for the creation of special seats (up to five) to represent Afro-Colombians, indigenous communities, Colombians living abroad, or other political minorities. Starting in 1994 a national district was created to select two seats for Afro-Colombians. This was expanded starting in 2002 to include one seat for indigenous persons, one for Colombians abroad, and one for political minorities.

This was later codified in the constitution in 2005, with the seats for Colombians abroad increasing to two in a 2013 reform. Starting in 2018 the number of seats for those abroad goes back to one and an ethnic minority in the San Andrés archipelago will get a special seat. Table 41.9 summarizes the provisions and the year they were added.

In the special constituencies for Afro-Colombians and for indigenous groups, the ballot gives voters the option of voting either in the regular constituency—i.e., the one-hundred-seat Senate district or their departmental district for Chamber—or instead voting in the special constituency (this is illustrated in Figures 41.5 and 41.6). Voters

## Table 41.9 Special Seats in the Colombian Congress

|      | Chamber Special Seats                                                                          | Senate Special Seats     |
| ---- | ---------------------------------------------------------------------------------------------- | ------------------------ |
| 1991 | None                                                                                           | Indigenous persons (2)   |
| 1994 | Afro-Colombians (2)                                                                            | Indigenous persons (2)   |
| 1998 | Afro-Colombians (2)                                                                            | Indigenous persons (2)   |
| 2002 | Afro-Colombians (2)<br>Indigenous persons (1)<br>Colombians abroad (1)                         | Indigenous persons (2)   |
| 2006 | Afro-Colombians (2)<br>Indigenous persons (1)<br>Colombians abroad (1)<br>Political minorities (1) | Indigenous persons (2)   |
| 2010 | Afro-Colombians (2)<br>Indigenous persons (1)<br>Colombians abroad (1)                         | Indigenous persons (2)   |
| 2014 | Afro-Colombians (2)<br>Indigenous persons (1)<br>Colombians abroad (2)                         | Indigenous persons (2)   |

*Source:* Authors' compilation from constitutional provisions.

choose at the polling place and do not have to belong to the minority group in question.[31] Colombians abroad, however, are treated as belonging to one global territorial district.

Building on the established concept of set-aside seats, the peace agreement with the FARC guerrillas, signed in 2016, proposes to create new seats to represent the political party that the FARC will form. This party will be guaranteed five seats in each chamber—with whatever seats they win via election being augmented up to five if they do not win them outright. The provisions will be in force only for the 2018 and 2022 elections.[32] The peace agreement further establishes transitional "peace constituencies," each consisting of a single seat to be contested by nonparty candidates in areas that were especially affected by the armed conflict (La Silla Vacia 2017). The precise details could yet change, given that as of late 2017 the peace accords were not fully implemented.

## Electing the National Executive

Direct election of the president dates to 1914. From that point until 1994, the president was elected via plurality to a four-year term. The 1991 constitution inserted an absolute majority requirement, with provision for a runoff between the top two if there was no majority in the first round. Under the 1886 constitution presidents could not stand for immediate re-election, but were eligible for nonconsecutive terms.[33] Under the 1991 constitution re-election was totally barred, but in 2005 the constitution was amended to allow for the immediate re-election of the president for a maximum of two terms. This led to Álvaro Uribe being the first popularly elected president in Colombian history to serve back-to-back terms (elected in 2002 and again in 2006). There was an attempt at an amendment in 2009 to allow Uribe to run for a third term, but it was blocked by the Constitutional Court. Juan Manuel Santos, Uribe's immediate successor, would go on to also serve two consecutive terms. However, the ability to be re-elected was removed in 2015, reverting the constitution to its original state on this matter.

Table 41.10 details the number of candidates who ran in each election since 1974, the effective number of presidential candidates, and the share of the vote won by the top two candidates. In the 1974–1990 period the effective number of candidates averaged 2.47, while in the majority-runoff era from 1994 on the average has been 3.11. Prior to 1990, the top two candidates dominated the field, combining for 87 percent or more of the vote. It is noteworthy that the 1990 election is the one that sees the spike in the number of candidates running (13), and a top-two share of just over 70 percent.

While the 1990 election was still in the plurality era, it was the first election in which there was a state-printed ballot, which may have lowered the barriers to entry for smaller party candidates (who would have been disadvantaged by the prior requirement to print and distribute their own ballots around the country). It was also the election marked by the participation in politics for the first time of a demobilized guerrilla group, the M-19, whose candidate, Antonio Navarro Wolf, won 12.6 percent of the vote. The election

### Table 41.10  Presidential Elections, 1974–2014

| | Absolute Number of Candidates | Effective Number of Candidates | Top Two Party Totals |
|---|---|---|---|
| 1974 | 6 | 2.36 | 87.58% |
| 1978 | 9 | 2.17 | 95.95% |
| 1982 | 5 | 2.51 | 87.65% |
| 1986 | 5 | 2.12 | 94.19% |
| 1990 | 13 | 3.17 | 71.52% |
| 1994 | 18 | 2.53 | 88.66% |
| 1998 | 13 | 3.15 | 69.78% |
| 2002 | 11 | 2.48 | 86.38% |
| 2006 | 7 | 2.22 | 84.37% |
| 2010 | 9 | 3.46 | 68.18% |
| 2014 | 5 | 4.77 | 55.00% |

*Source:* Registraduría National dEstado Civil and authors' calculations.

also featured a split in the Conservative Party into the National Salvation Movement and the Social Conservatives. This election thus marks the beginning of the fragmentation of the national party system, as well as the entry of new actors. It also coincided with a national movement to replace the country's constitution,[34] with the Constituent Assembly being elected in 1991 to carry out the task.[35] Thus, in terms of the relationship between presidential-election rules and the number of competitors (see Jones, this volume), we can say that the change from plurality rule to majority runoff followed from political fragmentation at the top, rather than was a cause of it. Nonetheless, the trend of an increasing number of entrants continued in subsequent elections until 2006, which, as noted previously, was the first one in which an incumbent was running. That the effective number of candidates was lower in both 2002 and 2006 than other elections after the implementation of the 1991 constitution is attributable to the popularity of Uribe, the only candidate to win the presidency in the first round since the majority requirement was introduced.

The 2014 elections (see Table 41.11) illustrate the basics of the current party system as described earlier. Interestingly, 2014 had the lowest number of candidates since 1986, but also had the lowest top-two vote share of all time. And while the number of candidates was smaller, a large number of parties participated under alliance tickets. Santos ran for re-election as part of a coalition of La U, Radical Change, and the Liberals. The Left ran a coalitional ticket of the Alternative Democratic Pole and the Patriotic Union. The second round was an almost ideal-type example of intraround coalition building: the

### Table 41.11  2014 Presidential Elections

| First Round (May) | | | |
|---|---|---|---|
| Óscar Iván Zuluaga | Democratic Center | 3,769,005.00 | 29.28% |
| Juan Manuel Santos Calderón | National Unity (La U/CR/PL) | 3,310,794.00 | 25.72% |
| Martha Lucía Ramírez | Conservative Party | 1,997,980.00 | 15.52% |
| Clara López | Alternative Democratic Pole/ Patriotic Union | 1,958,518.00 | 15.22% |
| Enrique Peñalosa | Green Party | 1,064,758.00 | 8.27% |
| Blank votes | | 770,543.00 | 5.99% |
| | | 12,871,598.00 | 100% |
| **Second Round (June)** | | | |
| Juan Manuel Santos Calderón | National Unity (La U/CR/PL) | 7,839,342 | 50.99% |
| Óscar Iván Zuluaga | Democratic Center | 6,917,001 | 44.99% |
| Blank votes | | 618,759 | 4.02% |
| Total Valid Votes | | 15,375,102 | 100.00% |

*Source:* Registraduría Nacional del Estado Civil and authors' calculations.

Conservatives overtly teamed up with the Democratic Center, while the Greens and the left alliance backed the National Unity Coalition.

Another element of presidential elections in Colombia has been the use of a type of open primary to nominate presidential candidates. This has occurred on a limited basis since 1990 when the Liberal Party first used an "internal consultation" (*consulta popular*) to select its candidate (Shugart 1992). The mechanism was deployed in the wake of the assassination of the party's presumptive nominee, Luis Carlos Galán, at a campaign event in 1989. The primary has been an intermittent feature of Colombian presidential elections since that time, with the Liberals using it in 1990, 1994, 2006, and 2009; the Greens and the Alternative Democratic Pole in 2009; and the Conservatives in 2010.

# Conclusion

Colombia's electoral system is one that had demonstrated a central notion of the electoral studies literature: that electoral rules matter to the political behavior of both those who vote and those who pursue votes. A main manifestation of this theoretical assumption is that parties will adapt to rules to capture the votes needed to win office.

As a case study, Colombia provides numerous examples of such adaptive behavior, as illustrated by the shift over time in both the effective number of parties and the absolute number of parties competing between 1974 and 2014 (as detailed in Table 41.2). Over that period of time we can see how major changes such as shifts in district magnitude for the Senate and the change to D'Hondt directly influenced the number of parties competing in elections. Specifically, too, these changes demonstrate the fact that groups of candidates understand the importance of party labels as a signaling device to attract voters. As such, the post-2003 rules allow parties to present either open or closed lists—probably the only electoral system in the world leaving this important matter to the discretion of parties. As we detailed, there are predictable patterns connecting the political context of a given party, district, and election to the choice of list type.

Colombia has maintained a competitive electoral democracy through decades in which the country has been beset with violence, both from left-wing guerrillas and from right-wing paramilitary forces. In an effort to strengthen democracy, Colombian elites and popular movements have promoted—and, as we have seen, sometimes enacted—significant institutional reforms. Thus, it is impossible to speak of an electoral system that is completely "stable"; there are ongoing proposals for reform, some of them connected to the ongoing peace process with guerrilla organizations. Yet the lack of stability in rules over recent decades has not meant that actors are unable to adapt to changes in rules in predictable ways. It is this process of reform and adaptation that makes Colombia a crucial case study for the way electoral systems function in their political context.

## Notes

1. These terms are explained later; see also Carey (this volume).
2. As discussed in detail later, a closed list means voters must vote for the party as a whole; the candidates are ranked by the party prior to the election. In an open list, voters may vote for a candidate on a list, and the candidates are elected from the list in the order of their vote totals. The only other country we know of that gives parties more than one option of how to organize their general-election lists is Denmark (see Elklit 2005), although a closed list is not one of the options for Danish parties.
3. The state did not start producing ballots until the May 1990 presidential election. Prior to that time, ballots were privately produced and distributed either by party (or, often, factional) operatives or via newspapers. For a history of the Colombian ballot see Taylor (2012). Analysis of the impact of ballot design on voter behavior in Colombia is further discussed in Pachón et al. (2017).
4. The right column of names for each office, headed "Suplentes," contains substitute candidates who would take the office if the elected principal resigned. We discuss substitute candidates briefly later.
5. The main difference is that governors and mayors are elected via plurality, whereas the presidency requires an absolute majority.

6. Colombia has been categorized as democratic, but "fractionalized" since 1995. See http://www.systemicpeace.org/polity/col2.htm (accessed April 2, 2017).

7. See Taylor (2009, 44–52).

8. Although the only truly competitive election was in 1970, which likely ended in electoral fraud when a Conservative faction (really, another party for all practical purposes and despite the rules of the National Front) called the National Popular Alliance (ANAPO) headed by the former dictator, Gustavo Rojas Pinilla, likely won the election, but the official candidate, Misael Pastrana was declared the winner.

9. Beyond the scope of this chapter, there were important changes to the powers of the presidency (Archer and Shugart 1997), as well as in the judiciary and decentralization of the political system, including the election of departmental governors. Direct election of mayors had already been introduced in the 1980s.

10. Since 1958, the only exceptions have been in 1970 and 1974 (when congressional and presidential elections were concurrent) and 1991 (when a special early election only for Congress was called in October under the newly enacted constitution).

11. Note that the votes for the Chamber are incomplete, as Bulletin 42 only contained 98.42 percent of the polling places having been counted. Final data are not available. The Senate data represent the final, certified vote count.

12. If the blank vote wins, new elections are called. In the case of mayor races, for example, a new contest requires all new candidates. This has happened on rare occasion (see El Pais 2011).

13. The effective number of parties is a size-weighted index of party system fragmentation. For details, see Shugart and Taagepera (this volume).

14. In 1982 Belasario Betancur won 46.69 percent of the vote, with the Liberal, Alfonso López, winning 40.96 percent, and the New Liberal, Luis Carlos Galan, winning 10.92 percent.

15. These included, but were not limited to, the National Salvation Movement, the National Conservative Movement, the New Democratic Force, Independent Conservatism, and the Progressive Force. Indeed, the mainline party itself demonstrated its own internal identity crisis by changing its name to the Social Conservative Party in the late 1980s/early 1990s (it would drop the "Social" from the label by the mid-1990s).

16. Note that seventeen of the Chamber and six of the Senate seats were elected on coalitional tickets where there may have been some repetition of party labels that elected candidates outside of those coalitions as well.

17. Pastrana was Bogotá's first elected mayor in 1988, as a Conservative. Further, his father, Misael, was a leader of the Conservative Party and was president from 1970 to 1974. During the Santos administration, Pastrana emerged as a key voice against the peace process and ally to Uribe.

18. He served in the Senate for 1986–1990, 1990–1991, and 1991–1994. He also was governor of Antioquia from 1995 to 1997. He ran in 2002 as "Uribe Presidente"/"Colombia First." In 2006 he simply used "Colombia First."

19. See Taylor (2009, 153 and n34) for details. See also Dudley (2004).

20. Such a division between chambers is not unique, as it is found in Paraguay and Uruguay as well.

21. From 1910 the law mandated some sort of representation of minority parties but did not specify the exact system to be used (see Baron 1915, 3–17; Eastman 1982, 226–227; and Mazzuca and Robinson 2006).

22. The clearest example of this can be found in the 1990 elections for the National Constituent Assembly, which used one national district (like the Senate rules starting in 1991). In that election, Liberal Party leaders decided to offer multiple lists rather than a unified list and dubbed the approach *Operación Avispa* or Operation: Wasp, insofar as the goal was to win by a swarm of small stings. As a result, while the unified AD/M-19 list won more votes (992,613 vs. 903,984), the Liberals won more seats, 22 to 19.
23. These were all two-seat winning lists, save for one list in Antioquia that won three seats in 1991.
24. Carey shows how parties in Hong Kong have followed a similar evolution under LR-Hare as their counterparts in Colombia decades earlier—presenting multiple lists to maximize their chances of winning seats "cheaply" via remainders.
25. See Taylor (2009, 125–128) for examples, the most prominent being the case of AD/M-19, which had been quite successful with a single list in 1991, but a combination of strategic errors and internal divisions doomed the party in subsequent elections. Radical Change also cost itself seats in 2002 with overnomination.
26. It might be argued that the 2002 high values were unsustainable and were likely to come down even with no electoral system reform. Obviously, this is not testable, but in any case, it was the highly fragmented election of 2002 that spurred the passage of a reform that had been in discussion since the 1998 election. Moreover, as we show later, the behavior of parties after the reform follows closely the incentives that we would expect to have been introduced by the new system.
27. This feature of the changed system is further demonstrated by the fact that the winners in 2006 are not the four candidates with the most votes, as the second Radical Change candidate has more votes than the second Liberal candidate. Yet the latter won a seat, due to his list having had significantly more votes.
28. The name of the third candidate is missing in the original data that we obtained from the electoral authority.
29. This candidate was an incumbent member who had been ranked second on Darío Córdoba's list and assumed the seat when it became vacant during the term of the Congress elected in 2002.
30. Based on replication data for Achury et al. (2017), generously provided by the authors, only 10 percent of deputies elected in the 2006–2014 period have been from closed lists.
31. In this way, the provisions for minorities are fundamentally different from those in New Zealand (where Maori voters can register to vote in special constituencies—see the chapter by Vowles) or India (where set-aside seats are restricted to candidates of the minority group, but with a single pool of voters—see the chapter by Ziegfeld).
32. The provisions are contained in section 3.2.1.1 of the accords. See https://draftable.com/compare/JjypTOknafBktqvc (accessed June 25, 2017).
33. This only happened once under the 1886 constitution: Alfonso López Pumarejo served from 1934 to 1938 and 1942 to 1946. The closest any other president came was López's son, Alfonso López Michelsen, who served as president from 1974 to 1978 and then ran, but lost, in the 1982 cycle.
34. Concurrent with the congressional election of March 1990, in which ballots were still distributed by campaign workers or printed in newspapers, was an unofficial plebiscite on calling for the Constituent Assembly. The ballot slips were referred to as Séptima Papeleta (seventh, after the ballots for various other offices being elected) and were counted by the electoral authorities under a presidential decree. See Taylor (2009, 54, 183–184) for more details and an example.

35. In a scene worthy of the magical realism made famous in the country's literature, the Constituent Assembly would have a three-person presidency that included Antonio Navarro Wolf of the M-19 and Álvaro Gómez Hurtado (National Salvation Movement), who had once been held hostage by the M-19.

## REFERENCES

Achury, Susan, Margarita Ramírez, and Francisco Cantú. "Endogenous Ballot Structures: The Selection of Open and Closed Lists in Colombia's Legislative Elections." *Electoral Studies* 49 (October 2017): 136–154.

Archer, Ronald P., and Matthew S. Shugart. "The Unrealized Potential of Presidential Dominance in Colombia." In *Presidentialism and Democracy in Latin America*, edited by Scott Mainwaring and Matthew S. Shugart, 110–159. Cambridge: Cambridge University Press, 1997.

Baron, Felipe. *La Reforma Electoral*. Bogotá: Minerva, 1915.

Batto, Nathan F. "Strategic Defection from Strong Candidates in the 2004 Taiwanese Legislative Election." *Japanese Journal of Political Science* 9, no. 1 (2008): 21–38.

Cox, Gary W., and Emerson Niou. "Seat Bonuses under the Single Nontransferable Vote System: Evidence from Japan and Taiwan." *Comparative Politics* 26, no. 2 (1994): 221–236.

Cox, Gary W., and Matthew S. Shugart. "In the Absences of Vote Pooling: Nomination and Allocation Errors in Colombia." *Electoral Studies* 14, no. 4 (1995): 441–460.

Dudley, Steven. *Walking Ghosts: Murder and Guerrilla Politics in Colombia*. New York: Routledge, 2004.

Eastman, Jorge M. "Seis Reformas Estructurales al Régimen Político: Resultados Electorales de 1930 a 1982." In Ministerio de Gobierno *Colección: "Legislación, Doctrina y Jurisprudencia."* Bogotá, Colombia: Impreso en la División de Edición del Departamento Administrativo Nacional de Estadística, DANE, 1982.

El Pais. "Voto en blanco supera a candidato ́ unico a alcaldía de Bello, Antioquia." *El Pais*, October 31, 2011. http://www.elpais.com.co/colombia/voto-en-blanco-supera-a-candidato-unico-a-alcaldia-de-bello-antioquia.html (accessed April 5, 2017).

Elklit, Jørgen. "Denmark: Simplicity Embedded in Complexity (or Is It the Other Way Round?)" In *The Politics of Electoral Systems*, edited by Michael Gallagher and Paul Mitchell, 453–472. Oxford: Oxford University Press, 2005.

Grofman, Bernard, Sung-Chull Lee, Edwin Winckler, and Brian Woodall, eds. *Elections in Japan, Korea, and Taiwan under the Single Non-Transferable Vote: The Comparative Study of an Embedded Institution*. Ann Arbor: University of Michigan Press, 1999.

La Silla Vacia. "Estas son las circunscripciones especiales," *La Silla Vacia*, April 26, 2017. http://lasillavacia.com/hagame-el-cruce/estas-son-las-circunscripciones-especiales-60690 (last accessed June 25, 2017).

Mazzuca, Sebastián, and James A. Robinson. "Political Conflict and Power-Sharing in the Origins of Modern Colombia." Cambridge, MA: National Bureau of Economic Research Working Paper Series, 2006.

Pachón, Mónica, Royce Carroll, and Hernando Barragán. "Ballot Design and Invalid Votes: Evidence from Colombia." *Electoral Studies* 48 (2017): 98–110.

Pachón, Mónica, and Matthew S. Shugart. "Electoral Reform and the Mirror Image of Interparty And Intraparty Competition: The Adoption of Party Lists In Colombia." *Electoral Studies* 29 (2010): 648–660.

Reed, Steven R. "Structure and Behaviour: Extending Duverger's Law to the Japanese Case." *British Journal of Political Science* 20, no. 3 (1990): 335–356.

Reed, Steven R. "Party Strategy or Candidate Strategy: How Does the LDP Run the Right Number of Candidates in Japan's Multi-Member Districts?" *Party Politics* 15, no. 3 (2009): 295–314.

República de Colombia. "Exposición de motivos: Proyecto de Acto Legislativo para la Reforma de la Política Colombiana y la Profundización de la Democracia," *Gaceta del Congreso*, no. 215, October 8, 1998, 7.

Shugart, Matthew S. "Leaders, Rank and File, and Constituents: Electoral Reform in Colombia and Venezuela," *Electoral Studies* 11, no. 1 (1992): 21–45.

Shugart, Matthew S., and J. M. Carey. *Presidents and Assemblies: Constitutional Design and Electoral Dynamics*. New York: Cambridge University Press, 1992.

Shugart, Matthew S., Erika Moreno, and Luis E. Fajardo. "Deepening Democracy by Renovating Political Practices: The Struggle for Electoral Reform in Colombia." In *Peace, Democracy, and Human Rights in Colombia*, edited by Christophe Welna and Gustavo Gallón. Notre Dame, IN: University of Notre Dame Press, 2007.

Shugart, Matthew S., and Rein Taagepera. *Votes from Seats: Logical Models of Electoral Systems*. New York: Cambridge University Press, 2017.

Taylor, Steven L. *Voting amid Violence: Electoral Democracy in Colombia*. Boston: Northeastern University Press, 2009.

Taylor, Steven L. "Colombian Voters and Ballot Structure: Error, Confusion, and/or 'None of the Above.'" *Latin Americanist* 56, no. 4 (December 2012): 111–130.

Taylor, Steven L. "The State of Democracy in Colombia: More Voting, Less Violence?" *Latin Americanist* 60, no. 2 (June 2016): 169–190.

Taylor, Steven L., Matthew S. Shugart, Arend Lijphart, and Bernard Grofman. *A Different Democracy: American Government in a Thirty-One Country Perspective*. New Haven, CT: Yale University Press, 2014.

UNODC. *Colombia: Monitoreo de territories afectados por cultivos ilícitos 2015*. Oficina de las Naciones Unidas contra la Droga y el Delito. 2016. https://www.unodc.org/documents/crop-monitoring/Colombia/Monitoreo_Cultivos_ilicitos_2015.pdf (accessed March 26, 2017).

# PART VIII

# ELECTORAL SYSTEMS IN THE CONTEXT OF NEW DEMOCRACIES

CHAPTER 42

······································································

# ELECTORAL SYSTEMS IN CONTEXT

## *Ukraine*

······································································

### ERIK S. HERRON

## INTRODUCTION

FOR election rules to exert expected psychological effects on voters, candidates, and parties, institutions should be durable and consistent. If political actors believe that the rules are likely to change or perceive that rules are unlikely to be enforced, they may pursue strategies and tactics that seem to be at odds with the electoral system's underlying incentive structure.[1] Ukraine provides a crucial case for the evaluation of electoral systems and their effects because the commitment by political actors to adjust to consistent rules and abide by them has been absent. Instead, political actors have regularly attempted to adjust the rules and test the limits of enforcement.

Ukraine has several features complicating the incentives that electoral systems produce: it is a relatively new and tenuous democracy, its party system is not yet institutionalized, no single electoral system has been used in three successive elections, and the most recent election cycle has been marred by foreign invasion. This chapter describes the electoral systems that have been in place, how they have influenced the evolution of the party system and other outcomes, and how conditions have intervened to undermine the incentives presented by institutional rules.

The chapter is divided into three sections to evaluate electoral systems and politics in Ukraine. The first section presents the context in which elections have occurred, describing how society and politics have developed since the end of the Soviet period. The second section describes electoral system choice and reform, discussing the Soviet inheritance and several waves of election rule reform that instituted majority runoff, mixed-member majoritarian (MMM), and nationwide proportional representation

(PR) rules.[2] The third section evaluates the consequences of electoral systems, assessing how the party system has changed over time.

# POLITICAL CONTEXT
# OF UKRAINE'S ELECTIONS

Ukraine's political trajectory has undulated since the collapse of the USSR. In its first decade of independence, Ukraine was a semiauthoritarian regime with some competition, but substantial restrictions on free and fair elections. As the second decade began, Ukraine moved toward regime change, and from 2005 to 2010, the country made halting progress toward democracy. After the 2010 presidential elections, authoritarian tendencies once again advanced. The ouster of the president in the wake of protests and regime repression in 2014 precipitated foreign invasion, Russia's annexation of one of Ukraine's regions, and ongoing violent conflict in two eastern regions. Despite all of these challenges, independent Ukraine has conducted seven parliamentary and five presidential elections.

Various measures of democratic quality illustrate how Ukraine's status has changed over time. While measures of democracy suffer from several problems (e.g., Munck and Verkuilen 2002), the recently released Varieties of Democracy (V-Dem) project[3] provides the widest range of criteria and permits scholars to customize evaluations of democratic quality. V-Dem scholars have also created several indexes to describe different types of democracy: electoral, liberal, deliberative, egalitarian, and participatory. With few exceptions, V-Dem's indexes suggest that Ukraine's conditions improved following the collapse of Communism, declined from the late 1990s until 2004, improved following the Orange Revolution until 2010, and then declined until 2014. The changes in democratic quality identified in the V-Dem data track closely with the key milestones in Ukraine's post-Soviet history.

Ukraine's first president, Leonid Kravchuk, was elected in 1991 during the Soviet Union's liberalization, but prior to its dissolution. Kravchuk, a Communist Party official who resigned from membership in the wake of the August 1991 coup attempt, oversaw Ukraine's transition from a Union Republic of the USSR to an independent state. His tenure was marked by allegations of corruption, economic difficulties, and increasing tensions with Russia. Kravchuk's relationship with his prime minister, Leonid Kuchma, also soured. Kuchma defeated Kravchuk in early presidential elections held in 1994.

The Kuchma era (1994–2004) was notable for the establishment of a semiauthoritarian regime. Kuchma and his allies permitted some political opposition and media activity but generally limited challenges to their power. While contestation was extended widely and opposition candidates could run for office, the use of government resources to benefit political parties and candidates associated with executive power undermined the success of antiregime politicians. In extreme cases, members of the opposition were threatened, subjected to violence, or killed. The most prominent incident occurred in 2000 when the journalist Heorhiy Gongadze was found murdered. Subsequent revelations of secret audio recordings taken in Kuchma's office implicated the president in the plan to eliminate Gongadze. An opposition movement, "Ukraine without Kuchma," emboldened by public reaction to Gongadze's death, conducted protests from late 2000 until the spring of 2001. While "Ukraine without Kuchma" was repressed and dissolved, it set the stage for larger-scale protests against the regime that would take place later.

As the scheduled 2004 presidential elections approached, the term-limited Kuchma selected a preferred successor, Viktor Yanukovych. Yanukovych faced an increasingly powerful opposition that grew from the "Ukraine without Kuchma" movement and achieved unexpected successes in the 2002 parliamentary elections. The leading opposition candidate, Viktor Yushchenko, was poisoned by dioxin during the campaign and faced increasingly malevolent tactics from pro-regime forces. Yanukovych and Yushchenko finished in the top two positions in the first round of the presidential election held in October 2004, and faced off in the second round held in November. Domestic and international observers documented widespread efforts to falsify results in the second round that inspired massive protest activity. Hundreds of thousands of demonstrators occupied the main square and street of the capital city, Kyiv,[4] in a popular uprising known as the Orange Revolution. The opposition set up a tent city and continued its protest for weeks until a compromise was reached: the second round of the election would be repeated. In December 2004, Yushchenko defeated Yanukovych and assumed the presidency in early 2005.

While the opposition won a short-term victory, it faced discord in its own ranks and a resurgent Yanukovych. Based on advice from foreign consultants, Yanukovych rebranded himself and the Party of Regions, and achieved significant success in the 2006 parliamentary election. The weak governing coalition collapsed in the summer of 2006, leading to a snap parliamentary election in 2007. In 2010, Yanukovych capitalized on the failures of the former opposition and gained a narrow victory in the presidential election over Yuliya Tymoshenko (Herron 2011).

After Yanukovych occupied the office of the presidency, he made policy decisions that undermined the democratic progress Ukraine had achieved in the half-decade since the failed effort to steal the election in 2004. Increased pressure on the media, growing corruption, and problematic local elections in 2010 accompanied policy decisions that some Ukrainians believed undermined sovereignty (e.g., the extended lease provided to Russia for Crimean military bases) (Herron and Boyko 2012).

Yanukovych attempted to navigate a difficult path between opening opportunities with Europe and running afoul of Russian government preferences for Ukraine to remain closely allied. These conflicts came to a head in late 2013 when Yanukovych was supposed to move forward on an Association Agreement with the European Union. Late in the process, Yanukovych reneged on his promise to sign the agreement, and large-scale protests engulfed the center of Kyiv. Unlike 2004's peaceful protests, the demonstrations grew violent, with government repression and violent counterattacks by some members of the protest movement. In February 2014, violence peaked when snipers killed dozens of protesters. Yanukovych fled the country, de facto abdicating the presidential office.

The interim government scheduled presidential elections in May 2014 and the newly elected president, Petro Poroshenko, called snap parliamentary elections in October of that year. At the same time, Russian military and security forces occupied Crimea, held an ersatz referendum, and annexed the peninsula. Russian intervention expanded to Ukraine's eastern regions of Donetsk and Luhansk, with Russian security forces using "hybrid warfare" tactics to covertly support supposedly indigenous insurgencies. The snap presidential and parliamentary elections were conducted under challenging circumstances: a direct threat to Ukraine's sovereignty, suffrage limited by occupation and active combat, restrictions on the choice set due to disarray in the party system, and the disintegration of many political networks that had functioned in the past.

Ukraine's post-Soviet elections took place in a constantly changing context. At times, the regime was semiauthoritarian, restricting activities by opposition politicians and the media, but not banning them outright. At other times, the regime was semidemocratic, conducting generally free and fair elections, but failing to address endemic problems of corruption. The most recent elections have been conducted in wartime conditions in parts of the country. In addition, the choice set regularly changed: no major party gained seats in every post-Communist contest. This instability was also reflected in the election rules: Ukraine modified its rules more than any other post-Soviet state, and perhaps more significantly than any other country since 1992. The following section tracks electoral system reform and discusses how and why the rules changed.

# ELECTORAL SYSTEMS IN UKRAINE, 1991–2016

As Ukraine began its transition from the Communist to the post-Communist era upon the USSR's collapse in December 1991, its electoral rules did not emerge *tabula rasa* from the minds of newly selected leaders. The institutional features of the late Soviet elections served as a point of departure.

The Soviet Congress of People's Deputies, selected in 1989, featured the first competitive elections since the consolidation of the political system under Josef Stalin in the late 1920s to early 1930s. For most of the Soviet period, elections were political theater, designed to showcase descriptive representation in an elected body with no real power to make meaningful policy changes. Elections during the early formation of the Soviet Union—from the October Revolution until the official foundation of the state in 1922—featured some competition. Non-Bolshevik candidates were banned from participation, but the election rules had not been standardized, producing a "delightful irregularity" across the country (Carson 1955, 9). With the codification of the Stalin Constitution in 1936, election rules were formalized and elections began to feature a single candidate (Swearer 1961). As the USSR entered into its twilight period in the 1980s, Mikhail Gorbachev instituted substantial reforms, including competitive elections for the newly created Congress of People's Deputies. Competitive Soviet elections were not multiparty elections; the Communist Party of the Soviet Union remained the only formally recognized political party. However, independent candidates contested and won seats, fostering the first open legislative debates in the USSR's history (Herron 2009).[5]

The Congress of People's Deputies elections paved the way for local legislative elections, and Ukrainians chose representatives for the regional parliament, the Verkhovna Rada, in 1990. Unlike the Congress of People's Deputies, which reserved one-third of its seats for selection by public organizations, all of the 450 seats in the Verkhovna Rada were allocated by majority-runoff rules in single-seat constituencies. The following year, Ukraine held direct presidential elections, shortly before the formal dissolution of the Soviet Union. The presidential and parliamentary elections held at the end of the Soviet period ultimately determined who would manage the transition; "founding" elections did not occur until 1994.[6]

In response to public protests and strikes, Ukrainian politicians agreed to hold early elections for the Verkhovna Rada in March 1994 and for president in June 1994. The Law on the Election of People's Deputies, initially codified in 1993, retained many elements of the Soviet-era election rules: citizens cast "negative" ballots in which they would strike off the name of any candidate whom they did not support (see Figure 42.1), and candidates needed to receive a majority of votes with a 50 percent

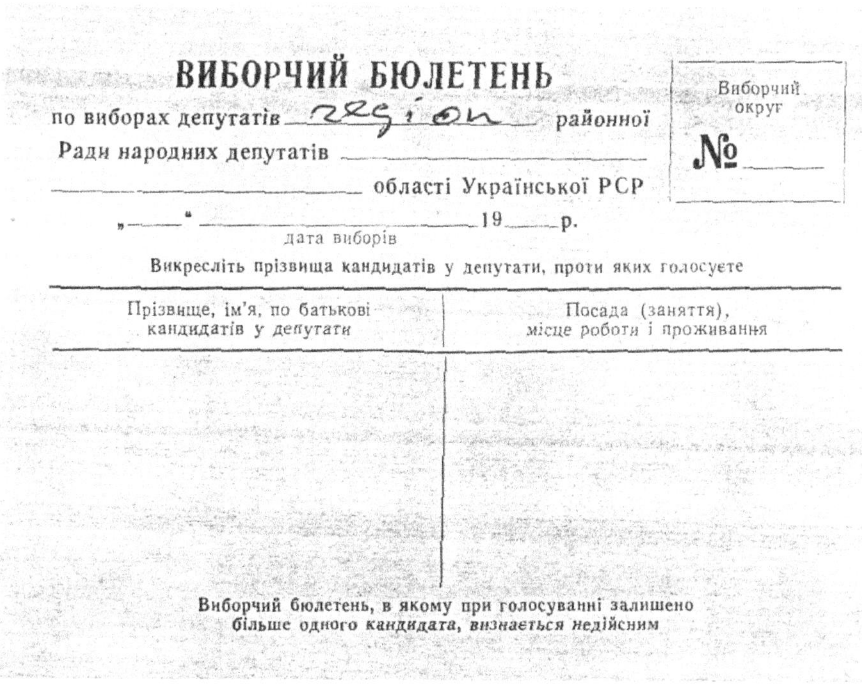

**ВИБОРЧИЙ БЮЛЕТЕНЬ**

по виборах депутатів region районної

Ради народних депутатів

області Української РСР

„ " 19 р.

дата виборів

Виборчий округ

№

Викресліть прізвища кандидатів у депутати, проти яких голосуєте

| Прізвище, ім'я, по батькові кандидатів у депутати | Посада (заняття), місце роботи і проживання |
|---|---|
| | |

Виборчий бюлетень, в якому при голосуванні залишено більше одного кандидата, визнається недійсним

**FIGURE 42.1.** Soviet-era Ukraine ballot.

Note: The ballot provides space for the candidate's name and personal information. The instructions indicate that voters should cross out the names of candidates they are voting against, and that ballots with more than one name identified for the office will be declared invalid.

turnout to win a seat in geographically defined districts. While proposals to institute a mixed-member electoral system were circulated at the time, these efforts failed. Some observers argued that Soviet-era rules were perpetuated to protect members of the political elite whose reputations could have been tarnished by associations with the Communist Party; majority-runoff rules allowed politicians to "hide" as non-affiliated independents.[7] Maintaining institutional rules designed for a single-party system caused significant complications in the competitive environment as only 338 of the 450 seats could be filled, requiring a series of later by-elections (Birch 1995, 1996; Bojcun 1995).

Relative to its peers in the post-Soviet space, Ukraine was a laggard in the development and codification of new formal institutions: its post-Soviet constitution was only ratified in 1996, last among the successor states. The constitution was followed by changes to the electoral system that eliminated the main features inherited from the Soviet period.

Prior to the 1998 elections, the new election law substantially modified the electoral system. One of the law's authors asserted that the new system emerged from careful study of the scholarly literature on elections, including consultations with experts. He also acknowledged that partisan interests influenced the choice as his party expected to improve its performance.[8] While the size of the assembly did not change, the 450 seats were divided into two for allocation purposes: half would be selected via national-level PR with a 4 percent threshold, and half would be selected in first-past-the-post (FPTP) single-seat constituencies. Candidates would be permitted to contest both ballots, running simultaneously in districts and on party lists, but a court decision deemed this provision unconstitutional.[9] The MMM system would remain in place for the next parliamentary elections, with some modifications to the rules instituted prior to the 2002 elections, including a formal prohibition on dual candidacy.

Concerns about election fraud, especially in constituency races, prompted the political opposition to more vigorously advocate for the adoption of a pure PR system. The mobilization success of the opposition movement encouraged reform advocates who believed that they could garner the votes needed to pass a new parliamentary election law prior to the 2002 elections. Arguing that constituency races were especially likely to produce results distorted by vote buying, intimidation, ballot-box stuffing, or other manipulation, election reformers proposed to allocate all seats by PR using a Hare quota and largest-remainders formula. Even President Leonid Kuchma acknowledged flaws in the MMM system at the time:

> I often ask myself if I didn't make a mistake by agreeing to a mixed [sic] electoral system for the last parliamentary elections . . . . The logic of the decision [was that] . . . elections on the party list would speed the development of blocs and coalitions, bringing greater clarity, direction, and simplicity to the party palette. It did not turn out this way. Instead, it was the opposite – there was a fragmentation of parties that was engineered by the electoral ambitions of their leadership.[10] (Herron 2000)

Despite Kuchma's concerns about issues with the implementation of Ukraine's MMM, he vetoed efforts to change the system to PR prior to the 2002 elections. However, in 2004, Kuchma proposed a series of constitutional reforms and assented to election reform in an effort to secure enough legislative support.[11] The law enacting PR passed, but the constitutional reform failed (see Herron 2007 and 2009 for a discussion).[12]

Election rule reform eliminated constituency races, lowered the electoral threshold, and required all candidates to contest seats as party affiliates. The 2006 parliamentary election used a single national district to allocate all 450 seats among parties that passed the 3 percent threshold. The snap election held in 2007 after the collapse of the governing coalition maintained the system with minor administrative changes.

After the 2010 presidential election elevated Viktor Yanukovych to the presidency, election reform returned to the agenda. Prior to the 2012 elections, the mixed-member majoritarian system was reinstated. While the initial statute included dual candidacy, its constitutionality was once again denied by the judiciary. The provisions finally implemented were similar to the 2002 version of MMM, albeit with a higher threshold for the party list ballot (5 percent).

The snap 2014 election rules included some minor revisions, but the broad contours of the electoral system were retained. However, the administration of the 2014 elections presented significant challenges. Russia's annexation of Crimea and infiltration of the eastern Ukrainian regions of Donetsk and Luhansk undermined the implementation of elections. Twenty-seven of the 225 districts designated for representation by single-seat constituency deputies could not hold elections (12 in Crimea, 9 in Donetsk, and 6 in Luhansk). The status of these territories also prevented millions of Ukrainian citizens from participating (Herron, Thunberg, and Boyko 2015). The actions of occupying forces undermined elections; not only did active combat threaten election administrators and voters, but also "insurgents" seized election equipment for use in their own sham elections. The absence of formal representation for many of Ukraine's regions raises questions about the viability of geographically defined constituencies in the current climate.

Discussions of election reform regularly occur among politicians and experts, and following the 2014 elections, new proposals emerged. The 2015 local elections featured a modified law that purported to introduce open-list proportional representation (OLPR). However, the basic features of this system did not conform to most variants of OLPR in use around the world. Regional council elections featured multiseat districts, but the ballots substantially constrained the choice set. Each multiseat district was further subdivided into smaller districts, and each ballot featured the name of the party, its leader, and a locally nominated candidate. Instead of having the option of voting for any party-affiliated candidate contesting the multiseat district, the ballot linked the party, its leader, and the candidate vote. Votes cast for the party in each district were aggregated to determine the overall seat allocation across parties. Within each party that passed the threshold, the designated party leader whose name was on all district ballots received the first seat. Seats were subsequently allotted to the local candidates based on the percentage of the vote that the party received in the district they were assigned.[13]

In 2016, proposals to institute a similar brand of OLPR in the Verkhovna Rada circulated. Most of the discourse in 2016 revolved around adoption of OLPR (or its improperly labeled variant) for the next elections. While parliamentary elections are not scheduled until 2019, the threat of early elections looms as the governing coalition is weak. Given past practices, further election reform efforts are likely to occur and changes to the law finalized close to the time of the scheduled election.[14]

# ELECTORAL SYSTEM EFFECTS

The previous sections have outlined political and social conditions, as well as the evolution of election laws, focusing on the post-Soviet era. Ukraine is a transitional state, wavering between authoritarian and democratic rule, with incomplete adaptation to the rule of law and a lack of commitment to maintaining institutional rules. The effects of these conditions can be observed in several areas, including the party system.

The party system exemplifies the fluidity of Ukrainian political life; the number and identity of parties contesting elections have regularly changed, with slow movement toward institutionalization. The description of the party system in Poland's early elections, presented in John Carey's chapter in this volume, reflects many of the dynamics present in Ukraine:

> At the initial democratic founding, expectations about [parties'] viability were ill-defined, and the choice set was bewildering. After the imposition of a rule establishing a clear benchmark for strategic alliances and voting, the set of viable choices narrowed, and actors updated expectations and behavior accordingly.

Like Poland, expectations about party viability were "ill-defined" and the choice set was also "bewildering." Unlike Poland, however, Ukraine's election rules were not established and maintained in a way that provided a "clear benchmark" for strategic behavior, the development of alliances, and the institutionalization of the party system.

Measures of party systems, such as the effective number of parties, have been linked to institutional and social factors.[15] While scholars have extended their assessments of the effects of electoral rules, several outcomes remain critical consequences attributed to electoral systems, including the effective number of parties, the development of individual parties, the ways in which parties interact, and the network of parties that survives over time.

As Ukraine began its political transition, it featured one institutionalized political party: the Communist Party of Ukraine (CPU). While the CPU was briefly banned from participation, it was formally registered in 1993. As the successor to the Soviet-era

Communist Party, the CPU had access to valuable resources, notably personnel, organizational capacity, and a meaningful "brand." The end of the ban on alternate political parties produced incentives for party formation, further enhanced by lack of clarity about which parties would succeed and the use of majority-runoff rules, followed by MMM, and then PR.

At the same time, competitive elections in the late Soviet period that banned alternative political parties "seeded" early electoral competition with independents. Because contesting elections as an unaffiliated candidate was the only way to gain ballot access outside the party apparatus in the late Soviet period, many new electoral participants registered as independents. Until the codification of PR in 2006, institutional rules supported participation by independent candidates; the opportunity returned in 2012. Consequently, in addition to emerging incentives for new party formation, Ukrainian politicians were also presented with a viable option to compete as formally unaffiliated candidates.

Table 42.1 shows the affiliations of the 5,608 candidates who contested in the first round of the 1994 founding elections. Ukrainian law differentiated the party membership of a candidate from the formal source of nomination, and these characteristics are featured in the table. One of the most notable characteristics of the 1994 elections is the substantial participation by candidates claiming no party membership, as well as those who were not nominated by a political party. These two categories of candidates are "independents," although nomination rather than membership is the more standard method to identify independents.

Regardless of how independent candidates are defined, they dominate the nominations. Almost three-quarters (4,109, or 73 percent) of candidates claimed membership in no political party. In addition, 3,495 (62 percent) candidates were nominated by voters and 1,498 (27 percent) were nominated by labor collectives. In short, the vast majority of candidates were not party affiliated. Among party-affiliated candidates, the Communist Party led the way with 381 members and 200 nominations, followed by a People's Rukh (230 members, 96 nominations), Socialist Party (172 members, 98 nominations), Republican Party (128 members, 83 nominations), and Democratic Party (73 members, 11 nominations). Twenty-three additional parties had members contesting, and thirteen additional parties or blocs nominated candidates. Independent candidates also experienced success in the election; among the 338 legislators selected during the initial round of voting, 136 (40 percent) were not affiliated with a political party by nomination.

Election administration rules, coupled with the incomplete democratic transition, also supported the proliferation of parties and candidates. Election commissions play important roles in managing the casting, counting, and compilation of ballots. In the 1990s, the semiauthoritarian regime used its "administrative resources"[16] in commissions to undermine opposition competitiveness. One method that developed to control commissions was the cultivation of "technical parties": formally registered political parties whose primary objective was to aid allied party control over commissions. Ukraine allocates commission positions to parties; when more parties seek representation than commissions can accommodate, a lottery determines who is seated. Liberal party

## Table 42.1  Party Affiliations, Verkhovna Rada Elections (1994)

| Membership | Number of Candidates | Nomination | Number of Candidates |
|---|---|---|---|
| Independent | 4,109 | Voters | 3,495 |
|  |  | Labor Collective | 1,498 |
| Communist Party | 381 | Communist Party | 200 |
| People's Rukh | 230 | People's Rukh | 96 |
| Socialist Party | 172 | Socialist Party | 98 |
| Republican Party | 128 | Republican Party | 83 |
| Liberal Party | 81 | Liberal Party | 35 |
| Democratic Party | 73 | Democratic Party | 11 |
| Peasant Party | 53 |  |  |
| Congress of Ukrainian Nationalists | 51 | Congress of Ukrainian Nationalists | 30 |
| Party of Democratic Rebirth | 48 | Party of Democratic Rebirth | 3 |
| Christian Democratic Party | 37 | Christian Democratic Party | 13 |
| Party of Greens | 36 |  |  |
| Social Democratic Party | 30 | Social Democratic Party | 1 |
| Conservative Republican Party | 27 | Conservative Republican Party | 10 |
| Labor Party | 26 | Labor Party | 13 |
| Civic Congress | 23 |  |  |
| Party of Justice | 15 | Party of Justice | 2 |
| Labor Congress | 14 | Labor Congress | 4 |
| Organization of Ukrainian Nationalists | 11 | Organization of Ukrainian Nationalists | 9 |
| State Independence Party | 9 |  |  |
| Liberal Democratic Party | 9 | Liberal Democratic Party | 3 |
| Slavic Unity Party | 8 |  |  |

## Table 42.1 Continued

| Membership | Number of Candidates | Nomination | Number of Candidates |
|---|---|---|---|
| Peasant Democratic Party | 7 | | |
| Constitutional Democratic Party | 6 | | |
| National Conservative Party | 6 | | |
| Economic Revival of Crimea Party | 5 | Economic Revival of Crimea Party | 1 |
| Party of Solidarity and Social Justice | 5 | | |
| Ukrainian Christian Democratic Party | 3 | Ukrainian Christian Democratic Party | 1 |
| Party of Free Peasants and Entrepreneurs | 2 | | |
| Beer Lovers Party | 2 | | |
| National Salvation Party | 1 | | |
| | | Party Bloc "Justice" | 2 |
| Total | 5,608 | | 5,608 |

*Data Source:* Central Electoral Commission of Ukraine. Author was provided the data.

registration rules, coupled with an incentive to flood the lottery with allied groups, facilitated a proliferation of "technical parties," especially in the 2000s (Boyko and Herron 2015). This practice further encouraged more parties to be formally registered, although most of these parties were hopeless electoral competitors by design.

In sum, social, political, and institutional conditions encouraged Ukraine's party system to develop in a peculiar manner. Politicians faced incentives to form parties to either contest seats or stack the deck on electoral commissions. But most of these parties were functionally limited and served as a kind of "front" organization to funnel resources and access without providing many of the benefits traditionally associated with party organizations. At the same time, many politicians saw clear advantages in maintaining formally independent status during election competitions; party system volatility, limited party-based resources, and the lack of a meaningful "brand" for most parties limited their value. Business sector connections were valuable substitutes and served some of the roles of traditional parties for nonaffiliated candidates (Hale 2006).[17] They also served as the foundation for local political machines that could effectively propel candidates to victory with or without formal party organizations (Herron and Sjoberg 2016).

The brief period of PR elections provided a shock to the system by eliminating access for independent candidates, and the party system began to stabilize with a few emergent parties developing more coherent electoral programs. Individual candidates often found "homes" on party lists under PR, subsequently abandoning those parties to run as independents or on other labels. While the PR interregnum generated institutional incentives for political parties to develop into functional organizations, most parties failed to move past personalistic orientations with limited ideological or programmatic coherence. It is worth noting that while parties contested in nationwide PR in two elections, the elections occurred in a short period of time from late March 2006 until late September 2007. Nationwide PR's short lifespan likely contributed to the failure of parties to institutionalize. The Euromaidan revolution, ouster of Yanukovych, and Russian occupation of Ukrainian territory beginning in late 2013 further shocked the system by denying suffrage to millions of voters, disrupting existing political networks especially active in the East and South of the country, and altering the election calendar with snap elections for president and parliament.

In sum, the evolution of Ukrainian electoral institutions and society has not laid a foundation for the incentives that one typically associates with electoral systems to become firmly embedded. Rather than adjusting to the incentives provided by stable institutional rules, politicians have altered the rules. They have further tested the limits by exploiting party registration and administrative regulations to gain advantages that violate the spirit if not the letter of the law for free and fair electoral competition. The remainder of this section describes party system outcomes.

Table 42.2 shows each parliamentary election that has taken place in the post-Soviet era, noting key election rules and results. The upper section of the table indicates how the overall system, formal threshold, and formulas have changed over time. The lower section of the table displays the number of seats that major parties received in each election. For all elections except 1994, the table shows the outcomes for parties that exceeded the formal threshold for the PR ballot. The 1994 results use 4 percent as a cutoff.

The table reveals several important consequences of elections in Ukraine. First, the total number of seats allocated in the initial round of the elections did not reach the total assembly size in all elections. In 1994, districts failed to reach the minimum vote threshold or the turnout threshold for results to be deemed legitimate. A series of by-elections did not fill all of the seats. In 1998 and 2012, elections in five districts were deemed invalid; by-elections filled vacant positions. In 2014, elections could not be held in occupied territories, and the seats remain unfilled at the time this chapter was completed in early 2017. These outcomes reveal some of the challenges of maintaining constituency-based races in a country facing social and political conditions like those in Ukraine. In the two elections where national-level PR allocated all seats, no positions were left vacant for long periods of time. Further, the PR ballot of the MMM system also yielded full seat allocation. Although the causes of incomplete seat allocation varied, from the participation and results requirements in 1994, to procedural inadequacies in some districts in 2002 and 2012, to foreign occupation and violent conflict in 2014, the

Table 42.2 Key Parliamentary Election Features and Results in Ukraine, 1994–2014

| | | 1994 | 1998 | 2002 | 2006 | 2007 | 2012 | 2014 |
|---|---|---|---|---|---|---|---|---|
| Rules | System | SSD | MMM | MMM | PR | PR | MMM | MMM |
| | PR Threshold | N/A | 4% | 4% | 3% | 3% | 5% | 5% |
| | SSD Formula | MR | Plurality | Plurality | N/A | N/A | Plurality | Plurality |
| Results | CPU | 86 | 123 | 65 | 21 | 27 | 32 | |
| | For United Ukraine | | | 121 | | | | |
| | Freedom | | | | | | 36 | |
| | Greens | | 19 | | | | | |
| | Hromada | | 23 | | | | | |
| | Interregional Reform Bloc | 15 | | | | | | |
| | Lytvyn Bloc | | | | | 20 | | |
| | Opposition Bloc | | | | | | | 29 |
| | Our Ukraine | | | 112 | 81 | 72 | | |
| | Party of Regions | | | | 186 | 175 | 183 | |
| | Peasant | 18 | | | | | | |
| | PDP | | 27 | | | | | |
| | People's Front | | | | | | | 82 |
| | Poroshenko Bloc | | | | | | | 127 |
| | Radical Party | | | | | | | 22 |
| | Rukh | 25 | 44 | | | | | |
| | PSP | | 17 | | | | | |
| | Self-Reliance | | | | | | | 33 |
| | SDPU(o) | | 18 | 27 | | | | |
| | Socialist | 14 | 34 | 22 | 33 | | | |
| | Tymoshenko Bloc/ Fatherland | | | 22 | 129 | 156 | 99 | 19 |
| | UDAR | | | | | | 40 | |
| | Independents | 136 | 102 | 72 | — | — | 47 | 94 |

(continued)

## Table 42.2  Continued

|               | 1994 | 1998 | 2002 | 2006 | 2007 | 2012 | 2014 |
|---------------|------|------|------|------|------|------|------|
| $N_s$ with Ind. | 4.15 | 6.32 | 5.35 | ----- | ----- | 3.99 | 5.01 |
| $N_s$ without Ind. | 4.52 | 5.64 | 4.38 | 3.41 | 3.30 | 3.34 | 4.04 |
| Total         | 338  | 445  | 450  | 450  | 450  | 445  | 422  |

*Note:* Parties listed in the table passed the PR threshold. Parties in 1994 surpassed 4 percent of the seats. The "Total" listed on the table refers to the total number of deputies chosen on Election Day, or in the case of 1994 during the first or second round. The totals do not include subsequent by-elections. The Socialist Party ran in a bloc with the Peasant Party in 2002.

The Effective Number of Legislative Parties ($N_s$) is based on the seat allocation reported by the Central Electoral Commission for each election. In one version of the Effective Number of Parties calculations, independents are included as a single party; in another, they are excluded from the calculations. Affiliations often change within parliament, and independent candidates tend to align with a parliamentary faction or deputy group.

*Sources:* Central Electoral Commission of Ukraine; Bojcun (1995); Birch and Wilson (1999).

consequence is the same: parliament does not have a full complement of deputies, and voters fail to have complete representation, in some cases for long periods of time.

Second, the party system remains inchoate. No single political party passed the threshold in every post-Communist election. The founding elections spawned dozens of formally registered political parties, but none of them have survived as major players in every election. Some of the political parties that participated in the 1994 elections remained viable for several elections, and a few are active today, albeit as minor parties. The Communist Party maintained viability throughout the post-Soviet period, only to be outlawed by the decommunization process in December 2015. It won seats in all but the 2014 elections, when its performance was hampered due to the loss of its parliamentary faction. The Socialist Party of Ukraine grew in popularity under Oleksandr Moroz but was abandoned electorally after it defected from the opposition ruling group to the Party of Regions group in the summer of 2006. Its dismal performance in the 2007 snap elections relegated it to an also-ran status.

Other political parties joined or split from coalitions with other party organizations. For example, People's Rukh, an early democratic party, suffered from internal disagreements and a split in the late 1990s, although it participated successfully in elections as part of a coalition with larger Western-oriented parties such as Our Ukraine. The Opposition Bloc, which gained twenty-nine seats in the 2014 parliamentary elections, was a successor to the Party of Regions that became dormant after the Euromaidan protests and abdication by Yanukovych.

Table 42.2 may overstate how much the party system has changed by focusing on labels rather than relationships among politicians. Many politicians from failed parties have found homes in other political parties. Most recently, former Party of Regions politicians were nominated by other parties for seats in the 2014 contest. At the same time, parties emerge and disappear regularly; among the six parties that gained seats in 2014, only one (Fatherland) was officially registered prior to 2010.

Although the mid-2000s were characterized by government instability, the elections held in this time period were judged the highest quality in Ukraine's independent history by international observers and seemed to be leading toward party system institutionalization. Ukraine's salient divisions were covered by competitive parties, with interests more sympathetic to state involvement in the economy and a closer relationship with Russia represented by the Party of Regions and Communist Party, and European, market-oriented interests represented by Our Ukraine and the Tymoshenko Bloc. Many parties remained personalistic, however, undermining their institutionalization. For example, while the Tymoshenko Bloc was perceived as oriented toward a Ukrainian national identity common in the western part of the country and an economic orientation focused on Europe, its titular leader emerged from a corrupt party of business interests and adopted populist rhetoric that sometimes diverged from Western market-oriented policies.

Third, nonaffiliated candidates continue to play a significant role in elections. Their prominence speaks, in part, to the general weakness of party organizations, but also to the advantages that some candidates seek to exploit in constituency races. Local business elites have been shown to seek office in constituency races, and their participation is associated with higher levels of reported election violations (Herron and Sjoberg 2016). While permitting independent candidates to participate expands the choice set for voters and allows ambitious politicians another way to gain ballot access, their presence is also associated with a higher level of instability. Moreover, party switches in parliament often involve independent candidates and have plagued the Rada, undermining coherent lawmaking (Herron 2002; Thames 2007).

In sum, the election rules, social conditions, and political environment have been conducive to the outcomes witnessed in Ukraine: a proliferation of formally registered parties, many of which are ephemeral or ersatz, and the strong lure of independent candidacy encouraging many election participants to remain unaffiliated during campaigns. Electoral systems contributed to this outcome in several ways. The rules Ukraine adopted—majority runoff, MMM, and PR—all encourage multiparty competition. The instability of rules, and the common expectation among politicians that election rules will change, discourages the establishment of consistent, long-term, programmatic alliances. Each new system presents different tactical advantages to exploit; retaining maximum flexibility in affiliations permits politicians to hedge their bets. Further, as political conditions have changed, some party labels have fallen out of favor. The ability to quickly disengage from these affiliations (e.g., Communist Party in 1994 and the Party of Regions in 2014) permits many politicians to cast off disadvantageous designations and successfully compete under different identities. Instability has encouraged politicians to take an especially short-term perspective on decision making, impeding the institutionalization of election rules and the party system.

# CONCLUSION

Ukraine's twenty-five-year experimentation with electoral systems has generated, in many ways, expected outcomes: a fluid political environment with a persistent failure by parties to institutionalize into functioning, programmatic organizations. Electoral system instability is not the sole cause of the system's failure to consolidate; endemic corruption, regime change, and an existential threat to its sovereignty have complicated the environment in which politicians operate.

Ukrainian politicians understand and respond to incentives, however. When the Communist Party monopoly was broken, many new political parties were formed. At the same time, the early success of independent candidates in the last Soviet and first independent elections showed that alternatives to ballot access via parties could yield rewards. The partisan organization of electoral commissions, and the use of those resources to influence elections, encouraged the formation of "technical parties" whose primary purpose was not to gain legislative seats. The rapid rise and fall of leaders in elections and popular uprisings has also encouraged politicians to develop short-term strategies and pursue tactics that allow them to hedge their bets. Until Ukraine adopts an approach like its neighbor, Poland, to impose "rule[s] establishing a clear benchmark for strategic alliances and voting," the system is likely to remain inchoate and unstable.

## NOTES

1. In addition, political actors make mistakes in the selection of institutional rules and the strategies to maximize their seat acquisition. Andrews and Jackman (2005) emphasize uncertainty in their assessment of electoral system choice and consequences.
2. By contrast, presidential election rules were stable over this time period, with a majority-runoff system in place. Local election rules varied, but are not the primary focus of this chapter.
3. See http:/www.v-dem.net.
4. This chapter uses transliterations based on Ukrainian-language names (e.g., Kyiv) rather than Russian-language transliterations (e.g., Kiev).
5. See http://www.nytimes.com/1989/05/31/world/soviet-tv-s-biggest-hit-200-million-watch-political-drama.html.
6. Some scholars treat the 1991 presidential election as the founding election (e.g., Birch 1995). Ukraine declared independence in August 1991; the subsequent referendum preceded the formal dissolution of the USSR by a few weeks in December 1991. I treat the 1994 elections as "founding" elections because they were the first held under the control of a formally independent Ukraine, free from any connection to the USSR because it no longer existed as a political entity.
7. This practice would continue in later elections with "technical parties" as well. In the 2014 parliamentary elections, forty elected deputies who were formally "independent" had been elected as nominees of the Party of Regions in earlier elections

(http://www.pravda.com.ua/rus/articles/2014/11/18/7044545/). The unaffiliated option allowed them to obscure their connections with the Party of Regions after it had fallen out of favor.

8. Author interview with Oleksandr Lavrynovych, 1999. At the time, Lavrynovych was a deputy associated with People's Rukh.

9. A Constitutional Court decision eliminated the dual-candidacy provision, but the ban was not implemented until the 2002 elections. The Constitutional Court ruled dozens of provisions as noncompliant but permitted the elections to move forward provided that the law would be altered for the next elections (Birch and Wilson 1999). The primary concern motivating the court to declare dual candidacy unconstitutional was that it treated candidates differently by providing unequal ballot access; independent candidates could not contest the PR race.

10. The quote was published on Leonid Kuchma's website, in an article entitled "About the Right and the Left." The quote was accessed in June 2000, but the site is no longer available. It was originally cited in Herron (2000).

11. The Communists and Socialists agreed to support constitutional reform if it was packaged with election rule reform. The antiregime opposition supported election reform but opposed constitutional reform.

12. However, constitutional reform was enacted as part of the negotiated settlement at the time of the Orange Revolution in late 2004.

13. For a description of similar systems, see Allen's chapter on Indonesia in this volume, the discussion of Slovenia in Cox (1997), and descriptions of the option occasionally used by parties in Denmark (Elklit 2005).

14. The 2015 local election law changed after the campaign had officially begun. In most cases, the laws were amended less than one year prior to the election.

15. See Ordeshook and Shvetsova (1994), Amorim Neto and Cox (1997), and Clark and Golder (2006) for a discussion of how institutional rules and social features fuel party system development. Also see Moser, Scheiner, and Stoll's and Shugart and Taagepera's chapters in this volume.

16. "Administrative resources" describes a wide range of tools that the ruling regime could use to influence elections, including control over electoral commissions, local government, and law enforcement. See Norris's chapter in this volume for more on election integrity and fraud.

17. Hale (2006) focuses on Russia, but the intersection of business and politics also occurred in Ukraine.

# References

Amorim Neto, Octavio, and Gary W. Cox. "Electoral Institutions, Cleavage Structures, and the Number of Parties." *American Journal of Political Science* 41, no. 1 (1997): 149–174.

Andrews, Josephine T., and Robert W. Jackman. "Strategic Fools: Electoral Rule Choice under Extreme Uncertainty." *Electoral Studies* 25, no. 1 (2005): 65–84.

Birch, Sarah. "The Ukrainian Parliamentary and Presidential Elections of 1994." *Electoral Studies* 14, no. 1 (1995): 93–99.

Birch, Sarah. "The Ukrainian Repeat Elections of 1995." *Electoral Studies* 15, no. 2 (1996): 281–282.

Birch, Sarah, and Andrew Wilson. "The Ukrainian Parliamentary Elections of 1998." 18, no. 2 (1999): 176–282.

Bojcun, Marko. "The Ukrainian Parliamentary Elections in March-April 1994." *Europe-Asia Studies* 47, no. 2 (1995): 229–249.

Boyko, Nazar and Erik S. Herron. "The Effects of Technical Parties and Partisan Election Management Bodies on Voting Outcomes." *Electoral Studies* 40 (2015): 23–33.

Carson, George B., Jr. *Electoral Practices in the USSR.* New York: Frederick A. Praeger, 1955.

Clark, William Roberts, and Matthew Golder. "Rehabilitating Duverger's Theory Testing the Mechanical and Strategic Modifying Effects of Electoral Laws." *Comparative Political Studies* 39, no. 6 (2006): 679–708.

Cox, Gary W. *Making Votes Count.* Cambridge: Cambridge University Press, 1997.

Elklit, Jorgen. "Denmark: Simplicity Embedded in Complexity (or Is It the Other Way Round)?" In *The Politics of Electoral Systems,* edited by Michael Gallagher and Paul Mitchell, 452–471. Oxford: Oxford University Press, 2005.

Hale, Henry E. *Why Not Parties in Russia? Democracy, Federalism, and the State.* Cambridge: Cambridge University Press, 2006.

Herron, Erik S. 2000. *Mixed Signals: Incentive Structures and Party Strategies in Mixed Electoral Systems.* Dissertation. East Lansing, Michigan State University.

Herron, Erik S. "Causes and Consequences of Fluid Faction Membership in Ukraine." *Europe-Asia Studies* 54, no. 4 (2002): 625–639.

Herron, Erik S. "State Institutions, Political Context, and Parliamentary Election Legislation in Ukraine, 2000-2006." *Journal of Communist Studies and Transition Politics* 23 (March 2007): 57–76.

Herron, Erik S. *Elections and Democracy after Communism?* New York: Palgrave MacMillan, 2009.

Herron, Erik S. "How Viktor Yanukovych Won: Reassessing the Dominant Narratives of Ukraine's 2010 Presidential Election." *East European Politics and Societies* 25 (February 2011): 47–67.

Herron, Erik S., and Nazar Boyko. "Reversing Democratic Revolutions: The Implications of Ukraine's 2010 Local Elections." *Journal of East European and Asian Studies* 3, no. 1 (2012): 79–100.

Herron, Erik S., and Fredrik Sjoberg. "The Impact of 'Boss' Candidates and Local Political Machines on Elections in Ukraine." *Europe-Asia Studies* 16, no. 6 (2016): 985–1002.

Herron, Erik S., Michael Thunberg, and Nazar Boyko. "Crisis Management and Adaptation in Wartime Elections: Ukraine's 2014 Snap Presidential and Parliamentary Elections." *Electoral Studies* 40 (December 2015): 419–429.

Munck, Gerardo L., and Jay Verkuilen. "Conceptualizing and Measuring Democracy." *Comparative Political Studies* 35, no. 1 (2002): 5–34.

Ordeshook, Peter C., and Olga V. Shvetsova. "Ethnic Heterogeneity, District Magnitude, and the Number of Parties." *American Journal of Political Science* 38, no. 1 (1994): 100–123.

Swearer, Howard R. "The Functions of Soviet Elections." *Midwest Journal of Political Science* 5, no. 2 (1961): 129–149.

Thames, Frank C. "Searching for the Electoral Connection: Parliamentary Party Switching in the Ukrainian Rada, 1998–2002." *Legislative Studies Quarterly* 32, no. 2 (2007): 223–256.

# CHAPTER 43

# ELECTORAL SYSTEMS IN CONTEXT

## *Indonesia*

NATHAN ALLEN

THE size of the country and the ambition of its attempts to engineer electoral outcomes make Indonesia a compelling case study. It is the world's largest country to use proportional representation (PR) to elect its national legislature, and its simultaneous, multilevel elections create the largest electoral event in the world in terms of participating candidates. As the world's most populous Muslim-majority country, Indonesia draws attention from those looking for institutional design lessons for other Islamic contexts. The country's institutional design process has produced some rare outcomes of interest for political science more broadly, including party formation rules that require parties to organize in all the country's provinces, a reverse-honeymoon presidential election cycle, and a directly elected nonpartisan national consultative body.

The literature on Indonesia's electoral systems is still in an adolescent stage. The initial studies and reviews focused largely on issues of electoral system design, producing a body of descriptive and analytical work exploring the origins of institutions and reform processes. As electoral results have accumulated, scholars have turned their attention to the effect of these institutional choices. This chapter provides an overview of core themes in the literature on both origins and outcomes, pointing to new directions for future research. First, I situate Indonesia's national legislative election in a broader political system that includes complex connections across time and levels of governance. Second, I examine the origins of the national electoral system, focusing on two trajectories of reform: one restricting opportunities for small parties and the other restricting the power of party leadership. Third, I examine the effects of the electoral system and look at whether electoral reforms have met their objectives. Finally, I conclude with an assessment of Indonesia's electoral system, its outcomes, and paths forward for research.

# A Multilevel Electoral System

A study of the Indonesian electoral system starts with a deceptively complex question: which electoral system? This examination will focus on the electoral system of the primary national legislative body—the People's Representative Council (Dewan Perwakilan Rakyat, DPR), one of two elected national bodies. The other is the Regional Representative Council (Dewan Perwakilan Daerah, DPD). DPR and DPD elections take place simultaneously every five years. Members of the DPR and DPD come together to constitute the supra-legislative body known as the People's Consultative Assembly (Majelis Permusyawaratan Rakyat, MPR), which has powers related to constitutional change and impeachment. The DPR has legislative, budgetary, and appointment powers, whereas the DPD is a largely advisory body.[1]

Indonesia is also a decentralized country, with two subnational levels of government—province and regency (kabupaten/kota)—each with their own elected legislatures. Table 43.1 presents the different electoral rules broken down by level of government. In an unusual move, the authors of Indonesia's decentralization laws bypassed the provincial-level governments and transferred wide powers to regencies (Turner et al. 2003). Subnational legislative elections for the provincial (Dewan Perwakilan

Table 43.1 The Electoral Systems of Indonesia

| Level of Government | Elected Office | Electoral System | Timing |
|---|---|---|---|
| National | People's Representative Council (DPR) | List proportional | Every 5 years |
| | Regional Representative Council (DPD) | Singe nontransferrable vote | Concurrent with DPR |
| | President and vice president | Majoritarian runoff | Approx. 3 months after DPR |
| Provincial | Regional People's Representative Council (DPRD I) | List proportional | Concurrent with DPR |
| | Governor and vice governor | Plurality | Every 5 years independent of DPR schedule |
| Regency | Regional People's Representative Council (DPRD II) | List proportional | Concurrent with DPR |
| | Regent/mayor and vice regent/mayor | Plurality | Every 5 years independent of DPR schedule |

A special exception for Jakarta requires a runoff if gubernatorial candidates receive less than 50% of the vote.

Rakyat Daerah—Provinsi, DPRD I) and regency (Dewan Perwakilan Rakyat Daerah—Kabupaten/Kota, DPRD II) take place on the same day as DPR and DPD elections.

All three levels of government also have corresponding direct executive elections. Prior to 2004, the MPR had the power to select the president. In the wake of a constitutional crisis, the executive branches at all levels were provided a separate mandate with direct elections. Presidential elections occurred for the first time in 2004 and took place several months after the national legislative elections. Direct subnational executive elections for governors and regents (Bupati/Walikota) were phased in over a staggered schedule starting in 2005. Though there has been some coordination of elections across subnational units, the timing of these contests remains independent of the legislative branch.

Indonesia's constitution distinguishes the participants of each electoral arena, limiting DPR and DPRD ballot access to political parties and DPD access to individuals. Only registered parties are allowed to run for DPR and DPRD elections, while parties are effectively prohibited from running for DPD elections, making it the largest elected nonpartisan body in the world. Candidates for the presidency and vice presidency run as a pair, and each executive pairing must be proposed by a party or a coalition of parties. The requirements for presidential ballot access have risen from 3 percent of seats or 5 percent of the popular vote in 2004 to 20 percent of seats or 25 percent of the popular vote in 2009. A similar nomination requirement exists for provincial- and regency-level executive elections, where candidates also run as a pair (e.g., regent and vice regent). However, nonpartisan pairs can attain ballot access by meeting a threshold of signed supporters, between 6.5 and 10 percent of residents depending on the region.

Indonesia's collection of electoral systems are interconnected, with no contest functioning independently of the broader system. On one day, voters will cast three list PR ballots for legislatures at three different levels of government, and then cast a single nontransferable vote for the DPD. Three months later, voters will cast a ballot for a combined presidential and vice presidential ticket whose eligibility was determined by the outcome of the national legislative contest. Depending on the result of the first round of voting, voters may be called on to cast a vote in a run-off presidential election. And sometime in the upcoming five years, voters will cast separate votes for prospective governors and regents whose access to the ballot was at least partially determined by results of subnational legislative elections.

# DESIGNING THE ELECTORAL SYSTEM

## Trajectories of Reform

There is a long-standing debate as to whether electoral institutions are the cause of party system outcomes or the outcome of an existing party system configuration (Benoit 2007; see also Colomer, this volume). Perhaps due to its standing as a relatively new democracy, scholars of Indonesia have focused on the politics of institutional design more than the outcomes of these choices. On the face of it, Indonesia appears to have a remarkably stable electoral system: PR was used in the country's first democratic election of 1955, resurrected by Suharto for six authoritarian-era elections between 1971 and 1997, and then kept in place for four free elections since 1999. Nevertheless, beneath the surface of PR, there has been considerable reform, particularly in the latest democratic era.

In terms of the causes of electoral system adoption and change, the Indonesian literature offers a veritable buffet of factors: the colonial example (Crouch 2010, 46); depth of existing sociocultural cleavages in 1955 (King 2003, 27); interests of party leaders to control their organizations (Evans 2003, 28; O'Rourke 2002, 199); issues of timing (Hosen 2004, 156–157); partisan gain (Crouch 2010, 46); partisan miscalculation (Horowitz 2013, 142); international influence (Horowitz 2013, 61); political engineering (Reilly 2006); the lessons of history (Horowitz 2013, 266); and so on. There is hardly a hypothesis of electoral system design that could not find some measure of support in Indonesia. Yet there is also a tendency in the literature to consider one rule at a time. Looking across instances of design, we see several broad patterns.

First, new regimes have adopted a comparatively "permissive" set of electoral rules, in that the mechanical features of the electoral system—and its attendant psychological effects—do little to block the entrance of parties into the legislature. Looking at the lead-up to elections in 1955, 1971, and 1999, the strategic logic of PR adoption was similar across time periods: it satisfied a diverse set of organized interests whose support was deemed critical for the stability of the new regime. Uncertainty regarding levels of public support also helped make a permissive proportional system the least risky of the alternatives.

Second, in terms of *interparty* competition, larger parties have modified rules to squeeze out smaller competitors and dissuade potential entrants (Crouch 2010, 78). After the founding election, victors seek to strengthen the rules, making the system increasingly more difficult to enter. The process was more abrupt and coercive in decades past: Sukarno seized power in the late 1950s and effectively terminated the electoral process, while Suharto forcibly consolidated the party system. In the current democratic period, the process is like a slowly turning vise, ratcheting the pressure on smaller competitors one electoral law at a time. The mechanisms, described later, include adjustments to the electoral formula, reductions of district magnitude, adoption of an increasingly strict legislative threshold, and an onerous set of ballot access rules.

Third, in terms of *intraparty* allocation and functions, another stream of reforms has restrained the power of the party's central leadership. The electoral system transitioned from a closed- to an open-list system. A gender quota was introduced and compliance standards tightened. These reforms have curbed party autonomy, constraining their candidate choices and reducing their ability to act as legislative gatekeepers by eliminating party control over allocation of seats to candidates.[2]

The two trajectories of reform—restrictive interparty rules and restrained intraparty functions—appear, at first, to be at odds: how can large parties manage to bend some electoral rules in their favor while simultaneously allowing other rules to restrict their autonomy and resources? Sherlock's (2009) explanation for the seemingly contradictory trends implicitly focuses on the contextual *act-contingent* motives for reform in post-Suharto Indonesia. Act-contingent motives consider the gain parties get for appearing to support (or at least not oppose) an electoral reform (Shugart 2008). Within Indonesia, there is a strong—and long-running—sentiment that political parties are a problem. "Antiparty" sentiment grew stronger in the chaotic period following the 1999 election and has continued on in the criticism of "cartel politics" (Johnson Tan 2002; Mietzner 2013). Reforms that conform to this spirit seek to snuff out the parties that can be eliminated and handcuff the rest. The need to conform with antiparty sentiment—or at least not cross it too blatantly—helps explain why electoral system reforms have been relatively consistent since 1999. A closer look at the moment of adoption and the two trajectories demonstrates the Indonesian pattern of reform while providing a description of the system.

## Choosing Proportional Representation, and Choosing It Again

Feith (1957, 3) notes that the initial adoption of PR in the 1950s occurred with no serious opposition. King (2003) saw the selection ultimately emanating from the fragmented configuration of societal forces, describing PR as "arguably the only political choice" (p. 27). It was not simply that the authors of the electoral law wanted to bring a diverse array of social groups into the system; the rules themselves were written by a fragmented, appointed legislature. The cabinet required parliamentary confidence, and parliament contained many small parties with an outsized influence concerned about their political fortunes (Feith 1954, 246). PR, with its promise of broad partisan representation, was the safest choice for the parties who happened to be crucial to writing the rules.

A similar dynamic emerged in the more authoritarian context of Suharto's electoral design choices (Gaffar 1992). In his early campaign to imprison and kill the members of the Indonesian Communist Party, and later to oust then-president Sukarno, Suharto enlisted a variety of social groups to assist him, including religious organizations, student leaders, and party elites. He sought to legitimize his executive power using constitutional procedures, which included promises of elections. Alternatives to PR were considered, with one faction of Suharto's supporters advocating a move to a single-seat district system with two controlled parties. PR was retained, in part, because it was more amenable to the existing parties whose participation Suharto valued for the sake of stability (Elson 2001, 183–185). The 1971 victory of Golkar, Suharto's hegemonic party, allowed Suharto to consolidate his regime, at which point he re-engineered the party system through a forced merger of the opposition.

Suharto's departure in 1998 prompted another re-examination of electoral rules. Interim president Jusuf Habibie, who was keen to place himself on the side of "reform," supported the work of a team of experts, known popularly as the Team of Seven, tasked with creating proposals for widespread electoral reform. The Team of Seven proposed transitioning from PR to a mixed-member proportional (MMP) system. The government forwarded a bill to the legislature, which was still dominated by Golkar. The opposition feared that Golkar stood to benefit from the transition to MMP, an assessment Golkar came to agree with following an internal evaluation of the proposed system (Woodward 2002, 222–223; O'Rourke 2002, 199; Hosen 2004, 156). The proposed reform faced strong resistance from opponents both inside and outside of the legislature. The ruling party worried that overriding objections would either cost them at the polls or cause a walkout by the opposition, thereby delegitimizing the result (Crouch 2010, 48; King 2003, 68). As the status quo system, PR prevailed.

## Restricting the System

Within the context of a PR system, Indonesia's electoral rules have become increasingly restrictive. In terms of districts and quotas, Indonesia conforms to Colomer's (2004, 3) "micro-mega rule": large parties prefer "smaller" institutions. The same desire to hobble smaller competitors is also apparent in legislative thresholds and ballot access rules.

### Districts

The original proposal to split the country into a modest number of districts was a matter of contentious debate in the 1950s (Feith 1954, 250). Small parties with diffuse support across the country pushed—unsuccessfully—for a single national constituency. There was no united opposition to the government proposal, however, as small regionally based parties separately sought to increase the number of districts to their advantage. In the end, the country was divided into sixteen districts. Suharto took a similar approach, creating electoral districts to follow provincial lines.

During the post-Suharto transition, district size again became a contentious issue. After backing down on an MMP system, Golkar proposed organizing electoral districts around the country's more than three hundred—and growing—regencies rather than provinces. As the opposition recognized, this was a move to a single-seat district system by stealth, as most regencies would only be awarded one legislative seat. The proposed district reform was rejected by parties fearing partisan disadvantage. Similar to Suharto-era elections, the country's 462 elected seats were distributed across twenty-seven provinces by population, with district magnitude ranging from four to eighty-two, briefly giving Indonesia a larger within-country magnitude variance than any other contemporary democracy.

In the lead-up to the 2004 election, a government-appointed electoral reform team proposed reducing district magnitude to make legislators more responsive to their constituents (Crouch 2010, 63; Horowitz 2013, 144). The range of permitted district magnitudes was eventually set from three to twelve, and the size of the elected DPR was expanded to 550 seats. Twelve of the more populous provinces were subdivided, and the country was left with sixty-nine districts. Another rule change in the lead-up to the 2009 election saw the legislature expand to 560 seats, the maximum permitted district size shrink to ten, and the number of districts increased to seventy-seven. This structure remained in 2014. Over the period of a decade, median district magnitude was brought down from ten to seven. On the island of Java—home to a majority of voters—median magnitude plunged from sixty to eight.

Where the reduction of district magnitude proved useful to larger parties, the drawing of boundaries and the distribution of seats have been more of an administrative process by electoral authorities than a point of partisan contention. The Suharto-era electoral system divided an equal number of seats between the island of Java and the outer islands, despite the fact that Java constituted more than 50 percent of the population. This distribution provided potentially rebellious regions with increased representation, and provided an advantage to Golkar. Since the transition, the regional imbalance has almost disappeared, to the benefit of parties with Javanese strongholds. In 2004, the electoral law required each seat correspond to between 325,000 and 425,000 residents, with exceptions related to the creation of new provinces. Though formal resident-to-seat requirements were removed from subsequent laws, the allocation of seats has not significantly changed. Electoral districts for national elections are formed around provincial and regency boundaries. The splitting of regencies provides potential opportunities for gerrymandering, since strategic actors have increased flexibility to combine their geographic support bases into electoral districts that allow them to maximize their anticipated representation in the legislature. Nonetheless, the stable composition of national districts has been the norm.

## Electoral Formula

All of Indonesia's national legislative elections, in both democratic and authoritarian eras, have used the Hare quota and largest remainders (LR-Hare; see Carey's chapter) to allocate seats. In 1999, parties were permitted to join apparentments. These were agreements announced in advance of the election that allowed parties to pool their remainder votes for the purposes of seat allocation. Known within Indonesia as "Stembus Accords," the apparentments proved unwieldy to administer for the newly constituted electoral authorities. Parties that had unexpectedly done well in an area sought to renege on their agreements, while others proposed ex post facto accords (King 2003, 90; Ellis 2000, 243). Facing myriad competing claims, the overburdened electoral authorities ended up ignoring the accords, to the protests of many smaller competitors, and they were not used in subsequent elections.

In 2009, the rules were significantly changed, though not clearly defined. There would be multiple stages of counting and allocation, creating a two-tier PR system with remainder pooling (as defined in the chapter by Gallagher and Mitchell). In the first stage, seats would be distributed within a district to all parties with 100 percent of quota. A second stage was added in which seats would then be distributed to all parties with 50 percent of quota. If there were any seats to still distribute, the remaining votes from the electoral districts within a province would be aggregated, where a new stage of distribution would commence. By moving from single-tier allocation by LR-Hare to this multistage remainder-pooling process, small parties would pick up fewer remainder seats, thereby benefiting larger parties.[3] Yet the rules were sufficiently complex that the Supreme Court and the Constitutional Court each held different interpretations of which votes should be transferred to the provincial stage of distribution (Butt 2015). In 2014, the complicated process was replaced with a district-level largest-remainder distribution similar to that used in 2004.

## Ballot Access

The two most important barriers to ballot access are organizational capacity and past electoral performance. In terms of organizational capacity, parties must satisfy the country's rules requiring a presence in a defined number of subnational units. The motivation for these requirements is twofold: an overriding concern for national integrity and a desire to limit the number of competitors (Crouch 2010, 47–48; King 2003, 51; Reilly 2006, 132; Horowitz 2013, 68). The electoral law passed in the lead-up to the 1999 election required all parties participating in the election to demonstrate an organizational presence in half of all regencies in half of all provinces. Enforcement of the regional requirement was loose in 1999, as electoral authorities preferred to include parties to avoid a perception that the outcome was engineered (Hosen 2004, 180–183).

The regional requirements have become more onerous since the founding election. For 2004, parties were required to demonstrate an organizational presence in two-thirds of regencies in two-thirds of all provinces. This was kept in place for the 2009 election. To attain ballot access in 2014, however, parties would have to demonstrate an organizational presence in 75 percent of regencies in 100 percent of Indonesia's provinces. Furthermore, the law added a new level of burden by requiring a presence in 50 percent of the relevant subregency units (kecamatan).

A second set of ballot access rules requires parties to meet a registration threshold based on performance in past elections. The Team of Seven proposed barring parties below an electoral performance benchmark from running in the next election (Woodward 2002, 200; King 2003, 51). After some expected pushback from smaller competitors, the registration threshold for competition in the subsequent election was set at 2 percent of national seats (or a similar percentage of subnational seats). In practice, most of the barred parties elided the law through a cosmetic change of name. In 2003, the party registration threshold was raised from 2 percent of all seats to 3 percent. However, the electoral law written in the lead-up to the 2009 election included a loophole allowing all those receiving at least one seat in 2004 to compete in the election.

## Electoral Thresholds

At the same time performance thresholds for party registration were loosened, Indonesia adopted a formal electoral threshold. The larger parties proposed a 5 percent national electoral threshold, though the threshold for 2009 was eventually set at 2.5 percent (Ziegenhain 2015, 94; Mietzner 2013, 161–162). Legal complaints from small parties were unable to remove the threshold, and their absence from the DPR after 2009 made it easier to bump the threshold up to 3.5 percent for the 2014 election.

# Curbing Party Autonomy

While one set of reforms squeeze out small parties, another set of intraparty reforms has reduced the autonomy of the central party leadership. Unlike the efforts to reduce the number of parties, the impetus for intraparty reforms came from outside the party system, and large parties had to be pressured into adopting gender quotas and providing a measure of "flexibility" in the party lists.

## Allocation to Legislators

Indonesia's first election in 1955 used a "flexible" list system. Parties nominated candidate lists, though only party symbols appeared on the ballot. Voters had the option of manually writing the name of a candidate who had received nomination. Candidates reaching quota were allocated seats; seats not allocated via written preference votes were distributed in accordance with list order. The return of controlled elections during Suharto's presidency eliminated this preference option.

When writing post-Suharto election laws, the Team of Seven sought to strengthen legislator–constituent ties through the introduction of an MMP system. As part of the compromise between PR and the mixed-member system, legislators injected a measure of plurality competition into the overarching framework of PR. Each candidate nominated within an electoral district would be assigned to a regency. Parties were to allocate their seats to the candidates from the regencies in which they had their strongest electoral performances, incentivising the cultivation of a local vote and thereby strengthening bonds between eventual legislators and their constituents. Under pressure from party organizations, however, electoral authorities allowed parties to circumvent the system through post hoc reassignment of candidates to regencies. As well, parties were permitted to choose the definitions of electoral performance that ensured their favored candidates were allocated seats (Ellis 2000, 242–244; Evans 2003, 128–130; King 2003, 91).

Following the 1999 election, it was clear that a new procedure to allocate seats to legislators was required. The government-appointed team assigned with devising reform favored strengthening legislator–constituent ties, which eventually led to a proposal for open-list PR (Horowitz 2013, 143; Crouch 2010, 63). The large parties initially opposed the open lists but eventually agreed to adopt a "flexible" list system. Voters were provided with the option of casting a preference vote for a particular candidate on a party's list, with candidate names appearing on the ballot. Candidates achieving a Hare quota within the district would receive a seat. Remaining seats would be distributed in the order determined by the party list. Given the modestly sized districts and the large number of competitive parties, achieving a Hare quota was a nearly impossible task, and only 2 of the 550 elected national legislators managed to cross this threshold. In practical terms, no party list was disturbed, in that the allocation of seats proceeded as it would have under a closed-list system.

In 2008, a rule change lowered the percentage of preference votes required to secure a seat from 100 percent of quota to 30 percent, making it easier for candidates to achieve the threshold needed to disturb the district-level list drawn up by party leadership. In the lead-up to election, several parties saw advantage in a pledge to allocate their seats based purely on preference votes. Candidates took the issue of seat allocation to the Constitutional Court, which ruled that all seats were to be distributed to those candidates receiving the most votes (Butt 2015). As a result of the court's decision, Indonesian elections would be an open-list contest, with copartisans competing for intraparty preference votes and preference votes solely determining the order of election.

## Gender Nomination Quotas

Control over candidate selection is a key power granted to party organizations. Parties must submit their lists of candidates for national office to the central electoral authorities for verification. The electoral authority reviews lists to ensure candidates meet minimal standards of eligibility. While the parties use different procedures to fill out their lists, the centralization of the verification process tends to empower the party's national office. List positions have been a valuable resource that party leaders have used for both party and personal enrichment (Haris and Sanit 2005; Sherlock 2009).

When the 1999 election resulted in a decline in women's representation in the legislature, the internal procedures of parties came under increased scrutiny. Since the composition of party lists played a significant role in allocation of seats, reformers focused on getting women on party lists. Many parties were initially reluctant to support the gender quota proposal, and opposition even came from the sitting female president, Megawati Sukarnoputri. Pressure from activists, the media, foreign nongovernmental organizations, and women legislators and ministers resulted in the adoption of a gender quota (Sherlock 2009, 14–16; Siregar 2006, 2–5; Shair-Rosenfeld 2012, 579–580; Bessel 2010, 227–228).

The initial quota, adopted in advance of the 2004 election, was not mandatory. Parties were to select candidates with "consideration" of attaining at least 30 percent of women's representation. Even though the nomination quota was voluntary, most major parties did alter internal practices in an effort to increase the representation of women. The gender quota was strengthened in the lead-up to the 2009 election. Parties would be required to run 30 percent women candidates. Furthermore, a "zipper" system was introduced, in which it was required that one of every three spots on a party list be occupied by a woman candidate. The "zipper" system sought to increase the proportion of women occupying desirable positions near the top of the party's list, under the assumption that allocation of seats would follow ballot order. The logic of the zipper system was undermined by the unanticipated transition to an open list, in which preference votes rather than list order would determine allocation of seats.

# EFFECTS OF THE ELECTORAL SYSTEM

Are the reforms put in since the transition working? Answering this question is complicated by the myriad motivations for adopting and changing the electoral rules. By necessity, some simplification is required. Next I focus on five goals: (1) a distribution of seats that is roughly proportional to the electoral vote; (2) a moderate number of parties; (3) a national party system where participants compete across the country, preventing conflict around geographically bounded identities; (4) strengthened ties between legislators and constituents; and (5) representation of women approaching 30 percent.

Electoral systems can have immediate effects (proximal) that result directly from an electoral rule or more distant effects (distal) that require multiple steps between the rule and the outcome (Scheiner 2008; Rae 1971). Indonesia's institutional designers have been successful in using blunt electoral rules with proximal effects to achieve straightforward goals, such as the elimination of small and regional parties. Achieving goals with a more complex sequence of steps between rules and outcomes, such as accountability of legislators to constituents and a consolidated party system, has been more difficult.

## Proportionality

In selecting proportional representation, there is an inherent preference in a system where electoral vote share closely tracks legislative seat share, though the restrictive drift of electoral rules indicates a willingness to trade off some level of proportionality for fewer parties. One simple means of tracking the conversion of votes into seats is Gallagher's proportionality index, where low values indicate that representation in the legislature reflects closely the distribution of votes in an election (1991; see also the chapter by Shugart and Taagepera). Values calculated for Indonesia's last four elections indicate a close match between vote shares and seat shares. The 1999 election had an index score of 3.3. The Gallagher index climbed to 4.5 in 2004, then to 6.7 in 2009. In 2014, the value dropped to 2.8, the lowest yet in the post-Suharto era.

Changes in proportionality track the dispersion of the electoral vote rather than adjustments to electoral rules. Between 1999 and 2014, the electoral system was made increasingly restrictive through reductions in district magnitude and the introduction of an electoral threshold, which could be expected to increase disproportionality. Nonetheless, the most proportional result (2014) occurred under the most restrictive system. This outcome reflected changes in the dispersion of the vote, specifically the drop in vote share for minor parties. In 2009, 18 percent of the electoral vote went to parties that received less than 3 percent of the vote. By contrast, only 2 percent of the vote went to similar-sized parties in 2014. The vote shifted to medium-sized parties that were able to reach the electoral threshold, thereby causing disproportionality to fall.

Although the allocation of seats does not significantly diverge from the electoral share of the parties at least at the national level, a large pool of votes do not get translated into seats at the district level. Votes received by a party that receives no seats in a district can be referred to as "wasted."[4] In Indonesia's first post-Suharto election, the median district-level wasted vote was 17 percent, and the maximum was 25 percent. In 2004, the median climbed slightly, to 20 percent, but reached a maximum of 58 percent. District-level wasted votes hit a peak in 2009, with the median wasted vote reaching 30 percent and the maximum rising to 62 percent. The median wasted vote dropped back to 18 percent in 2014, yet the maximum remained high, at 58 percent.

## The Number of Parties

Technocratic institutional designers and larger parties have shared the goal of restricting the representation of minor parties and consolidating the party system into a moderate number of competitors. An assessment of success depends on the metric used. On the one hand, small parties have been eliminated with blunt mechanical and administrative rule changes. In terms of ballot access, forty-eight national parties competed in 1999, twenty-four in 2004, thirty-eight in 2009, and twelve in 2014. The number of parties winning a seat in the legislature has also declined, from twenty-one in 1999 to sixteen in 2004, nine in 2009, and ten in 2014. Increasingly restrictive regional organizational requirements, and the enforcement of these requirements, have brought down the number of parties on the ballot, while the increasing legislative threshold and decreasing district magnitude reduced the number of parties attaining seats.

Despite the consolidation in competitors and total number of parties in the legislature, there has been a corresponding increase in the fragmentation of the legislative party system. The effective number of seat-winning parties ($N_S$) increased 50 percent between 1999 and 2004, jumping from 4.7 to 7.1. The legislative threshold helped bring $N_S$ down to 6.2 in 2009, but it climbed to a record high of 8.2 in 2014. Legislative fragmentation increased because Indonesians were spreading their votes over a greater number of parties. The effective number of vote-earning parties ($N_V$) almost doubled between 1999 and 2009, jumping from 5.1 in the founding election to 8.6 in 2004 and 9.6 in 2009. $N_V$ declined slightly to 8.9 in 2014. The drop in $N_V$ corresponded with a rise in $N_S$, as the electoral vote was consolidated in moderately sized parties capable of passing the electoral threshold.

Indonesian voters and elites have not responded to increasing institutional incentives to consolidate into a moderate number of parties. The mechanical effects of electoral rules are working as anticipated, and small parties have been gradually purged from the legislature. But Indonesia's increasingly restrictive electoral rules have produced little in the way of psychological effects, in which elites and voters act strategically in anticipation of mechanical effects. Between 1999 and 2009, voters increasingly supported marginal parties with little national power. Even after the minor competitors were blocked from the ballot, voters drifted toward a wide array of moderately sized parties rather than consolidating in a few large parties.

The weakness of the psychological effect can be seen in the lack of correlation between district-level electoral fragmentation and district magnitude, taken to be the "decisive" factor in determining party system outcomes (Taagepera and Shugart 1989). In low-magnitude districts, there is incentive to abandon preferred smaller parties for larger competitors with a viable chance of winning one of the few seats (Cox 1997). There is less incentive to abandon first choices in high-magnitude districts, as more competitors could win a seat.

However, there is no correlation between district magnitude and electoral fragmentation within Indonesia. Voters in low-magnitude districts spread their support widely, similar to voters in high-magnitude districts. Choi (2010) demonstrates that low district magnitude did not correlate with low electoral fragmentation in the elections of 1999, 2004, and 2009, a finding that held in 2014. Furthermore, the reduction of district magnitude across elections had no clear effect on party system fragmentation, which has increased. If district magnitude has had an effect on the party system, it has been subtle and generally overshadowed by other factors.

There are several explanations for why the party system is expanding while the electoral laws is becoming more restrictive. At the voter level, the conditions for strategic behavior, as laid out by Cox (1997, 76–80), are unlikely to exist. For one, accurate public information within a district is in short supply. There have only been a limited number of elections from which to form expectations of support levels, and many seemingly viable parties on the ballot. Parties, for their part, are constrained by regional requirement rules from strategically exiting hopeless races.

Another set of explanations suggests that Indonesian voters are not instrumentally rational in the short term when it comes to their legislative choices. Rather, Indonesian elites and voters use the national legislative elections to accomplish goals that go beyond representation in the DPR. One such answer focuses on the effect of presidentialism and the timing of elections. As Shugart and Taagepera (2017) explain, counterhoneymoon legislative elections—taking place late in a presidential term—tend to have a comparatively high effective number of parties as compared to concurrent elections or "honeymoon" elections that take place soon after a presidential contest. In a counterhoneymoon election, parties often use the legislative election to jockey for power in potential executive coalitions. This is the case in Indonesia, where politics at the legislative level are increasingly focused on issues of party leadership and presidential candidates (Choi 2010; Liddle and Mujani 2007; Tomsa 2010). Since the result of the DPR vote determines who has access to the presidential ballot, there is incentive to form—and vote for—parties supporting the presidential ambitions of an aspiring candidate. To support a run for the presidency, aspiring candidates form new parties to provide leverage in the coalition-making stage of presidential nominations.

The effect of the presidential ballot is seen by examining the individual parties over time. Six of the ten parties currently sitting in the DPR ran in the 1999 election. Of these, four are organized around religious identity or institutions.[5] On the secular end of the spectrum, the Indonesian Democratic Party of Struggle (Partai Demokrasi Indonesia

Perjuangan, PDI-P), the heir of Sukarnoist tradition, appeals to religious minorities and less devout voters. Golkar sits astride the religious–secular divide. All the parties had roots in either a religious network or a pre-existing New Order party.

Since 1999, the four successful new entrants are all vehicles for their leader's presidential ambitions. The Democratic Party (Partai Demokrat, PD) was formed in the lead-up to the 2004 election to support former general Susilo Bambang Yudhoyono's presidential run. Former Golkar personnel have also been responsible for the creation of three additional parties: Greater Indonesia Movement Party (Partai Gerakan Indonesia Raya, Gerindra), People's Conscience Party (Partai Hati Nurani Rakyat, Hanura), and the National Democrats (Nasional Demokrat, NasDem). These parties were formed to support the presidential ambitions of their respective leaders, Prabowo Subianto, Wiranto, and Surya Paloh. Similar to Golkar, all the presidential parties are catch-all parties with vague policy commitments.

A second institutional explanation for the increasing size of the party system looks at decentralization. The expanded power of the subnational governments has reduced the relative importance of national legislative elections. Even in areas where winning a national seat is unlikely, regional elites have had little incentive to withdraw or consolidate their efforts in a larger party as subnational seats offer valuable resources. Furthermore, aspiring governors and regents looking to cobble together a coalition to gain ballot access will often pay parties for their support (Buehler and Johnson Tan 2007). Accordingly, networks of politicians use existing party labels to gain access to the legislative ballot in efforts that are aimed at attaining subnational power more than winning national seats (Allen 2014). Given that Indonesian voters tend to support the same party for all three levels of office during legislative elections, these subnational efforts percolate up to affect the national election result.

The combined effects of the presidential and subnational elections reduce incentive for strategic behavior on the DPR ballot. District size, electoral formulas, and even legislative thresholds have had little effect on voters and elites because there are motivations that go beyond the immediate outcome of the national legislative election.

## Party System Nationalization

The regional requirements built into the party and electoral system laws exist to prevent partisan competition that divides the country along subnational identities. On one level, the goal is accomplished simply by requiring an organizational presence across multiple provinces. Outside of Aceh, no party exists that explicitly represents the interests of one particular region.[6] Organizing a regional party is not impossible, but prohibitively costly to dissuade any serious effort.

On the electoral level, Indonesia's parties are not nationalized when compared to other democratic countries. Jones and Mainwaring's (2003) Party Nationalization Score (PNS) provides a metric of how concentrated a party's electoral support is in a particular geographic unit, with low PNS indicating concentration.[7] PNSs in Indonesia, which

Table 43.2  Party Nationalization Scores

|      | Golkar | PDI-P | PKB | PAN | PPP | PKS | PD | Gerindra | Hanura | NasDem |
|------|--------|-------|-----|-----|-----|-----|----|----------|--------|--------|
| 1999 | 0.73 | 0.76 | 0.43 | 0.60 | 0.68 | 0.56 | | | | |
| 2004 | 0.80 | 0.69 | 0.59 | 0.70 | 0.76 | 0.67 | 0.74 | | | |
| 2009 | 0.83 | 0.64 | 0.61 | 0.74 | 0.71 | 0.75 | 0.82 | 0.83 | 0.78 | |
| 2014 | 0.80 | 0.73 | 0.72 | 0.76 | 0.75 | 0.78 | 0.80 | 0.88 | 0.83 | 0.80 |

*Sources of data:* 1999, 2004: Ken Kollman, Allen Hicken, Daniele Caramani, David Backer, and David Lublin. 2016. Constituency-Level Elections Archive. Produced and distributed by Ann Arbor, MI: Center for Political Studies, University of Michigan. 2009, 2014: *Komisi Pemilihan Umum* (General Elections Commission) website http://www.kpu.go.id/.

appear in Table 43.2, are similar to those in Jones and Mainwaring's "low nationalization" category, such as Peru, Brazil, and Canada.

Golkar and the presidential parties have the highest party nationalization scores. All of these catch-all parties can compete across the country and are capable of appealing to devout Muslim, religious minority, and secular voters. The Muslim parties have lower PNSs because they have trouble competing in provinces dominated by religious minorities. Though PNS values are low, there is a trend toward increasing nationalization. This is most pronounced within the Muslim parties, reflecting a process in which parties have declined in their regional strongholds while being forced by ballot access rules to compete across the country.

Regional requirements did not initially produce a set of nationalized parties. The tightening of regional party laws and the increasingly "presidential" orientation of the parties have, however, both contributed to increasing party nationalization. More significantly, region is not currently an enduring national-level cleavage, no separatist or regional parties exist, and communal election violence at the subnational level has been kept relatively low.

## Legislator–Constituent Ties

Strengthening ties between constituents and elected politicians was a consistent goal in the proposals forwarded by Team of Seven members during the transitional period. Reforms such as smaller districts and the introduction of a preference voting option were put in place to increase politicians' accountability to their constituents, thereby reducing the power of the party leadership.

Compared to other electoral reform objectives, strengthening the relationship between legislators and constituents was a diffuse goal without clearly identifiable preferred outcomes. There is little doubt that the move to open lists has had a significant effect on campaigns, increasing intraparty competition and leading to individualized electoral campaigns (Sherlock 2009, 4–10; Tomsa 2010, 143). One metric of increasing personalism is seen in the rising preference voting rate. When the optional preference ballot was introduced in 2004, approximately 52 percent of voters cast a vote for a particular candidate. With the introduction of a completely open list in 2009, this rose to 70 percent in 2009, and stayed steady at 71 percent in 2014.

Beyond increasing intraparty competition and electoral personalism, observers also point to a range of distal effects of the electoral reforms aimed at strengthening legislator–constituent ties. Assessments have found that the new system, among other things, enhanced accountability (Horowitz 2013, 185), solidified a move to "transactional" delivery of bribes and club goods (Aspinall 2014, 97), increased campaign costs (Mietzner 2015, 588), fragmented subnational party systems (Tomsa 2014), and "catalyzed the dissociation of voters from their parties" (Mietzner 2013, 43). Taken together, party organizations have been weakened, and the relationship between individual politicians and constituents plays an increasingly important role. The relationship is largely clientelist, however, which has likely undermined governance outcomes.

Within the context of an open-list PR system, Shugart, Valdini, and Suominen's (2005) cross-national work finds that low district magnitudes should lead to a lower individualized competition compared to higher-magnitude districts, where candidates must compete with a greater number of copartisans through the cultivation of a personal appeal. There is some support for this argument in the Indonesian case. After controlling for contextual factors, there is a positive relationship between district magnitude and preference voting rates within a district, though the effect is modest when compared to socioeconomic variables like ethnic fractionalization, urbanization, and the availability of subnational patronage (Allen 2015). At the level of individual candidates, incumbents receive a higher share of the personal vote, which indicates that advertising experience positively sets politicians apart from copartisans (Dettman, Pepinsky, and Pierskalla 2017). Notably, the incumbency advantage is largest in lower-magnitude districts, where there is less intraparty competition. Taken together, district magnitude correlates with both the level of individualized competition and the importance of certain individual candidate characteristics such as incumbency. The effect of district magnitude change has yet to receive sustained investigation, however.

## Women's Representation

Between 1999 and 2009—the period in which a quota was introduced—women's representation in the legislature doubled. Starting from a low of 9 percent in 1999, women's representation crept up to 11 percent in 2004, and jumped to 18 percent in 2009. In 2014, however, only 17 percent of legislators were women, indicating that the early gains of the present quota system may be complete.

The increase in women's representation was surprising considering initial worries that open lists would disadvantage women. Before the unanticipated switch to a fully open list, reformers put their hope in a "zipper" system, which afforded women many top positions, with the expectation that the allocation of seats to candidates would likely follow party list order. Open lists allowed voters to potentially "vote around" women candidates. Yet this did not become a significant problem in the 2009 election, and women's representation has risen with the more candidate-centered list.

The effect of the quota and its relative success are still debated. In a review of the quota's limitations, Noor (2015) finds that parties are likely selecting low-quality candidates simply to fill out lists, and recommends that a transition back to a closed-list system could improve women's representation. Shair-Rosenfield (2012) is cautiously optimistic, arguing that, in addition to the quota, experience with women incumbents has made Indonesian parties more likely to place women in top list positions and made voters more likely to support women. Although women's representation has yet to hit the 30 percent benchmark envisioned by the reformers, and falls far short of women's percentage of the population, the party quota for women candidates has clearly had some success.

## REFLECTIONS AND PATHS FORWARD

Indonesia's institutional designers have been moderately successful in using electoral rules to generate desired outcomes. The raw number of parties on the ballot and in the legislature has decreased, parties are increasingly nationalized, the percentage of women in the legislature increased after the quota, open lists are creating increased politician–constituent interaction, and electoral results are more proportional than they have ever been in the post-Suharto era. Through a circuitous route, Indonesia has arrived at the "electoral sweet spot" of low-magnitude PR, leaving it with an institutional structure that should tend to foster inclusion while facilitating accountable government (Carey and Hix 2011).

At the same time, voters and elites have not responded to institutional incentives to consolidate, and party system fragmentation has soared to new heights. It is routine for some districts in the outer islands to see more than half their voters support parties that receive no local representation in the national legislature. The new candidate-centered electoral rules have led to exploding campaign costs, placing pressure on successful politicians to fundraise through corrupt practices. After some initial gains, women's representation has slipped. And the proportionality of the system was only achieved through rules that eliminated small parties, making it extremely difficult for any new party lacking an oligarchic backer to ever achieve ballot access.

Indonesia's institutional configuration has produced a party system that functions reasonably well despite its obvious problems. While there has been a recent string of highly contentious executive contests, there has also been a long-term move to the center of the secular–religious divide, at least partially the result of parties having to form broad coalitions to compete in executive elections. Analysts point to weakening social roots and lack of programmatic platforms of parties as signs of dealignment, but this may also be a factor helping Indonesia avoid polarization (Johnson Tan 2015; Ufen 2008). Even though the party system has many competitors, it has avoided Sartori's (1976) "polarized pluralism," whereas the more consolidated system of the 1950s did not (Mietzner 2008). Broadly inclusive cabinets, which have been criticized for stifling accountability, have also helped the country avoid sharp executive–legislative conflict that some believe is endemic to multiparty presidential systems (Slater 2004; Mainwaring 1993).

The study of Indonesia's electoral system has been dominated by analysis of institutional choices. Given that Indonesia's electoral laws change with every election, this topic will continue to garner attention. Yet the accumulation of electoral data allows for increasing analysis of the effect of these laws. In particular, Indonesia's decentralized structure, executive elections, and regional requirements open important avenues for research about the impact of subnational elections on national vote choice, the strategic calculations made in anticipation of a presidential contest, and the evolution of party systems when parties are effectively prevented from "exiting" areas of electoral weakness. This is not to mention the quasi experiment offered by the court-mandated transition to a fully open-list system, the potential for comparison between partisan and nonpartisan bodies, and the enormous amount of subnational variance in institutions and outcomes. The continual process of electoral system reform raises the importance of empirically driven research in the Indonesian context.

## Notes

1. For more on Indonesia's constitution, see Indrayana (2008).
2. The elimination of state subsidies, which technically increased party autonomy from the state, also reduced the capacity of parties to function as independent organizations. For more on party financing, see Mietzner (2007, 2015).
3. For an explanation of the partisan consequence of quotas, see Gallagher (1992, 471–472).
4. Though other authors have used a similar measure of "wasted votes" (Tavits and Annus 2006), the term is not entirely accurate. Votes for a list that is "first loser" are not wasted, as we would not expect strategic desertion of a viable list, while votes for winning parties may be "wasted" in certain circumstances.
5. The United Development Party (Partai Persatuan Pembangunan, PPP), the National Mandate Party (Partai Amanat Nasional, PAN), the National Awakening Party (Partai Kebangkitan Bangsa, PKB), and the Prosperous Justice Party (Partai Keadilan Sejahtera, PKS).
6. Regional parties were permitted in Aceh as part of a peace deal signed between the Indonesian government and the Free Aceh Movement. See Barter (2011).
7. To construct PNSs, I aggregated electoral results at the provincial level.

# References

Allen, Nathan. W. "From Patronage Machine to Partisan Melee: Subnational Corruption and the Evolution of the Indonesian Party System." *Pacific Affairs* 87 (2014): 221–245.

Allen, Nathan. W. "Clientelism and the Personal Vote in Indonesia." *Electoral Studies* 37 (2015): 73–85.

Aspinall, Edward. "Parliament and Patronage." *Journal of Democracy* 25 (2014): 96–110.

Barter, Shane. J. "The Free Aceh Elections? The 2009 Legislative Contests in Aceh." *Indonesia* 91 (2011): 113–130.

Benoit, Kenneth. "Electoral Laws as Political Consequences: Explaining the Origins and Change of Electoral Institutions." *Annual Review of Political Science* 10 (2007): 363–390.

Bessell, Sharon. "Increasing the Proportion of Women in the Parliament: Opportunities, Barriers and Challenges." In *Problems of Democratisation in Indonesia: Elections, Institutions and Society*, edited by M. Mietzner and E. Aspinall, 219–242. Singapore: ISEAS, 2010.

Buehler, Michael, and P. J. Johnson Tan. "Party-Candidate Relationships in Indonesian Local Politics: A Case Study of the 2005 Regional Elections in Gowa, South Sulawesi Province." *Indonesia* 84 (2007): 41–69.

Butt, Simon. *The Constitutional Court and Democracy in Indonesia*. Leiden: Brill, 2015.

Carey, John. M., and S. Hix. "The Electoral Sweet Spot: Low-Magnitude Proportional Electoral Systems." *American Journal of Political Science* 55 (2011): 383–397.

Choi, Jungug. "District Magnitude, Social Diversity, and Indonesia's Parliamentary Party System from 1999 to 2009." *Asian Survey* 50 (2010): 663–683.

Colomer, Josep. M. "The Strategy and History of Electoral System Choice." In *The Handbook of Electoral System Choice*, edited by J. M. Colomer, 3–78. London: Palgrave Macmillan, 2004.

Cox, Gary. *Making Votes Count: Strategic Coordination in the World's Electoral Systems*. Cambridge: Cambridge University Press, 1997.

Crouch, Harold. *Political Reform in Indonesia after Soeharto*. Singapore: ISEAS, 2010.

Dettman, Sebastian., Thomas. B. Pepinsky, and J. H. Pierskalla. "Incumbency Advantage and Candidate Characteristics in Open-List Proportional Representation Systems: Evidence from Indonesia." *Electoral Studies* 48 (2017): 111–120.

Ellis, Andrew "The Politics of Electoral Systems in Transition: The 1999 Elections in Indonesia and Beyond." *Representation* 37 (2000): 241–248.

Elson, Robert. E. *Suharto: A Political Biography*. Cambridge: Cambridge University Press, 2001.

Evans, Kevin. R. *The History of Political Parties and General Elections in Indonesia*. Jakarta: Arise Consultancies, 2003.

Feith, Herbert. "Toward Elections in Indonesia." *Pacific Affairs* 27 (1954): 236–254.

Feith, Herbert. *The Indonesian elections of 1955*. Ithaca, NY: Cornell University Press, 1957.

Gaffar, Afan. *Javanese Voters: A Case Study of Election under a Hegemonic Party System*. Yogyakarta: Gadjah Mada University Press, 1992.

Gallagher, Michael. "Proportionality, Disproportionality and Electoral Systems." *Electoral Studies* 10 (1991): 33–51.

Gallagher, Michael. "Comparing Proportional Representation Electoral Systems: Quotas, Thresholds, Paradoxes and Majorities." *British Journal of Political Science* 22 (1992): 469–496.

Haris, Syamsuddin., and Arbi. Sanit. *Nomination and Selection Process of Indonesian Legislative Candidates*. Jakarta: Research Center for Politics—Indonesian Institute of Sciences, 2005.

Horowitz, Donald. *Constitutional Change and Democracy in Indonesia*. Cambridge: Cambridge University Press, 2013.

Hosen, Nadirsyah. *Reform of Indonesian Law in the Post-Soeharto Era (1998-1999)*. Wollongong, NSW: University of Wollongong, 2004.

Indrayana, Denny. *Indonesian Constitutional Reform 1999-2002: An Evaluation of Constitution-Making in Transition*. Jakarta: Kompas, 2008.

Johnson Tan, P. "Explaining Party System Institutionalization in Indonesia." In *Party System Institutionalization in Asia: Democracies, Autocracies, and the Shadows of the Past*, edited by A. Hicken and E. Kuhonta, 236–259. New York: Cambridge University Press, 2015.

Jones, Mark. P., and Scott. Mainwaring. "The Nationalization of Parties and Party Systems: Application to the Americas." *Party Politics* 9 (2003): 139–166.

King, Dwight. Y. *Half-Hearted Reform: Electoral Institutions and the Struggle for Democracy in Indonesia*. Westport, CT: Praeger, 2003.

Liddle, R. William, Mujani, S. "Leadership, Party, and Religion: Explaining Voting Behavior in Indonesia." Comparative Political Studies 40 (2007): 832–857.

Mainwaring, Scott. "Presidentialism, Multipartism, and Democracy: The Difficult Combination." *Comparative Political Studies* 26 (1993): 198–228.

Mietzner, Marcus. "Party Financing in Post-Soeharto Indonesia: Between State Subsidies and Political Corruption." *Contemporary Southeast Asia* 29 (2007): 238–263.

Mietzner, Marcus. "Comparing Indonesia's Party Systems of the 1950s and the Post-Suharto Era: From Centrifugal to Centripetal Inter-Party Competition." *Journal of Southeast Asian Studies* 39 (2008): 431–453.

Mietzner, Marcus. *Money, Power, and Ideology Political Parties in Post-Authoritarian Indonesia*. Singapore: NUS Press, 2013.

Mietzner, Marcus. "Dysfunction by Design: Political Finance and Corruption in Indonesia." *Critical Asian Studies* 47 (2015): 587–610.

Noor, Firman. "Electoral Reforms and Women's Representation in Indonesia: Successes, Challenges and the Way Forward." In *Improving Electoral Practices: Case Studies and Practical Approaches*, edited by R. Cordenillo, 163–179. Stockholm: International IDEA, 2015.

O'Rourke, Kevin.. *Reformasi: The Struggle for Power in Post-Soeharto Indonesia*. Crows Nest, Australia: Allen and Unwin, 2002.

Rae, Douglas. W. *The Political Consequences of Electoral Laws*. New Haven, CT: Yale University Press, 1971.

Reilly, Benjamin. *Democracy and Diversity: Political Engineering in the Asia-Pacific*. Oxford: Oxford University Press, 2006.

Sartori, Giovanni. *Parties and Party Systems: A Framework for Analysis*. Cambridge: Cambridge University Press, 1976.

Scheiner, Ethan. "Does Electoral System Reform Work? Electoral System Lessons from Reforms of the 1990s." *Annual Review of Political Science* 11 (2008): 161–181.

Shair-Rosenfield, Sarah. "The Alternative Incumbency Effect: Electing Women Legislators in Indonesia." *Electoral Studies* 31 (2012): 576–587.

Sherlock, Stephen. "Indonesia's 2009 Elections: The New Electoral System and the Competing Parties." CDI Policy Papers on Political Governance, Centre for Democratic Institutions, 2009.

Shugart, Matthew. S. "Inherent and Contingent Factors in Reform Initiation in Plurality Systems." In *To Keep or to Change First Past the Post?: The Politics of Electoral Reform*, edited by A. Blais, 7–60. Oxford: Oxford University Press, 2008.

Shugart, Matthew. S., and Rein. Taagepera. *Votes from Seats: Logical Models of Electoral Systems.* New York: Cambridge University Press, 2017.

Shugart, Matthew. S., Melody. E. Valdini, and Kati. Suominen. "Looking for Locals: Voter Information Demands and Personal Vote-Earning Attributes of Legislators under Proportional Representation." *American Journal of Political Science* 49 (2005): 437–449.

Siregar, Wahidah. Z. B. "Political Parties, Electoral System and Women's Representation in the 2004-2009 Indonesian Parliaments." Working Paper, Centre for Democratic Institutions, Canberra, 2006.

Slater, Dan. "Indonesia's Accountability Trap: Party Cartels and Presidential Power after Democratic Transition." *Indonesia* 78 (2004): 61–92.

Taagepera, R., and M. S. Shugart. *Seats and Votes: The Effects and Determinants of Electoral Systems.* New Haven, CT: Yale University Press, 1989.

Tan, Paige. J. "Anti-Party Reaction in Indonesia: Causes and Implications." *Contemporary Southeast Asia* 24 (2002): 484–508.

Tavits, Margit., and Taavi. Annus. "Learning to Make Votes Count: The Role of Democratic Experience." *Electoral Studies* 25 (2006): 72–90.

Tomsa, Dirk. "The Indonesian Party System after the 2009 Elections: Towards Stability?" In *Problems of Democratisation in Indonesia: Elections, Institutions and Society*, edited by M. Mietzner and E. Aspinall, 141–159. Singapore: ISEAS, 2010.

Tomsa, Dirk. "Party System Fragmentation in Indonesia: The Subnational Dimension." *Journal of East Asian Studies* 14 (2014): 249–278.

Turner, Mark., Owen. Podger, Maria. Sumardjono, and Wayan. K. Tirthayasa. *Decentralisation in Indonesia: Redesigning the State.* Canberra: Asia Pacific Press, 2003.

Ufen, Andreas. "From Aliran to Dealignment: Political Parties in Post-Suharto Indonesia." *South East Asia Research* 16 (2008): 5–41.

Woodward, Kathleen. E. *Violent Masses, Elites, and Democratization: The Indonesian Case.* Columbus, OH: Ohio State University, 2002.

Ziegenhain, Patrick. *Institutional Engineering and Political Accountability in Indonesia, Thailand and the Philippines.* Singapore: ISEAS, 2015.

...................................................................................................

# CHAPTER 44

# ELECTORAL SYSTEMS
# IN CONTEXT

*South Africa*

...................................................................................................

## KAREN E. FERREE

SOUTH AFRICA transitioned to democracy in April 1994 when the African National Congress (ANC) won a landslide election and took leadership of the national government, as well as seven of nine provincial governments. The electoral institutions guiding these elections emerged from a lengthy negotiation process, a key goal of which was the representation in parliament of the country's many diverse groups and political traditions. Reflecting these goals of inclusion and representation, South Africa's electoral institutions fell on the far end of the consensual/majoritarian spectrum: they combined parliamentary rules with an extreme form of proportional representation, one that would allow parties with as little as a quarter of 1 percent of the national vote to obtain a seat in the National Assembly. Such a design, endorsed by leading constitutional engineers as the most favorable to democracies with deep social divisions, is generally associated with the consensus-building coalition and minority governments of continental Europe (Lijphart 1999).

In spite of this highly proportional electoral system, South Africa has consistently experienced majoritarian outcomes. In the words of Gouws and Mitchell (2005, 353), it demonstrates "one party dominance despite perfect proportionality." The ANC has prevailed in national elections since 1994, winning over 60 percent of the vote in all elections to date and forming majority governments from 1999 on. The effective number of seat-winning parties in the national parliament has hovered at 2.3 or lower. The ANC has also won all but a handful of provincial races. The remainder of the electorate votes for a large and fluctuating set of opposition parties, some of which do not cross the (very low) threshold for representation at the national level. The most successful opposition party during the post-apartheid period has been the Democratic Alliance (DA), which typically wins less than 20 percent of the national vote and controls only one provincial legislature. Thus, although South Africa's highly proportional electoral system was adopted in part to ensure wide representation and coalition governments, South Africa has a low effective number of parties and majority party domination.

A very different institutional design, adopted in 2000, guides South Africa's municipal elections. These utilize a mixed-member electoral system, with ward-level seats elected according to plurality in single-seat districts, and municipality-wide multiseat districts elected through closed-list proportional representation (PR). Despite the mix of rules, these elections feature ANC dominance in both components of the system. Many parties compete in the races—as they do at the national level—but only a few win seats. The average effective number of parties is low (below two) in both the wards and the PR districts. The 2016 municipal elections suggested some erosion of the ANC's position as opposition parties pushed it out of majority control in a few large metropolitan municipalities, including Johannesburg. These shifts have rattled the ruling party and may auger larger changes, but should not be overstated: the ANC remains in control of more than three-quarters of South Africa's municipalities.

The concentration of support in a small number of parties does not confound the institutional logic of PR. As noted by Cox (1997), district magnitude puts a ceiling on the number of parties, not a floor. However, it falls short of the aspirations of many of those who endorsed proportional representation for South Africa and serves as a useful reminder of the limitations of constitutional engineering. Institutional factors may create the broad parameters within which party systems operate, but their effects on outcomes are rarely deterministic. South Africa's majoritarianism also begs an explanation for why the party system has resisted expansion in spite of highly permissive electoral rules.

Several contextual factors explain single-party dominance in South Africa. First, the formidable salience of racial cleavages in South Africa strongly impacts the party system. In the early post-apartheid period, the opposition parties with the most resources lacked legitimacy with black voters due to their roots in apartheid, which sharply limited their ability to win votes (Ferree 2011). Second, the ANC successfully unified most of the anti-apartheid movement in the early democratic period, starving alternative struggle parties of resources and organization (Ferree 2011). Third, once in power, the ANC exploited secondary electoral institutions like floor crossing and public financing rules to enhance its dominance (Booysen 2006; Gouws and Mitchell 2005; Booysen and Masterson 2009). Finally, like dominant parties everywhere, the ANC has used its control over the state's fiscal resources to encourage and reward loyalty (Kroth, Larcinese, and Wehner 2016). Combined, these factors enabled the ANC to prevent elite defections, present itself as the only reasonable option to govern the country, and preserve its dominance in spite of electoral rules that place virtually no constraints on the number of parties that can win seats. The South African case thus underlines the importance of putting electoral rules in their context. Electoral institutions shape party systems, but do so in combination with other factors, and sometimes in ways that defy simple expectations.[1]

# NATIONAL AND PROVINCIAL
# ELECTORAL RULES

South Africa is a parliamentary democracy, with parliamentary institutions at both the national and provincial levels. At the national level, it has a bicameral parliament, consisting of a ninety-seat upper house, the National Council of the Provinces (NCOP), and a four-hundred-seat lower house, the National Assembly. Parliament selects the head of state and government, the president, who then selects the cabinet. Parliament can dismiss the president and/or cabinet through a vote of no confidence, although this has not happened in the post-apartheid period.[2] South Africa also has nine provincial parliaments, which range in size from eighty seats in KwaZulu-Natal to thirty seats in Free State, Mpumalanga, and Northern Cape.[3] Provincial parliaments select provincial premiers, who select provincial cabinets, called executive councils. Provincial parliaments can dismiss executive councils and premiers through no-confidence votes.[4]

Elections for the National Assembly and the provincial legislatures have occurred concurrently every five years since 1994. Voters cast two ballots: one for the National Assembly and one for their provincial legislature. Concurrent elections, while the practice, are not constitutionally mandated. Election terms for the National Assembly are five years, but presidents can call for early elections if the National Assembly is dissolved prior to that.[5] The NCOP is filled through indirect election via the nine South African provincial legislatures; its primary purpose is to represent provincial interests in national government. Each provincial legislature sends ten delegates, including the provincial premier.

The voters of South Africa—citizens above the age of 18—elect the National Assembly using a two-tier compensatory proportional representation system, with closed party lists. Parties submit ranked lists of candidates to the Independent Electoral Commission (IEC). Parties have complete discretion over their lists, and internal party procedures for generating lists vary. Most consult with local branches to gather preferences, but party leadership retains a veto in all major parties.[6] Parties advertise the lists—which can include hundreds of names—prior to the election, but ballots do not include candidate names. Instead they feature the party name, symbol, and sometimes a photo of the leader. Voters cast one party vote and seats are allocated proportionally to parties according to the proportion of national votes won using the Droop quota with largest remainders (LR-Droop).[7]

In the seat allocation process, parties can submit up to ten lists: a national list (which is optional) and nine regional lists (one for each province). In the regional tier, 200 total seats are distributed over nine provincial multiseat constituencies proportional to provincial population. For example, based on its population, Western Cape received 23 of the 200 regional-to-national seats in 2009, Gauteng received 47 of the seats, Free State 12, and so on. These provincial allocations are distributed to parties proportionally based on their provincial vote totals in the national election using LR-Droop. Parties then allocate their seats to members based on the regional list for that province. The seats a party allocates from its regional lists are then summed across provinces and compared to the allocation of seats it is due based on its total national result. Any difference is topped up using the national list for the party. Thus, in 2009, the ANC won 266 of the 400 National Assembly seats based on its total national vote of 10,601,330. It secured 139 seats from the regional tier, and then received an additional 127 national-tier seats, which it allocated to members on its national list to bring it up to 266.[8]

The use of the two-tier list system affects how seats are distributed within parties, allowing more candidates to be seated from regional lists in provinces where the party has performed better, but does not alter the overall proportionality of the system as it is completely compensatory and the total number of seats a party receives reflects its performance in the national election. The system therefore acts *as if* it is one national district with a magnitude of four hundred. Large district magnitude, with no legal threshold for gaining representation, makes South Africa's electoral system one of the most proportional in the world. In 1994, parties needed just 48,712 votes to surpass the quota for a seat—or about 0.0025 percent of the vote. Based on the seat product model (see the chapter in this volume by Shugart and Taagepera), we would expect this electoral system to result in a very fragmented party system. Given that South Africa has a two-tier compensatory system, we would expect the effective number of seat-winning parties to be around 6.4,[9] which far exceeds its level in practice.

The provincial electoral system also employs closed-list proportional representation, with LR-Droop. Parties submit provincial lists to the IEC along with their national and regional-to-national lists. Election terms are five years, but elections can be called early if the provincial parliament is dissolved.[10] Provincial ballots resemble national ones, with party names, symbols, and images of leaders.

The interim constitution of South Africa established these electoral institutions in 1993 after a protracted series of negotiations.[11] They became permanent after the final constitution of 1996.[12] They replaced a strongly majoritarian, Westminster-like parliamentary system that employed plurality rule in single-seat districts. Legendary disproportionality characterized this system and facilitated the rise and consolidation of the National Party during the apartheid period (Faure 1996).[13] Adoption of South Africa's extreme PR rules reflected both dissatisfaction with the earlier majoritarian system and the context of the transition from apartheid.

In the early 1990s, as South Africa transitioned out of the apartheid, it faced deep challenges. Negotiations over a new constitution, including electoral rules for a nonracial democracy, took place against a backdrop of political conflict.[14] Race and poverty divided a country among the most unequal in the world. Civil war offered a frightening but plausible alternative to democratic transition. While negotiations primarily involved the ANC and National Party (NP), a wide set of additional actors and parties participated, some with antisystem inclinations. The Freedom Front and other extreme right groups teetered between participation in the new system and more violent strategies, as did parties representing ethnic and regional movements within the black population like the Inkatha Freedom Party (IFP). Moreover, both the ANC and the NP contained elements intent on derailing the process (Johnson and Schlemmer 1996).

While negotiations over the interim constitution periodically broke down over contentious details, the selection of the electoral system was one of the less controversial stages of the process, largely because of an early convergence of preferences of the main players (Lodge 2003). The NP and the representatives of other small political factions favored PR because it would increase their odds of survival (Faure 1996; Lodge 2003). With black South Africans representing 80 percent of the electorate, any party without black support would be a minority party. While the NP hoped to win black votes, it could hardly count on them, and indeed ultimately won few (Giliomee 1994). The ANC, expecting to win a majority of votes based on its popularity with black voters, initially opposed PR, viewing it as a last-ditch effort by white parties to hold on to power (Mattes 1994; Lodge 2003). By the early 1990s, however, the party had switched to embracing closed-list PR (Mattes 1994). This switch likely reflected several factors. The party believed it would obtain a majority independent of the rules, so compromising on this component of the constitution cost it little (Lodge 2003; Gouws and Mitchell 2005; Mattes 1994); Moreover, PR might allow it to secure seats for some of its less obviously electable members—for example, high-ranking whites and Indians with few links to actual black constituencies (Lodge 2003). Closed-list PR would also help party elites maintain discipline over backbenchers (Lodge 2003). And finally, the simplicity of party voting in a closed-list PR system had appeal to a party of newly enfranchised voters with limited education. Voters could find the party symbol and face of Nelson Mandela and put their mark in the correct place (Gouws and Mitchell 2005).

In adopting PR, South Africa followed the endorsements of prominent constitutional engineers like Arend Lijphart, who had longed advocated proportional rules as optimal for countries with deep racial and political fissures.[15] Extreme parties with antisystem tendencies might moderate with the promise of parliamentary representation. In contrast, a majoritarian system could freeze them out, stewing in their discontent. The hoped-for outcome of the design was consensual democracy, with a large multiparty system, coalition or minority governments, and the benefits such a system brings: inclusion, representation, moderation, and compromise (see also Reynolds 1998, 1999a; Sisk 1995). The interim constitution's mandate for a Government of National Unity, which involved leaders of the largest parties serving as deputy presidents in the cabinet, also reflected these goals.

Complaints about the electoral system periodically surface and discussions prior to the 1996 constitution debated the merits of moving to a different set of rules. A main criticism has been the lack of strong linkages between elected officials and constituents and the absence of incentives for constituency service (Mottiar 2005; Barkan 1998). The ANC made efforts to address these issues in 1994 by establishing an informal constituency system for elected members of parliament (MPs) and making resources available to support constituency service. However, absent an electoral linkage, these efforts amounted to little; few MPs keep staffed constituency offices (Barkan 1998). The ANC has not initiated more significant electoral reform.

# MUNICIPAL ELECTORAL RULES

Municipalities form the third and most local tier of government in South Africa. Legislation beginning in 1998 reformed the existing municipal map and established the structure, responsibilities, and electoral systems of municipal governments.[16] The first municipal elections under the new rules occurred in 2000, with subsequent elections in 2006, 2011, and 2016.[17] Municipal governments lead the "developmental crusade" in South Africa (Siddle 2011). The Municipal Structures Act of 1998 tasks them with the ambitious goal of overturning apartheid's legacy of poverty and uneven development. They provide highly valued local public goods like water, electricity, education, health, and housing; set and collect local taxes; and represent the most visible face of government to many voters. During the post-apartheid period, protests about local government performance have been frequent and widespread (Atkinson 2007; Siddle 2011). For these reasons, any treatment of South African electoral and party systems should include a discussion of the municipal level of government.

South African municipalities fall into three categories. Metropolitan municipalities (category A, or colloquially "metros") are large cities with high population densities and complex, developed economies. As of 2016, South Africa had eight metropolitan municipalities, including Cape Town, Durban, Tshwane (Pretoria), and Johannesburg. Local municipalities (category B) are smaller towns and surrounding rural areas. Most South African municipalities (207 in 2016) fall into category B. District municipalities (category C) combine and coordinate several local municipalities into a regional aggregation to capture economies of scale in service delivery. All category B local municipalities nest into overarching district municipalities (of which there were 44 as of 2016), and these two levels share responsibilities and authority for a particular area. Category A metros do not nest into a higher level.[18]

Municipal councils govern each type of municipality and range in size from three seats (in small local councils) to over two hundred (in large metros). Elections for councils occur every five years. Metropolitan and local municipalities employ mixed-member proportional (MMP) electoral systems, filling half the seats through single-seat plurality ward races, and the other half through municipality-wide closed-list proportional representation.[19] Voters cast two ballots in metro or local elections: one for a ward councilor and one for a municipal-level closed party list. Independent candidates can run in ward races, but not for PR seats. The Droop quota for the PR race is determined by dividing the total number of all party votes in the PR and ward races by the number of seats in the council (PR and ward) not filled by independent candidates and adding one.[20] To determine the total number of seats won by a party, its total votes (PR and ward) are divided by the quota. If this number exceeds the number of ward seats won, then it is compensated with PR seats using the largest-remainder system. District municipalities, on the other hand, fill 40 percent of their seats through a single district-wide PR election. Representatives selected from local councils fill the remaining 60 percent. Voters in local municipalities thus cast three ballots: one for ward representative, one in the PR race for the local municipality, and one in the PR race for the district council. In contrast, voters in metro municipalities cast only a ward vote and metro PR vote.

Although relatively little has been written on the process leading to these electoral rules, their adoption likely balanced the goal of maintaining proportionality while also injecting a degree of constituency representation into the local government system through ward councilors.[21] The rules also opened the door to independent candidates, a significant departure from the extreme party-centered nature of the national and provincial electoral rules (Nijzink and Piombo 2005, 77).[22]

Like the national and provincial electoral list PR systems, the PR half of South African municipal elections should enable a large number of parties to win seats. District magnitude varies by municipality. Some PR districts involve several dozen seats. Others are small, three to five seats. The mean council size from 2000 to 2011 was around sixteen seats, implying a mean PR district magnitude of eight.[23] Duvergerian logic suggests that the effective number of parties should be lower for ward elections versus municipal elections, especially over time as voters gain experience with the system.[24]

# THE SOUTH AFRICAN PARTY SYSTEM

While the guiding principle of South Africa's electoral system design was multipartism and consensual democracy, the predominant theme of the post-apartheid South African party system has been ANC dominance at all levels of government. The ANC frequently captures more than 60 percent of the vote in races small and large, and in many parts of the country regularly exceeds 80 percent of the vote. A secondary theme has been opposition fragmentation. The second-largest party typically wins 20 percent or less of the national vote, while a large and shifting set of smaller parties divide the remainder. Recent elections have seen ANC dominance fray somewhat, especially in urban areas, but the party continues to control national government, eight out of nine provinces, and most municipalities outside of Western Cape. Coalitions have been rare in South African government except at the municipal level, especially after the 2016 municipal elections, which produced coalition or minority governments in 13 percent of municipalities, including a handful of large metros like Johannesburg.[25]

Prior to the 1994 election, the ANC successfully unified the large majority of black voters, approximately 80 percent of the electorate, under its great tent.[26] By continuing to hold the loyalty of this group, the party has won national elections in South Africa by wide margins since 1994 (see Table 44.1). Indeed, in spite of South Africa's highly proportional electoral rules, there has only been one instance of coalition government at the national level: the Government of National Unity (GNU), which drew together the ANC, the National Party, and the IFP during the first parliament (1994–1999), and it transpired even though the ANC had a majority of seats in parliament.[27]

### Table 44.1 The National Party System

|                                    | 1994 | 1999 | 2004 | 2009 | 2014 |
|------------------------------------|------|------|------|------|------|
| Number of parties (votes)          | 19   | 16   | 21   | 26   | 29   |
| Number of parties (seats)          | 7    | 12   | 11   | 13   | 13   |
| Effective number of parties (seats) | 2.21 | 2.15 | 1.97 | 2.12 | 2.26 |
| Largest party                      | ANC  | ANC  | ANC  | ANC  | ANC  |
| Largest party vote percent         | 63   | 66   | 70   | 66   | 62   |
| Second-largest party               | NP   | DP   | DA   | DA   | DA   |
| Second-largest party Vote percent  | 20   | 10   | 12   | 17   | 22   |
| Coalition government?              | Yes  | No   | No   | No   | No   |

Calculations by author based on data from the Electoral Commission of South Africa's website at http://www.elections.org.za (accessed August 29, 2016).

### Table 44.2 The Provincial Party System

|                                          | 1994 | 1999 | 2004 | 2009 | 2014 |
|------------------------------------------|------|------|------|------|------|
| Average effective number of parties (seats) | 1.66 | 1.67 | 1.84 | 2.11 | 1.91 |
| Average number of parties (votes)        | 10   | 13   | 15   | 17   | 19   |
| Average number of parties (seats)        | 4.3  | 5.4  | 5    | 4.6  | 4.6  |
| Average ANC seat percentage              | 67   | 70   | 72   | 69   | 66   |
| ANC provinces                            | 7    | 7    | 7    | 8    | 8    |
| Opposition provinces                     | 2    | 0    | 0    | 1    | 1    |
| Coalition governments                    | 0    | 2*   | 2*   | 0    | 0    |

\*  Western Cape and KwaZulu Natal.

Calculations by author based on data from the Electoral Commission of South Africa's website at http://www.elections.org.za (accessed August 29, 2016).

The ANC has also dominated all but a few provincial legislatures: over five elections in nine provinces, only four provincial governments have featured majority control by a party other than the ANC: Western Cape in 1994, 2009, and 2014, and KwaZulu Natal in 1994. A handful of provincial coalitions also occurred in 1999 and 2004 as power shifted in Western Cape and KwaZulu-Natal (see Table 44.2). Of some note, the ANC's hold over Gauteng, the industrial heartland of the country with both Pretoria and Johannesburg, slipped to 54 percent in the 2014 election, the lowest ever. ANC support also dropped in traditional strongholds like Limpopo, Mpumalanga, and Free State. Recent erosions of

Table 44.3  The Municipal Party System

|  | 2000 | | 2006 | | 2011 | | 2016 | |
|---|---|---|---|---|---|---|---|---|
|  | Ward | PR | Ward | PR | Ward | PR | Ward | PR |
| Average effective number of parties (votes) | 1.7 | 1.8 | 1.7 | 1.9 | 1.8 | 2.0 | – | – |
| Average number of parties (votes) | 3.7 | 4.0 | 6.1 | 5.9 | 6.3 | 6.7 | – | – |
| ANC vote percentage | – | 59 | 64 | 66 | 61 | 63 | 53 | 55 |
| DA vote percentage | – | 22 | 16 | 16 | 24 | 24 | 27 | 27 |

Effective number of parties for 2000–2011 calculated by author using disaggregated data from the IEC; see details in Ferree et al. (2017). Calculations not completed for 2016. ANC and DA PR vote percentages for 2000 election reported by Electoral Institute of South Africa (EISA), "South African Local Election Results 2000: Proportional Representation Vote Comparison by Province," n.d. ANC and DA vote percentages for 2006 election reported by EISA, "South Africa: 2006 National Overview—Votes by Political Party," n.d. ANC and DA percentages for 2011 and 2016 on IEC webpage: http://www .elections.org.za/content/Elections/Municipal-elections-results/ (accessed August 29, 2016).

ANC dominance should be put in context, however: the party remained at 70 percent or above in all three provinces and still took an average of 66 percent of the seats across provincial legislatures.

Municipal elections present a more varied picture. The ANC dominates these elections in terms of control over municipal councils. Prior to 2016, opposition parties had firm footholds only in Western Cape, where the DA won control over half of the municipal councils in 2011, and KwaZulu Natal, where the IFP and smaller parties prevented the ANC from sweeping all municipalities. In 2016, the ANC lost majority control over a few large and important municipalities outside these provinces—Nelson Mandela Bay, Johannesburg, and Tshwane (Pretoria)—an outcome that filled newspaper headlines and induced jubilation in the opposition.[28] Nonetheless, the ANC continued to control over three-quarters of all municipalities in the country. Of some note, average ANC vote percentages have fallen below 70 percent of the vote in both ward and PR races since 2000, and in 2016, it won an all-time low of 53 percent of ward votes and 55 percent of PR votes (see Table 44.3).

The opposition divides a small pie of votes into many slivers. Since 1994, the opposition has featured one main party surrounded by a constellation of much smaller ones. The main opposition party generally wins no more than 20 percent of the vote in national elections, takes at most one provincial legislature, and controls less than 10 percent of all municipal councils.

Initially the primary opposition party was the former apartheid ruling party, the NP, which became the New National Party (NNP) in 1997. The NP won 20 percent of the votes in 1994 and controlled Western Cape.[29] In 1999, the Democratic Party (DP)—the descendent of apartheid-era opposition parties—eclipsed the NNP, but only won

10 percent of the vote overall.[30] The NNP and DP merged to form the DA prior to the 2000 local government elections,[31] and the DA has been the primary opposition party since then. The DA draws support largely from minority voters—primarily whites, but also increasingly coloureds and Indians. It won 12 percent of the national vote in 2004, 17 percent in 2009, and 22 percent in 2014. It has controlled Western Cape provincial governments since 2009, demonstrating its popularity among the white and coloured voters that make up most of the population there. It performed relatively well in the 2000 municipal elections, winning 22 percent of the ward and PR vote and taking control of a number of municipalities in Western Cape. In 2006, its performance flagged as its vote percentages dropped to 16 percent of the vote. It rebounded in 2011 and especially 2016, when it captured 27 percent of the vote and pushed the ANC out of majority control of key municipalities. Recent races suggest that the DA may be making some inroads into the black electorate—strong performances in Gauteng and Eastern Cape would require some degree of cross-over voting by blacks—but the majority of the black electorate, especially in rural areas, continues to avoid the party.

While the DA is the primary opposition party, South Africa features a large set of smaller single-digit and "micro" parties (Booysen 2006). The larger and more significant of these parties attract mostly black votes and modestly chip away at ANC control in one or more regions. They tend to flare up for a period of time and then collapse back into the ruling party or persist as one-man or -woman operations. The longest lasting and most significant of these has been the Inkatha Freedom Party (IFP). Under the leadership of Mangosutho Buthelezi, the IFP exploited its deep roots and patronage networks from the KwaZulu Bantustan (KZN) to take majority control over the KZN parliament in 1994.[32] It ruled in coalition with the ANC in 1999 and 2004. A significant and controversial player in the period leading up to elections and the early post-apartheid period, its importance has since waned.[33] It continues to win small municipalities in KZN (now competing with its own splinter, the National Freedom Party), but otherwise has little impact. Two other modestly successful parties that built on old Bantustan roots were the United Democratic Movement (UDM), led by Bantu Holomisa, and the United Christian Democratic Party (UCDP), led by Lucas Mangope. Both Holomisa and Mangope had previous incarnations as apartheid-era homeland leaders. The UDM drew votes from the ANC in Eastern Cape in 1999 and 2004 before retreating to obscurity (Piombo 1999). The UCDP was the second-largest party in the North West province in 1999 and 2004 but has had diminishing impact since then. Outside of the IFP (which presented a regional but not national challenge), none of these parties seriously threatened the ANC.

Beginning in 2009, a different type of opposition party emerged: one based more on ideology, with a broader, less regionally centered constituency. In 2009, the Congress of the People (COPE) formed out of elite splits in the ANC and opposition to the ascension of Jacob Zuma to party leadership at the divisive 2007 Polokwane ANC party conference. COPE initially appeared poised to draw significant high-level defections from the ANC in the run-up to the 2009 campaigns, and at one point predications suggested it might win as much as 40 percent of the vote (Ferree 2011, 215). It carved out a political space in the center of the spectrum, differentiating itself from the ANC less on policy and more on promises to implement programs more effectively and with less corruption. Although it initially appeared more dangerous to the ruling party than previous contenders, the ANC managed to stem elite defections and ran a strong campaign that ultimately cauterized COPE's impact, holding it to just 7.4 percent of the national vote and thirty National Assembly seats in 2009 (Ferree 2011). In 2014, COPE's support fell to under 1 percent of the vote and just three seats.

The 2014 election saw the emergence of the Economic Freedom Fighters (EFF). The populist EFF targets the left side of the political spectrum, campaigning on a hybrid ideology of African nationalism and socialism (Robinson 2014). In so doing, it taps into a deep river of African political tradition in South Africa that was largely quiescent during the early post-apartheid period. The EFF's leader, Julius Malema, formerly headed the Youth League of the ANC; known as brazen and twice convicted for hate speech, he was expelled from the ANC in 2012 amid controversy. The EFF quickly became popular in urban and semiurban communities in Gauteng, North West province, and Limpopo, where its radical economic message appeals to voters. It became the third-largest party in South Africa in the 2014 election, winning 6.4 percent of the vote and capturing twenty-five National Assembly seats. In the 2016 municipal elections, it increased its support to around 8 percent of the vote. While it is too early to tell whether the EFF will survive further election cycles, it represents a different and potentially more dangerous challenge to the ANC than its predecessors, with an ideological message that strongly resonates with an electorate weary from decades of high unemployment. The two-sided challenge of the EFF on the left and the DA on the right certainly represents something new for the ANC (Southall and Schulz-Herzenberg 2014). While the EFF and DA represent unlikely partners, they do periodically unite to oppose the ruling party and together they may force it into coalition government. Nonetheless, the ANC still has a very formidable hold on the electorate, with 62 percent of the national vote in 2014 and control of eight provinces and more than three-quarters of all municipalities.

In the aggregate picture, the number of parties winning votes in national elections has steadily increased since 1994, when 19 parties won votes, to 2014, when 29 did. The same trend applies to provincial elections: in 1994, an average of 10 parties won votes, whereas an average of 19 did in 2014. In fact, across every provincial legislature, the number of parties winning votes has increased in every single election since 1994. In this sense, South Africa's proportional system produces the expected outcome: a large (and growing) party system. However, while the number of parties competing in and winning votes has grown, the number of parties winning seats has not changed much at all. There was a big bump in parties winning seats in the National Assembly between 1994 and 1999 (from 7 to 12), but no significant change since. In the provincial elections, an average of 4.3 parties won seats in 1994; in 2014, it was 4.6. In terms of the effective number of parties, very little has changed: in the national party system, the effective number of seat-winning parties was 2.21 in 1994 and 2.26 in 2014, after a dip in the intervening years. In the provincial elections, the effective number of seat-winning parties ranged from 1.66 to 2.11. The low number of parties is not what we would expect for an extreme PR system.

Finally, while we might expect the size of ward party systems (with their single-seat plurality rules) to differ substantially from the size of municipal PR systems, this does not appear to be the case. As Table 44.3 shows, the average effective number of parties for each component of the municipal system was highly similar across the first three municipal elections: 1.7 versus 1.8 in 2000; 1.7 versus 1.9 in 2006; and 1.8 versus 2.0 in 2011. While the PR component produces slightly more parties, the overall pattern remains one of ANC dominance and low effective number of parties regardless of rules. Of some note, racial diversity drives the number of parties in *both* the single-seat district and PR sides of the system (Ferree et al. 2017), contradicting the well-known interactive hypothesis that social diversity should only shape party system outcomes in permissive electoral systems (Amorim-Neto and Cox 1997; Clark and Golder 2006; Ordeshook and Shvetsova 1994).[34] Ferree et al. (2017) suggest that the salience of racial divisions in South Africa may interfere with strategic behavior on the part of voters and parties, reducing defections from likely losers and preventing Duvergerian coordination. These results once again demonstrate the limits of institutional theories in South Africa.

# EXPLAINING SINGLE-PARTY DOMINANCE IN SOUTH AFRICA

With the exception of the single seat plurality rules that guide ward elections at the municipal level, South Africa's electoral rules place few constraints on its party system. Yet, while many parties win votes, few win more than a handful of seats, and power remains concentrated in the ruling ANC. Why? To explain single-party dominance in South Africa, one must look beyond the electoral rules to other features of the social and political context.

First, there is the formidable salience of racial cleavages in South Africa and the way in which these cleavages shape perceptions about parties. In the early post-apartheid period, the opposition parties with financial resources, ground organization, and campaign experience had little legitimacy with nonwhite voters, who made up the great majority of the country. The National Party had built the apartheid state, one of the most racially repressive institutions in the world, and it would take more than the release of Nelson Mandela and legalization of the ANC to reform its image in the black electorate. The Democratic Party was the latest manifestation of a series of parties that opposed apartheid "from within." These parties, which started with the Progressive Party in 1959, never captured much of the (all-white) vote, but did manage to periodically shine light on some apartheid-era abuses. While DP leaders hoped that this legacy would win the party black votes, it entered the apartheid period relatively unknown. Those black voters who did know it largely discounted its participation in the apartheid struggle. Thus, while the NP and DP had access to resources that many other opposition parties lacked, they entered the post-apartheid period with party images that significantly limited their appeal to most of the electorate. Most black voters saw them as exclusively "white," a label the Democratic Alliance inherited when it formed in 2000. As these perceptions of opposition parties fortified the ruling party's claim to being the only legitimate party to govern South Africa, it fought hard and successfully to preserve them (Ferree 2011).

Of some note, this explanation of how social factors impact the party system is distinct from those offered by prior theories, especially the interactive hypothesis. The interactive hypothesis suggests that large party systems require both permissive rules and significant social diversity. A small effective number of parties in a permissive system might therefore reflect a lack of social diversity. This is clearly not the explanation for South Africa. In addition to its four racial groups, it has thirteen ethnolinguistic groups. If social diversity and permissive rules are enough to generate a large party system, then South Africa should have one. Thus, the effects of social factors are not limited simply to "diversity." Beyond the size and number of groups, it is important to understand how particular cleavages drive political competition and shape the space of "legitimate" political organizations.

Second, the ANC successfully unified most of the anti-apartheid movement under its sweeping umbrella, monopolizing human capital, grassroots structures, and access to finance. Alternative opposition parties with struggle credentials existed during the early post-apartheid years. The Pan African Congress (PAC) had rich roots in the apartheid struggle and hopes of attracting significant support in the 1994 election, as did Azapo (the Azanian People's Organization). Without exception, however, these parties lacked financial, human, and organizational resources (Cooper 1994). They won slivers of the vote in early elections before fading into obscurity, prevented from capitalizing on their histories by resource constraints and internal squabbles. Other black opposition parties like the IFP, UDM, and UCDP had roots in the old Bantustan system and could build on existing patron-client networks. While they created greater headaches for the ANC, they were regional in nature, conservative, built on the support of only one ethnic group, and lacking in wider legitimacy. They too faded away as the ANC cemented its control over state structures. Finally, altogether new parties attempting to build themselves out of whole cloth faced formidable challenges on multiple fronts: acquiring money to run campaigns, building structures at the local level, developing attractive party labels, and finding viable candidates. The most obvious route to developing a new party may be to splinter away from an old one, but the experience of COPE, which was formed by ANC defectors who hoped to initiate a wave of additional defections, demonstrates the difficulty of following this path (Ferree 2011). The ruling party has ample means of punishing defectors, banishing them to political obscurity and curtailing their ability to move into lucrative careers in the private sector. More recently, the EFF also formed as a splinter from the ANC. It may ultimately draw more blood from the ruling party, but as of this writing, it is too early to say.

Third, the ANC has used its ability to shape secondary electoral institutions like floor-crossing rules and the public financing of political parties to tilt the playing field in its favor. Floor-crossing legislation in South Africa has followed an arc, from prohibition, to short periods in which it was permitted, back to prohibition. The primary effect of this arc of legislation was to cement ANC dominance and establish the DA as the largest opposition party. Party financing laws also favor the largest parties and deter efforts to form new ones, creating status quo bias in the party system. Both points are developed next.

The interim and 1996 constitutions prohibited floor crossing at all levels of government; MPs who did defect had to give up their seats.[35] In practice, the rule may have helped the ANC discipline its own members by eliminating exit options, allowing the party to "redeploy" members at the whim of party leadership (Gouws and Mitchell 2005; Lodge 1999). In spite of this convenience, in 2002–2003 the ruling party cooperated with the recently formed DA to amend the constitution to allow floor crossings at all levels of government. Crossing occurred during specific windows of time determined by the executive.[36] The first transfer window at the local level took place in October 2002; in provincial and national parliaments, it took place in March 2003. The ANC gained net seats at all levels of government by absorbing MPs from the NNP and other opposition parties during the initial floor-crossing periods. The DA also gained during the initial crossing windows, attracting the remaining representatives of the NNP to become the largest opposition party. The changes decimated the NNP and many smaller parties (Booysen 2006; Gouws and Mitchell 2005). The elections of 2004 further entrenched these patterns, as did later floor-crossing windows.[37] While enhancing ANC dominance, floor crossing also generated tensions within the party as defectors sometimes received higher positions on party lists than party stalwarts. After its contentious national conference at Polokwane in 2007, the party reversed its support of floor crossing and formally abolished it through an amendment of the constitution in January 2009 (Booysen and Masterson 2009).

Public financing of political parties provides another institutional resource for the ruling party. The Public Funding of Represented Political Parties Act (1997, 2(1)) established a fund to provide parties represented in the National Assembly and provincial legislatures with financial support. Parties receive funding proportional to their level of representation. The Independent Electoral Commission administers the fund and has the ability to audit and sanction parties that abuse their use of the money.[38] While public financing promotes transparency and regulation (as opposed to the private financing of parties, which is neither transparent nor well regulated in South Africa), it generates status quo bias in the party system. Because public financing is proportional to representation, the ANC's allocation dwarfs that of its competitors, reinforcing the advantages it already has as the ruling party. In 2009, for example, the ANC received over five times as much public financing as the second- and third-largest parties combined (Booysen and Masterson 2009, 415). Furthermore, because new parties do not receive funding until they gain representation, they face financial challenges during first campaigns. This reduces incentives for politicians to break away from existing (funded) parties to start new ones. Moreover, leaders of parties, even small ones, may be reluctant to merge with other parties if it means giving up an independent source of financing. As a result, public financing creates inertia in the party system, reinforcing existing patterns and levels of support.

Finally, in the tradition of dominant parties around the world (Magaloni 2006), the ANC used its control over the state's fiscal resources to encourage and reward loyalty. The party has delivered highly desired services to an electorate that previous governments massively underserved and neglected. While this may not guarantee voter loyalty (de Kadt and Lieberman forthcoming), it likely explains some of the electorate's continued support for the ruling party. The ANC also appears to engage in some resource targeting to areas that supported it in the past (Kroth, Larcinese, and Wehner 2016). Combined with the factors discussed earlier, these moves have helped ensure the ANC's hold over the South African electorate.

# Conclusion

South Africa's national electoral system, one of the most proportional in the world, was designed explicitly with the goal of ensuring representation in parliament for a wide variety of groups and parties. In spite of these rules, the ANC has dominated all levels of government, and the effective number of legislative parties in national, provincial, and municipal institutions is far lower than predicted by well-established institutional theories. South Africa thus represents a compelling puzzle for institutional theories and illustrates the way in which contextual factors impact the effects of institutions on the party system.

Ferree et al. (2014) distinguish two types of contextual effects. Context may winnow down the number of parties when electoral institutions are permissive. Alternatively, contextual factors may interfere with the strategic behavior necessary to generate coordination and reduce party number in restrictive systems. South Africa primarily demonstrates the former effect. Contextual factors drive down the number of parties, concentrating support in one major party in spite of electoral rules that impose few constraints and allow even very small parties to win seats. South Africa may also demonstrate the latter effect in its single-seat municipal ward elections, which appear to violate Duvergerian expectations when racial diversity is high. South Africa thus illustrates two primary avenues through which context can shape outcomes: winnowing and coordination inhibition.

The South African case also argues for the importance of a wider range of contextual variables. Existing "contextual" explanations for party systems generally focus on one of two factors: the age and/or institutionalization of the party systems and social diversity (Moser and Scheiner 2012).[39] Neither offers a sufficient explanation for South Africa. The relative youth of South Africa's democracy may offer a partial account for its party system. It is possible, even likely, that the dominance of the ANC will eventually crumble. Yet ANC dominance has persisted over twenty years and four national election cycles, and at some point, "youth" offers too thin an explanation for its success in holding on to power. The standard wisdom on how social diversity affects party systems is captured by the interactive hypothesis, which argues that large party systems require both permissive rules and high social diversity. Clearly, this hypothesis offers little insight into South Africa, which has a small party system in spite of both permissive rules and one of the most diverse societies on the planet.

South Africa's party system thus reflects factors beyond democratic age and social diversity. It refocuses attention not on the size and distribution of groups, but rather on the intensity of certain cleavages and how they shape the political terrain negotiated by parties. Social diversity may not shape the party system in a direct and linear way (more groups, more parties), but the *salience* of social divisions, specifically race, does clearly matter. Moreover, the South African case points to a fuller set of contextual factors including other types of institutions like floor-crossing legislation and party financing laws. Electoral rules are but one piece in a broad mosaic of rules and institutions that shape party system outcomes. More than anything, the case reveals the ways that dominant parties, once ensconced in power through some fortuitous confluence of factors, fortify their position by manipulating institutions, flows of resources, and perceptions of their opponents to bend the expectations generated by both constitutions and cleavages.

# Author's Note

All tables were prepared by the author specially for this chapter.

## Notes

1. On context and electoral rules, see Ferree, Powell, and Scheiner (2014) and Moser and Scheiner (2012).
2. See Republic of South Africa, Constitution of 1996, chap. 4 (Parliament) and chap. 5 (The President and National Executive). The constitution can be found online at http://www.gov .za/documents/constitution-republic-south-africa-1996 (accessed July 18, 2016).
3. These seat counts reflect the situation after the 2014 election. Information on the provincial legislatures can be found at Legislative Sector South Africa, "Legislatures," http://www.sals .gov.za/show.php?show=1 (accessed July 18, 2016).
4. Constitution of the Republic of South Africa, 1996, chap. 6 (Provinces).
5. Constitution of the Republic of South Africa, 1996, chap. 4 (Parliament), Sections 49 and 50. According to Section 50, the president must dissolve the National Assembly if three years have passed since the assembly was elected and the assembly adopts a resolution to dissolve with a supporting vote from a majority of its members. Section 50 also indicates that an acting president must dissolve the National Assembly if there is a vacancy in the office of president and the assembly has not elected a new president within thirty days of the occurrence of the vacancy.

6. See Ferree (2011, 184–186) and Lodge (1999).

7. The Droop quota is the number of valid votes divided by one plus the number of seats to be allocated. After application of the quota, the parties with the largest vote remainders (their votes minus votes used up already on quota seats) obtain the remaining seats. See the introduction to the volume for details.

8. For a clear explication of the arithmetic behind list allocations, see Manuel Álvarez-Rivera's "Election Resources on the Internet: The Republic of South Africa Electoral System," http://electionresources.org/za/system/ (accessed July 18, 2016). See also Faure (1996).

9. The Shugart-Taagepera formula is $N_S = 2.5^t(MS_B)^{1/6}$, where $t$ is the share of total seats allocated to the upper tier, and $MS_B$ is the product of the average magnitude of the basic tier and the total number of seats in that tier. In South Africa, both tiers have two hundred seats, so $t = 0.5$. The average magnitude of the basic tier is 22.22 and the total number of seats in that tier is two hundred.

10. Provincial legislatures are dissolved in a fashion similar to that of the National Assembly. The premier must dissolve the provincial legislature if three years have passed since it was elected and a majority of the legislature supports a resolution to dissolve.

11. More specifically, Schedule 2 of the interim constitution—Act 200 of 1993—and the Electoral Act of 1994. See Faure (1996).

12. The constitution of 1996, approved by the Constitutional Court on December 4, 1996, calls for proportional representation but does not stipulate details (Gouws and Mitchell 2005, 358, fn.10). It indicated that the 1999 election should be conducted according to the interim rules but required parliament to enact legislation for elections after 1999. The Electoral Act 73 of 1998 (Schedule 1) and Electoral Laws Amendment Act of 2003 provided this legislation.

13. Faure (1996, 90) notes that in the 1948 election, which put the National Party in power and marked the beginning of the apartheid period, the NP (and Afrikaner Verbond) won 42 percent of the vote and seventy-nine seats, while the United/Labour Parties won 52 percent of the vote and only seventy-one seats. During the 1961–1981 period, the NP held 75 percent of the seats in parliament with a far smaller percentage of the vote.

14. The negotiations were conducted at the Convention for a Democratic South Africa (Codesa), which ran between December 1991 and May 1992, when they broke down over disagreements between the ANC and NP. New negotiations started in April 1993 at the Multi-Party Negotiating Forum and culminated in the interim constitution and elections of April 1994. See Lodge (2003).

15. The choice of PR was not without intellectual critics, however. Horowitz (1991) questioned the consensus on proportional representation. He argued that an alternative vote (AV) system was preferable because it would create incentives for politicians to build coalitions and pursue "vote pooling," which would help bridge racial and ethnic divisions. Barkan (1998) registered a second critique, arguing that a constituency-based system was more appropriate for Africa's rural electorates, which needed a local, embedded elected representative. PR risked disconnecting the state from the population. Finally, Davis (2003), building off of Horowitz (1991) and Norris (2004), argued that PR encourages parties to engage in "bonding" campaign strategies (i.e., appealing to a narrow base), as opposed to "bridging" strategies that attempt to appeal to many groups and suggested PR has had this effect in South Africa.

16. The primary pieces of legislation include the Municipal Demarcation Act (No. 27 of 1998) and the Local Government Municipal Structures Act (No. 117 of 1998). There have been several amendments building on this legislation. Legislation can be accessed at http://www.gov.za/documents/acts (accessed August 23, 2016).

17. South Africa's first post-apartheid local government elections occurred in 1995, but these still were considered transitional as they used old boundaries.

18. For an overview, see Electoral Commission (2016).

19. Very small councils do not have wards, and hence the system here is pure PR. If there is an odd number of seats on the council, the number of ward seats is rounded up. Hence, a council with twenty-one seats would have eleven ward and ten PR seats. See Electoral Commission (2016, 72).

20. The formula is $\dfrac{V}{M-C}+1$, where $V$ is the total number of valid votes cast for all parties (in ward and PR races), $M$ is the number of seats on the metro or local council, and $C$ is the number of independent ward councilors elected in the election. See Section 12(1) of the Local Government Municipal Structures Act (p.70) and Electoral Commission (2016, 72).

21. Reynolds (1998) notes that options on the table for reforming the South African national electoral system in the late 1990s included a mixed-member proportional system like Germany's (see Zittel's chapter in this volume). This reform was obviously not adopted for the national system, but was reflected in the electoral system adopted for municipal elections.

22. The challenges facing independent candidates have nonetheless been significant. See Ndletyana (2007) for case studies of two candidates who stood as independents in the 2000 municipal elections, attempting to forge viable paths outside the main parties.

23. See Ferree, Gibson, and Hoffman (2017, Appendix Table 44.1).

24. The literature is somewhat divided on whether Duverger's law should hold in the district tier of mixed-member systems. Some have argued that parties may run extra candidates in the districts to help advertise and draw votes to their PR lists (see Ferrara, Herron, and Nishikawa 2005). Evidence has been mixed (Moser and Scheiner 2012). See Ferree et al. (2017) for an application to South Africa that suggests contamination effects are insignificant in that context. See the chapter in this volume by Herron, Nemoto, and Nishikawa for an extensive discussion of these issues.

25. Unless otherwise indicated, election results for this section come from the website of the Electoral Commission of South Africa: http://www.elections.org.za.

26. For more on the 1994 election, see Reynolds (1994) and Johnson and Schlemmer (1996). For a history of political opposition during the 1980s, see Lodge and Nasson (1991). Greenberg (2009) provides a fascinating inside account of the great difficulties the ANC faced in unifying the African electorate in the early 1990s.

27. An explicit effort to bring minority parties into cabinet through a rule guaranteeing any party with at least twenty (out of four hundred) seats the option of joining the government with one or more cabin portfolio, the GNU was a creature of the interim constitution. The final 1996 constitution of South Africa did not include similar provisions, and the ANC's strong margins have allowed it to form a series of majority governments from 2009 on.

28. Party control over municipal councils can be calculated from data available on the webpage of the Electoral Commission of South Africa: http://www.elections.org.za/content/Elections/Municipal-elections-results/ (accessed August 29, 2016).

29. See Giliomee (1994) for an account of the NP's 1994 campaign.

30. See Reynolds (1999b) and Lodge (1999).

31. Booysen (2006) offers a useful history of this period.

32. For accounts of the IFP see Hamilton and Mare (1994), Mare (1999), Piper (2005), and Piper (2014).

33. Violence between supporters of the IFP and supporters of the ANC resulted in hundreds of deaths in the province over more than a decade of conflict that started before the 1994 elections.

34. But see the chapters in this volume by Shugart and Taagepera and by Moser, Scheiner, and Stoll for caution about the applicability of this interactive hypothesis.

35. See Annexure A to Schedule 6 of the constitution, Item 23A(1) in the transitional constitution, and Section 47(5) of the final constitution.

36. Both the DA and the ANC had strategic motivations for pursuing the constitutional change. The DA supported relaxing the prohibition on floor crossing to allow its MPs—who still sat as members of either the DP or NNP—to officially convert to the newly formed DA. The ANC agreed, gambling that it could capture some of the support abandoning the sinking NNP. See Booysen (2006).

37. During the 2005 and 2007 windows, the ANC increased its parliamentary presence from 69.69 in 2004 to 74.25 percent by 2008. See Booysen and Masterson (2009).

38. Parties are not permitted to fund business ventures, pay representatives' salaries, or run campaigns with this money. Rather, the goal is to promote "continuous, vital links between the people and the organs of the state" through outreach, education, mobilization, and provision of information. EISA African Democracy Encyclopaedia Project, South Africa: Political Party Funding, https://www.eisa.org.za/wep/souparties2.htm (accessed August 19, 2016).

39. Also see the chapter by Moser, Scheiner, and Stoll in this volume.

## REFERENCES

Álvarez-Rivera, Manuel. "Election Resources on the Internet: The Republic of South Africa Electoral System," 2016, http://electionresources.org/za/system/ (accessed July 18, 2016).

Amorim Neto, Octavio and Gary W. Cox. "Electoral Institutions, Cleavage Structures, and the Number of Parties", *American Journal of Political Science* 41 (January 1997): 149–74.

Atkinson, Doreen. "Taking to the Streets: Has Developmental Local Government Failed in South Africa?" In *State of the Nation South Africa 2007*, edited by Sakhela Buhlungu, John Daniel, Roger Southall, and Jessica Lutchman, 53–77. Cape Town: Human Sciences Research Council, 2007.

Barkan, Joel. "Rethinking the Applicability of Proportional Representation for Africa." In *Elections and Conflict Management in Africa*, edited by Timothy D. Sisk and Andrew Reynolds, 57–70. Washington, DC: United States Institute of Peace, 1998

Booysen, Susan. "The Will of the Parties versus the Will of the People? Defections, Elections and Alliances in South Africa." *Party Politics* 12, no. 6 (2006): 727–746.

Booysen, Susan, and Grant Masterson. "South Africa." In *Compendium of Elections in Southern Africa 1989-2009: 20 Years of the Multiparty Democracy*, edited by Denis Kadima and Susan Booysen, 402–403. Johannesburg: EISA, 2009.

Clark, William Roberts, and Matt Golder. "Rehabilitating Duverger's Theory: Testing the Mechanical and Strategic Modifying Effects of Electoral Laws", *Comparative Political Studies* 39 (August 2006): 679–708.

Cooper, Saths. "The PAC and AZAPO." In *Election '94: The Campaigns, Results and Future Prospects*, ed. Andrew Reynolds, 117–120. New York: St. Martin's Press, 1994.

Cox, Gary. *Making Votes Count*. Cambridge: Cambridge University Press, 1997.

Davis, Gavin. "Bridges and Bonds: List Proportional Representation and Campaigns in South Africa." Working Paper No. 50, Centre for Social Science Research, Cape Town, 2003.

de Kadt, Daniel, and Evan S. Lieberman. "Nuanced accountability: Voter responses to service provision in South Africa." Forthcoming, *British Journal of Political Science*, forthcoming.

Electoral Commission of South Africa. "Municipal Election Results." n.d. http://www.elections .org.za/content/Elections/Municipal-elections-results/ (accessed May 5, 2017).

Electoral Commission of South Africa. "2016 Municipal Elections Handbook." 2016. http:// www.elections.org.za/content/Elections/2016-Municipal-Elections/2016-Municipal-Election-Publication/ (accessed August 19, 2016).

Electoral Institute of South Africa (EISA). "South Africa: Political Party Funding." African Democracy Encyclopaedia Project. n.d. https://www.eisa.org.za/wep/souparties2.htm (accessed August 19, 2016).

Electoral Institute of South Africa (EISA). "South African Local Election Results 2000: Proportional Representation Vote Comparison by Province." n.d. https://www.eisa .org.za/wep/sou2000results4a.htm (accessed August 29, 2016).

Electoral Institute of South Africa (EISA). "South Africa: 2006 National Overview—Votes by Political Party." n.d. https://www.eisa.org.za/wep/sou2006results2.htm (accessed August 29, 2016).

Faure, Murray. "The Electoral System." In *South Africa: Designing New Political Institutions*, edited by Murray Faure and Jan-Erik Lane, 89–104. London: Sage Publications, 1996.

Ferrara, Federico, Erik S. Herron, and Misa Nishikawa. *Mixed Electoral Systems: Contamination and Its Consequences*. New York: Palgrave Macmillan, 2005.

Ferree, Karen. *Framing the Race: the Political Origins of Racial-Census Elections*. Cambridge: Cambridge University Press, 2011.

Ferree, Karen E., G. Bingham Powell, and Ethan Scheiner. "Context, Electoral Rules, and Party Systems." *Annual Review of Political Science* 17 (2014): 421–439.

Ferree, Karen E., Clark C. Gibson, and Barak Hoffman. "Why the Salience of Social Divisions Matters in Party Systems: Testing the Interactive Hypothesis in South Africa." *Party Politics* (2017). Published online May 9, 2017. http://journals.sagepub.com/doi/pdf/10.1177 /1354068817705124.

Giliomee, Herman. "The National Party's Campaign for a Liberation Election." In *Election '94 South Africa*, edited by Andrew Reynolds, 43–72. New York: St. Martin's Press, 1994.

Gouws, Amanda, and Paul Mitchell. "South Africa: One Party Dominance Despite Perfect Proportionality." In *The Politics of Electoral Systems*, edited by Michael Gallagher and Paul Mitchell, 353–374. Oxford UK: Oxford University Press, 2005.

Greenberg, Stanley. *Dispatches from the War Room: In Trenches with Five Extraordinary Leaders*. New York: Thomas Dunne Books, St. Martin's Press, 2009.

Hamilton, Georgina, and Gerhard Mare. "The Inkatha Freedom Party." In *Election '94 South Africa*, edited by Andrew Reynolds. New York: St. Martin's Press, 1994.

Horowitz, Donald. *A Democratic South Africa?* Berkeley: University of California Press, 1991.

Johnson, R. W., and Lawrence Schlemmer. "Introduction: The Transition to Democracy." In *Launching Democracy in South Africa: The First Open Election, April 1994*, edited by R. W. Johnson and Lawrence Schlemmer, 1–15. New Haven, CT: Yale University Press, 1996.

Legislative Sector South Africa. "Legislatures." n.d. http://www.sals.gov.za/show.php?show=1 (accessed July 18, 2016).

Lijphart, Arend. *Patterns of Democracy: Government Forms and Performance in Thirty-Six Countries*. New Haven, CT: Yale University Press, 1999.

Lodge, Tom. *Consolidating Democracy: South Africa's Second Popular Election* Johannesburg: Witwatersrand University Press, 1999.

Lodge, Tom. "How the South African Electoral System Was Negotiated." *Journal of African Elections* 2, no. 1 (2003): 71–76.

Lodge, Tom, and Bill Nasson. *All Here and Now: Black Politics in South Africa in the 1980s*. London: C. Hurst and Company, 1991.

Magaloni, Beatriz. *Voting for Autocracy: Hegemonic Party Survival and Its Demise in Mexico*. Cambridge UK: Cambridge University Press, 2006.

Mare, Gerhard. "The Inkatha Freedom Party." In *Election '99 South Africa: From Mandela to Mbeki*, edited by Andrew Reynolds, 101–113. New York: St. Martin's Press, 1999.

Mattes, Robert. "The Road to Democracy: From 2 February 1990 to 27 April 1994." In *Election '94 South Africa*, edited by Andrew Reynolds, 1–22. New York: St. Martin's Press, 1994.

Moser Robert G., and Ethan Scheiner. *Electoral Systems and Political Context: How the Effects of Rules Vary Across New and Established Democracies*. Cambridge: Cambridge University Press, 2012.

Mottiar, Shauna. "Elections and the Electoral System in South Africa: Beyond Free and Fair Elections." CPS Policy Brief 39. Johannesburg: Centre for Policy Studies, 2005.

Ndletyana, Mcebisi. "Municipal Elections 2006: Protests, Independent Candidates, and Cross-Border Municipalities." In *State of the Nation: South Africa 2007*, edited by Sakhela Buhlungu, John Daniel, Roger Southall, and Jessica Lutchman, 95–113. Cape Town: HSRC Press, 2007.

Nijzink, Lia, and Jessica Piombo. "Parliament and the Electoral System: How Are South Africans Being Represented?" In *Electoral Politics in South Africa: Assessing the First Democratic Decade*, edited by Jessica Piombo and Lia Nijzink, 64–86. New York: Palgrave, 2005.

Norris, Pippa. *Electoral Engineering: Voting Rule and Political Behavior*. Cambridge: Cambridge University Press, 2004.

Ordeshook, Peter C., and Olga V. Shvetsova. "Ethnic Heterogeneity, District Magnitude, and the Number of Parties", *American Journal of Political Science* 38 (February 1994): 100–123.

Piombo, Jessica. "The UCDP, Minority Front, ACDP, and Federal Alliance." In *Election '99 South Africa: From Mandela to Mbeki*, edited by Andrew Reynolds, 133–146. New York: St. Martin's Press, 1999.

Piper, Laurence. "The Inkatha Freedom Party: Between the Impossible and the Ineffective." In *Electoral Politics in South Africa: Assessing the First Democratic Decade*, edited by Jessica Piombo and Lia Nijzink, 148–165. New York: Palgrave, 2005.

Piper, Laurence. "Inkatha Freedom Party: The Elephants' Graveyard." In *Election 2014: The Campaigns, Results, and Future Prospects*, edited by Collette Schulz-Herzenberg and Roger Southall, 89–103. Auckland Park, South Africa: Jacana Media, 2014.

Republic of South Africa. Constitution of 1996. n.d. http://www.gov.za/documents/constitution-republic-south-africa-1996 (accessed July 18, 2016).

Republic of South Africa. Municipal Demarcation Act (No. 27 of 1998). n.d. http://www.gov.za /documents/local-government-municipal-demarcation-act (accessed August 23, 2016).

Republic of South Africa. Local Government Municipal Structures Act (No. 117 of 1998). n.d. http://www.gov.za/documents/local-government-municipal-structures-act (accessed August 23, 2016).

Reynolds, Andrew. *Election '94 South Africa: The Campaigns, Results, and Future Prospects.* New York: St. Martin's Press, 1994.

Reynolds, Andrew. "Elections in Southern Africa: The Case for Proportionality, a Rebuttal." *In Elections and Conflict Management in Africa*, 71–80. Washington, DC: United States Institute of Peace Press, 1998.

Reynolds, Andrew. *Electoral Systems and Democratization in Southern Africa.* Oxford: Oxford University Press, 1999a.

Reynolds, Andrew. *Election '99 South Africa: From Mandela to Mbeki.* New York: St. Martin's Press, 1999b.

Robinson, Jason. "The Economic Freedom Fighters: Birth of a Giant?" In *Election 2014: The Campaigns, Results, and Future Prospects*, edited by Collette Schulz-Herzenberg and Roger Southall, 72–88. Auckland Park, South Africa: Jacana Media, 2014.

Siddle, Andrew M. "Decentralisation in South African Local Government: A Critical Evaluation," Doctoral Thesis, Graduate School of Business, University of Cape Town, South Africa, 2011.

Sisk, Timothy D. "Electoral System Choice in South Africa: Implications for Intergroup Moderation." *Nationalism and Ethnic Politics* 1, no. 2 (1995): 178–204.

Southall, Roger, and Collette Schulz-Herzenberg. "The Party System and Political Prospects in the Wake of Election 2014." In *Election 2014: The Campaigns, Results, and Future Prospects*, edited by Collette Schulz-Herzenberg and Roger Southall, 228–240. Auckland Park, South Africa: Jacana Media, 2014.

Kroth, Verena, Valentino Larcinese, and Joachim Wehner. "A Better Life for All?" Democratization and Electrification in Post-Apartheid South Africa." *Journal of Politics* 78, no. 3 (July 2016): 774–791.

# Index

Figures, tables, and notes are denoted by "*f*", "*t*", and "n" respectively.

Lightning Source UK Ltd.
Milton Keynes UK
UKHW030615150123
415322UK00007B/86